SOFTWARE PROJECT MANAGEMENT
Readings and Cases

Chris F. Kemerer

University of Pittsburgh

IRWIN

Chicago • Bogotá • Boston • Buenos Aires • Caracas
London • Madrid • Mexico City • Sydney • Toronto

Irwin Book Team

Publisher: *Tom Casson*
Senior sponsoring editor: *Rick Williamson*
Editorial assistant: *Carrie Berkshire*
Associate marketing manager: *Michelle Hudson*
Project supervisor: *Denise Santor-Mitzit*
Production supervisor: *Bob Lange*
Designer: *Larry J. Cope*
Prepress Buyer: *Charlene R. Perez*
Compositor: *Carlisle Communications, Ltd.*
Typeface: *10/12 Times Roman*
Printer: *R. R. Donnelley & Sons Company*

Library of Congress Cataloging-in-Publication Data

Kemerer, Chris F.
    Software project management : readings and cases / Chris F. Kemerer.
        p. cm.
    Includes index
    ISBN 0-256-18545-X
    1. Computer software--Development--Management.   2. Software engineering--Management.   I. Title.
QA76.76.D47K45   1997
005. 1'068—dc20   96–43010

Printed in the United States of America
1 2 3 4 5 6 7 8 9 0 DO 3 2 1 0 9 8 7 6

To AGK, LEK, and ARK

Preface

While the critical importance of information technology to business is widely recognized, progress in industry's ability to deliver the software necessary to provide information technology-related services has been slow, hampered, in part, to the early lack of research into these issues. Major software projects are typically a year or more late, and often several hundred percent over budget. Even firms for whom software development is their core process often fail in large and visible ways (e.g. Lotus Development Corporation's Release 3 of their 1-2-3 spreadsheet software). As a consequence of these real-world needs, there is an emerging research area in the area of software engineering management that straddles business and engineering schools. This research focuses on the development of models to better understand software development and tools to improve the productivity and quality of the process. For example, at the end of the 1980s, the federal government established the multi-million dollar Software Engineering Institute at Carnegie Mellon University in Pittsburgh, Pennsylvania, to focus research attention on this critical problem.

Despite this upsurge in research activity, this material has only slowly been making its way into university curricula. There are several reasons for this. In the not too distant past there was no established body of knowledge, and therefore little of substance to teach. Research has progressed considerably since these early days, but this knowledge has not been packaged in a way suitable for education.

In addition to the newness of this material, another significant barrier is the fact that this research exists at the interface between business school information systems departments and engineering school computer science departments. These factors, combined with the lack of suitable teaching materials, has meant that this important topic has not been able to be easily taught.

The primary intended audience for this book will be graduate and advanced undergraduate students, particularly those concentrating in Information Systems in business schools and Computer Science in engineering schools. In addition, students who anticipate careers with significant information technology interaction, even if only from a user perspective, are also often encouraged to gain exposure to this material so as to be better prepared to be part of a software development partnership team. There are two main ways this book will be employed in business school curricula, as the main required text in a course focused on software project management and as a required supplemental text in courses on systems analysis and design, information systems management, and information systems project courses.

In terms of primary courses, I have successfully taught this material in this format at MIT's Sloan School of Management, the Wharton School of the University of Pennsylvania, and the University of Pittsburgh's Katz Graduate School of Business. The Sloan course was aimed at MBA students, but with Sloan's open enrollment policy, I have taught students ranging from business school undergraduates, computer science undergraduates, and business school and computer science PhD students. At the Wharton School, this course has been taught both in an undergraduate version and a graduate version.

In terms of existing courses at other schools, this text could be used in courses with titles such as:

- Software Engineering Management
- Advanced Programming Methods
- Systems Analysis and Design
- Management of Information Systems
- Information Technology
- Systems Analysis
- Systems Design
- IS Project Course
- Project Management

I have found that the University of Pittsburgh's part-time MBA students, typically already employed in the information systems industry, readily adapt to the practical and applied nature of the material. This book should also find a ready audience in graduate or advanced undergraduate courses in software engineering in computer science departments. While my teaching has been in business schools, I have taught a significant fraction of students who were computer science majors that have enrolled in my course on software engineering management. They adapt very readily to this material, and, if anything, I suspect that this course is relatively more valuable to them in that it reflects a new set of concepts and priorities from a typical computer science course with its emphasis on pure theory or the building of small prototype systems.

In terms of existing courses at other schools, this text could be used as a main or supplemental text in courses with titles such as:

- Software Engineering Management
- Software Engineering
- Programming Methods
- Software Process Modeling
- Systems Design
- CS Project Course

As with the business school students, I expect that considerable demand exists for this practical material from students pursuing graduate and sometimes undergraduate CS degrees part-time while they work full-time. While I view the primary audience as university students, because of the book's format as a series of independent readings and because of the critical and timely nature of the material, I would expect considerable usage by practicing software developers and managers. In addition to its use as a teaching aid, particularly in aiding the transition of technical staff members to management positions, the book is also likely to serve a useful role as a standard industry reference, a book that contains the state of the art material on a variety of topics that will be encountered by managers at different points in their career.

Finally, for researchers and other authors in the field, let me offer a short note on the selection of articles for this volume. Even in a field as relatively new as this one there is much more material available than can fit within the covers of one book, which necessitates some difficult choices on the part of the editor. My goal here was primarily to provide a student text, and, in so doing, to balance fundamental articles with newer material to show the direction in which the field is moving. Therefore, the reader will find both "classic" articles, such as Fred Brooks' "No Silver Bullet," and work directly from the original source such as Albrecht and Gaffney's paper on Function Points, and more recently published work, such as the chapters on adoption of object-oriented techniques and on the SEI capability maturity model. Within the chapters there is a bias toward articles that employ quantitative approaches, as this is the emerging discipline of software engineering management. Finally, where it fit with the other objectives, I followed a pattern where the first article in the chapter would "set the stage," the second would focus on economic aspects, and the third would focus more on organizational aspects. This is designed to provide readers with a relatively broad view of the topic within a single chapter. The accompanying teacher's guide develops these themes in more depth for the instructor.

Chris F. Kemerer

Contents

Case Studies

Software Project Management Overview:

Software Engineering as a Discipline

INTRODUCTION

Chapter 1 introduces the topic of software project management through three related articles on software engineering as a Discipline. The central issue that all three of the articles address is why is the current practice in software project management so clearly seen as substandard. Why is it so difficult to deliver significant software products that meet their requirements on time and on budget? What contributions has the study of software engineering made to practice? How can we expect progress to be made in this area?

The chapter begins with a now famous essay by Fred Brooks on why software is so hard. He argues that most currently proposed solutions will not solve the problem, since they do not address its essence, only its accidental difficulties. Brooks effectively documents why the development of software is inherently different from other engineering endeavors and how past successes have dealt with only accidental difficulties, or are simply not able to be extrapolated to the next level of problems. He dissects a list of popular proposed solutions and argues that none address the essential difficulty of conceiving the appropriate system. He concludes with some practical advice that can help managers to do a better job in the near term.

The second article, authored by Mary Shaw of Carnegie Mellon University, takes the long view that the development of software engineering will take the same form as other engineering disciplines. Her general model depicts an evolution from craft to production (stimulated by demand and accomplished by the accumulation of knowledge in this area) and then evolves to engineering once the requisite science is developed in parallel and added. She documents the history of civil and chemical engineering as examples of her general model. She also documents successes as evidence that appropriate progress is being made, that computer science is developing the necessary science. She directly addresses some of Brooks's points.

A third point of view is provided by Victor Basili and John Musa. Like Shaw, they are positive, but take a shorter term (decade rather than century) perspective. They argue that progress has been made, but that more effort needs to be made to model and codify what has been learned. Their article directly supports the need for greater measurement, and the need for software engineering to learn from other disciplines besides computer science, including economics and psychology. They also provide a list of tools and approaches similar to Brooks, but argue that they are all good ideas, ideas that will move the profession forward.

NO SILVER BULLET:
ESSENCE AND ACCIDENTS
OF SOFTWARE ENGINEERING

Of all the monsters that fill the nightmares of our folklore, none terrify more than werewolves, because they transform unexpectedly from the familiar into horrors. For these, one seeks bullets of silver that can magically lay them to rest.

The familiar software project, at least as seen by the nontechnical manager, has something of this character; it is usually innocent and straightforward, but is capable of becoming a monster of missed schedules, blown budgets, and flawed products. So we hear desperate cries for a silver bullet—something to make software costs drop as rapidly as computer hardware costs do.

But, as we look to the horizon of a decade hence, we see no silver bullet. There is no single development, in either technology or in management technique, that by itself promises even one order-of-magnitude improvement in productivity, in reliability, in simplicity. In this article, I shall try to show why by examining both the nature of the software problem and the properties of the bullets proposed.

Skepticism is not pessimism, however. Although we see no startling breakthroughs—and indeed, I believe such to be inconsistent with the nature of software—many encouraging innovations are under way. A disciplined, consistent effort to develop, propagate, and exploit these innovations should indeed yield an order-of-magnitude improvement. There is no royal road, but there is a road.

Article by Fredrick P. Brooks, Jr. © 1987 IEEE. Reprinted, with permission, from (*IEEE Computer;* 20, 4, 10–19; April/1987).

The first step toward the management of disease was replacement of demon theories and humours theories by the germ theory. That very step, the beginning of hope, in itself dashed all hopes of magical solutions. It told workers that progress would be made stepwise, at great effort, and that a persistent, unremitting care would have to be paid to a discipline of cleanliness. So it is with software engineering today.

DOES IT HAVE TO BE HARD? ESSENTIAL DIFFICULTIES

Not only are there no silver bullets now in view, the very nature of software makes it unlikely that there will be any—no inventions that will do for software productivity, reliability, and simplicity what electronics, transistors, and large-scale integration did for computer hardware. We cannot expect ever to see twofold gains every two years.

First, one must observe that the anomaly is not that software progress is so slow, but that computer hardware progress is so fast. No other technology since civilization began has seen six orders of magnitude in performance-price gain in 30 years. In no other technology can one choose to take the gain in *either* improved performance *or* in reduced costs. These gains flow from the transformation of computer manufacture from an assembly industry into a process industry.

Second, to see what rate of progress one can expect in software technology, let us examine the difficulties of that technology. Following Aristotle,

I divide them into *essence,* the difficulties inherent in the nature of software, and *accidents,* those difficulties that today attend its production but are not inherent.

The essence of a software entity is a construct of interlocking concepts: data sets, relationships among data items, algorithms, and invocations of functions. This essence is abstract in that such a conceptual construct is the same under many different representations. It is nonetheless highly precise and richly detailed.

I believe the hard part of building software to be the specification, design, and testing of this conceptual construct, not the labor of representing it and testing the fidelity of the representation. We still make syntax errors, to be sure; but they are fuzz compared with the conceptual errors in most systems.

If this is true, building software will always be hard. There is inherently no silver bullet.

Let us consider the inherent properties of this irreducible essence of modern software systems: complexity, conformity, changeability, and invisibility.

Complexity

Software entities are more complex for their size than perhaps any other human construct because no two parts are alike (at least above the statement level). If they are, we make the two similar parts into a subroutine—open or closed. In this respect, software systems differ profoundly from computers, buildings, or automobiles, where repeated elements abound.

Digital computers are themselves more complex than most things people build: They have very large numbers of states. This makes conceiving, describing, and testing them hard. Software systems have orders-of-magnitude more states than computers do.

Likewise, a scaling-up of a software entity is not merely a repetition of the same elements in larger sizes, it is necessarily an increase in the number of different elements. In most cases, the elements interact with each other in some nonlinear fashion, and the complexity of the whole increases much more than linearly.

The complexity of software is an essential property, not an accidental one. Hence, descriptions of a software entity that abstract away its complexity often abstract away its essence. For three centuries, mathematics and the physical sciences made great strides by constructing simplified models of complex phenomena, deriving properties from the models, and verifying those properties by experiment. This paradigm worked because the complexities ignored in the models were not the essential properties of the phenomena. It does not work when the complexities are the essence.

Many of the classic problems of developing software products derive from this essential complexity and its nonlinear increases with size. From the complexity comes the difficulty of communication among team members, which leads to product flaws, cost overruns, schedule delays. From the complexity comes the difficulty of enumerating, much less understanding, all the possible states of the program, and from that comes the unreliability. From complexity of function comes the difficulty of invoking function, which makes programs hard to use. From complexity of structure comes the difficulty of extending programs to new functions without creating side effects. From complexity of structure come the unvisualized states that constitute security trapdoors.

Not only technical problems, but management problems as well come from the complexity. It makes overview hard, thus impeding conceptual integrity. It makes it hard to find and control all the loose ends. It creates the tremendous learning and understanding burden that makes personnel turnover a disaster.

Conformity

Software people are not alone in facing complexity. Physics deals with terribly complex objects even at the "fundamental" particle level. The physicist labors on, however, in a firm faith that there are unifying principles to be found, whether in quarks or in unified-field theories. Einstein argued that there must be simplified explanations of nature, because God is not capricious or arbitrary.

No such faith comforts the software engineer. Much of the complexity that he must master is arbitrary complexity, forced without rhyme or reason by the many human institutions and systems to which his interfaces must conform. These differ from interface to interface, and from time to time, not because of necessity but only because they were designed by different people, rather than by God.

In many cases, the software must conform because it is the most recent arrival on the scene. In others, it must conform because it is perceived as the most conformable. But in all cases, much complexity comes from conformation to other interfaces; this complexity cannot be simplified out by any redesign of the software alone.

Changeability

The software entity is constantly subject to pressures for change. Of course, so are buildings, cars, computers. But manufactured things are infrequently changed after manufacture; they are superseded by later models, or essential changes are incorporated into later-serial-number copies of the same basic design. Call-backs of automobiles are really quite infrequent; field changes of computers somewhat less so. Both are much less frequent than modifications to fielded software.

In part, this is so because the software of a system embodies its function, and the function is the part that most feels the pressures of change. In part it is because software can be changed more easily—it is pure thought-stuff, infinitely malleable. Buildings do in fact get changed, but the high costs of change, understood by all, serve to dampen the whims of the changers.

All successful software gets changed. Two processes are at work. First, as a software product is found to be useful, people try it in new cases at the edge of or beyond the original domain. The pressures for extended function come chiefly from

users who like the basic function and invent new uses for it.

Second, successful software survives beyond the normal life of the machine vehicle for which it is first written. If not new computers, then at least new disks, new displays, new printers come along; and the software must be conformed to its new vehicles of opportunity.

In short, the software product is embedded in a cultural matrix of applications, users, laws, and machine vehicles. These all change continually, and their changes inexorably force change upon the software product.

Invisibility

Software is invisible and unvisualizable. Geometric abstractions are powerful tools. The floor plan of a building helps both architect and client evaluate spaces, traffic flows, views. Contradictions and omissions become obvious. Scale drawings of mechanical parts and stick-figure models of molecules, although abstractions, serve the same purpose. A geometric reality is captured in a geometric abstraction.

The reality of software is not inherently embedded in space. Hence, it has no ready geometric representation in the way that land has maps, silicon chips have diagrams, computers have connectivity schematics. As soon as we attempt to diagram software structure, we find it to constitute not one, but several, general directed graphs superimposed one upon another. The several graphs may represent the flow of control, the flow of data, patterns of dependency, time sequence, namespace relationships. These graphs are usually not even planar, much less hierarchical. Indeed, one of the ways of establishing conceptual control over such structure is to enforce link cutting until one or more of the graphs becomes hierarchical.[1]

In spite of progress in restricting and simplifying the structures of software, they remain inherently unvisualizable, and thus do not permit the mind to use some of its most powerful conceptual tools. This lack not only impedes the process of design within one mind, it severely hinders communication among minds.

PAST BREAKTHROUGHS SOLVED ACCIDENTAL DIFFICULTIES

If we examine the three steps in software-technology development that have been most fruitful in the past, we discover that each attacked a different major difficulty in building software, but that those difficulties have been accidental, not essential, difficulties. We can also see the natural limits to the extrapolation of each such attack.

High-Level Languages

Surely the most powerful stroke for software productivity, reliability, and simplicity has been the progressive use of high-level languages for programming. Most observers credit that development with at least a factor of five in productivity, and with concomitant gains in reliability, simplicity, and comprehensibility.

What does a high-level language accomplish? It frees a program from much of its accidental complexity. An abstract program consists of conceptual constructs: operations, data types, sequences, and communication. The concrete machine program is concerned with bits, registers, conditions, branches, channels, disks, and such. To the extent that the high-level language embodies the constructs one wants in the abstract program and avoids all lower ones, it eliminates a whole level of complexity that was never inherent in the program at all.

The most a high-level language can do is to furnish all the constructs that the programmer imagines in the abstract program. To be sure, the level of our thinking about data structures, data types, and operations is steadily rising, but at an ever-decreasing rate. And language development approaches closer and closer to the sophistication of users.

Moreover, at some point the elaboration of a high-level language creates a tool-mastery burden that increases, not reduces, the intellectual task of the user who rarely uses the esoteric constructs.

Time-Sharing

Time-sharing brought a major improvement in the productivity of programmers and in the quality of their product, although not so large as that brought by high-level languages.

Time-sharing attacks a quite different difficulty. Time-sharing preserves immediacy, and hence enables one to maintain an overview of complexity. The slow turnaround of batch programming means that one inevitably forgets the minutiae, if not the very thrust, of what one was thinking when he stopped programming and called for compilation and execution. This interruption is costly in time, for one must refresh one's memory. The most serious effect may well be the decay of the grasp of all that is going on in a complex system.

Slow turnaround, like machine-language complexities, is an accidental rather an essential difficulty of the software process. The limits of the potential contribution of time-sharing derive directly. The principal effect of time-sharing is to shorten system response time. As this response time goes to zero, at some point it passes the human threshold of noticeability, about 100 milliseconds. Beyond that threshold, no benefits are to be expected.

Unified Programming Environments

Unix and Interlisp, the first integrated programming environments to come into widespread use, seem to have improved productivity by integral factors. Why?

They attack the accidental difficulties that result from using individual programs *together,* by providing integrated libraries, unified file formats, and pipes and filters. As a result, conceptual structures that in principle could always call, feed, and use one another can indeed easily do so in practice.

This breakthrough in turn stimulated the development of whole toolbenches, since each new tool could be applied to any programs that used the standard formats.

Because of these successes, environments are the subject of much of today's software-engineering research. We look at their promise and limitations in the next section.

HOPES FOR THE SILVER

Now let us consider the technical developments that are most often advanced as potential silver bullets. What problems do they address—the problems of essence, or the remaining accidental difficulties? Do they offer revolutionary advances, or incremental ones?

Ada and Other High-Level Language Advances

One of the most touted recent developments is Ada, a general-purpose high-level language of the 1980s. Ada not only reflects evolutionary improvements in language concepts, but indeed embodies features to encourage modern design and modularization. Perhaps the Ada philosophy is more of an advance than the Ada language, for it is the philosophy of modularization, of abstract data types, of hierarchical structuring. Ada is over-rich, a natural result of the process by which requirements were laid on its design. That is not fatal, for subsetted working vocabularies can solve the learning problem, and hardware advances will give us the cheap MIPS to pay for the compiling costs. Advancing the structuring of software systems is indeed a very good use for the increased MIPS our dollars will buy. Operating systems, loudly decried in the 1960s for their memory and cycle costs, have proved to be an excellent form in which to use some of the MIPS and cheap memory bytes of the past hardware surge.

Nevertheless, Ada will not prove to be the silver bullet that slays the software productivity monster. It is, after all, just another high-level language, and the biggest payoff from such languages came from the first transition—the transition up from the accidental complexities of the machine into the more abstract statement of step-by-step solutions. Once those accidents have been removed, the remaining ones will be smaller, and the payoff from their removal will surely be less.

I predict that a decade from now, when the effectiveness of Ada is assessed, it will be seen to have made a substantial difference, but not because of any particular language feature, nor indeed because of all of them combined. Neither will the new Ada environments prove to be the cause of the improvements. Ada's greatest contribution will be that switching to it occasioned training programmers in modern software-design techniques.

Object-Oriented Programming

Many students of the art hold out more hope for object-oriented programming than for any of the other technical fads of the day.[2] I am among them. Mark Sherman of Dartmouth notes on CSnet News that one must be careful to distinguish two separate ideas that go under that name: *abstract data types* and *hierarchical types.* The concept of the abstract data type is that an object's type should be defined by a name, a set of proper values, and a set of proper operations rather than by its storage structure, which should be hidden. Examples are Ada packages (with private types) and Modula's modules.

Hierarchical types, such as Simula-67's classes, allow one to define general interfaces that can be further refined by providing subordinate types. The two concepts are orthogonal—one may have hierarchies without hiding and hiding without hierarchies. Both concepts represent real advances in the art of building software.

Each removes yet another accidental difficulty from the process, allowing the designer to express the essence of the design without having to express large amounts of syntactic material that add no information content. For both abstract types and hierarchical types, the result is to remove a higher-order kind of accidental difficulty and allow a higher-order expression of design.

Nevertheless, such advances can do no more than to remove all the accidental difficulties from the expression of the design. The complexity of the design itself is essential, and such attacks make no change whatever in that. An order-of-magnitude gain can be made by object-oriented programming only if the unnecessary type-specification underbrush still in our programming language is itself nine-tenths of the work involved in designing a program product. I doubt it.

Artificial Intelligence

Many people expect advances in artificial intelligence to provide the revolutionary breakthrough that will give order-of-magnitude gains in software productivity and quality.[3] I do not. To see why, we must dissect what is meant by "artificial intelligence."

D.L. Parnas has clarified the terminological chaos:[4]

> Two quite different definitions of AI are in common use today. AI-1: The use of computers to solve problems that previously could only be solved by applying human intelligence. AI-2: The use of a specific set of programming techniques known as heuristic or rule-based programming. In this approach human experts are studied to determine what heuristics or rules of thumb they use in solving problems. . . . The program is designed to solve a problem the way that humans seem to solve it.
>
> The first definition has a sliding meaning. . . . Something can fit the definition of AI-1 today but, once we see how the program works and understand the problem, we will not think of it as AI any more. . . . Unfortunately I cannot identify a body of technology that is unique to this field. . . . Most of the work is problem-specific, and some abstraction or creativity is required to see how to transfer it.

I agree completely with this critique. The techniques used for speech recognition seem to have little in common with those used for image recognition, and both are different from those used in expert systems. I have a hard time seeing how image recognition, for example, will make any appreciable difference in programming practice. The same problem is true of speech recognition. The hard thing about building software is deciding what one wants to say, not saying it. No facilitation of expression can give more than marginal gains.

Expert-systems technology, AI-2, deserves a section of its own.

Expert Systems

The most advanced part of the artificial intelligence art, and the most widely applied, is the technology for building expert systems. Many software scientists are hard at work applying this technology to the software-building environment.[3,5] What is the concept, and what are the prospects?

An *expert system* is a program that contains a generalized inference engine and a rule base, takes input data and assumptions, explores the inferences derivable from the rule base, yields conclusions and advice, and offers to explain its results by retracing its reasoning for the user. The inference engines typically can deal with fuzzy or probabilistic data and rules, in addition to purely deterministic logic.

Such systems offer some clear advantages over programmed algorithms designed for arriving at the same solutions to the same problems:

- Inference-engine technology is developed in an application-independent way, and then applied to many uses. One can justify much effort on the inference engines. Indeed, that technology is well advanced.
- The changeable parts of the application-peculiar materials are encoded in the rule base in a uniform fashion, and tools are provided for developing, changing, testing, and documenting the rule base. This regularizes much of the complexity of the application itself.

The power of such systems does not come from ever-fancier inference mechanisms, but rather from ever-richer knowledge bases that reflect the real world more accurately. I believe that the most important advance offered by the technology is the separation of the application complexity from the program itself.

How can this technology be applied to the software-engineering task? In many ways: Such systems can suggest interface rules, advise on testing strategies, remember bug-type frequencies, and offer optimization hints.

Consider an imaginary testing advisor, for example. In its most rudimentary form, the diagnostic expert system is very like a pilot's checklist, just enumerating suggestions as to possible causes of difficulty. As more and more system structure is embodied in the rule base, and as the rule base takes more sophisticated account of the trouble symptoms reported, the testing advisor becomes more and more particular in the hypotheses it generates and the tests it recommends. Such an expert system may depart most radically from the conventional ones in that its rule base should probably be hierarchically modularized in the same way the corresponding software product is, so that as the product is modularly modified, the diagnostic rule base can be modularly modified as well.

The work required to generate the diagnostic rules is work that would have to be done anyway in generating the set of test cases for the modules and for the system. If it is done in a suitably general manner, with both a uniform structure for rules and a good inference engine available, it may actually reduce the total labor of generating bring-up test cases, and help as well with lifelong maintenance and modification testing. In the same way, one can postulate other advisors, probably many and probably simple, for the other parts of the software-construction task.

Many difficulties stand in the way of the early realization of useful expert-system advisors to the program developer. A crucial part of our imaginary scenario is the development of easy ways to get from program-structure specification to the automatic or semiautomatic generation of diagnostic rules. Even more difficult and important is the twofold task of knowledge acquisition: finding articulate, self-analytical experts who know *why* they do things, and developing efficient techniques for extracting what they know and distilling it into rule bases. The essential prerequisite for building an expert system is to have an expert.

The most powerful contribution by expert systems will surely be to put at the service of the inexperienced programmer the experience and accumulated wisdom of the best programmers. This is no small contribution. The gap between the best software engineering practice and the average practice is very wide—perhaps wider than in any other engineering discipline. A tool that disseminates good practice would be important.

"Automatic" Programming

For almost 40 years, people have been anticipating and writing about "automatic programming," or the generation of a program for solving a problem from a statement of the problem specifications. Some today write as if they expect this technology to provide the next breakthrough.[5]

Parnas[4] implies that the term is used for glamour, not for semantic content, asserting,

> In short, automatic programming always has been a euphemism for programming with a higher-level language than was presently available to the programmer.

He argues, in essence, that in most cases it is the solution method, not the problem, whose specification has to be given.

One can find exceptions. The technique of building generators is very powerful, and it is routinely used to good advantage in programs for sorting. Some systems for integrating differential equations have also permitted direct specification of the problem, and the systems have assessed the parameters, chosen from a library of methods of solution, and generated the programs.

These applications have very favorable properties:

- The problems are readily characterized by relatively few parameters.
- There are many known methods of solution to provide a library of alternatives.
- Extensive analysis has led to explicit rules for selecting solution techniques, given problem parameters.

It is hard to see how such techniques generalize to the wider world of the ordinary software system, where cases with such neat properties are the exception. It is hard even to imagine how this breakthrough in generalization could occur.

Graphical Programming

A favorite subject for PhD dissertations in software engineering is graphical, or visual, programming—the application of computer graphics to software design.[6,7] Sometimes the promise held out by such an approach is postulated by analogy with VLSI chip design, in which computer graphics plays so fruitful a role. Sometimes the theorist justifies the approach by considering flowcharts as the ideal program-design medium and by providing powerful facilities for constructing them.

Nothing even convincing, much less exciting, has yet emerged from such efforts. I am persuaded that nothing will.

In the first place, as I have argued elsewhere,[8] the flowchart is a very poor abstraction of software structure. Indeed, it is best viewed as Burks, von Neumann, and Goldstine's attempt to provide a desperately needed high-level control language for their proposed computer. In the pitiful, multipage, connection-boxed form to which the flowchart has today been elaborated, it has proved to be useless as a design tool—programmers draw flowcharts after, not before, writing the programs they describe.

Second, the screens of today are too small, in pixels, to show both the scope and the resolution of any seriously detailed software diagram. The so-called "desktop metaphor" of today's workstation is instead an "airplane-seat" metaphor. Anyone who has shuffled a lap full of papers while seated between two portly passengers will recognize the difference—one can see only a very few things at once. The true desktop provides overview of, and random access to, a score of pages. Moreover, when fits of creativity run strong, more than one programmer or writer has been known to abandon the desktop for the more spacious floor. The hardware technology will have to advance quite substantially before the scope of our scopes is sufficient for the software-design task.

More fundamentally, as I have argued above, software is very difficult to visualize. Whether one diagrams control flow, variable-scope nesting, variable cross-references, dataflow, hierarchical data structures, or whatever, one feels only one dimension of the intricately interlocked software elephant. If one superimposes all the diagrams generated by the many relevant views, it is difficult to extract any global overview. The VLSI analogy is fundamentally misleading—a chip design is a layered two-dimensional description whose geometry reflects its realization in 3-space. A software system is not.

Program Verification

Much of the effort in modern programming goes into testing and the repair of bugs. Is there perhaps a silver bullet to be found by eliminating the errors at the source, in the system-design phase? Can both productivity and product reliability be radically enhanced by following the profoundly different strategy of proving designs correct before the immense effort is poured into implementing and testing them?

I do not believe we will find productivity magic here. Program verification is a very powerful concept, and it will be very important for such things as secure operating-system kernels. The technology does not promise, however, to save labor. Verifications are so much work that only a few substantial programs have ever been verified.

Program verification does not mean error-proof programs. There is no magic here, either. Mathematical proofs also can be faulty. So whereas verification might reduce the program-testing load, it cannot eliminate it.

More seriously, even perfect program verification can only establish that a program meets its specification. The hardest part of the software task is arriving at a complete and consistent specification, and much of the essence of building a program is in fact the debugging of the specification.

Environments and Tools

How much more gain can be expected from the exploding researches into better programming environments? One's instinctive reaction is that the big-payoff problems—hierarchical file systems, uniform file formats to make possible uniform program interfaces, and generalized tools—were the first attacked, and have been solved. Language-specific smart editors are developments not yet widely used in practice, but the most they promise is freedom from syntactic errors and simple semantic errors.

Perhaps the biggest gain yet to be realized from programming environments is the use of integrated database systems to keep track of the myriad details that must be recalled accurately by the individual programmer and kept current for a group of collaborators on a single system.

Surely this work is worthwhile, and surely it will bear some fruit in both productivity and reliability. But by its very nature, the return from now on must be marginal.

Workstations

What gains are to be expected for the software art from the certain and rapid increase in the power and memory capacity of the individual workstation? Well, how many MIPS can one use fruitfully? The composition and editing of programs and documents is fully supported by today's speeds. Compiling could stand a boost, but a factor of 10 in machine speed would surely leave think-time the dominant activity in the programmer's day. Indeed, it appears to be so now.

More powerful workstations we surely welcome. Magical enhancements from them we cannot expect.

PROMISING ATTACKS ON THE CONCEPTUAL ESSENCE

Even though no technological breakthrough promises to give the sort of magical results with which

we are so familiar in the hardware area, there is both an abundance of good work going on now, and the promise of steady, if unspectacular progress.

All of the technological attacks on the accidents of the software process are fundamentally limited by the productivity equation:

$$time\ of\ task = \sum_i (frequency)_i \times (time)_i$$

If, as I believe, the conceptual components of the task are now taking most of the time, then no amount of activity on the task components that are merely the expression of the concepts can give large productivity gains.

Hence we must consider those attacks that address the essence of the software problem, the formulation of these complex conceptual structures. Fortunately, some of these attacks are very promising.

Buy Versus Build

The most radical possible solution for constructing software is not to construct it at all.

Every day this becomes easier, as more and more vendors offer more and better software products for a dizzying variety of applications. While we software engineers have labored on production methodology, the personal-computer revolution has created not one, but many, mass markets for software. Every newsstand carries monthly magazines, which sorted by machine type, advertise and review dozens of products at prices from a few dollars to a few hundred dollars. More specialized sources offer very powerful products for the workstation and other Unix markets. Even software tools and environments can be bought off-the-shelf. I have elsewhere proposed a marketplace for individual modules.[9]

Any such product is cheaper to buy than to build afresh. Even at a cost of one hundred thousand dollars, a purchased piece of software is costing only about as much as one programmer-year. And delivery is immediate! Immediate at least for products that really exist, products whose developer can refer products to a happy user. Moreover, such products tend to be much better documented and somewhat better maintained than home-grown software.

The development of the mass market is, I believe, the most profound long-run trend in software engineering. The cost of software has always been development cost, not replication cost. Sharing that cost among even a few users radically cuts the per-user cost. Another way of looking at it is that the use of n copies of a software system effectively multiplies the productivity of its developers by n. That is an enhancement of the productivity of the discipline and of the nation.

The key issue, of course, is applicability. Can I use an available off-the-shelf package to perform my task? A surprising thing has happened here. During the 1950s and 1960s, study after study showed that users would not use off-the-shelf packages for payroll, inventory control, accounts receivable, and so on. The requirements were too specialized, the case-to-case variation too high. During the 1980s, we find such packages in high demand and widespread use. What has changed?

Not the packages, really. They may be somewhat more generalized and somewhat more customizable than formerly, but not much. Not the applications, either. If anything, the business and scientific needs of today are more diverse and complicated than those of 20 years ago.

The big change has been in the hardware/software cost ratio. In 1960, the buyer of a two-million dollar machine felt that he could afford $250,000 more for a customized payroll program, one that slipped easily and nondisruptively into the computer-hostile social environment. Today, the buyer of a $50,000 office machine cannot conceivably afford a customized payroll program, so he adapts the payroll procedure to the packages available. Computers are now so commonplace, if not yet so beloved, that the adaptations are accepted as a matter of course.

There are dramatic exceptions to my argument that the generalization of software packages has changed little over the years: electronic spreadsheets and simple database systems. These powerful tools, so obvious in retrospect and yet so late in appearing, lend themselves to myriad uses, some quite unorthodox. Articles and even books now abound on how to tackle unexpected tasks with the spreadsheet. Large numbers of applications that would formerly have been written as custom programs in Cobol or Report Program Generator are now routinely done with these tools.

Many users now operate their own computers day in and day out on various applications without ever writing a program. Indeed, many of these users cannot write new programs for their machines, but they are nevertheless adept at solving new problems with them.

I believe the single most powerful software-productivity strategy for many organizations today is to equip the computer-naive intellectual workers who are on the firing line with personal computers and good generalized writing, drawing, file, and spreadsheet programs and then to turn them loose. The same strategy, carried out with generalized mathematical and statistical packages and some simple programming capabilities, will also work for hundreds of laboratory scientists.

Requirements Refinement and Rapid Prototyping

The hardest single part of building a software system is deciding precisely what to build. No other part of the conceptual work is as difficult as establishing the detailed technical requirements, including all the interfaces to people, to machines, and to other software systems. No other part of the work so cripples the resulting system if done wrong. No other part is more difficult to rectify later.

Therefore, the most important function that the software builder performs for the client is the iterative extraction and refinement of the product requirements. For the truth is, the client does not know what he wants. The client usually does not know what questions must be answered, and he has almost never thought of the problem in the detail necessary for specification. Even the simple answer—"Make the new software system work like our old manual information-processing system"—is in fact too simple. One never wants exactly that. Complex software systems are, moreover, things that act, that move, that work. The dynamics of that action are hard to imagine. So in planning any software-design activity, it is necessary to allow for an extensive iteration between the client and the designer as part of the system definition.

I would go a step further and assert that it is really impossible for a client, even working with a software engineer, to specify completely, precisely, and correctly the exact requirements of a modern software product before trying some versions of the product.

Therefore, one of the most promising of the current technological efforts, and one that attacks the essence, not the accidents, of the software problem, is the development of approaches and tools for rapid prototyping of systems as prototyping is part of the iterative specification of requirements.

A *prototype software system* is one that simulates the important interfaces and performs the main functions of the intended system, while not necessarily being bound by the same hardware speed, size, or cost constraints. Prototypes typically perform the mainline tasks of the application, but make no attempt to handle the exceptional tasks, respond correctly to invalid inputs, or abort cleanly. The purpose of the prototype is to make real the conceptual structure specified, so that the client can test it for consistency and usability.

Much of present-day software-acquisition procedure rests upon the assumption that one can specify a satisfactory system in advance, get bids for its construction, have it built, and install it. I think this assumption is fundamentally wrong, and that many software-acquisition problems spring from that fallacy. Hence, they cannot be fixed without fundamental revision—revision that provides for iterative development and specification of prototypes and products.

Incremental Development—Grow, Don't Build, Software

I still remember the jolt I felt in 1958 when I first heard a friend talk about *building* a program, as opposed to *writing* one. In a flash he broadened my whole view of the software process. The metaphor shift was powerful, and accurate. Today we understand how like other building processes the construction of software is, and we freely use other elements of the metaphor, such as *specifications, assembly of components,* and *scaffolding.*

The building metaphor has outlived its usefulness. It is time to change again. If, as I believe, the conceptual structures we construct today are too complicated to be specified accurately in advance, and too complex to be built faultlessly, then we must take a radically different approach.

Let us turn nature and study complexity in living things, instead of just the dead works of man. Here we find constructs whose complexities thrill us with awe. The brain alone is intricate beyond mapping, powerful beyond imitation, rich in diversity, self-protecting, and self-renewing. The secret is that it is grown, not built.

So it must be with our software systems. Some years ago Harlan Mills proposed that any software system should be grown by incremental development.[10] That is, the system should first be made to run, even if it does nothing useful except call the proper set of dummy subprograms. Then, bit by bit, it should be fleshed out, with the subprograms in turn being developed—into actions or calls to empty stubs in the level below.

I have seen most dramatic results since I began urging this technique on the project builders in my Software Engineering Laboratory class. Nothing in the past decade has so radically changed my own practice, or its effectiveness. The approach necessitates top-down design, for it is a top-down growing of the software. It allows easy backtracking. It lends itself to early prototypes. Each added function and new provision for more complex data or circumstances grows organically out of what is already there.

The morale effects are startling. Enthusiasm jumps when there is a running system, even a simple one. Efforts redouble when the first picture from a new graphics software system appears on the screen, even if it is only a rectangle. One always has, at every stage in the process, a working system. I find that teams can *grow* much more complex entities in four months than they can *build.*

The same benefits can be realized on large projects as on my small ones.[11]

Great Designers

The central question in how to improve the software art centers, as it always has, on people.

We can get good designs by following good practices instead of poor ones. Good design practices can be taught. Programmers are among the most intelligent part of the population, so they can learn good practice. Hence, a major thrust in the United States is to promulgate good modern practice. New curricula, new literature, new organizations such as the Software Engineering Institute, all have come into being in order to raise the level of our practice from poor to good. This is entirely proper.

Nevertheless, I do not believe we can make the next step upward in the same way. Whereas the difference between poor conceptual designs and good ones may lie in the soundness of design method, the difference between good designs and great ones surely does not. Great designs come from great designers. Software construction is a *creative* process. Sound methodology can empower and liberate the creative mind; it cannot inflame or inspire the drudge.

The differences are not minor—they are rather like the differences between Salieri and Mozart. Study after study shows that the very best designers produce structures that are faster, smaller, simpler, cleaner, and produced with less effort.[12] The differences between the great and the average approach an order of magnitude.

A little retrospection shows that although many fine, useful software systems have been designed by committees and built as part of multipart projects, those software systems that have excited passionate fans are those that are the products of one or a few designing minds, great designers. Consider Unix, APL, Pascal, Modula, the Smalltalk interface, even Fortran; and contrast them with Cobol, PL/I, Algol, MVS/370, and MS-DOS. (See Exhibit 1.)

Hence, although I strongly support the technology-transfer and curriculum-development efforts now under way, I think the most important single effort we can mount is to develop ways to grow great designers.

No software organization can ignore this challenge. Good managers, scarce though they be, are no scarcer than good designers. Great designers and great managers are both very rare. Most organizations spend considerable effort in finding and cultivating the management prospects; I know of none that spends equal effort in finding and developing the great designers upon whom the technical excellence of the products will ultimately depend.

My first proposal is that each software organization must determine and proclaim that great designers are as important to its success as great managers are, and that they can be expected to be similarly nurtured and rewarded. Not only salary, but the perquisites of recognition—office size, furnishings, personal technical equipment, travel funds, staff support—must be fully equivalent.

EXHIBIT 1 Exciting Versus Useful But Unexciting Software Products.

Exciting Products	
Yes	*No*
Unix	Cobol
APL	PL/I
Pascal	Algol
Modula	MVS/370
Smalltalk	MS-DOS
Fortran	

How to grow great designers? Space does not permit a lengthy discussion, but some steps are obvious:

• Systematically identify top designers as early as possible. The best are often not the most experienced.
• Assign a career mentor to be responsible for the development of the prospect, and carefully keep a career file.
• Devise and maintain a career-development plan for each prospect, including carefully selected apprenticeships with top designers, episodes of advanced formal education, and short courses, all interspersed with solo-design and technical-leadership assignments.
• Provide opportunities for growing designers to interact with and stimulate each other.

ACKNOWLEDGMENTS

I thank Gordon Bell, Bruce Buchanan, Rick Hayes-Roth, Robert Patrick, and, most especially, David Parnas for their insights and stimulating ideas, and Rebekah Bierly for the technical production of this article.

References

1. D.L. Parnas, "Designing Software for Ease of Extension and Contraction," *IEEE Transactions on Software Engineering,* Vol. 5, No. 2, March 1979, pp. 128–38.

2. G. Booch, "Object-Oriented Design," *Software Engineering with Ada,* 1983, Menlo Park, Calif.: Benjamin/Cummings.

3. *IEEE Transactions on Software Engineering* (special issue on artificial intelligence and software engineering), J. Mostow, guest ed., Vol. 11, No. 11, November 1985.

4. D.L. Parnas, "Software Aspects of Strategic Defense Systems," *American Scientist,* November 1985.

5. R. Balzer, "A 15-year Perspective on Automatic Programming," *IEEE Transactions on Software Engineering* (special issue on artificial intelligence and software engineering), J. Mostow, guest ed., Vol. 11, No. 11 (November 1985), pp. 1257–67.

6. *Computer* (special issue on visual programming), R.B. Graphton and T. Ichikawa, guest eds., Vol. 18, No. 8, August 1985.

7. G. Raeder, "A Survey of Current Graphical Programming Techniques," *Computer* (special issue on visual programming), R.B. Graphton and T. Ichikawa, guest eds., Vol. 18, No. 8, August 1985, pp. 11–25.

8. F.P. Brooks, *The Mythical Man-Month,* Reading, Mass.: Addison-Wesley, 1975, Chapter 14.

9. Defense Science Board, *Report of the Task Force on Military Software,* in press.

10. H.D. Mills, "Top-Down Programming in Large Systems," in *Debugging Techniques in Large Systems,* R. Ruskin, ed., Englewood Cliffs, N.J.: Prentice-Hall, 1971.

11. B.W. Boehm, "A Spiral Model of Software Development and Enhancement," 1985, TRW Technical Report 21-371-85, TRW, Inc., 1 Space Park, Redondo Beach, Calif. 90278.

12. H. Sackman, W.J. Erikson, and E.E. Grant, "Exploratory Experimental Studies Comparing Online and Offline Programming Performance," *Communications of the ACM,* Vol. 11, No. 1 (January 1968), pp. 3–11.

PROSPECTS FOR AN ENGINEERING DISCIPLINE OF SOFTWARE

The term "software engineering" was coined in 1968 as a statement of aspiration—a sort of rallying cry. That year, the North Atlantic Treaty Organization convened a workshop by that name to assess the state and prospects of software production. Capturing the imagination of software developers, the NATO phrase "software engineering" achieved popularity during the 1970s. It now refers to a collection of management processes, software tooling, and design activities for software development. The resulting practice, however, differs significantly from the practice of older forms of engineering.

WHAT IS ENGINEERING?

"Software engineering" is a label applied to a set of current practices for development. But using the word "engineering" to describe this activity takes considerable liberty with the common use of that term. The more customary usage refers to the disciplined application of scientific knowledge to resolve conflicting constraints and requirements for problems of immediate, practical significance.

Definitions of "engineering" abound. Although details differ, they share some common clauses:

- *Creating cost-effective solutions* . . . Engineering is not just about solving problems; it is about solving problems with economical use of all resources, including money.
- *. . . to practical problems* . . . Engineering deals with practical problems whose solutions matter to people outside the engineering domain—the customers.

Article by Mary Shaw. © 1990 IEEE. Reprinted, with permission, from (*IEEE Software;* 7, 11, 15–24; November/1990).

- *. . . by applying scientific knowledge* . . . Engineering solves problems in a particular way: by applying science, mathematics, and design analysis.
- *. . . to building things* . . . Engineering emphasizes the solutions, which are usually tangible artifacts.
- *. . . in the service of mankind.* Engineering not only serves the immediate customer, but it also develops technology and expertise that will support the society.

Engineering relies on codifying scientific knowledge about a technological problem domain in a form that is directly useful to the practitioner, thereby providing answers for questions that commonly occur in practice. Engineers of ordinary talent can then apply this knowledge to solve problems far faster than they otherwise could. In this way, engineering shares prior solutions rather than relying always on virtuoso problem solving.

Engineering practice enables ordinary practitioners so they can create sophisticated systems that work—unspectacularly, perhaps, but reliably. The history of development is marked by both successes and failures. The successes have often been virtuoso performances or the result of diligence and hard work. The failures have often reflected poor understanding of the problem to be solved, mismatch of solution to problem, or inadequate follow-through from design to implementation. Some failed by never working, others by overrunning cost and schedule budgets.

In current software practice, knowledge about techniques that work is not shared effectively with later projects, nor is there a large body of development knowledge organized for ready reference. Computer science has contributed some relevant theory, but practice proceeds largely independently of this organized knowledge. Given this track record, there are fundamental problems with the use of the term "software engineer."

Routine and Innovative Design

Engineering design tasks are of several kinds. One of the most significant distinctions separates routine from innovative design. Routine design involves solving familiar problems, reusing large portions of prior solutions. Innovative design, on the other hand, involves finding novel solutions to unfamiliar problems. Original designs are much more rarely needed than routine designs, so the latter is the bread and butter of engineering.

Most engineering disciplines capture, organize, and share design knowledge to make routine design simpler. Handbooks and manuals are often the carriers of this organized information. But current notations for software designs are not adequate for the task of both recording and communicating designs, so they fail to provide a suitable representation for such handbooks.

Software in most application domains is treated more often as original than routine—certainly more so than would be necessary if we captured and organized what we already know. One path to increased productivity is identifying applications that could be routine and developing appropriate support.

The current focus on reuse emphasizes capturing and organizing existing knowledge of a particular kind: knowledge expressed in the form of code. Indeed, subroutine libraries—especially of system calls and general-purpose mathematical routines—have been a staple of programming for decades. But this knowledge cannot be useful if programmers do not know about it or are not encouraged to use it. Furthermore, library components require more care in design, implementation, and documentation than similar components that are simply embedded in systems.

Practitioners recognize the need for mechanisms to share experience with good designs. This cry from the wilderness appeared on the Software Engineering News Group, a moderated electronic mailing list:

"In Chem E, when I needed to design a heat exchanger, I used a set of references that told me what the constants were . . . and the standard design equations. . . .

"In general, unless I, or someone else in my [software-] engineering group, has read or remembers and makes known a solution to a past problem, I'm doomed to recreate the solution. . . . I guess . . . the critical difference is the ability to put together little pieces of the problem that are relatively well known, without having to generate a custom solution for every application. . . .

"I want to make it clear that I am aware of algorithm and code libraries, but they are incomplete solutions to what I am describing. (There is no *Perry's Handbook for Software Engineering*.)"

This former chemical engineer is complaining that software lacks the institutionalized mechanisms of a mature engineering discipline for recording and disseminating demonstrably good designs and ways to choose among design alternatives. (*Perry's Chemical Engineering Handbook,* published by McGraw-Hill, is the standard design handbook for chemical engineering; it is about four inches thick and printed in tiny type on 8.5″ × 11″ tissue paper.)

Model for the Evolution of an Engineering Discipline

Historically, engineering has emerged from ad hoc practice in two stages: First, management and production techniques enable routine production. Later, the problems of routine production stimulate the development of a supporting science; the mature science eventually merges with established practice to yield professional engineering practice. Exhibit 1 shows this model.

The exploitation of a technology begins with craftsmanship: A set of problems must be solved, and they get solved any which way. They are solved by talented amateurs and by virtuosos, but no distinct professional class is dedicated to

EXHIBIT 1   Evolution of an Engineering Discipline. The lower lines track the technology, and the upper lines show how the entry of production skills and scientific knowledge contribute new capability to the engineering practice.

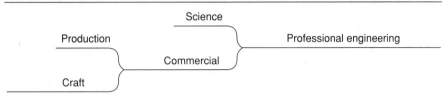

• Virtuosos and talented amateurs	• Skilled craftsmen	• Educated professionals
• Intuition and brute force	• Established procedure	• Analysis and theory
• Haphazard progress	• Pragmatic refinement	• Progress relies on science
• Casual transmission	• Training in mechanics	• Educated professional class
• Extravagant use of available materials	• Economic concern for cost and supply of materials	• Enabling new applications through analysis
• Manufacture for use rather than sale	• Manufacture for sale	• Market segmentation by product variety

problems of this kind. Intuition and brute force are the primary movers in design and construction. Progress is haphazard, particularly before the advent of good communication; thus, solutions are invented and reinvented. The transmission of knowledge between craftsmen is slow, in part because of underdeveloped communications, but also because the talented amateurs often do not recognize any special need to communicate.

Nevertheless, ad hoc practice eventually moves into the folklore. This craft stage of development sees extravagant use of available materials. Construction or manufacture is often for personal or local use or for barter, but there is little or no large-scale production in anticipation of resale. Community barn raisings are an example of this stage; so is software written by application experts for their own ends.

At some point, the product of the technology becomes widely accepted and demand exceeds supply. At that point, attempts are made to define the resources necessary for systematic commercial manufacture and to marshal the expertise for exploiting these resources. Capital is needed in advance to buy raw materials, so financial skills become important, and the operating scale increases over time.

As commercial practice flourishes, skilled practitioners are required for continuity and for consistency of effort. They are trained pragmatically in established procedures. Management may not know why these procedures work, but they know the procedures *do* work and how to teach people to execute them.

The procedures are refined, but the refinement is driven pragmatically: A modification is tried to see if it works, then incorporated in standard procedure if it does. Economic considerations lead to concerns over the efficiency of procedures and the use of materials. People begin to explore ways for production facilities to exploit the technology base; economic issues often point out problems in commercial practice. Management strategies for controlling development fit at this point of the model.

The problems of current practice often stimulate the development of a corresponding science. There is frequently a strong, productive interaction between commercial practice and the emerging science. At some point, the science becomes sufficiently mature to be a significant contributor to the commercial practice. This marks the emergence of engineering practice in the sense that we know it today—sufficient scientific basis to enable a core of educated professionals so they can apply the theory to analysis of problems and synthesis of solutions.

For most disciplines, this emergence occurred in the 18th and early 19th centuries as the common interests in basic physical understandings of natural science and engineering gradually drew together. The reduction of many empirical engineering techniques to a more scientific basis was essential to further engineering progress. And this liaison stimulated further advances in natural science. "An important and mutually stimulating tie-up between natural and engineering science, a development [that] had been discouraged for centuries by the long-dominant influence of early Greek thought, was at long last consummated," wrote historian James Kip Finch.[1]

The emergence of an engineering discipline lets technological development pass limits previously imposed by relying on intuition; progress frequently becomes dependent on science as a forcing function. A scientific basis is needed to drive analysis, which enables new applications and even market segmentation via product variety. Attempts are made to gain enough control over design to target specific products on demand.

Thus, engineering emerges from the commercial exploitation that supplants craft. Modern engineering relies critically on adding scientific foundations to craft and commercialization. Exploiting technology depends not only on scientific engineering but also on management and the marshaling of resources. Engineering and science support each other: Engineering generates good problems for science, and science, after finding good problems in the needs of practice, returns workable solutions. Science is often not driven by the immediate needs of engineering; however, good scientific problems often follow from an understanding of the problems that the engineering side of the field is coping with.

The engineering practice of software has recently come under criticism for lacking a scientific basis. The usual curriculum has been attacked for neglecting mathematics[2] and engineering science.[3] Although current software practice does not match the usual expectations of an engineering discipline, the model described here suggests that vigorous pursuit of applicable science and the reduction of that science to practice *can* lead to a sound engineering discipline of software.

Examples from Traditional Engineering

Two examples make this model concrete: the evolution of engineering disciplines as demonstrated by civil and chemical engineering. The comparison of the two is also illuminating, because they have very different basic organizations.

Civil Engineering: A Basis in Theory
Originally so-called to distinguish it from military engineering, civil engineering included all of civilian engineering until the middle of the 19th century. A divergence of interests led engineers specializing in other technologies to break away, and today civil engineers are the technical experts of the construction industry. They are concerned primarily with large-scale, capital-intensive construction efforts, like buildings, bridges, dams, tunnels, canals, highways, railroads, public water supplies, and sanitation. As a rule, civil-engineering efforts involve well-defined task groups that use appropriate tools and technologies to execute well-laid plans.

Although large civil structures have been built since before recorded history, only in the last few centuries has their design and construction been based on theoretical understanding rather than on intuition and accumulated experience. Neither the artisans of the Middle Ages nor of the ancient world showed any signs of the deliberate quantitative application of mathematics to determine the dimensions and shapes that characterizes modern civil engineering. But even without formal understanding, they documented pragmatic rules for recurring elements. Practical builders had highly developed intuitions about statics and relied on a few empirical rules.

The scientific revolution of the Renaissance led to serious attempts by Galileo Galilei, Filippo Brunelleschi, and others to explain structures and why they worked. Over a period of about 200 years, there were attempts to explain the composition of forces and bending of a beam. However, progress was slowed for a long time by problems in formulating basic notions like force, particularly the idea that gravity could be treated as just another force like all the others. Until the basic concepts were sorted out, it was not possible to do a proper analysis of the problem of combining forces (using vector addition) that we now teach to freshmen, nor was it possible to deal with strengths of materials.

Around 1700, Pierre Varignon and Isaac Newton developed the theory of statics to explain the composition of forces and Charles Augustin de Coulomb and Louis Marie Henri Navier explained bending with the theory of strength of materials. These now provide the basis for civil engineering. By the middle of the 18th century, civil engineers were tabulating properties of materials.

The mid-18th century also saw the first attempts to apply exact science to practical building. Pope Benedict ordered an analysis of St. Peter's dome in 1742 and 1743 to determine the cause of cracks and propose repairs; the analysis was based on the principle of virtual displacement and was carried out precisely (although the model is now known to fail to account properly for elasticity). By 1850, it was possible for Robert Stephenson's Britannia Tubular Bridge over the Menai Strait between Wales and England to be subjected to a formal structural analysis.

Thus, even after the basic theories were in hand, it took another 150 years before the theory was rich enough and mature enough to have direct utility at the scale of a bridge design.

Civil engineering is thus rooted in two scientific theories, corresponding to two classical problems. One problem is the composition of forces: finding the resultant force when multiple forces are combined. The other is the problem of bending: determining the forces within a beam supported at one end and weighted at the other. Two theories, statics and strength of materials, solve these problems; both were developed around 1700. Modern civil engineering is the application of these theories to the problem of constructing buildings.

"For nearly two centuries, civil engineering has undergone an irresistible transition from a traditional craft, concerned with tangible fashioning, towards an abstract science, based on mathematical calculation. Every new result of research in structural analysis and technology of materials signified a more rational design, more economic dimensions, or entirely new structural possibilities. There were no apparent limitations to the possibilities of analytical approach; there were no apparent problems in building construction [that] could not be solved by calculation," wrote Hans Straub in his history of civil engineering.[4]

You can date the transition from craft to commercial practice to the Romans' extensive transportation system of the first century. The underlying science emerged about 1700, and it matured to successful application to practice sometime between the mid-18th century and the mid-19th century. Exhibit 2 places civil engineering's significant events on my model of engineering evolution.

Chemical Engineering: A Basis in Practice

Chemical engineering is a very different kind of engineering than civil engineering. This discipline is rooted in empirical observations rather than in a scientific theory. It is concerned with practical problems of chemical manufacture; its scope covers the industrial-scale production of chemical

EXHIBIT 2   Evolution of Civil Engineering

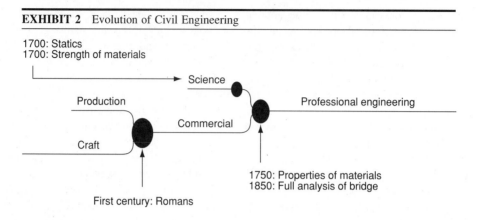

1700: Statics
1700: Strength of materials

Science

Production

Professional engineering

Commercial

Craft

First century: Romans

1750: Properties of materials
1850: Full analysis of bridge

goods: solvents, pharmaceuticals, synthetic fibers, rubber, paper, dyes, fertilizers, petroleum products, cooking oils, and so on. Although chemistry provides the specification and design of the basic reactions, the chemical engineer is responsible for scaling the reactions up from laboratory scale to factory scale. As a result, chemical engineering depends as heavily on mechanical engineering as on chemistry.

Until the late 18th century, chemical production was largely a cottage industry. The first chemical produced at industrial scale was alkali, which was required for the manufacture of glass, soap, and textiles. The first economical industrial process for alkali emerged in 1789, well before the atomic theory of chemistry explained the underlying chemistry. By the mid-19th century, industrial production of dozens of chemicals had turned the British Midlands into a chemical-manufacturing district. Laws were passed to control the resulting pollution, and pollution-control inspectors, called alkali inspectors, monitored plant compliance.

One of these alkali inspectors, G.E. Davis, worked in the Manchester area in the late 1880s. He realized that, although the plants he was inspecting manufactured dozens of different kinds of chemicals, there were not dozens of different procedures involved. He identified a collection of

functional operations that took place in those processing plants and were used in the manufacture of different chemicals. He gave a series of lectures in 1887 at the Manchester Technical School. The ideas in those lectures were imported to the US by the Massachusetts Institute of Technology in the latter part of the century and form the basis of chemical engineering as it is practiced today. This structure is called *unit operations;* the term was coined in 1915 by Arthur D. Little.

The fundamental problems of chemical engineering are the quantitative control of large masses of material in reaction and the design of cost-effective industrial-scale processes for chemical reactions.

The unit-operations model asserts that industrial chemical-manufacturing processes can be resolved into a relatively few units, each of which has a definite function and each of which is used repeatedly in different kinds of processes. The unit operations are steps like filtration and clarification, heat exchange, distillation, screening, magnetic separation, and flotation. The basis of chemical engineering is thus a pragmatically determined collection of very high-level functions that adequately and appropriately describe the processes to be carried out.

"Chemical engineering as a science . . . is not a composite of chemistry and mechanical and civil engineering, but a science of itself, the basis of which is those unit operations [that] in their proper sequence and coordination constitute a chemical process as conducted on the industrial scale. These operations . . . are not the subject matter of chemistry as such nor of mechanical engineering. Their treatment is in the quantitative way, with proper exposition of the laws controlling them and of the materials and equipment concerned in them," the American Institute of Chemical Engineers Committee on Education wrote in 1922.[5]

This is a very different kind of structure from that of civil engineering. It is a pragmatic, empirical structure—not a theoretical one.

You can date the transition from craft to commercial practice to the introduction of the LeBlanc process for alkali in 1789. The science emerged with the British chemist John Dalton's atomic theory in the early 19th century, and it matured to successful merger with large-scale mechanical processes in the 1890s. Exhibit 3 places chemical engineering's significant events on my model.

SOFTWARE TECHNOLOGY

Where does software stand as an engineering discipline? For software, the problem is appropriately an engineering problem: creating cost-effective solutions to practical problems, building things in the service of mankind.

Information-Processing as an Economic Force

The US computer business—including computers, peripherals, packaged software, and communications—was about $150 billion in 1989 and is projected to be more than $230 billion by 1992. The packaged-software component is projected to grow from $23.7 billion to $37.5 billion in this period, according to the Data Analysis Group's fourth-quarter 1989 forecasts. Services, including systems integration and in-house development, are not included in these figures.

Worldwide, software sales amounted to about $65 billion in 1989. This does not include the value of in-house development, which is a much larger activity. World figures are hard to estimate, but the cost of in-house software in the US alone may be in the range of $150 billion to $200 billion.[6] It is not clear how much modification after release (so-called "maintenance") is included in this figure. Thus, software is coming to dominate the cost of information processing.

The economic presence of information processing also makes itself known through the actual and opportunity costs of systems that do *not* work. Examples of costly system failures abound. Less obvious are the costs of computing that is not even tried: development backlogs so large that they discourage new requests, gigabytes of unprocessed raw data from satellites and space probes, and so

EXHIBIT 3   Evolution of Chemical Engineering

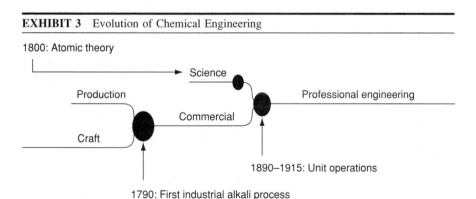

on. Despite very real (and substantial) successes, the litany of mismatches of cost, schedule, and expectations is a familiar one.

Growing Role of Software in Critical Applications

The US National Academy of Engineering recently selected the 10 greatest engineering achievements of the last 25 years.[7] Of the 10, three are informatics achievements: communications and information-gathering satellites, the microprocessor, and fiber-optic communication. Two more are direct applications of computers: computer-aided design and manufacturing and the computerized axial tomography scan. And most of the rest are computer-intensive: the Moon landing, advanced composite materials, the jumbo jet, lasers, and the application of genetic engineering to produce new pharmaceuticals and crops.

The conduct of science is increasingly driven by computational paradigms standing on equal footing with theoretical and experimental paradigms. Both scientific and engineering disciplines require very sophisticated computing. The demands are often stated in terms of raw processing power—"an exaflop (10^{18}) processor with teraword memory," "a petabyte (10^{15}) of storage," as one article put it[8] —but the supercomputing community is increasingly recognizing development, not mere raw processing, as a critical bottleneck.

Because of software's pervasive presence, the appropriate objective for its developers should be the effective delivery of computational capability to real users in forms that match their needs. The distinction between a system's computational component and the application it serves is often very soft— the development of effective software now often requires substantial application expertise.

Maturity of Development Techniques

Our development abilities have certainly improved over the 40 or so years of programming experience. Progress has been both qualitative and quantitative. Moreover, it has taken different forms in the worlds of research and practice.

One of the most familiar characterizations of this progress has been the shift from programming-in-the-small to programming-in-the-large. It is also useful to look at a shift that took place 10 years before that, from programming-any-which-way to programming-in-the-small. Exhibit 4 summarizes these shifts, both of which describe the focus of attention of the software research community.

Before the mid-1960s, programming was substantially ad hoc; it was a significant accomplishment to get a program to run at all. Complex software systems were created—some performed very well—but their construction was either highly empirical or a virtuoso activity. To make programs intelligible, we used mnemonics, we tried to be precise about writing comments, and we wrote prose specifications. Our emphasis was on small programs, which was all we could handle predictably.

We did come to understand that computers are symbolic information processors, not just number crunchers—a significant insight. But the abstractions of algorithms and data structures did not emerge until 1967, when Donald Knuth showed the utility of thinking about them in isolation from the particular programs that happened to implement them.

A similar shift in attitudes about specifications took place at about the same time, when Robert Floyd showed how attaching logical formulas to programs allows formal reasoning about the programs. Thus, the late 1960s saw a shift from crafting monolithic programs to an emphasis on algorithms and data structures. But the programs in question were still simple programs that execute once and then terminate.

You can view the shift that took place in the mid-1970s from programming-in-the-small to programming-in-the-large in much the same terms. Research attention turned to complex systems whose specifications were concerned not only with the functional relations of the inputs and outputs, but also with performance, reliability, and the states through which the system passed. This led to a shift in emphasis to interfaces and managing the programming process.

EXHIBIT 4 Significant Shifts in Research Attention

Attribute	1960 ± 5 years: programming any-which-way	1970 ± 5 years: programming -in-the-small	1980 ± 5 years: programming -in-the-large
Characteristic problems	Small programs	Algorithms and programming	Interfaces, management system structures
Data issues	Representing structure and symbolic information	Data structures and types	Long-lived databases, symbolic as well as numeric
Control issues	Elementary understanding of control flows	Programs execute once and terminate	Program assemblies execute continually
Specification issues	Mnemonics, precise use of prose	Simple input/output specifications	Systems with complex specifications
State space	State not well understood apart from control	Small, simple state space	Large, structured state space
Management focus	None	Individual effort	Team efforts, system lifetime maintenance
Tools, methods	Assemblers, core dumps	Programming language, compilers, linkers, loaders	Environments, integrated tools, documents

In addition, the data of complex systems often outlives the programs and may be more valuable, so we learned that we now have to worry about integrity and consistency of databases. Many of our programs (for example, the telephone switching system or a computer operating system) should *not* terminate; these systems require a different sort of reasoning than do programs that take input, compute, produce output, and terminate. In systems that run indefinitely, the sequence of system states is often much more important than the (possibly undesirable) termination condition.

The tools and techniques that accompanied the shift from programming-any-which-way to programming-in-the-small provided first steps toward systematic, routine development of small programs; they also seeded the development of a science that has matured only in the last decade. The tools and techniques that accompanied the shift from programming-in-the-small to programming-in-the-large were largely geared to supporting groups of programmers working together in orderly ways and to giving management a view into production processes. This directly supports the commercial practice of development.

Practical development proceeded to large complex systems much faster than the research community did. For example, the Sage missile-defense system of the 1950s and the Sabre airline-reservation system of the 1960s were successful interactive systems on a scale that far exceeded the maturity of the science. They appear to have been developed by excellent engineers who understood the requirements well and applied design and development methods from other (like electrical) engineering disciplines. Modern development methodologies are management procedures intended to guide large numbers of developers through similar disciplines.

The term "software engineering" was introduced in 1968 to name a conference convened by NATO to discuss problems of software production.[9] Despite the label, most of the discussion dealt with the challenge of progressing from the craft stage to the commercial stage of practice. In 1976, Barry Boehm proposed the definition of the term as "the practical application of scientific knowledge in the design and construction of computer programs and the associated documentation required to develop, operate, and maintain them."[10] This definition is consistent with traditional definitions of engineering, although Boehm noted the shortage of scientific knowledge to apply.

Unfortunately, the term is now most often used to refer to life-cycle models, routine methodologies, cost-estimation techniques, documentation frameworks, configuration-management tools, quality-assurance techniques, and other techniques for standardizing production activities. These technologies are characteristic of the commercial stage of evolution—"software management" would be a much more appropriate term.

Scientific Basis for Engineering Practice

Engineering practice emerges from commercial practice by exploiting the results of a companion science. The scientific results must be mature and rich enough to model practical problems. They must also be organized in a form that is useful to practitioners. Computer science has a few models and theories that are ready to support practice, but the packaging of these results for operational use is lacking.

Maturity of Supporting Science

Despite the criticism sometimes made by software producers that computer science is irrelevant to practical software, good models and theories *have* been developed in areas that have had enough time for the theories to mature.

In the early 1960s, algorithms and data structures were simply created as part of each program. Some folklore grew up about good ways to do certain sorts of things, and it was transmitted informally. By the mid-1960s, good programmers shared the intuition that if you get the data structures right, the rest of the program is much simpler. In the late 1960s, algorithms and data structures began to be abstracted from individual programs, and their essential properties were described and analyzed.

The 1970s saw substantial progress in supporting theories, including performance analysis and correctness. Concurrently, the programming implications of these abstractions were explored; abstract-data-type research dealt with such issues as:

• Specifications: abstract models and algebraic axioms.
• Software structure: bundling representation with algorithms.
• Language issues: modules, scope, and user-defined types.
• Information hiding: protecting the integrity of information not in the specification.
• Integrity constraints: invariants of data structures.
• Composition rules: declarations.

Both sound theory and language support were available by the early 1980s, and routine good practice now depends on this support.

Compiler construction is another good example. In 1960, simply writing a compiler at all was a major achievement; it is not clear that we really understood what a higher level language was. Formal syntax was first used systematically for Algol-60, and tools for processing it automatically (then called compiler compilers, but now called parser generators) were first developed in the mid-1960s and made practical in the 1970s. Also in the 1970s, we started developing theories of semantics and types, and the 1980s have brought significant progress toward the automation of compiler construction.

Both of these examples have roots in the problems of the 1960s and became genuinely practical in the 1980s. It takes a good 20 years from the time that work starts on a theory until it provides serious assistance to routine practice. Development periods of comparable length have also preceded the widespread use of systematic methods and technologies like structured programming, Smalltalk, and Unix, as Sam Redwine and colleagues have shown.[11] But the whole field of computing is only about 40 years old, and many theories are emerging in the research pipeline.

Interaction between Science and Engineering

The development of good models within the software domain follows this pattern:

We engineers begin by solving problems any way we can. After some time, we distinguish in those ad hoc solutions things that usually work and things that do not usually work. The ones that do work enter the folklore: People tell each other about them informally. As the folklore becomes more and more systematic, we codify it as written heuristics and rules of procedure. Eventually, that codification becomes crisp enough to support models and theories, together with the associated mathematics. These can then help improve practice, and experience from that practice can sharpen the theories. Furthermore, the improvement in practice let us think about harder problems—which we first solve ad hoc, then find heuristics for, eventually develop new models and theories for, and so on. Exhibit 5 illustrates this cycle.

The models and theories do not have to be fully fleshed out for this process to assist practice: The initial codification of folklore may be useful in and of itself.

This progression is illustrated in the use of machine language for control flow in the 1960s. In the late 1950s and the early 1960s, we did not have crisp notions about what an iteration or a conditional was, so we laid down special-purpose code, building each structure individually out of test and branch instructions.

EXHIBIT 5   Cycle of How Good Software Models Develop as a Result of the Interaction between Science and Engineering.

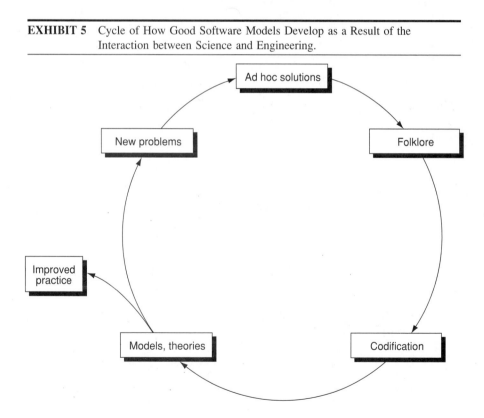

Eventually, a small set of patterns emerged as generally useful, generally easy to get right, and generally at least as good as the alternatives. Designers of higher level languages explicitly identified the most useful ones and codified them by producing special-purpose syntax. A formal result about the completeness of the structured constructs provided additional reassurance.

Now, almost nobody believes that new kinds of loops should be invented as a routine practice. A few kinds of iterations and a few kinds of conditionals are captured in the languages. They are taught as control concepts that go with the language; people use them routinely, without concern for the underlying machine code.

Further experience led to verifiable formal specifications of these statements' semantics and of the programs that used them. Experience with the formalization in turn refined the statements supported in programming languages. In this way, ad hoc practice entered a period of folklore and eventually matured to have conventional syntax and semantic theories that explain it.

Where Is Software?

Where, then, does current software practice lie on the path to engineering? It is still in some cases craft and in some cases commercial practice. A science is beginning to contribute results, and, for isolated examples, you can argue that professional engineering is taking place. (Exhibit 6 shows where software practice fits on my model.)

That is not, however, the common case.

There are good grounds to expect that there will eventually be an engineering discipline of software. Its nature will be technical, and it will be based in computer science. Although we have not yet matured to that state, it is an achievable goal.

The next tasks for the software profession are

• to pick an appropriate mix of short-term, pragmatic, possible purely empirical contributions that help stabilize commercial practice and
• to invest in long-term efforts to develop and make available basic scientific contributions.

The profession must take five basic steps on its path to becoming a true engineering discipline:

Understand the Nature of Expertise

Proficiency in any field requires not only higher order reasoning skills but also a large store of facts together with a certain amount of context about their implications and appropriate use. Studies have demonstrated this across a wide range of problem domains, including medical diagnosis, physics, chess, financial analysis, architecture, scientific research, policy decision making, and others, as Herbert Simon described in the paper "Human Experts and

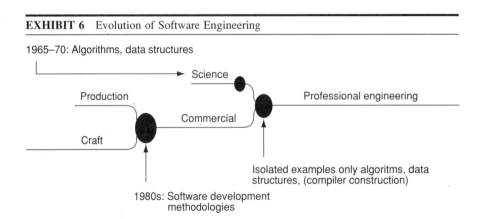

EXHIBIT 6 Evolution of Software Engineering

1965–70: Algorithms, data structures

Science

Production

Commercial

Craft

Professional engineering

Isolated examples only algoritms, data structures, (compiler construction)

1980s: Software development methodologies

Knowledge-Based Systems" presented at the 1987 IFIP Working Group 10.1 Workshop on Concepts and Characteristics of Knowledge-Based Systems.

An expert in a field must know about 50,000 chunks of information, where a chunk is any cluster of knowledge sufficiently familiar that it can be remembered rather than derived. Furthermore, in domains where there are full-time professionals, it takes no less than 10 years for a world-class expert to achieve that level of proficiency.[12]

Thus, fluency in a domain requires content and context as well as skills. In the case of natural-language fluency, E.D. Hirsch has argued that abstract skills have driven out content; students are expected (unrealistically) to learn general skills from a few typical examples rather than by a "piling up of information"; and intellectual and social skills are supposed to develop naturally without regard to the specific content.[13]

However, Hirsch wrote, specific information is important at all stages. Not only are the specific facts important in their own right, but they serve as carriers of shared culture and shared values. A software engineer's expertise includes facts about computer science in general, software design elements, programming idioms, representations, and specific knowledge about the program of current interest. In addition, it requires skill with tools: the language, environment, and support software with which this program is implemented.

Hirsch provided a list of some 5,000 words and concepts that represent the information actually possessed by literate Americans. The list goes beyond simple vocabulary to enumerate objects, concepts, titles, and phrases that implicitly invoke cultural context beyond their dictionary definitions. Whether or not you agree in detail with its composition, the list and accompanying argument demonstrate the need for connotations as well as denotations of the vocabulary.

Similarly, a programmer needs to know not only a programming language but also the system calls supported by the environment, the general-purpose libraries, the application-specific libraries, and how to combine invocations of these definitions effectively. The programmer must be familiar with the global definitions of the program of current interest and the rules about their use. In addition, a developer of application software must understand application-area issues.

Simply put, the engineering of software would be better supported if we knew better what specific content a software engineer should know. We could organize the teaching of this material so useful subsets are learned first, followed by progressively more sophisticated subsets. We could also develop standard reference materials as carriers of the content.

Recognize Different Ways to Get Information

Given that a large body of knowledge is important to a working professional, we as a discipline must ask how software engineers should acquire the knowledge, either as students or as working professionals. Generally speaking, there are three ways to get a piece of information you need: You can remember it, you can look it up, or you can derive it. These have different distributions of costs, as Exhibit 7 shows.

Memorization requires a relatively large initial investment in learning the material, which is then available for instant use.

Reference materials require a large investment by the profession for developing both the organization and the content; each student must then learn how to use the reference materials and then do so as a working professional.

Deriving information may involve ad hoc creation from scratch, it may involve instantiation of a formal model, or it may involve inferring meaning from other available information. To the extent that formal models are available, their formulation requires a substantial initial investment. Students first learn the models, then apply them in practice. Because each new application requires the model to be applied anew, the cost in use may be very high.[13]

Each professional's allocation of effort among these alternatives is driven by what he has already

---

EXHIBIT 7   Cost Distributions for the Three Ways to Get a Piece of Information

Method	Infrastructure cost	Initial-learning cost	Cost of use in practice
Memory	Low	High	Low
Reference	High	Low	Medium
Derivation	Medium-high	Medium	High

---

learned, by habits developed during that education, and by the reference materials available. Today, general-purpose reference material for software is scarce, although documentation for specific computer systems, languages, and applications may be extensive. Even when documentation is available, however, it may be underused because it is poorly indexed or because developers have learned to prefer fresh derivation to use of existing solutions. The same is true of subroutine libraries.

Simply put, software engineering requires investment in the infrastructure cost—in creating the materials required to organize information, especially reference material for practitioners.

Encourage Routine Practice

Good engineering practice for routine design depends on the engineer's command of factual knowledge and design skills and on the quality of reference materials available. It also depends on the incentives and values associated with innovation.

Unfortunately, computer-science education has prepared developers with a background that emphasizes fresh creation almost exclusively. Students learn to work alone and to develop programs from scratch. They are rarely asked to understand software systems they have not written. However, just as natural-language fluency requires instant recognition of a core vocabulary, programming fluency should require an extensive vocabulary of definitions that the programmer can use familiarly, without repeated recourse to documentation.

Fred Brooks has argued that one of the great hopes for software engineering is the cultivation of great designers.[15] Indeed, innovative designs require great designers. But great designers are rare, and most designs need not be innovative. Systematic presentation of design fragments and techniques that are known to work can enable designers of ordinary talent to produce effective results for a wide range of more routine problems by using prior results (buying or growing, in Brooks's terms) instead of always building from scratch.

It is unreasonable to expect a designer or developer to take advantage of scientific theories or experience if the necessary information is not readily available. Scientific results need to be recast in operational form; the important information from experience must be extracted from examples. The content should include design elements, components, interfaces, interchange representations, and algorithms. A conceptual structure must be developed so the information can be found when it is needed. These facts must be augmented with analysis techniques or guidelines to support selection of alternatives that best match the problem at hand.

A few examples of well-organized reference materials already exist. For example, the summary flowchart of William Martin's sorting survey[16] captured in one page the information a designer needed to choose among the then-current sorting techniques. William Cody and William Waite's manual for implementing elementary mathematical functions[17] gives for each function the basic strategy and special considerations needed to adapt that strategy to various hardware architectures.

Although engineering has traditionally relied on handbooks published in book form, a software engineers' handbook must be on line and interactive. No other alternative allows for rapid distribution of updates at the rate this field changes, and no other alternative has the potential for smooth integration with on-line design tools. The on-line incarnation will require solutions to a variety of electronic-publishing problems, including distribution, validation, organization and search, and collection and distribution of royalties.

Simply put, software engineering would benefit from a shift of emphasis in which both reference materials and case studies of exemplary software designs are incorporated in the curriculum. The discipline must find ways to reward preparation of material for reference use and the development of good case studies.

Expect Professional Specializations

As software practice matures toward engineering, the body of substantive technical knowledge required of a designer or developer continues to grow. In some areas, it has long since grown large enough to require specialization—for example, database administration was long ago separated from the corresponding programming. But systems programming has been resistant to explicit recognition of professional specialties.

In the coming decade, we can expect to see specialization of two kinds:

- internal specialization as the technical content in the core of software grows deeper and
- external specialization with an increased range of applications that require both substantive application knowledge and substantive computing knowledge.

Internal specialties are already starting to be recognizable for communications, reliability, real-time programming, scientific computing, and graphics, among others. Because these specialties rely critically on mastery of a substantial body of computer science, they may be most appropriately organized as postbaccalaureate education.

External specialization is becoming common, but the required dual expertise is usually acquired informally (and often incompletely). Computational specializations in various disciplines can be supported via joint programs involving both computer science and the application department; this is being done at some universities.

Simply put, software engineering will require explicit recognition of specialties. Educational opportunities should be provided to support them. However, this should not be done at the cost of a solid foundation in computer science and, in the case of external specialization, in the application discipline.

Improve the Coupling Between Science and Commercial Practice

Good science is often based on problems underlying the problems of production. This should be as true for computer science as for any other discipline. Good science depends on strong interactions between researchers and practitioners. However, cultural differences, lack of access to large, complex systems, and the sheer difficulty of understanding those systems have interfered with the communication that supports these interactions.

Similarly, the adoption of results from the research community has been impeded by poor understanding of how to turn a research result into a useful element of a production environment. Some companies and universities are already developing cooperative programs to bridge this gap, but the logistics are often daunting.

Simply put, an engineering basis for software will evolve faster if constructive interaction between research and production communities can be nurtured.

ACKNOWLEDGMENTS

This article benefited from comments by Allen Newell, Norm Gibbs, Frank Friedman, Tom Lane, and the other authors of articles in this special issue. Most important, Eldon Shaw fostered my appreciation for engineering. Without his support, this work would not have been possible, so I dedicate this article to his memory.

This work was supported by the US Defense Dept. and a grant from Mobay Corp.

Notes

1. J.K. Finch, *Engineering and Western Civilization,* McGraw-Hill, New York, 1951.

2. E.W. Dijkstra, "On the Cruelty of Really Teaching Computing Science," *Comm. ACM,* Dec. 1989, pp. 1,398–1,404.

3. D.L. Parnas, "Education for Computing Professionals," *Computer,* Jan. 1990, pp. 17–22.

4. H. Straub, *A History of Civil Engineering: An Outline from Ancient to Modern Times,* MIT Press, Cambridge, Mass., 1964.

5. F.J. van Antwerpen, "The Origins of Chemical Engineering," in *History of Chemical Engineering,* W.F. Furter, ed., American Chemical Society, Washington, D.C., 1980, pp. 1–14.

6. Computer Science and Technology Board, National Research Council, *Keeping the US Computer Industry Competitive,* National Academy Press, Washington, D.C., 1990.

7. National Academy of Engineering, *Engineering and the Advancement of Human Welfare: 10 Outstanding Achievements 1964–1989,* National Academy Press, Washington, D.C., 1989.

8. E. Levin, "Grand Challenges to Computational Science," *Comm. ACM,* Dec. 1989, pp. 1,456–1,457.

9. *Software Engineering: Report on a Conference Sponsored by the NATO Science Committee, Garmisch, Germany, 1968,* P. Naur and B. Randell, eds., Scientific Affairs Div., NATO, Brussels, 1969.

10. B.W. Boehm, "Software Engineering," *IEEE Trans. Computers,* Dec. 1976, pp. 1,226–1,241.

11. S.T. Redwine et al., "DoD-Related Software Technology Requirements, Practices, and Prospects for the Future," Tech. Report P-1788, Inst. Defense Analyses, Alexandria, Va., 1984.

12. S.T. Redwine et al., "DoD-Related Software Technology Requirements, Practices, and Prospects for the Future," Tech. Report P-1788, Inst. Defense Analyses, Alexandria, Va., 1984.

13. E.D. Hirsch, Jr., *Cultural Literacy: What Every American Needs to Know,* Houghton Mifflin, Boston, 1989.

14. M. Shaw, D. Giuse, and R. Reddy, "What a Software Engineer Needs to Know I: Vocabulary," tech. report CMU/SEI-89-TR-30, Carnegie Mellon Univ., Pittsburgh, Aug. 1989.

15. F.P. Brooks, Jr., "No Silver Bullet: Essence and Accidents of Software Engineering," *Information Processing 86,* pp. 1,069–1,076.

16. W.A. Martin, "Sorting," *ACM Computing Surveys,* Dec. 1971, pp. 147–174.

17. W.J. Cody, Jr., and W.M. Waite, *Software Manual for the Elementary Functions,* Prentice-Hall, Englewood Cliffs, N.J., 1980.

THE FUTURE ENGINEERING OF SOFTWARE: A MANAGEMENT PERSPECTIVE

There are many perspectives from which to view the future of software. This article focuses on the engineering process that underlies software development. This process is critical in determining what products are feasible. We support a quantitative approach and believe that software engineering must move in this direction to become a true engineering discipline and to satisfy the future demands for software development. Further, we want to spotlight some areas of software engineering that we believe have received less attention than they merit. We begin with a brief summary of how

Article by Victor R. Basili and John D. Musa. © 1991 IEEE. Reprinted, with permission, from (*IEEE Computer;* 20, 4, 90–96; September/1991).

information technology has affected both institutions and individuals in the past few decades.

The Past

In the 1960s, information technology penetrated institutions. This decade could be called the functional era, when we learned how to exploit information technology to meet institutional needs. Institutional functions began to interlink with software.

In the 1970s, the need to develop software in a timely, planned, and controlled fashion became apparent. This decade introduced phased life-cycle models and schedule tracking. It could be called the schedule era.

The 1980s might be named the cost era. Hardware costs continued to decrease, as they had from the early days of computing, and the personal computer created a mass market that drove software prices down as well. In this environment, information technology permeated every cranny of our institutions, making them absolutely dependent on it. At the same time, it became available to individuals. Once low-cost applications became practical and widely implemented, the importance of productivity in software development increased substantially. Various cost models came into use and resource tracking became commonplace.

The problem with these approaches to software development is their focus on single, isolated attributes. We did not understand the relations among functionality, schedule, and cost well enough to control trade-offs. We did not effectively define other attributes such as reliability, necessary for engineering a software product that satisfies a user's needs. We did not learn enough about how to engineer and improve products based on experience.

The Future

We believe the 1990s will be the quality era, in which software quality is quantified and brought to the center of the development process. This new focus on quality will be driven by the dependence of institutions on information processing. We can also expect software vendors to try to create new demand in the consumer mass market. Thus, home applications might expand rapidly in the nineties, although the time required for cultural acceptance of some applications could delay this past the turn of the century.

The consumer mass market, with its potential for large sales but rather unsophisticated users, increases the demands on quality. These demands, when satisfied, intensify competition in the institutional market because institutions can improve quality for their customers if better quality is available in the information systems they depend on. In the future, this overall intense competition will be international.

In this article we discuss software quality, software engineering that uses models and metrics to achieve quality, the processes needed to achieve software quality, and how to put these processes and technology into practice.

SOFTWARE QUALITY

Quality is not a single idea, but a multidimensional concept. The dimensions of quality include the entity of interest, the viewpoint on that entity, and the quality attributes of that entity. Entities include the final deliverable, intermediate products such as the requirements document, and process components such as the design phase. Example viewpoints are the final customer's, the developing organization's, and the project manager's. The quality attributes that are relevant in a given situation depend on both the entity and the viewpoint. For example, readability is an important quality attribute of a requirements document from the designer's viewpoint. Elapsed time is an important quality attribute of the design phase from the project manager's viewpoint. It is important to quantify these dimensions wherever possible.

Product Quality

The ultimate quality goal is user satisfaction. Therefore, we will consider quantitative specification of final product attributes that satisfy explicit and implicit user needs. The attributes most often named as significant are functionality, reliability, cost, and product availability date. Reliability often ranks first.

It is possible to reduce the list of attributes to three by taking a broad view of reliability as the probability (over an appropriate time period) that the product will operate without user dissatisfactions (denoted "failures"). In this view, if a function is missing when the user needs it, the event marks a failure. Thus, the attribute of functionality folds into the attribute of reliability.

The degree of quality is the closeness with which the foregoing attributes meet user needs. Competition makes it necessary to improve the match. It will increasingly force joint supplier-user setting of objectives and measurement to compare them with the results.

Software quality attributes are not independent; they influence each other. If we think of reliability in terms of failure intensity or failures per unit time, we can define a quality figure of merit as the reciprocal of the product of failure intensity, cost, and development duration. (The real relationship among the factors is probably somewhat more complex than simply taking their product, but this formulation will serve our purposes here.)

The quality figure of merit always characterizes the state of the art. Consequently, a lower failure intensity (increase in reliability) will generally require an increase in cost or development duration or both. As technology advances, the quality figure of merit increases and the lower failure intensity is achieved at lower cost or less development time or both.

Process Quality

Meeting quality objectives in the delivered product requires a suitable quality-oriented development process. You can view this process as a series of stages, each with feedback paths. In each stage, an intermediate supplier develops an intermediate product for an intermediate user—the next stage. Each stage also receives an intermediate product from the preceding stage. Each intermediate product will have certain intermediate quality attributes that affect the quality attributes of the delivered product, but are not necessarily identical to them. For example, in the design stage, designers are the users for the requirements specification. They develop the system architecture and unit specifications, defining them in a design document, which is their intermediate product. Important quality attributes of the design document are readability and completeness in meeting system requirements.

In addition to viewing the development process as a series of stages with intermediate products, we need to look at it as a semistructured cognitive activity of a social group. Human cognitive processes and social dynamics in software development affect product quality. For example, some evidence suggests that informal communication networks have much more impact than documents in the software development process.

We need models of the development process, measures of its characteristics, and practical mechanisms for obtaining those measures. We need to relate the measures to the quality attributes of the deliverable product. Then, we can control the development process and adjust it to meet the attribute objectives. For example, what are the appropriate methods for developing a product that must have high reliability and what leeway in cost or delivery is permissible to achieve it?

Finally, we need models of how users will employ the system and of the relative criticality of the various operations in this context.

ENGINEERING WITH MODELS AND METRICS

We have had quantitative approaches to the design and implementation of pure hardware systems for some time. Scheduling, cost estimation, and reliability technologies for hardware were fairly well developed by the 1960s, but similar technologies for software have lagged by 20 to 30 years. We believe this is due to lesser understanding of software development and the essential differences between hardware and software engineering (for example, the differences between production and development).

In spite of the complexity of the task, we must model, measure, and manage software development processes and products if we are to optimize the balance among quality attributes and satisfy user needs. Understanding where the time and effort are going and what processes provide the attributes needed for a more reliable product will help us refine models of quality attributes and the interrelationship between process and product.

To do this we must isolate and categorize the components of the software engineering discipline, define notations for representing them, and specify interrelationships among them as they are manipulated. The discipline's components consist of various processes and process components (for example, lifecycle models and phases, methods, techniques, tools), products (for example, code components, requirements, designs, specifications, test plans), and other forms of experience (for example, resource models, defect models, quality models, economic models).

We need to build descriptive models of the discipline components to improve our understanding of

1. The nature and characteristics of the processes and products.
2. The variations among them.
3. The weaknesses and strengths of both, and
4. Mechanisms to predict and control them.

We have models for some components. For example, there are several mathematical models of programs and modules, such as predicate calculus, functions, and state machines.

Cost and schedule models have moved from research and development into application. There are parameterized cost models for using historical data to predict the project costs. For example, many organizations are using or studying cost models like Cost Constructive Model (Cocomo).[1] Software Life-Cycle Management (Slim), Software Productivity, Quality, and Reliability Model (SPQR), and Estimacs.[2]

Software reliability engineering models are coming into practice.[2] The exponential and logarithmic nonhomogeneous Poisson models are the most widely used models in the industry today. Japan has made some use of S-curve models.

We have models and modeling notations for various life-cycle processes. These key modeling technologies form the basis for a quantitative approach to the engineering of software-based systems—enough to start the advance of software engineering from craft to science.

However, many more areas require models. For example, little work has been done in organizing and systematizing the practical knowledge accumulating in various application domains.

We need to screen the models that do exist. They often require more formal definition, further analysis, and integration to deepen our understanding of their components and interactions. We need to eliminate models that are not appropriate or useful.

Based upon analysis of these descriptive models, we must build prescriptive models that improve the products and the processes for creating them. Prescriptive models must relate to quality attributes. We must provide feedback for project control and learn to package successful experience.

Because the overall solutions are both technical and managerial, model-building requires the support of many disciplines. The next several sections focus on areas of technology that we believe will play an important role in deepening our understanding and attainment of software quality in the next decade.

Formal Methods

To improve our understanding of the software product itself and to enable the abstraction of its functionality, computer scientists have developed product models based on mathematical formalisms. These formalisms include predicate calculus, functions, and state machines (based on the work of R. Floyd, E. Dijkstra, C. Hoare, H. Mills, and others). These models have had theoretical value for many years, but they have not been used effectively in practice. This is largely due to the inability to scale them up to reasonable-size systems.

We are now beginning to see some practical application of formal methods in software development (for example, the Vienna Development Method, Z, and Cleanroom). They also may add to the associated discipline of correctness-oriented development. For an introduction to formal methods, see Wing.[3]

Design Methods

The 1980s brought a major breakthrough in software design with the introduction of object-oriented design methods, technologies, and languages.[4] This approach will continue to have a major effect on software design in the 1990s. For example, we expect object-oriented technologies to play a major part in the definition of integrated support environments. The notion of managing and designing systems by objects will be better defined and will change the way we think about systems. Object-oriented approaches, like functional decomposition approaches, will become part of the software engineer's set of intellectual tools. They have already begun to affect the creation of reusable software, and this effect is expected to increase as we learn more about software engineering and reuse.

Programming Languages

Languages that support object-oriented design and programming, in whole or in part, will continue to evolve (for example, Ada, Objective C, C++, Smalltalk). Notations will also evolve for formalizing higher level abstractions, such as requirements and specifications. The higher the level of these languages, the more likely they will become application oriented and specialized. For example, we will continue to see fourth-generation languages introduced for specific applications; we will also see more effective translation of these

higher order languages into executable forms. These notations will become basic tools in the engineering process for software.

Measurement Approaches

Measurement is associated with modeling. We must base measures on models to determine if they are performing as planned. In the past, measurement has been metric oriented, rather than model oriented. In other words, it has involved collecting data without an explicit goal, model, and context. For example, in analyzing a test process, project managers may collect data such as program size or number of defects. But they may be unable to compare the data to other projects unless the models used to specify the size and defect measures are documented with sufficient contextual information to interpret the data.

We have begun to see more organized approaches to measurement—approaches based on models and driven by goals.[5] These approaches integrate goals with models of the software processes, products, and quality perspectives of interest. They tailor these goals and models to the specific needs of the project and the organization. For example, if the goal is to evaluate how well a system test method detects defects, then models of the test process and defects must be available. Information that supports interpretation must be collected and integrated. For example, how effectively was the test method applied? How well did the testers understand the requirements? How many failures occurred after system test compared with similar projects?

Mechanisms for defining measurable goals have come into use. These include the goal/question/metric paradigm, the quality function deployment approach,[6] and the software quality metrics approach.[7] We expect the use of these frameworks to increase in the future.

Usage and Reduced-Operation Software

Software usage will guide software development. An operational profile, the set of expected user operations and their probabilities of occurrence, will be defined at the same time as the system requirements. Operations are akin to functions except that they also incorporate the concept of the environment. Operations are classified by criticality where appropriate. The operational profile, adjusted for criticality, will guide the setting of priorities and allocation of effort for the entire development process.

There is an excellent chance that we will see the emergence of reduced-operation software. ROS is the software analog of reduced instruction-set computing. It is based on the observation that most software has a few operations that are used most of the time and many operations that are used rarely. The rarely used operations eat up a large proportion of development, documentation, and maintenance costs. They also complicate the system, making user training much more difficult. The ROS approach avoids implementing as many of the rarely used operations as possible. In many cases, they can be replaced by sequences of more basic, frequently used operations. System and software designers might set up these sequences and document them for users or leave them for users to determine, since many users may never require them.

Reuse

In the past, reuse was limited mostly to the code level and based on individual experience. Interest and technology development have recently surged in this area. We can and must reuse all kinds of software experience, but reusing an object requires the concurrent reuse of the objects associated with it. For example, we have seen the development of faceted schemes, templates, and search strategies associated with reusable software components. Objects may have to be tailored for a particular project's needs; hence, reusable objects must be evaluated for reuse potential and processes must be established for enabling reuse.

Reuse will grow in the next decade based on better understanding of its implications and on development of supporting technology. Object-oriented design should make reuse easier.

Cognitive Psychology

Cognitive psychology is the study of problem solving. We can use its disciplines to study different intellectual activities in the software development process. To date, very little research based on cognitive psychology has been performed in software engineering, but there is substantial evidence of its promise. Software engineering, after all, is primarily a problem-solving activity. Unfortunately, few researchers are trained and experienced in both fields. The two fields also have significant cultural differences, which can make cross-fertilization difficult. For example, many software researchers pride themselves on the controlled discipline and logic they believe is central to their approach to problems. Cognitive psychologists sometimes focus on the deficits and weaknesses they find inherent in all human intellectual processes.

Application of cognitive psychology in software engineering has generally focused on the human-computer interface. This focus is implicit in computer-aided software engineering tools. CASE has championed such human-computer interface design principles as protecting users from mistakes, helping them navigate easily through the commands and data, providing for direct manipulation of objects (for example, screen editors), and using metaphors (for example, the "sheets of paper" metaphor of windows).

This tools-oriented work will undoubtedly continue, but we are likely to see more focus on the internal problem-solving activity of the individual and the methodologies and environmental factors that can enhance the quality and efficiency of this activity. For example, people are known to have limited short-term memory. Are there software development methods that deal with this limitation in a way that increases programmer productivity? Does this limitation tend to produce certain types of faults? If so, can we use that information to improve reliability and debug more efficiently?

Early work of Curtis, Krasner, and Iscoe[8] indicates that application domain knowledge is a principal factor in the wide performance differences among software developers. This belies the frequently held concept that software development is a domain-independent activity that can be abstracted and taught totally by itself. The findings argue for a certain degree of specialization among programmers. Attention must be given to organizing, publishing, and advancing knowledge in specific domains and to providing corresponding education, either formal or on-the-job.

A study of expert debuggers[9] shows that the stereotype of these people as isolated software "freaks" is not true. The best debuggers have excellent communication, negotiation, team building, and other social skills. They generally have a clear vision of the system's purpose and architecture. They typically cultivate an extensive network of experts they can call on. The career importance of these social skills indicates that education in these areas should start in the university and continue in the workplace.

Software Sociology

Most software projects are group activities, involving all the complexities of group dynamics, communication networks, and organizational politics. The study of group behavior in software development is in its infancy, but like the study of individuals, it promises to improve our understanding of the development process, particularly at the front end. Many observers believe that improving this phase of development could have the most impact on software quality and productivity.

Software developers commonly face inefficiencies and quality degradation that result from highly volatile requirements. Some change is unavoidable because user requirements evolve with time. However, poor communication accounts for much of this problem. Research on this problem[8] has shown that successful software development is a joint process in which the developer learns the application domain and user operations, and the user learns the design realities and available choices.

Negotiation and conflict resolution are inescapable parts of the process. Managing the learning and negotiation processes intelligently is critical to success. So is making decisions in a timely fashion. In fact, there is some indication that the percentage of unresolved design issues at a given point in the project life cycle may be a good indicator of progress and predictor of future trouble. Measures can play an important role in making the negotiation process concrete and the negotiated agreements specific.

Inadequate documentation has been blamed for many project problems that appear to stem from poor communication. However, documentation may not be the real culprit.[8] Many developers do not consider it possible to maintain documentation that is sufficiently current to meet their needs. They get their information through informal networks. This suggests that we devote more effort to encouraging, cultivating, maintaining, and supporting such networks.

IMPROVING SOFTWARE QUALITY

Engineering processes require models of the various entities within a discipline. The models must approximate reality and include a controlled feedback loop to monitor the differences between the models and reality. In software engineering, we have often not had enough models to complete the process. Where we do have models (for example, for costs and schedules), we do not sufficiently understand the relationship between them and the other discipline entities.

Models are necessary for focusing attention on the multiplicity of issues necessary for engineering a product. But so is a process that supports feedback, learning, and the refinement of the models for the environment.

Manufacturing has learned to control production using models and measurements of the process and product. Feedback processes, such as the Plan-Do-Check-Act cycle,[10] have provided quality-oriented processes for manufacturing. The Deming paradigm uses models and measures to control and engineer the characteristics of processes and products. The Plan phase sets up measures of quality attributes as targets and establishes methods for achieving them. The Do phase produces the product in compliance with development standards and quality guidelines. The Check phase compares the product with the quality targets. During the Act phase, problem reports become the basis for corrective action. Achieving the quality target is the gate to the next phase.

Although software development is fundamentally different from manufacturing, at some level the same principles apply. We need a closed-loop process with feedback to the project and the organization. The process must consider the nature of software development. The quality improvement paradigm[5] is an example approach. It can help in applying, evolving, tailoring, and refining various models and ranges of measurements in software development.

In QIP, *planning* requires models of the various software products and product quality attributes, processes and process quality attributes, and environmental factors. The models must be quantifiable and the measures for them must be set. Developers must understand particular project needs with respect to such factors as functionality, schedule, cost, and reliability. Project and corporate goals are set relative to measurements associated with the models. Unlike manufacturing, there is no single model of the process. Developers must choose the process to meet the mix of quality attributes required by a particular product's user.

Doing and *checking* require following the selected process and taking measurements to track conformance with the models. Because many models are primitive, we also need to track whether the model's predictions are valid and, if they are not, modify the models to come closer to reality.

Acting requires a closed-loop project cycle with feedback for modifying models as well as the processes. It involves analyzing and packaging the experience gained on a project so that it is available to other projects. Analysis includes a post-mortem review of the feedback data to evaluate the existing models, determine problems, record findings, and recommend future model improvements. Packaging involves implementing model improvements and storing the knowledge gained in an experience database available for future projects. This represents a closed-loop organization cycle that transfers learning from project to project.

Emphasis on the engineering process will help achieve quality goals for software development. It also supports the transfer of technology within and from outside an organization.

MAKING SOFTWARE ENGINEERING TECHNOLOGY MORE TRANSFERABLE

Transferring technology within an organization requires an evolutionary, experimental approach, similar to QIP. Such an approach bases improvements in software products and processes on the continual accumulation of evaluated experience (learning) in a form that can be effectively understood and modified (such as with experience models). Experience models must be integrated into an experience base that can be accessed and modified to meet the needs of new projects (reuse). The evolving process and product models can help in technology transfer. They represent what we know and can apply in the software development process.

This paradigm implies the separation of project development, which we can assign to a project organization, from the systematic learning and packaging of reusable experiences, which we can assign to a so-called *experience factory*.[5] The project organization's role is to deliver the systems required by the user, taking advantage of whatever experience is available. The experience factory's role is to monitor and analyze project developments; to package experience for reuse in the form of knowledge, processes, tools, and products; and to supply these to the project organization upon request.

In this sense, the experience factory is a logical organization, a physical organization, or both. It supports project developments by acting as a repository for experience, analyzing and synthesizing the experience, and supplying it to various projects on demand. The experience factory evaluates experience and builds models and measures of software processes, products, and other forms of knowledge. It uses people, documents, and automated support to do so.

TRANSFERRING SOFTWARE TECHNOLOGY INTO AN ORGANIZATION

There has been little success to date in transferring new software engineering methodologies and tools into active practice, despite the potential benefits of improving the development process in an industry of software's size and importance. This failure may be partly because software engineering is a process rather than a product. It is an abstract intellectual activity with limited visibility, which makes it much more difficult to transfer.

Also, research and practice in software engineering have been divided, both organizationally and by cultural values, impeding good communication.

Most practicing software engineers are not aware of all the possibilities for improvement that exist. Most researchers are not aware of the full range of problems that must be solved before new technologies can be applied in practice. Tools and methodologies are often difficult to learn or to use or both. Although most people realize that improvement means change in practice, few have been willing to deal with the cultural, motivational, and other factors that impede change.

The situation is not likely to change until researchers and practitioners deal explicitly with these factors, rather than leaving them to chance.[11] They must support change proactively.

Practitioners need to address the requirements and possibilities for improvement. Improvement requires widespread education in new methods, closely integrated with education in tools. We need methods and tools that are easy to learn and use.

The new technology must evolve and adapt as we gain experience with its use and continually evaluate its successes and failures. A concept like the experience factory can help with this.

A planned approach is necessary. Strategic planning identifies the goals for change and provides a basis for continuing evaluation of activities undertaken to achieve the goals. In general, this approach follows the classic phases of technology transfer: raising awareness, cultivating interest, and persuading someone to try the technology, followed by trial use and full adoption. Raising awareness typically involves the use of publications, talks before organizations, videos, and demonstrations at exhibits and meetings.

Market research is important in finding connections between project requirements and the opportunities offered by new technology. Then, technical research can find solutions to these requirements and extend available technology to seize the opportunities. Thus, technical and market research interact.

The development of training courses requires input from both marketing and technical research. However, courses are only part of the technology transfer process. Experts should present implementation workshops for the new technology. Consultants must be available to solve problems or, if a problem is not currently solvable, to stimulate research aimed at developing the technology needed for resolution.

The development of software tools should be seen as necessary to the application of a new technology and as an integral part of technology transfer.

It is useful for marketing personnel to attend training courses. They can facilitate connections between technical interests and project applications. This may involve uncovering and dealing with technological and cultural barriers to change. Technical marketing personnel can open communication channels, proactively soliciting user feedback that technology transfer personnel can use to improve tools, courses, consulting, research, and the marketing process itself.

These activities require a range of skills difficult to find in one person. Hence, building a team of people whose skills complement each other is essential, as is building trust and good communication within the team. In the future, we expect corporations to create technology transfer organizations specifically to improve and speed up the process of adopting software engineering technologies. These organizations will probably include a diverse group of professionals: researchers, educators, software developers, consultants, and marketing personnel. They will most likely associate closely with a research organization, but also have access to a training organization. They will cultivate extensive networks among practitioners. Technical improvement will depend on much more than technical factors alone.

We have tried to show why and how the 1990s will be the quality era for software. We believe that increasingly intense international competition will make it essential to specify and attain quantitative product characteristics in software-based systems. This will drive software engineering to become a true engineering discipline.

Existing technologies will become either better focused (reduced-operation software), more disciplined (reuse, measurement approaches), or more practical (formal development methods), providing more effective models for software development. The new disciplines of cognitive psychology and software sociology will enrich software technology.

Process and product models and other forms of structured experience will aid in the practical engineering of software. Feedback and learning through measurement based on these models will become fundamental. Software models will become corporate assets, used not only for improving quality but also for transferring technology. Companies will plan for efficient technology transfer.

The justification for any measure is its role in helping satisfy user needs, and the importance of the measure is its correlation with this satisfaction. The presence of measures indicates that a technology is being challenged in a healthy fashion, that it is responding positively, and that it is therefore maturing.

ACKNOWLEDGMENTS

We are indebted to Dieter Rombach, John Stampfel, Jar Wu, Pamela Zave, Marv Zelkowitz, and the reviewers for their helpful comments.

References

1. B. Boehm, *Software Eng. Economics,* Prentice Hall, Englewood Cliffs, N.J., 1981.

2. J.D. Musa, A. Iannino, and K. Okumoto, *Software Reliability: Measurement, Prediction, Application,* McGraw-Hill, New York, 1987.

3. J.M. Wing, "A Specifier's Introduction to Formal Methods," *Computer,* Vol. 23, No. 9, Sept. 1990, pp. 8–24.

4. B. Stroustrup, "What is Object-Oriented Programming?" *IEEE Software,* Vol. 5, No. 3, May 1988, pp. 10–20.

5. V.R. Basili, "Software Development: A Paradigm for the Future," *Proc. 13th Int'l Computer Software and Applications Conf.,* CS Press, Los Alamitos, Calif., Sept. 1989, pp. 471–485.

6. M. Kogure and K. Akao, "Quality Function Deployment and CWQC in Japan," *Quality Progress,* Vol. 16, Oct. 1983, pp. 25–29.

7. B.W. Boehm, J.R. Brown, and M. Lipow, "Quantitative Evaluation of Software Quality," *Proc. Second Int'l Conf. Software Eng.,* IEEE CS Press, Los Alamitos, Calif., Order No. 104 (microfiche only), 1976, pp. 592–605.

8. B. Curtis, H. Krasner, and N. Iscoe. "A Field Study of the Software Design Process for Large Systems," *Comm. ACM,* Vol. 31, No. 11, pp. 1,268–1,287.

9. T.R. Riedl et al., "Application of a Knowledge Elicitation Method to Software Debugging Expertise," to be presented at the Fifth Conf. Software Eng. Education, Software Eng. Inst., Oct. 1991.

10. W.E. Deming, *Out of the Crisis,* MIT Center for Advanced Eng. Study, MIT Press, Cambridge, Mass., 1986.

11. *Transferring Software Eng. Tool Technology,* S. Przybylinski and P.J. Fowler, eds., IEEE CS Press, Los Alamitos, Calif., Catalog No. 887, 1988.

Discussion Questions

1. Basili and Shaw are optimistic, and Brooks is pessimistic about progress in software engineering. Who do you find most believable?

2. Shaw cites HLL as evidence of progress, while Brooks says that we've hit declining marginal returns. Who do you believe? How might we try to assess the rate of progress here?

3. Note that both Shaw and Basili cite the need for application specialization. Will there be such a thing as discipline of software engineering in the future, or will this be like getting a degree in 'engineering' today?

4. Brooks seems self-contradictory when he says that a good way to go is mass market software (buy don't build) and giving staff members end user computing tools and turning them loose. The former implies some progress through specialization and the reliance on professional software developers, while the latter is a throwback to the 'every man a programmer'. How can these two views be reconciled?

5. Brooks notes that a major reason for software changes is change to accommodate change in hardware. What might this suggest about migrations from mainframes to distributed (client-server) environments?

Algorithmic Cost Estimation Models

INTRODUCTION

The first stage in any software project is planning, and a critical part of the management role is to estimate the project's cost. Cost estimation has proven to be a very difficult endeavor, with cost overruns of 100 to 200 percent not uncommon on software development projects and a significant number of projects abandoned before completion. The frequency of such reports should be particularly alarming given what must be a natural bias on the part of organizations and their managers to attempt to limit the distribution of such failure stories. This level of performance is not tolerated in any other area of the firm that is as critical to the day-to-day operation of the organization as information technology.

While the low accuracy of software cost estimation is becoming widely recognized, its consequences are sometimes overlooked. There are three main areas of impact of the inability to plan projects reliably: economic, technical, and organizational. The economic impacts are most obvious on projects that are grossly misestimated. The late realization that the project will not be completed anywhere near the budget often results in the project being canceled, with the associated waste of all work done to date. It has been estimated that as many as fifteen percent of large systems development projects never deliver anything, and initial misunderstandings of the scope of the project are clearly one cause of these failures.

While these economic problems are perhaps the most obvious negative result of underestimates, serious technical quality problems are also possible. When the budgeted end of the project draws near, but substantial additional work remains, the tendency is to scrimp on the final tasks in order to complete the project at or near the budget. Unfortunately, in the traditional systems development life cycle the last tasks are usually testing, documentation and training, and rushing these tasks yields systems that are less reliable and less well received by their ultimate users. In the absence of metrics to determine shippable quality, projects tend to stop testing and debugging and simply ship when the deadline arrives. While underestimation is not the only reason for these problems, it is clearly a contributing factor.

Finally, underestimation leads to a number of organizational problems as well. When an unrealistic deadline draws near additional pressures are brought to bear on the staff to complete the project in a hurry. Besides the likely short-term, detrimental effect on the quality of work produced, the long-term effect on morale is also costly. Staff may be pulled from other assignments in order to rescue the project in trouble, which can result in a worse problem than the original one (the so-called Brooks Law phenomenon: Adding staff to a late project makes it later). If this problem is pervasive, a 'crisis mentality' can develop where only projects of this type get any managerial attention.

In response to these cost estimation problems, a substantial amount of research has been directed at software cost estimation. An early and now classic paper by Bailey and Basili outlines what they term a *meta-model* for the cost estimation models. They outline the major general forms that such models take and discuss the issues that should be considered in developing a model for an individual organization. They also provide data for their own SEL model and compare their model with early models by Walston and Felix and by Boehm.

In the second article in the chapter, Barry Boehm provides an overview of this COnstructive COst MOdel (COCOMO), the most widely used algorithmic cost estimation model in industry. This article provides a brief overview of the cost estimation portion of his book, *Software Engineering Economics* (Prentice Hall, 1981). COCOMO pre-dicts the number of work months required based on an estimate of Delivered Source Instructions (DSI). Three basic formulas are given, corresponding to three increasingly difficult modes of development: organic, semi-detached, and embedded. All of the models contain a single exponential parameter which models software development as having diseconomies of scale. Boehm compares COCOMO with other cost models, especially models based on the Rayleigh distribution. A schedule model, estimating calendar months based on estimated work months as an input, is also provided. His book also provides detailed development of his intermediate and detailed models, which add productivity factors to adjust the size and estimates by project phase.

The final article by Kemerer provides a relatively more up-to-date tutorial and summary on software cost estimation models. It begins with a discussion of why misestimation is such a serious problem, causing technical, economic, and organizational problems on underestimated projects. Cost models are suggested as a remedy to this situation, and major models (COCOMO Rayleigh-curve based, and function point models) are introduced. (Function point models are explored in greater depth in chapter 4.) A review of software cost estimation model validation research is presented and summarized in a large table. Suggestions for practice in improving their estimation conclude the chapter.

A META-MODEL
FOR SOFTWARE DEVELOPMENT
RESOURCE EXPENDITURES

INTRODUCTION

Several resource estimation models for a software-producing environment have been reported in the

Article by John W. Bailey and Victor R. Basili. © 1981 IEEE. Reprinted, with permission, from (IEEE Fifth International Conference on Software Engineering, pp. 107–116.)

literature [1, 2, 3, 4, 5, 6, 7, 8, 9], each having been developed in a different environment, each having its particular strengths and weaknesses but with most showing fairly poor characteristics concerning portability to other environments. It is becoming apparent that it is not generally possible for one software development environment to use the algorithms developed at another environment to predict resource consumption. It is necessary for each environment to consider its own past productivity in order to estimate its future productivities. Traditionally, a good manager can estimate resource consumption for a programming project based on his past experience with that particular environment. A model should be able to do the same, and can serve as a useful aid to the manager in this estimating task.

However, if a manager uses a model developed at another environment to help him in his estimations, he will usually find that his intuitive estimates are better than any from the model. It would be advantageous for his software-development organization to generate a model of its own by duplicating the basic steps taken in the development of some outside environment's estimation model. The organization could parallel its own model's development with the development of the existing model, making decisions along the way with respect to which factors have an effect on its software environment, and could mold the newly emerging model to its specific environment. This is seen as an additional advantage over those models which are only "tuned" to the user's environment via a set of specified parameters, since in the latter case there may be no way to express certain peculiarities of the new environment in terms which the model can handle. When one considers in general how poorly a model from one environment fits another environment, it seems that such peculiarities are the rule rather than the exception. Unfortunately, there have been few attempts to reveal the steps taken in generating a resource estimation model which would be helpful to any organization wishing to establish a model for its own use.

This paper is a first attempt by the Software Engineering Laboratory of the University of Maryland at College Park to outline the initial procedures which we have used to establish this type of model for our environment. It is hoped that the framework for the model presented here is general enough to help another software development organization produce a model of its own by following a similar procedure while making decisions which mold the model to its own environment.

One basic approach will be outlined and developed here, but several variations will be discussed. The type of model used is based on earlier work of Walston and Felix at IBM Federal Systems Division and Barry Boehm at TRW in that it attempts to relate project size to effort. Some reasonable measure is used to express the size of a project, such as lines of source code, executable statements, machine instructions or number of modules, and a base-line equation is used to relate this size to effort. Then, the deviations of the actual projects from this prediction line are explained by some set of factors which attempt to describe the difference among projects in the environment. These factors may include measures of skill and experience of the programming team, use of good programming practices and difficulty of the project.

Several of the alternatives became apparent during our study and these are mentioned when appropriate even if they are not examined further here. Although some of the details and ideas used in this study may not pertain to other environments, it is hoped that enough possibilities are given to show the general idea of how the technique we used can be applied. The study now involves complete data on eighteen projects and sub-projects but was begun when we had complete data on only five projects. It is hoped that the presentation of our work will save other investigators who are developing a model some time or at least provide a point of departure for their own study.

Background

There exist many cost estimation models ranging from highly theoretical ones, such as Putnam's model [1], to empirical ones, such as the Walston and Felix [2] and the Boehm model [3]. An empirical model uses data from previous projects to evaluate the current project and derives the basic formulae from analysis of the particular data base available. A theoretical model, on the other hand, uses formulae based upon global assumptions, such as the rate at which people solve problems, the number of problems available for solution at a given point in time, etc. The work in this paper is empirical and is based predominantly on the work of Walston and Felix, and Barry Boehm.

The Software Engineering Laboratory (SEL) has worked to validate some of the basic relationships proposed by Walston and Felix which dealt with the factors that affect the software development process. One result of their study was an index computed with twenty-nine factors they judged to have a significant effect on their software development environment. As part of their study, they proposed an effort equation which was of the form $E = 5.2 * L^{91}$ where E is the total effort in man-months and L is the size in thousands of lines of delivered source code. Data from SEL was used to show that although the exact equation proposed by Walston and Felix could not be derived, the basic relationship between lines of code and effort could be substantiated by an equation which lay within one standard error of estimate for the IBM equation, and in a justifiable direction [10]. Barry Boehm has proposed a model that uses a similar standard effort equation and adjusts the initial estimates by a set of sixteen multipliers which are selected according to values assigned to their corresponding attributes. In attempting to fit an early version of this model, but with the SEL data, it was found that because of differing environments, a different base-line equation was needed, as well as a different set of environmental parameters or attributes. Many of the attributes found in the TRW environment are already accounted for in the SEL base-line equations, and several of the attributes in the SEL model which accounted for changes in productivity were not accounted for in the Boehm model, presumably because they had little effect in the TRW environment. Based upon this assumption and our experience with the IBM and TRW models, the meta-model proposed in this paper was devised.

The SEL Environment

The Software Engineering Laboratory was organized in August 1976. Beginning in November 1976, most new software tasks that were assigned by the System Development Section of NASA/Goddard Space Flight Center began submitting data on development progress to our data base. These programs are mostly ground support routines for various spacecraft projects. This usually consists of attitude orbit determinations, telemetry decommutation and other control functions. The software that is produced generally takes from six months to two years to produce, is written by two to ten programmers most of whom are working on several such projects simultaneously, and requires from six man-months to ten man-years of effort. Projects are supervised by NASA/GSFC employees and personnel are either NASA personnel or outside contractors (Computer Sciences Corporation).

The development facility consists of two primary hardware systems: a pair of S/360's and a PDP-11/70. During development of software systems users can expect turn-around time to vary from one or two hours for small, half-minute jobs, to one day for medium jobs (3 to 5 minutes, less than 600K), to several days for longer and larger jobs. The primary language used is FORTRAN although there is some application of assembler language.

THE META-MODEL

The meta-model described here is of the adjusted base-line type such as those proposed by Walston and Felix and Barry Boehm. Therefore, the basic approach is a two-step process. First, the effort expended for the average project is expressed as a function of some measure of size and, second, each project's deviation from this average is explained through the systematic use of a set of environmental attributes known for each project. The remainder of this paper will describe this process and will follow the format:

1. Compute the background equation
2. Analyze the factors available to explain the difference between actual effort and effort as predicted by the background equation
3. Use this model to predict the effort for the new project

The Background Equation

The background or base-line relationship between effort and size forms the basis for the local model. It is found by fitting some choice of curve through the scatter plot of effort versus size data. By definition, then, it should be able to predict the effort required to complete an average project, given its size. This average effort value as a function of size alone has been termed the "standard effort" throughout this paper. This section deals with:

1. Picking and defining measures of size and effort
2. Selecting the form of the base-line equation
3. Calculating an initial base-line for use in the model

In any given environment the decision of what size measure to use would have to depend initially upon what data is available. In our case, it was decided that size could be measured easily by lines of source code or by modules and that effort could be expressed in man-months. Consideration should also be given to the ease with which each measure can be estimated when the model is used to predict the effort required for future projects. The upper management in our programming environment was of the opinion that source lines with comments was the easier of the two readily available measures to predict. Also, it was decided that, based upon the data available and the ultimate use of the model, project effort would be defined to be measured from the beginning of the design phase through acceptance testing and to include programming, management and support hours.

In our data base, the total number of lines and modules as well as the number of new lines and new modules were available for the 18 projects and subprojects. Initially, we expressed effort in terms of each of the four size measures mentioned above. To do this, we used three forms of equations to fit the data, using both the raw data and logarithms of the data, which provided functions we hoped would express the basic relationship between size and effort that exists in our environment. The forms of the three types of equations were:

$$E = effort \qquad S = size$$

$$E = a * S + b \qquad (1)$$

$$E = a * S^b \qquad (2)$$

$$E = a * S^b + c \qquad (3)$$

Some difficulties were encountered when attempting to fit a conventional least-squares regression line through the raw data. One probable reason for this is that a correlation between the deviations from the prediction line and the size of the project could not easily be eliminated (heteroscedasticity). Rather than using a least-squares line with a single, arithmetic standard error of estimate which would be consistently large with respect to small projects and often too small when applying the equation to large projects, we opted for a prediction line which minimized the ratio between the predicted values for effort and each actual data point. In this way, the standard error is multiplicative and can be thought of as a percent error whose absolute magnitude increases as the project size increases. If, however, equations of the second or third form are derived by fitting a least-squares line through the logarithms of the data, the standard error automatically becomes multiplicative when converted back to linear coordinates.

The third form shown above was the most successful for us. It was in the form of an exponential fit but included a constant which removed the constraint that the prediction line pass through the origin. This line was not found by converting to logarithms but by an algorithm that selected the values which minimized the standard error of estimate when expressed as a ratio. The theory behind the implementation of this multiplicative standard error of estimate is described later. Although the size of our data base was not large enough to firmly support using this fit rather than a straight line, we are using it here primarily as an illustration, and therefore felt justified in retaining it.

Turning back to the measurement of size, it was noted that neither the equations based upon size in terms of new lines of code or new modules nor those based upon total lines of code or total modules captured the intuitive sense of the amount of work required for each project. It was felt that although using previously written code was easier than generating new code, the integration effort was still significant and should be accounted for. After examining the background relationships discussed above, another more satisfying measurement for size was derived. Instead of considering only the total lines or only the new lines to determine the size of a project, an algorithm to combine these sizes into one measure was selected. It was found that by computing the effective size in lines to be equal to the total number of new lines written plus 20% of any old lines used in the project, a base-line relationship of lower standard error could be derived. This new size measure will be called "developed lines" in this paper. The same technique was applied to numbers of modules and resulted in a measure of "developed modules." Other proportions of new and old sizes were tried as well as an algorithm which computed developed size based on a graduated mixture of new and old code where large projects counted a higher percentage of their re-used code in the developed size. Often, these equations did produce slightly better background relationships, but the improvement in standard error was judged not to be worth the added complexity. I was hoping that as long as some reasonable algorithm was selected which captured the size as measured by both the amount of new product as well as old product most of the remaining differences among the projects should be explainable by the varying environmental attributes.

At this point, the three base-line equations, based on the computed sizes of developed lines only, were:

E = effort in man-months of programming and management time

DL = number of developed lines of source code with comments (new lines with comments plus 20% of re-used lines)

Equation: Standard error of estimate*:

$$E = 1.36 * DL + 1.62 \qquad 1.269 \quad (4)$$

$$E = 1.86 * DL^{.93} \qquad 1.297 \quad (5)$$

$$E = 0.73 * DL^{1.16} + 3.5 \qquad 1.250 \quad (6)$$

Exhibit 1 shows how the exponential fit with constant for developed lines falls between those for new lines and total lines, hopefully doing a better job than either of the other two in relating a project's size to the resources consumed during its development. The remainder of this paper will deal entirely with this computed measure of size since it was our most successful expression for work output for a given project.

Exhibit 2 shows these three background prediction equations superimposed on the data points. It was decided to use equation 3, above, as the base-line throughout the remainder of the model generation since it achieved the best fit to the data points and suggested the intuitively satisfying fact that a project requires a minimum overhead effort (the Y-intercept of the function). Equation one, a straight line, does as well statistically, and could well have been adopted for simplicity. Since this is meant to be an illustration, however, and it was felt that the nonlinear relationship between size and effort was more common outside of our environment, equation three was adopted for use in this study. The remaining errors of estimation appear as the vertical distances between each point and the line. It is these distances in the form of ratios which we would like to explain in terms of the environmental attributes.

Project Factors

The next step in determining a model is to collect data about the programming environment of each project which captures the probable reasons why some projects took more effort and thereby consumed more resources than others when normalized for size. This data could include such factors as methodologies used during design and development, experience of the customer and of the programmers, managerial control during development, number of changes imposed during the

---

*Note that these are multiplicative factors. The predicted value given by the equation is multiplied and divided by this factor to get the range for one standard error of estimate. All standard errors of estimate (s.e.e.) in this paper are of this type.

EXHIBIT 1

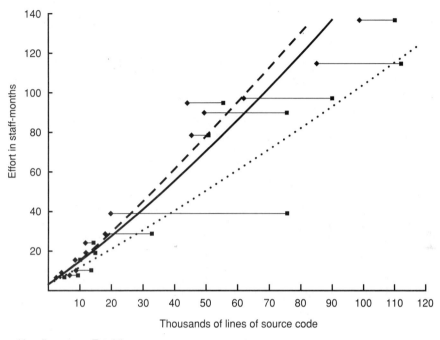

◆ New lines   ■ Total lines

development and type and complexity of the project. It is assumed that the correct application of information such as this can assist in explaining the variations observed among projects in terms of their productivities. The steps described in this section include:

1. Choosing a set of factors
2. Grouping and compressing this data
3. Isolating the important factors and groups
4. Incorporating the factors by performing a multiple regression to predict the deviations of the points from the computed base-line

In all, close to one hundred environmental attributes were examined as possible contributors to the variations among the productivities of the projects. Exhibit 3 shows a list of these factors as well as some others which we did not use. Thirty-six of the factors were those used by Walston and Felix, sixteen were used by Boehm and 30 others were suggested by our environment. Although we did not use all these factors, they are included to provide additional ideas for other investigators. It should be noted that it is not necessary to consider any factors which are constant for the set of projects currently in the data base since the influence of this factor will already be contained in the base-line relationship. If, however, a future project is rated differently in one of these categories, it may be necessary to reinstate it into the model.

The process of selecting attributes to use is largely a matter of what information is available. Since many of the projects we studied were completed when this investigation began, it was necessary to rely on project management for the information required. The inclusion of past projects was justified in order to establish as large a data base as possible, however, it made it

EXHIBIT 2

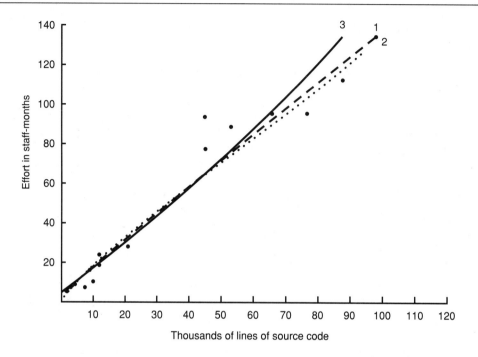

Thousands of lines of source code

necessary to be particularly careful about the consistency between the ratings for current projects and those for projects already completed. To maintain the integrity of the values of these attributes, all ratings produced by the vendor's management were examined by the customer's management and also by us. In this way we hoped to avoid the temptation to adjust ratings to reflect the known ultimate success of past projects.

Many of the attributes required no special work to assign a value, such as "Team Size" or "Percent Code: I/O," but most required imposing a scale of some kind. We decided that an exact scale was not possible or even necessary so a six-point subjective rating was used. This format was chosen by the managers who would be making the ratings since it conformed well with the information they had already collected about many of the attributes. Most of the factors, then, are rated on a scale from 0 to 5 with 5 being the most of that

particular attribute (whether it is "good" or "bad"). The most important point is that we tried to remain consistent in our ratings from project to project. The need for this was particularly noticeable when rating earlier projects in terms of development methodology. For instance, what may have been thought of as a "4" rating in "Formal Training" for a project which began coding over a year ago may actually be a "3" or even a "2" when compared with the increased sophistication of more recent projects. We found it necessary to re-scale a few of the attributes because of this consideration.

After a set of environmental factors is selected and the data collected, it is necessary to consider the number of these attributes versus the number of projects in the data base. It is not statistically sound to use a large group of factors to predict a variable with relatively few data points. Unless a very large number of projects is being used, it will

EXHIBIT 3

Walston and Felix:	*Boehm:*	*SEL:*
Customer experience	Required fault freedom	Program design language (development and design)
Customer participation in definition	Data base size	
Customer interface complexity	Product complexity	Formal design review
Development location	Adaptation from existing software	Tree charts
Percent programmers in design	Execution time constraint	Design formalisms
Programmer qualifications	Main storage constraint	Design/decision notes
Programmer experience with machine	Virtual machine volatility	Walk-through: design
Programmer experience with language	Computer response time	Walk-through: code
Programmer experience with application	Analyst capability	Code reading
Worked together on same type of problem	Applications experience	Top-down design
Customer originated program design changes	Programmer capability	Top-down code
Hardware under development	Virtual machine experience	Structured code
Development environment closed	Programming language experience	Librarian
Development environment open with request	Modern programming practices	Chief programmer teams
Development environment open	Use of software tools	Formal training
Development environment RJE	Required development schedule	Formal test plans
Development environment TSO		Unit development folders
Percent code structured		Formal documentation
Percent code used code review		Heavy management involvement and control
Percent code used top-down		
Percent code by chief-programmer teams		Iterative enhancement
Complexity of application processing		Individual decisions
Complexity of program flow		Timely specs and no changes
Complexity of internal communication		Team size
Complexity of external communication		On schedule
Complexity of data-base structure		TSO development
Percent code non-math I/O		Overall
Percent code math and computational		Reusable code
Percent code CPU and I/O control		Percent programmer effort
Percent code fallback and recovery		Percent management effort
Percent code other		Amount documentation
Proportion code real time of interactive		Staff size
Design constraints: main storage		
Design constraints: timing		
Design constraints: I/O capability		
Unclassified		

probably be necessary to condense the information contained in the whole set of factors into just a few new factors. This can be accomplished entirely intuitively, based on experience, or with the help of a correlation matrix or factor analysis routines. Although there is no absolute rule as to how many factors should be used to predict a given number of points, a rule of thumb might be to allow up to ten or fifteen percent of the number of data points. Strictly speaking, the adjusted r-squared values or the F-values should be observed as factors are added to the prediction equation via a multiple regression routine (described below) to avoid the mistake of using too many factors.

In our environment, we had data on 71 attributes which we suspected could affect the ultimate productivity of a project, but only 18 projects for which to see the results. We found it necessary, therefore, to perform such a compression of the data. Our next step, then, was to examine the attributes and group into categories those which we felt would have a similar effect on the project. As an aid to selecting potential groupings for analysis, a correlation matrix for all the attributes was studied. It was hoped that meaningful groups could be formed which would retain an intuitive sense of positive or negative contribution to the project's productivity. By studying the potential categorizations of the factors, and how they performed in potential models to predict developed lines, we settled upon three groups using 21 of the original attributes. The groups and their constituent attributes were:

Total Methodology
  Tree Charts
  Top Down Design
  Design Formalisms
  Formal Documentation
  Code Reading
  Chief Programmer Teams
  Formal Test Plans
  Unit Development Folders
  Formal Training

Cumulative Complexity
  Customer Interface Complexity
  Customer-Initiated Design Changes
  Application Process Complexity
  Program Flow Complexity
  Internal Communication Complexity
  External Communication Complexity
  Data Base Complexity

Cumulative Experience
  Programmer Qualifications
  Programmer Experience with Machine
  Programmer Experience with Language
  Programmer Experience with Application
  Team Previously Worked Together

We were particularly interested in using a methodology category due to the findings of Basili and Reiter [11] which implied improvement in the development process due to the use of a specific discipline. The methodology category was selected to closely coincide with the principles of the methodology used in the experiment. The complexity category was included to account for some of the known negative influences on productivity. The cumulative rating for each of these categories was merely a sum of the ratings of its constituents (each adjusted to a 0 to 5 scale). Although it was necessary to reduce the number of attributes used in the statistical investigation in this manner in order to give more meaningful results, the simple summing of various attributes loses some of the information which could be reflected in these categories. This is because even though one of the constituent attributes may be much more important than another, an unweighted sum will destroy this difference. One solution to this type of dilemma is to have many more data points, as mentioned before, and to use the attributes independently. Another would be to determine the relative effects of each attribute and to weight them accordingly. Without the necessary criteria for either of these solutions, however, we are forced to continue in this direction and to accept this trade-off.

Incorporating the Factors

The purpose of the attribute analysis is to explain the deviations displayed by each project from the derived background equation and, ultimately, to yield a prediction process where the attributes can be used to determine how far a project will "miss" the background equation, if at all.

The next step, then, is to compute these differences which must be predicted. A quantity based on the ratio between the actual effort expended and the amount predicted by the background equation was used as a target for the prediction. In this way, when the model is in use, the background equation can be applied to determine the standard effort (the amount needed if the project behaved as an average of the previous projects in the data base). Then, the attributes will be used to yield a ratio between this rough estimate and a hopefully more accurate expected value of the effort required.

The SPSS [12] forward multiple regression routine was used to generate an equation which could best predict each of the project's ratio of error. The actual ratio was converted to a linear scale with zero meaning the actual data point fell on the base-line. This was accomplished by subtracting one from all ratios greater than one and adding one to the negative reciprocals of those ratios which were less than one. For instance, if a project's standard effort was predicted to be 100 man-months and it actually required 150 man-months, this ratio would be 1.5. Subtracting one makes this project's target value 0.5. If however it had needed only 66.7 man-months, its ratio would be .667 which is less than one. Adding one to the negative reciprocal of this number gives a target value of −0.5. The assumption is that this scale tends to be symmetrical in that the first project had as many negative factors impact its productivity as the second project had positive.

In the first pass at using the multiple regression routine, we were using five attribute groups. Since the data base was not very large, we were cautious about assigning any useful significance to the results. We therefore recondensed the attribute data into the three groups shown above. The results of this attempt are described in a later section.

Variations on the Model

We noticed that it was possible to combine the two processes of first isolating a background equation and then applying the environmental attributes to explain deviations from that equation into a single procedure. To do this, a measure of size was included as a factor with the set of environmental attributes and the whole group was used to predict effort. As expected, size was always chosen first by the forward routine, since it correlated the best with effort for each project. This single process lacked the intuitively satisfying intermediate stage which related to a base-line relationship as a half-way point in the model's results, but it streamlined the model somewhat.

In order to preserve the possibility of an exponential relationship between size and effort, this method was used with the logarithms of the size and effort values. The output of the regression analysis would be of the form,

$$log(Effort) = A * log(Size) + B * attr1 + C * attr2 + \cdots + K \qquad (7)$$

This would convert to,

$$Effort = Size^{A} * 10^{(B * attr1 + C * attr2 + \cdots + K)} \qquad (8)$$

assuming, here, that log base 10 was used in the conversion.

A third template for a model was tried which attempted to eliminate nearly all of the reliance on the actual numerical values of our attribute ratings in order to legitimize some of our statistical analyzes. Only two of the attribute groups mentioned before were considered, "Complexity" and "Methodology." Each of these two ratings were transformed into two new ratings of binary values resulting in four new attributes, "High Methodology," "Low Methodology," "High Complexity," and "Low Complexity." The transformation was accomplished as follows: If a project's rating fell in the upper third of all projects, the value of the "High" binary attribute of that type was assigned a 1 while the value of the "Low" attribute for that type was assigned a 0. If the value fell in the middle third, both binary values were assigned a 0. If the value fell in the low third, the "Low" attribute was assigned a 1 while the "High" was assigned a 0. This reduced our assumptions about the data to the lowest level for statistical analysis. For illustration, call the four new binary attributes HM, LM, HC, LC for high and low methodology and high and low complexity. The result of the multiple regression analysis, then, would be in the form,

$$Effort = Size^A * 10^{(B * HM + C * LM + D * HC + E * LC + K)} \qquad (9)$$

Since the chance that any chosen attribute value will be 0 for a particular project is about ⅔, most of those terms on the right will drop out when the model is actually applied to a given project. Although we did not expect to achieve the same accuracy from this method, the simplicity of it was appealing.

APPLYING THE MODEL

As an illustration of the results obtained thus far for our environment, this section deals with the actual values of the data we used and the models we generated. It should serve as a useful guide and a summary of the steps we chose to follow. In order to include an illustration of the functioning of the completed model, one project, the most recently completed project, will be removed from the analysis while a new model is developed. This project will then be treated as a new data point in order to test and illustrate the performance of the model. Typically, the use of the model will involve the following steps:

1. Estimate size of new project
2. Use base-line to get standard effort
3. Estimate necessary factor values
4. Compute difference this project should exhibit
5. Apply that difference to standard effort

Exhibit 4 shows the eighteen projects and sub-projects currently in our data base with the measures of size previously discussed. As stated above, developed size is all of the newly written lines or modules plus 20% of the re-used lines or modules, depending on which size measure is being used. The developed size is what we chose to predict with the models generated. We also chose, as a base-line, the exponential equation with the constant term. The following illustration shows the development of the model with the first seventeen points in the data base. The base-line relationship between developed lines of code and effort was:

$$E = .72 * DL^{1.17} + 3.4 \text{ (s.e.e. } = 1.25) \quad (10)$$

The remaining information used about the projects is shown in Exhibit 4. The remaining error ratios from this line to each project's actual effort were computed and listed. These are the values which should be explained by the multiple regression analysis. When the model is in use, then, an error ratio can be derived by using the multiple regression equation which can then be applied to the base-line equation to provide what should be an even better estimate of effort than the base-line alone. As discussed, the three main categories of environmental attributes shown are the result of distilling many attributes.

The equations computed by the SPSS forward multiple regression routine which attempt to express the list of error ratios as functions of various of the attributes provided are:

$ER = Effort\ ratio\ (converted\ to\ linear\ scale)$

$METH = Methodology$

$CMPLX = Complexity$

$$ER = - .036 * METH + 1.0 \qquad (11)$$

$$ER = - .036 * METH + .006 * CMPLX + .86 \qquad (12)$$

To apply the model to the unused, eighteenth point, the base-line equation is first used to establish the standard effort. Since the estimated size of

EXHIBIT 4

Project	Effort (man-months)	Total Lines	New Lines	Developed Lines	Predicted Standard Effort	Effort Ratio Standard/ Actual	Method-ology	Complex-ity	Exper-ience
1	115.8	111.9	84.7	90.2	138.7	.835	30	21	16
2	96.0	55.2	44.0	46.2	65.8	1.459	20	21	14
3	79.0	50.9	45.3	46.5	66.2	1.194	19	21	16
4	90.8	75.4	49.3	54.5	79.0	1.150	20	29	16
5	39.6	75.4	20.1	31.1	42.9	.924	35	21	18
6	98.4	89.5	62.0	97.5	100.1	.982	29	29	14
7	18.9	14.9	12.2	12.8	17.5	1.082	26	25	16
8	10.3	14.3	9.6	10.5	14.7	.704	34	19	21
9	28.5	32.8	18.7	21.5	29.2	.977	31	27	20
10	7.0	5.5	2.5	3.1	6.2	1.128	26	18	6
11	9.0	4.5	4.2	4.2	7.4	1.220	19	23	12
12	7.3	9.7	7.4	7.8	11.4	.640	31	18	16
13	5.0	2.1	2.1	2.1	5.2	.957	28	19	20
14	8.4	5.2	4.9	5.0	8.2	1.025	29	21	14
15	98.7	85.4	76.9	78.6	118.8	.831	35	33	16
16	15.6	10.2	9.6	9.7	13.7	1.138	27	21	16
17	23.9	14.8	11.9	12.5	17.1	1.398	27	23	18
18	138.3	110.3	98.4	100.8	157.4	.879	34	33	16

the project was 101,000 lines, this standard effort value was 163 man-months with a range for one standard error of from 130 to 204 man-months. When the additional attributes are used to compute the error ratio as given by the multiple regression equations, the results (for each of the above equations) are:

$$ER = -0.224 \text{ and } ER = -0.166$$

Converting these numbers back to multiplicative factors means dividing the standard effort by 1.224 and by 1.166, respectively. When these ratios are applied to the standard effort value, the revised effort values are found to be 133 man-months with a range for one standard error from 115 to 154 man-months for the first equation, and 140 man-months with a range for one standard

error of from 121 to 162 man-months for the second equation. The actual effort for the project is known to have been 138 man-months.

Once any new project is added to the data base, at least the generation of the base-line relationship and the multiple regression analysis of the error ratios should be repeated. It may also be necessary to examine the factor groupings to see if they could be modified to increase the accuracy of the model or to include a previously unimportant attribute.

For our data, when this eighteenth point is added to the data base, the base-line equation becomes:

$$E = .73 * DL^{1.16} + 3.5 \text{ (s.e.e. = 1.25) (13)}$$

while the equations to predict the error ratio from the attributes become:

$$ER = -.035 * METH + .98$$
$$(s.e.e. = 1.16) \qquad (14)$$

$$ER = -.036 * METH + .009 * CMPLX$$
$$+ .80 \ (s.e.e. = 1.15) \qquad (15)$$

It should be remembered that the original choice of factors from the entire set, and the groupings of these factors, was done with regard to predicting size as measured by developed lines and was not so specifically tuned to predicting developed modules. It is reasonable to expect, then, that the results of the models generated to predict effort from the number of developed modules using these attribute groupings will be less accurate than those using the number of developed lines. If the objective had been to generate a model specifically suited to predicting modules, various adjustments would have been made during the early part of the model's development. Also, it is advisable to review the model each time a new project is completed and its data is added to the data base. In this way the model can be refined and kept up-to-date, and will be able to take into account changes in the overall programming environment.

Although we are not reporting here the actual values and equations generated in the development of the other forms of this basic model (described under "Variations on the Model," above) it became apparent that none of the model types is by far better than the rest, especially considering the fact that they all have differing amounts of statistical significance. In terms of a purely investigative study, all of them should probably be examined further. As more environmental information is added to the data base, it may be possible to reorganize the constituent groups involved in the environmental attributes and to produce better categories. Also, when several more projects are completed, it may be possible to justifiably expand the size of the set of variables used to predict the expected value in the multiple regression routine giving the potential for greater accuracy.

CONCLUSIONS

There is reason to believe that the techniques outlined here and used in our laboratory have potential in terms of producing a useful model which is specifically developed for use at any particular environment. The main difficulty seems to be in determining which environmental attributes really capture the reason for the differences in productivity among the projects. The use of too few of these attributes will mean less of the variation can possibly be explained, while the use of too many makes the analysis statistically meaningless. We found that it was necessary to stop including factors with the multiple regression analysis when the r-squared value indicated that we had explained no more than half of the variations among the error ratios. This would seem to indicate that there were considerably more influences upon the productivities of the projects than we managed to isolate. Simplifying the original idea for the model, however, which reduced the emphasis on the quality of the data did not weaken the accuracy of the model beyond useful proportions. This is particularly important when so much of the data which is essential to build the model is subjective and consequently nonlinear.

ACKNOWLEDGMENTS

The authors would like to thank Dr. Jerry Page of Computer Sciences Corporation and Frank McGarry of NASA/Goddard Space Flight Center for their invaluable help in providing the data for this study.

Research for this study was supported in part by National Aeronautics and Space Administration grant NSG-5123 to the University of Maryland. Computer time supported in part through the facilities of the Computer Science Center of the University of Maryland.

References

1. Putnam, L. "A General Empirical Solution to the Macro Software Sizing and Estimating Problem," *IEEE Transactions on Software Engineering*, Vol. 4, No. 4, 1978.

2. Walston, C., and C. Felix. "A Method of Programming Measurement and Estimation," *IBM Systems Journal*, Vol. 16, No. 1, 1977.

3. Boehm, Barry W. Draft of a book on Software Engineering Economics, to be published.

4. Lawrence, M.J., and D.R. Jeffery. "Inter-organizational Comparison of Programming Productivity," Department of Information Systems, University of New South Wales, March 1979.

5. Doty Associates, Inc. Software Cost Estimates Study Vol. 1, RADC TR 77-220, June 1977.

6. Wolverton, R. "The Cost of Developing Large Scale Software," *IEEE Transactions on Computers*, Vol. 23, No. 6, 1974.

7. Aron, J. "Estimating Resources for Large Programming Systems," NATO Conference on Software Engineering Techniques, Mason Charter, N.Y., 1969.

8. Carriere, W.M., and R. Thibodeau. "Development of a Logistics Software Cost Estimating Technique for Foreign Military Sales," General Research Corp., Santa Barbara, Calif., June 1979.

9. Norden, Peter V. "Useful Tools for Project Management," *Management of Production*, M.K. Starr, ed. Baltimore: Penguin Books, 1970, pp. 77–101.

10. Basili, V.R., and K. Freburger. "Programming Measurement and Estimation in the Software Engineering Laboratory," *Journal of Systems and Software*, Vol. 2, No. 1, 1981.

11. Basili, V.R., and R.W. Reiter, Jr. "An Investigation of Human Factors in Software Development," *Computer*, December 1979, pp. 21–38.

12. Statistical Package for the Social Sciences, Univac 1100 series manual.

SOFTWARE ENGINEERING ECONOMICS

I. INTRODUCTION

Definitions

The dictionary defines "economics" as "a social science concerned chiefly with description and analysis of the production, distribution, and consumption of goods and services." Here is another definition of economics which I think is more helpful in explaining how economics relates to software engineering.

Economics is the study of how people make decisions in resource-limited situations.

This definition of economics fits the major branches of classical economics very well.

Macroeconomics is the study of how people make decisions in resource-limited situations on a national or global scale. It deals with the effects of decisions that national leaders make on such issues as tax rates, interest rates, foreign and trade policy.

Microeconomics is the study of how people make decisions in resource-limited situations on a more personal scale. It deals with the decisions that individuals and organizations make on such issues as how much insurance to buy, which word processor to buy, or what prices to charge for their products or services.

Economics and Software Engineering Management

If we look at the discipline of software engineering, we see that the microeconomics branch of economics deals more with the types of decisions we need to make as software engineers or managers.

Clearly, we deal with limited resources. There is never enough time or money to cover all the good features we would like to put into our software products. And even in these days of cheap hardware

Article by Barry W. Boehm. © 1984 IEEE. Reprinted, with permission, from (*IEEE Transactions on Software Engineering*, SE-10, 1, 4–21; 1984).

and virtual memory, our more significant software products must always operate within a world of limited computer power and main memory. If you have been in the software engineering field for any length of time, I am sure you can think of a number of decision situations in which you had to determine some key software product feature as a function of some limiting critical resource.

Throughout the software life cycle,[1] there are many decision situations involving limited resources in which software engineering economics techniques provide useful assistance. To provide a feel for the nature of these economic decision issues, an example is given below for each of the major phases in the software life cycle.

- *Feasibility Phase:* How much should we invest in information system analyses (user questionnaires and interviews, current-system analysis, workload characterizations, simulations, scenarios, prototypes) in order that we converge on an appropriate definition and concept of operation for the system we plan to implement?
- *Plans and Requirements Phase:* How rigorously should we specify requirements? How much should we invest in requirements validation activities (automated completeness, consistency, and traceability checks, analytic models, simulations, prototypes) before proceeding to design and develop a software system?
- *Product Design Phase:* Should we organize the software to make it possible to use a complex piece of existing software which generally but not completely meets our requirements?
- *Programming Phase:* Given a choice between three data storage and retrieval schemes which are primarily execution time-efficient, storage-efficient, and easy-to-modify, respectively; which of these should we choose to implement?

---

[1] Economic principles underlie the overall structure of the software life cycle, and its primary refinements of prototyping, incremental development, and advancemanship. The primary economic driver of the life-cycle structure is the significantly increasing cost of making a software change or fixing a software problem, as a function of the phase in which the change or fix is made.

- *Integration and Test Phase:* How much testing and formal verification should we perform on a product before releasing it to users?
- *Maintenance Phase:* Given an extensive list of suggested product improvements, which ones should we implement first?
- *Phaseout:* Given an aging, hard-to-modify software product, should we replace it with a new product, restructure it, or leave it alone?

Outline of This Paper

The economics field has evolved a number of techniques (cost-benefit analysis, present value analysis, risk analysis, etc.) for dealing with decision issues such as the ones above. Section II of this paper provides an overview of these techniques and their applicability to software engineering.

One critical problem which underlies all applications of economic techniques to software engineering is the problem of estimating software costs. Section III contains three major sections which summarize this field:

III-A: Major Software Cost Estimation Techniques

III-B: Algorithmic Models for Software Cost Estimation

III-C: Outstanding Research Issues in Software Cost Estimation.

Section IV concludes by summarizing the major benefits of software engineering economics, and commenting on the major challenges awaiting the field.

II. SOFTWARE ENGINEERING ECONOMICS ANALYSIS TECHNIQUES

Overview of Relevant Techniques

The microeconomics field provides a number of techniques for dealing with software life-cycle decision issues such as the one given in the previous section. Exhibit 1 presents an overall master key to these techniques and when to use them.[2]

---

[2] The chapter numbers in Exhibit 1 refer to the chapters in [11], in which those techniques are discussed in further detail.

EXHIBIT 1   Master Key to Software Engineering Economics Decision Analysis Techniques

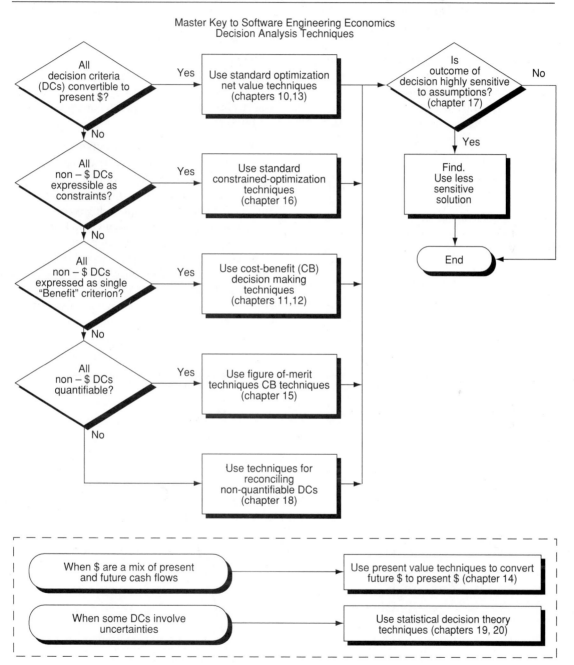

Master Key to Software Engineering Economics
Decision Analysis Techniques

As indicated in Exhibit 1, standard optimization techniques can be used when we can find a single quantity such as dollars (or pounds, yen, cruzeiros, etc.) to serve as a "universal solvent" into which all of our decision variables can be converted. Or, if the nondollar objectives can be expressed as constraints (system availability must be at least 98 percent; throughput must be at least 150 transactions per second), then standard constrained optimization techniques can be used. And if cash flows occur at different times, then present-value techniques can be used to normalize them to a common point in time.

More frequently, some of the resulting benefits from the software system are not expressible in dollars. In such situations, one alternative solution will not necessarily dominate another solution.

An example situation is shown in Exhibit 2, which compares the cost and benefits (here, in terms of throughput in transactions per second) of two alternative approaches to developing an operating system for a transaction processing system.

- *Option A:* Accept an available operating system. This will require only $80K in software costs, but will achieve a peak performance of 120 transactions per second, using five $10K minicomputer processors, because of a high multiprocessor overhead factor.
- *Option B:* Build a new operating system. This system would be more efficient and would support a higher peak throughput, but would require $180K in software costs.

The cost-versus-performance curve for these two options are shown in Exhibit 2. Here, neither option dominates the other, and various cost-benefit decision-making techniques (maximum profit margin, cost/benefit ratio, return on investments, etc.) must be used to choose between Options A and B.

In general, software engineering decision problems are even more complex than Exhibit 2, as Options A and B will have several important criteria on which they differ (e.g., robustness, ease of tuning, ease of change, functional capability). If these criteria are quantifiable, then some type of

---

EXHIBIT 2   Cost-Effectiveness Comparison, Transaction Processing System Options

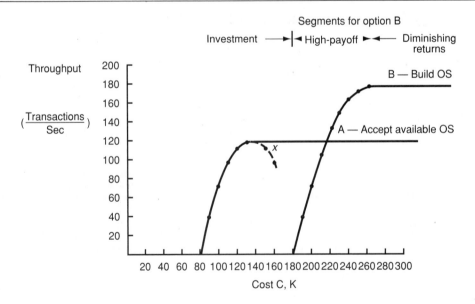

figure of merit can be defined to support a comparative analysis of the preferability of one option over another. If some of the criteria are unquantifiable (user goodwill, programmer morale, etc.), then some techniques for comparing unquantifiable criteria need to be used. As indicated in Exhibit 1, techniques for each of these situations are available, and discussed in [11].

Analyzing Risk, Uncertainty, and the Value of Information

In software engineering, our decision issues are generally even more complex than those discussed above. This is because the outcome of many of our options cannot be determined in advance. For example, building an operating system with a significantly lower multiprocessor overhead may be achievable, but on the other hand, it may not. In such circumstances, we are faced with a problem of *decision making under uncertainty,* with a considerable *risk* of an undesired outcome.

The main economic analysis techniques available to support us in resolving such problems are the following.

1. Techniques for decision making under complete uncertainty, such as the maximax rule, the maximin rule, and the Laplace rule [38]. These techniques are generally inadequate for practical software engineering decisions.
2. Expected-value techniques, in which we estimate the probabilities of occurrence of each outcome (successful or unsuccessful development of the new operating system) and complete the expected payoff of each option:

*EV = Prob(success) * Payoff (successful OS)*
*+ Prob(failure) * Payoff (unsuccessful OS).*

These techniques are better than decision making under complete uncertainty, but they still involve a great deal of risk if the Prob(failure) is considerably higher than our estimate of it.

3. Techniques in which we reduce uncertainty by *buying information*. For example, *prototyping*

is a way of buying information to reduce our uncertainty about the likely success or failure of a multiprocessor operating system; by developing a rapid prototype of its high-risk elements, we can get a clearer picture of our likelihood of successfully developing the full operating system.

In general, prototyping and other options for buying information[3] are most valuable aids for software engineering decisions. However, they always raise the following question: "how much information-buying is enough?"

In principle, this question can be answered via statistical decision theory techniques involving the use of Bayes' Law, which allows us to calculate the expected payoff from a software project as a function of our level of investment in a prototype or other information-buying option. (Some examples of the use of Bayes' Law to estimate the appropriate level of investment in a prototype are given in [11, ch. 20].)

In practice, the use of Bayes' Law involves the estimation of a number of conditional probabilities which are not easy to estimate accurately. However, the Bayes' Law approach can be translated into a number of *value-of-information guidelines,* or conditions under which it makes good sense to decide on investing in more information before committing ourselves to a particular course of action.

Condition 1: There exist attractive alternatives whose payoff varies greatly, depending on some critical states of nature. If not, we can commit ourselves to one of the attractive alternatives with no risk of significant loss.

Condition 2: The critical states of nature have an appreciable probability of occurring. If not, we can again commit ourselves without major risk. For situations with extremely high variations in

---

[3] Other examples of options for buying information to support software engineering decisions include feasibility studies, user surveys, simulation, testing, and mathematical program verification techniques.

payoff, the appreciable probability level is lower than in situations with smaller variations in payoff.

Condition 3: The investigations have a high probability of accurately identifying the occurrence of the critical states of nature. If not, the investigations will not do much to reduce our risk of loss due to making the wrong decision.

Condition 4: The required cost and schedule of the investigations do not overly curtail their net value. It does us little good to obtain results which cost more than they can save us or which arrive too late to help us make a decision.

Condition 5: There exist significant side benefits derived from performing the investigations. Again, we may be able to justify an investigation solely on the basis of its value in training, team-building, customer relations, or design validation.

Some Pitfalls Avoided by Using the Value-of-Information Approach

The guideline conditions provided by the value-of-information approach provide us with a perspective which helps us avoid some serious software engineering pitfalls. The pitfalls below are expressed in terms of some frequently expressed but faulty pieces of software engineering advice.

Pitfall 1: Always use a simulation to investigate the feasibility of complex realtime software. Simulations are often extremely valuable in such situations. However, there have been a good many simulations developed which were largely an expensive waste of effort, frequently under conditions that would have been picked up by the guidelines above. Some have been relatively useless because, once they were built, nobody could tell whether a given set of inputs was realistic or not (picked up by Condition 3). Some have been taken so long to develop that they produced their first results the week after the proposal was sent out, or after the key design review was completed (picked up by Condition 4).

Pitfall 2: Always build the software twice. The guidelines indicate that the prototype (or build-it-twice) approach is often valuable, but not in all situations. Some prototypes have been built of software whose aspects were all straightforward and familiar, in which case nothing much was learned by building them (picked up by Conditions 1 and 2).

Pitfall 3: Build the software purely top-down. When interpreted too literally, the top-down approach does not concern itself with the design of low level modules until the higher levels have been fully developed. If an adverse state of nature makes such a low level module (automatically forecast sales volume, automatically discriminate one type of aircraft from another) impossible to develop, the subsequent redesign will generally require the expensive rework of much of the higher level design and code. Conditions 1 and 2 warn us to temper our top-down approach with a thorough top-to-bottom software risk analysis during the requirements and product design phases.

Pitfall 4: Every piece of code should be proved correct. Correctness proving is still an expensive way to get information on the fault-freedom of software, although it strongly satisfies Condition 3 by giving a very high assurance of a program's correctness. Conditions 1 and 2 recommend that proof techniques be used in situations where the operational cost of a software fault is very large, that is, loss of life, compromised national security, major financial losses. But if the operational cost of a software fault is small, the added information on fault-freedom provided by the proof will not be worth the investment (Condition 4).

Pitfall 5: Nominal-case testing is sufficient. This pitfall is just the opposite of Pitfall 4. If the operational cost of potential software faults is large, it is highly imprudent not to perform off-nominal testing.

Summary: The Economic Value of Information

Let us step back a bit from these guidelines and pitfalls. Put simply, we are saying that, as software engineers:

"It is often worth paying for information because it helps us make better decisions."

If we look at the statement in a broader context, we can see that it is the primary reason why the software engineering field exists. It is what practically all of our software customers say when they decide to acquire one of our products: It is worth paying for a management information system, a weather forecasting system, an air traffic control system, an inventory control system, etc., because it helps them make better decisions.

Usually, software engineers are *producers* of management information to be consumed by other people, but during the software life cycle we must also be *consumers* of management information to support our own decisions. As we come to appreciate the factors which make it attractive for us to pay for processed information which helps *us* make better decisions as software engineers, we will get a better appreciation for what our customers and users are looking for in the information processing systems we develop for *them*.

III. SOFTWARE COST ESTIMATION

Introduction

All of the software engineering economics decision analysis techniques discussed above are only as good as the input data we can provide for them. For software decisions, the most critical and difficult of these inputs to provide are estimates of the cost of a proposed software project. In this section, we will summarize:

1. The major software cost estimation techniques available, and their relative strengths and difficulties;
2. Algorithmic models for software cost estimation;
3. Outstanding research issues in software cost estimation.

A. *Major Software Cost Estimation Techniques*

Exhibit 3 summarizes the relative strengths and difficulties of the major software cost estimation methods in use today.

1. *Algorithmic Models:* These methods provide one or more algorithms which produce a software cost estimate as a function of a number of variables which are considered to be the major cost drivers.
2. *Expert Judgment:* This method involves consulting one or more experts, perhaps with the aid of an expert-consensus mechanism such as the Delphi technique.
3. *Analogy:* This method involves reasoning by analogy with one or more completed projects to relate their actual costs to an estimate of the cost of a similar new project.
4. *Parkinson:* A Parkinson principle ("work expands to fill the available volume") is invoked to equate the cost estimate to the available resources.
5. *Price-to-Win:* Here, the cost estimate is equated to the price believed necessary to win the job (or the schedule believed necessary to be first in the market with a new product, etc.).
6. *Top-Down:* An overall cost estimate for the project is derived from global properties of the software product. The total cost is then split up among the various components.
7. *Bottom-Up:* Each component of the software job is separately estimated, and the results aggregated to produce an estimate for the overall job.

The main conclusions that we can draw from Exhibit 3 are the following.

- None of the alternatives is better than the others from all aspects.
- The Parkinson and price-to-win methods are unacceptable and do not produce satisfactory cost estimates.
- The strengths and weaknesses of the other techniques are complementary (particularly the algorithmic models versus expert judgment and top-down versus bottom-up).
- Thus, in practice, we should use combinations of the above techniques, compare their results, and iterate on them where they differ.

Fundamental Limitations of Software Cost Estimation Techniques

Whatever the strengths of a software cost estimation technique, there is really no way we can

EXHIBIT 3 Strengths and Weaknesses of Software Cost-Estimation Methods

Method	Strengths	Weaknesses
Algorithmic model	• Objective, repeatable, analyzable formula	• Subjective inputs
	• Efficient, good for sensitivity analysis	• Assessment of exceptional circumstances
	• Objectively calibrated to experience	• Calibrated to past, not future
Expert judgment	• Assessment of representativeness, interactions, exceptional circumstances	• No better than participants
		• Biases, incomplete recall
Analogy	• Based on representative experience	• Representativeness of experience
Parkinson	• Correlates with some experience	• Reinforces poor practice
Price to win	• Often gets the contract	• Generally produces large overruns
Top-down	• System level focus	• Less detailed basis
	• Efficient	• Less stable
Bottom-up	• More detailed basis	• May overlook system level costs
	• More stable	• Requires more effort
	• Fosters individual commitment	

expect the technique to compensate for our lack of definition or understanding of the software job to be done. Until a software specification is fully defined, it actually represents a range of software products, and a corresponding range of software development costs.

This fundamental limitation of software cost estimation technology is illustrated in Exhibit 4, which shows the accuracy within which software cost estimates can be made, as a function of the software life-cycle phase (the horizontal axis), or of the level of knowledge we have of what the software is intended to do. This level of uncertainty is illustrated in Exhibit 4 with respect to a human-machine interface component of the software.

When we first begin to evaluate alternative concepts for new software application, the relative range of our software cost estimates is roughly a factor of four on either the high or low side.[4] This range stems from the wide range of uncertainty we have at this time about the actual nature of the product. For the human-machine interface component, for example, we do not know at this time what classes of people (clerks, computer specialists, middle managers, etc.) or what classes of data (raw or pre-edited, numerical or text, digital or analog) the system will have to support. Until we pin down such uncertainties, a factor of four in either direction is not surprising as a range of estimates.

The above uncertainties are indeed pinned down once we complete the feasibility phase and settle on a particular concept of operation. At this stage, the range of our estimates diminishes to a factor of two in either direction. This range is reasonable

---

[4] These ranges have been determined subjectively, and are intended to represent 80 percent confidence limits, that is, "within a factor of four on either side, 80 percent of the time."

EXHIBIT 4   Software Cost Estimation Accuracy Versus Phase

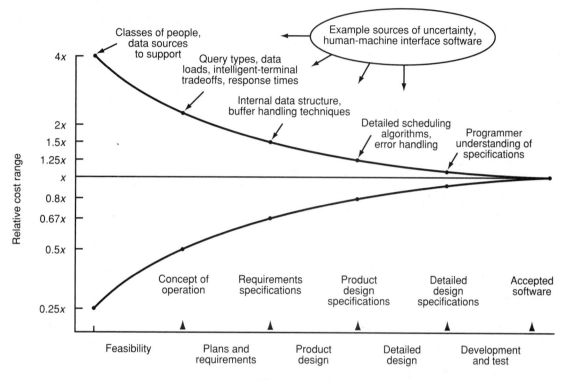

because we still have not pinned down such issues as the specific types of user query to be supported, or the specific functions to be performed within the microprocessor in the intelligent terminal. These issues will be resolved by the time we have developed a software requirements specification, at which point, we will be able to estimate the software costs within a factor of 1.5 in either direction.

By the time we complete and validate a product design specification, we will have resolved such issues as the internal data structure of the software product and the specific techniques for handling the buffers between the terminal microprocessor and the central processors on one side, and between the microprocessor and the display driver on the other. At this point, our software estimate should be accurate to within a factor of 1.25, the discrepancies being caused by some remaining sources of uncertainty such as the specific algorithms to be used for task scheduling, error handling, abort processing, and the like. These will be resolved by the end of the detailed design phase, but there will still be a residual uncertainty about 10 percent based on how well the programmers really understand the specifications to which they are to code. (This factor also includes such consideration as personnel turnover uncertainties during the development and test phases.)

B. Algorithmic Models for Software Cost Estimation

Algorithmic Cost Models: Early Development

Since the earliest days of the software field, people have been trying to develop algorithmic models to estimate software costs. The earliest attempts were simple rules of thumb, such as:

- on a large project, each software performer will provide an average of one checked-out instruction per man-hour (or roughly 150 instructions per man-month);
- each software maintenance person can maintain four boxes of cards (a box of cards held 2000 cards, or roughly 2000 instructions in those days of few comment cards).

Somewhat later, some projects began collecting quantitative data on the effort involved in developing a software product, and its distribution across the software life cycle. One of the earliest of these analyses was documented in 1956 in [8]. It indicated that, for very large operational software products on the order of 100,000 delivered source instructions (100 KDSI), that the overall productivity was more like 64 DSI/man-month, that another 100 KDSI of support-software would be required; that about 15,000 pages of documentation would be produced and 3000 hours of computer time consumed; and that the distribution of effort would be as follows:

Program Specs:	10 percent
Coding Specs:	30 percent
Coding:	10 percent
Parameter Testing:	20 percent
Assembly Testing:	30 percent

with an additional 30 percent required to produce operational specs for the system. Unfortunately, such data did not become well known, and many subsequent software projects went through a painful process of rediscovering them.

During the late 1950s and early 1960s, relatively little progress was made in software cost estimation, while the frequency and magnitude of software cost overruns was becoming critical to many large systems employing computers. In 1964, the U.S. Air Force contracted with System Development Corporation for a landmark project in the software cost estimation field. This project collected 104 attributes of 169 software projects and treated them to extensive statistical analysis. One result was the 1965 SDC cost model [41] which was the best possible statistical 13-parameter linear estimation model for the sample data:

$MM = -33.63$

$+ 9.15$ *(Lack of Requirements) (0-2)*

$+ 10.73$ *(Stability of Design) (0-3)*

$+ 0.51$ *(Percent Math Instructions)*

$+ 0.46$ *(Percent Storage/Retrieval Instructions)*

$+ 0.40$ *(Number of Subprograms)*

$+ 7.28$ *(Programming Language) (0-1)*

$- 21.45$ *(Business Application) (0-1)*

$+ 13.53$ *(Stand-Alone Program) (0.1)*

$+ 12.35$ *(First Program on Computer) (0-1)*

$+ 58.82$ *(Concurrent Hardware Development) (0-1)*

$+ 30.61$ *(Random Access Device Used) (0-1)*

$+ 29.55$ *(Difference Host, Target Hardware) (0-1)*

$+ 0.54$ *(Number of Personnel Trips)*

$- 25.20$ *(Developed by Military Organization) (0-1).*

The numbers in parentheses refer to ratings to be made by the estimator.

When applied to its database of 169 projects, this model produced a mean estimate of 40 MM and a standard deviation of 62 MM; not a very accurate predictor. Further, the application of the model is counterintuitive; a project with all zero ratings is estimated at minus 33 MM; changing language from a higher order language to assembly language adds 7 MM, independent of project size. The most conclusive result from the SDC study was that there were too many nonlinear aspects of software development for a linear cost-estimation model to work very well.

Still, the SDC effort provided a valuable base of information and insight for cost estimation and future models. Its cumulative distribution of productivity for 169 projects was a valuable aid for producing or checking cost estimates. The estimation rules of thumb for various phases and activities have been very helpful, and the data have been a major foundation for some subsequent cost models.

In the late 1960s and early 1970s, a number of cost models were developed which worked reasonably well for a certain restricted range of projects to which they were calibrated. Some of the more notable examples of such models are those described in [3], [54], [57].

The essence of the TRW Wolverton model [57] is shown in Exhibit 5, which shows a number of curves of software cost per object instruction as a function of relative degree of difficulty (0 to 100), novelty of the application (new or old), and type of project. The best use of the model involves breaking the software into components and estimating their cost individually. Thus, a 1000 object-instruction module of new data management software of medium (50 percent) difficulty would be costed at $46/instruction, or $46,000.

This model is well-calibrated to a class of near-real-time government command and control projects, but is less accurate for some other classes of projects. In addition, the model provides a good breakdown of project effort by phase and activity.

In the late 1970s, several software cost estimation models were developed which established a significant advance in the state of the art. These included the Putnam SLIM Model [44], the Doty Model [27], the RCA PRICE S model [22], the COCOMO model [11], the IBM-FSD model [53], the Boeing model [9], and a series of models developed by GRC [15]. A summary of these models, and the earlier SDC and Wolverton models, is shown in Exhibit 6, in terms of the size, program, computer, personnel, and project attributes used by each model to determine software costs. The first four of these models are discussed below.

The Putnam SLIM Model [44], [45]

The Putnam SLIM Model is a commercially available (from Quantitative Software Management, Inc.) software product based on Putnam's analysis of the software life cycle in terms of the Rayleigh distribution of project personnel level versus time. The basic effort macro-estimation model used in SLIM is

$$S_s = C_k K^{1/3} t_d^{4/3}$$

where

S_s = number of delivered source instructions

K = life-cycle effort in man-years

t_d = development time in years

C_k = a "technology constant."

Values of C_k typically range between 610 and 57,314. The current version of SLIM allows one to calibrate C_k to past projects or to estimate it as a function of a project's use of modern programming practices, hardware constraints, personnel experience, interactive development, and other factors. The required development effort, DE, is estimated as roughly 40 percent of the life-cycle effort for large systems. For smaller systems, the percentage varies as a function of system size.

The SLIM model includes a number of useful extensions to estimate such quantities as manpower distribution, cash flow, major-milestone schedules, reliability levels, and computer time and documentation costs.

The most controversial aspect of the SLIM model is its trade-off relationship between development effort K and between development time t_d. For a software product of a given size, the SLIM software equation above gives

$$K = \frac{constant}{t_d^4}.$$

For example, this relationship says that one can cut the cost of a software project in half, simply by increasing its development time by 19 percent

EXHIBIT 5   TRW Wolverton Model: Cost Per Object Instruction Versus Relative Degree of Difficulty

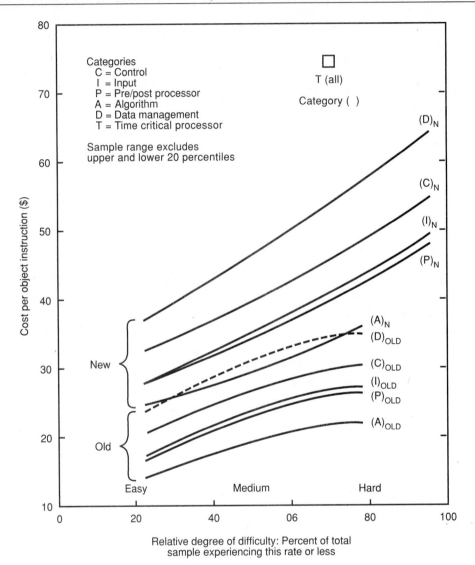

(e.g., from 10 months to 1 months). Exhibit 7 shows how the SLIM trade-off relationship compares with those of other models; see [11, ch. 27] for further discussion of this issue.

On balance, the SLIM approach has provided a number of useful insights into software cost esti-mation, such as the Rayleigh-curve distribution for one-shot software efforts, the explicit treatment of estimation risk and uncertainty, and the cube-root relationship defining the minimum development time achievable for a project requiring a given amount of effort.

EXHIBIT 6 Factors Used in Various Cost Models

Group	Factor	SDC, 1965	TRW, 1972	PUTNAM, SLIM	DOTY	RCA, PRICE S	IBM	BOEING, 1977	GRC, 1979	COCOMO	SOFCOST	DSN	JENSEN
SIZE ATTRIBUTES	Source Instructions	X		X	X	X	X	X		X	X	X	X
	Object Instructions	X	X		X	X							
	Number of Routines	X				X					X		
	Number of Data Items					X	X				X		
	Number of Output Formats								X	X		X	
	Documentation				X		X				X		X
	Number of Personnel			X			X	X			X		X
PROGRAM ATTRIBUTES	Type	X	X	X	X	X	X	X			X		X
	Complexity		X	X		X	X	X		X	X	X	X
	Language	X		X				X	X	X	X	X	
	Reuse			X		X		X	X	X	X	X	X
	Required Reliability			X		X		X	X	X	X		X
	Display Requirements				X						X		X
COMPUTER ATTRIBUTES	Time Constraint		X	X	X	X	X	X	X	X	X	X	X
	Storage Constraint			X	X	X	X		X	X	X	X	X
	Hardware Configuration	X				X							
	Concurrent Hardware Development	X			X	X	X			X	X	X	X
	Interfacing Equipment S/W										X	X	

EXHIBIT 6 *Cont.*

Group	Factor	SDC, 1965	TRW, 1972	PUTNAM, SLIM	DOTY	RCA, PRICE S	IBM	BOEING, 1977	GRC, 1979	COCOMO	SOFCOST	DSN	JENSEN
PERSONNEL ATTRIBUTES	Personnel Capability			X		X	X			X	X	X	X
	Personnel Continuity						X					X	
	Hardware Experience	X		X	X	X	X		X	X	X	X	X
	Applications Experience		X	X		X	X	X	X	X	X	X	X
	Language Experience			X		X	X		X	X	X	X	X
PROJECT ATTRIBUTES	Tools and Techniques			X		X	X	X		X	X	X	X
	Customer Interface	X					X				X	X	
	Requirements Definition	X			X		X				X	X	X
	Requirements Volatility	X			X	X	X		X	X	X	X	X
	Schedule			X		X				X	X	X	X
	Security						X				X	X	
	Computer Access			X	X		X	X		X	X	X	X
	Travel/Rehosting/Multi-site	X		X	X	X					X	X	
	Support Software Maturity			X		X				X		X	
CALIBRATION FACTOR													
EFFORT EQUATION	$MM_{NOM} = C(DSI)^X$ .X =		1.0		1.047		0.91	1.0		1.05–1.2		1.0	1.2
SCHEDULE EQUATION	$t_D = C (MM)^X$ .X =						0.35			0.32–0.38		0.356	0.333

68

EXHIBIT 7   Comparative Effort-Schedule Trade-off Relationships

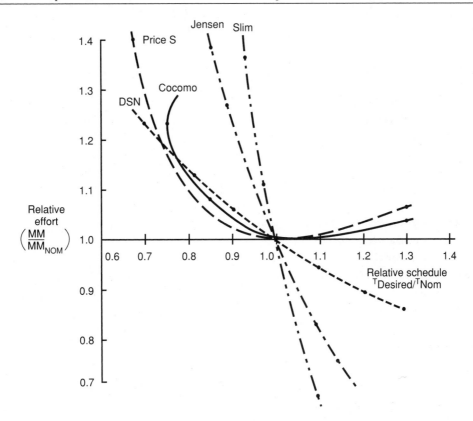

The Doty Model [27]

This model is the result of an extensive data analysis activity, including many of the data points from the SDC sample. A number of models of similar form were developed for different application areas. As an example, the model for general applications is

$$MM = 5.288 \ (KDSI)^{1.047}, \qquad for \ KDSI \geq 10$$

$$MM = 2.060 \ (KDSI)^{1.047}$$

$$\left(\prod_{j=1}^{14} f_j \right). \qquad for \ KDSI < 10.$$

The effort multipliers f_i are shown in Exhibit 8. This model has a much more appropriate func-

tional form than the SDC model, but it has some problems with stability, as it exhibits a discontinuity at KDSI = 10, and produces widely varying estimates via the f factors (answering "yes" to "first software developed on CPU" adds 92 percent to the estimated cost).

The RCA PRICE S Model [22]

PRICE S is a commercially available (from RCA, Inc.) macro cost-estimation model developed primarily for embedded system applications. It has improved steadily with experience; earlier versions with a widely varying subjective complexity factor have been replaced by versions in which a number of computer, personnel, and

---

EXHIBIT 8   Doty Model for Small Programs*

$$MM = 2.060\, I^{\,1.047} \prod_{j=1}^{j=14} f_j$$

Factor	f_j	Yes	No
Special display	f_1	1.11	1.00
Detailed definition of operational requirements	f_2	1.00	1.11
Change to operational requirements	f_3	1.05	1.00
Real-time operation	f_4	1.33	1.00
CPU memory constraint	f_5	1.43	1.00
CPU time constraint	f_6	1.33	1.00
First software developed on CPU	f_7	1.92	1.00
Concurrent development of ADP hardware	f_8	1.82	1.00
Timeshare versus batch processing, in development	f_9	0.83	1.00
Developer using computer at another facility	f_{10}	1.43	1.00
Development at operational site	f_{11}	1.39	1.00
Development computer different than target computer	f_{12}	1.25	1.00
Development at more than one site	f_{13}	1.25	1.00
Programmer access to computer	f_{14}	Limited	1.00
		Unlimited	0.90

* Less than 10,000 source instructions

---

project attributes are used to modulate the complexity rating.

PRICE S has extended a number of cost-estimating relationships developed in the early 1970s such as the hardware constraint function shown in Exhibit 9 [10]. It was primarily developed to handle military software projects, but now also includes rating levels to cover business applications.

PRICE S also provides a wide range of useful outputs of gross phase and activity distribution analyses, and monthly project cost-schedule-expected progress forecasts. Price S uses a two-parameter beta distribution rather than a Rayleigh curve to calculate development effort distribution versus calendar time.

PRICE S has recently added a software life-cycle support cost estimation capability called PRICE SL [34]. It involves the definition of three categories of support activities.

- *Growth:* The estimator specifies the amount of code to be added to the product. PRICE SL then uses its standard techniques to estimate the resulting life-cycle-effort distribution.
- *Enhancement:* PRICE SL estimates the fraction of the existing product which will be modified (the estimator may provide his own fraction), and uses its standard techniques to estimate the resulting life-cycle effort distribution.
- *Maintenance:* The estimator provides a parameter indicating the quality level of the developed code. PRICE SL uses this to estimate the effort required to eliminate remaining errors.

The COnstructive COst MOdel (COCOMO) [11]

The primary motivation for the COCOMO model has been to help people understand the cost conse-

EXHIBIT 9   RCA PRICE S Model: Effect of Hardware Constraints

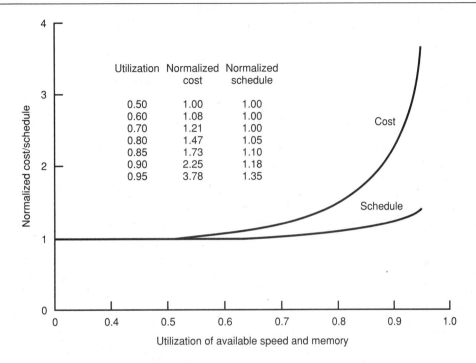

Utilization	Normalized cost	Normalized schedule
0.50	1.00	1.00
0.60	1.08	1.00
0.70	1.21	1.00
0.80	1.47	1.05
0.85	1.73	1.10
0.90	2.25	1.18
0.95	3.78	1.35

quences of the decisions they will make in commissioning, developing, and supporting a software product. Besides providing a software cost estimation capability, COCOMO therefore provides a great deal of material which explains exactly what costs the model is estimating, and why it comes up with the estimates it does. Further, it provides capabilities for sensitivity analysis and trade-off analysis of many of the common software engineering decision issues.

COCOMO is actually a hierarchy of three increasingly detailed models which range from a single macro-estimation scaling model as a function of product size to a micro-estimation model with a three-level work breakdown structure and a set of phase-sensitive multipliers for each cost driver attribute. To provide a reasonably concise example of a current state of the art cost estimation model, the intermediate level of COCOMO is described below.

Intermediate COCOMO estimates the cost of a proposed software product in the following way.

1. A nominal development effort is estimated as a function of the product's size in delivered source instructions in thousands (KDSI) and the project's development mode.

2. A set of effort multipliers are determined from the product's ratings on a set of 15 cost driver attributes.

3. The estimated development effort is obtained by multiplying the nominal effort estimate by all of the product's effort multipliers.

4. Additional factors can be used to determine dollar costs, development schedules, phase and activity distributions, computer costs, annual maintenance costs, and other elements from the development effort estimate.

Step 1—Nominal Effort Estimation:
First, Exhibit 10 is used to determine the project's development mode. Organic-mode projects typically come from stable, familiar, forgiving, relatively

EXHIBIT 10   COCOMO Software Development Modes

Feature	Mode		
	Organic	Semidetached	Embedded
Organizational understanding of product objectives	Thorough	Considerable	General
Experience in working with related software systems	Extensive	Considerable	Moderate
Need for software conformance with pre-established requirements	Basic	Considerable	Full
Need for software conformance with external interface specifications	Basic	Considerable	Full
Concurrent development of associated new hardware and operational procedures	Some	Moderate	Extensive
Need for innovative data processing architectures, algorithms	Minimal	Some	Considerable
Premium on early completion	Low	Medium	High
Product size range	< 50 KDSI	< 300 KDSI	All sizes
Examples	Batch data reduction Scientific models Business models Familiar OS, compiler Simple inventory, production control	Most transaction processing systems New OS, DBMS Ambitious inventory, production control Simple command-control	Large complex transaction processing systems Ambitious, very large OS Avionics Ambitious command-control

unconstrained environments, and were found in the COCOMO data analysis of 63 projects have a different scaling equation from the more ambitious, unfamiliar, unforgiving, tightly constrained embedded mode. The resulting scaling equations for each mode are given in Exhibit 11; these are used to determine the nominal development effort for the project in man-months as a function of the project's size in KDSI and the project's development mode.

For example, suppose we are estimating the cost to develop the microprocessor-based communica-tions processing software for a highly ambitious new electronic funds transfer network with high reliability, performance, development schedule, and interface requirements. From Exhibit 10, we determine that these characteristics best fit the profile of an embedded-mode project.

We next estimate the size of the product as 10,000 delivered source instructions, or 10 KDSI. From Exhibit 11, we then determine that the nominal development effort for this embedded-mode project is

$$2.8(10)^{1.20} = 44 \text{ man-months (MM)}.$$

EXHIBIT 11   COCOMO Nominal Effort and Schedule Equations

Development Mode	Nominal Effort	Schedule
Organic	$(MM)_{NOM} = 3.2(KDSI)^{1.05}$	$TDEV = 2.5(MM_{DEV})^{0.38}$
Semidetached	$(MM)_{NOM} = 3.0(KDSI)^{1.12}$	$TDEV = 2.5(MM_{DEV})^{0.35}$
Embedded	$(MM)_{NOM} = 2.8(KDSI)^{1.20}$	$TDEV = 2.5(MM_{DEV})^{0.32}$

(KDSI = thousands of delivered source instructions)

EXHIBIT 12   Intermediate COCOMO Software Development Effort Multipliers

Cost Drivers	Ratings					
	Very Low	Low	Nominal	High	Very High	Extra High
Product Attributes						
RELY Required software reliability	.75	.88	1.00	1.15	1.40	
DATA Data base size		.94	1.00	1.08	1.16	
CPLX Product complexity	.70	.85	1.00	1.15	1.30	1.65
Computer Attributes						
TIME Execution time constraint			1.00	1.11	1.30	1.66
STOR Main storage constraint			1.00	1.06	1.21	1.56
VIRT Virtual machine volatility*		.87	1.00	1.15	1.30	
TURN Computer turnaround time		.87	1.00	1.07	1.15	
Personnel Attributes						
ACAP Analyst capability	1.46	1.19	1.00	.86	.71	
AEXP Applications experience	1.29	1.13	1.00	.91	.82	
PCAP Programmer capability	1.42	1.17	1.00	.86	.70	
VEXP Virtual machine experience*	1.21	1.10	1.00	.90		
LEXP Programming language experience	1.14	1.07	1.00	.95		
Project Attributes						
MODP Use of modern programming practices	1.24	1.10	1.00	.91	.82	
TOOL Use of software tools	1.24	1.10	1.00	.91	.83	
SCED Required development schedule	1.23	1.08	1.00	1.04	1.10	

*For a given software product, the underlying virtual machine is the complex of hardware and software (OS, DBMS, etc) it calls on to accomplish its tasks

Step 2—Determine Effort Multipliers:

Each of the 15 cost driver attributes in COCOMO has a rating scale and a set of effort multipliers which indicate by how much the nominal effort estimate must be multiplied to account for the project's having to work at its rating level for the attribute.

These cost driver attributes and their corresponding effort multipliers are shown in Exhibit 12. The summary rating scales for each cost driver attribute are shown in Exhibit 13, except for the complexity rating scale which is shown in Exhibit 14 (expanded rating scales for the other attributes are provided in [11]).

The results of applying these tables to our microprocessor communications software example are shown in Exhibit 15. The effect of a software fault in the electronic fund transfer system could be a serious financial loss; therefore, the project's RELY rating from Exhibit 13 is High. Then, from Exhibit 12, the effort multiplier for achieving a High level of required reliability is 1.15, or 15 percent more effort than it would take to develop the software to a nominal level of required reliability.

The effort multipliers for the other cost driver attributes are obtained similarly, except for the Complexity attribute, which is obtained via Exhibit 14. Here, we first determine that communications processing is best classified under device-dependent operations (column 3 in Exhibit 14). From this column, we determine that communication line handling typically has a complexity rating of Very High; from Exhibit 12, then, we determine that its corresponding effort multiplier is 1.30.

Step 3—Estimate Development Effort:

We then compute the estimated development effort for the microprocessor communications software as the nominal development effort (44 MM) times the product of the effort multipliers for the 15 cost driver attributes in Exhibit 15 (1.35, in Exhibit 15). The resulting estimated effort for the project is then

$$(44\ MM)\ (1.35) = 59\ MM.$$

Step 4—Estimate Related Project Factors:

COCOMO has additional cost estimating relationships for computing the resulting dollar cost of the project and for the breakdown of cost and effort by life-cycle phase (requirements, design, etc.) and by type of project activity (programming, test planning, management, etc.). Further relationships support the estimation of the project's schedule and its phase distribution. For example, the recommended development schedule can be obtained from the estimated development man-months via the embedded-mode schedule equation in Exhibit 11:

$$T_{DEV} = 2.5(59)^{0.32} = 9\ months.$$

As mentioned above, COCOMO also supports the most common types of sensitivity analysis and trade-off analysis involved in scoping a software project. For example, from Exhibits 12 and 13, we can see that providing the software developers with an interactive computer access capability (Low turnaround time) reduces the TURN effort multiplier from 1.00 to 0.87, and thus reduces the estimated project effort from 59 MM to

$$(59\ MM)\ (0.87) = 51\ MM.$$

The COCOMO model has been validated with respect to a sample of 63 projects representing a wide variety of business, scientific, systems, real-time, and support software projects. For this sample, Intermediate COCOMO estimates come within 20 percent of the actuals about 68 percent of the time (see Exhibit 16). Since the residuals roughly follow a normal distribution, this is equivalent to a standard deviation of roughly 20 percent of the project actuals. This level of accuracy is representative of the current state of the art in software cost models. One can do somewhat better with the aid of a calibration coefficient (also a COCOMO option), or within a limited applications context, but it is difficult to improve significantly on this level of accuracy while the accuracy of software data collection remains in the "±20 percent" range.

A Pascal version of COCOMO is available for a nominal distribution charge from the Wang Institute, under the name WI-COMO [18].

EXHIBIT 13 COCOMO Software Cost Driver Ratings

Cost Driver			Ratings			
	Very Low	*Low*	*Nominal*	*High*	*Very High*	*Extra High*
Product attributes						
RELY	Effect: slight inconvenience	Low, easily recoverable losses	Moderate, recoverable losses	High financial loss	Risk to human life	
DATA		$\dfrac{\text{DBbytes}}{\text{Prog.DSI}} < 10$	$10 \leq \dfrac{D}{P} < 100$	$100 \leq \dfrac{D}{P} < 1000$	$\dfrac{D}{P} \geq 1000$	
CPLX	See Table 8					
Computer attributes						
TIME			≤ 50% use of available execution time	70%	85%	95%
STOR			≤ 50% use of available storage	70%	85%	95%
VIRT		Major change every 12 months Minor: 1 month	Major: 6 months Minor: 2 weeks	Major: 2 months Minor: 1 week	Major: 2 weeks Minor: 2 days	
TURN		Interactive	Average turnaround <4 hours	4–12 hours	>12 hours	

EXHIBIT 13 *Cont.*

Cost Driver	Very Low	Low	Nominal	High	Very High	Extra High
			Ratings			
Personnel attributes						
ACAP	15th percentile*	35th percentile	55th percentile	75th percentile	90th percentile	
AEXP	≤4 months experience	1 year	3 years	6 years	12 years	
PCAP	15th percentile*	35th percentile	55th percentile	75th percentile	90th percentile	
VEXP	≤1 month experience	4 months	1 year	3 years		
LEXP	≤1 month experience	4 months	1 year	3 years		
Project attributes						
MODP	No use	Beginning use	Some use	General use	Routine use	
TOOL	Basic microprocessor tools	Basic mini tools	Basic midi/maxi tools	Strong maxi programming, test tools	Add requirements, design, management, documentation tools	
SCED	75% of nominal	85%	100%	130%	160%	

*Team rating criteria: analyses (programming) ability, efficiency, ability to communicate and cooperate

EXHIBIT 14   COCOMO Module Complexity Ratings Versus Type of Module

Rating	Control Operations	Computational Operations	Device-dependent Operations	Data Management Operations
Very low	Straightline code with a few non-nested SP[a] operators: DOs, CASEs, IFTHENELSEs. Simple predicates	Evaluation of simple expressions: e.g., A = B + C * (D − E)	Simple read, write statements with simple formats	Simple arrays in main memory
Low	Straightforward nesting of SP operators. Mostly simple predicates	Evaluation of moderate-level expressions, e.g., D = SQRT (B**2 − 4, * A*C*)	No cognizance needed of particular processor or I/O device characteristics. I/O done at GET/PUT level. No cognizance of overlap	Single file subsetting with no data structure changes, no edits, no intermediate files
Nominal	Mostly simple nesting. Some intermodule control. Decision tables.	Use of standard math and statistical routines. Basic matrix/vector operations	I/O processing includes device selection, status checking and error processing	Multi-file input and single file output. Simple structural changes, simple edits
High	Highly nested SP operators with many compound predicates. Queue and stack control. Considerable intermodule control.	Basic numerical analysis: multivariate interpolation, ordinary differential equations. Basic truncation, roundoff concerns	Operations at physical I/O level (physical storage address translations: seeks, reads, etc.). Optimized I/O overlap	Special purpose subroutines activated by data stream contents. Complex data restructuring at record level
Very high	Reentrant and recursive coding. Fixed-priority interrupt handling	Difficult but structured N.A.: near-singular matrix equations, partial differential equations	Routines for interrupt diagnosis, servicing, masking. Communication line handling	A generalized, parameter-driven file structuring routine. File building, command processing, search optimization
Extra high	Multiple resource scheduling with dynamically changing priorities. Microcode-level control	Difficult and unstructured N.A.: highly accurate analysis of noisy, stochastic data	Device timing-dependent coding, micro-programmed operations	Highly coupled, dynamic relational structures. Natural language data management

[a] SP = structured programming

EXHIBIT 15   COCOMO Cost Driver Ratings: Microprocessor Communications Software

Cost Driver	Situation	Rating	Effort Multiplier
RELY	Serious financial consequences of software faults	High	1.15
DATA	20,000 bytes	Low	0.94
CPLX	Communications processing	Very High	1.30
TIME	Will use 70% of available time	High	1.11
STOR	45K of 64K store (70%)	High	1.06
VIRT	Based on commercial microprocessor hardware	Nominal	1.00
TURN	Two-hour average turnaround time	Nominal	1.00
ACAP	Good senior analysts	High	0.86
AEXP	Three years	Nominal	1.00
PCAP	Good senior programmers	High	0.86
VEXP	Six months	Low	1.10
LEXP	Twelve months	Nominal	1.00
MODP	Most techniques in use over one year	High	0.91
TOOL	At basic minicomputer tool level	Low	1.10
SCED	Nine months	Nominal	1.00
	Effort adjustment factor (product of effort multipliers)		1.35

Recent Software Cost Estimation Models

Most of the recent software cost estimation models tend to follow the Doty and COCOMO models in having a nominal scaling equation of the form $MM_{NOM} = c(KDSI)^x$ and a set of multiplicative effort adjustment factors determined by a number of cost driver attribute ratings. Some of them use the Rayleigh curve approach to estimate distribution across the software life-cycle, but most use a more conservative effort schedule trade-off relation than the SLIM model. These aspects have been summarized for the various models in Exhibit 6 and Exhibit 7.

The Bailey-Basili meta-model [4] derived the scaling equation

$$MM_{NOM} = 3.5 + 0.73 \ (KDSI)^{1.16}$$

and used two additional cost driver attributes (methodology level and complexity) to model the development effort of 18 projects in the NASA-Goddard Software Engineering Laboratory to within a standard deviation of 15 percent. Its accuracy for other project situations has not been determined.

The Grumman SOFCOST Model [19] uses a similar but unpublished nominal effort scaling equation, modified by 30 multiplicative cost driver variables rated on a scale of 0 to 10. Exhibit 6 includes a summary of these variables.

The Tausworthe Deep Space Network (DSN) model [50] uses a linear scaling equation ($MM_{NOM} = a(KDSI)^{1.0}$) and a similar set of cost driver attributes, also summarized in Exhibit 6. It also has a well-considered approach for determining the equivalent KDSI involved in adapting existing software within a new product. It uses the Rayleigh curve to determine the phase distribution of effort, but uses a considerably more conservative version of the SLIM effort-schedule trade-off relationship (see Exhibit 7).

EXHIBIT 16   Intermediate COCOMO Estimates Versus Project Actuals

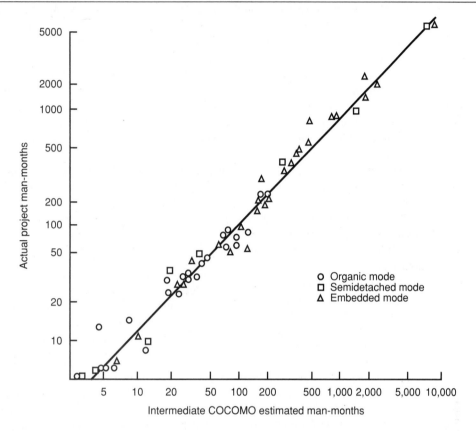

The Jensen model [30], [31] is a commercially available model with a similar nominal scaling equation, and a set of cost driver attributes very similar to the Doty and COCOMO models (but with different effort multiplier ranges); see Exhibit 6. Some of the multiplier ranges in the Jensen model vary as functions of other factors; e.g., increasing access to computer resources widens the multiplier ranges on such cost drivers as personnel capability and use of software tools. It uses the Rayleigh curve for effort distribution, and a somewhat more conservative effort-schedule trade-off relation than SLIM (Exhibit 7). As with the other commercial models, the Jensen model produces a number of useful outputs on resource expenditure rates, probability distributions on costs and schedules, etc.

Outstanding Research Issues in Software Cost Estimation

Although a good deal of progress has been made in software cost estimation, a great deal remains to be done. This section updates the state-of-the-art review published in [11], and summarizes the outstanding issues needing further research:

1. Software size estimation;
2. Software size and complexity metrics;
3. Software cost driver attributes and their effects;
4. Software cost model analysis and refinement;
5. Quantitative models of software project dynamics;
6. Quantitative models of software life-cycle evolution;
7. Software data collection.

1. *Software Size Estimation:* The biggest difficulty in using today's algorithmic software cost models is the problem of providing sound sizing estimates. Virtually every model requires an estimate of the number of source or object instructions to be developed, and this is an extremely difficult quantity to determine in advance. It would be most useful to have some formula for determining the size of a software product in terms of quantities known early in the software life cycle, such as the number and/or size of the files, input formats, reports, displays, requirements specification elements, or design specification elements.

Some useful steps in this direction are the function-point approach in [2] and the sizing estimation model of [29], both of which have given reasonably good results for small-to-medium sized business programs within a single data processing organization. Another more general approach is given by DeMarco in [17]. It has the advantage of basing its sizing estimates on the properties of specifications developed in conformance with DeMarco's paradigm models for software specifications and designs: number of functional primitives, data elements, input elements, output elements, states, transitions between states, relations, modules, data tokens, control tokens, etc. To date, however, there has been relatively little calibration of the formulas to project data. A recent IBM study [14] shows some correlation between the number of variables defined in a state-machine design representation and the product size in source instructions.

Although some useful results can be obtained on the software sizing problem, one should not expect too much. A wide range of functionality can be implemented beneath any given specification element or I/O element, leading to a wide range of sizes (recall the uncertainty ranges of this nature in Exhibit 4). For example, two experiments, involving the use of several teams developing a software program to the same overall functional specification, yielded size ranges of factors of 3 to 5 between programs (see Exhibit 17).

The primary implication of this situation for practical software sizing and cost estimation is that *there is no royal road to software sizing.* This is no magic formula that will provide an easy and accurate substitute for the process of thinking through and fully understanding the nature of the software product to be developed. There are still a number of useful things that one can do to improve the situation, including the following.

- Use techniques which explicitly recognize the ranges of variability in software sizing. The PERT estimation technique [56] is a good example.
- Understand the primary sources of bias in software sizing estimates. See [11, ch. 21].
- Develop and use a corporate memory on the nature and size of previous software products.

2. *Software Size and Complexity Metrics:* Delivered source instructions (DSI) can be faulted for being too low-level a metric for use in early sizing estimation. On the other hand, DSI can also be faulted for being too high-level a metric for precise software cost estimation. Various complexity metrics have been formulated to more accurately capture the relative information content of a program's instructions, such as the Halstead Software Science metrics [24], or to capture the relative control complexity of a program, such as the metrics formulated by McCabe in [39]. A number of variations

---

EXHIBIT 17   Size Ranges of Software Products Performing Same Function

Experiment	*Product*	*No. of Teams*	*Size Range (source-instr.)*
Weinberg & Schulman [55]	Simultaneous linear equations	6	33–165
Boehm, Gray, & Seewaldt [13]	Interactive cost model	7	1514–4606

of these metrics have been developed; a good recent survey of them is given in [26].

However, these metrics have yet to exhibit any practical superiority to DSI as a predictor of the relative effort required to develop software. Most recent studies [48], [32] show a reasonable correlation between these complexity metrics and development effort, but no better a correlation than that between DSI and development effort.

Further, the recent [25] analysis of the software science results indicates that many of the published software science "successes" were not as successful as they were previously considered. It indicates that much of the apparent agreement between software science formulas and project data was due to factors overlooked in the data analysis: inconsistent definitions and interpretations of software science quantities, unrealistic or inconsistent assumptions about the nature of the projects analyzed, overinterpretation of the significance of statistical measures such as the correlations coefficient, and lack of investigation of alternative explanations for the data. The software science use of psychological concepts such as the Stroud number have also been seriously questioned in [16].

The overall strengths and difficulties of software science are summarized in [47]. Despite the difficulties, some of the software science metrics have been useful in such areas as identifying error-prone modules. In general, there is a strong intuitive argument that more definitive complexity metrics will eventually serve as better bases for definitive software cost estimation than will DSI. Thus, the area continues to be an attractive one for further research.

3. *Software Cost Driver Attributes and Their Effects:* Most of the software cost models discussed above contain a selection of cost driver attributes and a set of coefficients, functions, or tables representing the effect of the attribute on software cost (see Exhibit 6). Chapter 24–28 of [11] contain summaries of the research to date on about 20 of the most significant cost driver attributes, plus statements of nearly 100 outstanding research issues in the area.

Since the publication of [11] in 1981, a few new results have appeared. Lawrence [35] provides an analysis of 278 business data processing programs which indicate a fairly uniform development rate in procedure lines of code per hour, some significant effects on programming rate due to batch turnaround time and level of experience, and relatively little effect due to use of interactive operation and modern programming practices (due, perhaps, to the relatively repetitive nature of the software jobs sampled). Okada and Azuma [42] analyzed 30 CAD/CAM programs and found some significant effects due to type of software, complexity, personnel skill level, and requirements volatility.

4. *Software Cost Model Analysis and Refinement:* The most useful comparative analysis of software cost models to date is the Thibodeau [52] study performed for the U.S. Air Force. This study compared the results of several models (the Wolverton, Doty, PRICE S, and SLIM models discussed earlier, plus models from the Boeing, SDC, Tecolote, and Aerospace corporations) with respect to 45 project data points from three sources.

Some generally useful comparative results were obtained, but the results were not definitive, as models were evaluated with respect to larger and smaller subsets of the data. Not too surprisingly, the best results were generally obtained using models with calibration coefficients against data sets with few points. In general, the study concluded that the models with calibration coefficients achieved better results, but that none of the models evaluated were sufficiently accurate to be used as a definitive Air Force software cost estimation model.

Some further comparative analyses are currently being conducted by various organizations, using the database of 63 software projects in [11], but to date none of these have been published.

In general, such evaluations play a useful role in model refinement. As certain models are found to be inaccurate in certain situations, efforts are made to determine the causes, and to refine the model to eliminate the sources of inaccuracy.

Relatively less activity has been devoted to the formulation, evaluation, and refinement of models to cover the effects of more advanced methods of software development (prototyping, incremental development, use of application generators, etc.) or to estimate other software-related life-cycle costs (conversion, maintenance, installation, training, etc.). An exception is the excellent work on software conversion cost estimation performed by the Federal Conversion Support Center [28]. An extensive model to estimate avionics software support costs using a weighted-multiplier technique has recently been developed [49]. Also, some initial experimental results have been obtained on the quantitative impact of prototyping in [13] and on the impact of very high level nonprocedural languages in [58]. In both studies, projects using prototyping and VHLL's were completed with significantly less effort.

5. *Quantitative Models of Software Project Dynamics:* Current software cost estimation models are limited in their ability to represent the internal dynamics of a software project and to estimate how the project's phase distribution of effort and schedule will be affected by environmental or project management factors. For example, it would be valuable to have a model which would accurately predict the effort and schedule distribution effects of investing in more thorough design verification, of pursuing an incremental development strategy, of varying the staffing rate or experience mix, of reducing module size, etc.

Some current models assume a universal effort distribution, such as the Rayleigh curve [44] or the activity distributions in [57], which are assumed to hold for any type of project situation. Somewhat more realistic, but still limited are models with phase-sensitive effort multipliers such as PRICE S [22] and Detailed COCOMO [11].

Recently, some more realistic models of software project dynamics have begun to appear, although to date none of them have been calibrated to software project data. The Phister phase-by-phase model in [43] estimates the effort and schedule required to design, code, and test a software product as a function of such variables as the staffing level during each phase the size of the average module to be developed, and such factors as interpersonal communications overhead rates and error detection rates. The Abdel Hamid-Madnick model [1], based on Forrester's System Dynamics world-view, estimates the time distribution of effort, schedule, and residual defects as a function of such factors as staffing rates, experience mix, training rates, personnel turnover, defect introduction rates, and initial estimation errors. Tausworthe [51] derives and calibrates alternative versions of the SLIM effort-schedule trade-off relationship, using an intercommunication-overhead model of project dynamics. Some other recent models of software project dynamics are the Mitre SWAP model and the Duclos [21] total software life-cycle model.

6. *Quantitative Models of Software Life-Cycle Evolution:* Although most of the software effort is devoted to the software maintenance (or life-cycle support) phase, only a few significant results have been obtained to date in formulating quantitative models of the software life-cycle evolution process. Some basic studies by Belady and Lehman analyzed data on several projects and derived a set of fairly general "laws of program evolution" [7], [37]. For example, the first of these laws states:

> "A program that is used and that as an implementation of its specification reflects some other reality, undergoes continual change or becomes progressively less useful. The change or decay process continues until it is judged more cost effective to replace the system with a recreated version."

Some general quantitative support for these laws was obtained in several studies during the 1970s, and in more recent studies such as [33]. However, efforts to refine these general laws into a set of testable hypotheses have met with mixed results. For example, the Lawrence [36] statistical analysis of the Belady-Lahman data showed that the data supported an even stronger form of the first law ("systems grow in size over their useful life"); that one of the laws could not be formulated precisely enough to be tested by the data; and that the other three laws did not lead to hypotheses that were supported by the data.

However, it is likely that variant hypotheses can be found that are supported by the data (for example, the operating system data supports some of the hypotheses better than does the applications data). Further research is needed to clarify this important area.

7. *Software Data Collection:* A fundamental limitation to significant progress in software cost estimation is the lack of unambiguous, widely used standard definitions for software data. For example, if an organization reports its "software development man-months," do these include the effort devoted to requirements analysis, to training, to secretaries, to quality assurance, to technical writers, to uncompensated overtime? Depending on one's interpretations, one can easily cause variations of over 20 percent (and often over a factor of 2) in the meaning of reported "software development man-months" between organizations (and similarly for "delivered instructions," "complexity," "storage constraint," etc.). Given such uncertainties in the ground data, it is not surprising that software cost estimation models cannot do much better than "within 20 percent of the actuals, 70 percent of the time."

Some progress towards clear software data definitions has been made. The IBM FSD database used in [53] was carefully collected using thorough data definitions, but the detailed data and definitions are not generally available. The NASA-Goddard Software Engineering Laboratory database [5], [6], [40] and the COCOMO database [11] provide both clear data definitions and an associated project database which are available for general use (and reasonably compatible). The recent Mitre SARE report [59] provides a good set of data definitions.

But there is still no commitment across organizations to establish and use a set of clear and uniform software data definitions. Until this happens, our progress in developing more precise software cost estimation methods will be severely limited.

IV. SOFTWARE ENGINEERING ECONOMICS BENEFITS AND CHALLENGES

This final section summarizes the benefits to software engineering and software management provided by a software engineering economics perspective in general and by software cost estimation technology in particular. It concludes with some observations on the major challenges awaiting the field.

Benefits of a Software Engineering Economics Perspective

The major benefit of an economic perspective on software engineering is that it provides a balanced view of candidate software engineering solutions, and an evaluation framework which takes account not only of the programming aspects of a situation, but also of the human problems of providing the best possible information processing service within a resource-limited environment. Thus, for example, the software engineering economics approach does not say, "we should use these structured structures because they are mathematically elegant" or "because they run like the wind" or "because they are part of the structured revolution." Instead, it says "we should use these structured structures because they provide people with more benefits in relation to their costs than do other approaches." And besides the framework, of course, it also provides the techniques which help us to arrive at this conclusion.

Benefits of Software Cost Estimation Technology

The major benefit of a good software cost estimation model is that it provides a clear and consistent universe of discourse within which to address a good many of the software engineering issues which arise throughout the software life cycle. It can help people get together to discuss such issues as the following.

- Which and how many features should we put into the software product?
- Which features should we put in first?
- How much hardware should we acquire to support the software product's development, operation, and maintenance?

- How much money and how much calendar time should we allow for software development?
- How much of the product should we adapt from existing software?
- How much should we invest in tools and training?

Further, a well-defined software cost estimation model can help avoid the frequent misinterpretations, underestimates, overexpectations, and outright buy-ins which still plague the software field. In a good cost-estimation model, there is no way of reducing the estimated software cost without changing some objectively verifiable property of the software project. This does not make it impossible to create an unachievable buy-in, but it significantly raises the threshold of credibility.

A related benefit of software cost estimation technology is that it provides a powerful set of insights on how a software organization can improve its productivity. Many of a software cost model's cost-driver attributes are management controllables: use of software tools and modern programming practices, personnel capability and experience, available computer speed, memory, and turnaround time, software reuse. The cost model helps us determine how to adjust these management controllables to increase productivity, and further provides an estimate of how much of a productivity increase we are likely to achieve with a given level of investment. For more information on this topic, see [11, ch. 33], [12] and the recent plan for the U.S. Department of Defense Software Initiative [20].

Finally, software cost estimation technology provides an absolutely essential foundation for software project planning and control. Unless a software project has clear definitions of its key milestones and realistic estimates of the time and money it will take to achieve them, there is no way that a project manager can tell whether his project is under control or not. A good set of cost and schedule estimates can provide realistic data for the PERT charts, work breakdown structures, manpower schedules, earned value increments, etc., necessary to establish management visibility and control.

Note that this opportunity to improve management visibility and control requires a complementary management commitment to define and control the reporting of data on software progress and expenditures. The resulting data are therefore worth collecting simply for their management value in comparing plans versus achievements, but they can serve another valuable function as well: they provide a continuing stream of calibration data for evolving a more accurate and refined software cost estimation models.

Software Engineering Economics Challenges

The opportunity to improve software project management decision making through improved software cost estimation, planning, data collection, and control brings us back full-circle to the original objectives of software engineering economics: to provide a better quantitative understanding of how software people make decisions in resource-limited situations.

The more clearly we as software engineers can understand the quantitative and economic aspects of our decision situations, the more quickly we can progress from a pure seat-of-the-pants approach on software decisions to a more rational approach which puts all of the human and economic decision variables into clear perspective. Once these decision situations are more clearly illuminated, we can then study them in more detail to address the deeper challenge: achieving a quantitative understanding of how people work together in the software engineering process.

Given the rather scattered and imprecise data currently available in the software engineering field, it is remarkable how much progress has been made on the software cost estimation problem so far. But, there is not much further we can go until better data becomes available. The software field cannot hope to have its Kepler or its Newton until it has had its army of Tycho Brahes, carefully preparing the well-defined observational data from which a deeper set of scientific insights may be derived.

References

1. T. K. Abdel-Hamid and S. E. Madnick, "A model of software project management dynamics," in *Proc. IEEE COMPSAC 82,* Nov. 1982, pp. 539–554.

2. A. J. Albrecht, "Measuring Application Development Productivity," in *SHARE-GUIDE,* 1979, pp. 83–92.

3. J. D. Aron, "Estimating resources for large programming systems," NATO Sci. Committee, Rome, Italy, Oct. 1969.

4. J. J. Bailey and V. R. Basili, "A meta-model for software development resource expenditures," in *Proc. 5th Int. Conf. Software Eng.,* IEEE/ACM/NBS, Mar. 1981, pp. 107–116.

5. V. R. Basili, "Tutorial on models and metrics for software and engineering," IEEE Cat. EHO-167-7, Oct. 1980.

6. V. R. Basili and D. M. Weiss, "A methodology for collecting valid software engineering data," Univ. Maryland Technol. Rep. TR-1235, Dec. 1982.

7. L. A. Belady and M. M. Lehman, "Characteristics of large systems," in *Research Directions in Software Technology,* P. Wegner, Ed. Cambridge, MA: MIT Press, 1979.

8. H. D. Benington, "Production of large computer programs," in *Proc. ONR Symp. Advanced Programming Methods for Digital Computers,* June 1956, pp. 15–27.

9. R. K. D. Black, R. P. Curnow, R. Katz, and M. D. Gray, "BCS software production data," Boeing Comput. Services, Inc., Final Tech. Rep., RADC-TR-77-116, NTIS AD-A039852, Mar. 1977.

10. B. W. Boehm, "Software and its impact: A quantitative assessment," *Datamation,* pp. 48–59, May 1973.

11. ———, *Software Engineering Economics.* Englewood Cliffs, NJ: Prentice-Hall, 1981.

12. B. W. Boehm, J. F. Elwell, A. B. Pyster, E. D. Stuckle, and R. D. Williams, "The TRW software productivity system," In *Proc. IEEE 6th Int. Conf. Software Eng.,* Sept. 1982.

13. B. W. Boehm, T. E. Gray, and T. Seewaldt, "Prototyping vs. specifying: A multi-project experiment," *IEEE Trans. Software Eng.,* to be published.

14. R. N. Britcher and J. E. Gaffney, "Estimates of software size from state machine designs," in *Proc. NASA-Goddard Software Eng. Workshop,* Dec. 1982.

15. W. M. Carriere and R. Thibodeau, "Development of a logistics software cost estimating technique for foreign military sales," General Res. Corp., Rep. CR-3-839, June 1979.

16. N. S. Coulter, "Software science and cognitive psychology," *IEEE Trans. Software Eng.,* pp. 166–171, Mar. 1983.

17. T. DeMarco, *Controlling Software Projects.* New York: Yourdon, 1982.

18. M. Demshki, D. Ligett, B. Linn, G. McCluskey, and R. Miller, "Wang Institute cost model (WICOMO) tool user's manual." Wang Inst. Graduate Studies, Tyngsboro, MA, June 1982.

19. H. F. Dircks, "SOFCOST: Grumman's software cost eliminating model," in *IEEE NAECON 1981,* May 1981.

20. L. E. Druffel, "Strategy for DoD software initiative," RADC/DACS, Griffiss AFB, NY, Oct. 1982.

21. L. C. Duclos, "Simulation model for the life-cycle of a software product: A quality assurance approach," Ph.D. dissertation, Dep. Industrial and Syst. Eng., Univ. Southern California, Dec. 1982.

22. F. R. Freiman and R. D. Park, "PRICE software model—Version 3: An overview," in *Proc. IEEE-PINY Workshop on Quantitative Software Models,* IEEE Cat. TH0067-9, Oct. 1979, pp. 32–41.

23. R. Goldberg and H. Lorin, *The Economics of Information Processing.* New York: Wiley, 1982.

24. M. H. Halstead, *Elements of Software Science.* New York: Elsevier, 1977.

25. P. G. Hamer and G. D. Frewin, "M. H. Halstead's software science—A critical examination," in *Proc. IEEE 6th Int. Conf. Software Eng.,* Sept. 1982, pp. 197–205.

26. W. Harrison, K. Magel, R. Kluczney, and A. DeKock, "Applying software complexity metrics to program maintenance," *Computer,* pp. 65–79, Sept. 1982.

27. J. R. Herd, J. N. Postak, W. W. Russell, and K. R. Stewart, "Software cost estimation study—Study results," Doty Associates, Inc., Rockville, MD, Final Tech. Rep. RADC-TR-77-220, vol. 1 (of two), June 1977.

28. C. Houtz and T. Buschbach, "Review and analysis of conversion cost-estimating techniques," GSA Federal Conversion Support Center, Falls Church, VA, Rep. GSA/FCSC-81/001, Mar. 1981.

29. M. Itakura and A. Takayanagi, "A model for estimating program size and its evaluation," in *Proc. IEEE 6th Software Eng.,* Sept. 1982, pp. 104–109.

30. R. W. Jensen, "An improved macrolevel software development resource estimation model," in *Proc. 5th ISPA Conf.,* Apr. 1983, pp. 88–92.

31. R. W. Jensen and S. Lucas, "Sensitivity analysis of the Jensen software model," in *Proc. 5th ISPA Conf.,* Apr. 1983, pp. 384–389.

32. B. A. Kitchenham, "Measures of programming complexity," *ICL Tech. J.,* pp. 298–316, May 1981.

33. ———, "Systems evolution dynamics of VME/B," *ICL Tech. J.,* pp. 43–57, May 1982.

34. W. W. Kuhn, "A software lifecycle case study using the PRICE model," in *Proc. IEEE NAECON,* May 1982.

35. M. J. Lawrence, "Programming methodology, organizational environment, and programming productivity," *J. Syst. Software,* pp. 257–270, Sept. 1981.

36. ——, "An examination of evolution dynamics," in *Proc. IEEE 6th Int. Conf. Software Eng.,* Sept. 1982, pp. 188–196.

37. M. M. Lehman, "Programs, life cycles, and laws of software evolution," *Proc. IEEE,* pp. 1060–1076, Sept. 1980.

38. R. D. Luce and H. Raiffa, *Games and Decisions.* New York: Wiley, 1957.

39. T. J. McCabe, "A complexity measure," *IEEE Trans. Software Eng.,* pp. 308–320, Dec. 1976.

40. F. E. McGarry, "Measuring software development technology: What have we learned in six years," in *Proc. NASA-Goddard Software Eng. Workshop,* Dec. 1982.

41. E. A. Nelson, "Management handbook for the estimation of computer programming costs," Syst. Develop. Corp., AD-A648750, Oct. 31, 1966.

42. M. Okada and M. Azuma, "Software development estimation study—A model from CAD/CAM system development experiences," in *Proc. IEEE COMPSAC 82,* Nov. 1982, pp. 555–564.

43. M. Phister, Jr., "A model of the software development process," *J. Syst. Software,* pp. 237–256, Sept. 1981.

44. L. H. Putnam, "A general empirical solution to the macro software sizing and estimating problem," *IEEE Trans. Software Eng.,* pp. 345–361, July 1978.

45. L. H. Putnam and A. Fitzsimmons, "Estimating software costs," *Datamation,* pp. 189–198, Sept. 1979; continued in *Datamation,* pp. 171–178, Oct. 1979 and pp. 137–140, Nov. 1979.

46. L. H. Putnam, "The real economics of software development," in *The Economics of Information Processing,* R. Goldberg and H. Lorin. New York: Wiley, 1982.

47. V. Y. Shen, S. D. Conte, and H. E. Dunsmore, "Software science revisited: A critical analysis of the theory and its empirical support," *IEEE Trans. Software Eng.,* pp. 155–165, Mar. 1983.

48. T. Sunohara, A. Takano, K. Uehara, and T. Ohkawa, "Program complexity measure for software development management," in *Proc. IEEE 5th Int. Conf. Software Eng.,* Mar. 1981, pp. 100–106.

49. SYSCON Corp., "Avionics software support cost model," USAF Avionics Lab., AFWAL-TR-1173, Feb. 1, 1983.

50. R. C. Tausworthe, "Deep space network software cost estimation model," Jet Propulsion Lab., Pasadena, CA, 1981.

51. ——, "Staffing implications of software productivity models," in *Proc. 7th Annu. Software Eng. Workshop,* NASA/Goddard, Greenbelt, MD, Dec. 1982.

52. R. Thibodeau, "An evaluation of software cost estimating models," General Res. Corp., Rep. T10-2670, Apr. 1981.

53. C. E. Walston and C. P. Felix, "A method of program-ming measurement and estimation," *IBM Syst. J.,* vol. 16, no. 1, pp. 54–73, 1977.

54. G. F. Weinwurm, Ed., *On the Management of Computer Programming.* New York: Auerbach, 1970.

55. G. M. Weinberg and E. L. Schulman, "Goals and performance in computer programming," *Human Factors,* vol. 16, no. 1, pp. 70–77, 1974.

56. J. D. Wiest and F. K. Levy, *A Management Guide to PERT/CPM.* Englewood Cliffs, NJ: Prentice-Hall, 1977.

57. R. W. Wolverton, "The cost of developing large-scale software," *IEEE Trans. Comput.,* pp. 615–636, June 1974.

58. E. Harel and E. R. McLean, "The effects of using a nonprocedural computer language on programmer productivity," UCLA Inform. Sci. Working Paper 3-83, Nov. 1982.

59. R. L. Dumas, "Final report: Software acquisition resource expenditure (SARE) data collection methodology," MITRE Corp., MTR 9031, Sept. 1983.

SOFTWARE COST ESTIMATION MODELS

INTRODUCTION

Practitioners have expressed concern over their inability to estimate accurately costs associated with software development. This concern has become even more pressing as costs associated with

Article by Chris F. Kemerer. Reprinted by permission of Butterworth-Heinemann Ltd. Copyright 1991

development continue to increase. As a result, considerable research attention is now directed at gaining a better understanding of the software development process as well as constructing and evaluating software cost estimating tools.

The purpose of this chapter is to provide prac-tising software development managers with an overview of work in the area of cost estimation models. The chapter is organized as follows. The first sections are a discussion of why estimation is a difficult problem, and why algorithmic models may be of use to the manager. Then an overview of three types of cost estimation models is presented. A review of empirical studies of these models follows this section. Finally, some recent research is summarized, and some suggestions for the practising manager are given. At the end of the chapter is a bibliography of the software cost estimation models literature for the reader who wishes to continue learning about this topic.

THE MANAGEMENT PROBLEM

It is a rare software development manager who can claim to be able to estimate accurately the costs associated with writing new systems. More likely, he falls into that unhappy category of typical developers who often underestimate large ($>60,000$ source lines of code) projects by anywhere from 100 to 200% (Jones, 1986b).

There are three main areas of impact of this inability to reliably plan projects: economic, technical and managerial. The economic impacts are most obvious on projects that are grossly misestimated. In the case of an internal systems department developing projects for its own firm, the late realization that the project will not be completed anywhere near the budget typically results in the project being cancelled, with the associated waste of all work done to date. Jones (1986b) has estimated that as many as 15% of large systems development projects never deliver anything, and initial misunderstandings of the scope of the project are clearly one cause of these failures. In the case of an outside contractor, underestimates will result in going back to the client, 'hat in hand', in an effort to secure additional funds. If the contract is on a fixed price basis, the contractor will be saddled with the cost of the overrun.

While these economic problems are perhaps the most obvious negative result of underestimates, serious technical problems are also possible. When the budgeted end of the project draws near, but substantial additional work remains, the tendency is to scrimp on the final tasks in order to complete the project at or near the budget. Unfortunately, in the systems development life cycle the last tasks are usually testing, documentation and training. Therefore, the result is systems that are less reliable and less well received by their ultimate users. While underestimation is not the only reason for these problems, it is clearly a contributing factor.

Finally, underestimation leads to a number of managerial problems as well. When an unrealistic deadline draws near additional pressures are brought to bear on the staff to complete the project in a hurry. Besides the likely short-term detrimental effect on the quality of work produced, the long-term effect on morale is also costly. Personnel are pulled from other assignments in order to 'save' the project in trouble, often resulting in a worse problem than the original one—the so-called 'Brooks Law' phenomenon (Brooks, 1975). If this problem is pervasive, then a sort of 'crisis mentality' can develop, where only projects of this type get any managerial attention. Also, staff turnover due to burnout can only increase.

DIFFICULTY OF SOFTWARE COST ESTIMATION

Given the costs associated with chronic underestimation described above, it is clear that management should desire to remedy this unfortunate situation. But to develop better estimates there needs to be some understanding of why software cost estimation is so difficult.

DeMarco has written a very readable book entitled *Controlling Software Projects* (1982), in which he outlines four reasons why software cost estimates are typically not accurate. The first of these is that developing an estimate is a complex task, requiring a significant amount of effort to do correctly. Unfortunately, a number of factors work against this ideal. Estimates are often done hurriedly, without an appreciation for the effort required to do a credible job. In addition, it is too often the case that an estimate is needed before clear specifications of the system requirements have been produced. Therefore, a typical situation is an estimator being pressured to quickly write an estimate for a system that he/she does not fully understand.

A second barrier to good estimates is the fact that the people developing the estimates (typically the project leader) generally do not have much experience at developing estimates, especially for large projects. Compounding this problem is the fact that few firms collect project data with which to check new estimates (more on this below). Therefore, project managers often start by doing a bad job and never get any better.

The third and fourth problems are related. They are an apparent human bias towards underestimation coupled with a management that asks for an estimate but often really desires a goal. One problem is that an estimator is likely to consider how long a certain portion of the system would take, and then to merely extrapolate this estimate to the rest of the system, thereby ignoring the nonlinear aspects of systems development including the overhead associated with coordinating a number of interconnected efforts. Another common underestimation problem is that the estimator, often the project manager or senior staff member, estimates the amount of time it would take him/her to do a task, forgetting the fact that in all likelihood, large portions of the system will be written by relatively more junior staff who will require more time. These underestimates are compounded by the fact that management typically tends to want to reduce the estimate to some degree, to make the bid look more attractive or to 'maximize productivity by reducing slack'. Therefore, an estimate that was probably too low to begin with gets further reduced.

AN ALTERNATIVE: ALGORITHMIC COST ESTIMATE ON MODELS

Boehm has defined a set of approaches to software cost estimation (1981). They include: expert judgment, analogy, top-down, bottom-up, and algorithmic models. The first four all suffer from the limits on human decision making capability described above. In situations such as these, ex-

plicit decision models are often recommended as an alternative or augmentation to the human decision maker (Tversky and Kahneman, 1974). Moreover, given that accurate software cost estimation is such a universal problem, it is not surprising that a large number of such models have been developed. Of course, the models are still subject to some human limitations in their use and interpretation, but the intent of these models is to provide a more unbiased, relatively independent source of cost estimates.

THREE STREAMS OF MODEL DEVELOPMENT

The first published papers in this area started to appear in the late 1960s and early 1970s, and a good history of some of the earliest models appears in Barry Boehm's book, *Software Engineering Economics* (1981) and see also Boehm (1984). Two types of models emerged from this early work, one of which might be termed the economic stream, represented by the work at TRW and IBM (Woverton, 1974; Walston and Felix, 1977) and the Rayleigh stream, best represented by the work of Putnam (1978 and 1979). A third stream, the function point stream, appears as early as 1979, but the majority of the work by Albrecht and others appears more recently (Albrecht, 1979; Albrecht and Gaffney, 1983; Jones, 1986a).

The Economic Stream

The economic stream of research is characterized by the development of economic production functions from data on past software development projects. The work on development of software cost is closely related to a number of studies investigating factors which influence software development productivity, such as the early work by Sackman et al., (1968), Gayle (1971), and Chrysler (1978). Much of the emphasis in the early cost estimation research was on the variables to be included, with much less emphasis on the input and output metrics or on the functional form of the model. For example, Walston and Felix (1977) investigated the effects of approximately 29 variables. Wolverton's seminal work (1974) might have had greater impact had he not chosen cost in dollars as the input (in contrast to the more common work-hours or work-months) and object lines of code (versus source lines of code) as the output.

However, by far the most popular and widely studied of the economic models is the COnstructive COst MOdel (COCOMO), developed by Barry Boehm of TRW and published in 1981. Based on his analysis of 63 software development projects, Boehm developed an easy-to-understand model that predicts the effort and duration of a project, based on inputs relating to the size of the resulting systems and a number of 'cost drivers' that Boehm believes affect productivity.

The popularity of this model in industry can probably be traced to two key factors. The first is that the model is available in the open literature as opposed to other proprietary models such as SLIM (Software Lifecycle Model), Estimacs, and RCA's Price. The second is that Boehm has written a textbook fully detailing the development and justification of the model.

A simplified version of the essential COCOMO effort equation for the basic model (the intermediate and detailed models discussed later) is of the form:

$$WM = C(KDSI)^k$$

where WM = number of work-months (= 152 working hours); C = one of three constant values depending upon 'development mode'; KDSI = thousands of 'delivered source instructions' (DSI); k = one of three constant values, depending upon 'development mode'.

Boehm defines delivered source instructions (DSI) as program instructions created by project personnel that are delivered as part of the final product. They exclude comments and unmodified utility software, and include job control language, format statements, and data declarations.

COCOMO supports three 'development modes' or broad project types. The best case is organic, where relatively small software teams work in a very familiar, in-house environment. The most difficult mode is embedded, where the project must work under severe constraints, such as strict conformance with pre-existing hardware or software. A third mode, which Boehm calls semi-detached, lies between those two extremes.

In Boehm's development of COCOMO he found that the basic model predicted effort within a factor of 1.3 only 29% of the time and within a factor of 2 only 60% of the time for his 63 project database. In an effort to improve the model's accuracy, he refined the equation to include the effects of 15 'cost drivers', which are attributes of the end product, the computer used, the personnel staffing, and the project environment. He believes that these 15 factors affect the project's productivity, and calls this version the intermediate model.

The new equations are:

$$MM = C(WDSI)$$

where

$$WDSI = (KDSI)^{e_i} \prod_{j=1}^{15} EM_j$$

and $WDSI$ = weighted delivered source instructions; e_i = exponent used for the ith development mode; EM_j = effort multiplier determined by the jth cost driver attribute.

The EM_js range from 0.7 (e.g., a product with very low complexity) to 1.66 (e.g., a project developed for a computer with a severe execution time constraint). Essentially, multipliers greater than 1 indicate factors that make the project team less productive than average, and multipliers less than 1 indicate factors that make the team more productive.

The COCOMO detailed model is very similar to the intermediate model except that the project is divided into four phases: product design, detailed design, coding/unit test, and integration/test. The 15 cost drivers are estimated and applied to each phase separately, rather than to the project as a whole.

The Rayleigh Stream

The Rayleigh curve has been used by a number of researchers, but has been most widely propagated through the proprietary SLIM estimating method developed in the late 1970s by Larry Putnam of Quantitative Software Management (1978 and 1979). SLIM depends upon a source line of code (SLOC, analogous to Boehm's DSI) estimate for the project's general size, then modifies this through the use of the Rayleigh curve model to produce its effort estimates. The user can influence the shape of the curve through two key parameters: the initial slope of the curve (the manpower buildup index = MBI) and a productivity factor (the technology constant or productivity factor = PF). An important (and somewhat controversial) feature of the model is its strict time/effort trade-offs, where attempts at reducing SLIM's 'minimum' time schedule are met with very large effort increases (Parr, 1980; Boehm 1981; Jeffery, 1987). The Rayleigh curve is a well-known exponentially declining curve used to model a number of developmental processes. Norden of IBM applied the curve to model research and development activities, and Putnam applied it to software development. The curve plots effort on the vertical axis and time on the horizontal axis. The equation describes a build-up followed by a slackening off for the software development cycle, where people are gradually added as they can become useful and then are transferred to other projects when the system is done, except for an ever decreasing maintenance staff.

While the Rayleigh curve describes the theoretical background behind the model, much of the estimating power of SLIM comes from its 'software equation', as follows:

$$S = cK^{1/3} \, t_d^{4/3}$$

where S = source statements, c = a technology constant (also known as the productivity factor); K = the life cycle effort; t_d = time of peak manpower.

Clearly, a higher value for the technology constant will allow more source statements (source lines of code) to be written with the same amount of effort in the same amount of time. Putnam refers to this technology constant as the 'funnel' through which all system development must pass.

The SLIM user has control over two key variables: the manpower buildup index ($MBI = K/t_d^2$) and the productivity factor ($PF = c$). MBI adjusts the slope of the initial part of the Rayleigh curve. The higher the value, the steeper the curve and the faster the buildup of staff on the project. This number establishes when t_d will be reached, and thus the 'minimum' time in which the project can be completed. The larger the c value, the higher the productivity rate. The SLIM user can choose these values either by calibrating the model with data from completed projects, or by answering a series of 22 questions from which SLIM will provide a recommended PF and MBI.

The Function Points Stream

One criticism of both the economic and Rayleigh type models is that they require the user to estimate the number of SLOC in order to get work-months and duration estimates. The function point measurement method was developed by Allan Albrecht at IBM and first published in 1979 (see also 1983). Albrecht was interested in the general problem of productivity measurement in systems development and created the function point method as an alternative to estimating SLOC. Albrecht's function points are at a more macro level than SLOC, capturing information like the number of input transaction types and the number of unique reports. He believes function points offer several significant advantages over SLOC counts. First, it is possible to estimate them early in the life cycle, about the time of the requirements definition document. This can be an important advantage for anyone trying to estimate the level of effort to be required on a software development project. Second, they can be estimated by a relatively non-technical project member. And finally, they avoid the effects of language and other implementation differences.

There are two steps involved in counting function points: (1) counting the user functions, and (2) adjusting for environmental processing complexity. There are currently five user function categories (although only four in Albrecht's original paper):

1. External input types.
2. External output types.
3. Logical internal file types.
4. External interface file types.
5. External inquiry types.

These are counted and weighted according to complexity, as shown in Exhibit 1. The total from this table is the number of function counts (FC).

$$FC = \sum_{i=1}^{5} \sum_{j=1}^{3} w_{ij} x_{ij}$$

where w_{ij} = weights and x_{ij} = counts.

Some guidelines for determining whether a user function is simple, average or complex have been provided by IBM (Albrecht, 1984). For example, for an external input type to be considered simple, it should reference no more than two file types and contain fewer than 16 data elements.

Albrecht also recognized that the effort required to provide a given level of functionality can vary depending upon the environment. For example, input transactions are harder to program if a lot of emphasis is placed on system throughput or end-user convenience. In response to this Albrecht has a list of 14 processing complexity characteristics that are to be rated on a scale from 0 (no influence) to 5 (strong influence). These environmental characteristics overlap only slightly with Boehm's cost drivers, which are heavily focused on project team capabilities and experience. The second step is to sum all the processing complexity points assigned. This number is then multiplied by 0.01 and added to 0.65 to obtain a weighting, as follows:

$$PCA = 0.65 + (0.01) \sum_{i=1}^{14} c_i$$

where PCA = *processing complexity adjustment, $0.65 \leq PCA \leq 1.35$, and c_i = complexity factors, $0 \leq c_i \leq 5$. This factor is then used in the final equation:*

$$FP = FC \, (PCA)$$

where FP = function points and FC = previously computed function counts.

The end result is that the function points can vary ±35% from the original function counts. Once the function points have been computed, they can be used to compare the proposed project with past projects in terms of its size. Through these comparisons an organization can begin to develop cost estimates, first based upon analogies, and later, as additional data are collected, through statistical analysis.

Since the development of function points, a number of proprietary models have adopted a function point type of approach, including Estimacs, (Rubin, 1985) and SPQR (Jones, 1986a). Symons has recently provided a critical evaluation of function points (Symons, 1988).

MODEL EVALUATION

The most critical question for a manager interested in using such a model is whether or not the estimates provided are sufficiently useful to justify the cost of using (and in some cases, purchasing) them. Ideally, a model would be easy to use and would provide estimates of sufficient accuracy that no other estimation efforts would be required. However, even models that fall short of this goal can provide sufficient benefits to merit management consideration, whether it be as useful benchmarks for estimates developed in the traditional

EXHIBIT 1   Function Count Weighting

	Simple	*Average*	*Complex*
External input	× 3	× 4	× 6
External output	× 4	× 5	× 7
Logical internal file	× 7	× 10	× 15
External interface file	× 5	× 7	× 10
External inquiry	× 3	× 4	× 6

fashion, or even to the extent that using the model requires the estimator to consider factors about the potential project that may influence his or her thinking.

Nonetheless, it would be useful for managers to understand what the software industry's experience has been with such models, in order to determine what are reasonable expectations in terms of their accuracy and ease of use.

One evaluation standard is the degree to which the model's estimated effort in man-months (MM_e) matches the actual effort (MM_a). If the models were perfect, then for every project, $MM_e = MM_a$. Clearly this will rarely, if ever, be the case.

There are several possible methods for evaluating the man-month estimates. A simple analysis approach would be to look at the difference between MM_e and MM_a. The problem with this absolute error approach is that the importance of the size of the error varies with project size. For example, on a 10-man-month project, an absolute error of 9 man-months would be likely to cause serious project disruption in terms of staffing, while the same error on a 1000-man-month project would be much less of a problem.

In light of this, Boehm and others have recommended a percentage error test, as follows:

$$\frac{MM_e - MM_a}{MM_a}$$

The test eliminates the problem caused by project size and better reflects the impact of any error. However, if one wishes to analyze a model's average performance over the entire set of projects, there is an additional problem. Errors can be of two types, underestimates, where $MM_e < MM_a$, and overestimates, where $MM_e > MM_a$. Both of these errors can have serious impacts on projects. Large underestimates will cause the project to be understaffed, and as the deadline approaches, project management may be tempted to add new staff members despite Brooks's Law. Overestimates can also be costly in that staff members, noting the project slack, become less productive (Parkinson's Law: 'Work expands to fill the time available for its

completion') or add so-called 'gold-plating', defined as additional systems features that are not required by the user.

In light of the seriousness of both types of errors, overestimates and underestimates, Conte, et al. (1986) have suggested a magnitude of relative error, or MRE test, as follows:

$$MRE = \frac{|MM_e - MM_a|}{MM_a}$$

Since the two types of errors do not cancel each other out when an average of multiple errors is taken, this is a widely used test.

Still another issue in interpreting the errors concerns bias. For example, a model developed in an environment less productive than the evaluation site, may generate errors that are biased towards overestimation. However, this model may be able to be recalibrated to approximate the evaluation site environment. What is important is that the estimates correlate with the actual results, i.e., bigger projects generate bigger estimates than smaller projects.

Albrecht and Gaffney (1983) and others (Behrens, 1983; Conte et al., 1986) have proposed linear regression as a means of measuring this correlation. Since Albrecht's method does not produce a man-month estimate directly, an alternative was needed to validate the function point method. His proposal was to perform a simple linear regression with man-months as the dependent variable and function points as the independent variable. He also performs regressions with lines of code as the dependent variable to show how function points could be used to generate a lines of code estimate for other models that require it. Regression is often used in this type of research by using actual man-months as the dependent variable and the man-months estimated by each model as the independent variable. The advantage of this method is that it can show whether a model's estimates correlate well with experience even when the MRE test does not. A 'perfect' score on the MRE test would be an error percentage of 0, while a 'perfect' score on Albrecht's test would be an R^2 of 1.00.

VALIDATION RESEARCH

A number of empirical studies have been done worldwide to validate the various cost estimation models. Validation is important to determine whether the models are likely to be of value. However, validation is difficult due to the need to capture large amounts of data about completed projects. These data may not have been captured contemporaneously, and therefore data collection may require researching historical projects or putting a mechanism in place to capture information about future projects. Both of these methods are labour- and time-intensive, particularly for larger projects, which happen to be of greatest interest since they are the most difficult to estimate.

Collecting data on large projects is particularly difficult, as most organizations are limited in the number of these projects they can do at one time, which limits the researcher's sample size. The only alternative is to collect data from multiple years, which may raise the issue of whether or not the projects all originate from the same sample. Nevertheless, as shown in Exhibit 2, a number of researchers have been able to perform such studies.

One of the first independent validations of any of these cost models was Golden et al.'s research on SLIM with four projects at Xerox (1981). They found some positive results in terms of SLIM's ability to predict both effort and duration, although the small sample showed a high amount of variance and therefore it is difficult to predict whether these generally positive results would hold for a larger sample. The authors also suggest the development of estimation models that do not require SLOC as an input.

A similar but somewhat more involved study was conducted by a group of researchers associated with Banker's Trust (Wiener-Ehrlich et al., 1984). They tested the fit of the Rayleigh curve

(the theoretical basis for the SLIM model, among others) to four data processing projects. In their first test they found that the Rayleigh curve tended to underestimate the time spent in the maintenance phase. Further analysis showed, however, that if maintenance was defined to only include so-called 'corrective' maintenance (Lientz and Swanson, 1980), then the Rayleigh curve predicted the maintenance phase equally well. The authors recommend that organizations collect their corrective maintenance data separately from their perfective and adaptive maintenance work to allow the use of the Rayleigh model, and to treat these latter two forms of maintenance as new projects.

In a series of two articles Kitchenham and Taylor (1984 and 1985) compared the results of the COCOMO and SLIM models on a large dataset of 33 British Telecom and ICL projects. They found that both of the models required calibration in order to accurately predict effort or duration in those environments. They recommended that firms collect sufficient data to allow calibration before implementing the models into their estimation process.

Rubin's research differs from the others in this study in that a hypothetical project was used, and therefore no comparison of estimates with actuals is possible (1985). However, it is an interesting comparison and overview of the inputs and output of these models, and can be seen as an update and improvement to the hypothetical test done by Mohanty (1981). One result was a wide variance in estimates for the same project, suggesting the need for calibration of the models.

Miyazaki and Mori's work (1985) calibrates the COCOMO model for 33 projects at Fujitsu in Japan. They found that COCOMO overestimated their application software projects, which were mostly written in COBOL. In addition to calibrating the major parameters of the model, they also eliminated three of the 15 cost drivers in order to improve the models' historical results.

Caccamese, et al. examined the performance of COCOMO and SLIM on three 'systems software' projects at Olivetti in Italy (1986). Like Kitchenham

EXHIBIT 2 Cost Estimation Models Validation Research

Description	Golden et al.	Wiener-Ehrlich et al.	Kitchenham and Taylor	Miyazaki and Mori	Caccamese et al.	Kemerer	Jeffery
Journal	Database	IEEE Trans on Soft. Engin.	Journals of Systems & Software	Proc. of 8th Intl. Conf. on Soft. Engin.	unpublished	Comm. of the Assoc. for Comp. Mach.	IEEE Trans. on Soft. Engin.
Year	1981	1984	1985	1985	1986	1987	1987
Models used	SLIM	Rayleigh (SLIM)	COCOMO, SLIM	COCOMO	COCOMO, SLIM	COCOMO, ESTIMACS, FP, SLIM	Rayleigh (SLIM)
Data source	Xerox	Bankers Trust Company	British Telecom, ICL	Fujitsu	Olivetti	Consulting firm	Software house, government, bank
Data origin	USA	USA	UK	Japan	Italy	USA	Australia
Number of projects	4	4	33	33	3	15	47
Type of projects	—	Data processing	Real time; operating systems	Application software	Systems software	Data processing	Data processing
Language(s) used	—	COBOL, BASIC, FORTRAN, MACRO	S3 (ALGOL), COBOL, Assembler	COBOL, PL/1, Assembler, FORTRAN	PASCAL, PLZ, LIMO	COBOL, Natural, BLISS	COBOL, PL/1
Average size	—	46.4 KSLOC	11.9 KSLOC	—	37 KSLOC	186.6 KSLOC	27.3 KSLOC
Average duration	12.7 months	—	11.7 months	—	24.4 months	14.3 months	15.7 months
Average effort	100 work-months	171 work-months	46.2 work-months	—	104.3 work-months	219.3 work-months	65.3 work-months
Analysis type	Data only	Graphical, regression	Regression	MRE, regression	Graphical	MRE, regression	Regression
Predictions tested	Effort, duration	Effort/phase	Effort, duration	Effort	Effort	Effort	Productivity vs elapsed time
Results	SLIM averaged within 10% of duration, and 42% of effort, with high variance	Rayleigh curve accurate if maintenance defined as corrective only	Calibration required; effort/phase poorly predicted	COCOMO overestimates; 3 cost drivers excluded to improve model	Effort/time not well-modelled; suggest system software development compressed	FP model validated; cost drivers not helpful; SLIM and COCOMO overestimate	No support for notion that productivity is reduced if time is reduced

ham and Taylor, they found that the effort per project phase predictions of both models did not fit their data well. The authors suggest that systems software development is possibly compressed relative to the projects which form the basis of the COCOMO and SLIM databases, even though their small sample does not allow this to be tested.

Kemerer's research (1987) compared both CO-COMO and SLIM as well as two newer, non-SLOC models, Estimacs and function points, on a dataset of 15 large data processing projects. Consistent with other researchers, Kemerer found that all of the models require calibration to the target environment, and that both COCOMO and SLIM tend to overestimate data processing applications. An important new result was that the function point model was validated on an independent dataset. Finally, this research found that the cost drivers and productivity factors of all four models contributed little to their accuracy, and suggests that additional work needs to be done in this area.

Jeffery (1987), working with a relatively large dataset, collected over a ten-year period, suggests that the strict time-effort relationships present in many of the cost estimation models, particularly the Rayleigh curve-based models, is not supported. His data show no support for the notion that productivity decreases as the project's duration is reduced. He suggests that loading (work-months divided by calendar months) may be a better measure than duration for the amount of project 'stress', a result suggested elsewhere as well (Banker et al., 1987).

RECENT RESEARCH

Some recent research has focused on (1) new methodologies for model development, (2) developing models designed for fourth generation language projects, and (3) new metrics for estimating earlier in the systems life cycle.

Madnick and Abdel-Hamid (1989) propose the use of systems dynamics (SD) to represent explicitly causal relationships in software development, one application of which is as a tool for software cost estimation. They develop an SD model which includes four subsystems: human resource management, software production, controlling, and planning. They propose that their model can be used as a simulation tool to test the estimated effect of changes in project management practices.

Verner and Tate (1988) provide one of the first pieces of research looking at estimation for fourth generation language (4GL) projects. Their case study suggests differences both in total effort and in distribution for 4GL projects.

Wrigley and Dexter (1988) develop an approach that uses some data model metrics and requirements analysis phase data to estimate the size of 4GL systems. In a test on 75 FOCUS programs, they found some statistically significant results in their models of system size.

In the future, one development that will aid the development of new models is the advent of computer-aided software engineering (CASE) tools. These tools designed to aid systems developers (by aiding in the preparation of structured analysis and design deliverables, for example) will greatly assist the cost estimation researcher in collecting design metrics such as the number of processes in a data flow diagram. The automation of such collection should reduce the barriers to new models based on analysis and design metrics.

RECOMMENDATIONS

Given the previous work in this area and the existence of a number of cost estimation models, how can a firm interested in using these models best proceed? While the exact steps will, of course, differ from firm to firm, the general strategy followed by the firms that have made the initial successes in this area has been to establish a separate team within the department with responsibility for the area of software cost estimation and related tasks (DeMarco, 1982). These permanent teams, variously referred to as the 'metrics council', 'high technology section', 'special studies team', 'productivity tools group', etc. have two broad goals: (1) to measurably improve productivity, and (2) to measurably improve software quality and reliability. To achieve these goals the group has a number of possible tasks related to the measurement and improvement of the management of software development within the firm. These tasks can include:

1. Collect and disseminate project data.
2. Calibrate/develop cost models.
3. Evaluate new technologies.
4. Act as change agents for new tools.
5. Assist/train project managers.
6. Build reusable code libraries.

The overriding concept is that the benefits arising from the investment in this staff group will be able to be leveraged over all of the firm's projects in terms of greater productivity and software quality. By acting as a central resource, the group can both quickly disseminate good ideas and can help project teams to avoid re-inventing the wheel or repeating past mistakes. By specializing in this area, they ensure that promising new ideas or technologies are not missed by the firm's project managers due to their pressing day-to-day concerns. In addition, the tools group will, over time, develop expertise in these areas which will enable them to evaluate or even develop technologies more efficiently than individual project teams.

The great advantage of such a group is the synergies that develop among all of the tasks. Collecting data on past projects in order to calibrate cost estimation models allows productivity trends to be tracked. The impact of changes in tool or methodology usage can then be measured, which will allow the identification of promising techniques. Tools that allow projects to be done with less effort can also lead to better estimates, since managers' estimation of smaller projects is typically better than larger ones. The typical role of acting as the librarian for the set of reusable code routines fits naturally with acting as the change agents to introduce newer tools, such as object-oriented approaches. Data collection provides a base for evaluating the impact of a change like a new language or something like knowledge-based systems technologies. Firms interested in estimating projects will require data in order to properly evaluate these impacts.

There are a number of guides to developing such a group. DeMarco's book, *Controlling Software Projects* (1982) was among the first to recommend this approach, and remains the most readable. A newer book, *Software Metrics: Establishing a Company-Wide Program* (1987) by Grady and Caswell, describes in great detail the exact process that Hewlett-Packard, one of the 'search for excellence' companies, used to establish their group. While the book's title seems limited to software metrics, all of the examples of the use of metrics are applications to cost estimation, productivity evaluation, and quality improvement.

The authors of these books take care to point out that developing such groups is painstaking and that the group's short term impact is likely to be minimal. However, the ultimate benefit of this approach towards software cost *estimation* improvement is that it will eventually lead to software cost *reduction,* which is a result well worth pursuing.

References and Bibliography

1. Albrecht, A. J. (1979) Measuring application development productivity. In *IBM Applications Development Symposium,* GUIDE/SHARE, pp. 83–92. [Albrecht's original exposition of the function points method]

2. Albrecht, A J. (1984) *AD/M productivity measurement and estimate validation,* CIS & A Guideline 313, IBM Corporate Information Systems and Administration. [Complete guide to using function points. Includes examples and recommendations on use]

3. Albrecht, A J. and Gaffney Jr., J. (1983) Software function, source lines of code, and development effort prediction: a software science validation. *IEEE Transactions on Software Engineering,* SE-9, 639–648. [Validation and update to the 1979 paper. Adds a fifth category to the four originally espoused]

4. Bailey, J. W. and Basili, V. R. (1981) A meta-model for software development resource expenditures. In *Proc. 5th International Conference on Software Engineering,* pp. 107–116. [Presentation of a model developed on 18 NASA/Goddard Space Flight Center software projects. Three variables, methodology, complexity, and experience are used to improve the model's ability to do cost estimation]

5. Banker, R., Datar, S. and Kemerer, C. (1987) Factors affecting software maintenance productivity. In *Proc. 8th International Conference on Information Systems,* Pittsburgh [Preliminary analysis of data on 65 software maintenance projects from a large commercial bank. An economic model of software maintenance is developed, and 15 factors affecting productivity are tested]

6. Banker, R. and Kemerer, C. Scale economies in new software development. *IEEE Transactions on Software Engineering* (in press, expected to appear in **15** (October 1989)). [Investigation of the effect of project scale on development productivity. It is suggested that *economies* of scale, in addition to the more commonly discussed *diseconomies* of scale, are present in new software development. A methodology for measuring these economies and for identifying the most productive scale size for an environment is presented and tested on eight datasets]

7. Basili, V. R. (ed.) (1980) *Tutorial on Models and Metrics for Software Management and Engineering,* IEEE Computer Society Press, New York [Useful complement to the Perlis, Sayward, Shaw collection]

8. Basili, V. R. (1981a) Resource models. In *Software Metrics,* MIT Press, Cambridge, MA., pp. 111–130 [Excellent survey of the software estimation models area]

9. Basili, V. R. (1981b) Data collection, validation, and analysis. In *Software Metrics,* MIT Press, Cambridge, MA, pp. 143–159 [Clearly addresses need for improved data collection of software metrics. Suggests an approach for implementing these tasks. Practitioner-oriented]

10. Basili, V. R. and Zelkowitz, M. (1978) Analysing medium-scale software development. In *Proc. 3rd International Conference on Software Engineering,* Institute of Electrical and Electronics Engineers, pp. 116–123 [Discussion of Software Engineering Laboratory at the University of Maryland with a case study applying the Rayleigh curve to two projects]

11. Behrens, C. A. (1983) Measuring the productivity of computer systems development activities with function points. *IEEE Transactions on Software Engineering,* SE-9, 648–642 [Empirical study within a life insurance organization using function points as output measures]

12. Boehm, B. W. (1973) Software and its impact: a quantitative assessment. *Datamation,* **19,** 48–59 [Interesting survey of the state of the art in 1973. Most of the issues and goals cited remain true today. Another call for software metrics research]

13. Boehm, B. W. (1981) *Software Engineering Economics,* Prentice-Hall, Englewood Cliffs, NJ [A widely cited text. Approximately divided into two-thirds discussion of Boehm's COCOMO model and other cost estimation topics and one-third other software metrics and application of quantitative methods]

14. Boehm, B. W. (1984) Software engineering economics. *IEEE Transactions on Software Engineering,* SE-10, 10–21 [A concise summary and update of his 1981 text]

15. Brooks, F. (1975) *The Mythical Man-month,* Addison-Wesley, Reading, Mass [Classic, very readable book concerning the author's experiences managing the OS/360 project and the lessons imparted on the management of large programming projects]

16. Caccamese, A., Cappello, L. and Dodero, G. (1986) A comparison of SLIM and COCOMO estimates versus historical man-power and effort allocation. *Unpublished paper* [Test of COCOMO and SLIM against three projects at Olivetti in Italy]

17. Callisen, H. and Colborne, S. (1984) A proposed method for estimating software cost from requirements. *Journal of Parametrics,* **4,** 33–40 [Exposition on preliminary work at developing a requirements analysis document syntax analyser for using an estimating tool]

18. Chrysler, E. (1978) Some basic determinants of computer programming productivity. *Communications of the ACM,* **21,** 472–483 [Empirical study of 36 COBOL programs using regression analysis to determine effects on productivity of programming task attributes and programmer experience levels]

19. Conte, S., Dunsmore, H. and Shen, V. (1986) *Software Engineering Metrics and Models,* Benjamin/Cummings, Reading, MA [Excellent recent textbook. Useful substitute for the 1981 Boehm text]

20. Crossman, T. D. (1979) Taking the measure of programmer productivity. *Datamation,* **25,** 144–147 [Description of empirical study done in COBOL

banking environment. The created micro measure of functionality was a good linear predictor of effort]

21. DeMarco, T. (1982) *Controlling Software Projects,* Yourdon Press, New York, NY [Excellent, highly readable text for practitioners on how best to do accurate project estimation and to develop a metrics data collection effort within a firm]

22. Elshoff, J. L. (1976) An analysis of some commercial PL/1 programs. *IEE Transactions on Software Engineering,* **SE2,** 113–120 [Early quantitative analysis of commercial software]

23. Ferens, D. V. (1984) Software support cost models: quo vadis? *Journal of Parametrics,* **4,** 64–99 [Anecdotal discussion of use of cost estimation models at the Air Force]

24. Ferens, D. V. and Whetstone, M. J. (1987) Software size estimation, the impossible dream? *Journal of Parametrics,* **7,** 57–67 [Results of a research effort directed at estimating eventual source lines of code (SLOC) from a number of functional characteristics such as complexity, reliability, quality of the specification, and the environment. Four databases containing 7, 26, 25, and 2 projects were used. Only a few statistically significant results were obtained]

25. Gaffney, J. E. (1984) Estimation of software code size based on quantitative aspects of function. *Journal of Parametrics,* **4,** 23–34 [A review of software models with a very general discussion of the possibilities and problems of using expert system technology to perform initial software sizing]

26. Gaffney, J. E. (1986) The impact of software development of using HOLs. *IEEE Transactions on Software Engineering,* **SE-12,** 496–499 [Brief article illustrating the problems in measuring productivity across projects using different languages and suggests using function points as an alternative measure]

27. Gayle, J. B. (1971) Multiple regression techniques for estimating computer programming costs. *Journal of Systems Management,* **22,** 13–16 [Early attempt at analysis of programming costs based on 18 data points. Significant cost predictors included programmer's experience, number of outputs produced, frequency of operation of the application, and distance of the programmer from the machine]

28. Golden, J. R., Mueller, J. R. and Anselm, B. (1981) Software cost estimating: craft or witchcraft. *Database,* **12,** 12–14 [A test of the SLIM software cost estimating model using four projects at Xerox]

29. Grady, R. B. and Caswell, D. L. (1987) *Software Metrics: Establishing a Company-wide Program,* Prentice-Hall, Englewood Cliffs, NJ [Recent practitioner-oriented book on Hewlett-Packard's experiences in setting up a corporate database for cost estimation and productivity measurement]

30. Houtz, C. A. (1985) Anatomy of a cost estimating model. In *Proc. Seventh Annual ISPA Conference* (1985) International Society of Parametric Analysts,

pp. 110–123 [Description of a federal government software conversion cost estimating model]

31. *IBM Estimating Application Development Projects Workbook* (1980) IBM Corporation, NAD Education Staff Services, East Irving, Texas [A self-paced tutorial on using IBM's Standard Task Method for estimating]

32. Jeffery, D. R. (1987) Time sensitive cost models in the commercial MIS environment. *IEEE Transactions on Software Engineering,* **SE-13,** 852–859 [Empircal analysis of time trade-offs in 47 Australian MIS projects completed in last ten years in four organizations. Uses stepwise regression to determine that projects do not support Rayleigh curve type model. Suggests that it is the maximum number of staff that is important and that loading not duration is the key]

33. Jones, C. (1986a) *Programming Productivity.* McGraw-Hill, New York [Up-to-date comprehensive survey of the factors affecting programmer productivity. Discussion illustrated with examples generated from Jones's SPQR estimation model]

34. Jones, C. (1986b) The productivity report card. *Software News,* **6,** 19 [Brief article noting some of the important general statistics regarding software development]

35. Kemerer, C. F. (1987a) An empirical validation of software cost estimation models. *Communications of the ACM,* **30,** 416–429 [Empirical test of four algorithmic cost estimating models on a database of 15 large completed software development projects]

36. Kemerer, C. F. (1987b) Management of software cost estimation. In *Proc. Royal Aeronautical Society's Symposium on Major Software Projects,* London, UK, 1987 [Early version of this chapter (Helpful comments from S. Madnick and C. Wrigley are gratefully acknowledged)]

37. Kitchenham, B. and Taylor, N. R. (1984) Software cost models. *ICL Technical Journal,* **5/84,** 73–102 [Test of COCOMO and SLIM on a database of 20 projects developed by British Telecom and ICL]

38. Kitchenham, B. and Taylor, N. R. (1985) Software project development cost estimation. *Journal of Systems and Software,* **5,** 267–278 [Further test of COCOMO and SLIM estimation models on a 33 project dataset collected at International Computer Laboratories and British Telecom. Neither model was found to be a good predictor for this dataset]

39. Lientz, B. P. and Swanson, E. B. (1980) *Software Maintenance Management,* Addison-Wesley, Reading, Mass [Classic book on Software Maintenance]

40. Madnick, S. and Abdel-Hamid, T. (1989) *The Dynamics of Software Development,* Prentice-Hall, Englewood Cliffs, NJ [Text describing a Systems Dynamics model of the software development process]

41. Masters, T. F. II. (1985) An overview of software cost estimating at the NSA. *Journal of Parametrics,* **5,** 72–84 [Anecdotal discussion of use of parametric software cost estimation models at the National Security Agency]

42. Miyazaki, Y. and Mori, K. (1985) COCOMO evaluation and tailoring. In *Proceedings of the 8th International Conference on Software Engineering*, pp. 292–299 [Calibration of the COCOMO model using 33 projects at Fujitsu in Japan]

43. Mohanty, S. (1981) Software cost estimation: present and future. *Software-Practice and Experience*, **11**, 103–121 [A comparison of 12 software cost estimating models on one sample project]

44. Parr, F. N. (1980) An alternative to the Rayleigh Curve Model for software development effort. *IEEE Transactions on Software Engineering*, **SE-6**, 291–296 [A criticism of Putnam's use of the Rayleigh curve for software development estimating]

45. Perlis, A., Sayward, F. and Shaw, M. (eds) (1981) *Software Metrics: An Analysis and Evaluation*, MIT Press, Cambridge, MA [Extremely useful collection of articles summarizing the then state of the art. Includes an extensive annotated bibliography]

46. Pinky, S. S. (1984) The effect of complexity on software trade off equations. *Journal of Parametrics*, **4**, 23–32 [Comparison of a number of parametric software cost estimation models on their complexity components]

47. Putnam, L. H. (1978) General empirical solution to the macro software sizing and estimating problem. *IEEE Transactions on Software Engineering*, **4**, 345–361 [Mathematical exposition of Putnam's SLIM model]

48. Putnam, L. and Fitzsimmons, A. (1979) Estimating software costs. *Datamation*, **25**, Nos. 10, 11, 12 [Non-mathematical exposition of Putnam's SLIM model. Article split over three issues]

49. Reese, R. M. and Tamulevicz, J. (1987) A survey of software sizing methodologies and tools. *Journal of Parametrics*, **7**, 36–56 [A concise summary of the difficulties involved in estimating the size of a software project. The paper describes the limitations of a number of methods, and illustrates them with examples from DeMarco's Bang, Albrecht's function points and RCA's PRICE-SZ. A combination of methods at different stages in the project is recommended]

50. Reeves, R. (1986) 2nd Annual COCOMO/WICOMO Software Users Meeting attracts international field to Wang Institute, *Software Engineering Notes*, **11**, No 3, 99, [Press release citing that COCOMO is the currently most widely used software cost estimating model]

51. Rubin, H. A. (1983) Macroestimation of software development parameters: the Estimacs system. In *SOFTFAIR Conference on Software Development Tools, Techniques and Alternatives*, IEEE [Most comprehensive description of Rubin's Estimacs model in the open literature]

52. Rubin, H. A. (1985) The art and science of software estimation: fifth generation estimators. In *Proceedings of the Seventh Annual ISPA Conference*, International Society of Parametric Analysts [Overview of estimation process and use of models. Suggests directions for future work in this area]

53. Rubin, H. A. (chair) (1985) A comparison of cost estimation tools (a panel session). In *Proc. 8th International Conference on Software Engineering*, IEEE Computer Society Press pp. 174–180 [Results of an estimation from a hypothetical system specification by the JS-2, SLIM, GECOMO and Estimacs system. The results were that the estimates varied significantly across models in terms of both effort and duration]

54. Sackman, H., Erikson, W. J. and Grant, E. E. (1968) Exploratory Experimental Studies Comparing Online and Offline Programming Performance. *Communications of the ACM*, **11**, No 1, 3–11, January (1968) [Seminal research noting the significant performance differences across individual programmers]

55. Sierevelt, H. (1968) Observations on software models. *Journal of Parametrics*, **6**, 51–74. Calibration of the PRICE-S software cost estimation model on four projects at Philips, Netherlands. Results were improved by not treating all work-months as equal, but rather by taking into account percentage of staff member's time dedicated to the project and the staff loading]

56. Symons, C. R. (1988) Function point analysis: difficulties and improvements. *IEEE Transactions on Software Engineering*, **14**, 2–11 [A critical evaluation of function points and some suggestions for extensions to address these problems]

57. Thebaut, S. M. (1983) *The Saturation Effect in Large Scale Software Development: Its Impact and Control*, PhD thesis, Purdue University [This thesis develops a co-operative programming model (COPMO) to demonstrate the effect of larger team sizes on software development projects. A comparison of this model with the COCOMO and SLIM models is also provided]

58. Tversky, A. and Kahneman, D. (1974) Judgement under uncertainty: heuristics and biases, *Science*, **5**, 1124–1131 [Classic article on the limitations of human information processing]

59. Verner, J. and Tate, G. (1988) Estimating size and effort in fourth generation development. *IEEE Software*, July, 15–22 [Results of a case study estimating the size and effort of a 4GL project using COCOMO and function points. Relative to a hypothesized COBOL development for the same system, a reduction in effort and a change in its distribution were noted]

60. Walston, C. E. and Felix, D. P. (1977) A method of programming measurement and estimation. *IBM Systems Journal*, **16**, 54–73 [Important early software estimation model. Uses regression to analyse 60 IBM projects]

61. Wiener-Ehrlich, W. K., Hamrick, J. R. and Rupolo, V. F. (1984) Modeling software behavior in terms of a formal life cycle curve: implications for software maintenance. *IEEE Transactions on Software Engineering*, **SE-10**, 376–383 [Application of Rayleigh curve to four

projects at Bankers Trust. Good fit except for maintenance, which was underestimated. Better fit if maintenance restricted to software repairs (one project's data)]

62.   Wolverton, W. R. (1974) Cost of developing large scale software. *IEEE Transaction on Computers,* **23,** 615–634 [Seminal work for much of the software cost estimation literature. Unfortunately, its use of object lines of code as an output measure has limited its transportability]

63.   Wrigley, C. and Dexter, A. (1988) A model for estimating information systems requirements size: preliminary findings. *Proc 9th International Conference on Information Systems.* November 30–December 3, 1988, 245–255 [Early report on effort to predict software size based on entity-relationship and other data from 15 programs written in a 4GL]

Discussion Questions

1. Based on the table in the Kemerer review chapter, software cost estimation models have not typically delivered accurately when used uncalibrated outside of their original environments. What factors might account for this?

2. If these cost estimation models don't give good answers, why should managers bother to use them?

Advanced Cost Estimation Models

INTRODUCTION

A relative wealth of research has been written on software cost estimation, due both to its critical managerial significance and the fact that this topic was one of the first undertaken by software engineering management researchers. Based, in part, on the work provided in Chapter 2, research has continued in two main directions: extending and validating the early work and providing alternative models to the algorithmic models exemplified by COCOMO and other Chapter 2 work.

In the first stream of work, Chris Kemerer (1987) provides an empirical validation of four cost estimation models: COCOMO, SLIM, ESTIMACS and Function Points on a new, independent dataset of fifteen large IS projects. This work showed that the models tended to overestimate required effort with relatively large percentage errors. However, the results were relatively correlated with actual effort, suggesting that they could be calibrated to local environments. The productivity variables in the models did not add much explanatory value, suggesting the need for further research in this area.

The second article, by Rajiv Banker and Chris Kemerer, challenges the notion of diseconomies of scale in software development, suggesting, in-stead, that either increasing or decreasing returns may be present. Their research tests this model on eight data sets using two different modeling approaches. The results on 5 of the 8 datasets suggest presence of both scale economies and diseconomies. The method they present allows practitioners to calculate their organization's Most Productive Scale Size (MPSS) from self-collected data. The main implication for practice is that project size should be treated as a productivity factor and scale size may influence the make or buy decision.

A second direction taken by modern software cost estimation research has been to provide alternative types of models for cost estimation. Steve Vicinanza, Mike Prietula, and Tridas Mukhopadhyay developed a knowledge-based or expert system for cost estimation using techniques from the artificial intelligence community. Their model was tested using 10 of 15 projects in the (Kemerer 1987) dataset. Their system performed better than either COCOMO or Function Points, but not quite as well as their human expert. Although this article provides no further independent validation, it does highlight the possibility of using knowledge-based approaches with the necessity to collect organizational data from relevant experts.

Another alternative to the algorithmic approach is provided by Tarek Abdel-Hamid and Stuart Madnick who use System Dynamics to develop a cost estimation model using data from a NASA project. Their model was able to replicate several common phenomenon such as Brooks's Law. Given this behavior, the author suggests that the model can be used as a project simulator to do "what if" analyses and training. Although their model was not validated on other data, it does suggest issues about the dynamic nature of software project management and the interaction of managerial decisions.

AN EMPIRICAL VALIDATION OF SOFTWARE COST ESTIMATION MODELS

INTRODUCTION

Practitioners have expressed concern over their inability to accurately estimate costs associated with software development. This concern has become even more pressing as costs associated with development continue to increase. As a result, considerable research attention is now directed at gaining a better understanding of the software-development process as well as constructing and evaluating software cost estimating tools.

This paper presents an empirical validation of four algorithmic models from the literature (SLIM, COCOMO, Function Points, and ESTIMACS) that are proposed as general software-development cost estimators. This research has built a database of completed software-development projects and focuses on comparing the actual costs with the *ex post* estimates obtained from the four models. Of particular interest is the comparison of the results of the four models' use of different measures (metrics) of the outputs underlying their productivity calculations.

Three research questions of interest to practitioners are addressed in this paper:

1. Are these software cost estimating models truly generalizable to environments other than that in which they were developed? If not, can they be easily calibrated to a typical business data-processing environment?

2. Are models that do not use source lines of code (SLOC) as an input as accurate as those that do? If so, then this could eliminate the need to attempt to estimate lines of code early in the project.

3. Are the models available in the open literature as accurate as proprietary models? If so, then this could allow practitioners to avoid the costs of purchasing the proprietary models.

Section 2 discusses the selection of the four models, followed by brief descriptions of the models. Section 3 describes the environment in which the data originated and compares this data set with that of other researchers. Section 4 describes the data-gathering and data-analysis methods, which leads directly into Section 5, "Results." Finally, Section 6 offers some summary conclusions and outlines extensions of this work.

2. BACKGROUND TO THE MODELS

2.1 Model Selection

A review of the literature revealed that the most interesting difference between estimation models is between models that use SLOC as the primary input versus models that do not. SLOC was selected early as a metric by researchers, no doubt due to its quantifiability and seeming objectivity. Since then an entire subarea of research has developed to determine the best method of counting SLOC [10, 12]. In response to this, and to practitioners' complaints about the difficulties in estimating SLOC before a project was well under way, new models have been developed that do not use SLOC as the primary input [2, 20].

The next step was to choose models that were well regarded in the current literature, and to winnow this selection down to a manageable number since each model's idiosyncrasies required the collection of different data. The approach to determining which models were well regarded was twofold: First, Barry Boehm (developer of the COCOMO model, a model eventually selected for this study) has written a widely cited book entitled *Software Engineering Economics* [5] in which he provides an analysis of eight important models. This list was used to generate candidates. The second step was a review of articles in the most recent issues of the *Journal of Parametrics,* a publication of the International Society of Parametric Analysts that devotes a large number of its pages to software estimation articles. This sampling validated whether the models cited in the Boehm study were well represented by their inclusion in other studies.

Boehm examines eight models (including COCOMO) in his evaluation. They are (1) SDC, (2) Wolverton, (3) SLIM, (4) Doty, (5) PRICE, (6) IBM-FSD, (7) Boeing, and (8) COCOMO [5, 16, 25, 27]. After examining this list of candidates, a review was undertaken of the most recent issues of the *Journal of Parametrics,* to determine the popularity of these models as demonstrated by their inclusion in other research. The results are presented in Exhibit 1 with an "X" signifying that a particular model was discussed or compared in that article [7, 9, 14, 15, 21].

From this list of candidates, COCOMO and SLIM seem to be the most widely reviewed. The

EXHIBIT 1   Journal of Parametrics Articles

	COCOMO	SLIM	PRICE
Callisen (12/84)	X		
Ferens (12/84)	X	X	X
Masters (3/85)	X	X	X
Pinsky (12/84)	X	X	
Rubin (6/85)	X	X	

PRICE model is also popular, but was developed primarily for use on aerospace applications and was therefore deemed unsuitable for the business applications that would comprise the database. Therefore, only COCOMO and SLIM were selected for this research.

All of the above analysis centered on SLOC models of one sort or another. This is to be expected since software effort estimation research began with these models and is a relatively young field. No similar comparisons for non-SLOC models were found, and in fact, only two models were discovered during the period when this research was being conducted. These two are the Function Points method, developed by Allan Albrecht at IBM in 1979 [2, 3], and the ESTIMACS model, developed by Howard Rubin of Hunter College and marketed by Management and Computer Services during the period when these data were being collected [20, 22]. Both of these models were selected, bringing the total number of models compared to four.

These four exhibit a certain symmetry, perhaps best illustrated in Exhibit 2. Therefore, some interesting comparisons can be made between not only

EXHIBIT 2   Model Categories

	Proprietary	Nonproprietary
SLOC	SLIM	COCOMO
Non-SLOC	ESTIMACS	Function Points

measurement methods, but between models that appear in the open literature and those that do not.

2.2 Models

Due to space limitations, the following are necessarily brief descriptions of the four models used in this paper. The interested reader is referred to the references provided for more detailed explanations.

2.2.1 *SLIM*

The SLIM estimating method was developed in the late 1970s by Larry Putnam of Quantitative Software Management [16, 17]. SLIM depends on an SLOC estimate for the project's general size, then modifies this through the use of the Rayleigh curve model to produce its effort estimates. The user can influence the shape of the curve through two key parameters: the initial slope of the curve (the "manpower buildup index" or MBI) and a productivity factor (the "technology constant" or PF). Since these are dimensionless numbers, the SLIM user has two options for choosing their values: The user can calibrate the model by inputting data from completed projects, or he or she can answer a series of 22 questions, from which SLIM will provide a recommended PF and MBI. The second method was chosen for this research due to the absence of a previously collected calibration database and the feeling that this would more accurately reflect the average user's experience.

2.2.2 *COCOMO*

The COnstructive COst MOdel (COCOMO) was developed by Barry Boehm of TRW and published in 1981 [5]. Based on his analysis of 63 software-development projects, Boehm developed an easy-to-understand model that predicts the effort and duration of a project, based on inputs relating to the size of the resulting systems and a number of "cost drivers" that Boehm believes affect productivity.

A simplified version of the essential COCOMO effort equation for the Basic Model (the Intermediate and Detailed Models are discussed later) is of the form

$$MM = C \, (KDSI)^k \, ,$$

where

MM = *number of man-months*[1]
    (= 152 *working hours*),

C = a constant,

$KDSI$ = *thousands of "delivered source instructions" (DSI), and*

k = a constant.

Boehm defines DSI as program instructions created by project personnel that are delivered as part of the final product. They exclude comments and unmodified utility software, and include job control language, format statements, and data declarations.

In Boehm's development of COCOMO, he found that the Basic Model predicted effort within a factor of 1.3 only 29 percent of the time and within a factor of 2 only 60 percent of the time for his 63-project database. In an effort to improve the model's accuracy, he refined the equation to include the effects of 15 "cost drivers," which are attributes of the end product, the computer used, the personnel staffing, and the project environment. He believes that these 15 factors affect the project's productivity and calls this version the Intermediate Model.

The COCOMO Detailed Model is very similar to the Intermediate Model except that the project is divided into four phases: Product Design, Detailed Design, Coding/Unit Test, and Integration/Test. The 15 cost drivers are estimated and applied to each phase separately, rather than to the project as a whole.

2.2.3 *Function Points*

The Function Points measurement method was developed by Allan Albrecht at IBM and first published in 1979 [2, 3]. Albrecht was interested in the general problem of productivity measure-

---

[1] "Man-months" is used in this paper in its vernacular sense of referring to all the hours worked on a project, whether by men or women.

ment in systems development and created the Function Points method as an alternative to estimating SLOC. Albrecht's Function Points are at a more macro level than SLOC, capturing things like the number of input transaction types and the number of unique reports. He believes Function Points offer several significant advantages over SLOC counts: First, it is possible to estimate them early in the life cycle, about the time of the requirements definition document. This can be an important advantage for anyone trying to estimate the level of effort to be required on a software-development project. Second, they can be estimated by a relatively nontechnical project member. And, finally, they avoid the effects of language and other implementation differences.

There are two steps involved in counting Function Points: (1) counting the use functions, and (2) adjusting for processing complexity. There are currently five user function categories:[2] external input types, external output types, logical internal file types, external interface file types, and external inquiry types. Albrecht recognized that the effort required to provide a given level of functionality can vary depending on the environment. For example, input transactions are harder to program if a lot of emphasis is placed on system throughput or end-user convenience. In response to this, Albrecht has a list of 14 processing complexity characteristics that are to be rated on a scale from 0 (no influence) to 5 (strong influence). The next step is to sum all the processing complexity points assigned. This number is then multiplied by 0.01 and added to 0.65 to obtain a weighting, as follows:

$$PCA = 0.65 + 0.01 \sum_{i=1}^{14} c_i$$

where PCA = processing complexity adjustment $(0.65 \leq PCA \leq 1.35)$, and c_i = complexity factors $(0 \leq c_i \leq 5)$.

---

[2] Albrecht's 1979 paper has only four, omitting External Interface File Types [2].

This factor is then used in the final equation:

$$FP = FC(PCA),$$

where FP = Function Points, and FC = previously computed Function Counts.

The end result is that the Function Points can vary ±35 percent from the original Function Counts. Once the Function Points have been computed, they can be used to compare the proposed project with past projects in terms of its size.

2.2.4 ESTIMACS

The ESTIMACS model was developed by Howard Rubin of Hunter College as an out-growth of a consulting assignment to Equitable Life. It is a proprietary system and, at the time the data were collected, was marketed by Management and Computer Services (MACS). Since it is a proprietary model, details, such as the equations used, are not available. The model does not require SLOC as an input, relying instead on "Function-Point-like" measures. The research in this paper is based on Rubin's paper from the 1983 IEEE conference on software development tools and the documentation provided by MACS [20, 22]. The 25 ESTIMACS input questions are described in these documents.

3. DATA

3.1 Data Source

The source for the project data for this research was a national computer consulting and services firm specializing in the design and development of data-processing software (hereafter referred to as the ABC consulting firm). Use of this consulting firm's data conveyed several advantages to this research.

First, because clients are charged by the hours spent on their projects, the consulting firm must maintain strict, auditable timekeeping records. Since a key element of this research is the comparison of estimated effort to actual effort, it was important that the measurement of actual effort be as accurate as possible.

Second, the projects in the database reflect a variety of data-processing applications, which should broaden the level of interest in the results, as opposed to, say, a database composed of all insurance or all defense contractor applications. However, within this framework there is a high level of consistency in both the quality of the staff and the methodologies employed, since all the projects were done by the same firm within the time span of a few years.

Third, as professional software developers, ABC is highly interested in software productivity. Since it is their primary business, as opposed to being relegated to a staff function as it might be in another industry, the ABC managers were highly motivated to provide good quality data and cooperate with the research.

3.2 Project Database

Projects selected possessed two attributes: First, they were medium to large in size, an explicit requirement of the models chosen [5, 19]. The average project size of this study is just under 200 KSLOC (SLOC stated in thousands), and the smallest project is 39 KSLOC, which was partly written in a fourth-generation language. Second, the project manager must have been available during the summer of 1985 to complete the data-collection form. (See Section 4 for more details.) This limited the database to fairly recent projects, which had the additional benefit of ensuring consistency in project methodology. The oldest project in the database was started in August 1981, and two-thirds of the projects started in 1983 or later.

Based on the above criteria, 15 projects qualified for inclusion in the study. The researcher or practitioner interested in large business applications is likely to find this data set to be a useful contribution for two reasons: First, in terms of sheer number of projects, it compares favorably with a number of other published studies [4, 7, 9,

11]. Second, and more important than the number of projects alone, is the content of the database. This database contains large business applications, 12 of which were written entirely in Cobol, the most widely used business data-processing language. By contrast, Boehm's 63-project database contains only 7 business applications, of which only 4 were written in Cobol. Albrecht's 1983 database contains 18 Cobol projects, but with an average size of only 66 KSLOC. The average size of Cobol applications in the ABC database is 221 KSLOC.

4. METHODOLOGY

4.1 Data-Collection Forms

The primary data-collection tools were three data-collection forms developed for this project. One form was designed to capture background information about the project (e.g., hardware manufacturer and model), as well as the ABC project number and the start and end dates.

After an analysis of each of the model's requirements, two additional consolidated metrics data-collection forms were devised. Although each of the models has its own set of data requirements, there is a fair amount of overlap in terms of the areas addressed as they relate to productivity. The questions were organized on the forms into broad categories, such as personnel attributes, rather than by models in order to help the respondent ensure consistency in his or her answers for all of the models. However, the questions were printed on the form verbatim from the original source documents whenever possible to minimize any effects of originality in the wording by the researcher.[3] The net result was a set of two data-collection forms, one "quantitative" (e.g., SLOC, database size) and one "qualitative" (e.g., complexity ratings). The intent of this procedure was to retain the

---

[3] The original source documents were, for SLIM, [19]; COCOMO, [5]; Function Points, [3]; and ESTIMACS, [22].

authenticity of the questions as asked in the original source documents, while providing some overall structure for the respondents.

4.2 Data-Collection Procedure

For each of the projects, there was an in-person meeting with the project manager who would be filling out the forms. The one exception to this procedure was a West Coast project manager who was already familiar with the metrics used. Data collection for that particular project was done via the mail and the telephone.

There were two main purposes to this labor-intensive approach. The first was to discuss each of the questions to ensure that it was understood and that each of the managers would answer consistently. The second purpose was to impress upon the managers the importance of their participation in this work. Given the amount of data requested (greater than 100 questions per project), this effort was believed necessary. The result was a large increase in the response rate compared to questionnaires distributed by the normal channels at ABC.

4.3 Data-Analysis Procedures

Once the forms were returned, they were checked for consistency. This was possible due to the redundancy of many of the questions from the different models. With the exception of the "Function-Point-like" questions of the ESTIMACS model, no questions were combined or consolidated.[4] This meant that it was possible to ensure that an answer about, say, project personnel skills for the COCOMO model was consistent with the answer for the similar question for the SLIM model. Next, the project identification information from the "Project Actuals" form was used to research the ABC accounting records to determine the level of effort expended. Finally, the

---

[4] See the ESTIMACS results section (Section 5.5) for discussion of this issue.

metrics data were input to each of the four models. For SLIM, COCOMO, and Function Points, this was done by the researcher. MACS staff offered to run a limited number of projects (without having access to the actual results) and to provide the estimates by telephone.

4.4 Error Analysis

The focus of this paper is on the degree to which the model's estimated effort (MM_{est}) matches the actual effort (MM_{act}). If the models were perfect, then for every project $MM_{est} = MM_{act}$. Clearly, this will rarely, if ever, be the case.

There are several possible methods for evaluating the man-month estimates. A simple analysis approach would be to look at the difference between MM_{est} and MM_{act}. The problem with this *absolute error* approach is that the importance of the size of the error varies with project size. For example, on a 10 man-month project, an absolute error of 9 man-months would be likely to cause serious project disruption in terms of staffing, whereas the same error on a 1000 man-month project would be much less of a problem.

In light of this, Boehm [5] and others have recommended a *percentage error* test, as follows:

$$Percentage\ Error = \frac{MM_{est} - MM_{act}}{MM_{act}}$$

This test eliminates the problem caused by project size and better reflects the impact of any error.

However, the analysis in this paper concentrates on the models' average performance over the entire set of projects. Errors can be of two types: underestimates, where $MM_{est} < MM_{act}$; and overestimates, where $MM_{est} > MM_{act}$. Both of these errors can have serious impacts on projects. Large underestimates will cause the project to be understaffed, and as the deadline approaches, project management will be tempted to add new staff members. This results in a phenomenon known as Brooks's law: "Adding manpower to a late software project makes it later" [6]. Otherwise productive staff are assigned to teaching the new team members, and with this, cost and schedule goals slip even further. Overestimates can also be costly in that staff members, noting the project slack, become less productive (Parkinson's law: "Work expands to fill the time available for its completion") or add so-called "gold plating," defined as additional systems features that are not required by the user [5].

In light of the seriousness of both types of errors, overestimates and underestimates, Conte et al. [8] have suggested a *magnitude of relative error,* or *MRE* test, as follows:

$$MRE = \left| \frac{MM_{est} - MM_{act}}{MM_{act}} \right|$$

By means of this test, the two types of errors do not cancel each other out when an average of multiple errors is taken, and therefore is the test used in this analysis.

Still another issue in interpreting the errors concerns bias. A model, because it was developed in an environment, say, less productive than ABC's, may generate errors that are biased toward overestimation. However, this model may be able to be recalibrated to approximate the ABC environment. What is important is that the estimates correlate with the actual results: that is, bigger projects generate bigger estimates than smaller projects.

Albrecht and others [3, 4, 8] have proposed linear regression as a means of measuring this correlation. Since Albrecht's method does not produce a man-month estimate directly, an alternative was needed to validate the Function Point method. His proposal was to perform a simple linear regression with man-months as the dependent variable and Function Points as the independent variable. He also performs regressions with SLOC as the dependent variable to show how Function Points could be used to generate an SLOC estimate for other models or methods that require it. Regression was used in this research for all of the models by using actual man-months as the dependent variable and the man-months estimated by each model as the independent variable. The advantage of this method is that it can show whether a model's estimates correlate well with experience even when the MRE test does not. A "perfect" score on the MRE test would be an error percentage of 0, whereas a "perfect" score on Albrecht's test would be an R^2 of 1.00.[5]

In summary, two tests are used to evaluate the models (as recommended by Theabaut [24]): the MRE test and regression. These tests have the advantage of not only being generally accepted in the literature, but of also having been proposed by some of the models' own developers.

5. RESULTS

5.1 Project Data

Exhibit 3 shows the background data on the projects. The "Months" figures are project durations in calendar months. The man-months ("MM") data refer to the total number of actual hours expended by exempt staff members (i.e., not including secretarial labor) on the project through implementation, divided by 152. This effort measure was the only output of the models that was evaluated, although several of them offer other features, such as project planning aids. The "KSLOC" figures follow Boehm's definition stated earlier (i.e., comments are not counted) with two exceptions.

One project (number 8) had reused code, and this was accounted for in the KSLOC data by counting a modified line as equivalent to a new line. In the KDSI data (used for COCOMO), Boehm's conversion formula for modified software was used [$]. This resulted in a KDSI count of 167 as opposed to the 200 KSLOC count shown above for project number 8.

The other exception is that Cobol nonprocedural statements are not specially weighted. Boehm

---

[5] In this analysis the more conservative $\bar{R}^2$, R^3 adjusted for degrees of freedom, was used, which results in slighter lower values than R^2.

EXHIBIT 3 Project Background

Project Number	Software	Hardware	Months	MM	KSLOC	SLOC/MM
1	Cobol	IBM 308X	17	287.00	263.80	884
2	Cobol	IBM 43XX	7	82.50	40.50	491
3	Cobol	DEC VAX	15	1,107.31	450.00	406
4	Cobol	IBM 308X	18	86.90	214.40	2,467
5	Cobol	IBM 43XX	13	335.30	449.90	1,338
6	Cobol	DEC 20	5	84.00	50.00	595
7	Bliss	DEC 20	5	23.20	43.00	1,853
8	Cobol	IBM 43XX	11	130.30	200.00	1,535
9	Cobol	IBM 308X	14	118.00	289.00	2,491
10	Cobol, Natural	IBM 308X	5	72.00	39.00	542
11	Cobol	IBM 308X	13	258.70	254.20	983
12	Cobol	IBM 43XX, 308X	31	230.70	128.60	557
13	Cobol	HP 3000, 88	20	157.00	161.40	1,028
14	Cobol	IBM 308X	26	246.90	164.80	667
15	Natural	IBM 308X	14	69.90	60.20	861
Mean			14.3	219.25	188.57	1,113
Standard deviation			7.5	263.00	136.82	689
Cobol mean					221.37	1,120
Cobol standard deviation					131.14	720

found this weighting necessary as only 4 of his 63 projects were Cobol, and as he states, some "pragmatic" procedure was required to make those projects fit his formula.[6] Since the project data in this research are overwhelmingly Cobol, no such pragmatic weighting was deemed necessary.

5.2 SLIM Results

SLIM was run using the default parameters provided by the model when the user answers the SLIM set of 22 questions. Exhibit 4 shows the actual man-months, the SLIM man-month esti-

mate,[7] and the error percentage. Also shown are the SLIM default PF, the default MBI, the calibrated PF, and the calibrated MBI. (The calibrated factors were obtained after the fact by using the SLIM "calibrate" function for use in later analyses.)

SLIM does not do well via the MRE test. The average percentage error is 772 percent, with the smallest error being 21 percent. In addition, the errors are all biased; effort is overestimated in all 15 cases. A possible explanation for this is that SLIM was originally developed using data from defense-related projects, including real-time systems. Productivity for these is typically less than

---

[6] See (5, p. 479). The unavailability of these data may make the COCOMO estimates slightly higher than they would be elsewhere.

[7] The SLIM man-month is 168 man-hours. All SLIM man-month estimates were converted to 152 man-hour man-months to aid comparison.

EXHIBIT 4   SLIM Data

Project Number	Actual MM	SLIM MM Estimate	SLIM error (%)	PF	MBI	Calibrated PF	Calibrated MBI
1	287.0	3,857.8	1,244.18	12	5	18	3
2	82.5	100.1	21.33	15	4	16	5
3	1,107.3	11,982.0	982.08	16	4	19	5
4	86.9	2,017.2	2,221.29	13	4	18	1
5	336.3	3,382.0	905.65	15	5	21	4
6	84.0	262.5	212.50	13	4	19	6
7	23.2	106.3	358.19	16	5	20	5
8	130.3	1,224.6	839.83	14	4	20	3
9	116.0	1,454.1	1,153.53	15	4	20	2
10	72.0	235.7	227.36	12	4	18	6
11	258.7	1,623.0	527.37	15	5	19	3
12	230.7	513.3	122.50	15	4	12	1
13	157.0	3,119.8	1,887.13	11	5	16	1
14	246.9	380.3	54.03	17	4	14	1
15	69.9	643.8	821.03	11	4	15	1
Mean (absolute values)	219.25	2,060.17	771.87	14.0	4.3	17.7	3.1
Standard deviation	263.06	3,014.77	661.33	1.9	0.5	2.6	1.9

that in the business data-processing systems developed by ABC [18, 23].

One possibility is that SLIM accurately reflects the project conditions, but is calibrated too high for the ABC environment. To evaluate this Albrecht's test was applied by means of a regression run with the SLIM estimate as the independent variable and the actual man-months as the dependent variable. The results were that the SLIM estimates correlated well with the actuals, generating an $\bar{R}^2$ of 87.8 percent, with a coefficient t statistic of 10.11.

$$\begin{array}{cc} \textit{Actual man-months} & \bar{R}^2 \\ = 4.9 + 0.082 \ (SLIM) & \overline{87.8\%} \\ (10.11) & \end{array}$$

The main input for SLIM is KSLOC, whose regression with actual man-months produced an $\bar{R}^2$

of only 48.5 percent, so the SLIM model seems to be adding information.

5.3 COCOMO Results

The results for the three COCOMO versions (Basic, Intermediate, and Detailed Models) appear in Exhibit 5. In the table "BAS" refers to the Basic Model, "INT" to the Intermediate Model, and "DET" to the Detailed Model. The "error %" columns are calculated by dividing the difference between the estimate and the actual man-months by the actual man-months.

All three COCOMO models did poorly according to the MRE percentage error test. The average error for all versions of the model was 601 percent, with the lowest single error being 83 percent. As was the case with SLIM, the estimates are biased; effort is overestimated in all 45 cases.

EXHIBIT 5   COCOMO Data

Project Number	Actual MM	COCOMO BAS	COCOMO-BAS Error (%)	COCOMO INT	COCOMO-INT Error (%)	COCOMO DET	COCOMO-DET Error (%)
1	287.00	1,095.10	281.57	917.56	219.71	932.96	225.07
2	82.50	189.40	129.58	151.66	83.83	151.19	83.26
3	1,107.31	5,497.40	396.46	6,182.65	458.35	5,818.75	425.49
4	86.90	1,222.30	1,306.56	558.98	543.25	566.50	551.90
5	336.30	1,466.00	335.92	1,344.20	299.70	1,316.04	291.33
6	84.00	393.60	368.57	313.36	273.05	312.24	271.71
7	23.20	328.40	1,315.52	234.78	911.98	234.51	910.82
8	130.30	925.30	610.13	1,165.70	794.63	1,206.17	825.69
9	116.00	3,231.00	2,685.34	4,248.73	3,562.70	4,577.62	3,846.22
10	72.00	181.60	152.22	180.29	150.40	181.36	151.89
11	258.70	1,482.20	472.94	1,520.04	487.57	1,575.68	509.08
12	230.70	691.00	199.52	558.12	141.92	584.37	153.30
13	157.00	891.20	467.64	1,073.47	583.74	1,124.36	616.15
14	246.90	511.00	106.97	629.22	154.85	663.84	168.87
15	69.90	295.30	322.46	133.94	91.62	130.72	87.01
Mean (absolute values)	219.25	1,226.72	610.09	1,280.85	583.82	1,291.75	607.85
Standard deviation	263.06	1,412.58	684.55	1,698.43	862.79	1,667.24	932.96

Again, this may be due to COCOMO's development on TRW's data. The average KSLOC/MM figure for Boehm's data is much lower than that for the ABC data, probably reflecting the composition of the type of systems developed by TRW and ABC. Again, it is possible that COCOMO is accurately reflecting the project conditions, but is calibrated too high for the ABC environment. In his book Boehm acknowledges the probable need for calibration of his model in a new environment [5].

To evaluate this Albrecht's regression test was run. The results were as follows:

Actual man-months
$$= 27.7 + 0.156 \ (COCOMO\text{-}Basic) \quad \dfrac{\bar{R}^2}{68.0\%}$$
(5.54)

Actual man-months
$$= 62.1 + 0.123 \ (COCOMO\text{-}Intermediate) \quad 59.9\%$$
(4.68)

Actual man-months
$$= 66.8 + 0.118 \ (COCOMO\text{-}Detailed) \quad 52.5\%$$
(4.06)

Paradoxically, the more advanced versions, COCOMO-Intermediate and COCOMO-Detailed, do not do as well as COCOMO-Basic in this instance. This implies that the cost drivers of the latter two models are not adding any additional explanation of the phenomenon. This is consistent with the results of Kitchenham and Taylor, who evaluated COCOMO on some systems programming

EXHIBIT 6   Function Points-MM Data

Project Number	Actual MM	Function Points	Function Counts	Albrecht FP MM Estimate	Albrecht MM Error (%)
1	287.00	1,217.10	1,010.00	344.30	19.96
2	82.50	507.30	457.00	92.13	11.68
3	1,107.31	2,306.80	2,284.00	731.43	−33.95
4	86.90	788.50	881.00	192.03	120.98
5	336.30	1,337.60	1,583.00	387.11	15.11
6	84.00	421.30	411.00	61.58	−26.69
7	23.20	99.90	97.00	−52.60	−326.73
8	130.30	993.00	998.00	264.68	103.13
9	116.00	1,592.90	1,554.00	477.81	311.90
10	72.00	240.00	250.00	−2.83	−103.93
11	258.70	1,611.00	1,603.00	484.24	87.18
12	230.70	789.00	724.00	192.21	−16.68
13	157.00	690.90	705.00	157.36	0.23
14	246.90	1,347.50	1,375.00	390.63	58.21
15	69.90	1,044.30	976.00	282.91	304.73
Mean (absolute values)	219.25	999.14	993.87	266.87	102.74
Standard deviation	263.06	569.60	577.17	202.36	112.11

and real-time systems projects developed by British Telecom and ICL [13].

In addition, a regression was run on the primary input to the COCOMO models, delivered source instructions, or KDSI. The result was an $\bar{R}^2$ of 49.4 percent, which is not as good a fit as any of the COCOMO models. Therefore, COCOMO seems to be adding information.

5.4 Function Points Results

In this section three separate analyses are performed. The first analysis compares the man-month predictions from Function Points to the actual man-months and is similar to the analysis done for the other models. In addition, two of Albrecht's other models are tested, one for predicting man-months from SLOC, and the other for predicting SLOC from Function Points.

5.4.1 *Function Points to Man-Month Results*

As shown in Exhibit 6, the average MRE is 102.74 percent, substantially better than either of the two SLOC-based models. This is probably due to the similarity of applications (business data processing) done by ABC and IBM's DP Services group, the source of Albrecht's data. The regression analysis of these estimates and the actual man-months was the following:

Actual (ABC) man-months
$= -37 + 0.96$ *(Function Points*
  (4.26) *estimated man-months)* $\dfrac{\bar{R}^2}{55.3\%}$

The regression analysis result from the ABC data is as follows:

ABC man-months
$= -122 + 0.341$ *(Function Points)*
  (4.28) $\dfrac{\bar{R}^2}{55.3\%}$

EXHIBIT 7   Cobol KSLOC-MM Data

Project Number	Actual MM	Albrecht SLOC MM Estimate	Albrecht MM Error (%)
1	287.00	613.67	113.82
2	82.50	81.90	−0.73
3	1,107.31	1,103.76	−0.32
4	86.90	515.85	493.61
5	336.30	1,103.51	228.13
6	84.00	105.61	25.72
8	130.30	479.91	268.32
9	116.00	702.00	505.18
11	258.70	615.16	137.79
12	230.70	301.74	30.79
13	157.00	383.59	144.33
14	246.90	392.08	58.80
Mean (absolute values)	260.30	533.23	167.29
Standard deviation	280.60	327.25	177.07

EXHIBIT 8   Function Points—COBOL KSLOC Data

Project Number	KSLOC	Albrecht KSLOC Estimate	Albrecht Error (%)
1	253.60	137.98	−45.59
2	40.50	53.73	32.66
3	450.00	267.33	−40.59
4	214.40	87.10	−59.37
5	449.90	152.28	−66.15
6	50.00	43.52	−12.96
8	200.00	111.38	−44.31
9	289.00	182.59	−36.82
11	254.20	184.74	−27.33
12	128.60	87.16	−32.22
13	161.40	75.52	−53.21
14	164.80	153.46	−6.88
Mean (absolute values)	221.37	128.07	38.17
Standard deviation	131.14	64.65	17.47

By way of comparison, in Albrecht's validation paper [3] he developed the following estimation equation from a data set of 24 projects:

$$\text{IBM man-months} = -88 + 0.355 \, (\text{Function Points}) \quad \frac{\bar{R}^2}{86.9\%}$$
$$(12.37)$$

Albrecht's equation developed using IBM data is strikingly similar to the equation using ABC data, differing primarily by the constant term. The results of an *F*-test comparing the two individual regressions with a single regression on all 39 data points revealed that the null hypothesis that the two models were the same could not be rejected at the 95 percent confidence level [26].

A similar regression was performed on the ABC Function Count data, the main input to Function Points.

$$\text{ABC man-months} = -111 + 0.333 \, (\text{Function Counts}) \quad \frac{\bar{R}^2}{53.8\%}$$
$$(4.16)$$

The difference between using Function Points, which include 14 factors that modify the Function Counts, and the Function Counts themselves, seems slight in this instance.

5.4.2 Source Lines of Code to Man-Month Results
Albrecht provides another model, showing the relationship for his data between Cobol KSLOC and man-months.

$$\text{IBM man-months} = -19.2 + 2.5 \, (\text{Cobol KSLOC}) \quad \frac{\bar{R}^2}{73.0\%}$$
$$(6.85)$$

The results are shown in Exhibit 7.

The average MRE of 167.3 percent is not as good as that generated by Function Points. The equivalent equation for the ABC data is the following:

$$\begin{array}{cc} ABC\ man\text{-}months & \bar{R}^2 \\ = -65 + 1.47\ (Cobol\ KSLOC) & \overline{41.9\%} \\ (2.99) & \end{array}$$

The results of an *F*-test are that we can reject the null hypothesis that the IBM and ABC models are the same at the 95 percent confidence level, but not at the 99 percent level.

5.4.3 *Function Points to Source Lines of Code Results*

Another validation that was performed was a check of Albrecht's claim of Function Points as a predictor of KSLOC. Albrecht provides the following model for estimating Cobol SLOC from Function Points:

$$\begin{array}{cc} IBM\ Cobol\ KSLOC & \bar{R}^2 \\ = -6.5 + 0.12\ (Function\ Points) & \overline{71.2\%} \\ (6.55) & \end{array}$$

The results are shown in Exhibit 8, and show an average MRE of 38.17 percent, with a large negative bias. The estimated relationship between the actual KSLOC and the estimates is the following:

$$\begin{array}{cc} ABC\ Cobol\ KSLOC & \bar{R}^2 \\ = 6 + 1.68\ (Function\ Points) & \overline{65.6\%} \\ (4.69)\ estimated\ KSLOC) & \end{array}$$

In general, these results seem to validate Albrecht's claims that Function Points do correlate well with eventual SLOC. The results for the ABC were as follows:

$$\begin{array}{cc} ABC\ Cobol\ KSLOC & \bar{R}^2 \\ = -5.0 + 0.20\ (Function\ Points) & \overline{65.6\%} \\ (4.69) & \end{array}$$

$$\begin{array}{cc} ABC\ Cobol\ KSLOC & \\ = -13.2 + 0.207\ (Function\ Counts) & 75.1\% \\ (5.85) & \end{array}$$

Although the IBM and ABC models are apparently fairly similar, the results of an *F*-test are that

EXHIBIT 9   ESTIMACS Data

Project Nnumber	Actuals MM	ESTIMACS	ESTIMACS Error (%)
1	287.00	230.26	−19.77
2	82.50	111.26	34.86
3	1,107.31	523.51	−52.72
4	86.90	234.59	169.95
5	336.30	687.63	104.47
8	130.30	389.26	198.74
10	72.00	67.20	−6.67
11	258.70	624.43	141.37
12	230.70	324.78	40.78
Mean (absolute values)	287.97	354.77	85.48
Standard deviation	322.48	219.66	70.36

we can reject the null hypothesis that the models are the same at the 99 percent level.

The second result is that, for the ABC data, the unmodified Function Counts have a higher correlation than the modified Function Points. This suggests that the functionality represented by Function Counts is related to eventual SLOC, but that the 14 "complexity adjustment" factors are not adding any information for this particular sample.

5.5 ESTIMACS Results

As explained in the "Methodology" section (Section 4), the procedure for testing ESTIMACS was to gather the data (excluding the actual man-months), send them to MACS, and receive the estimate. This procedure was performed on 9 of the 15 projects in the database. These 9 were simply the first projects for which data were collected. The data for ESTIMACS are presented in Exhibit 9.

The ESTIMACS average error is 85 percent, which includes some over and some under estimates, and is the smallest average error of the four models. This may be due to the similarity of the ESTIMACS application base (originally an insurance firm) and the ABC database, although this cannot be verified due to the proprietary nature of the ESTIMACS data. The regression data were as follows:

$$\text{Actual man-months} = 31 + 0.723 \, (ESTIMACS)$$
$$(1.50)$$

$$\frac{\bar{R}^2}{13.4\%}$$

Although the average error was less, the fit with the actual effort is worse than the other models. The *t* statistic is also less, although still significant at approximately the 92 percent confidence level.

To check the possibility that the 9-project subset estimated by ESTIMACS was somehow different from the 15-project data set as a whole, each of the models and its inputs were run against only that 9-project data set. The results were the following:

$$\text{Actual man-months} = 54.1 + 0.084 \, (SLIM)$$
$$(10.17)$$

$$\frac{\bar{R}^2}{92.8\%}$$

$$\text{Actual man-months} = 11.4 + 0.195 \, (COCOMO\text{-}Basic)$$
$$(10.82)$$

$$93.6\%$$

$$\text{Actual man-months} = 51 + 0.17 \, (COCOMO\text{-}Intermediate)$$
$$(12.24)$$

$$94.9\%$$

$$\text{Actual man-months} = 40.3 + 0.181 \, (COCOMO\text{-}Detailed)$$
$$(11.62)$$

$$94.4\%$$

$$\text{Actual man-months} = -203 + 0.451 \, (Function \ Points)$$
$$(4.63)$$

$$71.8\%$$

$$\text{Actual man-months} = -175 + 0.426 \, (Function \ Count)$$
$$(4.09)$$

$$66.2\%$$

$$\text{Actual man-months} = -94 + 1.67 \, (KDSI)$$
$$(2.90)$$

$$44.5\%$$

$$\text{Actual man-months} = -102 + 1.68 \, (KSLOC)$$
$$(2.83)$$

$$43.2\%$$

It does not appear that this 9-project subset was any more difficult to estimate than the full 15-project data set. In fact, SLIM, Function Points, and all three versions of COCOMO did better on the subset. Only KDSI and KSLOC did slightly worse, and these are not inputs to ESTIMACS. If anything, this suggests that the 6 projects not estimated by ESTIMACS were more difficult to accurately estimate than the original 9.

Another possibility may be related to how the input data for the ESTIMACS analysis were collected. Of the 25 required data items, 5 deserve special mention: (1) number of major business functions, (2) number of unique business inputs, (3) number of unique business outputs, (4) number of logical files, and (5) number of on-line inquiry types. These factors (which ESTIMACS collectively refers to as "volume") tend to drive most estimates.[8] Upon examining the ESTIMACS documentation, the last four of these questions sound exactly like the 1979 version of Albrecht's Function Points. For example, here are two direct quotations on the subject of inputs, the first by Albrecht and the second by Rubin:

> *External Input Types:* Count each unique user data or user control input type that enters the external boundary of the application being measured, and adds or changes data in a logical internal file type. An external input type should be considered unique if it has a different format, or if the external design requires a processing logic different from other external input types of the same format. . . . Do not include the input part of the external inquiry types as external input types, because these are counted as external inquiry types. [3]
>
> *Number of External Inputs:* How many unique logical business inputs will the system process? This is a count of the number of major data types that will enter the system from outside of it. In this

---

[8] Personal correspondence, P. Madden, July 1985.

way internal data base information is excluded from this total. On-line inquiry only screens are also excluded. Think in terms of major business communication transactions. Inputs counted should be unique in that they require different processing logic from other inputs. [22]

These two questions appear to address the same concept, and Albrecht's 1979 paper is cited in Rubin's 1983 paper. Therefore, in conducting this research, the Function Point definitions were used to answer the matching ESTIMACS questions. According to the MACS staff, however, this may result in overestimating these input quantities by a factor of three[9] or four.[10] How the difference is defined was not available from MACS, so "correct" use of the model may come only with experience. This begets the question of whether the use of Function Points for the "Function-Point-like" questions affected the model's performance. If the estimates had been uniformly high, then this would seem a likely possibility. However, given that the estimate errors ranged from −52.7 percent to +198.7 percent, this does not seem to be the case.

5.6 Sensitivity Analysis

As discussed in Section 3, this data set of 15 completed software projects is large relative to many other published studies. However, it is still small in terms of what researchers might like in order to assure that the results are robust. In particular, readers should note the sensitivity of the regression models to project number 3, which, although almost exactly equal to project number 5 in its KSLOC count, is several times larger in its actual man-months figure. Were this project to be dropped from the data set, almost all of the regression models on the new 14-point data set (particularly COCOMO's) would exhibit decreases in their $\bar{R}^2$, the measure of "goodness of fit." The sole exceptions to this were the KDSI and KSLOC regres-

sions, which exhibited very slight increases. This last result is likely due to the elimination of one of the two similarly sized projects (450 KSLOC) that had very different productivity rates. This would tend to make the remaining large project somewhat of an "anchor" for the regression.

A similar analysis was done for the 9-project "ESTIMACS subset." The results of the regressions run on the 8-project subset were that the $\bar{R}^2$ for SLIM, COCOMO, and ESTIMACS were all in the 38−49 percent range. The results for Function Points and Function Counts decreased to the 54−60 percent range, and the results for KSLOC and KDSI increase to the 56−59 percent range. Again, this last result is likely due to the elimination of one of the two similarly sized projects (450 KSLOC) that had very different productivity rates. As a test of this, the data were rerun on a 7-project subset without either of the largest projects. The models whose performance improved with the 8-project data set (ESTIMACS, KSLOC, KDSI) all worsened as a result. Therefore, the improvements seemed only related to the creation of project number 5 as a new "anchor." Consequently, project number 3 was not dropped, given no a priori reason for doing so, plus the new regression models' increased dependence on project number 5, the "new outlier" if project number 3 were dropped.

Owing to large differences in project productivity, variation such as the difference between project number 3 and project number 5 is not uncommon in project data. As an example, Albrecht's 24-project data set contains the following two projects:

	KSLOC	Man-Hours (in thousands)
Project number 1	130	102.4
Project number 2	318	105.2
24-project mean	61	21.9
24-project standard deviation	62	27.8

The difference between his largest project (number 2) and the next largest (number 1), in

---

[9] Personal correspondence, L. Kleeck, 7/18/85.

[10] Personal correspondence, P. Madden, 8/13/85.

terms of KSLOC, is 188, which is a difference of 3.03 standard deviations. The equivalent calculation for the ABC data is 2.93 standard deviations. The difference between Albrecht's largest project and the mean is 257, or 4.15 standard deviations, whereas the equivalent calculation for ABC is 3.38. Therefore, the ABC data have a less severe outlier problem than even Albrecht's data.

The existence of these outliers and large variations in productivity is not a particularly desirable situation from a research perspective. However, given the difficulty and cost in gathering this kind of data, the best available data are relatively small sets that are subject to this type of condition.

6. CONCLUSIONS

Having examined each model independently, it seems appropriate to summarize these results. Specifically, it is time to address the questions posed in the introduction to this paper to see what answers have been provided by this research. Of course, it will be important to bear in mind that these results stem from 15 projects developed by one firm, and overly broad generalizations are not possible. Rather, these results suggest certain hypotheses that may be verifiable with further research.

6.1 Implications for Practitioners

The first research question to be answered concerned the accuracy of the models outside their original environments and the ease with which they could be recalibrated to fit a new environment. One conclusion is that models developed in different environments do not work very well uncalibrated, as might be expected. Average error rates calculated using the MRE formula ranged from 85 to 772 percent, with many in the 500–600 percent range. This variation is most likely due to the degree to which the productivity of the environments where the models were developed matches the target (ABC) environment. This points out the need for organizations that wish to use algorithmic estimating tools to collect histori-

cal data on their projects in order to calibrate the models for local conditions.

After allowing for calibration, the best of the models explain 88 percent of the behavior of the actual man-month effort in this data set. This result alone probably justifies consideration of an algorithmic estimating method by a software manager who has sufficient data to calibrate it to his or her environment. In addition, there are benefits to the estimation task simply from the structure the models impose on the estimation process. Providing inputs for model parameters and sizing estimates requires a project team to carefully consider many important aspects of the upcoming project. Of course, as the model developers themselves point out, these models are adjuncts to, not substitutes for, a detailed estimate by task by the project management [3].

The second research question concerned the relative efficacy of SLOC models versus non-SLOC models. In terms of the MRE results, the non-SLOC models (Function Points and ESTI-MACS) did better, although this is likely due to their development in business data-processing environments similar to ABC's. In terms of the regression results, both of the SLOC models (CO-COMO and SLIM) had higher correlations than either ESTIMACS or Function Points. However, these data must be considered in light of an important implementation question. The SLOC counts were obtained *ex post* and are therefore likely to be much more accurate than SLOC counts obtained before a project begins. Although SLIM does provide a means for modeling this initial uncertainty (through a beta distribution approach), it is unlikely that a project manager could estimate SLOC counts with the degree of accuracy used in this research. Presumably, the variance between *ex ante* and *ex post* Function Point counts is less, although verifying this is an open research question.

An additional consideration is that Function Points and Function Counts can be used as predictors of KSLOC. In particular, Function Counts correlated with KSLOC at the level of 75.1

percent, which is similar to the correlations published by Albrecht [3], and is likely to be good enough to be of use to the software manager.

The third and final research question concerns the relation between the proprietary and the non-proprietary models. This question was not answered conclusively by this research, as the proprietary SLIM model outperformed (in its $\bar{R}^2$ value) the nonproprietary COCOMO model on this data set, while the nonproprietary Function Points model outperformed the proprietary ESTI-MACS model on this data set.

6.2 Directions for Future Research

This paper has provided several important research results regarding software metrics and models. First, Albrecht's model for estimating man-months of effort from Function Points has been validated on an independent data set. This is particularly significant in that Function Points has been proposed by IBM as a general productivity measure and prior to this there was only limited evidence for their utility from non-IBM sources [4].

One interesting research question raised by this Function Points result is the degree to which *ex ante* and *ex post* Function Points counts are similar. As pointed out in the previous section, the higher correlations generated by the SLOC-based models must be tempered by a recognition that, in practice, accurate *ex ante* SLOC estimates may be difficult to achieve. An interesting research question involves the degree to which initial misestimates change the results achieved by these models. A more general extension of this is, what impact do the estimates themselves have on projects? A recent paper by Abdel-Hamid and Madnick [1] discusses this issue from a systems dynamics perspective. The authors make the point that the effort required on a software-development project is in part a function of the estimate given at the beginning of the project. From this premise they devise a model (not shown in the cited paper) that presumably includes the estimate as an endogenous variable. They then develop an example to show that an estimate that was more accurate could also be more expensive in items of creating a bigger project.

Although an interesting example, one problem with it is that they draw the unsupported conclusion that the accuracy of software cost estimation models cannot be judged by their performance on historical (completed) projects. Clearly, *ex post* estimates cannot influence the project. Therefore, it seems reasonable to evaluate them by this method. It could be argued that software cost estimation models that do not include their own estimate are deficient, but this is a different conclusion than the one drawn by the authors. However, their idea of the effect of the estimate on a project is an interesting one, and further research should be done in this area.

Finally, although improving estimation techniques within the industry is a worthwhile goal, the ultimate question must concern how the productivity of software developers can be improved. These estimation and productivity questions are related in that the estimation models contain descriptions of what factors their developers believe affect productivity. How well do these models identify and reflect these factors?

The models researched in this study do not seem to capture productivity factors very well. There are several pieces of evidence to support this conclusion. The first is that the COCOMO-Intermediate and COCOMO-Detailed Models (the versions with the productivity factor "cost drivers") did not perform significantly better than the Basic Model and in fact correlated less well with actual man-months. Second, the raw Function Count data correlated as well as or better than the Function Point numbers, which reflect the 14 "processing complexity" adjustments. Third, ESTIMACS, with its 20 additional productivity-related questions, did less well than the similar Function Counts alone. Finally, the model that had the highest correlation, SLIM, has the problem that its questions designed to elicit productivity-related information uniformly generated PFs that were too low (the reason all the default estimates were too large) and MBIs that were too high. This was determined by comparing these values to the values that would have been obtained had the SLIM "calibrate" feature been used.

A reasonable conclusion from all this is that the models, although an improvement over their raw inputs for estimating project effort, do not model the factors affecting productivity very well. One possible extension of this research is to analyze the data in this study to attempt to determine the causes for the wide swings in accuracy of the estimates across projects. What characteristics make a project amenable to this type of estimation? What factors could be added to the models to enable them to do a better job on all of the projects? On the productivity side, the projects in this data set show a large amount of variance in terms of such traditional metrics as SLOC per man-month. Can these variations be traced to

productivity factors controllable by the software manager? What are the effects of modern programming practices, such as the use of fourth-generation languages, or AI techniques? Further research needs to be done to isolate and measure these factors affecting systems professionals' productivity if the profession is to meet the challenges of the future.

Acknowledgments

The author wishes to thank Fred Forman, Charles Kriebel, and Mary Shaw for their assistance with this paper. Additional thanks to Douglas Putnam of Quantitative Software Management and Patrick Madden of Management and Computer Services for permission to use their models during this research.

References

1. Abdel-Hamid, T., and Madnick, S. Impact of schedule estimation on software project behavior. *IEEE Softw. 3,* 4 (July 1986), 70–75.

2. Albrecht, A.J. Measuring application development productivity. In *Proceedings of the IBM Applications Development Symposium, GUIDE/SHARE* (Monterey, Calif., Oct. 14–17). IBM, 1979, pp. 83–92.

3. Albrecht, A.J., and Gaffney, J., Jr. Software function, source lines of code, and development effort prediction: A software science validation. *IEEE Trans. Softw. Eng. SE-9,* 6 (Nov. 1983), 639–648.

4. Behrens, C.A. Measuring the productivity of computer systems development activities with Function Points. *IEEE Trans. Softw. Eng. SE-9,* 6 (Nov. 1983), 648–652.

5. Boehm, B.W. *Software Engineering Economics.* Prentice-Hall, Englewood Cliffs, N.J., 1981.

6. Brooks, F.P. *The Mythical Man-Month.* Addison-Wesley, Reading, Mass., 1975.

7. Callisen, H., and Colborne, S. A proposed method for estimating software cost from requirements. *J. Parametrics 4,* 4 (Dec. 1984), 33–40.

8. Conte, S., Dunsmore, H., and Shen. V. *Software Engineering Metrics and Models.* Benjamin/Cummings, Menlo Park, Calif., 1986.

9. Ferens, D.V. Software support cost models: Quo vadis? *J. Parametrics 4,* 4 (Dec. 1984), 64–99.

10. Gaffney, J.E., Goldberg, R., and Misek-Falkoff, L. SCORE82 Summary. *Perform. Eval. Rev. 12,* 4 (Winter 1984–1985), 4–12.

11. Golden, J.R., Mueller, J.R., and Anselm, B. Software cost estimating: Craft or witchcraft. *Database 12,* 3 (Spring 1981), 12–14.

12. Jones, C. *Programming Productivity.* McGraw-Hill, New York, 1986.

13. Kitchenham, B., and Taylor, N.R. Software cost models. *ICL Tech. J. 4,* 1 (May 1984), 73–102.

14. Masters, T.F., II. An overview of software cost estimating at the NSA. *J. Parametrics 5,* 1 (Mar. 1985), 72–84.

15. Pinsky, S.S. The effect of complexity on software trade off equations. *J. Parametrics 4,* 4 (Dec. 1984), 23–32.

16. Putnam, L.H. General empirical solution to the macro software sizing and estimating problem. *IEEE Trans. Softw. Eng. SE 4,* 4 (July 1978), 345–361.

17. Putnam, L., and Fitzsimmons, A. Estimating software costs. *Datamation 25,* 10–12 (Sept.–Nov. 1979).

18. Quantitative Software Management. *Reference Notes for the DOD SLIM Software Cost Estimating Course.* Quantitative Software Management, McLean, Va., 1983.

19. Quantitative Software Management, *SLIM User Manual (IBM PC Version)* Draft copy ed. Quantitative Software Management, McLean, Va., 1984.

20. Rubin, H.A. Macroestimation of software development parameters: The Estimacs system. In *SOFTFAIR Conference on Software Development Tools, Techniques and Alternatives* (Arlington, Va., July 25–28). IEEE Press, New York, 1983, pp. 109–118.

21. Rubin, H.A. The art and science of software estimation: Fifth generation estimators. In *Proceedings of the 7th Annual ISPA Conference* (Orlando, Fla., May 7–9). International Society of Parametric Analysts, McLean, Va., 1985, pp. 56–72.

22. Rubin, H.A. Using ESTIMACS E. Management and Computer Services, Valley Forge, Pa., Mar. 1984.

23. Software Productivity Research. *SPQR / 20 User Guide*. Software Productivity Research, Cambridge, Mass., 1986.

24. Theabaut, S.M. Model evaluation in software metrics research. In *Computer Science and Statistics: Proceedings of the 15th Symposium on the Interface* (Houston, Tex., Mar.). 1983, pp. 277–285.

25. Walston, C.E., and Felix, C.P. A method of programming measurement and estimation. *IBM Syst. J. 16,* 1 (Jan. 1977), 54–73.

26. Weisberg, S. *Applied Linear Regression.* Wiley, New York, 1980.

27. Wolverton, W.R. Cost of developing large scale software. *IEEE Trans. Comput. C-23,* 6 (June 1974), 615–634.

SCALE ECONOMIES IN NEW SOFTWARE DEVELOPMENT

I. RESEARCH PROBLEM

Software development practitioners are faced with the problem of how to appropriately size new software development projects so as to maximize productivity. Unfortunately, much of the research in this area has arrived at apparently contradictory conclusions, namely that either economies of scale exist or that diseconomies of scale exist. This paper integrates these apparently contradictory results in a consistent framework, and empirically demonstrates that the existence of local scale economies or diseconomies depends upon the size of software development projects.[1] In addition, we provide a methodology for identifying the most productive scale size for a given software development environment.

A production process exhibits local increasing returns to scale if, at a given volume level, the marginal returns of an additional unit of input exceed the average returns. Economies of scale are thus present when average productivity is increasing, and scale diseconomies prevail when average productivity is decreasing. Reasons provided to explain the presence of economies of scale range from specialization of labor to phenomena such as learning curves. Software engineering researchers such as Boehm [14] have noted the presence of a number of factors in new software development that may contribute to economies of scale, such as software development tools like online debuggers or code generators. These tools may increase productivity, but the relatively large initial investment, both in purchase and in the organizational learning costs, may proscribe their use on small projects. Larger projects may also benefit from specialized personnel, whose expertise in a certain area (e.g., assembly language coding) may

Article by Rajiv D. Banker and Chris F. Kemerer. © 1989 IEEE. Reprinted, with permission, from (*IEEE Transactions on Software Engineering*; SE-15, 10, 416–429; 1989).

[1] In production economics, economies of scale are defined at specific volume levels in a production process, and are thus best described as *local*. It is therefore inappropriate to limit the characterization of a production process to only *global* economies (or diseconomies) of scale. In dealing with single input-single output production correspondences, we shall use the terms increasing returns to scale and scale economies interchangeably.

increase the project's overall productivity. Finally, all projects require a certain fixed investment in project management overhead. This type of overhead (e.g., status meetings and reports) does not increase directly with project size and therefore can be a source of economies of scale for larger projects.

In contrast to the reasons cited above, many authors have pointed out the possibility of diseconomies of scale on large software projects. Brooks [15] has suggested that the number of communication paths between project team members increases (at an increasing rate) with the number of team members.[2] This communication overhead is a clear case of nonlinear cost increase, and hence a factor that could contribute to diseconomies of scale. Somewhat analogously, Conte et al. [19] suggest that larger systems development projects will face more complex interface problems between system components. Boehm [14] points out that increasing the number of people also increases the chances for personality conflicts among team members. Jones [23] notes that many overhead activities, such as planning and documentation, grow at a faster than linear rate as project size increases. Another possible source of diseconomies of scale is project slack, which is likely to be larger on a larger project and may contribute to reduced productivity.

Given these contradictory hypotheses, how can researchers best model the software development production process? And, how can practicing software development managers appropriately size new software development projects so as to maximize average productivity? This paper addresses these questions and is organized as follows. Section II presents the empirical evidence for both the notion of economies of scale and the notion of diseconomies of scale in new software development. We integrate these two notions and suggest that in most organizations, the software development production process first exhibits local in-

creasing returns to scale, but decreasing returns set in for very large projects. We believe that one reason that this has not been shown by other researchers is due to the simple parametric models employed. We show in Section III, however, that in empirical applications even the more flexible parametric forms are limited in their ability to estimate the returns to scale. This motivates our use in Section IV of Data Envelopment Analysis as an alternative nonparametric modeling technique to identify the most productive scale size. Finally, the conclusions and suggestions for further research are presented in Section V.

II. EMPIRICAL EVIDENCE

A number of researchers have collected empirical data that support increasing returns to scale theories. The general approach of these researchers has been to estimate a function of the form:

$$y = a(x)^b$$

where y is the amount of input, typically professional work-hours, and x is the size of the project, typically measured in terms of source lines of code (SLOC) or Function Points (FP). This function is estimated by taking the logarithms of both sides and then estimating the resulting linear model using regression techniques.

$$ln\ (y) = a + b\ ln\ (x). \qquad (1)$$

An estimated exponent value b less than 1 indicates economies of scale, while an exponent greater than 1 indicates diseconomies of scale. This follows because the returns to scale measure is the *reciprocal* of ρ where

$$\rho = \frac{x}{y}\frac{dy}{dx} = b.$$

That is, marginal productivity (dx/dy) is greater than (less than) average productivity (x/y) if b is less than (greater than) one.

One of the earliest pieces of research to estimate this function was the work of Walston and Felix [28]. They collected data on 60 projects within

---

[2] The number of paths required is $n(n-1)/2$, where n is the number of project team members.

IBM's Federal Systems Division and estimated a function with an exponent of 0.91, a result that would indicate mild increasing returns to scale. Jeffery and Lawrence [22] and Vessey [27] have also reported economies of scale on small projects, although they have not published their data.

We have extended this analysis to a number of other published data sets. Using the 1978–1980 data from a Yourdon [20] survey of 17 projects from a variety of firms, we estimated an exponent of 0.72, indicating increasing returns to scale. Two other data sets that display exponents of approximately 0.95 are from Bailey and Basili's study [2] of 19 NASA/Goddard Space Flight Center projects and Behren's study [12] of 25 projects at Equitable Life Assurance Society.[3] Kemerer's [25] Function Point data from a commercial data processing consulting firm yield an estimated exponent of 0.85 (see Exhibit 1). In summary, the evidence for economies of scale comes from a number of sources representing a wide variety of application environments.

However, a number of researchers have provided empirical support for the notion of diseconomies of scale as well. Boehm's [14] 63 project COCOMO data set exhibits an exponent of 1.11. We estimated a high exponent of 1.49 for Albrecht and Gaffney's [1] 24 projects from IBM measured in Function Points. Two data sets that produce identical exponents of 1.06, showing mild decreasing returns to scale are Belady and Lehman's [13] 33 project data set from a large software house and Wingfield's [29] 15 project U.S. Army data set. Therefore, the empirical evidence for diseconomies of scale in new software development is at least as compelling as that for economies of scale.

Exhibit 1 summarizes the loglinear model analysis of the nine data sets, with five exhibiting increasing returns to scale and four exhibiting decreasing returns to scale. The returns to scale results reported in Exhibit 2 thus indicate that the con-

EXHIBIT 1 Kemerer [25] Data Set

Project	Hours	Func Pts	KSLOC
1	43624	1217.1	253.6
2	12540	507.3	40.5
3	168311	2306.8	450.0
4	13209	788.5	214.4
5	51118	1337.6	449.9
6	12768	421.3	50.0
7	3526	99.9	43.0
8	19806	993.0	200.0
9	17632	1592.9	289.0
10	10944	240.0	39.0
11	39322	1611.0	254.2
12	35066	789.0	128.6
13	23864	690.9	161.4
14	37529	1347.5	164.8
15	10625	1044.3	60.2
16	11552	1209.0	155.0
17	15048	1030.0	195.0

flicting theories about the presence of scale economies or diseconomies described in Section I are matched by conflicting empirical evidence obtained for different data sets. We reconcile this apparent contradiction by offering the hypothesis that for most software development "production processes" there exist increasing returns to scale for smaller projects and decreasing returns for very large projects. That is, average productivity is increasing as long as the project size is smaller than the "most productive scale size" (MPSS), and is decreasing for projects that are larger.[4] The actual MPSS may be different for different organizational settings.

The reasons for our above hypothesis stem from the conflicting arguments presented earlier in Section I for the presence of both economies and

---

[3] Behren's data set is not reported directly in his paper. However, a scatter graph is provided, which was enlarged and the data directly extrapolated. Note that the graph contains only 22 of the 25 reported data-points.

[4] Banker [3] provides a rigorous definition and discussion of the concept of most productive scale size (MPSS). We pursue this analysis further in Section IV.

EXHIBIT 2   Summary of Loglinear Models

DATA SET	n	Mean SLOC	Mean FP	b	t-statistic $H_0 : b = 1$
Behrens	22	n.a.	146	.94	−.32
Walston	60	20K	n.a.	.91	n.a.
Bailey	19	29K	n.a.	.95	−.73
Yourdon	17	34K	n.a.	.72	−1.21
COCOMO	63	67K	n.a.	1.11	1.30**
Albrecht	24	66K	648	1.49	2.57*
Belady	33	92K	n.a.	1.06	.60
Wingfield	15	180K	n.a.	1.06	.20
Kemerer	17	220K	1013	.85	−.79

*Significant at the 5 percent level for a one-tailed test.
**Significant at the 10 percent level for a one-tailed test.

EXHIBIT 3   Most Productive Scale Size (MPSS).

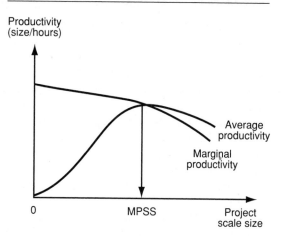

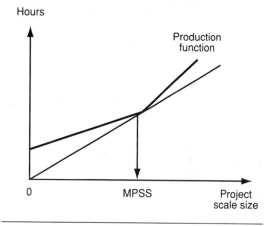

diseconomies of scale. Since most projects require a significant fixed investment in project management overhead, average productivity increases initially as the fixed overhead is spread over a larger project. Productivity increases on progressively larger projects may also come from the greater use of specialized personnel and tools, and possibly greater management attention. But, eventually the larger project size generally makes it more difficult to manage, and the marginal productivity of the project team is likely to decline. Increasing returns continue to prevail as long as marginal productivity remains greater than average productivity. At the most productive scale size (MPSS) marginal productivity equals average productivity, and beyond MPSS average productivity, being greater than marginal productivity, is declining and decreasing returns to scale prevail. This intuitive argument is depicted in Exhibit 3. We do not expect to observe situations where decreasing returns to scale prevail for smaller projects and increasing returns for larger projects. In the next two sections we reexamine eight[5] of the nine data

---

[5] Walston and Felix [28] report their estimated loglinear model, but do not present the actual data.

sets within the framework of less restrictive estimation models to provide empirical support for our hypothesis.

The MPSS will tend to differ across organizations. If the fixed overhead is large, or if the marginal productivity does not decline rapidly, increasing returns will continue to prevail for larger projects and the MPSS will be large. On the other hand, if the fixed overhead is relatively small or if the marginal productivity declines sharply, then the MPSS is small and decreasing returns set in at a lower scale level.

III. PARAMETRIC PRODUCTION FUNCTION ANALYSIS

The problem with the simple loglinear model of the previous research is that it does not allow for the possibility of increasing returns for some projects and decreasing for others. The estimated returns to scale are determined by a single parameter, the exponent b. But we require a more general model that allows for average productivity increases as the fixed project overhead gets spread over larger and larger projects, and after reaching the most productive scale size (MPSS), it allows for declining average productivity caused by negative factors affecting large projects such as the proliferation of communication paths. Rather than reject the parametric approach based only on the simple loglinear model, we first explore more flexible parametric forms that have been employed in empirical research in other production environments. Such a model that estimates MPSS would also be of use to software development managers because they can then identify the scale size where average productivity is maximized in their organization.

One possible method for generalizing the restrictive loglinear production function for new software development of previous research is by simply adding a logquadratic term as an independent variable. We can thus estimate the following translog function:[6]

$$ln\ (HOURS) = \beta_0 + \beta_1\ (ln\ (SIZE)) + \beta_2\ (ln\ (SIZE))^2. \quad (2)$$

Letting y equal HOURS and x equal SIZE, it is evident that the reciprocal of the returns to scale measure is given by ρ where

$$\rho = \frac{d\ ln\ y}{d\ ln\ x} = \frac{x\ dy}{y\ dx} = \beta_1 + 2\beta_2\ (ln\ x). \quad (3)$$

Therefore, if the estimated $\beta_2 > 0$ then increasing returns to scale prevail for $x < exp\ \{(1 - \beta_1)/2\beta_2\}$ and decreasing returns prevail for project sizes greater than the estimated MPSS given here by $x^* = exp\ \{(1 - \beta_1)/2\beta_2\}$. If, however, the estimated β_2 were negative then it would be inconsistent with our arguments above that the average productivity is decreasing for smaller projects, and increasing for larger projects.[7]

Hildenbrand [21], Varian [26], and Banker and Maindiratta [8] have argued that such a parametric approach imposes considerable untested structure on the production function. To provide evidence of robustness of their results, several empirical studies therefore estimate different parametrically specified functional forms.[8] For instance, in our present context an alternative specification may be the following quadratic form:

$$HOURS = \beta_0 + \beta_1\ (SIZE) + \beta_2\ (SIZE)^2. \quad (4)$$

Again letting y equal HOURS and x equal SIZE, the reciprocal of the returns to scale measure is given by ρ where:

$$\rho = \frac{x\ dy}{y\ dx} = \frac{x(\beta_1 + 2\beta_2 x)}{y}$$
$$= \frac{\beta_1 x + 2\beta_2 x^2}{\beta_0 + \beta_1 x + \beta_2 x^2}. \quad (5)$$

Therefore, $\rho > 1$ if and only if $\beta_2 x^2 > \beta_0$. If the estimated values of both β_0 and β_2 are positive then the MPSS is given by $x^* = \sqrt{\beta_0/\beta_2}$, with increasing returns for $x < x^*$ and decreasing returns for $x > x^*$. If estimated $\beta_0 < 0$ and $\beta_2 > 0$ then decreasing returns are exhibited for all $x > 0$,

---

[6] Christensen, Jorgenson, and Lau [18] note that the translog is a flexible functional form that provides a local second-order approximation to an arbitrary, twice-continuously-differentiable production function.

[7] Such contrary evidence appears in one of the eight data sets examined by us. See Exhibit 4. The validity of this inference is questionable, however, because of the high (0.9 · · ·) correlation between the two independent variables in the regression.

[8] We assume here that software development effort is determined primarily by the size metric. If other factors are also considered relevant, they can be included in the estimation model and the MPSS estimated based on the corresponding coefficient estimates.

EXHIBIT 4 Summary of Logquadratic Models

Data Set	β_0	β_1	β_2	R^2	MPSS*
Behrens	6.57	−.91	.21	57.7%	98.63 FP
	(1.61)	(−.49)	(1.00)		
Bailey	6.27	−.54	0.75	92.5%	21.47 KSLOC
	(13.82)	(−1.48)	(1.14)		
Yourdon	7.04	.17	.08	39.8%	148.41 KSLOC
	(2.62)	(.10)	(.33)		
COCOMO	6.56	.985	.05	73.8%	1.16 AKDSI
	(12.10)	(2.92)	(.38)		
Albrecht	3.60	.37	.09	73.6%	35.86 FP
	(.33)	(.11)	(.32)		
Belady	6.08	1.39	−.04	78.3%	N/A
	(5.59)	(2.31)	(−.53)		
Wingfield	20.90	−4.68	.57	55.4%	5.06 KSLOC
	(1.75)	(−.97)	(1.20)		
Kemerer	11.50	−1.55	.19	60.2%	739.68 FP
	(1.55)	(−.64)	(.99)		

MPSS ≡ estimated most productive scale size.
The t-statistics are presented in parentheses.
KSLOC ≡ thousands of source lines of code.
ADKSI ≡ thousands of adjusted delivered source instructions
FP ≡ function points

and if estimated $\beta_0 > 0$ and $\beta_2 < 0$ then increasing returns are exhibited for all $x > 0$. If the estimated values of both β_0 and β_2 are negative then decreasing returns correspond to small projects and increasing returns correspond to large projects, contrary to our earlier hypothesis.[9]

The empirical results for the eight available data sets for the logquadratic (translog) and the quadratic models are presented in Exhibits 4 and 5, respectively. Two empirical problems are encountered in practice. First, several researchers have observed that these so-called flexible parametric functional forms frequently violate reasonable regularity conditions, such as a monotonically increasing relation between inputs and outputs. See for instance, Caves and Christensen [16] and Barnet and Lee [11]. In our present context, the logquadratic models estimated for the Bailey and Wingfield data sets exhibit $dy/dx < 0$ (decreasing labor requirement for increasing project size) for smaller projects. Similar violation of this regularity condition is exhibited by the estimated quadratic models; for small projects by the Albrecht and Kemerer data sets and for large projects by the Bailey, COCOMO, and Belady data sets.

The second empirical problem is more serious for our objective of estimating returns to scale for new software development. The pairs of independent variables ln (SIZE) and (ln (SIZE))², and (SIZE) and (SIZE)², tend to be highly correlated.

---

[9] Negative estimates for both β_0 and β_2 occur in three of the eight data sets. See Exhibit 5. High correlation between the two variables (SIZE) and (SIZE)² suggests that returns to scale estimates are likely to be unstable. In fact, in all these three contrary cases, the estimated coefficients indicate that less hours are required for larger projects.

EXHIBIT 5   Summary of Quadratic Models

Data Set	β_0	β_1	β_2	R^2	MPSS*
Behrens	322 (.44)	4 (.39)	.029 (1.06)	58.4%	105.74 FP
Bailey	−1728 (−1.36)	517 (6.07)	−3.10 (−3.07)	88.6%	N/A
Yourdon	241 (.07)	261 (1.74)	−.90 (−.81)	42.8%	Increasing returns to scale for all observations
COCOMO	−31601 (−1.09)	2576 (6.28)	−1.51 (−3.12)	57.6%	N/A
Albrecht	8478 (1.87)	−14 (−1.09)	.034 (5.59)	94.9%	499.41 FP
Belady	−49442 (−.84)	2811 (3.17)	−2.50 (−1.76)	46.1%	N/A
Wingfield	81627 (.62)	13 (.01)	3.72 (1.31)	71.4%	148.13 KSLOC
Kemerer	26268 (1.95)	−59 (−2.35)	.049 (4.60)	81.8%	734.43 FP

The range of pairwise correlations was $0.967-0.999$ for ln (SIZE) and (ln (SIZE))^2 and $0.915-0.974$ for (SIZE) and (SIZE)^2 for the eight available data sets. This high level of collinearity implies that the confidence about interpreting the estimates of the coefficients β_1 and β_2 as the change in the dependent variable due to a change in the independent variables will be very low for both the logquadratic and the quadratic models.[10] Consequently, the estimates of these coefficients are likely to be unstable. See for instance Judge et al. [24]. The usual econometric methods, therefore, may not be appropriate for estimating the nature of returns to scale or the most productive scale size for these eight data sets.[11]

---

[10] The standard errors of the estimated coefficients are likely to be larger, and the corresponding *t*-statistics are less likely to be significant when the independent variables are highly correlated.

[11] The variance of the estimates of the returns to scale or MPSS measures depend on the variance and the covariance of the estimates of β_0, β_1, and β_2.

The high correlation between ln (SIZE) and (ln (SIZE))^2 is also of importance to the interpretation of the results of the estimation of the simple loglinear models reported in Exhibit 1. The estimated coefficient b in this case is likely to also pick up the effect of the omitted variable (ln (SIZE))^2, and therefore, the interpretation of b as the estimated returns to scale measure may not be appropriate.

IV. NONPARAMETRIC PRODUCTION FUNCTION ANALYSIS

Given these problems, and the limited *a priori* knowledge about the functional form of the production process underlying software development, specifying a parametric form for the production correspondence is difficult to substantiate theoretically or validate statistically. Also, it is not immediately apparent what restrictions these hypotheses, treated as axioms in the econometric approach, impose on the production correspondence [8], [21], [26]. Production economics theory indicates the need to employ a frontier notion for a production function, with deviations from the frontier occurring due to inefficiencies exhibited in individual observations [8], [9]. This differentiates between characteristics of the process and individual inefficiencies. Therefore, we propose to use Data Envelopment Analysis (DEA), a nonparametric approach to production frontier estimation developed by Charnes, Cooper, and Rhodes [17] and extended to a formal production economics framework by Banker, Charnes, and Cooper [4]. DEA does not impose a parametric form on the production function and assumes only that a monotonically increasing and convex[12] relationship exists between inputs and outputs, standard economic production function assumptions.[13] More formally, the following limited assumptions are made about the frontier production function $f(x)$:

1. *Monotonicity:* If $y = f(x)$, $y' = f(x')$ and $x \geq x'$, and $y \geq y'$.
2. *Convexity:* If $y = f(x)$, $y' = f(x')$ and $0 \leq \lambda \leq 1$ then $(1 - \lambda) y + \lambda y' \geq f[(1 - \lambda)x + \lambda x']$.
3. *Envelopment:* For each observation k, $k = 1$, $\cdots$, n, $y_k \geq f(x_k)$.
4. *Minimum Extrapolation:* If a function $g(\cdot)$ satisfies the monotonicity, convexity, and envelopment conditions, then $g(x) \leq f(x)$ for all x.

The estimation of the function $f(x)$ can be accomplished using linear programming techniques, and estimates of $f(x_j)$ obtained in this manner are maximum likelihood and consistent, see Banker [9]. The most productive scale size is estimated via the following linear programming

---

[12] The convexity assumption ensures that marginal productivity is decreasing so that decreasing returns for smaller projects are not followed by increasing returns for larger projects.

[13] Recent developments [10] in stochastic data envelopment analysis simultaneously consider deviations from the production frontier due to inefficiencies and also measurement errors. Evidence on the comparative application of the DEA and translog models is provided by Banker, Conrad, and Strauss [5].

model as in Banker [3] for the general case of multiple inputs and outputs.[14]

$$min \; \eta_A \qquad (6)$$

subject to

$$\sum_{k=1}^{n} \lambda_k x_{jk} \geq x_{jA} \quad j = 1, \cdots, J \qquad (6.1)$$

$$\sum_{k=1}^{n} \lambda_k y_{ik} \leq \eta_A y_{iA} \quad i = 1, \cdots, I \qquad (6.2)$$

$$\eta_A, \lambda_k \geq 0 \qquad (6.3)$$

where

x_{jk} = output j for observation k,

y_{ik} = input i for observation k, and

n = number of observations ($k = 1, 2, \cdots, n$).

The MPSS for the input-output mix given by (y_A, x_A), where $y_A \equiv (y_{1A}, \cdots, y_{iA}, \cdots, y_{IA})$, and $x_A \equiv (x_{1A}, \cdots, x_{jA}, \cdots, x_{JA})$, is computed as follows:

$$MPSS = \frac{x_A}{\eta_A \sum_{k=1}^{n} \lambda_k}.$$

In our present context, we are interested only in a single input–single output production correspondence, and the computational problem is consequently considerably simplified. The solution to the linear program in (6) is given by simply $\eta_A^* = x_A / M y_A$ where $M = \max_k \{x_k / y_k | k = 1, \cdots, n\}$ is the maximum observed average productivity across all observations. The most productive scale size is given by the project size x_M, say, for which $x_M / y_M \; (=M)$ is the largest for all observations. If

---

[14] Alternative models for estimating MPSS when some inputs or outputs are fixed or uncontrollable, or when some variables are measured on a categorical rather than on a continuous scale are described by Banker and Morey [6]. Banker and Maindiratta [7] discuss the estimation of other nonconvex technologies.

the maximum average productivity is also attained for some other observation, say M', with observed input-output pair $(x_{M'}, y_{M'})$, then the range of project sizes between $x_{M'}$ and x_M all represent MPSS.

The MPSS was calculated for the eight available data sets, and the results are reported in Exhibit 6 using the size metric chosen by each researcher. From a practitioner's viewpoint, the MPSS provides a project size goal in order to maximize the average productivity of future new software development projects. From a research perspective, it also allows the identification of both increasing and decreasing returns within these empirical data sets. Projects larger (smaller) than the MPSS correspond to decreasing (increasing) returns, respectively. Exhibit 6 shows the MPSS and the corresponding percentile value for the range of observed output data for each of the eight data sets. In five of the eight cases, the MPSS is within the interquartile range for the observed output data, thus indicating that both increasing and decreasing returns are present since there exist both smaller and larger projects than the MPSS at that site. It follows therefore that the

loglinear model may be an inadequate description of many new software development application environments.

V. CONCLUDING REMARKS

In this paper we have reconciled two opposing views regarding the presence of economies or diseconomies of scale in new software development. Our general approach provides for a production function model of software development that allows for both increasing and decreasing returns to scale. Through use of the DEA technique we have also shown how to identify the most productive scale size.

For the practitioner, our results contain a number of useful implications. In terms of project estimation, traditional algorithmic models have suggested a simple loglinear model with which to estimate eventual work-hours. While these models have some limited applicability, they ignore the possibility of improving project productivity by carefully selecting the scale of the project. Rather than taking the scale as exogenous, as most of these simple models do, managers could actively seek to identify the most productive scale size for their organization. In order to estimate models for their own environments, managers will need to collect input and output metrics for their own projects. As we have demonstrated the general model with both SLOC and Functions Points, the choice of particular metrics can be made by the individual manager. The only critical consideration is that these data be collected consistently and accurately.

Another application of the MPSS idea is that once managers have estimated the MPSS for their organizations' software development process, this information could be used as input to the make or buy decision. If a new system were estimated to be of a size very different from the MPSS, then that would be an additional factor to take into account in favor of buying the system rather than developing it in-house.

EXHIBIT 6   Most Productive Scale Sizes Using DEA

DATA SET	MPSS*	Percentile	Inter-quartile Range
Behrens	170.1 FP	68.2%	Yes
Bailey	7.8 KSLOC	26.3%	Yes
Yourdon	55.8 KSLOC	88.2%	No
COCOMO	15.0 Adjusted AKDSI	39.7%	Yes
Albrecht	199.1 FP	4.2%	No
Belady	35.1 KSLOC	66.7%	Yes
Wingfield	250.1 KSLOC	80.0%	No
Kemerer	1209.3 FP	64.7%	Yes

Percentile $\equiv$ percentage of projects less than or equal to the MPSS*.

Our results suggest that the MPSS varies widely across different application environments, and an interesting extension to this work would be to identify factors that contribute to some organizations' ability to successfully manage larger projects. Managers could also assess the effects on productivity of other scale-related factors, such as calendar duration and the number of new project team staff members.[15]

[15] Helpful comments from C. Beath, R. Davis, and participants at a research seminar at the University of Minnesota on an earlier version of this paper are gratefully acknowledged.

References

1. J. Albrecht and J. G. Gaffney, Jr., "Software function, source lines of code, and development effort prediction: A software science validation," *IEEE Trans. Software Eng.,* vol. SE-9, no. 6, pp. 639–648, Nov. 1983.

2. J. W. Bailey and V. R. Basili, "A meta-model for software development resource expenditures," in *Proc. 5th Int. Conf. Software Eng.,* 1981, pp. 107–116.

3. R. D. Banker, "Estimating most productive scale size using data envelopment analysis," *European J. Oper. Res.,* vol. 17, no. 1, pp. 35–44, July 1984.

4. R. D. Banker, A. Charnes, and W. W. Cooper, "Some models for estimating technical and scale inefficiencies in DEA," *Management Sci.,* vol. 30, no. 9, pp. 1078–1092, Sept. 1984.

5. R. D. Banker, R. F. Conrad, and R. P. Strauss, "A comparative application of DEA and translog methods: An illustrative study of hospital production," *Management Sci.,* vol. 32, no. 1, pp. 30–44, Jan. 1986.

6. R. D. Banker and R. C. Morey, "Efficiency analysis for exogenously fixed inputs and outputs," *Oper. Res.,* vol. 34, no. 4, pp. 513–521, July–Aug. 1986.

7. R. D. Banker and A. Maindiratta, "Piecewise loglinear estimation of efficiency production surfaces," *Management Sci.,* vol. 32, no. 1, pp. 126–135, Jan. 1986.

8. —, "Nonparametric analysis of technical and allocative efficiencies in production," *Econometrica,* vol. 56, no. 6, pp. 1315–1332, Nov. 1988.

9. R. D. Banker, "Maximum likelihood, consistency and data envelopment analysis," Carnegie Mellon Univ., Working Paper, 1987.

10. —, "Stochastic data envelopment analysis," *Management Sci.,* 1989, to be published.

11. W. A. Barnett and Y. W. Lee, "The global properties of the minflex Laurent, generalized Leontief and translog flexible functional forms," *Econometrica,* pp. 1421–1437, 1985.

12. C. A. Behrens, "Measuring the productivity of computer systems development activities with function points," *IEEE Trans. Software Eng.,* vol. SE-9, no. 6, pp. 648–652, Nov. 1983.

13. L. A. Belady and M. M. Lehman, "The characteristics of large systems," in *Research Directions in Software Technology,* P. Wegner, Ed. Cambridge, MA: MIT Press, 1979, pp. 106–138.

14. B. W. Boehm, *Software Engineering Economics.* Englewood Cliffs, NJ: Prentice-Hall, 1981.

15. F. P. Brooks, *The Mythical Man-Month.* Reading, MA: Addison-Wesley, 1975.

16. D. W. Caves and L. R. Christensen, "Global properties of flexible functional forms," *Amer. Econ. Rev.,* pp. 422–432, 1980.

17. A. Charnes, W. W. Cooper, and E. Rhodes, "Evaluating program and managerial efficiency: An application of data envelopment analysis to program follow through," *Management Sci.,* vol. 27, no. 6, pp. 668–697, June 1981.

18. L. R. Christensen, D. W. Jorgenson, and L. J. Lau, "Transcendental logarithmic production frontiers," *Rev. Econ. Stat.,* vol. 55, pp. 28–45, 1973.

19. S. Conte, H. Dunsmore, and V. Shen, *Software Engineering Metrics and Models.* Reading, MA: Benjamin/Cummings, 1986.

20. T. DeMarco, "Yourdon project survey: Final report," Yourdon, Inc., Tech. Rep., Sept. 1981.

21. W. Hildenbrand, "Short-run production functions based on microdata," *Econometrica,* vol. 49, no. 5, pp. 1095–1125, Sept. 1981.

22. D. R. Jeffery and M. J. Lawrence, "An inter-organisational comparison of programming productivity," in *Proc. 4th Int. Conf. Software Engineering,* 1979, pp. 369–377.

23. C. Jones, *Programming Productivity.* New York: McGraw-Hill, 1986.

24. G. G. Judge, W. E. Griffiths, R. C. Hill, and T. C. Lee, *The Theory and Practice of Econometrics.* New York: Wiley, 1980.

25. C. F. Kemerer, "An empirical validation of software cost estimation models," *Commun. ACM,* vol. 30, no. 5, pp. 416–429, May 1987.

26. H. Varian, "The nonparametric approach to production analysis," *Econometrica,* vol. 52, no. 3, pp. 579–597, 1984.

27. I. Vessey, "On program development effort and productivity," *Inform. Management,* vol. 10, pp. 255–266, 1986.

28. C. E. Walston and C. P. Felix, "A method of
     programming measurement and estimation," *IBM Syst.
     J.,* vol. 16, no. 1, pp. 54–73, 1977.

29. C. G. Wingfield, "USACSC experience with SLIM," U.S.
     Army Inst. for Research in Management Information and
     Computer Science, Tech. Rep. 360-5, 1982.

CASE-BASED REASONING
IN SOFTWARE EFFORT ESTIMATION

INTRODUCTION

Software is expensive to develop and is a major cost factor in corporate information systems budgets. The magnitude of software investments, estimated at more than $200 billion annually (Boehm 1987), impels management to carefully consider costs and benefits before committing the required resources to any potential software development project. Naturally, the accuracy of software project estimates has a direct and significant impact on the quality of the firm's software investment decisions.

When costs are underestimated, some projects are undertaken with an inflated impression of their worth to the firm, given the costs (i.e., estimation of effort) to develop them. Projects originally thought to be valuable may be subsequently judged improvident. Up to 15 percent of new development projects are abandoned mid-stream, largely due to cost overruns (Jones 1986). Underestimated projects that do reach completion are often released prematurely to meet the budget, omitting important features or system testing, and resulting in systems that are incomplete and unreliable (Kemerer 1989).

Project overestimation creates problems as well. Inflated project estimates may actually increase the project cost by putting less pressure on programmers to be productive (Abdel-Hamid and Madnick 1986). Additionally, projects possessing a real potential for benefit may be mistakenly rejected as too expensive, resulting in the cost of a missed opportunity to create value within the firm.

Consequently, both overestimation and underestimation may result in costly errors. Accurate project estimation can reduce these unnecessary costs and thereby increase the firm's efficiency (e.g., by making more appropriate resource allocation decisions of programmer's time) as well as their effectiveness (e.g., by making more appropriate cost/benefit project decisions). As software becomes increasingly expensive and critical to today's organizations, the consequences of misestimation become equally significant, further underscoring the need for accurate estimation techniques.

Methods of improving estimations have, for the most part, been based on analytical models. Although a wide number of such approaches have been generated, attempts at validating them have been largely unsuccessful. For example, uncalibrated models may average as much as 600 percent relative error (Kemerer 1987). Even with local calibration and attention, their use in industry is often restricted to the verification of estimates generated by manual techniques (Zelkowitz et al. 1984).

We propose that this type of (analytical) approach is not necessarily wrong, but that it is insufficient. Qualitative improvements in estimation accuracy will not come from the application of analytical models alone. Additional insights must be obtained from other sources. One such source is the people who have successfully adapted to the demands of the estimation task—the experts.

Previous research (Vicinanza, Mukhopadhyay and Prietula 1990) has suggested that expertise

Article by Steven Vicinanza, Michael J. Prietula, Tridas Mukhopadhyay. Reprinted with permission from the Eleventh International Conference on Information Systems.

at estimating software effort does exist and accurate estimates can be generated by highly experienced software development managers. The most accurate of the experts studied relied upon a distinct form of reasoning to solve the estimation problems. In particular, that expert utilized a form of analogical problem solving called case-based reasoning in which effort estimation was driven by recall of previously encountered software projects. The purpose of the current study is to construct a computational model demonstrating the analogical reasoning strategy used by the most accurate human estimator. Furthermore, this study explores the model's practical utility as a technique for estimating software effort.

We first summarize the current key research on software effort estimation. Next, we discuss the theory underlying the case-based reasoning approach. We then describe the reasoning model, called Estor, which instantiates the approach, and report on a test of Estor in which the accuracy of Estor's estimates are compared to those of Function Points, COCOMO, and the expert from whom the model was derived, on a common set of estimation problems. We conclude with a discussion of the implications to effort estimation and future research.

ESTIMATING SOFTWARE COSTS

Boehm (1981) describes a number of different cost estimation methods such as algorithmic models, expert judgment, analogy, and the traditional bottom-up approach, which is, perhaps, the method most widely practiced. Bottom-up estimating involves successively decomposing the development project into unit tasks until each unit or component of the project can be estimated by the individual responsible for the component's implementation. The familiarity of the project members with the components which they estimate leads to a high degree of accuracy in individual unit-task estimates. Unit-task costs can then be totalled to produce a final cost estimate. The major drawbacks of this approach include the tendency to neglect

system level costs and incidental activities such as reading, reviewing, meeting, and training. Moreover, a unit-task analysis cannot be performed in the absence of a sufficiently detailed software design. With the design of large software systems accounting for up to 40 percent of the total development cost (Conte, Dunsmore and Shen 1986, p. 6), it is often unreasonable to delay overall cost estimates until design completion.

An alternative method of estimating costs is the use of one or more algorithmic models. Cote, Boruque, Oligny, and Rivard (1988) have identified over twenty such software effort models in the literature including COCOMO (Boehm 1984), Doty (Herd et al. 1977), SLIM (Putnam 1978), PRICE-S (Frieman and Park 1979), ESTIMACS (Rubin 1983), and Function Points (Albrecht and Gaffney 1983). In general, algorithmic effort models use a combination of software size metrics and productivity factors to produce an estimate of the effort required to complete the project. The most common size metric used as input to these models is lines of code (LOC); however, other, more easily estimated size metrics such as Function Points, have also been used.

These models have the advantages of being objective (unbiased with respect to factors that are not parameters) and reliable (given the same inputs they always produce the same outputs). Although most require an estimate of software size such as LOC as input, they do not explicitly require a functional decomposition of the system and some, such as the Function Point model, have parameters that can be taken from a detailed requirements specification and do not require an LOC estimate.

Attempts have been made to seek independent validation for some of the algorithmic models. In general, these studies confirm that the accuracy of estimates generated by *uncalibrated* algorithmic models on independent project data sets is relatively low. Model calibration requires a sizable historical project database, which may not be available. A more fundamental problem with many quantitative models is that the estimation process is based on mathematical formulae whose parameters can be difficult for development managers to understand and manipulate. Consider the Function Point model, in which the total number of function points is calculated as a weighted combination of program size attributes (e.g., the number of external files). The weights assigned to each attribute have no inherent meaning to software managers—they are seemingly arbitrary multipliers which must be blindly applied to the project data. This lack of coherence between the actual task environment and the model may reduce managers' faith in the model's accuracy as well as their ability to manipulate the model to reflect the idiosyncrasies of their particular development environments. Given the problems with existing quantitative models, it is not surprising that their practical use is limited as a supplement to other methods (Zelkowitz et al. 1984).

Most alternative methods (see Boehm 1984) require the use of human expertise in one form or another to estimate development cost. Although the use of expert judgment is commonplace in industry (Wrigley and Dexter 1987), few researchers have generated empirical evidence on this approach. In the most direct examination of this method to date, Vicinanza, Mukhopadhyay, and Prietula (1990) report that experts given input parameters to COCOMO and Function Point models estimate effort with an average error as low as 32 percent. On the same project set, the Function Point and COCOMO models estimate with mean errors of 106 percent and 758 percent, respectively. Furthermore, the experts proved to be much more sensitive to factors affecting productivity than either COCOMO or Function Points, as evidenced by a markedly higher correlation between the experts' estimates and actual project efforts. Analogical reasoning was observed to be one strategy which was used to solve the estimation problem, and which produced accurate estimates. We have therefore focused our efforts on understanding and modeling this problem solving method.

MECHANISMS OF ANALOGY AND CASE-BASED REASONING

Analogical reasoning is a fundamental tool in the human problem solving repertoire (Sternberg 1977). As such, various aspects of this method have been studied in a wide variety of different task domains including natural language comprehension (Carbonell 1982), scientific discovery (Thagard and Holyoak 1985), dispute mediation (Kolodner, Simpson and Sycara-Cyranski 1985), accounting and tax problems (Marchant et al. 1989a), law (Marchant et al. 1989b), and business planning (Sullivan and Yates 1988). Within the context of software, Boehm (1984) recognizes it as a useful technique and Silverman (1985) identifies analogy as the primary method NASA systems designers use to estimate the size and execution time of new ground-based satellite control systems. Allen (1990) has applied case-based reasoning to the development of knowledge-bases describing orbital trajectory simulation systems. The empirical literature on analogical reasoning in software estimation is, however, virtually nonexistent.

General theories of analogical problem solving describe frameworks for understanding the processes that an expert using this type of reasoning should exhibit while developing project estimates. Nevertheless, these theories, broad in scope and covering a wide range of analogical reasoning situations, are too general for our purposes.

A more specific framework for studying analogical problem solving has been proposed by researchers building computational models of case-based reasoning (e.g., Kolodner, Simpson and Sycara-Cyranski 1985). At the most general level, analogical problem solving involves relating some previously solved problem or experience to a current, unsolved problem in a way that facilitates solution. The problem to be solved is referred to as the *target* of the analogy. The previous problem is called the *source* of the analogy. The formation of the analogy occurs when there is a perceived similarity between the source and target whose basis is dependent upon the problem solving domain context. Similar elements between the source and target are *mapped* to one another.

Whereas a general theory of analogical problem solving must accommodate the mapping of a source analog whose elements are syntactically remote from those of the target (i.e., across task domains), research into case-based reasoning has focused on a more common situation, where the source analog is drawn from the same general problem domain and has the same syntactic structure as the target. By constraining the source of the analogy to previously solved cases of the same problem class, the case-based framework provides a more explicit definition of the underlying cognitive processes we should expect to find in software cost estimation, a domain where the syntactic organization of the target case, a software project, is similar to that of previous cases, other software projects.

In case-based reasoning (e.g., Kolodner 1987), the problem solver, after creating a mental representation of the target problem, retrieves from long term memory one or more previous problem solving episodes, or cases, that have similar features. These cases are then evaluated and the most appropriate one is selected as the source analog. The mapping of source to target features is fairly straightforward, as a common set of features is shared among all cases. Then the solution that achieved the goal in the source problem is transferred to the target and subsequently modified to compensate for analogical elements whose mappings are not in correspondence.

The case-based approach to problem solving is appropriate in task domains that have no strong theoretical model and where the domain rules are incomplete, ill-defined, and inconsistent (Ashley and Rissland 1987). Viewed in terms of task adaptation, the structure of the task is always

changing and the appropriate knowledge adaptations cannot reflect deep causal principles, rather, those structures permit effective access to the most appropriate, similar experiences encountered and need not rely on underlying causal mechanisms (Prietula, Feltovich and Marchak 1989). As the domain of software effort estimation lacks a strong causal model based on deep principles and is situated within an often-changing, highly context-dependent task environment, the case-based approach evidenced by the expert should indeed be an appropriate strategy to bring to bear.

ESTOR: A CASE-BASED REASONING MODEL

In a prior study (Vicinanza, Mukhopadhyay and Prietula 1990), problem solving data was collected from highly experienced software managers, each individually estimating the effort required to complete each of ten software development projects. The software projects used in the study came from Kemerer (1987) and comprised 37 project factors and the actual development effort associated with each of the ten completed projects.

The projects represented medium to large data processing systems, ranged in size from 39,000 to 450,000 LOC, and required from 23 to 1,107 man-months of effort to complete. The COCOMO and Function Point inputs for these projects were converted into a suitable presentation format and used as stimulus materials.

Based on the magnitude of relative error, MRE (Conte, Dunsmore and Shen 1986) and the coefficient of determination (Albrecht and Gaffney 1983) measures of estimate accuracy, the most accurate expert was selected for protocol analysis. This individual was a software development manager at a very large software company, with ten years of total software management experience and nine of those years in data processing applications similar to the problem set projects.

The tape recorded protocol of the expert solving the first ten estimation problems was subjected to a process tracing analysis (Ericsson and Simon 1984; Newell and Simon 1972). Using the case-based reasoning form of analogical problem solving as a theoretical model, protocol segments were classified into the following categories:

- Knowledge acquisition and representation
- Analog retrieval and selection
- Source-target mapping
- Solution transfer
- Solution adjustment based on mapping non-correspondence

The utility of using this theoretical structure as a guide is that it enables the discrimination of a general cognitive mechanism (though one adapted for analogical functioning) from the knowledge needed to apply that mechanism to a specific domain. The computational model, Estor,[1] implements the five processes in a domain-independent form while the domain-specific knowledge obtained from the protocol analysis is contained in a separate knowledge-base. In fact, three distinct types of domain knowledge comprise that knowledge-base: representations of cases (i.e., software projects), knowledge to select the most relevant case, and knowledge to adjust the estimate based on the interaction between prior and current case representations. We will first discuss the generic case-based processes implemented by Estor and then describe the structure of the knowledge base.

Implementation of the Case-Based Reasoning Strategy

Estor incorporates a specific form of case-based analogical problem solving called *comparison-based reasoning* which employs five basic processes: construct, retrieve, transfer, map, and adjust.

The *construct* process is used to create an internal representation of the target problem. When our estimation task is performed by a human expert, the project attributes are retained in external memory on a set of index cards. Individual attribute values are entered into working memory by searching for that attribute's card and reading the value. In Estor, an external memory is simulated by reserving a portion of system memory to store definitions of target projects. For each project, the project's attributes are manually typed into the system and stored in individual project schemas. When the project is estimated, a pointer to the schema is stored in working memory and individual attributes are subsequently accessed symbolically using the pointer as a reference. Attribute symbols are hashed by the system to provide direct access to schema values.

To *retrieve* an appropriate source analog, Estor invokes a domain-specific case retrieval and selection heuristic. This heuristic can access all prior case knowledge, the domain knowledge, and the current case. In this implementation, the heuristic examines each project in the case knowledge-base and, one by one, calculates its function point distance (described later) to the target, and compares this value to the minimum distance stored in working memory (which is initialized to zero). If the current distance is less than or equal to the minimum, the new minimum is recorded in working memory as is a reference to the current project. When all prior cases have been examined, the project reference remaining in working memory becomes the source analog.

The next step is the *transfer* of the solution that achieved the goal in the source case to the target case. The human expert did this by writing down on scratch paper the base estimate. Adjustments were tracked by the expert on this external memory. In Estor, solution transfer is accomplished by referencing the effort attribute of the source project, bringing it into working memory, and transferring it to the effort attribute of the target project schema in external memory where it can be subsequently examined and manipulated.

The expert *mapped* the source and target by examining each target attribute, recalling its value on the source, and classifying it as either in correspondence or out of correspondence. The index cards for non-corresponding attributes were put in a separate pile which was then used to adjust the source effort. Estor performs this task by bringing each attribute of the source and target one by one into working memory, comparing them, and adding non-corresponding attributes to a list kept in external memory. A pointer to this list is maintained in working memory.

To *adjust* the estimate for a non-corresponding project attribute, the expert appeared to mentally simulate the effect of the target attribute value on the source project effort. This effect was then applied to the target project estimate. The processes behind this mental simulation were not evident in the protocol and are most likely quite complex. Therefore, the adjustment process is modeled by converting the results of the expert's mental simulation into production rules.

Each rule is represented by a rule schema which has slots for an identifier, a list of preconditions, an action, a comment, and a list of attributes for which the rule adjusts. The schemas are collected into a set in long term memory called the rule base. Rules are referenced by unique symbols which denote the segment of protocol from which they were extracted.

To perform adjustments on the list of non-corresponding attributes, Estor incorporates a production rule interpreter. The interpreter operates by creating a conflict set of rules in the rule base that will adjust for each non-corresponding attribute in the list. If the set contains more than one rule, then the conflict resolution mechanism must be invoked to prevent multiple adjustments to a single non-correspondence. The conflict resolution mechanism is based primarily on the specificity principle (Anderson 1983). Specificity gives preference to the production whose precondition set is more specific to the current situation and is a standard conflict resolution mechanism which has psychological support from spreading activation models of human cognition such as ACT* (Anderson 1983), as well as support from more utilitarian AI Production systems such as OPS5 (Forgy 1981).

The human expert provided a verbal protocol of the processes involved in estimation. Estor provides a trace of its behavior as well. At each step in project estimation, Estor logs the current process and the relevant memory elements being referenced. First, Estor displays the source project selected and the selection criteria used. It next indicates which rules comprise the conflict set and how the conflicts are resolved. Then, for each rule applied, Estor displays the rule name, why it is being applied, what the rule is doing, and the adjustment it is making to the estimate. When estimation is completed, Estor indicates which non-corresponding attributes were not adjusted by the rule base and gives the estimated effort.

Software Estimation Domain Knowledge

There are three distinct classes of domain knowledge required by Estor to develop effort estimates: case knowledge, case selection knowledge, and non-correspondence adjustment knowledge.

Case-knowledge reflects the episodic memory of previously encountered software projects, including the actual amount of effort required for each one. Before any analogical process can operate on a software project, the project must be put into an internal representation. The project abstraction created for this study comprises Function Point and COCOMO inputs. A project is thus represented as a set of attributes, called project factors, where each factor has a single value. Attribute values can be quantitative, such as the value for the attribute "lines of code," or qualitative, such as the value of the attribute "flexibility." Because of the highly contextual and bundled nature of this knowledge, the computational representation scheme selected was the schema or frame (Minsky 1975).

In Estor, project factors are represented as attributes (of a project schema) which can be instantiated with either numeric or symbolic data. The values of project attributes for *source* cases have been inferred from the verbal protocols. To reconstruct source cases, attributes of the target project which did not cause adjustment of the estimate were assumed to have identical values in the source project. Wherever an explicit adjustment was made for attribute non-correspondence, the indicated value difference is applied (in reverse) to the target to generate the assumed source attribute value. The expert relied primarily on three different source cases, two of which were successfully reconstructed from the protocols and formed the case base.

Case selection-knowledge permits the selection of an appropriate analog from the set of possible cases. The protocol analysis indicated that the expert used a combination of available size metrics to make this selection but the verbalization of this process in the protocol was inadequate for its reconstruction. As case retrieval and selection are intimately linked to the organization of episodic memory and employ subconscious cognitive processes (Shank 1982), it would be difficult if not impossible for the subject to provide us with an accurate description of the cognitive processing invoked by this task. This is generically called the "indexing problem" and though interesting research is proceeding (e.g., Hunter 1989; Kolodner 1989; Martin 1989), the results are not yet unequivocal and generalizable to any given domain. Therefore, Estor incorporates a plausible combination of the available function count data to discriminate among candidate source analogs. The function count similarity measure is represented by the sum of squares difference in function counts (i.e., number of external inputs, external outputs, external interface files, logical interface files, and external inquiry types) between the target and candidate source projects. The project which minimizes this difference is selected as the source analog.

Finally, *adjustment-knowledge* is brought to bear when non-correspondences arise in mappings between attributes of the source and target projects. To adjust the estimate for non-corresponding attributes, generalized domain knowledge is invoked in the form of interpreted production rules (Davis and King 1977). In contrast to case knowledge, this knowledge has a smaller granularity, is less context specific and requires particular invocation considerations, so interpreted production rules provide an acceptable form. The preconditions of these rules are sensitive to non-corresponding project attributes. Rule actions make the appropriate analogical inferences by adjusting the target project estimate to compensate for differences between the projects. Two examples (not in Smalltalk format) are shown in Exhibit 1.

The overall architecture of the system is illustrated in Exhibit 2. The knowledge base, or long-term memory, contains the domain-specific knowledge (case base, rule base, analog retrieval heuristic). The five reasoning processes (construct, retrieve, map, transfer, adjust) are implemented by the case-based analogical problem solver or inference engine. Information is transferred via a conceptual working memory into which symbolic references to memory structures and their values can be placed, manipulated, and accessed by the inference engine.

Exhibit 3 illustrates the contents of working, long-term, and external memory as a project is being estimated. External memory contains information relating to the target projects and the current estimation session. Working memory has been

---

EXHIBIT 1   Example Adjustment Rules

Rule 1.

IF

   Staff Size of Selected Base Project is small

   AND

   Staff Size of Target Project is large

THEN

   Increase the Effort Estimation of the Target Project by 20 percent

RULE 2.

IF

   Complexity of Target Project is two units > Selected Base Project

THEN

   Increase the Effort Estimation by adding back an among equal to the Base Estimate

EXHIBIT 2 Overall Architecture for Estor

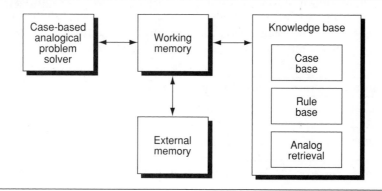

EXHIBIT 3 Regression Fit for Initial Ten Cases

Estimator	R-Square	α	β	Prob (2-tailed)
Expert	.95	−25.9	1.35	<.001
Estor	.95	19.1	1.00	<.001
COCOMO	.70	−14.0	.16	<.01
Function Points	.60	−38.4	1.08	<.01

elaborated with pointers to information needed by the current analogical reasoning process. This example depicts a snapshot of the system just before the conflict set of adjustment rules is to be created. At this instant, a target project has been identified, a source has been selected, and non-corresponding attributes have been identified. Pointers to these structures are referenced via working memory.

A COMPARISON OF PERFORMANCES

Method and Procedure

Estor provided estimates for the ten estimation problems described in the prior section as well as for five new projects of the same form. In addition, estimates of the five new problems were also obtained from a COCOMO and Function Point analysis (Kemerer 1987). Finally, the referent expert for the construction of Estor also solved the five new estimation problems. It should be noted that although Estor's domain knowledge was constructed from an analysis of the protocol for the referent expert, Estor was not otherwise based on any of the initial ten problems to which the expert was responding (i.e., the ten problems were not used as "training cases").

Results and Discussion

For all estimators, two primary data were used in the analysis: final estimates and derived MREs (magnitude of relative error[2]). The first analysis examined Estor's performance estimating the original ten projects. An analysis incorporating post-hoc Tukey tests was performed comparing Estor's mean MRE scores with the mean MRE scores obtained by the reference expert, CO-COMO and Function Points.

The results indicated that Estor performed better than COCOMO ($p<.05$), but not significantly better than the other estimators. A regression analysis was performed fitting a linear model to the relationship between the actual effort and estimated effort (Actual = α + β * Estimate). This analysis revealed an r^2 for (r^2 = .95) Estor equivalent to the r^2 of the referent expert and exceeding those of either COCOMO ($r^2 = .70$) or Function Points ($r^2 = .62$) for the same data (see Exhibit 3).

The overall architecture of the system is illustrated in Exhibit 4. The knowledge base, or long-term memory, contains the domain-specific knowledge (case base, rule base, analog retrieval heuristic). The five reasoning processes (construct, retrieve, map, transfer, adjust) are implemented by the case-based analogical problem solver or inference engine. Information is transferred via a

EXHIBIT 4   Illustration of Memory Contents During Estimation

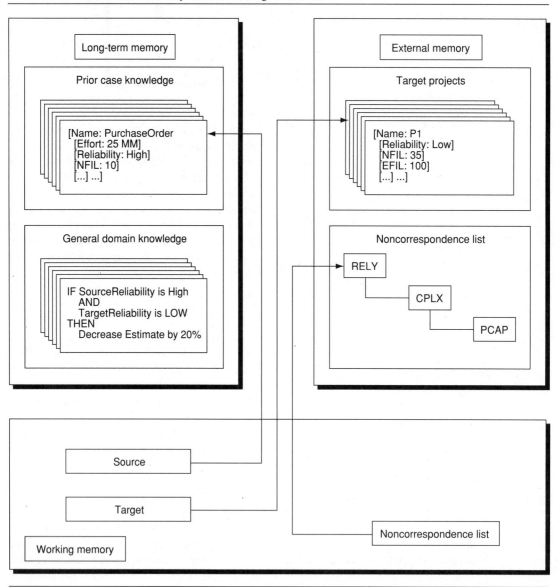

conceptual working memory into which symbolic references to memory structures and their values can be placed, manipulated, and accessed by the inference engine.

The second analysis focused on Estor's performance on the five new cases along with the referent expert, COCOMO and Function Points. Although there were not enough cases for a regression analysis, a Kruskal-Wallis one-way ANOVA by ranks indicated that differences in MRE scores did exist (KW = 10.98, p<.05). Alpha-adjusted multiple comparisons demonstrated that the referent expert had lower MREs than other estimators (p<.05) and that Estor and Function Points were lower than COCOMO (p<.05) but not significantly different themselves.

The third analysis pooled all of the data from the fifteen projects. An analysis of the MRE data yielded an overall estimator effect using the Kruskal-Wallis one-way ANOVA (KW = 33.22, p<.001). Alpha-adjusted multiple comparisons determined that the relationships among estimator MRE scores were quite similar to those obtained in the analysis of the five new cases—the referent expert had lower MREs than the other estimators (p<.05) and that Estor and Function Points were lower than COCOMO (p<.05). However, in this analysis Estor did have lower MRE scores than Function Points (p<.05). Exhibit 5 summarizes the results of the regression analysis for this data set. Note the variance explained in both Estor's and the referent expert's r^2 as well as similar adjustments to the intercept (plausibly establishing an anchor at the origin) and coefficients (β_{Estor} = 1.04, β_{Expert} = 1.32). Applying an r to z transformation (Sachs 1984), we compared the correlation coefficients noted in Exhibit 5. The results indicated that there was no difference between the referent expert and Estor (z = .98, ns) and no difference between COCOMO and Function Points (z = .55, ns). However, both the expert and Estor had significantly higher correlations than either COCOMO or Function Points (Estor > COCOMO, z = 2.23, p<.05).

EXHIBIT 5   Regression Fit for All Fifteen Cases

Estimator	R-Square	α	β	Prob (2-tailed)
Expert	.97	—	1.32	<.001
Estor	.94	—	1.04	<.001
COCOMO	.68	22.8	.15	<.001
Function Points	.55	−36.9	.96	<.01

A final, qualitative analysis begins to address the points of divergence between Estor and the referent expert by comparing aspects of the protocols generated during problem solving. The first difference between the two is in the retrieval of the source analog—the underlying case schema. The expert was able to use more of the information about both the target and candidate sources when retrieving a prior case from memory. As was previously noted, the verbal protocols contained little information about the cognitive processes involved in selecting a source project. Estor's retrieval heuristic, based primarily on function counts, was chosen by determining which project factors the subject was most often considering immediately before retrieving the source project. How the expert used this information and any additional information that was examined could not be determined from the verbal protocols. Consequentially, the selection heuristic in Estor did not always make the same choice of source analog as did the expert, resulting in different estimates because of subsequent differences in the initial base effort and non-correspondence mappings.

A second point of divergence between the two is in the selection of adjustment rules. Estor sometimes applied rules to mapping non-correspondences that were missed by the expert, often resulting in more accurate estimates than those of the expert. Unfortunately, this situation was more than compensated for by cases where there were insufficient rules in the knowledge base to make the needed analogical inferences. In fact, there were instances where no rules could be applied to map source to target. In these cases, Estor's estimates were much less accurate than those of the referent expert.

The identification of these points of divergence is important as it shows where the system can be modified to improve its performance. From the initial analysis, three basic improvements are a larger (though representative) case-base, a better selection heuristic, and a larger rule base to handle adjustments. These three represent the domain specific knowledge in the system. The basic analogical reasoning processes realized in the case-based reasoning model appear to be plausible and adequate to the task; furthermore, the specific addition of particular domain knowledge should significantly enhance performance.

CONCLUSION

This study has presented a model of case-based analogical software cost estimation and has described an instantiation of that model in the form of a computer program called Estor. We have demonstrated the plausibility of case-based reasoning as a form of problem solving employed by an expert and have illustrated the potential for improving the accuracy of software cost estimates through this form of deliberation. Estor did not perform quite as well as the human expert, but it did outperform existing algorithmic models on this data set. To be fair, it would almost certainly fail to accurately estimate projects from very different environments (e.g., embedded military systems) without additional domain knowledge. Given the underlying theoretical foundations for the fundamental process of analogical reasoning in uncertain domains, the case-based approach taken by Estor should be an appropriate one, so that modification of Estor would be through its domain knowledge and not the fundamental mechanisms. To test this proposition, we are adjusting Estor to address two additional and diverse environments: embedded military software (ADA) and traditional data-processing maintenance projects.

As the sample size for the analyses presented is limited, it is our intent that the validation study be viewed as an indicator of plausibility rather than an unequivocal verification of generalizability. Studies to validate the more general applicability of this approach are in progress.

Future research needs to be directed at three areas: domain knowledge improvement, model validation, and extension. The selection of the appropriate case from memory is a crucial component of the system's domain knowledge. The current heuristic is simplistic and might be improved by two methods. First, further study of how experts retrieve analog software projects (i.e., categorize) is needed to help understand this complex process in humans (e.g., Rips 1989). Second, empirical studies of differential system performance with various selection heuristics would provide useful data regarding optimal selection heuristic strategies for computer-based estimation. For example, evidence suggests that the selection problem should be addressed with domain-specific knowledge (Barletta and Mark 1988). We are in the process of performing such analyses. Finally, to be a complete cognitive model, Estor must improve its performance with the knowledge of results. Unlike existing algorithmic models which cannot learn from successive estimation runs, human experts are able to integrate the results of observing the development project into memory and make it available for future estimation. The current model is therefore being extended to incorporate this aspect of reasoning reflecting recent interest in analogical learning in humans and machines (e.g., Converse, Hammond and Marks 1989; Gentner 1989).

ACKNOWLEDGMENTS

We thank Chris F. Kemerer for providing us with the project data for this study, the anonymous reviewers for their helpful critiques, and Herbert A. Simon for his insightful comments and suggestions.

References

1. Abdel-Hamid, T., and Madnick, S. "Impact of Schedule Estimation on Software Project Behavior." *IEEE Software,* July, 1986.

2. Albrecht A. J., and Gaffney, J. "Software Function, Source Lines of Code, and Development Effort Prediction." *IEEE Transactions on Software Engineering,* SE9(6) 1983, pp. 639–648.

3. Allen, B. "Case-Based Reasoning in a Software Information System." Inference Corporation, Los Angeles, California. Manuscript submitted for publication, 1990.

4. Anderson, J. R. *The Architecture of Cognition.* Cambridge, Massachusetts: Harvard University Press, 1983.

5. Ashley, and Rissland, E. "Compare and Contrast: A Test of Expertise." In *Proceedings of AAAI-87,* 1987.

6. Barletta, R., and Mark, W. "Explanation-Based Indexing of Cases." In J. Kolodner (ed.), *Proceedings of a Workshop on Case-Based Reasoning,* Information Science and Technology Office, DARPA, 1988.

7. Boehm, B. W. "Improving Software Productivity." *IEEE Computer,* September, 1987, pp. 43–57.

8. Boehm, B. W. *Software Engineering Economics."* Englewood Cliffs, New Jersey: Prentice-Hall, 1981.

9. Boehm, B. W. "Software Engineering Economics." *IEEE Transactions on Software Engineering,* SE10, 1984, pp. 4–21.

10. Carbonell, J. "Metaphor: An Inescapable Phenomenon in Natural Language Comprehension." In W. Lehnert and M. Ringle (eds.), *Strategies in Natural Language Processing,* Hillsdale, New Jersey: Lawrence Erlbaum, 1982.

11. Converse, T.; Hammond, K.; and Marks, M. "Learning Modification Rules from Expectation Failure." *Proceedings of a Workshop on Case-Based Reasoning,* Information Science and Technology Office, DARPA, 1989.

12. Cote, V.; Bourque, P.; Oligny, S.; and Rivard, N. "Software Metrics: An Overview of Recent Results." *The Journal of Systems and Software,* 8, 1988, pp. 121–31.

13. Conte, S.; Dunsmore, H.; and Shen, V. *Software Engineering Metrics and Models.* Menlo Park, California: Benjamin/Cummings, 1986.

14. Davis, R., and King, J. "An Overview of Production Systems." In E. Elcock and D. Michie (eds.), *Machine Intelligence 8.* Cichester, England: Ellis Horwood, 1977.

15. Ericsson, K. A., and Simon, H. A. *Protocol Analysis: Verbal Reports as Data.* Cambridge, Massachusetts: MIT Press, 1984.

16. Forgy, C. "OPS5 User's Manual." Technical Report CMU-CS-81-135, Department of Computer Science, Carnegie Mellon University, 1981.

17. Frieman, F. R., and Park, R. D. "PRICE Software Model—Version 3: An Overview." In *Proceedings IEEE PINY Workshop on Quantitative Software Models,* 1979.

18. Gentner, D. "The Mechanisms of Analogical Learning." In S. Vosniadou and A. Ortony (eds.), *Similarity and Analogical Reasoning.* Cambridge, England: Cambridge University Press, 1989.

19. Herd, J. R.; Postak, J.; Russel, W.; and Steward, K. "Software Cost Estimation Study—Study Results." Final Technical Report RADC-TR-77-220, Volume 1, Doty Assoc., Rockville, Maryland, 1977.

20. Hunter, L. "Case-Based Planning: An Integrated Theory of Planning, Learning, and Memory." Unpublished Dissertation, Department of Computer Science, Yale University, 1989.

21. Jones, C. "The Productivity Report Card." *Software News,* Volume 6, Number 9, 1986, p. 19.

22. Kemerer, C. F. "An Empirical Validation of Software Cost Estimation Models." *Communications of the ACM,* Volume 30, Number 5, 1987, pp. 416–429.

23. Kemerer, C. F. "An Agenda for Research in the Managerial Evaluation of Computer-Aided Software Engineering (CASE) Tool Impacts." *Proceedings of the Twenty-Second Annual Hawaii International Conference on System Sciences,* IEEE Computer Society Press, 1989.

24. Kolodner, J. "Extending Problem Solving Capabilities Through Case-Based Inference." *Proceedings of the Fourth International Machine Learning Workshop,* 1987.

25. Kolodner, J. "Judging Which is the Best Case for a Case-Based Reasoner." *Proceedings of a Workshop on Case-Based Reasoning,* Information Science and Technology Office, DARPA, 1989.

26. Kolodner, J.; Simpson, R.; and Sycara-Cyransky, K. "A Process Model of Case-Based Reasoning in Problem Solving." *Proceedings of IJCAI-85,* 1985.

27. Marchant, G.; Robinson, J.; Anderson, U.; and Schadewald, M. "A Cognitive Model of Tax Problem Solving." *Advances in Taxation,* Volume 2, 1989a pp. 1–20.

28. Marchant, G.; Robinson, J.; Anderson, U.; and Schadewald, M. "Analogical Transfer and Expertise in Legal Reasoning." Forthcoming in *Organizational Behavior and Human Decision Processes,* 1989b.

29. Martin, C. "Direct Memory Access Parsing." Unpublished Dissertation, Department of Computer Science, Yale University, 1989.

30. Minsky, M. "A Framework for Representing Knowledge." In P. Winston (ed.), *The Psychology of Computer Vision.* New York: McGraw-Hill, 1975.

31. Newell, A., and Simon, H. *Human Problem Solving.* Englewood-Cliffs, New Jersey: Prentice-Hall, 1972.

32. Prietula, M.; Feltovich, P.; and Marchak, F. "A Heuristic Framework for Assessing Factors Influencing Knowledge Acquisition." *Proceedings of the Twenty-Second Hawaii International Conference on Systems Science,* IEEE Computer Society Press, 1989.

33. Putnam, L. H. "A General Empirical Solution to the Macro Software Sizing and Estimating Problem." *IEEE Transactions on Software Engineering,* SE4(4), 1978, pp. 345–361.

34. Rips, L. "Similarity, Typicality, and Categorization." In S. Vosniadou and A. Ortony (eds.), *Similarity and Analogical Reasoning.* Cambridge, England: Cambridge University Press, 1989.

35. Rubin, H. A. "Macroestimation of Software Development Parameters: The ESTIMACS System." *IEEE SOFTFAIR Conference on Software Development Tools, Techniques and Alternatives,* 1983.

36. Sachs, L. *Applied Statistics.* New York: Springer-Verlag, 1984.

37. Shank, R. *Dynamic Memory: A Theory of Reminding and Learning in Computers and People.* Cambridge, England: Cambridge University Press, 1982.

38. Silverman, B. "The Use of Analogs in the Innovation Process: A Software Engineering Protocol Analysis."

39. Sternberg, R. "Component Processes in Analogical Reasoning." *Psychological Review,* Volume 84, Number 4, 1977, pp. 353–378.

40. Sullivan, C., and Yates, C. "Reasoning by Analogy—A Tool for Business Planning." *Sloan Management Review,* Volume 29, Number 3, 1988, pp. 55–61.

41. Thagard, P., and Holyoak, K. "Discovering the Wave Theory of Sound: Inductive Inference in the Context of Problem Solving." *Proceedings of the Ninth International Joint Conference on Artificial Intelligence.* Palo Alto, California: Kaufmann, 1985.

42. Vicinanza, S.; Mukhopadhyay, T.; and Prietula, M. "Software Effort Estimation: A Study of Expert Performance." Manuscript submitted for publication, 1990.

43. Wrigley, C. D., and Dexter, A. S. "Software Development Estimation Models: A Review and Critique." *Proceedings of the ASAC Conference,* University of Toronto, 1987.

44. Zelkowitz, M.; Yeh, R.; Hamlet, R.; Gannon, J.; and Basili, V. "Software Engineering Practices in the US and Japan." *IEEE Computer,* June, 1984.

IEEE Transactions on Systems, Man, and Cybernetics, SMC-15(1), 1985, pp. 30–44.

Endnotes

1. Estor is implemented in Smalltalk/V from Digitalk, Inc.

2. MRE is calculated as 100 × | actual - estimate |/actual.

LESSONS LEARNED FROM MODELING THE DYNAMICS OF SOFTWARE DEVELOPMENT

The impressive improvements that are continuously being made in the cost-effectiveness of computer hardware are causing an enormous expansion in the number of applications for which computing is becoming a feasible and economical solution. This, in turn, is placing greater and greater demands for the development and operation of computer software systems. A conservative estimate indicates a hundredfold increase in the demand for software in the last two decades [32].

The growth of the software industry has not, however, been painless. The record shows that the development of software has been marked by cost overruns, late deliveries, poor reliability, and users' dissatisfaction [16, 34, 41].

In an effort to bring discipline to the development of software systems, attempts have been made since the early 1970s to apply the rigors of science and engineering to the software production process. This led to significant advances in the

Article by Tarek K. Abdel-Hamid and Stuart E. Madnick. Copyright 1989, Association for Computing Machinery, Inc. Reprinted by permission.

technology of software production (e.g., structured programming, structured design, formal verification, language design for more reliable coding, diagnostic compilers).

The managerial aspects of software development, on the other hand, have attracted much less attention from the research community [51]. Cooper [17] provides an insightful explanation for the reasons why:

> Perhaps this is so because computer scientists believe that management per se is not their business, and the management professionals assume that it is the computer scientists' responsibility.

This "deficiency" in the field's research repertoire may account for the persistence of the difficulties in producing software systems. A chief concern expressed is that, as of yet, we still lack a fundamental understanding of the software development process. Without such an understanding the possibility or likelihood of any significant gains on the managerial front is questionable [13, 30].

This article reports on a stream of research designed to address these concerns. Specifically, our goal is to develop a comprehensive model of the dynamics of software development that enhances our understanding of, provides insight into, and makes predictions about the process by which software development is managed. The following examples illustrate some of the critical management decisions that have been addressed in this research effort:

1. A project is behind schedule. Possible management actions include: revise completion date; hold to planned completion date, but hire more staff; hold to planned completion date, but work current staff overtime, etc. What are the implications of these alternatives?

2. How much of the development effort should be expended on quality assurance and how does that affect completion time and total cost?

3. What is the impact of different effort distributions among project phases (e.g., should the ratio of effort between development and testing be 80:20 or 60:40)?

4. What are the reasons for and implications of the differences between potential productivity, actual productivity, and perceived productivity?

5. Why does the "90% completion syndrome" chronically recur?

In the rest of this article we discuss the integrative dynamic model of software project management that has been developed. We will provide an overview of both the model's structure and its behavior followed by a discussion of the insights gained. We begin our presentation, however, by first presenting arguments for the necessity of an integrative and dynamic modeling approach in the study of software project management.

THE HIGH COMPLEXITY OF THE SOFTWARE PROJECT MANAGEMENT PROCESS

A simple view of the dynamics of project management is illustrated by the single-loop model shown in Exhibit 1 [45]. The model portrays how project work is accomplished through the use of project resources (manpower, facilities, equipment; see item 1 in Exhibit 1). As work (2) is accomplished on the project, it is reported (3) through some project control system. Such reports cumulate and are processed to create the project's forecast completion time (4) by adding to the current date the indicated time remaining on the job. Assessing the job's remaining time involves figuring out the magnitude of the effort (e.g., in man-days) believed by management to be remaining to complete the project, the level of manpower working on the project, and the perceived productivity of the project team. The feedback loop is completed (closed) as the difference, if any, between the scheduled completion date (5) and the forecast completion date (4) causes adjustments (6) in the magnitude or allocation of the project's resources (1). This new level of resources results in a new work rate (2) and the loop is repeated again.

What is attractive about the above model is that it is reasonable, simple, and manageable. It is the mental model that many project managers rely on

EXHIBIT 1   A Model of Software Project Management

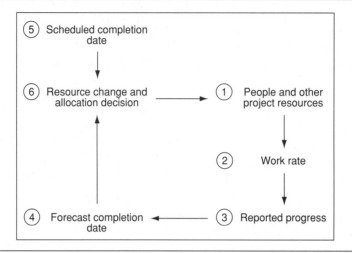

[45]. But is it an adequate model of the dynamics of software project management?

The software project management system is a far more complex conglomerate of interdependent variables that are interrelated in various nonlinear fashions. By excluding vital aspects of the real software project environment, the model depicted in Exhibit 1 could seriously misguide the unsuspecting software manager. To see how, let us consider just a few of the many typical decisions pondered in a software project environment.

Adding More People to a Late Project.   The mental picture of Exhibit 1 suggests a direct relationship between adding people resources and increasing the rate of work on the project, i.e., the higher the level of project resources, the higher the work rate. This ignores one vital aspect of software project dynamics, namely, that adding more people often leads to higher communication and training overheads on the project, which can in turn dilute the project team's productivity. Lower productivity translates into lower progress rates, which can, therefore, delay the late project even further. This, in turn, can trigger an additional round of work force additions and another pass around this vicious cycle. These dynamic forces create the phenomenon often referred to as Brooks' Law, i.e., adding more people to a late software project makes it later [15]. In Exhibit 2a we, therefore, amend Exhibit 1 by incorporating the vital link between the work force level and productivity.

Adjusting the Schedule of a Late Project. Another part of the real system that is ignored by Exhibit 1 concerns the impact of schedule pressures on the software developers' actions and decisions. For example, when faced with schedule pressures that arise as a project falls behind schedule, software developers typically respond by putting in longer hours and by concentrating more on the essential tasks of the job [25]. In one experiment, Boehm [14] found that the number of man-hours devoted to project work increased by as much as 100 percent. This additional link between schedule pressure and productivity is captured in Exhibit 2b.

The impact of schedule pressures on software development, however, is not limited to the above relatively direct role. Schedule pressures can also play less visible roles. For example, as Exhibit 2c suggests, schedule pressures can increase the error rate of the project team and thus the amount of rework on the project [31, 40].

EXHIBIT 2 Amendments to the Project Management Model

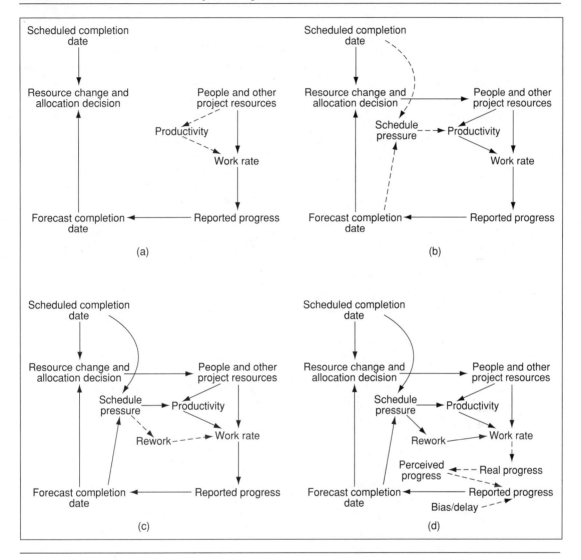

(a)

(b)

(c)

(d)

People under time pressure don't work better, they just work faster. . . . In the struggle to deliver any software at all, the first casualty has been consideration of the quality of the software delivered [19, p. 34].

The rework necessary to correct such software errors obviously diverts the project team's effort from making progress on new project tasks, and thus can have a significant negative impact on the project's progress rate.

How Late is a Late Software Project? Because software remains largely intangible during most of the development process, it is often difficult for project managers to assess real progress on the project [12]. To the extent that the perceived progress rate differs from the real progress rate, an error in perceived cumulative progress will gradually accumulate (Exhibit 2d). Furthermore, bias, often in the form of overoptimism, and delay in gathering and processing control information additionally distorts the reported progress. This undoubtedly poses yet another complication that is too real for the software project manager to exclude from a model of the process.

AN INTEGRATIVE SYSTEM DYNAMICS PERSPECTIVE OF SOFTWARE DEVELOPMENT

While the preceding discussion is still far less than a complete picture, it does illustrate that many variables, both tangible and intangible, impact the software development process. Furthermore, these variables are not independent, but are related to one another in complex fashions. Perhaps most importantly, understanding the behavior of such systems is complex far beyond the capacity of human intuition [45].

A major deficiency in much of the research to date on software project management has been the inability to integrate our knowledge of the microcomponents of the software development process such as scheduling, productivity, and staffing to derive implications about the behavior of the total socio-technical system. In the research effort described in this article we build upon and extend what has been learned about the microcomponents, to construct a holistic model of the software development process. It integrates the multiple functions of software development, including both the management-type functions (e.g., planning, controlling, staffing) as well as the software production-type activities (e.g., designing, coding, reviewing, testing).

A second unique feature of our modeling approach is the use of the feedback principles of system dynamics to structure and clarify the complex web of dynamically interacting variables. Feedback is the process in which an action taken by a person or thing will eventually affect that person or thing. Examples of such feedback systems in the software project environment have already been demonstrated in the preceding discussion and are evident in Exhibits 1 and 2.

The significance and applicability of the feedback systems concept to managerial systems has been substantiated by a large number of studies [45]. For example, Weick [48, p. 7] observes that

> The cause-effect relationships that exist in organizations are dense and often circular. Sometimes these causal circuits cancel the influences of one variable on another, and sometimes they amplify the effects of one variable on another. It is the network of causal relationships that impose many of the controls in organizations and that stabilize or disrupt the organization. It is the patterns of these causal links that account for much of what happens in organizations. Though not directly visible, these causal patterns account for more of what happens in organizations than do some of the more visible elements such as machinery, timeclocks, ...

One of the pioneering works in the field is Roberts' [44] published doctoral dissertation, which involved the development of a comprehensive system dynamics model of R&D project management. The model traces the full life cycle of a single R&D project and incorporates the interactions between the R&D product, the firm, and the customer. Roberts' work spurred a large number of system dynamics studies of project management phenomena. For example, Nay [33] and Kelly [26] extended Roberts' work in their research on multi-project environments. Richardson [42] took a different tack, focusing on the development group. His model reproduces the dynamics of a development group over an eight-year period as a continuous stream of products are developed and placed into production.

While the bulk of the system dynamics modeling work in the project management area has been devoted to the R&D environment, the applicability of the methodology to the domain of software production has been alluded to in the literature (e.g., [24, 28, 39]). Perhaps this should come as no surprise, since "the stages of research and development are similar in many respects to the stages of software analysis and design" [23]. In the remainder of this section we describe how the system dynamics modeling technique was extended to the software project domain.

Model Development and Structure

The model was developed on the basis of a field study of software project managers in five organizations. The process involved three information gathering steps:

First, we conducted a series of interviews with software development project managers in three organizations. The purpose of this set of interviews was to provide us with a first-hand account of how software projects are currently managed in software developing organizations. The information collected in this phase, complemented with our own software development experience, formed the basis for formulating a skeleton system dynamics model of software project management.

The second step was to conduct an extensive review of the literature. The skeleton model served as a useful road map in carrying out this literature review. When this exercise was completed, many knowledge gaps were filled, giving rise to a second much more detailed version of the model.

In the third, and final step:

> The model is exposed to criticism, revised, exposed again and so on in an iterative process that continues as it proves to be useful. Just as the model is improved as a result of successive exposures to critics a successively better understanding of the problem is achieved by the people who participated in the process [45, p. 6].

The setting for this was a second series of intensive interviews with software project managers at three organizations (only one of which was included in the first group).

Exhibit 3 depicts a highly aggregated view of the model's four subsystems, namely: (1) the human resource management subsystem; (2) the

software production subsystem; (3) the controlling subsystem; and (4) the planning subsystem. The figure also illustrates some of the interrelationships among the four subsystems. Similarities to Exhibit 2d can be recognized. Since the actual model is very detailed, containing over a hundred causal links, only a high-level description of the model can be presented in the limited space of this article. For a full discussion of the model's structure and its mathematical formulation the reader is referred to [1, 9].

Human Resource Management Subsystem

The human resource management subsystem captures the hiring, training, assimilation, and transfer of the human resource. The project's total work force is segregated into different types of employees, e.g., newly hired work force and experienced work force. Segregating the work force into such categories is necessary for two reasons. First, newly added team members are normally less productive (on the average) than the "old timers" [18]. Secondly, it allows us to capture the training process involved in assimilating the new members into the project team.

On deciding upon the total work force level needed, project managers consider a number of factors. One important factor, of course, is the project's completion date. As part of the planning subsystem (to be discussed later), management determines the work force level that it believes is necessary to complete the project on time. In addition, though, consideration is also given to the stability of the work force. Thus, before adding new project members, management contemplates the duration for which the new members will be needed. In general, the relative weights given to work force stability versus on-time completion is dynamic, i.e., will change with the stage of project completion. For example, toward the end of the project there could be considerable reluctance to bring in new people. This reluctance arises from the realization that there just wouldn't be enough time to acquaint the new people with the mechanics

EXHIBIT 3   Model Structure

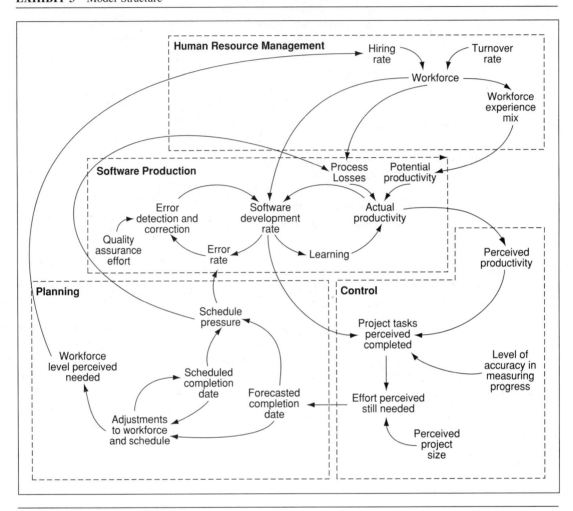

of the project, integrate them into the project team, and train them in the necessary technical areas.

Software Production Subsystem

This software production subsystem models the software development process. The operation and maintenance phases of the software life cycle are, thus, not included. The development life cycle phases incorporated include the designing, coding, and testing phases. Notice that the initial requirements definition phase is also excluded. There are two reasons for this. The primary reason relates to the desire to focus this study on the endogenous software development organization, i.e., the project managers and the software development professionals, and how their policies, decisions, actions, etc., affect the success/failure of software development. The requirements definition phase was, thus, excluded since in many environments the definition of user requirements is not totally within the control of the software development group [29]. As software is developed, it is also reviewed to detect any errors, e.g., using quality assurance activities such as structured walk-throughs. Errors detected through such activities are reworked.

The formulation of software productivity is based on the work of the psychologist Ivan Steiner [47]. Steiner's model can simply be stated as follows:

Actual Productivity
= Potential Productivity
− Losses Due to Faulty Process

Potential productivity is defined as "the maximum level of productivity that can occur when an individual or group . . . makes the best possible use of its resources." It is a function of two sets of factors, the nature of the task (e.g., product complexity, database size) and the group's resources (e.g., personnel capabilities, experience level, software tools). Losses due to faulty process refer to the losses in productivity incurred as a result of the communication and coordination overheads and/or low motivation.

Control Subsystem

Decisions made in any organizational setting are based on what information is actually available to the decision maker(s). Often, this available information is inaccurate. Apparent conditions may be far removed from the actual or true state, depending on the information flows that are being used and the amount of time lag and distortion in these information flows. Thus, system dynamicists go to great lengths to differentiate between actual and perceived model variables [21].

True productivity of a software project team is a good example of a variable that is often difficult to assess. To know what the true value of productivity is at a particular point in time requires accurate knowledge regarding the rates of accomplishment and resources expended over that period of time.

However, because software is basically an intangible product during most of the development process, "It is difficult to measure performance in programming . . . It is difficult to evaluate the status of intermediate work such as undebugged programs or design specification and their potential value to the complete project" [31, p. 57].

How, then, is progress measured in a software project's control system? Our own field study findings corroborate those reported in the literature, namely, that progress, especially in the earlier phases of software development, is typically measured by the actual expenditure of budgeted resources rather than by some count of accomplishments [19]. Baber [12, p. 188] explains:

> It is essentially impossible for the programmers to estimate the fraction of the program completed. What is 45% of a program? Worse yet, what is 45% of three programs? How is he to guess whether a program is 40% or 50% complete? The easiest way for the programmer to estimate such a figure is to divide the amount of time actually spent on the task to date by the time budgeted for that task. Only when the program is almost finished or when the allocated time budget is almost used up will he be able to recognize that the calculated figure is wrong.

When progress in software development is measured solely by the expenditure of budgeted resources, status reporting ends up being nothing more than an echo of the original plan.

As the project advances toward its final stages, work accomplishments become relatively more visible and project members become increasingly more able to perceive how productive the work force has actually been. As a result, perceived productivity gradually ceases to be a function of projected productivity and is determined instead on the basis of actual tasks developed.

Planning Subsystem

In the planning subsystem, initial project estimates (e.g., for completion time, staffing, man-days) are made at the beginning of the project using a variety of techniques [27]. These estimates are then revised, as necessary, throughout the project's life. For example, to handle a project that is perceived to be behind schedule, plans can be revised to add more people, extend the schedule, or do a little of both. Such planning decisions are driven by variables that can change dynamically throughout the project life cycle. For example, while it is common for management to respond to a delay in the early stages of the project by increasing staff level, there is often great reluctance to do that later in the life cycle. This reluctance arises from the realization that there just wouldn't be enough time to acquaint the new people with the mechanics of the project, integrate them into the project team, and train them in the necessary technical areas.

MODEL VALIDATION

Validation Tests Performed

The process of judging the validity of a system dynamics model includes a number of objective tests [43] all of which were performed to validate this model:

- *Face validity.* To test the fit between the rate/level/feedback structure of the model and the essential characteristics of the real system. This was confirmed by the software project managers involved in the study.
- *Replication of reference modes.* To test whether the model can endogenously reproduce the various reference behavior modes characterizing the system under study. Reference modes are the observed behavior patterns over time of important variables characterizing the system under study, including problematic behavior patterns and observed responses to past policies [43]. Reference modes reproduced by the model include: work force staffing patterns in the human resource management area [5], the "90% syndrome" in the control area [4], the impact of schedule compression on project cost and schedule in the planning area [6], and the deadline effect on software productivity in the software production area [10].

- *Extreme condition simulations.* To test whether the model behaves reasonably under extreme conditions or extreme policies. As noted by Forrester and Senge [22, p. 203].

> It is not an acceptable counterargument to assert that particular extreme conditions do not occur in real life and should not occur in the model; the nonlinearities introduced by approaches to extreme condition can have important effect in normal operating ranges. Often the nonlinearities in the transition from normal to extreme conditions are the very mechanisms that keep the extreme conditions from being reached.

To make the extreme condition tests, we examined each policy, represented by a rate equation in the model, traced it back through any auxiliary equations to the state variables, represented as state variables, on which the rate depends, and tested the implications of imaginary maximum and minimum values of each state variable and combination of state variables to determine the plausibility of the resulting rate equations. Examples of extreme conditions examined include: if the work force level reaches zero, then the software production rate must be zero; even if the turnover rate is set to extremely high values, the work force level should never become negative; if the size of the project is suddenly and dramatically increased, then adjustments in the workforce level and/or the schedule will not be instantaneous (delays will be incurred); if the error generation rate is set to zero, then no rework effort will be incurred but effort would still be allocated to QA and testing.

- *Case study.* After the model was completely developed, a case study was conducted at NASA's Goddard Space Flight Center (GSFC) to validate the model. (NASA was not one of the five organizations studied during model development.) The case study involved a simulation of one of GSFC's software projects, namely, the DE-A project.

DE-A Case Study

The objective of the DE-A project was to design, implement, and test a software system for processing

EXHIBIT 4   Model Simulation of the DE-A Project

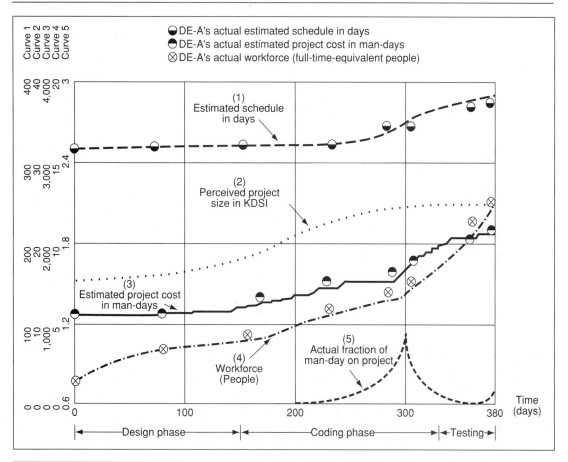

telemetry data and providing attitude determination and control for the DE-A satellite. The project's size was 24,000 delivered source instructions (24 KDSI), the development and target operations machines were the IBM S/360-95 and -75, and the programming language was FORTRAN. Initially, the project was estimated to require 1,100 man-days and to be completed in 320 working days. The actual results were 2,200 man-days and 380 days, respectively.

The model's DE-A simulation run is depicted in Exhibit 4. As shown, the model's results (represented by lines) conformed quite accurately to the project's actual behavior (represented by the circular points in the figure). Notice how project DE-A's management was inclined not to adjust the project's estimated schedule in days during most of the development phase of the project. Adjustments, in the earlier phases of the project, were instead made to the project's work force level. This behavior is not atypical. It arises, according to DeMarco [19, p. 10] because of political reasons:

> Once an original estimate is made, it's all too tempting to pass up subsequent opportunities to estimate by simply sticking with your previous numbers. This often happens even when you know

your old estimates are substantially off. There are a few different possible explanations for this effect: It's too early to show slip . . . If I re-estimate now, I risk having to do it again later (and looking bad twice). . . . As you can see, all such reasons are political in nature.

The work force pattern, on the other hand, is quite atypical. In the literature, work force buildup tends to follow a concave curve that rises, peaks, and then drops back to lower levels as the project proceeds toward the system testing phase [14]. Because NASA's launch of the DE-A satellite was tied to the completion of the DE-A software, serious schedule slippages were not tolerated. Specifically, all software was required to be accepted and frozen three months before launch. As this date was approached, pressures developed that overrode normal work force stability considerations. That is, project management became increasingly willing to pay any price necessary to avoid overshooting the three months before-launch date. This translated, as the figure indicates, into a management that was increasingly willing to add more people. (In [5] we investigate whether that staffing policy did or did not contribute to the project's late completion.)

On the other hand, various typical behavior patterns can be seen, such as the 90% completion syndrome [4, 19]:

> . . . estimates of the fraction of the work completed (increase) as originally planned until a level of about 80–90% is reached. The programmer's individual estimates then increase only very slowly until the task is actually completed [12, p. 188].

Its manifestation in the DE-A project is depicted in Exhibit 5. By measuring progress in the earlier phases of the project by the rate of expenditure of resources, status reporting ended up being nothing more than an illusion that the project was right on target. However, as the project approached its final stages (e.g., when 80 to 90% of the resources are consumed), discrepancies between the percentage of tasks accomplished and the percentage of re-

sources expended became increasingly more apparent. At the same time, project members became increasingly able to perceive how productive the work force has actually been. This resulted in a better appreciation of the amount of effort actually remaining. As this appreciation developed, it started to, in effect, discount the project's progress rate. Thus, although the project members proceeded toward the final stages of the project at a high work rate because of schedule pressures, their *net* progress rate slowed down considerably. This continued until the end of the project.

EXPERIMENTS UNDERTAKEN AND IMPLICATIONS OF RESULTS

"In software engineering it is remarkably easy to propose hypotheses and remarkably difficult to test them" [50, p. 57]. Many in the field have, thus, argued for the desirability of having a laboratory tool for testing ideas and hypotheses in software engineering [48].

The computer simulation tools of system dynamics provide us with such an experimentation vehicle. The effects of different assumptions and environmental factors can be tested. In the model system, unlike the real systems, the effect of changing one factor can be observed while all other factors are held unchanged. Internally, the model provides complete control of the system's organizational structure, its policies, and its sensitivities to various events.

Currently, the model is being used to study and predict the dynamic implications of managerial policies and procedures on the software development process in a variety of areas. This has produced three kinds of results: (1) Uncovered dysfunctional consequences of some currently adopted policies (e.g., in the scheduling area); (2) Provided support for managerial decision making (e.g., on the allocation of the quality assurance effort); and (3) Provided insight into software project phenomena (e.g., 90% syndrome and Brooks' Law).

EXHIBIT 5   Reported Percentage of Work Completed

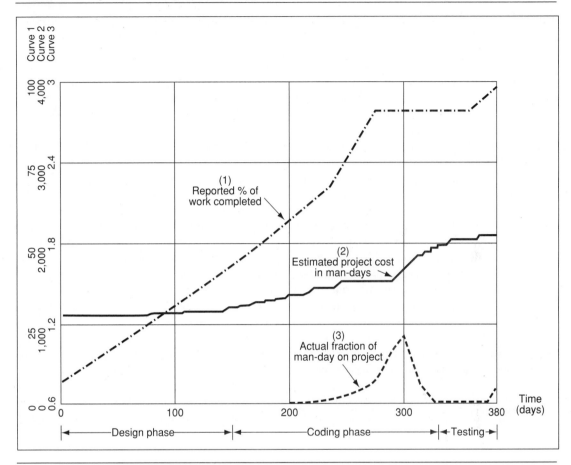

Dysfunctional Consequences of Some Current Policies

We investigated the project scheduling practices in a major U.S. minicomputer manufacturer [2]. In the particular organization, software project managers use Boehm's [14] COCOMO model to determine initial project estimates, which are then adjusted upward using a judgmental safety factor to come up with the project estimates actually used. In this organization, project managers were rewarded based upon how closely their project estimates matched actual project results. The pur-

pose of the experiment was to investigate the implications of this safety factor policy.

To test the efficacy of various safety factor policies, we ran a number of simulations on a prototypical software project that we will call project Example. Project Example's actual size is 64,000 DSI. At its initiation, however, it was incorrectly estimated to be 42.88 KDSI in size (that is, 33 percent smaller than 64 KDSI). This incorrectly perceived project size of 42.88 KDSI was the input used in COCOMO's estimation equations. We experimented with safety factor values ranging from 0 (the base run) to 100 percent. For a 50 percent safety factor, for example, the actual estimate used on the project would be (1 + 50/100) * COCOMO's estimates.

In Exhibit 6, the percent relative error in estimating man-days, defined as 100 × | Actual − Estimate | Actual, is plotted against different values of the safety factor. Notice that the safety factor policy seems to be working—the larger the safety factor, the smaller the estimation error.

The rationale for using a safety factor is based on the following assumptions:

1. Past experience indicates a strong bias among software developers to underestimate the scope of software projects [14].

2. One might think biases are the easiest of estimating problems to correct since they involve errors moving always in the same direction. But as [19] suggests, biases are almost by definition invisible; the same psychological mechanism that creates the bias (for example, the optimism of software developers) works to conceal it.

3. To rectify such bias, project managers often use a safety factor. Pietrasanta [37] observes that when project managers add contingency factors

(ranging, say, from 25 to 100 percent), they are saying in essence: I don't know all that is going to happen, so I'll estimate what I don't know as a percentage of what I do know.

In other words, the assumption is that safety factors are simply mechanisms to bring initial man-day estimates closer to true project size in man-days (see Exhibit 7a). Such an assumption cannot be contested solely on the basis of Exhibit 6 which provides only part of the story. Exhibit 7b presents a more complete picture; here, we used the model to calculate the actual man-days consumed by the project Example when different safety factors were applied to its initial estimate. The Exhibit 7a assumption is obviously invalidated. As we use higher safety factors, leading to increasingly generous initial man-days allocations, the actual amount of man-days consumed does not remain at some inherently defined value. In the base run, for example, project Example would be initiated with a man-day estimate of 2,359 man-days and would consume 3,795 man-days. When a 50 percent safety factor is used, leading to a 3.538 man-day initial estimate, Example ends up consuming not 3,795 man-days but 5,080 man-days.

EXHIBIT 6   Percentage of Relative Error in Estimating Actual Man-Days

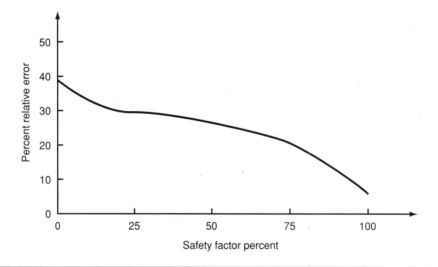

EXHIBIT 7 Differences between Assumed Man-Days and Actual Man-Days: (a) Comparison of Assumed Man-Days with Estimated Man-Days; (b) Comparison of Actual Man-Days with Estimated Man-Days

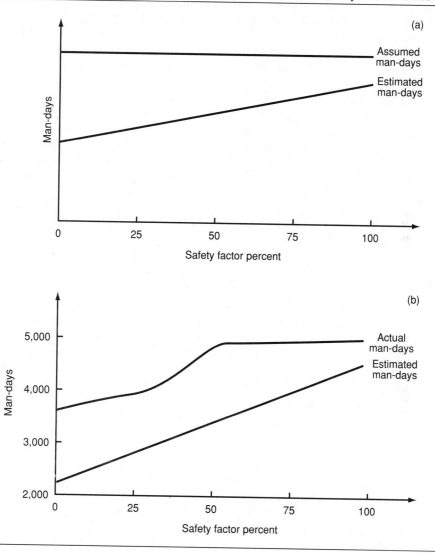

These results clearly indicate that by imposing different estimates on a software project we would, in a real sense, be creating different projects. This can be explained by realizing that schedules have a direct influence on decision-making behavior throughout a software project's life. In TRW's COCOMO model [14], for example, the project's average staff size would be determined by dividing the man-day estimate by the development time estimate (TDEV). Thus, a tight time schedule means larger work force. Also, scheduling can dramatically change manpower loading throughout the life of a project. For example, the work force level in some environments shoots upward toward the end of a late project when there are strict constraints on the extent to which the project's schedule is allowed to slip. Through its effects on the workforce level, a project's schedule also affects productivity (as illustrated in Exhibit 3). For example, a higher work force level means more communication and training overhead, affecting productivity negatively.

Productivity is also influenced by how tight or slack a project schedule is. If a project falls behind under a tight schedule, software developers often decide to work harder in an attempt to compensate for the perceived shortage and bring the project back on schedule. Conversely, man-day excesses could arise if project management initially overestimates a project; as a result, the project would be perceived ahead of schedule. When such a situation occurs, "Parkinson's law indicates that people will use the extra time for . . . personal activities, catching up on the mail, etc." [14]. Of course, this means that they become less productive.

One important managerial lesson learned from the above experiment is this: More accurate estimates are not necessarily "better" estimates. An estimation method should not be judged only on how accurate it is; it should also be judged on how costly the projects it creates are. For example, in one situation studied, we found that the estimation error which would have been 38 percent had been reduced to 9 percent by the safety factor policy. But, that policy resulted in a 43 percent cost increase in the project. For the first time management had a realization of the cost of their more accurate schedule estimation policy.

Provide Support for Management Decision Making

The quality assurance (QA) function has, in recent years, gained the recognition of being a critical factor in the successful development of software systems. However, because the use of QA tools and techniques can add significantly to the cost of developing software, the cost effectiveness of QA has been a pressing concern to the software quality manager. As of yet, though, this concern has not been adequately addressed in the literature.

We have investigated the trade-offs between the economic benefits and costs of QA in [6] and [8]. To do this, we used the model as a laboratory vehicle to conduct controlled experiments on QA policy. Effects considered in this experiment included error generation rate factors, such as schedule pressures and phase of project, and error detection factors, such as productivity, error types, error density. The results showed that the percent of the effort allocated to QA dramatically affects the total project cost. In one case studied (Exhibit 8a), the resulting total project cost ranged from 1,648 man-days to 5,650 man-days with the optimal QA allocation being 15 percent of the development effort.

Two important conclusions can be drawn from Exhibit 8a. The first, more generalizable conclusion, is that QA policy does have a significant impact on total project cost. At low values of QA expenditures, the increase in cost results from the high cost of the testing phase. On the other hand, at high values of QA expenditures, the excessive QA expenditures are themselves the culprit. The relationship between QA effort and the percentage of errors detected is shown in Figure 8b. Notice the "diminishing returns" of QA exhibited as QA expenditures extend beyond 10 to 15 percent of development effort. This type of behavior has been observed by others in the literature (e.g., [14, 46]).

The second important conclusion we can draw, concerns the 15 percent value for the optimal QA expenditure level. What, in our opinion, is really significant about this result is not its particular value, since this cannot be generalized beyond the DE-A software project used for this study, but rather the process of deriving it, namely, this article's integrative system dynamics simulation approach. Beyond controlled experimentation (which would be too costly and time consuming to be practical), as far as we know, this model provides the first capability to quantitatively analyze the costs/benefits of QA policy for software production. This, it is encouraging to note, is generalizable in the sense that one can customize the model for different software

EXHIBIT 8   Impact of Different QA Expenditure Levels: (a) Impact of Different QA Expenditure Levels on Project Cost; (b) Impact of Different QA Expenditure Levels on Percentage of Errors Detected

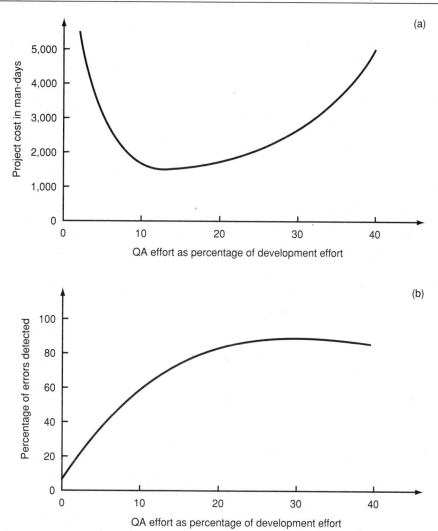

development environments to derive environment-specific optimality conditions.

New Insights into Software Project Phenomena

One oft-cited software project phenomenon is Brooks' Law, which states that adding manpower to a late software project makes it later [15]. Since its publication, Brooks' Law has been widely referenced in the literature even though it has not been formally tested. Furthermore, it has often been applied indiscriminately e.g., for applications-type projects as well as systems programming-type projects, both large and small [38], even though

Brooks was quite explicit in specifying the domain of applicability of his insights, to what he called "jumbo systems programming projects."

We have studied Brooks' Law in the context of medium-size applications-type projects in [5]. Recall the work force staffing pattern experienced on NASA's medium-sized DE-A project of Exhibit 4. It indicates that management is (implicitly if not explicitly) oblivious to the lesson of Brooks' Law. Because NASA's launch of the DE-A satellite was tied to the completion of the DE-A software, serious schedule slippages could not be tolerated. Specifically, all software was required to be accepted and frozen three months before launch. As the project slipped and this date approached, management reacted (or overreacted) by adding new people to the project to meet the strict launch deadline . . . as evidenced by the rising work force curve in the final stages of the project.

The lesson of Brooks' Law would, of course, suggest that by adding new people to the late DE-A project, management actually delayed it further. To test this hypothesis, we resimulated the DE-A project under different staffing policies. The experimental results showed that while adding more people to a late project of this type does cause it to become more costly, it does not always cause it to complete later. The increase in the cost of the project is caused by the increased training and communication overheads, which in effect decrease the average productivity of the work force and thus increase the project's cost in man-days. For the project's schedule to also suffer, the drop in productivity must be severe enough and late enough in the project's life cycle to render an additional person's net cumulative contribution to the project to be, in effect, a negative contribution. Our experimental results indicate that this happens only where management's willingness to add new staff members persists until the very final stages of the testing phase. In the particular case of the DE-A project where hiring did continue until the very end (as seen in Exhibit 4), our analysis indicates that the project period could have been

cut by two calendar weeks by curtailing hiring during the testing phase.

CONCLUSION

The objective of this research effort is to enhance our understanding of the software development process and how it is managed. There are two principal features that characterize our research paradigm, which we would like to reiterate in these concluding remarks. First, we emphasize the integrative perspective. We have attempted to demonstrate how the software management system is a conglomerate of interrelated and interdependent functions. Action taken by one subsystem (e.g., human resource management) can be traced throughout the entire management system (e.g., software production, planning, and control). The behavior of an individual subsystem in isolation may be very different from its behavior when it interacts with other subsystems (e.g., the lesson of Brooks' Law). Furthermore, differences in the environment and management policies between companies could explain why a software engineering technique that is effective in one organization may be ineffective in another organization [7].

Second, our research approach is grounded in the feedback systems principles of system dynamics. Feedback processes are universal in social systems in general. We have attempted to show how, when applied to software project management, they do provide a powerful lens to view and understand software project behavior. This is particularly important because:

> Most managers get into trouble because they forget to think in circles. I mean this literally. Managerial problems persist because managers continue to believe that there are such things as unilateral causation, independent and dependent variables, origins, and terminations [49, p. 86].

What is gained in understanding through the use of such a model to portray a portion of the real world is achieved by comprehending the law or laws built into the model. Hundreds of variables affect software development. Furthermore, these variables are not independent; many of them are related to one another. So far the many studies on the subject emphasize the difficulty and complexity of the process, but have done little to reveal a well-defined methodology or to delineate precise relationships among project variables [36]. We feel that the research paradigm presented in this article provides a viable vehicle.

If understanding is the intellectual outcome of a theoretical model, then prediction is its practical outcome. This model is also being used as an experimentation vehicle to study and predict the dynamic behavior of the software development process and of the implications of managerial policies and procedures pertaining to the development of software. The exercise produced three kinds of results: (1) uncovered dysfunctional consequences of some currently adopted policies (e.g., in the scheduling area); (2) provided guidelines for managerial policy (e.g., on the allocation of the quality assurance effort); and (3) provided new insights into software project phenomena (e.g., Brooks' Law).

These results are obviously limited by the model boundary selected for this study, our literature search, and our interviews. Our system dynamics software management model is not a model of small one-programmer-type projects nor large projects involving hundreds of software professionals over a period of several years. Instead, our research results specifically pertain to the domain of medium-sized projects that are 10,000 to 250,000 lines of code. Second, the type of projects investigated are the so-called organic type projects, i.e., projects conducted in familiar in-house environments [14]. Third, our current results are limited to projects that follow that traditional waterfall life cycle using third-generation programming languages. Finally, this approach is intended to provide a general understanding of the nature of the dynamic behavior of a project (e.g., how work force level and productivity change over time and why) rather than to provide point-

predictions (e.g., exactly how many errors will be generated.)

Finally, a note on possible future research directions. Two such research areas are particularly promising. The first involves extending this modeling approach to investigate, not the dynamics of a single software project, but rather to study the software development organization as a continuous stream of software products are developed, placed into operation, and maintained. A number of research questions are ripe for investigation, including: (1) the efficacy of different organizational structures (e.g., project, functional, and matrix); (2) personnel turnover, its costs (e.g., recruiting and training overheads), its benefits (e.g., access to new ideas and methodologies), and its causes (e.g., schedule pressures, maintenance load); and (3) the organizational/environmental determinants of productivity (e.g., standards, software tools, use of librarians, documentation requirements). Again, one needs to investigate both short-term as well as long-term implications. For example, an investment in developing powerful software development tools (e.g., compilers, automated testing tools) might hamper productivity in the short-run, but may lead to better software in the long-run.

Second, we are investigating the utility of incorporating AI-based modules into the model [11]. According to Nielsen [35], an expert-system form of representation for decision making can be particularly advantageous in situations where the actual system being modeled is not fully automated but, instead, relies upon human judgment or direct human intervention for a portion of its operation or behavior. "A knowledge-based programming approach may be used to capture the human element of the decision making, so that such knowledge may be appropriately reflected in the model" [35].

The management of software projects is such an application area. Capturing the decision-making process (e.g., in the staffing area) in a rule-based knowledge base, rather than using the traditional representation in procedural code has a number of benefits. For example, it allows for the incorporation of an explanation capability to the model.

The experiments that have been performed already, described in the previous section, illustrate the insights that can be gained from applying this paradigm to the myriad of concerns facing software development managers. Further work in these directions will help to resolve many more of these concerns.

ACKNOWLEDGMENTS

We appreciate the contribution of each of the individuals in the organizations providing perspectives and data to this research effort. In addition, we thank Robert Zmud and Chris Kemerer, whose suggestions have improved this article's organization and readability. Work reported herein was supported, in part, by NASA research grant NAGW-448.

References

1. Abdel-Hamid, T.K. The dynamics of software development project management: An integrative system dynamics perspective. Ph.D. dissertation, Sloan School of Management, MIT, 1984.

2. Abdel-Hamid, T.K., and Madnick, S.E. Impact of schedule estimation on software project behavior. *IEEE Softw. 3,* 4 (July, 1986).

3. Abdel-Hamid, T.K. The economics of software quality assurance: A simulation-based case study. *MIS Q.,* in press, 1988b.

4. Abdel-Hamid, T.K. Understanding the '90% syndrome' in software project management: A simulation-based case study. *J. Syst. Softw.,* in press, 1988c.

5. Abdel-Hamid, T.K. The dynamics of software project staffing: A system dynamics based simulation approach. *IEEE Trans. Softw. Eng. 15,* 2 (Feb. 1989a).

6. Abdel-Hamid, T.K. Investigating the cost schedule tradeoff in software development. *IEEE Softw.,* in press, 1989b.

7. Abdel-Hamid, T.K., and Madnick, S.E. On the porrtability of quantitative software estimation models. *Inf. Manag. 13,* 1 (Aug. 1987a), 1–10.

8. Abdel-Hamid, T.K., and Madnick, S.E. The economics of software quality assurance: A systems dynamics based simulation approach. *Annals of the Society of Logistics Eng. 1,* 2 (October 1987b), 8–32.

9. Abdel-Hamid, T.K., and Madnick, S.E. *Dynamics of Software Project Management.* Prentice-Hall, Englewood Cliffs, N.J.: in press, 1990.

10. Abdel-Hamid, T.K., and Madnick, S.E. Software productivity: Potential, actual, and perceived. *Syst. Dynamics Rev. 5,* 2 (Sum. 1989), 93–113.

11. Abdel-Hamid, T.K., and Sivasankaran, T.R. Incorporating expert system technology into simulation modeling: An expert-simulator for project management. In *Proceedings of the 1988 Society for Computer Simulation Multiconference,* February 3–5, 1988, pp. 268–274.

12. Baber, R.L. *Software Reflected.* North Holland, New York, 1982.

13. Basili, V.R. Improving methodology and productivity through practical measurement. Lecture at the Wang Institute of Graduate Studies, Lowell, Mass., November, 1982.

14. Boehm, B.W. *Software Engineering Economics,* Prentice-Hall, Englewood Cliffs, N.J., 1981.

15. Brooks, F.P. *The Mythical Man Month.* Addison-Wesley, Reading, Mass., 1978.

16. Buckley, F., and Poston, R. Software quality assurance. *IEEE Trans. Softw. Eng. 10,* 1 (Jan. 1984), 365–41.

17. Cooper, J.D. Corporate level software management. *IEEE Trans. Softw. Eng. SE-4,* No. 4 (July 1978), 319–325.

18. Cougar, J.D., and Zawacki, R.A. *Motivating and Managing Computer Personnel.* John Wiley, New York, 1980.

19. DeMarco, T. *Controlling Software Projects.* Yourdon Press, New York, 1982.

20. Devenny, T.J. An exploration study of software cost estimating at the electronics systems division. U.S. Department of Commerce, July, 1976.

21. Forrester, J.W. *Industrial Dynamics.* MIT Press, Cambridge, Mass., 1961.

22. Forrester, J.W., and Senge, P.M. Tests for Building Confidence in System Dynamics Models. In A.A. Legasto et al., Eds., *Studies in the Management Sciences: System Dynamics,* North-Holland, Amsterdam, 1980.

23. Gehring, P.F., and Pooch. V.W. Software development management. *Data Manag.* (Feb. 1977), 14–38.

24. Graham, A.K. Software design: Breaking the bottleneck. *IEEE Spectrum 19,* 3 (Mar. 1982), 43–50.

25. Ibrahim, R.L. Software development information system. *J. Syst. Manag. 29,* 12 (Dec. 1978), 34–39.

26. Kelly, T.J. The dynamics of R&D project management. Master's thesis, Sloan School of Management, MIT, 1970.

27. Kemerer, C.F. An empirical validation of software cost estimation models. *Commun. ACM 30,* 5 (May 1987), 416–428.

28. Lehman, M.M. Laws and conservation in large program evaluation. In *Proceedings of the Second Software Lifecycle Management Workshop* (Atlanta, Ga., Aug. 1978), pp. 21–22.

29. McGowan, C.L., and McHenry, R.C. Software Management. In P. Wegner, Ed., *Research Directions in Software Technology*. MIT Press, Cambridge, Mass., 1980.

30. McKeen, J.D. Successful development strategies for business application systems. *MIS Q. 7,* 3 (Sept. 1983).

31. Mills, H.D. *Software Productivity*. Little, Brown & Co., Boston, 1983.

32. Musa, J.D. Software engineering: The future of a profession. *IEEE Softw.* (Jan. 1985), 55–62.

33. Nay, J.N. Choice and allocation in multiple markets: A research and development systems analysis. Master's thesis, Department of Electrical Engineering, MIT, 1965.

34. Newport, J.P., Jr. A growing gap in software. *Fortune* (Apr. 28, 1986), 132–142.

35. Nielsen, N.R. Knowledge-based simulation programming. In *Proceedings of the National Computer Conference* (June 16–19, 1986), pp. 126–136.

36. Oliver, P. Estimating the Cost of Software. In J. Hannan, Ed., *Computer Programming Management*. Auerbach Publishers, Pennsauken, N.J., 1982.

37. Pietrasanta, A.M. Managing the Economics of Computer Programming. In *National Conference Proceedings of the ACM*, 1986.

38. Pressman, R.S. *Software Engineering: A Practitioner's Approach*. McGraw-Hill, New York, 1982.

39. Putnam, L.H. The Real Metrics of Software Development. *EASCON 80,* 1980.

40. Radice, A. Productivity Measures in Software. In R. Goldberg, Ed., *The Economics of Information Processing: Operations, Programming, and Software Models*. Volume II. Wiley, New York, 1982.

41. Ramamoorthy, C.V. et al. Software engineering: Problems and perspectives. *IEEE Comput. 17,* 10 (Oct. 1984), 191–210.

42. Richardson, G.P. Sources of rising product development times. Tech. Rep. D-3321-1, SD Group, MIT, 1982.

43. Richardson, G.P., and Pugh, G.L. III. *Introduction to System Dynamics Modeling with Dynamo*. The MIT Press, Cambridge, Mass., 1981.

44. Roberts, E.B. *The Dynamics of Research and Development*. Harper and Row, New York, 1964.

45. Roberts, E.B., Ed. *Managerial Applications of System Dynamics*. The MIT Press, Cambridge, Mass., 1981.

46. Shooman, M.L. *Software Engineering—Design, Reliability and Management,* McGraw-Hill, New York, 1983.

47. Steiner, I.D. *Group Process and Productivity*. Academic Press, New York, 1972.

48. Thayer, R.H. Modeling a software engineering project management system. Ph.D. Dissertation, Dept. of Computer Science, University of California, Santa Barbara, 1979.

49. Weick, K.E. *The Social Psychology of Organization*. 2nd ed. Addison-Wesley, Reading, Mass, 1979.

50. Weiss, D.M. Evaluating software development by error analysis. *J. Syst. Softw. 1,* 1 (1979), 57–70.

51. Zmud, R.W. Management of large software development efforts. *MIS Q. 4,* 2 (June 1980), 45–56.

Discussion Questions

1. Discuss reasons why software projects might exhibit economies of scale. Discuss reasons why software projects might exhibit diseconomies of scale. What is a likely impact of future advances in software development—will they make projects more or less likely to exhibit diseconomies of scale?

2. Kemerer (1989) summarizes several reasons why humans are poor estimators (tendency toward underestimation, management focus on goals not estimates, task complexity), yet Vicinanza et al. suggest using human experts to develop expert systems. Reconcile these two points of view.

3. Both Vicinanza et al. and Madnick/Abdel-Hamid propose relatively complex models that are hard to describe simply and have a large number of variables. How can managers become sufficiently comfortable with them to allow their results to guide their decision making?

4. The Madnick/Abdel-Hamid model has a large number of variables that could be expected to influence the course of a software project. Based on your experience or reading, are there major variables that are omitted?

Function Points

INTRODUCTION

As outlined in chapters 2 and 3, one approach to cost estimation is the function points (FPs) approach first presented at a conference in 1979 by Allan Albrecht and later formalized and validated by Albrecht and John Gaffney in 1983. The Albrecht and Gaffney article proposes FPs as an alternative to SLOC as a measure of the functionality (size) of a software system. The earlier (1979) work first proposed a simple four count measure without current complexity adjustments. In this extension, Albrecht and Gaffney standardized the measure around five attributes and added a list of fourteen complexity adjustments. The article then compares the FP counts on 24 projects to both SLOC and work-hours data on those projects. They argue that FPs provide a good correlation with both SLOC and work-hours and they further contrast COBOL and PL/1 development. They then go on to provide independent validation against 21 projects from 3 different sites. A detailed appendix describes how to count FPs.

An important critique of the proposed function point method was published a few years later by Charles Symons (1988). He argues that Albrecht's FP method has the following flaws: a range of simple/average/complex is insufficient to represent the range of true difficulty, internal complexity is

not represented, and the application boundary has a great influence on the final count. He proposes a variant approach labeled the 'Mark II method' for measuring three components (inputs, entity-types, and outputs) instead of the five of Albrecht. He proposes the idea of measuring entities rather than logical files. He also offers his own list of complexity factors. He presents validation for some limited data from nine systems which show that Mark II FPs are similar but tend to generate larger counts than Albrecht's. In the conclusion he raises an interesting point about the distinction between using FPs for estimating, where a user needs to continually adjust the model for changes in technology, versus using FPs for evaluation, where a user would want to keep a consistent measure so that any improvements in productivity over time can be documented. The long term contributions of this article are to point the way toward counting entities (soon to be the preferred approach), to impress the need to automate the counting (also a new development) and in general to point out flaws in the approach that have subsequently been noted.

One of the long standing concerns about Function Points is their degree of reliability. In particular, reliability in the FP context has two components:-

Given articles like Symons and others that propose variants on FP counting, would a system sized using two different counting methods produce a single, reliable answer (inter-method reliability)? Would two people independently counting the same system using the same method come up with the same number of FPs (inter-rater reliability)? The third article in this chapter presents the results of a field experiment set up to determine both the degree of relationship between the Albrecht FPs and the newer Entity-Relationship FPs and the degree of inter-rater reliability of both these methods. Data from 27 actual systems, averaging 450 FPs each, were analyzed and the results suggest that inter-rater reliability is quite high with differences averaging approximately 12%, and the null hypothesis of no difference not being able to be rejected. The conclusions are that managers can use FPs with relative confidence, they are much less subjective than is commonly believed, and that the new Entity-Relationship variation may be expected to provide similar counts to the original.

SOFTWARE FUNCTION, SOURCE LINES OF CODE, AND DEVELOPMENT EFFORT PREDICTION: A SOFTWARE SCIENCE VALIDATION

"FUNCTION POINTS" BACKGROUND

Albrecht [1] has employed a methodology for validating estimates of the amount of work-effort (which he calls work-hours) needed to design and develop custom application software. The approach taken is ". . . to list and count the number of external user inputs, inquiries, outputs, and master files to be delivered by the development project." As pointed out by Albrecht [1], "these factors are the outward manifestations of any application. They cover all the functions in an application." Each of these categories of input and output are counted individually and then weighted by numbers reflecting the relative value of the function to the user/customer. The weighted sum of the inputs and outputs is called "function points." Albrecht [1] states that the weights used were "determined by debate and trial." They are given in the section "Selection of Estimating Formulas."

The thesis of this work is that the amount of function to be provided by the application (program) can be estimated from an itemization of the major components of data to be used or provided by it. Furthermore, this estimate of function should be correlated to both the amount of "SLOC" to be developed and the development effort needed.

A major reason for using "function points" as a measure is that the point counts can be developed relatively easily in discussions with the user/customer at an *early* stage of the development process. They relate directly to user/customer requirements in a way that is more easily understood by the user/customer than "SLOC."

Another major reason is the availability of needed information. Since it is reasonable to expect that a statement of basic requirements includes an itemization of the inputs and outputs to be used and provided by the application (program) from the user's external view, an estimate may be validated early in the development cycle with this approach.

Article by Allan J. Albrecht and John E. Gaffney, Jr. © 1983 IEEE. Reprinted, with permission, from (*IEEE Transactions on Software Engineering;* SE-9, 6, 639–648; 1983).

A third reason is that "function points" can be used to develop a general measure of development productivity (e.g., "function points per work-month" or "work-hours per function point"), that may be used to demonstrate productivity trends. Such a measure can give credit for productivity relative to the amount of user function delivered to the user/customer per unit of development effort, with less concern for effects of technology, language level, or unusual code expansion occasioned by macros, calls, and code reuse.

It is important to distinguish between two types of work-effort estimates, a primary or "task-analysis" estimate and a "formula" estimate. The primary work-effort estimate should always be based on an analysis of the tasks to be done, thus providing the project team with an estimate *and a work plan*. This paper discusses "formula" estimates which are based solely on counts of inputs and outputs of the program to be developed, and not on a detailed analysis of the development tasks to be performed. It is recommended that such "formula" estimates be used only to validate and provide perspective on primary estimates.

"SOFTWARE SCIENCE" BACKGROUND

Halstead [2] states that the number of tokens or symbols N constituting a program is a function of η, the "operator" vocabulary size, and η, the "operand" vocabulary size. His software length equation is

$$N = \eta_1 \, log_2 \, \eta_1 + \eta_2 \, log_2 \, \eta_2.$$

This formula was originally derived to apply to a small program (or one procedure of a large program) or function, that is, to apply to the program expression of an algorithm. Thus, the number of tokens in a program consisting of a multiplicity of functions or procedures is best found by applying the size equation to each function or procedure individually, and summing the results.

Gaffney [3] has applied the software length equation to a single address machine in the following way. A program consists of data plus instruc-tions. A sequence of instructions can be thought of as a string of "tokens." At the machine code level, for a single address machine, "op. code" tokens, generally alternate with "data label" tokens. Exceptions do occur due to instructions that require no data labels. The "op. codes" may be referred to as "operators" and the "data labels" as "operands." Thus, in an instruction of the form "LA X", meaning, load accumulator with the content of location X, "LA" is the operator, and "X" is the operand. For single address machine level code, the case Gaffney [3] analyzes, one would expect to have approximately twice as many tokens (N) as instructions (I). That is, $I = 0.5N$. Gaffney [3] applied the Halstead software length equation to object code for the AN/UYK-7 military computer (used in the Trident missile submarine's sonar system, as well as other applications). He determined a value for the coefficient "b" in the equation "$I = bN$." It was $b = 0.478$, and the correlation between the estimate $I = 0.478N$ (where the estimate $\hat{N} = \eta_1 \, log_2 \, \eta_1 + \eta_2 \, log_2 \, \eta_2$), and the actual instruction count I, was 0.916. Thus, the data correlated closely with the estimate from the software length equation.

Gaffney's work presumed that the number of unique instruction types (η_1), or operator vocabulary size employed, as well as the number of unique data labels (η_2) or operand vocabulary size used, was known. However, η_1 need not be known in order for one to estimate the number of tokens N or the number of instructions I. An "average" figure for η_1 (and thus for $\eta_1 \, log_2 \, \eta_1$) can be employed, or the factor $\eta_1 \, log_2 \, \eta_1$ can be omitted, inducing some degree of error, of course. Indeed, Christiansen et al. [4] have observed that ". . . program size is determined by the data that must be processed by the program." Thus one could take several different approaches to estimating software (code) size. The data label vocabulary size (η_2) could be estimated. Alternatively, it is suggested that (η_2^*), the number of conceptually unique inputs and outputs, can be used as a surrogate for (η_2). The estimate for (η_2^*) should be relatively easy to determine early in the design cycle, from the itemization of external inputs and outputs found in a complete requirements definition or external system design.

Some data by Dekerf [5] supports the idea that I (and N) can be estimated as multiples of the variates $\eta_2 \log_2 \eta_2$ and $\eta_2^* \log_2 \eta_2^*$ (for example: $I = A \ \eta_2 \log_2 \eta_2$, where (A) is some constant). Dekerf counted tokens (N), operands (η_2), and conceptually unique inputs and outputs (η_2^*) in 29 APL programs found in a book [6] by Allen of the IBM System Science Institute in Los Angeles. Using Dekerf's data, we have found that the sample correlation between N and $\eta_2^* \log_2 \eta_2^*$ is 0.918 and between N and $\eta_2 \log_2$ is 0.988.

In the next sections, we demonstrate that these (and other) software science formulas originally developed for (small) algorithms only can be applied to large applications (programs), where (η_2^*) is then interpreted to mean the sum of overall external inputs and outputs to the application (program). "Function points" [1] can be interpreted as a weighted sum of the top level input/output items (e.g., screens, reports, files) that are equivalent to (η_2^*). Also, as is shown subsequently, a number of variates based on "function points" can be used as the measure of the function that the application (program) is to provide.

DP SERVICES DATA

Exhibit 1 provides data on 24 applications developed by the IBM DP Services organization. The language used in each application is cited. The counts of four types of external input/output elements for the application as a whole are given. The number of "function points" for each program is identified. The number of "SLOC," including comments (all the "SLOC" was new) that implemented the function required is identified. Finally, the number of work-hours required to design, develop, and test the application is given.

SELECTION OF ESTIMATING FORMULAS

Using the DP Services data shown in Exhibit 1, 13 estimating formulas were explored as functions of the 9 variates listed in Exhibit 2. A basis for their selection is now provided. "Function points" count (F) is the variable determined using Albrecht's methodology [1]. Albrecht uses the following average weights to determine "function points": number of inputs $\times$ 4; number of outputs $\times$ 5; number of inquiries $\times$ 4; number of master files $\times$ 10. Interfaces are considered to be master files. As stated in [1], the weighted sum of inputs, outputs, inquiries, and master files can be adjusted within a range of +/- 25 percent, depending upon the estimator's assessment of the complexity of the program. As an example of the calculation of the number of "function points," consider the data for "custom application one" in Exhibit 1. The number of function points is equal to

$$F = (25 \times 4) + (150 \times 5) + (75 \times 4) + (60 \times 10)$$
$$= 1750.$$

The current "Function Points Index Worksheet" being used in the IBM I/S organization is shown in Appendix A. The major changes from [1] are as follows.

1. Interfaces are separately identified and counted.
2. Provision is made for above average and below average complexities of the elements counted.
3. A more objective measure of processing complexity is provided.

"I/O count" (V) is the total program input/output count without the weights and processing complexity adjustment applied in "function points." Both function points and I/O count are treated as equivalent to Halstead's η_2^*, the unique input/output (data element) count. The "potential volume" formula $(F + 2) \log_2 (F + 2)$ was developed by Halstead [2]. The "information content" formula $(F \log_2 F)$, also used as a variate here, corresponds to $\eta_2^* \log_2 \eta_2^*$, an approximation to the factor $\eta_2 \log_2 \eta_2$ in Halstead's software length equation.

The origin of the "sort count" variate $(F/2) \log_2 (F/2)$ is as follows. Gaffney [7] estimated the number of conditional jumps in a program to be

$$J = (\eta_2^*/2) \log_2 (\eta_2^*/2)$$

EXHIBIT 1 DP Service Project Data

Custom Application Number	Language	Input/Output Element Counts				Function Points	Source Lines of Code (SLOC)	Work-Hours
		IN	OUT	FILE	INQ			
1	COBOL	25	150	60	75	1750	130K	102.4K
2	COBOL	193	98	36	70	1902	318K	105.2K
3	COBOL	70	27	12	—	428	20K	11.1K
4	PL/1	40	60	12	20	759	54K	21.1K
5	COBOL	10	69	9	1	431	62K	28.8K
6	COBOL	13	19	23	—	283	28K	10.0K
7	COBOL	34	14	5	—	205	35K	8.0K
8	COBOL	17	17	5	15	289	30K	4.9K
9	COBOL	45	64	16	14	680	48K	12.9K
10	COBOL	40	60	15	20	794	93K	19.0K
11	COBOL	41	27	5	29	512	57K	10.8K
12	COBOL	33	17	5	8	224	22K	2.9K
13	COBOL	28	41	11	16	417	24K	7.5K
14	PL/1	43	40	35	20	682	42K	12.0K
15	COBOL	7	12	8	13	209	40K	4.1K
16	COBOL	28	38	9	24	512	96K	15.8K
17	PL/1	42	57	5	12	606	40K	18.3K
18	COBOL	27	20	6	24	400	52K	8.9K
19	COBOL	48	66	50	13	1235	94K	38.1K
20	PL/1	69	112	39	21	1572	110K	61.2K
21	COBOL	25	28	22	4	500	15K	3.6K
22	DMS	61	68	11	—	694	24K	11.8K
23	DMS	15	15	3	6	199	3K	0.5K
24	COBOL	12	15	15	—	260	29K	6.1K

Note: "IN" = No. of inputs; "OUT" = No. of outputs; "FILE" = No. of master files; "INQ" = No. of inquiries.

if it is assumed that the η_2^* (total number of conceptually unique inputs and outputs) are equally divided between inputs and outputs. This is in keeping with the following observations: if $\eta_2^*/2$ were to symbolize the number of items to be sorted (by a data processing program), then the number of comparisons (and hence conditional jumps) required would be on the order of J, as just defined [8]. This form is used subsequently as the

"sort content" where either the variable "F" ("function point") or "V" (I/O count) is employed in the place of η_2^*.

DEVELOPMENT AND APPLICATION OF ESTIMATING FORMULAS

This section provides a number of formulas for estimating work hours and "SLOC" as functions

EXHIBIT 2   Estimating Variates Explored

		Dependent Variable Explored Source Lines of Code		
Independent Variate	*Formula Basis*	*PL/1*	*COBOL*	*Work-Hours*
1. Function Points	F	X	X	X
2. Function Sort Content	$(F/2) \log_2 (F/2)$	X		X
3. Function Potential Volume	$(F+2) \log_2 (F+2)$	X		
4. Function Information Content	$F \log_2 F$	X		X
5. I/O Count	V			X
6. Sort Count	$(V/2) \log_2 (V/2)$			X
7. Count Information Content	$V \log_2 V$			X
8. Source Lines of COBOL	SLOC			X
9. Source Lines of PL/1	SLOC			X

EXHIBIT 3   Summary Comparison of the SLOC Estimation Approaches

	Relative Error		Sample Correlation Between the Variables And Actual SLOC
Estimators of SLOC (1) Variables Used Were:	*Avg. (2)*	*Standard Deviation*	
1. Function Points (COBOL)	.229	.736	.854
2. Function Points (PL/1)	.003	.058	.997
3. Function Sort Content (PL/1)	.007	.057	.997
4. Function Potential Volume (PL/1)	−.002	.057	.997
5. Function Information Content (PL/1)	−.002	.057	.997

Notes:
   (1) The formulas used were:
       1. $\hat{S} = 118.7 \, (F) - 6{,}490$
       2. $\hat{S} = 73.1 \, (F) - 4{,}600$
       3. $\hat{S} = 13.9 \, (F/2) \log_2 (F/2) + 5{,}360$
       4. $\hat{S} = 6.3 \, (F+2) \log_2 (F+2) + 4{,}370$
       5. $\hat{S} = 6.3 \, (F \log_2 F) + 4{,}500$

   (2) $\dfrac{\hat{S}-S}{S}$, where $\hat{S}$ = estimate and S = actual SLOC

of "function points" (F), "input/output count" (V), and several of the variates cited in Exhibit 2, which themselves are functions of (F) and (V), as described in the previous section.

To demonstrate the equivalency of the various measures and also to show their effectiveness as estimators, correlations were performed on the combinations of variates checked in Exhibit 2. Exhibit 3 summarizes the results of using the variates checked to estimate "SLOC" in the Cobol and PL/1 applications (see Exhibit 1) as indicated. The estimating model relating "function points" to

PL/1 "SLOC" was found to be quite different from the model for Cobol. Significantly more Cobol "SLOC" are required to deliver the same amount of "function points" than are required with PL/1 "SLOC." The PL/1 data in particular closely approximate a straight line for all the measures. Any of the measures shown should be a good estimator for PL/1 "SLOC." In the next section, these measures are further validated using additional data from three other application development sites.

Exhibit 4 summarizes the results of using the variables checked in Exhibit 2 and SLOC to estimate work-effort. The correlations and standard deviations of the data for the estimating formulas, using I/O count (V) and function point count (F), shown suggest that any of them would be an effective "formula" estimate. The measures based on "I/O count" show slightly, but not significantly, better statistics than those based on "function points." The last two rows of Exhibit 4 summarize the results of using "SLOC" to estimate work-effort. It is shown that the estimating model based on the Cobol data is quite different from the model based on PL/1 data. Almost twice as much work-effort is required to produce a "SLOC" of PL/1 as is required to produce a "SLOC" of Cobol. However, Exhibit 3 shows that almost twice as much "function" is estimated to be delivered by an "SLOC" of PL/1 as is estimated to be delivered by an "SLOC" of Cobol. Therefore, it is advisable to keep these languages separated in estimating models based on "SLOC."

Exhibit 5 is a scatter plot of actual "function points" and work-hours data and estimation formula number 1 from Exhibit 4 plotted on the same graph.

EXHIBIT 4   Summary Comparison of the Work-Hours Estimation Approaches

| | (2) Relative Error | | Sample Correlation |
Estimators of Work-hours (1) Variables Used Were:	*Avg.*	*Standard Deviation*	*Between the Variables And Actual Work-Hours*
1. Function Points	.242	.848	.935
2. Function Sort Content	.192	.759	.945
3. Function Information Content	.194	.763	.944
4. I/O Count	.206	.703	.945
5. I/O Count Sort Content	.195	.630	.954
6. I/O Count Information Content	.195	.637	.954
7. Source Lines of Code (PL/1)	.023	.213	.988
8. Source Lines of Code (COBOL)	.323	.669	.864

Notes:
(1) The formulas used were:
   1. $\hat{W} = 54\ (F) - 13{,}390$
   2. $\hat{W} = 10.75\ (F/2) \log_2 (F/2) - 8{,}300$
   3. $\hat{W} = 4.89\ (F \log_2 F) - 8{,}762$
   4. $\hat{W} = 309\ (V) - 15{,}780$
   5. $\hat{W} = 79\ (V/2) \log_2 (V/2) - 8{,}000$
   6. $\hat{W} = 35\ (V \log_2 V) - 8{,}900$
   7. $\hat{W} = 0.6713\ (S) - 13{,}137,\ \text{PL/1}$
   8. $\hat{W} = 0.3793\ (S) - 2{,}913\ \text{COBOL}$

(2) $\dfrac{\hat{W} - W}{s}$, where $\hat{W}$ = estimated and W = actual work-hours

EXHIBIT 5   Function Points Versus Work-Hours

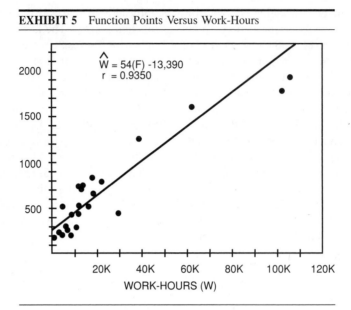

The correlations and standard deviations of linear models of "function points," "function sort content," "function information content," "I/O count," "I/O count," "I/O count sort content," and "I/O count information content," and "SLOC" are shown in Exhibit 4. Each model could be an effective tool for validating estimates. The early availability of elements that comprise "function points" and "I/O count" for an application suggest that this validation could be done earlier in the development schedule than validations based on estimated "SLOC."

VALIDATION

The previous section, and the related figure and tables, developed several estimating formulas and explored their consistency within the DP Services data used to develop the formulas. This section validates several SLOC estimation formulas developed from the DP Services data presented in Exhibit 1 against three *different* development sites. While it is *interesting* to note relations between "function points" and SLOC, it is *significant* to know that these relations hold also on a *different*

set of data than that employed to develop them originally. The excellent degree of fit obtained would tend to support the view that these (and the other) formulas not validated here have some degree of universality. Exhibit 6 presents four formulas developed from the DP Services data and the statistics of their validation on the data from the other three sites. Exhibit 7 provides the data from the three sites from which the statistics in Exhibit 6 are derived. The very high values of sample correlation between the estimated and actual SLOC for the 17 validation sites, listed in Exhibit 6 (i.e., >0.92) are most encouraging.

CONCLUSION

The "function point" software estimation procedure appears to have a strong theoretical support based on Halstead's software science formulas. Apparently, some of Halstead's formulas are extremely robust and can be applied to the major inputs and outputs of a software product at the top level. At least for the applications analyzed, both the development work-hours and application size in "SLOC" are strong functions of "function

EXHIBIT 6   Some Validation Statistics

SLOC Estimating Formula (2)	(3) Relative Error		Sample Correlation Between $\hat{S}$ and S
	Avg.	Standard Deviation	
$\hat{S}_1$	−.0753	.5438	.9367
$\hat{S}_2$	.2406	.5174	.9367
$\hat{S}_3$	−.0182	.4151	.9374
$\hat{S}_4$	.0629	.3983	.9289

Notes:
(1) For 'validation sites' 2, 3, 4, see detailed data in Exhibit 7.
(2) $\hat{S}_1 = 73.1F - 4600$ (based on the PL/1 cases)
$\hat{S}_2 = 53.2F + 12773$ (based on all 24 cases)
$\hat{S}_3 = 66F$ (a simplified model)
$\hat{S}_4 = 6.3F\log F + 4500$ (based on the PL/1 cases)
derived from the DPS data

(3) $\dfrac{\hat{S}-S}{S}$, where S = actual SLOC and $\hat{S}$ = estimated SLOC

points" and "input/output data item count." Further, it appears that basing applications development effort estimates on the amount of function to be provided by an application rather than an estimate of "SLOC" may be superior.

The observations suggest a two-step estimate validation process, which uses "function points" or "I/O count" to estimate, early in the development cycle, the "SLOC" to be produced. The work-effort would then be estimated from the estimated "SLOC." This approach can provide an early bridge between "function points," "software science" and "SLOC," until "function points" and "software science" have a broader supporting base of productivity data.

APPENDIX

A. Function Points Definitions

This section provides the basic definitions supporting the measurement, recording, and analysis of function points, work-effort, and attributes.

B. General

The following considerations are generally applicable to the specific definitions of function points, work-effort, and attributes in later paragraphs in this section.

1. Development Work-Product versus Support Work-Product:

Development productivity should be measured by counting the function points added or changed by the development or enhancement project. Therefore, we have the following.

Development Work-Product: The absolute value sum of all function points added or changed by the development or enhancement project. (Deleted function points are considered to be changed function points.)

Support productivity should be measured by counting the total function points supported by the support project during the support period. Therefore, we have the following.

Support Work-Product: The original function points of the application, adjusted for any changes

EXHIBIT 7   Validation of Some SLOC Estimating Equations

Application Number		Function Points F	PL/1 SLOC S	$\hat{S}_1$ KSLOC	$\hat{S}_2$ KSLOC	$\hat{S}_3$ KSLOC	$\hat{S}_4$ KSLOC
1. DPS -	4	759	54K	50.9	53.2	50.1	50.2
2.	14	682	42K	45.2	49.1	45.0	44.9
3.	17	606	40K	39.7	45.0	40.0	39.8
4.	20	1,572	110K	110.3	96.4	103.8	109.7
5. Site	2-1	803	31.0K	54.1	55.5	53.0	53.3
6.	2	335	31.4K	19.9	30.6	22.1	22.2
7.	3	685	23.3K	45.5	49.2	45.2	45.2
8.	4	1,119	126.6K	77.2	72.3	73.9	75.9
9.	5	712	40.9K	47.4	50.7	47.0	47.0
10.	6	261	19.9K	14.5	26.7	17.2	17.7
11. Site	3-1	1,387	120K	96.8	86.6	91.5	95.7
12.	2	1,728	120K	121.7	104.7	114.0	121.6
13.	3	2,878	150K	205.8	165.9	190.0	212.8
14. Site	4-1	2,165	123.2K	153.7	128.0	142.9	155.6
15.	2	236	16.3K	12.7	25.3	15.6	16.2
16.	3	3,694	195.0K	265.4	209.3	243.8	280.3
17.	4	224	41.0K	11.8	24.7	14.8	15.5
18.	5	42	6.5K	−1.5	15.0	2.8	5.9
19.	6	1,629	102.0K	114.5	99.4	107.5	114.0
20.	7	105	9.8K	3.1	18.4	6.9	8.9
21.	8	581	45.9K	37.9	43.7	38.3	38.1
Average Relative Error				−.060	.186	−.024	.051
Std. Deviation of Relative Error				.488	.480	.372	.358
Correlation With S				.938	.938	.938	.997

in complexity introduced, plus any function points added, minus any function points deleted by subsequent enhancement projects.

2. Measurement Timing:

To provide the work-product, work-effort, and attributes measures needed for each development project, enhancement project, and support project to be measured, the indicated measures should be determined at the following times in the application life cycle.

• The development work-product and attributes measures should be determined at the completion of the *external design phase* for each development and enhancement project (when the user external view of the application has been documented).

• The development work-product, work-effort, and attributes measures should be determined at the completion of the *installation phase* for each development and enhancement project (when the application is ready for use).

- The support work-product, work-effort, and attributes measures should be determined at the end of *each year* of support and use for each support project.

3. Application Boundaries:

Normally, as shown in Exhibit 5, a single continuous external boundary is considered when counting function points. However, there are two general situations where counting function points for an application in parts, is necessary.

a. The application is planned to be developed in multiple stages, using more than one development project.

This situation should be counted, estimated, and measured as *separate projects,* including all inputs, outputs, interfaces, and inquiries crossing *all* boundaries.

b. The application is planned to be developed as a single application using one development project, but it is so large that it will be necessary to divide it into subapplications for counting function points.

The internal boundaries are arbitrary and are for counting purposes only. The subapplications should be counted separately, but *none* of the inputs, outputs, interfaces, and inquiries crossing the *arbitrary internal* boundaries should be counted. The function points of the subapplications should then be summed to give the total function points of the application for estimation and measurement.

4. Brought-In Application Code:

Count the function points provided by brought-in application code (reused code), such as: an IBM, IUP, PP, or FDP; an internal shared application; or a purchased application if that code was selected, modified, integrated, tested, or installed by the project team. However, do *not* count the function points provided by the brought-in code that provided user function beyond that stated in the approved requirements.

Some examples are the following.

a. Do count the function points provided by an application picked up from another IBM site, or project, and installed by the project team.

b. Do *not* count the function points provided by software, such as IMS or a screen compiler, if that software had been made available by another project team.

c. Do *not* count ADF updates of *all* files if the user only required updates of *three* files, even though the capability may be automatically provided.

5. Consider All Users:

Consider *all* users of the application, since each application may have provision for many specified user functions, such as:

- end user functions (enter data, inquire, etc.)
- conversion and installation user functions (file scan, file compare discrepancy list, etc.)
- operations user functions (recovery, control totals, etc.).

C. Function Points Measure

After the general considerations described in the preceding paragraphs have been decided, the function points measure is accomplished in three general steps:

a. classify and count the five user function types;

b. adjust for processing complexity;

c. make the function points calculation.

The paragraphs in this section define and describe each of these steps. The first step is accomplished as follows.

Classify, to three levels of complexity, the following user functions that were made available to the user through the design, development, testing, or support efforts of the development, enhancement, or support project team:

a. external input types;

b. external output types;

c. logical internal file types;

d. external interface file types;

e. external inquiry types.

Then *list* and *count* these user functions. The counts should be recorded for use in the function points calculation, on an appropriate work-sheet.

The definitions of each of the user functions to be counted, and the levels of complexity, are provided in the following paragraphs.

1. External Input Type:

Count each unique user *data* or user *control* input type that enters the external boundary of the application being measured, and *adds* or *changes* data in a logical internal file type. An external input type should be considered unique if it has a different *format,* or if the external design requires a *processing logic* different from other external input types of the same format. As illustrated in Exhibit 5, include external input types that enter directly as transactions from the user, and those that enter as transactions from other applications, such as, input files of transactions.

Each external input type should be classified within three levels of complexity, as follows.

- *Simple:* Few data element types are included in the external input type, and few logical internal file types are referenced by the external input type. User human factors considerations are not significant in the design of the external input type.
- *Average:* The external input type is not clearly either simple or complex.
- *Complex:* Many data element types are included in the external input type, and many logical internal file types are referenced by the external input type. User human factors considerations significantly affect the design of the external input type.

Do *not* include external input types that are introduced into the application only because of the technology used.

Do *not* include input files of records as external input types, because these are counted as external interface file types.

Do *not* include the input part of the external inquiry types as external input types, because these are counted as external inquiry types.

2. External Output Type:

Count each unique user *data* or *control* output type that leaves the external boundary of the application being measured. An external output type should be considered unique if it has a different *format,* or if the external design requires a *processing logic* different from other external output types of the same format. As illustrated in Exhibit 5, include external output types that leave directly as reports and messages to the user, and those that leave as reports and messages to other applications, such as, output files of reports and messages.

Each external output type should be classified within three levels of complexity, using definitions similar to those for the external input types. For reports, the following additional complexity definitions should be used.

- *Simple:* One or two columns. Simple data element transformations.
- *Average:* Multiple columns with subtotals. Multiple data element transformations.
- *Complex:* Intricate data element transformations. Multiple and complex file references to be correlated. Significant performance considerations.

Do *not* include external output types that are introduced into the application only because of the technology used.

Do *not* include output files of records as external output types, because these are counted as external interface file types.

Do *not* include the output response of external inquiry types as external output types, because these are counted as external inquiry types.

3. Logical Internal File Type:

Count each major logical group of user *data* or *control* information in the application as a logical internal file type. Include each logical file, or within a data base, each logical group of data from the viewpoint of the user, that is *generated, used,* and *maintained* by the application. Count logical files as described in the external design, not physical files.

The logical internal file types should be classified within three levels of complexity as follows.

- *Simple:* Few record types. Few data element types. No significant performance or recovery considerations.

- *Average:* The logical internal file type is not clearly either simple or complex.
- *Complex:* Many record types. Many data element types. Performance and recovery are significant considerations.

Do *not* include logical internal files that are *not* accessible to the user through external input, output, interface file, or inquiry types.

4. External Interface File Type:

Files *passed* or *shared* between applications should be counted as external interface file types within *each* application. Count each major logical group of user *data* or *control* information that enters or leaves the application, as an external interface file type. External interface file types should be classified within three levels of complexity, using definitions similar to those for logical internal file types.

Outgoing external interface file types should also be counted as logical internal file types for the application.

5. External Inquiry Type:

Count each unique input/output combination, where an input causes and generates an immediate output, as an external inquiry type. An external inquiry type should be considered unique if it has a *format* different from other external inquiry types in either its input or output parts, or if the external design requires a *processing logic* different from other external inquiry types of the same format. As illustrated in Exhibit 5, include external inquiry types that enter directly from the user, and those that enter from other applications.

The external inquiry types should be classified within three levels of complexity as follows.

a. Classify the input part of the external inquiry using definitions similar to the external input type.

b. Classify the output part of the external inquiry type using definitions similar to the external output type.

3. The complexity of the external inquiry type is the greater of the two classifications.

To help distinguish external inquiry types from external input types, consider that the input data of an external inquiry type is entered only to direct the search, and no update of logical internal file types should occur.

Do *not* confuse a query facility as an external inquiry type. An external inquiry type is a direct search for specific data, usually using only a single key. A query facility provides an organized structure of external input, output, and inquiry types to compose many possible inquiries using many keys and operations. These external input, output, and inquiry types should *all* be counted to measure a query facility.

6. Processing Complexity:

The previous paragraphs define the external input, external output, internal file, external interface file, and external inquiry types to be listed, classified, and counted. The function points calculation describes how to use these counts to measure the standard processing associated with those user functions. This paragraph describes how to apply some general application characteristics to adjust the standard processing measure for processing complexity.

The adjustment for processing complexity should be accomplished in three steps, as follows.

a. The *degree of influence* of each of the 14 general characteristics, on the value of the application to the users, should be estimated.

b. The 14 degree of influence(s) should be summed, and the total should be used to develop an *adjustment factor* ranging from 0.65 to 1.35 (this gives an adjustment of +/− 35 percent).

c. The *standard processing measure* should be multiplied by the adjustment factor to develop the work-product measure called function points.

The first step is accomplished as follows.

Estimate the degree of influence, on the application, of each of the 14 general characteristics that follow. Use the degree of influence measures in the following list, and record the estimates on a work-sheet similar to Exhibit 8.

EXHIBIT 8 Function Points Calculation Worksheet

CI/S & A Guideline - Draft -

4.1 FUNCTION POINTS CALCULATION

Application: _____. Appl ID: _____.

Prepared by: _____ __/__/__. Reviewed by: _____ __/__/__.

Notes:

o Function Count:

Type ID	Description	Complexity			Total
		Simple	*Average*	*Complex*	
IT	External Input	__× 3 = __	__× 4 = __	__× 6 = __	_____
OT	External Output	__× 4 = __	__× 5 = __	__× 7 = __	_____
FT	Logical Internal File	__× 7 = __	__× 10 = __	__× 15 = __	_____
EI	Ext Interface File	__× 5 = __	__× 7 = __	__× 10 = __	_____
QT	External Inquiry	__× 3 = __	__× 4 = __	__× 6 = __	_____
FC			Total Unadjusted Function Points		_____

o Processing Complexity:

ID	Characteristic	DI	ID	Characteristic	DI
C1	Data Communications	_____	C8	Online Update	_____
C2	Distributed Functions	_____	C9	Complex Processing	_____
C3	Performance	_____	C10	Reuseability	_____
C4	Heavily Used Configuration	_____	C11	Installation Ease	_____
C5	Transaction Rate	_____	C12	Operational Ease	_____
C6	Online Data Entry	_____	C13	Multiple Sites	_____
C7	End User Efficiency	_____	C14	Facilitate Change	_____
PC			Total Degree of Influence		_____

o DI Values:

- Not present, or no influence	= 0		- Average influence	= 3
- Insignificant influence	= 1		- Significant influence	= 4
- Moderate influence	= 2		- Strong influence, throughout	= 5

PCA	Processing Complexity Adjustment	$= 0.65 + (0.01 \times PC)$	= _____.
FP	Function Points Measure	$= FC \times PCA$	= _____.

Degree of Influence Measures:

- Not present, or no influence if present   = 0
- Insignificant influence   = 1
- Moderate influence   = 2
- Average influence   = 3
- Significant influence   = 4
- Strong influence, throughout   = 5.

General Application Characteristics:

a. The *data* and control information used in the application are sent or received over *communication* facilities. Terminals connected locally to the control unit are considered to use communication facilities.

b. Distributed data or processing *functions* are a characteristic of the application.

c. Application *performance* objectives, in either response or throughput, influenced the design, development, installation, and support of the application.

d. A *heavily used* operational *configuration* is a characteristic of the application. The user wants to run the application on existing or committed equipment that will be heavily used.

e. The *transaction rate* is high and it influenced the design, development, installation, and support of the application.

f. On-line data entry and control functions are provided in the application.

g. The on-line functions provided, emphasize *end user efficiency.*

h. The application provides *on-line update* for the logical internal files.

i. Complex processing is a characteristic of the application. Examples are:

- many control interactions and decision points
- extensive logical and mathematical equations
- much exception processing resulting in incomplete transactions that must be processed again.

j. The application, and the code in the application, has been specifically designed, developed, and supported for *reusability* in other applications, and at other sites.

k. Conversion and *installation ease* are characteristics of the application. A conversion and installation plan was provided, and it was tested during the system test phase.

l. Operational ease is a characteristic of the application. Effective start-up, back-up, and recovery procedures were provided, and they were tested during the system test phase. The application minimizes the need for manual activities, such as, tape mounts, paper handling, and direct on-location manual intervention.

m. The application has been specifically designed, developed, and supported to be installed at *multiple sites* for multiple organizations.

n. The application has been specifically designed, developed, and supported to *facilitate change.* Examples are:

- flexible query capability is provided
- business information subject to change is grouped in tables maintainable by the user.

7. Function Points Calculation:

The previous paragraphs described how the function types are listed, classified, and counted; and how the processing complexity adjustment is determined. This paragraph describes how to make the calculations that develop the function points measures.

Using the definitions in paragraph C1, two equations have been developed to more specifically define the *development work-product* measure and the *support work-product* measure:

$$Development\ Work\text{-}Product\ FP\ Measure =$$
$$(Add + ChgA)$$
$$PCA2 + (Del)\ PCA1 = \underline{\quad}.$$
$$Support\ Work\text{-}Product\ FP\ Measure = Orig\ FP +$$
$$(Add + ChgA)\ PCA2 - (Del + ChgB)$$
$$PCA1 = \underline{\quad}.$$

Orig FP = adjusted FP of the application, evaluated as they were before the project started.

Add = unadjusted FP added to the application, evaluated as they are expected to be at the completion of the project.

ChgA = unadjusted FP changed in the
application, evaluated as they are
expected to be at the completion of
the project.

Del = unadjusted FP deleted from the
application, evaluated as they were
before the project started.

ChgB = unadjusted FP changed in the
application, evaluated as they were
before the project started.

PCA1 = the processing complexity adjustment
pertaining to the application before
the project started.

PCA2 = the processing complexity adjustment
pertaining to the application after
the project completion.

References

1. A. J. Albrecht, "Measuring application development productivity," in *Proc. IBM Applications Develop. Symp.,* Monterey, CA, Oct. 14–17, 1979; GUIDE Int. and SHARE, Inc., IBM Corp., p. 83.

2. M. H. Halstead, *Elements of Software Science.* New York: Elsevier, 1977.

3. J. E. Gaffney, "Software metrics: A key to improved software development management," presented at the Conf. Comput. Sci. Statist., 13th Symp. on Interface, Pittsburgh, PA, Mar. 1981; also Proceedings, Springer-Verlag, 1981.

4. K. Christensen, G. P. Fitsos, and C. P. Smith, "A perspective on software science," *IBM Syst. J.,* vol. 20, no. 4, pp. 372–387, 1981.

5. J.L.F. Dekerf, "APL and Halstead's theory of software metrics," in *APL81 Conf. Proc. ACM* (APL Quote Quad), vol. 12, Sept. 1981, pp. 89–93.

6. A. O. Allen, "Probability, statistics, and queueing theory—With computer science applications," in *Computer Science and Applied Mathematics Series.* New York: Academic, 1978.

7. J. E. Gaffney, "A comparison of a complexity—Based and Halstead program size estimates," presented at the 1979 ACM Comput. Sci. Conf., Dayton, OH, Feb. 1979.

8. D. F. Stanat and D. F. McAllister, *Discrete Mathematics in Computer Science.* Englewood Cliffs, NJ: Prentice-Hall, 1977, p. 265.

9. N. Pippenger, "Complexity theory," *Scientific Amer.,* p. 120, June 1978.

FUNCTION POINT ANALYSIS:
DIFFICULTIES AND IMPROVEMENTS

INTRODUCTION

The size of the task of designing and developing a business computerized information system is determined by the product of three factors (see Exhibit 1).

Article by Charles R. Symons © 1988. IEEE. Reprinted, with permission, from (*IEEE Transactions of Software Engineering;* 14, 1, 2–11; January/1988).

- The *information processing size,* that is some measure of the information processed and provided by the system.
- A *technical complexity factor,* that is a factor which takes into account the size of the various technical and other factors involved in developing and implementing the information processing requirements.

EXHIBIT 1 The Three Components of System Size

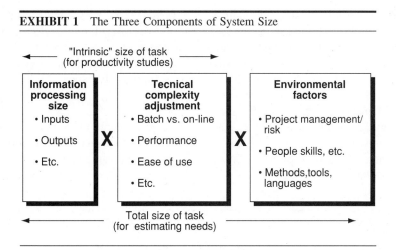

• *Environmental factors,* that is the group of factors arising from the project environment (typically assessed in project risk measures), from the skills, experience and motivation of the staff involved, and from the methods, languages, and tools used by the project team.

The first two of these factors are intrinsic to the size of the system in the sense that they result directly from the requirements for the system to be delivered to the user.

Allan Albrecht has described a method known as "Function Point Analysis" for determining the relative size of a system based on these first two factors [1]–[4]. The method has gained widespread acceptance in the business information systems community, for system size assessment as a component of productivity measurement, when system development or maintenance and enhancement activities are completed. Where historic productivity data are available, the method can also be used as an aid in estimating man-hours, from the point where a functional requirements specification is reasonably complete. For estimating purposes, the third group of environmental factors clearly also has to be taken into account.

The aims of this paper are:

• to critically review function point analysis,

• to propose some ways of overcoming the weaknesses identified,

• to present some initial results of measurements designed to test the validity of the proposed improvements.

While the paper contains some criticisms of Albrecht's Function Point method, the author wishes to acknowledge the substantial contribution made by Albrecht in this difficult area. The ideas in this paper are an evolutionary step, only made possible by Albrecht's original lateral thinking.

However, as Albrecht's method becomes ever more widely adopted, it will become a de facto industry standard. Before that happens it is important to examine the method for any weaknesses, and if possible to overcome them.

ALBRECHT'S FUNCTION POINT METHOD

In Albrecht's Function Point Method, the two components of the intrinsic size of a system are computed as summarized in the following:

1. The Information Processing Size is determined by first identifying the system components as seen by the end-user, and classifying them as five types, namely the external (or "logical") inputs, outputs, inquiries, the external interfaces to other systems, and the logical internal files. The components are each further classified as "simple," "average," or "complex," depending on the number of data elements in each type, and other factors. Each component is then given a number of points depending on its type and complexity [see Exhibit 2(a)] and the sum for all components is expressed in "Unadjusted Function Points" (or UFP's).

2. The Technical Complexity Factor is determined by estimating the "degree of influence" of some 14 component "General Application Characteristics" [see Exhibit 2(b)]. The degree of influence scale ranges from zero (not present, or no influence) up to five (strong influence throughout). The sum of the scores of the 14 characteristics, that is the total degrees of influence (DI), is converted to the "Technical Complexity Factor" (TCF) using the formula

$$TCF = 0.65 + 0.01 \times DI.$$

Thus each degree of influence is worth 1 percent of a TCF which can range from 0.65 to 1.35.

3. The intrinsic relative system size in Function Points (FP's) is computed from

---

EXHIBIT 2   (a) Unadjusted FP counting. (b) Technical Complexity Factor.

Description	Level of Information Processing Function			Total
	Simple	*Average*	*Complex*	
External Input	____ × 3 =____	____ × 4 =____	____ × 6 =____	____
External Output	____ × 4 =____	____ × 5 =____	____ × 7 =____	____
Logical Internal File	____ × 7 =____	____ × 10 =____	____ × 15 =____	____
Ext. Interface File	____ × 5 =____	____ × 7 =____	____ × 10 =____	____
External Inquiry	____ × 3 =____	____ × 4 =____	____ × 6 =____	____
			Total Unadjusted Function Points	____

(a)

ID	Characteristic	DI	ID	Characteristic	DI
C1	Data Communications	____	C8	On-line Update	____
C2	Distributed Functions	____	C9	Complex Processing	____
C3	Performance	____	C10	Re-Useability	____
C4	Heavily Used Configuration	____	C11	Installation Ease	____
C5	Transaction Rate	____	C12	Operational Ease	____
C6	On-Line Data Entry	____	C13	Multiple Sites	____
C7	End User Efficiency	____	C14	Facilitate Change	____
				Total Degree of Influence	____

TCF = 0.65 + 0.01 × (Total 'Degree of Influence')
DI Values
Not Present, or No Influence = 0
Insignificant Influence = 1
Moderate Influence = 2
Average Influence = 3
Significant Influence = 4
Strong influence, Throughout = 5

(b)

$$FP's = UFP's \times TCF.$$

Function Points are therefore dimensionless numbers on an arbitrary scale.

Albrecht's reasons for proposing Function Points as a measure of system size are stated (4) as:

- the measure isolates the intrinsic size of the system from the environmental factors, facilitating the study of factors that influence productivity,
- the measure is based on the user's external view of the system, and is technology-independent,
- the measure can be determined early in the development cycle, which enables Function Points to be used in the estimation process, and
- Function Points can be understood and evaluated by nontechnical users.

Another implied aim [2] is for a method which has an acceptably low measurement overhead.

FP ANALYSIS—A CRITICAL REVIEW

The following questions and difficulties have arisen in teaching and applying Albrecht's method.

Information Processing Size (Unadjusted FP's)

- Classification of all system component types (input, outputs, etc.) as simple, average, or complex, has the merit of being straightforward, but seems to be rather oversimplified. A system component containing, say, over 100 data elements is given at most twice the points of a component with one data element.
- The choice of "weights" [i.e., points per component type, see Exhibit 2(a)] has been justified by Albrecht as reflecting "the relative value of the function to the user/customer" [3] and "was determined by debate and trial." It seems a reasonable question to ask if the weights obtained by Albrecht from his users in IBM will be valid in all circumstances, and useful for size measurement in both productivity assessment and estimating. Some more objective assessment of the weights seems advisable. The weights also give rise to some surprising effects. Why for

example should an inquiry provided via a batch input/output combination gain more than twice as many points as the same inquiry provided on-line? Why should interfaces be of any more value to the user than any other input or output?

- Most of the UFP's for a system arise from its externally seen inputs, outputs, interfaces, and inquiries. Differences in *internal* processing complexity between systems are reflected in two ways. First, the classification of any input, output, inquiry, or interface as simple, average or complex depends in part on the number of logical file-types referenced from that component. As we shall see below, the latter is roughly related to internal processing complexity. (More recently guidelines have appeared [5] suggesting that "entities" should be counted rather than logical files.) Second, internal complexity appears as one of the 14 "General Application Characteristics," and can thus contribute up to 5 percent to the Technical Complexity Factor. All in all, the way internal complexity is taken into account seems to be rather inadequate and confused. Systems of high internal complexity studied by the author do not appear to have had their size adequately reflected by the FP method in the opinion of the designers of those systems.
- Finally, Function Points do not appear to be "summable" in the way one would expect. For example, if three systems, discrete but linked by interfaces, are replaced by a single integrated system providing the same transactions against an integrated database, then the latter system will score less FP's than the three discrete systems. (Arguably the integrated system should score more FP's because it maintains data currency better.) This result arises partly because the FP counting rules credit an interface to both the issuing and receiving system, and partly because the integrated file will generally score less than the three discrete files.

One of Albrecht's findings from studies of productivity has been a falloff in productivity by a factor of roughly 3, as system size increases from

400 to 2000 FP's [3]. This is a very important result if true, but the finding depends on the accuracy with which FP's reflect relative system size. Most of the above criticisms of the FP method point toward the conclusion that the FP scale underweighs systems which are complex internally and have large numbers of data elements per component, relative to simpler and therefore "smaller" systems. If the criticisms are valid and significant, then the falloff in productivity with system size may not be as serious as apparently observed. Clearly it is an important issue to resolve.

The Technical Complexity Factor

- The restriction to 14 factors seems unlikely to be satisfactory for all time. Other factors may be suggested now, and others will surely arise in the future. A more open-ended approach seems desirable. Also some of the factors, as currently defined, appear to overlap (e.g., those concerned with application performance, a heavily used hardware configuration for processing, and a high transaction rate); some reshuffling of the factors appears desirable.
- The weights ("degree of influence") of each of the 14 factors are restricted to the 0–5 range, which is simple, but unlikely to be always valid. One obvious example is the factor which reflects whether the system is intended for multisite implementation. In practice, initial development of such a system can easily cost a great deal more than it would if intended only for a single site. A re-examination of the TCF weights is therefore also desirable.

In summary the Albrecht FP method and especially the weights, were developed in a particular environment. With the benefit of experience and hindsight various questions arise about the validity of the method for general application, especially for the information processing size component. The GUIDE Project Team [5] has made steady progress in clarifying the detailed rules for FP counting to make them easier to apply, but has not questioned the underlying principles or weights. In the next section we will return to basic principles to develop an alternative approach for the information processing size component, then we will examine the calibration of the new UFP measure against practical data, and re-examine the calibration of Albrecht's Technical Complexity Factor. The resulting alternative approach will be referred to as the "Mark II" Function Point method, to distinguish it from Albrecht's method.

A NEW MEASURE OF INFORMATION PROCESSING SIZE ("MARK II" FUNCTION POINTS)

Given that we want a measure of Information Processing Size which is independent of technology (if that is possible) and is in terms which the system user will easily recognize, we will start with certain basic assumptions, namely:

- we will regard a system as consisting of logical "transaction-types," that is, of logical input/process/output combinations.
- Interfaces at this logical level will be treated as any other input or output. (If an input or output happens to go to or come from another application, and that fact increases the size of the task, then it should be reflected in the Technical Complexity Factor.)
- Inquiries will be considered just as any other input/process/output combination.
- The concept of a "logical file" is almost impossible to define unambiguously, particularly in a database environment, and at this level, the concept of "file" is not appropriate. The concept which correctly belongs at the logical transaction level is the "entity," that is anything (object, real, or abstract) in the real world *about which* the system provides information.

The other basic starting point is to establish the criterion which we will use to establish the size scale. As our aim is to obtain sizes which can be used for productivity measurement and estimating purposes, we will take the system size scale to be related explicitly to the *effort* to analyze, design, and develop the functions of the system. This is in contrast to Albrecht's aim of having a size which represents the "*value*" of function delivered to the user. The latter seems to be a more subjective criterion, and therefore less easy to verify or calibrate in practice.

The task then is to find properties of the input, process, and output components of each logical transaction-type which are easily identifiable at the stage of external design of the systems, are intelligible to the user, and can be calibrated so that the weights for each of the components are based on practical experience.

The most difficult component for which we need a size parameter is the process component. For this we rely on the work of McCabe [6] and others who have developed measures of software process complexity and shown for example that their measures correlate well with the frequency of errors found in the software. Such complexity measures are typically concerned with structural complexity, that is, they count and weight branches and loops. Sequential code between the branches and within loops does not add to complexity in this view. At the external design stage we do not know the processing structure of each logical transaction-type, and in any case this would be too complicated to assess and keep within the aims of method.

We do know however, from Jackson [7], that a well-structured function should match the logical data structure, which at this level is represented by the access path for the transaction through the system entity model. Since each step along the access-path through the entity model generally involves a selection or branch, or (if a one-to-many step) a loop, it seems a reasonable hypothesis that a measure of processing complexity is to count *the number of entity-types referenced by the transaction-type.* ("Referenced" means created, updated, read, or deleted.)

The above is a rather tenuous argument, and the result is a crude, first-order measure. Exhibit 3 shows an entity model for a simple order-processing system with a few logical transactions, and the num-

ber of entities referenced per transaction. Examples like this, and the experience of counting entity references per transaction in real systems, support this measure as a plausible hypothesis.

For the other (input and output) components of each logical transaction-type, we will take the number of data element types as being the measure of the size of the component. This is on the grounds that the effort to format and validate an input, and to format an output is in the first-order proportional to the number of data elements in each of those components, respectively. Exhibit 3 also shows illustrative numbers of input and output data element types for the order-processing transactions.

The net result of the above is that the Mark II formula for Information Processing Size expressed in Unadjusted Function Points becomes:

$$UFP's = N_I\, W_I + N_E\, W_E + N_O\, W_O$$

where

N_I = *number of input data element types,*

W_I = *weight of an input data element type,*

N_E = *number of entity-type references,*

W_E = *weight of an entity-type reference,*

N_O = *number of output data element types,*

W_O = *weight of an output data element type,*

and N_I , N_E , and N_O are each summed over all transaction-types.

(From now on whenever we refer to transactions, inputs, outputs, data elements, and entities, etc., it will be understood that we are referring to "types" unless it is necessary to distinguish between "types" and "occurrences.")

The next task is to attempt to determine the weights by calibrating this formula against practical data.

CALIBRATION OF MARK II FUNCTION POINTS

A first test and rough calibration of the Mark II Function Point method has been carried out using data collected from two Clients ("A" and "B") in

EXHIBIT 3 Example Analysis of an Order Processing System for Mark II Unadjusted Function Points (a) Entity Model. (b) Logical Transaction Analysis

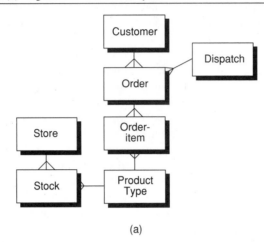

(a)

Transaction-Type	Input Data Elements	Entities Referenced		Output Data Elements
		Types	(Total)	
Add new customer	53	Customer	1	3
Check stock availability	20	Product-type store, stock	3	10
Process order-header	2	Customer order, dispatch	3	40
Process order-item	6	Order, dispatch, order-item product-type, store, stock	6	14
Cancel order-item	2	Customer, order, order-item product-type	4	15
Stock report by store & product	1	Store, product-type stock	3	21
Total	**84**		**20**	**103**

(b)

consultancy studies. In each case the objective of the study was to explore the use of function point analysis for productivity measurement, and in particular the merits of the Mark II versus the Albrecht method.

Both Clients selected six systems for assessment, which were of varying size and technology. No constraint was placed on system selection, other than that the system should be of a size requiring at least 3–4 months to develop, and that an expert should be available to explain the system.

Collection of data for each system and its analysis fell into three categories, namely

- Unadjusted Function Point data
- Technical Complexity Factor data
- development effort-data to calibrate the Mark II method.

Since the last of these three categories has parts in common with each of the first two, it will be described first.

Analysis of Development Effort Data

Of the 12 systems, 9 had been developed recently, and adequate data were available about the development effort for further analysis.

For calibration purposes, the project representatives were asked to analyze the man-hours which had been used for development, and break them down as shown in Exhibit 4. ("Development man-hours" were defined strictly according to Albrecht's rules.)

The first split required for each system is between the man-hours which had been devoted to the pure Information Processing Size, that is the effort devoted to analysis, design, and development purely to meet user requirements, and the man-hours needed for the work on the various parts of the Technical Complexity Factor. The effort devoted to the Information Processing Size was further broken down into the effort required to handle input, processing, and output, defined as follows.

Input	Data entry, validation, error correction.
Processing	Performing the updates and calculations from availability of valid input until output data are ready for formatting.
Output	Formatting and transmission of output to the output device.

This required breakdown of development man-hours is unusual. No records were available, and therefore the breakdowns given are subjective. The project representatives did not demur from the task however; percentage breakdown splits between input, process, and output varied considerably, examples given including 35 / 10 / 55, 25 / 65 / 10, 40 / 40 / 20, etc. The validity of this approach can only lie in its statistical basis. Data from the nine systems analyzed so far appear to behave reasonably, as will be seen below. As data from more systems are collected so the quality and credibility of the derived weights will improve.

The man-hours apportioned to the Technical Complexity Factor were similarly further broken down by spreading them across the 14 Albrecht factors, and other factors proposed by the author (see below). This "top-down" split had the possibility of some "bottom-up" cross-checking by the project representatives, although still subjectively, as again no records were available. For example it might result from a first breakdown that two man-days were apportioned to a particular TCF factor. At this bottom level, project representatives could often recall how much effort really went into this particular factor. So with some iteration the size of the TCF component of development

---

EXHIBIT 4   The Analysis of Project Development Time

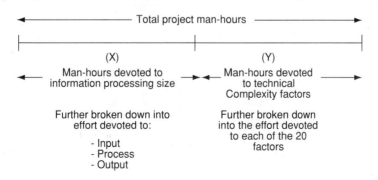

man-hours and its breakdown over the various factors was refined.

It should be emphasized that apart from prompting by the author on the required way of analysis, the development effort breakdown estimates are entirely those of the project representatives, working independently of each other, and without knowledge of the analysis which was to follow.

Collection and Analysis of UFP Data for Albrecht and Mark II Methods

All 12 systems were assessed according to the Albrecht and Mark II methods. First, for the Mark II method, an entity model of the system was derived, and at this point the "logical internal files" for Albrecht's method were identified and scored. Then each system was broken down into its logical transactions. The components of each transaction were classified for complexity and scored according to Albrecht's rules, and in parallel the counts of input and output data elements and entity references were collected for the Mark II method.

Early in the course of this work it became apparent that some counting conventions and definitions were needed for the Mark II method to ensure consistency and simplicity, such as have been developed by GUIDE [5] and Albrecht [4] in their "Current Practice" chapters. Space does not permit a full account of these conventions, and they may well evolve further. An outline of the main types of conventions is given in the Appendix.

With the total counts of input and output data elements, and entity references for all transactions in each system, such as illustrated in Exhibit 3, and the man-hours of development effort derived as in the section above, it was possible to calculate the "man-hours per count" data shown for all nine systems in Exhibit 5.

When examining Exhibit 5, one must bear in mind the variety of system types, sizes and technologies, and of environments involved, and the crudity of the estimates of the breakdown of development effort over input, process and output. One should particularly note the sensitivity of some of the component man-hour estimates to a

---

EXHIBIT 5   Estimated Man-Hours Per Count For Nine Development Projects

		Development Man-hours per Count			
Client	*System*	*Input Data Elements*	*Entity Refs*	*Output Data Elements*	*Technology*
A	1	1.30	12.9	1.31	Mainframe, Batch
	2	1.68	3.9	0.81	Mainframe, On-line
	3	1.67	3.0	0.97	Mini, On-line
	4	0.37[1]	8.0	2.17	Mainframe, Batch
B	7	0.52	0.25	0.21[2]	PC with DB Handler
	8	0.72	4.1	0.35	Mainframe, On-line
	9	1.37	5.1	0.35[3]	Mainframe, Mainly Batch
	10	2.4	3.2	0.87	Mainframe, On-line
	11	1.8	7.2	1.45	Fail-Safe Mini, On-line

Notes   1. This system obtained its input from another system. Little effort was required for input formatting and validation
2. This PC based system was unusual in producing very large numbers of documents with comparatively small variations across all document-types
3. This client had implemented special mainframe software to reduce the effort for preparing output

shift of a few percent between one category, e.g., input, and another, e.g., entity references.

In spite of these variations and uncertainties however, there is a clear pattern, and certain of the exceptionally high or low figures are explicable in terms of known project characteristics (the ringed figures in Exhibit 5).

To get a "normative" set of weights for combined Client A and B data, averages were taken of all the nonringed figures in Exhibit 5. These are

1.56 man-hours per input data element
5.9 "   "   " entity reference
1.36 "   "   " output data element.

These figures may be used directly as the weights in the Mark II UFP formula and could also have some value for future estimating purposes.

However, in order that the Mark II method produces UFP's comparable to Albrecht's, the Mark II scale was "pegged" to Albrecht's by scaling down the above weights so that the average

system size in UFP's for all 8 systems under 500 UFP's came out to be identical on both scales.

The Mark II formula for Information Processing Size on the basis of this data therefore becomes

$$UFP's = 0.44N_I + 1.67N_E + 0.38N_O .$$

The UFP sizes for all 12 systems, calculated according to this formula, were then plotted against the corresponding Albrecht UFP's (see Exhibit 6).

Two conclusions may be drawn in interpreting this graph. First, there is a general tendency for the Mark II method to give a larger information processing size relative to Albrecht's, as system size increases. More data are needed to confirm this trend, but the first results are in the direction expected from taking into account internal processing complexity in the Mark II method.

The second conclusion is that the Mark II method shows its sensitivity, especially in smaller systems, to relatively high or low average numbers

EXHIBIT 6   Albrecht Versus Mark II Unadjusted Function Points Comparison.

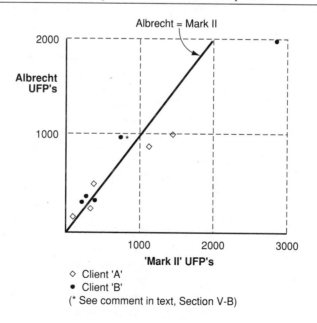

◇ Client 'A'
● Client 'B'
(* See comment in text, Section V-B)

of data elements per input or output component. The asterisked system in Exhibit 6 (system 11 in Exhibit 5) is unusual in having many transactions with exceptionally low counts of data elements per input and output relative to the amount of processing it carries out.

As to the Clients' interpretation of these data, Client A considered that the relative sizes of its systems and the derived productivity data were more plausible on the Mark II scale than on Albrecht's. Client B did not have sufficient feeling for the relative sizes to choose between the two methods. This Client did however prefer the Mark II method of analysis as giving more insight into the size measurement process.

Collection and Analysis of TCF Data According to Albrecht and Mark II Methods

The "Degree of Influence" of the 14 Albrecht Technical Complexity Factor components was scored for each system, using the scoring guidelines described by Albrecht [4] and Zwanzig [5]. A further five factors were proposed by the author, and project representatives were invited to nominate any other factors which they felt ought to be included in this category. The additional five factors are the needs

- to interface with other applications (project representatives suggested this should be broadened to include interfaces to technical software such as message switching),
- for special security features,
- to provide direct access for Third Parties,
- for documentation requirements, and
- for special user training facilities, e.g., the need for a training subsystem.

An additional factor suggested by project representatives was the need to define, select and install special hardware or software uniquely for the application.

Considerable debate took place about the criteria for what can be counted as a TCF component. The rule which evolved is that a TCF component *is a system requirement other than those concerned with information content, intrinsic to and affecting the size of the task, but not arising from the project environment.*

In total therefore 20 factors were scored on Albrecht's "Degree of Influence" scale, and in addition, for the 9 development systems, the actual effort devoted to each of these 20 factors was estimated by the project representatives.

Two analyses were performed to calibrate Albrecht's Degree of Influence scale against estimates of actual effort.

For the first analysis, the actual TCF was computed for each system from the formula

$$TCF \ (actual) = 0.65 \ (1 + Y/X)$$

where (see Exhibit 4)

Y = *man-hours devoted to Technical Complexity Factors*

X = *man-hours devoted to the Information Processing Size as measured by Unadjusted Function Points.*

Exhibit 7 shows the "TCF (actual)" plotted against the TCF derived from Albrecht's Degree of Influence scale for each of the 20 component factors. (Note the latter is not the pure Albrecht TCF, since Albrecht would only take 14 factors into account.)

In spite of the admitted roughness of the estimates going into the "TCF (actual)" figures, a clear pattern emerges from Exhibit 7. First, Albrecht's method of assessing a TCF appears to work, but the weight of each Degree of Influence should vary with the technology. For the systems whose points lie close to the line labeled (2) in Exhibit 7, a weight of 0.005 per Degree of Influence, or possibly less, is more appropriate than Albrecht's 0.01. In other words it seems to have taken less than half the effort to achieve these 20 technical complexity factors in practice than Albrecht's formula suggests. This correlates with the facts known about the systems lying along the line labeled (2). Client B has developed special software to simplify the development of on-line mainframe systems, while two of the other three sys-

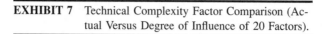

EXHIBIT 7   Technical Complexity Factor Comparison (Actual Versus Degree of Influence of 20 Factors).

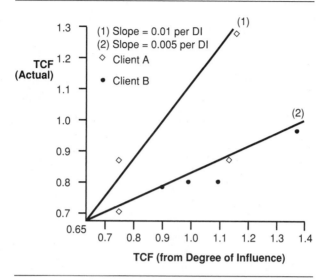

tems along this line are personal computer based, and built with a fourth generation language ("Natural"), respectively. In contrast Albrecht's formula was derived from projects developed with technology available in the late 1970s.

The second more detailed analysis attempted to correlate the Degree of Influence scores of individual TCF components against the estimated actual percentage development effort. Owing to the small number (9) of projects, the 20 components, and the roughness of the estimates, no firm conclusions can be drawn about the relative weights of the individual components. The following are first indications, but much more data will be needed to firm up these indications.

- Some grouping of Albrecht's components seems desirable; the distinctions made between his components 3, 4, and 5 concerned with performance, and 6, 7, and 8 concerned with on-line dialogs, were not completely clear to the project representatives.
- Components 11 (installation ease), 12 (operational ease), 14 (ease of changes) and 16 (secu-

rity) seem to require less effort per Degree of Influence than the other components.
- Component 19 (documentation) requires maybe double the effort per Degree of Influence of the other components.
- Component 9 (complex internal processing) does not strictly fit into the criteria for TCF components as now defined above. If this component is to stay, the guidelines for its scoring need to be more sharply defined.
- Component 13 (multiple-site implementation), as already noted, needs to be much more open-ended in its scoring.

CONCLUSIONS

The experience of applying Albrecht's Function Point Method and the alternative Mark II approach to a variety of systems has led to three groups of conclusions:

1. Albrecht versus Mark II Function Points.
2. Use of function points for productivity measurement and estimating.

3. Limitations of function points.

Albrecht Versus Mark II Function Points

The criticisms of Albrecht's Function Point method were given in the third section of this paper. The aim of the Mark II approach has been to overcome these weaknesses, particularly in the area of reflecting the internal complexity of a system. There will never be any "proof" that the Mark II approach gives superior results to that of Albrecht. Only the plausibility of the underlying assumptions, and judgment of many users on the results provided by both methods over a long period, will support one approach or the other.

As practitioners have gained experience in Albrecht's method in the last few years, it has evolved in the direction of the Mark II approach. First, the count of data elements has been introduced to make the complexity classification of inputs, outputs, etc., more objective. More recently the concept of "entities" has begun to replace "logical files." The remaining essential difference between the two methods is the way of looking at *data*. Albrecht's criterion for attributing UFP's to data is simply that the data is seen to exist in the system, regardless of how much of it is used; the Mark II approach attributes UFP's to data depending on its *usage* (create, update, read, delete) in transactions which form part of the system under study. Referring back to Albrecht's aims for Function Point Analysis, clearly it is the latter which is of "value" to the user. The *potential* value of stored data may be huge for a user, but it is only its actual value, resulting from use by transactions provided in applications, which can be measured by function points.

Other differences or similarities in practice between the two methods which are worthy of note are as follows.

- The Mark II approach requires an understanding of entity analysis, and rules are emerging (see Appendix) for entity counting conventions. For the Albrecht approach a knowledge of entity analysis is advisable, but no entity counting conventions have yet been published.

- The simplicity of the Mark II approach in having fewer variables than Albrecht's method in the UFP component has a number of advantages, such as greater ease of calibration against measurements or estimates, as shown in this paper. Also, if another hypothesis is made in the future for one of the UFP components, e.g., that the "size" of an input is proportional to, say, the number of data elements plus a constant, then it is easy to recalibrate the weights and explore the sensitivity of relative system sizes to the new hypothesis.

- There is a potential in the Mark II method for refining the measurement of the work-output in maintenance and enhancement activities which has not been tested so far. With Albrecht's method it is only possible to measure the total size of the changed system components. No distinction is possible between small and large changes to any single component. With the Mark II method, by recording the numbers of data elements changed, and counting references to entities which have been changed (or whose attributes have been changed), it should be possible to produce a measure of the size of the changes themselves (made to the changed components), that is, a measure more directly related to the work-output of maintenance and enhancement activities.

- The effort of counting data elements for each input and output means that FP measurement following the Mark II method may require 10–20 percent more effort than with Albrecht's method (which typically imposes about a one quarter percent overhead for system size measurement on the man-hours for a development project). Also the latter method may be applicable slightly earlier in the project life-cycle than the Mark II method, although it should be possible to produce reasonably accurate estimates of numbers of data elements per transaction for early sizing purposes.

Use of Function Points for Productivity Measurement and Estimating

An important conclusion illustrated by results from this study is that *function points are not a technology-independent measure of system size,* which was one of Albrecht's stated claims. The technology dependence is implicit in the weights used for the UFP and TCF components. This conclusion applies equally to the Albrecht and Mark II approaches. The conclusion for the TCF component is clearly illustrated in the results shown in Exhibit 7. In Exhibit 8 a hypothetical example is given for the size of error introduced into relative system size measurement by using an inappropriate set of weights, e.g., a set derived for a different technology from that actually being used.

A reasonable summary of the dependence of function points on technology is that the weights used by an organization in function point measurements imply a certain baseline or normative technology for that organization. If a system is built with a different technology, and its size is calculated with the organization's normative function point method, then the size calculated is the size the system would be if it were developed using the normative technology. This is clearly still very useful if the goal is to find out how productivity achieved with a new technology compares with that achieved with the normative technology. However

- if a new technology is introduced then sizes computed by function points cannot be reliably used for *estimating* unless a new set of weights is estimated or calibrated in line with the new technology, and
- if an organization changes its whole (normative) technology and it wants to continue to make fair size and productivity comparisons, then it must calibrate a new set of normative function point weights for the organization; clearly the latter will be necessary only at very infrequent intervals.

EXHIBIT 8   Example of Sensitivity of Function Points to Weights.

Suppose we have two systems, A and B, with the following characteristics

	N_I	N_E	N_O
System A	100	20	100
System B	100	20	20
Weights (conventional technology)	0.5	2	0.4

Then							
Size A	50	+	40	+	40	=	130
Size B	50	+	40	+	8	=	98
			Ratio Sizes A/B			=	1.33

But, if technology changes, such that weights should be

	0.5	2	0.2

Then							
Size A	50	+	40	+	20	=	110
Size B	50	+	40	+	4	=	94
			Ratio Sizes A/B			=	1.17

Conclusion: Use of the wrong set of weights may distort the ratio of sizes

---

Generally for estimating purchases in an organization, a historical pool of information on actual productivity achieved using function point methods would be an invaluable asset. However, variations in environmental factors, especially project risk, the learning difficulties of new technologies and the performance of individuals can be extremely important considerations when estimating.

Limitations of Function Point Analysis

For completeness it is important to understand certain limitations of function point analysis.

- The method is not as easy to apply in practice as it first appears. In particular, working back from an installed physical system providing an interactive dialog to derive the logical transactions, requires some experience. Also cases sometimes arise where it becomes a matter of subjective judgment whether subtypes of a logical transaction (e.g., those which have slightly different processing paths depending on input values) are counted as separate logical transactions, or whether the differences can be ignored. For some time to come therefore it will be best in any one organization if all measurements are supervised by one objective, experienced function point analyst. Such an analyst should accumulate and document cases and derive general rules such as given in the Appendix, which will help ensure consistency and objectivity in function point analysis.
- The suggestion has been made that it should eventually be possible to compute Mark II unadjusted function points automatically from a functional model of a system stored for example in a data dictionary. The difficulty with this is not so much automating the counting but, bearing in mind the previous limitation, ensuring that the model is correct and in a form suitable for FP counting. (However the benefits of this effort may be much wider than just the benefit of being able to count function points!)
- FP analysis works for installed applications, not for tools, or languages, such as a general purpose retrieval language. The distinction between these two classes of systems is not always absolutely clear. Applications provide preprogrammed functions where the user is invited to enter data and receives output data. Tools provide commands with which the user can create his or her own functions. Business information systems are usually applications, but may sometimes incorporate tools, or features with tool-like characteristics as well. Tools have a practically infinite variety of uses. The productivity of a group which supports a series of tools for use by others, for example an Information Center, can only be measured indirectly by sampling the productivity achieved by the end-users who apply the tools.
- A further limitation is that although in general FP analysis works for business applications it may not work for other types of applications, such as scientific or technical. This arises from its limited ability to cope with internal complexity. Again there is no absolute distinction between these different categories but internal complexity in business applications arises mainly from the processes of validation, and from interactions with the stored data. The Mark II method has aimed at reflecting these processes in a simple way. But scientific and technical applications typically have to deal with complex mathematical algorithms; FP analysis as currently defined has no reliable way of coping with such processes.

CONCLUDING REMARKS

The function point method as proposed by Albrecht has certain weaknesses, but it appears they can be overcome by adjustments to the counting method as outlined here in the Mark II approach. These methods still seem to offer one of the best lines of approach for an organization that wishes to study its trends in productivity and improve its estimating methods for the development and support of computerized business information systems.

APPENDIX
SUMMARY OF ENTITY AND DATA
ELEMENT COUNTING RULES

The following is a brief outline of the rules which have evolved, and which will probably evolve further, to simplify entity and data element counting, and to introduce more objectivity into the counting.

Entities

A distinction is made between three types of entities.

First, we count those entities with which the system is primarily concerned. These are typically the subjects of the main files or database of the system.

Second, we distinguish those things which data analysts frequently and rightly consider as entities, but about which the system holds typically only at most an identifying code, or name, and/or a description, and which are stored only to validate input. There are many possible rules to help distinguish such entities; information about them is usually held in files referred to as "system master tables" or "parameter tables." These are not included in our count of entity-references per transaction, on the grounds that their contribution to system size will be taken into account in the count of input data elements (which is considered to account for validation).

Third, entities about which information is produced only on output, for example in summary data reports, are also not counted. Their contribution to system size is considered to be reflected in the count of output data elements per transaction.

Data Elements

Several data element counting conventions are required; examples include:

- Data element *types* are counted, not data element occurrences.
- Conventions are needed for counting of dates (which may be subdivided), address fields (which may be multiline), and the like.
- Batch report jobs, whether initiated by an operator, or automatically at certain points in time, are considered to have always at least a one-data element input.
- Field labels, boxes, underlines, etc., should be ignored.

ACKNOWLEDGMENT

The author acknowledges with gratitude the permission of the two Clients A and B to use their data for this paper. He also wishes to thank Client staff for their patience, support, and enthusiasm in the collection and analysis of the data.

References

1. A. J. Albrecht, "Measuring application development productivity," in *Proc. IBM Applications Development Symp.,* GUIDE Int. and SHARE Inc., IBM Corp., Monterey, CA. Oct. 14–17, 1979, p. 83.

2. ——, "Function points as a measure of productivity," in *Proc. GUIDE 53 Meeting,* Dallas, TX, Nov. 12, 1981.

3. A. J. Albrecht and J. E. Gaffney, "Software function, source lines of code and development effort prediction: A software science validation," *IEEE Trans. Software Eng.,* vol. SE-9, no. 6, pp. 639–647, Nov. 1983.

4. A. J. Albrecht, "AD/M Productivity Measurement and Estimate Validation—Draft," IBM Corp. Information Systems and Administration, AD/M Improvement Program, Purchase, NY, May 1, 1984.

5. K. Zwanzig, Ed., *Handbook for Estimating Using Function Points,* GUIDE Project DP-1234, GUIDE Int., Nov. 1984.

6. T. J. McCabe, "A complexity measure," *IEEE Trans. Software Eng.,* vol. SE-2, no. 4, pp. 308–320, 1976.

7. M. Jackson, *Principles of Program Design.* London: Academic, 1975.

RELIABILITY OF
FUNCTION POINTS MEASUREMENT:
A FIELD EXPERIMENT

Software engineering management encompasses two major functions, planning and control, both of which require the capability to accurately and reliably measure the software being delivered. Planning of software development projects emphasizes estimation of appropriate budgets and schedules. Control of software development requires a means to measure progress on the project and to perform after-the-fact evaluations of the project, for example, to evaluate the effectiveness of the tools and techniques employed on the project to improve productivity.

Unfortunately, as current practice often demonstrates, both of these activities are typically not well performed. Software projects often run from 100 to 200+% over budget, due both to inadequate initial estimates and to managers' inability to accurately monitor the project's progress, owing in part to a lack of objective measures [19, 24]. Accurate measures of the complexity-adjusted size of the deliverables of a software project early in the lifecycle will permit the estimation of the relationships between the deliverables and the cost and time required to produce them. However, any error in the measurement of the deliverables will add to the errors involved in estimating the required resources. Therefore, a critical first step in software management is the use of reliable software size measures.

CURRENT MEASURES FOR SOFTWARE MANAGEMENT

While a large academic literature exists on software measures/metrics, there are essentially only two software size measures that are widely used in practice for software planning and control. These are the number of source lines of code (SLOC) delivered in the final system and the number of Function Points. SLOC, the older of the two measures, has been criticized in both its planning and control applications. In planning, the task of estimating the final SLOC count for a proposed system has been shown to be difficult to do accurately in practice [18]. In control applications, SLOC measures for evaluating productivity have weaknesses as well, in particular, the problem of comparing systems written in different languages [16].

An alternative software size measure was developed by Allan Albrecht of IBM [1, 2]. This measure, which he termed "function points" (hereafter FPs), is designed to size a system in terms of its delivered functionality, measured in terms of such objects as the numbers of inputs, outputs, and files.[1] Albrecht argued that these entities would be much easier to estimate than SLOC early in the software project lifecycle and would be generally more meaningful to nonprogrammers. In addition, for evaluation purposes, they would avoid the difficulties involved in comparing SLOC counts for systems written in different languages.

FPs have proven to be a broadly popular measure with both practitioners and academic researchers. Dreger [14] estimates that some 500 major corporations worldwide are using FPs, and, in a survey by the Quality Assurance Institute, FPs were found to be regarded as the best available MIS productivity measure [20]. They have also been widely used by researchers in such applications as cost estimation [17], software development productivity evaluation (5, 25], software maintenance productivity evaluation [4], software quality evaluation [11], and software project sizing [3].

[1] Readers unfamiliar with FPs are referred to Box A for an overview of FP definitions and calculations.

Box A.

Function Points Calculation

Readers interested in learning how to calculate Function Points are referred to one of the fully documented methods, such as the IFPUG Standard, Release 3.0 [27]. The following is a minimal description only. Calculation of Function Points begins with counting five components of the proposed or implemented system, namely, the number of external inputs (*e.g.,* transaction types), external outputs (*e.g.,* report types), logical internal files (files as the user might conceive of them, not physical files), external interface files (files accessed by the application but not maintained, *i.e.,* updated by it), and external inquiries (types of on-line inquiries supported). Their complexity is classified as being relatively low, average, or high, according to a set of standards that define complexity in terms of objective guidelines. Exhibit 1 is an example of such a guideline, in this case the table used to assess the relative complexity of External Outputs, such as reports.

To use this table in counting the number of FPs in an application, a report would first be classified as an External Output. By determining the number of unique files used to generate the report ("File Type Referenced"), and the number of fields on the report ("Data Element Types"), it can be classified as a relatively low-, average-, or high-complexity External Output. After making such determinations for each of the five component types, the number of each component type present is placed into its assigned cell

next to its weight in the matrix shown in Exhibit 2. Then, the total number of function counts (FCs) is computed as shown in Equation (1).

$$FC = \sum_{i=1}^{5} \sum_{j=1}^{3} W_{ij}X_{ij} \qquad (1)$$

where w_{ij} = weight for row *i*, column *j*, and x_{ij} = value in cell *i, j*.

The second step involves assessing the impact of 14 general system characteristics that are rated on a scale from 0 to 5 in terms of their likely effect for the system being counted. These characteristics are: (1) data communications, (2) distributed functions, (3) performance, (4) heavily used configuration, (5) transaction rate, (6) on-line data entry, (7) end user efficiency, (8) on-line update, (9) complex processing, (10) reusability, (11) installation ease, (12) operational ease, (13) multiple sites, and (14) facilitates change. These values are summed and modified then to compute the Value Adjustment Factor, or VAF:

$$VAF = 0.65 + 0.01 \sum_{i=1}^{14} c_i \qquad (2)$$

where c_i = value for general system characteristic *i*, for $0 < c_i <= 5$.

Finally, the two values are multiplied to create the number of Function Points (FP):

$$FP = FC(VAF). \qquad (3)$$

RESEARCH QUESTIONS IN FP RELIABILITY

Despite their wide use by researchers and their growing acceptance in practice, FPs are not without criticism. The first criticism revolves around the alleged low *interrater reliability* of FP counts, that is, whether two individuals performing an FP

count for the same system would generate the same result. The author of a leading software engineering textbook summarizes his discussion of FPs as follows: "The function-point metric, like LOC, is relatively controversial . . . Opponents claim that the method requires some 'sleight of hand' in that computation is based on subjective, rather than objective, data . . ." [21, p. 94].

EXHIBIT 1   Complexity Assignment for External Outputs [27]

	1–5 Data Element Types	6–19 Data Element Types	20+ Data Element Types
0–1 File Types Referenced	Low	Low	Average
2–3 File Types Referenced	Low	Average	High
4+ File Types Referenced	Average	High	High

EXHIBIT 2   Function Count Weighting Factors

	Low	*Average*	*High*
External Input	___× 3	___× 4	___× 6
External Output	___× 4	___× 5	___× 7
Logical Internal File	___× 7	___× 10	___× 15
External Interface File	___× 5	___× 7	___× 10
External Inquiry	___× 3	___× 4	___× 6

This perception of FPs as being unreliable has undoubtedly slowed their acceptance as a measure, as both practitioners and researchers may feel that in order to ensure sufficient measurement reliability either (a) a single individual would be required to count all systems or (b) multiple raters should be used for all systems and their counts averaged to approximate the "true" value [28]. Both of these options are unattractive in terms of either decreased flexibility or increased cost.

A second, related concern has developed more recently, due in part to FPs' growing popularity. A number of researchers and consultants have developed variations on the original method developed by Albrecht [13, 14, 23, 28] (also, C. Jones, Software Productivity Research, Inc., Feb. 20, 1988, mimeo, version 2). A possible concern with these variants is that counts using these methods may differ from counts using the original method [22, 30]. Jones has compiled a list consisting of 14 named variations and suggests that the values obtained using these variations might differ by as much as plus or minus 50% from the original Albrecht method (Software Productivity Research, Inc., Dec. 9, 1989, mimeo). If true, this lack of *intermethod reliability* poses several practical problems. From a planning perspective, one problem would be that for organizations adopting a method other than the Albrecht standard, the data they collect may not be consistent with those used in the development and calibration of a number of estimation models, (*e.g.,* see [2] and [17]). If the organization's data were not consistent with this previous work, then the estimated parameters of those models would no longer be directly usable by the organization. This would then force the collection of a large, internal dataset before FPs could be used to aid in cost and schedule estimation, which would involve considerable extra delay and expense. A second problem would be that for organizations that had previously adopted the Albrecht standard and desired to switch to another variation, the switch might render previously developed models and heuristics less accurate. From a control perspective, organizations using a variant method would have difficulty in comparing their *ex post* FP productivity rates to those of other organizations. For organizations that switched methods, the new data might be sufficiently inconsistent as to render trend analysis meaningless.

Finally, a related practical concern is the labor-intensive nature of FP counting. The originally developed procedure does not lend itself easily to automated data collection, and therefore another motivation for variant-counting methods is to develop an approach that would be automatable, perhaps through the use of computer-aided software engineering (CASE) tools. However, the question of the reliability of these new methods with the standard method remains. The conclusion of the preceding discussion is that the possibility of significant variations across methods poses a number of practical concerns, and there are currently only limited research results with which to guide practice in this area.

This article addresses the following specific research questions:

1. What is the interrater reliability of the standard FP-counting method?
2. What is the interrater reliability of a newer, alternative counting method?
3. What is the intermethod reliability of these two methods?

The approach taken was a field experiment involving more than 100 different total counts in a dataset with up to 27 actual commercial systems. Multiple raters and two methods were used to generate multiple counts of the systems, whose average size was 450 FPs. Briefly, the results of the study were (1) that the median difference in FP counts from pairs of raters using the standard method was approximately 12% and (2) that the correlation across the two methods was as high as 0.95 for the data in this sample. These results provide project managers with (1) objective measures of the degree of reliability of the measure and (2) evidence that the intermethod reliability is sufficiently high as to allow substitution of methods.

RESEARCH DESIGN AND PREVIOUS RESEARCH

Despite both the widespread use of FPs and the attendant criticism of their suspected lack of reliability, there has been only limited research on either the interrater question or the intermethod question. Perhaps the first attempt at investigating the interrater reliability question was made by members of the IBM GUIDE Productivity Project Group, the results of which are described by Rudolph as follows:

"In a pilot experiment conducted in February 1983 by members of the GUIDE Productivity Project Group ... about 20 individuals judged independently the function point value of a system, using the requirement specifications. Values within the range +/- 30% of the average judgment were observed ... The difference resulted largely from differing interpretation of the requirement specification. This should be the upper limit of the error range of the function point technique. Programs available in source code or with detailed design specification should have an error of less than +/- 10% in their function point assessment. With a detailed description of the system there is not much room for different interpretations" [25, p. 6].

Aside from this description, there has been no documented research until the study by Low and Jeffery [18], the first widely available, well-documented study of this question. Their research addressed only one of the two issues relevant to the current research, interrater reliability of FP counts. Their research methodology was a lab experiment using professional systems developers as subjects, with the unit of analysis being a set of program-level specifications. Two sets of program specifications were used in the experiment, both of which had been pretested with student subjects. For the interrater reliability question, 22 systems development professionals who counted FPs as part of their employment in 7 Australian organizations were used, as were an additional 20 inexperienced raters who were given training in the then-current Albrecht standard. Each of the experienced raters used his or her organization's own variation on the Albrecht standard (personal correspondence, R. Jeffery, Aug. 15, 1990). With respect to the interrater reliability research question Low and Jeffery found that the consistency of FP counts "appears to be within the 30 percent reported by Rudolph" within organizations, i.e., using the same method [18, p. 71].

Design of the Study

Given the Low and Jeffery research, a deliberate decision was made at the beginning of the current research to select an approach that would complement their work by (*a*) addressing the interrater reliability question using a different design and by (*b*) directly focusing on the intermethod reliability questions. The current work is designed to strengthen the understanding of the reliability of FP measurement, building on the base started by Low and Jeffery.

The area of overlap is the question of interrater reliability. Low and Jeffery chose a small group experiment, with each subject's identical task being to count the FPs implied from the two program specifications. Due to this design choice, the researchers were limited to choosing relatively small tasks, with the mean FP size of each program being 58 and 40 FPs, respectively. A possible concern with this design would be the external validity of the results obtained from the experiment in relation to real-world systems. Typical medium-sized application systems are generally an order of magnitude larger than the programs counted in the Low and Jeffery experiment [15, 29]. Readers whose intuition is that FPs are relatively unreliable might argue that the unknown true reliability is worse than that estimated in that experiment, since presumably it is easier to understand, and therefore count correctly, a small problem than a large one. On the other hand, readers whose intuition is that the unknown true reliability is better than that estimated in the experiment might argue that the experiment may have underestimated the true reliability since a single error,

such as omitting one file type, would have a larger percentage impact on a small total than a large one. Finally, a third opinion might be that both effects are present but that they cancel each other out, and therefore the experimental estimates are likely to be representative of the reliability of counts of actual systems. Given these competing arguments, validation of the results on larger systems is clearly indicated. Therefore, one parameter for the research design was to test interrater reliability using actual average-sized application systems.

A second research design question suggested by the Low and Jeffery results, but not explicitly tested by them, is the question of intermethod reliability. Reliability of FP counts was greater within organizations than across them, a result attributed by Low and Jeffery to possible variations in the methods used (personal correspondence, Aug. 15, 1990). As discussed earlier, Jones has also suggested the possibility of large differences across methods (Software Productivity Research, Inc., Dec. 9, 1989, mimeo). Given the growing proliferation of variant methods this question is also highly relevant to the overall question of FP reliability.

The goal of estimating actual medium-sized application systems required a large investment of effort on the part of the organizations and individuals participating in the research. Therefore, this constrained the test of intermethod reliability to a maximum of two methods to assure sufficient sample size to permit statistical analysis. The two methods chosen were (1) the International Function Point Users Groups (IFPUG) standard Release 3.0, which was the latest release of the original Albrecht method, [27] and (2) the Entity-Relationship approach developed by Desharnais [13].

The choice of the IFPUG 3.0-Albrecht Standard method (hereafter the "Standard method") was relatively obvious, as it is the single most widely adopted approach in current use, due in no small part to its adoption by the over 300-member IFPUG organization. Therefore, there is great practical interest in knowing the interrater reliability of this method. The choice of a second method was less clear-cut, as there are a number of competing variations. Choice of the Entity-Relationship method (hereafter "ER method") was suggested by a second concern often raised by practitioners. In addition to possible concerns about reliability, a second explanation for the reluctance to adopt FPs as a software measure is the perception that FPs are relatively expensive to collect, given the current reliance on labor-intensive methods [6]. Currently, there is no fully automated FP-counting system, in contrast to many such systems for the competing measure, SLOC. Therefore, many organizations have adopted SLOC not due to a belief in greater benefits, but due to the expectation of lower costs in collection. Given this concern, it would be highly desirable for there to be a fully automated FP collection system, and vendors are currently at work developing such systems. One of the necessary preconditions for such a system is that the design-level data necessary to count FPs be available in an automated format. One promising first step toward developing such a system is the notion of recasting the original FP definitions in terms of the widely used ER data-modeling approach. Many of the CASE tools that support data modeling explicitly support the ER approach, and therefore an FP method based on ER modeling seems to be a highly promising step toward the total automation of FP collection. Therefore, for all of the reasons stated above, the second method chosen was the ER approach.[2]

In order to accommodate the two main research questions, interrater reliability and intermethod reliability, the research design depicted in Exhibit 3 was developed and executed for each system in the dataset.

For each system i to be counted, four independent raters from that participating organization were assigned, two of them to the Standard method and two of them to the ER method. These raters were identified as Raters A and B (Standard

method) and Raters C and D (ER method) as shown in Exhibit 3.

The definition of reliability used in this article is that of Carmines and Zeller, who define reliability as concerning "the extent to which an experiment, test, or any measuring procedure yields the same results on repeated trials . . . This tendency toward consistency found in repeated measurements of the same phenomenon is referred to as reliability" [7, pp. 11–12].

Allowing for standard assumptions about independent and unbiased error terms, the reliability of two parallel measures, x and x', can be shown to be represented by the simple statistic, $\rho xx'$ [7]. Therefore, for the design depicted in Exhibit 3, the appropriate statistics are:[3]

$\rho (FP_{Ai}\ FP_{Bi}) =$ *interrater reliability for Standard method for System i*

$\rho (FP_{Ci}\ FP_{Di}) =$ *interrater reliability for ER method for System i*

$\rho (FP_{1i}\ FP_{2i}) =$ *intermethod reliability for Standard (1) and ER (2) methods for System i.*

EXHIBIT 3 Overall Research Design

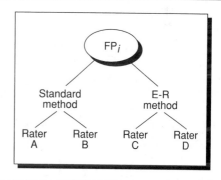

---

[3] In order to make the subscripts more legible, the customary notation $\rho_{xx'}$ will be replaced with the parenthetical notation $\rho(xx')$.

[4] For future reference of other researchers wishing to replicate this analysis, actual reported effort averaged 4.45 hours per system.

---

[2] Readers interested in the E-R approach are referred to [16]. However, a brief overview and example are provided in Box B.

Box B

Entity-Relationship Approach Summary

The following material is excerpted directly from the materials used by Raters C and D in the experiment and highlights the general approach taken in the ER approach to FP counting. Readers interested in further details regarding the experimental materials should see [9], and for complete details regarding the ER approach see [13].

"This methodology's definition of function point counting is based on the use of logical models as the basis of the counting process. The two primary models which are to be used are the "Data-Entity-Relationship" model and the "Data Flow Diagram." These two model types come in a variety of forms, but generally have the same characteristics related to Function Point counting irrespective of their form. The following applies to these two models as they are applied in the balance of this document.

"Data Entity Relationship Model (DER). This model typically shows the relationships between the various data entities which are used in a particular system. It typically contains "Data Entities" and "Relationships", as the objects of interest to the user or the systems analyst. In the use of the DER model, we standardize on the use of the "Third Normal Form" of the model, which eliminates repeating groups of data, and functional and transitive relationships. . . . Data Entity Relationship models will be used to identify Internal Entities (corresponding to Logical Internal Files) and External Entities (corresponding to Logical External interfaces).

"Data Flow Diagrams (DFD). These models typically show the flow of data through a particular system. They show the data entering from the user or other source, the data entities which are used, and the destination of the information out of the system. The boundaries of the system are generally clearly identified, as are the processes which are used. This model is frequently called a "Process"model. The level of detail of this model which is useful is the level which identifies a single (or small number) of individual business transactions. These transactions are a result of the decomposition of the higher-level data flows typically at the system level, and then at the function and subfunction level. Data Flow Diagrams will be used to identify the three types of transactions which are counted in Function Point Analysis (External Inputs, External Outputs and Inquiries)." The following is an example of the documentation provided to count one of the five function types, Internal Logical Files.

"Internal Logical Files—Definition. Internal entity types are counted as Albrecht's internal file types. An entity-type is internal if the application built by the measured project allows users to create, delete, modify and/or read an implementation of the entity-type. The users must have asked for this facility and be aware of it. All attributes of the entity-type, elements that are not foreign keys, are counted. We also count the number of relation types that the entity-type has. The complexity is determined by counting the number of elements and the number of relationships:

Guidance.

- Entities updated by application are counted as logical internal files.
- Complexity is based on the number of relationships in which the entity participates as well as the number of DETs.
- When considering an Entity-Relationship chart, be sure to consider the real needs of the application. For instance, frequently attributes required are attributes of the relationship rather than the entities, thus requiring a concatenated key to satisfy the requirement. The related entities may or may not be required as separate USER VIEWS."

EXHIBIT 4   Complexity Assignment for Internal Logic Files, ER Method

	1–19 Data Attribute Types in the Entity	*20–50 Data Attribute Types in the Entity*	*51+ Data Attribute Types in the Entity*
1 Relationship or other Entity Type	Low	Low	Average
2–5 Relationships or other Entity Types	Low	Average	High
6+ Relationships or other Entity Types	Average	High	High

While this design addresses both major research questions, it is a very expensive design from a data collection perspective. Collection of FP counts for one medium-sized system was estimated to require four work hours on the part of each rater.[4] Therefore, the total data collection cost for each system, i, was estimated at 16 hours, or two work days per system. A less expensive alternative would have been to use only two raters, each of whom would use one method and then recount using the second method, randomized for possible ordering effects. Unfortunately, this alternative design would suffer from a relativity bias, whereby raters would tend to remember the answer from their first count, and thus such a design would be likely to produce artificially high correlations [7, ch. 4]. Therefore, the more expensive design was chosen, with the foreknowledge that this would likely limit the number of organizations willing and able to participate, and therefore limit the sample size.

DATA COLLECTION

The pool of raters came from organizations that are members of the International Function Point Users Group (IFPUG), although only a small fraction of the raters are active IFPUG members. The organizations represent a cross section of U.S., Canadian, and U.K. firms both public and private, and represent a wide spectrum of industries. As per the research agreement, their actual identities will not be revealed; however, characterizations of participants by industry SIC codes and

by system type are shown in Box C. The first step in the data collection procedure was to send a letter to an information systems contact person at each organization explaining the research and inviting participation. The contacts were told that each system would require four independent counts, at an estimated effort of four hours per count. Based on this mailing, information systems contacts at 63 organizations expressed interest in the research and were sent a packet of research materials. The contacts were told to select recently developed medium-sized applications, defined as those that required from one to six work years of effort to develop. After a follow-up letter, and, in some cases, follow-up telephone call(s), usable data were ultimately received on 27 systems. The only direct benefit promised to the participants was a report comparing their data with the overall averages. Using the classification scales developed by Jones [16] the vast majority of applications can be described as being interactive MIS-type systems, typically supporting either Accounting/Finance or Manufacturing-type applications (Box C).

Experimental Controls

A number of precautions were taken to protect against threats to validity, the most prominent being the need to ensure that the four counts were done independently. First, in the instructions to the site contact the need for independent counts was repeatedly stressed. Second, the packet of research materials contained four separate data collection forms, each uniquely labeled A, B, C, and D for

Box C.

Data Background

EXHIBIT 5   Data by Industry

Industry	Percentage
Conglomerate	16%
Agriculture, Forestry & Fishing	5%
Mining	5%
Construction	0%
Manufacturing	26%
Transportation, Communication, Electric, Gas & Sanitary	11%
Wholesale & Retail Trade	5%
Finance, Insurance & Real Estate	16%
Services	5%
Government	11%

EXHIBIT 6   Data by System Type

System Type (Source: [16])	Percentage
Batch MIS application	15%
Interactive MIS application	70%
Scientific or mathematical application	0%
Systems software or support application/utility	11%
Communications of telecommunications application	0%
Embedded or real-time application	0%
Other or DNA	4%

was felt that this was an important step to reduce the possibility of inadvertent collusion through the sharing of manuals across raters, where the first rater might make marginal notes or otherwise give clues to a second reader as to the first rater's count. Fourth, and finally, four individual envelopes, prestamped and preaddressed to the researcher, were enclosed so that immediately on completion of the task the rater could place the data collection sheet into the envelope and mail it to the research team in order that no postcount collation by the site contact would be required. Again, this added some extra cost to the research, but was deemed to be an important additional safeguard. Copies of all of these research materials are available in [9] for other researchers to examine and use if desired to replicate the study.

One additional cost to the research of these precautions to assure independence was that the decentralized approach led to the result that not all four counts were received from all of the sites. Exhibit 7 summarizes the number of sets of data for which analysis of at least one of the research questions was possible.

In Exhibit 7 the first column shows the type of data. The row labeled A $\wedge$ B indicates that data from both the A and B rater were received. Since both of these raters used the Standard method, the interrater reliability for this method can be assessed using these data. The second row is similar, except that it applies to the ER method. The third row refers to systems for which all four counts were received and can be used as originally designed to measure intermethod reliability. This set will be referred to as the *Quadset* to indicate that all four counts were present. The four row refers to systems for which at least one A or B count exists and at least one C or D count exists. These data can also be used to test intermethod reliability and will be referred to as the *Fullset*. The Fullset naturally includes all of the systems in the Quadset.

These counts reflect the data after the removal of five systems' data that were deemed unusable for purposes of the study. Data for two systems were not used as only one count for each system

immediate distribution to the four raters. Third, four FP manuals were included, two of the Standard method (labeled Method I) and two of the ER method (labeled Method II). While increasing the reproduction and mailing costs of the research, it

EXHIBIT 7   Summary of Primary Data Collected

Counts Received:	Systems	Observations	Research Question
A $\wedge$ B	27	54	Standard method Interrater reliability
C $\wedge$ D	21	42	ER method Interrater reliability
A $\wedge$ B $\wedge$ C $\wedge$ D	17	68	Intermethod reliability ("Quadset")
(A $\vee$ B) $\wedge$ (C $\vee$ D)	26	90	Intermethod reliability ("Fullset")

(an A in one case and a D in the other) was received, and therefore no comparison of any kind could be made. Data for two other systems, one an average of 3,590 FPs, and the other of 2,294 FPs, approximately 9.1 and 5.3 standard deviations above the mean for the interrater sample respectively, were also excluded, on the grounds that they reflected large systems rather than the medium-size (one to six work years) systems requested. Finally, data for a fifth system for which independence of the raters was in doubt were also excluded.[5]

Posttest of Random Assignment Assumption

Given that the four raters were assigned to one of the two methods by the site contact, one possible concern might be that their assignment may have been biased in some way. For example, if raters A and B had greater FP-counting experience, on average, than raters C and D, then any comparison of methods would be simultaneously testing the methods hypothesis and a hidden experience hypothesis [18]. Given the number of field sites involved, assignment of raters could not be rigorously controlled *a priori,* other than through the instructions given to the site contact. This lack of direct control over random assignment is typical in field experimentation [10, p. 6]. Therefore, *ex post* tests of independent variables that could be postu-

lated to have some effect were done, and the results of these tests are presented in Exhibits 8 & 9.

As shown in Exhibit 8, the average overall experience of the raters, in terms of their systems development experience, their experience in counting FPs, and the percentage of raters who were involved with the development or maintenance of the system being counted, was relatively consistent across all four groups. The results of one-way ANOVA tests for both rater differences and method differences (where A and B represent the Standard method and C and D represent the ER method) did not support rejecting the null hypothesis of zero difference between the mean levels of experience. In addition, the Scheffe multiple-comparison procedure was run on the full raters-nested-within-methods model, with the same result that no statistically significant difference was detectable at even the $\alpha = 0.10$ level for any of the possible individual cases (*e.g.,* A vs B, A vs C, A vs. D, B vs. C . . .) [26]. Therefore, later tests of possible methods effects on FP count data will be assumed to have come from randomly assigned raters with respect to relevant experience.

In addition to experience levels, another factor that might be hypothesized to affect FP measurement reliability might be the system source materials with which the rater has to work. As suggested by Rudolph [25], three levels of such materials might be available: (1) requirements analysis phase documentation, (2) external design phase documentation (e.g., hard copy of screen designs, reports, file layouts, and so forth), and (3) the completed system, which could include access

---

[5] It should be noted that the correlations of the counts for two of these three latter systems were extremely high, and their exclusion in the interests of conservatism has the effect of reducing the overall reliability measures for the dataset.

EXHIBIT 8 Check of Rater and Method Assignment Randomness, Experience

Experience Type:	A Raters Mean or %	B Raters Mean or %	C Raters Mean or %	D Raters Mean or %	ANOVA F-test, by Rater	ANOVA F-test, by Method	Scheffe Test, α = 0.10
Systems Development	11.3 yrs.	9.7 yrs.	10.9 yrs	11.2 yrs	F = 0.21 (p = 0.89)	F = 0.08 (p = 0.77)	Negative, all cases
Function Points	1.3 yrs.	1.5 yrs.	1.7 yrs	1.7 yrs	F = 0.41 (p = 0.75)	F = 0.96 (p = 0.33)	Negative, all cases
This Application System	6%	19%	15%	13%	F = 0.76 (p = 0.52)	F = 0.08 (p = 0.78)	Negative, all cases

EXHIBIT 9 Check of Rater and Method Assignment Randomness, Materials

Source Materials Type:	A Raters %	B Raters %	C Raters %	D Raters %	ANOVA F-test, by Rater	ANOVA F-test, by Method	Scheffe Test, α = 0.10
Requirements Analysis Documentation (level I)	11%	6%	14%	14%	F = 0.37 (p = 0.78)	F = 0.82 (p = 0.37)	Negative, all cases
Detailed Design documentation (level II)	68%	66%	64%	67%	F = 0.03 (p = 0.99)	F = 0.03 (p = 0.87)	Negative, all cases
Completed System (level III)	21%	28%	23%	19%	F = 0.22 (p = 0.88)	F = 0.23 (p = 0.63)	Negative, all cases

to the actual source code. Each of the raters contributing data to the study was asked which of these levels of source materials he or she had access to in order to develop the FP count. The majority of all raters used design documentation ("level II"). However, some had access only to level-I documentation, and some had access to the full completed system, as indicated in Exhibit 9. In order to assure that this mixture of source materials level was unbiased with respect to the assigned raters and their respective methods, ANOVA analysis as per Exhibit 8 was done, and the results of this analysis are shown in Exhibit 9.

Similar to the results for experience levels, it appears that access to source materials was sufficiently similar for each rater group as to rule this out as a probable source of bias. Therefore, later tests of possible methods effects on FP count data will be assumed to have come from randomly assigned raters with respect to source material.

MAIN RESEARCH RESULTS

For each of the three research questions three sets of data are presented: (a) the average counts from each approach, (b) a Pearson correlation coefficient, and (c) a paired t-test of the null hypothesis of zero difference between the results.

1. *Standard method.*

$$H_0: \overline{FP}_A - \overline{FP}_B = 0$$

Based on the research design described earlier, the average value for the A raters was 436 (standard deviation of 345), and for the B raters it was 464 (383), with $n = 27$. The results of a test of interrater reliability for the standard method yielded a Pearson correlation coefficient (ρ) = 0.80, (p = 0.0001), suggesting a strong correlation between FP counts of two raters using the standard method. The results of a paired t-test of the null hypothesis that the difference between the means is equal to 0 was only −0.61 (p = 0.55), indicating no support for rejecting the null hypothesis. The power of this test for revealing the presence of a large difference, assuming it was to exist, is approximately 90% [8, Table 2.3.6].[6] Therefore, based on these results, there is clearly no statistical support for assuming the counts are significantly different.

2. *Entity-Relationship method.*

$$H_0 : \overline{FP}_C - \overline{FP}_D = 0$$

The same set of tests was run for the two sets of raters using the ER method, *mutatis mutandis*. For $n = 21$, values of $\overline{FP}_C$ and $\overline{FP}_D$ were 476 (381) and 411 (323) respectively. Note that these values are not directly comparable to the values for $\overline{FP}_A$ and $\overline{FP}_B$, as they come from slightly different samples. The reliability measure is $\rho(FP_{Ci}\ FP_{Di})$ = 0.74 (p = 0.0001), not quite as high as for the Standard method, but nearly as strong a correlation. The results of an equivalent t-test yielded a value of 1.15 (p = 0.26), again indicating less reliability than the Standard method, but still well below the level where the null hypothesis of no difference might be rejected. The power of this test is approximately 82%.

---

[6] All later power estimates are also from this source, *loc. cit.*

3a. *Intermethod reliability results.*
Quadset analysis ($n = 17$)

The test of intermethod reliability is a test of the null hypothesis:

$$H_0: \overline{FP}_1 - \overline{FP}_2 = 0$$

$$where\ \overline{FP}_1 = \sum_{i=1}^{n} \frac{FP_{Ai} + FP_{Bi}}{2}$$

$$and\ \overline{FP}_2 = \sum_{i=1}^{n} \frac{FP_{Ci} + FP_{Di}}{2}$$

At issue here is whether FP raters using two variant FP methods will produce highly similar (reliable) results, in this particular case the two methods being the Standard method and the ER method. In the interests of conservatism, the first set of analyses uses only the 17 systems for which all four counts, A, B, C, and D, were obtained. This is to guard against the event, however unlikely, that the partial response systems were somehow different. The values for $\overline{FP}_1$ and $\overline{FP}_2$ were 418 (322) and 413 (288), respectively, and yielded a $\rho(FP_{1i}\ FP_{2i})$ = 0.95 (p = 0.0001). The t-test of the null hypothesis of no difference resulted in a value of 0.18 (p = 0.86), providing no support for rejecting the hypothesis of equal means. These results clearly speak to a very high intermethod reliability. However, the conservative approach of only using the Quadset data yielded a smaller sample size, thus reducing the power of the statistical tests (e.g., the relative power of this t-test is 74%). To increase the power of the test in order to ensure that the preceding results were not simply the result of the smaller sample, the next step replicates the analysis using the Fullset data, those for which at least one count from the Rater A and B method and at least one count from the Rater C and D method were available.

3b. *Intermethod reliability results.*
Fullset analysis ($n = 26$)

The results from the Fullset analysis, while somewhat less strong than the very high values reported for the Quadset, still show high correlation, and since the Fullset test has greater power to detect differences, should they exist, greater confidence can be placed in the result of no difference. The values of $\overline{FP}_1$ and $\overline{FP}_2$ were 403 (303) and 363 (252), respectively, and yielded a $\rho(FP_{1i} FP_{2i}) = 0.84$ (p = 0.0001). The *t*-test of the null hypothesis was 1.25 (p = 0.22), with a power of 89%. Thus, it is still appropriate not to reject the null hypothesis of no difference across these two methods, and, based on the Fullset analysis, not rejecting the null hypothesis can be done with increased confidence.

Managerial Results and Discussion

From the statistical results summarized in Exhibit 10 it can be concluded that both the interrater and intermethod reliability of FPs are high. From the point of view of practicing managers some additional information that might be helpful in using FPs is the average magnitude of the differences across raters and methods. For example, one use of such data would be in performing sensitivity analysis on FP counts that are used for performing project estimates. Given a single FP count, what might be an appropriate range to use to adjust for possible differences that may have resulted from getting an FP count from a different analyst?

1. *Interrater results.* A plot of the Rater A versus Rater B counts is shown as Exhibit 11. It should be noted that the dashed line is the 45-degree line representing a perfect match (A = B) rather than a line that has been fitted to the data. One clear outlier is present, but its data have not been excluded from any of the data analysis. As a practical test the percentage differences for the standard method across raters for any single pair of raters is simply

$$\left| \frac{FP_A - FP_B}{FP_A} \right|.$$

The median value for all 27 pairs of raters using the standard method is 12.22%. Due to the presence of a single large outlier, the mean value is greater (26.53%). Similarly, the interrater result for the ER method can be computed by substituting FP_C for FP_A and FP_D for FP_B. The median value for the 21 pairs of raters using the ER method is 20.66%. Again, the mean value is higher (38.85%). A plot of Rater C vs. Rater D is shown as Exhibit 12.

The interrater error for the ER method was almost twice that of the Standard method. There are a number of possible explanations for this difference. The first, and easiest to check, is whether the slightly different samples used in the analysis of the two methods (the 27 systems used by the Standard method and the 21 systems used by the ER method) may have influenced the results. To check this possibility, both sets of analyses were rerun, using only the Quadset of 17 systems for which all four counts were available. This sub-analysis generated a median percentage error of 11.51% for the Standard method and a median percentage error of 20.66% for the ER method, so it appears as if the difference cannot simply be attributed to a sampling difference.

EXHIBIT 10   Summary of Reliability Statistics

	Interrater, Standard method	Interrater, ER method	Intermethod, Quadset	Intermethod, Fullset
n (Systems, Counts)	27, 54	21, 42	17, 68	26, 90
$\rho(xy)$; p	0.80 (0.0001)	0.74 (0.0001)	0.95 (0.0001)	0.84 (0.0001)
paired *t*-test; p	−0.61 (0.55)	1.15 (0.26)	0.18 (0.86)	1.25 (0.22)
$1 - \beta$ (power)	0.90	0.82	0.74	0.89

EXHIBIT 11   Interrater Results, Standard Method (A vs. B)

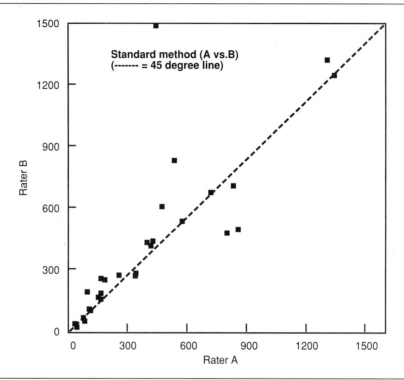

More likely explanations stem from the fact that the ER approach, while perhaps the most common data-modeling approach in current use, is still unfamiliar enough to cause errors. Of the raters contributing data to the study, 23% of the C and D raters reported having no prior experience or training in ER modeling, and thus were relying solely on the experimental documentation provided. Thus, the comparison of the Standard and ER methods results shows the combined effects of both the methods themselves, and their supporting manuals. Therefore, the possibility of the test materials, rather than the method *per se,* being the cause of the increased variation, cannot be ruled out by the study.

An additional hypothesis has been suggested by Allan Albrecht. He notes that the ER approach is a user functional view of the system, a view that is typically captured in the requirements analysis documentation, but sometimes does not appear in the detailed design documentation. To the degree that this is true, and to the degree that counters in this study used the detailed design documentation to the exclusion of using the requirements analysis documents, this may have hindered use of the ER method (personal correspondence, A.J. Albrecht, Sept., 1990). A similar possibility is that the application system's documentation used may not have contained ER diagrams, thus creating an additional intermediate step in the counting process for those raters using the ER method in order to create these diagrams, or their equivalents, which could have contributed to a greater number of errors and hence a wider variance. Finally, given that the raters typically had significant experience with prior IFPUG standards, their better performance using the Standard method may be

EXHIBIT 12   Interrater Results, E-R Method (C vs. D)

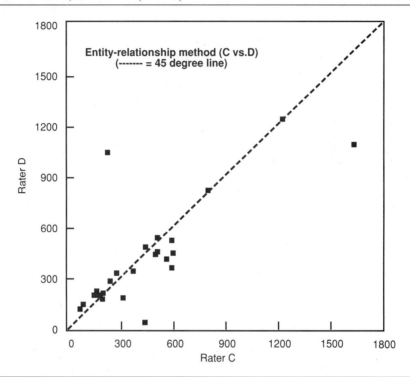

partly attributable to their possibly greater comfort with this approach than the newer, ER approach.

Ultimately, the interrater reliability results for the ER method are the least practically meaningful of the three major results, as hand counting using the ER approach should be seen as only an intermediate step toward their eventual automation.

2. *Intermethod results.* The percentage error calculations for the intermethod results are, for the Quadset, a median of 17.95% (average = 17.75%) and for the Fullset, a median of 18.91% (average = 23.01%). Plots of the average Standard Method count vs. the average ER method count are shown as Exhibits 13 (Quadset) and 14 (Fullset). The intermethod results are the first documented study of this phenomenon and thus provide a baseline for future studies. The variation across the two methods is similar to that obtained across raters and thus does not appear to be a major source of error *for these two methods.* Of course, these results cannot necessarily

be extended to pairwise comparisons of two other FP method variations, or even of one of the current methods and a third method. Determination of whether this result represents typical, better, or worse effects of counting variations must await further validation. However, as a practical matter, the results should be encouraging to researchers or vendors who might automate the ER method within a software engineering tool, thus addressing both the reliability and the data collection cost concerns. The results also suggest that organizations choosing to adopt the ER method now, although at some risk of possible lower interrater reliability, are likely to generate FP counts that are sufficiently similar to counts obtained with the Standard method so as to be a viable alternative. In particular, an analysis of the Quadset data revealed a mean FP count of 418 for the Standard method and 413 for the ER method, indistinguishable for both statistical and practical purposes.

EXHIBIT 13 Intermethod Results (Quadset)

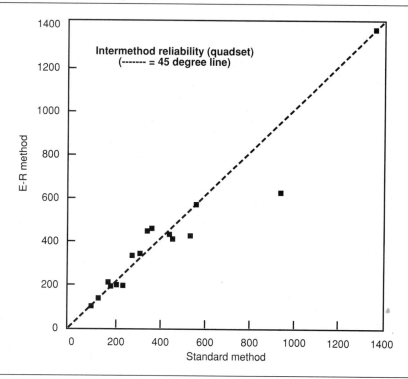

CONCLUDING REMARKS

If software development is to fully establish itself as an engineering discipline, then it must adopt and adhere to the standards of such disciplines. A critical distinction between software engineering and other, more well-established branches of engineering, is the clear shortage of well-accepted measures of software. *Without* such measures the managerial tasks of planning and controlling software development and maintenance will remain stagnant in a craft'-type mode, whereby greater skill is acquired only through greater experience, and such experience cannot be easily communicated to the next project for study, adoption, and further improvement. *With* such measures software projects can be quantitatively described, and the managerial methods and tools used on the projects ot improve productivity and quality can be evalu-

ated. These evaluations will help the discipline grow and mature, as progress is made at adopting those innovations that work well, and discarding or revising those that do not.

Currently, the only widely available software measure that has the potential to fill this role for MIS projects in the near future is Function Points. This experiment has shown, contrary to some speculation and limited prior research, that both the interrater and intermethod reliability of FP measurement are sufficiently high that their reliability should not pose a practical barrier to their continued adoption and future development.

The collection effort for FP data in this research averaged approximately 1 work hour per 100 FPs and can be expected to be indicative of the costs to collect data in actual practice, since the data used in this research were actual commercial systems.

EXHIBIT 14   Intermethod Results (Fullset)

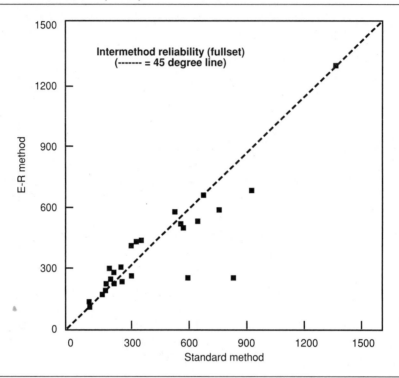

For large systems this amount of effort is nontrivial and may at least partially account for the relative paucity of prior research on these questions. Clearly, further efforts directed toward developing aids to greater automation of FP data collection should continue to be pursued. However, even the current cost is small relative to the large sums spent on software development and maintenance in total, and managers should consider the time spent on FP collection and analysis as an investment in process improvement of their software development capability. Such investments are also indicative of true engineering disciplines, and there is increasing evidence of these types of investments in leading-edge software firms in the U.S. and in Japan [12]. Managers wishing to quantitatively improve their software development and maintenance capabilities should adopt or extend software measurement capabilities within their organizations. Based on this experiment, FPs offer a reliable yardstick with which to implement this capability.

ACKNOWLEDGMENTS

Helpful comments were received from A. Albrecht, N. Campbell, J. Cooprider, B. Dreger, P. Guinan, J. Henderson, R. Jeffery, C. Jones, M. Keller, W. Orlikowski, D. Reifer, A. Rollo, H. Rubin, E. Rudolph, W. Rumpf, G. Sosa, C. Symons, N. Venkatraman, and J. Verner. Finally, special thanks are due to my research assistant, M. Connolley.

References

1. Albrecht, A.J. Measuring application development productivity. In *GUIDE/SHARE: Proceedings of the IBM Applications Development Symposium* (Monterey, Calif.), 1979, pp. 83–92.

2. Albrecht, A.J. and Gaffney, J. Software function, source lines of code, and development effort prediction: A software science validation. *IEEE Trans. Softw. Eng. SE-9*, 6 (1983), 639–648.

3. Banker, R.D. and Kemerer, C.F. Scale economies in new software development. *IEEE Trans. Softw. Eng. SE-15*, 10 (1989), 416–429.

4. Banker, R.D., Datar, S.M. and Kemerer, C.F. A model to evaluate variables impacting productivity on software maintenance projects. *Manage. Sci. 37*, 1 (1991), 1–18.

5. Behrens, C.A. Measuring the productivity of computer systems development activities with Function Points. *IEEE Trans. Softw. Eng. SE-9*, 6 (1983), 648–652.

6. Bock, D.B. and Klepper, R. FP-S: A simplified Function Point counting method. Working Paper, Southern Illinois Univ., at Edwardsville, Ill., 1990.

7. Carmines, E.G. and Zeller, R.A. *Reliability and Validity Assessment.* Sage Publications, Beverly Hills, Calif., 1979.

8. Cohen, J. *Statistical Power Analysis for the Behavioral Sciences.* Academic Press, New York, N.Y., 1977.

9. Connolley, M.J. An empirical study of Function Points analysis reliability, Masters thesis, MIT Sloan School of Management, Cambridge, Mass., 1990.

10. Cook, T.D. and Campbell, D.T. *Quasi-Experimentation: Design and Analysis Issues for Field Settings.* Houghton-Mifflin, Boston, 1979.

11. Cooprider, J. and Henderson, J. A multi-dimensional approach to performance evaluation for I/S development. Working Paper 197, MIT Center for Information Systems Research, Cambridge, Mass., 1989.

12. Cusumano, M. and Kemerer, C.F. A quantitative analysis of US and Japanese practice and performance in software development. *Manage. Sci. 36*, 11 (1990), 1384–1406.

13. Desharnais, J.-M. Analyse statistique de la productivite des projets de developpement en informatique a partir de la technique des points de fonction (English version). Masters thesis, Universite du Quebec, Montreal, 1988.

14. Dreger, J.B. *Function Point Analysis,* Prentice-Hall, Englewood Cliffs, N.J., 1989.

15. Emrick, R.D. Software development productivity second industry study. In the *1988 International Function Point Users Group Spring Conference Proceedings* (Dallas, Tex.). IFPUG, Westerville, Ohio, pp. 1–44.

16. Jones, C. *Programming Productivity.* McGraw-Hill, New York, 1986.

17. Kemerer, C.F. An empirical validation of software cost estimation models. *Commun. ACM 30*, 5 (May 1987), 416–429.

18. Low, G.C. and Jeffery, D.R. Function Points in the estimation and evaluation of the software process. *IEEE Trans. Softw. Eng. 16*, 1 (1990), 64–71.

19. Maglitta, J. It's reality time. *Computerworld* (1991), 81–84.

20. Perry, W.E. The best measures for measuring data processing quality and productivity. Tech. Rep. Quality Assurance Institute, 1986.

21. Pressman, R.S. *Software Engineering: A Practitioner's Approach.* McGraw-Hill, New York, 1987.

22. Ratcliff, B. and Rollo, A.L. Adapting Function Point analysis to Jackson system development. *Softw. Eng. J.* (1990), 79–84.

23. Rubin, H.A. Macroestimation of software development parameters: The estimacs system. In *IEEE SOFTFAIR Conference on Software Development Tools, Techniques and Alternatives.* IEEE, New York, N.Y., 1983.

24. Rubin, H.A. Measure for measure. *Computerworld* (1991), 77–79.

25. Rudolph, E.E. Productivity in computer application development. Working Paper 9, Univ. of Auckland, Dept. of Management Studies, Auckland, New Zealand, 1983.

26. Scheffe, H. *Analysis of Variance.* John Wiley & Sons, New York, 1959.

27. Sprouls, J. *IFPUG Function Point Counting Practices Manual Release 3.0.* International Function Point Users Group, Westerville, Ohio, 1990.

28. Symons, C.R. Function Point analysis: Difficulties and improvements. *IEEE Trans. Softw. Eng. 14*, 1 (1988), 2–11.

29. Topper, A. CASE: A peek at commercial developers uncovers some clues to the mystery. *Computerworld, 24*, 15 (1990), 61–64.

30. Verner, J.M., Tate, G., Jackson, B. and Hayward, R.G. Technology dependence in Function Point analysis: A case study and critical review. In *Proceedings of the 11th International Conference on Software Engineering.* 1989, pp. 375–382.

Discussion Questions

1. FPs are proposed as an improvement to SLOC as an estimation tool due to their earlier availability. What further criticisms could you make of SLOC?

2. Given the criticisms of SLOC, why was this originally chosen as a measure?

3. What are some of the limitations of FPs as presented in the 1983, Albrecht and Gaffney article?

4. Besides aiding cost and schedule estimation, how might FP be practically applied?

5. FPs have been criticized as being useful only for business applications. What changes might be made to make these metrics more general and therefore more applicable to a wider range of software applications?

6. In the Kemerer article, much discussion is devoted to the issue of standard measures. Why might this matter to a manager?

Risk Management

INTRODUCTION

Risk management is a much broader topic than just software projects. Numerous books have been written about the subject. This chapter focuses on a very small subset of articles about software specific risk factors and strategies to mitigate those risks.

Many articles in the business press articles highlight a number of examples of significant software project failures. Many of the examples are from systems developed by contractors, some of which have ended up in litigation. Many common symptoms are noted: large projects, new technologies, lack of detailed project planning, lack of user/management oversight/inexperienced staffs, radical business change. From a review of these past project failures, a number of risk factors can be identified, which can then be used as a checklist in planning future projects.

Barry Boehm has taken this approach a step further and developed an approach to software project risk management. Boehm divides risk management into risk assessment and risk control, and offers a number of steps within each of these categories. For each step, a short list of techniques are outlined, with some examples from actual projects at TRW. A set of useful tables and figures illustrate these techniques, including a 'top 10' list of project risk factors.

The article by Richard Fairley follows up on these techniques and demonstrates their application on a telecommunications software project. He makes significant use of the COCOMO cost estimation model to estimate the impact of risk factors on budget and schedule, and demonstrates the use of statistical distributions to provide a likely range of probable outcomes. From this information he then develops contingency plans and documents what actions project management actually take on the project.

Finally, this chapter ends with a practice oriented article written by Tom Gilb in his typical tongue in cheek style. Beyond the humor, however, this article serves as a useful reminder of how a schedule is consistently the driving force on projects, and how this emphasis results in suboptimal performance on other dimensions. It further points out the opportunities created by the problem of inadequately specified systems in terms of reducing project deliverables in order to meet schedules. Gilb suggests using evolutionary development in order to rationally achieve this balance. Finally, it contains other pragmatic advice, such as the use of Fagan inspections and software metrics in order to improve project management performance.

Reminders of the consequences of mismanagement of software project risk are plentiful. Some excellent examples are found in Glass, R., "The Anatomy of a Runaway," *The Software Practitioner,* 2, (6): 1–10, (November–December 1992). A detailed description of the Westpac Banking Corporation's Core System Redevelopment and a number of mini-cases are described in Winsberg, P. and D. Richards, "The one that got away," *Computerworld In Depth,* XXVI, (15): 83–85, (1992).

SOFTWARE RISK MANAGEMENT: PRINCIPLES AND PRACTICES

Like many fields in their early stages, the software field has had its share of project disasters: the software equivalents of the Beauvais Cathedral, the *HMS Titanic,* and the "Galloping Gertie" Tacoma Narrows Bridge. The frequency of these software-project disasters is a serious concern: A recent survey of 600 firms indicated that 35 percent of them had at least one runaway software project.[1]

Most postmortems of these software-project disasters have indicated that their problems would have been avoided or strongly reduced if there had been an explicit early concern with identifying and resolving their high-risk elements. Frequently, these projects were swept along by a tide of optimistic enthusiasm during their early phases that caused them to miss some clear signals of high-risk issues that proved to be their downfall later.

Enthusiasm for new software capabilities is a good thing. But it must be tempered with a concern for early identification and resolution of a project's high-risk elements so people can get these resolved early and then focus their enthusiasm and energy on the positive aspects of their product.

Current approaches to the software process make it too easy for projects to make high-risk commitments that they will later regret:

• The sequential, document-driven waterfall process model tempts people to overpromise software capabilities in contractually binding requirements specifications before they understand their risk implications.

• The code-driven, evolutionary development process model tempts people to say, "Here are some neat ideas I'd like to put into this system. I'll code them up, and if they don't fit other people's ideas, we'll just evolve things until they work." This sort of approach usually works fine in some well-supported minidomains like spreadsheet applications but, in more complex application domains, it most often creates or neglects unsalvageable high-risk elements and leads the project down the path to disaster.

At TRW and elsewhere, I have had the good fortune to observe many project managers at work firsthand and to try to understand and apply the factors that distinguished the more successful project managers from the less successful ones. Some successfully used a waterfall approach, others successfully used an evolutionary development approach, and still others successfully orchestrated complex mixtures of these and other approaches involving prototyping, simulation, commercial software, executable specifications, tiger teams, design competitions, subcontracting, and various kinds of cost-benefit analyses.

One pattern that emerged very strongly was that the successful project managers were good *risk managers.* Although they generally didn't use such terms as "risk identification," "risk assessment," "risk-management planning," or "risk monitoring," they were using a general concept of risk

Article by Barry W. Boehm, © 1991 IEEE. Reprinted, with permission, from (IEEE Software; 1, 32–41 January/1991).

exposure (potential loss times the probability of loss) to guide their priorities and actions. And their projects tended to avoid pitfalls and produce good products.

The emerging discipline of software risk management is an attempt to formalize these risk-oriented correlates of success into a readily applicable set of principles and practices. Its objectives are to identify, address, and eliminate risk items before they become either threats to successful software operation or major sources of software rework.

BASIC CONCEPTS

Webster's dictionary defines "risk" as "the possibility of loss or injury." This definition can be translated into the fundamental concept of risk management: risk exposure, sometimes also called "risk impact" or "risk factor." Risk exposure is defined by the relationship

$$RE = P(UO) * L(UO)$$

where RE is the risk exposure, P(UO) is the probability of an unsatisfactory outcome and L(UO) is the loss to the parties affected if the outcome is unsatisfactory. To relate this definition to software projects, we need a definition of "unsatisfactory outcome."

Given that projects involve several classes of participants (customer, developer, user, and maintainer), each with different but highly important satisfaction criteria, it is clear that "unsatisfactory outcome" is multidimensional:

- For customers and developers, budget overruns and schedule slips are unsatisfactory.
- For users, products with the wrong functionality, user-interface shortfalls, performance shortfalls, or reliability shortfalls are unsatisfactory.
- For maintainers, poor-quality software is unsatisfactory.

These components of an unsatisfactory outcome provide a top-level checklist for identifying and assessing risk items.

A fundamental risk-analysis paradigm is the decision tree. Exhibit 1 illustrates a potentially risky situation involving the software controlling a satellite experiment. The software has been under development by the experiment team, which understands the experiment well but is inexperienced in and somewhat casual about software development. As a result, the satellite-platform manager has obtained an estimate that there is a probability P(UO) of 0.4 that the experimenters' software will have a critical error: one that will wipe out the entire experiment and cause an associated loss L(UO) of the total $20 million investment in the experiment.

The satellite-platform manager identifies two major options for reducing the risk of losing the experiment:

- Convincing and helping the experiment team to apply better development methods. This incurs no additional cost and, from previous experience, the manager estimates that this will reduce the error probability P(UO) to 0.1.
- Hiring a contractor to independently verify and validate the software. This costs an additional $500,000; based on the results of similar IV & V efforts, the manager estimates that this will reduce the error probability P(UO) to 0.04.

The decision tree in Exhibit 1 then shows, for each of the two major decision options, the possible outcomes in terms of the critical error existing or being found and eliminated, their probabilities, the losses associated with each outcome, the risk exposure associated with each outcome, and the total risk exposure (or expected loss) associated with each decision option. In this case, the total risk exposure associated with the experiment-team option is only $2 million. For the IV & V option, the total risk exposure is only $1.3 million, so it represents the more attractive option.

Besides providing individual solutions for risk-management situations, the decision tree also provides a framework for analyzing the sensitivity of preferred solutions to the risk-exposure parameters.

EXHIBIT 1 Decision Tree for Whether to Perform Independent Validation and Verification to Eliminate Critical Errors in a Satellite-Experiment Program. L(UO) is the Loss Associated With an Unsatisfactory Outcome, P(UO) is the Probability of the Unsatisfactory Outcome, and CE is a Critical Error

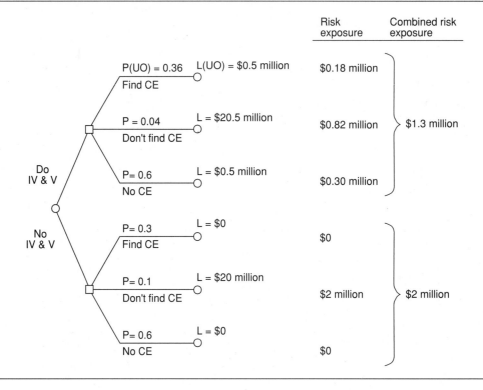

Thus, for example, the experiment-team option would be preferred if the loss due to a critical error were less than $13 million, if the experiment team could reduce its critical-error probability to less than 0.065, if the IV & V team cost more than $1.2 million, if the IV & V team could not reduce the probability of critical error to less than 0.075, or if there were various partial combinations of these possibilities.

This sort of sensitivity analysis helps deal with many situations in which probabilities and losses cannot be estimated well enough to perform a precise analysis. The risk-exposure framework also supports some even more approximate but still very useful approaches, like range estimation and scale-of-10 estimation.

RISK MANAGEMENT

As Exhibit 2 shows, the practice of risk management involves two primary steps each with three subsidiary steps.

The first primary step, risk assessment, involves risk identification, risk analysis, and risk prioritization:

- Risk identification produces lists of the project-specific risk items likely to compromise a project's success. Typical risk-identification techniques include checklists, examination of decision drivers, comparison with experience (assumption analysis), and decomposition.
- Risk analysis assesses the loss probability and loss magnitude for each identified risk

EXHIBIT 2   Software Risk Management Steps

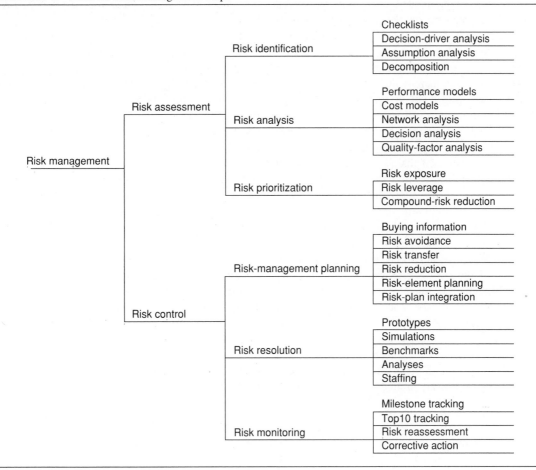

item, and it assesses compound risks in risk-item interactions. Typical techniques include performance models, cost models, network analysis, statistical decision analysis, and quality-factor (like reliability, availability, and security) analysis.

- Risk prioritization produces a ranked ordering of the risk items identified and analyzed. Typical techniques include risk-exposure analysis, risk-reduction, leverage analysis (particularly involving cost-benefit analysis), and Delphi or group-consensus techniques.

The second primary step, risk control, involves risk-management planning, risk resolution, and risk monitoring.

- Risk-management planning helps prepare you to address each risk item (for example, via information buying, risk avoidance, risk transfer, or risk reduction), including the coordination of the individual risk-item plans with each other and with the overall project plan. Typical techniques include checklists of risk-resolution techniques, cost-benefit analysis, and standard risk-management plan outlines, forms, and elements.

- Risk resolution produces a situation in which the risk items are eliminated or otherwise resolved (for example, risk avoidance via relaxation of requirements). Typical techniques include prototypes, simulations, benchmarks, mission analyses, key-personnel agreements, design-to-cost approaches, and incremental development.
- Risk monitoring involves tracking the project's progress toward resolving its risk items and taking corrective action where appropriate. Typical techniques include milestone tracking and a top-10 risk-item list that is highlighted at each weekly, monthly, or milestone project review and followed up appropriately with reassessment of the risk item or corrective action.

In addition, risk management provides an improved way to address and organize the life cycle. Risk-driven approaches, like the spiral model of the software process, avoid many of the difficulties encountered with previous process models like the waterfall model and the evolutionary development model. Such risk-driven approaches also show how and where to incorporate new software technologies like rapid prototyping, fourth-generation languages, and commercial software products into the life cycle.

SIX STEPS

Exhibit 2 summarized the major steps and techniques involved in software risk management. This overview article covers four significant subsets of risk-management techniques: risk-identification checklists, risk prioritization, risk-management planning, and risk monitoring. Other techniques have been covered elsewhere.[3,4]

Risk-Identification Checklists

Exhibit 3 shows a top-level risk-identification checklist with the top 10 primary sources of risk on software projects, based on a survey of several experienced project managers. Managers and system engineers can use the checklist on projects to help identify and resolve the most serious risk items on the project. It also provides a corresponding set of risk-management techniques that have been most successful to date in avoiding or resolving the source of risk.

If you focus on item 2 of the top-10 list in Exhibit 3 (unrealistic schedules and budgets), you can then move on to an example of a next-level checklist: the risk-probability table in Exhibit 4 for assessing the probability that a project will overrun its budget. Exhibit 4 is one of several such checklists in an excellent US Air Force handbook[5] on software risk abatement.

Using the checklist, you can rate a project's status for the individual attributes associated with its requirements, personnel, reusable software, tools, and support environment (in Exhibit 4, the environment's availability or the risk that the environment will not be available when needed). These ratings will support a probability-range estimation of whether the project has a relatively low (0.0 to 0.3), medium (0.4 to 0.6), or high (0.7 to 1.0) probability of overrunning its budget.

Most of the critical risk items in the checklist have to do with shortfalls in domain understanding and in properly scoping the job to be done—areas that are generally underemphasized in computer-science literature and education. Recent initiatives, like the Software Engineering Institute's masters curriculum in software engineering, are providing better coverage in these areas. The SEI is also initiating a major new program in software risk management.

Risk Analysis and Prioritization

After using all the various risk-identification checklists, plus the other risk-identification techniques in decision-driver analysis, assumption analysis, and decomposition, one very real risk is that the project will identify so many risk items that the project could spend years just investigating them. This is where risk prioritization and its associated risk-analysis activities become essential.

The most effective technique for risk prioritization involves the risk-exposure quantity described earlier. It lets you rank the risk items identified and determine which are most important to address.

EXHIBIT 3   Top 10 Software Risk Items

Risk Item	*Risk-Management Technique*
Personnel shortfalls	Staffing with top talent, job matching, team building, key personnel agreements, cross training.
Unrealistic schedules and budgets	Detailed multisource cost and schedule estimation, design to cost, incremental development, software reuse, requirements scrubbing.
Developing the wrong functions and properties	Organization analysis, mission analysis, operations-concept formulation, user surveys and user participation, prototyping, early users' manuals, off-nominal performance analysis, quality-factor analysis.
Developing the wrong user interface	Prototyping, scenarios, task analysis, user participation.
Gold-plating	Requirements scrubbing, prototyping, cost-benefit analysis, designing to cost.
Continuing stream of requirements changes	High change threshold, information hiding, incremental development (deferring changes to later increments).
Shortfalls in externally furnished components	Benchmarking, inspections, reference checking, compatibility analysis.
Shortfalls in externally performed tasks	Reference checking, preaward audits, award-fee contracts, competitive design or prototyping, team-building.
Real-time performance shortfalls	Simulation, benchmarking, modeling, prototyping, instrumentation, tuning.
Straining computer-science capabilities	Technical analysis, cost-benefit analysis, prototyping, reference checking.

One difficulty with the risk-exposure quantity, as with most other decision-analysis quantities, is the problem of making accurate input estimates of the probability and loss associated with an unsatisfactory outcome. Checklists like that in Exhibit 4 provide some help in assessing the probability of occurrence of a given risk item, but it is clear from Exhibit 4 that its probability ranges do not support precise probability estimation.

Full risk-analysis efforts involving prototyping, benchmarking, and simulation generally provide better probability and loss estimates, but they may be more expensive and time-consuming than the situation warrants. Other techniques, like betting analogies and group-consensus techniques, can improve risk-probability estimation, but for risk prioritization you can often take a simpler course:

assessing the risk probabilities and losses on a relative scale of 0 to 10.

Exhibits 5 and 6 illustrate this risk-prioritization process by using some potential risk items from the satellite-experiment project as examples. Exhibit 5 summarizes several unsatisfactory outcomes with their corresponding ratings for P(UO), L(UO), and their resulting risk-exposure estimates. Exhibit 6 plots each unsatisfactory outcome with respect to a set of constant risk-exposure contours.

Three key points emerge from Exhibits 5 and 6:

- Projects often focus on factors having either a high P(UO) or a high L(UO), but these may not be the key factors with a high risk-exposure combination. One of the highest P(UO)s comes from item G (data-reduction errors), but the fact

EXHIBIT 4 Quantification of Probability and Impact for Cost Failure

	Probability		
Cost Drivers	*Improbable (0.0–0.3)*	*Probable (0.4–0.6)*	*Frequent (0.7–1.0)*
Requirements			
Size	Small, noncomplex, or easily decomposed	Medium to moderate complexity, decomposable	Large, highly complex, or not decomposable
Resource constraints	Little or no hardware-imposed constraints	Some hardware-imposed constraints	Significant hardware-imposed constraints
Application	Nonreal-time, little system interdependency	Embedded, some system interdependencies	Real-time, embedded, strong interdependency
Technology	Mature, existent, in-house experience	Existent, some in-house experience	New or new application, little experience
Requirements stability	Little or no change to established baseline	Some change in baseline expected	Rapidly changing, or no baseline
Personnel			
Availability	In place, little turnover expected	Available, some turnover expected	Not available, high turnover expected
Mix	Good mix of software disciplines	Some disciplines inappropriately represented	Some disciplines not represented
Experience	High experience ratio	Average experience ratio	Low experience ratio
Management environment	Strong personnel management approach	Good personnel management approach	Weak personnel management approach
Reusable software			
Availability	Compatible with need dates	Delivery dates in question	Incompatible with need dates
Modifications	Little or no change	Some change	Extensive changes
Language	Compatible with system and maintenance requirements	Partial compatibility with requirements	Incompatible with system or maintenance requirements
Rights	Compatible with maintenance and competition requirements	Partial compatibility with maintenance, some competition	Incompatible with maintenance concept, noncompetitive
Certification	Verified performance, application compatible	Some application-compatible test data available	Unverified, little test data available
Tools and environment			
Facilities	Little or no modification	Some modifications, existent	Major modifications, nonexistent
Availability	In place, meets need dates	Some compatibility with need dates	Nonexistent, does not meet need dates
Rights	Compatible with maintenance and development plans	Partial compatibility with maintenance and development plans	Incompatible with maintenance and development plans
Configuration management	Fully controlled	Some controls	No controls
Impact	Sufficient financial resources	Some shortage of financial resources, possible overrun	Significant financial shortages, budget overrun likely

EXHIBIT 5   Risk Exposure Factors for Satellite Experiment Software

Unsatisfactory Outcome	*Probability of Unsatisfactory Outcome*	*Loss Caused by Unsatisfactory Outcome*	*Risk Exposure*
A. Software error kills experiment	3–5	10	30–50
B. Software error loses key data	3–5	8	24–40
C. Fault-tolerant features cause unacceptable performance	4–8	7	28–56
D. Monitoring software reports unsafe condition as safe	5	9	45
E. Monitoring software reports safe condition as unsafe	5	3	15
F. Hardware delay causes schedule overrun	6	4	24
G. Data-reduction software errors cause extra work	8	1	8
H. Poor user interface causes inefficient operation	6	5	30
I. Processor memory insufficient	1	7	7
J. Database-management software loses derived data	2	2	4

that these errors are recoverable and not mission-critical leads to a low loss factor and a resulting low RE of 7. Similarly, item I (insufficient memory) has a high potential loss, but its low probability leads to a low RE of 7. On the other hand, a relatively low-profile item like item H (user-interface shortfalls) becomes a relatively high-priority risk item because its combination of moderately high probability and loss factors yield a RE of 30.

- The RE quantities also provide a basis for prioritizing verification and validation and related test activities by giving each error class a significance weight. Frequently, all errors are treated with equal weight, putting too much testing effort into finding relatively trivial errors.
- There is often a good deal of uncertainty in estimating the probability or loss associated with an unsatisfactory outcome. (The assessments are frequently subjective and are often the product of surveying several domain experts.) The

amount of uncertainty is itself a major source of risk, which needs to be reduced as early as possible. The primary example in Exhibits 5 and 6 is the uncertainty in item C about whether the fault-tolerance features are going to cause an unacceptable degradation in real-time performance. If P(UO) is rated at 4, this item has only a moderate RE of 28, but if P(UO) is 8, the RE has a top-priority rating of 56.

One of the best ways to reduce this source of risk is to buy information about the actual situation. For the issue of fault tolerance versus performance, a good way to buy information is to invest in a prototype, to better understand the performance effects of the various fault-tolerance features.

Risk-Management Planning

Once you determine a project's major risk items and their relative priorities, you need to establish a set of risk-control functions to bring the risk items

EXHIBIT 6   Risk-Exposure Factors and Contours for the Satellite-Experiment Software. RE is the Risk Exposure, P(UO) the Probability of an Unsatisfactory Outcome, and L(UO) the Loss Associated With that Unsatisfactory Outcome. The Graph Points Map the Items From Table 3 Whose Risk Exposure Are Being Assessed

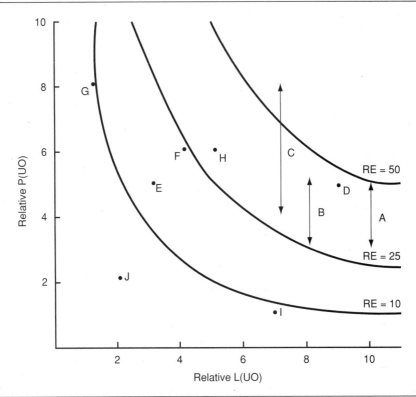

under control. The first step in this process is to develop a set of risk-management plans that lay out the activities necessary to bring the risk items under control.

One aid in doing this is the top-10 checklist in Exhibit 6 that identifies the most successful risk-management techniques for the most common risk items. As an example, item 9 (real-time performance shortfalls) in Exhibit 3 covers the uncertainty in performance effect of the fault-tolerance features. The corresponding risk-management techniques include simulation, benchmarking, modeling, prototyping, instrumentation, and tuning. Assume, for example, that a prototype of representative safety features is the most cost-

effective way to determine and reduce their effects on system performance.

The next step in risk-management planning is to develop risk-management plans for each risk item. Exhibit 7 shows the plan for prototyping the fault-tolerance features and determining their effects on performance. The plan is organized around a standard format for software plans, oriented around answering the standard questions of why, what, when, who, where, how, and how much. This plan organization lets the plans be concise (fitting on one page), action-oriented, easy to understand, and easy to monitor.

The final step in risk-management planning is to integrate the risk-management plans for each risk

---

EXHIBIT 7   Risk-Management Plan for Fault-Tolerance Prototyping

---

1. Objectives (the "why")
   - Determine, reduce level of risk of the software fault-tolerance features causing unacceptable performance.
   - Create a description of and a development plan for a set of low-risk fault-tolerance features.
2. Deliverables and milestones (the "what" and "when").
   - By Week 3.
     1. Evaluation of fault-tolerance options
     2. Assessment of reusable components
     3. Draft workload characterization
     4. Evaluation plan for prototype exercise
     5. Description of prototype
   - By Week 7.
     6. Operational prototype with key fault-tolerance features.
     7. Workload simulation
     8. Instrumentation and data reduction capabilities.
     9. Draft description, plan for fault-tolerance features.
   - By Week 10.
     10. Evaluation and iteration of prototype
     11. Revised description, plan for fault-tolerance features
3. Responsibilities (the "who" and "where")
   - System engineer: G. Smith
     Tasks 1, 3, 4, 9, 11. Support of tasks 5, 10
   - Lead programmer: C. Lee
     Tasks 5, 6, 7, 10. Support of tasks 1, 3
   - Programmer: J. Wilson
     Tasks 2, 8. Support of tasks 5, 6, 7, 10
4. Approach (the "how")
   - Design-to-schedule prototyping effort
   - Driven by hypotheses about fault-tolerance-performance effects
   - Use real-time operating system, add prototype fault-tolerance features
   - Evaluate performance with respect to representative workload
   - Refine prototype based on results observed
5. Resources (the "how much")
   $60K—full-time system engineer, lead programmer, programmer (10 weeks)*(3 staff)*$2k/staff-week)
   $0—three dedicated workstations (from project pool)
   $0—two target processors (from project pool)
   $0—one test coprocessor (from project pool)
   $10K—contingencies
   $70K—total

---

item with each other and with the overall project plan. Each of the other high-priority or uncertain risk items will have a risk-management plan; it may turn out, for example, that the fault-tolerance features prototyped for this risk item could also be useful as part of the strategy to reduce the uncertainty in items A and B (software errors killing the experiment and losing experiment-critical data). Also, for the overall project plan, the need for a 10-week prototype-development and -exercise period must be factored into the overall schedule, to keep the overall schedule realistic.

Risk Resolution and Monitoring

Once you have established a good set of risk-management plans, the risk-resolution process consists of implementing whatever prototypes, simulations, benchmarks, surveys, or other risk-reduction techniques are called for in the plans. Risk monitoring ensures that this is a closed-loop process by tracking risk-reduction progress and applying whatever corrective action is necessary to keep the risk-resolution process on track.

Risk management provides managers with a very effective technique for keeping on top of projects under their control: *Project top-10 risk-item tracking.* This technique concentrates management attention on the high-risk, high-leverage, critical success factors rather than swamping management reviews with lots of low-priority detail. As a manager, I have found that this type of risk-item-oriented review saves a lot of time, reduces management surprises, and gets you focused on the high-leverage issues where you can make a difference as a manager.

Top-10 risk-item tracking involves the following steps:

- Ranking the project's most significant risk items.
- Establishing a regular schedule for higher management reviews of the project's progress. The review should be chaired by the equivalent of the project manager's boss. For large projects (more than 20 people), the reviews should be held monthly. In the project itself, the project manager would review them more frequently.
- Beginning each project-review meeting with a summary of progress on the top 10 risk items. (The number could be seven or 12 without loss of intent.) The summary should include each risk item's current top-10 ranking, its rank at the previous review, how often it has been on the top-10 list, and a summary of progress in resolving the risk item since the previous review.

- Focusing the project-review meeting on dealing with any problems in resolving the risk items.

Exhibit 8 shows how a top-10 list could have worked for the satellite-experiment project, as of month 3 of the project. The project's top risk item in month 3 is a critical staffing problem. Highlighting it in the monthly review meeting would stimulate a discussion by the project team and the boss of the staffing options: Make the unavailable key person available, reshuffle project personnel, or look for new people within or outside the organization. This should result in an assignment of action items to follow through on the options chosen, including possible actions by the project manager's boss.

The number 2 risk item in Exhibit 8, target hardware delivery delays, is also one for which the project manager's boss may be able to expedite a solution—by cutting through corporate-procurement red tape, for example, or by escalating vendor-delay issues with the vendor's higher management.

As Exhibit 8 shows, some risk items are moving down in priority or going off the list, while others are escalating or coming onto the list. The ones moving down the list—like the design-verification and -validation staffing, fault-tolerance prototyping, and user-interface prototyping—still need to be monitored but frequently do not need special management action. The ones moving up or onto the list—like the data-bus design changes and the testbed-interface definitions—are generally the ones needing higher management attention to help get them resolved quickly.

As this example shows, the top-10 risk-item list is a very effective way to focus higher management attention onto the project's critical success factors. It also uses management's time very efficiently, unlike typical monthly reviews, which spend most of their time on things the higher manager can't do anything about. Also, if the higher manager surfaces an additional concern, it is easy to add it to the top-10 risk-item list to be highlighted in future reviews.

EXHIBIT 8 Project Top-10 Risk Item List for Satellite Experiment Software

Risk item	Monthly ranking			Risk-Resolution Progress
	This	Last	No. of months	
Replacing sensor-control software developer	1	4	2	Top replacement candidate unavailable
Target hardware delivery delays	2	5	2	Procurement procedural delays
Sensor data formats undefined	3	3	3	Action items to software, sensor teams; due next month
Staffing of design V & V team	4	2	3	Key reviewers committed; need fault-tolerance reviewer
Software fault-tolerance may compromise performance	5	1	3	Fault-tolerance prototype successful
Accommodate changes in data bus design	6	—	1	Meeting scheduled with data-bus designers
Test-bed interface definitions	7	8	3	Some delays in action items; review meeting scheduled
User interface uncertainties	8	6	3	User interface prototype successful
TBDs in experiment operational concept	—	7	3	TBDs resolved
Uncertainties in reusable monitoring software	—	9	3	Required design changes small, successfully made

IMPLEMENTING RISK MANAGEMENT

Implementing risk management involves inserting the risk-management principles and practices into your existing life-cycle management practices. Full implementation of risk management involves the use of risk-driven software-process models like the spiral model, where risk considerations determine the overall sequence of life-cycle activities, the use of prototypes and other risk-resolution techniques, and the degree of detail of plans and specifications. However, the best implementation strategy is an incremental one, which lets an organization's culture adjust gradually to risk-oriented management practices and risk-driven process models.

A good way to begin is to establish a top-10 risk-item tracking process. It is easy and inexpensive to implement, provides early improvements, and begins establishing a familiarity with the other risk-management principles and practices. Another good way to gain familiarity is via books like my recent tutorial on risk management[3] which contains the Air Force risk-abatement pamphlet[5] and other useful articles, and Robert Charette's recent good book on risk management.[4]

An effective next step is to identify an appropriate initial project in which to implement a top-level life-cycle risk-management plan. Once the organization has accumulated some risk-management experience on this initial project, successive steps can deepen the sophistication of the risk-management techniques and broaden their application to wider classes of projects.

Exhibit 9 provides a scheme for implementing a top-level life-cycle risk-management plan. It is presented in the context of a contractual software acquisition, but you can tailor it to the needs of an internal development organization as well.

EXHIBIT 9   Framework for Life-Cycle Risk Management

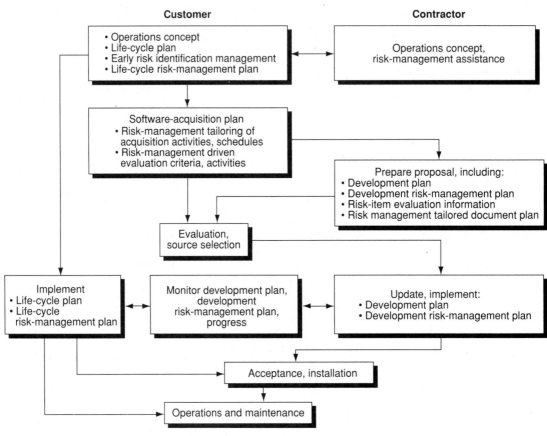

You can organize the life-cycle risk-management plan as an elaboration of the "why, what, when, who, where, how, how much" framework of Exhibit 7. While this plan is primarily the customer's responsibility, it is very useful to involve the developer community in its preparation as well.

Such a plan addresses not only the development risks that have been the prime topic of this article but also operations and maintenance risks. These include such items as staffing and training of maintenance personnel, discontinuities in the switch from the old to the new system, undefined responsibilities for operations and maintenance facilities and functions, and insufficient budget for planned life-cycle improvements or for corrective, adaptive, and perfective maintenance.

Exhibit 9 also shows the importance of proposed developer risk-management plans in competitive source evaluation and selection. Emphasizing the realism and effectiveness of a bidder's risk-management plan increases the probability that the customer will select a bidder that clearly understands the project's critical success factors and that has established a development approach that satisfactorily addresses them. (If the developer is a noncompetitive internal organization, it is equally important for the internal customer to require and review a developer risk-management plan.)

The most important thing for a project to do is to get focused on its critical success factors.

For various reasons, including the influence of previous document-driven management guidelines, projects get focused on activities that are not critical for their success. These frequently include writing boilerplate documents, exploring intriguing but peripheral technical issues, playing politics, and trying to sell the "ultimate" system.

In the process, critical success factors get neglected, the project fails, and nobody wins.

The key contribution of software risk management is to create this focus on critical success factors—and to provide the techniques that let the project deal with them. The risk-assessment and risk-control techniques presented here provide the foundation layer of capabilities needed to implement the risk-oriented approach.

However, risk management is not a cookbook approach. To handle all the complex people-oriented and technology-driven success factors in projects, a great measure of human judgment is required.

Good people, with good skills and good judgment, are what make projects work. Risk management can provide you with some of the skills, an emphasis on getting good people, and a good conceptual framework for sharpening your judgment. I hope you can find these useful on your next project.

References

1. J. Rothfeder, "It's Late, Costly, and Incompetent—But Try Firing a Computer System," *Business Week,* Nov. 7, 1988, pp. 164–165.

2. B.W. Boehm, "A Spiral Model of Software Development and Enhancement," *Computer,* May 1988, pp. 61–72.

3. B.W. Boehm, *Software Risk Management,* CS Press, Los Alamitos, Calif., 1989.

4. R.N. Charette, *Software Engineering Risk Analysis and Management,* McGraw-Hill, New York, 1989.

5. "Software Risk Abatement," AFSC/AFLC pamphlet 800–45, US Air Force Systems Command, Andrews AFB, Md., 1988.

RISK MANAGEMENT FOR SOFTWARE PROJECTS

Many software projects fail to deliver acceptable systems within schedule and budget. Many of these failures might have been avoided had the project team properly assessed and mitigated the risk factors, yet risk management is seldom applied as an explicit project-management activity. One reason risk management is not practiced is that very few guidelines are available that offer a practical, step-by-step approach to managing risk. To address this deficiency, I have created a seven-step process for risk management that can be applied to all types of software projects.

I base the process on several years of work with numerous organizations to identify and overcome risk factors in software projects. My clients and I have used a variety of risk-management techniques within the framework of the process. I describe one set of techniques here, which incorporates regression-based cost modeling, but other techniques, such as decision theory, risk tables, and spiral process models, are equally applicable.[1]

ELEMENTS OF RISK MANAGEMENT

The seven steps of my risk-management process are

1. *Identify risk factors.* A risk is a potential problem; a problem is a risk that has materialized. Exactly when the transformation takes place is somewhat subjective. A schedule delay of one week might not be cause for concern, but a delay of one month could have serious consequences. The important thing is that all parties who may be affected by a schedule delay agree in advance on the point at which a risk will become a problem. That way, when the risk does become a problem, it is mitigated by the planned corrective actions. In identifying a risk, you must take care to distinguish symptoms from underlying risk factors. A potential schedule delay may in fact be a symptom of difficult technical issues or inadequate resources.

Whether you identify a situation as a risk or an opportunity depends on your point of view. Is the glass half full or half empty? Situations with high potential for failure often have the potential for high payback as well. Risk management is not the same as risk aversion. Competitive pressures and the demands of modern society require that you take risks to be successful.

2. *Assess risk probabilities and effects on the project.* Because risk implies a potential loss, you must estimate two elements of a risk: the probability that the risk will become a problem and the effect the problem would have on the project's desired outcome. For software projects, the desired outcome is an acceptable product delivered on time and within budget. Factors that influence product acceptability include delivered functionality, performance, resource use, safety, reliability, versatility, ease of learning, ease of use, and ease of modification.

Depending on the situation, failure to meet one or more of these criteria within the constraints of schedule and budget can precipitate a crisis for the developer, the customer, and/or the user community. Thus, the primary goal of risk management is to identify and confront risk factors with enough lead time to avoid a crisis.

The approach I describe here is to assess the probability of a risk by computing probability distributions for code size and complexity and use them to determine the effect of limited target memory and execution time on overall project

effort. I then use Monte Carlo simulation to compute the distribution of estimated project effort as a function of size, complexity, timing, and memory, using regression-based modeling.

This approach uses estimated effort as the metric to assess the impact of risk factors. Because effort is the primary cost factor for most software projects, you can use it as a measure of overall project cost, especially when using loaded salaries (burdened with facilities, computer time, and management, for example).

3. *Develop strategies to mitigate identified risks.* In general, a risk becomes a problem when the value of a quantitative metric crosses a predetermined threshold. For that reason, two essential parts of risk management are setting thresholds, beyond which some corrective action is required, and determining ahead of time what that corrective action will be. Without such planning, you quickly realize the truth in the answer to Fred Brooks' rhetorical question, "How does a project get to be a year late?" One day at a time.[2]

Risk mitigation involves two types of strategies. *Action planning* addresses risks that can be mitigated by immediate response. To address the risk of insufficient experience with a new hardware architecture, for example, the action plan could provide for training the development team, hiring experienced personnel, or finding a consultant to work with the project team. Of course, you should not spend more on training or hiring than would be paid back in increased productivity. If you estimate that training and hiring can increase productivity by 10 percent, for example, you should not spend more than 10 percent of the project's personnel budget in this manner.

Contingency planning, on the other hand, addresses risks that require monitoring for some future response should the need arise. To mitigate the risk of late delivery by a hardware vendor, for example, the contingency plan could provide for monitoring the vendor's progress and developing a software emulator for the target machine.

Of course, the risk of late hardware delivery must justify the added cost of preparing the

Regression-Based Cost Modeling

You develop a regression-based cost model by collecting data from past projects for relationships of interest (like software size and required effort), deriving a regression equation, and incorporating additional cost factors to explain deviations of actual project costs from the costs predicted by the regression equation.

A commonly used approach to regression-based cost modeling is to derive a linear equation in the log-log domain (log Effort, E, as a linear slope-intercept function of log Size, S) that minimizes the residuals between the equation and the data points for actual projects. Transforming the linear equation, $\log E = \log a + b * \log S$, from the log-log domain to the real domain gives you an exponential relationship of the form $E = a * S^b$. Exhibit 1 illustrates this approach, where E is measured in person-months and S is measured in thousands of lines of source code (KLOC).

As the exhibit shows, it is not untypical to observe wide scatter in actual project data, which indicates large variations in the effort predicted by the regression equation and the actual effort. Residual error is one measure of the variations. A large residual error means that factors in addition to size exert a strong influence on required effort. If size were a perfect predictor of effort, every data point in Exhibit 1 would lie on the line of the equation, and the residual error would be zero.

The next step in regression-based cost modeling is to identify the factors that cause variations between predicted and actual effort. We might, by examining our past projects, determine that 80 percent of the variation in required effort for projects of similar size and type can be explained by variations in stability of the requirements, familiarity of the development team with the application domain, and involvement of users during the development cycle. As illustrated in Exhibit 2, you can assign weighting factors to these variables to model their effects.

EXHIBIT 1   Derivation of a Regression-Based Cost Model

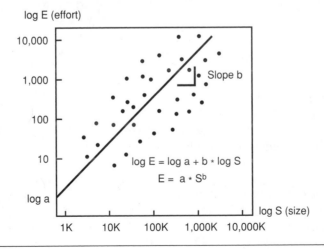

Regression-Based Cost Modeling (*Cont.*)

The regression-based cost model is then of the form:

$$Effort = (a * Size^b) * EAF$$

where EAF is the effort-adjustment factor, which is the product of the effort multiplier values from Exhibit 2.

According to the table, high requirements volatility, medium application experience, and low user involvement would result in an EAF of 1.56 (1.2 * 1.0 * 1.3); low requirements volatility, medium application experience, and high user involvement would result in an EAF of 0.64 (0.8 * 1.0 * 0.8). The former situation would require 56 percent more effort than the nominal estimate, while the latter would require 36 percent less effort than the nominal case.

Using effort multipliers to adjust an estimate implies that factors not accounted for in the model do not change from past projects to the one being estimated. For example, the model presented in Exhibits 1 and 2 does not incorporate factors such as personnel capabilities or stability of the development environment. If these factors should change, the corresponding impacts (positive or negative) must be incorporated into the estimate for a future project. Failure to do so increases risk.

Examples. Barry Boehm's Cocomo (Constructive Cost Model) is perhaps the best known example of a regression-based cost model. Cocomo is based on data from 63 projects, collected by Boehm during the mid-to-late 1970s. He clustered the data into three groupings, which he called modes. He then derived two linear equations for each mode in the log-log domain; one equation for estimated effort as a function of software size and one for estimated development time as a function of estimated effort.

Boehm and his colleagues identified 15 cost drivers as those factors that contributed most to the observed variations in effort and schedule for software projects of similar size and mode. The ranges of cost-driver values were derived by expert judgment using a Delphi procedure.

Boehm illustrated, by example, how to construct a regression-based cost model; hence the name of the model. The model does not work without recalibration to allow for differences in Boehm's environment and the environment of interest, however. When organizations use the equations and tables without doing so, the estimates may be seriously skewed. *Cocomo equations and tables should not be used as published without recalibrating the model in the local environment.*

Automation concerns. Several tools are available that automate regression-based cost modeling. One of the best tool sets, for versatility and ease of use, is from the Softstar Systems Company of Amherst, New Hampshire. The Softstar tools include a tool (Calico) for entering local project data and deriving regression equations tailored to the local environment, a tool (Dbedit) to edit the effort and schedule distribution tables, cost-driver values, hours per work-month, and other factors; and the estimation tool (CoStar), which uses the outputs from Calico and Dbedit as the basis for estimates.

EXHIBIT 2 Effort Multipliers for a Software Project

Cost Driver	*Effort Multiplier*		
	Low	Medium	High
Requirements volatility	0.8	1.0	1.2
Application experience	1.4	1.0	0.7
User involvement	1.3	1.0	0.8

contingency plan, monitoring the situation, and implementing the plan's actions. If the cost is justified, plan preparation and vendor monitoring might be implemented immediately, but the action to develop an emulator might be postponed until the risk of late delivery became a problem (the vendor's schedule slipped beyond a predetermined threshold). This brings up the issue of sufficient lead time. When do you start to develop the emulator? The answer lies in analyzing the probability of late delivery. As that probability increases, the urgency of developing the emulator becomes greater.

4. *Monitor risk factors.* You must monitor the values of risk metrics, taking care that the metrics data is objective, timely, and accurate. If metrics are based on subjective factors, your project will quickly be reported as 90 percent complete and remain there for many months. You must avoid situations in which the first 90 percent of the project takes the first 90 percent of the schedule, while the remaining 10 percent of the project takes another 90 percent of the schedule.

5. *Invoke a contingency plan.* A contingency plan is invoked when a quantitative risk indicator crosses a predetermined threshold. You may find it difficult to convince the affected parties that a serious problem has developed, especially in the early stages of a project. A typical response is to plan on catching up during the next reporting period, but most projects never catch up without the explicit, planned corrective actions of a contingency plan. You must also specify the duration of each contingency plan to avoid contingent actions of interminable duration. If the team cannot solve the problem within a specified period (typically one to two weeks), they must invoke a crisis-management plan.

6. *Manage the crisis.* Despite a team's best efforts, the contingency plan may fail, in which case the project enters crisis mode. There must be some plan for seeing a project through this phase, including allocating sufficient resources and specifying a drop-dead date, at which time management must reevaluate the project for more drastic corrective action (possibly major redirection or cancellation of the project).

7. *Recover from a crisis.* After a crisis, certain actions are required, such as rewarding personnel who have worked in burnout mode for an extended period and reevaluating cost and schedule in light of the drain on resources from managing the crisis.

I illustrate these seven steps for a project to implement a telecommunications protocol. The project, which is actually a composite of several real projects, gave me the opportunity to explore key risk-management issues, such as the likelihood that an undesired situation might occur, the resulting effect of the risk situation, the cost of mitigating the risk, the degree of urgency in mitigation, and the lead time required to avoid a crisis.

CASE STUDY

The project's goal was to implement a telecommunications protocol for a network gateway using a 10-MHz microprocessor with a 256-Kbyte memory. The project had several constraints that challenged risk management. The project team could not enlarge the memory because the processor was provided by the customer and its use was mandatory. The maximum execution time for message processing was 10 ms.

Risk Identification

I used a regression-based cost model to identify and assess the impact of risk factors on estimated project effort. The box on pp. 231–232 describes regression-based cost modeling in more detail, as well as some tools for automating it. For the telecom project, I used a regression-based cost model for real-time telecommunications systems on microprocessors, which I had developed for the client, using historical data from similar projects.

The regression equation I derived to relate effort to product size is

$$Effort = 3.6 * (Size)^{1.25} * EAF$$

where EAF is the effort-adjustment factor. EAF is the product of 15 cost factors taken from Barry Boehm's Cocomo model.[3] Required software reliability (Rely), ratio of database size to source-code size (Data), software complexity (Cplx), execution time constraint on the target machine (Time), memory constraint on the target machine (Stor), volatility of the development machine and software (Virt), response time of the development environment (Turn), analyst capability (Acap), applications experience for the development team (Aexp), programmer capability (Pcap), team experience on the development environment (Vexp), team experience with the programming language (Lexp), use of modern programming practices (Modp), use of software tools (Tool), and required development schedule (Sced).

Using these cost drivers as a checklist for the telecom project, I identified five risk factors and added one (Size):

- *Cplx.* Effect of algorithmic complexity
- *Time.* 10-ms timing constraint
- *Stor.* 256K memory of the target processor
- *Vexp.* Lack of experience with the target processor
- *Tool.* Lack of adequate software tools for the target processor
- *Size.* Uncertainty in estimated code size.

These six factors are interrelated: If the algorithms are complex, code size is likely to increase; if size increases, more memory and execution time will be required. With more experience on the target processor architecture and with better software tools, the team might better control the code size, execution time, and memory requirements.

Probability and Effects Assessment

According to evidence from similar projects and some analysis, I estimated that the size of the telecom project's code would be no less than 9 KLOC and no more than 15 KLOC, with the most likely size being approximately 10 KLOC, as Exhibit 4a shows. Exhibit 4b is the probability-density function for the probable effect of algorithmic complexity (Cplx) on project effort. As the exhibit shows, I estimated the most likely impact to be 1.3, with a normal distribution of 1.0 to 1.6. The function for Cplx models the impact that uncertainty in target-

EXHIBIT 3   Effects of Limited Memory and Time on Project Effort

Memory used	Stor	Time used	Time
Less than 50%	1.00	Less than 50%	1.00
70%	1.06	70%	1.11
85%	1.21	85%	1.30
95%	1.56	95%	1.66

machine experience (Vexp) and lack of tools (Tool) will have on the ability to control the complexity of the program that implements the communication algorithms. I used these probability-density functions to derive a distribution of probable project effort, as the box on p. 236 describes.

Thus, the risk factors to be modeled are software size, algorithmic complexity, and the memory and execution-time constraints of the target machine. To assess the effect of uncertainty in size, complexity, execution time, and the memory constraint on the required effort, I constructed a probabilistic cost model and used Monte Carlo simulation. The simulation model is of the form

$$Effort = 3.6 * (Size)^{1.25} * EAF \qquad (1)$$

where EAF is the product of Stor, Time, and Cplx, and where Size and Cplx are modeled by the probability distributions in Exhibit 4. Stor and Time are dependent on Size.

I determined values for Stor by first randomly selecting a value from the inverse probability distribution for Size. I then used a code-expansion factor of 16 (based on a ratio of 1 to 4 for source-to-object instructions and 1 to 4 for object instructions to object bytes), multiplied by Size, and divided by 256K (the memory size) to get the percentage of memory used. That is,

$$Percentage\ of\ memory =$$
$$100 * [16 * SIZE]/256 \qquad (2)$$

For example, I determined that the percentage of memory used is 93.75 when Size is 15 KLOC. Exhibit 3 shows values of Stor and Time taken from Cocomo.[3] In the first two columns are the values

EXHIBIT 4 Two Probability Distribution Curves for the Telecom Project. *(A) Size Distribution and (B) Effect of Algorithmic Complexity (Cplx) on Project Effort*

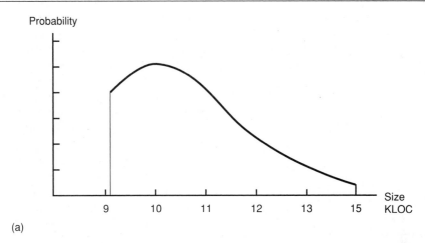

(a)

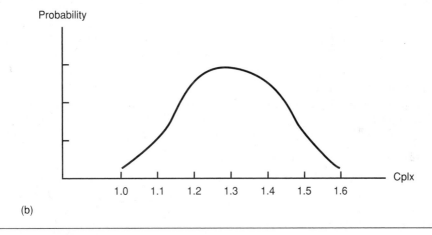

(b)

of Stor for various percentages of use. From the table, I interpolated that Stor is approximately 1.55 when the percentage of memory is 93.75.

The last two columns of Exhibit 3 show how execution time affects project effort. Time, which is also dependent on Size, is modeled as

$$\text{Percentage of time} = 100 * [(1/2) * (1/3) * (4 * \text{SIZE})] / 10 \qquad (3)$$

where 1/2 is the average cycle time in milliseconds for instruction processing on the target processor (five clock ticks at 10 MHz); a third of the object bytes are instructions executed by the main timing loop (an assumption) and the remainder are data cells and exception-handling code; and 4 * Size is the expansion factor from source instructions to object instructions. I then divide Time by 10 ms (the timing constraint) to determine the percentage of time. The percentage of time is 100 when Size is 15 KLOC.

Although, as this analysis shows, the timing constraint dominates the memory constraint, I tracked both factors because the assumption used

Probability-Density and Distribution Functions

Probability-density functions [$p(x)$] are the continuous counterparts of discrete probability histograms (the relative number of times you can expect event x to occur). A probability-distribution function is the integral of $p(x)$. Integrating $p(x)$ from negative infinity to Y is the probability that x will be less than or equal to Y:

$$P(x \leq Y) = \int_{-\inf}^{Y} p(x)dx$$

where $p(x)$ is the lognormal distribution function in Exhibit 4 in the main text, for example. The integral $P(Y \leq x \leq Z)$ is the continuous counterpart of summing the values of a discrete probability histogram from Y to Z:

$$P(Y \leq x \leq Z) = \int_{Y}^{Z} p(x)dx$$

This integral is the probability that x will be in the range Y to Z; for example, the probability that Size will be in the range of 10,000 to 12,000 lines of code is:

$$P(10 \leq size \leq 12) = \int_{10}^{12} p(x)dx$$

where $p(x)$ is the probability-density function in Exhibit in the main text.

The inverse distribution function, P–1(x), provides values of x that correspond to given values of P(x). Inverse probability-distribution functions are used in Monte Carlo simulation to compute values of x that correspond to randomly selected probability values, P(x).

In practice, you can calculate $P^{-1}(x)$ by table lookup for certain well-defined probability distributions (Z tables for normal distributions, for example) or by sampling techniques such as the Latin Hypercube sampling method.[1]

Monte Carlo simulation is a technique for modeling probabilistic situations that are too complex to solve analytically. Probability distributions are specified for the input variables to the model. A random number generator is used to select independent sample points from the inverse probability distributions for each of the input variables. These sample values are used to compute one point on the specified output distribution(s). Repeating the process a few hundred to a few thousand times produces a histogram that approximates the resultant probability distributions to any desired degree of accuracy.

Until recently, Monte Carlo simulation was the province of modeling specialists. Introduction of PC-based and Macintosh-based simulation packages has made Monte Carlo simulation accessible to anyone who knows statistics and PCs. Two tools for Monte Carlo simulation are @Risk from Palisade Corp. of Los Angeles and Crystal Ball from Decisioneering Corp. of Denver, both of which run in conjunction with a spreadsheet. For the telecom project described in the main text, I used Crystal Ball, to specify probability distributions for the variables in the cells of the spreadsheet, randomly select values from them, and calculate result values according to the spreadsheet equations.

References

1. R. Inman and J. Helton, "An Investigation of Uncertainty and Sensitivity Analysis Techniques for Computer Models," *Risk Analysis,* Jan. 1988, pp. 71–90.

to derive the percentage of time equation (Time) was not certain and because both Stor and Time affect project effort. In reality, memory could become the dominant factor.

To compute the probable effort for the telecom project, I used Monte Carlo simulation and the Crystal Ball simulation tool from Decisioneering Corp., which randomly selected data points from the inverse probability-distribution functions for Size and Cplx and used the value of Size along with Exhibit 3 to determine values for Time and Stor. The tool then used the values of Size, Cplx, Time, and Stor in the regression equation to compute a point on the probability-density histogram for effort. The tool should repeat this computation at least a few hundred times to produce a reasonable approximation of the probability-density function for estimated effort.

Exhibit 6 shows the probable effort for the telecom project converted to dollars, because effort was the primary driver of this project's cost. The conversion factor was a loaded salary of $10,000 per person month, loaded meaning that indirect and overhead costs are included. The right vertical axis indicates the actual number of times the tool computed a given cost. The left vertical axis indicates the probability of that cost occurring, as computed by the ratio of the number of occurrences to total occurrences.

The summation of probabilities up to any given dollar amount is the probability that the project can be completed for that amount of money or less. Exhibit 5 presents some estimated costs and associated probabilities. For example, it is 70 percent probable that the project can be completed for $600,000 or less (60 person months of effort at $10,000 per person month). This cost might involve scheduling six people for 10 months or five people for 12 months.

As illustrated in Exhibits 5 and 6, low complexity and a small product size, with associated small values of Time and Stor, would result in low cost. If the product is large and complex, the resulting cost would be high.

The next issue to face is commitment to a schedule and budget. To distinguish estimates from commitments, I used the equation

$$Commitment = Estimate + Contingency$$

That is, the difference between estimate and commitment is the contingency reserve for the project. In this case, the contingency reserve is for dealing with the impact of uncertainty in source-code size and complexity, and the resulting effects of timing and memory constraints on estimated effort.

In one organization I work with, project teams and management routinely set their development schedules and budgets at 70 percent probability of success, but commit to their customers at 90 percent. The 20 percent difference is a contingency reserve for each project.

Risk Mitigation

Boehm recommends avoidance, transfer, and acceptance as potential risk-mitigation strategies.[1] For the telecom project, avoidance techniques might be to buy more memory or a faster processor or to decline the project. Transfer techniques might include implementing the lowest layers of the communications protocol in hardware, placing the top levels of the protocol on a network server, or subcontracting the work to specialists in communication software. Acceptance techniques require that all affected parties (customers, users, managers, developers), publicly acknowledge the risk factors and accept them. They also involve preparing action, contingency, and crisis-management plans for the identified risks.

EXHIBIT 5   Probable Cost of Effort for the Telecom Project

Percentile	Cost
50th	$570K
70th	$600K
85th	$667K
95th	$762K

EXHIBIT 6   Probability Density of Cost for the Telecom Project

---

Probability   300 trials   Frequency

.04 — 12
.03 — 9
.02 — 6
.01 — 3

Dollars

382K   477K   572K   667K   762K   857K

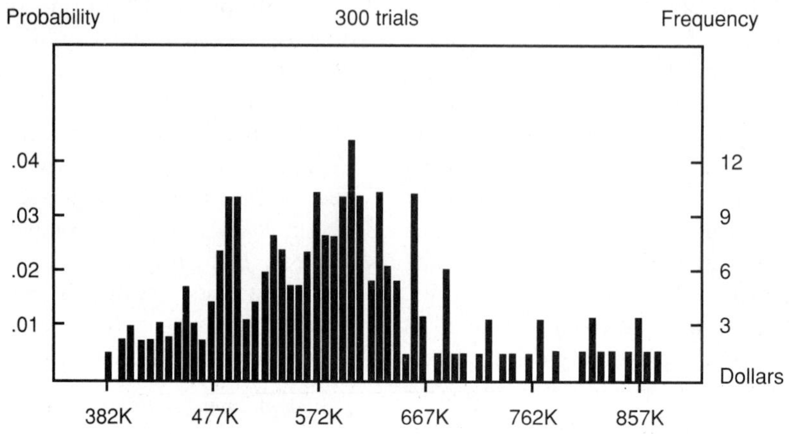

Action Planning

To mitigate the risks of insufficient experience with the target processor, the project manager might provide training for the present staff or hire additional, more experienced personnel as consultants or staff. To deal with the lack of adequate software tools, the manager might acquire more effective tools and provide training. However, he or she would have to evaluate the risk caused by inadequate tools against the risk of insufficient knowledge of the replacement tools.

I used Boehm's Cocomo cost drivers to determine investment strategies for training, consultants, and tools. If training and consultants are expected to lower the effort multiplier for target-machine experience by 10 percent, six percent of this could be invested in training and consultants to produce a four percent savings in estimated project cost.

Another action plan is to investigate the possibility of buying more memory and/or a faster processor. For the telecom project, the existing processor and memory were provided by the customer and thus required (as in government-furnished equipment), although buying your way out of potential software problems with more and better hardware is sometimes a feasible alternative.

This solution might also involve buying some of the software rather than building it all. However, buying commercial off-the-shelf software is not without risk, especially if you are going to incorporate it into a larger system.

The size and complexity of software in the telecom project were factors for which no immediate actions were apparent: the communication protocols were specified, the team had to use the specified hardware and algorithms, and they could not prioritize requirements and eliminate those that were desirable, but not essential.

Contingency Planning

Contingency planning involves preparing a contingency plan, a crisis-management plan, and a crisis-recovery procedure. Contingency plans address the risks not addressed in the action plans. A crisis-management plan is the backup plan to be used if the contingency plan fails to solve a problem within a specified time. A crisis-recovery procedure is invoked when the crisis is over, whether the outcome is positive or negative.

The contingency plan for the telecom project is concerned with controlling the timing budget and memory use on the target processor. It takes into consideration that the probable source size truncates at 15 KLOC, which the code expansion factor of 16 dictates if the major timing loop is to execute in no more than 10 ms.

Thus, preparation of a contingency plan involves

- *Specifying the nature of the potential problem.* For the telecom project this was the effect of memory size and execution time on project effort and schedule.
- *Considering alternative approaches.* For the telecom project, these included building a prototype, using memory overlays, using a faster processor, buying more memory, or pursuing incremental development and monitoring the timing and execution-time budgets. Another approach that is usually considered is to eliminate unessential (desirable but not vital) requirements. However, there are no unessential requirements in a communications protocol.
- *Specifying constraints.* For the telecom project, these were a memory size of 256 Kbytes, an execution time of 10 ms, and the mandatory use of the existing processor and memory.
- *Analyzing alternatives.* Building a prototype would require that the team know how to scale up timing and memory requirements. Using memory overlays would have incurred an unacceptable penalty on execution time. Using a faster processor wasn't possible because use of the current processor was mandatory. Buying more memory wasn't feasible because the processor's address space was limited to 256 Kbytes.
- *Selecting an approach.* Thus, only the last alternative was viable: pursue incremental development and monitor the allocated memory and timing budgets. To do this, the team had to partition the design into a series of builds, allocate memory and timing budgets to each build, and track actual versus budgeted amounts of time and memory for each demonstrated build as the product evolved. A contingency plan was to be invoked when the performance index for

actual versus budgeted memory or execution time exceeded a predetermined threshold.

In allocating the timing and memory budgets, the team held back a contingency reserve. According to equations 2 and 3, a code size of 15 KLOC would result in 93.75 percent use of memory and 100 percent use of execution time. Backsolving equation 3 showed that developers needed to limit the code size to 13.5 KLOC if they wished to hold 10 percent of the execution time in reserve.

The next step was to form the contingency plan, which involves specifying

- *Risk factors.* In the telecom project, these were the 10-ms timing constraint and the 256-Kbyte memory constraint.
- *Tracking methods.* For the telecom project, these were weekly demonstrations of incremental builds and the monitoring of the memory and execution-time budgets.
- *Responsible parties.* For the telecom project, two members of the project team were assigned to monitor performance indices and execute the contingency plan if necessary.
- *Thresholds.* The conditions under which the contingency plan would be invoked. The threshold for the telecom project was a performance index greater than 1.1 for budgeted memory or budgeted execution time.
- *Resource authorizations.* The responsible parties in the telecom project were to be allowed unlimited overtime for two weeks to solve the memory and/or execution-time problem.
- *Constraints.* For the telecom project, the project manager specified that recovery efforts were not to affect the ongoing activities of other project personnel.

Two items in the contingency plan are particularly important: the threshold for initiating the plan (10 percent overrun) and the time limit allotted to fix the problem (two weeks). Because 10 percent of the timing budget is to be withheld, exceeding the performance index for memory or time by less than 10 percent would still yield an acceptable system. A more conservative approach would have been to set the threshold at five percent, while retaining the same 10 percent contingency reserve.

Risk Monitoring and Contingency Planning

To compute the performance indices specified in the contingency plan, the responsible parties compared the actual amount of resources used (time or memory) to the budgeted amount for each incremental build using

$$PI = \Sigma \, (AA/BA)$$

where AA is the actual amount of time or memory required to implement the current build, BA is the cumulative amount of time or memory budgeted for all builds up to and including the current build, and the summation is over all system elements in the current build.

Each weekly build adds functionality to the previous build, so the performance indices track overall growth of time and memory use as the implemented features evolve. Periodically demonstrating implemented capabilities is the only way to accurately track the timing and memory budgets for an evolving software product.

Because software is not a physical entity, there are no physical laws or mathematical theories to guide the development of engineering models that will let us design software to specified levels of reliability, performance, or resource use. The lack of a scientific basis for software design, in terms of traditional engineering parameters, also makes it impossible to scale the results of prototyping and simulation to a full-scale system. This inability, more than any other factor, differentiates software engineering from the traditional engineering disciplines. The only recourse in software is the approach taken in the telecom project: design partitioning, allocation of resource budgets, incremental development, monitoring of budgeted vs. demonstrated values, and contingency plans to control conformance of actual capabilities to requirements.

Crisis Management

A crisis is a show-stopper. All project effort and resources must be dedicated to resolving the situation. You can define some elements of crisis management, such as the responsible parties and drop-dead date, before the crisis materializes, but you may not be able to formulate the exact details until the crisis occurs.

The elements of crisis management are to

- *Announce and generally publicize the problem.* For the telecom project, a crisis was said to occur if the contingency plan failed to resolve the overrun of memory or timing budget within two weeks. A crisis occurred after the team had implemented half the required functions, overrun the memory budget by 12 percent, and two weeks of contingency actions had not fixed the problem.
- *Assign responsibilities and authorities.* Both of the responsible parties and two other team members stopped all other work to concentrate on the problem. The crisis team had access to all necessary resources, subject to the project manager's approval.
- *Update status frequently.* The project team held daily 15-minute stand-up meetings at 11:00 am and 6:00 pm.
- *Relax resource constraints.* Management dedicated all needed resources to solving the problem, including flying in two additional target machines. They also provided resources to support personnel working around the clock, including catering meals and providing sleeping facilities on site.
- *Have project personnel operate in burnout mode.* The crisis team worked as many hours as were humanly possible. All other project personnel were on 24-hour call to assist them until the problem was solved.
- *Establish a drop-dead date.* Efforts to resolve the problem were not to continue longer than 30 days. If the problem was not solved by then, marketing and upper management would reevaluate project

Using COTS: A Different Set of Risks

An increasingly popular approach to constructing software systems is to purchase commercial off-the-shelf packages from vendors and integrate them rather than build all the needed components. In many cases this buy-and-integrate strategy is a viable approach to constructing a system. However, many organizations are so enamored with this latest silver bullet that they overlook the inherent risk factors:

- *Integration.* Integrating data formats and communication protocols of various packages can be tricky. In some cases, it may take more effort to integrate the packages than to build the components from scratch. In other cases, subtle "gotchas" in a package may render it useless in your environment, and they may not be apparent until you have already invested substantial effort in the integration.
- *Upgrading.* There are often difficulties in upgrading a vendor's package. The new version may not have the same interface or feature set as the old version. The data formats and communication protocols may be different, and the new version may require more memory and run more slowly than the old version. If you stay with the old version, the vendor will eventually stop supporting it.
- *No source code.* If you need to enhance the system, you may only have the object code. In most cases, vendors are understandably reluctant to provide source code. In the rare instances that they do, the code is usually so difficult to understand that it is very difficult to modify correctly.
- *Vendor failures or buyouts.* What happens to your system if the vendor goes out of business or is bought out? In some cases, purchasers of COTS have made vendors place the source code in escrow, to be available should the vendor's business fail or be acquired by another company. Again, however, having the source code does not guarantee that anyone can understand it well enough to modify it.

I am not advocating that you never buy COTS, of course, merely that you be aware of the risks.

---

feasibility. As it turned out, the team resolved the crisis before the 30-day deadline.
- *Clear out unessential personnel.* Management requested that all personnel not assigned to the telecom project continue with normal work activities, as long as they did not interfere with the crisis team's work.

One of the most important steps in crisis management is to set a drop-dead date because no one can sustain this kind of effort indefinitely. If the timing problem had not been fixed in 30 days, management would have stopped crisis mode and reconsidered earlier approaches that had been rejected because of project constraints, such as using a different processor or subcontracting the work to telecommunication specialists. They might also have considered moving the upper levels of the protocol to a network server, or even canceling the project altogether.

Crisis Recovery

It is important to examine what went wrong, evaluate how the budget and schedule have been affected, and reward key crisis-management personnel.

As part of crisis-recovery, you should

- *Conduct a crisis postmortem.* This gives you the opportunity to fix any systemic problems that may have precipitated the crisis and to document any lessons learned. For the telecom project, the postmortem revealed that the design was overly complex in a key area and that a simpler design would have yielded a smaller, faster program. The root cause was the team's overall lack of experience in designing software for the target processor.

- *Calculate cost to complete the project.* It is important to know how the crisis has affected the project's budget and schedule. To determine this, I used a technique developed by Karen Pullen of Mitre Corp.,[4] which involves multiplying the expected percentage of total effort for each type of work activity by the actual percentage of completion for each activity. This gave me the current percentage of project completion.

Exhibit 7 shows the status of the telecom project after the crisis. Exhibit 8 summarizes the effort distribution among activities for similar projects. The information in Exhibit 7 indicates an incremental development process; that is, each activity is progressing in parallel with the others. This is consistent with the approach the telecom project team took: Build the product in stages and compare budgeted to actual memory and timing.

Had they taken a waterfall approach, they would have designed all the requirements before beginning coding and completed all coding before beginning acceptance testing. The disadvantage of the waterfall approach is that you don't know if you have an acceptable product until the end of the

EXHIBIT 8   Distribution of Telecom Project Effort

Activity	Percent
Design	17
Coding	26
Code testing	35
Integration	10
Acceptance testing	12

project. The team would have had to wait too long to find out if the software would fit in available memory and run within an acceptable time—this risk was unacceptable.

Exhibits 7 and 8 show that the project was 90 percent complete with 17 percent of the estimated project effort (design); 75 percent complete with 26 percent of the effort (coding), and so on. Therefore, the project was 56 percent complete at crisis recovery.

$$90(.17) + 75(.26) + 50(.35)$$
$$+ 20(.10) + 14(.12) = 56$$

From project data, I knew that 36 person-months of effort had been expended when the crisis occurred. Therefore, 28 person-months of effort would be required to complete the project, assuming the tasks completed were representative of the remaining tasks. However, the remaining work may be more or less difficult than the work already done, so this assumption must be checked for validity.

Also, I knew that the team had expended six calendar months of a 10-month schedule, with a current staffing level of six people (36/6). Using six people, *and assuming that effort to date was representative of future effort and that no further crises would arise,* the project could be completed in another five months (28/6). This would result in an overall development cycle of 11 months (6+5), plus the time spent on preparing and executing contingency plans and managing the crisis. In the end, the 10-month project was completed in 12

EXHIBIT 7   Current Status of the Telecom Project

Project Activity	Degree of Completeness
Requirements designed	27 to 30 designed (90%)
Design elements coded	75 of 100 coded (75%)
Coded modules tested	50 of 100 tested (50%)
Tested modules integrated	20 of 100 integrated (20%)
Requirements tested	4 of 30 tested (14%)

months with 68 person-months of effort. Referring to Exhibits 5 and 6, we see that the project was completed at the 87th percentile of probable effort.

- *Update plans, schedules, and work assignments.* Time and resources have been expended on the contingency plan and crisis management, so original project budget and schedule are likely invalid. For the telecom project, management added 12 person-months to the budget ($120,000) and extended the project schedule by two months. The contingency plan remained in effect but was not invoked again.
- *Compensate workers for extraordinary efforts.* Bonuses and overtime pay are appropriate forms of compensation. However, there is no substitute for resting, regrouping, and recharging. This means time off. The amount of time depends on the level of stress encountered during the crisis. Project managers should factor in that time off when they replan project schedules and assignments. Each member of the telecom project's crisis team was given three days off to recover.

- *Formally recognize outstanding performers and their families.* This may include formal letters of commendation, accelerated promotions, and letters to the families of those who worked around the clock. Free dinners and weekend vacations are other ideas. For the telecom project's crisis team, management provided letters of appreciation and dinner certificates.

Many techniques can be used to implement the seven steps of risk management. I have illustrated one approach. Others are certainly possible. Risk management is an ongoing process continually iterated throughout the life of a project; some potential problems never materialize; others materialize and are dealt with; new risks are identified and mitigation strategies are devised as necessary; and some potential problems submerge, only to resurface later. Following the risk-management procedures illustrated here can increase the probability that potential problems will be identified, confronted, and overcome before they become crisis situations.

References

1. B. Boehm, *Tutorial: Software Risk Management,* IEEE CS Press, Los Alamitos, Calif., 1989.
2. F. Brooks, *The Mythical Man-Month,* Addison-Wesley, Reading, Mass., 1975.
3. B. Boehm, *Software Engineering Economic,* Prentice-Hall, Englewood Cliffs, N.J., 1981.
4. K. Pullen, "Uncertainty Analysis with Cocomo," *Proc. Cocomo Users Group,* Software Eng. Institute, Pittsburgh, Pa., 1987.

DEADLINE PRESSURE:
HOW TO COPE
WITH SHORT DEADLINES,
LOW BUDGETS AND
INSUFFICIENT STAFFING LEVELS

THE PROBLEM

The Problem As Viewed By the Project Manager's Manager

The big boss wants it.

A deadline has been established.

The pressure to deliver something, on time, is on.

There may well be some clear reason for the particular date chosen. It may be specified in a contract. It may be synchronized with other product developments. But, it could just be an arbitrary guesstimate. It could have simply been a rash promise by the project manager, made to impress his boss.

It is probable that the big boss *really:*

- would like to get even earlier delivery - of something, - has no clear unambiguous definition of *what* is to be delivered, - might accept later delivery of *parts* of the package, - has been misunderstood, as to what and when, - hasn't told the project manager what he really wants, yet, - is in the process of deciding differently about what and when.

All of these represent potential opportunities for relief of deadline pressure.

The Problem As Viewed By the Project Manager

The project manager is caught between the pressures from above, and the finite productive capacity below him. You might wonder how intelligent people can voluntarily accept such lack of control over both their destiny and reputation.

Article by Tom Gilb. Reprinted with permission from *Information Processing*, pp. 293–299, Gilb, T., "Deadline Pressure: How to Cope with Short Deadlines, Low Budgets and Insufficient Staffing Levels", 1986, Elsevier Science B. V., Amsterdam, The Netherlands.

The project manager feels that the demands from above are unreasonable. Further, that the resources, in terms of people, talent, budget, machinery and time for getting the job done, are inadequate.

But, the project manager is there to do as well as can be expected under the circumstances. And he will try to do so with the least pain to himself.

The project manager, either through ineptitude, or experience and cunning, has made sure that the *exact nature* of the project deliveries are *perfectly unclear.* This has the effect of allowing him to deliver something, really anything that is ready by the "deadline", and claim on-time delivery. Who can prove otherwise?

The Problem As Viewed By the Project Professional

The people working for the project manager—the ones that have to do the real work—are perfectly prepared to let their boss worry about deadlines, as long as they can do whatever they most enjoy doing, the way they enjoy doing it. They realize that the project manager doesn't dare fire them or take similar drastic action (like training them) because that would destroy the project schedule.

Of course, as individuals each one of them would very much like to make a brilliant recognized contribution to the project. The problem is they are not sure what the project is all about, and they are pretty sure that somebody else will snatch the glory from them anyway. Better to save those brilliant efforts for when one starts one's own company.

If the project fails, they might get promoted to project manager. But the important thing is to not be *seen* to threaten the project.

The Problem As Viewed By the Customer/User

The recipient of the project output probably needs the results "yesterday". Your deadline, as project manager, is probably viewed as the longest acceptable wait time until the product is ready.

The "customer" might very well be willing to wait longer for 90% of the project results, if only 10% were delivered on time. They might even be willing to let some of that 10% be delivered later if 1% were delivered *much* earlier. It is perfectly possible that *they* really don't need 99% of what has been asked for. There are a lot of people out there who have a vested interest in building new systems, rather than improving old ones.

THE SOLUTIONS

Redefine the Problem

I have never yet walked into a project of any kind, anywhere in the world where I felt that the project deliveries were fully and completely defined.

I'm not saying that all projects should be *perfectly* defined in advance. There are both good and bad reasons for incomplete requirements specification. However, this lack-of-specification situation gives us a powerful tool for relieving deadline pressure, because it can put us in a position to "clarify" or "detail" the specifications in such a way as to make the delivery task easier.

Gerald M. Weinberg, in our book "Humanized Input"[1] made use of this principle when he formulated his "Zeroth Law of Unreliability".

"If a system doesn't have to be reliable, it can meet any other objective."

If a quality, like reliability, is not clearly specified—you can deliver the project earlier—if you "interpret" the quality requirement as "whatever it happens to be when the deadline arrives". This, coupled with an innocent "Ohhh! You wanted *more* than two minutes between failures!", after the first complaints arrive, will solve the deadline problem initially. You are of course prepared to discuss a new schedule and project for enhancing quality to the required levels—now clarified for the first time.

Whether or not "reliability" is defined is irrelevant. There are a large number of quality attributes[2] which probably have a dramatic influence on cost and schedule. You only need *one* of them to be unclearly specified to give you the opening you need.

The more quality requirement specifications that are added, the more uncertainty is introduced into the schedule estimation problem. In fact with ten or more demanding state-of-the-art quality requirements—you can be certain that the project can *never* be delivered.

The trick is to get the client to specify what they "dream of", rather than what they will want to pay for or wait for. They will always be tempted into this trap, and you will always have an excuse for non-delivery.

Don't Work Harder, Work Smarter

It is natural, when faced with deadline pressure, to consider various ways of working harder. More overtime, reducing employee vacations, working weekends. Such a response is designed to give the *impression* of trying to meet the deadlines. But, let's face it, working harder defeats the *real* purpose of life, whatever it is.

There is no certainty that hard work will help the deadline at all. The real *problem* is the individual who made a promise for a deadline, without considering whether it was realistic at all. Unfortunately, this person is often the Chief Executive of the company.

So, you have to work smarter. This involves doing things mentioned elsewhere in this paper, such as,

- redesigning for evolutionary delivery,
- using Inspection of requirements and high-level design to find problems while they are small ones,
- formally identifying the real goals, measurably,
- sub-contracting the work to someone else.

Refuse! Make Counter-Threats

Have you ever considered refusing to accept the deadline which someone is trying to impose upon you? You can do so under the guise of loyalty to your boss. But do it in writing. An oral refusal can too easily be misunderstood or misused. Here is an example of a diplomatic formulation:

"I must unfortunately decline, at the present moment, to accept full responsibility for meeting the suggested deadline. I sincerely believe that this would result in you (your boss!) getting blamed for non-delivery at a later date. The project is as yet not clearly defined (it never is) and it is by no means clear that we have the resources (you never will) to complete it on the suggested schedule to the quality expected by the customer. We must not be caught making promises we cannot keep, no matter how great the pressure. What we will promise is to do the very best we can to deliver as early as possible, with the resources we have or are later granted."

If this diplomatic attempt to avoid responsibility doesn't work, don't worry. The project is sure to be late, or some kind of a disaster. You can then prove that you were wise enough to disclaim responsibility in advance. If, by some miracle everything succeeds, you can safely assume that your disclaimer will be forgotten in the euphoria of success. And *if* it is remembered, you can safely say that it was luck or that certain factors became *clearer* after it was written.

If Necessary, Use the Counter-Threat

A diplomatic disclaimer might not be enough to fool your boss. The "counter-threat" ploy may be necessary. The objective is to scare people into *not* imposing a really *serious* deadline. It might be along the following lines. (do not copy this text exactly each time—someone might get suspicious).

"I cannot but note the deadline that you have felt it necessary to impose. We will naturally do our very best to meet it. However, in your own interest please note the following problems which may occur as a result.

1. There is very little real chance of meeting this deadline. Can we afford the damage to our reputation?

2. If we do try to deliver something by this date it will most certainly have a quality level below what people will expect. Can we afford this damage to our reputation?

3. The attempt to meet an impossible deadline, upon which we have not been consulted or agreed to, will result in severe stress to our staff. We risk that our best people (who do all the real work) leaving us in frustration.

We do of course want to cooperate in any way we can to make a realistic plan, and to help estimate realistic resources for doing a job which will not threaten our standing as responsible professionals in the eyes of customers or the public."

Redefine the Solution

If these tactics fail, don't despair! There are many avenues of rescue open to you. One is to redefine the solution so that it is easier to achieve than the one you were landed with.

This can be a dangerous path because solutions are often "Holy Cows" for somebody. However—just as often—the solutions are accidental and nobody really cares about the detailed solution type—as long as they achieve their real objectives. Somebody (you of course,) has to take the initiative to change the solution so that the deadline can be met.

The steps are as follows:

1. Trap your boss or customer into declaring that the proposed *deadline is extremely critical* (if it is not, your problem dissolves anyway).

2. Entice them into agreeing that the *results* of the project are more critical than the *means* by which it is accomplished. Few managers will admit to anything else. Establish in formal measurable terms the results to be accomplished (savings of time and money, improved service or sales etc.).

3. Show them that the presently suggested solution does not *guarantee* the achievement of these results. (No solution is ever guaranteed anyway.)

4. Then, *find an alternative solution* which at least looks far more safe in terms of getting the results. For example, such a solution is likely to be based on *existing and known products or technologies,* modified for your purposes. Possibly you can get some *outside instance* to *guarantee the deadline* for the modifications—in which case the monkey is off your back.

Naturally, you offer to manage the new effort. This gets you a reputation for sheer heroism in the face of impossible odds. When it's all over, you can take the credit for the successful solution.

Define the Solution Yourself

Of course "redefining" the solution might seem a bit too much for the cases where no clear solution has yet been defined. In this case you should make use of such an opportunity to get control over the solution definition before others do. They might suggest something which *cannot* be achieved within the deadline.

There is one *cardinal rule* when defining *solutions.* Make sure you have a *clear idea of the objectives* which *top management* has. This is likely to be *different* from what your boss told you the goals were.

Next, you want to do what engineers call "design to cost". This simply means that you must find a solution architecture which ensures that you deliver the results as expected. It is vital that you are prepared to go outside your normal specialty discipline to achieve this.

For example you may be a software engineer. The requirement may be for "zero defects" software. You may not feel capable of producing that within the deadline. So, you must be prepared to swallow your pride—but deliver a solution.

You must, for example, find a ready-made solution with "zero defect" (or near to it, because perfection is mighty hard to find in practice). Or, you need to find some reputable sub-supplier who will guarantee the result on time.

They will not of course be able to do it—but you can blame them afterwards. *Your* job amounts to writing a clear specification of what they will be attempting to deliver by the deadline. You should get them to guarantee this in a contract, or at least a letter or in writing.

You might feel more like a legal person than a technical person at this point, but remember—legal people cannot write technical specifications—and they don't care about your deadline pressure.

Get Somebody Else To Do It

There is an important strategy of making sure it is *someone else* who is under the deadline pressure. Remember, management doesn't really care who does things, as long as they get done. If you can, make a strong case for letting somebody else do the job—then pressure is off your back.

It is important that you consider taking main contractor responsibility. That is, you find, then you control, the sub-contractor. This gives you something to do and to look busy with—but of course the sub-contractor does all the real work. You just sit there with a whip.

THE TECHNOLOGIES OF THE SOLUTIONS

Evolutionary Delivery

The most powerful practical technique I have experienced for getting control over deadline pressure is evolutionary delivery[3]. The evolutionary delivery method is based on the simple observation that not everything is needed all at one initial delivery or deadline.

An example: The New Taxation System.

In one concrete case, a national taxation on-line system—we had a deadline six months hence. The initial project plan was to use a staff of one hundred technical people (programmers) for probably (nobody knew) three years to complete delivery of a totally new design. I worked out an alternative design based on making use of all the *old data and programs,* with a few politically interesting frills thrown in.

This idea alone, guarantees you will meet any deadline—but it is not nearly as much fun for the technologists who want to play with new toys. In this case there were ninety-eight programmers who wanted to learn a totally new programming language.

I made sure that I kept my eye on the essential *deadline* idea—that the Finance Minister was to see the new system in action personally in exactly six months. The new system was the old system, on a new computer mainly. Secondarily a "while-you-wait" access to their base of taxation data was desired. We provided a way using a copy of their current data. The Finance Minister had to wait one full second to get the data, using binary search on disks, with my modified solution, as opposed to 1/10th of a second with the previously committed 300 work-year solution.

They argued for a full three months about whether my simplistic solution could possibly work in such a large and complex environment. Then, using a handful of people they actually delivered successfully in three months.

USING FAGAN'S INSPECTION METHOD

"A stitch in time saves nine" says the old folk wisdom. Many of the problems in meeting deadlines for large projects are caused by the tail end backlash. This is the penalty you pay for *poor quality control in the early stages of design and planning.* The small details that were overlooked come back to haunt you—as you desperately try to fix the problems that pop up when you try to meet required quality levels or performance levels for delivery.

Conventional quality control [4] methods insist that "inspection" of product and process quality is a vital pre-requisite for being able to maintain the required cost and quality attributes of almost any development. Around 1972 Michael E. Fagan, of IBM in Kingston New York, began to transfer these methods to quality control of IBM software products. Nobody had tried to do this until then. In fact it was his training as a quality control hardware engineer which gave him the basic idea of applying "inspection" to software. It was an uphill battle at IBM, but very successful [5]. Although the method is widely recognized internationally, it will still take many more years before it is widely used.

The aspect of Inspection which is interesting in connection with *deadline pressure* is that it seems to have these repeatable general characteristics:

1. Delivery of major software projects is achieved in about 15% to 35% [6] less calendar time than otherwise. This saving can also be translated into cost or work-power savings if desired[7].

2. The quality (in terms of defects removed) is measurably improved (by as much as one or two orders of magnitude) while this saving is made.

3. Improvements are cumulative, for several years. This is due to a process of management analysis of the time and defect statistics generated by inspection—combined with management taking change action to improve productivity [8].

Why Does Inspection Save Time and Cost?

It would be too much to explain all the details of inspection here. But, the basic reason why inspection saves resources is simple.

1. It can be used at *early stages* of design and planning—before conventional product testing can be used. Sixty percent of software bugs *exist already at this stage,* according to a TRW Study [9]. It identifies and cleans up defects which would cause much larger later repair costs. IBM data indicates as much as eighty-two times[10] more to correct software errors found late at the customer site, as opposed to early at design stages, if they were not found until much later.

2. The *statistical data* collected during the inspection process is carefully *analyzed.* This is much like Financial Directors analyze accounting data to get insights into a company's operational weakness. It is then used to suggest, and confirm the results of, major changes to the entire development or production process.

If the *changes are implemented early enough in a project, they can impact the deadline* of that project. If the changes are implemented late, or even after the project is completed—they can at least improve your ability to perform better on the *following* projects.[11]

Attribute Specification

Another technology for getting some control over deadlines and other resource constraints is, as indicated above, setting formal *objectives for quality and resources* in a formal *measurable* way.

The major reason why this impacts resources is that at the high levels of qualities desired by any user, even small improvements in a quality level, can cost disproportional resources.

So for example it took Bell Labs several years to move the best levels of availability they could report[12] from 99.9% to 99.98% for computerized telephone switching systems. The difference "0.08%" does not seem like a significant number in considering a project deadline. Both the above measures of system availability are "extremely high state of the art levels" if described in mere words. But that "little difference" cost Bell Labs (or AT&T) about eight years of research and development.

It is obviously vital for management to know exactly what levels their projects are aiming for in relation to the *state of the art limits*. If they don't have full control over those factors, then they do not have control over meeting deadlines.

Here are some *principles of attribute specification:*

1. All critical attributes of quality and resources should be established as *measurable and testable* requirements.

2. Any *single critical attribute* which management *fails to control,* is likely to be the Achilles Heel of the project—threatening cost and time resources.

3. All attributes should be specified at at least *two parameters*. The *worst acceptable case* for any system delivery—and the *"planned level"*— the one you *hope* to get together with the others.

4. It is also quite useful to document, for all critical attributes, the *"present system levels"* and the known *engineering limits* or *"state of the art limits"*. It is particularly these which give manage-

ment a warning of unreasonable *planned* levels— and thus of impending schedule or cost problems.

5. Even with a first attempt at specification, *be prepared to iterate towards a balanced specification* of all the demands throughout the design and development process.

AN EXAMPLE OF ACTUAL APPLICATION OF THE PRINCIPLES OF THIS PAPER ON A LARGE PROJECT

One large (multi-thousand work-years, years of effort, $100 million dollars cost) software project in Europe asked me what they could do to avoid overrunning their deadline, a year from then, by more than two years.

Part of my advice was to break the project down, even at this late stage, into *evolutionary deliveries*. In this case the software critical to the initial and high-volume products to go before the very low volume product software which had been coupled to the same deadline.

Another part of my advice was to use Fagan's Inspection method on their work.

A third component of my advice was to define the worst case quality levels and performance levels *more precisely*. They had to differentiate between those software components which *needed high quality levels,* and those that were not as critical. Most of the volume of the software was not as critical as the central "real-time" components— and they had failed to make that distinction in their planning! They were quite simply committed to far too high a quality level, too early, for too much of their project product.

THE RESULTS

After eleven months, in November 1985, one month *before* the "impossible deadline", this group reported to me that their first useful delivery had been operating for two continuous weeks without any problems. There were certainly many reasons for this, not all of which I have depth knowledge. But evolutionary extraction was certainly a key element.

SUMMARY

Let me sum up what I have tried to say, as guiding principles of resisting deadline pressure.

1. *The Deadline Mirage.* Rethink the deadline given to you—it may not be real.

2. *The Solution Mirage.* Rethink the solution handed to you—it may be in the way of on-time delivery.

3. *The Other Viewpoint.* Rethink the problem from other people's point of view—it will help you simplify your problem and convince them to agree with you.

4. *The Expert Trap.* Don't trust the experts blindly—they will cheerfully lead you to disaster. Be skeptical and insist on proof and guarantees.

5. *The All-at-once Trap.* Remember, nobody *needs* all of what they asked for by the deadline—they would simply like you to provide the miracle if possible.

6. *The Real-Needs Principle.* Don't damage your credibility by bowing to pressure to make impossible promises. Increase your credibility by fighting for solutions which solve the real needs of your bosses and clients.

7. *The Ends Dictate The Means.* If the deadline is critical and seems impossible otherwise—don't be afraid to change the solution.

8. *The Principle of Conservation of Energy.* If deadlines are critical, make maximum use of existing systems and "known technology"—avoid research-into-unknowns during your project.

9. *The Evolutionary Delivery Principle.* Any large project can be broken down into a series of earlier and smaller deliverables—don't give up—even if you have to change the technical solution to make it happen. Keep your eye on results—not technologies.

10. *The "don't blame me" Principle.* If you succeed using these principles, take the credit—give your boss and these ideas some credit in a footnote. If you fail—you obviously didn't apply these principles correctly (don't mention my name, mention your boss's if you must blame somebody. Management is always at fault.)

References

1. T. Gilb & G. M. Weinberg, *Humanized Input: Techniques for Reliable Keyed Input,* QED Information Sciences, Inc., 170 Linden St., Wellesley Mass USA 02181. ISBN 0-89435-073-0, 1984.

2. Gilb, T., *Principles Of Software Engineering Management,* Addison-Wesley, ca. 1987. This contains chapters on quantitative definitions of software qualities, as well as chapters on Inspection and Evolutionary Delivery discussed in this paper.

3. Tom Gilb, *Evolutionary Delivery versus the Waterfall Model,* ACM Software Engineering Notes, July 1985, p. 49–61.

4. See for example J M Juran (Editor), Quality Control Handbook, Third Edition, McGraw Hill, ISBN 0-07-033175-8, 1974.

5. In 1979 Fagan was awarded a $50 thousand personal "Outstanding Contribution Award" by IBM in recognition of the success of his variant of the method in improving IBM software quality and cost.

6. See for example the 35% difference measured on about 30 of 60 projects at IBM Federal Systems Division, as reported in IBM Systems Journal Number One 1977 (Felix and Walston article).

7. Other examples of savings are reported in M E Fagan, "Design and code inspections to reduce errors in program development", IBM Systems Journal Number Three 1976, page 182–211.

8. These points are supported by various IBM Technical publications authored by Horst Remus of IBM San Jose from 1978 to 1983.

9. T. A. Thayer et al, Software Reliability, North-Holland, TRW Series 2. 1978, ISBN 0-444-85217-4. Page 80.

10. According to data collected by the author at IBM Santa Teresa Labs from Ken Christiansen in 1979. Another factor observed by IBM earlier was 62 x. Same principle as "An ounce of prevention is worth a pound of cure."

11. R. A. Radice et al, *A Programming Process Architecture,* IBM SJ Vol. 24, No. 2, p. 79–90. also, C. L. Jones, *A process-integrated approach to defect prevention,* p. 151–167.

12. Communications of ACM about mid 1984, as I recall.

Discussion Questions

1. Both the Rothfeder and Mehler articles describe a number of failed projects. What aspects do these projects have in common? (Two useful collections are: Mehler, M., "Reining in Runaway Systems", *Information Week*, (351): 20–24, (December 16 1991) and Rothfeder, J., "It's Late, Costly, and Incompetent—But Try Firing a Computer System", *Business Week*, p. 164–165, (November 7, 1988).

2. Failure often seems linked to the use of new technologies. If this is well known, why do people persist in repeating this mistake?

3. Most of the examples in the Rothfeder and Mehler articles are projects done by outside system integration firms. Are these firms simply not very good, and thus account for many failures?

4. Boehm discusses a wide array of techniques for risk management. Which ones do you feel offer the most promise? Which ones do you feel would be easiest to use?

5. Gilb suggests that schedule considerations dominate other performance aspects in software development, even though rationally people might rank this below other concerns, such as reliability, functionality, and cost. Discuss why this might be the case.

Lifecycle Models

INTRODUCTION

A tremendous amount of work has gone into so-called lifecycle models of software development. In this view a prescriptive process is laid out, starting with systems concept activities like requirements analysis, moving on to systems design activities which are then followed by development of the operational system. These models come in a large variety of permutations in both the number and naming of the various stages, but in general all feature the notion that a significant amount of planning and analysis should precede the physical development of the system, and that, to the degree possible, iteration from a more advanced stage back to a previous stage should be avoided. In this chapter three articles present insights into the lifecycle concept and how it has evolved. Like some other chapters in this volume, these three articles mirror the pattern of first, what is the technical issue, second, why do managers need to understand this issue, and finally, how do these issues actually play out in practice.

As will be seen in Chapter 7, lifecycle models have come under much criticism in light of opportunities to employ prototyping in an iterative approach to systems development. The first two articles in this chapter may be viewed, in part, as attempts to salvage the most valuable portions of the lifecycle approach.

In the first article, Barry Boehm, as a prelude to presenting his "spiral model", does an excellent job of concisely presenting the history and rationale behind the development of the lifecycle approach. He then presents a refinement to this approach that addresses many of its shortcomings and adds explicit recognition of activities that can be performed so as to minimize project management risks. It is a useful companion piece to Boehm's article on risk management from Chapter 5 and it may be helpful to read the two articles as a set.

In a brief but important essay, David Parnas and Paul Clements address the critique of the lifecycle models acknowledging that such models will always be idealizations of what will go on during a software development project. However, they go on to point out why viewing the problem this way still adds considerable value to the process. Their advice is essential reading for any manager thinking about modifying his or her organization's current process model.

Finally, lifecycle process models have supported a number of systems development "methodologies", most notably historically structured analysis and design and information engineering. These approaches have had to evolve and adapt as the lifecycle approach has changed. Ed Yourdon's short piece from Datamation a number of years ago succinctly traces these effects on structured analysis. It serves as a useful reminder that any proposed methodology will always be subject to ongoing forces of change in the form of new conceptualizations of the software development process and of advances in the technology. Therefore any approaches adopted by management must be sufficiently flexible to endure these forces.

A SPIRAL MODEL
OF SOFTWARE DEVELOPMENT
AND ENHANCEMENT

"Stop the life cycle—I want to get off!"
"Life-cycle Concept Considered Harmful."
"The waterfall model is dead."
"No, it isn't, but it should be."

These statements exemplify the current debate about software life-cycle process models. The topic has recently received a great deal of attention.

The Defense Science Board Task Force Report on Military Software[1] issued in 1987 highlighted the concern that traditional software process models were discouraging more effective approaches to software development such as prototyping and software reuse. The Computer Society has sponsored tutorials and workshops on software process models that have helped clarify many of the issues and stimulated advances in the field (see "Further reading").

The spiral model presented in this article is one candidate for improving the software process model situation. The major distinguishing feature of the spiral model is that it creates a *risk-driven* approach to the software process rather than a primarily *document-driven* or *code-driven* process. It incorporates many of the strengths of other models and resolves many of their difficulties.

This article opens with a short description of software process models and the issues they address. Subsequent sections outline the process steps involved in the spiral model; illustrate the application of the spiral model to a software project, using the TRW Software Productivity Project as an example; summarize the primary advantages and implications involved in using the spiral model and the primary difficulties in using it at its current incomplete level of elaboration; and present resulting conclusions.

BACKGROUND ON SOFTWARE PROCESS MODELS

The primary functions of a software process model are to determine the *order of the stages* involved in software development and evolution and to establish the *transition criteria* for progressing from one stage to the next. These include completion criteria for the current stage plus choice criteria and entrance criteria for the next stage. Thus, a process model addresses the following software project questions:

1. What shall we do next?
2. How long shall we continue to do it?

Consequently, a process model differs from a software method (often called a methodology) in that a method's primary focus is on how to navigate through each phase (determining data, control, or "uses" hierarchies; partitioning functions; allocating requirements) and how to represent phase products (structure charts; stimulus-response threads; state transition diagrams).

Why are software process models important? Primarily because they provide guidance on the

Article by Barry W. Boehm. © 1988 IEEE. Reprinted, with permission, from (*IEEE Computer,* 5, 61–72; May/1988).

order (phases, increments, prototypes, validation tasks, etc.) in which a project should carry out its major tasks. Many software projects, as the next section shows, have come to grief because they pursued their various development and evolution phases in the wrong order.

Evolution of Process Models

Before concentrating in depth on the spiral model, we should take a look at a number of others: the code-and-fix model, the stage-wise model and the waterfall model, the evolutionary development model, and the transform model.

The Code-and-Fix Model

The basic model used in the earliest days of software development contained two steps:

1. Write some code.
2. Fix the problems in the code.

Thus, the order of the steps was to do some coding first and to think about the requirements, design, test, and maintenance later. This model has three primary difficulties:

1. After a number of fixes, the code became so poorly structured that subsequent fixes were very expensive. This underscored the need for a design phase prior to coding.
2. Frequently, even well-designed software was such a poor match to users' needs that it was either rejected outright or expensively redeveloped. This made the need for a requirements phase prior to design evident.
3. Code was expensive to fix because of poor preparation for testing and modification. This made it clear that explicit recognition of these phases, as well as test-and-evolution planning and preparation tasks in the early phases, were needed.

The Stagewise and Waterfall Models

As early as 1956, experience on large software systems such as the Semi-Automated Ground Environment (SAGE) had led to the recognition of these problems and to the development of a stage-wise model[2] to address them. This model stipulated that software be developed in successive stages (operational plan, operational specifications, coding specifications, coding, parameter testing, assembly testing, shakedown, system evaluation).

The waterfall model,[3] illustrated in Exhibit 1, was a highly influential 1970 refinement of the stagewise model. It provided two primary enhancements to the stagewise model:

1. Recognition of the feedback loops between stages, and a guideline to confine the feedback loops to successive stages to minimize the expensive rework involved in feedback across many stages.
2. An initial incorporation of prototyping in the software life cycle, via a "build it twice" step running in parallel with requirements analysis and design.

The waterfall model's approach helped eliminate many difficulties previously encountered on software projects. The waterfall model has become the basis for most software acquisition standards in government and industry. Some of its initial difficulties have been addressed by adding extensions to cover incremental development, parallel developments, program families, accommodation of evolutionary changes, formal software development and verification, and stagewise validation and risk analysis.

However, even with extensive revisions and refinements, the waterfall model's basic scheme has encountered some more fundamental difficulties, and these have led to the formulation of alternative process models.

A primary source of difficulty with the waterfall model has been its emphasis on fully elaborated documents as completion criteria for early requirements and design phases. For some classes of software, such as compilers or secure operating systems, this is the most effective way to proceed. However, it does not work well for many classes of software, particularly interactive end-user

EXHIBIT 1   The Waterfall Model of the Software Life Cycle

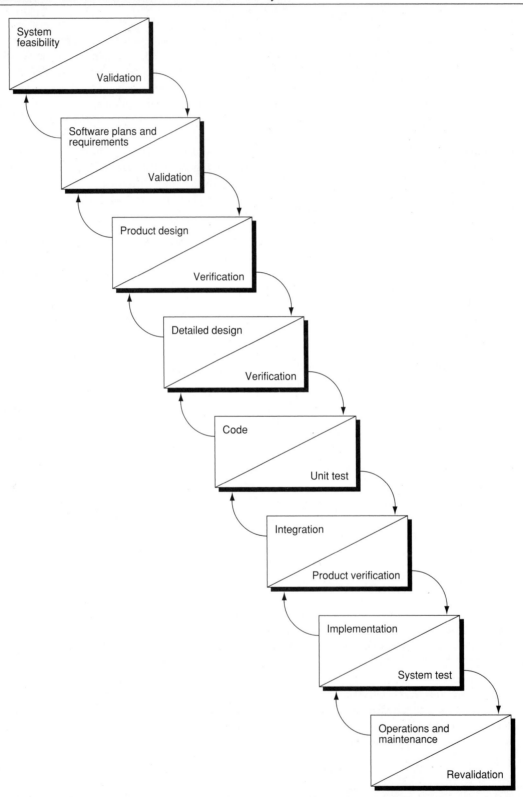

applications. Document-driven standards have pushed many projects to write elaborate specifications of poorly understood user interfaces and decision-support functions, followed by the design and development of large quantities of unusable code.

These projects are examples of how waterfall-model projects have come to grief by pursuing stages in the wrong order. Furthermore, in areas supported by fourth-generation languages (spreadsheet or small business applications), it is clearly unnecessary to write elaborate specifications for one's application before implementing it.

The Evolutionary Development Model

The above concerns led to the formulation of the *evolutionary development* model,[4] whose stages consist of expanding increments of an operational software product, with the directions of evolution being determined by operational experience.

The evolutionary development model is ideally matched to a fourth-generation language application and well matched to situations in which users say, "I can't tell you what I want, but I'll know it when I see it." It gives users a rapid initial operational capability and provides a realistic operational basis for determining subsequent product improvements.

Nonetheless, evolutionary development also has its difficulties. It is generally difficult to distinguish it from the old code-and-fix model, whose spaghetti code and lack of planning were the initial motivation for the waterfall model. It is also based on the often-unrealistic assumption that the user's operational system will be flexible enough to accommodate unplanned evolution paths. This assumption is unjustified in three primary circumstances:

1. Circumstances in which several independently evolved applications must subsequently be closely integrated.

2. "Information-sclerosis" cases, in which temporary work-arounds for software deficiencies increasingly solidify into unchangeable constraints on evolution. The following comment is a typical example: "It's nice that you could change

those equipment codes to make them more intelligible for us, but the Codes Committee just met and established the current codes as company standards."

3. Bridging situations, in which the new software is incrementally replacing a large existing system. If the existing system is poorly modularized, it is difficult to provide a good sequence of "bridges" between the old software and the expanding increments of new software.

Under such conditions, evolutionary development projects have come to grief by pursuing stages in the wrong order: evolving a lot of hard-to-change code before addressing long-range architectural and usage considerations.

The Transform Model

The "spaghetti code" difficulties of the evolutionary development and code-and-fix models can also become a difficulty in various classes of waterfall-model applications, in which code is optimized for performance and becomes increasingly hard to modify. The transform model[5] has been proposed as a solution to this dilemma.

The transform model assumes the existence of a capability to automatically convert a formal specification of a software product into a program satisfying the specification. The steps then prescribed by the transform model are

- a formal specification of the best initial understanding of the desired product;
- automatic transformation of the specification into code;
- an iterative loop, if necessary, to improve the performance of the resulting code by giving optimization guidance to the transformation system;
- exercise of the resulting product; and
- an outer iterative loop to adjust the specification based on the resulting operational experience, and to rederive, reoptimize, and exercise the adjusted software product.

The transform model thus bypasses the difficulty of having to modify code that has become poorly structured through repeated reoptimizations, since the modifications are made to the specification. It also avoids the extra time and expense involved in the intermediate design, code, and test activities.

Still, the transform model has various difficulties. Automatic transformation capabilities are only available for small products in a few limited areas: spreadsheets, small fourth-generation language applications, and limited computer-science domains. The transform model also shares some of the difficulties of the evolutionary development model, such as the assumption that users' operational systems will always be flexible enough to support unplanned evolution paths. Additionally, it would face a formidable knowledge-base-maintenance problem in dealing with the rapidly increasing and evolving supply of reusable software components and commercial software products. (Simply consider the problem of tracking the costs, performance, and features of all commercial database management systems, and automatically choosing the best one to implement each new or changed specification.)

THE SPIRAL MODEL

The spiral model of the software process (see Exhibit 2) has been evolving for several years, based on experience with various refinements of the waterfall model as applied to large government software projects. As will be discussed, the spiral model can accommodate most previous models as special cases and further provides guidance as to which combination of previous models best fits a given software situation. Development of the TRW Software Productivity System (TRW-SPS), described in the next section, is its most complete application to date.

The radial dimension in Exhibit 2 represents the cumulative cost incurred in accomplishing the steps to date; the angular dimension represents the progress made in completing each cycle of the spiral. (The model reflects the underlying concept that each cycle involves a progression that addresses the same sequence of steps, for each portion of the product and for each of its levels of elaboration, from an overall concept of operation document down to the coding of each individual program.) Note that some artistic license has been taken with the increasing cumulative cost dimension to enhance legibility of the steps in Exhibit 2.

A Typical Cycle of the Spiral

Each cycle of the spiral begins with the identification of

- the objectives of the portion of the product being elaborated (performance, functionality, ability to accommodate change, etc.);
- the alternative means of implementing this portion of the product (design A, design B, reuse, buy, etc.); and
- the constraints imposed on the application of the alternatives (cost, schedule, interface, etc.).

The next step is to evaluate the alternatives relative to the objectives and constraints. Frequently, this process will identify areas of uncertainty that are significant sources of project risk. If so, the next step should involve the formulation of a cost-effective strategy for resolving the sources of risk. This may involve prototyping, simulation, benchmarking, reference checking, administering user questionnaires, analytic modeling, or combinations of these and other risk-resolution techniques.

Once the risks are evaluated, the next step is determined by the relative remaining risks. If performance or user-interface risks strongly dominate program development or internal interface-control risks, the next step may be an evolutionary development one: a minimal effort to specify the overall nature of the product, a plan for the next level of prototyping, and the development of a more detailed prototype to continue to resolve the major risk issues.

If this prototype is operationally useful and robust enough to serve as a low-risk base for future product evolution, the subsequent risk-driven steps would be the evolving series of

EXHIBIT 2 Spiral Model of the Software Process

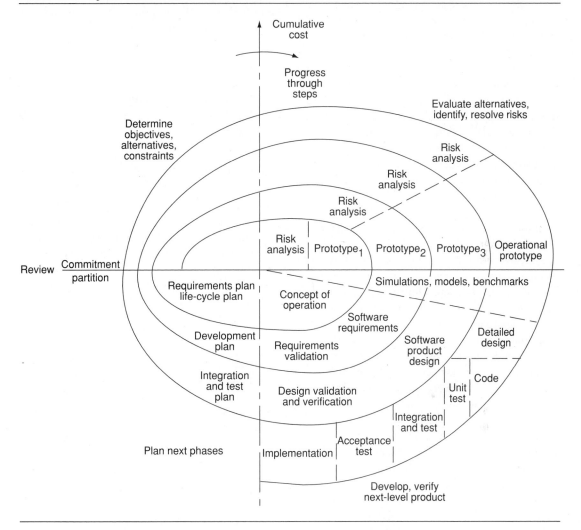

evolutionary prototypes going toward the right in Exhibit 2. In this case, the option of writing specifications would be addressed but not exercised. Thus, risk considerations can lead to a project implementing only a subset of all the potential steps in the model.

On the other hand, if previous prototyping efforts have already resolved all of the performance or user-interface risks, and program devel-opment or interface-control risks dominate, the next step follows the basic waterfall approach (concept of operation, software requirements, pre-liminary design, etc. in Exhibit 2), modified as appropriate to incorporate incremental develop-ment. Each level of software specification in the exhibit is then followed by a validation step and the preparation of plans for the succeeding cycle. In this case, the options to prototype, simulate, model, etc. are addressed but not exercised, leading to the use of a different subset of steps.

This risk-driven subsetting of the spiral model steps allows the model to accommodate any appropriate mixture of a specification-oriented, prototype-oriented, simulation-oriented, automatic transformation-oriented, or other approach to software development. In such cases, the appropriate mixed strategy is chosen by considering the relative magnitude of the program risks and the relative effectiveness of the various techniques in resolving the risks. In a similar way, risk-management considerations can determine the amount of time and effort that should be devoted to such other project activities as planning, configuration management, quality assurance, formal verification, and testing. In particular, risk-driven specifications (as discussed in the next section) can have varying degrees of completeness, formality, and granularity, depending on the relative risks of doing too little or too much specification.

An important feature of the spiral model, as with most other models, is that each cycle is completed by a review involving the primary people or organizations concerned with the product. This review covers all products developed during the previous cycle, including the plans for the next cycle and the resources required to carry them out. The review's major objective is to ensure that all concerned parties are mutually committed to the approach for the next phase.

The plans for succeeding phases may also include a partition of the product into increments for successive development or components to be developed by individual organizations or persons. For the latter case, visualize a series of parallel spiral cycles, one for each component, adding a third dimension to the concept presented in Exhibit 2. For example, separate spirals can be evolving for separate software components or increments. Thus, the review-and-commitment step may range from an individual walk-through of the design of a single programmer's component to a major requirements review involving developer, customer, user, and maintenance organizations.

Initiating and Terminating the Spiral

Four fundamental questions arise in considering this presentation of the spiral model:

1. How does the spiral ever get started?
2. How do you get off the spiral when it is appropriate to terminate a project early?
3. Why does the spiral end so abruptly?
4. What happens to software enhancement (or maintenance)?

The answer to these questions involves an observation that the spiral model applies equally well to development or enhancement efforts. In either case, the spiral gets started by a hypothesis that a particular operational mission (or set of missions) could be improved by a software effort. The spiral process then involves a test of this hypothesis: at any time, if the hypothesis fails the test (for example, if delays cause a software product to miss its market window, or if a superior commercial product becomes available), the spiral is terminated. Otherwise, it terminates with the installation of new or modified software, and the hypothesis is tested by observing the effect on the operational mission. Usually, experience with the operational mission leads to further hypotheses about software improvements, and a new maintenance spiral is initiated to test the hypothesis. Initiation, termination, and iteration of the tasks and products of previous cycles are thus implicitly defined in the spiral model (although they're not included in Exhibit 2 to simplify its presentation).

USING THE SPIRAL MODEL

The various rounds and activities involved in the spiral model are best understood through use of an example. The spiral model was used in the definition and development of the TRW Software Productivity System (TRW-SPS), an integrated software engineering environment.[6] The initial mission opportunity coincided with a corporate initiative to improve productivity in all appropriate corporate operations and an initial hypothesis that software engineering was an attractive area to investigate. This led to a small, extra "Round 0" circuit of the spiral

---

EXHIBIT 3 Spiral Model Usage: TRW Software Productivity System, Round 0

Objectives	Significantly increase software productivity
Constraints	At reasonable cost Within context of TRW culture • Government contracts, high tech., people oriented, security
Alternatives	Management: Project organization, policies, planning, control Personnel: Staffing, incentives, training Technology: Tools, workstations, methods, reuse Facilities: Offices, communications
Risks	May be no high-leverage improvements Improvements may violate constraints
Risk resolution	Internal surveys Analyze cost model Analyze exceptional projects Literature search
Risk resolution results	Some alternatives infeasible • Single time-sharing system: Security Mix of alternatives can produce significant gains • Factor of two in five years Need further study to determine best mix
Plan for next phase	Six-person task force for six months More extensive surveys and analysis • Internal, external, economic Develop concept of operation, economic rationale
Commitment	Fund next phase

---

to determine the feasibility of increasing software productivity at a reasonable corporate cost. (Very large or complex software projects will frequently precede the "concept of operation" round of the spiral with one or more smaller rounds to establish feasibility and to reduce the range of alternative solutions quickly and inexpensively.)

Exhibits 3, 4, and 5 summarize the application of the spiral model to the first three rounds of defining the SPS. The major features of each round are subsequently discussed and are followed by some examples from later rounds, such as preliminary and detailed design.

Round 0: Feasibility Study

This study involved five part-time participants over a two- to three-month period. As indicated in Exhibit 3, the objectives and constraints were expressed at a very high level and in qualitative terms like "significantly increase," "at reasonable cost," etc.

Some of the alternatives considered, primarily those in the "technology" area, could lead to development of a software product, but the possible attractiveness of a number of non-software alternatives in the management, personnel, and facilities areas could have led to a conclusion not to embark on a software development activity.

The primary risk areas involved possible situations in which the company would invest a good deal only to find that

• resulting productivity gains were not significant, or
• potentially high-leverage improvements were not compatible with some aspects of the "TRW culture."

EXHIBIT 4   Spiral Model Usage: TRW Software Productivity System, Round 1

Objectives	Double software productivity in five years
Constraints	$10,000 per person investment
	Within context of TRW culture
	• Government contracts, high tech., people oriented, security
	Preference for TRW products
Alternatives	Office: Private/modular/ . . .
	Communication: LAN/star/concentrators/ . . .
	Terminals: Private/shared; smart/dumb
	Tools: SREM/PSL-PSA/ . . .; PDL/SADT/ . . .
	CPU: IBM/DEC/CDC/ . . .
Risks	May miss high-leverage options
	TRW LAN price/performance
	Workstation cost
Risk resolution	Extensive external surveys, visits
	TRW LAN benchmarking
	Workstation price projections
Risk resolution results	Operations concept: Private offices, TRW LAN, personal terminals, VAX
	Begin with primarily dumb terminals; experiment with smart workstations
	Defer operating system, tools selection
Plan for next phase	Partition effort into software development environment (SDE), facilities, management
	Develop first-cut, prototype SDE
	• Design-to-cost: 15-person team for one year
	Plan for external usage
Commitment	Develop prototype SDE
	Commit an upcoming project to use SDE
	Commit the SDE to support the project
	Form representative steering group

The risk-resolution activities undertaken in Round 0 were primarily surveys and analyses, including structured interviews of software developers and managers, an initial analysis of productivity leverage factors identified by the constructive cost model (Cocomo)[7]; and an analysis of previous projects at TRW exhibiting high levels of productivity.

The risk analysis results indicated that significant productivity gains could be achieved at a reasonable cost by pursuing an integrated set of initiatives in the four major areas. However, some candidate solutions, such as a software support environment based on a single, corporate, maxicomputer-based time-sharing system, were found to be in conflict with TRW constraints requiring support of different levels of security-classified projects. Thus, even at a very high level of generality of objectives and constraints, Round 0 was able to answer basic feasibility questions and eliminate significant classes of candidate solutions.

The plan for Round 1 involved commitment of 12 man-months compared to the two man-months invested in Round 0 (during these rounds, all participants were part-time). Round 1 here corresponded fairly well to the initial round of the spiral model shown in Exhibit 2, in that its intent was to

---

EXHIBIT 5   Spiral Model Usage: TRW Software Productivity System, Round 2

Objectives	User-friendly system
	Integrated software, office-automation tools
	Support all project personnel
	Support all life-cycle phases
Constraints	Customer-deliverable SDE $\rightarrow$ Portability
	Stable, reliable service
Alternatives	OS: VMS/AT&T Unix/Berkeley Unix/ISC
	Host-target/fully portable tool set
	Workstations: Zenith/LSI-11/ . . .
Risks	Mismatch to user-project needs, priorities
	User-unfriendly system
	• 12-language syndrome; experts-only
	Unix performance, support
	Workstation/mainframe compatibility
Risk resolution	User-project surveys, requirements participation
	Survey of Unix-using organizations
	Workstation study
Risk resolution results	Top-level requirements specification
	Host-target with Unix host
	Unix-based workstations
	Build user-friendly front end for Unix
	Initial focus on tools to support early phases
Plan for next phase	Overall development plan
	• for tools: SREM, RTT, PDL, office automation tools
	• for front end: Support tools
	• for LAN: Equipment, facilities
Commitment	Proceed with plans

---

produce a concept of operation and a basic life-cycle plan for implementing whatever preferred alternative emerged.

Round 1: Concept of Operations

Exhibit 4 summarizes Round 1 of the spiral along the lines given in Exhibit 3 for Round 0. The features of Round 1 compare to those of Round 0 as follows:

- The level of investment was greater (12 versus 2 man-months).
- The objectives and constraints were more specific ("double software productivity in five years at a

cost of $10,000 a person" versus "significantly increase productivity at a reasonable cost").

- Additional constraints surfaced, such as the preference for TRW products (particularly, a TRW-developed local area network (LAN) system).
- The alternatives were more detailed ("SREM, PSL/PSA or SADT, as requirements tools etc." versus "tools"; "private/shared" terminals, "smart/dumb" terminals versus "workstations").
- The risk areas identified were more specific ("TRW LAN price-performance within a $10,000-per-person investment constraint" versus "improvements may violate reasonable-cost constraint").

- The risk-resolution activities were more extensive (including the benchmarking and analysis of a prototype TRW LAN being developed for another project).
- The result was a fairly specific operational concept document, involving private offices tailored to software work patterns and personal terminals connected to VAX superminis via the TRW LAN. Some choices were specifically deferred to the next round, such as the choice of operating system and specific tools.
- The life-cycle plan and the plan for the next phase involved a partitioning into separate activities to address management improvements, facilities development, and development of the first increment of a software development environment.
- The commitment step involved more than just an agreement with the plan. It committed to apply the environment to an upcoming 100-person testbed software project and to develop an environment focusing on the testbed project's needs. It also specified forming a representative steering group to ensure that the separate activities were well-coordinated and that the environment would not be overly optimized around the testbed project.

Although the plan recommended developing a prototype environment, it also recommended that the project employ requirements specifications and design specifications in a risk-driven way. Thus, the development of the environment followed the succeeding rounds of the spiral model.

Round 2: Top-Level Requirements Specification

Exhibit 5 shows the corresponding steps involved during Round 2 defining the software productivity system. Round 2 decisions and their rationale were covered in earlier work[6] ; here, we will summarize the considerations dealing with risk management and the use of the spiral model:

- The initial risk-identification activities during Round 2 showed that several system requirements hinged on the decision between a host-target system or a fully portable tool set and the decision between VMS and Unix as the host operating system. These requirements included the functions needed to provide a user-friendly front-end, the operating system to be used by the workstations, and the functions necessary to support a host-target operation. To keep these requirements in synchronization with the others, a special minispiral was initiated to address and resolve these issues. The resulting review led to a commitment to a host-target operation using Unix on the host system, at a point early enough to work the OS-dependent requirements in a timely fashion.
- Addressing the risks of mismatches to the user-project's needs and priorities resulted in substantial participation of the user-project personnel in the requirements definition activity. This led to several significant redirections of the requirements, particularly toward supporting the early phases of the software life-cycle into which the user project was embarking, such as an adaptation of the software requirements engineering methodology (SREM) tools for requirements specification and analysis.

It is also interesting to note that the form of Exhibits 4, 5, and 6 was originally developed for presentation purposes, but subsequently became a standard "spiral model template" used on later projects. These templates are useful not only for organizing project activities, but also as a residual design-rationale record. Design rationale information is of paramount importance in assessing the potential reusability of software components on future projects. Another important point to note is that the use of the template was indeed uniform across the three cycles, showing that the spiral steps can be and were uniformly followed at successively detailed levels of product definition.

Succeeding Rounds

It will be useful to illustrate some examples of how the spiral model is used to handle situations arising in the preliminary design and detailed design of components of the SPS: the preliminary design specification for the requirements traceability tool (RTT), and a detailed design rework or go-back on the unit development folder (UDF) tool.

The RTT Preliminary Design Specification

The RTT establishes the traceability between itemized software requirements specifications, design elements, code elements, and test cases. It also supports various associated query, analysis, and report generation capabilities. The preliminary design specification for the RTT (and most of the other SPS tools) looks different from the usual preliminary design specification, which tends to show a uniform level of elaboration of all components of the design. Instead, the level of detail of the RTT specification is risk-driven.

In areas involving a high risk if the design turned out to be wrong, the design was carried down to the detailed design level, usually with the aid of rapid prototyping. These areas included working out the implications of "undo" options and dealing with the effects of control keys used to escape from various program levels.

In areas involving a moderate risk if the design was wrong, the design was carried down to a preliminary-design level. These areas included the basic command options for the tool and the schemata for the requirements traceability database. Here again, the ease of rapid prototyping with Unix shell scripts supported a good deal of user-interface prototyping.

In areas involving a low risk if the design was wrong, very little design elaboration was done. These areas included details of all the help message options and all the report-generation options, once the nature of these options was established in some example instances.

A Detailed Design Go-Back

The UDF tool collects into an electronic "folder" all artifacts involved in the development of a single-programmer software unit (typically 500 to 1000 instructions): unit requirements, design, code, test cases, test results, and documentation. It also includes a management template for tracking the programmer's scheduled and actual completion of each artifact.

An alternative considered during detailed design of the UDF tool was reuse of portions of the RTT to provide pointers to the requirements and preliminary design specifications of the unit being developed. This turned out to be an extremely attractive alternative, not only for avoiding duplicate software development but also for bringing to the surface several issues involving many-to-many mappings between requirements, design, and code that had not been considered in designing the UDF tool. These led to a rethinking of the UDF tool requirements and preliminary design, which avoided a great deal of code rework that would have been necessary if the detailed design of the UDF tool had proceeded in a purely deductive, top-down fashion from the original UDF requirements specification. The resulting go-back led to a significantly different, less costly, and more capable UDF tool, incorporating the RTT in its "uses-hierarchy."

Spiral Model Features

These two examples illustrate several features of the spiral approach.

- It fosters the development of specifications that are not necessarily uniform, exhaustive, or formal, in that they defer detailed elaboration of low-risk software elements and avoid unnecessary breakage in their design until the high-risk elements of the design are stabilized.
- It incorporates prototyping as a risk-reduction option at any stage of development. In fact, prototyping and reuse risk analyses were often used in the process of going from detailed design into code.
- It accommodates reworks or go-backs to earlier stages as more attractive alternatives are identified or as new risk issues need resolution.

Overall, risk-driven documents, particularly specifications and plans, are important features of the spiral model. Great amounts of detail are not necessary unless the absence of such detail jeopardizes the project. In some cases, such as with a product whose functionality may be determined by a choice among commercial products, a set of weighted evaluation criteria for the products may be preferable to a detailed pre-statement of functional requirements.

Results

The Software Productivity System developed and supported using the spiral model avoided the identified risks and achieved most of the system's objectives. The SPS has grown to include over 300 tools and over 1,300,000 instructions; 93 percent of the instructions were reused from previous project-developed, TRW-developed, or external-software packages. Over 25 projects have used all or portions of the system. All of the projects fully using the system have increased their productivity at least 50 percent; indeed, most have doubled their productivity (when compared with cost-estimation model predictions of their productivity using traditional methods).

However, one risk area—that projects with non-Unix target systems would not accept a Unix-based host system—was underestimated. Some projects accepted the host-target approach, but for various reasons (such as customer constraints and zero-cost target machines) a good many did not. As a result, the system was less widely used on TRW projects than expected. This and other lessons learned have been incorporated into the spiral model approach to developing TRW's next-generation software development environment.

EVALUATION

Advantages

The primary advantage of the spiral model is that its range of options accommodates the good features of existing software process models, while its risk-driven approach avoids many of their difficulties. In appropriate situations, the spiral model becomes equivalent to one of the existing process models. In other situations, it provides guidance on the best mix of existing approaches to a given project; for example, its application to the TRW-SPS provided a risk-driven mix of specifying, prototyping, and evolutionary development.

The primary conditions under which the spiral model becomes equivalent to other main process models are summarized as follows:

- If a project has a low risk in such areas as getting the wrong user interface or not meeting stringent performance requirements, and if it has a high risk in budget and schedule predictability and control, then these risk considerations drive the spiral model into an equivalence to the waterfall model.

- If a software product's requirements are very stable (implying a low risk of expensive design and code breakage due to requirements changes during development), and if the presence of errors in the software product constitutes a high risk to the mission it serves, then these risk considerations drive the spiral model to resemble the two-leg model of precise specification and formal deductive program development.

- If a project has a low risk in such areas as losing budget and schedule predictability and control, encountering large-system integration problems, or coping with information sclerosis, and if it has a high risk in such areas as getting the wrong user interface or user decision support requirements, then these risk considerations drive the spiral model into an equivalence to the evolutionary development model.

- If automated software generation capabilities are available, then the spiral model accommodates them either as options for rapid prototyping or for application of the transform model, depending on the risk considerations involved.

- If the high-risk elements of a project involve a mix of the risk items listed above, then the spiral approach will reflect an appropriate mix of the process models above (as exemplified in the TRW-SPS application). In doing so, its risk-avoidance features will generally avoid the difficulties of the other models.

The spiral model has a number of additional advantages, summarized as follows:

It Focuses Early Attention on Options Involving the Reuse of Existing Software. The steps involving the identification and evaluation of alternatives encourage these options.

It Accommodates Preparation for Life-Cycle Evolution, Growth, and Changes of the Software Product. The major sources of product change are included in the product's objectives, and information-hiding approaches are attractive architectural design alternatives in that they reduce the risk of not being able to accommodate the product-charge objectives.

It Provides a Mechanism for Incorporating Software Quality Objectives into Software Product Development. This mechanism derives from the emphasis on identifying all types of objectives and constraints during each round of the spiral. For example, Exhibit 5 shows user-friendliness, portability, and reliability as specific objectives and constraints to be addressed by the SPS. In Exhibit 3, security constraints were identified as a key risk item for the SPS.

It Focuses on Eliminating Errors and Unattractive Alternatives Early. The risk-analysis, validation, and commitment steps cover these considerations.

For Each of the Sources of Project Activity and Resource Expenditure, It Answers the Key Question, "How Much is Enough?" Stated another way, "How much of requirements analysis, planning, configuration management, quality assurance, testing, formal verification, etc. should a project do?" Using the risk-driven approach, one can see that the answer is not the same for all projects and that the appropriate level of effort is determined by the level of risk incurred by not doing enough.

It Does Not Involve Separate Approaches for Software Development and Software Enhancement (or Maintenance). This aspect helps avoid the "second-class citizen" status frequently associated with software maintenance. It also helps avoid many of the problems that currently ensue when high-risk enhancement efforts are approached in the same way as routine maintenance efforts.

It Provides a Viable Framework for Integrated Hardware-Software System Development. The focus on risk-management and on eliminating unattractive alternatives early and inexpensively is equally applicable to hardware and software.

Difficulties

The full spiral model can be successfully applied in many situations, but some difficulties must be addressed before it can be called a mature, universally applicable model. The three primary challenges involve matching to contract software, relying on risk-assessment expertise, and the need for further elaboration of spiral model steps.

Matching to Contract Software

The spiral model currently works well on internal software developments like the TRW-SPS, but it needs further work to match it to the world of contract software acquisition.

Internal software developments have a great deal of flexibility and freedom to accommodate stage-by-stage commitments, to defer commitments to specific options, to establish minispirals to resolve critical-path items, to adjust levels of effort, or to accommodate such practices as prototyping, evolutionary development, or design-to-cost. The world of contract software acquisition has a harder time achieving these degrees of flexibility and freedom without losing accountability and control, and a harder time defining contracts whose deliverables are not well specified in advance.

Recently, a good deal of progress has been made in establishing more flexible contract mechanisms, such as the use of competitive front-end contracts for concept definition or prototype fly-offs, the use of level-of-effort and award-fee contracts for evolutionary development, and the use of design-to-cost contracts. Although these have been generally successful, the procedures for using them still need to be worked out to the point that acquisition managers feel fully comfortable using them.

Relying on Risk-Assessment Expertise

The spiral model places a great deal of reliance on the ability of software developers to identify and manage sources of project risk.

A good example of this is the spiral model's risk-driven specification, which carries high-risk elements down to a great deal of detail and leaves low-risk elements to be elaborated in later stages; by this time, there is less risk of breakage.

However, a team of inexperienced or low-balling developers may also produce a specification with a different pattern of variation in levels of detail: a great elaboration of detail for the well-understood, low-risk elements, and little elaboration of the poorly understood, high-risk elements. Unless there is an insightful review of such a specification by experienced development or acquisition personnel, this type of project will give an illusion of progress during a period in which it is actually heading for disaster.

Another concern is that a risk-driven specification will also be people-dependent. For example, a design produced by an expert may be implemented by non-experts. In this case, the expert, who does not need a great deal of detailed documentation, must produce enough additional documentation to keep the non-experts from going astray. Reviewers of the specification must also be sensitive to these concerns.

With a conventional, document-driven approach, the requirement to carry all aspects of the specification to a uniform level of detail eliminates some potential problems and permits adequate review of some aspects by inexperienced reviewers. But it also creates a large drain on the time of the scarce experts, who must dig for the critical issues within a large mass of noncritical detail. Furthermore, if the high-risk elements have been glossed over by impressive-sounding references to poorly understood capabilities (such as a new

synchronization concept or a commercial DBMS), there is an even greater risk that the conventional approach will give the illusion of progress in situations that are actually heading for disaster.

Need for Further Elaboration of Spiral Model Steps

In general, the spiral model process steps need further elaboration to ensure that all software development participants are operating in a consistent context.

Some examples of this are the need for more detailed definitions of the nature of spiral model specifications and milestones, the nature and objectives of spiral model reviews, techniques for estimating and synchronizing schedules, and the nature of spiral model status indicators and cost-versus-progress tracking procedures. Another need is for guidelines and checklists to identify the most likely sources of project risk and the most effective risk-resolution techniques for each source of risk.

Highly experienced people can successfully use the spiral approach without these elaborations. However, for large-scale use in situations where people bring widely differing experience bases to the project, added levels of elaboration—such as have been accumulated over the years for document-driven approaches—are important in ensuring consistent interpretation and use of the spiral approach across the project.

Efforts to apply and refine the spiral model have focused on creating a discipline of software risk management, including techniques for risk identification, risk analysis, risk prioritization, risk-management planning, and risk-element tracking. The prioritized top-ten list of software risk items given in Exhibit 6 is one result of this activity. Another example is the risk management plan discussed in the next section.

Implications: The Risk Management Plan

Even if an organization is not ready to adopt the entire spiral approach, one characteristic technique that can easily be adapted to any life-cycle model provides many of the benefits of the spiral

EXHIBIT 6 A Prioritized Top-Ten List of Software Risk Items

Risk Item	Risk Management Techniques
1. Personnel shortfalls	Staffing with top talent, job matching; teambuilding; morale building; cross-training; pre-scheduling key people
2. Unrealistic schedules and budgets	Detailed, multisource cost and schedule estimation; design to cost; incremental development; software reuse; requirements scrubbing
3. Developing the wrong software functions	Organization analysis; mission analysis; ops-concept formulation; user surveys; prototyping; early users' manuals
4. Developing the wrong user interface	Task analysis; prototyping; scenarios; user characterization (functionality, style, workload)
5. Gold plating	Requirements scrubbing; prototyping; cost-benefit analysis; design to cost
6. Continuing stream of requirement changes	High change threshold; information hiding; incremental development (defer changes to later increments)
7. Shortfalls in externally furnished components	Benchmarking; inspections; reference checking; compatibility analysis
8. Shortfalls in externally performed tasks	Reference checking; pre-award audits; award-fee contracts; competitive design or prototyping; teambuilding
9. Real-time performance shortfalls	Simulation; benchmarking; modeling; prototyping; instrumentation; tuning
10. Straining computer-science capabilities	Technical analysis; cost-benefit analysis; prototyping; reference checking

approach. This is the Risk Management Plan summarized in Exhibit 7. This plan basically ensures that each project makes an early identification of its top risk items (the number 10 is not an absolute requirement), develops a strategy for resolving the risk items, identifies and sets down an agenda to resolve new risk items as they surface, and highlights progress versus plans in monthly reviews.

The Risk Management Plan has been used successfully at TRW and other organizations. Its use has ensured appropriate focus on early prototyping, simulation, benchmarking, key-person staffing measures, and other early risk-resolution techniques that have helped avoid many potential project "show-stoppers." The recent US Department of Defense standard on software management, DoD-Std-2167, requires that developers produce and use risk management plans, as does its counterpart US Air Force regulation, AFR 800-14.

Overall, the Risk Management Plan and the maturing set of techniques for software risk management provide a foundation for tailoring spiral model concepts into the more established software acquisition and development procedures.

We can draw four conclusions from the data presented:

1. The risk-driven nature of the spiral model is more adaptable to the full range of software project situations than are the primarily document-driven approaches such as the waterfall model or the primarily code-driven approaches such as evolutionary development. It is particularly applicable to very large, complex, ambitious software systems.

EXHIBIT 7   Software Risk Management Plan

---

1. Identify the project's top 10 risk items.
2. Present a plan for resolving each risk item.
3. Update list of top risk items, plan, and results monthly.
4. Highlight risk-item status in monthly project reviews.
   • Compare with previous month's rankings, status.
5. Initiate appropriate corrective actions.

---

2. The spiral model has been quite successful in its largest application to date: the development and enhancement of the TRW-SPS. Overall, it achieved a high level of software support environment capability in a very short time and provided the flexibility necessary to accommodate a high dynamic range of technical alternatives and user objectives.

3. The spiral model is not yet as fully elaborated as the more established models. Therefore, the spiral model can be applied by experienced personnel, but it needs further elaboration in such areas as contracting, specifications, milestones, reviews, scheduling, status monitoring, and risk-area identification to be fully usable in all situations.

4. Partial implementations of the spiral model, such as the Risk Management Plan, are compatible with most current process models and are very helpful in overcoming major sources of project risk.

ACKNOWLEDGMENTS

I would like to thank Frank Belz, Lolo Penedo, George Spadaro, Bob Williams, Bob Balzer, Gillian Frewin, Peter Hamer, Manny Lehman, Lee Osterweil, Dave Parnas, Bill Riddle, Steve Squires, and Dick Thayer, along with the *Computer* reviewers of this article, for their stimulating and insightful comments and discussions of earlier versions of the article, and Nancy Donato for producing its several versions.

References

1. F.P. Brooks et al., *Defense Science Board Task Force Report on Military Software,* Office of the Under Secretary of Defense for Acquisition, Washington, DC 20301, Sept. 1987.

2. H.D. Benington, "Production of Large Computer Programs," *Proc. ONR Symp. Advanced Programming Methods for Digital Computers,* June 1956, pp. 15–27. Also available in *Annals of the History of Computing,* Oct. 1983, pp. 350–361, and *Proc. Ninth Int'l Conf. Software Engineering,* Computer Society Press, 1987.

3. W.W. Royce, "Managing the Development of Large Software Systems: Concepts and Techniques," *Proc. Wescon,* Aug. 1970. Also available in *Proc. ICSE 9,* Computer Society Press, 1987.

4. D.D. McCracken and M.A. Jackson, "Life-Cycle Concept Considered Harmful," *ACM Software Engineering Notes,* Apr. 1982, pp. 29–32.

5. R. Balzer, T.E. Cheatham, and C. Green, "Software Technology in the 1990s: Using a New Paradigm," *Computer,* Nov. 1983, pp. 39–45.

6. B.W. Boehm et al., "A Software Development Environment for Improving Productivity," *Computer,* June 1984, pp. 30–44.

7. B.W. Boehm, *Software Engineering Economics,* Prentice-Hall, 1981, Chap. 33.

A RATIONAL DESIGN PROCESS: HOW AND WHY TO FAKE IT

THE SEARCH FOR THE PHILOSOPHER'S STONE: WHY DO WE WANT A RATIONAL DESIGN PROCESS?

A perfectly rational person is one who always has a good reason for what he does. Each step taken can be shown to be the best way to get to a well defined goal. Most of us like to think of ourselves as rational professionals. However, to many observers, the usual process of designing software appears quite irrational. Programmers start without a clear statement of desired behavior and implementation constraints. They make a long sequence of design decisions with no clear statement of why they do things the way they do. Their rationale is rarely explained.

Many of us are not satisfied with such a design process. That is why there is research in software design, programming methods, structured programming, and related topics. Ideally, we would like to derive our programs from a statement of requirements in the same sense that theorems are derived from axioms in a published proof. All of the methodologies that can be considered "top down" are the result of our desire to have a rational, systematic way of designing software.

This paper brings a message with both bad news and good news. The bad news is that, in our opinion, we will never find the philosopher's stone. We will never find a process that allows us to design software in a perfectly rational way. The good news is that we can fake it. We can present our system to others as if we had been rational designers and it pays to pretend to do so during development and maintenance.

Article by David Lorge Parnas and Paul C. Clements. © 1986 IEEE. Reprinted, with permission, from (*IEEE Transactions on Software Engineering*, v. SE-12, n. 2, pp. 251–257).

WHY WILL A SOFTWARE DESIGN "PROCESS" ALWAYS BE AN IDEALIZATION?

We will never see a software project that proceeds in the "rational" way. Some of the reasons are listed below:

1. In most cases the people who commission the building of a software system do not know exactly what they want and are unable to tell us all that they know.

2. Even if we knew the requirements, there are many other facts that we need to know to design the software. Many of the details only become known to us as we progress in the implementation. Some of the things that we learn invalidate our design and we must backtrack. Because we try to minimize lost work, the resulting design may be one that would not result from a rational design process.

3. Even if we knew all of the relevant facts before we started, experience shows that human beings are unable to comprehend fully the plethora of details that must be taken into account in order to design and build a correct system. The process of designing the software is one in which we attempt to separate concerns so that we are working with a manageable amount of information. However, until we have separated the concerns, we are bound to make errors.

4. Even if we could master all of the detail needed, all but the most trivial projects are subject to change for external reasons. Some of those changes may invalidate previous design decisions. The resulting design is not one that would have been produced by a rational design process.

5. Human errors can only be avoided if one can avoid the use of humans. Even after the concerns are separated, errors will be made.

6. We are often burdened by preconceived design ideas, ideas that we invented, acquired on related projects, or heard about in a class. Sometimes we undertake a project in order to try out or use a favorite idea. Such ideas may not be derived from our requirements by a rational process.

7. Often we are encouraged, for economic reasons, to use software that was developed for some other project. In other situations, we may be encouraged to share our software with another ongoing project. The resulting software may not be the ideal software for either project, i.e., not the software that we would develop based on its requirements alone, but it is good enough and will save effort.

For all of these reasons, the picture of the software designer deriving his design in a rational, error-free way from a statement of requirements is quite unrealistic. No system has ever been developed in that way, and probably none ever will. Even the small program developments shown in textbooks and papers are unreal. They have been revised and polished until the author has shown us what he wishes he had done, not what actually did happen.

WHY IS A DESCRIPTION OF A RATIONAL IDEALIZED PROCESS USEFUL NONETHELESS?

What is said above is quite obvious, known to every careful thinker, and admitted by the honest ones. In spite of that we see conferences whose theme is the software design process, working groups on software design methods, and a lucrative market for courses purporting to describe logical ways to design software. What are these people trying to achieve?

If we have identified an ideal process, but cannot follow it completely, we can still follow it as closely as possible and we can write the documentation that we would have produced if we had followed the ideal process. This is what we mean by "faking a rational design process."

Below are some of the reasons for such a pretense:

1. Designers need guidance. When we undertake a large project we can easily be overwhelmed by the enormity of the task. We will be unsure about what to do first. A good understanding of the ideal process will help us to know how to proceed.

2. We will come closer to a rational design if we try to follow the process rather than proceed on an ad hoc basis. For example, even if we cannot know all of the facts necessary to design an ideal system, the effort to find those facts before we start to code will help us to design better and backtrack less.

3. When an organization undertakes many software projects, there are advantages to having a standard procedure. It makes it easier to have good design reviews, to transfer people, ideas, and software from one project to another. If we are going to specify a standard process, it seems reasonable that it should be a rational one.

4. If we have agreed on an ideal process, it becomes much easier to measure the progress that a project is making. We can compare the project's achievements to those that the ideal process calls for. We can identify areas in which we are behind (or ahead).

5. Regular review of the project's progress by outsiders is essential to good management. If the project is attempting to follow a standard process, it will be easier to review.

WHAT SHOULD THE DESCRIPTION OF THE DEVELOPMENT PROCESS TELL US?

The most useful form of a process description will be in terms of work products. For each stage of the process, this paper describes

1. What product we should work on next.
2. What criteria that product must satisfy.
3. What kind of persons should do the work.
4. What information they should use in their work.

Management of any process that is not described in terms of work products can only be done by mindreaders. Only if we know which work products are due and what criteria they must satisfy, can we review the project and measure progress.

WHAT IS THE RATIONAL DESIGN PROCESS?

This section describes the rational, ideal software design process that we should try to follow. Each step is accompanied by a detailed description of the work product associated with that step.

The description of the process that follows includes neither testing nor review. This is not to suggest that one should ignore either of those. When the authors apply the process described in this paper, we include extensive and systematic reviews of each work product as well as testing of the executable code that is produced. The review process is discussed in [1] and [17].

Establish and Document Requirements

If we are to be rational designers, we must begin knowing what we must do to succeed. That information should be recorded in a work product known as a requirements document. Completion of this document before we start would allow us to design with all the requirements in front of us.

Why Do We Need a Requirements Document?

1. We need a place to record the desired behavior of the system as described to us by the user; we need a document that the user, or his representative, can review.

2. We want to avoid making requirements decisions accidentally while designing the program. Programmers working on a system are very often not familiar with the application. Having a complete reference on externally visible behavior relieves them of any need to decide what is best for the user.

3. We want to avoid duplication and inconsistency. Without a requirements document, many of the questions it answered would be asked repeatedly throughout the development by designers, programmers and reviewers. This would be expensive and would often result in inconsistent answers.

4. A complete requirements document is necessary (but not sufficient) for making good estimates of the amount of work and other resources that it will take to build the system.

5. A requirements document is valuable insurance against the costs of personnel turnover. The knowledge that we gain about the requirements will not be lost when someone leaves the project.

6. A requirements document provides a good basis for test plan development. Without it, we do not know what to test for.

7. A requirements document can be used, long after the system is in use, to define the constraints for future changes.

8. A requirements document can be used to settle arguments among the programmers; once we have a complete and accurate requirements document, we no longer need to be, or consult, requirements experts.

Determining the detailed requirements may well be the most difficult part of the software design process because there are usually no well-organized sources of information.

What Goes Into the Requirements Document?

The definition of the ideal requirements document is simple: it should contain everything you need to know to write software that is acceptable to the customer, and no more. Of course, we may use references to existing information, if that information is accurate and well organized. Acceptance criteria for an ideal requirements document include the following:

1. Every statement should be valid for all acceptable products; none should depend on implementation decisions.

2. The document should be complete in the sense that if a product satisfies every statement, it should be acceptable.

3. Where information is not available before development must begin, the areas of incompleteness should be explicitly indicated.

4. The product should be organized as a reference document rather than an introductory narrative about the system. Although it takes considerable effort to produce such a document, and a reference work is more difficult to browse than an introduction, it saves labor in the long run. The information that is obtained in this stage is recorded in a form that allows easy reference throughout the project.

Who Writes the Requirements Document?

Ideally, the requirements documents would be written by the users or their representatives. In fact, users are rarely equipped to write such a document. Instead, the software developers must produce a draft document and get it reviewed and, eventually, approved by the user representatives.

What Is the Mathematical Model Behind the Requirements Specification?

To assure a consistent and complete document, there must be a simple mathematical model behind the organization. The model described here is motivated by work on real-time systems but, because of that, it is completely general. All systems can be described as real-time systems—even if the real-time requirements are weak.

The model assumes that the ideal product is not a pure digital computer, but a hybrid computer consisting of a digital computer that controls an analog computer. The analog computer transforms continuous values measured by the inputs into continuous outputs. The digital computer brings about discrete changes in the function computed by the analog computer. A purely digital or purely hybrid computer is a special case of this general module. The system that will be built is a digital approximation to this hybrid system. As in other areas of engineering, we can write our specification by first describing this "ideal" system and then specifying the allowable tolerances. The requirements document treats outputs as more important than inputs. If the value of the outputs is correct, nobody will mind if the inputs are not even read. Thus, the key step is identifying all of the outputs. The heart of the requirements document is a set of mathematical functions described in tabular form. Each table specifies the value of a single output as a function of external state variables.

How Is the Requirements Document Organized?

Completeness in the requirements document is obtained by using separation of concerns to obtain the following sections:

Computer Specification. A specification of the machines on which the software must run. The machine need not be hardware—for some software this section might simply be a pointer to a language reference manual.

Input/Output Interfaces. A specification of the interfaces that the software must use in order to communicate with the outside world.

Specification of Output Values. For each output, a specification of its value in terms of the state and history of the system's environment.

Timing Constraints. For each output, how often, or how quickly, the software is required to recompute it.

Accuracy Constraints. For each output, how accurate it is required to be.

Likely Changes. If the system is required to be easy to change, the requirements should contain a definition of the areas that are considered likely to change. You cannot design a system so that everything is equally easy to change. Programmers should not have to decide which changes are most likely.

Undesired Event Handling. The requirements should also contain a discussion of what the system should do when, because of undesired events, it cannot fulfill its full requirements. Most requirements documents ignore those situations; they leave the decision about what to do in the event of partial failures to the programmer.

It is clear that good software cannot be written unless the above information is available. An example of a complete document produced in this way is given in [9] and discussed in [8].

Design and Document the Module Structure

Unless the product is small enough to be produced by a single programmer, one must give thought to how the work will be divided into work assignments, which we call modules. The document that should be produced at this stage is called a module guide. It defines the responsibilities of each of the modules by stating the design decisions that will be encapsulated by that module. A module may consist of submodules, or it may be considered to be a single work assignment. If a module contains submodules, a guide to its substructure is provided.

A module guide is needed to avoid duplication, to avoid gaps, to achieve separation of concerns, and most of all, to help an ignorant maintainer to find out which modules are affected by a problem report or change request. If it is kept up-to-date, this document, which records our initial design decisions, will be useful as long as the software is used.

If one diligently applies "information hiding" or "separation of concerns" to a large system, one is certain to end up with a great many modules. A guide that was simply a list of those modules, with no other structure, would help only those who are already familiar with the system. The module guide should have a tree structure, dividing the system into a small number of modules and treating each such module in the same way until all of the modules are quite small. For a complete example of such a document, see [3]. For a discussion of this approach and its benefits, see [6, 15].

Design and Document the Module Interfaces

Efficient and rapid production of software requires that the programmers be able to work independently. The module guide defines responsibilities, but it does not provide enough information to permit independent implementation. A module interface specification must be written for each module. It must be formal and provide a black box picture of each module. Written by a senior designer, it is reviewed by both the future implementors and the programmers who will use the module. An interface specification for a module contains just enough information for the programmer of another module to use its facilities, and no more. The same information is needed by the implementor.

While there will be one person or small team responsible for each specification, the specifications are actually produced by a process of nego-

tiation between implementors, those who will be required to use it, and others interested in the design, e.g., reviewers. The specifications include

1. a list of programs to be made invokable by the programs of other modules (called "access programs");

2. the parameters for the access programs;

3. the externally visible effects of the access programs;

4. timing constraints and accuracy constraints, where necessary;

5. definition of undesired events.

In many ways this module specification is analogous to the requirements document. However, the notation and organization used is more appropriate for the software-to-software interface than is the format that we use for the requirements.

Published examples and explanations include [1, 2, 5, 11].

Design and Document the Uses Hierarchy

The "uses" hierarchy [13] can be designed once we know all of the modules and their access programs. It is conveniently documented as a binary matrix where the entry in position (A, B) is true if and only if the correctness of program A depends on the presence in the system of a correct program B. The "uses" hierarchy defines the set of subsets that can be obtained by deleting whole programs without rewriting any programs. It is important for staged deliveries, fail soft systems, and the development of program families [12]. The "uses" hierarchy is determined by the software designers, but must allow the subsets specified in the requirements document.

Design and Document the Module Internal Structures

Once a module interface has been specified, its implementation can be carried out as an independent task except for reviews. However, before coding the major design decisions are recorded in a document called the module design document [16]. This document is designed to allow an efficient review of the design before the coding begins and to explain the intent behind the code to a future maintenance programmer.

In some cases, the module is divided into submodules and the design document is another module guide, in which case the design process for that module resumes at the "Design and Document the Module" step above. Otherwise, the internal data structures are described; in some cases, these data structures are implemented (and hidden) by submodules. For each of the access programs, a function [10] or LD-relation [14] describes its effect on the data structure. For each value returned by the module to its caller, another mathematical function, the abstraction function, is provided. This function maps the values of the data structure into the values that are returned. For each of the undesired events, we describe how we check for it. Finally, there is a "verification," an argument that programs with these properties would satisfy the module specification.

The decomposition into and design of submodules is continued until each work assignment is small enough that we could afford to discard it and begin again if the programmer assigned to do it left the project.

Each module may consist of one or more processes. The process structure of the system is distributed among the individual modules.

When one is unable to code in a readable high-level language, e.g., if no compiler is available, pseudocode must be part of the documentation. It is useful to have the pseudocode written by someone other than the final coder, and to make both programmers responsible for keeping the two versions of the program consistent [7].

Write Programs

After all of the design and documentation has been carried out, one is finally ready to write actual executable code. Because of the preparatory work, this goes quickly and smoothly. The code should not include comments that are redundant with the documentation that has already been written. It is unnecessary and makes maintenance of the system more expensive. Redundant comments increase the likelihood that the code will not be consistent with the documentation.

Maintain

Maintenance is just redesign and redevelopment. The policies recommended here for design must be continued after delivery or the "fake" rationality will disappear. If a change is made, all documentation that is invalidated must be changed. If a change invalidates a design document, it and all subsequent design documents must be faked to look as if the change had been the original design. If two or more versions are being maintained, the system should be redesigned so that the differences are confined to small modules. The short term costs of this may appear high, but the long term savings can be much higher.

WHAT IS THE ROLE OF DOCUMENTATION IN THIS PROCESS?

What is Wrong with Most Documentation Today? Why is it Hard to Use? Why is it Not Read?

It should be clear that documentation plays a major role in the design process that we are describing. Most programmers regard documentation as a necessary evil, written as an afterthought only because some bureaucrat requires it. They do not expect it to be useful.

This is a self-fulfilling prophecy; documentation that has not been used before it is published, documentation that is not important to its author, will always be poor documentation.

Most of that documentation is incomplete and inaccurate, but those are not the main problems. If those were the main problems, the documents could be easily corrected by adding or correcting information. In fact, there are underlying organizational problems that lead to incompleteness and incorrectness and those problems, which are listed below, are not easily repaired.

Poor Organization

Most documentation today can be characterized as "stream of consciousness," and "stream of execution." "Stream of consciousness" writing puts information at the point in the text that the author was writing when the thought occurred to him. "Stream of execution" writing describes the system in the order that things will happen when it runs. The problem with both of these documentation styles is that subsequent readers cannot find the information that they seek. It will therefore not be easy to determine that facts are missing, or to correct them when they are wrong. It will not be easy to find all the parts of the document that should be changed when the software is changed. The documentation will be expensive to maintain and, in most cases, will not be maintained.

Boring Prose

Lots of words are used to say what could be said by a single programming language statement, a formula, or a diagram. Certain facts are repeated in many different sections. This increases the cost of the documentation and its maintenance. More importantly, it leads to inattentive reading and undiscovered errors.

Confusing and Inconsistent Terminology

Any complex system requires the invention and definition of new terminology. Without it the documentation would be far too long. However, the writers of software documentation often fail to provide precise definitions for the terms that they use. As a result, there are many terms used for the same concept and many similar but distinct concepts described by the same term.

Myopia

Documentation that is written when the project is nearing completion is written by people who have lived with the system for so long that they take the major decisions for granted. They document the small details that they think they will forget. Unfortunately, the result is a document useful to people who know the system well, but impenetrable for newcomers.

How Can One Avoid These Problems?

Documentation in the ideal design process meets the needs of the initial developers as well as the needs of the programmers who come later. Each of the documents mentioned above records requirements or design decisions and is used as a reference document for the rest of the design. However, they also provide the information that the maintainers will need. Because the documents are used as reference manuals throughout the building of the software, they will be mature and ready for use in the later work. The documentation in this design process is not an afterthought; it is viewed as one of the primary products of the project. Some systematic checks can be applied to increase completeness and consistency.

One of the major advantages of this approach to documentation is the amelioration of the Mythical Man Month effect [4]. When new programmers join the project they do not have to depend completely on the old staff for their information. They will have an up-to-date and rational set of documents available.

"Stream of consciousness"and "stream of execution" documentation is avoided by designing the structure of each document. Each document is designed by stating the questions that it must answer and refining the questions until each defines the content of an individual section. There must be one, and only one, place for every fact that will be in the document. The questions are answered, i.e., the document is written, only after the structure of a document has been defined. When there are several documents of a certain kind, a standard organization is written for those documents [5]. Every document is designed in accordance with the same principle that guides our software design: separation of concerns. Each aspect of the system is described in exactly one section and nothing else is described in that section. When documents are reviewed, they are reviewed for adherence to the documentation rules as well as for accuracy.

The resulting documentation is not easy or relaxing reading, but it is not boring. It makes use of tables, formulas, and other formal notation to increase the density of information. The organizational rules prevent the duplication of information. The result is documentation that must be read very attentively, but rewards its reader with detailed and precise information.

To avoid the confusing and inconsistent terminology that pervades conventional documentation, a system of special brackets and typed dictionaries is used. Each of the many terms that we must define is enclosed in a pair of bracketing symbols that reveals its type. There is a separate dictionary for each such type. Although beginning readers find the presence of !+terms+!, %terms%, #terms#, etc., disturbing, regular users of the documentation find that the type information implicit in the brackets makes the documents easier to read. The use of dictionaries that are structured by types makes it less likely that we will define two terms for the same concept or give two meanings to the same term. The special bracketing symbols make it easy to institute mechanical checks for terms that have been introduced but not defined or defined but never used.

FAKING THE IDEAL PROCESS

The preceding describes the ideal process that we would like to follow and the documentation that would be produced during that process. The process is "faked" by producing the documents that we would have produced if we had done things the ideal way. One attempts to produce the documents in the order that we have described. If a piece of information is unavailable, that fact is noted in the part of the document where the information should go and the design proceeds as if that information were expected to change. If errors are found, they must be corrected and the consequent changes in subsequent documents must be made. The documentation is our medium of design and no design decisions are considered to be made until their incorporation into the documents. No matter how often we stumble on our way, the final documentation will be rational and accurate.

Even mathematics, the discipline that many of us regard as the most rational of all, follows this procedure. Mathematicians diligently polish their proofs, usually presenting a proof very different from the first one that they discovered. A first proof is often the result of a tortured discovery process. As mathematicians work on proofs, understanding grows and simplifications are found. Eventually, some mathematician finds a simpler proof that makes the truth of the theorem more apparent. The simpler proofs are published because the readers are interested in the truth of the theorem, not the process of discovering it.

Analogous reasoning applies to software. Those who read the software documentation want to understand the programs, not to relive their discovery. By presenting rationalized documentation we provide what they need.

Our documentation differs from the ideal documentation in one important way. We make a policy of recording all of the design alternatives that we considered and rejected. For each, we explain why it was considered and why it was finally rejected. Months, weeks, or even hours later, when we wonder why we did what we did, we can find out. Years from now, the maintainer will have many of the same questions and will find his answers in our documents.

An illustration that this process pays off is provided by a software requirements document written some years ago as part of a demonstration of the ideal process [9]. Usually, a requirements document is produced before coding starts and is never used again. However, that has not been the case for [9]. The currently operational version of the software, which satisfies the requirements document, is still undergoing revision. The organization that has to test the software uses our document extensively to choose the tests that they do. When new changes are needed, the requirements document is used in describing what must be changed and what cannot be changed. Here we see that a document produced at the start of the ideal process is still in use many years after the software went into service. The clear message is that if documentation is produced with care, it will be useful for a long time. Conversely, if it is going to be extensively used, it is worth doing right.

CONCLUSION

It is very hard to be a rational designer; even faking that process is quite difficult. However, the result is a product that can be understood, main-

tained, and reused. If the project is worth doing, the methods described here are worth using.

ACKNOWLEDGMENT

R. Faulk, J. Shore, D. Weiss, and S. Wilson of the Naval Research Laboratory provided thoughtful reviews of this paper. P. Zave and anonymous referees provided some helpful comments.

References

1. D.L. Parnas, D.M. Weiss, P.C. Clements, and K.H. Britton, "Interface Specifications for the SCR (A-7E) Extended Computer Module," NRL Memorandum Report 5502, December 31, 1984 (major revisions to NRL Report 4843).

2. K.H. Britton, R.A. Parker, and D.L. Parnas, "A Procedure for Designing Abstract Interfaces for Device-Interface Modules," in *Proceedings of the Fifth International Conference on Software Engineering,* 1981.

3. K.H. Britton and D.L. Parnas, "A-7E Software Module Guide," NRL Memorandum Report 4702, December 1981.

4. F.P. Brooks, Jr., *The Mythical Man-Month: Essays on Software Engineering.* Reading, Mass.: Addison-Wesley, 1975.

5. P. Clements, A. Parker, D.L. Parnas, J. Shore, and K. Britton, "A Standard Organization for Specifying Abstract Interfaces," NRL Report 8815, June 14, 1984.

6. P. Clements, D. Parnas, and D. Weiss, "Enhancing Reusability with Information Hiding," in *Proceedings of the Workshop on Reusability in Programs,* September 1983, pp. 240–47.

7. H.S. Elovitz, "An Experiment in Software Engineering: The Architecture Research Facility as a Case Study," in *Proceedings of the Fourth International Conference on Software Engineering,* September 1979.

8. K.L. Heninger, "Specifying Software Requirements for Complex Systems: New Techniques and Their Application," *IEEE Transactions on Software Engineering,* Vol. SE-6, January 1980, pp. 2–13.

9. ———, J. Kallander, D.L. Parnas, and J. Shore, "Software Requirements for the A-7E Aircraft," NRL Memorandum Report 3876, November 27, 1978.

10. R.C. Linger, H.D. Mills, B.I. Witt, *Structured Programming: Theory and Practice.* Reading, Mass.: Addison-Wesley, 1979.

11. A. Parker, K. Heninger, D. Parnas, and J. Shore, "Abstract Interface Specifications for the A-7E Device Interface Module," NRL Memorandum Report 4385, November 20, 1980.

12. D.L. Parnas, "On the Design and Development of Program Families," *IEEE Transactions on Software Engineering,* Vol. SE-2, March 1976.

13. ———, "Designing Software for Ease of Extension and Contraction," in *Proceedings of the Third International Conference on Software Engineering,* May 10–12, 1978, pp. 264–77.

14. ———, "A Generalized Control Structure and Its Formal Definition," in *Communications of the ACM,* Vol. 26, No. 8, August 1983, pp. 572–81.

15. ———, P. Clements, and D. Weiss, "The Modular Structure of Complex Systems," in *Proceedings of the Seventh International Conference on Software Engineering,* March 1984, pp. 408–17.

16. S. Faulk, B. Labaw, and D. Parnas, "SCR Module Implementation Document Guidelines," NRL Technical Memorandum 7590-072:SF:BL:DP, April 1, 1983.

17. D.L. Parnas and D.M. Weiss, "Active Design Reviews: Principles and Practices," in *Proceedings of the Eighth International Conference on Software Engineering,* August 1985, pp. 132–36.

WHAT EVER HAPPENED
TO STRUCTURED ANALYSIS?

I believe it's time to restate the case for structured analysis.

Approximately 90% of the worldwide professional data processing community is at least superficially familiar with the basic concepts of structured analysis, design, and programming. About half the dp organizations in this country make some effort to use it in their development projects.

But many others that tried to use classic structured analysis, vintage 1978, lost interest, sometimes finding it more of a hindrance than a help. Today, only about 10% of the dp organizations in North America practice structured techniques in a disciplined fashion.

The importance of structured systems development for large and complex systems has been obscured by such recent advancements as prototyping, fourth generational languages, and personal computing facilities. Nevertheless, as is well known, personal computers and workstations can be used to assist programmers and systems analysts in their work.

To most people, classic structured analysis is associated with dataflow diagrams, or bubble diagrams, of the sort shown in Exhibit 1. There is still debate about whether the bubbles should be round, oval, or rectangular; whether the lines connecting the bubbles should be curved or straight; and a variety of other cosmetic issues. But almost everyone agrees that a central idea behind structured analysis is the use of graphs to communicate the system requirements to the end user.

To many people, the term structured analysis also implies a certain methodological process: a step-by-step series of activities that, when finished, will lead to a desired result—in this case, a complete specification of the user's requirements for a new system.

Article by Edward Yourdon. Reprinted, with permission, from (*Datamation*, June 1, 1986, pp. 133–138.)

The methodology commonly associated with structured analysis is shown in Exhibit 2.

Like a lot of popular ideas, structured analysis is a concept that has a long history and a number of proponents who can claim—with varying degrees of accuracy—to have created it. Many read the theory for the first time in Tom DeMarco's book, *Structured Analysis and Systems Specification* (Yourdon Press, 1978). In addition, my former colleagues, Chris Gane and Trish Sarson, contributed to the development of the idea of structured analysis in their book, *Structured Systems Analysis,* (Prentice-Hall, 1979).

Doug Ross and his colleagues at Softech, Waltham, Mass., developed a structured analysis variant known as SADT. Ken Orr and Jean-Dominique Warnier developed their own approach, which emphasizes data modeling more than function modeling. Michael Jackson developed program and system design methods that bear his name. Dozens of other researchers, writers, and consultants contributed the basic concepts of structured analysis, which began to emerge in the late 1970s.

With the publication of textbooks by Gane & Sarson, DeMarco, Warnier, Orr, Jackson, and others in the late 1970s, structured analysis and a variety of other software engineering techniques became firmly entrenched in the software industry.

Many organizations made a valiant effort to use structured analysis but eventually abandoned it altogether. Others spent a long time incorporating structured analysis into standard manuals only to find, years later, that no one followed it. Still others who used structured analysis happily in the late 1970s and early 1980s became convinced later on that tools like fourth generation languages and prototyping packages were better.

What happened to the revolutionary fervor with which structured analysis was accepted a relatively few short years ago?

EXHIBIT 1   The Elements of a Dataflow Diagram

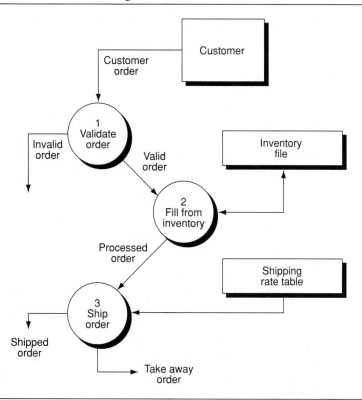

REASONS FOR REVERSAL

I believe three problems caused this reversal. The first is that people became frustrated with the amount of manual labor that was required to develop structured analysis models.

The use of structured analysis on real-world projects requires dozens, if not hundreds, of dataflow diagrams like the one shown in Exhibit 1. Any reasonable systems analyst is willing to draw a diagram once. Drawing a hundred such diagrams is a different matter, especially because each diagram typically has to be revised and redrawn several times as the analyst and the end user change the model. The overwhelming tedium of drawing and redrawing has led many well-intentioned analysts to abandon structured analysis altogether.

Systems analysts have traditionally been forced to use manual techniques—like walkthroughs, inspections, and careful personal scrutiny—to determine whether the large collection of dataflow diagrams and related documents (data dictionaries, process specifications, etc.) was complete and internally consistent. It is cheaper to correct a user-analyst misunderstanding while systems analysis is still under way than it is to allow the misunderstanding to remain undetected until final system testing. But this isn't much comfort to the analyst who has to scrutinize dozens of dataflow diagrams to see if anything is missing.

Another problem is that people became frustrated with their inability to apply classical structured analysis to complex, real-time systems.

Over the past decade, most textbooks and training materials for structured analysis and structured

EXHIBIT 2   Overview of the Analysis Activity

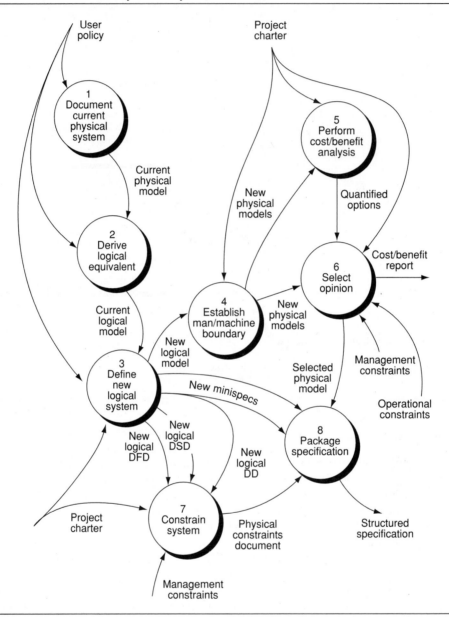

design have assumed the analyst was involved in building a straightforward, business-oriented information system on a batch computer system—e.g., a payroll or accounting system for a mainframe. Little or no guidance was provided to people building systems involving networks of mainframes, minis, micros, and smart, on-line terminals. Today, hardly anyone builds simple, batch, mainframe systems—except, perhaps, in university computer science courses.

The final problem is that people were lured away from structured analysis by the promises of prototyping tools and fourth generation languages.

Fourth generation languages have been advertised as tools that can improve productivity by a factor of 10. From the perspective of systems analysis—the business of determining system requirements—4GLS can sometimes be seen as a practical way of implementing Fred Brooks's adage that one should be prepared to build a system, throw it away, and then build the right system.

Similarly, prototyping tools can be used effectively to provide the end user with a tangible, satisfying mock-up of the system he thinks he wants. In the right circumstances—for example, small- to medium-sized projects, with cooperative users, etc.—4GLS and prototyping packages are powerful, effective tools that should definitely be used by the system developer.

PACKAGES HAVE BEEN OVERSOLD

Unfortunately, 4GLS and prototyping packages have been oversold. Even worse, they were sometimes presented as tools that rendered structured analysis obsolete. A reasoned, evenhanded presentation of the relative advantages and disadvantages of prototyping and structured analysis was presented by Bernard Boar in his book, *Application Prototyping* (Addison-Wesley, 1984).

But other books, like James Martin's *Application Development without Programmers* (Prentice-Hall, 1982), portrayed structured analysis as an obsolete technology of the 1970s. Unfortunately, it seems this idea was widely accepted.

But structured analysis is not obsolete. In fact, the concept of structured analysis has been developing since it was first formulated in the late 1970s. Attitudes about it are changing as well. For example, software quality and productivity are now considered by many to be very important.

People have given lip service to the importance of developing superior, reliable, maintainable software (on schedule and under budget) ever since the 1960s. Until recently, however, nobody cared enough to do anything about it. Indeed, many organizations still don't care enough—they tolerate sloppy, undocumented, bug-infested, low-quality, unmaintainable systems.

And what is equally bad, they sacrifice long-term issues of reliability and maintainability for the short-term expediency of getting a system into operation, regardless of whether it actually serves the user's needs.

But now, more and more end users, top executives, and others are demanding top-quality systems. Even if there were no further developments in the technology of structured analysis, this demand is sufficient reason for the techniques to be used more widely than in the past.

Just as important, the modeling tools of structured analysis have been improved. As mentioned, classic structured analysis was primarily developed for non-real-time business information systems. One version of structured analysis placed more emphasis on function modeling and less on data modeling. Another version took the opposite approach, emphasizing data modeling over function modeling.

It has become increasingly evident, however, that there are three important dimensions of complexity: functions, data, and time-dependent behavior. If a system is complex in one dimension but relatively simple in the other two (for example, a batch inquiry system with no processing or updating of data), then the classic forms of structured analysis are sufficient.

Classic methods are inadequate for modeling systems that have complex functions and complex data. Structured analysis isn't useful in modeling real-time systems either.

New methods of applying structured analysis have closed this gap. In *Structured Development for Real-Time Systems* (Yourdon Press, 1985), authors Stephen Mellor and Paul Ward offer a comprehensive view of modeling systems that are complex in all three of the dimensions shown in Exhibit 3.

Increasingly, we are finding that big systems have complexities in all three dimensions. Banking and insurance systems, for example, not only have increasingly complex data and functions (which must be modeled accurately during the systems analysis phase), but also have thousands of on-line terminals with response-time requirements that are becoming more and more stringent. Similarly, today's real-time systems often contain hundreds of thousands, if not millions, of lines of code to carry out increasingly complex functions. The tools of structured analysis have evolved to model real-time systems. Early textbooks' simple data structure diagrams, which detail data and their component attributes, have been replaced by more appropriate entity-relationship diagrams, which depict relationships among high-order groupings of data, i.e., entities. The modeling of time-dependent behavior is now carried out with state-transition diagrams, which depict the various states of a system and the conditions that lead to a change from one state to another.

DIAGRAM HAS EVOLVED

Equally important, the classic dataflow diagram shown in Exhibit 1, which depicts the processes that affect data from start to finish in a system or subsystem, has itself evolved—dashed lines indicate signals or interrupts and dashed bubbles symbolize control processes, which exist to synchronize and coordinate the activities of other functions.

Each of these three modeling tools—the dataflow diagram, the entity-relationship diagram, and the state-transition diagram—provides a way to

---

EXHIBIT 3 Three Dimensions of Systems Complexity

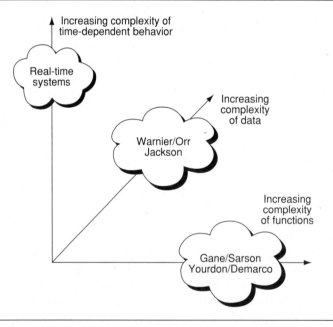

emphasize one critical aspect of a system (and deemphasize the others). For example, the dataflow diagram highlights the functions in the system and the interfaces between them, but says little about stored data.

If the three different views of the system are not consistent, there is a danger of getting into a position analogous to that of the three blind men who touched different parts of an elephant and came to three different conclusions about the nature of the beast.

To maintain consistency, we need cross-checking rules to ensure the three models do not conflict. One such rule is that each data store on a dataflow diagram should correspond to an object on an entity-relationship diagram, and vice versa. We need similar cross-checking rules to ensure that the dataflow diagram and the state-transition diagram are also consistent with each other.

There have also been changes in the process of structured analysis. Specifically, we have deemphasized the practice of modeling the existing system. Users of structured analysis who follow the methodology suggested by Exhibit 3 often start out by modeling the system that is scheduled to be replaced. While there were good reasons to model the existing system, there are even more compelling reasons to stop the practice.

For one thing, systems people tended to spend far too much time on this phase of the project. Authors Steve McMenamin and John Palmer, in their book *Essential Systems Analysis* (Yourdon Press, 1984), refer to this phenomenon as the "current physical tarpit." Others call it "analysis paralysis."

In reaction, my company has virtually eliminated the concept. We took this somewhat drastic step because we realized that modeling the current system often turned out to be politically dangerous. We had seen too many projects canceled because the user got impatient after spending 12 months modeling a system that was about to be thrown away.

Perhaps the most exciting recent development in structured analysis is the availability of pc-based workstations that help automate the systemsanalyst's job.

CASE WILL CHANGE INDUSTRY

Just as CAD/CAM technology has helped revolutionize various engineering disciplines over the past 25 years, so CASE (computer aided software engineering) technology will help revolutionize the software industry. At present, there are an estimated 6,000 CASE workstations installed in the U.S.—or about one for every 100 programmers and analysts. By 1990, 10% of professional programmers and analysts should be equipped with this kind of technology—by 1995, that figure should grow to 90%.

The software development profession, if one charitably accepts the notion that it is a profession, is not even 30 years old. The term software engineering was first used in 1968, less than 20 years ago. Structured analysis is less than 10 years old, and even 10 years ago, it wasn't widely known.

Perhaps it is unreasonable to expect that structured analysis concepts would develop smoothly and be put into widespread practice—without objections, problems, and false starts. As Capers Jones, the noted software productivity guru, has pointed out, it took the military 75 years to switch from muskets to rifles.

But I am impatient, and I think systems analysts, MIS organizations, and even whole companies are also impatient to see structured analysis and related software engineering techniques used far more aggressively. I believe the next three years will be seen as a major turning point in the conscious—no, passionate!—adaptation of such techniques.

Two factors will speed the use of structured analysis. First, more and more systems developed in the 1960s and 1970s are dying of old age. They simply can't be patched, extended, upgraded, or tinkered with much longer. The agony of the analyst trying to distill corporate policy and end-user requirements from old, undocumented programs is such that it is absolutely essential to develop formal, rigorous, maintainable models of the system's requirements.

Second, a new generation's top executives and middle management realize they can't ignore the issues of building information systems because their companies' strategies and abilities to compete may utterly depend on those systems.

Eventually, I expect structured analysis to merge with artificial intelligence. Work in natural language processing will be applied to the dreary job of writing minispecs or process specifications that define each piece of business policy in an information system. Expert systems will be used to create expert analysts, i.e., programs that know what questions to ask the nontechnical end user who wants a new information system.

But this is still some years away. In the meantime, we have much work to do to apply vintage 1986 structured analysis technology to the systems that will be built during the next five years. There are still a few Luddites who avoid using any formal, structured approach. I expect them to disappear by the end of the decade.

In fact, even those who practice 1978 structured analysis are probably doomed as well in view of the new concepts, additional modeling tools, and rapidly evolving CASE workstation technology. Structured analysis is not yet a mature discipline, but it has moved beyond its infancy. Those who can take advantage of the ongoing evolution of the technology have much to gain.

Discussion Questions

1. Boehm's Spiral Model seems to be a 'meta-model' that encompasses both lifecycle (waterfall) and other process models. Therefore, it appears as if any organization could easily adopt it. What obstacles do you think, in practice, would need to be overcome before it could be adopted?

2. Parnas and Clements stress the difficulty of documenting the requirements task well. To what degree do you believe that this task is inherently difficult versus an argument that would say it is only difficult for the traditional systems development role players?

3. Yourdon notes that one of the problems with the widescale adoption and greater assimilation of structured analysis is that "people were lured away . . . by the promise of prototyping tools and fourth generation languages". How does this relate to Brooks's article in Chapter 1 on silver bullets? Was structured analysis a silver bullet? Why or why not?

4. Imagine that it is a number of years in the future, and someone writes an article entitled "What Ever Happened to Object Oriented Analysis?" In what ways might such an article resemble the Yourdon article? In what ways might it differ?

Chapter

7

Prototyping

INTRODUCTION

By the end of the 1970s, a large body of anecdotal evidence suggested that the great investment in systems development life cycle models created projects that were very expensive, took a great deal of time to produce, but still tended to produce systems that were often not what the users wanted and therefore required significant amounts of rework effort to be made satisfactory. At a conference at Georgia State University in 1980 Daniel McCracken and Michael Jackson wrote a short 'minority dissenting opinion' that soon became something of an instant classic. In their essay they note that the traditional SDLC allows only a very limited role for users primarily in requirements definition, and that it also assumes (unrealistically, in their opinion) that these requirements can be defined completely and errorlessly at the project's inception. They advocate allowing for prototyped development both as a possible means of requirements specification only (throwaway prototyping) and as a possible development strategy (evolutionary development).

Much time has passed since this seminal essay and a significant amount of experience has accrued with prototyping. Gordon and Bieman, as part of a four year study, document results from 39 case studies, primarily from secondary data collection. They summarize and characterize the observations of participants in these projects as to the effects of the prototyping approach on both product and process.

They are careful to note that, despite the characterization of these projects as successful in the overwhelming majority of the cases, prototyping possesses its own set of possible difficulties. They provide a thoughtful list of recommended managerial actions to help avoid these pitfalls. Gordon and Bieman's extensive use of secondary data illustrates the importance of the community's documentation of experience, particular with newer technologies and methods.

Another recent collection of case studies of prototyped projects comes from three authors from Germany. In their article, Lichter, Schneider-Hufschmidt, and Zullighoven report on five case studies that they have had the opportunity to personally observe. Prototypes are typically categorized as either 'throwaway', designed to be used to assist the requirements analysis and design but then discarded, or 'evolutionary', where the prototype eventually becomes the operational system. Lichter et al. further divide the throwaway category into 'exploratory prototypes', used for exploring problem design options (due to user uncertainty) and 'experimental prototypes', used for analysis of alternative designs (e.g. interfaces). Interestingly, three of the five case studies are reported as relatively unsuccessful. Lichter et al. note that a common theme in these failures is the absence of significant user involvement, despite the fact that user involvement is a central tenet of the prototyping approach.

LIFE CYCLE CONCEPT
CONSIDERED HARMFUL

The authors were among the participants at an invitational conference held in September of 1980 at the Georgia State University to study the topic "Systems Analysis and Design: A Plan for the 80s."[1]

We found the conference and workshop stimulating and useful, and we support many of its processes and conclusions.

However, we came to the meeting unprepared for the stultifying effect of the organizers' decision to structure the group's work around the concept of a system development life cycle.

The life cycle concept as promulgated in pre-conference mailings was that systems development consists of the following ten steps:

1. Organizational analysis
2. Systems evaluation
3. Feasibility analysis
4. Project plan
5. Logical design (produces general design specifications)
6. Physical design (produces detailed design specifications)
7. Program design
8. Implementation
9. Operation
10. Review and evaluation

Most attendees apparently found the life cycle concept comfortable. Several pointed out that there are many variations on the basic theme, but asserted

Written by Daniel D. McCracken and Michael A. Jackson. © Association of Computing Machinery. Reprinted, with permission, from (*ACM Software Engineering Notes*, v. 7 n. 2, pp. 29–32, April 1982).

---

[1] The published report, with the same title, is available from Elsevier North-Holland, New York, 1981, 553 pp. The meeting was organized by the Institute for Certification of Computer Professionals (ICCP), and sponsored by the Computer Society of the Institute of Electrical and Electronics Engineers (IEEE-CS), the Association for Computing Machinery (ACM), ICCP, and Georgia State University. The body of this paper is printed in the report under the title "A Minority Dissenting Position."

that all life cycle concepts can be mapped onto each other. We would be interested in a demonstration of the latter assertion, which we doubt is true in any strict sense; if it *is* true, then we believe that the life cycle concept is probably, on balance, harmful. We adduce three groups of criticism.

1. Any form of life cycle is a project management structure imposed on system development. To contend that *any* life cycle scheme, even with variations, can be applied to *all* system development is either to fly in the face of reality or to assume a life cycle so rudimentary as to be vacuous.

The elaborate life cycle assumed as the basis for this conference may have seemed to be the only possible approach in the past when managing huge projects with inadequate development tools. (That it seemed to be the only choice, obviously did not prevent many such projects from failing.) It is foolish to use it as the basis for a certification effort that may be hoped to have a significant impact on the education of systems analysts for the next decade or more. During that time it seems highly probable to us that new development methodologies and implementation techniques will force—or rather permit—a complete reevaluation of the assumptions built into the life cycle way of thinking.

2. The life cycle concept perpetuates our failure so far, as an industry, to build an effective bridge across the communication gap between end-user and systems analyst. In many ways it constrains future thinking to fit the mold created in response to failures of the past. It ignores such factors as the following, all of which are receiving rapidly increasing attention from both researchers and practitioners:

• The widest possible development of systems by end-users themselves, limited only by the (rapidly improving) availability of development tools suited to the purpose. This is, of course, the optimum response to the communication gap: eliminate the need for communication.

• Heavy end-user involvement *in all phases* of the application development process—not just requirements specification, but design and implementation also.

- An increasing awareness that systems requirements cannot ever be stated fully in advance, not even in principle, because the user doesn't *know* them in advance—not even in principle. To assert otherwise is to ignore the fact that the development process itself changes the user's perceptions of what is possible, increases his or her insights into the applications environment, and indeed often changes that environment itself. We suggest an analogy with the Heisenberg Uncertainty Principle: any system development activity inevitably changes the environment out of which the need for the system arose. System development methodology *must* take into account that the user, and his or her needs and environment, change during the process.

What we understand to be the conventional life cycle approach might be compared with a supermarket at which the customer is forced to provide a complete order to a stock clerk at the door to the store, with no opportunity to roam the aisles— comparing prices, remembering items not on the shopping list, or getting a headache and deciding to go out for dinner. Such restricted shopping is certainly possible and sometimes desirable—it's called mail order—but why should anyone wish to impose that restricted structure on *all* shopping?

3. The life cycle concept rigidifies thinking, and thus serves as poorly as possible the demand that systems be responsive to change. We all know that systems and their requirements inevitably change over time. In the past, severely limited by inadequate design and implementation tools as we were, there was little choice but to freeze designs much earlier than desirable and deal with changes only reluctantly and in large packets. The progress of system development thus moved along a kind of sawtooth, with a widely separated set of points being designated "completion of implementation," "completion of first set of modifications," etc. The term "life cycle," if it has any linguistic integrity at all, seems an odd way to describe this process. To impose the concept on emerging methods in which much

greater responsiveness to change is possible, seems to us to be sadly shortsighted.

Here, as sketches only, are two scenarios of system development processes that seem to us to be impossible to force into the life cycle concept without torturing either logic or language or both.

1. (Prototyping.) Some response to the user's earliest and most tentative statement of needs is provided for experimentation and possibly even productive use, extremely early in the development process—perhaps 1% of the way into the eventual total effort. Development proceeds step-by-step *with the user,* as insight into the user's own environment and needs is accumulated. A series of prototypes, or, what is perhaps the same thing, a series of modifications to the first prototype, evolves gradually into the final product. Formal specifications may *never* be written. Or, if specifications are needed, perhaps to permit a re-implementation to improve performance, the prototype itself furnishes the specifications.

This mode of operation is emphasized by some writers as being fundamental to the concept of Decision Support Systems; we believe it has even wider applicability.

2. A process of system development done by the end-user and an analyst in this sequence: implement, design, specify, redesign, re-implement. The user is provided with an implementation tool *and one version of a system thought to be potentially useful.* By a process of experimentation, in occasional consultation with the analyst, the *user* carries out— essentially in parallel—the following activities:

- Learning the capabilities of the implementation tool.
- Designing the desired system.
- Specifying the desired system.

The *analyst* then works from the "specification," which in fact consists of a running functional model of the system, to produce a design that is implemented by a programmer in some conventional language.

We claim that neither of these scenarios, nor many others that are readily imaginable, can be "mapped onto" the life cycle reproduced at the beginning of this note, or onto any other life cycle that is not vacuous. The life cycle concept is simply unsuited to the needs of the 1980s in developing systems.

RAPID PROTOTYPING:
LESSONS LEARNED

Selecting an appropriate development approach is crucial to building a successful software system. Although the waterfall model remains the most common life-cycle paradigm, interest in evolutionary methods such as rapid prototyping is growing. But is this approach actually being used? If so, how effective is it?

In an attempt to answer these questions, we launched a study four years ago that involved collecting data on as many published case studies of rapid prototyping as we could find and determining commonalities.

In another publication, we documented the effects of rapid prototyping on software quality. [1] Here we extend that work to include not only its effects on the product, but also its influence on the software process itself, in areas like development effort and costing. The study is continuing, and we hope to publish additional results in the near future.

The box titled Survey Scope and Rationale describes our evaluation approach. Finding rapid prototyping case studies was not easy. There are many books and research papers on the subject, but few report actual experience. We found only 22 sources of published case studies that include information on the technique's effectiveness. We supplemented these with solicited first-hand accounts, as the box describes. In total, we analyzed the results of 39 studies.

Our overall objective is to use the studies to develop guidelines on how to use rapid prototyping effectively. An important goal is to compare the use of the two main prototyping methodologies: *throwaway,* in which the prototype is discarded and not used in the delivered product, and *evolutionary,* in which all or part of the prototype is retained. In presenting our results, we pay special attention to factors that contribute to the selection of one prototyping method over another.

Our results show that developers considered rapid prototyping a success in 33 of the 39 cases. Of the remaining six, three were described as failures and three did not claim success or failure. We suspect some bias in this number, however, because people are often reluctant to report failures, but even with this bias, the results clearly show that rapid prototyping is a viable development tool. Some of the successful sources address intermediate difficulties encountered and perceived disadvantages.

Another surprise, in light of most attitudes about evolutionary prototyping, [2] was that of the 39 studies, 22 used evolutionary prototyping, while only eight used throwaway (the rest did not state a choice).

The studies reflect military (12), commercial (17), and academic (10) applications. After evaluating the data for common experiences and opinions, we tallied the commonalities to identify recurring themes. We were able to group these into three areas:

- *Product attributes.* These include ease of use, match with user needs, performance, design quality, maintainability, and number of features. Although design quality and maintainability are closely related, many studies reported the two separately. In some instances, the authors were able to observe maintenance and so report specifically about it. In other cases, there were maintenance tools.
- *Process attributes.* These include effort, degree of end-user participation, cost estimation, and expertise requirements. There were fewer

Article by V. Scott Gordon and James M. Bieman. © 1995 IEEE. Reprinted, with permission, from (*IEEE Software;* 12.1, 85–95; January/1995).

commonalities in this area, perhaps because prototyping itself is a process, and it may not have occurred to authors to report other process effects.

- *Problems.* These include performance, end-user misunderstandings, maintenance, delivery of a throwaway prototype, budgeting, and prototype completion and conversion. Authors rarely described actual occurrences of these problems, but many detailed the steps they took to avoid them. As part of our data analysis, we matched stated problems with solutions from other sources.

PRODUCT ATTRIBUTES

Exhibit 1 shows the six product attributes commonly affected by prototyping. For each attribute, the figure indicates case studies that experienced a positive or negative impact. The box titled Survey Scope and Rationale gives the corresponding studies. We also indicate the relative number of studies

in which the particular effect was not observed or discussed. The relatively high number of unreported effects reflects the diversity of reporting methods among the case studies.

The first three product attributes—ease of use, user needs, and number of features—can be considered usability factors. The remaining three (performance, design quality, and maintainability) are structural issues.

Usability Factors

Users have an opportunity to interact with the prototype, and give direct feedback to designers. Consequently, difficulties with the interface are quickly revealed. Seventeen of our case studies reported improvements in ease of use as a direct result of rapid prototyping; none reported negative effects. After working with a prototype, one user in an academic study soon tired of retyping

EXHIBIT 1   How Case-Study Developers Perceive the Effect of Rapid Prototyping on the Product. Referenced Case Studies Appear in the Box Titled Survey Scope and Rationale

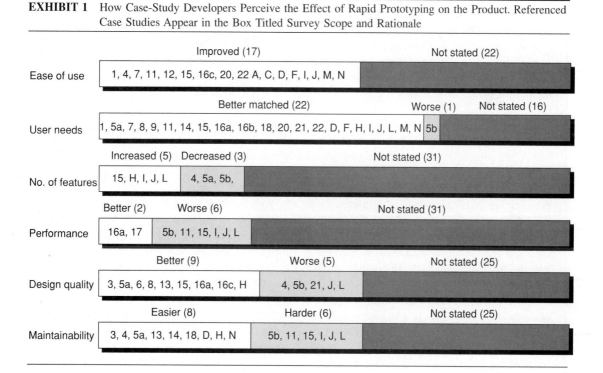

Survey Scope and Rationale

The 39 case studies included in our analysis describe particular software projects and discuss how prototyping helped or hindered development. In an effort to obtain a good cross-section of practical use, we combined published case studies with more focused surveys of individuals who claimed to have been involved in software-development projects that used rapid prototyping. Consequently, the case studies come from a variety of sources—each with their own motivations and goals—and few addressed all the effects worth tracking.

To obtain some degree of corroboration among the studies, we have tried to locate the effects that were observed in at least three case studies. Thus, when reviewing the results by effect, we incurred a preponderance of "not stated" responses. Perhaps we could decrease this number in the future by doing a controlled study, where we knew in advance what effects would be tracked.

The case studies are described below. Each is identified by a number (published) or letter (anonymous), which is used as a reference in the figures in the main text.

Case-study analysis Case studies varied in degree of rigor. Four sources observed multiple teams (or projects) and presented one set of conclusions based on careful quantitative measurements of the results. Six sources described projects that involved no customer; the goal was simply to create a system for the developers. We avoided drawing strong conclusions about the clarity of requirements or successful analysis of user needs when a project did not involve a separate user.

More often, the cases offer subjective conclusions and suggestions in a less specific, more qualitative manner, acquired from personal experience in a single project. The case studies have varied objectives and intended audiences.

One study may report difficulty with a particular rapid-prototyping activity, while another may suggest a remedy for the same problem. Some of the studies include a minimal amount of quantitative measurement interspersed with judgments.

The published sources listed below represent a variety of organizations in academic, military, and commercial environments: AT&T, General Electric, Rand, Mitre, Martin Marietta, Los Alamos National Laboratory, Tektronix, Rome Air Force Base, Hughes, government divisions, and others. The anonymous sources also represent a sampling from these three environments.

Some cases involve separate prototyping and development teams. Ten cases are projects conducted at universities, with only three being student projects. Twelve describe military projects, and the remaining 17 describe other professional software development. (Note that two sources describe multiple projects.)

Attribute selection The lack of commonalities, the diverse reporting methods, and the varying terminology made attribute selection difficult. We began by identifying attributes (effects) that appeared in three or more sources and used these attributes in our analysis. We then tallied the attributes, along with relevant opinions, observations, and suggestions. We emphasized conclusions that were reached by multiple sources independently.

Although the terminology in the case studies differs, we tried to standardize on the definitions suggested by Bob Patton [1] and B. Ratcliff [2] because we found their terms to be the ones most consistent with the terms used in the case studies. Some terminology remains general because the authors concentrate on different details, and because the software systems described in the case studies are themselves so diverse. "Design quality," for example, can mean many things, depending on

Survey Scope and Rationale (*Cont.*)

the nature of the system or the designer's point of view. One source may illustrate improve–ment in design quality by specifically listing improvements in code structure, reducing patches, and increasing flexibility, while other sources list different items or none at all.

Although we could have included additional attributes, or subdivided attributes into more specific categories, we did not because the results would have been less clear and there would have been fewer commonalities among the studies. We did not include attributes that the case studies did not mention, even if we thought they might be useful. Also, we omitted some attributes that would have been interest-ing to observe, such as cohesion, coupling, cyclomatic complexity, and product lifespan, because of insufficient data in the case studies.

PUBLISHED CASE STUDIES

1. *Commercial study.* The author investigates 12 information-systems development projects using the prototyping approach in six organi-zations. He also presents an experiment in-volving nine student groups, in which some groups used prototyping and some used specification. The experiment confirmed the findings of the investigation.—M. Alavi, "An Assessment of the Prototyping Approach to Information Systems Development," *Comm. ACM,* June 1984, pp. 556–563.

2. *Commercial study.* The authors describe a methodology for applying object-oriented technology to switching systems and dis-cuss the advantages of using an object-oriented approach in conjunction with prototyping.—E. Arnold and D. Brown, "Object-Oriented Software Technologies Ap-plied to Switching System Architectures and Software-Development Processes," *Proc. Int'l Switching Symp.,* 1990, pp. 97–106.

3. *Military study.* Evolutionary prototyping using object-oriented programming is shown to be an effective way to develop a medium-to-large (50,000 LOC) signal-processing system.—B. Barry, "Prototyping a Real-Time Embedded System in Smalltalk," *Proc. OOPSLA,* ACM Press, New York, 1989, pp. 255–265.

4. *Academic study.* Seven student teams de-veloped the same product: three used pro-totyping, and four used specification. The authors compare the two techniques.—B. Boehm, T. Gray, and T. Seewaldt, "Proto-typing Versus Specifying: A Multiproject Experiment," *IEEE Trans. Software Eng.,* May 1984, pp. 290–302.

5 a,b. *Commercial studies.* Both cases involve the use of the Ingres database system. Project 5a involved rewriting a resource-control system for tracking the cost of soft-ware projects. It was completed and the sys-tem implemented to the apparent satisfaction of all parties. Project 5b in-volved developing a requirements document generator. It was criticized by various parties and eventually abandoned.—J. Connell and L. Brice, "The Impact of Implementing a Rapid Prototype on System Maintenance," *Proc. AFIPS,* IEEE CS Press, Los Alamitos, Calif., 1985, pp. 515–524.

6. *Academic study.* The authors describe their experiences applying prototyping tech-niques to the development of programming languages with advanced features.—R. Ford and C. Marlin, "Implementation Pro-totypes in the Development of Program-ming Language Features," *Software Eng. Notes,* Dec. 1982, pp. 61–66.

7. *Commercial study.* The author describes a case study using Promis, a large process-management and information system devel-oped at General Electric to fabricate inte-grated circuits, and tracks the progress of

Survey Scope and Rationale (*Cont.*)

prototyping and subsequent development. —H. Gomaa, "The Impact of Rapid Prototyping on Specifying User Requirements," *Software Eng.: Notes,* Apr. 1983, pp. 17–28.

8. *Military study.* The author describes a large multiphase software- and hardware-development effort in Ada that used incremental development techniques (with rapid prototyping) and object-oriented design.—M. Goyden, "The Software Lifecycle with Ada: A Command and Control Application," *Proc. Tri-Ada,* ACM Press, New York, 1989, pp. 40–55.

9. *Commercial study.* The authors describe how small clinical research programs were developed and evaluated for users who have difficulty clearly expressing their computing needs. Rapid prototyping provided a positive environment, in which users were more willing to participate and better able to express their views.—G. Groner et al., "Requirements Analysis in Clinical Research Information Processing: A Case Study," *Computer,* Sept. 1979, pp. 100–108.

10. *Commercial study.* The author describes 48 Fortune 1000 companies and evaluates the feasibility of discarding prototypes. Although most of the companies use throw-away prototyping, the author concludes that evolutionary prototyping is preferable.—T. Guimaraes, "Prototyping: Orchestrating for Success," *Datamation,* Dec. 1987, pp. 101–106.

11. *Academic study.* The author demonstrates the suitability of rapid prototyping for the development of CAD systems and for object-oriented development. The focus is on the application rather than the merits of prototyping in general.—R. Gupta et al., "An Object-Oriented VLSI CAD Frame-work: A Case Study in Rapid Prototyping," *Computer,* May 1989, pp. 28–36.

12. *Military study.* The authors track the development of a small prototype messaging system that uses Lisp. Focus is on the role of the prototype, prototyping efforts in general, and reuse of prototype code.—C. Heitmeyer, C. Landwehr, and M. Cornwell. "The Use of Quick Prototypes in the Secure Military Message Systems Project," *Software Eng. Notes,* Dec. 1982, pp. 85–87.

13. *Academic study.* The author describes how rapid-prototyping methodologies were used to develop a prototyping language, EPROL, and a prototyping system, EPROS.—S. Hekmatpour, "Experience with Evolutionary Prototyping in a Large Software Project," *Software Eng. Notes,* Jan. 1987, pp. 38–41.

14. *Military study.* The authors propose a new methodology for rapid prototyping, called software storming, which involves an intense week of videotaped interaction between software designers and users.—P. Jordan et al., "Software Storming: Combining Rapid Prototyping and Knowledge Engineering," *Computer,* May 1989, pp. 39–48.

15. *Academic study.* The authors compare specification and prototyping in a controlled study using student teams. Effort curves were smoother for the prototyping teams, reducing the "deadline effect" common in software development.—W. Junk, P. Oman, and G. Spencer, "Comparing the Effectiveness of Software Development Paradigms: Spiral-Prototyping vs. Specifying," *Proc. Pacific Northwest Software Quality Conf.,* PNSQC, Portland, 1991, pp. 3–18.

16a-c. *Commercial studies.* Describes five cases, three of which are used in the study reported in this article. Project 16a involved an expert system to support a customer-advice service. Project 16b involved a distributed database accessed via a wide-area network. Project 16c involved a real-time control system for quality assurance of a chemical process. The authors

Survey Scope and Rationale (*Cont.*)

attempt to highlight commonalities between the cases, and in the process show that prototyping has advantages over specification. Project 16b can be characterized as large.—H. Lichter et al., "Prototyping in Industrial Software Projects: Bridging the Gap Between Theory and Practice," *Proc. ICSE,* IEEE CS Press, Los Alamitos, Calif., 1993, pp. 221–229.

17. *Academic study.* The author introduces CAPS, a computer-aided prototyping system that is essentially an integrated set of computer-aided software tools, and describes its application to the development of a medical system.—Luqi, "Software Evolution through Rapid Prototyping," *Computer,* May 1989, pp. 13–25.

18. *Military study.* Evolutionary prototyping is shown to have advantages over specifying, even on large (100,000 LOC) projects. The authors point out that a significant portion of delivered military systems do not meet original needs and that prototyping can greatly improve this situation.—C. Martin et al., "Team-Based Incremental Acquisition of Large-Scale Unprecedented Systems," *Policy Sciences,* Feb. 1992, pp. 57–75.

19. *Military study.* The author describes a prototyping environment at the Rome Air Development Center, concentrating on a heavily I/O intensive application. There was a significant decrease in development time as a direct result of prototyping.—W. Rzepka, "A Requirements Engineering Testbed: Concept, Status and First Results," in *Proc. Hawaii Conf. System Sciences: Vol. II,* IEEE CS Press, Los Alamitos, Calif., 1989, pp. 339–347.

20. *Academic study.* The authors describe how retaining prototype code and using a special-purpose prototyping language can be useful for small software projects.—E. Strand and W. Jones, "Prototyping and Small Software Projects." *Software Eng. Notes,* Dec. 1982, pp. 169–170.

21. *Military study.* The author describes how a major ($100 million) military project was successfully implemented using rapid prototyping in a CICS development environment. The study provides insights into how prototyping affects management techniques and the development process in general.—D. Tamanaha, "An Integrated Rapid Prototyping Methodology for Command and Control Systems: Experience and Insight," *Software Eng. Notes,* Dec. 1982, pp. 387–396.

22. *Academic study.* The author describes experiences implementing Backus's FFP System using rapid prototyping. The need for certain functionality became apparent while exercising the prototype.—M. Zelkowitz, "A Case Study in Rapid Prototyping," *Software Practice and Experience,* Dec. 1980, pp. 1037–1042.

ANONYMOUS SOURCES

A. *Academic study.* Employees at a major university describe the development of an online registration system using a special-purpose prototyping environment. They report improved customer satisfaction, ease of use, and ease of training as a direct result of rapid prototyping.

B. *Academic study.* A researcher at a major university reports satisfaction with using Scheme as a prototyping language to produce a working campus-support system in C.

C. *Commercial study.* An engineer at a large telecommunications firm describes problems with rapid prototyping that stemmed from management not understanding the limits of a prototype. The problems resulted in development hardships and premature announcements of delivery dates.

Survey Scope and Rationale (*Cont.*)

D. *Military study.* An engineer at a large military contractor reports substantially improved product quality, reduced effort, lower maintenance costs, and faster delivery as a direct result of using rapid prototyping. Leveraging with off-the-shelf products helped greatly.

E. *Commercial study.* An engineer at a large data-processing firm reports that prototyping has been quite effective. Recommendations include using an object-oriented approach and throwaway prototyping and carefully selecting an appropriate prototyping language.

F. *Military study.* An engineer at a large military division describes the successful development of small government systems through the use of rapid prototyping. Some results include reuse of typically half the prototype, improved product quality, and better matching with user needs. Some people became upset when their ideas were quickly discredited by experiences with the prototype.

G. *Military study.* An engineer at a small software company reports prototyping worked well in a small project for developing low-level system software. One observation was that you can bid lines-of-code-per-day at a higher rate. Another is that prototyping works only if experienced engineers are available.

H. *Military study.* An engineer at a small military contractor that develops all products using prototyping reports on the use of special prototyping tools that require fewer programming skills to master than typical programming environments.

I. *Commercial study.* An engineer at a large manufacturer reports on the use of evolutionary prototyping to develop very large software systems for workstations. The ability to overlap some of the requirements, design, and coding tasks has improved productivity.

J. *Commercial study.* An engineer at a large communications-and-control contractor describes how proof-of-concept prototypes are developed in Smalltalk, and then the final products are developed using evolutionary prototyping with C. Although total effort has decreased and the product is easier to use, design quality and performance have sometimes suffered because design standards are not rigorous enough.

K. *Military study.* A consultant for a defense contractor reports how rapid prototyping was used for internal support software, but misunderstandings between engineers and marketing staff, along with difficulties in scheduling and costing, have led the company to return to specification.

L. *Commercial study.* An engineer at a large electronics firm describes how operating systems are developed using the Rapid prototyping language. The interface between Rapid and C was the "messiest" part of the final system, but overall the project was successful.

M. *Commercial study.* An engineer at a small software company reports that the organization successfully used rapid prototyping on several nonmilitary internal development projects and that users are much happier with products developed with prototyping methods.

N. *Commercial study.* An engineer at a large communications firm reports that rapid prototyping improved quality, increased user participation, and made final products easier to use. However, developers are often pressured into reusing a throwaway prototype. The engineer recommends carefully defining the prototype's scope and definition.

References

1. B. Patton, "Prototyping—A Nomenclature Problem," *Software Eng. Notes,* Apr. 1983, pp. 14–16.

2. B. Ratcliff, "Early and Not-So-Early Prototyping—Rationale and Tool Support," *Proc. Compsac,* IEEE CS Press, Los Alamitos, Calif., 1988, pp. 127–134.

definitions for each run. This was valuable information for modifying the design.

One commercial developer found that prototyping helped reveal misunderstandings between developers and users. Sometimes users are not sure they want certain functions implemented until they can actually try them, or they may not know they need certain features until actual use exposes an omission or inconvenience. A commercial study found that prototyping helped ensure that the nucleus of the system is right. One academic developer found prototypes useful because "omissions of functions are . . . difficult . . . to recognize in formal specifications." [Case study 20]

In working with the prototype, users may also find certain features or terminology confusing. Thus prototyping helps ensure that the first implementation (after the prototype) will meet user needs, especially when the prototype includes the user interface. One academic developer states

"The traditional model of software development relied on the assumption that designers could stabilize and freeze the requirements. In practice, however, the design of accurate and stable requirements cannot be completed until users gain some experience with the proposed software system." [Case study 17]

These findings are consistent with Fred Brooks' famous maxim, [3]"plan to throw one away; you will, anyhow."

The effect of prototyping on the number of features in a final system is less clear. Only eight studies reported any data in this area. Thus, the evidence neither supports nor refutes the intuitive notion that prototyping gives the end user a license to demand more and more functionality.

As Exhibit 1 shows, five cases report that the prototype increased the number of features (in one case, features increased but the author failed to observe the effect). Authors saw the increase as the result of

- special-purpose prototyping languages, which made it easy to add new features,
- internal software development, which tends to require less time for baselining requirements and

thus more time for considering additional features, and
- users' demand for more and more functionality, because the prototype lets them visualize increased functionality without considering the cost of adding features.

These authors viewed the increase as a negative effect. One military developer commented "The customer goes crazy adding features and making changes."

In contrast, three studies report a decrease in features as a result of prototyping. In these studies, prototyping caused critical components to be emphasized and noncritical ones to be suppressed, thus reducing the total number of features. One academic study reports that prototyping "fostered a higher threshold for incorporating marginally useful features. . . ." [Case study 4] As a result only the most important features were included in the final product.

One military developer suggested that contractors consider incorporating some mechanism for increasing the cost of the final product when the user requests extra functionality. This might mean costing the prototype phase separately from the rest of development.

Structural Factors

In this area, prototyping has more opportunity to produce negative effects. The effect on system performance, for example, depends partly on the prototype's scope. When the prototype focuses solely on the user interface, system performance is likely to be unaffected. When it is used to examine various design alternatives, the outcome can vary.

Sometimes prototyping can lead to better system performance because it is easier to test several design approaches. As one military developer put it, ". . . with large and complex systems, one's intuition is often a poor guide for identifying the performance-critical regions that will require optimization." [Case study 8] Prototyping can also provide insights into alternative design approaches. One academic developer found that the prototype let the team assess early on the techniques needed to implement specific features.

Evolutionary prototyping, however, can lead to problems when performance is not adequately measured and either inefficient code is retained in the final product or the prototype demonstrates functionality that is unrealizable under normal usage loads. One commercial developer cited "design baggage" as a reason for performance problems. Another academic developer suggested considering performance "as early as possible if [the prototype] is to evolve into the final system." [Case study 11] The case studies contain more evidence of performance problems for evolutionary prototypes than for throwaways.

Design-quality effects are also mixed. More sources indicated an improvement in design, quality for both kinds of prototyping, but others report that evolutionary prototyping can result in a less coherent design and more difficult integration. Still others state that the iterative design-modify-review process can yield a better overall design. Three sources reported more lines of code, while four reported fewer lines. However, neither side interpreted this as good or bad.

Quality also suffers when, during evolutionary prototyping, design standards are not enforced in the prototype system. Even when produced with good tools, a design can suffer when developers fail to remove remnants of discarded design alternatives. One commercial developer cited documentation with no design of system procedures and control flows. To avoid these problems, the same developer recommended using a design checklist for each section of incorporated code.

Quality can also be improved by limiting the scope of the prototype to a particular subset (often the user interface), and by including a design phase with each iteration of the prototype. Another option is to completely discard the prototype.

Maintainability effects are similar to those observed for design quality. More studies cite better maintainability than worse. Four described successful maintenance of prototyped systems, even for large projects. (It is with some trepidation that we use the term "large" at all, since it means different things to different people. However, in this article, "large" refers to systems of 100,000-plus lines of code.) The high degree of modularity required for successful evolutionary prototyping can generate easily maintainable code, because such a system is more likely to contain reusable and replaceable functional modules. On the flip side, including hastily designed modules in the final system could cause problems. Indeed, for evolutionary prototyping specifically (not shown in the exhibit), more sources observe worse maintainability.

Maintenance costs can also go down simply because the final system more accurately reflects user needs. Maintenance often involves correcting invalid requirements or responding to changing requirements. Rapid prototyping can help reduce this type of maintenance because it is likely that user needs will have been better met.

Summary

Overall, we find that software product effects are generally positive, with certain problems related primarily to evolutionary prototyping. We found, however, that developers can use evolutionary prototyping effectively, even for large projects. One academic developer even stated that, for small contracts, throwaway prototyping was economically infeasible compared with evolutionary. Nonetheless, quality attributes such as performance, design quality, and maintainability can suffer during evolutionary prototyping if developers fail to take steps to avoid potential problems, as we describe later.

Unfortunately, the sample size for throwaway prototyping is too small to be statistically useful in evaluating its specific effect on structural factors. (Only two authors of the eight addressed questions on individual attributes.)

PROCESS ATTRIBUTES

Exhibit 2 lists the four process attributes. Again, the exhibit indicates which case studies observed either a positive or negative effect.

EXHIBIT 2   How Case-Study Developers Perceive the Effect of Rapid Prototyping on the Development Process. Referenced Case Studies Appear in the Box Titled Survey Scope and Rationale

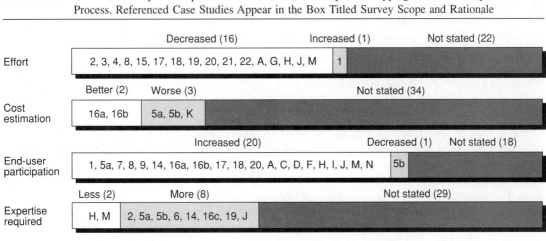

Although the studies discuss other process attributes, such as interface design and language selection, there is less commonality than for product attributes. We do, however, briefly cover these attributes apart from the four in Exhibit 2 because our overall goal is to describe the effective use of rapid prototyping.

Effort and Estimation

One of the most commonly cited benefits of rapid prototyping is that it can decrease development effort. Most of the case studies support this notion. In some instances, the decrease is dramatic. One military study reports a reduction of 70 percent. An academic study reports a reduction of 45 percent. One military project team observed a productivity of 34 lines of code per day, more than six times the estimate for typical military software systems. As one military developer put it, "A buck buys more software now than before." [Case study H]

There are various reasons for this positive effect. Faster design is possible when requirements are clearer or more streamlined. Also, in evolutionary prototyping, part (or all) of the prototype can be leveraged, so the requirements and development efforts tend to overlap.

In one commercial case, development effort increased. The reasons cited were frequent changes in user requirements, which tended to frustrate the designers, and a failure to establish explicit procedures for managing and controlling the prototyping effort. Another commercial developer also suggested the lack of an organized methodology as a possible cause of wasted effort, although it is not clear that this was actually ever observed. In both these cases, prototyping might have decreased development effort if the techniques to manage it had been more effective.

Another commercial study reported an increase in development effort because prototyping revealed that the initial set of requirements was inadequate, and they had to be extended. We think it is unfair to call this a case of increased effort, however, because prototyping actually *prevented* significant wasted effort in the long run.

In viewing cost estimation in a rapid-prototyping environment, the general mood is one of skepticism. One commercial developer observed that the early availability of visible outputs can cause users and managers to be "easily seduced into believing that [subsequent phases] can be skimped on" [Case study 5b] and will be easy to complete. As a result, projects can be underbid. One military consultant cited a case in which a two-year project was sold to management as a six-week project! Most case studies, however, did not address cost estimation in much detail. For that reason, it is difficult to draw any conclusions about the effects of prototyping in this area.

Three sources (two commercial and one military) did offer some suggestions, though. Managers can use rapid prototyping in a contract environment as a separately costed proof-of-concept item. The prototype can be used to test feasibility and/or cost-effectiveness, allowing a customer to abandon a project at a greatly reduced expense. It also gives the developer a chance to better estimate (or abandon) a project that might have been underbid with specification. Developers using proof-of-concept prototyping may have to bid actual development of a complete system separately. Bernard Boar [2] gives a number of suggestions for keeping cost estimates under control.

Human Factors and Staffing

As Exhibit 2 shows, most studies reported greater end-user participation in requirements definition. This is not surprising, since users are likely to be more comfortable with a prototype than a specification—which, as one commercial developer noted, can be dull reading. A military source also noted that documentation can be "open to interpretation; [whereas] sample display output is more definitive." [Case study 8] Thus the prototype makes it easier for users to make well-informed suggestions.

As we described earlier, increased user participation has a positive effect on the product by increasing the likelihood that user needs will be met. In fact, lack of sufficient user participation can negate some prototyping benefits. One source describes a case in which the customer's management purposely excluded end users from interacting with the prototype. The intent was to hide the inappropriate allocation of personnel (in a particu-

lar division's favor) for as long as possible. Another source observed the same technique, calling it "staff rationalization."

This dangerous political maneuver can be avoided simply by making sure that end users remain actively involved. Because a main advantage of rapid prototyping is in revealing actual requirements, developers should insist on prototype interaction with end users, not just with middle management.

A military developer noted another political difficulty that can surface when using rapid prototyping: "Sometimes our prototype proved that [a particular person's] idea wasn't so great. Result: one upset person/organization." [Case study F]

Eight case studies considered an experienced, well-trained team essential for successful prototyping, because prototyping often involves high-level design decisions about complex programming tasks. Problems can result when inexperienced team members are forced to make such decisions. One case specifically described a project that failed in part because temporary student programmers were thrown into a rapid-prototyping environment. Other case studies indicated that prototyping would not have been successful without highly experienced engineers.

Two cases did use entry-level programmers effectively, attributing their success to the availability of good prototyping tools. However, the failed project that had inexperienced teams was using a fourth-generation-language environment, contradicting the suggestion that having good tools is sufficient; good tools do not guarantee a good system design.

Other Effects

One common use of rapid prototyping is to develop a user interface. Various tools exist exclusively for quick development of user-friendly environments, for example Next's Interface Builder and Emultek Corp.'s Rapid. These tools naturally fit into a rapid-prototyping methodology. When special-purpose prototyping tools are used, product maintainability may depend on these tools remaining available.

Early emphasis on the user interface can produce either positive or negative effects, depending on the system being developed.

On the one hand, early development of a prototype gives users the chance to test-drive the software. This aids in clarifying requirements, matching user needs, and creating an easier-to-use product.

On the other hand, there may be a tendency to design the entire system from the user interface. This can be dangerous because the user interface may not characterize the best overall system structure. Thus, a user-interface prototype should be considered part of a requirements specification, not a basis for system design. Again, discarding the prototype is an option, but is only helpful when the prototype's performance is unimportant—*not* the case when the goal is to evaluate the performance of a particular design.

Another attribute that affects prototyping is language selection. Most case studies agreed on the importance of choosing a language suitable for prototyping, but there was much less agreement on what language to choose; in 38 cases, there were 26 languages! The most popular language was Lisp, and it was used in only four cases. Object-oriented methods are receiving increased attention for rapid prototyping, [4] six sources identify object-oriented methods (three used Small-talk) as being particularly well-suited for prototyping. One commercial study even cited the reverse relationship: ". . . the OO life-cycle almost always includes prototyping." [Case study E]

Two sources cited problems with special-purpose prototyping languages, especially when the language is interpreted rather than compiled. Here, the potential for evolutionary prototyping to result in performance problems is more clear.

PROBLEMS

Most of the studies described successful projects, so there is less direct data on prototyping problems. However, many authors described anticipating and avoiding particular situations. In a few cases, the project could have avoided the reported problem by using a suggestion described in another source. Thus, we were able to see common problems and match them with possible solutions.

Performance

When prototyping is used to evaluate design alternatives, early measurement of performance is important, and delays in addressing problems can result in design problems that may be costly to repair later.

A prototype can also demonstrate functionality that is not possible under real-time constraints, and this problem may not be discovered until long after the prototype phase is complete. One academic source suggested avoiding this problem by using an open-systems environment, which would make it easier to integrate faster routines when necessary.

End-User Misunderstandings

Given too much access to the prototype, end users may equate the incompleteness and imperfections in a prototype with shoddy design. In two cases, this effect contributed to the project's ultimate failure. In another case, rapid prototyping was abandoned as a suitable development method because it gave users the unrealistic expectation that there would be a complete and working system in a short time.

Insufficient knowledge of rapid-prototyping techniques is not limited to users. Sales staff may pass along inappropriate expectations to customers after seeing "working" prototypes. Users then understandably become skeptical or upset when told that development will take longer than they were led to believe. In the studies, high user expectations were typically fueled by too much or too little access to the prototype.

By limiting user interaction to a more controlled setting, developers can keep user expectations at reasonable levels. Users should be clearly told that they are interacting with a mock-up, not a working system, and that the purpose is to clarify requirements. Sometimes developers might want to limit interaction to specific sequences and administer them personally. Further, developers should not oversell the prototype in an effort to impress the customer.

Finally, organizations must train sales and managerial staff to properly understand (and convey) the nature and purpose of the prototyping phase and the prototype itself.

Code Maintainability

Certainly, a prototype developed quickly, massaged into the final product, and then hurriedly documented can be very difficult to maintain or enhance. Adding to that is the failure to reevaluate a prototype design before starting to implement the final system. The result is a product that inherits patches from the prototype phase.

To avoid these pitfalls, developers should include documentation criteria in a design checklist, which will help ensure that the prototype is completely documented. Other sources suggested conducting frequent reviews and using object-oriented technology. Discarding the prototype is also an option.

Prototyping can decrease system maintainability when the use of a special-purpose prototyping language results in maintenance engineers having to deal with the prototyping language, the target language, and the interface between them. Complexity can increase, even when system design is good. A prototyped system can become impossible to maintain if it was developed using tools that are not available to maintenance engineers.

Delivering a Throwaway

One of the perils of throwaway prototyping is that the prototype may not *get* thrown away. This surprisingly common problem occurs when managers who agree to throwaway prototyping later decide it costs too much to "redo" the system and try to massage the prototype into the product. The resulting system often lacks robustness, is poorly designed, and is not maintainable.

Managers can avoid this problem by maintaining a firm commitment to whatever prototyping

paradigm was initially chosen. When a prototype is slated for disposal, then it is best to do so because it was probably not designed with retention in mind. Developers can do their part by fully defining the prototype's scope and purpose.

Budgeting

Three cases described scenarios in which projects were underbid. Because visible outputs are quickly available, managers and salespersons may believe that development is all downhill from here. This breeds overconfidence, which in turn can result in underbidding.

In the case in which the two-year project was presented as a six-week project, management believed that prototyping would achieve fast, working results. Again, organizations must train sales and managerial staff to understand the nature and purpose of the prototyping phase and the prototype itself and to make the distinction between a prototype and a complete system.

Completion and Conversion

Prototype development can be time consuming, especially when the purpose and scope of the prototype is not initially well-defined. Boar [2] describes how inadequately narrowing scope can lead to "thrashing" or "aimless wandering" through tasks. Six of the studies support this. Suggested solutions include using a disciplined approach to schedule prototyping activities, carefully defining the prototype's scope, and keeping entry-level programmers out of a rapid-prototyping environment.

Prototyping languages are often used to ease the implementation of a particular system aspect. For example, if the prototype is developed to test user-interface options, the developer will want a language that provides convenient I/O.

However, converting the prototype into the final system may require significant effort and time. This problem is exacerbated when a separate prototyping language is used, especially if the ultimate target language does not have the same simple I/O handling. Another example is the use of an object-oriented language such as Smalltalk with a target language that does not have inheritance.

A few sources observed cost or time overruns. Carefully defining the prototype's scope and systematically comparing the features of both prototyping and target languages can help avoid this problem.

Large Systems

As we noted earlier, opinions vary widely on what constitutes a large software system. In one case study, the author described a 200-line system as large! Although some researchers might claim that our definition of large (100,000 LOC) is more suited to the medium range, few would argue that it is small. To distinguish between medium and small projects, we used whatever description the case study reports used and avoided selecting a specific boundary.

Exhibit 3 shows a breakdown of projects by size. We find no support for the common notion that evolutionary prototyping is dangerous for large projects. In fact, all seven case studies that used evolutionary prototyping with systems of more than 100,000 LOC reported success!

Many case-study authors suggested that problems with evolutionary prototyping will grow in proportion to system size, although the data they report does not provide any direct confirmation of this.

Nonetheless, evolutionary prototyping on large projects can pose problems. It can yield a system filled with patches—hastily designed prototype modules that become the root of later problems. The same problems that challenge performance and maintenance will become more pronounced as the system grows. The same solutions apply, such as using an object-oriented approach or limiting prototyping to user-interface modules, which are less likely to involve important structural design decisions.

Our study identified several surprising prototyping trends and debunked several myths about the approach. For example, we found that rapid prototyping is indeed appropriate for large systems, and there seems to be more successful use of evolutionary prototyping than throwaway. However, with evolutionary prototyping, developers must be careful to address performance issues early in the process, particularly if parts of the prototype are to be included in the final system.

The study also underlined prototyping's potential problems. The most serious are poor design quality and maintainability (especially when using evolutionary prototyping), underbidding, and misunderstandings between developers and users. All of these can be remedied by carefully defining the purpose and scope of the prototype and acting in accordance with its limitations. 91 organizations can further reduce design problems by using experienced, rather than entry-level, programmers whenever prototyping activities involve design decisions. Finally, to avoid creating unrealistic expectations about prototyping, any end-user interaction with the prototype should be carefully monitored.

We recognize that our data is somewhat incomplete. We hope in future work to conduct follow-up surveys of both our published case studies and anonymous sources. We encourage authors of case studies to contact us with updated information. We are also seeking additional case studies, especially descriptions of rapid prototyping in failed software projects.

Our results show that rapid prototyping has had a number of positive effects on both the software product and development process and that it can be used successfully in a variety of situations. We hope that the successes and failures reported here will help those who are now considering this technique.

EXHIBIT 3   Distribution of Case Studies by System Size

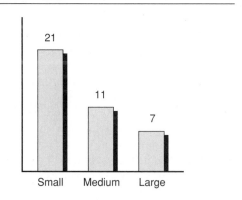

References

1. V. Gordon and J. Bieman, "Reported Effects of Rapid Prototyping on Industrial Software Quality," *Software Quality F.,* June 1993, pp. 93–110.

2. B. Boar, *Application Prototyping—A Project Management Perspective,* American Management Assoc. Membership Publications Division, New York, 1985.

3. F. Brooks, *The Mythical Man-Month,* Addison-Wesley, Reading, Mass., 1975.

4. K. Auer et al., "From Prototype to Product?" *Proc. OOPSLA,* ACM Press, New York, 1989, pp. 482–484.

PROTOTYPING IN INDUSTRIAL SOFTWARE PROJECTS—BRIDGING THE GAP BETWEEN THEORY AND PRACTICE

I. INTRODUCTION

In view of the problems associated with software development and the criticism aimed at traditional life cycle plans, prototyping has, in recent years, increasingly become an approach that is adopted to improve the planning and success of software projects [17]. Many experience reports on prototyping presented in publications are based on investigations that were done in an academic context, e.g., student projects or parts of experimental projects [1], [2]. Experience reports that have been published (see, e.g., [6], [10], [23], [24]) are, in our opinion, of restricted validity since their conceptual background and their definition of prototyping have not been clearly stated.

What has been lacking so far is documented experience with the use of prototyping in industrial software production backed with a thorough understanding of the respective concepts. This paper tries to close this gap by presenting the analysis of the results obtained from case studies of industrial software projects in which explicit use of prototypes was made with a differing understanding of the underlying concepts.

Article by Horst Lichter, Matthias Schneider-Hufschmidt, and Heinz Züllighoven. ©1994 IEEE. Reprinted, with permission, from (*IEEE Transactions on Software Engineering;* 20, 11, 825–832; November/1994).

Our major concern was to analyze the experience gained in the projects and the major pitfalls of the use of prototyping and, in particular, to juxtapose these pros or cons and the claims made for prototyping in the literature. Our analysis is not limited to "success stories" because we feel that understanding the limits and problems of prototyping will help to make full use of the obvious advantages. Our experience with prototyping goes well beyond the analyzed projects. We can draw on the results of many discussions with practitioners—results that we have collected during our own research and consulting work.

We have organized this paper as follows: in Section II we introduce the basic prototyping terminology and concepts. Section III briefly describes the projects analyzed in our investigation. In Section IV we compare the projects according to some essential criteria. In Section V we present our results and findings. Section VI contains our conclusions.

II. PROTOTYPING CONCEPTS

The term Prototyping has been used with various semantics in the literature [21]. Even in recent publications it has been stated that the terms prototype and prototyping are as vaguely defined as the concepts behind their use [6], [18]. Klingler in [16] lists a multitude of attributes and properties that have been used in the literature to characterize these terms. The first consequence of this apparent vagueness is that "anything goes." There is also, however, the implicit assumption that a method that cannot be defined exactly cannot serve as the conceptual basis for professional software development. Consequently, orthogonal concepts like object-oriented design or even the use of languages like Ada, have been proposed as alternative solutions.

Floyd in [7] presented a first set of definitions of the term prototyping and its various meanings. These definitions have been refined and consolidated during the last few years. On this basis and on the background of practical experiences, an understanding of the concepts behind the term "prototyping" has been developed [5]. We have adopted these concepts and want to present the essential definitions and our conclusions for software design.

As a starting point we want to give a first impression of our understanding of the term *prototyping* and the principles we see behind it as follows.

- *Prototyping* is an *approach* based on an evolutionary view of software development, affecting the development process as a whole.
- *Prototyping* involves producing *early* working versions ("prototypes") of the future application system and experimenting with them.

Prototyping provides a *communication basis* for discussions among all groups involved in the development process, especially between users and developers. In addition, prototyping enables us to adopt an approach to software construction based on *experiment* and *experience*.

A. Kinds of Prototypes

Three major activities of the software development process can be influenced by the construction of prototypes: starting the project, analyzing the business needs, designing and constructing the software system. To illustrate the way in which we see the relationship between prototype and these activities, we distinguish between the following *kinds of prototypes:*

- A *presentation prototype* supports the initiation of a software project. It is of major importance whenever an explicit contract is to be set up between a client and a software manufacturer. This may even be within the same company or institution. During acquisition, a presentation prototype is used to convince the client that the future application system is either feasible or that its user interface and handling is in line with user requirements. In most cases the presentation prototype is developed to show the user's view of the envisaged system, i.e., it will present important aspects of the user interface. Furthermore, if the technical solution of a problem is unclear, the presentation prototype may present functional details to convince the customer of the possibility of solving his problem.
- We use the term *prototype proper* to describe a provisional operational software system that is constructed parallel to the information system model. A prototype of this sort is generally designed to illustrate specific aspects of the user interface or part of the functionality and helps to clarify the problem in hand.
- We call a prototype that is designed chiefly to help clarify construction-related questions facing the development team a *breadboard*. A breadboard is derived from the information system model or the software specification. This kind of prototype is also encountered in traditional software projects, although the experimental approach associated with it is seldom given explicit recognition. Users are generally excluded from the evaluation of breadboards. To this extent, the use of breadboards is a restricted form of prototyping.
- If a prototype is used not only for experimental testing of an idea or for "illustrative purposes," but is actually used in the application area itself as the core of the application system, it is known as a *pilot system* [22]. In such cases, there ceases

to be any strict distinction between the prototype and the application system. After reaching a certain degree of "sophistication," the prototype is implemented as a pilot system and enhanced in cycles. Whereas defining the development framework, i.e., specifying the software development goals, is a joint task performed by both developers and users. The various pilot system increments should be geared exclusively to user priorities.

B. Goals of Prototyping

In a software project various issues arise and can be answered by building prototypes. Here, we focus on the major problems arising in typical *development situations,* problems which prototyping is designed to help solve. Following [7], we distinguish between several different goals of prototyping:

- *Exploratory Prototyping* is used where the problem in hand is unclear. Initial ideas are used as a basis for clarifying user and management requirements with respect to the future system. Here, equal consideration is given to changes in work content and to the type and scope of computer support. Particular importance is attached to examining a variety of design options as not to restrict ideas prematurely to one specific approach (a problem which prototyping cannot eliminate). The developers gain insight into the application area and into the users' work tasks and the problems they face.
- *Experimental Prototyping* focuses on the technical implementation of a development goal. Through experimentation the users are able to further specify their ideas about the type of computer support required. The developers, for their part, are provided with a basis for appraisal of the suitability and feasibility of a particular application system. An essential aspect here is the communication between users and developers on technical problems and questions about software ergonomics.
- *Evolutionary Prototyping* is not merely used as a tool in the context of a single development

project; it is a continuous process for adapting an application system to rapidly changing organizational constraints. This means that software development is no longer seen as a self-contained project, but as a process continuously accompanying the application. One consequence of this is that the role of the developers changes. They are no longer the "protagonists" of a self-contained project. Instead, they become technical consultants working continuously in close cooperation with the users to improve the application system.

This classification is to a large extent orthogonal to the taxonomy described in Section II-A. While Section II-A distinguishes prototypes as "products," the goals of prototyping are concerned with characteristics of the prototyping "process." Certain strong relations exist, however, between process and product. For instance, an evolutionary prototyping process will eventually lead to a pilot system.

C. Prototype Construction Techniques

Developing prototypes is also a technical process which can be realized in different ways. In professional software development we frequently find two approaches related to specific construction techniques.

If we see software construction as the design and implementation of many layers, ranging from the user interface to the base layer (normally the operating system or a data base query language), the subdivision into horizontal and vertical prototyping begins to make sense [19].

- In *horizontal prototyping* only specific layers of the system are built, e.g., the user interface layer with its forms and menus, or functional core layers, such as data base transactions.
- In *vertical prototyping* a chosen part of the target system is implemented completely ("down prothrough all layers"). This technique is appropriate where the system's functionality and implementation options are still open.

When considering the differences between horizontal and vertical prototyping, it should not be forgotten that it is the software development method that determines the layers of the software. It is by no means "natural" for the user interface to constitute the top software layer or to be located in precisely one layer.

A further criterion for classifying prototypes is the relationship between the prototype and the application system [9]. Here, many different views are taken:

- A prototype is part of the application system specification: The application system is built based on an accepted prototype. The prototype serves specification purposes only and is not used as a building block in the application system itself; it is a "throwaway."
- Prototypes are enhanced to produce the application system: As the use of workstations and very high level languages (VHLL) for commercial applications become increasingly widespread, technical differences between prototypes and application systems are gradually disappearing. Available building blocks like window systems or components for error recovery simplify the gradual transition from prototype to application system.
- Prototypes serve to clarify problems only: One extreme view is to build prototypes merely for the purposes of acquiring knowledge, with no intention of building an application system, at least for the time being. This form of prototyping is frequently encountered in research and development institutes and universities. One may even find this approach in commercial data processing, if, within a feasibility study, the fundamental decision has to be made as to whether a software system is to be developed at all.

In the following sections, we want to discuss several opinions about the use and advantages of prototyping that can be frequently found in the literature and contrast them with the results found in our investigation.

III. A CASE STUDY OF INDUSTRIAL PROTOTYPING PROJECTS

First, we give a short overview of our investigation and the projects analyzed. The goal of our project evaluation was

- to find out whether prototyping approaches have been used successfully in industrial environments,
- to identify critical factors for the success or failure of such projects, and
- to infer advice for future prototyping projects to enhance the chances of success.

A. How the Investigation was Organized

For our investigation we have selected projects according to the following criteria:

- The projects had to be of an industrial nature; this excluded research projects.
- The developers and users had to be two different parties; internal company development projects were not considered.
- The use of prototyping had to be explicitly provided for in the project planning; this excluded projects in which an unsatisfactory result was subsequently labeled a prototype.

The projects selected ranged from a large-scale project with a total development budget of 240 person-years to small projects in the order of 2 person-years. The development teams involved in the projects included both the computer departments of large industrial corporations and small to medium-sized software manufacturers.

The investigation was done in two steps. First, we interviewed the developers while the projects were running. In these interviews we gathered information on the following topics: the application area of the project, the people involved in the development, the development process and use of prototyping, the kinds of prototypes built. A second interview was conducted after the projects were completed.

This procedure results in the several advantages. For instance, the information about prototyping obtained from the developers during the development process was less likely to be contrived. In the second interviews we obtained information concerning the following aspects:

- How do the developers estimate the influence of prototyping on the quality of the development process and on the quality of the constructed software.
- Was the product development completed and the product accepted by the client, or was the project abandoned.

B. Project Descriptions

In this section, we briefly characterize the projects which we have analyzed during our investigation. The projects are described in more detail in [15].

Project 1—A Customer Advice System: A public service company contracted the development of a sales support system for the configuration of complex systems which must adhere to many legal rules. The advice system was to be used by the sales employees, not by customers. The system offers an initial configuration which can be modified according to the needs and preferences of the customers.

The reason behind the decision to start the project was the inconsistent quality of the advice given. Also, changes in the market due to the appearance of competitors meant that more flexibility was needed in determining the range of services offered.

During this project different kinds of prototypes were built: a presentation prototype for the purpose of project acquisition, several breadboards, and finally a pilot system which was eventually delivered to the customer. The entire development was organized as an evolutionary prototyping process.

The first prototype was intended to demonstrate the system's feasibility; its main purpose, however, was project acquisition. It exceeded what we have called the pure presentation prototype, implementing important features of the application system's functionality. This prototype not only served

as a specification, but also formed the technical core for the further development of the system.

The second prototype modeled additional parts of the functionality as well as the user interface. This prototype proper was extended until, by the end of the main project phase, it was ready for delivery to the client and subsequently has been installed in the user organization as a pilot system.

In addition, small prototypes were built as breadboards to evaluate technical decisions like the selection of the appropriate knowledge representation.

Various problems could be traced back to the conversion of the demonstration prototype to a building block of the subsequent prototypes. For instance, system components which became redundant due to modifications in the system design could still be found in the final system. Nevertheless, the final prototype was delivered to the customer.

Project 2—A Distributed Information System: In this project a client commissioned the construction of a software system to ensure communication and exchange of information among several computers distributed throughout Germany. It proved impossible, however, to produce a detailed task description—only a rudimentary description was possible.

The task description, such as was available, called for the development of a distributed information system. The system was to comprise a distributed database and the necessary applications software—again distributed over several computers. The computers were linked together with a wide area network. A commercial database system was to form the technical base of the information system.

The decision to use prototyping was based on the following considerations: only a vague requirements definition was available; several user groups had to be taken into account when fixing the requirements; and the client had stipulated that the user interface had to be taken as the point of departure for the system specification. A prototype, consisting of a large number of screen forms, was to be used to analyze the design of the user interface. Also, parallel to this, the functional requirements identified during the prototyping process were described and discussed with the users.

Since the target system was implemented using the same development environment and language as the prototype it was planned to integrate all the screen forms generated for the prototype in the target system—aiming at cutting down the development effort. The resulting prototype can be characterized as a pilot system implementing the user interface combined with a prototype proper aimed at modeling the underlying functionality. Both system components were developed using an evolutionary approach.

After the implementation of the target system was completed, it turned out that the functionality of the system had not been sufficiently modeled by the interface prototype. Thus, the user management decided not to put the system into final use.

Project 3—A Planning System: In the heating and plumbing industry, a large portion of the activities are concerned with system planning. Traditionally the jobs involved are carried out on a team basis using manual equipment and aids such as drawing boards, sketches, construction drawings, spreadsheets, and lists of materials.

In addition to these traditional manual techniques, engineering firms are increasingly using personal computer programs, each offering solutions for specific planning tasks, e.g., for calculating pressure losses. Since these programs only support individual work tasks, and also due to the lack of application programs available for other jobs, it is not possible to combine them to allow integrated computer support of the whole planning process.

It was against this background that the idea of building an integrated planning system for projects in the heating and plumbing industry was born. The projected system was to make available all the required design tools in the form of an integrated toolkit for project planning.

The use of prototyping served two different purposes: to improve the sometimes poor communication with the future users and the clients; and to help in situations where it was otherwise impossible to assess risks due to the development team's lack of experience with projects of this sort.

The initial presentation prototype served to give the client's representatives a realistic impression of the software engineering options for solving their problems. This prototype showed, with the help of a planning scenario specially developed for the purpose, the way the planning system was to work and the tasks it was to perform. The functionality was simulated in each case by simply clipping data from a CAD system into a window in which it could be scrolled, as well as calling some predefined dialog sequences. The prototype managed to convey something of the flavor of the potential interaction features, although it was not meant, at this stage, to model the actual structure of the future system.

Besides the presentation prototype, a series of functional prototypes were developed. The prototypes were developed using an evolutionary prototyping approach and the process culminated in an installable pilot system. The prototypes served as the main means of communication between the developers and the clients. The prototypes were, therefore, presented to the clients at the end of each development step, approximately every 3-4 months. This enabled the clients to keep control on the manner in which work was progressing and, at the same time, to evaluate the prototype. Occasionally, other potential users were invited to participate in the evaluation process. The system currently runs successfully in a small number of pilot installations.

Project 4—A Document Management System: A publishing house annually issues a series of related documents. An important feature of these documents is the fact that their structure, and to some extent their content as well, remains constant throughout several editions. Also, the documents are simultaneously published in several languages. The management, revision, and production of the manuscripts is an area as yet practically untouched by computer support.

A software manufacturer developed a prototype of a system to support the activities described above. The prototype was primarily intended to model the functional features of the system; it was not proposed to develop a suitable user interface.

Since the prototype was designed mainly to demonstrate the implementability of technical and organizational requirements, it can be considered a prototype proper implemented using experimental prototyping. In regard to its scope, it can be looked on as a purely functional prototype demonstrating, in a narrower sense, all the essential aspects of the system's functionality, but lacking a user interface of its own. Compared with the projected application system the prototype was limited regarding data formats and data quantities as well as some of its functional aspects. The prototype was also equipped with an input/output interface to facilitate its construction, testing, and evaluation. Nevertheless, the interactive component was not subject to evaluation. Although the system was technically implemented, the lack of end user involvement led to acceptance problems which prevented the system from being installed.

Project 5—A Process Control System: In this project, a client requested the development of a process control system for machine tools. This control system was to be implemented on a given hardware platform with the help of a rule-based system. In the project, it was proposed to build a series of prototypes. The first prototype, an example of an experimental prototype, was intended to model both the user interface and major aspects of the functionality. The project was set up for evolutionary prototyping, the last prototype planned as the final system.

During the development of the first prototype many problems became apparent:

- There had been insufficient contact between the client, the users, and the developers during construction of the prototype. This meant that not enough consideration was given to the users' requirements and the future users' level of training.
- The client was unable to give the developers a clear enough idea of what he expected from the

system. This created a gap between what the client wanted and what the prototype could provide.
- The integration of the application system into the existing work environment had not been taken into consideration. During development of the prototype, it became apparent that the hardware environment stipulated by the client did not meet the requirements for the user interface.

This analysis of a developed prototype led to the decision to abandon the whole project.

IV. COMPARISON OF THE PROJECTS

Exhibit 1 shows the comparison of the analyzed projects according to a list of essential criteria which was set up before starting the investigation.

The different columns of the exhibit characterize the five selected projects while the rows document our findings across the entire set of projects. The first two rows try to summarize the technical and organizational framework for the different projects, i.e., tools used and people involved. The third and fourth rows characterize the different prototypes and their development process following our classification scheme described in Sections II-A and II-B.

The last three rows show the results of the evaluation of the projects. The row labeled "Main reason for prototyping" mainly reflects the opinion of the developers. The "Success of the project" has been judged by end users and developers in the second study, while the "Main problems" of the projects reflect our evaluation of the analyzed projects.

V. ANALYSIS OF THE PROJECTS—THE LESSONS LEARNED

In each of the projects analyzed, the prototypes used exhibited specific characteristics and effects on the software development process. We have tried to generalize the results obtained, thus enabling these findings to be drawn on for other projects. In doing so, we found that existing claims about prototyping were in some cases substantiated, but others called for qualification. We also succeeded in identifying benefits and pitfalls that

EXHIBIT 1   Summary of the Project Evaluation

	Customer Advice System (Project 1)	Distributed Information System (Project 2)	Planning System (Project 3)	Document Management System (Project 4)	Process Control System (Project 5)
Tools supporting prototyping	Prolog	form editor	interface builder	——	expert system shell
Groups involved	developers, management, user representatives	developers, users	developers, users	developers	developers, users
Kinds of prototypes developed	acquisition pt, pt proper, pilot system, breadboards	user interface pt	demo pt, functional pt, pilot system, breadboards	functional pt	pt proper
Goals of prototyping	evolutionary, experimental	experimental, evolutionary	exploratory, evolutionary	evolutionary	exploratory, evolutionary
Main reason for prototyping	unclear functionality and specification	user interface development	unclear functionality	unclear functionality	company strategy
Success of the project	system in use, accepted by the users	abandoned due to internal management decision	pilot system under construction	never put into use	abandoned after about 50% of the budget had been spent
Main problems	lack of user involvement, poor project planning	milestone planning not appropriate	unclear requirements	lack of user involvement	hardware decisions taken too early

have so far been given little or no consideration in the prototyping discussion.

In the following Section we will contrast characteristics of the prototyping concept with the findings of our study. As we have been dealing with this topic in research and practice for years, we will also bring in our own experiences where appropriate.

A. Beyond Interface Prototyping

Studying the literature, we find that various papers consider prototyping, in essence, to center on the rapid development of user interfaces (see, e.g., [9]). The background for most of the underlying experiences is, however, the area of database systems. In this area, the functionality of an application system is largely prescribed and experience in using computers for similar problems is already available. Here, the frequently propagated form of "horizontal prototyping" is probably the best solution. On the other hand, project 2 showed that where a system's functionality is still largely unclear, is precisely the point at which prototyping must come in. The same holds when the system platform has to be changed from menu-driven mainframe applications to interactive workstation applications with graphical interfaces.

A development process which starts with the prototyping of the user interface and continues with the implementation of the functional system kernel cannot be recommended uniformly. Only after the question which the prototype is supposed to answer has been stated clearly, can the right methodological approach be chosen. For many standard applications the user interface is the essential component designed by prototyping. Occasionally, however, in a project dealing with specific technical solutions, modeling of the user interface can be dispensed with altogether (see project 4).

B. Prototyping as Part of a Development Strategy

Looking at the various cases of our study, prototyping obviously does not offer any support for structuring the software development process. This has also been stated in many publications (see, for example [13], [26]). As a consequence, this frequently serves as a justification for using prototyping approaches as integrated parts of conventional software development life cycles. In this view, prototyping is usually restricted to the so-called early phases. This is in line with the opinion of [4]: *Hence plan to throw one away, you will anyhow.* The underlying assumption is that a running prototype supplies the necessary knowledge to implement a complete application system following a life-cycle based methodology.

Our analysis shows that this assumption is problematic.

- Project 2 showed that control techniques developed for traditional life-cycle oriented software development tend to hinder software projects using prototyping approaches.
- Contractual enforcement of milestones and deliverables and the results of consecutive prototyping cycles rarely fit together.
- The effort necessary for explicit evaluation of prototypes by end users is often ignored or underestimated (as done in projects 4 and 5).

- Project 3 showed that specific phases necessary for prototyping should be foreseen during the project planning and the budget estimates. These phases include the necessary development effort for the reimplementation of presentation prototypes, the evaluation of pilot systems, and the cyclic enhancement of these systems.

Failure to take this additional overhead into account often leads to projects which cannot be completed in the estimated time or budget. Factors that prove an obstacle to prototyping are the financing of projects on a flat-rate basis and the performance of project planning and control using traditional life cycle plans. When planning and financing a project of this sort, it is important to recognize the real possibility of testing design options. Otherwise, different design options can not be evaluated due to financial or time constraints (see project 5).

We think that software developers should take another view of prototyping. While the realization of self-contained software projects becomes less and less important [20], the main task for software engineers will be the evolutionary adaptation of existing information processing infrastructures to the changing needs of their organizations [8], and thereby a need for a more experience-based and evolutionary strategy arises.

C. Prototyping and End-User Involvement

The importance of end-user involvement in the prototyping process is, to our astonishment, still an open question. This holds especially true in the U.S. literature, although many advocates of prototyping will cite user involvement among the top benefits of prototyping [6]. While most European approaches will primarily focus on user-oriented forms of prototyping [14], the North American focus seems to be on getting something working quickly, almost independently of either the type of user involvement or the quality of the final prototype (see most contributions in [12]). Nevertheless, choosing both the right type of user involvement and the proper systems architecture is crucial to the success of a project ([3] and project 3).

Beyond the general approach to end-user involvement, there are substantial problems in getting the users involved. Often user management is reluctant to allow the actual end users of an application system to participate in the evaluation of prototypes, let alone in discussions on design options. There are generally two reasons for this reluctance:

- Frequently, the implicit goal of a development project (i.e., one which the user management is not ready to openly admit) is staff rationalization (as in project 4). In order to keep those affected from obtaining the relevant information for as long as possible, they are excluded from the development process altogether.
- Also, quite apart from this, representatives of intermediate management in the user organization in particular believe that they are in a better position to assess the necessary functionality and potential design options than the future end users of a system. We found this to be the case in projects 1 and 5. Although management may sometimes have a better grasp of the underlying problems, this attitude strikes us as being a mere variant of the traditional developers' conviction: "We know what the users *really* want."

Our analysis of all projects showed that the involvement of "real" end users is of major importance for the success or failure of a prototyping project. Lack of participation of end users in the development process almost invariably leads to nonoptimal systems not well accepted by their users. Using other sources (e.g., user management) as input for a prototyping process is problematic because these sources usually supply their own view of the users' needs which may not agree totally with what real users need.

User involvement is only part of the story. Many developers expect far too much from the users concerning creativity and innovative ideas about the technical design of a prototype. This applies particularly to prototypes evaluated by the users under "laboratory conditions." Since the users still lack experience in everyday use of the system, they seldom can make suggestions for the design of technical aspects of the system that do not yet exist. Their suggestions are generally confined to criticism of what already exists. The situation usually changes (see projects 2 and 3) once a pilot system is installed at their place of work. Then, not only inconvenient and impracticable features of a prototype are identified, but also the absence of features needed to perform a particular task. Here, the developers should not make the mistake of encouraging the users to voice all the ideas and wishes that come into their heads when evaluating a prototype as this may result in the incorporation of absolutely every conceivable function or interface design option into the requirements specification.

User involvement is not just a necessary add-on to existing development methods. User involvement implies a totally different view. The experience and knowledge of clients and end users of an application system are important inputs for the design process which should be preserved and enhanced. Therefore, the integration of all these groups as application domain experts should be a central point of system engineering.

D. Choosing the Right Kind of Prototype

Whenever a prototyping project is established, one has to decide which kinds of prototypes will be developed. In our experience a good "mixture" of presentation prototypes, prototypes proper, breadboards, and pilot systems may be necessary for a successful system development. Project 3 is an example of this system development approach.

It is not only terminologically important to separate provisional presentation prototypes from subsequent prototypes proper. In the literature, scarcely any attention has been paid so far to the important role played by presentation prototypes in project acquisition. This fact is totally at odds with empirical findings in this area (e.g., project 1, 3, or 5). It is crucial that only these presentation prototypes will be developed in the "quick-and-dirty" sense. Our experiences and project 1 show that the expectations of clients often enforce the evolution of such a "quick-and-dirty" prototype into the final system. The adoption of these prototypes as technical building blocks in the further course of the development process becomes something of a problem, if not disastrous for the project as a whole. The very nature of these prototypes makes them unsuitable as a sound basis for producing a high-quality software architecture appropriate to the problem at hand. Therefore, presentation prototypes should be explicitly designed as throwaways to prevent the advantages offered by prototyping from having a detrimental effect on the future application system (see project 3).

Another topic worth addressing is the importance of breadboards in developing creative solutions and design options. Projects 1 and 3 show that this has a considerable potential for innovative ideas that remains as yet untapped. All the projects in which the developers were not confined to everyday routine development work, but also had scope to experiment and "play around" with breadboards produced concepts and design ideas which, though frequently not incorporated into the current system version, nevertheless formed or might form the basis for subsequent revisions.

We think that the quality of all prototypes, other than demonstration prototypes, should not be neglected during the design process. The architecture of prototypes has to match the fundamental architecture of the envisaged application system independently of the purpose of the prototype (Goma states the opposite opinion in [9].) If this requirement is not met in favor of fast construction and early rapid modifications, the resulting systems become incomprehensible, hard to maintain, and unusable for evolutionary development [25].

VI. CONCLUSIONS AND OUTLOOK

The case studies have clearly indicated that building a prototype without further considerations about the kind of prototype used and the aspects covered might lead to problems. It became obvious as well that end user involvement is of crucial importance in clarifying the requirements and essential features of a system.

A third type of finding was related to the technical support for software development. The expectation that more or better development tools would be a remedy to all problems of systems engineering could not be fulfilled (see project 5). It is not enough to develop software in increasingly shorter time periods and with less program errors. Experiences from the area of fourth-generation languages [11] show that the central problem to be solved is the difference between application knowledge and information processing knowledge. This difference is clearly visible at the gap between application-specific models and the resulting software architectures. This gap cannot be bridged by end user programming since end users, although they have the necessary application knowledge, usually do not have sufficient understanding of technical dependencies and structural properties of large application systems.

An extended understanding of the prototyping methodology might help to reach a solution. Ideally, prototypes cover two aspects of the system being developed: the semantics of the application and the architecture of the software. If both aspects are modeled in the prototyping process, this can considerably ease the problems of system design. A fact which clearly emerged was that the developers must have sufficient knowledge of the application area and the work environment (see project 3). Application domain analysis is, therefore, a necessary prerequisite for successful prototyping, and it is imperative that users as application domain experts participate throughout a prototyping project.

References

1. B. I. Blum, "Application systems prototyping," in *Prototyping—State of the Art Report,* M. E. Lipp, Ed. New York: Pergamon Infotech Ltd., 1986, pp. 3–14.

2. B. W. Boehm, T. E. Gray, and T. Sandewaldt, "Prototyping versus specifying: A multi-project experiment," *IEEE Trans. Software Eng.,* vol. SE-10, pp. 290–303, 1984.

3. M. Bourke, "Actual experience in prototyping," in *Prototyping—State of the Art Report,* M. E. Lipp, Ed. New York: Pergamon Infotech Ltd., 1986, pp. 15–26.

4. F. P. Brooks, *The Mythical Man Month.* Reading, MA: Addison Wesley, 1975.

5. R. Budde, K. Kautz, K. Kuhlenkamp, and H. Züllighoven, *Prototyping—An Approach to Evolutionary System Development.* Heidelberg, Germany: Springer-Verlag, 1992.

6. J. M. Carey and J. D. Currey, "The prototyping conundrum," *Datamation,* pp. 29–33, June 1, 1989.

7. C. Floyd, "A systematic look at prototyping," in *Approaches to Prototyping,* Budde *et al.,* Ed. Heidelberg, West Germany: Springer-Verlag, 1984, pp. 105–122.

8. _____ , "Outline of a paradigm change in software engineering" in *Computers and Democracy—A Scandinavian Challenge,* G. Bjerknes *et al.,* Eds. Avebury, 1987.

9. H. Goma, "Prototypes—Keep them or throw them away?," in *Prototyping—State of the Art Report,* M. E. Lipp, Ed. New York: Pergamon Infotech Ltd., 1986, pp. 41–54.

10. S. Gordon and J. Bieman, "Rapid prototyping and software quality: Lessons From industry," Dept. of Computer Science, Colorado State Univ., Tech. Rep. CS-91-113, 1991.

11. F. J. Grant, "The downside of 4GLs," *Datamation,* pp. 99–104, July 15, 1985.

12. HICSS, "Rapid software prototyping," in *Proc. 25th Hawaii Int. Conf. Syst. Sci.,* 1992, pp. 470–567.

13. D. Iggulden, "Prototyping developments," in *Prototyping—State of the Art Report,* M. E. Lipp, Ed. New York: Pergamon Infotech Ltd., 1986, pp. 55–63.

14. IT&P, "Software prototyping," special issue of *Info. Technol. People,* vol. 8, no. 4, 1992.

15. A. Kieback, H. Lichter, M. Schneider-Hufschmidt, and H. Züllighoven, "Prototyping in industriellen Software-Projekten," *Erfahrungen und Analysen, Informatik-Spektrum,* vol. 15, no. 2, pp. 65–77, Apr. 1992.

16. D. E. Klingler, "The ten commandments of prototyping," *J. Info. Syst. Management,* pp. 66–72, Summer 1988.

17. K. Lantz, *The Prototyping Methodology.* Englewood Cliffs, NJ: Prentice-Hall, 1986.

18. M. E. Lipp, "Analysis," in *Prototyping—State of the Art Report,* M. E. Lipp, Ed. Pergamon Infotech Ltd., 1986, pp. 129–184.

19. H. C. Mayr, M. Bever, and P. C. Lockemann, "Prototyping interactive application systems," in *Approaches to Prototyping,* Budde *et al.,* Eds. Heidelberg, West Germany: Springer-Verlag, 1984, pp. 105–122.

20. B. Meyer, *Object-Oriented Software Construction.* Englewood Cliffs, NJ: Prentice Hall, 1988.

21. B. Patton, "Prototyping—A nomenclature problem," *ACM SIGSOFT Software Eng. Notes,* vol. 8, no. 2, pp. 14–16, 1983.

22. G. Rzevski, "Prototypes versus pilot systems: Strategies for evolutionary information system development," in *Approaches to Prototyping,* Budde *et al.,* Eds. Heidelberg, West Germany: Springer-Verlag, 1984, pp. 341–356.

23. M. G. Sobol and A. Kagan, "Which systems analysts are more likely to prototype?," *J. Info. Syst. Management,* pp. 36–43, Summer 1989.

24. G. Tillmann, "Prototyping for the right results," *Datamation,* pp. 42–45, Apr. 1, 1989.

25. J. Trenouth, "A survey of exploratory software development," *The Computer J.,* vol. 34, no. 2, pp. 153–163, 1991.

26. R. S. Weinberg, "Prototyping and the systems development life cycle," *J. Info. Syst. Management,* pp. 47–53, Spring 1991.

Discussion Questions

1. An advertisement for a software product that once ran in the trade press had a big picture of a duck-billed platypus with the caption, "It's poorly planned, over-designed, and lays eggs. It has a lot in common with most custom software." What could it mean to "over-design" software? What negative impacts could this have?

2. Gordon and Bieman, while reporting that 33 of their 39 projects were classified as 'successful', caution the reader about a possible bias in these results. What might account for this bias and how do Gordon and Bieman compensate?

3. In the Lichter et al. study they find a significant number of failed prototyping projects (3 of the 5 studied). This result is in contrast to typical results reported in the literature, e.g., Gordon and Bieman. What might account for this result?

Chapter

8

Process Tools and their Adoption—CASE Tools Application

INTRODUCTION

Within the broad scope of the process models outlined in the previous chapters, over the years a wide variety of process tools have been proposed to support and improve the software development process. One of the most important early categories of tools was Computer Aided Software Engineering tools, or CASE. This chapter and its companion chapter, Chapter 9 on Object Oriented Methods, follow the same general outline. The first article introduces the technology, the second suggests its application, and the third illustrates issues in the tool's adoption.

CASE tools are a subject about which much has been written, and therefore, the selection of a single article to describe this technology is a daunting task. However, the first article, by John Henderson and Jay Cooprider fills this role admirably. They set out on an ambitious project to categorize and analyze the functionalities provided by both then current and future generations of CASE tools. As such, their framework generalizes above the tools of only one or a few vendors. Most importantly, because of their approach of collecting data from experts about what functionalities might be desirable (rather than simply what was

currently available, their model both allows them to point out deficiencies in the current generation of tools and has considerable staying power. Of course, their model is limited to planning and design aids, and therefore does not, for example, discuss issues around code generation or support for the testing phase. However, it is the early stages of the life cycle that are widely believed to be the greatest leverage points in improving software development and, therefore, Henderson and Cooprider made the appropriate choice in making the necessary limit to the scope of their research.

The second article in this chapter by Chris Kemerer, focuses on the evaluation and implementation of new software process technologies, such as CASE, with an emphasis on how the learning or experience curve can be measured and managed. The article is motivated by the numerous observations of the failure of integrated CASE tools to be successfully assimilated into an organization's normal practices. One proposed reason for this general lack of success is management's failure to understand the investment required in learning in order for the technology to be successful. Kemerer contrasts learning in the software development setting with those that have historically been studied by learning curve researchers. Multiple learning curve models are proposed along with a discussion of potential difficulties in their application.

A third article by Wanda Orlikowski employs a different research technique to answer questions relating to the organizational changes both in support of and due to the implementation of CASE tools. Her research approach involves an in-depth qualitative investigation of a single organization's adoption of CASE tools with a focus on the social relationship changes associated with this implementation. She finds that the adoption of CASE tools institutionalized two separate cultures within the organization and precipitated some possibly unanticipated shifts in power between these two groups. This article makes for insightful reading for anyone anticipating the adoption of new software process technologies. A later article she wrote, entitled "CASE Tools as Organizational Change: Investigating Incremental and Radical Changes in Systems Development." won the best paper of the year in *MIS Quarterly* for 1993. This article, which is more theoretical in its primary contribution, contrasts the original data with observations from a second organization.

DIMENSIONS OF I/S PLANNING AND DESIGN AIDS: A FUNCTIONAL MODEL OF CASE TECHNOLOGY

Information technology is playing an increasingly integral role in the competitive strategies of many organizations. As this trend continues, it is not surprising that there is growing emphasis on the ability of organizations to plan, design and implement critical information systems. A major strategy to improve the effectiveness of these processes is the use of computer-based planning and design aids. However, there is little empirical evidence that using this technology provides a significant performance impact. One factor limiting research on the impact of technology on planning and design is the manner in which this technology has been conceptualized for measuring usage behavior. This research develops a functional model of I/S planning and design support technology that distinguishes three general functional dimensions:

Production Technology, Coordination Technology and Organizational Technology. An empirical analysis is used to test the robustness of the proposed model and its ability to discriminate among current design aids in a meaningful way. Implications for the use of this model in the study of I/S planning and design processes are discussed.

INTRODUCTION

In today's business environment, a critical management issue is "time-to-market": the length of time it takes an organization to convert a product concept into a viable product that is available in a specific market. The Xerox Corporation, for example, argues that their improved ability to manage time-to-market while retaining or improving quality has been a major factor in their efforts to rebuild their competitiveness (Harvard Business School, 1988). Extending this notion, Hewlett-Packard focuses on the "time-to-break-even" as a

Article by John C. Henderson and Jay G. Cooprider. © 1990, The Institute of Management Sciences. Reprinted, with permission, from (*Information Systems Research*, v. 1 n. 3, pp. 227–254).

measure of success for product development (personal communication with author, 1988). This perspective directly incorporates aspects of quality and maintainability while highlighting the criticality of rapid response.

It is not surprising that the I/S function within a business faces this same challenge. As information technology becomes an integral part of an organization's competitive strategy, the I/S function faces increased demands to improve the "time-to-market" for I/S products and services. In fact, researchers and practitioners such as Hackathorn and Karimi (1988), Kull (1984), Brooks (1987) and others have suggested that the inability of the I/S function to reduce the backlog of demand for systems products and meet the increasing demand for new I/S products represents a significant management challenge.

While many factors affect an organization's ability to deliver high quality products in a short time frame (Ancona and Caldwell 1987), a key way to address this issue is the use of computer-aided planning and design tools. We see, for example, Xerox, Ford and many other organizations focusing on the role of CAD/CAM technologies as one way to radically enhance their capacity to quickly develop and deliver products to specific markets. Similarly, we have seen the growth of a major industry that seeks to deliver comparable design aid technology to the I/S function. Sometimes referred to as CASE (Computer Assisted Software Engineering), this technology is targeted at those who wish to use automation to affect the timing, cost and quality of products and services delivered by the I/S function. Beck and Perkins (1983), for example, found that 56 out of the 97 organizations they surveyed used automated tools as a means of improving their I/S planning and design processes.

However, the impact of these tools on the productivity of software developers and, ultimately, on time-to-market is unclear. Semprevivo (1980) and Necco et al. (1987), for example, have reported that design aid technology improves the productivity of designers. In contrast, Card et al.

(1987) and Lempp and Lauber (1988) found that, after controlling for factors such as experience and task complexity, the use of software development aids had no significant effect on productivity, and had only a relatively weak effect on quality.

Such conflicting results could be attributed to many factors. For example, some of the studies address productivity impacts on narrowly defined tasks such as the encoding of specifications or the development of flow representations (Case 1985). In contrast, other studies examine the entire system design life cycle (Card et al. 1987). Perhaps more fundamental is the lack of a clear definition of *design aid usage*. It is often unclear whether usage refers to access (e.g., such technology was available to the team) or, in fact, measures actual usage behavior. Further, it is not clear that the level of aggregation defined by usage variables in most studies provides sufficient precision to actually predict performance impact. For example, if a macro usage variable is employed (e.g., "did I use this package"), teams may indicate similar design aid usage levels but actually utilize quite different subsets of functionality. As a result, the impact of the technology can easily be mixed, leading to an overall assessment across design teams that indicates little or no impact.

The need to better define and measure technology usage behavior suggests a need to develop a model of design aid technology that corresponds more closely to key designer behaviors. That is, rather than define this technology in economic terms (e.g., costs), technology terms (e.g., PC-based or networked), or other more general terms (e.g., having an embedded design language or structured code compiler), we must develop a model of design aid technology that is functionality oriented. Such a model would then provide a way to directly relate usage of a tool to design team performance.

The existing literature on I/S planning and design offers a starting point. Hackathorn and Karimi (1988) and Welke and Konsynski (1980) differentiate between design methodologies and design tools. Methodologies define the logical disciplines underlying I/S planning and design activities, while tools instantiate these principles in a software application. Hackathorn and Karimi (1988), Beck and Perkins (1983) and others support the notion that software engineering and information engineering involve the application of sound engineering principles to the task of I/S planning and design. Understanding these principles offers one means of mapping the functions of design aid technology onto key usage behaviors.

The difficulty lies in the diverse set of concepts, principles and subsequent methodologies that could be used to generate a design aid environment. Chikofsky and Rubenstein (1988), for example, claim that there is, as yet, no clearly accepted definition of CASE technology that satisfies this diverse range of design concepts and methodologies. In a similar vein, Osterweil (1981) recognizes this inherent diversity and argues that a research program in software engineering must address the full range of design related activities. He states

> The task of creating effective environments is so difficult because it is tantamount to understanding the fundamental nature of the software processes. A specific environment does not merit the name unless it provides strong, uniform support for the entire process it is intended to facilitate; that is not possible unless the process is fully appreciated and understood. (Osterweil, p. 36)

In the following sections, we describe the development of a functional model of design aid technology. We refer to this as a functional CASE technology model (FCTM). However, it is important to realize that we use the term *CASE* in a broad sense, encompassing a wide range of planning and design activities. This interpretation is consistent with an emerging view of CASE that emphasizes the focus of design attention upon the entire programming environment (Holt et al. 1983, Acly 1988). We begin by presenting the results of a series of in-depth interviews with leading academic and industry designers of CASE products

concerning the range of possible CASE functionality. Past research on CASE functionality is then used to organize these functionalities into general dimensions of CASE technology. The ability of these dimensions to serve as a model of CASE technology is evaluated empirically through both a Q-sort study of I/S planners and designers (familiar with CASE technology) and the use of the dimensions to characterize the strengths and weaknesses of commercially available CASE products. Finally, implications for the use of this functional model in research on the impact of CASE technology are discussed.

A FUNCTIONAL CASE TECHNOLOGY MODEL (FCTM)

There are several reviews of the range of functionality found across various CASE environments. Hackathorn and Karimi (1988), for example, categorize CASE technology in terms of the range of the design life cycle addressed and the extent to which the environment provides for a range of support from conceptual to explicit design techniques. The functionality of the CASE technology is then implied by the method(s) incorporated in the environment and the aspect of planning and development for which the support environment is targeted. Thus, a tool that embraces the Gane-Sarson method (Gane and Sarson 1979) could be expected to provide features such as functional decomposition or data flow diagrams. Of course, the tool might provide much more in the context of communications or analysis. Such distinctions, however, are not clear.

Reifer and Montgomery (1980) provide a more general schema. They begin with a general model of design having three components: input, process, and output. Each component is decomposed until a set of 52 functions is identified. They argue that this taxonomy permits classification of all current software development tools (at the time of their study) and allows easy comparison and evaluation of tools. While one could argue the validity of such an ambitious claim, their taxonomy does provide a direct linkage to design behavior. For example, they identify features such as tuning, structure checking, scheduling, auditing and editing. Clearly, such a model can be linked to the actual behaviors of designers. Similar approaches are discussed by Rajaraman (1982) and Houghton and Wallace (1987).

These models, however, appear limited. For example, the functionality associated with teams is not clearly identified. Features such as those found in COLAB (Stefik et al. 1987) or PLEXSYS (Konsynski et al. 1984) that support groups through structured processes for brainstorming, communication, voting, negotiation or other key team behaviors appear to be lacking. To the extent that improving the "time-to-break-even" will involve the use of teams (as suggested by Ancona and Caldwell 1987, Cooprider and Henderson 1990 and others), there is a need to incorporate these functions into CASE and into any functional model of planning and design technology.

In this research, we pursued an objective consistent with prior research that attempts to characterize the key dimensions of design support technology. That is, we developed a functional model of design support (CASE) technology. To achieve this objective, we used a four step process. First, leading designers of CASE-related technology were interviewed to generate a set of critical functions that *could* be of value to an I/S planner or designer. The specific functional definitions discussed in the interviews were required to correspond to observable design behaviors. Second, 25 practicing designers familiar with CASE technology reviewed the complete set of generated functions to refine ambiguous items and reduce any obvious redundancies. Third, based on a review of the design literature, a classification scheme was developed as a basis for sorting each specific functionality generated during the interview process. This Q-sort was done by an independent group of 34 I/S designers experienced in CASE technology. The intent of this step was to evaluate

the robustness of the model. Finally, the model was used to evaluate currently available CASE products. This step represents one test of the model's ability to adequately represent and discriminate between actual CASE environments.

In the first step, open-ended interviews with leading CASE designers (both academics and practitioners) were used to develop a list of possible CASE functionalities. A total of eleven interviews, each lasting from two to three hours, were conducted. Each interview subject had extensive personal involvement in CASE technology research or had actual development experience with a range of commercial CASE products. Subjects included three academics and eight practitioners.

In the interviews, we provided each subject with a list of functionalities extracted from the literature. To ensure adequate discussion, the lists were divided into five sections. The subjects reviewed each functional description, noting any ambiguity or bias in its definition. At the end of each section, problems with definitions were discussed and new functionalities added. The order of presentation of each section was randomized across subjects.

A total of 124 distinct functionalities was generated via the interview process. The second step involved a clarification procedure to combine or eliminate vague or redundant functional definitions. In this effort, three to five expert users for each of eight existing CASE products were asked to evaluate their product using the 124 functionalities. Each subject indicated the ease of use of a given function on a one-to-five scale, with one being "very difficult to use or nonexistent" and five "very easy to use or essentially automatic." The reliability of each functional definition can be assessed by analyzing the variance (or correlation) across subjects for a given product. If the definition is unambiguous, subject experts should assign the same ease of use rating to a given function. Functional definitions with high variance or low interrater reliability (below 0.8) were reviewed and eliminated or refined. As a result of this process, 98 distinct functionalities were defined.

The third step in the process involved developing a model that reflected the scope of these 98 functions. This model, called the *Functional CASE Technology Model* (FCTM), was developed in a two-stage process. First, a review of relevant design literature was used to define a general a priori model. Then, a new set of 34 expert CASE users sorted each of the 98 functionalities into one of the a priori dimensions defined by this model. The extent to which this Q-sort process results in a consistent sorting pattern across subjects is taken as evidence that the a priori model is a meaningful abstraction and can be used to represent a wide range of CASE functionality. That is, the model represents more than a unique artifact of the researchers' interpretation of existing literature.

An alternative approach for developing such a model is discussed by Sherif and Sherif (1967). In this approach, the subject is asked to manually cluster similar attributes, thereby developing a subject-specific model. The models generated by a set of subjects can then be analyzed for underlying similarities, and form the basis for generating an overall model. The strength of this approach lies in the ability to eliminate the bias created by an a priori model. Such an approach requires extensive time and may result in dimensions that have little theoretical grounding. In this case, the time demand for a clustering task of 98 items far exceeded the time subjects were willing to provide. Further, years of both theoretical and empirical research on I/S planning and design provide a basis for developing an a priori model. Given these two factors, the Q-sort testing strategy was utilized.

The final step tests this model by using it to discriminate between actual CASE products. In the following section, each dimension of the FCTM is described and the results of the Q-sort process are provided. The section concludes with a summary of the adequacy of this model. The third section then uses the model to evaluate actual products and discusses the implications of these results. Finally, the fourth section summarizes the findings of this research and discusses the implications for future research.

Two Dimensions of CASE Technology

Reviews of the organizational literature on technology (Fry 1982, Fry and Slocum 1984, Slocum and Sims 1980, Withey et al. 1983) reveal a diversity of approaches to the measurement of technology. Perrow (1967) defines technology as the actions used to transform inputs into outputs. In that context, technology is a production variable, affecting the way inputs are converted to desired outputs. Economists have long characterized technology as production technology concerned with creating, processing, and handling physical goods. Thus, as illustrated in Exhibit 1, one perspective of CASE technology is to view it as an underlying production technology.

This perspective on planning and design technology focuses on the actions used to transform inputs to outputs (Kottemann and Konsynski 1984). At an individual level, Simon (1976, 1981) argues that bounded rationality ultimately limits the capacity of human information processing and, hence, the transformation process. This information processing perspective is often used to characterize the planning and design task (Thomas and Carroll 1979) and provides a basis to characterize the production dimension of design aid technology. We define *production technology* as *functionality that directly impacts the capacity of an individual(s) to generate planning or design decisions and subsequent artifacts or products.*

A second perspective that has been used to evaluate technology is coordination. Williamson (1975) notes that constraints on human information processing can arise from the bounded rationality of a particular agent, and from the communication requirements stemming from the interaction between agents. Bakos and Treacy (1986) also identify the need to reflect both bounded rationality of individuals and communication costs in a general model of information technology. Thompson (1967) argues that coordination is needed when interdependence occurs among business processes. Interdependence implies that the performance of one or more discrete

EXHIBIT 1   Two Functional Dimensions of I/S Planning and Design Technology

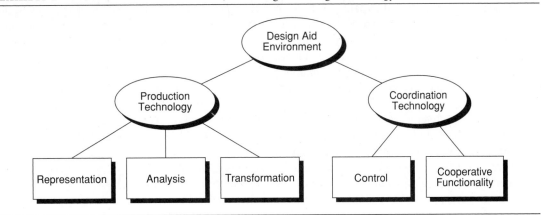

operations has consequences for the completion of others. The concept of interdependence is a fundamental principle in designing organizations (McCann and Galbraith 1981, Galbraith 1977, Thompson 1967). Different types of interdependence create different coordination structures between the participants involved.

Winograd and Flores (1987) claim that in all but the most routinized jobs, a worker requests and initiates actions that affect the economic, political or physical conditions of those around him. They describe organizations as "networks of directives and commissions" and state that the coordination of action is of central importance in this work environment. Given this characterization of organizations, they suggest that a major benefit can be gained from technology used within organizations to request, create and monitor commitments.

Malone (1988) defines coordination as "the additional information processing performed when multiple, connected actors pursue goals that a single actor pursuing the same goals would not perform." Applying these ideas about coordination to programming environments, Holt et al. (1983) suggest that a coordination system can serve as an appropriate foundation of CASE technology. Malone, Winograd and Flores, Holt et al. and other researchers have identified a major role of com-

puter technology: better enabling or supporting coordination activities. Consistent with this perspective, we define *coordination technology* as *functionality that enables or supports the interactions of multiple agents in the execution of a planning or design task.* Since a design team consists of multiple agents with a variety of goals and skills, coordination technology may emerge as an important dimension of CASE technology.

Taken together, we conceptualize design aid technology as a combination of production and coordination technology. In the following we will build from these two perspectives of technology to characterize the components of CASE technology. In each section we will examine relevant research on I/S planning and design aids and define these two major dimensions in terms of distinct subdimensions or components (Exhibit 1).

Production Technology: Representation

The first component of production technology is labeled *representation* to emphasize the notion of abstracting or conceptualizing a phenomenon. Schon (1984), Zachman (1986) and others have identified the process of evolving abstractions and presenting them in an understandable form as an essential activity in planning and design. Zachman (1986) lists categories of functionality such as process flow diagrams, functional charting or entity modeling that reflect alternative means to represent concepts or phenomena. Kottemann and Konsynski (1984) identify a hierarchy of knowledge representation that includes names or labels, domain set specifications, association or relations mapping and complete meaning that suggests the need for a range of representation functionalities. From our perspective, each of these categories suggests the need for specific functionality to support the process of generating an external representation of a planning or design concept.

Specifically, the *representation* component is defined as *functionality to enable the user to define, describe or change a definition or description of an object, relationship or process.* Our interviews resulted in a range of functionalities that appear to operationalize this conceptual component. These functionalities will be detailed in the next section, but some general observations might be made. The generated representation functionalities reflect a general notion of knowledge representation and acquisition. For example, functionalities such as the ability to describe a process in terms of an information flow or the ability to represent an organization's authority relationships reflect basic requirements to represent knowledge.

A second aspect of the representation dimension reflects requirements for adapting or changing representations, and for storing or retrieving representations. For example, the ability to combine many entity or process representations into a single complex object supports the user in an adaptation or change task.

Finally, the ability to use alternative modes of representation (e.g., text versus visual representation) is reflected. In fact, as suggested by Konsynski et al. (1984), our subjects viewed the ability to shift between alternative representations as an important type of functionality.

Production Technology: Analysis

The dimension of analysis reflects the problem-solving and decision-making aspects of planning and design. Simon (1981) portrays design as a problem-solving process and emphasizes the criticality of tasks involving evaluation of multiple alternatives and choices made by the designer. In a similar vein, we define the *analysis* component to be *functionality that enables the user to explore, simulate, or evaluate alternate representations or models of objects, relationships or processes.*

Similar to the functional building blocks of a decision support system (Keen and Scott Morton 1978, Treacy 1981, Sprague and Carlson 1982), the analysis functionalities reflect the need to compare, simulate, evaluate, ask "what if" with respect to a criteria, and choose or optimize. It is interesting to note that some functional definitions imply an embedded intelligence in the design aid. For example, the ability to suggest problem resolutions based on previously used solutions reflects the use of expert system and AI concepts in the development of design aids.

In each case, the functionality in this dimension assumes the existence of a knowledge base (often a model) and seeks to manipulate this knowledge in order to investigate alternatives, resolve conflicts or support a choice. It is a proactive analysis process that builds upon or adds to knowledge. Thus, we would expect the result of using analysis functionality to be the enhancement or adjustment of a given representation (i.e., the use of modeling functionality). The significant interaction between these two dimensions suggests that they constitute components of the more general dimension of production technology.

Production Technology: Transformation

The nature of planning and design has been conceptualized as a process or series of transformations (Kottemann and Konsynski 1984, Zachman 1986). A transformation is an internally complete and consistent change in a design concept or artifact. The need for completeness and consistency reflects the attribute that a transformation is a non-random purposeful activity and, hence, is repeatable. For example, converting a logical data model into a set of definitions represented in the language of a given data base system constitutes a transformation.

In general, the notion of transformation has been the mechanism to represent important aggregates or chunks of design activity. At a macro level, the system design life cycle describes a series of design transformations. Researchers such as Zachman (1986) and Hackathorn and Karimi (1988) have suggested a range of transformations that are central to I/S planning and design processes. We define the component of *transformation* to be *functionality that executes a significant planning or design task, thereby replacing or substituting for a human designer/planner.*

This dimension of CASE technology reflects a straightforward capital/labor substitution. It differs from *analysis* in replacing human activity rather than only providing support. The distinction is analogous to decision support systems vs. process automation. Of course, transformation technology can enhance the overall performance of humans by allowing redistribution of human resources. Still, at task level, the intent of transformation functionality is direct substitution for the human resource.

As might be expected, the bulk of the generated transformation functionalities address activities late in the design cycle (e.g., code generation). They often depend on a minimum set of functions being available in the representation component. However, as we will discuss in the fourth section, current technology often does not effectively link these two functional components.

The ability to deliver transformation functionality often implies embedding intelligence into the CASE technology. For example, the ability to automatically normalize a data model is an emerging type of transformation functionality that makes extensive use of expert systems and AI technology. As we see increased use of intelligent CASE technology, we might expect to see new types of functionality emerge for this dimension.

Coordination Technology: Control

The focus of the components of technology discussed thus far has been production-oriented. That is, the technology has provided a direct impact on the ability of an individual to produce aspects of the design. In this capacity, the technology represents a classic productivity-enhancing investment; i.e., a capital/labor tradeoff. Through the investments in technology, the task of a designer is accomplished with fewer resources.

However, the use of technology to reduce the cost of coordination can enable a design team to achieve new levels of efficiency and effectiveness. For example, Applegate et al. (1986) and Stefik et al. (1987) describe technology that is intended to improve the productivity of meetings in part through enhanced communication functionality. Such technology can not only affect the efficiency or effectiveness of a given meeting, but also improve the team's decision making or problem solving processes throughout the design life cycle.

Our interviewees identified a range of technology that focused on the need to effectively coordinate individuals. It was interesting to note that during the interviews, subjects seemed to shift from conceptualizing the planning or design process as an individual activity to one involving a group or team. When this shift occurred, the design aid functionality discussed reflected issues such as the need to exchange information, enforce policies or security measures, or understand or resolve conflicts.

It is not surprising that one aspect of design aid technology that emerges from the design literature reflects a component of coordination—control. This component reflects a notion of a manager/employee or principal/agent relationship in a planning or design process. That is, design activities involve an explicit or implicit contract to deliver a product or service to a customer for a given price. In order to ensure that the contract is fulfilled, a control system or monitoring system is required. Similarly, within the activities of a design team, a project leader may contract with an individual. Again, the project leader requires some information to ensure that this individual executes the contract in the intended way.

In addition to the need to monitor, the principal or manager may want to impose restrictions on the activities of a given agent or employee. For example, he/she may want to restrict access to particular data or prevent changes to some aspect of an existing or proposed system. At a more abstract level, the project leader needs the ability to communicate project goals (even the means to achieve these goals) and to ensure that the resources of the team are allocated in a manner that best achieves the goals.

Of course, requirements to control the activities of a group have long been recognized by the developers of computer-aided design technology. Houghton and Wallace (1987), Reifer and Montgomery (1980) and others identify a range of functionality spanning notions of project management, configuration control, and access control. We define the *control* component to be *functionality that enables the user to plan for and enforce rules, policies or priorities that will govern or restrict the activities of team members during the planning or design process.*

Two general types of relations appear in this component—resource management and access control. Resource management is the functionality that enables a manager to ensure that the behavior of individuals and, therefore, the resource utilization by the design team, is consistent with organization goals. The capability to budget, to identify a critical path or set of activities, to monitor progress or service levels, or to communicate or enforce appropriate goals are examples of this type of functionality. It is functionality that supports a range of traditional control activities. As will be discussed later, the potential for CASE technology to enable effective internal control (i.e., substitute individual control behavior for managerial control) has major implications for performance.

A second type of functionality involves access or change control. Issues of security and access must be carefully managed. Access control functionality includes configuration control, authorization management, and the ability to identify and audit the activity of designers, particularly when these activities change existing work or directly pertain to a team policy. In essence, these types of functionality assume that the design team utilizes

and produces a valuable asset. Hence, access to those assets must be monitored and controlled.

Coordination Technology: Cooperative Functionality

The control dimension addresses the need to establish and enforce goals, policy, procedures, standards and priorities during a design process. It is the traditional concept of manager/employee that assumes the need to enforce a work contract. Information is required both to ensure effective execution of task and to monitor the contract.

An alternative mode of coordination assumes that the participants operate at a peer-to-peer level. In this mode, the interaction among individuals is based on a shared set of goals and a perception of mutual gain from a given interaction. Thus, cooperative behavior is not enforced by a set of rules. Rather, such interaction reflects a sense of peer involvement where exchange is often voluntary.

Davis and Smith (1983), Henderson (1988) and Malone (1988) describe the concept of cooperative behavior in this manner. For example, Davis and Smith (1983) argue that the need for cooperation among experts arises from shared goals and a knowledge interdependence among the experts with respect to these goals. In this research we define the component of *cooperative functionality as functionality that enables the user to exchange information with another individual(s) for the purpose of influencing (affecting) the concept, process or product of the planning/design team.*

The interview process generated a range of functionalities that are modeled as cooperative functionality. These functionalities reflect the role of CASE technology as both a communication channel and a facilitation aid. Reifer and Montgomery (1980) identify communication functionality as an important aspect of computer-aided design technology. In a group context, communication is a key issue. The basic cooperative functionalities address the need for a range of communication functions, from basic messaging to enhancements such as the ability to attach a note to a diagram. This functionality provides a platform for electronic interaction among members of a team.

The second class of cooperative functionality uses technology to help facilitate group interaction. This includes functionality that provides for electronic brainstorming or manages the degree of anonymity of input (i.e., votes). Applegate et al. (1986) describe technology that provides this type of functionality. The user of PLEXSYS technology can choose between several structured group processes and adapt the technology to the execution of the particular approach chosen. The technology impacts the process through efficiency (e.g., the ability to capture the output of a brainstorming session) and by changing parameters of the group process within an efficiency level. For example, the technology can permit a significantly larger group size than is often associated with a brainstorming session. To the extent that participation and involvement affect the success of a project, this increased capacity could have significant benefits. These functionalities, particularly those which implement structured group processes, have aspects of control embedded in them. For example, electronic brainstorming enforces an interaction protocol on the members of the team. This association between control and cooperative functionality is to be expected since they are both components of the common dimension of coordination. The key distinction is that cooperative functionality assumes a peer relationship among participants and is based on a concept of sharing. It is a conduit or enabler of information exchange. Control functionality, in contrast, assumes that a hierarchical relationship exists and provides a mechanism to exchange the information necessary to establish, monitor and enforce this hierarchy. Each relates to coordination but does so from a different perspective.

A Third Dimension of CASE Technology: Organizational Technology

Simon (1976) notes that the bounds of rationality can be increased not only by increasing individual computational power, but also by institutionalizing organization-wide standards or procedures to help individual performance. This capability, which we refer to as organizational technology, can be described as organization-wide mechanisms through which an organization provides "institutionalized help" to individuals and groups to overcome the cognitive burdens of information processing. March and Simon (1958) argue that by establishing organization infrastructures, which they call standard operating procedures, the organization can reduce burdens of information processing because search procedures are automated to some extent in the standard operating procedures. Similarly, Galbraith (1977) argues that implementing a vertical information system and the implied standards of data and language associated with such a system can increase the information processing capacity of the firm.

Organizational technology is viewed in this context as an institutionalized support technology. Recent research in areas such as Organizational Decision Support Systems (King and Star 1990) and the use of I/S for creating an "information economy" (Zmud et al. 1986) has highlighted the need to differentiate the characteristics of information technology support for organizational processes (e.g., organizational decision making) from group and individual processes. The feedback that we received from our interviews supported the need to distinguish organizational technology from the other technology dimensions. A given design team performs its work within a larger organizational context as it interacts with other teams or stakeholders in order to obtain resources, make decisions, and exchange inputs and outputs. In this regard, organizational technology is concerned with the environment in which these interactions occur. In this light, we define *organizational technology* as *functionality and associated policy or procedures that determine the environment in which production and coordination technology will be applied to the planning and design process.* Instantiating any production or coordination technology requires decisions to conform to or deviate from standards of technology and procedures. These decisions affect the ability of organizations to support the design process. Decisions to deviate from standards, for example, reduce the ability to use specific production or coordination technologies as well as the ability of teams to use these functions *across* design teams or processes.

Our interviews and our empirical analysis revealed some confusion about the functionality definitions within the organizational technology dimension. One explanation for this confusion is that this dimension is not completely independent of the production and coordination dimensions. Rather, organizational technology enables the use of the production and coordination technology. For example, the organizational technology reflected in a standard design methodology will affect the dimensions of production (e.g., what diagrams/models are used) and coordination (e.g., providing a common language for teams to communicate results). For this reason, Exhibit 2 shows organizational technology as affecting production and coordination rather than as a separate, independent dimension.

Organizational Technology: Support

One component of the organizational technology dimension addresses the skills required to use technology, rather than directly focusing on specific planning and design tasks. At issue is the range of support required to help the design aid user learn about and utilize the design aid in the most effective way. We refer to this component as *support technology,* and define it to be *functionality to help an individual user understand and use a planning and design aid effectively.*

Our interviewees considered support functionality to be an essential part of gaining impact from the use of CASE. They identified functions ranging from passive functionality (e.g., an on-line help function) to proactive functionality that uses domain knowledge or past user behavior patterns to diagnose or recommend appropriate action (e.g., explaining why a particular functionality should be used in a particular situation).

Many characteristics of "user friendly" systems incorporate these types of support functionality. For example, Houghton and Wallace (1987)

EXHIBIT 2   Organizational Technology: A Third Dimension of I/S Planning and Design Technology

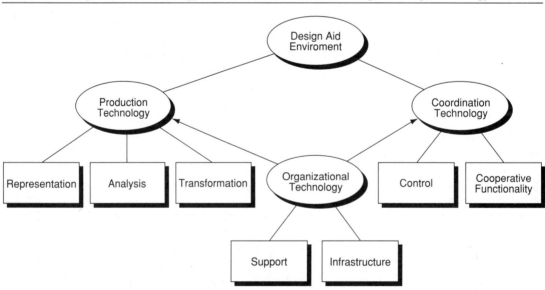

describe a range of support functions that reflect the range of skills of a typical user population (expert to novice). It should be noted that general interface technology is not incorporated as a support function. For example, the use of a mouse or point-and-click is a feature that affects the (physical or mental) effort necessary to exercise a functionality. As such, this aspect of the design environment should be incorporated into the ease of use measure of a set of functions.

Organizational Technology: Infrastructure

Computer-based design tools can provide organization-wide infrastructures for the development of complex software. Often, complex software is built module by module by several design teams. If the teams do not proceed carefully, the idiosyncrasies of an undisciplined team can lead to expensive failure. Design aid tools can help the design team manage the complexities of development by providing a common foundation for the development of I/S. As a result, the organization gains the potential to introduce parallelism and time-share scarce talent among teams. The infrastructure enforces the use of consistent techniques throughout the organization.

However, because enforcement of organization-wide infrastructure comes primarily by limiting what design teams can do with the tools, there is the possibility that an inflexible infrastructure can stand in the way of designing effective systems. Therefore, while the ultimate power of infrastructure technology lies in the ability to widen as far as possible the range of solutions and approaches that can be handled by the design team, the actual impact of this component on the development process is unclear.

Ultimately, the ability to develop and sustain an organizational infrastructure requires the use of standards. As suggested above, standards offer the potential to increase organizational flexibility and to limit the creative process of planning and design. For example, Lempp and Lauber (1988) argue that the issue of emerging standards for computer-aided design technology and practice are of strategic concern to organizations that depend upon information technology.

A major purpose of the infrastructure functionality component is to provide portability of skills and data. Portable skills and data are promoted through standardized relationships among various activities of the design life cycle. The ability to introduce simultaneous design processes is enhanced. For example, adopting a standard structure for representing the knowledge generated in a design process increases the ability to share this knowledge with other teams. Similarly, it provides a basis to train designers about what knowledge is available and how other teams function. As a result, increased organizational performance can be achieved by a given team's ability to anticipate when coordination is required.

The interviewees generated few examples of functionality that could be thought of as standards, and so this technology component was not included in our subsequent analyses. However, during debriefing with organizations, the importance of a technology infrastructure was frequently emphasized. The discussion of infrastructure functionality often reflected system utilities and architectures. For example, one functionality focused on the ability to port between technology platforms, while another highlighted the ability to function in a highly distributed environment. The need for consistency of the data definition storage structure with emerging standards for a central repository was also mentioned frequently.

In essence, the discussions brought out the need to incorporate a dimension of design aid technology that reflects the potential to support organization change and flexibility. As such we define the *infrastructure* component of organizational technology as *functionality standards that enable portability of skills, knowledge, procedures, or methods across planning or design processes.*

Summary

In the previous sections, we have introduced three general dimensions and seven components of planning and design technology. Specifically, we preresented production, coordination and organizational technologies as the relevant dimensions. We characterized production as being composed of three components (representation, analysis and transformation); coordination, as two components (control and cooperative functionality); and organizational technology, as two components (support and infrastructure). Additionally, we described organizational technology as a primary enabler of the production and coordination technology dimensions rather than as an independent dimension.

Several observations seem appropriate. A distinction often made between design support environments is the ease of use of a functionality. For example, two design aid environments may both support data flow diagramming. They may differ significantly in the ease of use that they provide for this functionality. Ease of use can be viewed as a measure of the effort required to exercise the functionality and, thus, as a relative measure of cost. Combining a functional model with the notion of ease of use will permit the researcher to explore the usability of CASE technology.

Secondly, the level of functional *specificity* reflects the goal of creating a correspondence between the functional model and usage behavior. For example, interviewees rejected as too general the use of "documentation" as a type of functionality. Rather, discussions indicated that documentation is a passive form of representation that requires particular functionality. However, the need to develop a parsimonious model in a research setting (particularly one that requires users of a system to describe their usage behaviors) argues against a micro model. The functionality described herein reflects the subjects' judgment as to an appropriate level of aggregation.

Finally, there is no claim that the list of 98 functionalities which we described above and will detail in the next section does not represent an exhaustive set of functionalities for planning and design technology. Rather, the functional set specified for each component is viewed as spanning or reflecting the scope of the component. As we will discuss, the convergence found in the Q-sort process and the ability to discriminate across actual products support the conclusion that these functionalities can be meaningfully grouped under the proposed definitions of the components.

EVALUATING THE FCTM

A final concern in the development of the functionality items is the ability to reliably associate a particular functionality with actual CASE products. As discussed in the previous section, a reliability check resulted in a total of 98 functions forming the pool with which we define the functional dimensions described above. In the following sections, a Q-sort test is used to examine the robustness of the proposed model. The test consists of giving independent experts in CASE technology the definitions of each component[1] and asking them to sort the 98 functions into these categories. To the extent that the subjects sort the functions in the same way, there is evidence that the proposed model is a meaningful characterization of a wide range of CASE technology. A second test then examines the extent to which the model actually discriminates among CASE products in an interesting and useful way. The following sections present the results of this Q-sort and the application of the model to evaluate eight commercially available CASE products.

An Empirical Analysis of the FCTM

A summary of the results of the Q-sort test is shown in Exhibit 3. A total of 34 subjects not involved in the previous development of this model sorted the functionalities according to the definitions described in the previous section. The results were tabulated based on the category receiving the most frequent assignments. As Exhibit 3 shows, 50 functionalities were assigned to the Production Technology dimension, 26 to

---

[1] As discussed, the infrastructure component resulted from feedback during debriefing. Thus, it is not included in the Q-sort test.

EXHIBIT 3 Summary Profile of Components of Design Aid Technology

Component	Number of Functionalities Associated by a Majority of Respondents	Number of Additional Functionalities Associated by a Plurality of Respondents	Total Number of Functionalities
Representation	9	9	18
Analysis	17	2	19
Transformation	11	2	13
Production Technology:	37	13	50
Control	12	4	16
Cooperative Functionality	9	1	10
Coordination Technology:	21	5	26
Support	13	9	22
Organizational Technology:	13	9	22

Coordination Technology, and 22 to Organizational Technology.

The detailed results of the Q-sort test are shown in the right-hand columns of Exhibits 4A–4F. In these exhibits, the functionalities are listed in the order of declining frequency among the 34 subjects. Following the description of each functionality is the percentage of the respondents who sorted that functionality into the relevant component. For example, looking at item 1 in Exhibit 4A, 88% of the respondents sorted "represent a design in terms of process or flow models" into representation.

A second aspect of the model can also be examined with this data. Even if assignments do not indicate agreement on a primary component, there may be agreement on the more general dimensions of production, coordination or organizational technology. If this is true, there is support for the premise that these general dimensions adequately reflect CASE technology. The final three columns of Exhibits 4A–4F show the percentage of respondents sorting the specific functionality into the production dimension (*representation, analysis,* or *transformation*), the coordination dimension (*control* or *cooperative functionality*), and organizational dimension (*support*). For example, function 15 of Exhibit 4A ("Map the existing systems onto a functional description of the organization") was sorted by only 42% of the respondents into the representation component, but fully 94% of the respondents placed it into the general production technology dimension (that is, sorted it into *representation, analysis,* or *transformation*).

A simple chi-square goodness of fit test (with a 0.05 level of significance) is used to test the hypothesis that assignments are random. The results of this simple test is shown in Exhibit 4 at both the component level (i.e., the six components that were used in the sort) and at the dimension level (i.e., production, coordination and organizational). At the component level, there are only two functions for which the chi-square test of uniform distribution is not rejected (transformation #13 and support #22). Although this is a weak test, it does support the conclusion that the six components do differ significantly. At the dimension level, only

EXHIBIT 4 Detailed Profile of Components of Design Aid Technology

EXHIBIT 4A Functionalities of Representation (Production Technology)

	% Selecting Component: Representation	*% Selecting Dimension:*		
		Prod.	*Coord.*	*Org.*
1. Represent a design in terms of process or flow models	(88%)	94%	3%	3%
2. Represent a design in terms of data models	(82%)	94%	3%	3%
3. Construct several types of models (data, process, functional, . . .)	(77%)	91%	0%	9%
4. Customize the language or conventions used for representation	(70%)	76%	15%	9%
5. Represent relationships between information requirements & goals	(68%)	91%	9%	0%
6. Represent authority relationships of target system's organization	(65%)	82%	9%	9%
7. Provide the option of drawing diagram lines exactly where wanted	(65%)	73%	9%	18%
8. Combine many entities or processes into a single complex object	(59%)	85%	3%	12%
9. Show an object's attributes by selecting it in a diagram	(52%)	82%	0%	18%
10. Maintain descriptions of existing systems to interact with target	(47%)	76%	18%	6%
11. Provide flexible naming conventions	(47%)	56%	18%	26%*
12. Maintain a single master definition of each process, object, etc.	(44%)	62%	26%	12%*
13. Move between different types of models	(44%)	70%	9%	21%
14. Redraw a diagram so that it is uncluttered and easy to read	(42%)	79%	3%	18%
15. Map the existing systems onto a functional organizational desc.	(42%)	94%	6%	0%
16. Combine structurally equivalent processes or objects	(35%)	91%	0%	9%
17. Simultaneously display several screens showing different versions	(34%)	59%	16%	25%*
18. Choosing a first-cut model from among stored generic models	(30%)	70%	6%	24%

*Failed chi-square test for 3 dimensions.

EXHIBIT 4B   Functionalities of Analysis (Production Technology)

	% Selecting Component: Analysis	% Selecting Dimension:		
		Prod.	*Coord.*	*Org.*
1. Test for consistency between a process model and a data model	(85%)	91%	9%	0%
2. Check for the structural equivalence of objects or processes	(82%)	91%	0%	9%
3. Check for unnecessary or redundant model connections	(79%)	88%	9%	3%
4. Detect inconsistencies in models, definitions, etc.	(79%)	88%	9%	3%
5. Identify the design impact of proposed changes in a design	(79%)	88%	6%	6%
6. Search the design for similar objects	(74%)	88%	0%	12%
7. Use analytical decision aids to measure performance	(73%)	88%	6%	6%
8. Detect and analyze system errors from execution of target system	(73%)	88%	6%	6%
9. Identify schedule impacts of a proposed design change	(70%)	82%	18%	0%
10. Search design for complex relationships	(68%)	70%	12%	18%
11. Suggest problem resolutions based on previously used solutions	(65%)	76%	3%	21%
12. Estimate the process/performance characteristics of a design	(64%)	76%	15%	9%
13. Search design for objects with specified characteristics	(59%)	70%	6%	24%
14. Simulate the production environment of the target system	(58%)	88%	3%	9%
15. Identify where predefined criteria or rules have been violated	(56%)	65%	35%	0%
16. Trace relationships between detailed specs and planning efforts	(50%)	76%	18%	6%
17. Identify the differences between separate versions of an object	(50%)	65%	20%	15%*
18. Recommended a gen'l model incorporating many limited perspectives	(41%)	88%	3%	9%
19. Perform an operation on only a portion of a design	(35%)	82%	9%	9%

*Failed chi-square test for 3 dimensions.

EXHIBIT 4C   Functionalities of Transformation (Production Technology)

	% Selecting Component: Transformation	% Selecting Dimension:		
		Prod.	*Coord.*	*Org.*
1. Generate executable code from a screen mockup	(91%)	94%	3%	3%
2. Generate executable code in several procedural languages	(91%)	94%	3%	3%
3. Generate code compatible with a variety of physical environments	(79%)	85%	12%	3%
4. Generate standard code for generic programs	(79%)	82%	9%	9%
5. Generate executable versions of a design for testing/evaluation	(79%)	94%	3%	3%
6. Convert a logical specification into a physical one	(74%)	97%	0%	3%
7. Transform a high-level representation into a more detailed one	(68%)	97%	0%	3%
8. Provide documentation as a by-product of design	(59%)	74%	0%	26%
9. Perform reverse engineering	(59%)	91%	0%	9%
10. Generate screen mockups	(53%)	94%	6%	0%
11. Import data from and export data to external files/packages	(50%)	56%	31%	13%
12. Create templates for tasks and deliverables	(38%)	50%	38%	12%*
13. Propagate a change in an object to all places the object appears	(32%)	70%	21%	9%* **

*Failed chi-square test for 3 dimensions.

**Failed chi-square test for 6 components.

twelve functions failed to reject the test of a random assignment. Again, this supports the conclusion that these dimensions differ.

A more specific review of the assignment patterns is even more revealing. For *representation,* only nine of the eighteen items received more than 50% as a primary selection. However, all nine of the functions below 50% appear to have consensus as general production functionalities.

The sorting results for *analysis* appear more consistent, with seventeen of nineteen functions receiving more than 50% primary assignments. Again, the two items below 50% appear to reflect general production functionality with a fairly uni-

form distribution across representation, analysis and transformation.

The *transformation* component has 11 of 13 functions exceeding 50%. In general, the functions appear to be clearly within the production dimension. The two functions that fall below 50% are ambiguous. Both functions 12 and 13 fail to reject the chi-square test at the dimension level, suggesting that there is significant overlap between the production and control aspects of these functions.

In the *control* component, 12 of 16 functions receive more than 50% primary assignments. This distribution of assignments suggests support of this component and a consensus with respect to the

---

EXHIBIT 4D Functionalities of Control (Coordination Technology)

	% Selecting Component: Control	% Selecting Dimension:		
		Prod.	Coord.	Org.
1. Specify who can review various parts of the design work	(79%)	6%	94%	0%
2. Provide project management information	(79%)	15%	82%	3%
3. Maintain a record of who is responsible for each part of project	(71%)	6%	82%	12%
4. Maintain a record of changes made in the design	(65%)	9%	82%	9%
5. Provide management information for more than one project	(64%)	15%	82%	3%
6. Specify who can modify various parts of the design work	(64%)	12%	85%	3%
7. "Freeze" a portion of a design to protect it from changes	(62%)	15%	79%	6%
8. Manage the quality assurance path for a project	(55%)	9%	85%	6%
9. Alter rules that control the way certain functions are performed	(55%)	24%	67%	9%
10. Provide assistance in analyzing project management priorities	(52%)	33%	55%	12%
11. Estimate how long a specific task or project will take	(52%)	36%	52%	12%*
12. Remind members of team about approaching deadlines	(52%)	6%	85%	9%
13. Follow rules in merging separate versions of models, diagrams, etc.	(49%)	27%	70%	3%
14. Produce metrics for comparing projects (complexity, quality, etc.)	(49%)	30%	52%	18%*
15. Maintain list of requirements for design and how satisfied	(46%)	49%	45%	6%*
16. Temporarily ignore a problem/inconsistency so work can continue	(29%)	41%	32%	27%*

*Failed chi-square test for 3 dimensions.

---

coordination dimension. For the four functions not receiving more than 50% assignment, function 13 appears to reflect a general coordination perspective, while functions 14, 15 and 16 fail to reject the chi-square test for differences at the dimension level. These functions appear to have overlap with *support* and *analysis,* suggesting a significant level of ambiguity in their functional descriptions.

The *cooperative functionality* component received only ten assignments, but nine of those

EXHIBIT 4E   Functionalities of Cooperative Functionality (Coordination Technology)

	% Selecting Component: Cooperative Functionality	*% Selecting Dimension:*		
		Prod.	*Coord.*	*Org.*
1. Maintain a dialogue with other users of the tools	(91%)	3%	91%	6%
2. Allow a group of users to work simultaneously on a single task	(91%)	6%	91%	3%
3. Send messages to others who use the tools	(88%)	3%	91%	6%
4. Allow concurrent use by several users of dictionary/diagram/etc.	(85%)	6%	91%	3%
5. Provide group interaction support (brainstorming, NGT, etc.)	(85%)	9%	88%	3%
6. Attach electronic notes to objects for others to read	(62%)	20%	65%	15%
7. Allow giving of anonymous feedback or input	(53%)	6%	88%	6%
8. Notify designer if a change is made in design that affects his work	(53%)	9%	88%	3%
9. Build a catalog of macros that other users can access	(50%)	24%	50%	26%
10. Help the designer and end user evaluate design alternatives	(41%)	47%	44%	9%*

*Failed chi-square test for 3 dimensions.

received more than 50% as a primary assignment. In general, these functions appear to reflect a coordination perspective, but subjects distinguished them from the control component. Function 10 did not receive more than a 50% primary assignment and also failed to reject the chi-square test at the dimension level. This function shows significant overlap with both analysis and support.

Finally, the *support* component had 22 functionalities, with only thirteen of the 22 receiving primary assignment. This component appears to be difficult for subjects to clearly differentiate. Although there are six functions that have strong agreement as support, the remaining functions reflect aspects of both production and coordination. Two of the nine functions receiving less than

50% primary assignment fail the chi-square test. Function 21 fails to reject the test at the dimension level and function 22 fails to reject at the weaker component level test. The sort pattern across those assignments with less than a 50% primary sort appears to reflect significant overlap with at least one other dimension. These results could suggest a need to refine the definition for the support component. An alternative explanation is reflected in Exhibit 2. The organizational dimension of technology affects the support environment primarily through its impact on the production and coordination dimensions. Because of this, it is often difficult to isolate the functionalities of organizational and support technology from those of production and coordination.

EXHIBIT 4F Functionalities of Support (Organizational Technology)

	% Selecting Component: Support	*% Selecting Dimension:*		
		Prod.	*Coord.*	*Org.*
1. Provide aids for quick references to basic commands/functions	(97%)	3%	0%	97%
2. Provide on-line help for a specified command/feature	(94%)	3%	3%	94%
3. Provide instructional materials for learning the tools	(91%)	3%	6%	91%
4. Provide context-specific on-line help	(88%)	6%	6%	88%
5. Identify external sources of information on specific topics	(84%)	16%	0%	84%
6. Provide options about how to interact with the tools	(76%)	21%	3%	76%
7. Build templates or examples of work for use in tutorials/demos	(59%)	18%	23%	59%
8. Explain why an action or alternative has been recommended	(55%)	42%	3%	55%
9. "Browse" in other segments of the tool while using graphics mode	(50%)	47%	3%	50%
10. Explain why part of a design has been identified as inconsistent	(50%)	47%	3%	50%
11. Anticipate user's mistakes from his pattern of previous errors	(50%)	32%	18%	50%
12. Allow the undoing of a series of commands	(50%)	41%	9%	50%
13. Generate outputs in a variety of media	(50%)	26%	24%	50%
14. Incorporate new command "macros" into command structure	(49%)	39%	12%	49%
15. Generate presentation-quality printed reports and documents	(47%)	38%	15%	47%
16. Provide individual change pages of documents	(43%)	24%	33%	43%
17. Graphically magnify a model to see greater levels of detail	(38%)	59%	3%	38%
18. Build a general access library of customized models	(35%)	35%	30%	35%
19. Prepare, edit, store, send and retrieve documents	(32%)	53%	15%	32%
20. Store versions of a design for later "roll-back"	(32%)	38%	30%	32%
21. Link a design to a library of models/systems for testing	(30%)	49%	21%	30%*
22. Develop, run & store completely customized reports	(29%)	59%	12%	29%**

*Failed chi-square test for 3 dimensions.

**Failed chi-square test for 6 components.

In summary, the sorting results provide support for each of the component concepts. Only 13 of the 98 functions fail to reject the chi-square test at the dimension or component level. Twenty-seven functions receive less than 50% as a primary sort. However, 13 of these 27 have support as their first or second choice, reflecting the difficulty with the separation of this component. Of the remaining 14 functions, eight reflect a general production perspective and one a general coordination perspective, thereby providing additional support for the dimension level concepts.

As the next step in the analysis, the technology components are used to compare eight commercially available CASE products. The comparison will be used to determine if the FCTM provides a useful tool to evaluate potential CASE environments.

Comparison of CASE Products

In this section, the FCTM is used to characterize eight commercially available CASE products. The products were selected in an attempt to cover the full span of the system development life cycle. The life cycle was divided into three general categories: planning, design and construction. Two prod-ucts that appear to target each of these were selected for comparison. In addition, two products that purport to provide integration across all three components were selected for evaluation. To ensure that the products did reflect these components, 25 expert users were asked to indicate the level of support provided by the product for the seven tasks shown in Exhibit 5. These perceptions support the conclusion that the tools selected for evaluation span the life cycle and have distinctive product features.

Exhibit 6 provides a summary of the product evaluations. In each case, three to five expert users of a product were asked to evaluate its ease of use with respect to the 98 functions. A five-point scale (see Exhibit 6) was used for evaluation. A function was considered to exist if the average response of the subjects was greater than 3.0.

Several observations can be drawn from Exhibit 6. First, the model differentiates across products in an expected way. For example, the products that target planning and conceptual design have the focus of their functionality on representation while they are relatively weak on transformation. Similarly, those products targeting construction provide higher levels of transformation functionality and are weaker on representation.

EXHIBIT 5   Life Cycle Coverage by Product

| | Product | | | | | | | |
Design Activity	A	B	C	D	E	F	G	H
I/S Planning	4.5	3.71	1.88	2.8	2.0	1.1	3.5	2.4
Requirement Definition	3.25	3.86	4.0	3.3	2.8	1.8	4.5	3.2
Conceptual Design	3.0	3.57	4.50	3.67	2.8	2.3	4.8	4.0
Detailed Design	2.0	2.29	3.63	3.0	4.0	3.4	4.6	4.6
Implementation	1.33	1.86	2.1	1.6	4.6	4.7	3.1	3.1
Testing	1.0	1.43	1.6	1.0	3.2	4.3	2.2	1.7
Maintenance	2.0	1.43	2.5	1.8	4.2	4.8	3.9	2.5

Scale:	1	2	3	4	5
	very little support	some support	adequate support	good support	extensive support

EXHIBIT 6   Summary of Product Evaluations

CASE Tool	I Representation 18 Possible	%	II Analysis 19 Possible	%	III Transformation 13 Possible	%	IV Control 16 Possible	%	V Cooperative Functionality 10 Possible	%	VI Support 22 Possible	%
A	7	39	5	26	2	15	0	0	1	10	4	18
B	5	28	2	11	1	8	0	0	1	10	3	14
C	11	61	3	16	2	15	3	19	2	20	8	36
D	9	50	5	26	2	15	0	0	0	0	8	36
E	2	11	0	0	5	38	0	0	3	30	1	5
F	3	17	4	21	7	54	1	6	2	20	5	23
G	13	72	5	26	4	31	9	56	4	40	14	64
H	10	56	3	16	4	31	0	0	3	30	8	36
Total Used	17	94	9	47	11	85	9	56	4	40	17	77

Example

The user can instruct the tools to redraw a diagram on the screen so that it is uncluttered and easy to read.

1	2	3	4	5
Does Not Exist or is Very Difficult to Use	Difficult to Use	Adequate Ease of Use	Easy to Use	Very Easy to Use Essentially Automatic

Secondly, only one product provides significant coverage for control functionality. Further, all products are weak on cooperative functionality. This result suggests that current products may have a limited impact on team performance.

Thirdly, the products do provide support functionality, but there is significant variation across products. As we will discuss, a more detailed analysis shows that there exists a general level of support in the form of basic help commands, but the availability of advanced, intelligent support functionality is quite limited.

A final observation is reflected in the summary "total used" row in Exhibit 6. This row indicates the number and percentage of the total possible functions that appear in at least one product. The results suggest that claims for integration and coverage by CASE products are at best limited to

notions of production technology. There is a significant gap between possible and available functionality in coordination, analysis and intelligent forms of support. Even within the production dimension, the degree of support can vary significantly.

A detailed listing of the available functionality of the eight CASE tools is shown in Exhibit 7. As with Exhibit 6, a particular functionality is considered to exist for a specific product if the expert users of that product rate the ease of use of the functionality as being greater than 3.0. One can use Exhibit 7 to compare specific functionality across products. For example, the support functionalities of "provide on-line help" and "quick reference to basic commands" (#1 and #2) are generally available across the life cycle. However, more sophisticated or intelligent support such as

EXHIBIT 7 Detailed Listing of CASE Tool Functionality

CASE Tool	A-Representation 1 2 3 4 5 6 7 8 9 10 11 12 13 14 15 16 17 18	B-Analysis 1 2 3 4 5 6 7 8 9 10 11 12 13 14 15 16 17 18 19	C-Transformation 1 2 3 4 5 6 7 8 9 10 11 12 13
A	X · · · X · X X X · X X · · · X · ·	X · · · · · · · · X · X · X X X · · ·	· · · · · · · X · X · · X
B	· · · X · · · X X · X X X · · · · ·	· · · · · · · · · · · X · X · · · · X	· · · · · · · · · · · · X
C	X X X X · X X X X · X X X · · · · ·	· · · · · X · · · · · X · X X · · · ·	· · · · · · · · X X · · ·
D	X X X · · X · X X · X X X · · · X ·	X · · · · X · · · · · X · X X · · X ·	· · · · · · X · · · · X ·
E	· · · · · · · X · · X · · · · · · ·	· · · · · · · · · · · · · · · · · · ·	X · X X · · · X X X · · ·
F	· · · · X · X · · · X X · · · · · ·	· · X · · X · · · · · X X · · · · · ·	X · · X X X X X X X X X ·
G	X X X · · X X X X X X X X · · · X X	· · · · · X · · · · · X · X X X · X ·	· · · · X · · · X X X · ·
H	X X X · · X X · · X · X X · · X · X	· · · · · · · · · · · X · · · · · X X	· · · · X · · X X X X · X

CASE Tool	D-Control 1 2 3 4 5 6 7 8 9 10 11 12 13 14 15 16	E-Cooperative Functionality 1 2 3 4 5 6 7 8 9 10	F-Support 1 2 3 4 5 6 7 8 9 10 11 12 13 14 15 16 17 18 19 20 21 22
A	· · · X · X · · · · · · · · · ·	· · · · · X · · · ·	X X X X · · · · · · · · · · · · · · · · · ·
B	· X · · · · · · · · · · · · · ·	· · · X · · · · · ·	X X · · · X · · · · · · · · · · · · · · · ·
C	· · · · X · X X · · · · · · · ·	· · · · · X · · X ·	X X X X X · · · · X · · · X · · X X X · · X
D	· · · · · · · · · · · · · · · ·	· · · · · · · · · ·	X X X X · · · · X X · · X · · X · · · · · ·
E	· · · · · · · · · · · · · · · ·	· · · X X · · X · ·	· · · · · · · · · · · · · · X X · · · · · ·
F	· · · X · · · · · · · · · · · ·	· · X · X · · · X ·	· · · · · · · · · · · · · · · X X · · · · ·
G	X · X X · X X X · · X X · · X ·	· · · X X · · · X X	X X X X X · · · · · · · X · X X X X X X X X
H	X X X · · X X · · · · · · X · ·	· · · X X · · · X ·	· X · · · · · · · · · · X · · X · · X X · ·

An "X" indicates that the average ease-of-use rating for that functionality was greater than 3.0.

"the ability to anticipate user mistakes based on past errors" (#11) is totally lacking.

These results suggest that the FCTM is a meaningful way to characterize design aid technology. While clearly not the only possible perspective, this model does appear to reflect a reliable and valid model for a wide range of functionality, and it does differentiate across products. In the following section, we discuss the implications of the FCTM and possible items for future research.

IMPLICATIONS AND FUTURE RESEARCH

This research has led to the development of a model of design aid technology with three general dimensions: production, coordination and organization. Each of these general dimensions is composed of a number of sub-dimensions. Production technology consists of representation, analysis and transformation; coordination technology, of control and cooperative functionality; and organizational technology, of support and infrastructure. A Q-sort technique was used to map specific functionalities onto these components and their related dimensions. The results of this analysis suggest a reasonably strong consensus among those involved in the sorting process, implying that these dimensions provide a useful mechanism for categorizing major functionalities. Further, when this model is applied to existing products, meaningful differences are revealed.

The results of applying the FCTM to current products highlight two significant limitations (at least for the products included in this study). First, the products support a relatively weak level of analysis functionality. Since the ability to support the critical thinking process of design is crucial, these results suggest that increasing the level of analysis technology holds strong promise. Second, the products provide a limited amount of support for cooperative activities in the design process. The potential ability of these tools to assist in the coordination of the activities of multiple designers within and across teams provides a major area for enhancing the functionality of these tools.

Our debriefings strongly emphasized the importance of the organizational dimension of technology. This emphasis suggests that users of design aids must pay careful attention to the availability of support and the building of technology infrastructures through the use of standards and relevant support functionality.

The selection of a design aid tool requires a fitting of functionality with the characteristics of the user's design task. In this sense, one cannot conclude that coverage across all functionality is inherently valuable. Rather, one must recognize how specific functionality addresses the behavior of a designer or design team. One interpretation is that the relative value of the identified dimensions and even the specific functionalities within a dimension may not be equal across all task environments. Therefore, one important line of future research would be to empirically establish the organizational and specific design activities that increase the importance of specific functionalities or dimensions.

This research represents an initial attempt at examining the underlying dimensions of design aid technology in a systematic way. While the results of the work are encouraging, there are some concerns that should be noted. The methodology used was a limited test of the construct validity of the dimensions and their components. Future research should provide for a more formal testing of the underlying validity of these technology dimensions. The model presented in this research provides a meaningful representation as interpreted by a large number of expert designers and users. Clearly, one has to be concerned that this consensus approach might reflect a bias of the design community that would omit or understate innovative or emerging functionality. Nevertheless, the degree of convergence shown by the data and its usefulness for classifying present products indicates that it is a meaningful starting point.

A primary focus for future research involves the measurement of the usage behavior of actual design teams with respect to the dimensions of technology described in the FCTM. By using the FCTM as a basis for conceptualizing usage behavior, the relationship between the usage behavior of design teams and their actual performance can be empirically demonstrated. In this way, the FCTM will provide a meaningful way to characterize the performance impacts of I/S planning and design aids.

ACKNOWLEDGMENTS

This research was funded by the Management in the 1990s project. The authors wish to thank the reviewers for their comments and suggestions.*

---

*John King, Associate Editor. This paper was received October 19, 1988, and has been with the authors 8 months for 2 revisions.

References

1. Abdel-Hamid, T. K. and S. E. Madnick, "Impact of Schedule Estimation on Software Project Behavior," Working Paper No. 127, Center for Information Systems Research, Massachusetts Institute of Technology, Cambridge, MA, 1985.

2. Acly, E., "Looking Beyond CASE," *IEEE Software* (March 1988), 39–43.

3. Adelson, B. and E. Soloway, "The Role of Domain Experience in Software Design," *IEEE Transactions on Software Engineering*, SE-11:11 (Nov. 1985), 1351–1360.

4. Ancona, D. G. and D. F. Caldwell, "Management Issues Facing New-Product Teams in High-Technology Companies," in *Advances in Industrial and Labor Relations*, 4, D. Lewin, D. B. Lipsky and D. Sockell (eds.), Jai Press Inc., Greenwich, CT (1987), 199–221.

5. Andriole, S. J., *Software Development Tools: A Source Book*, Petrocelli Books, Princeton, NJ, 1986.

6. Applegate, L. M., B. R. Konsynski, and J. F. Nunamaker, "A Group Decision Support System for Idea Generation and Issue Analysis in Organizational Planning," in *Proc. Conf. Computer-Supported Cooperative Work*, Austin, TX (December 3–5, 1986), 16–34.

7. Bakos, J. Y. and M. E. Treacy, "Information Technology and Corporate Strategy: A Research Perspective," *MIS Quart.*, 10, 2 (1986), 107–119.

8. Banker, R. D., S. M. Datar, and C. F. Kemerer, "Factors Affecting Software Maintenance Productivity: An Exploratory Study," *Proc. Eighth Internat. Conf. Information Systems*, Pittsburgh, PA, (December 6–9, 1987), 160–175.

9. Beck, L. L. and T. E. Perkins, "A Survey of Software Engineering Practice: Tools, Methods, and Results," *IEEE Transactions on Software Engineering*, SE-9, 5 (September 1983), 541–561.

10. Brooks, F. P., Jr., "No Silver Bullet: Essence and Accidents of Software Engineering," *IEEE Computer*, 20, 4 (April 1987), 10–19.

11. Bruns, G. and S. L. Gerhart, "Theories of Design: An Introduction to the Literature," MCC Technical Report Number STP-068-86, Microelectronics and Computer Technology Corporation, Austin, TX, 1986.

12. Card, D. N., F. E. McGarry, and G. T. Page, "Evaluating Software Engineering Technologies," *IEEE Transactions of Software Engineering*, SE-13, 7 (July 1987), 845–851.

13. Case, A. F., Jr., "Computer-Aided Software Engineering (CASE): Technology for Improving Software Development Productivity," *Data Base*, 17, 1 (Fall 1985), 35–43.

14. Chikofsky, E. J. and B. L. Rubenstein, "CASE: Reliability Engineering for Information Systems," *IEEE Software* (March 1988), 11–16.

15. Connor, A. J. and A. F. Case, Jr., "Making A Case for CASE," *Computerworld* (July 9, 1986), 45–46.

16. Cooprider, J. G. and J. C. Henderson, "Technology-Process Fit: Perspectives on Achieving Prototyping Effectiveness," *Proc. 23rd Hawaii Internat. Conf. System Sciences* (January 1990), 623–630.

17. Dart, S. A., R. J. Ellison, P. H. Feiler, and A. N. Habermann, "Software Development Environments," *IEEE Computer*, 20, 11 (November 1987), 18–28.

18. Davis, R. and R. G. Smith, "Negotiation as a Metaphor for Distributed Problem Solving," *Artificial Intelligence*, 20, 1 (January 1983), 63–109.

19. Durfee, E. H. and V. R. Lesser, "Using Partial Global Plans to Coordinate Distributed Problem Solvers," *Proc. 10th Internat. Joint Conf. Artificial Intelligence*, Milan, Italy (August 23–28, 1987), 875–883.

20. ————, ———— and D. D. Corkill, "Coherent Cooperation Among Communicating Problem Solvers," *IEEE Transactions on Computers*, C-36, 11 (November 1987), 1275–1291.

21. Frenkel, K. A., "Toward Automating the Software-Development Cycle," *Comm. ACM*, 28, 6 (June 1985), 578–589.

22. Fry, L., "Technology-Structure Research: Three Critical Issues," *Academy of Management J.,* 25 (1982), 532–552.

23. Fry, L. W. and J. W. Slocum, Jr., "Technology, Structure, and Workgroup Effectiveness: A Test of a Contingency Model," *Academy of Management J.,* 27, 2 (June 1984), 221–246.

24. Galbraith, J. R., *Organization Design,* Addison-Wesley, Reading, MA, 1977.

25. Gane, C. and T. Sarson, *Structured Systems Analysis: Tools and Techniques,* Prentice-Hall, Inc., Englewood Cliffs, NJ, 1979.

26. Glass, R. L. "Recommended: A Minimum Standard Software Toolset," *ACM SIGSOFT Software Engineering Notes,* 7, 4 (October 1982), 3–13.

27. Hackathorn, R. D. and J. Karimi, "A Framework for Comparing Information Engineering Methods," *MIS Quart.,* 12, 2 (June 1988), 203–220.

28. Hanson, S. J. and R. R. Rosinski, "Programmer Perceptions of Productivity and Programming Tools," *Comm. ACM,* 28, 2 (February 1985), 180–189.

29. Harvard Business School, "Xerox Corporation: Executive Support Systems," Harvard Business School Case #N9-189-134, Harvard University, Cambridge, MA, April 1989.

30. Henderson, J. C., "Involvement as a Predictor of Performance in I/S Planning and Design," Working Paper No. 175, Center for Information Systems Research, Massachusetts Institute of Technology, Cambridge, MA, August 1988.

31. Holt, A., H. Ramsey, and J. Grimes, "Coordination System Technology as the Basis for a Programming Environment," *Electrical Comm.,* 57, 4 (1983), 307–314.

32. Honda, K., M. Azuma, A. Komatubara, and Y. Yokomizo, "Research on Work Environment for Software Productivity Improvement," *IEEE Proceeding of 9th COMPSAC Computer Software & Applications Conference,* Chicago, IL (October 9–11, 1985), 241–248.

33. Houghton, R. C., Jr. and D. R. Wallace, "Characteristics and Functions of Software Engineering Environments: An Overview," *ACM SIGSOFT Software Engineering Notes,* 12, 1 (January 1987), 64–84.

34. Keen, P. G. W. and M. S. Scott Morton, *Decision Support Systems: An Organizational Perspective,* Addison-Wesley, Reading, MA, 1978.

35. Kemerer, C. F., "Software Production Economics: Theoretical Models and Practical Tools," Working Paper No. 168, Center for Information Systems Research, Massachusetts Institute of Technology, Cambridge, MA, 1988.

36. King, J. L. and S. L. Star, "Conceptual Foundations for the Development of Organizational Decision Support Systems," *Proc. 23rd Annual Hawaii Internat. Conf. on System Sciences* (January 1990), 143–151.

37. King, W. R., "Evaluating an Information Systems Planning Process," working paper, Graduate School of Business, University of Pittsburgh, Pittsburgh, PA, 1984.

38. Konsynski, B. R., J. E. Kottemann, J. F. Nunamaker, Jr. and J. W. Stott, "PLEXSYS-84: An Integrated Development Environment for Information Systems," *J. Management Information Systems,* 1, 3 (Winter 1984–85), 64–104.

39. Kottemann, J. E. and B. R. Konsynski, "Dynamic Metasystems for Information Systems Development," *Proc. Fifth Internat. Conf. Information Systems,* Tucson, AZ (November 28–30, 1984), 187–204.

40. Kull, D., "To Raise Productivity Work Smarter, Not Harder," *Computer Decisions,* 16, 3 (March 1984), 164–189.

41. Lempp, P. and R. Lauber, "What Productivity Increases to Expect from a CASE Environment: Results of a User Survey," in *Productivity: Progress, Prospects and Payoff, Proc. 27th Annual Technical Symposium,* Gaithersburg, MD (June 9, 1988), 13–19.

42. Malone, T. W., "What is Coordination Theory?" Working Paper #2051-88, Sloan School of Management, Massachusetts Institute of Technology, Cambridge, MA, 1988.

43. March, J. G. and H. A. Simon, *Organizations,* John Wiley & Sons, New York, NY, 1958.

44. Martin, C. F., "Second-Generation CASE Tools: A Challenge to Vendors," *IEEE Software* (March 1988), 46–49.

45. McCann, J. and J. R. Galbraith, "Interdepartmental Relations," in *Handbook of Organizational Design,* 2, P. C. Nystrom and W. H. Starbuck (eds.), Oxford University Press, New York, NY (1981), 60–84.

46. McIntyre, S. C., B. R. Konsynski, and J. F. Nunamaker, Jr., "Automating Planning Environments: Knowledge Integration and Model Scripting," *J. Management Information Systems,* 2, 4 (Spring 1986), 49–69.

47. Necco, C. R., C. L. Gordon, and N. W. Tsai, "Systems Analysis and Design: Current Practices," *MIS Quart.,* 11, 4 (December 1987), 461–476.

48. Osterweil, L., "Software Environment Research: Directions for the Next Five Years," *IEEE Computer,* 14, 4 (April 1981), 35–43.

49. Perrow, C., "A Framework for the Comparative Analysis of Organizations," *American Sociological Rev.,* 32, 2 (April 1967), 194–208.

50. Rajaraman, M. K., "A Characterization of Software Design Tools," *ACM SIGSOFT Software Engineering Notes,* 7, 4 (October 1982), 14–17.

51. Reifer, D. J. and H. A. Montgomery, "Final Report, Software Tool Taxonomy," Management Consultants Report No. SMC-TR-004, National Bureau of Standards, #NB795BCA0273, June 1980.

52. Schon, D. A., "Problems, Frames and Perspectives on Designing," *Design Studies,* 5, 3 (July 1984), 132–136.

53. Semprevivo, P., "Incorporating Data Dictionary/ Directory and Team Approaches into the Systems Development Process," *MIS Quart.,* 4, 3 (September 1980), 1–15.

54. Sherif, M. and C. W. Sherif, "The Own Categories Procedure in Attitude Research," in *Readings in Attitude Theory and Measurement,* M. Fishbein (ed.), John Wiley and Sons, New York, NY (1967), 190–198.

55. Simon, H. A., *Administrative Behavior: A Study of Decision-Making Processes in Administrative Organization,* 3rd ed. The Free Press, New York, NY, 1976.

56. ————, *The Sciences of the Artificial,* 2nd ed. The MIT Press, Cambridge, MA, 1981.

57. Slocum, J. W., Jr. and H. P. Sims, Jr., "A Typology for Integrating Technology, Organization, and Job Design," *Human Relations,* 33, 3 (March 1980), 193–212.

58. Sprague, R. H., Jr. and E. D. Carlson, *Building Effective Decision Support Systems,* Prentice-Hall, Englewood Cliffs, NJ, 1982.

59. Stefik, M., G. Foster, D. G. Bobrow, K. Kahn, S. Lanning, and L. Suchman, "Beyond the Chalkboard: Computer Support for Collaboration and Problem Solving in Meetings," *Comm. ACM,* 30, 1 (January 1987), 32–47.

60. Thomas, J. C. and J. M. Carroll, "Psychological Study of Design," *Design Studies,* 1, 1 (July 1979), 5–11.

61. Thompson, J. D., *Organizations in Action,* McGraw-Hill, New York, NY, 1967.

62. Treacy, M. E., "Toward a Behaviorally Grounded Theory of Information Value," *Proc. Second Internat. Conf. Information Systems,* Cambridge, MA (December 7–9, 1981), 247–257.

63. Wasserman, A. I., "Automated Tools in the Information System Development Environment," in *Automated Tools for Information Systems Design,* H. J. Schneider and A. I. Wasserman (eds.), North-Holland Publishing Co., New York, NY (1982), 1–9.

64. Weiderman, N. H., A. N. Habermann, M. W. Borger, and M. H. Klein, "A Methodology for Evaluating Environments," *Proc. ACM SIGSOFT/SIGPLAN Software Engineering Symposium on Practical Software Development Environments,* Palo Alto, CA (December 9–11, 1986), 199–207.

65. Welke, R. J. and B. R. Konsynski, "An Examination of the Interaction Between Technology, Methodology and Information Systems: A Tripartite View," *Proc. First Internat. Conf. Information Systems,* Philadelphia, PA (December 8–10, 1980), 32–48.

66. Williamson, O. E., *Markets and Hierarchies,* Free Press, New York, NY, 1975.

67. Winograd, Terry and Fernando Flores, *Understanding Computers and Cognition,* Ablex Publishing Company, Norwood, NJ, 1986.

68. Withey, M., R. L. Daft, and W. H. Cooper, "Measures of Perrow's Work Unit Technology: An Empirical Assessment and a New Scale," *Acad. Management J.,* 26, 1 (March 1983), 45–63.

69. Zachman, J. A., "A Framework for Information Systems Architecture," Report No. G320-2785, IBM Los Angeles Scientific Center, Los Angeles, CA, 1986.

70. Zmud, R. W., A. C. Boynton, and G. C. Jacobs, "The Information Economy: A New Perspective for Effective Information Systems Management," *Data Base* (Fall 1986), 5–16.

HOW THE LEARNING CURVE
AFFECTS CASE TOOL ADOPTION

With the rising cost of software development, tools for integrated computer-aided software engineering offer solutions to productivity and quality problems that plague the profession. But while most software developers accept the idea that integrated CASE can help lower costs and increase productivity, the state of practice is less optimistic. Organizations tend to adopt integrated CASE only in a limited form or they abandon a good percentage of the technology soon after it is implemented.

One study shows that one year after introduction, 70 percent of CASE tools and techniques are never used, 25 percent are used by only one group, and five percent are widely used, but not to capacity. In a different survey of more than 200 leading organizations, less than 25 percent of the staff were using front-end CASE tools. In another survey of 63 leading organizations, only 24 percent were using CASE at all. Another study reports that one organization is not using 80 to 90 percent of the CASE tool packages it purchased.[1]

Yet there is an obvious need for such tools. The already high demand for software continues to grow, and there is a shortage of qualified software developers. Indeed, one cause of quality shortfalls in delivered software could very well be the participation of marginally qualified individuals in its development. So with this relatively scarce supply of software-development labor, it makes good sense to substitute development capital in the form of CASE tools. Some think of this as software development's favorable evolution from a craft-type activity to one more closely resembling an engineering or manufacturing operation.[2]

So why aren't organizations embracing the idea of integrated CASE in more than just theory? One problem is that the first project written with an integrated CASE tool typically fails to deliver improved results. Academicians and practitioners say that the learning curve, described in the box titled Learning-Curve Model: A Flexible Measurement Tool, can partially explain this phenomenon. But merely identifying learning as a source of the problem is not enough. Managers need more information to justify their investment in CASE technology. They need a way to predict the extent of the learning curve and data to estimate its parameters so that they can determine their return on investment or similar measures for CASE tool adoption.

Ultimately, knowing the factors that favorably influence the rate of learning, not merely the observed learning rate, will be what managers find the most useful. But a necessary first step is the ability to measure the current state of the process.

INFLUENCE OF LEARNING CURVES

Integrated CASE tools have raised the stakes of the learning issue. Because these tools cover the entire life cycle, there is more to learn, and therefore the study of learning—and the learning-curve phenomenon—is becoming especially relevant.

One interpretation of the learning curve is that initial projects are relatively more expensive than later projects and are even likely to be more expensive than projects produced under the old technology. In a survey of more than 60 sites, W. Bruce Chew and colleagues translated this effect into the *S* curve in Exhibit 1.[3] The curve, which represents actual performance, dips below 0 on the relative performance scale, indicating that performance on initial projects with the new

Article by Chris F. Kemerer. © 1992 IEEE. Reprinted, with permission, from (*IEEE Software;* 9, 5, 23–28; 1992).

EXHIBIT 1 Performance Over Time with Learning Effect

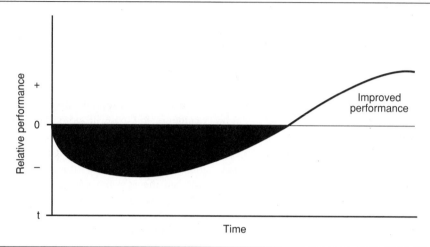

technology is worse than performance on projects with the old technology. This effect eventually wears off, but it is not what adopters of process innovations usually expect. They often project a zero increase in performance followed by a rise that eventually plateaus. Thus, they are disappointed when expected benefits do not materialize as soon as planned and may abandon the technology before realizing any net benefit.

Adding to the confusion is that CASE tools are relatively new, and there is no published data on the learning-curve effect—although a number of observers have postulated a model like Exhibit 1. The problem for CASE tool adopters is that no one agrees on how the learning curve is likely to affect tool adoption. For example, a model from Software Productivity Research predicts that the *S* curve for CASE tools crosses the 0 relative productivity level in about six months. A near identical graph from the Gartner Group shows the *S* curve for integrated CASE tools crossing after more than a year. A mix and match of vendor solutions reach the same level only after more than two years. On the other extreme is a survey of CASE users by CASE Research Corp., which found that more than one-third of all back-end (lower) CASE users claimed full proficiency in only one to two months. Finally, a report in *CASE Outlook,* while

noting the absence of quantitative studies, nonetheless offers the following prediction: " . . . plan on a productivity reduction of 50 percent for six months, parity for the next six months, and 30 percent to 50 percent improvement thereafter [including tool-specific learning-curve effects]."[1]

Clearly, the industry has only contradictory evidence to provide CASE tool adopters—which may be part of the reason the tools aren't being adopted very quickly. (The difference may also be because time is chosen as the model's axis instead of projects, which more accurately reflects how learning occurs.) This view of learning emphasizes costs, rather than the traditional learning benefits, as the box titled Learning Curve Model: A Flexible Measurement Tool describes. The goal of this article is to go beyond that view and show how learning-curve models can help managers in adopting integrated CASE tools.

ADAPTING MODELS TO INTEGRATED CASE

Although there are many learning-curve models, it is not easy to adapt them to estimating learning curves for integrated CASE tools. A number of issues—both theoretical and those having to do with implementation—present formidable

Learning-Curve Model: A Flexible Measurement Tool

Part of adopting an industrial process is to go through a learning curve that measures the rate at which the average unit cost of production decreases as the cumulative amount produced increases. Learning curves do not relate solely to individual learning, although some authors have attempted to restrict it in this way, using terms like "experience curves" or "progress functions" to denote group or organizational learning. But more often "learning curve" is used in the broadest sense, as it is in this article.

Learning curves are also not restricted to the measurement of low-skill labor; their effects have been observed in skills like heart surgery, for example.

Several factors contribute to the learning curve, including

- labor efficiency, both in production and management;
- improved methods and technology;
- product redesign, with the reduction or elimination of costly features;
- production standardization, with a reduction in the number of setups or changes; and
- effects from economies of scale.

These factors are sometimes characterized as autonomous learning (automatic gains from learning by doing) and induced learning (conscious efforts by managers to observe and improve the process).

Software development exhibits all these factors. Production standardization, for example, is exhibited by organizations that batch small maintenance changes into a few releases. This might also be interpreted as an effect from economies of scale. Greater experience with tools and applications has also been widely suggested as improving software-development productivity.

Much has been written about learning curves. Louis Yelle gives a comprehensive review.[1] Three models are the most established:

the traditional model (with variants) to estimate average unit cost and more recently a model developed by Linda Argote and colleagues and a model by Paul Adler and Kim Clark.

Traditional Model

The earliest industrial learning curve is the Wright or cumulative-average curve, represented by

$$y = \alpha X^{-\beta} + \epsilon \quad \beta > 0$$

where y is the average cost, α is the cost of the first unit, X is the total number of units, and β is the learning rate parameter, which can be estimated using least-squares regression after taking logarithms of both sides:

$$ln\ y = ln\ \alpha - \beta\ ln\ X$$

β is sometimes expressed in percent, which reflects the percentage of decline in average cost with each doubling of cumulative volume:

$$\beta = \frac{ln(\%)}{ln\ 2}$$

Typical percentage rates observed in practice are from 70 to 95 percent. Exhibit 2 shows the curve for an 80-percent learning rate.

Smaller percentages indicate a relatively steeper learning curve, implying more rapid cost decreases. Therefore, when learning-curve researchers refer to steep learning curves, they are actually referring to a favorable event—as opposed to the popular use of the term, which implies something bad to overcome.

Recent Research

The learning-curve model has been successfully used in a variety of settings and continues to be the source of significant research. Recent effort has focused on managing both the transfer and loss of learning.

Learning-Curve Model: A Flexible Measurement Tool (*Cont.*)

The transfer of learning is the study of how knowledge gained at one site or installation is transferred to others. This transfer can be either internal, as from a pilot or leading-edge facility to the rest of the organization, or external, as in attempting to bootstrap on the efforts of other firms.

Adler and Clark describe three types of internal learning transfer: across the development/manufacturing interface, from start-up operations to other facilities, and ongoing cooperation between facilities. In all three cases, they find evidence of sharing but also suggest that more could be done to contribute to this.

Argote and colleagues examined transfer across shipyards building Liberty ships in World War II.[2] They found that, while there was some evidence of initial learning transfer (shipyards starting later generally showed higher initial levels of productivity than earlier shipyards), no other significant learning transfers seemed to take place.

Thus both Adler and Clark and Argote and colleagues show that the transfer of learning across organizations is limited.

A topic mentioned in the learning-curve literature but rarely studied is the loss of learning, or forgetting. The literature generally assumes a steady production process after start-up, with continuing benefits until the process is replaced. Recent experimental research conducted at Florida State University by Charles Bailey suggests that forgetting is a significant loss in procedural tasks that are interrupted for long periods. He found that the amount of forgetting was a function of the amount learned and the passage of time, but not the learning rate. The study by Argote and colleagues also noted forgetting, referring to it as the lack of persistence of learning. Their results suggest that cumulative output overstates the gains to be had from learning when the process has been significantly interrupted.

References

1. L. Yelle, "The Learning Curve: Historical Review and Comprehensive Survey," *Decision Sciences,* Feb. 1991, pp. 302–328.

2. L. Argote, S. Beckman and D. Epple, "The Persistence and Transfer of Learning in Industrial Settings," *Management Science,* Vol. 36, No. 2, pp. 140–154.

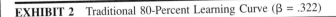

EXHIBIT 2   Traditional 80-Percent Learning Curve ($\beta = .322$)

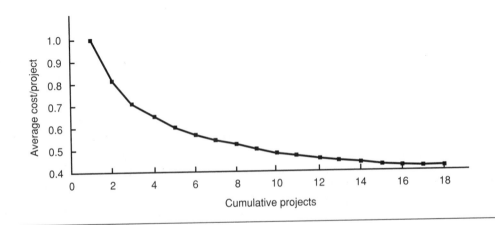

obstacles to using traditional models, which were created to predict the performance of manual workers performing repetitive tasks. Users of integrated CASE tools are essentially knowledge workers performing tasks, that (at least at first approximation) are not so repetitive.

Theoretical Issues

These issues include sensitivities peculiar to knowledge work, the diversity of tasks, and the confusion between tool learning curves and learning curves for supporting technologies.

Knowledge-Work Sensitivities

Although all the original applications of learning curves involved manual tasks, there was no reason to believe similar effects would not be found in knowledge work—tasks like system design and analysis. Such effects are arguably stronger for tasks that are not physically constrained. Airframe construction and printed-circuit-board assembly, for example, ultimately encounter physical constraints such as maximum speed of operation, especially if safety is a priority. So a natural assumption is because knowledge work does not have these binding constraints, traditional learning-curve models will apply at least equally well.

Unfortunately, it doesn't work out that way. Classic learning-curve models assume production categories are either

- large lots or batches of relatively low cost units (like semiconductors) or
- tens or hundreds of very large identical or nearly identical units (like airplanes or ships).

Software projects have elements of both, but fall neatly into neither. A software project can be viewed as the production of many relatively atomic units (like source lines of code or function points). However, these tend to be aggregated into units with nonuniform granularity—program size varies widely, for example—which correspond to odd-size batches. This view obviously disrupts the classic learning-curve model.

On the other hand, if the unit of analysis is the software project itself, roughly corresponding to airplanes in the second category, the units are clearly not identical. This issue of the repetitive versus nonrepetitive nature of software development is receiving a lot of attention because it relates directly to software reusability. Software developers tend to treat each project as unique, when, in fact, research suggests that less than 15 percent of the code created is actually unique, novel, or specific to individual applications.[4]

An appropriate approach may be, then, to treat each project as a batch—in which the batch size is a measure of software size—and adjust the model to account for a possible wide variation in batch size. A modeling approach similar to that for a microeconomic production process may be quite suitable. In this approach, learning is merely one independent variable, which together with other variables (like the amount of input), is given equal opportunity to influence the result.

For example, slightly modifying the model of Argote and colleagues gives you

$$ln\ q_t = \alpha + \beta\ ln\ K_{t-1} + \chi\ ln\ L_t + d\ ln\ W_t + \epsilon$$
$$K_t = \lambda K_{t-1} + q_t$$

where q_t is the output in time period t, K_t is knowledge gained during t, L_t is the labor input during t, W_t is the capital input during t, and λ is a depreciation of the knowledge parameter.

In this model the effects of learning (K_t) are separable from other possible effects, such as changes in the mix of capital and labor inputs or in scale.

Task Diversity

Systems-development tasks can be anything from requirements analysis to testing and documenting source code. These diverse tasks are likely to reflect different rates of learning, and be supported to different degrees by the integrated CASE tool. The issue here is how much the task mix differs from project to project. If it differs markedly and if different tasks exhibit highly different rates of learning, the results may be anomalous. There are several ways to avoid this. One is to take great care in selecting as homogeneous a set of projects as possible to model. Another is to incorporate additional variables in the model to account for this mix discrepancy. Finally, discrete tasks within the project can be modeled separately. Each of these suggestions, whether done together or separately, carries with it some practical difficulties.

Another problem is caused by how CASE tools provide different levels of support for different project tasks. For example, John Henderson and Jay Cooprider found that current tools differ significantly in their ability to support cooperative design activities.[5]

With this different level of support, plus a possible mix of activities across projects, an earlier project may be (anomalously) more productive because a particular life-cycle phase or task within a phase was both significant and relatively well supported. A later project, on the other hand, might be relatively unlucky on both counts. Moreover, an earlier project may use a different version of the integrated CASE tool.

Tool Versus Supporting Methods

The distinction between learning the integrated CASE tool and learning the underlying or supporting methodology has received some attention in both the trade press and academic writing. Texas Instruments' Information Engineering Facility and Knowledgeware's Information Engineering Workbench are examples of learning the tools, while information engineering is an example of learning a supporting methodology. Distinguishing types of learning is fundamental to such notions as "readiness for integrated CASE," in which developers are recommended to delay adopting integrated CASE tools until they are fully comfortable with the underlying methodology.[6]

This distinction suggests using separate models to track the individual rates of learning and to track variables relating to the training received by the staff assigned to integrated CASE projects. Although research has documented the importance of training to learning,[7] organizations tend to underinvest in training. To estimate the benefit of training, managers can adopt a version of Paul Adler and Kim Clark's model:

$$ln\frac{q_t}{l_t} = ln\ \alpha + \beta\ ln\ X_{t-1} + \chi\ ln\ T_{t-1} + \epsilon$$

where q_t over l_t is productivity during time period t and T_{-1} is the cumulative hours spent in training during $t-1$.

Implementation Issues

After the functional form of the learning-curve model is established, work can proceed on empirically validating models in integrated CASE settings. The three biggest tasks in implementation are locating a suitable data site, collecting the data, and validating the results.

Finding a Suitable Site

The best place to start looking for a site is in organizations that have already adopted integrated CASE tools. But this is no easy task for several reasons.

- Even if a suitable site can be found, most organizations simply do not collect the performance data necessary to quantitatively evaluate learning about integrated CASE tools. Work-hour data by project, if captured at all, may reflect sloppy or even incorrect bookkeeping. Staff members or managers may not report actual work hours if doing so will put a project over budget. Even worse, they may charge them to another project or to an overhead account, which will further compound the error if data is used for future planning.
- If an organization *does* keep detailed project data, it won't do much good unless management has also kept detailed data by person or by project phase. It is easy to imagine a situation in which a new project n is expected to demonstrate the effect of learning but, because not enough members of project $n-1$'s team are transferred to the new project, they cannot. Without data on who charged the hours (and their level of experience with the integrated CASE tool), researchers cannot readily discern

this scenario.[8] Some sites may have several integrated CASE projects going on in parallel, which create multiple organizational learning curves unless management makes a significant effort to transfer the knowledge gained.

- Even if organizations have collected a lot of data already, other data will probably be required to carefully construct a learning curve. Practitioners are understandably concerned about demanding anything extra from an already overburdened IS staff.

Given these problems, finding a site with enough completed integrated CASE projects and a relatively similar set of team members may seem like an impossible task. But the number of suitable sites is growing, albeit slowly, as integrated CASE catches on. Because modern technology and modern process and product measurement often go hand in hand, organizations that have adopted such tools are more likely to have modern measurement practices as well. Moreover, integrated CASE tools aren't cheap. Senior management has probably mandated the implementation of measurement to monitor the process as a prerequisite of adoption.

Thus, while practical data problems are significant impediments for most organizations to implement these models, they may prove much less formidable to early adopters of integrated CASE technology.

Collecting Data

To minimize the effect on staff, researchers may have to limit the sample to a small group of hopefully representative projects. To reach a sufficient sample size, they can either use data from completed projects or wait for data from future projects. The first option requires much care to ensure accurate data. Collecting historical data is often particularly problematic because many IS departments have high turnover. It is not at all unusual to begin collecting data on a completed project only to discover that the project manager or some other key individual no longer works there. Such projects may have to be excluded from

analysis because records require interpretation or supplements from these key informants.

If researchers opt to use data from future projects, they should be aware that individuals collecting the data may perceive alternative uses (particularly managerial control) for it. For example, self-reported data on source lines of code or function points may be misrepresented to give the impression of high personal productivity.

Another problem in collecting future data is that the average-size firm may take a long time to generate enough new projects to make data collection meaningful. This is particularly true in evaluations of integrated CASE tools because many tools are designed to be of the greatest (perhaps any) value only on large systems. A firm is likely to do these large systems projects only infrequently, and of course, being large, they take a long time to complete.

A third problem is that the waiting period for data collection—given integrated CASE's slow adoption and relatively quick abandonment—puts research results at risk. Changes in the site's business or technology may obscure any meaningful results. As time passes, new versions of the tool will become available. These later versions may aid performance by providing more functions or greater ease of use, or they may actually hinder learning because they become more complex. Which effect dominates clearly depends on the site and tools.

An additional danger of long-term data collection is the loss of learning when tool adoption is interrupted.

Validating Results

A final implementation problem is assessing the validity of the results once the research is complete. Integrated CASE tools, like other new technologies, are likely to be initiated in only one or a few specially selected pilot projects. These pilot projects may or may not be representative of systems projects as a whole.

If volunteers are solicited, there will clearly be some selection bias toward rapid technology adopters or simply staff members who are dissatisfied with their current work. Even if management selects pilot projects, the Hawthorne effect—the tendency for workers to show increased productivity under any new situation in which their performance is being monitored—may still dominate. It may, therefore, be difficult to get a representative sample, and later projects may be sufficiently different to obscure learning effects.

Of course, the ultimate problem with any field study may be its external validity. Even if researchers can show the effect of an integrated CASE tool and support a causal relationship with statistical data, they cannot assume that the results will extend to other firms, even similar ones. The implementation of integrated CASE tools at one organization may have been well received by staff eager for its use, well educated in theoretical background, and gently introduced to tool mechanics through excellent training and ongoing support. The same tool at another site may have been received with hostility, with the staff feeling it had been forced on them by management.

Staff acceptance is only one example of how organizations may differ, and therefore how a tool can fail to have the same impact across sites. Differences in applications mix, technical environment, personnel, management, users, backlog, organizational structure, and history can also affect results. For example, the makeup of project team members and their experience with new technologies plays an important role. The culture of the organization—in particular, the degree of local resistance to change—is also a factor. It is important to collect learning-curve data at many sites to test the effects of differences in these environmental conditions.

Learning-curve models clearly have much to offer organizations. Besides being able to quantitatively document the productivity effects of integrated CASE tools by factoring out the learning costs, managers can use model results to estimate future projects with greater accuracy. Without this depth of understanding, managers are likely to make less-than-optimal decisions about integrated CASE and may abandon the technology too soon.

Data from the models has other, more sophisticated, uses as well, which could lead to a greater understanding of how learning occurs, what factors affect it, and how learning time can be shortened—all of which are instrumental in reducing tool-adoption costs. For example, managers can control, and to some extent anticipate, most of the benefits associated with learning.

An important research benefit would be to look at how the emerging discipline of software engineering can benefit from the knowledge these types of models provide, with emphasis on the underlying concepts of formal models developed in other, more mature engineering disciplines. Learning-curve work could provide insight into how researchers could usefully adapt concepts developed in other domains to aid the understanding of software delivery.

Another useful general outcome would be to prove the value of process measurement to software engineering. While much lip service is given to the need for and importance of measurement, its adoption has been slow and easily abandoned. But if managers continue to apply the results of measurement programs, their value will be justified and investment in them sustained. With a sound measurement base many other software-engineering process improvements may be possible. Therefore, the knowledge gained from a greater understanding of the software-technology adoption process will aid the implementation of not only integrated CASE, but also potential innovations like object-oriented technologies.

Finally, much has been written about the nationwide trend toward a service-sector economy. One related issue is the low productivity of service-sector work and the general inability to effectively measure and increase it. Software development falls in the high end of the service-sector categories, an area of increasing concern and importance for worldwide competitiveness. Increasing the understanding of software development could benefit other high-end service-sector categories as well.

ACKNOWLEDGMENTS

Research support from MIT's Center for Information Systems Research and helpful comments from three anonymous referees on an early draft of this article are gratefully acknowledged.

References

[1] C. Kemerer, "Learning Curve Models for Integrated CASE Tool Management," Working Paper 231, MIT Center for Information Systems Research, Cambridge, Mass., Nov. 1991.

[2] M. Shaw, "Prospects for an Engineering Discipline of Software," *IEEE Software,* Nov. 1990, pp. 15–24.

[3] W. Chew, D. Leonard-Barton, and R. Bohn, "Beating Murphy's Law," *Sloan Management Rev.,* Spring 1991, pp. 5–16.

[4] T.C. Jones, "Reusability in Programming: A Survey of the State of the Art," *IEEE Trans. Software Engineering,* May 1984, pp. 488–494.

[5] J. Henderson and J. Cooprider, "Dimensions of IS Planning and Design Aids: A Functional Model of CASE Technology," *Information Systems Research,* Sept. 1990, pp. 227–253.

[6] J. Nosek, G. Baram, and G. Steinberg, "Ease of Learning and Using CASE Software: An Empirical Evaluation," working paper, Temple University, Computer and Information Sciences Dept., Philadelphia, Mar. 1990.

[7] P. Adler and K. Clark, "Behind the Learning Curve: A Sketch of the Learning Process," *Management Science,* Mar. 1991, pp. 267–281.

[8] R. Banker, S. Datar, and C. Kemerer, "A Model to Evaluate Variables Impacting Productivity on Software Maintenance Projects," *Management Science,* Jan. 1991, pp. 1–18.

DIVISION AMONG THE RANKS: THE SOCIAL IMPLICATIONS OF CASE TOOLS FOR SYSTEM DEVELOPERS

INTRODUCTION

Today we are seeing tremendous interest and investment in the automation of the systems development process. This trend towards Computer-Aided Software Engineering (CASE) tools is an attempt to remedy the apparent lack of computer-based support for systems developers, a lack to which many of the ills of the systems building process have been attributed. CASE tools are software programs which automate or support tasks typically constituting information systems development practice. There is no general agreement as to what functionality a CASE tool should provide, but most would agree that CASE tools comprise some subset of the following elements: screen and report design aids, text and diagram editors, data modeling tools, data dictionaries, code generators, testing and debugging tools. The

Article by Wanda J. Orlikowski. Reprinted, with permission, from *(Tenth International Conference on Information Systems,* pp. 199–210, December/1989).

major advantages that have been advertised for CASE tools include increased responsiveness to user needs in the face of changing requirements, increased systems development productivity, decreased systems development time, enhanced system quality, standardization, ability to replace project personnel easily, and the capability to solve larger and more complex problems (Case 1985; Freedman 1986; Stamps 1987).

While some of these benefits may be realizable, the mechanisms through which CASE tools are successfully implemented are not identified. There are few, if any, detailed analyses of actual CASE tool implementations, and little empirical data is available on the organizational effects of using automated means to develop systems. Most discussions of CASE tools focus on technical and project management criteria with little discussion, and hence little understanding, of the social implications of using CASE tools. Information technology, as is by now well accepted, can never be deployed in a vacuum. Its form and function are always influenced by the social context within which it is embedded (Boland 1979; Kling and Scacchi 1982; Markus 1983; Weick 1984) and it invariably exerts a reciprocal influence on that context (Giddens 1984). Similarly, we can expect that the information technology deployed to support/automate systems development (CASE tools) will interact with the organizational context, introducing perturbations into the social relations surrounding tool development and use. Drawing on an empirical study, this paper recounts how the deployment of CASE tools in systems development changed social relations among developers, providing insight into some organizational changes triggered by automating systems development.

The following section provides background to the research study, outlining the organizational context and history within which CASE tools were introduced. Section three investigates the structural changes engendered by CASE tools and describes the behavioral response of system developers. Section four discusses the meanings of these changes for the developers in terms of their perspectives and subculture affiliations. Section five reviews the findings, recasting them in terms of a more general, social theory. The paper concludes by outlining some implications for practice and for future research into the social issues surrounding CASE tools.

BACKGROUND TO THE RESEARCH

The Research Study

The discussion in this paper draws on a research study that investigated the automation of the systems development process in a large, northeastern software consulting firm (henceforth known as the Beta Consulting Corporation). The software consulting firm, in operation since the 1960s, employs about 600 consultants and develops computer-based information systems for its clients across various industries: financial services, manufacturing, retail, and government. These information systems are typically large, transaction-processing applications used by clients to support their major administrative activities. Beta's operations are organized by project, with project teams varying from around ten to over a hundred personnel, and projects extending from a few months to a number of years in duration. Project costs range from a hundred thousand to a few million dollars. As a consequence of the growing demand for large, complex, integrated application software, Beta has—over the last two decades—attempted to streamline as much of its systems development practice as possible. The most recent and visible manifestation of this strategy is the construction and deployment of CASE tools within project teams. This shift towards computer-based systems development support in Beta dates back more than five years, in contrast to most firms which have not yet seriously committed to CASE.[1]

The findings discussed here are part of a larger research study that focused on the organizational changes that accompanied Beta's implementation of CASE tools in its systems development operations (Orlikowski 1988). The study employed ethnographic techniques (Agar 1980; Van Maanen 1979, 1988) such as observation of participants, interaction with CASE tools, documentation review, social contact, unstructured and semi-structured interviews. It was executed over eight months within Beta and in those client sites where Beta developers were building application systems. In the first phase of the research, historical data on the Beta corporation and its systems development practices was gathered from published material (in-house and trade press), and from interviews with senior managers who had been involved in Beta's traditional systems development, as well as its adoption of a computer-based systems development process.

With some background information on Beta and its practices, five different application projects (four large and one small) were selected for in-depth analyses. Projects were not selected at random but were strategically identified to guarantee exposure to the use of CASE tools in all major phases of the systems development life cycle (requirements analysis, conceptual design, detailed design, implementation, and testing). An average of four weeks was spent on each project, observing and interviewing team members in their daily systems development work, and in their interaction with each other and the CASE tools. There were 120 interviews conducted, each lasting an average of one and a half hours. Participation in the research was voluntary and while the particular projects examined were selected by Beta's senior management, individuals within projects were invited to participate in the study by the researcher alone. These individuals spanned Beta's hierarchic levels from the most junior analysts and programmers to senior project managers.[2] Other key informants, such as the senior recruiting officer, the director of research and development, sales directors, major client managers, and former Beta employees, were identified and sought out both within and outside Beta. Data was also collected throughout the study at monthly (all day) division meetings and in project training sessions on CASE tools.

Beta has not diffused its CASE tools on a corporate-wide basis, but has followed a phased implementation with major offices first adopting the tools, followed by the smaller offices. Because offices regularly share personnel to take advantage of slack resources, it was possible to find developers having differential exposure to the CASE tools. Thus, on the projects studied, there were developers who had never used CASE tools before, as well as developers who were four and five year veteran tool users. This differential exposure to tool use facilitated a natural contrast that revealed interesting insights into how systems developers perceive and interact with CASE tools.

Project Teams Before the Use of CASE Tools

The history of project team composition in Beta indicates that gradually over the last two decades a partitioning between functional and technical expertise was established within system development

teams.[3] This partitioning, however, was only institutionalized with the introduction of CASE tools during the last five years, when a number of structural changes underscored the division among the project team members, accentuating relations of power and dependence. Before proceeding to the discussion of these organizational changes, the evolution of project team relations in Beta over time is sketched out.

In the late 1960s, Beta personnel working on systems development projects were not differentiated by expertise so much as by what stage in the systems development process they serviced. Thus, some people specialized in the upfront conceptual work of systems specification, performing information requirements determination and systems analysis, while others conducted actual system implementations via functional and technical design, programming, testing, and installation. While this type of specialization did lead to differentiated knowledge and experience, the lines were not drawn along functional and technical expertise. Largely as a result of the unanticipated weaknesses of this temporal schism—having two different teams develop a single system for a client often resulted in many development inefficiencies[4] as well as duplicate client negotiations—the tasks of the development process were bundled together, so that a single team carried a project through in its entirety.

A division of labor which encouraged functional and technical specialization quickly emerged within such a single project team structure. This specialization was driven by the size and complexity of applications that Beta began to develop and was encouraged by the software engineering tenets gaining ascendancy in the early 1970s. Even as different tasks were assigned to various team-appointed specialists, all the tasks concerned the building of an application—the target system—for the current client. None of the project team members were responsible for supporting the activities of other team members. Hence, dependencies on the project resulted from coordinating disparate tasks, rather than from a differential distribution of resources. Functional and technical specializations on teams were informally negotiated and sustained, were temporary (lasting only the duration of a project), and were not officially recognized by Beta's structural apparatus (its hierarchy, assignment mechanism, promotion and reward schedule). In the early 1970s, Beta did not formally differentiate its personnel along lines of expertise.

RESPONDING TO CASE TOOLS AND STRUCTURAL CHANGE

Setting the Stage for CASE Tools

In the mid-1970s, however, information technology became increasingly integrated, diverse and technically complex, encompassing different hardware and software standards, sophisticated operating systems, database management systems, networks, and multiple computer configurations. Beta recognized that in order to deliver "leading edge" systems, project teams would have to augment their level of technical expertise. Senior Beta management formally designated some individuals as the firm's technical "experts" and a separate division within Beta was formed to house them. Personnel for the technical division were specifically recruited from computer science schools and were not assigned to particular project teams. Instead of spending time on clients' sites building application systems, they were located at Beta's headquarters to research new technological innovations and to serve as general technical consultants to projects on an as-needed basis. This latter responsibility required them to travel to projects for a few days at a time to provide the technical knowledge that local project teams lacked. While the technical expertise of these specialists was formally recognized by Beta, little power accrued to them as their involvement with projects was minor, and it is project engagements that earn revenues and hence influence within Beta. The technical specialists were generally perceived as advisors and referred to as the "consultants' consultants." The technical expertise furnished was strictly concerned with the hardware and software environment within which application systems were being built. There was, as yet, no notion of using information technology to support systems development work.

Beta's systems development practice grew and the demand for technically complex application systems increased. Time pressure on technical specialists limited even further their already sporadic contact with project teams and, as a result, their contributions to local systems development efforts were shortlived and superficial. The general sentiment from local project managers was that these technical specialists were too inexperienced in functional matters, too focused on narrow technologies, and too removed from the daily exigencies of projects to benefit applications development. Out of these pressures and frustrations, the concept of "localized technical groups" emerged in Beta about ten years ago. Each local office now develops its own cadre of technical experts—consultants specializing in technical matters—to support client projects specific to each local office through close and daily involvement in systems development.

By establishing local technical groups, Beta personnel in local offices are formally differentiated by functional or technical expertise. Like their functional counterparts, technical consultants are assigned to client projects on a full-time basis. Each project team now comprises two distinct types of personnel: the "functional team" (drawn from the general pool of local functional consultants), and the "technical team" (drawn from the local technical group). Initially, functional consultants developed application systems while technical consultants supported their functional colleagues in the technical aspects of application development. Technical consultants were the experts on CICS, VM/CMS, IMS, ADABAS, UNIX, telecommunications, performance tuning, the technical feasibility of various proposed designs, and so on. They were largely uninvolved in developing application systems, playing a staff role to the functional consultants' line role. In particular (with the rare exception of applications based on sophisticated telecommunications networks or esoteric systems software), they did not represent significant components on a project's critical path.

Enter CASE Tools

With the growing sophistication of systems being demanded by clients, and the consequent increased system development time-frames and project costs, Beta management decided that local technical consultants should develop capabilities to support the project teams. At first, these capabilities comprised what came to be known as the technical architecture.[5] Senior managers in Beta realized that they could leverage their projects by allowing a few of the technical consultants to build the generic, technical foundation for all of a project's application programs, rather than have each functional consultant develop their own. They found they could avoid duplicated effort and the inevitable inconsistencies that arise when team members work in isolation. In this way, time was saved and the work was easier to correct, validate, and refine (thus improving the quality of the product). There was also less need for functional consultants to be technically knowledgeable before they could develop application systems.

This represents somewhat of a shift in the work performed by technical consultants on projects, changing from a purely advisory role to one that builds a substantial portion of the application system under development for the client. This technical architecture built by the technical team does not strictly constitute CASE tools, as it forms part of the client's application system rather than a technology owned by Beta. However, it clearly was its forerunner, as in practice it amounts to information technology that assists functional consultants' development work by eliminating their need to build complex technical procedures in their programs.

In the early 1980s, the idea of fully-fledged CASE tools, in-house technology dedicated to supporting systems developers, had taken hold in Beta and over time a number of different CASE tools were developed on separate Beta projects and quickly diffused throughout the firm. As CASE tools became more widely known throughout Beta, they began to be a common feature of all large system development projects, mediating many systems development practices. Concomitantly, the role of technical consultants on projects began to change. Not only were they responsible for providing technical advice and building the technical architecture, they were now also responsible for setting up, modifying, and maintaining Beta's CASE tools at each client site.[6]

Structural Changes Following CASE Tools

As the technical architecture and CASE tools became more critical to the systems development process, the technical team responsible for them began to play a pivotal role on each project. Reflecting this change in scope, the technical contingent on projects increased in size (from some five percent of the project team members to about twenty percent). The use of technical architectures and CASE tools radically changed the dependence relations of the project team. Whereas before, the functional consultants called on the technical team on an as-needed basis, now they had to rely on the technical consultants to set up the tools and the architecture before they could perform any substantive work. The technical team's installation of tools and building of the technical architecture had become key stages on the critical path of systems development projects. Further, the technical team had to become more intimately involved in analysis and design decisions. That is, the structure of the technical architecture and CASE tools were constraints on possible application designs, while the conceptual systems design influenced the content of the technical architecture and CASE tools implemented. The technical team began to assume more of a production role as opposed to its prior, purely support role, which had not involved any direct involvement in applications development work.

The division of labor on systems development projects had changed, with functional consultants relinquishing many technical tasks to the technical consultants, whose involvement in project activities had shifted from the periphery to the center. Accompanying the increased visibility and activity of the technical team had come increased responsibility and power as the functional team became heavily dependent on the technical team, whose activities facilitated their productive work.

MEDIATING THE MEANING OF STRUCTURAL CHANGE

Following the increased dependence of project teams on a technical infrastructure (technical architecture and CASE tools), project social relations became polarized around two very different perspectives: the technical and the functional. Each of these perspectives represents a separate subculture that has formed within Beta, reflecting different perceptions of and interactions with clients, project goals, and systems development activities in general. The strength of the polarization was surprising given the fairly strong and relatively homogeneous corporate culture that pervades Beta, but it adds support to Riley's (1983) contention that multiple subcultures develop even within a more overarching culture. The following discussion examines how the norms, orientations, and interests of the different subcultures mediated individuals' understanding of and actions towards CASE tools and each other.

Functional Subculture

Functional Perspective

Functional consultants perform the substantive work of Beta's systems development practice. They do not perceive themselves as "system developers," but as "business consultants" who develop functional solutions for client business problems through the medium of information technology. The medium is considered less important than the functionality that is provided. Infor-

mation technology is apprehended as the means through which valued ends are achieved, rather than an end in itself. Hence, the information technology used by functional consultants is valued for its instrumental contribution to their work. Their general stance towards human activity (Schein 1987, pp. 101–102) reflects a results orientation, that is, a focus on "doing" (achievement and accomplishment) rather than a focus on "being" (process and development). Their time orientation is the present and their context local. They concentrate their energies on building a system for the current situation and completing the immediate project. Their attitude towards information technology (both the CASE tools and the actual technology used to build client application systems) reflects their results orientation and instrumentalism; they objectify it. Thus, functional consultants, even though they use information technology as a raw material in their work—building and fashioning a system for clients out of an amalgam of hardware and software—appear to be unaware of, or to ignore, the often arbitrary and nontechnical aspects of information technology. They treat CASE as a neutral, abstract object, that facilitates rational and deliberate manipulation and that can be deployed across client contexts, application domains, and problem types.

Conflict Over Expertise

When local technical groups were first initiated within Beta and technical consultants joined project teams to provide technical advice, functional consultants appreciated the support and service they received from these "*backroom guys*,"[7] who resolved tricky technical issues in the systems being built, thereby helping functional consultants achieve their desired ends. The central role of the functional consultants as primary producers of application systems was not threatened or challenged. There was little felt dependence on the technical consultants, who kept a low profile and whose advice dealt with the information technology itself. The technical consultants did not in any substantial way shape the direction or content of work performed by functional consultants.

With the implementation of CASE tools on projects came a change in the responsibilities and role of technical consultants. Perceptions among functional consultants and relations between the technical and functional teams have been noticeably affected. The technical consultants are now seen to perform many development functions. They are no longer the *"technical gurus"* offering backstage advice; they have moved firmly into center stage, both in terms of the importance of their work to the project and in terms of the financial investment their work represents to Beta and its clients. The functional consultants feel somewhat upstaged and less in control of the exigencies of their work. The activities of the technical consultants are now on the critical path of the project, so they directly influence and constrain the work of functional consultants. Functional consultants are acutely aware of their dependence on the technical team, whose tools and technical architecture they are required to employ. A functional manager commented on the change.

> The technical team had no formal role on the team before tools. They did technical advising and resolved technical issues. Now they are the key part of the project, building and running the engine that everyone works off.

There is resentment that the technical consultants no longer provide support to the functional consultants, who still regard themselves as the main actors. Technical consultants are perceived as having *"stolen the show"* and *"doing their own thing,"* with little or no regard for the needs or activities of the functional players. A functional consultant expressed the sense of abandonment generally felt by the functional team.

> Now (after CASE tools were introduced) there is a distinct lack of communication between the technical and functional teams, because we have mutually exclusive tasks and motivations. Before we worked on the same thing. Their focus was on providing technical support and expertise as needed and demanded by us, the functional team. They provided a service; they were the internal

consultants. Now they produce a product, the program shells and the bridges, and they are less concerned with support. There has been a big change in roles between the two teams. The onus for solving technical problems is now a functional responsibility. The technical team feel they have other things to do than support us. But we feel they are there to support us. . . . There is a concern that they are getting too caught up in the design, that they may dictate the design. It is important that the tech team assume an advisory role and not drive the design.

Such different perceptions indicate that functional and technical consultants have well-defined yet opposing expectations of each others' roles and responsibilities, resulting in conflict over expertise and the bounds of legitimate action. A subtle territorialism has emerged within Beta which is manifest in the stereotyping and subcultural activities engaged in by the groups of consultants.

Stereotyping the Technical Consultants

There is a deeply felt sense among the functional team that the technical consultants are just interested in the technology and in *"hacking"* the most elegant design or code without regard for what support the functional teams needs, or when. One functional consultant commented on the technical team's attitude by noting:

> The technical team should rely more on the functional team than they do. They have their own ideas and don't want to know the functional story. They are not open to criticism. They feel some ownership of the tools and so are very defensive. I guess that's human nature . . . they just don't want to know that their tools are defective or weak.

A lot of "finger pointing" is apparent, with each team using the other as a scapegoat when things go wrong. Typical comments from functional consultants about the technical team included:

> The technical team don't understand what we need. . . . They're the ivory tower. . . . They never give us what we want.

Stereotyping is rampant, as a functional manager explained.

> There really is an us-them mentality. The functional team view the technical team as restrictive, while the latter view the former as unrealistic in terms of budgets, efficiency, volumes.

Losing Autonomy

Functional consultants feel that they have lost autonomy by having to follow the dictates of the technical team and being forced to conform to the language of the CASE tools. In particular, now that systems development work consists primarily of interaction with CASE tools, the functional consultants' designs and code are subject to review by the technical team. This generates much resentment. A functional senior analyst's view is typical.

> Without the tech team we would never have made the CASE tools work.... But there is some resistance to their presence. When one of them would ask us to change the name of something, we'd resent it. Who are they to tell us what to do?

With the CASE tools mediating systems development activities, many of the tasks previously handled by analysts are now automated. For example, screens and reports are "ergonomically" designed by the tools on receipt of the data items to be displayed and up to 75 percent of the program code for standard, transaction processing systems is generated by the tools on receipt of a few customizing parameters. Functional consultants no longer engage in many detailed design and implementation processes. They resent being excluded from decisions which directly impact the form and functioning of the application systems they are constructing for clients. In particular, the functional consultants object to the technical team developing and installing technical architecture and CASE tools without consulting them, taking exception to having to use technology they did not help design. While some of this resentment may have existed before the onset of tools with the systems software that functional consultants used, this software was typically perceived as "in the

background," and hence as dissociated from application work. CASE tools, however, directly confront the functional consultants in the performance of their work, being very much in the "foreground" of systems development work, mediating almost everything the functional team does. A functional consultant commented on the resentment that he and his peers feel towards what they perceive as elitism among the technical consultants.

> Tools have developed a tech team of egotists, who feel they have all the knowledge, and that the more they can keep hidden from us, the more knowledge and power they have and can keep.

Asserting Control

The loss of autonomy that the functional analysts feel relative to the technical team frustrates their ambitions to get the job done. The frustration and tension can sometimes lead to rebellious action, to a defiance of Beta's norms that require team play, cooperation, and conformity. A number of functional consultants described resorting to sabotage of the CASE tools in order to reassert their sense of control. For example, on a particularly technically complex project with many CASE tools rigidly enforced by the technical team, the control over systems development work was so effective that, as one functional manager stated,

> [It] drove people on the functional team to break the tools right and left. As soon as things started going wrong with the tools, we circumvented them so that we could get on with our work.

A functional consultant recounted a similar tale on another project. His story is worth citing in full.

> On this project, the tech team had set up two kinds of ids to use the system. The one was a technical or powerful id which allowed you to romp around in the operating system, create files, etc. The other was an id for the functional people, for the coders, which only gave you access to the coding panel (a menu of options to use the CASE tools) where you could only edit or browse files, compile programs, print program listings, and you could not test some programs, look at some files, or create new files. So

we were very restricted functionally, and we found this extremely limiting to our work. But the tools were often causing a lot of unnecessary work. For example, they would time and date stamp the object modules when they were compiled and the test data when they were generated. And these time and date stamps were often out of sync. And if they were out of sync the tools wouldn't let you do anything like use the data to run an object module, so we would have to run to the tech team each time so they could fix things up. The tech team was reluctant to give us technical ids or their passwords so we could use their ids and fix up things ourselves. They thought we'd wreak havoc. But somehow technical passwords were gotten hold of. Some people looked over the tech consultants' shoulders; I had a friend on the tech team so I could get hold of his. And we used these powerful ids to go into the system and we changed our own ids to give us more power, so we had greater functional capability. And we could get on with our work. Of course when all this came out, a big political stink blew up. We were told we weren't team players. But eventually we convinced the tech team that we needed to manipulate a little more of the files. In the end they created a three-tiered system, with those who were fully technical like the tech team having all access, some who were semi-technical like us, who did functional work but needed to sometimes go around the tools, and then the fully functional types like coders who only did application work and only used the coding panels.

So a partial victory had been won for the functional consultants who forced the technical team to give them more computer capability, but the access given was very much on the technical team's terms. The technical consultants managed to regain the control that had been temporarily usurped. They did not give the functional team more powerful ids, which would have given the functional consultants control over when and how to use or bypass the tools. Instead the technical team modified the functional consultants' coding panels so that for a few simple functions the functional consultants could exit the tools to do a few restricted actions outside the realm of the tools. However, this only allowed them to do a little more than they were able to do before their revolt.

More importantly it did not give them the option to choose when and how to use the tools.

Rebellions such as these are not common within Beta. The strong corporate culture and ideology of teamwork discourages dissension among the functional consultants, who are concerned with personal career advancement and do not want to be labeled as "troublemakers." However, when rebellious action by functional consultants does occur, it is particularly revealing. On the one hand, it indicates how frustrating task restrictions can be to people with the appropriate expertise who realize that things could be done differently. On the other hand, it demonstrates that, socialization, corporate culture, and career ambitions notwithstanding, individuals can and do act in ways that undermine mechanisms of organizational control.

Technical Subculture

Technical Perspective
Technical consultants are typically attracted to Beta because of their dual interest in technology and business. For their first few years in the firm, however, business interests play a secondary role, as the specialization of roles on projects demands that they focus on technology. Most technical consultants are more than happy to oblige. While they acknowledge that the purpose of projects is to solve functional problems, they welcome the opportunity to concentrate exclusively on the computer medium and leave the business details to their functional counterparts. Many see the technology as the means through which they can express and display their creativity and a way for them to learn new technical skills which are highly prized (among their peers and in the larger "hacker" occupational culture to which they feel some affiliation). In this sense, exploiting the technology becomes an end in itself. Technical consultants are process oriented, intent on action rather than results. Information technology is more than just instrumentally important to the technical consultants in the execution of their tasks. It carries motivational significance as well. Technical

consultants are less focused on the immediate client problem and more interested in finding a unique and elegant solution to the technical problems at hand. While their time orientation is somewhat in the present, it also tends to look beyond the current project to a more abstract, timeless level where technical architectures and CASE tools are perfectible according to some absolute criteria. Technical consultants commonly rationalize why they spend inordinate amounts of time recreating a routine or macro by claiming that their products will be reused on future Beta projects in other clients' sites. Hence (they argue) their work transcends present-time and client-specific boundaries. That such reuse is not commonly realized in practice seems of little consequence to their motivation.

The context of technical consultants' work is defined by the particular hardware and software configuration of the current client's installation. While this context is specific to projects, it is stripped of social or functional content by the technical consultants' exclusive emphasis on the technology. Their attitude towards information technology reflects their greater involvement in process: the technology (both CASE tools and the information technology used to build application systems) is created and manipulated, and hence is not objectified. It is not perceived as a tool for getting their work done, but rather as constituting the arena on which their work is played out.

Akin to their functional counterparts, technical consultants do not see themselves as system developers. While they do subscribe to the "consultant" image, they augment this with a constant reference to their status as technical innovators. This self-image allows them to differentiate themselves from the other team members. One technical senior analyst noted,

> The contribution of technical people to Beta is that we are crusaders. We find out all the neat things done in the labs and we figure out how to import these into our monolithic development environment and procedures.

An aspect of Beta that helps to keep the technical analysts motivated is their participation in a strong and active technical community. Part of this community is tied to the computer "hacker" culture beyond Beta (Turkle 1984) with which the technical consultants identify. Technical consultants pride themselves on being creative, which explains their dislike for the functional consultants' preoccupation with getting the application *"out the door."* Technical consultants are heavily involved with the technology and they can often avoid interacting with their colleagues and users if they wish. A technical senior analyst remarked:

> I prefer to just do the technical stuff. I get quicker feedback that way. You do something and then when you're finished it goes away. You don't have users coming back all the time with changes.

There is a strong identification with being special and different from the rest of the consultants in Beta. One technical manager remarked:

> All the technical people are so arrogant. We are the spoilt rotten brats in Beta. We're told we are so wonderful and we tend to believe it. We think functional work is so easy anyone can do it.

One means through which technical consultants reinforce their difference is by maintaining their own internal communication system. One of the local technical groups publishes a regular newsletter, *The Technical Times,* which is distributed to all technical consultants in Beta and which contains reprints of topical articles,[8] transcripts of presentations given at Beta meetings, and some notes by senior technical managers. Another way of sustaining the technical culture is through monthly local technical group meetings, which usually comprise presentations of the latest technology, research and design innovations so as to keep the technical consultants technologically stimulated. One such meeting, for example, spanned a whole day and was devoted to the latest user interface technologies, with a number of vendors bringing in their products and giving hands-on demonstrations.

Interspersed among the demonstrations were presentations by guest speakers and in-house personnel on issues in ergonomic design and the dimensions of the person-machine interface. Such meetings and communications serve to strengthen the shared meanings, values, and norms of the technical subculture, as well as providing a forum in which to transmit and reinforce such shared meanings and interests. The result is a reaffirmation of technical consultants as special and different from the rest of the consultants in the organization. This subculture identity in turn helps to sustain the polarization of consultants on the project teams.

Discounting the Functional Consultants

The technical consultants tend to stereotype other team members (whether functional consultants or client data processing personnel) as "tool users" and hence as having little understanding of the information technology underlying the tools. This allows the technical consultants to rationalize their need to hide the tools from these "*user types.*" On projects, the status of actors in Beta and client organizational hierarchies is less important than actors' ability to wield technical control. On one project, for example, a junior technical consultant, who had been with Beta for barely a year, was able to limit the discretion of functional consultants (two and three years his senior) and client data processing personnel (with five to eight years technical experience) through his authorization of their CASE tool user profiles. His attitude is evident in this rationále he gave for restricting the computer capability of other team members.

> You show them *[the non-technical members of the team]* the functions of the tool gradually, not all at once, as you want to get them going as fast as possible. So you don't show them things they won't need, or things that are too complicated as you don't want to confuse them. So the principle is show them as little as possible.

In other circumstances, this technical consultant's approach might be taken as evidence of a careful

teacher who does not want to overwhelm his/her students. However, on this particular project, all the functional team members and client data processing personnel were technically experienced. It seems that the technical team's world-view engenders a perception of other team members as necessarily incompetent without tools. The consultant's attitude is typical of most technical consultants, whatever the reality of their functional team's experience and knowledge.

This dim view of their functional contemporaries is, however, becoming a self-fulfilling prophecy. The functional consultants' lack of exposure to technical issues coupled with Beta providing little technical training to new recruits is creating a growing pool of technically illiterate functional consultants. This has the desired effect of increasing the use of CASE tools on projects (hence increasing Beta's project leveraging factor) while reinforcing the functional team's dependence on the technical team. It also has an unanticipated consequence, as it requires technical consultants to be responsive to the now more-dependent functional consultants. Technical consultants find themselves performing technical support tasks (repairing databases, installing new versions of tools, creating backup copies of software and data, training tool users, and answering technical questions) when they would prefer to be building advanced and complex technical routines. A technical manager remarked:

> With the tools and technical architecture we completely hide CICS and DB2 from the programmers, and can get incredible productivity from them. But we also get uneducated programmers, who can't handle the smallest technical problem, and at the first sign of trouble they go screaming for the tech team.

Resisting the Results Orientation

Notwithstanding the extensive control that technical consultants have over the conditions under which the functional team operates, the inherent results orientation of the Beta culture causes much frustration among technical consultants. For technical consultants, Beta's results orientation is a major restriction on their creativity and a constraint on their ability to refine the technical infrastructure they construct and maintain. They feel that a results orientation is myopic and that such a short-term strategy inhibits the development of good technical solutions. Given the dependence of the whole team on the CASE tools, the technical team's mandate is to get the tools operational on the current computer environment as soon as possible, in any way possible. But this does not allow sufficient time for technical consultants to develop the smart, elegant solutions they would like to. A technical consultants commented that

> The budgetary restrictions on the project cause problems in scope; they force a narrow view on the tech team. This is frustrating for us, the technical team, as we see and know what should be done to improve, refine, and generalize the tools we carry around from project to project, but we can't do that. . . . So it is frustrating for the technical types who may have great ideas, but who don't have the time to develop or implement them.

It is interesting to look at this issue of results orientation from the other side. A functional senior analyst felt that a belief in the *"technical fix"* pervaded Beta's technical consultants.

> There is a preoccupation with tools in Beta, particularly from the technical groups. They are always in search of the golden goose that will save time and money. But that's just too simple.

Another functional consultant remarked on technical team priorities.

> There is a feeling that they *[the technical consultants]* do not want to release stuff until it is perfect. . . . But right now we need basic transportation. And we would rather they give us something to walk with, and then they can enhance it later to give us a racing car.

The standoff between these two orientations reflects the functional interest in results and the technical interest in technological innovation. It is a conflict that has to be managed constantly and

the burden of this falls on the shoulders of the project managers, who must support their functional analysts in getting the project completed on time and within budget, but must also keep their technical analysts motivated to provide a reliable, efficient and useful system infrastructure.

Summary of CASE Tools Research Study

The deployment of CASE tools in Beta triggered structural changes within the project teams, which institutionalized the existing, formalized fragmentation of expertise into technical and functional groupings. Such a duality of interests, orientations, skills, and tasks on projects undermines the homogeneity of the Beta "team" ideology by breeding subcultures and territorialism. It results in tension and conflict on project teams that sometimes lead to eruptions. The functional consultants seem typically to lose out in these confrontations, as CASE tools are the stated policy of Beta, and the technical consultants, as implementors of this stated policy, have legitimacy and Beta's resources on their side. Rebellion by functional consultants is a way for them to reassert the autonomy they feel the technical team has usurped. In time, such resentment may diminish as new functional consultants enter Beta and take the presence of a powerful technical team for granted. Not being aware of the prior division of labor, and not having been exposed to projects where technical consultants were the "backroom guys," these functional consultants are unlikely to feel a loss of control, centrality, and territory.

The following section re-examines the findings described above by interpreting them in terms of a broader social theoretic framework so as to derive more general insight into relations between technical experts and functional workers around the deployment of information technology.

THEORETICAL INTERPRETATION

The introduction of CASE tools in information systems development can be understood as an instance of the more general phenomenon increasingly pervading contemporary organizations: the deployment of information technology in core production activities. In the particular instance of CASE tools in Beta, the production work being mediated by information technology is the development of information systems and the particular information technology being deployed is a set of capabilities that support/automate the activities of systems development. Recognizing this, the specific findings about social relations on project teams using CASE tools can be articulated in terms of the more generic organizational processes of which they are a microcosm.

The insight provided by this study pertains to changes in the division of labor and the relations of dependency on project teams following the introduction of CASE tools. This suggests that any substantial mediation of production work by information technology can be expected to lead to changes in the division of labor and patterns of dependency among the actors involved. Introducing information technology commits a production process to a technically complex infrastructure of hardware, software, and procedures that necessarily involves new forms of expertise. As a result, specialized skills are needed to ensure the reliable and effective mediation of production by information technology. At least two ways of providing these skills are possible.

1. If the existing production/functional personnel are able to adequately manipulate the information technology, they will be required to integrate technical skills into their work. In this case, functional workers also become technical experts and social relations among workers need not be disrupted (although disruptions may result from the role conflict, ambiguity, and overload that such an infusion of new tasks and skills could engender within individuals). While this may appear to be upskilling of work, in that the workers now acquire technical skills, it need not be. Job upskilling only occurs if the new skills increase the discretion and autonomy of the workers on their jobs. If the skills are required just so that workers can perform the same tasks they executed before (with the same level of autonomy), there has been no up-

skilling of work. It is important to note that the relationship posited here refers to work and not to workers. The processes of deskilling affecting jobs are not synonymous with those affecting individuals (Attewell 1985; Lee 1981). For example, while a particular task may be deskilled by being made simpler and more routine, the particular job incumbents may not be deskilled for they may now work at the more skilled aspects of the job, with the deskilled task being executed by a different set of workers (who may well find that their jobs have been upskilled).

2. Given the extreme specialization of roles commonly experienced in organizations, however, it is unlikely that functional workers will have the capability, resources, or inclination to develop and maintain the information technology that facilitates their daily work, end-user computing notwithstanding. As the demand for and supply of sophisticated and complex computer capability escalates in advanced industrial economies, it is probable that the information technology deployed in production work will be beyond the scope of the average end-user. In this case, functional workers will merely use the information technology, while outside expertise in the form of technical specialists will be imported into the production process to develop and maintain it. New technical expertise and new technology-management tasks are introduced into a given production process and the existing division of labor and patterns of dependency will certainly be affected, as evidenced in Beta's experiences.

In Beta's case, changes in tasks and expertise are reflected through changes in social relations among project team members. Rephrasing in more general terms, social relations among the key actors in the production arena will be affected as a consequence of deploying information technology in production. Power is a feature of all forms of social relations (Giddens 1976, p. 112), so that one of the ways in which the nature of change in social relations can be investigated is through studying shifts in power relations among key actors. Power is the means of getting things done and, as such, actors mobilize different resources that they bring to bear on their social interaction. It is through differential possession of and access to these resources that power is exercised. In the light of the findings presented above, it is expected that in the context of production work mediated by information technology, technical expertise and unrestricted access to information technology become significant resources around which power is mobilized. The study of Beta further demonstrates that CASE tools, as central elements in social interaction, generate conflict between functional and technical consultants on the project teams. Given differences among technical and functional workers in perceptions, interests, and work-pressures, the differential distribution of technical resources can be expected to lead to or accentuate social conflicts around any production process being mediated by information technology.

By deploying information technology in production, traditional bases of expertise and authority (hence power) in the existing production process are threatened. With the increased dependence on technical expertise, conflict arises between the newly arrived technical experts and the established functional workers whose expertise and authority is challenged and changed through the mediation of production work by information technology. How this conflict is played out across various production arenas remains open to empirical elaboration. The technical experts may triumph, institutionalizing their technocratic dominance, or production workers may reassert control through their continued resistance to the technical dependence that is now inherent in their computer-mediated production tasks. Different outcomes will be generated across different contexts and different outcomes may be generated over time within the same context. While such outcomes can never be predicted unequivocally, we can determine the likelihood of different patterns of response based on an understanding of contexts, actors, and resources. For example, it is expected that where production workers have established

legitimacy and influence—say they are accredited professionals (physicians or lawyers)—it is more likely that institutionalized bases of authority will persist, even in the face of information technology. On the other hand, where production workers have little credibility beyond the confines of their employing organization—as in the case of Beta's functional consultants—the infringement of authority by technical specialists is more probable.

In Beta, there was a shift of power to technical experts as prior, more established functional bases of power were undermined. While the technical consultants exercised considerable control over the circumstances under which functional consultants worked, their power was not inviolate. Functional consultants, as knowledgeable and capable agents, occasionally were able to recognize the constraints on their behavior and take action to subvert the power of the technical consultants. Thus, by refusing to conform to the tools and the "team" way of doing things, such functional workers reasserted their agency, underscoring the notion that power is always relational—not a static property of an individual or institution—and not only realized through social interaction (Giddens 1984). They also risked their status and job security. The message here is that, when provoked sufficiently, individuals can and do rebel against structural and technological imperatives.

The frequency with which "power struggles" occur, and the extent to which functional workers resist the conditions of the power asymmetry in their work context, will determine the amount of dominance technical experts amass. Where such resistance is weak or sporadic, the differential distribution of technical resources will be reproduced over time. Where technical experts are able to generate outcomes by affecting the conduct of functional workers—through the application of technical knowledge or manipulation of information technology—such reproduction will occur. Through their action or lack thereof, technical and functional actors thus recreate the conditions of their dependence relationship. In time, such power asymmetries become institutionalized into structures of domination. However—and this point must be stressed—such patterns of domination are not deterministic and where actors deliberately take action that challenges existing conditions and resource distributions, they have the potential to transform rather than reproduce the power asymmetry. While dissension was present at Beta, it was not sufficiently strong or organized enough to achieve transformation and, as was seen, the technical experts' dominance was sustained (at least for the time period examined by the current study). Notwithstanding this, it is possible that in the future within Beta, as CASE tools become more general, reliable and simple to use, the functional workers will lose their reliance on technical experts. This would attenuate the power of the technical experts as the value of resources will have eroded. The existing patterns of domination will in such circumstances not be reproduced and new social structures will emerge.

CONCLUSIONS

This paper has sketched out the ways in which social relations on project teams can be disrupted and changed as a consequence of deploying CASE tools. The findings suggest implications for practice as well as directions for future research. Practitioners introducing CASE tools into systems development efforts need to recognize that such implementation will affect social relations among project team members, reflecting the changes that result when any significant mediation of work by information technology is realized. Being sensitive to the potential disruption is an important first step in managing the changes that CASE tools will inevitably bring to the development process.

More research is needed to determine the conditions under which tensions between functional and technical project personnel may be mitigated and when they are exacerbated. Of particular interest is determining how systems development tasks are distributed among the three sets of

agents: application developers, tool facilitators, and the actual CASE tools. Little is known about the longevity of the disruptions and whether the territorialism, resentment, and rebellion are transitory or more deeply rooted disjunctures. There is some preliminary evidence for a generational effect, which leads to the speculation that as CASE tools become more fully part of the systems development "landscape," they will become more institutionalized, and systems developers will be socialized into taking them for granted. As such, tools may lose their potency as overt symbols of power and harbingers of territorial threat. Less conflict may result.

Changing the social relations around the systems development process, while clearly affecting the actors directly involved, will also likely affect the indirect actors—the users—who ultimately are the consumers of the final product. CASE tools are often touted as increasing user participation. How use of tools changes social relations between users and system developers, and across different levels of users, contexts, and time, are significant areas of future research. This study examined the use of CASE tools in a software consulting firm, but CASE tools are also being implemented with increasing rapidity in traditional data processing environments. While relations between tool users and tool facilitators in such environments are anticipated to resemble those discussed above, the unique practices of in-house systems development provide a set of dimensions that may alter the social relations affected by CASE tools. How the various shifts in system development tasks, responsibility, and authority—occasioned by CASE tools—are interpreted and acted on across different organizational contexts will require comparative investigations over time to determine how changes are institutionalized.

As production processes become mediated by information technology, new technical expertise is introduced into the production work. An important issue arising from this, not explored in the current discussion, concerns the management of the new expertise. Given that production work is central to the operation of an organizational unit, mediation of this work by information technology means that the expertise responsible for maintaining the integrity of that mediation is critical to the ongoing functioning of the unit. A key question here is how does the existing authority structure integrate the new forms of expertise without undermining its power?

In general, the social relations view used here to interpret the automation of systems development processes promises to be a useful perspective within which to understand the interdependent and dynamic social changes engendered by the deployment of information technology in organizations.

References

1. Agar, M. H. *The Professional Stranger,* New York: Academic Press, 1980.

2. Attewell, P. "The De-Skilling Controversy." Working Paper, Sociology Department, State University of New York, Stony Brook, New York, 1985.

3. Boland, R. J. "Control, Causality and Information Systems Requirements." *Accounting, Organizations and Society,* Volume 4, Number 4, 1979, pp. 259–272.

4. Carlyle, R. E. "Where Methodology Falls Short?" *Datamation,* Volume 34, December 1988, pp. 179–191.

5. Case, A. F. "Computer-Aided Software Engineering: Technology for Improving Software Development Productivity." *DataBase,* Fall 1985, pp. 35–43.

6. Freedman, D. H. "Programming without Tears." *High Technology,* April 1986, pp. 38–45.

7. Giddens, A. *The Constitution of Society: Outline of the Theory of Structure,* Berkeley, California: University of California Press, 1984.

8. Giddens, A. *New Rules of Sociological Method,* New York: Basic Books Inc., 1976.

9. Kling, R., and Scacchi, W. "The Web of Computing: Computer Technology as Social Organization." *Advances in Computers,* Volume 21, 1982, pp. 1–90.

10. Lee, D. J. "Skill, Craft and Class: A Theoretical Critique and a Critical Case." *Sociology,* February 1981, pp. 56–78.

11. Markus, M. L. "Power, Politics, and MIS Implementation." *Communications of the ACM,* Volume 26, 1983, pp. 430–444.

12. Orlikowski, W. J. *Information Technology and Post-Industrial Organizations: An Exploration of the Computer-Mediation of Production Work,* Unpublished Doctoral Dissertation, Stern School of Business, New York University, 1988.

13. Riley, P. "A Structurationist Account of Political Culture." *Administrative Science Quarterly,* Volume 28, 1983, pp. 347–414.

14. Schein, E. H. *Organizational Culture and Leadership.* San Francisco: Jossey-Bass, 1987.

15. Stamps, D. "Cranking Out Productivity." *Datamation,* July 1, 1987, pp. 55–58.

16. Turkle, S. *The Second Self: Computers and the Human Spirit,* New York: Simon & Schuster, 1984.

17. Van Maanen, J. "The Fact of Fiction in Organizational Ethnography." *Administrative Science Quarterly,* Volume 24, 1979, pp. 539–550.

18. Van Maanen, J. *Tales from the Field,* Chicago: University of Chicago Press, 1988.

19. Weick, K. E. "Theoretical Assumptions and Research Methodology Selection." In W. F. McFarlan, Editor, *The Information Systems Research Challenge,* Boston Massachusetts: Harvard Business School Press, 1984, pp. 111–132.

ENDNOTES

1. It is estimated that, in the U.S. to date, only seven or eight percent of information system workers have been exposed to CASE tools (Carlyle 1988).

2. Beta has a single career path with the stages junior analyst (two years), senior analyst (two years), junior manager (4 years), project manager (2 to 3 years), and senior project manager.

3. Functional expertise refers to knowledge of an industry, such as aerospace or banking, and knowledge of functional areas, such as production, marketing or sales. Technical expertise refers to knowledge of software products, such as operating systems or database management systems, and familiarity with various hardware platforms.

4. Development inefficiencies were due to misinterpretation, ambiguity, rework, and multiple, separate learning curves.

5. The technical architecture is that set of software modules common to most programs of an application system and which is typically technically complex (e.g., screen mapping, screen communication, database I/O, macros).

6. CASE tools in Beta emerged out of individual project endeavors and are not general enough to be fully portable across multiple environments. As each of Beta's clients has a unique hardware and software environment, the CASE tools have to be adapted at each client installation to fit the particular computer configuration at hand.

7. Comments in italics constitute statements made by Beta personnel during the field study.

8. A recent issue included, for example, the articles "The Rise of Techno-Nationalism" by Robert Reich reprinted from *The Atlantic* and "No Silver Bullet" by Fred Brooks Jr. reprinted from *IEEE Computer.*

Discussion Questions

1. Henderson and Cooprider's model identifies three broad types of technologies: Production, Coordination, and organizational. Vendors and early adopters of CASE technologies tended to focus almost exclusively on the Production aspects. Why might this be?

2. Kemerer cites several sources of conflicting estimates about the time required to successfully adopt and receive value from CASE tools. What factors could account for such differing estimates?

3. Orlikowski's article suggests some unanticipated downsides to CASE tool implementation. If you wanted to criticize the approach taken that developed these results, what arguments might you offer?

4. One of the impacts of CASE tools are the effects on project staffing. Of the two arguments for the impacts of CASE tools, de-skilling (the enforcement of constraints that limit creativity) or up-skilling (the elimination of the routine structured work by the tool, thereby freeing more time for the creative work), which do you find more persuasive?

Process Tools and their Adoption—Object Oriented Application

INTRODUCTION

The most recent major process tools to achieve widespread discussion are Object Oriented tools. This approach, which represents a radical departure from prior methods, has been cited as holding great promise to change the entire structure of software development and, in particular, greatly increase the level of software reuse, which is the subject of Chapter 10. Similar to Chapter 8 on CASE tools, the first article of this chapter introduces the technology, the second suggests its application or managerial potential, and the third illustrates issues in the tool's adoption.

The first article by Robert Fichman and Chris Kemerer describes a variety of proposed methods for Object Oriented analysis and design. A separate framework for describing these approaches is provided for both analysis and design. These matrices are then completed for a sample of Object Oriented approaches, but also for the previous generations of traditional approaches, specifically Modern Structured Analysis and Design and Information Engineering. This allows the reader with some familiarity with either of these previous

approaches to begin to understand how OO approaches differ. In addition, it suggests the ways in which organizations might best try to migrate to these new approaches.

The second article by Cox lays out the managerial promise of the OO approach. In it he describes how software development must undergo a change on the order of the change wrought by the original industrial revolution. In particular, he makes the analogy to the craft era of manufacturing, where individual components were hand made. He describes how that approach was overtaken by the industrial revolution, with its notion of mass-produced interchangeable parts. Much like the Chapter 1 article by Mary Shaw (which appeared in the same issue of *IEEE Software* as the Cox article), Cox argues that software development will also progress to this next stage, with substantial improvements in productivity, quality, and cycle times.

The final article, again by Fichman and Kemerer, provides a gentle introduction to the technology followed by an analysis of how likely and/or rapid such an evolution to an object-oriented assembly of software components would be. They combine theory from the traditional, organizational communication view of technology adoption with newer theory from the economics of technologies with increasing returns to adoption such as software process tools. They argue that widespread adoption of OO by in-house information systems departments is by no means easy or even obvious. However, they go on to suggest leading indicators that would show that OO is making significant progress on the way to becoming a dominant software process technology.

OBJECT-ORIENTED AND CONVENTIONAL ANALYSIS AND DESIGN METHODOLOGIES: COMPARISON AND CRITIQUE

Although the concepts underlying object-orientation as a programming discipline go back two decades, it's only in the last few years that object-oriented analysis (OOA) and object-oriented design (OOD) methodologies have begun to emerge. Object orientation certainly encompasses many novel concepts, and some have called it a new paradigm for software development. Yet, the question of whether object-oriented methodologies represents a radical change over such conventional methodologies as structured analysis remains a subject of much debate.

Yourdon has divided various object-oriented methodologists into two camps, *revolutionaries* and *synthesists*.[1] Revolutionaries believe that object orientation is a radical change that renders conventional methodologies and ways of thinking about design obsolete. Synthesists, by contrast, see object orientation as simply an accumulation of sound software engineering principles that adopters can graft onto their existing methodologies with relative ease.

On the side of the revolutionaries, Booch[2] states

Let there be no doubt that object-oriented design is fundamentally different from traditional structured design approaches: it requires a different way of thinking about decomposition, and it produces software architectures that are largely outside the realm of the structured design culture.

Coad and Yourdon[3] add

We have no doubt that one could arrive at the same results [as Coad and Yourdon's OOA methodology produces] using different methods; but it has also been our experience that the thinking process, the discovery process, and the communication between user and analyst are fundamentally different with OOA than with structured analysis.

On the side of the synthesists, Wasserman, Pircher, and Muller[4] take the position that their object-oriented structured design (OOSD) methodology is essentially an elaboration of structured design. They state that the "foundation of OOSD is structured design" and that structured design "includes most of the necessary concepts and notations" for OOSD. Page-Jones and Weiss[5] take a similar position in stating that

The problem is that object orientation has been widely touted as a revolutionary approach, a complete break with the past. This would be fascinating if it were true, but it isn't. Like most engineering developments, the object-oriented approach is a refinement of some of the best software engineering ideas of the past.

Article by Robert G. Fichman and Chris F. Kemerer. © 1993 IEEE. Reprinted, with permission, from (*IEEE Computer;* 25, 10, 20-39; Winter/1993).

Factors to Consider

One of the most important assessments a company must make in considering the adoption of a technical innovation is where the innovation falls on the incremental-radical continuum in relation to its own current practice. Incremental innovations introduce relatively minor changes to an existing process or product and reinforce the established competencies of adopting firms. Radical innovations are based on a different set of engineering and scientific principles, and draw on new technical and problem-solving skills.

If object-oriented analysis and design comes to be regarded as a radical change by most organizations, then a strong, negative impact on the ultimate rate of adoption of the technology can be expected. Compared with incremental change, implementation of radical change involves greater expense and risk, and requires different management strategies. Many development groups have already invested considerable resources in conventional methodologies like structured analysis/structured design or information engineering. These investments can take many forms, including training in the specifics of the methodology, acquisition of automated tools to support the methodology, and repositories of analysis and design models accumulated over the course of employing the methodology.

On an industry-wide level, vendors have been actively developing more powerful tools to support conventional methodologies, and a growing pool of expertise now exists in the use of these tools. To the extent that object orientation is a radical change, investments in conventional methodologies will be lost: Staff will have to be retrained, new tools will have to be purchased, and a likely expensive conversion process will be necessary.

Implementation of radically new technologies also involves a much greater element of risk because the full range of impacts is typically unknown. Moreover, the implementation of a radically new methodology requires different strategies to manage this risk and to overcome other implementation barriers (such as resistance to change).

The radical-versus-incremental debate is crucial to assessing the future of object orientation and formulating a transition strategy, but unfortunately no comprehensive analyses have been performed comparing leading object-oriented methodologies with conventional methodologies. Two surveys of object-oriented methodologies have been compiled, but these only cover either analysis[6] or design[7], and neither draws specific comparisons with conventional methodologies. Loy[8] provides an insightful commentary on the issue of conventional versus object-oriented methodologies, although no specific methodologies are compared.

The current research fills the gap left by other surveys by analyzing several leading conventional and object-oriented analysis and design methodologies, including a detailed point-by-point comparison of the kinds of modeling tools provided by each. A review (described below in greater detail) was performed that resulted in the selection of six analysis methodologies and five design methodologies. The analysis methodologies were

- DeMarco structured analysis,
- Yourdon modern structured analysis,
- Martin information engineering analysis,
- Bailin object-oriented requirements specification,
- Coad and Yourdon object-oriented analysis, and
- Shlaer and Mellor object-oriented analysis.

The design methodologies were

- Yourdon and Constantine structured design,
- Martin information engineering design,
- Wasserman et al. object-oriented structured design,
- Booch object-oriented design, and
- Wirfs-Brock et al. responsibility-driven design.

Incremental or Radical?

We conclude that the object-oriented analysis methodologies reviewed here represent a radical change over process-oriented methodologies such as DeMarco structured analysis but only an incremental change over data-oriented methodologies such as Martin information engineering. Process-oriented methodologies focus attention away from the inherent properties of objects during the modeling process and lead to a model of the problem domain that is orthogonal to the three essential principles of object orientation: encapsulation, classification of objects, and inheritance.

By contrast, data-oriented methodologies rely heavily on the same basic technique—information modeling—as each of the three OOA methodologies. The main differences between OOA and data-oriented conventional methodologies arise from the principle of encapsulation of data and behavior: OOA methodologies require that all operations be encapsulated within objects, while conventional methodologies permit operations to exist as subcomponents of disembodied processes. At the level of detail required during analysis, however, we conclude that expert information modelers will be able to learn and apply the principle of encapsulation without great difficulty.

Regarding design methodologies, we conclude that object-oriented design is a radical change from *both* process-oriented and data-oriented methodologies. The OOD methodologies we review here collectively model several important dimensions of a target system not addressed by conventional methodologies. These dimensions relate to the *detailed* definition of classes and inheritance, class and object relationships, encapsulated operations, and message connections. The need for adopters to acquire new competencies related to these dimensions, combined with Booch's uncontested observation that OOD uses a completely different structuring principle (based on object-oriented rather than function-oriented decomposition of system components), renders OOD as a radical change.

CONVENTIONAL METHODOLOGIES

A systems development methodology combines tools and techniques to guide the process of developing large-scale information systems. The evolution of modern methodologies began in the late 1960s with the development of the concept of a systems development life cycle (SDLC). Dramatic increases in hardware performance and the adoption of high-level languages had enabled much larger and more complicated systems to be built. The SDLC attempted to bring order to the development process, which had outgrown the ad hoc project control methods of the day, by decomposing the process into discrete project phases with "frozen" deliverables—formal documents—that served as the input to the next phase.

Structured Methodologies

The systems development life cycle concept gave developers a measure of control, but provided little help in improving the productivity and quality of analysis and design per se. Beginning in the 1970s, structured methodologies were developed to promote more effective analysis and more stable and maintainable designs. Early structured methodologies were largely *process-oriented,* with only a minor emphasis on modeling of entities and data. This emphasis on processes seemed natural, given the procedural programming languages and batch, file-based applications commonplace at the time. Although many authors contributed to the so-called structured revolution, our review concentrates on the critical contributions of Yourdon and Constantine[9], DeMarco[10], and Ward and Mellor[11].

Yourdon and Constantine structured design provided a method for developing a system architecture that conformed to the software engineering principles of modularity, loosely coupled modules, and module cohesion. The structure chart (see the sidebar, "Tools for structured methodologies") was the primary tool for modeling a system design. (Although the emphasis of structured design was on creating a module architecture, the methodology also suggested dataflow diagrams for modeling processes and hierarchy diagrams for defining data structure.)

DeMarco's seminal work enlarged the structured approach to encompass analysis. DeMarco

Tools for Structured Methodologies

Dataflow Diagram (DFD)—Depicts processes (shown as bubbles) and the flow of data between them (shown as directed arcs). DFDs are usually organized into a hierarchy of nested diagrams, where a bubble on one diagram maps to an entire diagram at the next lower level of detail. Does not depict conditional logic or flow of control between modules.

Data-Dictionary—A repository of definitions for data elements, files, and processes. A precursor to the more comprehensive "encyclopedias."

Entity-Relationship Diagram (ERD)—Depicts real-world entities (people, places, things, concepts) and the relationships between them. Various notations are used, but usually entities are portrayed as boxes and relationships as arcs, with different terminating symbols on the arcs to depict cardinality and whether the relationship is mandatory or optional.

Hierarchy Diagram—A simple diagram that shows a top-to-bottom hierarchical decomposition of data files and data items (enclosed within boxes) connected by undirected arcs.

Mini-Spec—A structured-English specification of the detailed procedural logic within a process; performs the same function as the traditional flowchart. A mini-spec is developed for each process at the lowest level of nesting in a set of DFDs.

State-Transition Diagram—Depicts the different possible states of a system or system component, and the events or messages that cause transitions between the states.

Structure Chart—Depicts the architecture of a system as a hierarchy of functions (boxes) arranged in a tree-like structure. Identifies interconnections between functions, and input and output parameters. Does not depict control structures like condition, sequence, iteration, or selection.

---

prescribed a series of steps for performing structured analysis, flowing from modeling of existing systems (using dataflow diagrams) to modeling of the system to be developed (using dataflow diagrams, mini-specifications, and a data dictionary). Although modeling of data was not ignored, the emphasis was on modeling processes. The ultimate goal of structured analysis and design was to create a top-down decomposition of the functions to be performed by the target system.

Continuing in the structured tradition, Ward and Mellor recommended significant extensions to structured analysis to better support modeling of real-time systems. Their methodology added entity-relationship diagrams and state-transition diagrams to the structured analysis toolset. Entity-

relationship diagrams illustrate the structure of entities and their interrelationships, while state-transition diagrams focus on system and subsystem states and the events that caused transitions between states.

In recognition of the evolution of systems, languages, and tools over the past two decades, Yourdon[12] updated structured analysis under the name *modern structured analysis*. Modern structured analysis differs from DeMarco's original work in several respects: It no longer recommends modeling of current implemented systems; it adds a preliminary phase to develop an "essential model" of the system; it substitutes a technique known as "event partitioning" for top-down functional decomposition as the preferred technique for constructing dataflow diagrams; it places more emphasis on information modeling (via entity-relationship diagrams) and behavior modeling (via state-transition diagrams); and it encourages prototyping.

These updates have served to blur somewhat the one-time clear distinctions between structured methods and the data-oriented methods that we describe next.

Information Engineering

In the late 1970s and early 1980s, planning and modeling of data began to take on a more central role in systems development, culminating in the development of data-oriented methodologies such as information engineering. The conceptual roots of data-oriented methodologies go back to the 1970s with the invention of the relational database model and entity-relationship modeling, although it took several years for mature data-oriented methodologies to emerge.

The data-oriented approach has two central assumptions:

1. Organizational data provides a more stable foundation for a system design than organizational procedures.

2. Data should be viewed as an organizational resource independent of the systems that (currently) process the data.

One outgrowth of the data-oriented approach was the creation of a new information systems subfunction, data administration, to help analyze, define, store, and control organizational data.

Martin[13] information engineering is a comprehensive methodology that extends the data-oriented approach across the entire development life cycle. While structured methods evolved backwards through the life cycle from programming, information engineering evolved forward through the life cycle from planning and analysis. Martin defines information engineering as consisting of four phases:

1. Information strategy planning,
2. Business area analysis,
3. System design, and
4. Construction

Information engineering distinguishes activities that are performed on the level of a business unit (planning and analysis) from those that are project-specific (design and construction). Compared with structured methods, information engineering recommends a much broader range of analysis techniques and modeling tools, including enterprise modeling, critical success-factors analysis, data modeling, process modeling, joint-requirements planning, joint-applications design, time-box methodology, and prototyping (see the sidebar, "Tools for Martin information engineering").

Information engineering describes planning as an organization-wide activity that develops an enterprise model and a high-level data architecture. Business area analysis attempts to capture a more detailed understanding of business activities and their interdependencies, using such tools as data-model diagrams, decomposition diagrams, process-dependency diagrams, and entity-process matrices. The design phase builds on the results of prior phases and produces a detailed model of a target system consisting of process-decomposition diagrams, process-dependency diagrams, dataflow diagrams, action diagrams, and data-structure diagrams. System construction, the last phase of information engineering, consists of translating the models from the design phase to an operational system—ideally using a code generator.

OBJECT-ORIENTED ANALYSIS METHODOLOGIES

As with traditional analysis, the primary goal of object-oriented analysis is the development of an accurate and complete representation of the problem domain. We conducted a literature search to identify well-documented, broadly representative OOA methodologies first published in book form or as detailed articles in refereed journals from 1980 to 1990. This search resulted in the selection of three methodologies from Coad and Yourdon[3], Bailin[14], and Shlaer and Mellor[15,16]. Numerous OOA methodologies have emerged in recent years. Since no more than a few methodologies could be

Tools for Martin Information Engineering

Action Diagram—Used to depict detailed procedural logic at a given level of detail (for example, at a system level or within individual modules). Similar to structured English, except graphical constructs are used to highlight various control structures (condition, sequence, iteration, and selection).

Bubble Chart—A low-level diagram used as an aide to normalization of relational tables. Shows attributes (depicted as bubbles) and the functional dependencies between them (depicted as directed arcs).

Dataflow Diagram (DFD)—Conforms to the conventional notation and usage for dataflow diagrams (see the sidebar, "Tools for structured methodologies").

Data-Model Diagram—Depicts data entities (boxes) and their relational connections (lines). Shows cardinality and whether the connections are optional or mandatory. Similar to the entity-relationship diagram.

Data-Structure Diagram—Shows data structures in a format appropriate to the database management system to be used for implementation.

Encyclopedia—A more comprehensive version of the data dictionary that serves as an integrated repository for modeling information from all development phases, including the enterprise model; organizational goals, critical success factors, strategies, and rules; data models and data definitions; process models and process definitions; and other design-related information. Automated support is assumed.

Enterprise Model—A model that defines, at a high level, the functional areas of an organization and the relationships between them. It consists of text descriptions of functions (usually an identifiable business unit such as a department) and processes (a repetitive, well-defined set of tasks that support a function).

Entity-Process Matrix—Cross-references entities to the processes that use them.

Process-Decomposition Diagram—A hierarchical chart that shows the breakdown of processes into progressively increasing detail. Similar to the conventional tree diagram, except a particularly compact notation is used to fir many levels on one page.

Process-Dependency Diagram—A diagram consisting of processes (depicted by bubbles) and labeled arcs. It shows how each process depends on the prior execution of other processes. Similar to a dataflow diagram, except conditional logic and flow of control is also depicted.

State-Transition Diagram—Conforms to the conventional notation and usage for state-transition diagrams (see the sidebar, "Tools for structured methodologies").

---

compared in depth, two criteria—maturity (first published prior to 1990) and form of publication (book or refereed journal)—were used to select among them. Several methodologies were identified that did not meet these criteria (see Fichman and Kemerer[17]) although this should not be taken to mean they are inferior to those that did. Object-oriented analysis is, of course, quite young; it is much too early to predict which (if any) of the current methodologies will come to be recognized as standard works in the field. The goal here is to provide a detailed comparison of representative methodologies at a single point in time, not a comprehensive review.

The three methodologies are presented in the order of their similarity to conventional methodologies. Bailin's methodology is viewed as most similar, followed by Coad and Yourdon's, and then Shlaer and Mellor's.

Bailin Object-Oriented Requirements Specification

Bailin developed object-oriented requirements specification (OOS) in response to a perceived incompatibility between conventional structured analysis and object-oriented design. Outwardly, the method resembles structured analysis in that a system decomposition is performed using a dataflow diagram-like notation. Yet, there is an important difference: Structured analysis specifies that functions should be grouped together only if they are "constituent steps in the execution of a higher level function," while OOS groups functions together only if they "operate on the same data abstraction[14]." In other words, functions cannot exist as part of disembodied processes, but must be subordinated to a single entity. (Bailin uses the term entity rather than object for stylistic reasons only; the terms are assumed to be interchangeable.) This restriction is used to promote encapsulation of functions and data.

Two distinctions are central to OOS. First, Bailin distinguishes between *entities,* which possess underlying states that can persist across repeated execution cycles, and *functions,* which exist solely to transform inputs to outputs and thus have no underlying states remembered between cycles. Entities can be further decomposed into subentities or functions, but functions can only be decomposed into subfunctions.

Second, Bailin distinguishes between two classes of entities, *active* and *passive*. Active entities perform operations (on themselves or other entities) important enough to be considered in detail during the

analysis phase, while passive entities are of lesser importance and can therefore be treated as a "black box" until the design phase. These distinctions are important because, as we show below, active entities, passive entities, and functions are each modeled differently during the analysis process.

The OOS methodology consists of a seven-step procedure:

1. *Identify key problem domain entities.* Draw dataflow diagrams and then designate objects that appear in process names as candidate entities.

2. *Distinguish between active and passive entities.* Distinguish between entities whose operations are significant in terms of describing system requirements (active entities) versus those whose detailed operations can be deferred until design (passive). Construct an entity-relationship diagram (ERD).

3. *Establish dataflows between active entities.* Construct the top-level (level 0) entity-dataflow diagram (EDFD). Designate each active entity as a process node and each passive entity as a dataflow or data store.

4. *Decompose entities (or functions) into subentities and/or functions.* This step is performed iteratively together with steps 5 and 6. Consider each active entity in the top-level EDFD and determine whether it is composed of lower level entities. Also consider what each entity does and designate these operations as functions. For each of the subentities identified, create a new EDFD and continue the decomposition process.

5. *Check for new entities.* At each stage of decomposition, consider whether any new entities are implied by the new functions that have been introduced and add them to the appropriate EDFD, reorganizing EDFDs as necessary.

6. *Group functions under new entities.* Identify all the functions performed by or on new entities. Change passive to active entities if necessary and reorganize EDFDs as appropriate.

7. *Assign entities to appropriate domains.* Assign each entity to some application domain, and create a set of ERDs, one for each domain.

The end result of OOS is an entity-relationship diagram, together with a hierarchy of entity-dataflow diagrams (see the sidebar "Tools for Bailin object-oriented requirements specification"). Bailin's methodology conforms to the essential principals of object orientation, although explicit object-oriented terminology is not used. (Loy[8] lists three principles that distinguish object orientation from other approaches: encapsulation of attributes, operations, and services within objects; classification of object abstractions; and inheritance of common attributes between classes.) The entity-relationship diagrams capture a classification of objects as well as opportunities for inheritance, and Bailin's functions map to the object-oriented concept of encapsulated services.

Coad and Yourdon Object-Oriented Analysis

Coad and Yourdon[3] view their OOA methodology as building "upon the best concepts from information modeling, object-oriented programming languages, and knowledge-based systems." OOA results in a five-layer model of the problem domain, where each layer builds on the previous layers. The layered model is constructed using a five-step procedure:

1. *Define objects and classes.* Look for structures, other systems, devices, events, roles, operational procedures, sites, and organizational units.

2. *Define structures.* Look for relationships between classes and represent them as either general-to-specific structures (for example, employee-to-sales manager) or whole-to-part structures (for example, car-to-engine).

3. *Define subject areas.* Examine top-level objects within whole-to-part hierarchies and mark these as candidate subject areas. Refine subject areas to minimize interdependencies between subjects.

4. *Define attributes.* Identify the atomic characteristics of objects as attributes of the object. Also look for associative relationships between objects and determine the cardinality of those relationships.

5. *Define services.* For each class and object, identify all the services it performs, either on its own behalf or for the benefit of other classes and objects.

The primary tools for Coad and Yourdon OOA are class and object diagrams and service charts (see the sidebar, "Tools for Coad and Yourdon object-oriented analysis"). The class and object diagram has five levels, which are built incrementally during each of the five analysis steps outlined above. Service charts, which are "much like a [traditional] flow chart," are used during the service definition phase to represent the internal logic of services." In addition, service charts portray state-dependent behavior such as preconditions and triggers (operations that are activated by the occurrence of a predefined event).

Coad and Yourdon explicitly support each of the essential principles of object orientation. The class

---

Tools for Bailin Object-Oriented Requirements Specification

Entity-Relationship Diagram—Conforms to the conventional notation and usage for entity-relationship diagrams (see the sidebar, "Tools for structured methodologies").

Entity-Dataflow Diagram (EDFD)—A variant on the conventional dataflow diagram wherein each process node contains either an active entity or some function related to an active entity, rather than disembodied processes. Active entities and functions are enclosed within bubbles. Bubbles are connected to each other and to data stores by labeled arcs containing dataflows. Dataflows and data stores are passive entities.

Entity Dictionary—A repository of entity names and descriptions, analogous to the data dictionary of DeMarco structured analysis.

Tools for Coad and Yourdon Object-Oriented Analysis

Class and Object Diagram—A complex diagram consisting of five layers, each adding a level of detail. The layers are (1) class and object layer, which shows classes and objects enclosed within boxes with rounded corners, (2) structures layer, which connects classes and objects with arcs to show generalization-specialization and whole-part inheritance relationships, (3) subjects layer, which adds a border around closely related classes, (4) attributes layer, which adds a list of attributes inside the class and object boxes and identifies associative relationships between objects, and (5) service layer, which adds a list of services inside the class and object boxes and provides arcs showing message connections between boxes.

Object-State Diagram—A simple diagram that shows all the possible states of an object and the allowed transitions between states. States are enclosed within boxes and transitions are represented as directed, unlabeled arcs between states.

Service Chart—A flowchart-like diagram that depicts the detailed logic within an individual service, including object-state changes that trigger or result from the service.

and objects diagram (levels 1, 2, and 4) provides an object classification and identifies potential inheritance relationships. In addition, encapsulation of objects is modeled through the concept of exclusive services. Coad and Yourdon OOA is similar to modern structured analysis (MSA) and information engineering in its emphasis on information modeling, but differs in providing constructs for modeling exclusive services and message connections.

Shlaer and Mellor Object-Oriented Analysis

Shlaer and Mellor developed their object-oriented analysis methodology over the course of several years of consulting practice in information modeling. Although information modeling forms the foundation of the method, two other views of the target system are prescribed as well: a state model and a process model. This three-way view of the system, contained in interrelated information, state, and process models, is proposed as a complete description of the problem domain. Shlaer and Mellor advocate a six-step procedure:

1. *Develop an information model.* This model consists of objects, attributes, relationships, and multiple-object constructions (based on is-a, is-part-of, and associative relationships). (The term object, as used by Shlaer and Mellor, is equivalent to the conventional notion of an entity, that is, a person, place, thing, or event that exists in the real world.)

2. *Define object life cycles.* The focus here is on analyzing the life cycle of each object (from creation through destruction) and formalizing the life cycle into a collection of states (some predefined condition of an object), events (signals that cause transitions from state to state), transition rules (which specify the allowable transitions between states), and actions (activities or operations that must be done by an object upon arrival in a state). This step also defines *timers,* mechanisms used by actions to generate a future event. The primary tool during this step is the state model. (See the sidebar, "Tools for Shlaer and Mellor object-oriented analysis.")

3. *Define the dynamics of relationships.* This step develops a state model for those relationships

Tools for Shlaer and Mellor Object-Oriented Analysis

Action-Dataflow Diagram (ADFD)—Similar to DFDs, except ADFDs are used to model elementary "action" processes rather than to create a top-down functional decomposition of the entire system. Standard DeMarco notation is used, except additional notations are provided to show control flows and to show conditionality in the execution of dataflows and control flows.

Domain Chart—A simple diagram that illustrates all domains relevant to the implementation of an OOA model. Domains are enclosed within bubbles and are connected by directed arcs. These arcs represent bridges between domains. Four types of domains are identified: application, service, architectural, and implementation.

Information Structure Diagram—A variant on the entity-relationship diagram that shows objects (boxes) connected by relationships (labeled arcs). Attributes are listed within object boxes. Relationship conditionality and multiplicity are also shown.

Object and Attribute Description—A text description of an object, including object name, object description, object identifier, a list of attributes, and descriptions of each attribute.

Object-Access Model—Shows the synchronous interactions between state models at the global system level. Synchronous interactions occur when one state model accesses the instance data of another object via an accessor process. State models (enclosed in ovals) are connected to each other by directed arcs labeled with the accessor process.

Object-Communication Model—Shows the asynchronous interactions between state models and external entities at the global system level. State models (enclosed in ovals) are connected to each other and to external entities (enclosed in boxes) by directed arcs labeled with communicating events.

Process Description—A narrative description of a process. A process description is needed for every process appearing on an action-dataflow diagram.

Relationship Specification—A text description of each relationship, including the name of the relationship (from the point of view of each object), conditionality (required or optional), multiplicity (one-to-one, one-to-many, many-to-many), a general description of the relationship, and identification of the attributes (foreign keys) through which the relationship is formalized.

State Model—State models conform to the conventional notation for state-transition diagrams (see the sidebar, "Tools for structured methodologies"), except they are used to model the states of problem domain entities. (Traditional STDs, by contrast, model the states of a system, system component, or process.)

Subsystem Access Model—Shows synchronous interactions between object-access models (one OAM exists for each subsystem). Directed, labeled arcs represent synchronous processes flowing between OAMs (enclosed in boxes).

Subsystem Communication Model—Shows asynchronous interactions between object-communication models (one OCM exists for each subsystem). Directed, labeled arcs represent asynchronous events flowing between OAMs (enclosed in boxes).

Subsystem Relationship Model—Shows relationships between information models (where each subsystem has exactly one information model). Information models (enclosed in boxes) are connected by undirected arcs (labeled with relationships).

between objects that evolve over time (dynamic relationships). For each dynamic relationship, an associative object is defined in the information model. Special assigner state models are defined for relationships in which there may be contention between object instances for resources of another object instance.

4. *Define system dynamics.* This step produces a model of time and control at the system level. An object-communication model (OCM) is developed to show asynchronous control (akin to simple message passing). An object-access model is developed to show synchronous control (instances where one object accesses the instance data of another through an accessor process). Shlaer and Mellor also describe a procedure for tracing threads of control at a high level (by following events on the OCM) and at a more detailed level (by creating a thread-of-control chart for individual actions).

5. *Develop process models.* For each action, an action-dataflow diagram is created that shows all of the processes for that action, and the data flows among the processes and data stores. (Standard DeMarco notation for DFDs is used, except additional notations are provided to show control flows and to show conditionality in the execution of dataflows and control flows.) OOA defines four types of processes (accessors, event generators, transformations, and tests) and provides guidelines for decomposing actions into these constituent processes.

6. *Define domains and subsystems.* For large problems, it can be useful to decompose the subject matter into conceptually distinct domains. Four types of domains are identified: application, service, architectural, and implementation. In addition, it is sometimes useful to decompose the application domain into multiple subsystems.

Shlaer and Mellor provide implicit, rather than explicit, support for the three essential principles of object orientation—classification, inheritance, and encapsulation. The objects and relationships contained in the information structure diagram, while not identical to object-oriented

concepts of classification and inheritance, can easily be mapped to these concepts during design. (Regular entities and parent entities engaged in is-a style relationships correspond to classes and superclasses, respectively, and identify candidate inheritance relationships. The is-part-of-style relationships correspond to whole-to-part class relationships.) The requirement that each action process (and associated dataflow diagram) be associated with exactly one object preserves encapsulation of those operations.

COMPARISON OF ANALYSIS METHODOLOGIES

The conventional and OOA methodologies reviewed here can be compared along 11 modeling dimensions; these dimensions represent the superset of dimensions supported by the individual methodologies (see Exhibit 1). Since the various methodologists tend to use widely divergent terminology and notations for similar concepts, Exhibit 1 presents the dimensions at a level that captures essential similarities and differences between the methodologies. We examined the concepts and notations advocated by each methodology in detail to determine those that were variants on the same basic idea. (For example, Coad and Yourdon's concept of a generalization-specialization relationship between objects is viewed as essentially the same as the is-a style or subtype/supertype entity relationships described in the other analysis methodologies. When used as part of an OOA methodology, generalization-specialization and is-a relationships are both intended to identify candidate opportunities for inheritance.)

Object-Oriented Versus Conventional Analysis

As Exhibit 1 shows, object-oriented analysis covers many of the same dimensions as Yourdon MSA and Martin information engineering, although there is a marked contrast between OOA and DeMarco structured analysis. MSA, information engineering, and all of the object-oriented methodologies provide a variety of tools for modeling

EXHIBIT 1   Comparison of Analysis Methodologies

Component	DeMarco Structured Analysis	Yourdon Modern Structured Analysis	Martin Information Engineering	Bailin Object-Oriented Requirements Specification	Coad and Yourdon Object-Oriented Analysis	Shlaer and Mellor Object-Oriented Analysis
1. Identification/ classification of entities*	Not supported	Entity-relationship diagram	Data-model diagram	Entity-relationship diagram	Class and objects diagram layer 1	Information-structure diagram
2. General-to-specific and whole-to-part entity-relationships	Not supported	Entity-relationship diagram	Data-model diagram	Entity-relationship diagram	Class and objects diagram layer 2	Information-structure diagram
3. Other entity-relationship (creates, uses, etc.)	Not supported	Entity-relationship diagram	Data-model diagram	Entity-relationship diagram	Class and objects diagram layer 4	Information-structure diagram
4. Attributes of entities	Data dictionary	Data dictionary	Bubble chart	Not supported	Class and objects diagram layer 4	Information-structure diagram
5. Large-scale model partitioning	Dataflow diagram	Event-partitioned dataflow diagram	Subject databases	Domain-partitioned entity-relationship diagrams	Class and objects diagram layer 3	Domain chart; subsystem communication, access, and relationship models
6. States and transitions**	Not supported	State-transition diagram	Not supported	Not supported	Object-state diagram; service chart	State model

entities. These include tools for defining entity relationships and attributes (see Exhibit 1, rows 1 through 4) and partitioning large models by grouping naturally related entities (row 5). MSA, Coad and Yourdon OOA, and Shlaer and Mellor OOA support modeling of states (row 6), although within MSA states are modeled at the level of a system or system component, while in the OOA methodologies states are modeled at the level of problem domain entities (objects). DeMarco structured analysis, MSA, Coad and Yourdon OOA, and Shlaer and Mellor OOA provide tools for defining the detailed logic within functions or services (row 7).

EXHIBIT 1   Comparison of Analysis Methodologies (*Cont.*)

Component	DeMarco Structured Analysis	Yourdon Modern Structured Analysis	Martin Information Engineering	Bailin Object-Oriented Requirements Specification	Coad and Yourdon Object-Oriented Analysis	Shlaer and Mellor Object-Oriented Analysis
7. Detailed logic for functions/ services	Mini-specification	Mini-specification	Not supported	Not supported	Service chart	Action dataflow diagram; process descriptions
8. Top-down decomposition of functions***	Dataflow diagram	Dataflow diagram	Process-decomposition diagram	Not Supported	Not supported	Not Supported
9. End-to-end processing sequences	Dataflow diagram	Dataflow diagram	Process-dependency diagram	Not supported	Not supported	Not supported
10. Identification of exclusive services	Not supported	Not supported	Not supported	Entity-dataflow diagram	Class and objects diagram layer 5	State model, action-data-flow diagram
11. Entity communication (via messages or events)	Not supported	Not supported	Not supported	Entity-dataflow diagram	Class and objects diagram layer 5	Object communication model; object-access model

*For stylistic reasons, the term entity, when it appears in this column, is intended to encompass the terms entity (as used in conventional methodologies and by Bailin), object (as used by Shlaer and Mellor), and class (as used by Coad and Yourdon).

**Conventional STDs as used in Yourdon's MSA describe the states of a system or system component, whereas Shlaer and Mellor's state model and Coad and Yourdon's object-state diagram describe the states of problem domain entities. STDs are not an integral part of information engineering because they are thought to be too detailed for the analysis phase, although Martin allows that they may be used occasionally.

***Bailin does provide some support for decomposition of functions via entity-dataflow diagrams, but functions are decomposed only at the lowest levels of the diagram rather than at all levels.

The most important differences between object-oriented and conventional analysis methodologies ultimately stem from the object-oriented requirement of encapsulated operations. Conventional methodologies provide tools to create a functional decomposition of operations (row 8) and to model end-to-end processing sequences (row 9). A functional decomposition of systems violates encapsulation because operations can directly access a multitude of different entities and are not subordinated to any one entity; so it is appropriate that no object-oriented methodology provides support here. It is less clear why none of the OOA methodologies as reviewed here provide an explicit model of end-to-end processing sequences, since there is no inherent incompatibility between this view of a system and object orientation. This issue is discussed further in the concluding section.

All the OOA methodologists recognize a need to develop some sort of model of system operations, albeit in a way that preserves encapsulation. As a result, each methodology provides new tools, or variants on conventional tools, for modeling operations as exclusive services of objects (row 10). Row 11 illustrates a further distinction between object-oriented and conventional analysis that arises from the need in object orientation for active communication between entities. (Entities communicate explicitly in an object-oriented system, whereas in a conventional system, entities are passive data stores manipulated by active, independent procedures.)

OOA Methodology Similarities

The three OOA methodologies illustrated in Exhibit 1 overlap significantly, although different notations and terminology are used for essentially the same concepts. These stylistic differences obscure the fact that, in each of the three methodologies, entities (objects) and relationships establish a foundation for later stages of analysis. Bailin uses a standard ERD notation, which includes the idea of subtype/supertype relationships, as well as any number of user-defined relationships. Shlaer and Mellor's information structure diagrams are similar in terms of content to ERDs. While neither of these methodologies specifically mentions such object-oriented notions as inheritance and object classification, ERDs do, in fact, capture candidate instances of these sorts of relationships using subtype/supertype constructs.

Dynamic entity connections and using-style relationships are also captured in ERDs through such relationship types as creates, destroys, uses, and modifies. Unlike the other two methodologies, Coad and Yourdon refer explicitly to object-oriented concepts such as inheritance and object de-

composition. Nonetheless, layers 1, 2, and 4 of the class and objects diagram can easily be mapped to an ERD notation, and these three layers serve essentially the same purpose as an ERD. (The objects and classes identified in level 1 map to the ERD concept of an entity. The generalization-specialization relationships defined in level 2 correspond to subtype/supertype relationships in an ERD. The wholepart structures defined in level 2 and the associative relationships identified in layer 4 correspond to general relationships in an ERD.)

OOA Methodology Differences

The clearest differences between the methodologies occur in three areas:

1. depiction of entity states,
2. definition of exclusive services, and
3. attention to attribute modeling.

Shlaer and Mellor place the most emphasis on modeling entity states and devote an entire phase of their methodology to defining entity life cycles and depicting them in state models. Coad and Yourdon also model entity states, although this does not appear to be a significant component of the methodology. (Coad and Yourdon's service chart contains much of the same information as Shlaer and Mellor's state model, although it also contains procedural logic unrelated to entity states and transitions. Coad and Yourdon recommend the use of an object-state diagram where helpful, but this diagram does not explicitly name the events that trigger transitions. The object-state model is referred to only sparingly, and does not appear to be a significant component of the final system model.) Bailin has no formal means of depicting entity states and transitions, although he notes that state-transition diagrams are being considered as one possible extension of the method.

Coad and Yourdon and Shlaer and Mellor provide the most detailed representations of exclusive services. In Coad and Yourdon, exclusive services are assigned to objects in layer 5 of the class and objects diagram, and the procedural logic contained in each service is defined in detail in an associated service chart. Shlaer and Mellor also identify exclusive services, which they term *actions*. Actions are identified on state models (object specific) and are defined in detail in the action-dataflow diagram (ADFD) and corresponding process descriptions. The primary tool for modeling Bailin's functions—the entity-dataflow diagram—contains much less detail than Coad and Yourdon's service chart or Shlaer and Mellor's ADFD with process descriptions.

The methodologies differ substantially in their level of attention to attribute modeling. Bailin places a very low emphasis on defining attributes of entities; in fact, he makes no mention of attribute modeling at all. Coad and Yourdon devote a phase to identifying attributes, although not to the extent of ensuring that attributes are normalized within entities. Shlaer and Mellor provide the most emphasis on attribute modeling of the three methodologies, including extensive guidance for describing and normalizing attributes.

Finally, Shlaer and Mellor support some concepts not addressed by Coad and Yourdon or Bailin. These include

1. a distinction between asynchronous and synchronous control,
2. the use of timers to generate future events, and
3. the concept of a dynamic relationship and its role in handling contention between concurrent processes.

OOA: Incremental Versus Radical Change

With regard to the incremental versus radical debate, object-oriented analysis does represent a radical departure from older process-oriented methodologies such as DeMarco structured analysis, but is only an incremental change from data-oriented methodologies like Martin information engineering. Exhibit 1 shows that OOA methodologies typically model six dimensions of the problem domain not contained in a structured analysis model (see rows 1-3, 6, 10-11) and do not model two process-oriented dimensions (rows 8-9)

that form the foundation of a DeMarco structured analysis model. OOA decomposes the problem domain based on a classification of entities (objects) and their relationships, while structured analysis provides a decomposition based on processes. Developers schooled in DeMarco structured analysis will find the competencies they developed in the construction of hierarchies of DFDs to be, for the most part, irrelevant. Meanwhile, a whole new set of competencies relating to the classification and modeling of entities will have to be developed.

The revolutionaries quoted in the introduction rightly observe that object orientation is fundamentally at odds with the process-oriented view of systems favored by structured methodologies during the 1970s. However, they ignore important changes in these same methodologies over the course of the 1980s towards a more balanced view of data and processes. OOA methodologies only model two dimensions of the problem domain not modeled by Yourdon MSA or Martin information engineering (see Exhibit 1, rows 10-11).

All the OOA methodologies reviewed here contain a heavy information modeling component, and potential adopters with a strong information modeling background should require only limited exposure to absorb the notational differences between conventional information modeling diagrams and the variants developed by OOA methodologists. The idea of shifting from disembodied processes (modeled in dataflow diagrams) to encapsulated services will be more challenging. However, at the level of detail required for analysis, this conceptual shift can probably be absorbed without great difficulty. Shlaer and Mellor OOA, with its emphasis on modeling object life cycles, appears to represent the most significant change of the three OOA methodologies.

OBJECT-ORIENTED DESIGN METHODOLOGIES

Design is the process of mapping system requirements defined during analysis to an abstract representation of a specific system-based implementation, meeting cost and performance constraints. As was done with OOA methodologies, we conducted a literature search to identify broadly representative OOD methodologies first published in book form or as detailed articles in refereed journals from 1980 to 1990. This resulted in the selection of three methodologies from Booch[2], Wasserman et al.[4], and Wirfs-Brock et al.[18] Implementation-specific methodologies, such as those targeted at real-time systems using the Ada language, were excluded from consideration.

We present the methodologies in an order based on their similarities to conventional methodologies. Wasserman et al. draws most heavily on structured design and is presented first, followed by Booch, and Wirfs-Brock et al.

Wasserman et al. Object-Oriented Structured Design

Object-oriented structured design (OOSD) was developed by Wasserman, Pircher, and Muller. The methodology provides a detailed notation for describing an *architectural design,* which they define as a high-level design that identifies individual modules but not their detailed internal representation. Wasserman et al. state that the overall goal of OOSD is to provide a standard design notation that can support every software design, including both object-oriented and conventional approaches.

OOSD offers a hybrid notation that incorporates concepts from previous work from several areas, including structure charts from structured design; Booch's notation for Ada packages and tasks; hierarchy and inheritance from object orientation; and the concept of monitors from concurrent programming. However, as Wasserman et al. observe, OOSD does not provide a detailed procedure for developing the design itself.

The primary tool for OOSD is the object-oriented structure chart (see the sidebar, "Tools for Wasserman et al. object-oriented structured design"). This chart takes the symbols and notations from conventional structure charts, including modules, data parameters, and control parameters, and adds notations for such object-oriented constructs as objects and classes (called "information clusters" by the authors), methods, instantiation, exception handling, generic definitions (similar to abstract classes), inheritance, and concurrency. Object-oriented structure charts can be used to show multiple inheritance, message passing, polymorphism, and dynamic binding. OOSD also supports the concept of a monitor, which is useful in depicting the asynchronous processes typically found in real-time systems.

Although OOSD is intended primarily for architectural design, the authors state that OOSD provides a foundation for representing design decisions associated with the physical design. The authors recommend that annotations be used to reflect the idiosyncrasies of individual implementation languages, while preserving the generic character of basic symbols. For example, OOSD includes optional Ada language-specific annotations to provide for packages, sequencing, and selective activation.

Tools for Wasserman et al. Object-Oriented Structured Design

Object-Oriented Structure Chart—An updated version of the classical structure chart that adds notations for objects and classes ("information clusters"), methods, visibility, instantiation, exception handling, hidden operations, generic definitions (abstract classes), inheritance, and concurrency. The charts can also be used to show multiple inheritance, message passing, polymorphism, dynamic binding, and asynchronous processes.

Booch Object-Oriented Design

Booch pioneered the field of object-oriented design. As originally defined in the early 1980s, Booch's methodology was Ada language specific, but it has been significantly expanded and generalized since then. Booch views his methodology as an alternative to, rather than an extension of, structured design.

Although Booch describes a host of techniques and tools to assist design, ranging from informal lists to formal diagrams and templates, he is reluctant to prescribe a fixed ordering of phases for object-oriented design. Rather, he recommends that analysts work iteratively and incrementally, augmenting formal diagrams with informal techniques as appropriate to the problem at hand. Nevertheless, Booch does delineate four major steps that must be performed during the course of OOD:

1. *Identify classes and objects.* Identify key abstractions in the problem space and label them as candidate classes and objects.

2. *Identify the semantics of classes and objects.* Establish the meaning of the classes and objects identified in the previous step using a variety of techniques, including creating "scripts" that define the life cycles of each object from creation to destruction.

3. *Identify relationships between classes and objects.* Establish class and object interactions, such as patterns of inheritance among classes and patterns of cooperation among objects. This step also captures visibility decisions among classes and objects.

4. *Implement classes and objects.* Construct detailed internal views of classes and objects, including definitions of their various behaviors (services). Also, allocate objects and classes to modules (as defined in the target language environment) and allocate programs to processors (where the target environment supports multiple processors).

The primary tools used during OOD are

- class diagrams and class templates (which emphasize class definitions and inheritance relationships);

- object diagrams and timing diagrams (which stress message definitions, visibility, and threads of control);
- state-transition diagrams (to model object states and transitions);
- operation templates (to capture definitions of services);
- module diagrams and templates (to capture physical design decisions about the assignment of objects and classes to modules); and
- process diagrams and templates (to assign modules to processors in situations where a multiprocessor configuration will be used).

(See the sidebar, "Tools for Booch object-oriented design.")

Booch OOD provides the widest variety of modeling tools of the OOD methodologies reviewed here. Although he does not prescribe a fixed sequence of design steps, Booch does provide a wealth of guidance on the design process by describing in detail the types of activities that must be performed and by working through the design of five hypothetical systems from different problem domains.

Wirfs-Brock et al. Responsibility-Driven Design

Wirfs-Brock, Wilkerson, and Wiener developed their responsibility-driven design (RDD) methodology during several years of internal software development experience in various corporate settings. RDD is based on a client-server model of computing in which systems are seen as being composed of collections of *servers* that hold private responsibilities and also render services to *clients* based on contracts that define the nature and scope of valid client-server interactions.

To map these terms to more conventional object-oriented terminology, clients and servers are different kinds of objects, while services and responsibilities correspond to methods. Contracts and collaborations are metaphors for the idea that, to preserve encapsulation, some objects must be willing to perform certain tasks (such as modify-

Tools for Booch Object-Oriented Design

Class Diagram/Template—Shows the existence of classes (enclosed in dotted-line "clouds") and their relationships (depicted by various kinds of directed and undirected arcs) in the logical design of a system. Relationships supported include uses, instantiates, inherits, metaclass, and undefined.

Module Diagram/Template—Documents the allocation of objects and classes to modules in the physical design of a system. Only needed for languages (such as Ada) that support the idea of a module as distinct from objects and classes.

Object Diagram/Template—Used to model some of dynamics of objects. Each object (enclosed in solid line "clouds") represents an arbitrary instance of a class. Objects are connected by directed arcs that define object visibility and message connections.

Does not show flow of control or ordering of events.

Operation Template—Structured text that provides detailed design documentation for operations.

Process Diagram/Template—Used to show the allocation of processes to processors in the physical design of a system. Only for implementations in multiprocessor environments.

State-Transition Diagram—Shows the states (depicted by circles) of a class, the events (directed arcs) that cause transitions from one state to another, and the actions that result from a state change.

Timing Diagram—A companion diagram to the object diagram, shows the flow of control and ordering of events among a group of collaborating objects.

---

ingthe values of their own internal variables) for the benefit of other objects, and that some kinds of services require several objects to work together to achieve the desired result.

Their methodology is responsibility driven because the focus of attention during design is on contracts between clients and server objects. These contracts spell out what actions each object is responsible for performing and what information each object is responsible for sharing. Wirfs-Brock et al. contrast their approach with what they term data-driven object-oriented design methodologies (they cite no specific authors), which are said to emphasize the design of data structures internal to objects and inheritance relationships based on common attributes. In contrast, the responsibility-

driven approach is intended to maximize the level of encapsulation in the resulting design. Data-driven design is said to focus more on classes and inheritance, while responsibility-driven design focuses more on object interactions and encapsulation.

Like Booch, Wirfs-Brock et al. recommend an incremental/iterative approach to design, as opposed to rigid phases with fixed deliverables. RDD provides for a six-step procedure spread across two phases. An exploration phase finds candidate classes, responsibilities, and collaborations. A second analysis phase builds hierarchies, defines subsystems, and defines protocols. The steps are

1. *Find classes.* Extract noun phrases from the requirements specification and build a list of candidate classes by looking for nouns that refer to physical objects, conceptual entities, categories of objects, and external interfaces. Attributes of objects and candidate superclasses are also identified.

2. *Find responsibilities and assign to classes.* Consider the purpose of each class and examine the specification for action phrases to find candidate responsibilities. Assign responsibilities to classes such that system intelligence is evenly distributed, behaviors reside with related information, and responsibilities are shared among related classes.

3. *Find collaborations.* Examine responsibilities associated with each class and consider which other classes are needed for collaboration to fulfill each responsibility.

4. *Define hierarchies.* Construct class hierarchies for kind-of-inheritance relationships such that common responsibilities are factored as high as possible and abstract classes do not inherit from concrete classes. Construct contracts by grouping together responsibilities used by the same clients.

5. *Define subsystems.* Draw a collaborations graph for the complete system. Look for frequent and complex collaborations and identify these as candidate subsystems. Classes within a subsystem should support a small and strongly cohesive set of responsibilities and should be strongly interdependent.

6. *Define protocols.* Develop design detail by writing design specifications for classes, subsystems, and contracts. Construct the protocols for each class (the signatures for the messages to which each class responds).

Tools used throughout the design process include

- Class cards (steps 1, 2 and 3);
- Hierarchy diagrams (step 4);
- Venn diagrams (step 4);
- Collaborations graphs (steps 4 and 5);
- Subsystem cards (step 5);
- Class specifications (step 6); and
- Subsystem specifications (step 6).

(See the sidebar, "Tools for Wirfs-Brock et al. responsibility-driven design.")

In advocating an approach that emphasizes the dynamic behavior and responsibilities of objects rather than their static class relationships, RDD provides a significant contrast to Booch OOD and to the OOA methodologies reviewed earlier. Unlike these other methodologies, the initial steps of RDD do not focus on establishing a hierarchy of classes, but rather attempt to construct a close simulation of object behaviors and interactions.

COMPARISON OF DESIGN METHODOLOGIES

Object-Oriented Design Versus Conventional Design

The distinctions between conventional and object-oriented development, some of which were identified in the discussion of analysis methodologies, are amplified during design due to the growing importance of implementation-specific issues (see Exhibit 2). None of the conventional methodologies support the definition of classes, inheritance, methods, or message protocols, and while it may not be necessary to consider these constructs explicitly during object-oriented analysis, they form the foundation of an object-oriented design (Exhibit 2, rows 6 through 10). In addition, while conventional and object-oriented methodologies both provide tools that define a hierarchy of modules (row 1), a completely different method of decomposition is employed, and the very definition of the term module is different.

In conventional systems, modules—such as programs, subroutines, and functions—only contain procedural code. In object-oriented systems, the object—a bundling of procedures and data—is the primary unit of modularity. Structured design and information engineering both use function-oriented decomposition rules, resulting in a set of procedure-oriented program modules. OOD methodologies, by contrast, employ an object-oriented decomposition resulting in collections of methods encapsulated within objects.

Tools for Wirfs-Brock et al. Responsibility-Driven Design

Class Cards—A physical card used to record text describing classes, including name, superclasses, subclasses, responsibilities, and collaborations.

Class Specification—An expanded version of the class card. Identifies superclasses, subclasses, hierarchy graphs, collaborations graphs. Also includes a general description of the class, and documents all of its contracts and methods.

Collaborations Graph—A diagram showing the classes, subsystems, and contracts within a system and the paths of collaboration between them. Classes are drawn as boxes. Subsystems are drawn as rounded-corner boxes enclosing multiple classes. Collaborations are directed arcs from one class to the contract of another class.

Hierarchy Diagram—A simple diagram that shows inheritance relationships in a lattice-like structure. Classes (enclosed within boxes) are connected by undirected arcs that represent an inheritance relationship. Superclasses appear above subclasses.

Subsystem card—A physical card used to record text describing subsystems, including name and a list of contracts.

Subsystem Specification—Contains the same information as a class specification, only at the level of a subsystem.

Venn Diagram—Used to show the overlap of responsibilities between classes to help identify opportunities to create abstract superclasses. Classes are depicted as intersecting ellipses.

The greatest overlap between conventional and object-oriented design methodologies is between Booch OOD and information engineering. Both methodologies provide a tool for defining end-to-end processing sequences (row 4), although Booch's timing diagram contains much less detail than information engineering's data-dependency diagram. Both methodologies provide for a detailed definition of procedural logic.

Booch recommends the use of a generic program definition language (PDL) or structured English, while information engineering recommends the use of a graphical action diagram for this purpose. Finally, for information-intensive applications, Booch recommends that a normalization procedure be used for designing data. This normalization procedure is very similar to the one employed by information engineering.

OOD Methodology Differences

The most notable differences among the three OOD methodologies have to do with

1. data design,
2. level of detail in describing the process of OOD, and
3. level of detail provided by diagram notations.

Booch, as mentioned above, employs a detailed procedure (where appropriate) for designing the data encapsulated within objects. In fact, Booch[2] sees many parallels between database design and OOD:

> In a process not unlike object-oriented design, database designers bounce between logical and physical design throughout the development of the database . . . The ways in which we describe the elements of a database are very similar to the ways

EXHIBIT 2 Comparison of Design Methodologies

Component	Yourdon and Constantine Structured Design	Martin Information Engineering	Wasserman et al. Object-Oriented Structured Design	Booch Object-Oriented Design	Wirfs-Brock et al. Responsibility-Driven Design
1. Hierarchy of modules (physical design)	Structure chart	Process-decomposition diagram	Object-oriented structure chart	Module diagram	*Not supported*
2. Data definitions	Hierarchy diagram	Data-model diagram; data-structure diagram	Object-oriented structure chart	Class diagram	Class specification
3. Procedural logic	*Not supported*	Action diagram	*Not supported*	Operation template	Class specification
4. End-to-end processing sequences	Dataflow diagram	Dataflow diagram; process-dependency diagram	*Not supported*	Timing diagrams	*Not supported*
5. Object states and transitions	*Not supported*	*Not supported*	*Not supported*	State-transition diagram	*Not supported*
6. Definition of classes and inheritance	*Not supported*	*Not supported*	Object-oriented structure chart	Class diagram	Hierarchy diagram
7. Other class relationships (instantiates, uses, etc.)	*Not supported*	*Not supported*	Object-oriented structure chart	Class diagram	Class specification
8. Assignment of operations/ services to classes	*Not supported*	*Not supported*	Object-oriented structure chart	Class diagram	Collaborations graph; class specification
9. Detailed definition of operations/ services	*Not supported*	*Not supported*	*Not supported*	Operations template	Class specification
10. Message connections	*Not supported*	*Not supported*	Object-oriented structure chart	Object diagram and template	Collaborations graph

in which we describe the key abstractions in an application using object-oriented design.

Wasserman et al. and Wirfs-Brock et al., by contrast, say little on the issue of data design or normalization.

Wirfs-Brock et al. provide a very thorough description of the design process, which they break into 26 identifiable design activities spread across six steps. Booch offers less in the way of explicit, step-wise design procedures, although he does provide a wealth of implicit guidance, using a detailed description of five hypothetical design projects. Wasserman et al., by contrast, assume that the particulars of an implementation environment will dictate what kinds of procedures and quality metrics are best; they do not offer a procedural description of OOSD.

Wasserman et al. and Booch both provide a comprehensive and rigorous set of notations for representing an object-oriented design. Wirfs-Brock et al. provide a less detailed notation in their RDD methodology, and do not address such concepts as persistence, object instantiation, and concurrent execution. The authors claim that RDD is appropriate for object-oriented and conventional development projects alike; this may explain the lack of attention to implementation issues that are more closely associated with object orientation.

OOD: Incremental Versus Radical Change

Regarding the incremental-versus-radical debate, object-oriented design is clearly a radical change from both process-oriented methodologies and data-oriented methodologies (Yourdon and Constantine structured design and Martin information engineering, respectively). Exhibit 2 shows that the number of modeling dimensions on which conventional and object-oriented methodologies overlap ranges from a maximum of four out of 10 (information engineering and Booch OOD) to as few as one out of 10 (structured design and Wirfs-Brock OOD). Although conventional methodologies such as information engineering support a data-oriented view in modeling the problem

domain during analysis, they use a function-oriented view in establishing the architecture of program modules during design. As a result, not only is the primary structuring principle for program code different—functions versus objects—but at least half of the specific dimensions of the target system model are different.

Object-oriented design requires a new set of competencies associated with constructing detailed definitions of classes and inheritance, class and object relationships, and object operations and message connections. The design tradeoffs between maximizing encapsulation (by emphasizing object responsibilities) versus maximizing inheritance (by emphasizing commonalties among classes) are subtle ones. Designing classes that are independent of the context in which they are used is required to maximize reuse, and here again, very subtle design decisions must be made[19]. As mentioned in the introduction, the important point is not whether object-oriented concepts are radically new in some absolute sense, but rather whether they are radically new to the population of potential adopters. The idea of building systems devoid of global-calling programs, where everything literally is defined as an object, will certainly be a radical concept to designers schooled in conventional design methodologies.

TRANSITION FROM ANALYSIS TO DESIGN

Analysis is usually defined as a process of extracting and codifying user requirements and establishing an accurate model of the problem domain. Design, by contrast, is the process of mapping requirements to a system implementation that conforms to desired cost, performance, and quality parameters. While these two activities are conceptually distinct, in practice the line between analysis and design is frequently blurred. Many of the components of an analysis model have direct counterparts in a design model. In addition, the process of design usually leads to a better understanding of requirements, and can uncover areas where a change in requirements must be negotiated to support desired performance and cost constraints. In recognition of these realities, most current methodologies recommend that analysis and design be performed iteratively, if not concurrently.

One of the frequently cited advantages of object orientation is that it provides a smoother translation between analysis and design models than do structured methodologies. It is true that no direct and obvious mapping exists between structured analysis and structured design:

> Anyone involved with [structured design] knows that the transition from the analysis model to the design model can be tricky. For example, in moving from a dataflow diagram view of the system to creating design-structure charts the modeler is forced to make a significant shift in perspective. There are strategies to assist in the matter (transform analysis, transaction analysis, etc.), but it remains a difficult task because the mapping is not truly isomorphic[6].

With object orientation, the mapping from analysis to design does appear to be potentially more isomorphic, as a comparison of Exhibits 1 and 2 reveals. Every analysis model component supported by at least one OOA methodology can be mapped to a similar (albeit usually more detailed) component supported by at least one design methodology. Rows 1-3, 4, 5, 6, 7, 10, and 11 in Exhibit 1 correspond to rows 6-7, 2, 1, 5, 9, 8 and 10 in Exhibit 2, respectively.

Only two object-oriented methodologists provided detailed procedures encompassing both analysis and design (Coad and Yourdon[20] and Rumbaugh et al.[21]). Shlaer and Mellor also briefly describe a procedure for translating OOA into OOD. Development groups that do not elect to adopt a single methodology spanning analysis and design will face the problem of matching up incompatible terminology and notations from different methodologists. The blurring between analysis and design is a particularly acute issue because the somewhat arbitrary line between analysis and design is drawn in different places by

different methodologists. Of the OOA methodologies, Coad and Yourdon's and Shlaer and Mellor's seem to encroach the most on design. Coad and Yourdon explicitly identify inheritance relationships (usually considered a design activity) and provide for a formal and detailed specification of the logic within services. Shlaer and Mellor provide for complete normalization of attributes and advocate detailed modeling of entity life cycles. Of the design methodologies reviewed here, Wirfs-Brock et al. RDD appears to encroach the most on analysis in that it assumes that only an English-language specification (rather than a full-analysis model) is the input to the methodology.

OVERALL CRITIQUE

Object-oriented methodologies are less mature than conventional methodologies, and may be expected to undergo a period of expansion and refinement as project experience uncovers gaps in modeling capabilities or misplaced assumptions. Three areas currently stand out as candidates for further development work. To begin with, a rigorous mechanism is needed for decomposing very large systems into components, such that each component can be developed separately and subsequently integrated. Second, tools for modeling end-to-end processing sequences that involve multiple objects are either cumbersome or wholly lacking. Third, in the area of reuse, much is made of designing in reuse ("sowing" reuse), but no more than passing mention is made of techniques or procedures for finding and exploiting existing models, domain knowledge, or components ("harvesting" reuse). The first two areas are ones where object-oriented methodologies lack functionality provided by conventional methodologies, while the third area lacks support in both object-oriented and conventional methodologies.

System Partitioning/Object Clustering

Traditional methodologies, such as structured analysis and information engineering, provide mechanisms for creating a natural, coarse-grained decomposition of systems (nested processes in the case of structured analysis, and subject databases in the case of information engineering). This decomposition is essential because many projects are too large to be developed by a single team within the desired time frame and, hence, must be divided into components and assigned to multiple teams working in parallel. To be most beneficial, the decomposition must be performed early in the development process, which also suggests it must be created in top-down fashion rather than bottom-up. In addition, the decomposition must create natural divisions between components and allow for a rigorously defined process of subsequent reintegration of the components.

The most coarse-grained, formally defined entities in object orientation are objects and classes. While objects and classes certainly provide a powerful mechanism for aggregating system functionality, they are usually defined in a bottom-up fashion as common characteristics get factored to ever higher levels in an inheritance structure. In addition, very large systems, even after this factoring process has been completed, may still consist of hundreds of top-level classes. De Champeaux[22] notes

> While the analysis of a toy example like the popular car cruise control system yields only a "flat" set of objects [classes], the analysis of . . . an airline system or a bank will yield "objects" [classes] at different abstraction levels.

The objects and classes, even at the highest level, are too fine-grained and defined too late in the development process to provide a basis for partitioning large development projects. This limitation has apparently been recognized by several methodologists; they have responded by inventing high-level constructs for clustering related object classes. These constructs include subject areas[3], domains[16], systems[16,18], and ensembles[22].

Two of these constructs—Coad and Yourdon's subject areas and the Wirfs-Brock et al. subsystems—appear to be very similar conceptually and provide a starting point for partitioning

object-oriented models. Yet they are quite informally defined, and they provide little indication of how individually developed system components might interact. Shlaer and Mellor's concepts of domains and subsystems are better developed, and four of the methodology's diagrams are devoted to modeling the interactions between domains and between application domain subsystems (domain, chart, subsystem relationship model, subsystem communication model, and subsystem access model).

De Champeaux's *ensembles* and *ensemble classes*[22] are the most rigorously defined of the clustering mechanisms. Ensembles are analogous to conventional objects, while ensemble classes are analogous to conventional classes. An ensemble is a flat grouping of objects (or other ensembles) that naturally go together—usually because they participate in whole-to-part relationships. An automobile, for example, is an ensemble consisting of an engine, doors, wheels, etc. Ensembles have many of the same characteristics as conventional objects, including attributes, states and transitions, and the capability of interacting with other objects and ensembles.

De Champeaux distinguishes ensembles from objects on this basis: Ensembles can have *internal parallelism* while objects cannot. That is, ensembles may consist of subordinate objects or ensembles that each exhibit behaviors in parallel during system execution. Objects, by contrast, are assumed to exhibit only sequential behaviors (for example, as modeled in a finite-state machine.)

De Champeaux distinguishes ensembles from other clustering mechanisms (such as, the Wirfs-Brock et al. subsystems) in that they are more than just conceptual entities; they exist during system execution and may have persistent attributes. It is less clear how ensembles differ from the conventional notion of a compound or composite object[2], except that ensembles seem to be a more general concept than composite objects. That is, an ensemble might refer to a cluster of related entities, such as a fleet of ships that would not ordinarily be viewed as a composite object in the real world.

Yet, in terms of how they behave, ensembles and composite objects appear to be quite similar. De Champeaux notes that the constituents of an ensemble only interact directly with each other or with the encompassing ensemble. An ensemble hides the details of constituents that are irrelevant outside of the ensemble, and acts as a gateway that forwards messages or triggers to external objects and ensembles. Likewise, Booch recommends that when using composite objects, the encapsulating object should hide the details of the constituent objects and mediate between constituent objects and external objects[2].

Although De Champeaux's use of ensembles seems promising on a conceptual level, actual project experiences will tell whether or not ensembles provide a practical basis for partitioning large projects. An interesting question for language designers is whether ensembles, or some similar construct, should be explicitly supported, for example, through mechanisms that limit the allowable patterns of interaction between ensembles, their constituents, and external objects to just those envisioned by de Champeaux.

End-to-End Process Modeling

Many problem domains contain global processes that impact many objects and involve the serial or parallel execution of numerous intermediary steps between initiation and conclusion. Examples of such processes include the ordering process for a manufacturer, daily account reconciliation in a bank, and monthly invoice processing by a long-distance telecommunications carrier. Conventional methodologies provide well-established tools such as dataflow diagrams (see the "Tools for structured methodology" sidebar) and process-dependency diagrams (see the sidebar, "Tools for Martin information engineering") for modeling these sorts of processes.

None of the object-oriented methodologies reviewed here provide a specific model for describing global processes end to end, although individual parts of the process are modeled piecemeal

using such concepts as operations[2,4], services[3], actions and processes[16] and responsibilities[18]. (Shlaer and Mellor describe a procedure for following threads of control, but this procedure spans several different diagrams and seems rather cumbersome. In any case, no distinct view of end-to-end processing—devoid of extraneous information—is provided.)

Bailin supports the idea of using dataflow diagrams (and presumably, global process modeling as well) during analysis, but only to help achieve a better understanding of objects. The resulting diagrams serve only as an intermediate representation and are not part of the object-oriented specification[14].

Booch's timing diagram (see the sidebar, "Tools for Booch object-oriented design") is the closest that any of the methodologies come to supporting a distinct view of end-to-end process modeling. Yet this diagram contains very little expressive power compared with, for example, information engineering's process-dependency diagram. A timing diagram only shows flow of control information, whereas a process-dependency diagram shows flow of control, flow of data, and conditional execution. Bailin also recognizes the need for end-to-end process modeling and has listed composition graphs (similar to timing diagrams in terms of expressive power) as a possible extension of his methodology. (Note that the most recent Bailin methodology refers to compositions graphs as "stimulus-response diagrams.")

This lack of support for global processes is not surprising since the concept of a global process, not subordinated to any individual object, seems to be at odds with the spirit of object orientation. In fact, Booch[2] and de Champeaux[22] both warn against the use of even throw-away dataflow models, for fear that it will irrevocably bias subsequent object modeling towards a "function" orientation.

Still, there is no reason to believe that complicated business processes and the system components that automate them will no longer exist simply because one adopts object orientation. Nor is elimination of end-to-end processes listed by any methodologist as a precondition for adopting object orientation. Thus, it would seem that a separate tool is needed to arrange the mosaic of encapsulated services into a model that illustrates sequencing, conditional execution, and related ideas for certain key global processes.

Harvesting Reuse

One of the most persistently claimed advantages of object orientation is that it enables pervasive levels of software reuse. If properly applied, object-oriented mechanisms such as encapsulation, inheritance, polymorphism, and dynamic binding certainly obviate many technical barriers to reuse of program code. In addition, it has been claimed that object orientation opens the way to reuse of design models, or frameworks[7], and even analysis models from relevant problem domains[6]. At the level of analysis and design, reuse can take two basic forms: reuse of components from previously developed analysis and design models, and reuse of abstractions of previously implemented program components.

Even within an object-oriented implementation environment, achieving high levels of reuse is by no means automatic; virtually all object-oriented methodologists emphasize that reuse must be designed into an application from the start. This emphasis on sowing reuse is not surprising; however, it is curious how little attention object-oriented methodologists pay to harvesting reuse during analysis and design. Analysis and design consume more resources than programming, and perhaps more importantly, development budgets and management decisions—both of which should be strongly influenced by anticipated levels of reuse—are set early in the development process.

Of the methodologies described here, only two address the issue of harvesting reuse from beyond the confines of the project at hand. Coad and Yourdon refer to the need to examine previous analysis models for reusable components and also provide a procedure for merging existing design or program components with new applications[20].

Like Coad and Yourdon, Booch emphasizes the importance of seeking reusable software components from existing class libraries during design. Yet, neither author provides specific guidance on how to find or evaluate existing components.

De Champeaux and Faure[6] and Caldiera and Basili[19] discuss the issue of harvesting reuse at the level of analysis and design. De Champeaux and Faure recommend a repository-based approach to managing reuse. They suggest that the software development process can be seen as a process of creating and modifying three cross-referenced repositories with analysis, design, and implementation components. In this view, the analysis components serve as annotations to the design and implementation components and may point to alternative realizations of the same requirements (for example, with different performance parameters). They further suggest that these annotations could be the basis for a smart library transversal mechanism. This mechanism could assist in identifying candidate reusable components.

Caldiera and Basili provide a much more thorough examination of the issue of harvesting reuse, especially in the areas of identifying and qualifying software components. They suggest a model for project organization where application developers are segregated from "reuse specialists." Reuse specialists work in a "component factory" and are responsible for the development and maintenance of a repository of reusable components. The component factory is responsible for identifying, qualifying, and tailoring reusable components for subsequent integration—by application developers—into ongoing applications development projects.

Object-oriented analysis and design methodologies are rapidly evolving, but the field is by no means fully mature. None of the methodologies reviewed here (with the possible exception of Booch OOD) has—as of this writing—achieved the status of a widely recognized standard on the order of the conventional methodologies of Yourdon and Constantine or DeMarco. Object-oriented methodologies will continue to evolve, as did conventional methodologies before them, as subtler issues emerge from their use in a wide array of problem domains and project environments. As discussed above, three areas—system partitioning, end-to-end process modeling, and harvesting reuse—appear to be especially strong candidates for further development work. In the meantime, adopters of current object-oriented methodologies may need to develop their own extensions to contend with these issues, or alternatively, limit application of the methodologies to problem domains where these issues are of lesser importance.

Compared with object-oriented methodologies, conventional methodologies fall at different places along the incremental-radical continuum. Developers schooled only in structured analysis circa 1978 can be expected to have great difficulty making the transition to OOA, while those with an information modeling background will find much of OOA to be based on familiar concepts.

During design, all conventional methodologies revert to a process-oriented view in establishing the architecture of program modules, and as a result, object orientation will likely be viewed as radical change by developers schooled in any of the conventional design methods reviewed here. Since organizations will have to adopt object-oriented design methodologies to end up with object-oriented implementations, a move to an object-oriented environment in general may be seen predominantly as a radical change.

Object orientation is founded on a collection of powerful ideas—modularity, abstraction, encapsulation, reuse—that have firm theoretical foundations. In addition, trends in computing towards complex data types and complex new forms of integrated systems seem to favor the object model over conventional approaches.

Although little empirical evidence exists to support many of the specific claims made in favor of object orientation, the weight of informed opinion among many leading-edge practitioners and academics favors object orientation as a "better idea" for software development than conventional approaches. Organizations that are able to absorb this radical change may well find themselves in a significantly stronger competitive position vis-a-vis those incapable of making the transition.

References

[1] E. Yourdon, "Object-Oriented Observations," *Am. Programmer,* Vol. 2, No. 7-8, Summer 1989, pp. 3–7.

[2] G. Booch, "What Is and What Isn't Object-Oriented Design?" *Am. Programmer,* Vol. 2, No. 7-8, Summer 1989, pp. 14–21.

[3] P. Coad and E. Yourdon, *Object-Oriented Analysis,* 2nd edition, Prentice Hall, Englewood Cliffs, N.J., 1991.

[4] A. I. Wasserman, P. A. Pircher, and R. J. Muller, "An Object-Oriented Structured Design Method for Code Generation," *Software Eng. Notes,* Vol. 14, No. 1, Jan. 1989, pp. 32–55.

[5] M. Page-Jones and S. Weiss, "Synthesis: An Object-Oriented Analysis and Design Method," *Am. Programmer,* Vol. 2, No. 7-8, Summer 1989, pp. 64–67.

[6] D. De Champeaux and P. Faure, "A Comparative Study of Object-Oriented Analysis Methods," *J. Oriented-Oriented Programming,* Vol. 5, No. 1, 1992, pp. 21–33.

[7] R. J. Wirfs-Brock and R. E. Johnson, "Surveying Current Research in Object-Oriented Design," *Comm. ACM,* Vol. 33, No. 9, Sept. 1990, pp. 104–124.

[8] P. H. Loy, "A Comparison of Object-Oriented and Structured Development Methodologies," *ACM SIGSoft Software Eng. Notes,* Vol. 15, No. 1, Jan. 1990, pp. 44–48.

[9] E. Yourdon and L. Constantine, *Structured Design: Fundamentals of a Discipline of Computer Programming and Design,* 2nd edition, Prentice Hall, New York, 1979.

[10] T. DeMarco, *Structured Analysis and System Specification,* Yourdon Inc., New York, 1978.

[11] P. T. Ward and S. J. Mellor, *Structured Development of Real-Time Systems,* Yourdon Press, Englewood Cliffs, N.J., 1985.

[12] E. Yourdon, *Modern Structured Analysis,* Yourdon Press, Englewood Cliffs, N.J., 1989.

[13] J. Martin, *Information Eng., Books I, II, and III,* Prentice Hall, Englewood Cliffs, N.J., 1990.

[14] S. C. Bailin, "An Object-Oriented Requirements Specification Method," *Comm. ACM,* Vol. 32, No. 5, May 1989, pp. 608–623.

[15] S. Shlaer and S. J. Mellor, *Object-Oriented Analysis: Modeling the World in Data,* Yourdon Press, Englewood Cliffs, N.J., 1988.

[16] S. Shlaer and S. J. Mellor, *Object Life Cycles: Modeling the World in States,* Yourdon Press, Englewood Cliffs, N.J., 1992.

[17] R. G. Fichman and C. F. Kemerer, "Object-Oriented Analysis and Design Methodologies: Comparison and Critique," MIT Sloan School of Management, Center for Information Systems Research Working Paper No. 230, Nov. 1991.

[18] R. Wirfs-Brock, B. Wilkerson, and L. Wiener, *Designing Object-Oriented Software,* Prentice Hall, Englewood Cliffs, N.J., 1990.

[19] G. Caldiera and V. Basili, "Identifying and Qualifying Reusable Software Components," *Computer,* Vol. 24, No. 2, Feb. 1991, pp. 61–70.

[20] P. Coad and E. Yourdon, *Object-Oriented Design,* Prentice Hall, Englewood Cliffs, N.J., 1991.

[21] J. Rumbaugh et al., *Object-Oriented Modeling and Design,* Prentice Hall, Englewood Cliffs, N.J., 1991.

[22] D. De Champeaux, "Object-Oriented Analysis and Top-Down Software Development," *Proc. European Conf. Object-Oriented Programming, Lecture Notes in Computer Science,* P. America, ed., Springer-Verlag, Geneva, 1991, pp. 360–376.

PLANNING THE SOFTWARE INDUSTRIAL REVOLUTION

The possibility of a software industrial revolution, in which programmers stop coding everything from scratch and begin assembling applications from well-stocked catalogs of reusable software components, is an enduring dream that continues to elude our grasp. Although object-oriented programming has brought the software industrial revolution a step closer, commonsense organizational principles like reusability and interchangeability are still the exception, not the rule.

According to historian Thomas Kuhn[1], science does not progress continuously, by gradually extending an established paradigm. It proceeds as a series of revolutionary upheavals. The discovery of unreconcilable shortcomings in an established paradigm produces a crisis that may lead to a revolution in which the established paradigm is overthrown and replaced.

The software crisis is such a crisis, and the software industrial revolution is such a revolution.

Article by Brad J. Cox. © 1990 IEEE. Reprinted, with permission, from (*IEEE Software;* November/1990).

The familiar process-centric paradigm of software engineering, where progress is measured by advancement of the software-development process, entered the crisis stage 23 years ago when the term "software crisis" was first coined. The paradigm that may launch the Information Age is the same one that launched the Manufacturing Age 200 years ago. It is a product-centric paradigm in which progress is measured by the accretion of standard, interchangeable, reusable components, and only secondarily by advancing the processes used to build them.

SOFTWARE CRISIS

The gunsmith shop in colonial Williamsburg, Va., is a fascinating place to watch gunsmiths build guns as we build software: by fabricating each part from raw materials and hand-fitting each part to each assembly. When I was last there, the gunsmith was filing a beautifully proportioned wood screw from a wrought iron rod that he'd forged on the anvil behind his shop, cutting its threads entirely by hand and by eye. I was fascinated by how he tested a newly forged gun barrel—charging it with four times the normal load, strapping it to a log, and letting it rip from behind a sturdy shelter—not the least hindered by academia's paralyzing obsession that such testing "only" reveals the presence of defects, not their absence.

The cottage-industry approach to gunsmithing was in harmony with the economic, technological, and cultural realities of colonial America. It made sense to expend cheap labor as long as steel was imported at great cost from Europe. But as industrialization drove materials' costs down and demand exceeded what the gunsmiths could produce, they began to experience pressure to replace the cottage-industry gunsmith's process-centered approach with a product-centered approach: interchangeable parts to address the consumer's demand for less costly, easily repaired products.

The same inexorable pressure is happening today as the cost of hardware plummets and demand for software exceeds our ability to supply it. As irresistible force meets immovable object, we experience the pressure as the software crisis: the awareness that software is too costly, of insufficient quality, and its development nearly impossible to manage.

Insofar as this pressure is truly inexorable, nothing we think or do will stand in its path. The software industrial revolution will occur, sometime, somewhere—whether our value system is for it or against it—because it is our consumers' values that govern the outcome. It is only a question of how quickly and of whether we or our competitors will service the inexorable pressure for change.

SOFTWARE INDUSTRIAL REVOLUTION

Contrary to what a casual understanding of the Industrial Revolution may suggest, the displacement of cut-to-fit craftsmanship by high-precision interchangeable parts didn't happen overnight and it didn't happen easily. The heroes of this revolution were not the cottage-industry gunsmiths, who

actually played almost no role whatsoever, for or against. The value system of the craftsman culture, so palpable in that Williamsburg gunsmith, was too strong. They stayed busy in their workshops, filing on their iron bars, and left it to their consumers to find another way.

It was actually the ultimate consumer of ordnance products. Thomas Jefferson, who found the solution in 1785 during a visit to France before his presidency. Congress supported his proposal with remarkable steadfastness through 25 years of unsuccessful attempts, such as Ely Whitney's pioneering effort, until John Hall finally succeeded in 1822. An additional 24 years were to elapse before what was then called armory practice spread to private contractors—a half century! This may be a fundamental time constant of such revolutions, since similar lags occurred in the telephony, phonograph, automobile, steamboat, railroad, and other industries. On this time scale, the distinction between evolution and revolution can be exceedingly hard to discern.

Two Imperatives

Although I certainly hope that events will prove me wrong, I fear that the software industrial revolution will take as long, or even longer. Exhibit 1 represents where we are today by juxtaposing two hotly contested imperatives as to how to escape the software crisis[2,3].

The first viewpoint is the intangibility imperative, which is most common in computer-science circles. Its advocates view software as a solitary, mental, abstract activity akin to mathematics. For example, James Fetzer [3] attributed the following expression of this viewpoint to C.A.R. Hoare: "The construction of computer programs is a mathematical activity like the solution of differential equations, that programs can be derived from their specifications through mathematical insight, calculation, and proof, using algebraic laws as simple and elegant as those of elementary arithmetic."

But this viewpoint is hardly unique to academics. Most programmers will really readily to this

EXHIBIT 1 Software Is a Hybrid, Halfway Between an Abstract Idea and a Physical, Tangible Thing. It Lies at the Overlap of Two Imperatives: Tangibility and Intangibility

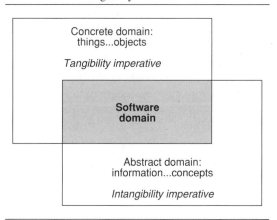

Concrete domain:
things...objects

Tangibility imperative

Software domain

Abstract domain:
information...concepts

Intangibility imperative

quote, by one of Apple's most creative programmers, which compares programming to novel writing, another solitary, mental, abstract activity: "Reusing other peoples's code would prove that I don't care about my work. I would no more reuse code than [Ernest] Hemingway would have reused other authors' paragraphs."

The opposing viewpoint is the tangibility imperative, which is most common in software-engineering circles. Its advocates counter that although software is like mathematics or novel writing in many ways, the intangibility imperative works best for problems that do not exceed the abilities or the longevity of an individual. Intangibles are notoriously hard to produce by committee. Furthermore, the intangibility imperative concentrates power in the hands of those with the abstract reasoning skills to comprehend an intangible product: the producers. The consumers are left powerless, unable to contribute the financial and legal resources that are needed to drive deep-seated cultural and technological changes.

This drive to empower the consumer is making software as accessible and immediate as everyday tangible objects underlies the recent enthusiasm for

direct manipulation (iconic) user interface browsers, personal workstations, and other techniques for making software more tangible, less abstract, and more approachable by nonprogrammers.

Hybrid Approach

The recent enthusiasm for object-oriented technologies are particularly interesting in that both camps embrace it, but for opposite reasons—the tangibility advocates for encapsulation and dynamic binding; intangibility advocates for inheritance and static binding. This apparent convergence but actual convergence is responsible for much of the confusion as to what the term means.

This article does not propose that either imperative should eliminate the other. Software really is an abstract/concrete swamp, a hybrid for which dual perspectives can be useful as first-order approximations to a complex reality. Rather, it proposes a paradigm shift to a new frame of reference in which both imperatives coexist, each predominating at different times and places.

I've emphasized the tangibility imperative throughout this article because of the need to begin building and using commercially robust repositories of trusted, stable components whose properties can be understood and tabulated in standard catalogs, like the handbooks of other mature engineering domains.

The intangibility imperative will always retain its current role as the primary tool of solitary, mental creativity, and will acquire even greater utility for predicting how trusted, quantifiable components, the raw materials of a mature software engineering discipline, will behave when assembled and placed under load.

OBJECT-ORIENTED TECHNOLOGIES

Objects are turning up all over! There are object-oriented databases, drawing programs, telephone switching systems, user interfaces, and analysis and design methods. And, oh yes, there are object-oriented programming languages. Lots of them, of every description, from Ada at the conservative right to Smalltalk at the radical left, with C++ and Objective-C somewhere in between. And everyone is asking, "What could such different technologies possibly have in common? Do they have anything in common? What does 'object-oriented' really mean?"

What does any adjective mean in this murky swamp we call software? No one is confused when adjectives like "small" or "fast" mean entirely different things in nuclear physics, gardening, and geology. But in our murky world of intangible abstractions, it is all too easy to lose your bearings, to misunderstand the context, to confuse the very small with the extremely large. So the low-level modularity/binding technologies of Ada and C++ are confused with the higher level ones of Smalltalk, and all three with hybrid environments like Objective-C. And visually intuitive, nonsequential technologies like Fabrik[4] and Metaphor Computer System's Metaphor are summarily excluded for being iconic rather than textual and for not supporting inheritance—forgetting that the same is true of tangible everyday entities that are indisputably objects.

Such confusion is not surprising. The denizens of the software domain, from the tiniest expression to the largest application, are as intangible as any ghost. And because we invent them all from first principles, everything we encounter there is unique and unfamiliar, composed of components that have never been seen before and will never be seen again and that obey laws that don't generalize to future encounters. Software is a place where dreams are planted and nightmares harvested, where terrible demons compete with magical panaceas, a world of werewolves and silver bullets.

As long as all we can know for certain is the code we ourselves wrote during the last week or so, mystical belief will reign over quantifiable reason. Terms like "computer science" and "software engineering" will remain oxymorons—at best, content-free twaddle spawned of wishful thinking and, at worst, a cruel and selfish fraud on the consumers who pay our salaries.

In the broadest sense, "object-oriented" refers to an objective, not a technology for achieving it. It means wielding all the tools we can muster, from well-proven antiques like Cobol to missing ones like specification languages, to enable our consumers by letting them reason about our products via the commonsense skills we all use to understand tangible objects.

But because reverting to this broader meaning might confuse terminology even further, I use a separate term—software industrial revolution—to mean what "object-oriented" has always meant to me: transforming programming from a solitary cut-to-fit craft into an organizational enterprise like manufacturing. This means letting consumers at every level of an organization solve their own software problems just as home owners solve plumbing problems: by assembling their own solutions from a robust commercial market in off-the-shelf subcomponents, which are in turn supplied by multiple lower level echelons of producers.

Clearly, software products are different from tangible products like plumbing supplies, and the differences are not small. However, there is a compelling similarity: Except for small programs that a solitary programmer builds for personal use, both programming and plumbing are organizational activities. Both are engaged in by people like those who raised the pyramids, flew to the Moon, repair their plumbing, and build computer hardware—ordinary people with the common sense to organize as producers and consumers of each other's products instead of reinventing everything from first principles.

VALUE RIGIDITY

Robert Pirsig has related a powerful analogy that well describes the basic problem we software developers face today: the need to think about our values and reevaluate them, rather than rigidly hold on to them even when ultimately fatal. Pirsig wrote[5], "The most striking example of value rigidity I can think of is the old South Indian monkey trap, which depends on value rigidity for its effectiveness. [The trap is simply a coconut shell with a hole in it, baited with food.] The monkey reaches in and is suddenly trapped—by nothing more than his own value rigidity. He can't revalue the food. He cannot see that freedom without food is more valuable than capture with it. The villagers are coming to get him and take him away. They're coming closer . . . closer . . . now!

"There is a fact this monkey should know: If he opens his hand he's free. But how is he going to discover this fact? By removing the value rigidity that rates food above freedom. How is he going to do that? Well, he should somehow try to slow down deliberately and go over ground that he has been over before and see if things he thought were important really were important, and well, stop yanking and just stare at the coconut for a while. Before long he should get a nibble from a little fact wondering if he is interested in it."

The software industrial revolution, like all revolutions, is as much cultural as technological. It involves not only tools but values: deeply held beliefs about the nature of software, our role in its construction and use, and ultimately our ideals of good versus bad. Revolutions happen so slowly—and often displace one group by another—because of value rigidity, the inability to relax the pursuit of an older good to gain a newer one. Examples of potential value-rigidity traps abound:

- Programs must be provably correct, as opposed to compliant to specification within a stated tolerance.
- We should focus on solutions that will bear fruit quickly, within a manager's 12-month planning horizon.
- Seamless panaceas are better than kits of diverse tools.
- Software is a closed universe in which all potential interactions between the parts of that universe can be declared when these parts are created by their compiler.

Consider the last two of these in more detail. The closed-universe model surfaces as the belief that compile-time type checking is universally "better."

The preference for panaceas instead of tools surfaces as the belief that early and late binding are mutually exclusive panaceas, that the language designer should choose one at the expense of the other rather than providing many binding technologies that the user can choose from according to the job at hand.

To see how these value systems keep us trapped in the software crisis, consider the program in Exhibit 2. This program was written according to the closed-universe model: Everything is declared in advance so the compiler can prevent a supposedly common kind of error through strong type checking.

But in return, this programmer has given up the opportunity to escape the software crisis by building a market in reusable software components, such as Set. To see why, shift your focus from the assembly to the parts that make it up—from the application to the Set class. For Set's add: method

---

EXHIBIT 2 This Program Computes the Number of Unique Words in a Document. It Turns Tokens Produced By the GetWord Subroutine Into Instances of Word (Current-Word) and Adds These to an Instance of Set (UniqueWords), Relying on the Set to Discard Duplicates. As Written Here, the Application is Strictly Type-Checked at Compile Time. A More Flexible Solution Would Have Been to Declare CurrentWord to be of Type Id Rather Than Word* to Delay Binding Until Runtime

---

```
Set* uniqueWords;
Word* currentWord;
uniqueWords = [Set new];
while (getWord(buf) !=EOF) {
    currentWord = [Word str:buf];
    [uniqueWords add:current-
Word];
}
printf("unique words = %d\n",
    [uniqueWords size]);
```

to be consistent with the type declaration in the application (Word*currentWord), the compiler must insist that the formal argument of Set's add: method, aMember, be declared as Word*, ByteArray*, or AbstractArray*, depending on which declares the messages that add: will send to aMember. The closed-universe model forces Set's designer to anticipate what consumers will use Set for—at compile time—when Set is produced by the compiler, rather than at runtime, when it is used by installing it into its reuse environment.

But what about consumers whose set members are not implemented as a subclass of AbstractArray? Why not sets of Wrenches or sets of Unicorns? Why not sets of Sets? A commercial Set must be reusable for members of any class, regardless of how its consumer chose to implement them—regardless of the members' inheritance hierarchy.

But this involves an open-universe model in which Set's members are checked not when Set is compiled, but when it is used—when it is drawn from a library of compiled code and first encounters its members at runtime. Set must be written so its members may be chosen after Set has been compiled, packaged in a library, and delivered in binary form through the market in software components.

In Objective-C, the syntax for doing this is to replace the offending type declaration, Word*, with the anonymous type name, id. This instructs the compiler that the add: method is prepared to deal with instances of any class, excluding only types other than id. Because type checking and binding are now deferred until runtime, a Set can be compiled once and for all and distributed in binary form for reuse as a commercial software component. By relaxing our frantic grasp on the compile time type-checking bait, we've taken a step toward freedom from the software crisis.

The point of this example is not that runtime type checking and anonymous types are better or worse than the converse. Although the example used dynamic binding to attach members to set as it used static binding to build the getWord( ) subroutine. The example shows that seamless panaceas—languages that do not offer multiple modularity/binding technologies—prevent these markets by failing to provide modularity/binding technologies suitable for users at different levels of the producer/consumer hierarchy.

Strongly coupled languages like Ada and C++ are deficient insofar as they do not also support loosely coupled modularity/binding technologies like screwing, bolting, welding, soldering, pinning, riveting, and mortising. And loosely coupled environments like Smalltalk are deficient insofar as they fail to support tightly coupled modularity/binding technologies like forging and casting. Hybrid environments like Objective-C and CLOS, and analogous ones that could be based on Cobol, Ada, Pascal, or C++, support multiple modularity/binding technologies and tools to be picked up or laid aside according to the job at hand.

SOFTWARE ARCHITECTURE

It is easy to see how interchangeable parts could help in manufacturing. But manufacturing involves replicating a standard product, while programming does not. Programming is not an assembly-line business but a built-to-order one, more akin to plumbing than gun manufacturing.

But the principles of standardization and interchangeability pioneered for standard products apply directly to build-to-order industries like plumbing. They enabled the markets of today where all manner of specialized problems can be solved by binding standardized components into new and larger assemblies.

Mature industries like plumbing are less complex than ours, not because software is intrinsically more complicated, but because they—and not we—have solved their complexity, nonconformity, and changeability problems by using a producer/consumer hierarchy to distribute these problems across time and organizational space. The plumbing supply market lets plumbers solve only the complexities of a single level of the producer/consumer hierarchy without having to think about lower levels, for example, by reinventing pipes, faucets, thermostats, and water pumps from first principles.

Kuhn has pointed out that the crucial test of a new paradigm is whether it reveals a simpler structure for what was previously chaotic. Certainly, the process-centric software universe is chaotic today. The process-centric paradigm requires that only one process be "right," so each new contender must slug it out for that coveted title, "standard"—rapid prototyping versus Mil-Std-2167, object-oriented versus structured. Ada versus Smalltalk, C++ versus Objective-C. Different levels of the producer/consumer hierarchy are not permitted to use specialized tools for their specialized tasks, skills, and interests, but must fit themselves to the latest panacea.

But by focusing on the nature of the *products* of these languages and methodologies, rather than on them as processes significant unto themselves, a simpler pattern emerges that is reminiscent of the distinct integration levels of hardware engineering (shown in Exhibit 3). The hardware community's monumental achievements are largely due to the division of labor made possible by the loosely coupled modularity/binding technologies shown in this figure.

Card-level pluggability lets users plug off-the-shelf cards to build custom hardware solutions without having to understand soldering irons and silicon chips. (Pluggability is the ability to bind a component into a new environment dynamically, when the component is used, rather than statically, when it is produced.) Chip-level pluggability lets vendors build cards from off-the-shelf chips without needing to understand the minute gate and block-level details that their vendors must know to build silicon chips. Each modularity/binding technology encapsulates a level of complexity so the consumer needn't know or care how components from a lower level were implemented—just how to use them to solve the problem at hand.

Each integration level in this figure already exists in software, scattered among competing languages. Asking "What is object-oriented?" is like asking for a context-independent meaning of "small." Just as it is proper that "small" means entirely different things for atoms, spark plugs, automobiles, and traffic jams, it is proper that "object" mean different things at each integration level.

EXHIBIT 3   Hardware Engineering's Levels of Integration Are a Good Model for Software Engineering. "Object-Oriented" Means Different Things at Different Levels of Integration. The Pies Show the Extent to Which Several Popular Languages Support Work at Each Level

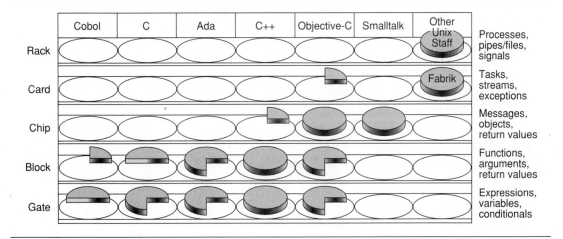

COMMERCIAL EXAMPLE

My company, Stepstone, was founded seven years ago to pursue the ideas in this article on a commercial scale. Its mission is providing pluggable chip-level software components to C system builders who realize that building large systems (rack-level objects) with only the modularity/binding technologies that C provides is equivalent to wafer-scale integration, something that hardware engineering can barely accomplish to this day.

However, C did not support pluggability, so we built an enabling technology: a C preprocessor to support a loosely coupled chip-level modularity/binding technology within C's gate- and block-level technologies.

The goal of this extended language, Objective-C, was not to be yet another language nor, as originally envisioned, to repair C's long-standing deficiencies (subsequent versions have since addressed many of these deficiencies by supporting ANSI improvements, even for older C compilers that don't provide them). It was to provide enabling technology for building the Objective-C system-building environment and a multilevel market in software components.

Stepstone's experience amounts to an experimental study of the software-components market strategy in action.

The good news is that, with substantial libraries now in the field and others on the way, the chip-level software-components market concept has been tried and proven sound for diverse applications in banking, insurance, factory automation, battlefield management, CAD/CAM, CASE, and others. The component libraries have proven to be flexible enough, and easy enough to learn and use, that they have been used to build highly graphical applications in all of these domains, and sufficiently portable that it has been possible to support them on most hardware and software platforms during this era of rapid platform evolution.

The bad news is that this experiment has shown that it is exceedingly difficult, even with state-of-the-art technologies, to design and build compo-

nents that are both useful and genuinely reusable, to document them so customers can understand them, to port them to an unceasing torrent of new hardware platforms, to ensure that recent enhancements or ports haven't violated some existing interface, and to market them to a culture whose value system, like the Williamsburg gunsmith, encourages building everything from first principles.

A particularly discouraging example of this value system is that, in spite of the time and money we've invested in libraries and environmental tools like browsers, Objective-C is still thought of as yet another programming language to be compared with Ada and C++, rather than as the tiniest part of a much larger environment of ready-to-use software components and tools.

This experiment has also shown that chip-level objects are only a beginning, not an end. The transition from how the machine forces programmers to think to how everyone expects tangible objects to behave is not a single step but many. At the gate and block levels of Exhibit 3, "object-oriented" means encapsulation and sometimes inheritance, but the dynamism of everyday objects has been intentionally relinquished in favor of machine-oriented virtues like computational efficiency and static binding.

At the intermediate (chip) level, the open-universe model of everyday experience is introduced. At this level, all possible interactions between parts and the whole do not have to be known and declared in advance, when the universe is created by the compiler.

THE NEXT STEP

But on the scale of any significant system, gate-, block-, and even chip-level objects are extremely small units of granularity—grains of sand where bricks are needed. Furthermore, since chip-level objects are no less procedural than conventional expressions and subroutines, they are just as alien to nonprogrammers. Until invoked by passing them a thread of control from outside, they are as inert as conventional data, quite unlike the objects of everyday experience.

Fabrik[4] pioneered a path that I hope the object-oriented world will soon notice and follow. Because Fabrik was written in Smalltalk, it consists internally of chip-level objects. But externally, it projects a higher level kind of object, a card-level object, to the user. These higher level objects communicate, not synchronously through procedural invocation, but asynchronously by sending chip-level objects through communication-channel objects such as Streams. They amount to a new kind of object that encapsulates a copy of the machine's thread of control on a software card, along with the chip-level objects used to build that card. Software cards are objects of the sort that programmers call lightweight processes: objects that operate as coroutines of one another, not subroutines.

Because software cards can operate concurrently, they admit a tangible user interface (as Exhibit 4 shows) that is uniquely intuitive for nonprogrammers and, for this reason alone, more fundamentally object-oriented than the procedural, single-threaded languages of today. Like the tangible objects of everyday experience, card-level objects provide their own thread of control internally, they don't communicate by procedural invocation, they don't support inheritance, and their user interface is iconic, not textual.

By adding these, and probably other architectural levels, each level can cater to the needs, skills, and interests of a particular constituency of the software-components market. The programmer shortage can be solved as the telephone-operater shortage was solved: by making every computer user a programmer.

PRODUCT-CENTERED PARADIGM

Once Congress mandated interchangeable parts for government-purchased equipment, technologies

---

EXHIBIT 4 Example of How a Nonprogrammer Might Construct a Banking Application by Assembling Software Cards, or Dataflow Modules

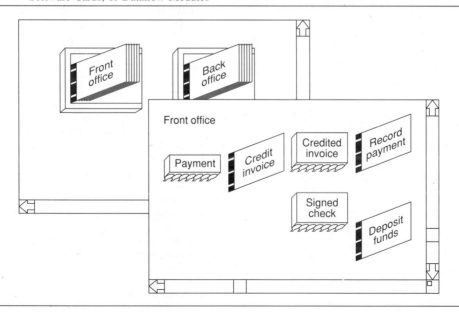

for building them followed posthaste. The first phase focused on water-powered tools like Blanchard's pattern lathe. This lathe represents the mainstream approach of the software community until now: the search for processes that can transform progressively higher level descriptions of the problem, like the gun-stock pattern that guides this lathe, into concrete products that are correct by construction.

Today, this lathe stands in the American History Museum in Washington. D.C. but its stands there to point out that the crucial innovation that made interchangeable parts possible was not only the elimination of cut-to-fit craftsmanship by tools like this lathe. The crucial discovery was made, not by Blanchard, but by John Hall, who realized that implementation tools were insufficient unless supplemented by specification tools capable of determining whether parts complied to specification within tolerance. The museum reinforces this point by displaying a box of hardened steel inspection gauge in the same exhibit with Blanchard's lathe.

This discovery has not yet occurred as software. Although it is easy to find articles with specification in their title, they usually mean implementation, as in "automatically generating code from specifications." Although such higher level implementation tools are clearly worthwhile. It is misleading to call them specification languages, because this obscures the absence of true specification technologies in software—the rulers, protractors, calipers, micrometers, and gauges of manufacturing. Programmers continue to rely exclusively on implementation technologies, be they ultrahigh-level programming languages—tools of certainty like the Blanchard lathe—or lower level languages—tools of risk like the rasps, files, and spokeshaves that it displaced.

Confusing Implementation and Specification

The confusion of implementation and specification is particularly prominent in that most fashionable of object-oriented features: inheritance. As used in object-oriented-language circles, inheritance is the Blanchard lathe of software—a powerful and important tool for creating new classes from existing ones, but not nearly as useful for specifying static properties like how they fit into their environment, and useless for describing dynamic properties like what these classes do.

Rather than laboriously building each new class by hand, inheritance copies functionality from a network of existing classes to create a new class that is, until the programmer begins overriding or adding methods, correct by construction. Such hierarchies show how a class's internals were constructed. They say nothing, or worse, mislead, about the class's specification—the static and dynamic properties that the class offers its consumers.

For example, Exhibit 5 shows the implementation hierarchy for a Semaphore class that inherits four existing classes. Compare this implementation hierarchy with the following facts:

- Semaphores are a kind of Queue only from the arcane viewpoint of their author. This hierarchy

EXHIBIT 5   Implementation Hierarchy Showing How New Classes Are Implemented from Existing Ones. However, it Provides a Misleading Picture of What the Customer Is Interested In: the Specification of What the Classes Do

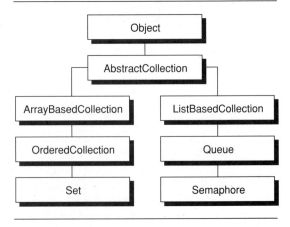

resulted from a speed optimization of no interest to consumers, who should view them as scheduling primitives with only wait and signal methods. How will the producer tell the consumer to avoid some, many, or all of those irrelevant and dangerous methods being inherited from all four superclasses? And if such static issues are handled statically, where will dynamic ones be handled?—the vital question of what Semaphore does.

- This hierarchy says explicitly that OrderedCollection is similar to Set and dissimilar to Queue. However, exactly the opposite is true. Queue is functionally identical to OrderedCollection. I carefully hand-crafted Queue to have each of OrderedCollection's methods, each with precisely the same semantics, to show that encapsulation lets a class's internals be revised without affecting its externals. But how will the consumer discover that OrderedCollection and Queue provide the same functionality—that they are competing implementations of precisely the same specification? And how will any commercially significant differences, like time/space trade-offs, be expressed independently of these similarities?

Parallel Tools

Manufacturing handles this issue by providing two separate classes of tools: implementation tools for the producer's side of the interface and specification tools for the consumer's side. Shouldn't we do likewise? Shouldn't conceptual aids like inheritance be used on both sides, but separately, just as Blanchard's lathe and Hall's inspection gauges deal with different views of the same object's interface? Shouldn't Semaphore's consumer interface be expressed in an explicit specification hierarchy as in Exhibit 6, independently of the producer's implementation hierarchy?

Just as a measuring stick is not a higher level saw, a specification tool is not a higher level implementation tool. Specification is not the implementation tool's job. Separating the two would eliminate performance as a constraint on

EXHIBIT 6 Specification Hierarchy for the Example in Exhibit 5. This Specification Hierarchy Uses the Names of Test Procedures, Not Classes, That Verify (Gauge) Whether an Implementation Compiles to a Specification Within a Tolerance Embodied in Each Test

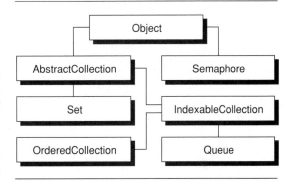

the specification tool, letting knowledge representation shells that already support rich conceptual relationships be used as a basis for a specification-language compiler. The two tools can be deployed as equal partners, both central to the development process, as in Exhibit 7.

The primitives of the specification language are ordinary test procedures—predicates with a single argument that identifies the putative implementation to be tested. A test procedure exercises its argument to determine whether it behaves within its specification's tolerence. For example, a putative duck is an acceptable duck upon passing the isADuck gauge. The specification compiler builds this gauge by assembling walksLikeADuck and quacksLikeADuck test procedures from the library. The compiler is simply an off-the-shelf knowledge-representation tool for invoking the appropriate test procedures stored in the test-procedure library.

How It Works

The test-procedure libraries play the role in software as elsewhere—defining the shared vocabulary that makes producer/consumer dialogue

EXHIBIT 7 A Development Process in Which Specification Is Given the Same Emphasis as Implementation

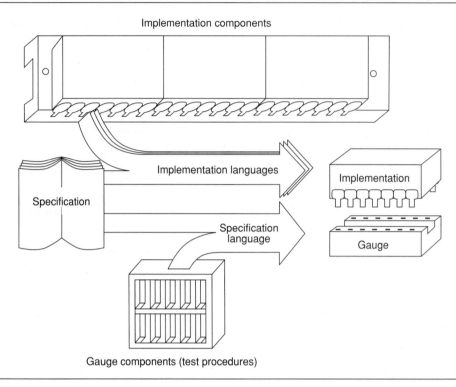

Implementation components

Implementation languages

Specification

Specification language

Implementation

Gauge

Gauge components (test procedures)

possible. For example, in "I need a pound of roofing nails," "pound" is defined by a test procedure involving a scale, and "nail" by a test procedure involving shape recognition by the natural senses. Test procedures are particularly crucial in software because of the natural senses' inability to contribute to the specification of otherwise intangible software products like Stack or Set. Making software tangible and observable, rather than intangible and speculative, is the first step to making software engineering and computer science a reality.

Test procedures collect operational, or indirect, measurements of what we'd really like to know, the product's quality as perceived by the customer. They monitor the consumer's interface, rather than our traditional focus on the producer's interface

(by counting lines of code, cyclomatic complexity, Halstead metrics, and the like). This knowledge of how product quality varies over time can then be fed back to improve the process through statistical quality-control techniques, as described by W. Edwards Deming[6], that play such a key role today in manufacturing.

Implications

The novelty of this approach is threefold:

- applying inheritance concepts not only to implementation, but to specification and testing, thus making the specification explicit,
- preserving test procedures for reuse across different implementations, versions, or ports through an inheritance hierarchy, and

- distributing the specifications and test procedures between producers and consumers to define a common vocabulary that both parties can use for agreeing on software semantics.

The implications could be immense, once we adjust to the cultural changes that this implies: a shift in power away from those who produce the code to those who consume it—from those who control the implementations to those who control the specifications. Three implications are:

- Specification/testing languages could lead to less reliance on source code, new ways of documenting code for reuse, and fundamentally new ideas for classifying large libraries of code so it can be located readily in reference manuals, component catalogs, and browsers.
- Specification/testing languages could free us from our preoccupation with standardized processes (programming languages) and our neglect of standardized products (software components). Producers would be freed to use whatever language is best for each task, knowing that the consumer will compile the specification to determine whether the result is as specified.
- Specification/testing languages can provide rigor to open-universe situations when compile-time type checking is not viable. For example, in the set example described earlier, the implementation-oriented declaration Abstract-Array* was too restrictive because sets should work for members that are not subclasses of AbstractArray. However, the anonymous type id is unnecessarily permissive because sets do impose a protocol requirement that you'd like to check before runtime. But because specification/testing tools can induce static meanings (isADuck) from dynamic behavior (quacksLikeADuck), why not feed this back to the language as implementation-independent type declarations? This amounts to a new notion of type that encompasses both the static and dynamic properties, rather than the static implementation-oriented meaning of today.

At Stepstone, implementing software components has never been a big problem, but making

them tangible to consumers has been. The marketing department experiences this in explaining the value of a component to potential customers. Customers experience it when they try to find useful components in libraries that are organized by inheritance hierarchies and not by specification hierarchies. And the development team experiences it when changing a released component in any fashion, such as when porting it to a new machine, repairing a fault, or extending it with new functionality.

Without tools to express the old specification independently from the new and then determine if the old specification is intact while independently testing the new one, development quickly slows to a crawl. All available resources become consumed in quality assurance.

Of course, intangible software components are quite different from the tangible components of gunsmithing and plumbing, and the differences go even beyond the abstract/concrete distinction of Exhibit 1. The most fundamental differences include

- complexity, nonconformity, and mutability,
- intangibility (invisibility),
- single-threadedness, and
- ease of duplication.

This list originated in a list Fred Brooks[7] provided to distinguish "the inescapable essence of software, as opposed to mere accidents of how we produce software today." I added two properties that he neglected to mention: single-threadedness and ease of duplication. However, I did not do this to reinforce his implication that the software crisis is an inescapable consequence of software's essence. I did it to argue that all the items on this list are only obstacles that can, and will, be overcome:

- A robust software-components market addresses the complexity, nonconformity, and mutability obstacle by providing an alternative to implementing everything from first principles.
- Object-oriented programming technologies at each of the many levels of Exhibit 3 address the

intangibility obstacle, particularly if supported by a specification technology as in Exhibit 5.

- Ultrahigh-level (card- and rack-level) object-oriented languages also address the intangibility obstacle by providing nonprocedural objects that nonprogrammers can manipulate via direct-manipulation user interfaces.
- Card-and rack-level languages address the single-threadedness obstacle by relaxing the relentlessly procedural, single-control-thread restrictions of the gate-, block-, and chip-level languages of today.

The problem, of course, is the absence of easy technological solutions to the ease-of-duplication obstacle, which stands ready to undercut any assault we might mount on the others by inhibiting the growth of a commercially robust software-components market. Such markets will be weak as long as it is difficult for component producers to guarantee income commensurate to their invest-ments by controlling the ability to replicate copies.

But as long as the pressure for change increases as the software crisis grows ever more severe, so-lutions to even this last obstacle will be sought—and they will be found, either by us or our competitors. Ideally, the solutions will be technical. Perhaps they will be legal, economic, and policy sanctions im-posed by our consumers. Perhaps they will be the kind of sheer determination that the free-enterprise system is famous for inspiring.

I only wish that I were as confident that the changes will come quickly or that we, the current software-development community, will be the ones who make it happen. Or will we stay busy at our terminals, filing away at software like gun-smiths at iron bars, and leave it to our consumers to find a solution that leaves us sitting there?

References

1. T. Kuhn, *The Structure of Scientific Revolutions,* Univ. of Chicago Press, Chicago, 1962.

2. E. Dijkstra, "The Cruelty of Really Teaching Computer Science," *Comm. ACM,* Dec. 1989, pp. 1,398–1,404.

3. J. H. Fetzer, "Program Verification: The Very Idea," *Comm. ACM,* Sept. 1988, pp. 1,048–1,063.

4. D. Ingalls et al., "Fabrik: A Visual Programming Environment," *Proc. Object-Oriented Programming, Systems, Languages, and Applications Conf.,* ACM, New York, 1988.

5. R. M. Pirsig: *Zen and the Art of Motorcycle Maintenance: An Inquiry into Values,* Quill William Morrow, New York, 1974.

6. W. E. Deming, *Out of the Crisis,* Center for Advanced Engineering Study, Massachusetts Inst. of Technology, Cambridge, Mass., 1989.

7. F. P. Brooks, "No Silver Bullet: Essence vs. Accidents of Software Engineering," *Computer,* April 1987, pp. 10–19.

ADOPTION OF SOFTWARE ENGINEERING PROCESS INNOVATIONS: THE CASE OF OBJECT ORIENTATION

Organizations increasingly rely on information technology (IT) both to perform their day-to-day operations and as a source of new products and services. The popular focus has been on hardware components, and that story has been overwhelmingly positive: the new technologies that come to market are cheaper, more reliable, and more portable than previous ones.

However, much less has been written about the software side of IT, and what has been written has not been positive. We commonly read that software is late, over budget, and of poor quality. Specific examples of software in the news are almost always negative—microcomputer software vendors that deliver releases late, federal government systems projects that never reach the implementation stage, and the recent telephone system outage that was blamed on a Texas supplier who "changed only three or four lines of the program."[1]

This imbalance has reached such proportions that it has been termed the software crisis. Software production represents the single biggest obstacle to the successful use of IT in organizations; all precepts such as "using IT for strategic advantage," "reengineering the business," and "informating the workplace" become mere slogans if the necessary software is not properly delivered on time.

Into this void have rushed a multitude of vendors and consultants offering solutions to the crisis. A quick review of trade press magazines will reveal articles on such topics as computer-aided software engineering (CASE), rapid applications development, cleanroom software engineering, software factories, and object-oriented (OO) approaches. All of these represent *software engineering process technologies,* that is, means by which an application software product is created (hereafter "software process technologies").[2] The idea that process technologies in general are critical sources of economic success is gaining acceptance.[3] However, the problem with this rich set of software process technologies is that they may be technically incompatible, or, if not, then at least sufficiently expensive and requiring significantly large changes in an organization's operation that they are unlikely to be successfully adopted at the same time.

How, then, can the chief information officer (CIO) of a large business application development organization choose which, if any, of these new software process technologies to adopt? Unfortunately, the choice of a new approach is rendered very difficult by the lack of unbiased information sources. All of the technologies are shrouded in new vocabularies and explainable only by a self-selected cadre of experts.

Moreover, many previous technologies have been so oversold that it is now sometimes difficult to tell legitimate enthusiasm from marketing hype. Fred Brooks has even coined a term for such oversold software process innovations—silver bullets.[4] One of Brooks's silver bullets is artificial intelligence (AI) expert systems. These were supposed to solve many problems, not just software development, and they merited at least two cover stories in *Business Week* over the past decade, perhaps the only software process technology to merit such general press attention. However, according to Brooks and others, the gains delivered by this technology have been much less than promised.[5] In contrast to the initial waves of enthusiasm, it now appears that relatively few new systems in business organizations are being developed using this technology and that their use remains plateaued at a small niche of applications, most of them limited to diagnostic tasks.

This is not to say that AI expert systems are a poor technology, just that they did not meet the inflated expectations. The critical point is that AI expert systems have not become a dominant software process technology. An intuitive test of technology dominance is whether the majority of organizations developing applications software would choose this technology in developing or replacing their core applications. For example, third-generation software languages such as CO-BOL, FORTRAN, and C are dominant over their predecessor second-generation assembly languages in that second-generation languages are now relegated to highly specialized portions of applications and are not chosen as the primary software process technology for programming if any other alternative is available.

The reason that a CIO should care about sorting out which new software process technologies are likely to be dominant is that the costs of choosing a nondominant technology can be substantial. In particular, even technologies that offer some technical advantages over their predecessors may not end up dominating because they fail to achieve a critical mass. And once an organization commits to a technology that then fails to become dominant, it faces a number of additional problems, such as:

- Difficulties in hiring experienced staff;
- Limited enhancements to core technology available on the market;
- Few complementary products available;
- Third-party training opportunities less available;

- Lack of accumulated wisdom in the industry as to how best to improve the technology's performance; and
- Possible loss of vendor support.

Given the significant learning and adoption start-up costs, and the increased risk of failure, these additional burdens may make the adoption of a nondominant technology extremely expensive in the long run.

The question remains: How can you choose tomorrow's dominant software process technology from today's list of candidates? Arguably, the leading candidate at the moment is the object-oriented approach. Although some of the key ideas of OO date back to late 1960s computer science research, it is in the past six years that OO has become a popular research topic and that commercial products have become widely available for its use. Recently OO was featured on the cover of *Business Week* as the key to "making software simple."[6] The central ideas of OO fit well with previous advances in software engineering, and proponents argue that the approach lends itself to the assembly of previously developed, well-tested components into software systems, thereby avoiding the labor-intensive and less reliable approach of building everything from scratch.

Will OO become the dominant software process technology of the future for in-house business application development? Our thesis is that for any software process technology to become dominant, it must first overcome a series of obstacles to adoptability. In particular, we evaluate adoption from two perspectives: diffusion of innovations and economics of technology standards. There is a rich academic and practical history of studying the diffusion of innovations, that is, the adoption of technology by individuals and their organizations, and of sorting out the characteristics of those innovations that have been successfully adopted. The economics of technology standards perspective examines technologies that have significant increasing returns to adoption. That is, the benefits of adoption largely depend on the size (past, present, and future) of the community of other adopters. Technologies have a greater likelihood of success to the degree that barriers to adoption are lowered.

In the sections that follow, we describe these two points of view and apply them to three past software process technologies (structured analysis and design methodologies, production fourth-generation languages, and relational database management systems). We construct a framework that evaluates the likelihood of dominance based on the technology's adoptability for both individual organizations and for whole communities or industries. And, finally, we introduce OO and analyze it in terms of the framework. We find that object-oriented technology faces considerable hurdles to both individual and industry adoption.

PERSPECTIVES ON TECHNOLOGY ADOPTION

Why are some innovations adopted more rapidly than others? This simple question has been the subject of intense study by innovation diffusion researchers. Object orientation qualifies as an innovation—some say a radical one—in software engineering process technology; as a result, the vast body of literature on the diffusion of innovations (DOI) is a natural starting point in the search for clues about the technology's ultimate disposition. DOI researchers have typically studied the technology adoption decisions of individuals or organizations without taking into account community issues that strongly affect the innovation's inherent economic value.

Yet, community effects are likely to be crucial for software engineering process innovations because the benefits of adoption usually depend on the size of the current and future network of other adopters. (For example, widespread adoption of a software engineering process innovation increases the likelihood of the availability of complementary software tools.) Fortunately, a second line of research, in the area of the economics of technology standards, is focused on the role of community

effects on technology adoption. Hence, for the purposes of the current analysis, we will use these two complementary perspectives.

Diffusion of Innovations

DOI research has been broadly defined as the study of how innovations spread through a population of potential adopters over time.[7] From the DOI perspective, diffusion is predominantly a process of communication; when and how a potential adopter learns about an innovation are important determinants of whether that individual will adopt. Other factors include the characteristics of the adopters and the means employed by vendors and change agents to persuade them to adopt.

To address the broader question of the likely rate of adoption of a specific innovation across an entire population, one must look to attributes of the innovation itself. Everett Rogers reviewed hundreds of diffusion studies and identified five generic innovation attributes that influence rates of adoption: (1) relative advantage, (2) compatibility, (3) complexity, (4) trialability, and (5) observability.[8] Although Rogers's synthesis is based mostly on studies of adoptions by individuals (e.g., of consumer goods), Van de Ven and others have argued that innovation attributes also play an important role in adoptions by organizations.[9] In fact, these researchers maintain that innovation attributes take on a broader role in the context of organizational adoption of complex technologies, affecting not only the initial decision to adopt, but also the ease of traversing later stages of adoption such as implementation, adaptation, and routinization. Hence, the analysis of innovation attributes provides a basis for assessing not only the likely rate of adoption across a population, but also the technology's comparative "adoptability" within individual firms (i.e., the overall ease of reaching a state of routinized use).

Exhibit 1 briefly defines Rogers's five innovation attributes, tailored somewhat to better fit the context of organizational adoption of complex technologies.[10] With the exception of complexity,

---

EXHIBIT 1   Attributes of Innovations

Relative Advantage	The innovation is technically superior (in terms of cost, functionality, "image," etc.) than the technology it supersedes.
Compatibility	The innovation is compatible with existing values, skills, and work practices of potential adopters.
Complexity	The innovation is relatively difficult to understand and use.
Trialability	The innovation can be experimented with on a trial basis without undue effort and expense; it can be implemented incrementally and still provide a net positive benefit.
Observability	The results and benefits of the innovation's use can be easily observed and communicated to others.

"high" values of the attribute are favorable to easier implementation within a given organization.

The explanations for the relative advantage, compatibility, and complexity attributes are straightforward enough: organizations are more likely to be willing and able to adopt innovations that offer clear advantages, that do not drastically interfere with existing practices, and that are easier to understand. Trialability and observability are both related to risk. Adopters look unfavorably on innovations that are difficult to put through a trial period or whose benefits are difficult to see or describe. These characteristics increase the uncertainty about the innovation's true value.

Economics of Technology Standards

The traditional DOI approach is a valuable but incomplete view of the dynamics of technologies, which, like software process technologies, are subject to the phenomenon of *increasing returns to adoption*.[11] Increasing returns to adoption means that the benefits of adopting an innovation largely depend on the size (past, present, and future) of the community of other adopters. Even though the DOI perspective recognizes the effects of community adoption on how potential adopters *perceive* a technology (e.g., by increasing social pressure to adopt), community adoption levels also affect the *inherent* value of any class of technology that has large increasing returns to adoption.

Economists have identified several sources of increasing returns to adoption, but the three most applicable to software process technologies are *learning by using, positive network externalities,* and *technological interrelatedness.* Learning by using means that a technology's price-performance ratio improves rapidly as a community of adopters (vendors and users) accumulates experience in developing and applying the technology. Positive network externalities (sometimes called network benefits) means that the immediate benefits of use are a direct function of the number of current adopters. (The classic example here is the telephone network, where the number of people available to call depends on the number of previous subscribers.) Technological interrelatedness means that a large base of compatible products—and hence a large base of likely adopters—is needed to make the technology worthwhile as a whole.

Several economists have developed analytical models to predict the circumstances under which technologies subject to increasing returns to adoption are likely to achieve critical mass and be widely adopted as a standard.[12] Among them, Farrell and Saloner have noted that a group of adopters, facing a decision to adopt a new and technically superior standard, may still fail to adopt in numbers necessary to achieve critical mass because of each adopter's reluctance to be the first to pay either of two early adoption penalties: *transient incompatibility costs* (because of delays in achieving a satisfactory network for the new technology) and *risk of stranding* (because of failure to ever achieve a critical mass of adoption).[13]

These two penalties can cause "excess inertia" to develop around an existing technology and prevent the adoption of an otherwise superior new technology.[14] A well-known example of this situation is the persistence of the inefficient QWERTY layout for typewriter keyboards (designed in the late 1800s to slow typists down sufficiently to avoid key jamming) despite the later invention of many superior keyboard layouts.

What determines whether a technology will achieve critical mass? Several factors have been identified by economists: (1) prior technology "drag," (2) investment irreversibility, (3) sponsorship, and (4) expectations (see Exhibit 2).

The reasoning behind these factors is as follows. When a prior technology exists that has already developed a mature adoption network (i.e., it has a large installed base), the disparity in short-term benefits between the old and new technologies is likely to be large, even though the new technology may hold more promise in the long term. Hence the mere existence of a prior technology's installed base represents a "drag" on the community's progress toward switching to the new technology because few adopters are willing to absorb the transition costs associated with joining a small, immature network. When adoption requires large,

irreversible investments, this reluctance grows even stronger because a substantial risk premium must be added to adoption costs to take into account the chance of being stranded should a satisfactory network never develop for the new technology.

If prior technology drag and irreversible investments were the only relevant factors, dominant technologies might never be overturned. There are, however, two common ways that a new technology can overcome the head start of a prior technology: strong sponsorship and positive expectations. Sponsors can tip the cost-benefit equation in favor of the new technology by actively subsidizing early adopters, by making credible commitments to develop the technology regardless of the initial adoption rate, and by setting standards that ensure that a single network will emerge around the new technology instead of a pastiche of smaller, potentially incompatible networks (with correspondingly diffused network benefits).

Expectations about a technology's chances for dominance are also a crucial dimension in the technology standards view, for expectations largely drive critical mass dynamics. Early in the development cycle, promising new technologies typically enjoy a kind of "honeymoon" period during which some firms join an immature network assuming that widespread adoption will occur later. If not enough firms hold these positive expectations to begin with, or if the honeymoon

---

EXHIBIT 2   Economic Factors Affecting Technology Adoption

Prior Technology Drag	A prior technology provides significant network benefits because of a large and mature installed base.
Irreversibility of Investments	Adoption of the technology requires irreversible investments in areas such as products, training, and accumulated project experience.
Sponsorship	A single entity (person, organization, consortium) exists to define the technology, set standards, subsidize early adopters, and otherwise promote adoption of the new technology.
Expectations	The technology benefits from an extended period of widespread expectations that it will be pervasively adopted in the future.

period is cut short unexpectedly, then critical mass is unlikely to be achieved.

What determines the length and robustness of a new technology's honeymoon period? Positive characteristics include a strong scientific base and a clear match between the technology's unique strengths and apparent industry trends. For example, in the software industry, data-oriented design methodologies emerged at the same time many organizations were beginning to view data as a shared corporation resource. Such characteristics can lend an air of inevitability to a technology. On the negative side, widely publicized adoption "horror stories," substantial improvements to the existing dominant technology, or the rise of a new, even more promising substitute technology can cut the honeymoon period short.[15] Also, the expectation that the technology itself is soon to be significantly improved can induce inertia in potential adopters.

The technology standards approach to adoption of new technologies complements the DOI approach in three key ways. First, it defines a special class of innovations, those subject to increasing returns to adoption, to which software process technologies clearly belong. Second, it identifies several communitywide factors (e.g., prior technology drag) that are not included in the DOI view and that have an impact on the adoption of such technologies. Third, it predicts different patterns of adoption for technologies subject to increasing returns to adoption. According to the DOI perspective, innovation attributes may distinguish whether the cumulative adoption of an innovation is a steep or gently rolling S-curve, but in any case adoption should still follow an S-curve. The technology standards perspective, by contrast, sees adoption much more dichotomously: if a technology achieves critical mass within some reasonable period of time (during its honeymoon period), it will become dominant. Otherwise, the tide of expectations about the technology will turn among "swing voters," those who will consider adoption only if they expect the technology to dominate, and adoption will abruptly plateau or even turn negative as adopters discontinue use. Therefore, both perspectives add value to our discussion.

EXAMPLES OF SOFTWARE ENGINEERING INNOVATIONS

The two perspectives described above have been useful in explaining adoption in many industries, but how accurately do they describe the speed and pattern of adoption for historical innovations in software engineering?

To answer this question, we examined three recent candidates for dominance in the realm of software engineering: (1) structured analysis and design methodologies (hereafter "structured methodologies"), (2) production fourth-generation languages (4GLs), and (3) relational database management systems (RDBs). Each of these innovations was intended to revolutionize a different segment of the software engineering discipline—analysis and design, coding and testing, and data management, respectively. And, like object orientation, each was preceded by tremendous publicity. Exhibit 3 provides an overview of these technologies.

- **Structured Methodologies.** In the mid-1970s, structured methodologies (such as DeMarco structured analysis and Yourdon/Constantine structure design) emerged to replace the informal analysis and design practices of the day with an engineering style dedicated to rigorous procedures, formal diagrams, and measures of design quality. These methodologies went beyond the mere adoption of a systems development life cycle and prescribed very specific schedules of tasks and activities.
- **Production 4GLs.** Although a wide variety of special-purpose 4GLs had previously existed, it was not until the early 1980s that a new breed of production 4GLs became commercially available. Production 4GLs, unlike end-user query-oriented 4GLs like FOCUS and RAMIS II, are those languages such as Natural, ADS/Online, and IDEAL that were designed to support development of large-scale business systems, a domain that was then dominated by COBOL.
- **RDBs.** Commercial RDBs emerged in the early 1980s as an alternative to the hierarchical and network model databases such as IMS and IDMS. Although RDBs and production

EXHIBIT 3   Software Engineering Innovations

	Structured Methodologies	*Production 4GLs*	*RDBs*
General Goals	Bring engineering-style rigor to the process of systems analysis and design.	Substantially reduce the quantity of program code in typical business applications and eliminate the applications backlog.	Make databases more easily accessible and more flexible to meet changing requirements.
Prior Technology	Informal, "homegrown" analysis and design methodologies.	3GLs, especially COBOL.	Hierarchical and network database models.
Key Characteristics	Decomposition of systems development into a sequence of well-defined, mandatory activities. Formal, standard techniques and diagrams for eliciting user requirements and representing candidate designs. Metrics for judging system design quality.	Nonprocedural constructs for screen management, menus, reports, and graphics generation. Many built-in language functions (mathematical and statistical calculations, searching for character strings, etc.). High-level control clauses to facilitate structured programming (e.g., "select case").	Data represented as Mself-contained tables of values. Relationships between tables created by shared values instead of programmer-defined links. Data manipulated via powerful set-level operators (select, join, project, etc.).
Notable Example	DeMarco Structured Analysis	Natural	Oracle
Early Predictions	A revolution in software engineering. Significant reduction in systems maintenance costs. Elimination of large-scale development fiascoes.	The long-awaited death knell for COBOL. Ten-to-one improvements in programmer productivity. Applications development "without programmers."	Domination of database market. Improved database design stability and flexibility due to increased data independence. Nontechnical users develop their own queries.
Adoption History	Slow acceptance as the sanctioned approach to systems development in most large companies. Significant resistance to use in practice.	3GLs still dominant for business applications. 4GLs in danger of becoming "stranded" in face of newer technologies (CASE, code generators, object orientation).	Rapidly adopted as dominant technology for new development after some early "growing pains." Gradual conversion of existing installed base of applications.

4GLs emerged concurrently, and some vendors bundled the two technologies together, most vendors took a mix-and-match approach wherein a production 4GL could be used with nonrelational databases, and a relational database could be accessed via 3GLs, especially COBOL.

Because the adoption context is important, the analysis below assumes a large, technologically capable information systems department of a business organization during the early adoption window for the respective innovations—a typical early adopter. For structured methodologies, the early adoption window occurred in the mid-1970s when they were proposed as a replacement for informal (or no) processes. For production 4GLs and RDBs, this window was the early 1980s, when they were slated to replace 3GLs and earlier database models, respectively.

The point of studying prior technological innovations is that their adoption trajectories can be used to test dominance theories. Of the three technologies, only RDBs have proven to be dominant in the sense that they replaced the prior technology for new development activities. It is unlikely that an organization would routinely proceed with developing a new application using an older generation (nonrelational) database model, whereas organizations continually choose the older, third-generation languages for new development. Similarly, structured methodologies have not reached the stage of widespread routinized use. Many organizations still cling to ad hoc methods within the life cycle approach or have abandoned the life cycle altogether for prototyping approaches that make no use of structured methods. The lack of adoption of structured methods has even been cited as a major barrier to the adoption of integrated CASE tools.

Analysis from DOI Perspective

According to the DOI view, an innovation's adoption rate and ease of implementation are largely determined by its degree of relative advantage, compatibility, complexity, trialability, and observ-

ability. Of the three software process innovations, structured methodologies stand out as having faced particularly difficult challenges on these terms. Although structured methodologies (like any legitimate candidate to dominance) offered relative advantages over informal methodologies, relatively high complexity and relatively low compatibility, trialability, and observability raised substantial barriers to rapid widespread adoption.

Structured methodologies were largely incompatible with the practices of most development groups because they overturned the "craft-oriented" values of experienced project managers of the 1970s, who had individually acquired an idiosyncratic array of guidelines during their apprenticeships. Structured methodologies had other compatibility problems as well. They required adopters to learn an extensive new skill set, and they changed many standard work practices associated with project organization and developer-client interactions (such as requiring that greater resources be devoted to a project's analysis and design phases). In addition, structured methodologies were far more complicated than the ad hoc methods they replaced. Entire books were devoted to presenting the details, including procedural guidance, diagram notations, and diagram construction rules.

Structured methodologies were also difficult to put through a trial period because of significant upfront training costs. But as the benefits of structured methodologies were mainly improved system maintainability and avoidance of development fiascoes, an extended trial period was needed to allow time for these benefits to unfold. Finally, structured methodologies suffered from low observability because it was difficult to describe concretely how benefits such as higher maintainability were to be achieved.

In summary, the DOI view would have suggested a slow and problematic adoption of structured methodologies, owing to relatively low compatibility, high complexity, low trialability, and low observability.

Production 4GLs and RDBs, on the other hand, would have rated much more favorably, suggesting comparatively rapid and smooth diffusion. By the 1980s, programming languages had evolved through three previous technology "generations," and it was reasonable to assume that these new languages, optimistically called the fourth generation, would enjoy similar success. Vendors and the business press were reporting productivity gains of ten-to-one; indeed, one industry guru *defined* 4GLs in this way. RDBs enjoyed the advantage of a respected theoretical foundation and near universal acclaim in the academic community as a simpler, more elegant data model that was also more robust to change. Therefore, the relative advantages of production 4GLs and RDBs were perceived as being particularly high.

Production 4GLs and RDBs did not have the compatibility problems that structured methodologies had. Adoption of production 4GLs and RDBs required a more straightforward substitution of new skills for old, with no major changes in work organization or reductions in autonomy for system developers. Although some idiosyncratic 3GL skills were lost with production 4GLs, the effect was less severe than with structured methodologies. In addition, inherently high complexity was not a problem. Production 4GLs were intended to simplify programming by letting the machine do more of the work, which is not to say that production 4GLs were simple to use in some absolute sense, but rather that they were simpler to use than alternative languages like COBOL. Likewise, RDBs were much simpler to use than first-generation database systems, with relatively intuitive select and joint join commands replacing arcane pointer references.

Although production 4GLs and RDBs required upfront investments in software and training comparable to structured methodologies, it was possible to demonstrate value on a single pilot project. As a result, the costs of experimenting with either technology could be kept at reasonable levels. Finally, production 4GLs were highly observable because adopters could draw concrete comparisons between applications written in a production 4GL and a third-generation language (e.g., number

of work hours). RDBs, by contrast, suffered from lower observability because it was difficult to describe in concrete terms how they would achieve greater flexibility and data independence.

In summary, 4GLs and RDBs faced many fewer obstacles to adoption than did structured methodologies, and therefore the DOI view would have suggested more rapid and smooth adoption of these two technologies.

However, only RDBs have become dominant. Although the DOI view accounts for the fate of structured methodologies, it does not effectively discriminate between 4GLs and RDBs and, therefore, would have been an inadequate single explanation of dominance.

Analysis from Economics of Technology Standards Perspective

The three technologies under discussion are all subject to increasing returns to adoption; they become much more valuable to individual adopters to the extent that others adopt. Widespread adoption leads to faster maturation (learning by using), wider availability of qualified personnel (positive network externalities), and a larger array of complementary products and services (technological interrelatedness). Hence, the technology standards view is appropriate for analyzing the communitywide adoptability of these three technologies. As described earlier, four factors largely determine whether a technology will achieve critical mass and become a dominant technology: prior technology drag, irreversibility of investments, sponsorship, and expectations.

Production 4GLs stand out among the three technologies as having faced especially severe obstacles from the economics of technology standards view. Production 4GLs faced extensive prior technology drag, required large irreversible investments, were poorly sponsored, and had diminished expectations (due to publicity surrounding adoption fiascoes and the lack of a strong scientific base).

When introduced in the early 1980s, production 4GLs were a textbook case of an innovation facing a monolithic installed base, namely, the COBOL programming language. Forgoing the COBOL standard meant missing out on a large network of experienced personnel and compatible tools (e.g., database systems). Hence, prior technology drag was especially high.

Adoption of production 4GLs required largely irreversible investments in staff training and software—specialized assets that lose most or all of their value should the investment project be abandoned later. Naturally, organizations are reluctant to incur the risk associated with such investments, especially when the investment pertains to technologies that, like most software engineering innovations, require a critical mass of other adopters to achieve full benefits over the long term.

Lack of sponsorship also created a hurdle for 4GLs. A dominant sponsor can advance the adoption of a technology by promoting a unified standard, by subsidizing early adopters, or by making a credible commitment to develop the technology even in the face of expected delays in widespread adoption. In the case of production 4GLs, many languages emerged—none supported by a dominant sponsor. Production 4GLs even lacked a single authority figure to define exactly what capabilities a production 4GL should provide.

Finally, expectations worked against community adoption. Production 4GLs were developed primarily by innovators in the commercial sector and suffered from a lack of scientific support or more objective boosterism from the academic community. Perhaps more damaging, 4GLs experienced some widely publicized adoption fiascoes, such as the infamous New Jersey Department of Motor Vehicles case.[16]

In summary, the economics of technology standards view offers an explanation for the failure of 4GLs to achieve critical mass because of high prior technology drag, large irreversible investments, relatively poor sponsorship, and rapidly diminished expectations.

Structured methodologies and RDBs, on the other hand, would have rated much more favor-

ably from the economics of technology standards view. On the first and most important dimension—prior technology drag—structured methodologies were an attempt to impose order on chaos and thus faced essentially no installed base. RDBs faced an installed base of first-generation database systems, although not one so mature and ubiquitous as COBOL. In addition, the first-generation database market was fragmented, meaning that the benefits associated with joining the network of any given database product (e.g., IMS, or IDMS) were correspondingly reduced.

As with production 4GLs, RDBs and structured methodologies required largely irreversible investments in staff training. Additionally, adoption of RDBs required the purchase of expensive software. This suggests that the irreversible investments dimension is not a significant discriminator among any of the three technologies. On the sponsorship dimension, RDBs had a founding father in E. F. Codd who clearly established the criteria for database management systems (DBMS) to qualify as fully relational. Structured methodologies also had easily identifiable founding fathers (e.g., Ed Yourdon and Tom DeMarco, among others). Although none of the three technologies was strongly sponsored in the traditional sense of a single organization encouraging adoption, RDBs and structured methodologies had widely recognized leaders defining the technology and proselytizing for widespread adoption, and they therefore rank relatively higher than production 4GLs on this dimension.

With an unassailable scientific base and near universal support in the academic community, RDBs benefited from high expectations. In addition, the strengths of RDBs—data independence and greatly simplified information retrieval—complemented industry trends toward more data-intensive applications. Structured methodologies were certainly in line with the trend in the 1970s toward large-scale development projects, and they also escaped widely publicized disasters. Therefore, production 4GLs rated the poorest on this dimension.

To summarize, compared with production 4GLs, RDBs faced a much less well-established installed base and had the advantage of positive expectations and a strong sponsor to push forward a cohesive definition of the technology. Structured methodologies had effectively no installed base to overcome, required less in the way of irreversible investments, and were somewhat better sponsored. Hence, other things being equal, the economics of technology standards view would have implied a relatively easy community adoption of structured methodologies and RDBs.

Again, however, only RDBs have actually become dominant. Therefore, the economics of technology standards view, although accurately reflecting the fate of production 4GLs, does not effectively discriminate between structured methodologies and RDBs and therefore would have been an inadequate single explanation of the ultimate dispositions of these technologies.

FRAMEWORK FOR ASSESSING SOFTWARE ENGINEERING PROCESS TECHNOLOGIES

To summarize, the DOI perspective rates production 4GLs highly but fails to take into account the effects of increasing returns to adoption present in software process technologies. The economics of technology standards perspective rates structured methodologies highly but fails to consider the delays caused by low organizational adoptability. Of the three, only RDBs have become a dominant technology, and only RDBs rate highly on both criteria. This suggests that it may be necessary to consider both perspectives in order to accurately forecast the likelihood of the innovation dominance.

Exhibit 4 illustrates a unified framework for assessing the likelihood of software engineering technologies becoming dominant. The vertical axis reflects the DOI view of organizational adoptability. The horizontal axis reflects the economics of technology standards perspective of community adoptability. The space defined by the two con-

tinuums can be simplified by dividing each in half and creating four quadrants, each of which implies a distinctive adoption trajectory.

This framework effectively explains the adoption patterns of these three past software engineering process innovations. Production 4GLs diffused rapidly to a number of organizations but never displaced 3GLs as the dominant choice for new development, except possibly in some niche applications. 3GLs are still the language of choice for code generators, which may imply that a plateau has been reached for production 4GL adoption. Structured methodologies, almost twenty years after their introduction, are still being adopted very slowly, as evidenced by the difficulty in introducing CASE tools that are tied to these methodologies. RDBs became a dominant technology during the 1980s and now represent the vast majority of new implementations of large-scale business systems.

WHAT IS OBJECT ORIENTATION?

Object-oriented technologies are being touted as tomorrow's software process technology. In this section, we give a very brief introduction to OO as it is portrayed by its advocates. The section is designed as a primer to these ideas for the CIO or equivalent.

A daunting lexicon has developed around object-oriented technology, partly because the object-oriented approach touches all aspects of software engineering and partly because many of the concepts associated with OO have no direct analogs in the world of conventional systems development (see Exhibit 5 for a list of key terms). Yet the essence of the object-oriented approach can be captured by two principles for structuring systems: storing data and related operations together within objects (encapsulation) and sharing commonalities between classes of objects (inheritance). Advocates of OO claim that adherence to these ideas advances such long-standing software engineering goals as abstraction, modularity, and reuse.

EXHIBIT 4   Software Engineering Process Technologies Adoption Grid

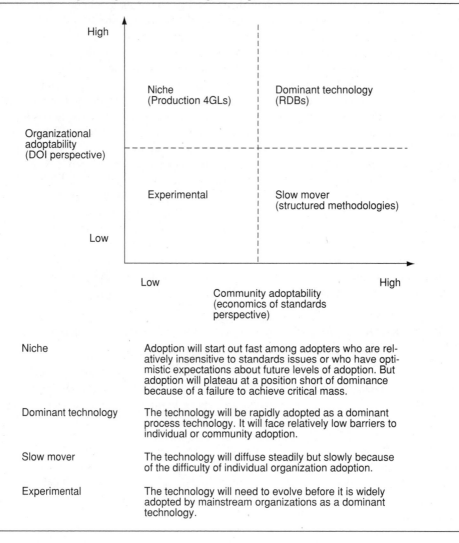

Niche	Adoption will start out fast among adopters who are relatively insensitive to standards issues or who have optimistic expectations about future levels of adoption. But adoption will plateau at a position short of dominance because of a failure to achieve critical mass.
Dominant technology	The technology will be rapidly adopted as a dominant process technology. It will face relatively low barriers to individual or community adoption.
Slow mover	The technology will diffuse steadily but slowly because of the difficulty of individual organization adoption.
Experimental	The technology will need to evolve before it is widely adopted by mainstream organizations as a dominant technology.

Designers achieve *encapsulation* by placing a set of data and all the valid operations on that data together inside a metaphorical "capsule" called an object. The logic behind encapsulation is simple: as there is usually a limited number of sensible operations for any given data structure, why not restrict processing to only these operations and put them together with the data in one place? Although this seems reasonable, it is not how traditional systems are organized. In a traditional system, the various operations associated with any given set of data (edits, calculations, transformations, update logic, and so forth) are typically repeated, more or less consistently, in many otherwise independent

---

EXHIBIT 5   Object-Oriented Terminology

Class	An abstract definition or template for a collection of objects that share identical structure and behavior.
Encapsulation	Enclosing a data structure and all operations that access the structure inside a "capsule" or object, which prevents direct access to the data by means other than those operations.
Information Hiding	A design principle that states that the internal structure of a given module should be a black box that stays hidden from other modules. Information hiding insulates other modules from changes that affect a given module's internal representation but not its external interface.
Inheritance	A mechanism that allows objects from different but related classes to share common characteristics (variable and method definitions) by placing those common characteristics in higher-level classes and creating links to those classes.
Message Passing	The practice of using explicit messages sent from one object to another as the only form of object communication. A message consists of an object identifier, a method name, and a set of arguments.
Method	A small program associated with an object that performs an atomic and cohesive operation, usually on that object's data.
Object	An abstraction of a real-world object that encapsulates a set of variables and methods corresponding to the real-world object's attributes and behaviors.
Polymorphism	A programming mechanism that allows the same message protocol to be sent to objects from distinct yet similar classes to invoke a common action. For example, polymorphism allows the same PRINT message protocol to be sent to a document or spreadsheet rather than having separate message protocols for each.
Variable	An item of data associated with an object.

---

application programs. To take a simple example, variants on an "update customer balance" operation might appear in a billing program, a cash processing program, and a credit processing program. Traditional systems are designed this way because they were developed prior to the widespread advocacy of encapsulation and because conventional languages make encapsulation, as a primary structuring principle, awkward to achieve.

Inheritance in OO is something like inheritance in the real world. To take a particularly literal example, a sporting dog inherits attributes (physical characteristics) and behaviors (pointing and retrieving) from its parents. Likewise, within an object-oriented system, classes of software objects inherit common variables and methods from an-

cestor classes. The net result of inheritance is that developers can avoid coding redundancies by placing each operation at the appropriate level in a hierarchy of system modules (object classes). For example, suppose that employees are classified as hourly or salaried. With inheritance, a designer places common data and operations in a parent "employee" class and unique characteristics (e.g., regarding compensation) in two subclasses, "hourly employee" and "salaried employee." This avoids the need to either (a) create a single set of data and operations with extra logic to handle differences between kinds of employees or (b) create two separate and largely redundant sets of data and operations (one for each employee type). As with encapsulation, inheritance is rarely used in traditional systems development because conventional programming languages make it difficult to be implemented as a primary structuring principle.

Advocates of OO have argued that encapsulation and inheritance can advance the software engineering goals of abstraction, modularity, and reuse (see Exhibit 6). These qualities in turn can drastically reduce system development and maintenance cost while improving system flexibility and quality. Not surprisingly, computer scientists have been seeking better ways to promote these three qualities for decades.

Abstraction is a tool for managing complexity. Designers promote abstraction of computer systems (or any other technical artifact) by emphasizing details that are important to the user while suppressing details that are unnecessary for the task at hand. For example, consider the different level of detail required to explain a combustion engine to a driver, mechanic, or physicist. Encapsulation promotes abstraction by making it easier to define objects in terms of *what they do* instead of *how they do it*. OO advocates believe inheritance is potentially even more powerful for promoting abstraction. One of the best ways to create useful abstractions is to describe some idea first in its most general form, followed by progressively specific versions (e.g., mammal, canine, sporting dog, retriever). This is precisely what an inheritance hierarchy does—it defines a hierarchical taxonomy of object classes from most general (at the top of the hierarchy) to most specific (at the bottom).

Modularity is a powerful tool for managing large problem domains. In fact, the structured programming movement in the late 1960s and early 1970s was largely an attempt to develop methods to improve the extent and quality of

---

EXHIBIT 6   Software Engineering Goals

Abstraction	Abstraction is a "simplified description or specification of a system that emphasizes some of the systems details or properties while suppressing others."* The evolution of software engineering can be seen as a stream of improved software abstraction mechanisms, beginning in the 1950s with the invention of symbolic assemblers and continuing over the next three decades with the invention of callable procedures, stepwise refinement, structured programming, and, especially successive generations of higher-level programming languages.
Modularity	Modularity is the principle of decomposing program logic into a collection of well-defined, self-contained units (modules) rather than creating a single, monolithic program. Ideally, modules should be loosely coupled and highly factored. Loosely coupled modules have a minimum of interdependencies, which means that an individual module can be modified or extended without causing a cascade of related changes. Factoring, the practice of putting one thing in one place, seeks to eliminate duplicate code across similar but not quite identical modules. By eliminating redundant coding efforts, factoring reduces the size of development and maintenance projects and avoids the creeping inconsistencies that may appear over time in modules that share redundant code.
Reuse	Software reuse means applying a piece of program code for some purpose beyond what is was originally intended for. Subroutine libraries, program skeletons, and cutting-and-pasting code from one program to another are all forms of reuse. The reuse of software eliminates the need to redundantly develop software, thereby improving productivity, and allows the use of tested and proven components, thereby improving quality.

*M. Shaw, "Abstraction Techniques in Modern Programming Languages," *IEEE Software,* October 1984, pp. 10–26.

modularity in delivered systems. The net result of high-quality modularity is to localize system functionality so that changes can be made to one part of a system without a cascade of related changes. This cascade of changes (the so-called ripple effect) can be devastating; in many systems, hundreds or thousands of programs may be interdependent because of program code redundancies or, more subtly, the sharing of common data. (A seemingly minor change to the meaning or structure of data can ripple across all programs that share the data.) Encapsulation promotes a looser coupling of modules by disallowing sharing of data and limiting the range of module interdependencies to their external interfaces. Inheritance, when properly used, provides an elegant tool for extracting logic common to a group of classes at one level and placing it in a single, higher-level "superclass."

Reuse is the well-known principle of avoiding extra work by not reinventing the wheel. Although software reuse is perhaps the most persistently claimed advantage of object orientation, it has existed in one form or another since the early days of programming. But although conventional approaches allow for reuse of code, object orientation provides mechanisms that facilitate and enforce reuse. Encapsulation promotes information hiding, which reduces the burden of describing and finding reusable components—a significant obstacle to reuse in a large-scale environment. Inheritance plays an even more important role. Each time a new class is defined in an inheritance structure, this implicitly enforces reuse of operations from the parents of the new class. Finally, encapsulation and inheritance can both support reuse indirectly by improving system modularity. When system components are highly modular, they are much easier to reassemble in new combinations to support a new context.

In summary, object orientation is a software engineering process innovation whose essential principles—encapsulation and inheritance—have been claimed to lead to systems that are more abstract, more modular, and more reusable.

OBJECT ORIENTATION: WHERE DOES IT FIT?

Where does object orientation fit on the new framework? Is it more likely to become a dominant technology or to end up in the slow mover, niche, or experimental categories? To answer this question, we must analyze object orientation along the dimensions of organizational adoptability and community adoptability.

Organizational Adoptability

Like production 4GLs and RDBs, object orientation rates highly on perceived relative advantage. The practitioner literature has taken an almost uniformly positive tone toward OO, and a strong body of theoretical evidence supports the approach. Proponents have argued that object orientation promotes abstraction, modularity, and reuse, all of which are long-standing objectives of the software engineering field. It is fair to assume, then, that many potential adopters will develop favorable opinions of the advantages of object orientation based on positive reviews in the literature and their own assessments of the technology's potential merits.

As in the case of structured methodologies, however, compatibility appears to be a significant pitfall. Object orientation is a new development model and requires new skills in analysis, design, and programming that replace, rather than build on, those associated with conventional development.[17] In addition, several authors have noted that successful reuse requires marked changes in culture and values.[18] It has been observed that to maximize reuse, developers must learn to assemble applications using objects developed by others. This means that developers must learn to trust classes they did not develop and to overcome the "not invented here" bias. Furthermore, OO adoption as an organization's standard approach will likely require a restructuring of development teams. Some proponents have suggested the need to institutionalize reuse through creation of a new function similar to data administration that administers and controls the common repository of reusable components.[19] Others have gone so far as to suggest that object orientation requires the creation of new categories of developers—class "producers" who develop the foundation classes in the repository and class "consumers" who assemble existing components into new applications.[20]

Object orientation, as a process technology, also rates unfavorably on the complexity dimension, even relative to other complex software engineering technologies like structured methodologies. To be successful with OO as a software engineering process technology, an adopter must absorb a new lexicon, new development methodologies, and new development tools. The need to master such concepts as encapsulation, inheritance, information hiding, polymorphism, and many others beyond those presented in Exhibit 5 represents a significant barrier to achieving an overall understanding of object orientation and its proper application.

Object orientation, as a process technology, is also difficult to put through a trial period. As with the structured methodologies, production RDBs, and 4GLs, OO will require substantial upfront expenditures on software and training in order to conduct meaningful pilot projects. Many of the ultimate benefits of object orientation come from the repository of reusable components, which may take many years to create.[21] In the meantime, adopters are likely to experience an initial productivity decline because of the extra initial effort to design modules for reuse.

As a software engineering process innovation, object orientation is largely a "black box" technology—unless one mistakenly equates object orientation, as many do, with iconic user interfaces. The benefits of object orientation resist direct observation, and few organizations collect and track the software metrics required to demonstrate increased reuse, improved maintainability, or incremental improvements in productivity. As a result, object orientation suffers from low observability.

In summary, object orientation rates comparably with structured methodologies, the least favorable

of the three previously reviewed technologies, on ease of adoption, with high relative advantage, but equal or lower ratings on compatibility, complexity, trialability, and observability.

Community Adoptability

For object orientation, the rival entrenched technology is not just a language generation or a database model, but the entire procedural paradigm for software development. It is therefore difficult to imagine a more compelling instance of prior technology drag in software engineering. New approaches have been proposed in every segment of software engineering: analysis (OOA), design (OOD), programming (OOP), and databases (OODBMS). Full object orientation also requires more extensive irreversible investments than production 4GLs or RDBs because of a substantially larger training burden and a wider array of potential software purchases (i.e., CASE tools to support analysis and design, new programming languages, and a new DBMS).

Object orientation does have a sponsor, the Object Management Group (OMG). OMG, a consortium of over two hundred technology vendors and users, performs all of the roles of a traditional technology sponsor: coordination of standards, subsidization of early adopters (e.g., through technology-sharing agreements), and general promotion of the technology (e.g., through seminars and technology fairs). However, an industry consortium is a relatively weak type of sponsor as it is subject to defections and even disbandment if the vendor participants decide it is in their interest to do so. In addition, standards generated by committee generally take longer to form than de facto or other unilateral standards and may therefore be less successful. For both these reasons, a consortium can be a weaker sponsor than a single vendor or other source.

Object orientation possesses many of the characteristics that lead to an extended period of favorable expectations. Object technology has a strong scientific base and enjoys widespread support in the academic community as a "better way" to develop software. It provides powerful mechanisms for software modularity and abstraction; these can be seen as central to most software engineering advances to date. In addition, object technology is aligned with many current technology trends. It appears well suited to event-driven graphical user interfaces, multimedia systems (voice, imaging, animation), and highly parallel processing (e.g., for full text searching and retrieval). These kinds of applications tend to require complex multilevel data structures and data encapsulation, both of which are difficult to implement within the procedural paradigm, but they play to the particular strengths of object orientation. However, production 4GLs also had high positive expectations, reflected in their very name, which implied an inevitability to their replacing 3GLs. In addition, OO faces a more sophisticated and skeptical adoption community as the passing years have provided a larger array of proposed software process technologies that failed to live up to early expectations.

In summary, object orientation rates about the same as production 4GLs, the lowest of the previously reviewed software engineering innovations, from the economics of technology standards view. Object orientation faces an even more thoroughly entrenched standard (the procedural paradigm) and requires a more extensive investment in irreversible assets than production 4GLs. Although expectations for OO are currently positive, they were similarly positive for 4GLs when first introduced. While object orientation does appear to be better sponsored than production 4GLs, this sponsorship is in the form of a potentially fragile consortium.

The combined ratings on ease of both individual and community adoption place object orientation in the experimental quadrant of the framework. This suggests that further development of the technology will be needed before widespread adoption will occur.

CONCLUSIONS

The poor state of software development practice has engendered a large number of proposed process technology improvements. Managers seeking advice on new software process technologies should learn from the lessons of technological change in other domains while recognizing the relatively unique features of software process technologies. The two-dimensional framework combines the work on diffusion of innovations and economics of technology standards to create a method for evaluating the potential of technology dominance. As we have shown, the framework offers an explanation for the adoption trajectory of previous technologies in analysis and design, coding and testing, and data management. Object orientation, the latest widely touted software process technology, rates unfavorably on both scales relative to these prior technologies and thus is unlikely to become the dominant software process technology for large in-house business application developers without significant changes.

What are the risks for the CIO of ignoring the framework when evaluating software process technologies? The primary risk associated with early adoption of niche technologies is being stranded on a technological "spur" away from the main track of technology development; the primary risk associated with early adoption of slow movers is implementation failure or the need to weather an extended period of transient incompatibility costs while waiting for a robust network to emerge. For some organizations, under some circumstances, these risks may be acceptable. Companies facing a wave of crucial new development projects that cannot feasibly be done with current technologies might consider a particularly well-suited niche technology—with the understanding that an expensive redevelopment or conversion may become necessary sooner (e.g., within five to ten years) rather than later (e.g., within ten to twenty years). Companies that are facing a major system replacement decision, that have a successful track record in adopting "bleeding edge" technologies, *and* that have the resources to support a robust internal training program might consider adopting a slow mover.

The risks of full-scale organizational adoption of current OO technology include both of the above, given its predicted trajectory into the experimental cell of the matrix. It will prove difficult to make the technology a routine part of software development. And, even if the organization successfully adopts the technology, the crucial benefits that accrue from a large network of users may never develop, given the barriers to industry adoption. The organization may end up locked into a stranded technology, finding it difficult to hire experienced staff, to purchase complementary tools, and in general to achieve the benefits that adopters of dominant process technologies enjoy.

Having said this, in the immediate future, there will no doubt be a series of OO success stories— some genuine and others overstated for dramatic effect, as vendors and early adopters try to encourage a bandwagon. In assessing these stories, however, managers must consider several key questions. First, to what degree is the system truly "object oriented"? As with expert systems, a new technology often accrues a certain status so that vendors quickly give the new label to all their technologies within reach, whether or not they actually deserve it. Second, who did the development? Results achieved by handpicked internal stars or a team of industry consultants cannot be generalized to an entire IS development organization. Third, what kind of system was developed? Here again, a stand-alone application in a specialized domain might not be representative of the broader range of large business-oriented systems that comprise the core applications of most IS organizations. And finally, has the adopting company truly made the transition to routinized use, where OO has become the default technology for new applications? All too many software innovations end up as "shelfware" after promising pilot projects, because of the difficulty in replicating the success of one team across the entire organization.

But isn't it desirable to be different from your competitors? Wouldn't being a first mover in adopting OO provide a competitive advantage as many proponents suggest? This is unlikely. Publicly available technologies rarely provide a *sustainable* competitive advantage in and of themselves: they require mating with some other relatively unique organizational competence, otherwise all competitors would also adopt the technology and quickly close the gap. In fact, in the case of OO, first movers will be in the ironic position of having to hope they are quickly followed, so that critical mass will be reached and the technology will become dominant. Meanwhile—even assuming dominance eventually is achieved—the benefits of being a first mover (e.g., riding the internal learning curve sooner, building general innovative capabilities, and attracting leading-edge personnel) could easily be outweighed by disadvantages (e.g., joining an immature network with high transient incompatibility costs, adopting an early and less favorable technology vintage, and experiencing a loss of trained staff to other companies). As a result, instances of first-mover advantages for corporate IS departments are likely to be rare. (For software vendors, however, an alternative scenario exists where heavy initial investment in OO could trigger a virtuous cycle of increased market share and resulting increased economics of scale.)

The framework we have described outlines the likely diffusion pattern at the time the ratings are performed. The most appropriate time to perform the assessment is during the technology's first widespread commercial availability. It is possible that, over a period of years, ratings on individual dimensions could evolve enough to move a technology's trajectory to a different cell. Having said that, such a move is probably unusual given the rapid arrival of new technologies and the inevitable loss of uncritical media attention typically bestowed on an emerging technology. Technologies can be new and exciting only once; premature deployment and excessive claims about benefits can be very damaging.[22] However, some speculation on the possibility of OO's trajectory changing is clearly appropriate, both for proponents who wish to increase the adoption rate of their technology and for potential adopters who wish to track the progress of this technology for signs of increasing likelihood of its widescale adoption.

On the positive side, better than expected growth in the demand for applications that fit well with the OO approach is likely to increase OO's relative advantage. Thus a growth in multimedia applications and the demand for applications running in client-server environments would clearly help. New tools that reduce the technology's complexity or make OO more compatible with existing techniques would also be positive steps. Adoption of OO techniques in university programs would enable the next generation of software engineers to avoid the compatibility trap. Favorable trade press coverage about OO success stories and the absence of widely publicized OO disasters would further improve the technology's observability and would improve the general level of expectations. The ability of the Object Management Group to maintain the coalition and generate some initial successes on standards would solidify its position as external sponsor of the technology.

On the negative side, slow progress on the above-mentioned fronts will be warning signs that OO's potential for dominance is limited. Additionally, wide-scale adoption of OO is threatened by growth from competing technologies, such as CASE (specifically CASE templates), which offers many of the same advantages of productivity, quality, and reuse. Rapid progress in this or other areas may sharply reduce OO's honeymoon period. Finally, the development of a newer, yet-to-be-announced technology could supplant the current interest in OO, riding the same wave of enthusiasm that currently benefits OO.

Our conclusion that object orientation has low prospects for becoming dominant in large in-house IS organizations is in sharp contrast to the enthusiastic touting we hear in the trade press.[23] We see many obstacles in object orientation's way. Some of these can be worked around with an appropriate adoption strategy, while others depend on communitywide actions beyond any individual adopting organization's control. For vendors and other OO proponents, this framework offers a clear agenda for the future by outlining several avenues where an aggressive, coordinated effort is needed to lower obstacles to individual and communitywide adoptability.

Notes

We received helpful comments on earlier versions of this paper from S. Brobst, E. Brynjolfsson, J. Quillard, W. Orlikowski, J. Rockart, W. Stevens, L. Votta, and participants at the UCLA Information Systems Colloquium. We gratefully acknowledge the funding provided for this work by Credit Suisse and the MIT Center for Information Systems Research.

1. M. L. Carnevale, "DSC Says Software Change Led to Phone Outages," *Wall Street Journal,* 10 July 1991, p. 5.

2. The innovation literature distinguishes *process* technology innovations from *product* innovations. A process innovation is one that changes the production process, that is, the way a product is produced. Most industrial tools, when first introduced, are simultaneously process and product innovations—a product innovation for the tool producer and a process innovation for the tool consumer. For example, for a DBMS vendor, a new RDB offering is a product innovation; for a systems developer, RDB technology is a process innovation that, among other things, involves the purchase of a product. As this article is targeted at consumers rather than producers of software technologies, we define them as process innovations. For further reading on the topic of process and product innovations, see:
W. J. Abernathy and J. M. Utterback, "Patterns of Industrial Innovation," *Technology Review,* June-July 1978, pp. 40–47.

3. L. Thurow, "Who Owns the Twenty-First Century?" *Sloan Management Review,* Spring 1992, pp. 5–17.

4. F. P. Brooks, "No Silver Bullet: Essence and Accidents of Software Engineering," *IEEE Computer* 20 (1987): 10–19.

5. W. M. Bulkeley, "Bright Outlook for Artificial Intelligence Yields to Slow Growth and Big Cutbacks," *Wall Street Journal,* 5 July 1990, pp. B1, B3.

6. "Software Made Simple," *Business Week,* 30 September 1991, pp. 92–100.

7. E. M. Rogers, *Diffusion of Innovations* (New York: Free Press, 1983).

8. Ibid., ch. 6.

9. See, for example:
    J. E. Eveland and L. G. Tornatzky, "The Deployment of Technology," in *The Processes of Technological Innovation,* eds. L. G. Tornatzky and M. Fleischer (Lexington, Massachusetts: Lexington Books, 1990), pp. 117–148;
    T. H. Kwon and R. W. Zmud, "Unifying the Fragmented Models of Information Systems Implementation" in *Critical Issues in Information Systems Research,* eds. J. R. Boland and R. Hirshheim (New York: John Wiley & Sons, 1987);
    D. Leonard-Barton, "Implementation Characteristics of Organizational Innovations," *Communication Research* 15 (1988): 603–631;
    G. C. Moore, "End-User Computing and Office Automation: A Diffusion of Innovations Perspective," *Infor* 25 (1987): 214–235;
    J. M. Pennings, "Technological Innovations in Manufacturing," in *New Technology as Organizational Change,* eds. J. M. Pennings and A. Buitendam (Cambridge, Massachusetts: Ballinger, 1987), pp. 197–216; and
    A. H. Van de Ven, "Managing the Process of Organizational Innovation" in *Changing and Redesigning Organizations,* ed. G. P. Huber (New York: Oxford University Press, 1991).

10. We use Rogers's five innovation attributes mainly because they are familiar in the DOI field. Van de Ven, Moore, and Kwon and Zmud also use Rogers's definitions, although others have provided alternative taxonomies of the salient attributes of complex organizational technologies. Leonard-Barton identifies transferability, organizational complexity, and divisibility. Pennings identifies concreteness, divisibility, and cost. Eveland and Tornatzky identify trialability, lumpiness, adaptability, degree of packaging, and the "hardness" of the underlying science. In most cases, these attributes can be mapped to one or more of Rogers's original five attributes, at least as they are used here.

11. W. B. Arthur, "Competing Technologies: An Overview," in *Technical Change and Economic Theory,* ed. G. Dosi (New York: Columbia University Press, 1987).

12. See:
    Arthur (1987);
    J. Farrell and G. Saloner, "Competition, Compatibility, and Standards: The Economics of Horses, Penguins, and Lemmings," in *Product Standardization and Competitive Strategy,* ed. H. L. Gabel (Amsterdam: North-Holland, Elsevier Science, 1987);
    M. L. Katz and C. Shapiro, "Technology Adoption in the Presence of Network Externalities," *Journal of Political Economy* 94 (1986): 822–841.

13. Farrell and Saloner (1987).

14. Ibid.

15. N. Rosenberg, "On Technological Expectations," in *Inside the Black Box: Technology and Economics* (New York: Cambridge University Press, 1982).

16. G. Rifkin and M. Betts, "Strategic Systems Plans Gone Awry," *Computerworld,* 14 March 1988, pp. 1, 104–105.

17. R. Fichman and C. Kemerer, "Object-Oriented and Conventional Analysis and Design Methodologies: Comparison and Critique," *IEEE Computer* 25 (1992): 20–39.

18. See S. Atre, "The Scoop on OOPS," *Computerworld,* 17 September 1990, pp. 1115–1116;
    J. Moad, "Cultural Barriers Slow Reusability," *Datamation,* November 1989, pp. 87–92; and
    M. Stewart, "Object Projects: What Can Go Wrong," *Hotline on Object-Oriented Technology* 2 (1991): 15–17.

19. Moad (1989).

20. Stewart (1991).

21. Atre (1990).

22. Rogers (1983) notes that unfulfilled expectations about an innovation's benefits are a primary cause of subsequent discontinuance. Leonard-Barton has argued that discontinuers can become influential "negative" opinion leaders, and that entrenched opinions about an early technology generation are hard to overturn, even when later and more viable technology generations become available. See:
    D. Leonard-Barton, "Experts as Negative Opinion Leaders in the Diffusion of a Technological Innovation," *Journal of Consumer Research,* 11 March 1985, pp. 914–926.

23. As mentioned previously, adoption context is important to the ratings. In some segments, such as CAD/CAM, CASE, operating systems, and simulation-oriented applications more obviously suited to OO's strengths, a different classification may result.

Discussion Questions

1. Choose a new OO analysis or design approach and complete a new column on one of Fichman and Kemerer's matrices. How well does the approach you have chosen match up to the earlier approaches shown in their article?

2. In Chapter 1 Fred Brooks includes OO tools on his list of "non silver bullets" for the software engineering crisis. How might Cox respond to this article?

3. Compare and contrast Cox's view of software development evolution with Shaw's from Chapter 1.

4. Use Fichman and Kemerer's framework to evaluate any other software process technology with which you may be familiar. How does it rate? How well does this match your perception of its penetration in the industry?

Chapter

10

Management of Software Reuse

INTRODUCTION

Software reuse has long been an attractive concept in software engineering. As a product, software has characteristics that distinguishes it from more typical products, particularly manufactured goods. In manufacturing, a typical goal is to efficiently produce multiple copies of what are essentially, or nearly so, identical units. Each of these units has a positive marginal cost associated with it. In software, the primary resources are devoted toward producing ("designing", in the broad sense of the term) the first unit, while the "manufacturing" of additional units is seen as costly beyond the costs of the media. The presumption, then, is that each piece of software to be written is somehow different than what is already available. This presumption, while essentially true, masks the fact that there is much commonality across software, particularly in domains that have been subject to at least some software support for any length of time. In fact, at least one author has suggested that, on average, as little as 15% of well-understood applications may, in fact, be unique[1]. This underlying notion has spanned a great amount of thought about how to capture previous work products when developing new pieces of software. This work is well-documented in collections devoted exclusively to software reuse such as Biggerstaff and Perlis's *Software Reusability* and Freeman's *Tutorial: Software Reusability*. Four managerially oriented articles are provided in this chapter. The first provides an overview of software reuse, the middle two present the business case for reuse, and the final chapter documents the practical experiences of an organization that implemented a systematic reuse effort.

Barnes and Bollinger take an appropriately expansive view of reuse as the reuse of human problem solving. This is in contrast to much of the technical literature in software reuse which views the problem narrowly as reuse of code. After explaining the essential concepts, Barnes and Bollinger outline three general steps toward maximizing the benefit to cost ratio of reuse: (1) increase the total level of reuse, (2) decreasing the average cost of reuse, and (3) decrease the cost of investment in reusable components. They also outline two broad strategies. They term one strategy adaptive; the reuse of relatively large structures by making small changes to them. The other strategy

---

[1]Jones, T. C., "Reusability in Programming: A Survey of the State of the Art." *IEEE Transactions on Software Engineering*, SE-10(5): 488–494 (1984).

is termed compositional reuse, the assembly of relatively small structures to create new wholes. Examples of the former can be seen in approaches such as CASE tool templates[2], and examples of the latter in approaches such as object orientation.

The second article in this chapter, by Wayne Lim, provides a quantitative assessment of two multi-year endeavors at Hewlett-Packard to increase software reuse. Lim documents the significant increases in both product quality (in terms of reduced number of defects) and development productivity (in terms of delivered lines of code) at both Hewlett-Packard sites. While many authors acknowledge that reuse is not free, due both to the cost of reuse and to the additional costs to make a component more easily reusable, Lim actually quantifies this investment and performs a net present value calculation to show the significant positive ROI for software reuse. This article won the best paper of the year award from *IEEE Software* for 1994.

In a similar fashion, Banker and Kauffman document the experience of a large financial services firm in their use of an integrated CASE tool specifically designed to promote reuse. They studied twenty projects completed by this firm over a two year period and measured their productivity in terms of the number of Function Points produced per effort required (see Chapter 4). They are able

---

[2]Hofman, J. D. and J. F. Rockart, "Application Templates: Faster, Better, and Cheaper Systems." *Sloan Management Review*, 36(1): 49–60 (1994).

to show that productivity improved significantly from the first year to the second, supporting some of the CASE tool learning curve ideas from Chapter 8. They also develop a new reuse ratio, in terms of the number of the tool's "objects" (not to be confused with an object-oriented approach) that are reused.

The final article, by Apte et al., documents the experience of a commercial bank in implementing a systematic reuse program. In contrast to the previous two articles, the Apte et al. piece is relatively more limited in the quality of its quantitative benefits results, which are based primarily on estimates. However, the Apte et al. article makes an important contribution in terms of its documentation of the organizational factors that they found to either promote or inhibit reuse. They illustrate the need for top management support, since the total program was phased in over a five year period. The need for top management support is further sustained by Apte et al.'s clear explication of the conflicts faced by project managers in terms of the strong incentives provided by deadlines and budgets to deliver today's project as soon and as cheaply as possible, in contrast to the extra time and effort required to develop software for reuse. The authors argue strongly for the need to provide these project managers and their staff with incentives to both contribute to, and, in many cases, reuse from, a software library. They further emphasize the critical role played by documentation in promoting the use of library components.

MAKING REUSE COST-EFFECTIVE

There has been quite a bit of debate in the last few years on the merits of software reuse. One reason for this continuing debate has been a question of scope: Should software reuse be defined narrowly in terms of one or a few specific methods (such as libraries of scavenged parts), or should it be defined broadly so it includes widely differing methods and processes?

The question of scope is important, since it really asks whether the concept of software reuse provides any major insight into the software-development process. A narrow definition implies that reuse is simply another development technique that, like many other techniques, is helpful in some contexts and inappropriate in many others. A broad definition implies that reuse incorporates one or more general principles that should be recognized and addressed explicitly in the software-development process.

We believe that reuse is in fact one of the fundamental paradigms of development and that, until it is better understood, significant reductions in the cost of building large systems will simply not be possible. We base this assertion primarily on our belief that:

The defining characteristic of good reuse is not the reuse of software per se, but the reuse of human problem solving.

A SCARCE RESOURCE

By "human problem solving," we mean those non-repetitive, nontrivial aspects of software development and maintenance that cannot easily be formalized or automated using current levels of expertise.

Article by Bruce H. Barnes and Terry Bollinger. © 1991 IEEE. Reprinted, with permission, from (*IEEE Software;* 1, 13–24; January/1991).

Unlike many other hardware and software resources used in development, human problem solving cannot readily be multiplied, multiplexed, accelerated, or enhanced. Problem solving thus shares many of the characteristics of precious metals in the materials-processing industry: It must be used judiciously, replaced by less expensive resources when possible, and recovered for further use whenever feasible.

If human problem solving is viewed as a scarce resource then the three techniques of judicious use, replacement, and recovery correspond fairly closely to project planning, automation, and reuse:

- Good planning reduces the loss of human problem solving by minimizing redundant and dead-end work, by enhancing communication of solutions among developers, and by helping development groups select environments that support worker productivity.
- Automation is the classic process of tool building, in which well-understood work activities such as the conversion of formulas into assembly code are replaced with less costly automated tools such as compilers.
- Reuse multiplies the effectiveness of human problem solving by ensuring that the extensive work or special knowledge used to solve specific development problems will be transferred to as many similar problems as possible. Reuse differs from judicious planning in that it can actually amplify available problem-solving resources, just as automation can amplify the effect of well-understood, formally defined work activities.

Broad-Spectrum Reuse

If the key feature of effective software reuse is the reuse of problem-solving skills, it follows that reuse should not be restricted to source code. Any work product that makes problem solutions readily accessible to later projects is a good candidate for reuse. (A work product is any explicit, physical result of a work activity in the development and maintenance process.)

Examples of potentially reusable work products are requirements specifications, designs, code modules, documentation, test data, and customized tools.

This idea of *broad-spectrum* reuse[1] is particularly important because it has the potential to reduce costs substantially. It can reduce costs because reusing an early work product can greatly increase the likelihood of reuse of later work products developed from it.

For example, although reusing code modules from a custom database system can certainly reduce costs, reusing the system's overall functional specification could lead to the reuse of the entire set of designs, code modules, documentation, test data, and associated user experience that were developed from that specification. The chances of cost-effective reuse are much higher, both because more work products are reused and because the effort needed to adapt and integrate those work products into a new environment is greatly diminished.

Curiously, informal reuse of early work products is actually very common, but it often is not recognized because it masquerades as code-level reuse. Informal reuse of early work products occurs primarily when highly experienced developers use their familiarity with the functionality and design of a code module set to adapt those modules to new, similar uses[2].

This powerful form of reuse is feasible only when developers can use their familiarity with early work products to zero in on the code modules that were derived from those products. The fact that these early work products may reside entirely within the developers' memories does not diminish their importance. Indeed, such situations point out the importance of automated support for reuse early in the life cycle. You need only have those developers retire or quit to discover how inefficient true code-level reuse is by comparison!

Reuse and Automation

Thinking of effective software reuse as problem-solving reuse provides a good general heuristic for judging a work product's reuse potential. For example, modules that solve difficult or complex problems (like hardware-driver modules in an operating system) are excellent reuse candidates because they incorporate a high level of problem-solving expertise that is very expensive to replicate.

In contrast, a set of Unix date-and-time routines that differ only in their output formats are generally poor reuse candidates. You can program such format variants easily in Unix by using a stream editor such as Sed to modify the output of the standard date-and-time function. This approach is very flexible, and it requires little problem-solving skill beyond specifying the desired output formats and familiarity with a standard Unix tool. Trying to anticipate all the possible variants of date-and-time formats would in effect place a costly reuse technique (building a large library of variants) in direct competition with an existing automated method (generating variants by directly specifying output formats).

This example leads to a general rule:

Reuse should complement automation, not compete with it.

Automation and reuse are complementary in that automation tries to transfer as much work as possible to the computer, while reuse tries to make the most efficient use of work activities that cannot be fully automated.

Automated problem solving may one day help reduce the need for the human variety, but until that day arrives, software reuse offers a practical, high-potential approach to stretching the critical development resource of human problem solving.

REUSE AS AN INVESTMENT

If reuse is a vital component of the development process, what then is the best approach to understanding it and increasing its efficiency? First and foremost, we must recognize that reuse has the same cost and risk characteristics as any financial investment. Exhibit 1 illustrates why reuse should be viewed as an investment and introduces the reuse-investment relation.

Reuse-Investment Relation

The left side of this relation, the producer side, represents all the investments made to increase reusability. Reuse investments are any costs that do not directly support the completion of an activity's primary development goals but are instead intended to make one or more work products of that activity easier to reuse. For example, labor hours devoted specifically to classifying and placing code components in a reuse library are a reuse investment, since those hours are intended primarily to benefit subsequent activities.

Reuse investments should not be confused with the costs of making software maintainable, since maintainability costs are an integral part of building deliverable products. Instead, the completion of maintenance investments is the starting point for reuse investments. This distinction is particularly important because maintenance technology overlaps extensively with reuse technology. The threshold between these two costs is best defined in terms of global objectives, rather than in terms of specific technologies.

The right side of the reuse-investment relation, the consumer side, shows the cost benefits accrued as a result of earlier reuse investments. For each activity that applies reuse, the benefit is simply a measure in dollars of how much the earlier investment helped (or hurt) the activity's effectiveness.

To calculate the reuse benefit, you must first estimate the activity's cost without reuse and compare that to its cost with reuse. For example, if an activity placed several reusable components in a library, a subsequent activity would estimate its reuse benefit by comparing total development costs without reusing those components to total development costs when the reusable components are fully exploited.

You find the *total reuse benefit* by estimating the reuse benefit for *all* subsequent activities that profit from the reuse investment, even if those activities occur in the distant future. It is vital that you include all activities that benefit from a

---

EXHIBIT 1   Reuse-Investment Relation

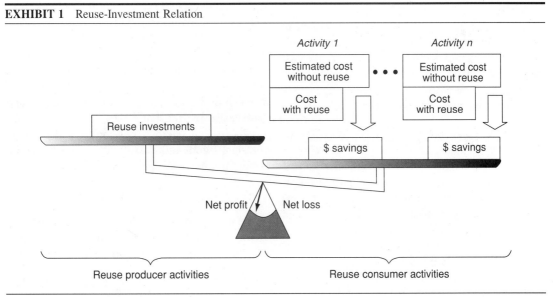

reuse investment, because it is this total benefit that determines the maximum level of reuse investment that you can apply economically to a set of work products.

In short, reuse investment is cost effective only when

$$R < B$$

where R is the total reuse investment and B is the total cost benefits. B is in turn defined as

$$B = \sum_{i=1}^{n} b_i = \sum_{i=1}^{n} [e_i - c_i]$$

where b_i is the benefit from reuse investment for activity i, e_i is the estimated cost of activity i without exploiting reuse, c_i is the cost of activity i when reuse investment is exploited, and n is the number of activities affected by the investment.

If an early estimate of the total reuse benefit indicates that it will be very small, you should make only a very limited investment in reuse technologies (beyond those needed to meet maintenance requirements). If estimates indicate that the total benefit will be very great, you should make substantial investments in advanced reuse technologies.

In either case, the failure of a development group to acknowledge the constraints of the reuse-investment relation could be disastrous from a cost perspective. After all, of what use is a very impressive, very advanced suite of reusable software if no one ever gets around to reusing it?

PRODUCERS AND CONSUMERS

In Exhibit 1, activities that work to increase the reusability of work products are called reuse producer activities and activities that seek to reduce costs through reuse of work products are called reuse consumer activities. We intentionally used terminology with strong commercial implications because the underlying processes behind software reuse and commercial software marketing are strikingly similar.

Vendors of commercial software achieve net cost benefits only when their products are purchased (reused) enough times to cover development costs, just as reuse producers achieve a net benefit only when their work products are reused enough times to cover investment costs. Most reuse producers (vendors) and reuse consumers (buyers) differ from their commercial counterparts primarily in that the transfer of products between them takes place within a single company or project, rather than across company or organizational boundaries.

The producer/consumer reuse model is rich in both managerial and technical implications. One obvious managerial implication is that organizations that fail to provide some form of payback incentives to producer projects are unlikely to succeed at reuse, since producers will, in effect, be penalized for making overhead expenditures that do not directly contribute to their development project.

Indeed, it is likely that one of the most significant inhibitors of reuse in the software industry is a lack of incentive strategies to encourage coordinated reuse investments. Without such incentives, reuse becomes a scavenger hunt, where each reuse customer must bear the full cost of finding, understanding, and modifying work products to meet his needs.

Scavenging is an extremely inefficient form of reuse because it duplicates reengineering costs each time the product is reused. Well-planned investments made up front by producers can make it much easier for consumers to find, understand, and customize the parts they need. Also, reuse producers can build in reusability, which avoids the significantly more costly task of reengineering reusability into existing work products.

MAKING REUSE COST-EFFECTIVE

Another way to express the reuse-investment relation is to define a *quality-of-investment measure,* Q, which is simply the ratio of reuse benefits to reuse investments:

$$Q = B/R$$

where R is the total reuse investment and B is the total cost benefits resulting from reuse investment.

The Q measure is just another way of saying, "Try to get the most for your money." If Q is less than 1 for a reuse effort, there was a net financial loss; if Q is significantly greater than 1, the reuse investment provided good returns.

In the case of commercial products, Q can become very large due to the many reuses (sales) afforded by commercial marketing. The commercial-marketing comparison again points out an important issue: Reuse investments are most likely to pay off when they are applied to high-value work products. Applying expensive reuse technologies to low-value work products is not at all likely to produce reuse winners, although in some cases such a strategy may result in particularly spectacular failures.

If the key to making reuse cost-effective is to increase the Q measure, how is such an increase best accomplished? The variables in the reuse-investment relation suggest three major strategies for increasing Q:

- Increase the level of reuse.
- Reduce the average cost of reuse.
- Reduce the investment needed to achieve a given reuse benefit.

We have developed ways to implement these strategies, and in the process we uncovered a few surprising implications about how reuse is closely linked to the general problem of developing high-quality software.

INCREASING REUSE

The first strategy for increasing Q is to increase the level of consumer reuse. However, the likely level of consumer reuse for a work product depends strongly on the product's intrinsic value. Components that incorporate a high level of unique expertise are far more likely to have a large reuse market than are weak products that lack distinctive features.

Increasing the number of actual instances of reuse thus should be viewed primarily as an analysis task, to identify the relative merit of investing in a set of work products. By performing such an analysis early in development, you can avoid low-value investments and more accurately determine the potential of high-value products.

Reuse Instances

A *reuse instance* occurs whenever a work product is actually reused in a subsequent development activity. Due to the strong (roughly linear) dependence of Q on the overall level of reuse, if you have low expectations for the number of reuse instances, you should keep the average level of reuse investment per unit of code low. But if you expect many reuse instances, the project may merit much more extensive reuse investments per unit of code.

In estimating reuse instances, an important first step is simply to ask questions. Often, if you ask the specifiers and architects of a new system to make an order-of-magnitude guess of the number of reuse instances (one? 10? 1,000?), they can do so with little difficulty. Even such rough approximations can help you avoid costly overinvestments.

Reuse and Competition

The process of estimating reuse instances for a software component is linked to the much broader problem of understanding the commercial software market. This is because all forms of reuse are essentially competitive: Any group that wants to reuse software must decide whether to take that software from a corporate reuse library or buy it. If the quality of library software is low, if it requires extensive adaptation, or if it is poorly documented, it is entirely possible that a similar commercial product with an initially higher cost could in the long run prove to be less costly than the equivalent "free" software.

This means that reuse investors should be careful not to inflate instance estimates with reuse opportunities that are real but that are likely to be filled by products from other sources. As an extreme example, very few developers should seriously consider making a custom file system reusable, since this would place them in direct competition with a very advanced commercial market for database-management systems. A realistic estimate of the number of reuse instances in this case should be very low, perhaps zero.

You can greatly reduce the risks of mistakenly competing with external markets if you apply the principle that good software reuse is actually good problem-solving reuse. Most companies are particularly skilled in one or more problem-solving areas, which gives them important competitive advantages. A company that builds software for the National Aeronautics and Space Administration may have special expertise in flight-dynamics algorithms, for example. If a persistent need for this type of expertise is expected, the company might well find it profitable to build reusability into its flight-dynamics software. A rule of thumb summarizes such situations:

Build reusable parts for local expertise; buy reusable parts for outside expertise.

Variants Analysis

Estimating reuse instances is the simplest form of a more general type of analysis that we call *variants analysis*. Variants analysis is to reusable software what requirements analysis is to traditional once-only software. Its objective is to quantify requirements for reuse investment up front, just as requirements analysis attempts to quantify requirements for functionality up front.

As in reuse-instance estimation, variants analysis in its simplest form consists simply of asking questions—explicitly examining how future development or maintenance efforts may use updated or altered versions of the current project's functional requirements.

More elaborate forms of variants analysis require a structured format to record such information. By analogy with requirements specifications, these repositories of information about likely future variants are called variants specifications.

Variants Specifications

A variants specification is a requirements specification extended to include the best available information on how the activity's work products are likely to be reused.

To help designers translate these specifications into reusable products, they are stated in terms of product variants—functional variations of the primary product. Product variants can be described in many ways, ranging from explicit descriptions of multiple products to parameterized, generic requirements.

Unlike a requirements specification, a variants specification tries to describe an objective that is inherently heuristic—it must express a set of best guesses as to which of a potentially infinite range of product variants is most likely to be needed in the future.

This likelihood of use can be described in terms of a probability percentage, which may range from 100 percent for products that are specifically required as part of the product delivery, through moderate values (10 percent) for variants that are fairly good reuse candidates, to potentially very low values (0.01 percent) for product variants that are not likely to be needed but that could be very valuable if they are ever actually reused.

You can also use such likelihood-of-use percentages to set priorities, where a 100-percent rating would indicate a customer requirement that must be met to fulfill contractual obligations, while lower ratings would determine the relative value of variants.

Because variants specifications describe sets of software products, you can make them as simple or as elaborate as you want. If you describe only one product (all requirements have 100-percent priority), the variants specification is identical to a (simplistic) requirements specification. Better is a group of variants specifications that correspond to a typical requirements specification.

Although requirements specifications are not usually viewed in terms of reuse, they normally contain some variants requirements phrased in terms of modularity and portability. For example, a requirement that a product must be portable across Digital Equipment Corp., IBM, and Sun computers is a variants requirement, because it says in effect that there is a very high probability that the customer will reuse (port) the product to one or more environments.

Reuse, Maintenance, and Good Design

Besides reusability, there is another intriguing reason explicit variants analysis could be a useful addition to the development process.

A key feature of a well-designed architecture is that it be easy to maintain, since such systems are more likely to have a long useful life span and less likely to be expensive to support. However, software maintenance is itself a form of reuse-with-replacement, in which new variants of entire systems are created and then substituted for the original systems.

From this perspective, the problem of creating a well-designed system is fundamentally a problem of anticipating its most likely variants and of applying design techniques that will ensure that the most likely variants will also be the least expensive to build during maintenance—in other words, variants analysis. Current design approaches apply general rules that, while they usually result in designs that support the necessary variants, lack the specificity provided by an explicit variants analysis.

If variants analysis is in fact a hidden dimension of good software design, then a better understanding of how to build highly reusable software could simultaneously lead to a more quantitative understanding of what makes a particular design "good" or "bad." It would also imply that good design may be a more relative concept than is generally recognized. A design that supports long-term maintenance very well in one corporate environment could simultaneously be badly mismatched to the long-term needs of a different corporate environment.

REDUCING COST

The second technique for increasing the investment-quality measure Q is to reduce the average cost of reusing work products by making them easy and inexpensive to reuse. Just as commercial vendors try to make their packages easy to adapt to the environments of many customers, reuse producers need to encourage reuse of their products by making them easy to find, adapt, and integrate into new systems.

How much a reuse producer can invest in such efforts will depend both on expected levels of reuse and the availability of appropriate reuse technologies. Reducing the cost of reuse thus depends to a large degree on selecting technologies that adequately support the needs of reuse customers while constraining reuse investment costs to acceptable levels.

Classifying Reuse Technologies by Cost

To select reuse technologies on the basis of cost versus power, you first must compare them in these terms. Exhibit 2 shows some ballpark approximations of how various code-specific reuse technologies compare in terms of costs versus power[3]. (Comparable sets of reuse technologies for noncode work products such as designs and requirements specifications do not yet exist. This is a curious deficiency, since the development of such broad-spectrum reuse technologies may eventually prove to be a profitable enterprise.) The diagram has three dimensions: reuse investment costs, component generality, and cost to reuse.

Reuse Investment Costs

The reuse investment cost is the total cost to the producer to make parts readily available for reuse. Comparing technologies along this dimension alone will help eliminate major classes of reuse technologies as too costly. For example, program generators (exemplified by operating-system Sysgen programs) are very powerful and easy to use but require large investments[4]. You can justify

EXHIBIT 2   Cost-Based Selection of Reuse Technologies. Component Generality Refers to the Number of Readily Available Variations of a Part; Producer Cost is the Total Cost of Making Parts Readily Available to Later Developers

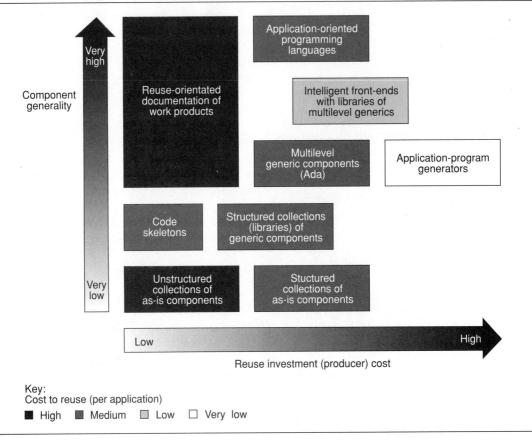

Key:
Cost to reuse (per application)
■ High   ■ Medium   □ Low   □ Very low

such investments only if you anticipate many potential reuse instances, such as is true for operating-system installations.

Component Generality

The component-generality dimension introduces the concept of the relative power of a reuse technology, expressed in terms of how many variations of a part can readily be obtained by applying that technology. Generality measures how well a particular technology can cover the needs of an application area. Because very few parts can be reused without some modification, a technology that provides large suites of easy-to-reuse, predefined variants greatly increases the total number of reuse opportunities.

But building generality into reusable parts tends to be expensive and labor-intensive. While Ada's generic procedures are undeniably more flexible and reusable than conventional Fortran-like procedures, they are also significantly harder to build.

Generative methods are an extreme example of component generality. In effect, these methods allow the synthesis of reusable parts from application-specific languages in much the same way that compilers allow the synthesis of object-code modules from higher level languages. Although generative methods provide high levels of generality and ease of use, they require extensive analysis and preparation. Their high investment cost thus makes them appropriate only when you anticipate very many reuse instances.

Cost to Reuse

The cost to reuse is the total cost to the reuse consumer of finding, adapting, integrating, and testing a reusable component. In the simplest cases, you can minimize the cost to reuse by identifying a plausible level of reuse investment and choosing the corresponding reuse technology that has the lowest cost to reuse.

Thus, if a reuse producer group has identified the need for a moderate level of reuse investment and has adequately characterized the likely reuse instances, it might choose to use Ada generics, for example, to implement its reusable components.

The key phrase, however, is "adequately characterized." The problem is that the generality of Ada generics is comparatively low, because they primarily substitute data types rather than modify functionality. If future reuse instances are poorly characterized, this means that highly specific generalizations could easily miss the target of actual future needs. Alternately, the total costs of generalization could become excessive as the developers try to use an overly restrictive technique to cover a very broad range of conceivable reuse instances.

REDUCING INVESTMENT COSTS

The prospect of overextending a reuse technology brings up the third strategy for increasing the Q measure: reducing investment costs. Just as a reuse technology that is not general enough can be unduly expensive for reuse consumers, a technology that is either overextended or more general than necessary can result in excessive costs to the reuse producer.

What you need is a way to analyze the information provided by variants analysis more carefully, so the level of generality provided by reuse technologies will match future expected needs.

The starting point for this matching is the concept of *instance spaces,* which let you define the generality level of reusable components more precisely. The instance space of a component or other work product is the full set of variants that can be retrieved at reasonable cost (defined as less than the equivalent full development cost) by a reuse consumer.

Exhibit 3 shows an instance space for an Ada generic component. An important feature of an instance space is that it makes no difference whether a specific instance of a part is actual (a part in a library) or virtual (a potential but as-yet-unrealized instantiation). Because they abstract out the issue of whether a part is physical, instance spaces let you compare highly diverse reuse technologies such as code libraries and generative methods.

Instance-space abstraction also takes manual methods into account, since they can be classified as having very large instance spaces (people can program nearly anything in time) but high consumer costs (programming is more expensive than, say, building new procedures with Ada generics).

Matching Generality to Needs

In variants analysis, you characterize consumer needs in terms of product variants. Characterizing variants this way lets you compare the results of variants analysis to the instance spaces of generalized components or work products.

Exhibit 4 shows such a comparison, including the three groups of instances that normally result from an intersection of variants and instance spaces. These three groups are labeled in terms of how they are perceived by reuse consumers: extensive-adaptation instances, moderate- to minimal-adaptation instances, and unused instances.

- Extensive-adaptation instances are actually accessed and used by consumers, but they are so

---

EXHIBIT 3   Instance Spaces

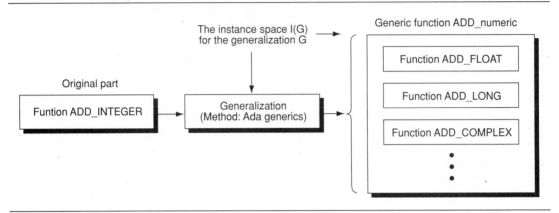

difficult to adapt that the cost benefits are negligible or possibly even negative. These instances represent lost opportunities where a reusable part could have provided cost benefits, but its generalization failed to anticipate the needs of the consumer adequately.

- Moderate- to minimal-adaptation instances represent significant cost benefits to one or more customers. In these cases, the part was generalized so it was easy to retrieve and adapt.
- Unused instances are a large category that, while they should be expected in any application, should be controlled by reuse producers to prevent overinvestment. Many low-cost unused instances are generally acceptable and even desirable as insurance, but many unused instances created with expensive technologies could easily result in reuse-investment losses.

Comparing instance spaces to variants analysis works best when the product is relatively small. Otherwise, the size of the instance space becomes so large that it becomes impractical to directly characterize the moderate- to minimal-adaptation instances.

Even for small components, the instance spaces are typically so large that they are better handled by specifying characteristics than by explicitly enumerating all possible instances. Thus, you would characterize the moderate- to minimal-adaptation instance space for the Ada generic example of Exhibit 3 by specifying key constraints, such as the potential need for any legal scalar variant of the routine, the exclusion of matrix-algebra variants, and the need for a particular range of computational accuracies.

Again, the most important reason to perform such characterizations is to encourage reuse investment decisions based explicitly on expected needs, instead of on habit or what's easiest to do. For example, if you could firmly establish that the generic addition routine in Exhibit 3 would never be reused in any applications requiring complex algebra, you could avoid the extra expense of generalizing that routine to include complex addition. Conversely, if the routine was part of a larger package for which conversion to matrix algebra was plausible, the extra effort to add hooks for such conversion might be worthwhile.

Mixing Reuse Technologies

You need not pick just one reuse technology for a set of components. In fact, it is more likely that the best and most economical coverage of consumer needs will be provided by two or more reuse technologies.

EXHIBIT 4   Cost Objectives in Building Highly Reusable Software

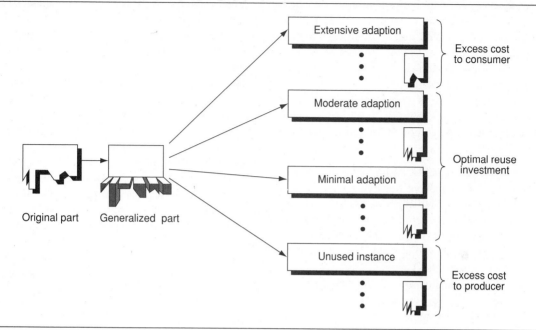

Original part   Generalized part

Extensive adaption — Excess cost to consumer

Moderate adaption

Minimal adaption — Optimal reuse investment

Unused instance — Excess cost to producer

The reason for this is related to risk reduction. In most cases, you will be able to describe likely consumer variants only in broad terms. While you may be able to state firmly that there will be many instances of reuse within a broad set of variants, you may not know where in that set those instances will fall. Ada generics are a simple example of this situation, since they involve cases where the need for new data types is well established but the exact definition of those data types cannot be known until the consumer actually needs a new routine.

Such late-binding situations are best covered by reuse technologies that provide a high level of generality, but they are relatively costly to the consumer. An example of such a technology is reuse-oriented documentation, which amounts to simply ensuring that the results of variants analysis are embedded as documentation throughout a development effort's work products.

On the other hand, instances that are very good candidates for reuse should be handled using technologies that pass the lowest possible cost to the reuse consumer. Moving costs to the producer for such sure-bet cases is nearly always appropriate, since the developer of a system can usually generalize its work products far more cheaply than later reuse consumers can reengineer them.

In these cases of certain reusability, it may be inappropriate to invest in large amounts of costly generality, because the target reuse instances are already well characterized. An extreme example is a reuse variant that is fully specified and is 100-percent certain to be needed. In this case, the ideal reuse strategy would be to build the reuse instance at the same time the primary product is built.

REUSE STRATEGIES

Although instance spaces help represent the diversity and quality of reusable parts, they rapidly become intractably large and difficult to characterize as the complexity of reusable components increases.

What we need is a way to introduce modularity into the design of reusable systems so the instance-space size can be made more tractable. Modular reuse strategies should take a divide-and-conquer approach that supports both the design of new, highly reusable systems and the analysis of existing, potentially reusable systems.

The starting point is to recognize that you can view reuse (and development) as the construction of new systems by combining two forms of functionality:

- Invariant functionality, which is the set of components (or component fragments) that are used without change. Mathematical routines are common examples. By definition, invariant functionality alone cannot create a new system, since it lacks the customization needed to meet a new set of requirements.
- Variant functionality, which is the set of new functionality (software) that must be added to customize invariant components. Variant functionality may be as simple as a set of arguments passed to a parameterized package, or as complex as full, from-scratch, new-system development.

Mixing Variant and Invariant Functionality

Regardless of how simple or complex a system is, it will always contain some mix of these two functionality types. Invariant functionality provides the kernel of functionality around which new systems are constructed; variant functionality provides the novel functionality that lets a system address a new set of needs.

The objective of reuse-intensive development is not to do away with the variant component, since that would, in effect, prevent any new needs from being addressed. The objective of effective reuse-intensive development is the creation of invariant components that help focus the development of variant functionality into very precise, succinct statements of the differences between the old and new systems.

Paradoxically, then, reuse-intensive development is best accomplished by focusing more on how to change software effectively than on how to keep it from changing. Well-focused mechanisms for expressing variant functionality will do far more to keep large sections of code invariant than will arbitrary attempts to build around existing code components.

The concept of variant and invariant functionality can readily be extended to noncode work products by analyzing how they can be built by combining baseline components of various sizes and types. As with executable code, the objective in building, say, a highly reusable system specification is to develop a set of baseline components that support concise, succinct descriptions of how new specifications differ from existing ones. Technologies such as hypertext are being applied toward this type of objective[5], but far more work on characterizing the features of "good" variant and invariant components of noncode work products must be done.

Two Fundamental Strategies

If reusable systems are always constructed from some mix of invariant and variant functionality then the way in which they are combined is an important criterion for evaluating a system's reuse characteristics. This observation leads immediately to the definition of two broad, complementary reuse strategies, which are shown in Exhibit 5:

- Adaptive reuse uses large frame structures as invariants and restricts variability to low-level, isolated locations within the overall structure[6]. Examples include changing arguments to parameterized modules, replacing low-level I/O modules, and altering individual lines of code within modules. Adaptive reuse is similar to maintenance in that both try to isolate changes to minimize their system-wide impact.
- Compositional reuse uses small parts as invariants and variant functionality as the glue that links those parts[7,8]. Examples include constructing systems from parts in a reuse library and programming in high-level languages. As its name implies, compositional reuse is similar to

EXHIBIT 5   Fundamental Reuse Strategies. (A) Adaptive Reuse; (B) Compositional Reuse

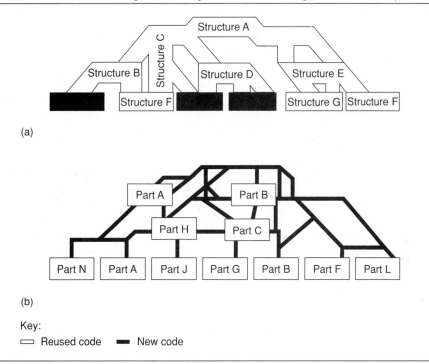

(a)

(b)

Key:

☐ Reused code   ■ New code

conventional programming, in which individual functions of moderate complexity are composed according to some grammar to create new, more powerful functions.

Differences

In terms of cost and component-generality characteristics, adaptive and compositional reuse are strikingly different. For example, because adaptive reuse tries to keep most of the overall structure invariant, it tends to be application-specific and comparatively inflexible, but it helps keep both producer and consumer reuse costs under control.

By contrast, compositional reuse can be very flexible if the initial set of reusable components is sufficiently rich and generalized. However, constructing such a generalized component set (such

as the functions in an application-specific language) can be very expensive for the reuse producer. Also, consumer costs for compositional reuse tend to rise rapidly as the complexity of the constructed software increases; when compositional reuse is extended too far, it begins to look more and more like conventional programming.

Coverage Level

For compositional reuse, we make a further distinction based on the coverage level of part sets. Coverage level refers to the ability of a set of parts to address an application area without forcing the consumer to use a lower level language such as Ada or Cobol. There are two major coverage types:

• Full-coverage sets are sufficiently rich and complete to let you solve new problems within a

well-defined application area using only those reusable parts. Examples of full-coverage sets include application-specific languages and abstract data types implemented with Ada packages.
- Partial-coverage sets provide representative parts that act as examples of the component types needed to solve problems in an application area. However, partial-coverage sets are not sufficiently generalized to let you solve all problems in that application area without resorting to the use of lower level languages. A library is a good example of a partial-coverage set, because the parts in it usually are neither highly generalized nor complete in their coverage of a problem area.

Partial-coverage sets are likely to be much less expensive to produce, but they are also more likely to be expensive to reuse because the parts they contain are hard to understand, modify, and test.

Combining Strategies

By themselves, neither adaptive nor compositional reuse strategies are general enough to cover the full range of potentially reusable structures. However, the structured combination of these two approaches creates hybrid strategies much broader in coverage. Exhibit 6 shows the two major hybrid approaches.

- Full-coverage hybrid reuse uses an adaptive framework to keep overall costs down and "bubbles" of full-coverage compositional sets at key locations to provide flexibility.

Unix's Termcap package demonstrates this concept nicely, even though it was not designed as a reuse technology. With Termcap, you build drivers for new terminal types using interface descriptions written in the special-purpose Termcap language. These interface definitions are actually examples of compositional reuse, since the Termcap language allows ready access to (reuse of) a complex suite of general-purpose driver routines. Because you can handle hardware variations with a specialized minilanguage that strongly encapsulates such variations, you can transfer (adaptively reuse) higher level programs that use Termcap among systems with few or no changes.

- Partial-coverage hybrid reuse is very similar to the full-coverage hybrid, but it allows the bubbles to be either full-coverage or partial-coverage—they need not be fully generalized for handling the problem area they address.

Many types of maintenance are equivalent to partial-coverage hybrid reuse, since they are based on localized modification of components that have never been fully generalized.

EXHIBIT 6   Hybrid Reuse Strategies. (a) Full-Coverage Hybrid; (b) Partial-Coverage Hybrid

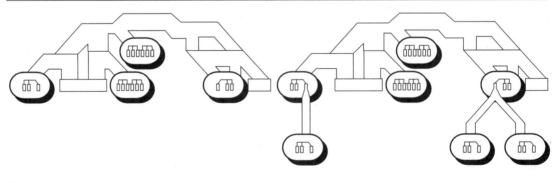

(a)   (b)

Cutting Costs

Partial-coverage hybrid reuse provides the best overall framework for defining the divide-and-conquer approach that is our motive for exploring reuse strategies. Partial-coverage hybrid reuse keeps the overall structure invariant, so producers can focus on smaller, more precisely defined problem areas. Reuse investments in those problem areas then can produce minilanguage sets that permit the flexibility consumers need.

When variants analysis indicates a need for extensive generalization (Termcap's terminal-interface problem, for example), producers can invest in expensive technologies such as application-specific languages or program generators. When needs are clearly identified but full generalizations are not justified due to poor characterizations or limited numbers of expected reuse instances, producers can provide partial-coverage sets such as localized libraries.

It is the ability to combine such techniques within the partial-coverage hybrid framework that makes it a good strategy for keeping producer costs in check.

REUSE AND PARAMETERIZATION

When we say that highly generalized parts define minilanguages for solving specialized problems, we don't mean to imply that these languages are true general-purpose languages—they are not. But designers use them in a way similar to general-purpose languages. Thus, sets of reusable graphics routines are a minilanguage for constructing and modifying diagrams; libraries of mathematical routines are minilanguages for dealing with mathematical problems.

From this perspective, good sets of reusable parts should possess the same general characteristics of expressive power and ease of composition that are the hallmarks of good programming languages.

Producers and consumers can further reduce reuse costs by designing appropriate, well-structured minilanguages. While this language design is identical to the task of generalizing parts, the language-design perspective places a much stronger emphasis on the integration of parts. The minilanguages that

result should define clear and succinct problem solutions through the composition of a relatively small number of objects and operators.

The design of optimal minilanguages can be assisted by recognizing a curious equivalence that has significant consequences. The equivalence is this:

All parameterizations can be interpreted as minilanguages, and all minilanguages can be interpreted as parameterizations.

Parameters as Programs

At first glance, the statement that parameterizations and languages are in some way equivalent seems outlandish, particularly if it encompasses data parameterizations. After all, what does the passing of two complex numbers to a Fortran subroutine for complex division have to do with expressing a problem in a minilanguage?

Actually, quite a bit. A Fortran complex-division subroutine is a formal system for solving problems in a very small, very precisely defined domain: division of complex numbers. There are only two terms in this domain's minilanguage, which may be paraphrased as "define the dividend to be (value)" and "define the divisor to be (value)."

These terms are "coded" with a simple positional notation, but the semantic interpretation implied by the paraphrased versions most definitely must be met to obtain valid results.

Ironically, such routines are not usually thought of as defining small languages precisely because of their effectiveness: They are very succinct and directly address the key variability (new data values) needed to solve problems in their domains. In Ada, you can make this equivalence more obvious through the use of named parameters that help preserve such semantic implications.

Programs as Parameters

Looking at the equivalence from the other side, you can view a compiler as a formal system for interpreting program parameter values. Like any other parameter, a program consists of a string of binary data that has a specific meaning when passed to the formal system (compiler) for which it was constructed.

The key way in which a program differs from a traditional set of parameter values is that instead of defining a problem solution in terms of many relatively independent terms, a program uses comparatively few highly interrelated terms.

There is no rigid boundary between low-complexity schemes in which parameters are fairly independent and high-complexity cases in which they are highly interrelated. For example, some application-specific languages such as database-report generators often provide ways to specify common "programs" (reports) with very simple, parameter-like specifications.

Also, conventional parameterization schemes may include language-like features to reduce the number of necessary parameters. For example, many Unix tools such as Grep and Sed use parameterizations that range in complexity from the passing of simple flags for commonly needed variants of their functionality to the passing of complicated, program-like character strings for customizing their behavior in very specific ways.

Limits of Parameterization

Exhibit 7 shows that extreme parameterization does not necessarily lead to a more understandable or reusable system, since extreme parameterization is functionally equivalent to developing a highly generalized mini-language.

Very high levels of parameterization tend to approach what we call the Turing limit, the point at which the parameterization becomes so extensive that it is comparable in power to a general-purpose language. "Turing" refers to the fact that a fully generalized minilanguage permits construction of any desired program, and thus is akin to a Turing machine. At best, a parameterization scheme that has reached the Turing limit will be as complex as a general-purpose language, and it could easily be far more complex.

EXHIBIT 7   Limits of Parameterization in Reuse

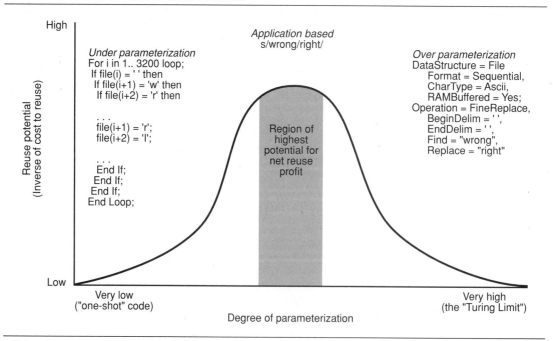

At that point, the reuse potential of a component effectively becomes nil, since it would probably be easier and less costly to redevelop the component in the original language.

As Exhibit 7 shows, the best payoff in parameterization comes from finding combinations of parameters that cover common application variabilities while simultaneously requiring the least possible specification efforts from consumers. Just as many manufacturing disciplines have developed sets of complementary parts that can be adjusted and combined to produce wide ranges of useful products, good software-parameterization schemes should provide versatile tool kits of options by which the needs of later consumers can be succinctly specified.

Options that are very likely to be needed should be made as simple to specify as possible, while increasingly less likely variations should be made to require proportionally larger specification efforts. At the lower end of this domain-specificity continuum is the language itself, in which variations with very low priorities can be coded directly.

WHAT'S NEXT?

We need consistent, broad-spectrum methodologies that integrate reuse analysis and development methods across the development life cycle.

In fact, life-cycle integration is likely to be one of the key factors that makes reuse truly effective. After all, if the first thing developers see in their programming environments are compilers, the first thing they will be tempted to do is to write code. If the first thing they see are lists of existing parts that may match their needs, the first thing they will be tempted to do is reuse. Put more colloquially, if you want to lose weight you should put the healthy food at the front of the fridge and the junk food at the back.

Reuse-Oriented Automation

Exhibit 8 shows the broad structure of a tool that would use instance spaces as the basis for presenting reusable components to reuse consumers[9] and that would implement separation concepts similar to those of Vic Basili and Dieter Rombach's reuse factory[10].

The idea is to deemphasize how reusable parts are retrieved or created and emphasize the cost of retrieving them. Incorporating cost issues at such a fundamental level would let the system take a much more active role in making reuse decisions. For example, consumers who reuse early work products such as specifications or designs would receive cost quotes that would indicate the strong relative cost advantages for their selections. This type of "shop around" approach would encourage reuse consumers to select development paths that make the best possible use of existing work products.

For some time, reuse has suffered from an image problem. Anyone who has ever gone to an auto salvage yard to pick up a spare part for his old car "knows" what reuse is, and the image that it thus invokes is not altogether favorable.

The theme we most want to convey is that reuse is not a trivial concept. As a mechanism for preserving and guiding the use of that most expensive of resources, human creativity and ingenuity, software reuse is a field that merits careful attention both from managers interested in the bottom line and from researchers interested in better understanding that most curious of symbiotic relationships, the one that exists between humans and computers.

References

1. M.D. Lubars, "Wide-Spectrum Support for Software Reusability," in *Software Reuse: Emerging Technology,* Will Tracz, ed., CS Press, Los Alamitos, Calif., 1988, pp. 275–281.

2. V.R. Basili and H.D. Rombach, "Towards a Comprehensive Framework for Reuse: A Reuse-Enabling Software Evolution Environment," Tech. Report CS-TR-2158, Dept. of Computer Science, Univ. of Maryland, College Park, Md., Dec. 1988.

3. T. Biggerstaff and C. Richter, "Reusability Framework, Assessment, and Directions," *IEEE Software,* March 1987, pp. 41–49.

EXHIBIT 8   Reuse Abstraction: Separating Requests from Methods

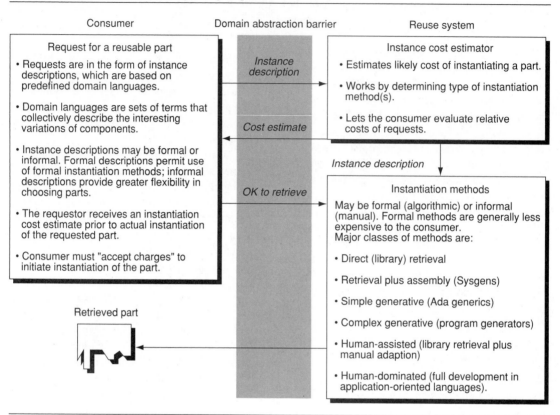

Consumer   Domain abstraction barrier   Reuse system

Request for a reusable part

- Requests are in the form of instance descriptions, which are based on predefined domain languages.

- Domain languages are sets of terms that collectively describe the interesting variations of components.

- Instance descriptions may be formal or informal. Formal descriptions permit use of formal instantiation methods; informal descriptions provide greater flexibility in choosing parts.

- The requestor receives an instantiation cost estimate prior to actual instantiation of the requested part.

- Consumer must "accept charges" to initiate instantiation of the part.

Instance description

Cost estimate

OK to retrieve

Instance description

Instance cost estimator

- Estimates likely cost of instantiating a part.

- Works by determining type of instantiation method(s).

- Lets the consumer evaluate relative costs of requests.

Instantiation methods

May be formal (algorithmic) or informal (manual). Formal methods are generally less expensive to the consumer.
Major classes of methods are:

- Direct (library) retrieval

- Retrieval plus assembly (Sysgens)

- Simple generative (Ada generics)

- Complex generative (program generators)

- Human-assisted (library retrieval plus manual adaption)

- Human-dominated (full development in application-oriented languages).

Retrieved part

---

4. F.J. Polster, "Reuse of Software through Generation of Partial Systems," *IEEE Trans. Software Eng.,* March 1986, pp. 402–416.

5. L. Latour and E. Johnson, "Seer: A Graphical Retrieval System for Reusable Ada Software Modules," *Third Int'l Conf. Ada Applications and Environments,* IEEE, Piscataway, N.J., May 1988, pp. 105–113.

6. P.G. Bassett, "Frame-Based Software Engineering," *IEEE Software,* July 1987, pp. 9–16.

7. M.A. Simos, "The Domain-Oriented Software Life Cycle: Towards an Extended Process Model for Reusability," in *Software Reuse: Emerging Technology,* Will Tracz, ed., CS Press, Los Alamitos, Calif., 1988, pp. 354–363.

8. M. Lenz, H.A. Schmid, and P.F. Wolf, "Software Reuse through Building Blocks," *IEEE Software,* July 1989, pp. 34–42.

9. T. Bollinger and B.H. Barnes, "Reuse Rules: An Adaptive Approach to Reusing Ada Software," *Proc. Artificial Intelligence and Ada Conf.,* George Mason Univ., Fairfax, Va., 1988, pp. 14-1–14-8.

10. V.R. Basili and H.D. Rombach, "The TAME Project: Towards Improvement-Oriented Software Environments," *IEEE Trans. Software Eng.,* June 1988, pp. 758–773.

EFFECTS OF REUSE
ON QUALITY, PRODUCTIVITY,
AND ECONOMICS

Although not a new concept, reuse as a means of improving software quality and productivity has been aggressively pursued only recently. Hewlett-Packard has found that reuse can have a significant and largely positive effect on software development. This article presents metrics from two HP reuse programs that document the improved quality, increased productivity, shortened time-to-market, and enhanced economics resulting from reuse.

In this article, *work products* are the products or by-products of the software-development process: for example, code, design, and test plans. *Reuse* is the use of these work products without modification in the development of other software. *Leveraged reuse* is modifying existing work products to meet specific system requirements. A *producer* is a creator of reusable work products, and the *consumer* is someone who uses them to create other software. *Time to market* is the time it takes to deliver a product from the time it is conceived.

Our experience with reuse, which includes multiple reuse programs in different divisions within the company, has been largely positive. Because work products are used multiple times, the accumulated defect fixes result in a higher quality work product. Because the work products have already been created, tested, and documented, productivity increases because consumers of reusable work products need to do less work. However, increased productivity from reuse does not necessarily shorten time-to-market. To reduce time-to-market, reuse must be used effectively *on the critical path* of a development project, the chain of activities

that determine the total project duration. Finally, we have found that reuse allows an organization to use personnel more effectively because it leverages expertise. Experienced software specialists can concentrate on creating work products that less experienced personnel can then reuse.

However, software reuse is not free. It requires resources to create and maintain reusable work products, a reuse library (if necessary), and reuse tools. To help evaluate the costs and benefits of reuse, we have developed an economic analysis method, which we have applied to multiple reuse programs at HP. I present the results from two of these programs here.

TWO CASE STUDIES

The first reuse program is within the Manufacturing Productivity section of HP's Software Technology Division, which produces large-application software for manufacturing resource planning. The MP section's reuse program started in 1983 and is ongoing. The original motivation for pursuing reuse was to increase engineering productivity to meet critical milestones[1]. The MP section has since discovered that reuse also eases the maintenance burden and supports product enhancement.

MP engineers practiced reuse by using generated code and other work products such as application and architecture utilities and files. The data reported here reflects only the use of reusable work products, not generated code. Total code size for the 685 reusable work products was 55,000 lines of noncomment source statements. The reusable work products were written in Pascal and SPL, the Systems Programming Language for the HP 3000 computer system. The development and

Article by Wayne C. Lim. © 1994 IEEE. Reprinted, with permission, from (*IEEE Software;* 11, 5, 23–30; 1994).

target operating system was MPEXL, the Multiprogramming Environment.

The second program is within the San Diego Technical Graphics Division, which develops, enhances, and maintains firmware for plotters and printers. The STG reuse program began in 1987 and continues to the present. Among the program's goals, as described in an internal report, were lowering development costs by reducing duplication and providing consistent functionality across products. The reusable work product analyzed here is 20,000 noncomment source statements written in C. The development operating system was HPUX and the target operating systems were PSOS and an internal one.

FINDINGS

At HP, we collected data from these two reuse programs and conducted a *reuse assessment*—an analytical and diagnostic method used to evaluate both qualitative and quantitative aspects of a reuse program. As part of this assessment, data on the improved quality, productivity, and economics attributable to reuse is analyzed and documented. Exhibit 1 summarizes the productivity, quality, and time-to-market benefits from reuse.

Quality

Because work products are used multiple times, the defect fixes from each reuse accumulate, resulting in higher quality. More important, reuse provides incentives to prevent and remove defects earlier in the life cycle because the cost of prevention and debugging can be amortized over a greater number of uses[2].

Exhibit 2 summarizes the quality results. The MP section's data shows a defect-density rate for reused code of about 0.9 defects per thousand noncomment source statements (KNCSS) (not shown in figure) compared to 4.1 defects/KNCSS for new code. Using reused code in combination with new code (in which 68 percent of the product was from reused work products) resulted in 2.0 defects/KNCSS, a 51 percent reduction in defect density compared to new code. If we take into account the effects of generated code, we achieve a total defect-density reduction of 76 percent compared to new code.

The STG division also reported a positive experience with reuse. They estimated the actual defect-density rate for reused code to be 0.4 defects/KNCSS (not shown in figure), compared

EXHIBIT 1 Quality, Productivity, and Time-to-Market Profiles

Organization	Manufacturing Productivity	San Diego Technical Graphics
Quality	51% defect reduction	24% defect reduction
Productivity	57% increase	40% increase
Time to market	Data not available	42% reduction

EXHIBIT 2 Effect of Reuse on Software Quality—As Measured by Defects Per Thousand Noncomment Source Statements—in New Code Only Versus New Code Combined With Reused Code, in Two Development Efforts Participating in the Two HP Reuse Programs Analyzed

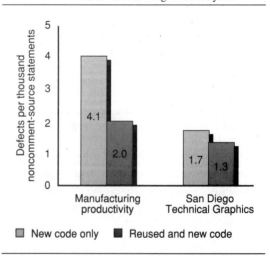

to 1.7 defects/KNCSS for new code. A product that incorporated the STG reusable work product had a 31 percent reuse level and a defect-density rate of about 1.3 defects/KNCSS, a 24 percent reduction in defect density.

Productivity

Reuse improves productivity because the life cycle now requires less input to obtain the same output. For example, reuse can reduce labor costs by encouraging specialization in areas such as user interfaces. Because of their experience, specialists usually accomplish tasks more efficiently than nonspecialists. Or productivity may increase simply because fewer work products are created from scratch. For example, if the reused work products are already documented and tested, the new product requires less work in these areas. Reuse can also improve a product's maintainability and reliability, thereby reducing maintenance labor costs.

In general, reuse improves productivity by reducing the amount of time and labor needed to develop and maintain a software product. As Exhibit 3 shows, another similar project in the MP section reported a productivity rate of 0.7 KNCSS/engineering month for new code. Its product, which was composed of 38 percent reused code, had a productivity rate of 1.1 KNCSS/engineering month, a 57 percent increase in productivity over development from scratch.

The STG division estimates a productivity rate of 0.5 KNCSS/engineering month for new code. In contrast, its released product comprising 31 percent reused code had a productivity rate of 0.7 KNCSS/engineering month, a 40 percent improvement.

Another firmware division within HP has been tracking the reuse ratio to the productivity rates in the development of their products. As Exhibit 4 shows, by 1987 several products had already exceeded their 1990 productivity goal of 2.0 KNCSS/engineering month with greater than 70

EXHIBIT 3 *Effect of Reuse on Productivity—As Measured by Thousands of Noncomment Source Statements Produced Per Engineering Month—in New Code Only Versus New Code Combined With Reused Code, in Two Development Efforts Participating in the Two HP reuse programs analyzed*

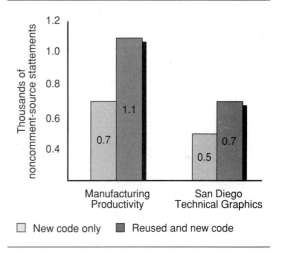

percent reuse. And they were well above their projected productivity rates. It should be noted that the reuse ratio calculation used in this division,

$$reuse\ ratio = ([directly\ reused\ KNCSS + modified\ KNCSS]/\ product\ total\ KNCSS) \times 100$$

includes leveraged reuse of code as well.

Time to Market

The STG division reports that the same development effort using the reusable work product required only 21 calendar months compared to an estimated 36 calendar months had the reusable work product not been used, a reduction of 42 percent. Suitable data showing elapsed time was not available for the MP product.

EXHIBIT 4   Firmware Productivity in a Third HP Division, Measured From 1985 Through 1990. Using Reuse, the Division Had Set a Productivity Goal of Two Thousand Noncomment Source Statements Per Engineering Month By 1990 (Dotted Line). The Division Exceeded Its Goal With the Release of Product D in 1987. The Numbers in Brackets Associated With Each Product are the Percentage of Reused Code in the Product and the Thousands of Noncomment Source Statements Actually Produced Each Engineering Month. Note That the Ratio Used Here Includes Leveraged Code, Which is Reused Code That has Been Modified

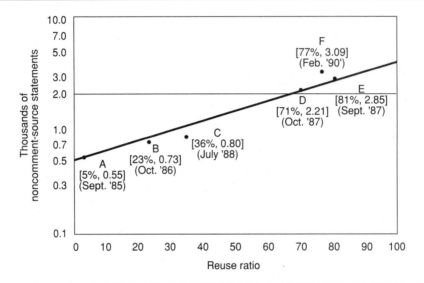

REUSE COSTS

In general, the costs of reuse include creating or purchasing reuse work products, libraries, tools, and implementing reuse-related processes. I will not explicitly describe them here, but will include them in aggregate form in the next section. In this section, I focus on the incremental cost to create a reusable work product.

Techniques to create reusable work products range from reengineering existing work products to be reusable to intentionally developing new work products for reuse. Exhibit 5 summarizes some relevant findings. Johan Margono and Lynn Lindsey, citing experience on the US Federal Aviation Administration's Advanced Automation System project, have shown that the relative cost of creating a reusable code component is about twice

that of creating a nonreusable version, and the costs to integrate reused components into new products ranged from 10 to 20 percent of the cost of creating a nonreusable version[3]. John Favaro cites findings that the relative cost of producing a reusable component ranged from 120 to 480 percent of the cost of creating a nonreusable version, and integration costs ranged from 10 percent to 63 percent of the cost of creating a nonreusable version[4].

Experience at HP in the STG graphics firmware domain has shown that the cost of creating reusable firmware is 111 percent of the cost of creating a nonreusable version, and integration costs were 19 percent of the cost of creating a nonreusable version.

Exhibit 6 shows the percent increase in engineering months by life-cycle phase (except maintenance) in creating a reusable software work product in the STG division. The data shows that

EXHIBIT 5   Cost to Produce and Reuse

Domain	Air-Traffic-Control System	Menu- and Forms-Management System	Graphics Firmware
Relative cost to create reusable code	200%	120 to 480%	111%
Relative cost to reuse	10 to 20%	10 to 63%	19%

EXHIBIT 6   Additional Effort in the San Diego Technical Graphics Division to Create the Reusable Work Product, By Phase. Investigation Is the Initial Analysis of User Requirements, Product Risks, and Benefits; External Design Is the Detailed Analysis of User Requirements and Definition of the Product's External View; Internal Design Is the Translation of External Design into Detailed Design of System and Modules; Code Includes Coding Through Unit Testing; Test Is Integration and System Test Through Alpha and Beta Test; and Repair Is the Repair of Defects Discovered During Test Phase. Maintenance Is Not Included

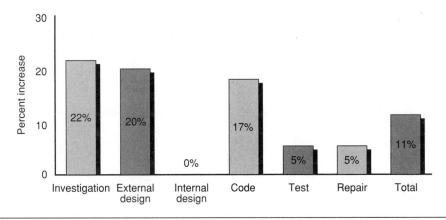

the most significant increases were in the investigation and external design phases. This is because the producer of the work product required a greater amount of time to understand the multiple contexts in which the work product will be reused. Margono has also cited additional costs by life cycle phase in producing reusable code[5]. He found that analysis and top-level design required 10 percent more than normally incurred in that phase (15 percent more for complex components), in the detailed design phase, 60 percent more, and in the code and unit test phases, 25 percent more.

REUSE ECONOMICS

An important aspect of software reuse is the economic return the organization receives for its efforts. Bruce Barnes, Terry Bollinger, Tom Durek, John Gaffney, and Shari Lawrence Pfleeger have done pioneering research in reuse economics. Gaffney and Durek present a relative cost model that describes development with reuse as a proportion of a baseline project[6]. Barnes, Bollinger, and Pfleeger[7,8] determine the cost/benefit by subtracting the producer investment costs of making

ing work products reusable from the consumer development costs saved net of adaptation costs.

The technique of economic analysis used for the two HP reuse projects is the well-established net-present-value method[9]. Net present value takes the estimated value of reuse benefits and subtracts from it associated costs, taking into account the time value of money[10]. This model contributes to the field of reuse economics by recognizing the potential increased profit from shortened time-to-market and accounting for risk. Because the economic benefit derived from shortened time-to-market is difficult to assess, the overall economic benefit shown for each HP reuse program is conservative. The model is also meant to be applied over the entire life cycle, including maintenance.

An economic analysis may be performed for a reuse program or a given reusable work product. We begin with economic analyses at the program level.

Program Savings

Exhibit 8a shows the economic analysis for the MP section's reuse program calculated over 10 years; Exhibit 8b shows the same type of analysis for the STG division's program over eight years (the final year uses estimated costs and benefits). Exhibit 7 summarizes the experience of these two projects. To account for the time value of money, we discounted the cash flows at a 15 percent discount rate.

By creating reusable work products periodically as the opportunity arose, the MP section pursued an incremental investment strategy. Its reuse program required about 26 engineering months (about $0.3 million) as startup expenses, including work-product creation and engineer training, for six products. Because no reuse-specific tools were purchased, engineers' time constituted the majority of the expense. Ongoing

---

EXHIBIT 7   Reuse Program Economic Profiles

Organization	Manufacturing Productivity	San Diego Technical Graphics
Time horizon	1983–1992 (10 years)	1987–1994 (8 years) 1994 data estimated
Start-up resources required	26 engineering months (start-up costs for six products) $0.3 million	107 engineering months (about three engineers for three years) $0.3 million
Ongoing resources required	54 engineering months (about one-half engineer for nine years) About $.3 million	99 engineering months (about one to three engineers for five years) About $0.7 million
Gross cost	80 engineering months ($1.0 million)	206 engineering months ($2.6 million)
Gross savings	328 engineering months ($4.1 million)	446 engineering months ($5.6 million)
Return on investment (savings/cost)	410%	216%
Net present value	125 engineering months ($1.6 million)	75 engineering months ($0.9 million)
Break-even year (recoup start-up costs)	Second year	Sixth year

EXHIBIT 8 Reuse Cost-Benefit Analysis by Program. (A) Manufacturing Productivity Section Over 10 Years; (B) San Diego Technical Graphics Division Over Eight Years

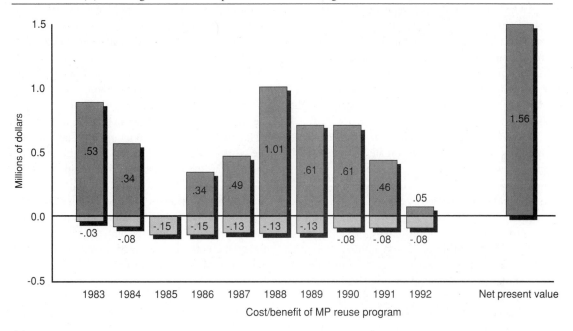

(a)

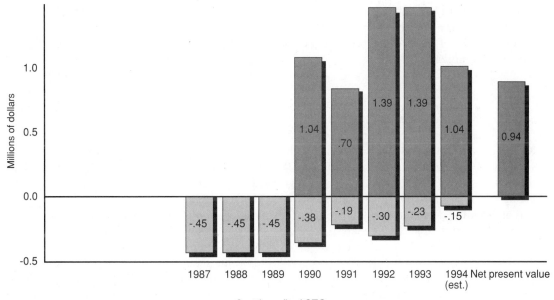

(b)

☐ Benefit ■ Cost

expenses, such as the maintenance of the reusable work products, were about $0.7 million, for gross expenses of about $1.0 million. The gross savings during this period was $4.1 million, for a return on investment of 410 percent. A net-present-value analysis indicates a savings of $1.6 million. The break-even point occurs in the second year.

The STG division devoted the time of three engineers for three years to create its reuse work product, which was used by development projects in subsequent years. Startup resources—again, mostly engineers' time—were $1.3 million, and ongoing expenses were also about $1.3 million. The gross costs of $2.6 million are offset by gross savings of $5.6 million. So the return on investment is 216 percent, and the net present value is $0.9 million. The break-even point occurs in the sixth year.

To compare the economic performance of the two reuse programs, we also determined the MP section's return over eight years (1983–1990). Its return on investment for this time period was 422 percent, with a net present value of 1.4 million. These figures can be directly compared to the STG division's return of 216 percent and net present value of $0.9 million.

Product Savings

Exhibit 9a shows an analysis of 15 reusable work products—ranging in size from 58 to 2257 NCSS—created in the MP section, indicating the savings a consumer receives from reuse. In the MP section, the savings ranged from 0.2 to 4.0 engineering days. Exhibit 9b shows an economic analysis from the perspective of the producer for the same 15 work products. This analysis attempts to answer the question, "Is it worthwhile for me as a producer to create this reusable work product?" The results range from a gain of 43.3 engineering days to a loss of 31.5 engineering days (the 31.5 engineering-day loss was the result of fewer than expected reuses and higher than expected maintenance costs). These figures do not include overhead costs, such as the manager's time, only the

direct time spent by the producer to create the reusable work product.

Exhibit 10 shows the analysis from the perspective of the STG consumer at the work-product level. In the first year, the time required for the consumer to understand, adapt, and integrate the reusable work product is $0.07 million. The savings to the consumer in the initial year from not having to create the functionality that the reusable work product provides is $0.36 million. In the second year, the consumer avoids having to repair defects that he would have otherwise had to had he created the functionality from scratch. This cost avoidance is $0.06 million. Using a 15 percent discount rate to take into account the time value of money, the net value received by a consumer with each reuse of this work product is $0.35 million.

DECISION SUPPORT

You can also use this economic model to determine the economic viability for work products under consideration to be made reusable. Exhibit 11 displays the results of such an analysis for four potential work products in the MP section. These results were determined using the same cost-benefit model described earlier. Such an analysis helps personnel decide which work products are economically worthwhile to create and, for resource-constrained producers, the sequence in which they should be created.

In this example, all four work products are economically worthwhile to create because their net present values are positive. The areas of the circles are proportional to their net present values. The number of reuses to break even (recover creation costs) ranges from one to eight. An economic ranking of these work products suggests that producers create the work products in the following sequence: 1, 2, 4, and 3. In prioritizing the creation of reusable work products, producers should also take into consideration other factors such as the schedules of the consumer projects.

While the overall economics for the two reuse projects have been positive, economic analysis for one of the programs indicates that creating some

EXHIBIT 9   Net Present Value of 15 Work Products—as Measured in Days Saved—From the Manufacturing Productivity Section. (A) NPV Received by Work-Product Consumer; (B) NPV Provided By Work-Product Producer to the Organization

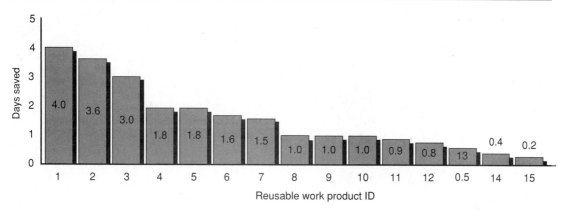

(a)

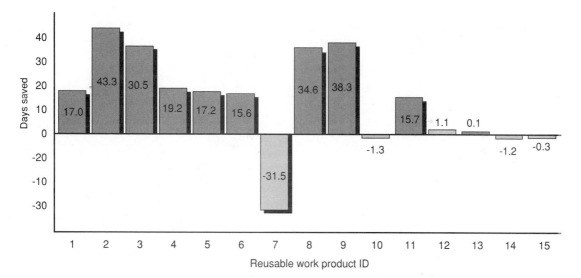

(b)

☐ Benefit   ■ Cost

of the work products has resulted in an overall economic gain and a few have resulted in a loss. Performing cost-benefit analyses for potential work products helps determine which work products should be created or reengineered to be reusable.

The data collected for these two programs have been used to initiate other reuse programs across HP. In addition, the results have been distributed as an example of start-up and ongoing costs and benefits of reuse for managers considering reuse in their divisions.

EXHIBIT 10   Net Present Value—as Measured in Millions of Dollars—Received By the Consumers of the Work Product from the San Diego Technical Graphics Division

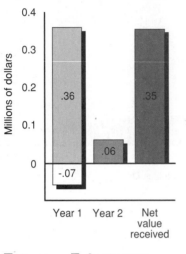

Savings ☐ Cost to reuse ☐
Net value received ■

ACKNOWLEDGMENTS

I thank Jack Cassidy, Sylvia Kwan, Joe Mueller, Alvina Nishimoto, Masahiro Yokokawa, and their teams for their help with collecting data and permission to publish this information. Additional acknowledgments to the HP Corporate Reuse team for their comments on previous versions of this article. Earlier versions of this work were presented at the 1992 Pacific Northwest Quality Conference and the 2nd International Workshop on Software Reuse.

EXHIBIT 11   A "Reuse Value Map" of Work Products Under Consideration to be Designed for Reuse in the Manufacturing Productivity Section. In This Case, the Total Potential Savings—the Portfolio NPV—is $167.7 Thousand

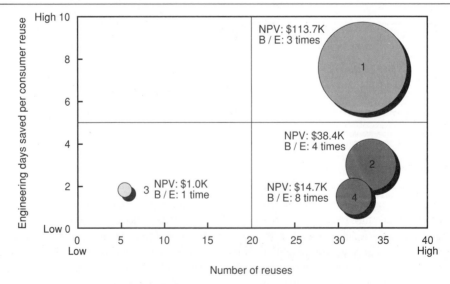

References

1. A. Nishimoto, "Evolution of a Reuse Program in a Maintenance Environment," *Proc. 2nd Irvine Software Symp.,* University of California, Irvine, Calif., 1992, pp. 89–108.

2. M.D. Lubars, "Affording Higher Reliability Through Software Reusability," *Software Eng. Notes,* Oct. 1986, p. 39.

3. J. Margono and L. Lindsey, "Software Reuse in the Air Traffic Control Advanced Automation System," *Proc. Software Reuse and Reengineering Conf.,* Nat'l Inst. for Software Quality and Productivity, Washington, D.C., 1991.

4. J. Favaro, "What Price Reusability," *Proc. First Symp. on Environments and Tools for Ada,* ACM, New York, 1990, pp. 115–124.

5. J. Margono, and T. Rhoads, "Software Reuse Economics: Cost-Benefit Analysis on a Large-Scale Ada Project," *Proc. Int'l Conf. Software Eng.,* CS Press, Los Alamitos, Calif., 1992, pp. 338–348.

6. J.E. Gaffney and T.A. Durek, "Software Reuse—Key to Enhanced Productivity: Some Quantitative Models," Tech. Report SPC-TR-88-015, Software Productivity Consortium, Herndon, Va., 1988.

7. B.H. Barnes and T.B. Bollinger, "Making Reuse Cost-Effective," *IEEE Software,* Jan. 1991, pp. 13–24.

8. T.B. Bollinger and S.L. Pfleeger, "The Economics of Software Reuse," Tech. Report CTC-TR-89-014, Contel Technology Center, Chantilly, Va., 1989.

9. W. Lim, "A Cost-Justification Model for Software Reuse," *Proc. 5th Annual Workshop for Institutionalizing Software Reuse,* University of Maine, Orono, 1992.

10. R. Brealey and S. Myers, *Principles of Corporate Finance,* McGraw-Hill, New York, 1981.

REUSE AND PRODUCTIVITY IN INTEGRATED COMPUTER-AIDED SOFTWARE ENGINEERING: AN EMPIRICAL STUDY

INTRODUCTION

In 1988, Boehm and Papaccio estimated that by the early 1990s, firms would be spending in excess of $125 billion per year on software in their efforts to remain competitive. To control these spiralling costs, many firms are turning to computer-aided software engineering (CASE) products in hopes of realizing improvements in productivity and system quality. Although expenditures on CASE were reported to be rapidly rising (*Software Magazine,* 1988), and firms continue to view CASE as holding out considerable promise for delivering gains

Article by Rajiv D. Banker and Robert J. Kauffman. Reprinted by special permission from the MIS Quarterly, Volume 15, Number 3. Copyright 1991 by the Society for Information Management and the Management Information Systems Research Center at the University of Minnesota.

(Loh and Nelson, 1989), investment in CASE has tended to be a leap of faith: the performance gains have been very difficult to identify and measure (Davis, 1988; Voelckner, 1988), and unsubstantiated claims of productivity improvements are widespread. For example, IBM has claimed 20 percent to 30 percent gains for its AD/Cycle (Sperling, et al., 1989), and Sony claims to have achieved 600 percent gains in a limited range of applications (Gabel, 1989). Popular press estimates top out at around 10,000 percent in gains (Breidenbach, 1989; Clemons, 1991), but the impact of such high-end claims is offset by others who report little or no gains at all (McGuff, 1989). Moreover, in a recent survey of 196 CASE-using firms conducted by *Software Magazine,* 74 percent responded that they did not have a productivity measurement program in place (Knight, 1989). Clearly, many firms have not yet begun to even measure the impact of CASE.

CASE technologies involve significant automation of the software development life cycle. Currently available tools fall into three categories: lower CASE, upper CASE, and integrated CASE. *Lower CASE* provides support for the later life cycle stages, especially code construction and testing. *Upper CASE* offers assistance during the early life cycle stages of analysis and design. *Integrated CASE* (ICASE) tools, by contrast, support both the earlier and later stages of the life cycle. Depending upon the specific ICASE tool that is considered, developers will have access to a variety of automated software engineering facilities. Some of these include specialized report painting and user screen design tools, code reuse search facilities, automated documentation preparation facilities, multiple code generators, code debugging tools, links to existing 3GL code libraries, entity-relationship (E/R) and data flow diagrammers (DFD), and software version distribution control facilities.

At the heart of an investment program in ICASE is management's desire to improve development productivity and software maintainability. In this article, some empirical evidence is presented about the viability of implementing an information systems (IS) strategy that enables a firm to produce high functionality software that could not have been produced in a cost-effective manner with traditional development methods. The cornerstone of this strategy was the deployment of an ICASE tool that emphasizes software reusability. The benefits of constructing reusable software were recently discussed by Kim and Stohr (1991) and Nunamaker and Chen (1989a). Apte, et al. (1990) present a case study of a large commercial bank's experiences with this software reusability-based approach. However, there is a lack of generally accepted methods for creating and implementing reusable software (Lenz, et al., 1987), and little research has been done to document the gains that a reusability approach can produce (Biggerstaff and Richter, 1987; Parker and Hendley, 1988).

Moreover, little work has been done to determine the leverage that object-oriented development methods may provide in improving development efficiency.

The empirical results presented in this article are intended to provide some initial evidence about the gains from reuse. They are based on an analysis of data collected in a two-year field study of software development at the First Boston Corporation, a large investment bank in New York City. The firm deployed an ICASE tool called High Productivity Systems (HPS) that was meant to support and integrate activities involved in the development of multi-platform, cooperative processing or client-server architecture applications. Such applications achieve levels of functionality beyond what can be produced using traditional development approaches. This architecture is increasingly seen in the industry as a prerequisite to manage growing hardware costs while optimizing processing performance for local decision making, trades processing, and large-scale database searches and financial optimization at the mainframe level.[1]

Twenty-one software development projects were studied in depth (though one project was later omitted from the formal analysis as an outlier). The applications that resulted now form First Boston Corporation's new trades processing architecture (NTPA), a set of core software applications that provide much of the bank's trades processing, securities inventory management, trades commission processing, real-time pricing of financial instruments, and general ledger accounting capabilities.

The principal contributions of this research are:

1. Description of an IS strategy that relies on software reusability so that high functionality, cooperative processing software can be produced in a cost-effective manner.
2. Documentation of an order of magnitude gain in software development productivity that

---

[1]For additional background information on cooperative processing and the client-server architecture, refer to Desmond (1989) and Edelstein (1989).

appears to be associated with the deployment of an ICASE tool that supports reusability in software development.

3. Demonstration of the use of a new reuse measurement approach for software development productivity that is generalizable to other organizations that deploy ICASE with the objective of supporting reusability.

HPS AT FIRST BOSTON: AN IS STRATEGY INVOLVING ICASE AND REUSABLE SOFTWARE

This section discusses the rationale for the IS strategy pursued by the First Boston Corporation, the characteristics of the ICASE tool and the software development environment in which it was implemented. Also presented are the research questions that later sections of this article address through empirical analysis.

The Need for a New IS Strategy

The 1980s were characterized by rapid technological change and increasing competition for major American investment banks. The First Boston Corporation's investment banking business required more sophisticated software applications and growing computer hardware power for high-speed securities and money market transactions processing, immediate access to and processing of large mainframe databases for use with real-time financial analytics, local access and customized analysis of distributed databases for financial market traders, and management and control of the firm's cash balances and securities inventory. Similar to those of its competitors, First Boston's systems increasingly were required to operate seamlessly 24 hours a day across three platforms—microcomputers, minicomputers and mainframes—in support of global investment banking and money market trading activities.

The trend in the investment banking industry has been in the direction of applications software that achieves a higher level of functionality for the user than in prior generations. Much of this is

aimed at giving traders added capabilities to realize a profit in highly competitive markets. For example, at First Boston *high functionality software* was expected to offer the trader the ability to:

1. Consolidate multiple digital feeds of market information into a single trader workstation;
2. Support real-time, computer-based financial optimization analytics for trading decisions with respect to existing (e.g., index arbitrage and option pricing) and newly created (e.g., synthetic options, and multi-instrument hedging) financial instruments;
3. Provide a user-friendly, windowing interface that traders could customize for their own needs; and,
4. Deliver consolidated and unbundled information on customer accounts and trader positions for risk management purposes.

Gene Bedell, the firm's CIO at the time, believed that First Boston's strategic necessity was to deliver systems that could attain such high levels of functionality. Because bringing high functionality systems into production rapidly was not possible with traditional development methods, maintaining the status quo of traditional software development methods would be a losing strategy (Clemons, 1991). In the absence of more productive development methods, the IS operations would blunt the firm's ability to deliver and support innovative financing products in a timely manner.

Characteristics of the IS Strategy

Bedell recognized that First Boston's IS operations needed to build software in a way that growing system complexity and system size would not lead to increasingly uncontrolled growth in development and maintenance costs. Bedell also recognized that increasingly complex interfaces were needed between cooperative processing platforms and that this would create major development bottlenecks. First, the functionality that had to be built was substantial, and the larger the system the more cost prohibitive it would be to deliver (Conte, et al., 1986). Second, the firm would need to retain three sets of highly skilled and highly paid developers—one set for each of the three processing platforms. The only way to avoid this "software trap" was to consider automating software development (Feder, 1988).

Bedell's next move was just that: to recommend that First Boston consider CASE as the major component of its IS strategy. But after a range of vendor-supplied lower and upper CASE tools available on the market were tested, Bedell's technical staff concluded that none would offer the right mix of power and flexibility to build the high functionality, cooperative processing systems that were needed to take the bank into the mid-1990s. Piecemeal application of specific CASE tools to individual phases of the software development life cycle would make it difficult to effectively link the phase-by-phase products of development, and there would likely be little positive impact on productivity.

Bedell's alternative strategy to cope with this "functionality risk" was to build an ICASE tool *in-house* (Clemons, 1991). Although the investment posed a major risk to the firm, First Boston subsequently committed $65 million for a new software development methodology and a new architecture of investment of investment banking software applications in late 1986, one year before the stock market crashed.[2] This investment would lay the foundation for High Productivity Systems (HPS), the firm's ICASE tool, and a set of core applications for First Boston called the New Trades Processing Architecture. (Exhibit 1 expands on the business strategy/IS strategy link that led to First Boston's investment in HPS.)

The Technical Vision Behind the IS Strategy

In early 1986, the First Boston Corporation gathered together a team of senior IS and user managers to make a set of recommendations regarding the firm's technology and systems. They reached

an important conclusion: the firm would implement a *reusability approach* to rebuild and upgrade the capabilities of the existing information systems architecture in a way that their basic building blocks—objects and modules—could be reused repeatedly. Vivek Wadhwa, later to become the firm's top technical specialist, was hired to implement and expand on this technical vision, which also was meant to reduce the bank's reliance on costly language-specialized programmers by making it possible to develop software that could run on any of the three platforms with a single "rules language." This rules language would be defined within HPS. Code generators would then process this HPS code so that run-time COBOL, PL/1, and C and other code would result for each of the three major development platforms, effectively screening developers from the complexity of the development environment. Wadhwa believed that this approach, when combined with special facilities to provide the platform-to-platform communications links called "middleware," would lead to the development of NTPA systems at an affordable cost. (For a description of some representative NTPA systems, refer to Exhibit 2.)

HPS: An ICASE Tool to Support the IS Strategy

HPS supports reusability because it is an *object-based* ICASE tool. The object types include programs, rules, output screens, user reports, data fields, and 3GL components, among others.[3] In

---

[2]The costs would later rise as high as $100 million (Schwartz, 1990).

---

[3]This term is used to distinguish development environments like HPS and should not be confused with the object-oriented approach. The primary differences are that object-based development does not allow for instances of object classes to be "classes" themselves, nor would objects in object-based development have any special "inheritance properties." (See Booch, 1989, for additional details on the distinctions, and Meyer, 1988, or a discussion of the object-oriented paradigm of software construction.) Thus, in HPS development object types, such as a "screen" or a "_" parallel abstract data types or classes in the object-oriented paradigm. Instances of HPS object types might include a "CLIENT_INPUT_SCREEN" or a "COMMISSION_CALCULATION_RULE." These parallel

EXHIBIT 1   An Analysis of the Business Strategy/IS Strategy Link for the First Boston Corporation

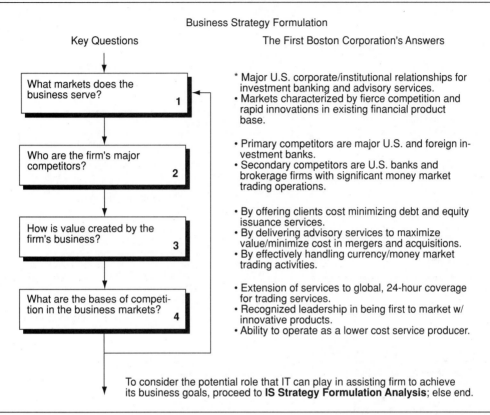

Business Strategy Formulation

Key Questions   The First Boston Corporation's Answers

What markets does the business serve? **1**

* Major U.S. corporate/institutional relationships for investment banking and advisory services.
• Markets characterized by fierce competition and rapid innovations in existing financial product base.

Who are the firm's major competitors? **2**

• Primary competitors are major U.S. and foreign investment banks.
• Secondary competitors are U.S. banks and brokerage firms with significant money market trading operations.

How is value created by the firm's business? **3**

• By offering clients cost minimizing debt and equity issuance services.
• By delivering advisory services to maximize value/minimize cost in mergers and acquisitions.
• By effectively handling currency/money market trading activities.

What are the bases of competition in the business markets? **4**

• Extension of services to global, 24-hour coverage for trading services.
• Recognized leadership in being first to market w/ innovative products.
• Ability to operate as a lower cost service producer.

To consider the potential role that IT can play in assisting firm to achieve its business goals, proceed to **IS Strategy Formulation Analysis**; else end.

order to make the reusability approach possible, HPS development was coupled with a centralized repository for reusable objects. The structure of the data stored in the repository is based on an implementation of the entity-relationship attribute model, originally developed for database design (Chen, 1976; Chen and Sibley, 1991; Teory, et al., 1986). Specifications for the objects used to construct an application are stored in a central repository where they become available to other developers. The repository includes all the definitions of the data and objects that make up the organization's business. The motivation for having a single repository for all such objects is similar to that for having a single database for all data: all objects need only be written once, no matter how many times they are used. When they are used and reused in various combinations, repository objects form the functionality that represents the information systems processing capability of the firm.[4]

"instances" of object classes in object-oriented development; however, in HPS an instance of an object is unable to act as a class and would not include any "inheritance" capabilities.

[4]For additional background on repositories, see the following: Banker and Kauffman (1991), Chen and Sibley (1991), Fisher (1990), and Hazzah (1989).

EXHIBIT 1 *(Cont.)*

IS Strategy Formulation Analysis

Business Strategy/IS Strategy Link

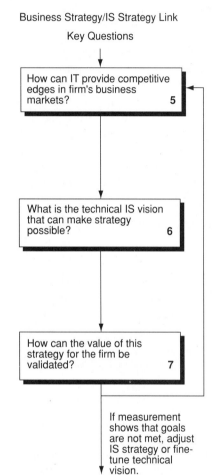

Key Questions	The First Boston Corporation's Answers
How can IT provide competitive edges in firm's business markets? **5**	• Implement the following: •• control software maintenance costs. •• rapidly deploy new products. •• manage hardware use/control costs. •• develop customized user interfaces for trader workstation applications. •• enable creation of multi-tier cooperative processing applications. •• reduce functionality risk in software development and react to changing business environment.
What is the technical IS vision that can make strategy possible? **6**	• Develop HPS ICASE so that it emphasizes reusability and controls software costs. • Define a very simple language that will enable rapid prototyping across three hardware platforms. • Automatically generate code for various platforms in five languages. • Deliver a centralized repository for storage of reusable software. • Provide diagraming and screen painting tools to facilitate some of the labor-intensive tasks in construction.
How can the value of this strategy for the firm be validated? **7**	• Implement a software/hardware metrics program that includes measurement of: •• **extent of software reuse.** •• **software development productivity.** •• software quality. •• average time to prototype. •• average cost for executed MIP across multiple tiers. •• marginal value of high functionality applications in business use.

If measurement shows that goals are not met, adjust IS strategy or fine-tune technical vision.

Return to **Business Strategy Formulation Analysis**

In addition, HPS provides diagramming and "painting" facilities for enterprise modeling and analysis and design; it provides code generators for five development languages; and it also offers tools for debugging code and managing versions of the same application. The coverage of the HPS tool set across the systems development life cycle is depicted in Appendix 1.

Software Development Performance at First Boston Corporation

Prior to 1987, First Boston did not have a formal program in place for tracking software development productivity. However, First Boston's senior IS managers informed us that some IS consulting firms had reported productivity of about eight to

EXHIBIT 2 Representative Applications from First Boston Corporation's New Trades Processing Architecture (NTPA)

Application Name	Description
Dealer's Clearance	Designed to improve operational and treasury management productivity by automating settlement, providing online, real-time display of clearances, and projected end-of-day securities and cash balance positions.
General Ledger Interface	A table-driven, self-balancing system that automatically posts entries from every transaction processing system included in NTPA. As a result, manual reconciliations are never required.
Firm Inventory/Foreign Securities & Currencies	Maintenance information for firm-wide management of foreign securities and currencies. Tracks individual trade lots and can determine profit and loss using various trading accounting bases.
Floor Broker	Manages fee and discount information for all brokers used by the firm. The system maintains payment histories linked to exchange, broker, and trading volume.
Product Master	This system supports identification of financial products across business areas. It enables each business group to classify and process securities according to its own business requirements, and it allows trading areas to establish new product types in the process of conducting business.
Real-Time Firm Inventory	Trading management uses this system to monitor trading positions, exposures, and intraday profit and loss by product, account, desk, department, or the entire organization. This system also enables traders to set up and monitor a strategy by linking several positions.

10 function points per person month at large financial institutions. (*Function points* is a popular productivity metric for software development that is discussed in more detail later in the article. For example, Capers Jones estimates function point productivity levels in the range of eight function points per person month for MIS business applications (Bouldin, 1989).) In addition, several project managers that we interviewed had worked in the IS development areas of other large financial institutions. They indicated that First Boston's traditional software development performance prior to the deployment of HPS was similar to those other firms. They also believed the IS consulting firms' estimates were applicable to the pre-HPS deployment environment at First Boston.

To obtain additional background information on the extent to which ICASE enabled the firm's reusability approach to deliver productivity benefits, interviews were conducted with seven managers who had overseen NTPA development projects at First-Boston. When the development of multi-tiered (co-operative processing), high functionality applications using traditional tools was compared with using HPS, the interviewees estimated that:

1. Full life-cycle traditional development would take 115 percent longer on average (std. dev. = 73.4%) to complete;
2. The construction phase alone would take 121 percent longer on average (std. dev. = 101.9%); and ,
3. Maintenance and enhancement also would take 121 percent longer on average (std. dev. = 71.6%).

The project managers indicated that reusable software was essential for such productivity gains to be possible. Yet the firm had not measured development productivity in an HPS environment, so their estimates were not confirmed.

Because high productivity gains from software reusability were believed to be essential to First Boston's IS strategy, this article addresses three principal research questions:

1. What was the level of reuse observed in software development projects?
2. Did reusability lead to any significant productivity gains during the first two years of the deployment of the HPS ICASE tool?
3. Did the evolving features of the HPS tool set and the organization's adaptation to the new development environment influence reuse and productivity gains?

Systematic evidence documenting product gains from software reusability is the essential first step in this research because this source of productivity gains forms the very foundation of the IS strategy at the research site. In this first study, however, we did not test other important aspects of the firm's IS strategy—for example, the value of the high functionality user interface offered to the trader and the importance of real-time connections across multiple processing platforms. Nor did we attempt to verify claims as to whether downstream maintenance costs would be lower, whether higher quality would be created, or whether using HPS would drive down the skill level at which a developer becomes productive.

The answers to these research questions regarding First Boston's experience with ICASE should be of general interest to practitioners and the IS research community alike. At present, there is little descriptive information available about reuse levels in ICASE environments. Nor is there much evidence to assist our understanding of the extent of the leverage that reuse creates in making software development operations more efficient. And, because every vendor's software development tools are evolving at a rapid rate, we believe that it is important for all firms that deploy CASE tools to gauge how development performance will shape up in the presence of a changing and imperfect tool set.

A DESCRIPTIVE MODEL FOR REUSABILITY AND ICASE DEVELOPMENT PRODUCTIVITY

This section presents a model relating development productivity to the deployment of an ICASE methodology that emphasizes reuse. Specifically discussed are the motivation for this model, the constructs it involves, and the measures for the constructs. This model does not attempt to capture all aspects of the deployment of ICASE: it focuses on the leverage that reuse creates on productivity.

Background for Model Development

A series of semi-structured interviews were initially conducted with five senior managers and seven project managers who managed the development of various aspects of the First Boston Corporation's New Trades Processing Architecture. The interviews probed how the firm's ICASE tool affected development productivity under a variety of development scenarios. Project managers reported that:

1. The single most important feature of the ICASE tool was its ability to store reusable objects in a centralized repository.
2. Software reuse under HPS required experienced developers to learn new skills; however, relatively inexperienced developers seemed to learn about reuse quite rapidly. Project managers reported that it took only two months to become productive as an HPS developer, and after about six months the learning curve flattened out.
3. The reliable performance of the development tools offered within HPS and the stability of the overall development environment over a longer period of time were believed to be more important than the skill levels of individual developers.
4. During the first year after ICASE was deployed, not all of the key pieces were in place, and this meant that not all kinds of application projects were equally well supported. For example, batch

systems tended to be heavy in one object type called "components." These are 3GL library routines whose integration was not well handled early in version 1 of HPS. In addition, the relatively early availability of an HPS screen-painting facility within version 1 tended to enhance development productivity for on-line, real-time applications. These contained more user screens than applications with mostly batch processing functions.

Overall, reuse was believed to be the major factor affecting development productivity. These observations are supported by a growing literature on productivity and software reuse (Apte, et al., 1990; Moad, 1990; Nunamaker and Chen, 1989a; 1989b; Norman and Nunamaker, 1989; Scacchi, 1989).

The interview findings led us to build into our model characteristics that differ from traditional software development productivity models in several ways. The *extent of observed reuse* should be explicitly incorporated to capture the leverage on development labor consumed in boosting output functionality. Because the ICASE tool that was deployed at the First Boston Corporation is object-based, reuse occurs as reuse of *repository objects* (e.g., rules, screens, and reports, and 3GL components—which can also be used as though they were repository objects, though technically they are not) that were created for other applications or earlier for the same application.

The *maturity of the ICASE tool set* also should be incorporated as a predictor of the extent of reuse and software development productivity, especially when major changes in its capabilities change with the deployment of new versions of the tool. In addition, the initial deployment of ICASE is as likely to result in reduced productivity as it is to deliver on the promise of productivity gains. Initially, it is unlikely that all of the bugs in the tool will be worked out nor that all of the ICASE tool's planned capabilities will be in place. In addition, development staff will need to be retrained, and project managers will need to refine

elements of their management tactics to effect project control. Finally, with the deployment of a new ICASE tool—especially one that is repository-based—it will be necessary to establish a base of reusable code in the repository.

Although the firm's software development staff varied in its levels of traditional software development experience, most had little exposure to HPS when the construction of the NTPA applications was initiated. The maximum amount of experience that anyone had with HPS was about one year. All of the projects examined were managed under a common management structure; most project personnel worked on multiple projects to broaden their experience, and the HPS rules language was constant across projects. Interviews with project managers and team members also indicated that experience and skills did not vary significantly across projects.

The Descriptive Model

A descriptive model was proposed for evaluating the impact of reuse in ICASE development that utilizes five constructs: software development labor consumed, the application functionality produced, the extent of reuse, the nature of the ICASE tool set at the time an application was developed, and the characteristics of the application under development. (See Exhibit 3.)

New Objects Built

The descriptive model employs an *object reuse* metric that can be applied to a range of object-based and object-oriented development environments and can be readily measured.[5] Our metric fits First Boston's ICASE environment well because software development essentially involves constructing and reusing objects, thereby reducing the amount of new software that must be written.

---

[5]For a more comprehensive discussion of software reuse metrics, see Banker, et al. (1990a).

EXHIBIT 3   Conceptual and Estimation Models

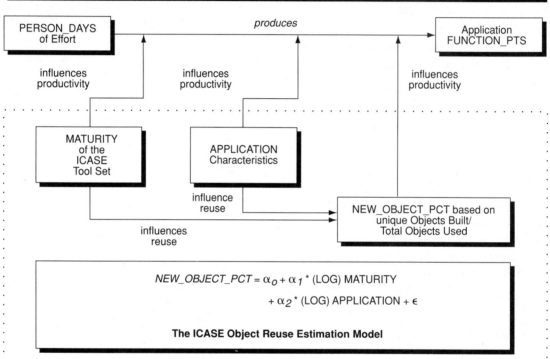

The ICASE Development Productivity Estimation Model

$$\text{FUNCTION\_POINTS} = e^{\beta_0} * \text{PERSON\_DAYS}^{\beta_1} * \text{NEW\_OBJECT\_PCT}^{\beta_2}$$

$$* \text{MATURITY}^{\beta_3} * \text{APPLICATION}^{\beta_4} * \zeta$$

PERSON_DAYS
of Effort

produces

Application
FUNCTION_PTS

influences
productivity

influences
productivity

influences
productivity

MATURITY
of the
ICASE
Tool Set

APPLICATION
Characteristics

influence
reuse

NEW_OBJECT_PCT based on
unique Objects Built/
Total Objects Used

influences
reuse

$$\textit{NEW\_OBJECT\_PCT} = \alpha_0 + \alpha_1 * (\text{LOG}) \text{ MATURITY}$$

$$+ \alpha_2 * (\text{LOG}) \text{ APPLICATION} + \epsilon$$

The ICASE Object Reuse Estimation Model

Both repository objects and 3GL components (which are also considered to be objects in this environment) are reusable within applications and across their boundaries. The metric we employed is defined as:

$$\textit{New Object PCT} =$$
$$\frac{\textit{Number Unique Objects Built for Application}}{\textit{Total Number of Objects Comprising Application}}$$

NEW_OBJECT_PCT (new object percentage) provides a measure of the portion of the total number of objects that comprise an application that must be built for the first time.[6] The total number of objects in an application is based on the number of different situations in which a program uses an object. As a result, multiple executions of the same object in the same situation are not

---

[6]An alternative is to weight each object by counting the number of function points it represents. However, this approach is not readily applied in practice because functionality spans multiple objects.

counted. The computation of NEW_OBJECT _PCT is illustrated in Appendix 3.

The ICASE Object Reuse Model

The extent of new code that must be constructed (NEW_OBJECT_PCT) is likely to be influenced by the stability and length of time the ICASE tools have been in place (MATURITY) and the features of the ICASE tool that offer support for building systems with different characteristics (APPLICATION). Reuse may be limited for applications with certain characteristics, especially when an object with highly specialized functionality is required that is not already stored in the repository. These relationships are depicted in the ICASE Object Reuse Model in Exhibit 3.

The ICASE Development Productivity Model

Software development effort, operationalized as PERSON_DAYS of effort, is the primary driver of the overall amount of functionality that is delivered in a software development project, operationalized in terms of FUNCTION_POINTS. Functionality delivered by the software development process is influenced by three project factors:

1. ICASE tool set MATURITY, a binary variable indicating whether a project was one of 13 built in the first year (and primarily built with HPS version 1) or one of seven built in the second year of the tools' deployment (and mostly built with HPS version 2, which expanded on the capabilities of the earlier version);[7]

2. NEW_OBJECT_PCT, a variable representing the portion of new code that had to be developed in a project;

3. APPLICATION type, a binary variable indicating a batch processing or an online, real-time application. Although we chose to focus on only two application types in this research, this variable more generally is meant to capture how the characteristics of an application interact with the available development tools to result in code reuse and the production of software functionality.

The variables are defined in more detail in Exhibit 4. The relationships among these variables are labeled as the ICASE Development Productivity Model in Exhibit 3. A more general model, based on additional experience with other organizations that have deployed CASE, could employ other operationalizations of the variables we selected and may also involve additional variables not considered here.

SOFTWARE DEVELOPMENT PRODUCTIVITY RESEARCH FROM AN ICASE PERSPECTIVE

This section discusses two aspects of the prior literature on software development performance evaluation that guided our development of the descriptive model ICASE productivity and reuse: metrics in software development productivity research, and measurement of code reuse.

Metrics for Software Development Performance Assessment

Much has been written in recent years regarding the modeling and measurement of software development productivity (Banker and Kemerer, 1989; Banker, et al., 1991; Davis, 1988; Gaffney, 1986; Grammas and Klein, 1985; Kang and Levy, 1989; Nunamaker and Chen, 1989b; Scacchi, 1989). Evaluation of development productivity involves measuring inputs consumed in the process of planning, designing, documenting, building, testing,

---

[7] The reader should recognize that the operationalization we selected is in some sense the best surrogate for MATURITY that was available. While we expect that CASE tools mature gradually over time, as new capabilities are deployed and come into increasing use among developers, normally an upgrade from an old version to a new one involves a significant number of changes. When First Boston's software development managers characterized projects as "Year 1" or "Year 2" development efforts, they not only were indicating that a Year 2 project had started at a certain point in time, they were also indicating that the composition of the tool set used to build the project had changed from Year 1.

EXHIBIT 4   Definitions of Variables in the Estimation Models

Variable Name	*Definition*
Object Reuse Estimation Model	
NEW_OBJECT_PCT	Number of unique objects built for the application divided by the total number of objects comprising the application (UNIQUE OBJECTS/OBJECTS USED).
MATURITY	A binary variable that takes the value e if a project is a "Year 2/HPS Version 2 Project" and 1 if a project is a "Year 1/HPS Version 1 Project."
APPLICATION	A binary variable that takes the value e if a project results in an online, real-time application, and 1 if it is a batch application.
α_0, α_1, α_2	Model parameters to be estimated.
ϵ	A normally distributed error term.
ICASE Development Productivity Estimation Model	
FUNCTION_POINTS	An output metric for the size of the software product that is delivered.
PERSON_DAYS	An input metric for development effort in person days.
OBJECT_REUSE	Number of unique objects built for the application divided by the total number of objects comprising the application (UNIQUE OBJECTS/OBJECT USED).
MATURITY	A binary variable that takes the value e if a project is a "Year 2/HPS Version 2 Project" and 1 if a project is a "Year 1/HPS Version 1 Project."
β_0, β_1, β_2, β_3	Model parameters to be estimated.
ζ	A log-normally distributed error term.

Note: Taking logs of the MATURITY and APPLICATION variables results in the values 1 and 0, respectively, when these variables have the observed values of e and 1. The usual interpretation of a binary variable is maintained.

and implementing, as well as comparing the resulting functionality. The standard approach is to gauge project development productivity across the entire life cycle. This approach is often represented as a "black box" production process, in which consumption of labor results in developed code delivering the functionality of a software application.

Software development labor is the primary input that drives functionality delivered in a software project. Software development productivity is often measured using the input-output ratio:

$$Productivity =$$
$$\frac{Size\ of\ Application\ Developed}{Labor\ Consumed\ During\ Development}$$

Two popular ways of measuring the size of the output of a software development project have emerged over the years: counting *source lines of code*[8]

---

[8]SLOC can be thought of in terms of the code that forms the procedure division of a Cobol program because this is what creates the functionality of an application developed using this language.

(SLOC) (Jones, 1986; 1988) and performing *function point analysis* (Albrecht and Gaffney, 1983; Low and Jeffrey, 1990; Sprouls, 1990; Symons, 1988). SLOC is not an appropriate metric for this study because HPS generates code in five different languages, making the resultant measures incomparable across applications and with manually written SLOC.

The function point analysis methodology gauges the size of an application in terms of its functionality. The metric that results—function points—incorporates two intermediate measures: function counts (FC) and a complexity multiplier (CM). Function counts aggregate the number and relative complexity of data input types, output types, file types, external interface types, and external inquiry types. Function counts are then adjusted using a complexity multiplier representing the impact of 14 dimensions (FACTORS) of the application's implementation environment. This yields function points. (Additional introductory details on function point analysis are provided in Appendix 2.)

The function points method offers an attractive metric because it abstracts from the programming languages used in different development projects. Firms that use function points for productivity comparisons are also supported by the existence of national and international user groups that define the standards for implementing the methodology to ensure that software development productivity results are comparable across organizations. As a result, function points currently enjoy support among *Fortune 500* firms (Bouldin, 1989; Dreger, 1989; IFPUG, 1988; Sprouls, 1990) and receive continued attention by the academic research community (Kemerer, 1990; Symons, 1988). There is currently no other common metric that emphasizes functionality as much as function points or supports better software development comparisons, and so we have chosen to adopt it in this research.

On the input side, labor is clearly the primary ingredient; all other capital inputs, such as the ICASE tool or the hardware used, are invariant across projects. The measures most often employed for labor are days or months of effort.

Measurement of Software Reusability

Prior research has investigated numerous project factors that influence software development productivity (Banker, et al., 1991). The relevant ones include project management practices, application type, development staff experience, the programming language used, and the stability of the development platform and user requirements (e.g., in terms of project size or function points). In software projects developed using HPS, the *level of reuse* (conceivably a project management practice) was believed to be the major factor deserving attention (Gaffney and Durek, 1989; Jones, 1984). If extensive reuse can increase productivity by an order of magnitude or more, as has been reported in the popular press, it would yield significant cost reductions in software development operations.

Reused code is also present to some degree in traditionally developed projects. For example, it is common for a developer to identify a piece of code that has similar functionality and then adapt or "template" it to meet a specific need. Successful reuse programs have been stymied in many organizations, however, because of weaknesses in the methodologies used (Horowitz and Munson, 1984; Mathis, 1986), problems with training and top management support (Biggerstaff and Richter, 1987; Tracz, 1987), and motivational reasons when developers and project managers feel that a methodology change endangers jobs (Kemerer, 1989; Nezlek and Leitheiser, 1991; Wong, 1987). Assessing the level of reuse in a 3GL programming environment is also difficult. Although certain types of explicit reuse (for example, modules from code libraries) are easy to identify, most of the code that might be reused is hidden within programs where it cannot be readily identified.

Unfortunately, prior research on reuse provides little guidance as to how to construct a relevant metric for reuse. The bulk of the work has focused on how to exploit the available technology to increase the level of reuse in 3GL and 4GL environments. (Some representative references include Horowitz and Munson, 1984; Jones, 1984; Kernighan, 1984; Lanergan and Grasso, 1984; and Matsumoto, 1984.) We identified just two studies that made concrete suggestions regarding the measurement of reuse. Standish (1984) proposed that reuse should be measured at the line of code level. Neighbors (1984) argued that reuse should be abstracted from the level of source code into some meta-language that relates to the problem. This idea fits better with the ICASE tool development environment examined in this field study because the repository objects can be thought of as the elements of the meta-language. In fact, in the HPS environment systems developers reuse entire objects rather than specific lines of code, and such reuse is more appropriately referred to as *object reuse*.

AN ESTIMATION MODEL FOR OBJECT REUSE AND ICASE DEVELOPMENT PRODUCTIVITY

Data Collection

Data were obtained on person months from First Boston's software development labor charge-out records for 21 projects. Labor was charged out by PERSON_DAYS to the various phases of a software development project, and a normal person month was conservatively viewed as having 18 PERSON_DAYS. Interviews were conducted with project managers wherever possible to review project charge-out data and examine their project worksheets. When a project manager had left the bank, the labor data were unavailable or too sketchy to give a picture of the overall level of effort, or the documentation was not in order, the project was eliminated from further consideration. Also investigated, in addition to the 21 projects, was the feasibility of obtaining data on other NTPA projects. However, one project for which other information was available could not be evaluated because of a lack of records about the amount of labor consumed; six more were not

documented in a manner that would enable us to measure functionality.

Nearly all the information needed to analyze FUNCTION_POINTS for an application was obtained from the functional and technical specification documentation stored in the central repository. HPS also provided a facility for printing out a hierarchically decomposed diagram of application modules. This greatly assisted function point and object reuse analysis because the documentation we examined was effectively standardized.

Manual collection and cross-checking of function points data is very costly. The collection of function points was coordinated by a single person who was on site at First Boston for three months. He initially trained and provided feedback on function point analyses conducted by two other members of the research team, who were also involved in performing object reuse analysis and conducting project manager interviews. Function point complexity measures were obtained directly from the project managers who had built and implemented the projects.[9] Function point estimates for the projects were checked by performing a recount. Any discrepancies were later resolved in discussion between project members. Our findings were consistent with the recent results of Kemerer (1990), who found that function point estimation tends to vary little more than plus

---

[9] The median value of the sum of the raw application complexity scores (FACTORS) was 36, implying that on average FUNCTION_COUNTS would be adjusted by a complexity multiplier (CM) of:
CM = .65 + (.01 * FACTORS) = .65 + (.01 * 36) = 1.01
to arrive at FUNCTION_POINTS. (See Appendix 2 for details.) In addition:
* The upper quartile value of FACTORS = 55 (a CM of 1.20); the lower quartile value of FACTORS = 29 (CM of 0.94).
* The median value of CM for online applications = 1.15; the median value of CM for batch processing applications = 0.91. The results are robust with respect to this relatively subjective measure. When the model was estimated substituting FUNCTION_COUNTS for FUNCTION_POINTS, the results did not change much.

EXHIBIT 5   An Overview of the Data Set

Project #	Person Days Labor (A)	Function Points (B)	Function Points/ Person Month (B/A)*	Online or Batch Application Type	New Object Pct	Year 1 or Year 2 Project? (Maturity)
1	1068	2250.08	37.93	ONLINE	23.2%	YEAR 1
2	737	170.56	4.17	BATCH	100.0%	YEAR 1
3	492	300.14	10.98	BATCH	54.3%	YEAR 1
4	2193	632.96	5.20	BATCH	71.9%	YEAR 1
5	520	264.60	9.16	ONLINE	35.1%	YEAR 1
6	1294	1273.70	17.71	BATCH	61.0%	YEAR 1
7	295	352.50	21.51	BATCH	49.3%	YEAR 1
8	471	494.08	18.88	ONLINE	48.1%	YEAR 1
9	136	97.92	12.96	BATCH	93.1%	YEAR 1
10	426	148.41	6.27	BATCH	96.2%	YEAR 1
11	862	385.14	8.04	BATCH	69.0%	YEAR 1
12	147	1092.00	133.71	ONLINE	44.8%	YEAR 1
13	230	241.82	18.93	ONLINE	45.7%	YEAR 1
14	686	3812.40	100.03	ONLINE	26.6%	YEAR 2
15	376	1772.40	84.85	ONLINE	34.7%	YEAR 2
16	469	3475.20	133.38	ONLINE	29.2%	YEAR 2
17	85	135.00	28.59	ONLINE	78.1%	YEAR 2
18	648	5876.25	163.23	ONLINE	23.1%	YEAR 2
19	233	3712.80	286.83	ONLINE	16.1%	YEAR 2
20	416	886.58	38.38	BATCH	32.8%	YEAR 2

or minus 10 percent when different people do the counting.

Our final sample of 20 projects excluded one project among the initial 21 that was believed to be an outlier. This project exhibited a very low level of productivity that was attributed to changing functional specifications and interruption of the development schedule. The data set examined in this research compare favorably in size with other studies that used data sets employing function points as the output metric (for example, Albrecht and Gaffney, 1983 (24 obs.); Behrens, 1983 (22 obs.); and Kemerer, 1987 (17 obs.)).

Detailed data and summary statistics for object reuse and productivity for the 20 projects are shown in Exhibit 5.

Projects ranged in size from a minimum of about 98 to a maximum of 5,876 FUNCTION _POINTS. The PERSON_DAYS of labor expended on these projects also varied, with a low of 85 and a high of 2,193 days, respectively. The value of NEW_OBJECT_PCT ranged from 100 percent (indicating there was no reuse because each newly built object was used just once) to 16.1 percent (indicating the project involved 83.9 percent reuse).

EXHIBIT 5   *(Cont.)*

Project #	Person Days Labor (A)	Function Points (B)	Function Points/ Person Month (B/A)*	Online or Batch Application Type	New Object Pct	Year 1 or Year 2 Project? (Maturity)
			Descriptive Statistics			
MEAN	589.2	1368.7	57.0**	_____	51.6%**	_____
STDDEV	489.3	1630.0	73.4	_____	25.7%	_____
MAXIMUM	5876.0	2193.0	286.8	_____	100.0%	_____
MINIMUM	97.9	85.0	4.2	_____	16.1%	_____
COUNT	_____	_____	_____	BATCH: 9	_____	YEAR 1:13
				ONLINE: 11	_____	YEAR 2:7

Correlation Matrix

	PERSON DAYS	FUNCTION POINTS	APPLICATION TYPE	NEW OBJECT PCT	MATURITY
PERSON DAYS	1.000				
FUNCTION POINTS	.043	1.000			
APPLICATION TYPE	−.326	.511	1.000		
NEW OBJECT PCT	.096	−.683	−.653	1.000	
MATURITY	−.336	.576	.533	−.515	1.000

*We used a conservative estimate of 18 PERSON_DAYS in a PERSON_MONTH of software development to determine function point productivity; i.e.:
FUNCTION_POINTS/PERSON_MONTH = FUNCTION_POINTS/PERSON_DAY* 18.

**The means for FUNCTION_POINTS/PERSON_MONTH and NEW_OBJECT_PCT reported in this table are simple averages. We report more meaningful *project size-weighted average values for the means* of FUNCTION_POINTS/ PERSON_MONTH and NEW_OBJECT_PCT in Exhibits 6 and 7.

An Econometric Model for Object Reuse and CASE Productivity Estimation

The estimation model we employed to represent the descriptive model is shown below.

$$NEW\_OBJECT\_PCT =$$
$$\alpha_0 + \alpha_1 * LOG\ (MATURITY) +$$
$$\alpha_2 * LOG\ (APPLICATION) + \epsilon \qquad [1]$$

$$LOG\ (FUNCTION\_POINTS) =$$
$$\beta_0 + \beta_1 * LOG\ (PERSON\_DAYS) + \beta_2 *$$
$$LOG\ (NEW\_OBJECT\_PCT) + \beta_3 * LOG$$
$$(MATURITY) + \beta_4 * LOG\ (APPLICATION)$$
$$+ LOG\ (\zeta) \qquad [2]$$

In equation 1, NEW_OBJECT_PCT is estimated as a function of the logarithms of the MATURITY of the ICASE tool in the development environment and the type of APPLICATION being developed. Equation 2, presented in its loglinear estimation form, extends prior multiplicative models of software development productivity (e.g., Albrecht and (e.g., Albrecht and Gaffney, 1983; Bailey and Basili, 1981; Banker and Kemerer, 1989; Behrens, 1983; Belady and Lehman, 1979; Boehm, 1981; DeMarco, 1981; Kemerer, 1987; Walston and Felix, 1977; Wingfield, 1982) to incorporate software reusability. It captures the intuition expressed in the descriptive model.

The error terms of the two models are likely to be correlated (i.e., $COV(\epsilon, \log(\zeta)) \neq 0$), as they relate to the same projects. For this reason, we employed *seemingly unrelated regression* (SUR) to estimate the joint model. Estimation of the two equations together as a SUR model, using an iterative method devised by Zellner (1962), results in statistical efficiency gains.[10]

DISCUSSION OF EMPIRICAL RESULTS

Results and Interpretation of the Estimation Model

The results of the estimation of the ICASE object reuse and development productivity models for 20 projects are shown below.

$$NEW\_OBJECT\_PCT =$$
$$\alpha_0 + \alpha_1 * MATURITY \quad + \quad \alpha_2$$
$$\mathbf{0.71} \quad - \mathbf{0.12} \qquad\qquad \mathbf{-0.27}$$
$$.001 \qquad .11 \qquad\qquad\quad .003$$
$$*APPLICATION \qquad\qquad\qquad [3]$$

---

[10]SUR would not result in statistical efficiency gains if the set of dependent variables in equation 2 was identical to, or a linear transformation of, the set of dependent variables in equation 1. Note, however, that PERSON_DAYS appears only in the right hand side of equation 2. It is also worthwhile to point out that the presence of NEW_OBJECT_PCT as a dependent variable in equation 1 and as an independent variable in equation 2 does not eliminate the statistical efficiency gains of the joint estimation or render the use of SUR inappropriate. For additional details, see Judge, et al. (1985), pp. 466–471.

$$LOG\ (FUNCTION\_POINTS) =$$
$$\beta_0 \quad + \quad \beta_1 * LOG\ (PERSON\_DAYS)$$
$$\mathbf{1.45} \quad \mathbf{0.55}$$
$$.10 \quad .001$$
$$+\ \beta_2 * LOG\ (NEW\_OBJECT\_PCT) + \beta_3$$
$$\mathbf{-1.92} \qquad\qquad\qquad\qquad \mathbf{0.40}$$
$$.001 \qquad\qquad\qquad\qquad\qquad .11$$
$$* LOG\ (MATURITY) + \beta_4 * LOG\ (APPLICATION)$$
$$\mathbf{-0.04}$$
$$46 \qquad\qquad\qquad [4]$$

Note: The one-tailed significance level is shown below the coefficient estimate, which is shown in bold. The correlation between the estimates for ϵ and $LOG(\zeta)$ was 62.4 percent, supporting the need for our SUR estimation approach.

Equation 3. The negative estimated coefficient of the variable APPLICATION ($\alpha_2 = -0.27$, .003 level) indicates that batch processing applications development required more new code to be developed, and thus less reuse, on average than online, real-time projects. In addition, the coefficient for MATURITY ($\alpha_1 = -0.12$, .11 level) was also negative, suggesting that the development of new application functionality required increasingly less new code in Year 2. The estimated value of the intercept is also noteworthy ($\alpha_0 = 0.71$, .001 level). The intercept is significantly less than 1.00, providing evidence that HPS has a beneficial effect overall in reducing the proportion of new objects that must be built in application development.

Equation 4. The results of the estimation of Equation 4 show that PERSON_DAYS of effort ($\beta_1 = 0.55$, .001 level) are substantially leveraged by object reuse ($\beta_2 = -1.92$, .001 level) and the MATURITY of the ICASE environment ($\beta_3 = 0.40$, .11 level) in the production of FUNCTION_POINTS. Again, a substantial amount of learning was occurring between Year 1 and Year 2 in the use of HPS. The variable for APPLICATION type ($\beta_4 = -0.04$, .46 level) was not significant at conventional levels, suggesting that if there is an effect on productivity, it occurs largely through reuse.[11] The coefficient for NEW_OBJECT_PCT($\beta_2 = -1.92$, .001 level) has a very straightforward interpretation in the original multiplicative model: it can be interpreted as a 1.92 percent productivity gain associated with a 1 percent decrease in the value of NEW_OBJECT_PCT (or a 1 percent increase in reuse) in the range of project sizes that we observed. The β_3 parameter ($\beta_3 = 0.40$, .11 level) estimate can be interpreted in a similar way. The impact of an additional year of organizational experience with the CASE tool is to amplify the productivity of development labor by a factor of

e$^{.40}$ = 1.49 times, because the value of the binary MATURITY variable is e to indicate Year 2.

The presence of diseconomies of scale for development labor ($\beta_1 = 0.55$, .001 level) suggests that higher productivity can be achieved with smaller-size projects. (Note: In our multiplicative model, a coefficient estimate of greater than 1 indicates the presence of scale economies, an estimate of 1.0 indicates constant returns to scale, and an estimate of less than 1 indicates diseconomies of scale.) This is probably due to the considerable complexity of managing large software projects in a new development environment.

---

[11]When we estimated this model without the APPLICATION type variable in Equation 4, we found that the estimated coefficient of NEW_OBJECT_PCT rose to about—1.57, yet the estimated coefficients of the other variables were largely unaffected. This suggests that APPLICATION type affected productivity through reuse.

Was the IS Strategy Delivering Software Development Performance Gains?

The average productivity and object reuse by application type and year are presented in Exhibits 6 and 7. Their implications for the performance of

---

EXHIBIT 6   Year 1 and Year 2 Productivity Comparisons

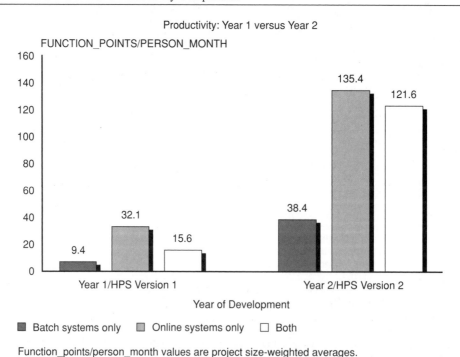

Productivity: Year 1 versus Year 2

FUNCTION_POINTS/PERSON_MONTH

Year of Development

■ Batch systems only   ■ Online systems only   □ Both

Function_points/person_month values are project size-weighted averages.

EXHIBIT 7   Year 1 and Year 2 Reuse Comparisons

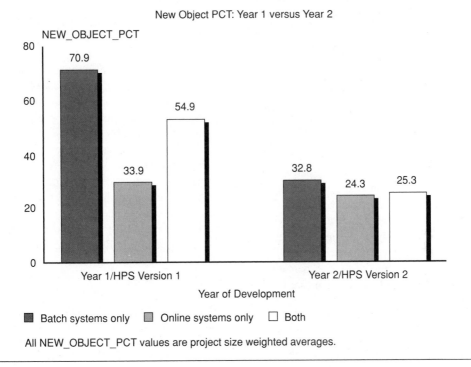

New Object PCT: Year 1 versus Year 2

All NEW_OBJECT_PCT values are project size weighted averages.

the firm's IS strategy are discussed in the remainder of this section.[12]

As can be seen in Exhibit 5, it appears there is greater productivity in the development of online, real-time systems, with a range of between 9.1 and 287.8 function points per person month. The proportion of new objects built (NEW_OBJECT-_PCT) ranged from 16.1 percent to 48.1 percent, equivalent to reuse levels of 83.1 percent and 51.9 percent respectively. Batch system development

productivity, by contrast, ranged between 4.2 and 38.4 function points per person month. One application, Project #2, exhibited no reuse at all. And the smallest proportion of new objects built for a batch application was observed for Project #20. In this instance, NEW_OBJECT_PCT was 32.8 percent, consistent with a 67.2 percent level of reuse.

Differences between Year 1 and Year 2 project productivity performance are also evident from the weighted averages (see Exhibit 6, which presents averages weighted for project size). Online application project development productivity grew from 32.1 to 135.4 function points per person month, and batch development productivity also grew from 9.4 to 38.4 function points per person month. The combined averages for online and batch projects evidenced an order of magnitude of growth, from 15.6 to 121.6 function points per

---

[12]A potential approach to the analysis of these data would have been to conduct simple t-tests to gauge whether *significant differences* exist between the means for the productivty results by application type in Years 1 and 2, and for the NEW_OBJECTPCT numbers as well. However, such a test would not fairly represent the characteristics of our structural model, especially because of the existence of scale diseconomies and correlated error terms.

person month between Years 1 and 2. If the estimated figure of 8 function points per person month is used for traditional development prior to the deployment of HPS, there appear to have been efficiency gains that were made during the first year of development.

The overall weighted average for proportion of new objects built (NEW_OBJECT_PCT) for the 20 projects was 39.8 percent. The weighted average NEW_OBJECT_PCT among Year 1 projects was 54.9 percent, which fell to 25.3 percent for Year 2 projects. The construction of new code was minimized among online projects at 24.3 percent of the total application objects in Year 2. The big potential for additional gains appears to have been in the creation of batch processing projects, however. Although our data set only includes one observation from Year 2 batch development, NEW_OBJECT _PCT fell from 70.9 percent to 32.8 percent. This suggests that potential efficiency gains are available from the HPS version 2 tool set for batch development.

CONCLUSION

This section reviews the major results of our research and discusses their generalizability, as well as the generalizability of the model employed to obtain them.

Major Findings at the First Boston Corporation

This article reports on the productivity gains that can result from the implementation of an IS strategy that was consciously adopted to promote the development and delivery of customizable and rapidly deployable, high functionality cooperative processing software applications, while controlling software development costs. The First Boston Corporation's investment in HPS was the solution to this problem, and the technical vision behind it involved three important related elements:

1. Emphasis on software reusability and automated code generation;
2. Storage of reusable software in a centralized object repository;

3. Integration of the CASE tool set across the development life cycle.

The evidence we presented suggests that the deployment of HPS was an essential first step in achieving the goals that senior management had set, and that effective software reuse was a precondition for this success. The levels of productivity reported represent an order of magnitude gain over the eight to 10 function points per person month productivity estimates for prior development at First Boston and for Capers Jones' national sample of MIS business applications (Bouldin, 1989). Further, the results of our economic model of ICASE reuse and productivity are of special interest: they offer evidence to confirm the importance of software reusability in the achievement of improved productivity, despite the increasing functionality and complexity of the software applications that were built.

The productivity gains that we observed were indeed substantial—high enough, in fact, to provide First Boston's senior software development managers with confirmation that the technical vision they implemented to support the firm's IS strategy was working well. First Boston's software development performance also exceeded Capers Jones' estimates for development productivity of 15 function points per person month prior to the maturation of a newly deployed CASE tool (Bouldin, 1989). In fact, the firm is likely to be achieving an even higher level of software development productivity than initially estimated by software development project managers. This kind of feedback reinforces the importance of implementing a software metrics program to track reusability and productivity, the final step we recommend in our analysis of the link between IS strategy and business strategy (see Exhibit 1). First Boston's investment in HPS was undertaken with the intent of obtaining competitive advantage in operations with high functionality software, while at the same time controlling software development costs. Interestingly, First Boston Corporation sold its NTPA software in 1988 to Kidder

Peabody (Arend, 1988), a large investment banking competitor, thus creating an opportunity for senior management to generate additional cash flows to defray the costs of implementing its IS strategy.

On the Generalizability of the Model and Results

One of the most important questions for practitioners who read this article is: How generalizable is the modeling approach employed by this research? In addition, to what extent is First Boston's experience with a software reusability strategy, improved productivity, and ICASE tools likely to be transferrable to other organizations? And, overall is CASE necessary to obtain the kind of productivity gains reported in this article?

Although prior literature on software development productivity was utilized for deciding on how to model what we saw and how to derive results from the descriptive model that emerged, we emphasize one of the limitations of this study: it investigates a model of software development productivity that is specific to what was learned about ICASE and reuse *at First Boston*. Thus, as a next step it would be valuable to examine additional data from other sites that have deployed HPS to determine whether reuse, application type, and the maturity of the ICASE tool set have similar productivity effects. But even this effort would only yield information about a single tool. Some preliminary insights are presented below.

The Case of Carter Hawley Hale, Inc. Carter Hawley Hale (CHH), a large Los Angeles-based retailing firm, is one such site from which additional conclusions might be drawn about our modeling approach and the efficacy of a reusability strategy involving HPS. The firm purchased HPS to support a software reusability strategy in its corporate systems development activities. Although we are unable to offer any quantitative information on development productivity or reuse levels, this model would be testable in the CHH environment, because the HPS tool set continues

to be upgraded over time, and learning effects are still observed as developers' use of the tool set matures. In addition, reuse at CHH is primarily object-based; CHH bought only the tool, not the NTPA systems as in Kidder Peabody's case (below). There also is preliminary evidence that the reusability strategy is working well. CHH, recently struggling with financial difficulties, filed for protection from creditors under Chapter 11 early in 1991. Although HPS had only recently been implemented at the firm, management decided to use it to enable deployment of a crucial, high functionality creditor claims management system in a short period of time, while under great pressure to cut software development costs.

The Case of Kidder Peabody. Additional conclusions can be drawn about the generalizability of our model from Kidder Peabody's experience with HPS. Kidder Peabody is a firm that has taken the reusability strategy even farther. Its purchase of NTPA was made with the idea that NTPA would be customized from First Boston's reusable object building blocks and repository models of core investment banking industry systems for use in a different organizational environment with different business requirements. In this case, not only would reuse be object-based, it would also be *model-based*,[13] leading to additional gains in productivity that were not possible in First Boston's primary development activities, and which would not be adequately addressed by the model we proposed. Because this kind of development is similar to system enhancement in traditional software engineering, it points out the need for a model that can meaningfully measure performance when reuse extends to the design phase (Lanergan and Grasso, 1984) or the maintenance/enhancement phase of development (Basili, 1990; Rombach, 1991).

Application Type and ICASE Tool Set Feature Evaluation. Because some shortcomings of HPS' handling of batch development were

---

[13]Personal communication with Vivek Wadhwa, Seer Technologies, July 10, 1991.

eliminated with the release of version 2, examining batch versus online systems development now would only be of interest to determine how well the capabilities of the ICASE tool set have developed. Management, however, also may want to examine other aspects of the applications that they build to determine how well the ICASE tools support development. We expect that no ICASE tool will support all tasks equally well, and inclusion of a relevant operationalization of the application type variable could help to confirm other strengths or weaknesses. Thus, with a more general treatment, the application-type variable should continue to be of interest to those who do single tool/single site, single tool/multi-site, or multi-tool/single site research on CASE productivity.

The Reuse Model. One of the most generalizable aspects of the model that we present is the inclusion of reuse as a driver for productivity. Equally important, however, is the realization that high levels of reuse are not automatic when repository and object-based ICASE tools are deployed. One researcher recently pointed out that "[r]euse is enabled by some development process and both reusable components and the reuse process employed need to be tailored to and integrated into that development process model" (Rombach, 1991, p. 89). Thus, a useful model for CASE productivity evaluation is likely to require a model for software reuse evaluation embedded within it.

Although we identified application type and ICASE maturity as drivers for reuse in the First Boston model, a larger set of factors must be considered in a more general model to evaluate reuse (Banker, et al., 1990). The factors would include:

1. Technical qualities of the tool (e.g., ease of reusable object identification and retrieval, and functionality of reusable objects);
2. Development team characteristics (e.g., size of the team, expert-novice composition, and relative knowledge of the repository);
3. Organizational factors (e.g., an incentive system to promote reuse by developers, and project reuse level targets); and,

4. Architectural factors (e.g., the extent to which reusability is leveraged in systems planning, and whether the development environment integrates reusability across life cycle phases).

Note that each of these classes of variables offers management an opportunity to redesign the systems development environment to promote reuse in a cost-effective manner (Barnes and Bollinger, 1991; Bollinger and Pfleeger, 1990). Considering such variables will become increasingly important in the future as firms move forward from merely implementing ICASE to maximizing its effectiveness.

The Reuse Metric. The reuse metric that we have presented, NEW_OBJECT_PCT, is readily generalized. It can represent the percentage of new code developed in a variety of software engineering environments. For example, this metric could be operationalized as "new lines of CASE code," "new objects built" in other entity relationship attribute object-based tools (such as IEF), or "new objects classes" built in object-development (Rubin, 1990). We should also point out that a more immediate metric for reuse is given by 1 - NEW_CODE_PCT, and that this metric can also be employed where management's focus is on the level of reuse, rather than the level of new code built.

Clearly, this research is only a first step in developing an understanding of reuse and productivity in ICASE environments. Additional work at other sites is needed to probe the impacts of other tools that are based on entity relationship attribute data modeling, as well as those that are based on object-oriented data modeling (Chen and Sibley, 1991). We make no claim that the model presented in this article is a general model, though we argued that it can be generalized along a number of dimensions. Nor have we shown that ICASE is a prerequisite for reuse, since high levels of reuse could be obtained from CASE tools that do not integrate the entire life cycle. (In fact, a repository may be more important.) However, the capabilities that ICASE provides to integrate phase-specific outputs for use across the life cycle may well be necessary to translate the potential that a reusability strategy offers into meaningful software development productivity gains.

ACKNOWLEDGMENTS

We wish to thank Mark Baric, Gene Bedell, Tom Lewis, and Vivek Wadhwa of Seer Technologies for providing us access to data on software development projects and offering their own and their managers' time. We also thank Charles Wright, Eric Fisher, and Vannevar Yu for assistance with the collection of the software project data. We acknowledge four anonymous reviewers, Macedonio Alanis, Cynthia Beath, Eric Clemons, Rosann Collins, Gordon Davis, Gordon Everest, Jean Kauffman, Chris Kemerer, Rachna Kumar, Dani Zweig, and the participants of research seminars at the University of Minnesota, New York University, the University of Pennsylvania, the University of Rochester, and the University of California, Irvine for their helpful comments and suggestions. Finally, we thank the National Science Foundation (grant #SES-8709044) for partial funding of data collection.

References

1. Albrecht, A. J. and Gaffney, J. E. "Software Function, Source Lines of Code, and Development Effort Prediction: A Software Science Validation," *IEEE Transactions on Software Engineering* (9:6), November 1983, pp. 639–647.

2. Apte, U., Sankar, C. S., Thakur, M., and Turner, J. "Reusability Strategy for Development of Information Systems: Implementation Experience of a Bank," *MIS Quarterly* (14:4), December 1990, pp. 421–431.

3. Arend, M. "Kidder, First Boston Get on Each Other's CASE," *Wall Street Computer Review,* September 1988, pp. 86–90.

4. Bailey, J. W. and Basili, V. R. "A Meta-model for Software Development Resource Expenditures," *Proceedings of the 5th International Conference on Software Engineering,* 1981, pp. 107–116.

5. Banker, R. D. and Kauffman, R. J. "Automated Software Metrics, Repository Evaluation and the Software Asset Management Perspective," working paper, Center for Information Systems, Stern School of Business, New York University, New York, NY, 1991.

6. Banker, R. D. and Kemerer, C. F. "Scale Economies in New Software Development," *IEEE Transactions on Software Engineering* (15:10), October 1989, pp. 1199–1205.

7. Banker, R. D., Fisher, E., Kauffman, R. J., Wright, C., and Zweig, D. "Automating Software Development Productivity Metrics," working paper, Center for Research on Information Systems, Stern School of Business, New York University, New York, NY, 1990a.

8. Banker, R. D., Kauffman, R. J., and Morey, R. C. "Measuring Gains in Operational Productivity from Information Technology: A Study of the Positran Deployment at Hardee's Inc.," *Journal of Management Information Systems,* Fall 1990b.

9. Banker, R. D., Datar, S., and Kemerer, C. "A Model to Evaluate Variables Impacting the Productivity of Software Maintenance," *Management Science* (37:1), January 1991, pp. 1–18.

10. Barnes, H. B. and Bollinger, T. "Making Software Reuse Cost Effective," *IEEE Software* (8:1), January 1991.

11. Basili, V. "Viewing Maintenance as Reuse-Oriented Software Development," *IEEE Software* (7:1), January 1990, pp. 19–25.

12. Behrens, C. A. "Measuring the Productivity of Computer Systems Development Activities with Function Points," *IEEE Transactions on Software Engineering* (9:6), November 1983, pp. 648–651.

13. Belady, L. A. and Lehman, M. M. "The Characteristics of Large Systems," in *Research Directions in Software Technology,* P. Wegner (ed.), MIT Press, Cambridge, MA, 1979, pp. 106–138.

14. Biggerstaff, T. and Richter, C. "Reusability Framework, Assessment and Directions," *IEEE Software* (4:2), March 1987, pp. 41–49.

15. Boehm, B. *Software Engineering Economics,* Prentice-Hall, Englewood Cliffs, NJ, 1981.

16. Boehm, B. and Papaccio, P. N. "Understanding and Controlling Software Costs," *IEEE Transactions on Software Engineering* (14:10), October 1988, pp. 1462–1477.

17. Bollinger, T. B. and Pfleeger, S. L. "Economics of Reuse: Issues and Alternatives," *Information and Software Technology* (32:10), December 1990.

18. Booch, G. "What Is and What Isn't Object-Oriented Design," *Ed Yourdon's Software Journal* (2:7–8), Summer 1989, pp. 14–21.

19. Bouldin, B. M. "CASE: Measuring Productivity—What Are You Measuring? Why Are You Measuring It?" *Software Magazine* (9:10), August 1989, pp. 30–39.

20. Breidenbach, S. "Developers Dump Hosts for PC LANs," *Network World,* March 20, 1989.

21. Chen, M. and Sibley, E. H. "Using a CASE-Based Repository for Systems Integration," *Proceedings of the 1991 Hawaii International Conference on Systems Sciences,* IEEE, January 1991, pp. 578–587.

22. Chen, P. P. "The ER Model Toward a Unified View of Data," *ACM Transaction on Database Systems* (1:1), 1976, pp. 9–36.

23. Clemons, E. "Evaluating Investments in Strategic Information Technologies," *Communications of the ACM,* January 1991.

24. Conte, S. D., Dunsmore, H. D., and Shen, S. Y. *Software Engineering Metrics and Models,* Benjamin Cummings, Reading, MA, 1986.

25. Davis, G. B. "Commentary on Information Systems: Productivity Gains from Computer-Aided Software Engineering," *Accounting Horizons* (2:2), June 1988, pp. 90–93.

26. DeMarco, T. "Yourdon Project Survey: Final Report," Yourdon Inc., Technical Report, 1981.

27. Desmond, J. "Tools Are Needed for Race to the Desktop," *Software Magazine* (9:9), July 1989.

28. Dreger, J. B. *Function Point Analysis,* Prentice-Hall, Englewood Cliffs, NJ, 1989.

29. Edelstein, H. "Cooperative Processing Applications Expanding in Number," *Software Magazine* (11:2), December 1989, pp. 39–45.

30. Feder, B. "The Software Trap: Automate—Or Else," *Business Week,* May 9, 1988.

31. Fisher, J. T. "IBM's Repository: Can Big Blue Establish OS/2 EE as the Professional Programmer's Front End?" *DBMS,* January 1990, pp. 42–49.

32. Gabel. "A Yen for Just-in-time Decisions Aids Sony's Drive for Coprocessing," *Computerworld,* April 10, 1989.

33. Gaffney, J. E., Jr. "Estimation of Software Code Size Based on Quantitative Aspects of Function (with Application of Expert Systems Technology)," working paper, IBM Federal Systems Division, Advanced Technology Department, Gaithersburg, MD, 1986.

34. Gaffney, J. E., Jr. and Durek, T. A. "Software Reuse—Key to Enhanced Productivity: Some Quantitative Models," *Information and Software Technology* (31:5), June 1989, pp. 258–267.

35. Grammas, G. W. and Klein, J. R. "Software Productivity as a Strategic Variable," *Interfaces* (15:3), May-June 1985, pp. 116–126.

36. Hazzah, A. "Making Ends Meet: Repository Manager," *Software Magazine,* December 1989, pp. 59–72.

37. Horowitz, E. and Munson, J. "An Expansive View of Reusable Software," *IEEE Transactions on Software Engineering* (SE-10:3), September 1984, pp. 477–487.

38. IFPUG. *Proceedings of the International Function Points Users Group,* International Function Point Users' Group, 1988.

39. Jones, T. C. "Reusability in Programming: A Survey of the State of the Art," *IEEE Transactions on Software Engineering* (SE-10:5), September 1984, pp. 484–494.

40. Jones, T. C. *Programming Productivity,* McGraw-Hill, New York, NY, 1986.

41. Jones, T. C. "A New Look At Languages," *Computerworld,* November 7, 1988.

42. Judge, G. G., Griffiths, W. E., Hill, R. C., Lutkepohl, H., and Lee, T.-C. *The Theory and Practice of Econometrics, Second Edition,* John Wiley and Sons, New York, NY, 1985.

43. Kang, K. C. and Levy, L. S. "Software Methodology in the Harsh Light of Economics," *Information and Software Technology* (31:5), June 1989, pp. 239–249.

44. Kemerer, C. F. "An Empirical Valuation of Software Cost Estimation Models," *Communications of the ACM,* May 1987.

45. Kemerer, C. F. "An Agenda For Research in the Managerial Evaluation of Computer-Aided Software Engineering (CASE) Tool Impacts," *Proceedings of the 22nd Hawaii International Conference on Systems Sciences,* Kailuo-Kona, HI, January 1989.

46. Kemerer, C. F. "Reliability of Function Points Measurement: A Field Experiment," working paper, Sloan School of Management, MIT, Boston, MA, December 1990.

47. Kernighan, B. W. "The UNIX System and Software Reusability," *IEEE Transactions on Software Engineering* (SE-10:5), September 1984, pp. 513–518.

48. Kim, Y. and Stohr, E. A. "Software Reuse: Issues and Research Directions," working paper, Center for Research on Information Systems, Stern School of Business, New York University, New York, NY, June 1991.

49. Knight, J. "CASE Up On MIS Agenda," *Software Magazine,* August 1989, pp. 32–36.

50. Lanergan, R. G. and Grasso, C. A. "Software Engineering with Reusable Designs and Code," *IEEE Transactions on Software Engineering* (SE-10:5), September 1984, pp. 498–501.

51. Lenz, M., Schmid, H. A., and Wolfe, P. F. "Software Reuse Through Building Blocks," *IEEE Software* (4:4), July 1987, pp. 34–42.

52. Loh, M. and Nelson, R. R. "Reaping CASE Harvests," *Datamation,* July 1, 1989, pp. 31–33.

53. Low, G. C. and Jeffery, D. R. "Function Points in the Estimation and Evaluation of the Software Process," *IEEE Transactions on Software Engineering* (16:1), January 1, 1990, pp. 64–71.

54. Mathis, R. F. "The Last 10 Percent," *IEEE Transactions on Software Engineering* (SE-12:6), June 1986, pp. 705–712.

55. Matsumoto, Y. "Some Experiences in Promoting Reusable Software: Presentation in Higher Abstract Levels," *IEEE Transactions on Software Engineering* (SE-10:5), September 1984, pp. 502–512.

56. McGuff, F. P. "Cost Cutting Revisited, *Computerworld,* July 17, 1989.

57. Meyer, B. *Object-Oriented Software Construction,* Prentice-Hall, New York, NY, 1988.

58. Moad, J. "Cultural Barriers Slow Reusability," *Datamation,* November 15, 1989, pp. 87–92.

59. Neighbors, J. M. "The DRACO Approach to Constructing Software from Reusable Components," *IEEE Transactions on Software Engineering* (SE-10:5), September 1984, pp. 564–574.

60. Nezlek, G. S. and Leitheiser, R. L. "Towards Developing a Coherent Research Framework to Measure CASE Effectiveness," *Proceedings of the 24th Hawaii International Conference on Systems Sciences,* January 1991, pp. 438–445.

61. Norman, R. J. and Nunamaker, J. F., Jr. "CASE Productivity Perceptions of Software Engineering Professionals," *Communications of the ACM* (32:9), September 1989, pp. 1102–1108.

62. Nunamaker, J. F., Jr. and Chen, M. "Software Productivity: A Framework of Study and an Approach to Reusable Components," *Proceedings of the 22nd Hawaii International Conference on Systems Sciences,* Kailua-Kona, HI, January 1989a, pp. 959–968.

63. Nunamaker, J. F., Jr. and Chen, M. "Software Productivity: Gaining Competitive Edges in an Information Society," *Proceedings of the 22nd Hawaii International Conference on Systems Sciences,* Kailua-Kona, HI, January 1989b, pp. 957–958.

64. Parker, J. and Hendley, B. "The Re-usage of Low Level Programming Knowledge in the UNIVERSE Programming Environment," in *Software Engineering Environments,* P. Brereton (ed.), Halstead Press, New York, NY, 1988.

65. Rombach, H. D. "Software Reuse: A Key to the Maintenance Problem," *Information and Software Technology* (33:1), January/February 1991.

66. Rubin, K. "Reuse in Software Engineering: An Object-Oriented Perspective," *Proceedings of COMPCON,* 1990, pp. 340–346.

67. Scacchi, W. "Understanding Software Productivity: A Comparative Empirical Review," *Proceedings of the 22nd Hawaii International Conference on System Sciences,* Kailua-Kona, HI, January 1989, pp. 969–977.

68. Schwartz, E. "IBM Sets Sights on Financial Services," *Computer Systems News,* March 19, 1990.

69. *Software Magazine.* "CASE Growth Will Skyrocket," March 1988, p. 16.

70. Sperling, E., Schwartz, E., and Gerber, C. "IBM Makes CASE for Coding," *Computer Systems News,* September 25, 1989.

71. Sprouls, J. (ed.). *IFPUG Function Point Counting Practices Manual, Release 3.0,* International Function Point Users Group, Westville, OH, 1990.

72. Standish, T. A. "An Essay on Software Reuse," *IEEE Transactions on Software Engineering* (SE-10:5), September 1984, pp. 494–497.

73. Symons, C. R. "Function Point Analysis: Difficulties and Improvements," *IEEE Transactions of Software Engineering* (14:1), January 1988, pp. 2–10.

74. Teory, T. Y., Yang, D., and Fry, J. P. "A Logical Design Methodology for Relational Database Using the Extended Entity-Relationship Model," *ACM Computing Surveys* (18:2), June 1986, pp. 197–222.

75. Tracz, W. "Software Reuse: Motivations and Inhibitors," *Proceedings of COMPCON 87,* San Francisco, CA, February 1987, pp. 358–363.

76. Voelckner, J. "Automating Software: Proceed with Caution," *IEEE Spectrum,* July 1988.

77. Walston, C. E. and Felix, C. P. "A Method of Programming Measurement and Estimation," *IBM Systems Journal* (16:1), 1977, pp. 54–73.

78. Wingfield, C. G. "USACSC Experience with SLIM," US Army Institute for Research in Management Information and Computer Science, Technical Report 360–5, 1982.

79. Wong, W. "Management Overview of Software Reuse," Technical Report PB87-109856, National Bureau of Standards, Gaithersburg, MD, 1987.

80. Zellner, A. "An Efficient Method for Estimating Seemingly Unrelated Regressions and Tests for Aggregation Bias," *Journal of the American Statistical Association* (57), 1962, pp. 348–368.

The High Productivity Systems (HPS) ICASE Development Tool Set

HPS, the object and repository-based ICASE tool studied in this research, provides support across the systems development life cycle through a series of integrated tools, as shown below: The HPS application development platform consists of the following features:

- A central DB2-based repository, with PS/2-based local development repositories;
- A technical documentation generator and manager;

- Reuse enabling facilities and management tools;
- Project level security and control;
- Source code library management facilities.

HPS promotes reuse. Developers can search the centralized repository by object type, object name, or keywords that contain an object's description. Once identified, objects can be reused to create functionality in new applications.

EXHIBIT 8   Case Development Tool Set

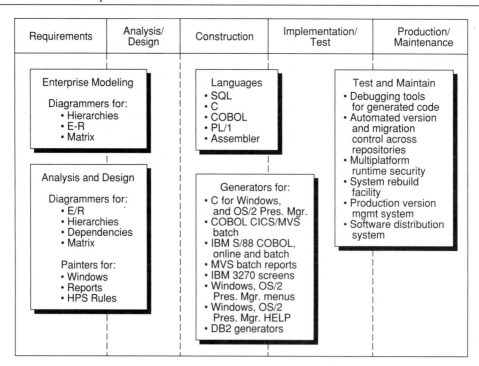

492

An Overview of the Function Point Analysis Methodology

The function point analysis methodology for the measurement of the size of a software project is based on the identification of functions performed by the software. The methodology was originally developed by Allan Albrecht at IBM. Since then, the methodology has developed, with the help of a national users group, into an operationally well-defined methodology (Dreger, 1989). It continues to gain in popularity, despite the extent of the effort required to analyze a system of moderate size, because of its robustness across different programming environments and its usability as an early life cycle labor estimation tool. (For a description of the International Function Point Users Group Standard, Release 3.0, the interested reader is referred to Sprouls, 1990.)

Function point analysis has two primary components: function counts and complexity measures. *Function counts* (FC) represent a basic measure of the user functionality of a system, independent of the technical features of implementation. The *complexity modifier* (CM) expression provides the final adjustment to the function count obtained to reflect the degree of technical difficulty involved in implementing a system.

EXHIBIT 9   Function Point Calculation

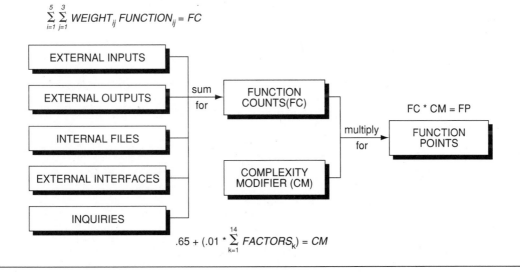

$$\sum_{i=1}^{5}\sum_{j=1}^{3} WEIGHT_{ij}\ FUNCTION_{ij} = FC$$

$$.65 + (.01 * \sum_{k=1}^{14} FACTORS_{k}) = CM$$

Function counts are broken down into five FUNC-TION types (i = 1 to 5): external inputs, external outputs, internal files, external interfaces, and inquiries. An application's function count is the sum of the scores an application achieves on each of the external function types. Function counts are determined by applying WEIGHTS (j = 1 to 3; LOW/MEDIUM/HIGH) from a set of tabulated values that represent the number of file types referenced and data elements associated with each occurrence of a FUNCTION type.

The function points method also includes 14 technical FACTORS (k) for implementation that are rated on a scale of "0" to "5." A complexity measure of "0" represents the absence of a factor and thus no adjustment to the original function count, while a "1" means that the technical complexity factor was expected to play an important role in influencing labor consumption. Examples of the factors include batch/online systems, complexity of mathematical logic, required level of reliability, and stability of the development environment. From the above formula, we see that function points are mainly based on function counts. When a system exhibits an average level of development environment complexity, the complexity modifier (CM) will take on the value 1. Less than average complexity reduces functionality, while greater than average complexity increases it.

An Illustration of the New Object Percentage Metric

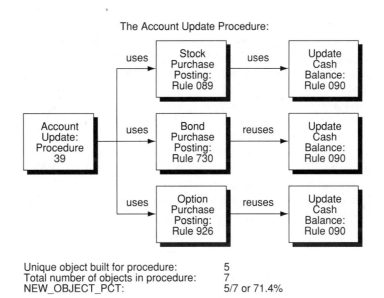

The Account Update Procedure:

	uses	Stock Purchase Posting: Rule 089	uses	Update Cash Balance: Rule 090
Account Update: Procedure 39	uses	Bond Purchase Posting: Rule 730	reuses	Update Cash Balance: Rule 090
	uses	Option Purchase Posting: Rule 926	reuses	Update Cash Balance: Rule 090

Unique object built for procedure: 5
Total number of objects in procedure: 7
NEW_OBJECT_PCT: 5/7 or 71.4%

Appendix 3 illustrates a software reuse metric called NEW_OBJECT_PCT that measures the extent of the new code that must be developed for an ACCOUNT UPDATE PROCEDURE. In this example, no objects from prior applications are used for development; however, the UPDATE CASE BALANCE RULE 090—built for the first time here—is reused twice. This results in a NEW _CODE_PCT of 71.4 percent. If the CASH BALANCE UPDATE RULE 090 had been available in the repository from a prior software development effort, this would result in a reduction of NEW_OBJECT_PCT to 57.1 percent. Note that we exclude multiple calls to the same object (e.g., control structure in traditional programming that involves a loop or recursion) in our calculation of reuse.

REUSABILITY-BASED STRATEGY FOR DEVELOPMENT OF INFORMATION SYSTEMS: IMPLEMENTATION EXPERIENCE OF A BANK

INTRODUCTION

Information systems are the backbone of the products and services offered by financial institutions and hence are viewed as important ingredients of their success. Information system trends over the last two decades point to the development of application software as a particularly critical task facing the managers of information systems. A review of these trends reveals that hardware and communications technologies have made tremendous strides in terms of increased processing power, reduced size, and lower prices. For example, productivity in semiconductors and communications industries has increased at the rates of 65 percent and 100 percent per year, respectively, over the last two decades. However, the technology of software development, displaying a productivity growth rate of only 5 percent per year, has not kept pace and is recognized as being the primary bottleneck in creating appropriate information systems capability (Gruman, 1988). Considering the magnitude of the software development costs—estimated at $125 billion in the USA in 1990 (Boehm, 1988)—the criticality of software productivity growth assumes even greater importance.

The concept of reusability is seen as an important approach for improving software productivity and has received a great deal of attention in the software engineering literature. The main theme

conveyed in research literature is that the concept of reusability is certainly feasible and has great potential for delivering substantial benefits. One of the advantages of reusing software is that well-used modules have tended to be thoroughly tested and very rarely give rise to errors (Ince, 1988). In addition, software reusability is believed to lead to improved maintainability, quality, portability, and software productivity (Bassett, 1987; Wong, 1986).

However, while reusability is a strategy of great promise, its promise has been largely unfulfilled (Biggerstaff and Richter, 1987; Parker and Hendley, 1988). The main inhibiting factors have been the absence of a clear reusability strategy (Biggerstaff and Richter, 1987) and the lack of specific top-management support, which can lead to resistance from project managers and programmers (Tracz, 1987). This resistance to implementing reusability is possibly due to the view held by some project managers and developers that reusability will lead to reduction in their budget and staff (Wong, 1986).

The reusability concept is not being implemented to the degree that it deserves because of several other reasons (Ramamoorthy, et al., 1988; Woodfield, et al., 1987):

1. Software systems are often not initially designed for software reusability. This makes the task of identifying the reusable components within the existing code extremely difficult.
2. Integrating multiple components in one application is difficult because of a large number

Article by Uday Apte, Chetan S. Sankar, Meru Thakur, and Joel E. Turner. Reprinted by special permission from the *MIS Quarterly*, Volume 14, Number 4. Copyright 1990 by the Society for Information Management and the Management Information Systems Research Center at the University of Minnesota.

of bugs that occur when there are interface problems.

3. With deadlines near, the priority of programmers is to fix bugs in programs quickly, making the programmers less amendable to using reusable components.
4. Investment needed to develop software reuse systems, to develop tools and methods to support both the creation and use of component libraries, and to train users is an inhibiting factor.

A generally accepted methodology for creating and implementing reusability is still lacking (Lenz, et al., 1987). An asset-based system development methodology has been recently proposed by Karimi (1990). The proposed method required integration of data and process modeling through the use of semantic modeling techniques and tools. This method emphasizes reusability at the design rather than at the code level. It is interesting to note that the reusability project described in our paper independently arrived at, and used during the prototype development, a methodology that is, in essence, equivalent to the asset-based methodology.

Practical experience with reuse has been scant, and very little has been reported in the literature. Few reusability systems that are in widespread use are based upon numerical computations and subroutine libraries for input/output and string manipulation (Horowitz and Munson, 1984; Shriver, 1987). The software productivity system at TRW has promoted software reuse and tool integration (Wartik and Panedo, 1986). An interesting result of a study of reusability at Raytheon Company showed that 40 to 60 percent of the program code was repeated in more than one application (Frank, 1981). Most studies of software reuse agree that about one-half of code from one application is reusable in another (Biggerstaff and Perlis, 1984). An early example of implementing reusability can be seen in Japanese software factories, where the benefits have justified the cost of developing reusable parts (Matsubara, et al., 1981). GTE data services used several incentives to encourage reuse—a quarterly newsletter describing its benefits, a $50 reward for programmers whose components were reused within a year, and making successful reuse a part of the project manager's job evaluations and a condition of pay raises.

This paper describes the experience of a large bank, well known for its information systems capability, in implementing a reusability-based strategy for development of information systems. First, the bank's rationale in choosing the reusability strategy is discussed. Then, the implementation strategy is described in two stages: (1) building a prototype to investigate the feasibility and attractiveness of the reusability concept for the bank, and (2) its subsequent implementation using a library of reusable entities and a programmer's workbench. Finally, the lessons the bank learned in implementing software reusability are presented and future directions are suggested.

INFORMATION SYSTEMS STRATEGY OF A BANK

The banking industry has undergone a period of turbulence in the last decade that promises to persist in the foreseeable future (Sametz, 1984). The major changes affecting the industry have been in the areas of government regulation, technology changes, and consumer preferences.

Deregulation of the banking industry has increased the scope of permissible activities for financial and non-financial institutions, has relaxed geographic restrictions, and has gradually phased out the ceilings on interest rates payable on deposits. All these changes have increased the intensity of competition by expanding the range of services being provided by banks and other financial institutions.

Technological advances in both the computer and telecommunications industry have improved the economies of scale and scope and are having a profound impact on the functioning of a bank. Technology has given banks an ability to handle a large volume of transactions at a declining average unit cost, to support geographically dispersed operations through distributed processing, and to offer new products and delivery channels, such as automated teller machines (ATMs), bank-by-phone, automated clearinghouse, etc.

Customers' preferences and attitudes have also changed. Customers are more prone to shopping for the optimum balance of risk and return on their deposits, and are becoming more discerning in their evaluation of services. This has added to the competitive pressures on the industry.

These changes have put pressure on profit margins in the banking industry, and cost containment in all areas, including information systems, is becoming strategically important. Competitive forces have also led banks to change their product development activities. The ability to offer new products quickly to customers is becoming more critical, and the movement toward technology-based differentiation of products and delivery channels is becoming more pronounced.

Timely introduction of products requires that the corresponding applications be developed in a like manner. It is also necessary that this application development be carried out without disrupting the systems supporting existing products. At the same time, new software development and maintenance activities are also becoming increasingly more expensive. Senior information systems management is, therefore, becoming highly sensitized to the need for new ways to improve the efficiency of software development and maintenance.

Critical Success Factors

Recognition of the above factors in the early 1980s led senior information systems management at the bank to identify the following critical success factors for application systems:

1. The cost of developing and maintaining software must be reduced.
2. New applications must be developed in a timely manner.
3. The application systems as a whole must be flexible enough to evolve in a controlled manner.

Investigation into the various options available to realize these factors led to the concept of the reusability of code aided by software engineering tools, including formal methodologies for structured analysis and design of code. A review of the bank's products and services had previously revealed that they were based on a small set of basic transactions, such as open account, accrue interest, etc. Therefore, if a set of reusable programs could be created to capture these basic transactions, it was conjectured that it would be possible to recreate the significant portion of a bank's applications systems over time through the reusable software.

Use of a library of reusable software could save considerable development costs and improve the quality of software and maintenance of software products. Development costs would be reduced because some software would not have to be developed. Reusable software would also allow timely development of applications. Being a one-time development activity, it would be easier to ensure that the reusable modules belonging to the library were of extremely high quality. Because new software would be composed of these high-quality modules, the final quality of the software would be high, and this would mean lower maintenance costs over the life of a system. The maintenance and enhancement of applications could also become easier because, in many cases, maintenance would need to be performed only on a single copy of the reusable component. By allowing better system maintenance and enhancement, the reusable code could improve flexibility of application systems. Thus, it was felt that reusability of software would satisfy all the critical success factors.

In 1982 an information system strategy based on reusability of software was proposed, and subsequently, an 18-month research and prototyping effort to examine and confirm the feasibility and attractiveness of the proposed strategy was commissioned by senior information systems management. A project team was then assembled to work on this project.

PROTOTYPE PROJECT: OBJECTIVES, METHODOLOGY AND RESULTS

The project team began its work on the prototype by addressing the following major research questions:

1. What are the main characteristics that determine the applicability, or non-applicability, of a software reusability concept to a given application system?
2. How does one identify the reusable components of code from existing application systems?
3. Is it feasible to recreate multiple applications from reusable software, and what is the extent of reusability that can be achieved?

The concepts developed and results of the work performed by the team are described below in three subsections that parallel these research questions.

Reuse of Code: Manufacturing Approach to Software Development

To address the first question, the project team developed a concept that it labelled a "manufacturing approach" to software development. This approach involved viewing application development activities as a production operation, with completed application software as the product. This viewpoint suggests the use of a simple, yet powerful, operations management concept of the matching of products and processes (Hayes and Wheelwright, 1979). The concept recommends using a job shop-type process for producing customized, one-of-a-kind products, while using a component assembly line approach for producing standardized, large-volume products.

Within the context of application development, program types (i.e., products) can be organized along a continuum from decision support systems (DSS), to management information systems (MIS) to transaction processing systems (TPS). The development approaches can be arranged from a craft approach to a manufacturing approach. The craft approach implies an unstructured activity in which a few skilled analysts/programmers assume responsibility for developing the system. The

EXHIBIT 1 Application Type/Development Approach Matrix

	Program Types	
Development Approaches	Decision Support	Transaction Processing
Craft	X	
Manufacturing		X

manufacturing approach implies piecing together applications from previously constructed reusable components. Exhibit 1 illustrates the suggested matching of development approaches and program types. The craft approach is well-suited for one-of-a-kind situations such as those found in decision support applications. In contrast, the manufacturing approach, or the reusability of software approach, would make sense in a high-volume, transaction processing type of banking application (e.g., demand deposit, credit card, installment loan, etc.) where a good deal of commonality exists among applications.

Development and use of the manufacturing approach concept helped identify the appropriate development approach for programs in each application system.[1] The programs that could be implemented under the manufacturing approach were selected and targeted for further analysis in order to identify reusable components. These components, representing commonly used processing steps within a particular group of applications, would thus act as a set of "building blocks."

A prerequisite to choosing reusable building blocks is that the set of targeted applications should display a sufficient degree of commonality.

---

[1] In the banking industry, application systems are organized according to the products they support. Each application typically consists of several programs that individually perform the different tasks necessary to support a product. Thus, an application system consists of programs of various types, ranging from TPS to DSS.

This requires that transactions involved in underlying products or services also have a sufficient degree of commonality. For example, deposit products such as savings accounts and money market accounts involve similar transactions. Our observation was that this condition was met to a larger degree by the retail banking business. The wholesale and international banking and trust business had products that each displayed a substantial amount of uniqueness. It was, therefore, concluded that the concept of reusability, at a business function level, was applicable more on the retail banking side.

Methodology for Identifying Reusable Components

Identifying reusable components was the first critical task in the prototype effort. The project team used both analytical and empirical methods in parallel to accomplish this.

The *empirical method* of the study involved examination of the bank's processing needs by interviews with system users and by a detailed review of current application systems. Although the project team studied all banking products and application systems, it concentrated its efforts on those products and programs that were considered to be most appropriate for the application of reusability. The interviews and application reviews were followed by an exercise to identify parts of programs that were used in more than one application and were based on similar processing logic.

The *analytical method* of study involved examining the fundamental relationships between a financial institution and its customers, and describing the basic financial services and supporting transactions associated with these relationships. Based on this examination, the reusable components required to support the common transactions were designed. We observed that a degree of commonality existed within the group of deposit products and within the group of loan products.

Two kinds of reusable components were identified at the banking function level: monetary and non-monetary. Monetary components addressed all monetary transactions that by definition have an impact on account balances (e.g., deposit to account, interest accrual, etc.). Non-monetary components addressed all other important transactions performed in a bank (e.g., open account, renew account, etc.).

In addition to the banking industry's specific components, the team also identified components related to the general data processing functions (e.g., sorting, database access, etc.) or to transaction management (e.g., creating transaction log, maintaining control totals, etc.). We found that developing reusable components of this type hinged on the standardization of data.

Exhibit 2 shows examples of relationships between the account types (or bank's products) and reusable components. The "renew account" component is relevant to certificates of deposit but does not apply to checking and savings accounts. Similarly, interest must be calculated for savings

EXHIBIT 2   Reusable Components and Banking Products

	Component Type			
	Monetary		*Non-Monetary*	
Products	*Deposit to Account*	*Calculate Interest*	*Open Account*	*Renew Account*
Interest-free checking	X		X	
Savings	X	X	X	
Certificates of Deposit	X	X	X	X

and certificates of deposit, whereas it need not be calculated for an interest-free checking account.

The analytical and empirical methods proved complementary to each other. The analytical method provided a conceptual framework for organizing and identifying the components, whereas the empirical method supplied the details necessary in specifying components in terms of the data elements and the processing logic used.

Prototype Development

The end result of the analytical and empirical work was the identification and specification of reusable components. An entity-relationship-based enterprise data model was also developed for the bank. A high-level design of all transaction processing systems was created using this data model and the data flow methodology. A prototype of a selected subset of the bank's product was then constructed using a highly productive fourth generation language.

In the prototype development effort, about 30 reusable components were identified and developed. Each component was found to be reused, on average, in approximately eight different products. These reusable components accounted for an estimated 60 percent of the software needed to construct an existing or new banking product. The study also found that the components under the monetary category could be reused in their entirety across different products. These components provided the highest form of reusability that could be achieved. Nonmonetary transaction components shared processing logic, although they were not always identical in terms of the data elements used. Developing reusable components for the nonmonetary transactions, therefore, hinged on resolving the differences in naming and formatting the underlying data elements and in creating a unified enterprise data model.

In summary, the prototype validated the feasibility of the software reusability approach. It also confirmed that the use of a standardized reusable code would result in both strategic benefits (e.g., increasing the bank's capability for timely response to market opportunities) and operational benefits (e.g., reducing and controlling system development and maintenance costs).

EXPERIENCE IN IMPLEMENTING THE SOFTWARE REUSABILITY CONCEPT

Subsequent to the completion of the prototype in mid-1984 and its successful presentation and demonstration, senior information systems management decided to implement the proposed concepts and created a small organization for that purpose. This organization was given an explicit charter to improve programmer productivity through reusable software, and one of the first projects undertaken by the unit was the establishment of a reusable entity library (REL). In approving the REL project a "sunset" clause was set. The clause stated that the success of the project would be measured in terms of the actual usage of the REL entities. If, after a reasonable time, usage did not match expectations, the effort would be redirected or curtailed. This library was made available in early 1986 and was later enhanced to create a standard application development environment, termed *programmer workbench,* in 1988. These two projects are described in the next subsections.

Phase 1: The Reusable Entity Library

Very early in the REL project, the team realized that the biggest obstacles, and yet prerequisites for success, were successfully persuading managers at all levels and training programmers to think in terms of reusable programming constructs. These two tasks were not easy but were accomplished through multiple activities.

The benefits of reusability are not immediate for any programming team working under deadlines and coping with day-to-day operational problems. In fact, most project managers tend to focus on upfront learning costs, which may lead to productivity loss in the short term and cause potential delays, rather than on reduced development cost and time and on the downstream benefits of higher-quality systems that have reduced maintenance costs.

The banking function-level reusable entities were already identified and specified as part of the prototype effort. It would have been feasible to create a library of entities based on these specifications, but developing a complete retail banking application such as a demand deposit system from scratch, using these entities was simply out of the question. These systems represent an investment of literally hundreds of millions of dollars, and although the current systems may not be perfect, with regular maintenance they seem to work satisfactorily. Therefore, to recreate existing applications just to make use of reusable components was clearly risky and unjustified.

A study of programmer activities at the bank indicated that a typical programmer spent about 25 percent of available time on new application development, about 60 percent on maintenance and enhancement of old programs, and about 15 percent on user support and operations. Hence, limiting the application of the reusability concept to software alone was deemed short-sighted because it would have addressed only about one quarter of a programmer's activities. Therefore in defining the REL project, a broad definition of reusable entity was adopted. This definition included any software or procedure that could be used by system developers in all stages of the system life cycle. Examples of reusable entities include subprograms, utilities, parameter-driven CLISTS, JCL, file definitions, etc. The design of REL addressed both the technical and managerial issues and was completed by early 1985. This design divided the REL implementation into three logical functions that had to be in place for the project to succeed: reusable software development, online documentation, and management reporting.

Reusable Software Development

This function involved establishing a set of documentation and programming standards for the reusable entities and setting up a process for populating the library with reusable entities. An effort was made to make the process as market-driven as possible. To kick off the process, the team solicited participation of technical representatives from all major programming areas. The primary responsibility of these representatives was to survey their individual areas for candidate entities to be included in the library. All surveys were analyzed, and the suggested entities were prioritized on the basis of their expected benefits. The team had the responsibility of developing and introducing the "high hitter" entities, i.e., entities that had high benefits and were suggested by the most application areas. A total of eight entities were developed in the first round, either through new development or through retrofitting of existing components. This process has been repeated every year since then and has become the modus operandi for populating the REL.

Online Documentation

This function involved setting up a "system shell" for helping programmers discover information related to the functionality and use of entities belonging to the REL. Online documentation was critical to the success of the REL because getting programmers to use the library depended, to a large extent, on successfully fulfilling the informational requirements needed by an average programmer. A set of utilities was designed and established for this purpose. These utilities related to the establishment of an online document listing the contents of the library and a keyword search facility for producing summary abstracts of the entities. In addition to this online documentation, the REL was also promoted through presentations, seminars, and management memos to all major programming areas.

Management Reporting

The major purpose of this function was to set up a process for tracking the usage of entities by programming areas. Quarterly usage reports were produced to help senior management monitor the project in terms of the economic benefits achieved. These reports were also used as a basis for an incentive scheme that encouraged programmers to use the REL. The scheme was based on recognizing and rewarding the teams that made above-average use of the REL.

The first version of the REL design was in place by the end of 1985. The initial release of the library in early 1986 consisted of approximately 20 entities. The number of entities grew to 40 by the year end. Over time, the entity usage grew steadily from approximately 200 usages in mid-1986 to over 3,000 usages per month by the end of 1987.

Although the initial objectives of the reusability project during the prototype phase were primarily to identify and implement reusable components in functionally similar banking applications, we found that programmer demand and the big payoffs were in developing common utilities that helped programmers alleviate their daily operational "bottlenecks." The requests received from technical representatives dealt with managing code in a multi-site environment, handling turnover procedures, interfacing with core systems (e.g., general ledger, output services, etc.), automatically enforcing programming standards, and improving programming efficiency.

The team estimated the benefit potential of each entity by computing the dollar value of the time saved per entity use. As expected, a wide distribution of benefits was observed. For example, only a few dollars were saved by using an entity that determined the optimal blocking factor for a particular I/O medium, but the use of an entity for interfacing a purchased package with the bank's standard printing utility resulted in savings of thousands of dollars.

The library achieved the break-even volume of operation in the third quarter of 1987 and met the usage expectations of senior management. It was estimated that the library contributed about a quarter of a million dollars in benefits in 1987. In terms of the manpower used, about five man-years were spent developing the REL, with half that amount spent in 1987 alone.

Phase II: The Programmer Workbench

The analysis of the entity usage of REL showed that increase in usage was directly linked to the number of entities in the library. In late 1987, usage had levelled off in the range of 3,000 to 4,000 per month. The main reason for this levelling off,

determined through informal programmer feedback, was that the information utilities supporting the library shell were fast becoming inadequate for the task of presenting the contents of the library to the programmer community in an increasingly complex application development environment. The bank had recently introduced a new relational DBMS and a new teleprocessing monitor, and had reorganized its development activities into three separate sites. Thus, as the introduction of additional entities occurred, the cost of finding, understanding, and using entities had increased to a point where it seemed to have imposed a negative influence on programmer productivity.

The team's solution was to develop a programmer's workbench to provide a single consistent application development environment for all programmers. The workbench would provide a consistent framework for housing all reusable entities. All screens, help facilities, and interfaces were made consistent across all entities, and thus the cost of learning the features of a new entity and operating in a new environment were minimized. The workbench shielded the programmer as much as possible from the idiosyncrasies of the actual operating environment. The programmer would only select the actual entity of interest, and the workbench would create the necessary conditions (in terms of required JCL, job class parameters, etc.) for the entity to work properly in the current operating environment. The workbench design used a hierarchy of menus for beginning users, with the added capability for experienced users to access desired functions directly through the use of function keys.

The programmer workbench project was started in the third quarter of 1987 and was implemented in the second quarter of 1988. The initial release raised the REL usage from about 3,000 to 6,000 per month. Since then, the functionality and contents of the workbench have been continuously enhanced; today the REL usage is over 20,000 per month, and about 900 distinct users log on to it. A graph depicting the increase in usage over the last four years is shown in Exhibit 3. A recent benefit calculation showed that the programmer workbench

EXHIBIT 3   Entity Usage (Quarterly)

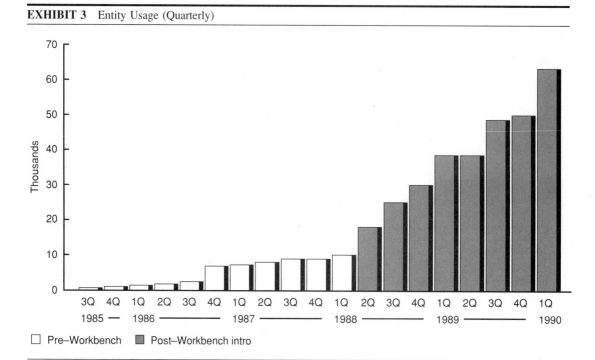

☐ Pre–Workbench   ■ Post–Workbench intro

has saved the bank over $1.5 million in development costs in 1989.

LESSONS LEARNED IN IMPLEMENTING SOFTWARE REUSABILITY

The workbench/reusability effort is an ongoing project at the bank. The current scope of the project is somewhat broader than the one envisioned during the project startup. Nevertheless, the experience gained in implementing software reusability during the last eight years has taught several valuable lessons. This section discusses our recommendations for implementing reusability.

Reusability Improves Productivity and Cost Performance

Based on our experience in implementing reusability at the bank, the strategic and operational benefits of reusability are clear. Reuse of standard, well-tested, off-the-shelf software components im-

proves programmer productivity and saves significant cost in developing software. The high quality of reusable components also reduces application maintenance in the long run. In terms of the investment costs of the reusability strategy, the bank has spent little more than $1 million over the last five years. In comparison, the benefits realized during the same time period, in terms of avoided development costs, are more than $2 million, with an annual savings of approximately $1.5 million in 1989 alone. Thus, from a cost containment viewpoint, implementing software reusability has proven to be an attractive proposition.

With reduction in time required for software design, development, testing, and implementation the overall software productivity has also improved. The case for strategic benefits of enabling quicker introduction of new products is, in our opinion, also quite strong. But, not having concrete and quantifiable proof, this benefit should be viewed as a strongly plausible hypothesis that remains to be proven.

Reusability Comes in Many Flavors

One of the main lessons the team learned is that, from a broad perspective, reusability should ideally be viewed as a productivity enhancement tool. The low growth in software productivity and the general shortage of quality programming resources are proving to be the main bottlenecks in using information systems in the bank. We feel that promoting reusability, in its broadest sense, is an important tool for alleviating that bottleneck.

Traditionally, the work on reusability has focused on isolating functional commonality across application systems. This viewpoint mainly addresses the coding aspects of a programmer's job. However, coding is not the only task a programmer performs. The process of software development and maintenance involves a number of fairly standard processes that must be repeated for each project. Some of these typical programmer activities include business modeling, data analysis, conforming to standards, testing, and turnover procedures. Wherever possible, these activities should be considered as candidates for the application of reusability. After all, from a business perspective, the management is interested in developing a high quality system that is delivered on time and within budget.

At the bank, reusable entities have been classified into five groups. We view the banking function-level software reusability as a high-level one, whereas the reusable entities that deal with operational/informational aspects of a programmer's job are viewed as the lower-level ones.[2] The entity groups listed below are arranged from a high to low level in terms of standard system life cycles—development, testing, implementation.

Banking Function Entities: This group consists of common banking functions such as interest calculation routines, date routines, etc.

Application Development Entities: These entities help software development and include utilities for manipulation and scanning of data and files, source code development, code restructuring and quality analysis, and screen generation. They create standard interfaces to accounting and reporting systems (such as general ledger) and to various DP processes (such as input/output, teleprocessing monitors, etc.).

Application Testing and Maintenance Entities: These relate to activities such as online and batch testing, test data generation, scripting, and flow pathing.

Operations and Standards Entities: These activities deal with responsibilities such as conforming to software standards, requests for computing resources, generation of run books for scheduling dependencies of programs, and procedures for a program's turnover to operations.

Application Management Entities: These include traditional project management, resource allocation, and status reporting activities associated with software development. Also included in this group are activities important to operations function such as monitoring the on-call responsibility.

Information Utilities: These deal with information required by software developers and include items such as manuals, entity information, training, bulletin boards, and hotlines.

Our hypothesis is that the benefit per usage of high-level reusable entities is higher than the low-level entities. But it should be noted that the high-level entities are more difficult to identify and develop, are likely to be used with lower frequency, and are, in general, more difficult to implement. The lower-level entities, on the other hand, give smaller benefits per usage, but are easier to develop and implement. Lower-level entities are also used with higher frequency and are more easily accepted by programmers. Hence, in implementing reusability, it is advisable to implement lower-level entities in the beginning.

Another difference between higher-level entities and lower-level entities is that the value of the former is related to the size (in lines of code) of the module; however, the value of the latter is

---

[2] In using the terms high or low, we do not intend to convey a meaning that high-level reusability is better than the low-level one.

determined primarily by the time it saves the programmer in completing a particular procedure, not necessarily by the size of the reusable entity.

The Major Challenges Are Not Technical But Managerial

Persuading managers and programmers to buy into the concept of reusability involves a major change from traditional practices. This change is not likely to be automatic, and we feel that the entire exercise is more likely to fail from a lack of management commitment and programmer interest than from any technical reasons.

Securing senior management's approval is relatively easy. Because of their long-term, strategic viewpoint, the benefits of reusability are evident to them. But middle-level managers, including direct managers of programmers, are more resistant to the concept. The difficulty in obtaining buy-in is possibly due to their short-term planning horizon and their performance evaluation, which emphasize meeting the target completion dates and budgeted costs. These factors make them reluctant to accept any new process that implies a certain amount of up-front learning costs for their programmers and a possible delay in project completion. Thus, from an implementation viewpoint, it is important that these managers be specifically kept in mind in marketing the reusability concepts through such means as presentations, seminars, and senior management memos.

Getting programmers to use the reusable software is, of course, the most important prerequisite for success. As we found in our experience with the programmer workbench, meeting the information requirement of programmers and making reusable components an integral part of a standard software development environment is key to the success of reusability.

Implementing Reusability: Other Considerations

In implementing reusability, it is important that the applications targeted for potential use of reusable software are transaction processing types. In the

bank's case, it was found that this reusable software was more applicable to the simple, retail banking products as opposed to the more complex wholesale banking or trust products.

As discussed earlier, it is advisable to implement lower-level entities in the beginning of a reusability project. Programmers will then immediately realize that reusability helps them solve their operational problems and improve their productivity. An important consideration for improving programmers' usage of reusable entities is to provide a monetary or other suitable incentives.

As in any project dealing with new concepts, achieving a few success stories early in the game is very important, and starting with the lower-level reusable entities is a good way to ensure that. The high-risk, high-payoff entities in the form of reusable software modules can always be implemented once the programmers and their managers have bought into the concept of reusability.

CONCLUSIONS AND FUTURE DIRECTION

This project has provided important insights in strategic and operational implementation of reusability in software development. Although the initial objectives were primarily to identify and implement reusable components in functionally similar banking applications, the project team found that programmer demand and the big payoffs were in developing reusable entities that helped programmers alleviate their daily operational "bottlenecks." Developing the programmer's workbench so it would provide a consistent software development environment for housing all reusable entities proved to be a successful approach. Initially it was difficult to get the buy-in from programmers and their direct managers, and it was essential to market the reusability concept to these managers. Achieving a few success stories early in the implementation proved to be very important, and starting with the lower-level reusable entities ensured that objective.

The present goal of the programmer workbench/reusability project is to integrate existing mainframe-based CASE tools into the platform to enhance its capability as an integrated software development environment. The project team is also excited about the developments in PC/ workstation technology. Plans to position the workstation and REL to better utilize these technologies and to possibly migrate to these platforms over the next several years are currently underway.

References

1. Bassett, P. G. "Frame-based Software Engineering," *IEEE Software* (4:4), July 1987, pp. 9–16.

2. Biggerstaff, T. and Perlis, A. "Forward: Special Issue on Software Reusability," *IEEE Transactions on Software Engineering* (10:5), September 1984, pp. 474–476.

3. Biggerstaff, T. and Richter, C. "Reusability Framework, Assessment and Directions," *IEEE Software* (4:2), March 1987, pp. 41–49.

4. Boehm, B. W. and Papaccio, P. N. "Understanding and Controlling Software Costs," *IEEE Transactions on Software Engineering* (14:10), October 1988, pp. 1462–1477.

5. Frank, W. L. "What Limits to Software Gains?" *Computerworld*, May 4, 1981, pp. 65–70.

6. Gruman, G. "Early Reuse Practice Lives Up To Its Promise," *IEEE Software* (5:11), 1988, pp. 87–91.

7. Hayes, R. and Wheelwright, S. "Link Manufacturing Process and Product Life Cycles," *Harvard Business Review* (57:1), January-February 1979, pp. 133–140.

8. Horowitz, E. and Munson, J. B. "An Expansive View of Reusable Software," *IEEE Transactions on Software Engineering* (10:3), September 1984, pp. 477–487.

9. Ince, D. *Software Development: Fashioning the Baroque*, Oxford University Press, New York, NY, 1988.

10. Karimi, J. "An Asset-Based Systems Development Approach to Software Reusability," *MIS Quarterly* (14:2), June 1990, pp. 179–198.

11. Lenz, M., Schmid, H. A., and Wolfe, P. F. "Software Reuse Through Building Blocks," *IEEE Software* (4:4), July 1987, pp. 34–42.

12. Matsubara, T., Sasaki, O., Nakajim, K. Takezawa, K., Yamamoto, S., and Tanaka, T. "SWB System: A Software Factory," in *Software Engineering Environments*, H. Hunke (ed.), North-Holland Publishing Company, Amsterdam, 1981, pp. 305–318.

13. Parker, J. and Hendley, B. "The Re-Usage of Low-Level Programming Knowledge in the UNIVERSE Programming Environment," in *Software Engineering Environments*, P. Brereton (ed.), Halsted Press, New York, NY, 1988.

14. Ramamoorthy, C. V., Garg, V. and Prakash, A. "Support for Reusability in Genesis," *IEEE Transactions on Software Engineering* (14:8), August 1988, pp. 1145–1154.

15. Sametz, A. (ed.). *The Emerging Financial Industry*, Lexington Books, Lexington, MA, 1984.

16. Shriver, B. D. "Reuse Revisited," *IEEE Software* (4:1), January 1987, p. 5.

17. Tracz, W. "Software Reuse: Motivations and Inhibitors," *Proceedings of COMPCON 87*, San Francisco, CA, February 1987, pp. 358–363.

18. Wartik, S. P. and Penedo, M. H. "Fillin: A Reusable Tool for Form-Oriented Software," *IEEE Software* (3:2), March 1986, pp. 61–69.

19. Wong, W. "Management Overview of Software Reuse," Technical Report PB87-109856/XAB, National Bureau of Standards, Gaithersberg, MD, 1986.

20. Woodfield, S. N., Embley, D. W., and Scott D. T. "Can Programmers Reuse Software?" *IEEE Software* (4:4), July 1987, pp. 52–59.

Discussion Questions

1. Barnes and Bollinger's adaptive reuse (reusing relatively large structures by making small changes) sounds similar to software maintenance projects, whereby a large structure (the previous version of the system) is "reused" by modifying it. However, software reuse is widely regarded as an activity worth promoting, whereas often organizations seek to minimize their expenses for software maintenance. What accounts for these two differing interpretations?

2. At Lim's two Hewlett-Packard sites, the benefits of reuse seemed greater at the Manufacturing Productivity site than the San Diego Technical Graphics site. Provide some speculation as to why this might have been.

3. Banker and Kauffman observe a much higher average rate of productivity, as measured by the number of Function Points delivered per person-month in Year 2 versus Year 1 in their data set (see Exhibit 6). What factors might account for this?

4. Apte et al.'s emphasis on the incentives issues in software reuse might lead to a proposal to form a separate organizational unit charged with developing materials for reuse and helping other developers to find and use them. These "creators" would then be a distinct group from the "assemblers" or, in Barnes and Bollinger's term, "consumers". What managerial issues might arise in such an organizational design?

Software Maintenance

INTRODUCTION

Perhaps the most important topic in software engineering management in terms of its economic significance is software maintenance; what the IEEE defines as "the modification of a software product after delivery to correct faults, to improve performance or other attributes, or to adapt the product to a changed environment". This activity typically requires half or more of the staff resources in software development organizations, and tends to grow as new applications are developed and added at a rate that exceeds that of the retirement of application software. The articles in this chapter follow the common format of an introductory article followed by an article that highlights an issue in the managerial economics of the activity, followed by a piece highlighting organizational aspects of the problem.

The 1987 survey article by Schneidewind, while naturally somewhat dated, still retains a solid achievement in describing and categorizing the major issues in software maintenance. He particularly emphasizes the disconnection between software maintenance's practical importance and the emphasis placed on it in software engineering research, which tends to be limited. (Interestingly, it is this paucity of research that keeps Schneidewind's survey from becoming rapidly obsolescent.) He goes on to highlight possible productive avenues for future work and research.

In the second article, Banker et al. examine the relationship between maintenance costs and software complexity in an empirical study of 65 maintenance projects in a commercial bank. They develop an econometric model and find a statistically significant relationship between what they term "accidental complexity" and productivity. More than a simple statistical relationship, their model allows them to estimate that this accidental complexity is very costly to the firm, and further suggests that the results of the model provide support for the argument that so-called "quick and dirty" development is very expensive in the long run.

The final article is by Burt Swanson and Cynthia Beath. Swanson is well-known in the software maintenance community for his pioneering study at the end of the 1970s with Lientz which characterized the maintenance activity in several hundred organizations and developed a three way typology that is still used today. This more recent work focuses on how firms organize for maintenance. They propose a format with a dedicated maintenance group (known as an "L" type organization) which would allow maintenance to develop as a professional activity within the firm, rather than a poor stepchild to new development. They provide the results of twelve case studies, including several that have adopted a hybrid form of this type of organization.

THE STATE OF
SOFTWARE MAINTENANCE

INTRODUCTION

To gauge the state of software maintenance, ask yourself these questions:

- How many articles have appeared in this TRANS-ACTIONS on the subject of maintenance in the last couple of years? Answer: none between August 1985 and November 1986, inclusive, and few prior to this period in the history of the TRANSACTIONS. However, before rushing to judgement about the "guilt" of TSE, realize that it is not unique in this regard among technical journals.

Some additional questions to ponder:

- How many computer science departments have a course in maintenance?
- How many doctoral dissertations have there been in maintenance?

To work in maintenance has been akin to having bad breath. Yet, examine the "Problem" below and ask yourself whether there is any justification for this neglect. But, first, a disclaimer, followed by some definitions so that we may proceed from a common reference point.

The information which follows represents a selected overview of the state of the software maintenance field. Since this is a survey paper, it is difficult to cover every aspect of the field, given time and page limitations. We apologize for any significant work which may not be covered.

Article by Norman F. Schneidewind. ©1987 IEEE. Reprinted, with permission, from (*IEEE Transactions on Software Engineering;* SE-13, 3, 303-310; March/1987).

Definitions

Maintenance: Modification of a software product after delivery to correct faults, to improve performance or other attributes, or to adapt the product to a changed environment [1].

Maintainability: The ease with which a software system can be corrected when errors or deficiencies occur, and can be expanded or contracted to satisfy new requirements [2].

Why Is There a Maintenance Problem?

There is a maintenance problem because [3]:

- 75–80 percent of existing software was produced prior to significant use of structured programming.
- It is difficult to determine whether a change in code will affect something.
- It is difficult to relate specific programming actions to specific code.

The main problem in doing maintenance is that we cannot do maintenance on a system which was not designed for maintenance. Unless we design for maintenance, we will always be in a lot of trouble after a system goes into production.

In addition, there is the very significant personnel problem concerning the myth that there is no challenge for creative people in maintenance.

According to Zvegintzov, most software is immortal (immoral?). He says that all surveys of the distribution of effort between new systems and present systems show about a 50–50 split [4]. This is the case because of the following important considerations:

- Functions are added, not replaced.
- Every new function must be tied into the present system.
- Systems are not totally replaced, except for overriding economic or technical reasons.
- Organizations strive for compatibility in systems, not perfection.

Specifically, Lientz and Swanson report from a survey of data processing managers in 487 data processing organizations that: departments spend about half of their application staff time on maintenance; over 40 percent of the effort in supporting an operational application system is spent on providing user enhancements and extensions; the average application system is between three and four years old, consists of about 55 programs and 23,000 source statements, and is growing at a rate of over 10 percent a year; and about one-half man-year is allocated annually to maintain the average system [5].

If all programs to be maintained were well documented and cleanly structured, and used third-normal form data models and data dictionaries for generating the programmer's data, the task of the maintainer would be much easier. The problem for most maintainers is that they have to maintain ill-documented code that is covered with patches with no comprehensible structure and that has data representations buried in the program code. It is a major detective operation to find out how the program works, and each attempt to change it sets off mysterious bugs from the tangled undergrowth of unstructured code [2].

Why Is Maintenance Hard?

Maintenance is hard because [6]:

- We cannot trace the product nor the process that created the product.
- Changes are not adequately documented.
- Lack of change stability (See Metrics Section below).
- Ripple effect of making changes.

- Myopic view that maintenance is strictly a post-delivery activity.

One consequence of this lack of attention to maintainability requirements during design is loss of traceability. This is defined as the ability to identify the technical information which pertains to a software error detected during the operational phase (or other postrequirements phase) and thereby trace the error to the applicable design specifications and user requirements statements [7].

Why Is Maintenance Expensive?

In the early days of programming, when programmers' salaries were an almost insignificant percentage of the data processing budget, when programmers spent most of their time writing new programs, and when machine resources were expensive, the mark of a well written program was efficiency. Twenty years later, when programmers' salaries consume the majority of the data processing budget, when programmers spend most of their time maintaining programs, and when hardware is cheap, a new standard for well written programs has emerged: how maintainable are they, especially for future generations of programmers [8]?

Should Existing Code Be Discarded?

If existing code is so bad, why should it be retained? Belady believes that we cannot and should not declare "old" software obsolete or not worth studying [9]. This collection of functions is an important asset, embodying a wealth of experience, and constitutes an inventory of "ideas" for identifying the building blocks of future systems. Even if the code itself is inelegant and possibly not reusable, a study of the specifications and identification of the most frequently used components could reveal a set of generic classes of algorithms and functions which could be usable in future systems.

MODELS

Do We Have the Wrong Model for Maintenance?

Since the software industry does not seem to have a good understanding of and model for maintenance, it is worthwhile to consider some proposed models which provide insight into the maintenance process. Lehman suggests that change is intrinsic in software, and must be accepted as a fact of life, and since software undergoes change throughout its life, there is no reason to distinguish maintenance from initial development. Evolutionary development is inevitable [10], [11]. Furthermore, the very act of installing software changes the environment; pressures operate to modify the environment, the problem, and technological solutions. Changes generated by users and the environment and the consequent need for adapting the software to the changes is unpredictable and cannot be accommodated without iteration. Programs must be more alterable and the resultant change process must be planned and controlled. According to Lehman, large programs are never completed, they just continue to evolve. In other words, with software, we are dealing with a moving target and that, in effect, "maintenance" is performed continuously. Lehman suggests that the word "maintenance" not be used and that the term "program evolution" be used instead. If this model of the software process is correct, it suggests that change activity and change management should be an integral part of development and all other phases of the life of software. In this view, a change would be no more associated with "maintenance" than with development.

Do Requirements End in the Requirements Phase?

Lehman's view seems to be supported by Lientz and Swanson [12]. They state that the approach which is in vogue of getting requirements right before starting the design may be based on the fallacious assumption that requirements are fixed.

The reality is that requirements change continually, often in response to organizational change. These changes are more likely to emanate from experience in the use of the system than from an abstract specification in the early design of the system. The major problem in requirements assessment may not be the development of a complete, consistent and unambiguous specification, prior to design, but, rather, the evolution of requirements which allow a timely response of the software to organizational change. Requirements assessment during maintenance may be as demanding as during development.

Is the Life Cycle Model Appropriate for Maintenance?

The traditional view of the software life cycle has done a disservice to maintenance by depicting it solely as a single step at the end of the cycle. In fact, it would be more accurately portrayed as 2nd, 3rd, . . . , nth round development [13]. The traditional view also fosters the idea that structured techniques are best applied to development, whereas their application to maintenance is equally valid.

In contrast, the traditional view of maintenance is that it is an activity confined to the postdelivery phase, is not directly related to development, and has its own special requirements.

METHODS FOR IMPROVING MAINTENANCE

Software maintenance authors have made many suggestions for improving the maintainability of software. These suggestions can be classified into three categories: design approach, maintenance practices, and management.

What Design Approaches Are Needed?

Software design practices should include criteria for maintainability [14]. These criteria are the following:

- Design software with maintainability in mind.
- Develop design criteria for achieving maintainability.

- Simplicity should outweigh completeness.
- Change management should be used to:

—Limit the effects in the maintenance phase of a change made in the design phase.
—Determine ripple effects on other modules of making a change to a common module:

- global variables.
- modules which invoke or are invoked by a common module.

—Determine the effect on a module of making a change to a local variable.

- Evaluate the design for excessive complexity.

Another design approach to aid maintenance describes the design in terms of parts and the interconnections of those parts [15]. With parts interconnections as the focal point of the design and documentation, the system maintainer can more readily judge the possible ripple effect of change. Three levels—system, assembly, and component—are shown in list and graphical form, where each succeeding level provides a more detailed description of the previous level. A parts list and connections list is shown for each level. The parts list shows functions and the data associated with the functions. The connections list shows the input/output relationships between functions and data.

What Maintenance Practices Are Needed?

Maintainability can be significantly improved if the following practices are used [16], [14], [17], [18]:

- Change Management:
—Make easiest changes first.
—Change one module at a time.
—Inspect proposed changes for each type of side effect.
—Run regression tests after every change.
- Produce guidelines for modifying and retesting software.
—Provide information to support assessment of the impact of a change in various parts of the software.

What Other Practices Are Needed?

- Identify source statements which have been changed with a number which is associated with the change request.
- Learn to *read* programs (alien code).
- Keep diaries of bugs and maintenance issues.
- Centralize variable declarations in a program.

—Use abstract data types to define the legitimate types and values which objects of a type may assume and a set of operations which may be performed on that type.

- Centralize symbolically defined and referenced database definitions in a computer processible data dictionary.
- Since it can be taken for granted that software will evolve and change, each programmer in the process should give consideration to the next programmer in the life cycle.

One of the major sources of error in making maintenance modifications arises when neither the program nor the documentation reveal that sections of a program that are far apart are related. As suggested by Letovsky and Soloway, this may cause the programmer to make assumptions about the plans of a program which are based purely on local information. This can lead to an inaccurate understanding of the program as a whole [19]. Their solution to this problem is to provide answers to the two questions: What information needs to be provided to the reader of the program?

When and how should this information be provided?

Easily accessible information is needed to form correct interpretations of delocalized plans. What is needed is to move from documenting the code itself to documenting the plans in the code. A tool which may provide this capability is under development.

What Management Policies Are Needed?

Some guidelines offered by McClure [14] for improving the management of maintenance are the following:

- Involve maintainers in design and testing.

- Put the same emphasis on the use of standards in maintenance as in design.
- Rotate personnel between design and maintenance.
- Make design documentation available to maintainers at design time.
- Carry over the use of design tools into maintenance.
- Use configuration management and change request procedures.
- Establish a liaison between users and maintenance.

Boehm suggests the following for maximizing the motivation and, hence, productivity of maintenance personnel [20]:

- Couple software objectives to organizational goals.
- Couple software maintenance rewards to organizational performance.
- Integrate software maintenance personnel into operational teams.
- Create a discretionary perfective maintenance budget.
- Create the perquisites of software ownership.
  —Participation by maintenance personnel in: development standards creation, development reviews, and acceptance test preparation.
- Rectify the negative image of software maintenance.

The reader can see that the objective of these guidelines is to *integrate* design and maintenance—to reverse the current procedure of considering and managing these activities in disparate and separate functions.

What Tools Are Needed?

Tools are needed in maintenance to look for (and hopefully find) structure [2]:

- Looking for structure. Several types of structure need to be understood:
  —Procedural structure.
  —Control structure.
  —Data structure.
  —Input/output structure.

- Understanding data aliases:
  —Data may be referred to by several names.
- Following data flow:
  —Where do data originate? where are they used?
- Following control flow:
  —The consequences of executing each path must be understood.
- Understanding versions of a program:
  —How does a change affect different versions of a program?

Tools are available which address the above areas. These consist of displaying the following [2]:

- Structure Chart: Shows hierarchy and call/called relationships.
- Data Trace: Origins, uses, and modifications of variables.
- Control Trace: Shows control flow statements and indicates how a destination can be reached from a given origin.
- Version Comparisons: Statements which differ between two versions of a program are highlighted. Additionally, the following tool capabilities are useful for maintenance [21]:
- Stored test execution information giving dynamic behavior of a program.
- Test cases to exercise modified sections of a program.
- Symbolic and actual execution information.

An interesting tool is one designed to restructure unstructured code. One tool of this type is called structured retrofit, involving the restructuring of Cobol programs [22]. The application of this kind of tool rests on the premise that with 7 out of 10 programmers involved in maintenance, and costs for this activity soaring, maintenance must be made easier and, hence, less costly. Furthermore, the argument is made that even if the code is bad, the logic of the design may not be bad. In other words, the design concept was good but its implementation was poor. Since this poor code is meeting user requirements but is difficult and costly to maintain, it should be salvaged, where feasible.

The structured retrofit procedure consists of the following steps:

- Scoring: Programs are evaluated as candidates for restructuring by scoring them against the following criteria:
  —Degree of structure.
  —Level of nesting.
  —Degree of complexity.
  —Breakout of verb utilization.
  —Analysis of potential failure modes.
  —Trace of control logic.

However, even if a program scores low on the above criteria but still runs with little time required for maintenance, it will not be retrofitted.

- Compilation: Programs which are to be retrofitted are compiled. Programs which do not compile cleanly are referred to others for resolution. Programs continue in the retrofit process only if they compile cleanly.
- Restructuring: Programs that are unstructured are put through this process to make them structured. The resulting program will produce the same transformation on the same input data as the original program.
- Formatting: Programs are made more readable through the formatting process. They are then recompiled to pick up possible syntax errors.
- Validation: The same inputs are applied to the original and restructured programs and the outputs are compared on a bit-by-bit basis by a file-to-file compare utility.
- Optimization: The code is optimized to reduce overhead which may have been introduced by the restructuring process.

It is claimed that structured retrofit has been able to restructure 60 percent of programs offered automatically, another 20 percent with some manual intervention, and 20 percent cannot be restructured cost-effectively.

METRICS

In order to perform maintenance effectively, we must be able to measure the effects of design approaches on maintenance and, especially important, be able to measure the effects of maintenance approaches on future maintenance!

Ideally, we want maintenance to improve software. Our minimum objective is that maintenance should have a neutral effect. Unfortunately, too often, maintenance makes software worse, due to unforseen ripple effect. In order to minimize ripple effect, software must be stable. Stability must be achieved at design time, not during the maintenance phase. Stability in design is achieved by minimizing potential ripple effect caused by interaction between modules (i.e., a change to a module causes undesirable changes to other modules). The definitions and concepts applicable to achieving design stability were developed by Yau and Collofello [23]; these are the following:

- Program stability: Quality attribute indicating the resistance to the potential ripple effect which a program would have when it is modified.
- Module stability: A measure of the resistance to the potential ripple effect of a modification of the module on other modules in the program.
- Logical stability: Measure of resistance to impact of modification on other modules in terms of logical considerations.
- Performance stability: Measure of resistance to impact of modification on other modules in terms of performance considerations.
- "Maintenance activity" is a change to a single variable.
- Intramodule change propagation involves flow of changes within the module as a consequence of a modification.
- Intermodule change propagation involves flow of changes actoss modules as a consequence of a modification.
- Intramodule change propagation is utilized to identify the set of interface variables which are affected by logical ripple effect as a conse-

quence of a modification to a variable definition in a module. This requires an identification of which variables constitute the module's interfaces and the potential intramodule change propagation among the variables in the module.

- Once an interface variable is affected by a change, the flow of changes may cross module boundaries and affect other modules. Interface change propagation is used to identify the set of modules involved in intermodule change propagation as a consequence of affecting an interface variable in a module.
- Measure the complexity of affected modules to analyze the possible relationship between complexity and vulnerability to ripple effect.
- Compare stability of alternate versions of module for the purpose of making a design choice. (However, there may be no time available to design alternatives.)
- Use as predictor of amount of maintenance required.
- Reject request for maintenance if it involves modifying unstable modules.
- Restructure modules with poor stability.

The measure of design stability of a module, proposed by Yau and Collofello [23], [24], is the reciprocal of the total number of assumptions made by other modules about the given module. If the given module has poor design stability and it is modified, it is likely to produce undesirable effects on other modules, which either invoke, share global data with, or are invoked by the given module. The rationale of this metric is that modules which cause large ripple effects, if modified, are among the modules with poor design stability. This definition of stability only applies to modular software. This point illustrates one of the difficulties in trying to improve maintenance: much of the existing software which must be maintained is not modular!

More information needs to be captured in a metric than just the effects of a change to a single variable or the effects of changes to a set of variables. What is needed is the effects of changes on other aspects of a program, such as documentation. Also, since all assumptions are not equally important, this metric

could possibly be improved by weighting the assumptions. Although this metric addresses an important aspect of maintainability dealing with assumptions that are made about interfaces between modules, it is silent on the subject of intramodule design characteristics. Despite these limitations, this metric would be very useful, primarily, for deciding among design alternatives for *new* software.

An approach to assessing the difficulty of *maintaining* a program is to quantify program difficulty as the sum of the difficulties of the constituent parts [25]. A Maintainability Analysis Tool was developed to analyze the difficulty of understanding and maintaining Fortran programs by assigning weights, which represent relative difficulty of understanding, to various program attributes, such as syntactic elements (e.g., parameter) and syntactic attributes (e.g., name in COMMON). The numeric weights and factors are summed for a program to yield a measure of difficulty. Obviously, there can be a lot of subjectivity involved in assigning weights and measures.

A strategy for determining whether to continue to *maintain* software is to focus on modules which may be candidates for rewriting. These error prone modules need to be identified. One method for identifying error prone modules is to have maintenance personnel record information about: 1) which modules were changed, 2) how much effort was involved in making the changes, and 3) reasons for making the changes [26].

Another aspect of applying metrics to maintenance is the establishment of criteria for determining whether maintenance is being *performed* effectively. Arnold and Parker [27] established the following criteria for 40 telemetry processing projects at the NASA/Goddard Space Flight Center:

- Desired effort distribution: Distribution of maintenance effort between enhancements/restructurings and fixes.
- Desired frequency distribution: Distribution of reports approved for action between enhancements/restructurings and fixes.
- Completion rates: Rates for enhancements/restructurings and fixes.

- Effort per change: Labor time limits for enhancements/restructurings and fixes.

MAINTENANCE INFORMATION MANAGEMENT

Since maintenance usually involves having to understand what someone else did to the code, information about the characteristics of the code and specifications (if they exist) are essential to doing an effective job of maintenance. Important elements of the information base are: control flow information, data flow information, and declaration information [28]. This information base should be established as part of every *design* and *maintenance* activity.

STANDARDS

In general, development standards have been inappropriate for use in maintenance [29]. Of greater concern is the fact that standards efforts have not addressed maintenance.

Although no standards exist for maintenance, management guides are available from the National Bureau of Standards, which provide methodologies and procedures for conducting an effective maintenance program [30], [31]. Among the recommendations of [30] are the following:

- Develop a software maintenance plan.
- Recognize improvement of maintainability.
- Elevate maintenance visibility in the organization.
- Reward maintenance personnel; provide a career path and training.
- Establish and enforce standards.

The major conclusion of [31] is that, in addition to developing software with maintenance in mind, software must also be maintained with maintenance in mind!

MAINTENANCE OF EXISTING CODE

This activity involves maintaining software which has not been modularly designed. It dominates maintenance work.

Restructuring

As reported above, in the description of the structured retrofit system, unstructured code can be converted to a structured format. Due a proof by Jacopini and Bohm, any computable algorithm in any language, can be represented by a structured graph. This result is the basis for restructuring programs. Unstructured programs typically have graphs whose nodes are so connected that the graph cannot be effectively partitioned into independent regions. However, by means of a graph simplification process, an unstructured program can be rendered into a structured form. The original unstructured program is parsed into an abstract syntax tree. Several tree to tree transformations are performed to reduce the tree to a few simple control flow expressions. When the tree is sufficiently simple, it is transformed into a control flow graph. This simplification process terminates when the topology of the graph represents a structured algorithm.

Although the method sounds impressive there are problems in restructuring when the program has GOTO's. In addition, an enormous amount of machine time may be required to develop new control graphs representing the new structure [8]. However, if it is determined that restructuring is more economical than rewriting, it is clear that restructuring is only feasible when an automated method such as this is used.

It is not always feasible to make unstructured code look like structured code and more readable by using structured documentation. In a study conducted by Schneidewind [32] to analyze the effectiveness of documentation for maintenance purposes, where the documentation had been created with the intent of making the software more readable and understandable by showing a 'hierarchical structure' of unstructured code, it was found that the new documentation did not always tell the truth about the code logic as represented by the program listing. The reason for this was that the hierarchical documentation could not faithfully describe software which was unstructured. Lesson learned: the code must also be restructured.

Recovering the Design with Abstract Specifications

For situations in which no specifications exist, a technique called Maintenance by Abstraction is claimed to allow one to recover the design by using the following steps [33]:

- Inspect the code.
- Propose a set of abstractions (directed graph representations of the code).
- Choose the most suitable set of abstractions.
- Construct a specification from the abstractions.

The recovered design (i.e., the specification derived above) is then applied to the Transformation-based Maintenance Model. The directed graph representation of the code is examined to find nodes representing design decisions such that the order of design decisions can be reversed—for the purpose of making maintenance changes—in a way that will not affect the final implementation. It appears that this complex procedure would only be cost effective on large programs.

The IBM Federal Systems Division is upgrading the Federal Aviation Administration National Airspace System, 20 year old, 100,000 line, en route software by modeling programs as either function abstractions (transforms a value in input domain to output range) or data abstractions (class of data objects and the set of operations performed on them) [34]. Function abstractions can also be regarded as entities which do not retain data across invocations and data abstractions as entities which do retain data. The abstractions were used by the designer to determine the required change (added, deleted, and updated functions as needed).

SURVEYS

To provide a feel for the characteristics of maintenance as practiced in various organizations, results from several surveys are presented briefly below.

In a survey of 487 data processing organizations, it was found that most maintenance is perfective (55 percent): performed to enhance performance, improve maintainability, or improve executing efficiency. This is followed by adaptive maintenance (25 percent): performed to adapt software to changes in the data requirements or processing environments. Lastly, there is corrective maintenance (20 percent): performed to identify and correct software failures, performance failures, and implementation failures [12].

Chapin [35] reports that from a limited survey of users of fourth generation languages that although these languages are beneficial for development, their use may make maintenance more difficult and expensive. One reason he cites for this situation is that interprogram and intersystem communication of data with these languages is often obscure, thus rendering the effect of a maintenance action unclear.

In another survey by Chapin [36], he reports on information collected from supervisory personnel closest to software maintenance work. The survey consisted of 260 questionnaires collected from 123 data processing installations; there were 769 responses across the various questions. The biggest problems identified were poor documentation and inadequate staff. With regard to the latter, there is a problem in matching the characteristics of the software to be maintained with appropriate personnel.

PROGNOSIS

Much of the problem will remain of being condemned to maintain existing, nonstructured code for a long time into the future—perhaps 20 years. This situation will only change when two things happen: 1) software development environments become so effective and programmer productivity becomes so great that it will be more economical to develop new systems than to maintain old systems; 2) organizations want to do business in *new* ways. Thus the decision will not be over the cost of reprogramming or redesign, but about whether organizations will adapt their information systems to support the organization's survival in a changing world. In the interim, restructuring techniques will be an important tool for attempts to convert a "sow's ear into a silk purse." In making the restructuring decision, only relevant costs should be considered. The fact that a lot of money has been spent in the past is irrelevant to making a decision about the future. These are sunk costs; only future costs should be considered. The cost to rewrite, redesign, or develop a new system *are* relevant costs.

On the personnel front, there is hope. Software engineers are being sensitized to the need for considering maintainability in their designs. More academics will do research in maintenance when academic administrators recognize the importance of maintenance. Computer science programs will contain a course on maintenance when academics themselves recognize the importance of maintenance!

APPENDIX

The following lists some information about an important conference and a special interest group in the field of software maintenance:

Conference

The first conference in software maintenance, sponsored by technical societies, was the Software Maintenance Workshop, held at the Naval Postgraduate School, Monterey, CA, December 6–8, 1983 [37]. It was sponsored by the IEEE Technical Committee on Software Engineering of the IEEE Computer Society, National Bureau of Standards, and the Naval Postgraduate School, and in cooperation with the ACM Special Interest Group on Software Engineering.

The second conference was the Conference on Software Maintenance–1985, held at the Sheraton Inn Washington–Northwest, Washington, DC, November 11–13, 1985. It was sponsored by the same organizations as above, minus the Naval Postgraduate School, and with the addition of the Data Processing Management Association, and in cooperation with the Association for Women in Computing, and the Software Maintenance Association.

Special Interest Group

The Software Maintenance Association (SMA) is a special interest group in the field. For information about this organization and a maintenance newsletter, contact:

Nicholas Zvegintzov
141 Marks Place, #5F
Staten Island, NY 10301
(718) 981 -7842.

References

1. *An American National Standard IEEE Standard Glossary of Software Engineering Terminology,* ANSI/IEEE Standard 729, 1983.

2. J. Martin and C. McClure, *Software Maintenance: The Problem and Its Solutions.* Englewood Cliffs, NJ: Prentice-Hall, 1983.

3. D. P. Freedman and G. M. Weinberg, "A checklist for potential side effects of a maintenance change," in *Techniques of Program and System Maintenance,* Girish Parikh, Ed. Ethotech., Inc., 1980, pp. 61–68.

4. N. Zvegintzov, "Nanotrends," *Datamation,* pp. 106–116, Aug. 1983.

5. B. P. Lientz and B. E. Swanson, "Problems in application software maintenance," *Commun. ACM,* vol. 24, no. 11, pp. 763–769, Nov. 1981.

6. N. F. Schneidewind, "Quality metrics standards applied to software maintenance" (Abstract), in *Proc. Comput.*

Standards Conf. 1986 (Addendum), IEEE Comput. Soc., May 113–15, 1986.

7. M. B. Kline and N. F. Schneidewind, "Life cycle comparisons of hardware and software maintainability," in *Proc. Third Nat. Rel. Conf.,* Birmingham, England, Apr./May 1981, p. 4A/3/1–4A/3/14.

8. E. Bush, "The automatic restructuring of COBOL," in *Proc. Conf. Software Maintenance–1985.* Washington, DC: IEEE Comput. Soc. Press, Nov. 1985, pp. 35–41.

9. L. A. Belady, "Evolved software for the 80's," *Computer,* vol. 12, no. 2, pp. 79–82, Feb. 1979.

10. M. M. Lehman, "Programs, life cycles, and laws of software evolution," *Proc. IEEE,* vol. 68, no. 9, Sept. 1980.

11. ___, "Program evolution," Dep. Computing, Imperial College of Science and Technology, London SW7 2BZ, England, Res. Rep. DoC 82/1, Dec. 1982.

12. B. P. Lientz and E. B. Swanson, *Software Maintenance Management*. Reading, MA: Addison-Wesley, 1980.

13. J. R. McKee, "Maintenance as a function of design," in *AFIPS Conf. Proc.,* vol. 53, 1984 Nat. Comput. Conf., pp. 187–193.

14. C. L. McClure, *Managing Software Development and Maintenance*. New York: Van Nostrand, 1981.

15. J. Silverman, N. Giddings, and J. Beane, "An approach to design-for-maintenance," in *Proc. Software Maintenance Workshop,* R. S. Arnold, Ed. Washington, DC: IEEE Comput. Soc. Press, Dec. 1983, pp. 106–110.

16. R. L. Glass and R. A. Noiseux, *Software Maintenance Guidebook,* Englewood Cliffs, NJ: Prentice-Hall, 1981.

17. J. B. Munson, "Software maintainability: A practical concern for lifecycle costs," *Computer,* vol. 14, no. 11, pp. 103–109, Nov. 1981.

18. E. Yourdon, "Structured maintenance," in *Techniques of Program and System Maintenance,* Girish Parikh, Ed. Ethotech, Inc., 1980, pp. 211–213.

19. S. Letovsky and E. Soloway, "Delocalized plans and program comprehension," *IEEE Software,* vol. 3, no. 3, pp. 41–49, May 1986.

20. B. Boehm, "The economics of software maintenance," in *Proc. Software Maintenance Workshop,* R. S. Arnold, Ed. Washington, DC: IEEE Comput. Soc. Press, Dec. 1983, pp. 9–37.

21. Z. Kishimoto, "Testing in software maintenance and software maintenance from the testing perspective," in *Proc. Software Maintenance Workshop,* R. S. Arnold, Ed. Washington, DC: IEEE Comput. Soc. Press, Dec. 1983, pp. 166–117.

22. M. J. Lyons, "Salvaging your software asset (tools based maintenance)," in *AFIPS Conf. Proc.,* 1981 Nat. Comput. Conf., pp. 337–341.

23. S. S. Yau and J. S. Collofello, "Some stability measures for software maintenance," *IEEE Trans. Software Eng.,* vol. SE-6, pp. 545–552, Nov. 1980.

24. ____, "Design stability measures for software maintenance," *IEEE Trans. Software Eng.,* vol. SE-11, pp. 849–856, Sept. 1985.

25. G. M. Berns, "Assessing software maintainability," *Commun. ACM,* vol. 27, no. 1, pp. 14–23.

26. H. Schafer, "Metrics for optimal maintenance management," in *Proc. Conf. Software Maintenance–1985.* Washington, DC: IEEE Comput. Soc. Press, 1985, pp. 114–119.

27. R. S. Arnold and D. A. Parker, "The dimensions of healthy maintenance," in *Proc. 6th Int. Conf. Software Eng.* Washington, DC: IEEE Comput. Soc. Press, Sept. 1982, pp. 10–27.

28. J. S. Collofello and J. W. Blaylock, "Syntactic information useful for software maintenance," in *AFIPS Conf. Proc.,* vol. 54, 1985 Nat. Comput. Conf., pp. 547–553.

29. N. F. Schneidewind, "Usability of military standards for the maintenance of embedded computer software," in *Advisory Group for Aerospace Research & Development Conf. Proc. 330, Software for Avionics,* North Atlantic Treaty Organization, The Hague, Netherlands, Sept. 6–10, 1982, pp. 21–1–21–6.

30. J. A. McCall, M. A. Herdon, and W. M. Osborne, "Software Maintenance Management," Nat. Bureau Standards, NBS Special Publ. 500-129, Oct. 1985.

31. R. J. Martin and W. M. Osborne, "Guidance of software maintenance," Nat. Bureau Standards, NBS Special Publ. 500-106, Dec. 1983.

32. N. F. Schneidewind, "Evaluation of maintainability enhancement for the TCP/TSP Revision 6.0 Update .20," Naval Postgraduate School, Rep. NPS54-82-004, Feb. 1982.

33. G. Arango, "TMM: Software maintenance by transformation," *IEEE Software,* vol. 3, no. 3, pp. 27–39, May 1986.

34. R. N. Britcher and J. J. Craig, "Using modern design practices to upgrade aging software systems," *IEEE Software,* vol. 3, no. 3, pp. 16–24, May 1986.

35. N. Chapin, "Software maintenance with fourth-generation languages," *ACM Software Engineering Notes,* vol. 9, no. 1, pp. 41–42, Jan. 1984.

36. ____, "Software maintenance: A different view," in *AFIPS Conf. Proc. 54,* Nat. Comput. Conf., 1985, pp. 509–513.

37. R. S. Arnold, N. F. Schneidewind, and N. Zvegintzov, "A software maintenance workshop," *Commun. ACM,* vol. 27, no. 11, pp. 1120–1121, 1158.

SOFTWARE COMPLEXITY
AND MAINTENANCE COSTS

While the link between the difficulty in understanding computer software and the cost of maintaining it is appealing, prior empirical evidence linking software complexity to software maintenance costs is relatively weak [21]. Many of the attempts to link software complexity to maintainability are based on experiments involving small pieces of code, or are based on analysis of software written by students. Such evidence is valuable, but several researchers have noted that such results must be applied cautiously to the large-scale commercial application systems that account for most software maintenance expenditures [13, 17]. Furthermore, the limited large-scale research that has been undertaken has generated either conflicting results or none at all, as, for example, on the effects of software modularity and software structure [6, 12]. Additionally, none of the previous work develops estimates of the actual cost of complexity, estimates that could be used by software maintenance managers to make the best use of their resources. While research supporting the statistical significance of a factor is, of course, a necessary first step in this process, practitioners must also have an understanding of the practical magnitudes of the effects of complexity if they are to be able to make informed decisions.

This study analyzes the effects of software complexity on the costs of Cobol maintenance projects within a large commercial bank. It has been estimated that 60 percent of all business expenditures on computing are for maintenance of software written in Cobol [16]. Since over 50 billion lines of Cobol are estimated to exist worldwide, this also suggests that their maintenance represents an information systems (IS) activity of considerable economic importance. Using a previously developed economic model of software maintenance as a vehicle [2], this research estimates the impact of software complexity on the costs of software maintenance projects in a traditional IS environment. The model employs a multidimensional approach to measuring software complexity, and it controls for additional project factors under managerial control that are believed to affect maintenance project costs.

The analysis confirms that software maintenance costs are significantly affected by software complexity, measured in three dimensions: module size, procedure size, and branching complexity. The findings presented here also help to resolve the current debate over the functional form of the relationship between software complexity and the cost of software maintenance. The analysis further provides actual dollar estimates of the magnitude of this impact at a typical commercial site. The estimated costs are high enough to justify strong efforts on the part of software managers to monitor and control complexity. This analysis could also be used to assess the costs and benefits of a class of computer-aided software engineering (CASE) tools known as restructurers.

PREVIOUS RESEARCH AND CONCEPTUAL MODEL

Software Maintenance and Complexity

This research adopts the ANSI/IEEE standard 729 definition of maintenance: modification of a software product after delivery to correct faults, to improve performance or other attributes, or to

Article by Rajiv D. Banker, Srikant M. Datar, Chris F. Kemerer, and Dani Zweig. Copyright 1990, Association for Computing Machinery, Inc. Reprinted by permission from (*Communication of the ACM*, v. 36, n. 11, pp. 81–94 November/1993).

adapt the product to a changed environment [28]. Research on the costs of software maintenance has much in common with research on the costs of new software development, since both involve the creation of working code through the efforts of human developers equipped with appropriate experience, tools, and techniques. Software maintenance, however, is fundamentally different from new systems development in that the software maintenance must interact with an existing system. The goal of the current research is to identify the factors affecting the assimilation process and thereby increase (decrease) the amount of effort required to perform the maintenance task. In particular, the current research focuses on measuring the impact of the existing source code aspects believed to affect the amount of effort required.

Basili defines software complexity as "... *a measure of the resources expended by another system while interacting with a piece of software. If the interacting system is people, the measures are concerned with human efforts to comprehend, to maintain, to change, to test, etc., that software* " [4, p. 232]. Curtis et al. similarly define this concept as psychological complexity: "*Psychological complexity refers to characteristics of software which make it difficult to understand and work with*" [15, p. 96]. Both of these authors note that the lack of use of structured programming techniques is believed to increase the cognitive load on a software maintainer. In the current research this will simply be referred to as software complexity, with the focus being on correctable software com-

plexity (i.e., complexity that results from specific syntactical choices made by the developer).

Factors that increase maintainer effort will increase project cost, since maintenance costs are most directly a function of the professional labor component of maintenance projects. Therefore, this research is designed to measure the impact of aspects of software complexity of the existing system that affect the cost of maintenance by increasing or decreasing the amount of maintainer effort to comprehend the software, while controlling for project factors that may also affect performance. Given the growing economic importance of maintenance, several researchers have attempted to validate hypotheses relating to complexity. However, researchers have not been able to empirically test the impact of complexity on maintenance effort while controlling for additional factors known to affect costs, such as project size and maintainer skill [19, 31]. The main research objective in this article is investigating the relationship between existing software complexity and maintenance costs. However, in order to properly understand this relationship, the effects of project factors will be controlled for. Exhibit 1 presents a simplified view of the conceptual model that will be tested in this research.

Modularization

Researchers have employed many measures in attempts to operationalize the concept of software complexity. The consensus is that there is no single best metric of software complexity [5, 13,

EXHIBIT 1   Software Maintenance Project Costs Conceptual Model

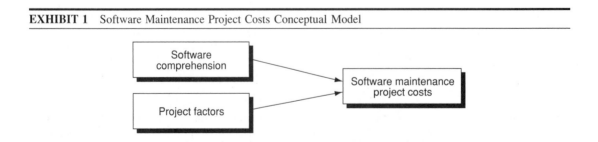

27]. However, two main concepts have emerged—modularity and branching.

Schneidewind estimates that 75- to 80% of existing software was produced prior to significant use of structured programming [28]. A key component of structured programming approaches is *modularity,* defined by Conte et al. as "the programming technique of constructing software as several discrete parts" [13, p. 197]. Structured programming proponents argue that modularization is an improved programming style, and therefore, the absence of modularity is likely to be a significant practical problem. A number of researchers have attempted to empirically validate the impact of modularity on either software quality or cost with data from actual systems (see Exhibit 2).

In terms of positive impacts of greater modularity, perhaps the first widely disseminated field research in this area was by Vessey and Weber [30]. They studied repair maintenance in Australian and U.S. data processing organizations and used subjective assessments of the degree of modularity in a large number of Cobol systems. In one data set they found that more modular code was associated with fewer repairs; in the other data set no effect was found. In a later study, Korson and Vaishnavi [24] conducted four experiments comparing the time required to modify two alternative versions of a piece of software, one modular and one monolithic. In three of the four cases the modular version was significantly easier to modify.

Card et al. [12] reached the opposite conclusion. They tested the impact of module size and strength (cohesion) on programming effort, measured as programmer hours per executable statement. They found that effort decreased as the size of the module increased. However, effort decreased as strength increased, but increases in strength were associated with decreases in module size. They concluded that nothing definitive could be stated about the impact of module size. A study by An et al. [1] analyzed changed data from two releases of Unix. They found the average size of unchanged modules (417 lines of C) was larger than that of changed modules (279 lines of C). Unfortunately, they did not provide any analysis to determine if this difference was statistically significant.

An alternative hypothesis is that modules that are either too large or too small are unlikely to be optimal. If the modules are too large they are

EXHIBIT 2   Previous Field Research on Modularity

Year	Researchers	Language	Dependent Variable	Conclusions[a]
1983	Vessey and Weber	Cobol	# of Repairs	Unidirectional ⇑
1984	Bowen	Algol, CMS, and others	McCabe, Halstead metrics	Suggests two-way relationship
1984	Boydston	Assembler, PLS	Effort	Suggests two-way relationship
1985	Card, et al.	Fortran	Effort	Unidirectional ⇓
1986	Korson and Vaishnavi	Pascal	Effort	Unidirectional ⇑
1987	An, et al.	C	Change data	Unidirectional ⇓
1989	Lind and Vairavan	Pascal, Fortran	Normalized change data	Suggests two-way relationship

[a] For unidirectional test, "⇑" indicates that greater modularity (more, smaller modules) improved performance and "⇓" indicates that less modularity (fewer, larger modules) improved performance. Several of the analyses in these unidirectional studies also found no significant results in either direction. A two-way relationship is one in which both positive and negative deviations from optimal module size reduce performance.

unlikely to be devoted to single purpose. If the modules are too small then much of the complexity will reside in the interfaces between modules and therefore they will again be difficult to comprehend. In contrast to the unidirectional studies cited previously, a few researchers have suggested the possibility of bidirectional effects. For example, Conte et al. note that: *"The degree of modularization affects the quality of a design. Over-modularization is as undesirable as under-modularization"* [13, p. 109]. In an analysis of secondary data, Bowen compared the number of source lines of code (SLOC)/module with a set of previously proposed maximum desirable values of two well-known metrics, McCabe's V(G) and Halstead's [10]. He concluded that the optimal values of SLOC/module differed across languages, but that all were much lower than the Department of Defense's (DoD's) proposed standard of 200 SLOC/module. In his suggestions for future research, he notes the following:

> More research is necessary to derive and validate upper and lower bounds for module size. Module size lower bounds, or some equivalent metric such as coupling have been neglected; however, they are just as significant as upper bounds. With just a module size upper bound, there is no way to dissuade the implementation of excessively small modules, which in turn introduce inter-module complexity, complicate software integration testing, and increase computer resource overhead.[10, p. 331]

Boydston undertook a study of completed systems programming projects at IBM whose main purpose was to gain greater accuracy in cost estimation [11]. One additional analysis he performed (p. 155) was to attempt to estimate the optimum SLOC/module ratio for new code, based on the hypothesis that *"Complexity of programming increases as the lines of code per module and the number of modules to interface increase."* In other words, extremes of either a very small number of large modules or a very large number of small modules would both be unlikely to be optimal. His regression analysis developed multiple, nonlinear functions of workmonths as a function of the number of new modules,

with SLOC held constant. He concludes that "*. . . as a project gets larger, the additional complexity of larger modules has to be balanced by the increasing complexity of information transfer between modules*" (p. 159). However, his model does not control for any noncode factors.

While not examining maintenance cost directly, Lind and Vairavan obtained empirical evidence supporting the hypothesis of a nonextreme optimum value for module size (i.e., that the best-sized modules were those that were neither too big nor too small) [25]. They analyzed the relationship between the change rate (number of changes per 100 lines of code, a surrogate for cost) vs. a discrete (categorical) lines-of-code-based variable. Their five discrete SLOC categories were 0–50, 50–100, 100–150, 150–200, and 200+. They found that minimum change rates occurred in the 100 to 150 range, a result they describe (p. 652) as indicating the "*. . . program change density declines with increasing metric values up to a certain minimum value . . . beyond this minimum value, the program change density actually increases with an increase in the value of the metrics.*"

The results of these previous studies can be summarized as follows. Researchers testing for unidirectional results (i.e., that either smaller modules or larger modules were better) have found either contradictory results or none at all. Other researchers have suggested that a U-shaped function exists, that is, modules that are either too small or too large are problematical. In the case of many small modules, more intermodule interfaces are required. In the case of a few large modules, these modules are less likely to be devoted to a single purpose.[1] However, researchers who suggest the U-shaped curve hypothesis provide either limited data or none at all linking size and cost. In

---

[1] Interfaces are relevant because they have been shown to be among the most problematical components of programs [6]. Modules not devoted to a single purpose have been shown to result in a larger number of errors and therefore higher amounts of repair maintenance, which can be interpreted as increased cost [12, 30].

EXHIBIT 3   Software Level Hierarchy

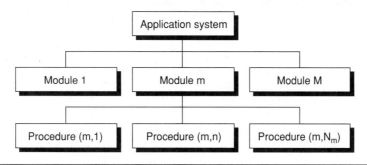

general they also do not provide a model for determining the optimum module size.[2]

The most recent research includes an earlier study at the current research site where 35 application systems were analyzed to develop a basis for selecting among dozens of candidate software metrics that the research literature has suggested [32]. Exhibit 3 shows the relationship among the three software levels identified in this research. An *application system* has *M modules*. In turn, each module *m* has N_m *procedures*. Exhibit 4 provides the definitions for these levels.

Previous research investigating a large number of proposed software complexity metrics has found them to be variations on a small number of orthogonal dimensions [27]. An analysis of software complexity metrics at this research site identified three major groups: procedure-level modularity, module-level modularity, and branching [32]. Despite their apparent similarities, previous research has suggested that the two kinds of modularity represent independent aspects of software complexity [14]. A commercial static code analyzer was used to compute these metrics. Given the high levels of correlation within (but not across) complexity metric

groups, a representative metric from each group was selected, based in part on the ease with which it could be understood by software maintenance management and its ease of collection. This approach has been recommended by previous research [27].

The first metric is the average size in executable statements of a module's procedures (PROCSIZE). There is an almost universal tendency to associate large procedure size with poor procedure-level modularity. However, intuitively, neither extreme is likely to be effective. If modules are broken into too many small procedures, complexity could rise, and in this case increasing the average procedure size would be expected to be beneficial.

Module length, in executable statements (MODLSIZE) was selected as the metric of module-level modularity [5].[3] The effect of this complexity metric is expected to depend on the application systems being analyzed. As discussed in the survey of previous research, it is generally believed that large modules will be more difficult to understand and modify than small ones, and maintenance costs will be expected to increase with average module size. As with procedures, however, a system can be composed of too many small modules. If modules are too small, a maintenance project will spread out over many modules

---

[2] Boydston [11] does extrapolate from his data set to suggest a specific square root relationship between number of new lines of code and number of modules for his Assembler and PLS language data.

[3] This metric was found to be uncorrelated with PROCSIZE (Pearson correlation coefficient = .10).

with the attendant interface problems. Therefore, complexity could decrease as module size increases. Thus two specific research hypotheses concerning modularity are proposed:

> HYPOTHESIS 1. *Controlling for other factors known to affect software maintenance costs, the costs will depend significantly on average procedure size as measured by PROCSIZE, with costs rising for applications whose average procedure size is either very large or very small.*

> HYPOTHESIS 2. *Controlling for other factors known to affect software maintenance costs, the costs will depend significantly on average module size as measured by MODLSIZE, with costs rising for applications whose average module size is either very large or very small.*

Branching. Previous work has suggested that control constructs (branching) are expected to have a significant impact on comprehension [15].

Structured programming is a design approach that limits programming constructs to three basic means of branching through a piece of software. Because it is difficult to comply with these structures using the GOTO syntax found in older programming languages, this approach is sometimes colloquially referred to as GOTO-less programming. A review of work in this area before 1984 was conducted by Vessey and Weber [31]. While few negative results have been found, they note the absence of significant results is as frequent as a finding of positive results. They attribute this outcome, in part, to the researchers' not having adequately controlled for other factors. They also note the difficulty of achieving such control, particularly in nonlaboratory real-world settings.

More recently, Gibson and Senn have investigated the impact of software structure using a laboratory experiment [17]. They found that more

---

EXHIBIT 4   Source Code Definitions

Level	*Definition*
Application system	A set of modules assigned a common name by the research site, typically performing a coherent set of tasks in support of a given department and maintained by a single team. References to this term refer only to the source code, not to the JCL. 'Application' or 'system,' if used separately, mean the same thing.[b]
Module	A named, separately compilable file containing Cobol source code. A module will typically, though not necessarily, perform a single logical task or set of tasks. INCLUDE modules and COPY files were the only modules not included, since they contain only Cobol source code but not the headers that allow it to be run on its own.
Procedure	The range of a PERFORM statement. For example, if paragraphs are labeled sequentially, the statement PERFORM D THRU G invokes the procedure consisting of paragraphs D, E, F, G, and the paragraphs invoked by these paragraphs.[c]
Paragraph[d]	The smallest addressable unit within a piece of Cobol software. A sequence of Cobol-executable statements preceded by an address/identification label.

[b] Application systems can be described as being composed of 'programs,' but the current research has analyzed the data at a finer level of detail, the module, and the program construct has not been used in the current research.

[c] The possibility exists, in Cobol, that procedures will overlap. (e.g., PERFORM D THRU G and PERFORM E THRU J will have at least E, F, and G in common.) This research followed previous work by Spratt and McQuilken in defining the union of overlapping procedures to be a single procedure to prevent double counting [29]. Such overlaps were relatively rare at this site, however, with the result that this research design decision results in no practical difference. Spratt and McQuilken use the term "components" instead of procedures, but the latter term will be used throughout this article.

[d] This construct is not used directly in this research, but is defined here as it is used in the definition of procedure.

structured versions of the same piece of software required less time to maintain on average. They also found that maintainers' subjective assessments of the complexity of the existing systems were not very accurate, a result they attribute to the maintainers' inability to separate task complexity from existing systems complexity. They recommend using objective measures of systems complexity to remedy this defect. However, the expected results from their experiments did not hold in all cases. In addition, as noted by the authors, laboratory experimentation is not a substitute for field research: *"Further research is needed to determine whether the relationships observed in this tightly controlled experiment exist in live settings "* (p. 357). In particular, laboratory experimentation is unlikely to provide estimates of the actual cost impacts of ill-structured programs in commercial settings.

In a recent pilot study of seven maintenance projects on Fortran and Pascal-based real-time systems, Gill and Kemerer found that maintainer productivity decreased as existing systems complexity increased, as measured by complexity density, a size-adjusted measure of branching complexity [18]. However, their model does not control for any noncode factors. The authors also note the need to validate these results on a larger sample of commercial systems. Therefore, the question of a negative impact of excessively complex branching on maintenance costs has only limited empirical support, and there is a need for further research.

In the current research the initial candidate metric chosen for branching was the proportion of the executable statements that were GOTO statements (GOTOSTMT). This branching metric is normalized for module size, so that it would not be confounded with MODLSIZE. This metric is also a measure of module divisibility, since the degree to which a module can be divided into small and simple procedures depends directly on the incidence of branching within the module. Highly divisible modules (modules with low values of GOTOSTMT) should be less costly to maintain,

since a maintainer can deal with manageable portions of the module in relative isolation.

While the density of GOTO statements (GOTOSTMT), like other candidate control metrics examined, is a measure of divisibility,[4] it does not distinguish between more and less serious structure violations. A branch to the end of the current paragraph, for example, is unlikely to make that paragraph much more difficult to comprehend, while a branch to a different section of the module may. However, none of the existing structure metrics examined clearly differentiate between the two cases. In addition, the modules analyzed have a large incidence of GOTO statements (approximately 7 per 100 executable statements). If only a relatively small proportion of these seriously affect maintainability then the GOTOSTMT metric may be too noisy a measure of branching complexity. At this research site over half of the GOTOs in these modules (19 GOTOs out of 31 in the average module) are used to skip to the beginning or end of the current paragraph. Such branches would not be expected to contribute noticeably to the difficulty of understanding a module (in most high-level languages other than Cobol they would probably not be implemented by GOTO statements). Therefore, a metric such as GOTOSTMT, which does not distinguish between these and the approximately 40% less benign branch commands, will be unlikely to be managerially useful.

To avoid this problem, a modified metric was computed, GOTOFAR, which is the density of the GOTO statements that extend outside the boundaries of the paragraph and that can be expected to seriously impair the maintainability of the software.[5] Since the automated static code analyzer was not able to compute this metric, it was computed manually. Due to the large amount of

---

[4] Each GOTO command makes a module more difficult to understand by forcing a programmer to consider multiple portions of the module simultaneously.

[5] This is believed to be similar in concept to Gibson and Senn's [17] elimination of "long jumps in code (GOTOs)."

EXHIBIT 5   Software Maintenance Project Cost Model

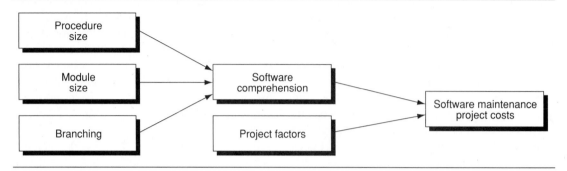

---

data collection effort and analysis this computation required, the metric was manually computed by a single analyst for a random sample of approximately 50 modules per application system. This random sample consisted of approximately 1,500 modules in total, or approximately 30% of all modules in the total data set.[6]

Therefore, the third research hypothesis is:

HYPOTHESIS 3. Controlling for other factors known

---

[6] A later sensitivity analysis regression using GOTOSTMT instead of GOTOFAR lends credence to the belief that the excluded branch commands represent a noise factor. The estimated effect of GOTOSTMT had the same relative magnitude as that of GOTOFAR, but the standard error of the coefficient was 4 times as large.

to affect software maintenance costs, software maintenance costs will depend significantly on the density of branching as measured by GOTOFAR, with costs rising with increases in the incidence of branching.

Exhibit 5 presents the full conceptual model. Exhibit 6 summarizes the software complexity variables used in the model.

Project Factors[7]

The research model has two main components, one consisting of factors related to existing source code complexity, and one of controllable project

---

[7] This section draws heavily on work presented in [2].

EXHIBIT 6   Software Complexity Variables

Name	Variable	Measurement	References
PROCSIZE	Average size of a module's procedures	A count of the number of noncomment SLOC in a module divided by the number of procedures	[32]
MODLSIZE	Average size of an application's modules	A count of the number of noncomment SLOC in the application divided by the number of modules.	[5, 32]
GOTOFAR	Density of the nonbenign GOTO statements	A normalized count of the GOTO statements which extend outside the boundaries of the paragraph	[17, 32]

factors that are believed to affect maintenance costs. While the current research focuses on assessing the effect of software complexity on maintenance costs, it is necessary to control for project factors (such as task size and the skill of the developers) known to affect these costs [19, 31]. The most significant of these is the size of the maintenance task. Excluding task size or other relevant factors would result in a misspecification of the model and incorrect inferences about the impact of software complexity on costs.[8] To control for this factor and for other project factors known to affect costs, the research began with a previously developed economic model of software maintenance. The initial data collection procedures and model development are described in detail in [2] and [22]. They will only be summarized here.

Basic Maintenance Cost Model

This model adopts the standard cost model formulation developed in the software engineering literature [3, 9]:

$$Effort = f(Size, Other\ Cost\ Drivers)$$

Exhibit 7 summarizes the measures of the maintenance function used based on the model developed in [2]. The unit of analysis for this model is the project as defined by the research site. Each maintenance project has its own task requirements and its own budget. Exhibit 8 shows the project factors that are included in the model for each project. The output of the software maintenance process is the modified system, and therefore measures of the size of the additions and changes need to be included in the model. Measures of size in a maintenance context are the size of the portions of the system that were added or changed by the maintenance project. While SLOC added or changed is the most widely used measure of size, function points (FPs) added or changed are gaining in acceptance [3]. FPs have an additional advantage of including a measure of *task* complexity.[9]

The SKILL variable is important, as previous research has found large differences in ability between top-rated developers and poorer ones [9]. All maintainers in the organization at the research site are rated on a numerical scale, and the measure used in the model is the percentage of hours that were charged to the project by staff who were

---

[8] It should be noted that this research's inclusion of factors other than complexity militates *against* finding any statistical effect resulting from complexity, in contrast to previous research that examines the effect of complexity without controlling for other factors. While the model presented does not possess undesirable multicollinearity, no empirical model of this type has factors that are completely orthogonal. Therefore, inclusion of the other factors partially reduces any effect found for the complexity factors, making this a conservative test of the complexity hypotheses.

---

[9] This should not be confused with the application software complexity that is the focus of this research. Task complexity in FPs includes such factors as whether the project will be held to above average reliability standards, or whether the operational system will run in a distributed environment.

EXHIBIT 7   Cost Drivers

Activity	Measured By	Mediated By
Analysis/design	Function points (FPs) added or changed by the project	Maintainer skill Maintainer application experience Structured analysis/design methodology use
Coding/testing	Source lines of code (SLOC) added or changed by the project	Operational quality Hardware response time Application source code complexity (3 measures)

EXHIBIT 8   Maintenance Model Project Factor Variables [2]

Name	Variable	Measurement	References
HOURS	Effort	Number of hours charged to the project. This information was obtained from the project billing files, which were collected contemporaneously with the project.	[3] [9]
FP	Task magnitude and task complexity	The number of function points added or changed by the maintenance project.	[3]
SLOC	Task magnitude	The number of source lines of code added or changed by the maintenance project.	[9]
SKILL	Maintainer skill	The percentage of developer hours billed by the most highly skilled (by formal management evaluation) class of developers. This variable is distinct from the following one, which depends on the developer's experience with a specific application system.	[9]
LOWEXPER	Maintainer application experience	The extensive use (over 90% of hours billed to the project) of developers lacking experience with the application being modified. (A binary variable.)	[9, 20]
METHOD	Structured analysis/ design method use	The use of a structured design methodology (a binary variable). This is expected to have an adverse effect on single-project performance, although it is meant to reduce costs to the organization in the long run.	[2]
QUALITY	Operational quality	A measure (on a three-point scale of low/average/high quality) of the degree to which the completion of the project was followed by a change in the number of operational errors. This measure was based on information obtained from the site's error logs.	[2, 22]
RESPONSE	Hardware response time	The availability of a fast-turnaround programming environment. (A binary variable.)	[9, 20]

---

highly rated. The SKILL variable is often neglected in research due to the practical difficulties involved in collecting these data. These practical difficulties include the fact that formal personnel ratings may not always be available, and, even if collected by the organization, may not be made available to researchers for confidentiality reasons. For the current work strict control over these data were guaranteed to the research site by the researchers.

A personnel-related variable distinct from ability is LOWEXPER [9, 20]. Even a good developer is at a disadvantage when faced with an unfamiliar system, as time must be expended in comprehending the software and becoming familiar with it.

METHOD, the use of a structured analysis and design methodology, is meant to increase developer performance. However, previous research has shown that such methods add costs in the short term at this site [2]. QUALITY may also be important, as it has been suggested that doing a careful job of error-free programming will cost more than a rushed job, although benefits will be realized in the long term. Conversely, some researchers believe that careful and systematic programming may not take longer, with some even arguing that it should be less expensive. The measure used here was one of operational quality, the degree to which the system operates smoothly after the maintenance project's changes are placed into production. The measure was generated from data on abnormal ends and user problem reports collected on an ongoing basis by the research site. Data from the two-month period following implementation were compared with data from the previous 12 months' trend. Statistically significant deviations from the previous mean resulted in above or below average operational quality ratings [22]. The RESPONSE variable is included as there has been some evidence that fast-turnaround environments enhance developer performance, an effect that is likely to be seen in maintenance work as well.

Based on the software economics literature the effects of these factors are believed to be proportional, rather than absolute [3, 9]. Thus they are weighted by project size, either FP added or changed or SLOC added or changed, depending on whether they are thought to be associated more strongly with the analysis/design phase or with the coding/testing phase of the project [2]. Skill and application experience are weighted by FPs, as it was believed their impact would be felt most strongly during analysis/design, where the greatest amount of leverage from capability and experience would be obtained. Use of the structured analysis/design methodology is also clearly associated with the analysis and design phase, measured here by FPs. Operational quality was weighted by SLOC, as the types of errors represented by the operational quality measure used reflect poor coding technique and/or insufficient testing. Response time was also weighted by SLOC, as it seems more relevant to coding/testing activities than to analysis/design work, since the latter is not dependent on access to machine cycles. Finally, all complexity measures are weighted by SLOC, since the impact of existing code complexity would be felt most strongly during coding/testing

rather than analysis/design. As noted earlier, any collinearity that may exist between the weighted complexity metrics and other independent variables that have been weighted by SLOC will cause the model to underestimate the significance of the complexity metric variable. Therefore, the following analysis is a conservative test.

STATISTICAL MODEL AND RESULTS

The previous section described the selection of the variables in the model, including both the existing source code complexity variables and the project factors. In this section, following a brief description of the research site, the statistical model and its results are presented, followed by tests of the research hypotheses.

The Research Site

Data were collected at a major regional bank with a large investment in computer software. The bank's systems contain over 18 million lines of code. Almost all are written in the Cobol programming language, and are running on large IBM mainframe computers. The software is organized into large application systems (e.g., demand deposits), which have an average size of 226,000 SLOC.[10] Some of the bank's major application systems were written in the mid-1970s and are generally acknowledged to be more poorly designed and harder to maintain than recently written software.

Given that Cobol and IBM are the most widely used software and hardware in commercial information systems (IS), this software environment appears to be a typical commercial data processing environment. Thus, the research results should apply to other commercial environments, especially those with financial services transaction processing systems. The projects analyzed were homogeneous in that they all modified Cobol systems, and therefore

---

[10] Mean = 226 KSLOC, standard deviation = 185 KSLOC, min = 54 KSLOC, max = 702 KSLOC.

the results are not confounded by the effects of multiple programming languages.

Sixty-five software maintenance projects from 17 major application systems were analyzed. These projects were carried out between 1985 and 1987. An average project took about 1,000 hours (at an accounting cost of $40 per hour) and added or changed approximately 5,000 SLOC.

Statistical Model

The statistical model is described by:

$$HOURS = \beta_0 + \beta_1 *FP +$$
$$\beta_2 *SLOC + \beta_3 *FP*FP +$$
$$\beta_4 *SLOC*SLOC +$$
$$\beta_5 *FP*SLOC +$$
$$\beta_6 *FP*SKILL +$$
$$\beta_7 *FP*LOWEXPER +$$
$$\beta_8 *FP*METHOD +$$
$$\beta_9 *SLOC*QUALITY +$$
$$\beta_{10} *SLOC*RESPONSE +$$
$$\beta_{11} *SLOC*PROCSIZE +$$
$$\beta_{12} *SLOC*PROCSIZE^2 +$$
$$\beta_{13} *SLOC*MODLSIZE +$$
$$\beta_{14} *SLOC*MODLSIZE^2 +$$
$$\beta_{15} *SLOC*GOTOFAR + \epsilon$$

This model, without the five complexity terms (the terms associated with parameters β_{11} through β_{15}), has been previously validated at the research site. The relationships between maintenance costs and procedure size and between maintenance costs and module size are expected to be U-shaped, rather than monotone, with costs being lowest for some optimal size and higher for larger or smaller sizes. The squared terms PROCSIZE^2 and MODL-SIZE^2 are included to model this effect.

In this model project costs (measured in developer HOURS) are primarily a function of project size, measured in FPs and in SLOC. To model the known nonlinearity of development costs with respect to project size, not only FP and SLOC are included, but also their second-order terms. This

approach is expected to result in a high degree of multicollinearity among the size variables (the terms associated with parameters β_1 through β_5) which will make the interpretation of their coefficients difficult [3]. The multicollinearity among the size variables, however, is not of concern for examining the current research hypotheses relating to the impact of complexity, since the complexity variables are not collinear with the size variables. Exhibit 9 presents the summary statistics for this data set. The values given for the complexity metrics are application system averages. The model was estimated using ordinary least squares (OLS) regression, since the OLS assumptions were satisfied in the context of the estimation. The statistical results from two-tailed tests are presented in Exhibit 10 with the complexity metric variables in bold type. The summary statistical results are as follows:

$$F_{15, 49} = 28.63 \ (p < .0001), R^2 = 89.76\%, \ Adjusted \ R^2 = 86.62\%.$$

Although not all project factor variables are significant for this sample, none of the project factor variables are eliminated in order to achieve a more

---

EXHIBIT 9   Maintenance Project Summary Statistics (65 Projects)

Variable	Mean	Stand. Deviation	Min	Max
HOURS	937	718	130	3342
FP	118	126	8	616
SLOC	5416	7230	50	31060
SKILL	65	34	0	100
LOWEXPER	.66	.48	0	1
METHOD	.32	.47	0	1
QUALITY	2.06	.58	1	3
RESPONSE	.65	.48	0	1
MODLSIZE	681	164	382	1104
PROCSIZE	43	18	13	87
GOTOFAR	0.024	0.016	0.0	0.07

parsimonious fit. The interest in the current research is in assessing the *marginal* impact of adding the complexity metrics to an earlier version of the model (see [2]). The Belsley-Kuh-Welsch multicollinearity diagnostics (see [8]) indicated that the complexity metrics are not significantly confounded with the other regression variables. Thus, their coefficients may be interpreted with relative confidence. Also the residuals and the absolute residuals were uncorrelated with size. The latter result supports the homoskedasticity assumption in regression analysis. The former supports the decision to model the complexity effects in the regression as proportional ones rather than use the unweighted metrics alone. If the complexity effects were not proportional to project magnitude, use of the weighted metrics would cause the model to overestimate the costs of large projects, resulting in residuals negatively correlated with size.

Tests of the Research Hypotheses

Hypothesis 1 was that maintenance costs would be significantly affected by procedure size. This general hypothesis is confirmed by an F-test on the joint effect of the two PROCSIZE terms:

$$P(H_0 : \beta_{11} = \beta_{12} = 0) < 0.0001$$
$$as\ F_{2,\ 49} = 14.20.$$

A U-shaped relationship between PROCSIZE and software maintenance costs was hypothesized, and the data confirm this relationship, given that the two coefficients are significantly different from zero and that the linear term is negative and the squared term is positive. The minimum of the U-shaped curve may be computed by dividing the negated coefficient of the linear term by twice that of the quadratic term.[11] At this site the minimum-cost procedure size was computed to be $(0.0106/(2*0.00012)) = 44$ executable statements PROCSIZE (see Exhibit 10).

This value is very close to the mean (43) and to the median (40) for this organization. However, individual applications vary in average PROCSIZE from 13 to 87 executable statements.

As is often the case in this type of estimation there was a high degree of multicollinearity between the linear term and the quadratic term. This means that the estimates of the two individual coefficients (and hence the minimum point) are to be taken with caution. To test the robustness of this calculation the analysis was repeated using a model that replaced the linear and quadratic PROCSIZE terms with two linear variables, representing positive and negative deviations from a conjectured optimum respectively.[12] This model was repeatedly estimated using a different conjectured optimum value each time. The results consistently showed cost increases resulting from deviations in either direction from the minimum point. This sensitivity analysis supports the results shown in Exhibit 10 suggesting a bidirectional (U-shaped) relationship.

Hypothesis 2, that costs increase for both large or small values of MODLSIZE, was not supported, as the conditions described in the discussion for PROCSIZE were not met. Since the coefficients for both the linear and quadratic MODLSIZE variables are in the same direction, they are likely picking up each other's effects, and therefore the individual t-test values are low. However, a hypothesis that maintenance costs are not significantly affected by module size can be rejected:

$$P(H_0: \beta_{13} = \beta_{14} = 0) = 0.0076$$
$$as\ F_{2,\ 49} = 5.39$$

which supports the notion that MODLSIZE, as suggested by previous research, is a variable worthy of managerial attention. A similar insight is obtained from a simplified version of the model that excludes the MODLSIZE^2 term. There the coefficient for the SLOC *MODLSIZE term = $-.00012$, t = -3.32 (p = .0017). This result can be interpreted in the traditional way, that is, the effect

---

[11] This can easily be seen by differentiating with respect to x the quadratic equation $y = ax + bx^2$, and setting $dy/dx = 0$ which yields $x = a/2b$.

---

[12] This can be seen as measuring the relationship as a 'V' rather than a 'U.'

EXHIBIT 10 Regression Results

Variable	β	Coefficient	Standardized βs	t	p
Intercept	0	333	0	4.96	.0001
Project size					
FP	1	3.152	.554	1.98	.0533
SLOC	2	0.342	3.448	5.01	.0001
FP*FP	3	.009	.774	2.80	.0072
SLOC*SLOC	4	−2.8E-6	−.743	−0.92	.3614
FP*SLOC	5	−.0001	−.439	−1.29	.2026
Project Environment					
FP*SKILL	6	−.049	−.64	−3.48	.0011
FP*LOWEXPER	7	.122	.02	0.18	.8578
FP*METHOD	8	1.764	.228	3.03	.0039
SLOC*QUALITY	9	.027	.575	2.74	.0085
SLOC*RESPONSE	10	−.019	−.196	−1.17	.2486
Software complexity					
SLOC*PROCSIZE	11	−.0106	−5.404	−4.85	.0001
SLOC*PROCSIZE^2	12	.00012	3.708	5.30	.0001
SLOC*MODLSIZE	13	−.0011	−.774	−1.36	.1815
SLOC*MODLSIZE^2	14	−4.4E-10	−.077	−0.09	.9279
SLOC*GOTOFAR	15	1.317	.401	3.25	.0021

at this site tended to be linear over the observed range of module sizes (controlling for project factors) with costs decreasing as module size increases.[13]

It should be noted, however, that while these data do not support a U-shaped relationship, they are not necessarily inconsistent with such a hypothesis. The observed linear relationship is consistent with the data falling on the downward sloping arm of this U, with the possibility that

costs would again begin to rise had sufficiently large modules been available. Therefore, if there is a U-shaped relationship, the turning point appears to be outside the range of data collected at this site. Further empirical work at other research sites will be required for this alternative interpretation to be verified.

Hypothesis 3 was that maintenance costs would be significantly affected by the density of branch instructions within the modules. This hypothesis is confirmed.

$$P(H_0: \beta_{15} = 0) = 0.0021 \text{ as } t_{49} = 3.25.$$

Software maintenance costs are seen to increase linearly with an increase in the number of long GOTO statements, as defined earlier.

---

[13] With this simplified model it is noteworthy that while concern over modularity typically focuses on large modules, at this site the systems that cost more to maintain tended to have modules that were too small.

IMPLICATIONS FOR SOFTWARE MAINTENANCE MANAGEMENT

Through the preceding analysis the effect of software complexity on software maintenance costs has been estimated. While it is a firmly established article of conventional wisdom that poor programmingstyle and practices increase programming costs, little empirical evidence has been available to support this notion. Consequently, efforts and investments meant to improve programming practices have relied largely on faith. The current research has extended an existing model of software maintenance and used it as a vehicle to confirm the significance of the impact of software complexity on project costs and to estimate its magnitude.

This model provides managers with estimates of the benefits of improved programming practices that can be used to justify investments designed to improve those practices. Given these data and estimates relating software complexity and costs, the form of the model allows inference about the productivity of software maintainers. Productivity is typically defined as the ratio of output to input. Since the model controls for task side (output) variables on the RHS (right-hand side), any LHS (left-hand side) increases in required inputs that are associated with increases in complexity can be interpreted as decreases in productivity. Therefore, the model results may be interpreted to mean that *increased existing software complexity significantly decreases the productivity of software maintainers*. This result accords with strongly held intuition. The current research also provides actual estimates of the magnitude and significance of this effect, results that have generally not been available, particularly for commercial applications involving actual maintenance activities and controlling for project factors believed to affect productivity.

This model enables managers to estimate the *benefits* of improving software development and maintenance practices, and to justify investments designed to improve those practices. In the following illustrative computations, the impact of a one-standard deviation change in the value of each of the complexity variables is computed for a project of 5416 SLOC (the site mean) with average complexity values. The effects of PROCSIZE on HOURS is estimated in the regression model as follows:

$$0.00012*PROCSIZE^2*SLOC - 0.0106*PROCSIZE*SLOC$$

Solving this equation once for the mean value of PROCSIZE (43) and once for a one-standard deviation increase in PROCSIZE (to 61), and then subtracting the first result from the second results in a difference of 183.28 hours, or an increase of 20% of the average project cost of 937 hours. A similar calculation for a decrease of one standard deviation in PROCSIZE (to 25) is 25%.[14] The calculations for MODLSIZE and GOTOFAR are similar, and the results are shown in Exhibit 11.

Another way to use the results of the model for managerial planning is to estimate the aggregate

---

[14] Note that these results are not symmetric as the site mean is not identical to the optimum value.

EXHIBIT 11   Estimated Cost Impacts

Name	Mean, Std. Dev.	*Impact of 1 Std. Dev. Variation . . .* *. . . in Hours*	*. . . As a % of Total*
PROCSIZE	43, 18	183, 238	20%, 25%
MODLSIZE	681, 164	98	10%
GOTOFAR	.024, .016	114	12%

cost impact to the organization of software complexity. To do this a manager might postulate the following question: What would be the estimated cost savings if the more complex systems were improved, not to some *optimal* level, but merely to the current *average* level of all systems?

The measurement of the individual systems and the model can be used to develop such an estimate. The first step is to note that the current actual projects have an average cost of 937 hours. The second step is to modify the data set in the following manner: test each of the three complexity variables for each of the 65 projects to determine whether it is of higher complexity than average. If it is, replace that value with the average complexity value. If not, leave it unchanged. Once this transformation of the data is complete, the model is used to estimate the cost of hypothetical projects based on the transformed data, which gives a predicted cost of 704 hours for an average project, a 25% savings over the actual situation.

In order to determine the estimated dollar value to the organization of this reduction in complexity, a "back-of-the-envelope" calculation of the estimated aggregate possible savings can be done. Two assumptions are necessary for this calculation to be valid, (1) that the projects studied represent a typical mix (believed to be the case), and (2) that maintenance projects represent 70% of the budget (also true for this site). The result is that improving the site's more poorly written systems, not to optimality, but merely to the level of the site's average complexity, could result in an aggregate savings of more than 17% (.25* .7) of the applications software budget, which at this site translates into a savings of several million dollars in the year following such an improvement.

These quantified impacts of complexity can help software maintenance managers make informed decisions regarding preferred managerial practice. For example, one type of decision that could be aided by such information is the purchase of CASE tools for code restructuring. The benefits of these tools have generally had to be taken on faith. The current analysis, however, indicates that the magnitude of the economic impact of software complexity is sufficiently great that many organizations may be able to justify the purchase and implementation of CASE tools for code restructuring on the basis of these estimated benefits.

More generally, a common belief in the long-term importance of good programming practice has not been powerful enough to stand in the way of expedience when "quick-and-dirty" programming has been perceived to be needed immediately. An awareness of the magnitude of the cost of existing software complexity can combat this tendency. The cost of software complexity at this research site is the legacy of the practices of previous years.

Taken together, these ideas show how, through the use of the model developed here, managers can make decisions *today* on systems design, systems development, and tool selection and purchase that depend on system values that will affect *future* maintenance. This model can be a valuable addition to the traditional exclusive emphasis on software development project schedules and budgets because it allows for the estimation of full life-cycle costs. Given the significant percentages of systems resources devoted to maintenance, improving managers' ability to forecast these costs will allow them to be properly weighted in current decision making.

As with any empirical study, some limitations of these research results must be observed. The results were found to exist in a site which, due to its size, software tools, hardware tools, and application type, is typical of a large number of commercial IS applications, particularly financial transaction processing systems. However, additional studies at other sites, especially maximally dissimilar sites with applications such as real-time command and control applications should be done before claims can be made about the overall generalizability of these results. Also, values of specific parameters, such as the optimal number of SLOC/module, are likely to differ with programming languages,[15] particularly nonthird-generation languages.

---

[15] Although it is interesting to note that the optimal value of statements/module found here for Cobol code, 44, is similar to

In summary, this research suggests that considerable economic benefits can be expected from adherence to appropriate programming practices. In particular, aspects of modern programming practice, such as the maintenance of moderate procedure size and the avoidance of long branching, seem to have great benefits. The informed use of tools or techniques that encourage such practices should have a positive net benefit.

CONCLUDING REMARKS

This study has investigated the links between software complexity and software maintenance costs. On the basis of an analysis of software maintenance projects in a commercial application environment, it was confirmed that software maintenance costs are significantly affected by the levels of existing software complexity. In this study, software maintenance costs were found to increase with increases in the complexity of a system's implementation, as measured by its average procedure size, average module size, and its branching complexity.

Historically, most models of software economics have focused on new development. Therefore, they have not used software complexity metrics. After controlling for project factors believed to affect maintenance costs, the analysis at this site suggests that high levels of software complexity account for approximately 25% maintenance costs or more than 17% of total lifecycle costs. Given the extremely high cost of maintenance in commercial applications, the neglect of software complexity is potentially a serious omission.

The results presented here are based on a detailed analysis of maintenance costs at a site judged to be typical of traditional transaction processing environments. These types of environments account for a considerable percentage of today's software maintenance costs. Based on this analysis, the aggregate cost of poor programming practice for industry as a whole is likely to be substantial.

APPENDIX A.
DATA COLLECTION AND ANALYSIS IN A COMMERCIAL MAINTENANCE ENVIRONMENT

The main body of this research presents a generalizable model that has been estimated in a specific environment. Researchers and practitioners who are interested in validating this work in other environments will need to follow a series of three steps: data requirements analysis; metrics selection; data modeling and interpretation.

Data requirements analysis begins with determining the research goals that will drive the modeling process. This is, in many ways, the most critical of the three steps. In the current research the focus was on measuring the impact of complexity on maintenance productivity, and therefore the data requirements included cost (effort), project size, application complexity, and other nonsize project factors (See Exhibit 2 in the text.)[16] Each of these may require multiple metrics, as was done in the current research. In particular, the use of the two size variables and their second order terms in the current model, while requiring additional observations, does allow for a better fit of the data.

There are a number of sources for use in determining an appropriate set of complexity metrics from the universe of available metrics, for example, the work by Basili and Weiss [7]. Despite the large number of metrics proposed in the literature, most of them are highly correlated and a relatively small number will cover the major identified dimensions. In the current work the emphasis has been on metrics that reflect the adherence (or its lack) to structured programming precepts, and that are relatively easy for maintainers to understand and use.

Finally, it is very important not to lose sight of the need to collect data on the other project factors. These factors are likely to have a significant impact on the results, and failure to include them is likely to result in a misspecified model.

---

the maximum size heuristic used at Toshiba in Japan for Fortran code, 50 (See [26], pp. 45–52).

---

[16] In other environments the center of the investigation might be on other areas, such as defect detection and prevention, which would generate a different list.

The appropriate measures are likely to be highly site specific, but the general areas are likely to include project size (in a maintenance environment, functionality added or changed), staffing process or tool variables, and project quality. A data site that has already devoted some time to formal project cost estimation is likely to have a head start on what the important factors are likely to be.

Once the data requirements are determined, great care must be taken in data collection to ensure the data accurately represent the project experience. (Some of these issues are discussed in [23].) Generally speaking, *ex post* collection of metrics is often difficult, and the final sample size will typically be significantly smaller than the initial universe of projects selected. This phenomenon should be taken into account when outlining the scope of the research effort, and, in particular, when specifying the model. A significant amount of effort will need to be devoted to initial data collection, both on the part of the research team

and on team members from the project being studied, in order to locate and verify data on completed projects. Organizations that follow a disciplined methodology in their software development and maintenance will generally have more success at collecting these data than organizations that do not.

Given careful attention to the earlier steps, model estimation can proceed quite directly. The general form of the model used in the current research, a multiplicative formulation, is a general model that can be expected to be applicable in a wide variety of software engineering settings. Interpreting the model results can proceed as described in the main text. Feedback of these results to the participants at the data site is a critical step as a check to ensure that there are no extramodel factors influencing the results. Additionally, this feedback can help to ensure that the results of the model are actually used to modify and improve the process of software maintenance at the site.

References

1. An, K. H., Gustafson, D. A. and Melton, A. C. A model for software maintenance. *Conference on Software Maintenance* (1987), pp. 57–62.

2. Banker, R. D., Datar, S. M. and Kemerer, C. F. A model to evaluate variables impacting productivity on software maintenance projects. *Manage. Sci.* 37, 1 (1991) 1–18.

3. Banker, R. D. and Kemerer, C. F. Scale economies in new software development. *IEEE Trans. Softw. Eng. SE-15,* 10 (1989), 416–429.

4. Basili, V. R. Quantitative software complexity models: A panel summary. In V. R. Basili, Ed., *Tutorial on Models and Methods for Software Management and Engineering,* IEEE Computer Society Press, Los Alamitos, Calif, 1980.

5. Basili, V. R. and Hutchens, D. H. An empirical study of a syntactic complexity family. *IEEE Trans. Softw. Eng. SE-9,* 6 (1983), 664–672.

6. Basili, V. R. and Perricone, B. Software errors and complexity: An empirical investigation. *Commun. ACM 27,* 1 (1984), 42–52.

7. Basili, V. R. and Weiss D. M. A methodology for collecting valid software engineering data. *IEEE Trans. Softw. Eng. SE-10,* 6, 728–738.

8. Belsley, D. A., Kuh, E. and Welsch, R. E. *Regression Diagnostics.* Wiley and Sons, New York, 1980.

9. Boehm, B., *Software Engineering Economics.* Prentice-Hall, Englewood Cliffs, N.J., 1981.

10. Bowen, J. B. Module size: A standard or heuristic? *J. Syst. Softw. 4* (1984) 327–332.

11. Boydston, R. E., Programming cost estimate: Is it reasonable? In *Proceedings of the Seventh International Conference on Software Engineering* (1984), pp. 153–159.

12. Card, D. N., Page, G. T. and McGarry, F. E. Criteria for software modularization. In *Proceedings of the Eighth International Conference on Software Engineering* (1985), pp. 372–377.

13. Conte, S. D., Dunsmore, H. E. and Shen, V. Y. *Software Engineering Metrics and Models.* Benjamin-Cummings, Reading, Mass., 1986.

14. Curtis, B., Shepperd, S. and Milliman, P. Third time charm: Stronger prediction of programmer performance by software complexity metrics. In *Proceedings of the Fourth International Conference on Software Engineering* (1979), pp. 356–60.

15. Curtis, B., Sheppard, S. B., Milliman, P., Borst, M. A. and Love T. Measuring the psychological complexity of

software maintenance tasks with the Halstead and McCabe metrics. *IEEE Trans. Softw. Eng. SE-5*, 2 (1979), 96–104.

16. Freedman, D. H. Programming without tears. *High Tech, 6*, 4 (1986), 38–45.

17. Gibson, V. R. and Senn, J. A. System structure and software maintenance performance. *Commun. ACM 32*, 3 (1989), 347–358.

18. Gill, G. K. and Kemerer, C. F. Cyclomatic complexity density and software maintenance productivity, *IEEE Trans. Softw. Eng. 17*, 12 (1991), 1284–1288.

19. Gremillion, L. L. Determinants of program repair maintenance requirements. *Commun. ACM 27*, 8 (1984), 826–832.

20. Jeffery, D. R. and Lawrence, M. J. Managing programming productivity. *J. Syst. Softw. 5* (1985), 49–58.

21. Kearney, J. et al. Software complexity measurement. *Commun. ACM 29*, 11 (1986), 1044–1050.

22. Kemerer, C. F. Measurement of software development productivity. Ph.D. thesis, Carnegie Mellon University, 1987.

23. Kemerer, C. F. An agenda for research in the managerial evaluation of computer-aided software engineering tool impacts. In *Proceedings of the Twenty-Second Hawaii International Conference on System Sciences,* (Jan. 1989), pp. 219–228.

24. Korson, T. D. and Vaishnavi, V. K. An empirical study of the effects of modularity on program modifiability. In

25. Lind, R. and Vairavan K. An experimental investigation of software metrics and their relationship to software development effort. *IEEE Trans. Softw. Eng. 15*, 5 (1989), 649–653.

26. Matsumura, K., Furuva, K., Yamashiro, A. and Obi, T. Trend toward reusable module component: Design and coding technique 50SM. In *Proceedings of the Eleventh Annual International Computer Software and Applications Conference (COMPSAC).* (Tokyo, Japan, Oct. 7–9 1987), pp. 45–52.

27. Munson, J. C. and Koshgoftaar, T. M. The dimensionality of program complexity. In *Proceedings of the International Conference on Software Engineering* (1989), pp. 245–253.

28. Schneidewind, N. F. The state of software maintenance, *IEEE Trans. Softw. Eng. SE-13*, 3 (1987), 303–310.

29. Spratt, L. and McQuilken, B. Applying control-flow metrics to COBOL. In *Proceedings of the Conference on Software Maintenance* (1987), pp. 38–44.

30. Vessey, I. and Weber, R. Some factors affecting program repair maintenance: An empirical study. *Commun. ACM 26*, 2 (1983), 128–134.

31. Vessey, I. and Weber, R. Research on structured programming: An empiricist's evaluation. *IEEE Trans. Softw. Eng. SE-10*, 4 (1984), 394–407.

32. Zweig, D. Software complexity and maintainability. Ph.D. thesis, Carnegie Mellon University, 1989.

Empirical Studies of Programmers, E. Soloway, and S. Ivengar, Eds., Ablex, Norwood, N.J., 1986.

DEPARTMENTALIZATION IN SOFTWARE DEVELOPMENT AND MAINTENANCE

Software maintenance—the correction, adaptation, and perfection of operational software [37]—has been a relatively neglected subject in the literature of software engineering and management. Attention has instead focused primarily on improved techniques for new system development. The virtues of these techniques are often held to include ease of maintenance on implementation. However, such claims are seldom validated through empirical study. It has not been shown that the maintenance burden is reduced by user involvement, prototyping, or the use of fourth generation development techniques. Systems beget systems; better systems generate more systems, subject data bases,

Article by E. Burton Swanson and Cynthia Mathis Beath. Copyright 1990, Association for Computing Machinery, Inc. Reprinted, with permission, from *(Communication of the ACM,* v. 33, n. 6, pp. 658–667, June/1990).

and strategic information systems. The installed software base grows larger and more diversified as end user developed systems, third party developed systems, and purchased packages are added. The maintenance burden grows too. (For background, see [10, 11, 30, 35, 47].)

The allocation of organizational resources to new system development and installed system maintenance has rarely been studied as a joint problem. Among the few studies which touch upon this issue are those of Lientz et al. [28] and Lientz and Swanson [26, 27], who report, based on their surveys of application software maintenance, that information systems (IS) organizations generally devote about the same amount of effort to maintenance as to new system development. Lientz and Swanson [26] also report that the expenditure of staff time to maintain a system tends to increase with both its age and size. Further, growth in size averages a substantial 10 percent per year, a finding which closely parallels that of Belady and Lehman [6] in their classic study of the growth of Operating System/360 over successive releases. In both studies, the provision of additional features and functionality is found to largely account for the common pattern of growth. Thus, older systems tend to be larger and harder to maintain; one reason for the increased difficulty is they have been enhanced to meet the needs of their users. (See also related studies by [20, 21, 42].)

The mature IS organization is therefore responsible for a substantial accumulation of installed application systems, which undergoes continuous growth and "evolution" [6, 7, 25], and which must be managed in conjunction with the acquisition and development of those new systems to which the organization also commits itself. With growth in the size of the IS organization often limited by management fiat despite continued growth in the size of the application system portfolio, the proper organization of work to carry out the joint tasks of maintenance and development is a subject of substantial management interest (see [15, 46]).

IS productivity in system development and maintenance is recognized to be a major concern

[23]; the typical organizational backlog of programs to be written stretches to a period of three years or more [24, 32]. The business risks of failure both in development and maintenance are also significant. A notorious case of such failure is Bank of America's attempt to develop a new trust accounting system at an estimated cost of $80 million; among many difficulties the staff bore the brunt of working concurrently on both the new system and the older operational system it was designed to replace [16]. The frequently reported failures of critical operational software also illustrate the risks involved (see [22]).

Two issues form the crux of the organizational problem: The first is whether the individual professional analyst or programmer should divide his or her time between maintenance and new system development work. Here, the matching of the motivating potential of the work to the "growth need strength" of the individual is an important consideration in any assignment, according to Couger and Colter [13], who found that development work has higher motivating potential than does maintenance work. The second issue, which arises only where it is decided that an individual should not divide his or her time between the two tasks, is whether or not maintenance staff should be organized as a separate department. In this case, considerations of productivity gains through specialization, efficiency of communication, and management control have been suggested to be of primary importance [38]. This article will focus on the departmentalization issue.[1]

We begin by presenting three alternative bases for departmentalization of the systems staff. The strengths and weaknesses of the three alternatives are discussed. Then, data taken from a set of twelve case studies are used to describe current

---

[1] While users have significant roles to play in both development and maintenance activities, we are concerned here with the standing organization of the technical staff. Of course, if technical staffs are decentralized to user organizations, similar questions of organization structure might arise and could be addressed using the logic presented in this article.

departmentalization practice. In subsequent discussion, an historical interpretation of the pattern of practice is suggested, and it is argued that a life cycle based organizational form, in which maintenance is organized separately from new system development, deserves closer scrutiny by IS management. Implications for current practice and further research are drawn in conclusion.

ALTERNATIVE BASES FOR DEPARTMENTALIZATION

Issues in the organization of work have long been studied by management and organizational researchers, as well as by other social scientists interested in the impacts of organizational practice on society. Classical management theory, dating from the early 1900s, originating in Adam Smith's 18th century work, provides much of the contemporary theoretical vocabulary. (For a review, see Galbraith [17].) Among its basic concepts are the horizontal division of labor among workers based upon specialization; and the vertical division of labor between workers and managers, and among levels of management, typically based on principles of command and control. Closely related is the concept of departmentalization, the aggregation of work roles to form groups, units, departments and divisions. Galbraith [17], whose information-processing theory of organization design we draw upon here, suggests three fundamental bases for departmentalization: input resources (grouping by function, technical specialty, or process), outputs (grouping by product, market, or customer) and physical location.

Our own analysis of application software development and maintenance suggests that three particular bases for the division of labor and the departmentalization of systems staff are of importance:
Work type: systems analysis versus programming
Application type: application group A versus application group B
Life cycle phase: development versus maintenance

Here the term "versus" indicates simply that a formal distinction is made for the purpose of organizing work. As we shall indicate, these bases relate closely to organizing around inputs or outputs as described by [17].

Division of labor by work type implies job specialization according to distinctive work skills. Historically, the most common work type distinction has been between systems analysis and programming, with systems analysts specializing in the functional specification of a system, and programmers in its computer-based implementation [12]. Where departmentalization is also based on this specialization—systems analysts and programmers are organized into separate departments—the organization may similarly be said to have a work type (W-type) form (also referred to in the general management literature as a "functional" form; see [46]). The W-type form corresponds to the concept of departmentalizing around input resources. Its distinguishing feature is concurrent multidepartment responsibility for a system's development or maintenance. This is necessary even though systems analysis precedes programming within the task sequence because analysis as a whole is iterative and continuous.

Division of labor by application type constitutes the second basic alternative. Here, the distinction is between individuals being assigned work on one system or group of systems versus their being assigned work on another system. Specialization is in the knowledge associated with the domain of application, rather than in certain work skills. Such a domain often, though not always, maps closely to one or more user departments. (In some instances, the domain may be integrative across departments.) Where departmentalization is also based on application domain, the organization may similarly be said to have an application type (A-type) form which corresponds closely to the "product" form discussed in the general management literature. The A-type form corresponds to the concept of departmentalizing around outputs. Its distinguishing feature is that a single department is responsible for the development and maintenance of a system over the system's life.

A third alternative is the division of labor by life cycle phase. The distinction here is typically between development work on new systems or on new versions of installed systems, and maintenance work on installed systems [37]. Specialization is in the skills and management of the development or maintenance phases of the life cycle. Where departmentalization is also based on this distinction—developers and maintainers are organized into separate departments or work units—the organization may similarly be termed a life cycle based (L-type) organization. Less obviously than the A-type form, the L-type form also corresponds to the concept of departmentalizing around outputs. In this case, the development unit focuses upon software products as its output, while the maintenance unit concentrates on service to users of installed systems. The important distinguishing feature of the L-type form is the transfer of responsibility for a system's development and maintenance between departments at the time the system becomes operational.

The L-type form, based on a distinction between development and maintenance work, is an idea that has been around for years (see [34]). It may be employed in several variations. Among these are the centralized development unit with decentralized maintenance at multiple installation locations; the location of a "fire fighting" maintenance team within the computer operations unit [38]; and the integration of maintenance into the user organization [8].

The choice of any particular organizational structure necessitates trading off the strengths and weaknesses of the three alternatives, (i.e., departmentalization by work type, application type, or life cycle phase). In Exhibit 1 we summarize these basic trade-offs. Following Galbraith's [17] theory of organization design, focal strengths and weaknesses of the three forms are presented in terms of their knowledge development and information processing implications. Uncertainty in the development and maintenance tasks is understood to be the basis of information and communication requirements within the IS organization, both laterally and hierarchically. Increased uncertainty requires that the IS organization find ways to increase its capacity to process information, or reduce its need for information. The preferred IS organizational form is in gen-

EXHIBIT 1   Trade-Offs Among Alternative
Organizational Forms

W-Type   Departmentalization by work type
(systems analysis versus programming)

Focal strength: development and
specialization of programming
knowledge and skills

Focal weakness: costs of coordination
between systems analysts and
programmers

A-Type   Departmentalization by application
domain (application group A versus
application group B)

Focal strength: development and
specialization of application knowledge

Focal weakness: costs of coordination
and integration among application
groups

L-Type   Departmentalization by life-cycle phase
(development versus maintenance)

Focal strength: development and
specialization of service orientation and
maintenance skills

Focal weakness: costs of coordination
between development and maintenance
units

eral that which is best matched to the task uncertainty faced. (See [17, 45] for details.)

The unique strength of the W-type form, in which programmers and systems analysts are organized into separate departments, is the development and specialization of programming skills. Here, the role of the systems analyst is to buffer the programmer from the user, allowing the programmer to focus on translating specifications into software. Where programming is a formidable task—as it is where machine constraints are tight and the programming language is close to that of the machine—the development of programming knowledge and skills may be critical and the advantage of the W-type form decisive. However, the weakness of the W-type form is also significant. Costs of coordination between systems analysts and programmers may be substantial for two reasons: the software specification bears the burden of formally mediating work between the two departments, often with considerable difficulty; and resulting interdependency problems between the departments may require frequent and costly resolution within the management hierarchy. These costs may, of course, be moderated where software specification is relatively straightforward and few problems need resolution. However, where software specification is particularly problematic and subject to ambiguity or instability, the weakness of the W-type form may be its undoing.

The A-type form in which departmentalization is based on application type has its own unique strength and weakness. Its strength is the development and specialization of application knowledge [15]. In contrast to the W-type form in which specialization focuses on inputs, such as programming skills, specialization in the case of the A-type form focuses on outputs, (i.e., upon the functionality of the applications). To the extent that applications share substantial communality within areas, such specialization is likely to be particularly important. However, there is a weakness here regarding the cost of coordinating and integrating across application areas. An overall information architecture may be needed to formalize application interdependence and autonomy. A strategy may also be required to establish priorities for resource claims across domains. However, such formal mechanisms will not always suffice. Where application areas are strongly interdependent, the resulting frequent conflicts, problems, and ambiguities will require resolution by the management hierarchy, at significant further costs.

In the case of the L-type form, in which development and maintenance are organized as separate departments, the particular strength is in the specialization and provision of services in support of day-to-day business operations which rely on installed information systems. These services, which focus on improving the value of installed systems

to their users, have historically taken a back seat to new system development. In particular, the system development life cycle has focused almost entirely upon aspects of the task that precede system installation and maintenance. In the IS organization, maintenance has been a background rather than a foreground task. But where the installed base of systems is large and mature, the advantages of specializing in the maintenance and enhancement of their services may be substantial. Like the other forms, the L-type form has a weakness. It is in the cost of coordination during implementation and in transferring responsibility for development and maintenance between departments. Here again, it will be necessary for the management hierarchy to resolve problems, especially in coordinating a system replacement; as with the A-type form, the costs may be significant.

No form is perfect. Fortunately, the three alternatives are by no means mutually exclusive as bases for organizing, and thus their strengths and weaknesses can be balanced through combination. For example, an individual work assignment may consist wholly of maintenance programming of a single application system or subsystem. In the case of departmentalization, IS organizations may combine two or even all three of the basic alternatives into a hybrid form. In deciding whether and how to combine the basic alternatives IS organizations have an opportunity to trade off the pluses and minuses of the three forms, if they so choose.

How do IS organizations currently make choices among alternative forms? What hybrid forms, if any, are employed, with what frequencies? What stresses and strains result with what implications? The design choices of 12 contemporary IS organizations will now be presented and analyzed to illuminate current practice.

A STUDY OF CURRENT PRACTICE

A set of 12 cases on application software maintenance was recently developed as part of an ongoing research project. These cases focus on the comparative maintenance environments of IS organizations, and on alternative IS management strategies for maintenance of the application system portfolio, including alternative approaches to organization design; task definition and assignment; work technique; and policies for coordination and control.

Development of the cases concluded in the summer of 1985. Among the participating organizations were four high technology manufacturers, two food and beverage producers, one oil company, a retail grocery firm, an aerospace company, a research and development laboratory, a public utility, and a university. Six of the organizations are based in southern California; the rest are dispersed throughout the U.S. Significant diversity among the participants, in terms of organizational size and type, was sought. The sample is not representative of a specific population. Rather, its purposes are intentionally exploratory and the appropriate logic of comparative analysis is that of theoretical replication, where each case is roughly analogous to a separate experiment [44], in which a single research question is studied from several different experimental vantage points. Thus, diversity among participants may be compared to variety among experimental arrangements, with the expectation that the findings should also be rich across cases.

Questionnaires, on-site interviews, and reviews of organizational documents were used in data gathering. Both quantitative and qualitative data were obtained, following a common protocol [40]. Together, the cases appear in Swanson and Beath [41]. Selected data are presented in Exhibit 2.

EXHIBIT 2 Twelve Cases in Information Systems Organization

Org	Staff	Dep	Span	Form	M-Sys	D-Sys	R-Sys	M-Role	D-Role	S-Role
1	148	6	6.4	A-L	51	16	4	38%	59%	3%
2	102	4	7.5	L-A	81	22	9	28%	62%	10%
3	7	1	2.5	L-A	33	11	11	100%	0%	0%
4	67	6	10.2	A	14	3	0	34%	16%	42%
5	46	3	5.6	A-L	103	15	10	26%	48%	26%
6	266	18	13.8	A	89	21	11	42%	31%	27%
7	45	4	2.8	A	28	5	3	31%	38%	31%
8	19	1	5.3	A	33	6	3	26%	16%	58%
9	117	9	12.0	A	22	0	0	100%	0%	0%
10	102	8	11.8	A	30	3	2	0%	0%	100%
11	118	5	8.8	A-W	25	10	6	44%	28%	28%
12	108	4	3.5	A-L	171	0	0	93%	7%	0%

Notes: Organizations are numbered in the sequence in which the cases were prepared. Staff counts represent application development and maintenance personnel only. Department (Dep) counts represent units reporting to first-level managers. Span of control (span) is the average number of staff reporting to a first-level manager or supervisor. Organizational forms refer to the predominate basis of departmentalization: the A-type organizations are departmentalized by application type; A-L type organizations include subordinated maintenance and/or new system development units; the A-W type organization includes subordinated analyst and programmer units; the L-A type organizations are departmentalized according to maintenance and new system development, with subunits subordinated according to application type. Numbers of systems maintained (M-Sys), new systems under development (D-Sys), and replacement systems among the new systems under development (R-Sys) are based on differing levels of system definition across organizations. Numbers of maintainers (M-role) spend two-thirds or more of their effort on maintenance; developers (D-role) spend two-thirds or more of their effort on new system development; others (S-role) split their efforts between maintenance and development more evenly.

Across the 12 cases, classification of the organizational forms employed is based on the three basic forms discussed earlier: the work type (W-type); the application type (A-type); and the life cycle based (L-type) forms. Both pure and hybrid forms are identified, with the latter described in terms of principal and subordinate bases of departmentalization as explained in Exhibit 2. Remarks on each of the cases included in Exhibit 3 explain each instance of the forms and provide additional perspective. Considerable diversity is seen to exist, and it is further apparent that various temporal and contextual factors (e.g., company reorganization or strategic realignment) also shape the organizational design choices. (Zmud, [46], makes a similar argument.)

Overall, the A-type form is represented in all 12 cases, and is the primary basis of departmentalization in 10 instances. The L-type form is currently represented in five cases, though most frequently as a subordinate basis of departmentalization. The W-type form appears only once in a subordinate role. While the A-form dominates current practice, the less-recognized L-form is well represented.

The cases provide a good illustration of the ways in which IS organizations seek to strike a balance among the advantages and disadvantages of the three principal forms. Half the cases present hybrid forms. In several cases, transitions between forms occurred prior to or subsequent to the data gathering. Organization 1 has recently changed from L-A form to A-L form. In the words of one manager, however, this "was probably a mistake." (A task force was appointed at this site to examine the issue, and subsequent to our study, the department returned to an L-A form.) Organization 5, which used an L-A form for about 14 years, recently changed to A-L, retaining many desirable features of their L-A form in the process. Organizations 11 and 12 are both in the process of establishing groups dedicated to maintenance. Small groups dedicated to the maintenance of an important or problematic system were found at other organizations.

On balance, the predominant trade-off that concerns IS managers is between (a) forms in which

most of the application staff members split their time between maintenance and development (the A and A-W forms in our cases), and (b) forms in which development and maintenance staff are separated to some extent (the L-A and A-L forms in our cases).

We analyzed the data of Exhibit 2 to compare these two alternatives—the more traditional A or A-W forms with the two L-forms (L-A and A-L). Specifically, we asked whether separating maintenance and development (as in the two L-forms) was related to (i) organizational size; (ii) management span of control; (iii) application portfolio maturity, as indicated both by systems maintained as a proportion of the total under new development and maintenance, and by replacement systems as a proportion of the total under new development; and (iv) the percentages of staff effort allocated to development and maintenance. No statistically significant differences were found, except for the percentages of staff effort allocated to development and maintenance.[2] Here it was found that relatively more staff time was allocated to development work, on average, where development and maintenance were organized separately. Exhibit 4 summarizes.

Interpretation of Exhibit 4 is by no means straightforward. Our own interpretation provides for an almost paradoxical finding. While caution is in order, given the sample, we believe that separating maintenance from development is associated with a focusing of managerial attention on maintenance, with the result that the maintenance staff is more efficient and more productive at maintaining systems. Therefore, more resources are available for development work. Of course,

---

[2] Unpaired T-tests were used to compare six A and A-W form cases to three L-A and A-L form cases. Three cases were excluded from the analysis—Organizations 3, 9, and 12—because in each case no development was being performed at the time due to various organizational exigencies. T-values and significance levels were: Development work (D-role plus half of S-role), T = -4.68. $p + .001$; Maintenance work (M-role plus half of S-role), $t = 5.62$, $p = .001$.

EXHIBIT 3 Remarks on Organizational Forms

Org Form		Remarks

1 A-L Maintenance has a significant profile in this organization. Of six departments, four are responsible for application systems grouped by user functional areas. A fifth is responsible for development of a major new system. A sixth provides planning and technical support. Within departments, staff are assigned to either new system development or maintenance. A few years ago, maintenance was centralized as a separate department. Now, management is weighing whether to return to this arrangement.

2 L-A Maintenance is a major function in this organization. Of four departments, two work primarily on new system development, with division of labor by user area. A third maintains systems developed by the first two. A fourth develops and maintains systems for another area of use. Management considers the arrangement cost-effective, but worries about the "stigma of maintenance" and its effects.

3 L-A A single small department works wholly on maintenance and local plantsite support. Within the department, two supervisors are responsible for distinct application groups. New systems are developed and supplied by the parent organization. A major group of Manufacturing Resource Planning (MRP) systems is soon to be implemented, and one supervisor is working full time on the project.

4 A Of six departments in this organization, four develop and maintain systems according to area of application. Within one of these, a team of five individuals maintains a major system. However, this reflects the scale of the system, more than a commitment to maintenance organization. Two other departments develop and maintain supporting common systems. Management envisions a transition to a distributed processing environment with user-developed applications.

5 A-L Management in this organization believes that maintenance and development appeal to different types of people. Maintenance was once centralized. Now two departments develop and maintain systems for distinct user divisions. Within each, separate staffs are associated with maintenance and new system development. Each has its own supervisor. A third department develops and maintains office systems.

6 A This large organization is departmentalized by groups of applications. Eighteen units are formed within five departments under one manager. There is no formal distinction between maintenance and new system development staff. Enhancement of existing systems occupies a substantial proportion of staff time, and the age and maintainability of applications is a concern. User dissatisfaction with the backlog of work is also a problem.

7 A In this organization, four departments develop and maintain systems grouped by area of application. Responsibility for production systems, as opposed to new systems, is a formal requirement for career advancement. However, there is no division of labor based on maintenance versus development, and, in fact, the distinction is blurred. Responsibility for production systems includes their further development.

8 A In this organization, the systems staff is departmentalized by area of application. Each of three groups has full responsibility for development and maintenance with its area of jurisdiction. Necessarily, more time is spent on maintenance than on development, but an attempt is made to spread development opportunities equitably. Responsibility for the maintenance of several systems critical to business operations is reserved for senior people.

9 A This new organization is responsible for the development and maintenance of manufacturing information systems, and reports directly to the manager or manufacturing. It has just been spun off from a large, centralized IS function. New system development is frozen during the present transition period. Staff include programmers as well as analysts who formerly worked in user departments. All now work as programmer/analysts. Departmentalization is by area of application.

EXHIBIT 3 *(Cont.)*

Org	Form	Remarks
10	A	This organization is departmentalized by area of application into two major groups. Each unit within a group is responsible for both development and maintenance. Staff tend to split their efforts evenly between the two tasks. Nearly half the systems in the current portfolio are more than ten years old. New system development is motivated by changes in the core business technology supported.
11	A-W	This organization consists of five departments, four of whose supervisors divide development and maintenance responsibility for the applications portfolio. Systems are allocated to supervisors by client area, for the most part. Separate staffs for programming and systems analysis exist within each department. Analysts tend to work in a liaison role between users and programmers.
12	A-L	New system development is currently frozen in this large organization, while the business seeks a major new government contract. Three departments are responsible for systems grouped by area of application. A fourth department provides system support, which will shortly include acceptance of all systems put into production, as well as primary responsibility for corrective maintenance in the event of operational difficulties.

other interpretations are conceivable. The firms in our sample with separate maintenance departments may simply be understaffing maintenance, or they may have relatively smaller maintenance burdens for reasons we have not considered. In any case, a more systematic study of this issue is clearly needed.

How do we account for the pattern of organizational practice found here? Why does the A-form dominate while the W-form is barely represented? What features of the L-form account for its apparent efficiencies, and what are its overall benefits and costs when examined in more depth? What are the likely implications for the future? We will now turn to these questions.

DISCUSSION

We suggest a process of historical change underlies current IS departmentalization practice. During the early years in which IS organizations emerged, almost three decades ago, division of labor was frequently based on work type, by distinguishing between the programming and systems analysis tasks [43]. Because systems were typically constructed in lower-level languages (fre-

quently, assembler languages) and utilized an expensive and scarce computing resource, the programmer's task was to work close to the machine, while systems analysts inherited the problem of mediating between the programmers and users who knew little if anything of computing technology. Overall task uncertainty derived in large part from the computing resource and its efficient deployment, and the development of computing expertise was critical.

Over the years, however, as user organizations have become more computer-sophisticated, and as computer technology itself has become more user-friendly, the systems analysis task (and with fourth-generation tools, even the programming task) has increasingly been shared between IS and user organizations. Moreover, because programming work no longer takes place so close to the machine, and because the mediating role of systems analysis spans less of a knowledge gap, the distinctive features of both jobs have become blurred even within IS; apparently this basis for the division of labor has eroded. Increasingly, more individuals possess the skills necessary for both roles, and the integrated programmer/analyst job is now a realistic alternative. For example, at

EXHIBIT 4   Comparison of Allocation of Effort

When maintenance receives managerial attention, in A-L or L-A form organizations, relatively more resources are available to be used for development than in A or A-W form organizations.

A and A-W form organizations
(N = 6)

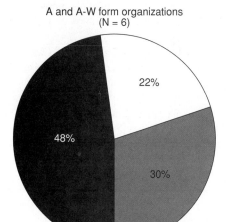

A-L and L-A form organizations
(N = 3)

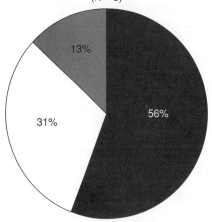

☐ >2/3 time doing maintenance

▨ Doing both maintenance and development

■ >2/3 time doing development

Note:
Cases 3, 9 and 12 are excluded here. Case 3 (L-A form) does only maintenance work; development is done at corporate headquarters. Case 9 (A-form) and Case 12 (A-L form) are currently doing only maintenance due to other organizational factors.

Organization 9 a recent reorganization has merged programmers with analysts, who formerly worked in user departments. The new department hopes for "synergism in the programmer/analyst activity."

Also, since the early years, the IS organization has gradually shifted its task focus to its application outputs. Beyond the automating of routine accounting procedures, the application domain has been extended to almost all corners of the enterprise. Certain applications have further come to be recognized as strategic[33]. Therefore, task uncertainty for the systems staff has increasingly derived less from computing resources than from complexities and risks associated with applications. Development of these applications has accordingly required the nurturing of application expertise among systems staff, and as a substantial and diversified base of applications has been accumulated, increased specialization by application type has been pursued. Thus, the application domain has come to constitute the predominant basis for departmentalization in today's IS organization.

Nevertheless, as depicted earlier, a significant number of organizations do make use of the life cycle based alternative in which a distinction between system development and maintenance forms at least some basis for departmentalization. Use of this alternative may also be on the rise. A recent study in the UK (cf. [36]) found the percentage of IS departments that organize maintenance into separate groups was significantly higher (40 percent vs. 16 percent) than the level found by Lientz and Swanson [26]. Why should use of the life cycle based alternative persist? In our view, L-forms (here, the L-A and A-L forms; more generally, any form that separates developers from maintainers) offer certain important advantages for the contemporary IS organization. Diversity among applications is not the only source of task uncertainty for the systems staff; a more important source of uncertainty may lie in the immediate organizational impacts of installed applications.

This suggests that the overall strengths and weaknesses of L-forms should be examined more closely. Based on the present study, in addition to

---

EXHIBIT 5   The Life Cycle Based on
Organizational Form
(Departmentalization by Maintenance
and Development)

Overall Strengths

1. Clear accountability for both maintenance expenses and the investment costs of new system development.

2. Buffering of new system development personnel from the intermittent demands of maintenance.

3. Facilitation of software quality assurance, in that the maintenance unit is motivated to require a meaningful acceptance test prior to accepting responsibility for a system.

4. Supports a focus on improved level of service to the user, by means of maintenance specialization.

5. Increased productivity in maintenance, through concentration of system familiarity.

Overall Weaknesses

1. Potential status differential between development and maintenance units, with consequential degradation of maintenance work and demotivation of those who perform it.

2. Loss of knowledge about system in transferring it from development to maintenance.

3. Costs of coordinating between the development and maintenance units during implementation period, especially where new systems are replacement systems.

4. Increased costs of system acceptance.

5. Possible duplication of communication channels to user organizations.

---

drawing from other related work, we present our own assessment. As summarized in Exhibit 5, five overall strengths and five weaknesses are suggested. We discuss each briefly. As a matter of practical interest, we include mentioning ways in which adopters of L-forms may attempt to compensate for its weaknesses. In doing so, we do not mean to suggest that L-forms are in general superior, but rather they need to be more deeply examined and more broadly understood.

Strengths

A first strength of the L-forms is *clear accountability for both maintenance expenses and the investment costs of new system development,* which has long been a problem for IS management. When personnel are assigned both maintenance and new system development work, they have some discretion in the charging of their time between the two classes of activity. Our case observations suggested that under- or overcharging to maintenance is commonplace and follows the management pressures of the moment. Campaigns to "reduce the time spent on maintenance" or "meet those development targets" may thus be deceptive in their appearance of success. L-form departmentalization puts an end to this situation, and gives better visibility to both maintenance expenses and the costs of new system development.

Buffering of new system development staff from the intermittent demands of maintenance is a further advantage of L-forms, our studies suggest. Maintenance problems are by their nature largely unpredictable, and they play havoc with the more orderly process of new system development. A manager at Organization 10 complained that a major problem for developers was being drawn into "answering user questions" about installed systems, which he noted, was "the biggest chunk of maintenance." At Organizations 1, 2 and 5 we were told that maintenance had been separated from development in part to buffer the development staffs from the demands of maintenance, allowing the developers to concentrate on their projects. Many failures to deliver new systems on schedule have been attributed to the siphoning off of staff time to meet the exigencies of maintenance. With an L-form this drain is much more apparent and can be more easily resisted.

Facilitation of software quality assurance is also supported by the L-forms. The maintenance unit is clearly motivated to require a meaningful acceptance test prior to assuming responsibility for a newly-developed system. At Organization 12, an elite group "possessing the best talent within IS," is being formed to provide the first line of support for installed systems. Of necessity, this group is expected to design and administer acceptance criteria for new systems. These criteria may be more or less formal, our case studies indicate, depending upon the working relationships between the maintenance and new system development work units. Acceptance tests provide leverage for assuring that quality standards are not unduly compromised by the pressures of new system development schedules and budgets.

A focus on an improved level of user service, particularly regarding responsiveness to user requests for maintenance, is also encouraged by L-form departmentalization. In contrast to new system development, which orients itself more toward delivering a software product, maintenance is by its nature a service activity, undertaken largely in response to a continuing stream of user requests. Thus, maintenance managers at Organization 5 pointed with pride to the "big in-basket and big out-basket" aspect of maintenance. Centralization of maintenance also allows users and IS to more closely evaluate responsiveness in meeting these IS requests.

Where user service is particularly important, pockets of staff dedicated to maintenance are often found in an otherwise A-form organization. At Organization 8, for example, the IS department's principal mission is to provide high reliability operations of a few critical applications in a highly dynamic business environment. Maintenance of critical systems is reserved for a small group of highly skilled senior people who have developed elaborate and reliable techniques for making changes and retesting these systems while providing continuous service to their users.

Finally, *productivity gains in maintenance* may also apparently be achieved through specialization and L-form departmentalization, as originally suggested by Mooney [31]. Why might this be the

case? Recall that familiarity with systems is fundamental to maintenance [1, 26]. Where staff split their time between maintenance and new system development, more staff must generally be assigned to maintain a given portfolio of systems with the consequence that their collective familiarity is more fragmented. We suspect fragmented familiarity is difficult to deploy and sustain. Loss of efficiency follows.

Separate maintenance groups may also be more efficient because their analysts and programmers develop expertise in maintenance and because their managers learn how to manage maintenance. At Organization 9, for example, after the manager began distributing a simple report of processing times and maintenance assignments for a group of systems, processing times for the systems were cut by half. Centralization of maintenance also makes it easier to justify investment in modern maintenance tools, such as restructuring or code analyzer packages.

Weaknesses

These strengths of L-forms are clearly compelling. However, against these strengths there are a number of weaknesses.

A potential status differential between the new system development and maintenance units is a first concern. Among the most discussed subjects in the literature is the low status and motivating potential of maintenance work ([13, 29, 34]). To the extent that maintenance is seen as undesirable work, an L-form is disadvantaged, in that it creates two classes of citizens in system development and maintenance. When an L-A form was adopted 14 years ago at Organization 5, it was feared that everyone might quit. They did not. But at Organization 2, which uses an A-L form, the maintenance manager's principal worry is morale.

Some argue that maintenance is inherently less motivating than new system development, because, for example, the hours are unpredictable and it involves routine work with older technology. Others disagree, arguing that maintenance offers at least as great a work challenge, involving, for example, expert troubleshooting under substantial operational pressure requiring a sensitive, experienced touch. Among our cases, for instance, at Organizations 5, 11 and 12, management's experience is that some people prefer maintenance work to development work. Our own view, based on the case studies, is that managerial attitudes and traditional IS career paths may explain much of the present motivational differential where it exists. At Organization 10 (A-type), for example, the IS manager told us he believes that maintenance work is not as challenging as development; his lower level managers told us that development assignments had more impact on upward career movement. Similarly, at Organization 2 where the maintenance manager worries about morale, IS management's attention is on development, and a common career path is from operations, through maintenance, and "up" to development.

Too many careers begin or end in maintenance. Newcomers are often initiated in maintenance before advancing to new system development. Similarly, oldtimers skilled in earlier technologies too frequently find themselves retired to the maintenance pastures. At Organization 11 (A-W form), managers try to avoid the "second-class citizen syndrome" by rotating maintenance assignments, but they are reluctant to do this if it means sacrificing in-depth knowledge of a system. So, some maintenance assignments drift on indefinitely.

Career paths in which responsibility for a major installed system is recognized as a significant and necessary mid-career achievement might do much to alleviate the current motivational issue. At Organization 7, an A-type organization where management nevertheless devotes attention and resources to maintenance, a period of responsibility for a "production" (installed) system is a prerequisite for advancement to management. (See [2, 4, 5, 18].)

Investment in new maintenance technology should also contribute to motivation, in that staff skills may be upgraded. In fact, managerial attention to maintenance in almost any form seems to alleviate some of the morale problem.

Loss of knowledge about systems in transferring them from new system development to maintenance is a second potential disadvantage of L-forms. As discussed earlier, knowledge about a system is fundamental to its efficient maintenance. To mitigate against this loss, the use of maintenance escorts is recommended [26]. At Organizations 2 and 5, maintainers sometimes participate in development projects and then rejoin the maintenance staff to maintain the system. An even simpler approach, also used at Organization 5, is for developers to take a few days to teach the maintainers the general data flow of the new system.

The costs of coordinating between the new system development and maintenance units, especially for replacement systems, is a related disadvantage of L-forms. Here the problem is not so much the permanent loss of knowledge about the system in transferring responsibility from development to maintenance as it is the temporary sharing of knowledge needed to effect a smooth changeover. Where the new system replaces one or more existing systems, as it increasingly does (see Exhibit 2), this process is particularly delicate and trouble-prone. Required coordination costs may, however, be moderated by employing implementation teams as lateral integrating mechanisms [17, 38].

Increased costs of system acceptance by the maintenance unit must also be weighed against the quality benefits associated with acceptance tests. When systems are turned over to L-form maintenance units, some acceptance criteria established by that unit typically must be met. Documentation must be complete, all functions must be implemented, loose ends must be tied up. Sometimes meeting these acceptance criteria will require short-term investments which have unpredictable long-term value—documentation may never again need to be referenced or functions agreed to in specifications may ultimately not be needed. In A-type organizations these costs may be avoided or simply postponed until much later.

In L-form units, our studies suggest, acceptance costs may be moderated over time by the growth of mutual trust between departments, founded on their long-term relationship. In Organization 5, trust between units evolved over the 14 year period in which maintenance was centralized, and acceptance standards and methods were worked out in cooperation with the system development unit, eventually easing the acceptance process. Over time, the development group improved its compliance with standards and the maintenance group gained a better understanding of which standards were really important to them.

Finally, *possible duplication of communication channels to user organizations* is a concern with L-forms. Users must work with both new system development and maintenance units. Nevertheless, the costs of such duplication may be offset by other considerations. For example, the use of separate channels to resolve maintenance and new system development issues may be more effective in practice in that the integrity of each process is less easily compromised. However, we have no direct evidence that this is so from our cases.

CONCLUSION

In our view, the most significant insight in the above analysis lies in the trade-offs among the classical system parameters of quality, schedule, and budget. The most compelling advantage of the L-forms may be their potential for quality assurance and improved user service, which may have been neglected in application systems work due to the pressures of schedules and budgets associated with new system development. Adoption of an organizational form in which maintainers are separated from developers brings about a shift of emphasis to improved quality assurance and user service, we believe. This shift is also responsive to rising user expectations for information services, which have been fueled by user experiences with microcomputer products and services available in the marketplace.

Because of its quality and productivity improvement potential, we believe an L-form structure, in some variation, deserves consideration by many IS organizations, especially those with mature, well-developed application system portfolios, where

services to day-to-day business operations are of central importance. At the same time, we would caution the unwary manager against seizing upon an L-form as a general solution to problems of IS productivity and service. Good organization design makes a difference in IS, as it does elsewhere, but organization design is more than organization structure [17]. The benefits of a separate maintenance unit are also dependent on good management at the head of the maintenance unit, recognition and rewards for its members, and viable systems acceptance criteria, our research suggests.

Most of the IS managers in our cases are attempting to derive some of the benefits of an L-form arrangement while maintaining the benefits they have achieved with A-form designs. Both forms are ways of departmentalizing around outputs. In the L-forms, the output focus is user service; with A-forms, it is software products. Since both of these are important outputs of the IS department, some combination of approaches seems appropriate. As possible combinations we note the various L-A and A-L forms, and also the design adopted at Organization 7, where an A-type form is combined with explicit managerial commitment to the installed system base.

Much remains to be learned about organization design for IS. Additional research is needed to investigate the relative productivity and quality benefits of A-forms and L-forms. Of particular interest may be the user's response to differences in form. The task for IS researchers, in our view, is to accompany practitioners in their various organizational redesigns: they will observe their reforms as experiments, as originally suggested by Campbell [9], to better reveal the complex workings of the organizational process in the variety of settings in which it unfolds so that future practice may continue to be better informed.

ACKNOWLEDGMENTS

We are grateful to Chris Kemerer and to three anonymous reviewers and the department editor for their helpful comments on earlier versions of this article.

References

1. Bankar, R. D., Datar, S. M., and Kemerer, C. F. Factors affecting software maintenance productivity: An exploratory study. In *Proceedings of the Eighth International Conference on Information Systems* (Pittsburgh, Dec. 6–9, 1987), pp. 160–175.

2. Baroudi, J. J. The impact of role variables on IS personnel work attitudes and intentions. *MIS Q. 9,* 4 (1985), 341–356.

3. Baroudi, J. J., and Ginzberg, M. J. Impact of the technological environment on programmer/analyst job outcomes. *Commun. ACM 29,* 6 (1986), 546–555.

4. Bartol, K. M. Turnover among DP personnel: A causal analysis. *Commun. ACM 26,* 10 (1983), 807–811.

5. Bartol, K. M., and Martin, D. C. Managing information systems personnel: A review of the literature and managerial implications. *MIS Q.,* Special Issue (1982), 49–70.

6. Belady, L. A., and Lehman, M. M. A model of large program development, *IBM Syst. J. 15,* 3 (1976), 225–252.

7. Bendifallah, S., and Scacchi, W. Understanding software maintenance work. *IEEE Trans. Softw. Eng. SE-13,* 3 (1987), 311–323.

8. Boehm, B. The economics of software maintenance. Software Maintenance Workshop, Naval Postgraduate School, Monterey, Calif., Dec. 6–8, 1983, in R. S. Arnold (Ed.), Software Maintenance Workshop Record, IEEE Computer Science Press, N.Y., 9–37.

9. Campbell, D. T. Reforms as experiments. *Am. Psych. 24,* 4 (1969), 409–429.

10. Canning, R. G., Ed. That maintenance 'iceberg'. *EDP Analyzer,* (Oct. 1972), 1–14.

11. Canning, R. G., Ed. Easing the software maintenance burden. *EDP Analyzer* (Aug. 1981), 1-14.

12. Cheney, P. H., and Lyons, N. R. Information systems skill requirements: A survey. *MIS Q. 4,* 1 (1980), 35–43.

13. Couger, J. D., and Colter, M. A. *Maintenance Programming: Improved Productivity Through Motivation.* Prentice-Hall, Englewood Cliffs, N.J., 1985.

14. Couger, J. D., and Zawacki, R. A. *Motivating and Managing Computer Personnel.* Wiley Press, New York, 1980.

15. Dickson, G. W., and Wetherbe, J. C. *The Management of Information Systems.* McGraw-Hill, New York, 1985.

16. Frantz, D. BofA's plans for computer don't add up. *L.A. Times* (Feb. 7, 1988), 1 ff.

17. Galbraith, J. *Designing Complex Organizations.* Addison-Wesley, Reading, Mass., 1973.

18. Ginzberg, M. J., and Baroudi, J. J. MIS careers—A theoretical perspective. *Commun. ACM 31,* 5 (1988), 586–594.

19. Goldstein, D. K., and Rockart, J. F. An examination of work-related correlates of job satisfaction in programmer/analysts. *MIS Q. 8,* 2 (1984), 103–115.

20. Gremillion, L. L. Determinants of program repair maintenance requirements. *Commun. ACM 27,* 8 (1984), 826–832.

21. Guimaraes, T. Managing application program maintenance expenditures. *Commun. ACM 26,* 10 (1983), 739–746.

22. Haffner, K. Is your computer secure? *Bus. Week* (Aug. 1, 1988), 64–72.

23. Izzo, J. E. *The Embattled Fortress: Strategies for Restoring Information Systems Productivity.* Jossey-Bass, San Fran., Calif., 1987.

24. Kim, C., and Weston, S. Software maintainability: perceptions of EDP professionals. *MIS Q. 12,* 2 (1988), 167–185.

25. Lehman, M. M. Programs, life cycles, and laws of software evolution. In *Proceedings of the IEEE. Special Issue on Software Engineering, 68,* 9 (Sept. 1980), 1060–1076.

26. Lientz, B. P., and Swanson, E. B. *Software Maintenance Management.* Addison-Wesley, Reading, Mass., 1980.

27. Lientz, B. P., and Swanson, E. B. Problems in application software maintenance. *Commun. ACM 24,* 11 (1981), 763–769.

28. Lientz, B. P., Swanson, E. B., and Tompkins, G. E. Characteristics of application software maintenance. *Commun. ACM 21,* 6 (1978), 466–471.

29. Liu, C. C. A look at software maintenance. *Datamation 22,* 11 (1976), 51–55.

30. Martin, J., and McClure, C. L. *Software Maintenance: The Problem and Its Solutions.* Prentice-Hall, Englewood Cliffs, N.J., 1983.

31. Mooney, J. W. Organized program maintenance. *Datamation 21,* 2 (1975), 63–64.

32. Port, O. The software trap: Automate—Or else. *Bus. Week Special Report,* (May 9, 1988), 142–154.

33. Porter, M. E., and Millar, V. E. How information gives you competitive advantage. *Harvard Bus. Rev. 63,* 4 (1985), 149–160.

34. Riggs, R. Computer systems maintenance. *Datamation 15,* 9 (1969), 227, 231–2.

35. Schneidewind, N. F. The state of software maintenance. *IEEE Trans. Softw. Eng. SE-13,* 3 (1987), 303–310.

36. Software Maintenance News. *Numbers from England, 7* (July 1989), 8.

37. Swanson, E. B. The dimensions of maintenance. In *Proceedings of the Second International Conference on Software Engineering* (San Fran., Calif., Oct. 13–15, 1976), pp. 492–497.

38. Swanson, E. B. Organizational designs for software maintenance. In *Proceedings of the Fifth International Conference on Information Systems* (Tucson, Ariz., Nov. 28–30, 1984), pp. 63–72.

39. Swanson, E. B., and Beath, C. M. The demographics of software maintenance management. In *Proceedings of the Seventh International Conference on Information Systems* (San Diego, Calif., Dec. 15–17, 1986), pp. 313–326.

40. Swanson, E. B., and Beath, C. M. The use of case study data in software management research. *J. Syst. Softw. 8* (1988), 63–71.

41. Swanson, E. B., and Beath, C. M. *Maintaining Information Systems in Organizations.* Wiley, Chichester, England, 1989.

42. Vessey, I., and Weber, R. Some factors affecting program repair maintenance. *Commun. ACM 26, 2* (1983), 128–134.

43. Willoughby, T. C. Staffing the MIS function. *Comput. Surveys, 4,* 4 (1972), 241–259.

44. Yin, R. K. Case Study Research: Design and Methods. Sage, Beverly Hills, Calif., 1984.

45. Zmud, R. W. Management of large software development efforts. *MIS Q. 4,* 2 (1980), 45–55.

46. Zmud, R. W. Design alternatives for organizing information systems activities, *MIS Q. 8,* 2 (1984), 79–93.

47. Zvegintzov, N. Immortal software. *Datamation* (June 15, 1984), 170–180.

Discussion Questions

1. Schneidewind clearly points out that too little software engineering research is conducted on the maintenance issue. Suggest some reasons why this might be the case.

2. Swanson and Beath suggest that a separate "L-type" organization will improve productivity through greater application familiarity on the part of full-time maintainers, yet also note that some knowledge of the application will be lost during the hand-off from development to maintenance. Which effect do you feel will predominate?

Software Capability Maturity Model

INTRODUCTION

The underlying theme of most of the articles in this collection is that software development must adopt a greater engineering process focus and a necessary part of such an evolution is the greater use of measurement. Many of these ideas come together in Watts Humphrey's Capability Maturity Model (CMM), probably the most well known idea to come out of more than a decade's work at the DOD's Software Engineering Institute (SEI) in Pittsburgh. It therefore serves as a useful capstone chapter for this collection. The first article is Humphrey's original, article-length statement of the CMM. A second article describes one organization's experiences with the CMM, and a final, more recent article summarizes the criticism and evolution of the model since its inception.

Humphrey adopts a strong process view, develops a five stage prescriptive framework that he argues will help an organization identify their highest priority problem areas, and suggests ways in which their process can be improved. The five stages are: (1) Initial—processes are ad hoc, there is little formal project management, no separate Quality Assurance group, and poor change control. (2) Repeatable—compared to Initial, here com-mitment control (schedules and budgets) has been achieved to some degree. Most organizations are either at the Initial or Repeatable stages. (3) Defined—the organization has a process group, an architecture, and a set of well-followed methods. (4) Managed—the organization has process measures (not simply product measures), a process database, and feedback systems to continually improve. (5) Optimizing—in this organization the data tune the software development process and they have completely adopted a continuous improvement paradigm. Humphrey also has a book length treatment of the material, *Managing the Software Process*. Modifications to the original model have also been published by the SEI.[1]

Humphrey was a co-author a few years later of a case study at Hughes Aircraft where they describe the process they followed to improve from a level 2, Repeatable organization to a level 3, Defined organization. Key changes focused on higher levels

---

[1] Paulk, M. C., B. Curtis, M. B. Chrissis and C. V. Weber, (1993), "Capability Maturity Model, Version 1.1", *IEEE Software, 10, 7,* 18–27.

of training and centralizing responsibility for the software process. The authors report quantifiable benefits in terms of risk reduction, budget adherence, as well as intangible benefits in terms of morale and a common culture or language. They caution, however, that senior management commitment is required, since process improvement is a long term effort. They estimate that it will take an organization approximately two years to advance one level.

Saiedian and Kuzara provide a useful review of the CMM, its evolution, and of criticisms of the CMM. They provide a summary of the model and highlight the difference in its application as a Software Process Assessment, which organizations perform primarily to determine how they might improve their process, and Software Capability Evaluations (SCE), which are official 'audits' of an organization's process to determine its maturity level, potentially for the purpose of determining an organization's eligibility to bid on certain government contracts. They summarize many positive case studies (including the Hughes article included in this collection), as well as a set of critiques about the framework that include critiques of the design of the method as well as its application.[2] The authors' summary that the CMM is likely to lead to better software at lower cost, but that the transition is not without difficulties or risks, serves as a useful summary and closing to this collection.

---

[2] See especially Bollinger, T. B. and C. McGowan, (1991), "A Critical Look at Software Capability Evaluations", *IEEE Software, 8, 4,* 25–41 and the response from the SEI, Humphrey, W. S. and B. Curtis, (1991), "Comments on 'A Critical Look' ", *IEEE Software, 8,* 4, 42–48.

CHARACTERIZING THE SOFTWARE PROCESS: A MATURITY FRAMEWORK

The amount of money spent on software in the US grows approximately 12 percent each year, and the demand for added software functions grows even faster. Software is a major and increasing portion of US Defense Dept. procurement costs, and software often adversely affects the schedules and effectiveness of weapons systems.

In recognition of the need to improve the development of military software, the Defense Dept. has launched several initiatives on software reli-

Article by Watts S. Humphrey. © 1988, IEEE. Reprinted, with permission, from (*IEEE Software.* 5, 3, 73–79; March/1988).

ability, maintainability, and testing, including the Ada Joint Program Office and the STARS program. The Defense Dept. formed the Software Engineering Institute at Carnegie Mellon University in 1984 to establish standards of excellence for software engineering and to accelerate the transition of advanced technology and methods into practice.

One SEI project is to provide the Defense Dept. with some way to characterize the capabilities of software-development organizations. The result is this software-process maturity framework, which can be used by any software organization to assess its own capabilities and identify the most important areas for improvement.

IDEAL SOFTWARE PROCESS

It is worthwhile to examine the characteristics of a truly effective software process. First, it is predictable: Cost estimates and schedule commitments are met with reasonable consistency and the quality of the resulting products generally meet user needs.

Statistical Control

The basic principle of software process management is that if the development process is under statistical control, a consistently better result can be achieved only by improving the process. If the process is not under statistical control, sustained progress is not possible until it is.[1]

When a process is under statistical control, repeating the work in roughly the same way will produce roughly the same result.

W.E. Deming, in his work with the Japanese industry after World War II, applied the concepts of statistical process control to industry.[1] While there are important differences, these concepts are just as applicable to software as they are to automobiles, cameras, wristwatches, and steel. A software-development process that is under statistical control will produce the desired results within the anticipated limits of cost, schedule, and quality.

Measurement

The basic principle behind statistical control is measurement. As Lord Kelvin said a century ago, ". . . when you can measure what you are speaking about, and express it in numbers, you know something about it; but when you cannot measure it, when you cannot express it in numbers, your knowledge is of a meager and unsatisfactory kind; it may be the beginning of knowledge, but you have scarcely in your thoughts advanced to the stage of science. . . ."[2]

There are several factors to consider in measuring the programming process. Perhaps most important is that the mere act of measuring human processes changes them. Since people's fears and motivations are involved, the results must be viewed in a different light than data on natural phenomena.

It is also essential to limit the measurements to those few items that will really be used. Measurements are both expensive and disruptive; overzealous measuring can degrade the processes we are trying to improve.

DEVELOPMENT-PROCESS IMPROVEMENT

An important first step in addressing software problems is to treat the entire development task as a process that can be controlled, measured, and improved. We define a process as a sequence of tasks that, when properly performed, produces the desired result. Clearly, a fully effective software process must consider the relationships of all the required tasks, the tools and methods used, and the skill, training, and motivation of the people involved.

To improve their software capabilities, organizations must take five steps:

1. understand the current status of their development process or processes,
2. develop a vision of the desired process,
3. establish a list of required process improvement actions in order of priority,
4. produce a plan to accomplish these actions, and
5. commit the resources to execute the plan.

The maturity framework developed at the SEI addresses these five steps by characterizing a software process into one of five maturity levels. By establishing their organization's position in this maturity structure, software professionals and management can more readily identify those areas where improvement actions are most likely to produce results.

PROCESS MATURITY LEVELS

As Exhibit 1 shows, the five levels of process maturity are:

1. Initial. Until the process is under statistical control, no orderly progress in process improvement is possible.

EXHIBIT 1   The Five Levels of Process Maturity

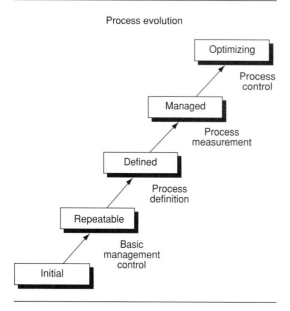

- represent a measure of improvement that is reasonable to achieve from the prior level,
- suggest interim improvement goals and progress measures, and
- make obvious a set of immediate improvement priorities, once an organization's status in this framework is known.

While there are many other elements to these maturity-level transitions, the basic objective is to achieve a controlled and measured process as the scientific foundation for continuous improvement. This structure is intended to be used with an assessment and management methodology, as outlined in the box titled "How to Use this Framework".

INITIAL PROCESS

The Initial Process could properly be called ad hoc, and it is often even chaotic. Here, the organization typically operates without formalized procedures, cost estimates, and project plans. Tools are neither well integrated with the process nor uniformly applied. Change control is lax and there is little senior management exposure to or understanding of the problems and issues. Since problems are often deferred or even forgotten, software installation and maintenance often present serious problems.

While organizations at this level may have formal procedures for project control, there is no management mechanism to ensure they are used. The best test is to observe how such an organization behaves in a crisis. If it abandons established procedures and reverts to merely coding and testing, it is likely to be at the Initial Process level. After all, if the techniques and methods are appropriate, they must be used in a crisis and if they are not appropriate, they should not be used at all.

One reason organizations behave chaotically is that they have not gained sufficient experience to understand the consequences of such behavior. Because many effective software actions such as design and code reviews or test data analysis do not appear to directly support shipping the product, they seem expendable.

2. Repeatable. The organization has achieved a stable process with a repeatable level of statistical control by initiating rigorous project management of commitments, cost, schedule, and changes.

3. Defined. The organization has defined the process, to ensure consistent implementation and provide a basis for better understanding of the process. At this point, advanced technology can usefully be introduced.

4. Managed. The organization has initiated comprehensive process measurements, beyond those of cost and schedule performance. This is when the most significant quality improvements begin.

5. Optimizing. The organization now has a foundation for continued improvement and optimization of the process.

These levels have been selected because they

- reasonably represent the actual historical phases of evolutionary improvement of real software organizations,

How to Use This Framework

This process-maturity structure is intended to be used with an assessment methodology and a management system.[1-3]

Assessment lets you identify the organization's specific maturity status. A management system establishes a structure for actually implementing the priority actions necessary to improve the organization. Once its position in this maturity structure is defined, the organization can concentrate on those items that will let it advance to the next level.

When, for example, a software organization does not have an effective project-planning system, it may be difficult or even impossible to introduce advanced methods and technology. Poor project planning generally leads to unrealistic schedules, inadequate resources, and frequent crises. In such circumstances, new methods are usually ignored, and the focus is on coding and testing.

Using this maturity framework, the SEI has developed an assessment questionnaire and methodology, a portion of which is shown in Exhibit 2.[4,5] The questionnaire has been reviewed by more than 400 governmental and industrial organizations. Also, it has been completed by more than 50 programming professionals from nearly as many software organizations.

The SEI has also used the assessment methodology to conduct in-depth technical reviews of 25 programming projects in four large programming organizations.

Through this work, the assessment methodology and questionnaire have evolved, but the five-level maturity framework has remained essentially unchanged. We have found that it portrays, with reasonable accuracy, the status and problems as seen by the managers and professionals in the organizations reviewed.

These early results indicate that the model reasonably represents the state of such organizations and provides a mechanism to rapidly identify the key improvement issues they face. At this time, the data is too limited to provide any more detailed information as to maturity distribution by industry, organization size, or type of work.

References

1. W.S. Humphrey, *Managing for Innovation— Leading Technical People,* Prentice-Hall, Englewood Cliffs, N.J., 1987.

2. R.A. Radice et al., "A Programming Process Study," *IBM Systems J.,* Vol. 24, No. 2, 1985, pp. 91–101.

3. R.A. Radice et al., "A Programming Process Architecture," *IBM Systems J.,* Vol. 24, No. 2, 1985, pp. 79–90.

4. W.S. Humphrey and D.H. Kitson, "Preliminary Report on Conducting SEI-Assisted Assessments of Software Engineering Capability," Tech. Report SEI-87-TR-16, Software Eng. Inst., Pittsburgh, July 1987.

5. W.S. Humphrey and W.L. Sweet, "A Method for Assessing the Software Engineering Capability of Contractors," Tech. Report SEI-87-TR-23, Software Eng. Inst., Pittsburgh, Sept. 1987.

It is much like driving an automobile. Few drivers with any experience will continue driving for very long when the engine warning light comes on, regardless of their rush. Similarly, most drivers starting on a new journey will, regardless of their hurry, pause to consult a map. They have learned the difference between speed and progress.

In software, coding and testing seem like progress, but they are often only wheel-spinning. While they must be done, there is always the

---

EXHIBIT 2   A Portion of the SEI's Assessment Questionnaire

2.3. Data Management and Analysis

Data management deals with the gathering and retention of process metrics. Data management requires standardized data definitions, data management facilities, and a staff to ensure that data is promptly obtained, properly checked, accurately entered into the database, and effectively managed.

Analysis deals with the subsequent manipulation of the process data to answer questions such as, "Is there a relatively high correlation between error densities found in test and those found in use?" Other types of analyses can assist in determining the optimum use of reviews and resources, the tools most needed, testing priorities, and needed education.

2.3.1. Has a managed and controlled process database been established for process metrics data across all projects?

2.3.2. Are the review data gathered during design reviews analyzed?

2.3.3. Is the error data from code reviews and tests analyzed to determine the likely distribution and characteristics of the errors remaining in the product?

2.3.4. Are analyses of errors conducted to determine their process related causes?

2.3.5. Is a mechanism used for error cause analysis?

2.3.6. Are the error causes reviewed to determine the process changes required to prevent them?

2.3.7. Is a mechanism used for initiating error prevention actions?

2.3.8. Is review efficiency analyzed for each project?

2.3.9. Is software productivity analyzed for major process steps?

---

danger of going in the wrong direction. Without a sound plan and a thoughtful analysis of the problems, there is no way to know.

Organizations at the Initial Process level can improve their performance by instituting basic project controls. The most important are:

• Project management. The fundamental role of a project-management system is to ensure effective control of commitments. This requires adequate preparation, clear responsibility, a public declaration, and a dedication to performance.[3]

For software, this starts with an understanding of the job's magnitude. In any but the simplest projects, a plan must then be developed to determine the best schedule and the resources required.

In the absence of such an orderly plan, no commitment can be better than an educated guess.

• Management oversight. A disciplined software-development organization must have senior management oversight. This includes review and approval of all major development plans before official commitment.

Also, a quarterly review should be conducted of facility-wide process compliance, installed-quality performance, schedule tracking, cost trends, computing service, and quality and productivity goals by project. The lack of such reviews typically results in uneven and generally inadequateimplementation of the process as well as in frequent overcommitments and cost surprises.

- Quality assurance. A quality-assurance group is charged with assuring management that the software-development work is actually done the way it is supposed to be done. To be effective, the assurance organization must have an independent reporting line to senior management and sufficient resources to monitor performance of all key planning, implementation, and verification activities. This generally requires an organization of about 5 to 6 percent the size of the development organization.
- Change control. Control of changes in software development is fundamental to business and financial control as well as to technical stability. To develop quality software on a predictable schedule, the requirements must be established and maintained with reasonable stability throughout the development cycle. Changes will have to be made, but they must be managed and introduced in an orderly way.

While occasional requirements changes are needed, historical evidence demonstrates that many of them can be deferred and phased in later. If all changes are not controlled, orderly design, implementation, and testing is impossible and no quality plan can be effective.

REPEATABLE PROCESS

The Repeatable Process has one important strength over the Initial Process: It provides commitment control.

This is such an enormous advance over the Initial Process that the people in the organization tend to believe they have mastered the software problem. They do not realize that their strength stems from their prior experience at similar work. Organizations at the Repeatable Process level thus face major risks when they are presented with new challenges.

Examples of the changes that represent the highest risk at this level are:

- New tools and methods will likely affect how the process is performed, thus destroying the

relevance of the intuitive historical base on which the organization relies. Without a defined process framework in which to address these risks, it is even possible for a new technology to do more harm than good.
- When the organization must develop a new kind of product, it is entering new territory. For example, a software group that has experience developing compilers will likely have design, scheduling, and estimating problems if assigned to write a control program. Similarly, a group that has developed small, self-contained programs will not understand the interface and integration issues involved in large-scale projects. These changes again destroy the relevance of the intuitive historical basis for the organization's work.
- Major organization changes can be highly disruptive. In the Repeatable Process organization, a new manager has no orderly basis for understanding what is going on and new team members must learn the ropes through word of mouth.

The key actions required to advance from the Repeatable Process to the Defined Process are:

1. Establish a process group. A process group is a technical group that focuses exclusively on improving the software-development process. In most software organizations, people are entirely devoted to product work. Until someone is given a full-time assignment to work on the process, little orderly progress can be made in improving it.

The responsibilities of process groups include defining the development process, identifying technology needs and opportunities, advising the projects, and conducting quarterly management reviews of process status and performance. Typically, the process group should be about 1 to 3 percent the size of the development organization. Because of the need for a nucleus of skills, groups smaller than about four are unlikely to be fully effective. Small organizations that lack the experience base to form a process group should address these issues through specially formed committees of experienced professionals or by retaining consultants.

2. Establish a software-development process architecture that describes the technical and management activities required for proper execution of the development process.[4] The architecture is a structural decomposition of the development cycle into tasks, each of which has entry criteria, functional descriptions, verification procedures, and exit criteria. The decomposition continues until each defined task is performed by an individual or single management unit.

3. If they are not already in place, introduce a family of software-engineering methods and technologies. These include design and code inspections, formal design methods, library-control systems, and comprehensive testing methods. Prototyping should also be considered, along with the adoption of modern implementation languages.

DEFINED PROCESS

With the Defined Process, the organization has achieved the foundation for major and continuing progress. For example, the development group, when faced with a crisis, will likely continue to use the Defined Process. The foundation has now been established for examining the process and deciding how to improve it.

As powerful as the Defined Process is, it is still only qualitative: There is little data to indicate what is going on or how effective the process really is. There is considerable debate about the value of software-process measurements and the best ones to use. This uncertainty generally stems from a lack of process definition and the consequent confusion about the specific items to be measured. With a defined process, we can focus the measurements on specific tasks. The process architecture is thus an essential prerequisite to effective measurement.

The key steps[3,4] to advance to the Managed Process are:

1. Establish a minimum, basic set of process measurements to identify the quality and cost

parameters of each process step. The objective is to quantify the relative costs and benefits of each major process activity, such as the cost and yield of error detection and correction methods.

2. Establish a process database with the resources to manage and maintain it. Cost and yield data should be maintained centrally to guard against loss, to make it available for all projects, and to facilitate process quality and productivity analysis.

3. Provide sufficient process resources to gather and maintain this data and to advise project members on its use. Assign skilled professionals to monitor the quality of the data before entry in the database and to provide guidance on analysis methods and interpretation.

4. Assess the relative quality of each product and inform management where quality targets are not being met. An independent quality-assurance group should assess the quality actions of each project and track its progress against its quality plan. When this progress is compared with the historical experience on similar projects, an informed assessment generally can be made.

MANAGED PROCESS

In advancing from the Initial Process via the Repeatable and Defined Processes to the Managed Process, software organizations typically will experience substantial quality improvements. The greatest potential problem with the Managed Process is the cost of gathering data. There are an enormous number of potentially valuable measures of software development and support, but such data is expensive to gather and maintain.

Therefore, approach data gathering with care and precisely define each piece of data in advance. Productivity data is generally meaningless unless explicitly defined. For example, the simple measure of lines of source code per development month can vary by 100 times of more, depending on the interpretation of the parameters. The code count could include only new and changed code or all shipped instructions. For modified programs, this can cause a ten-times variation. Similarly, you can use noncomment, nonblank lines, executable instructions, or equivalent assembler instructions, with variations again of up to seven times.[5] Management, test, documentation, and support personnel may or may not be counted when calculating labor months expended. Again, the variations can run at least as high as seven times.[6]

When different groups gather data but do not use identical definitions, the results are not comparable, even if it made sense to compare them. The tendency with such data is to use it to compare several groups and put pressure on those with the lowest ranking. This is a misapplication of process data.

First, it is rare that two projects are comparable by any simple measures. The variations in task complexity caused by different product types can exceed five to one. Similarly, the cost per line of code of small modifications is often two to three times that for new programs. The degree of requirements change can make an enormous difference, as can the design status of the base program in the case of enhancements.

Process data must not be used to compare projects or individuals. Its purpose is to illuminate the product being developed and to provide an informed basis for improving the process. When such data is used by management to evaluate individuals or teams, the reliability of the data itself will deteriorate. The US Constitution's Fifth Amendment, which protects against self-incrimination, is based on sound principles: Few people can be counted on to provide reliable data on their own performance.

The two fundamental requirements to advance from the Managed Process to the Optimizing Process are:

1. Support automatic gathering of process data. Some data cannot be gathered by hand, and all manually gathered data is subject to error and omission.

2. Use this data to both analyze and modify the process to prevent problems and improve efficiency.

OPTIMIZING PROCESS

In varying degrees, process optimization goes on at all levels of process maturity. With the step from the Managed to the Optimizing Process, however, there is a paradigm shift. Up to this point, software-development managers have largely focused on their products and will typically only gather and analyze data that directly relates to product improvement. In the Optimizing Process, the data is available to actually tune the process itself. With a little experience, management will soon see that process optimization can produce major quality and productivity improvements.

For example, many errors can be identified and fixed far more economically by code inspections than through testing. Unfortunately, there is little published data on the costs of finding and fixing errors.[7] However, I have developed a useful rule of thumb from experience: It takes about one to four working hours to find and fix a bug through inspections and about 15 to 20 working hours to find and fix a bug in function or system test. It is thus clear that testing is not a cost-effective way to find and fix most bugs.

However, some kinds of errors are either uneconomical or almost impossible to find except by machine. Examples are errors involving spelling and syntax, interfaces, performance, human factors, and error recovery. It would thus be unwise to eliminate testing completely because it provides a useful check against human frailties.

The data that is available with the Optimizing Process gives us a new perspective on testing. For most projects, a little analysis shows that there are two distinct activities involved. The first is the removal of bugs. To reduce this cost, inspections should be emphasized together with any other cost-effective techniques. The role of functional and system testing should then be changed to one of finding symptoms that are further explored to see if the bug is an isolated problem or if it indicates design problems that require more comprehensive analysis.

In the Optimizing Process, the organization has the means to identify the weakest elements of the process and fix them. At this point in process improvement, data is available to justify the application of technology to various critical tasks and numerical evidence is available on the effectiveness with which the process has been applied to any given product. We no longer need reams of paper to describe what is happening because simple yield curves and statistical plots provide clear and concise indicators. It is now possible to assure the process and hence have confidence in the quality of the resulting products.

People in the Process

Any software-development process is dependent on the quality of the people who implement it. Even with the best people, however, there is always a limit to what they can accomplish. When engineers are already working 50 to 60 hours a week, it is hard to see how they could handle the vastly greater challenges of the future.

The Optimizing Process helps in several ways:

- It helps managers understand where help is needed and how best to provide the people with the support they require.
- It lets professionals communicate in concise, quantitative terms. This facilitates the transfer of knowledge and minimizes the likelihood of their wasting time on problems that have already been solved.
- It provides the framework for the professionals to understand their work performance and to see how to improve it. This results in a highly professional environment and substantial productivity benefits, and it avoids the enormous amount of effort that is generally expended in fixing and patching other people's mistakes.

The Optimizing Process provides a disciplined environment for professional work. Process discipline must be handled with care, however, for it can easily become regimentation. The difference between a disciplined environment and a regimented one is that discipline controls the environment and methods to specific standards while regimentation defines the actual conduct of the work.

Discipline is required in large software projects to ensure, for example, that the people involved use the same conventions, don't damage each other's products, and properly synchronize their work. Discipline thus enables creativity by freeing the most talented software professionals from the many crises that others have created.

The Need

There are many examples of disasters caused by software problems, ranging from expensive missile aborts to enormous financial losses. As the computerization of our society continues, the public risks due to poor-quality code will become untenable. Not only are our systems being used in increasingly sensitive applications, but they are also becoming much larger and more complex.

While proper questions can be raised about the size and complexity of current systems, they are human creations and they will, alas, continue to be produced by humans—with all their failings and creative talents. While many of the currently promising technologies will undoubtedly help, there is an enormous backlog of needed functions that will inevitably translate into vast amounts of code.

More code means increased risk of error and, when coupled with more complexity, these systems will become progressively less testable. The risks will thus increase astronomically as we become more efficient at producing prodigious amounts of new code.

As well as being a management issue, quality is an economic one. It is always possible to do more inspections or to run more tests, but it costs time and money to do so. It is only with the Optimizing Process that the data is available to understand the costs and benefits of such work. The Optimizing Process thus provides the foundation for significant advances in software quality and simultaneous improvements in productivity.

There is little data on how long it takes for software organizations to advance through these maturity levels toward the Optimizing Process. Based on my experience, transition from level 1 to level 2 or from level 2 to level 3 take from one to three years, even with a dedicated management commitment to process improvement. To date, no complete organizations have been observed at levels 4 or 5.

To meet society's needs for increased system functions while simultaneously addressing the problems of quality and productivity, software managers and professionals must establish the goal of moving to the Optimizing Process.

This software-development process-maturity model reasonably represents the actual ways in which software-development organizations improve. It provides a framework for assessing these organizations and identifying the priority areas for immediate improvement. It also helps identify those

places where advanced technology can be most valuable in improving the software-development process.

The SEI is using this model as a foundation for a continuing program of assessments and software process development. These assessment methods have been made public[8,9], and preliminary data is now available from several dozen software organizations.

Exhibit 3 shows the maturity distribution of these organizations and the three leading problems faced at each level. At level one, the distribution is shown by quartile. There is not yet sufficient data to provide this detail for levels 2 or 3. As further data is gathered, additional reports will be published on the results obtained.

EXHIBIT 3 Early Results from Several Dozen Software Organizations Queried by the SEI Shows the Maturity Distribution and the Three Leading Problems Faced at Each Level. At Level One, the Distribution Is Shown by Quartile. There is Not Yet Sufficient Data to Provide This Detail for Levels 2 or 3. To Date, No Complete Organizations Have Been Observed at Levels 4 or 5

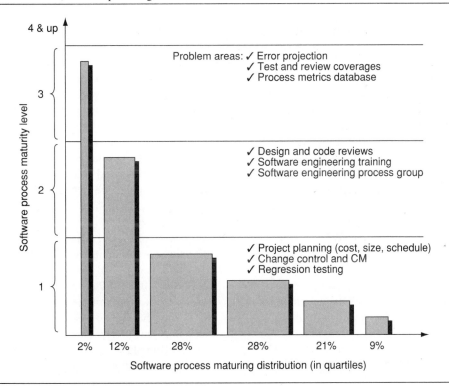

References

1. W.E. Deming, "Quality, Productivity, and Competitive Position," tech. report, MIT Center for Advanced Eng. Study, Cambridge, Mass., 1982.

2. J.R. Dunham and E. Kruesi, "The Measurement Task Area," *Computer,* Nov. 1983, pp. 47–54.

3. W.S. Humphrey, *Managing for Innovation: Leading Technical People,* Prentice-Hall, Englewood Cliffs, N.J., 1987.

4. R.A. Radice et al., "A Programming Process Architecture," *IBM Systems J.,* Vol. 24, No. 2, 1985, pp. 79–90.

5. M.L. Shooman, *Software Engineering: Design, Reliability, and Management,* McGraw-Hill, New York, 1983.

6. R.W. Wolverton. "The Cost of Developing Large-Scale Software," *IEEE Trans. Computers,* June 1974, pp. 615–636.

7. M.L. Shooman and M.I. Bolsky, "Types, Distribution, and Test and Correction Times for Programming Errors," *Proc. Int'l Conf. Reliable Software,* IEEE, New York, 1975, pp. 347–357.

8. W.S. Humphrey and D.H. Kitson, "Preliminary Report on Conducting SEI-Assisted Assessments of Software-Engineering Capability," Tech. Report SEI-87-TR-16, Software Eng. Inst., Pittsburgh, July 1987.

9. W.S. Humphrey and W.L. Sweet, "A Method for Assessing the Software Engineering Capability of Contractors," Tech. Report SEI-87-TR-23, Software Eng. Inst., Pittsburgh, Sept. 1987.

SOFTWARE PROCESS IMPROVEMENT AT HUGHES AIRCRAFT

In 1987 and 1990, the Software Engineering Institute conducted process assessments of the Software Engineering Division of Hughes Aircraft in Fullerton, Calif. The first assessment found Hughes' SED to be a level 2 organization, based on the SEI's process-maturity scale of 1 to 5, where 1 is worst and 5 is best.[1]

This first assessment identified the strengths and weaknesses of the SED, and the SEI made recommendations for process improvement. Hughes then established and implemented an action plan in accordance with these recommendations. The second assessment found the SED to be a strong level 3 organization.

The assessment itself cost Hughes about $45,000, and the subsequent two-year program of improvements cost about $400,000. Hughes found that the investment improved working conditions, employee morale, and the performance of the SED as measured in project schedule and cost. Hughes estimates the resulting annual savings to be about $2 million.

In this article, we outline the assessment method used, the findings and recommendations from the initial assessment, the actions taken by Hughes, the lessons learned, and the resulting business and product consequences.

We write this article in the broad interest of software-process improvement, particularly its costs and benefits. Because its assessments are confidential, the SEI cannot publicize costs and benefits until it has amassed a large body of data. So, during the second assessment in 1990, Watts Humphrey and Terry Snyder agreed to write an article—Humphrey to provide material on the assessment process and Hughes to provide material on results and benefits.

Written by Watts S. Humphrey, Terry R. Snyder, and Ronald R. Willis. © 1991 IEEE. Reprinted , with permission, from (*IEEE Software;* 8, 4, 11–23; July/1991).

Background

The SED is one division in Hughes' Ground Systems Group. Although it is the largest dedicated software organization in the Ground Systems Group and provides contract support for many other divisions, there are other (project-related) software organizations in the group.

The SED, formed in 1978, primarily works on US Defense Dept. contracts. It employs about 500 professionals. Of these, 41 percent have 10 to 20 years experience in software and 12 percent have 20 or more years experience. The assessments described here examined only the work of the SED in Fullerton; the findings and recommendations are pertinent only to that organization. However, Hughes has capitalized on this experience to launch a broader process-improvement effort.

At the time of the 1990 assessment, the SEI had conducted 14 assessments and observed 18 self-assessments. As a result, it had gained a great deal of experience on effective methods for identifying the actual state of practice in software organizations. It is thus our opinion that the overall effect of misunderstandings and errors on these assessments was modest.

ASSESSMENT PROCESS

A process assessment helps an organization characterize the current state of its software process and provides findings and recommendations to facilitate improvement. The box titled "SEI Process Assessment Procedures," explains the SEI's process-improvement paradigm, its supporting process-maturity structure, and the principles of process assessment.

Hughes Assessments

The two Hughes assessments were conducted by teams of SEI and Hughes software professionals. In both assessments, all the team members were experienced software developers. The 1987 assessment was conducted by a team of seven: one from Hughes and six from the SEI. The 1990 assessment team included nine professionals: four from Hughes and five from the SEI. Two of the authors, Watts Humphrey and Ronald Willis, were members of both teams.

The SED team members prepared a list of candidate projects for review by the entire assessment team during training. The entire team then selected projects that it felt reasonably represented the development phases, typical project sizes and applications, and the major organization units. Six projects were reviewed in the 1987 assessment and five in 1990. Only one project was included in both assessments.

Before the assessment, the Hughes SED manager, Terry Snyder, and the SEI's process-program director, Watts Humphrey, signed confidential agreements covering the ground rules for the assessments. The key points in these agreements were:

- The SEI and the assessment team members were to keep the assessment results confidential. Hughes could use the assessment results in any way it chose.
- The SED manager agreed to participate in the opening and closing assessment meetings.
- In addition to the regular team members, the SED manager agreed that Hughes would provide needed support to handle the assessment arrangements and to lead the work on the follow-up action plan.
- The SED manager also committed Hughes to developing and implementing appropriate action plans in response to the assessment recommendations. If Hughes deemed that action was not appropriate, it was to explain its reasons to the assessment team.

After the SEI agreed to consider conducting an assessment:

- A commitment meeting was held with the SEI and the SED manager and his staff to agree on conducting the assessment and to establish a schedule.
- For both assessments, Hughes and the SEI selected the assessment team members, and the

SEI Process Assessment Procedures

To make orderly improvement, development and maintenance organizations should view their process as one that can be controlled, measured, and improved. This requires that they follow a traditional quality-improvement program such as that described by W. Edwards Deming[1].

For software, this involves the following six steps:

1. Understand the current status of their process.
2. Develop a vision of the desired process.
3. Establish a list of required process-improvement actions in priority order.
4. Produce a plan to accomplish these actions.
5. Commit the resources and execute the plan.
6. Start over at step 1.

The SEI has developed a framework to characterize the software process across five maturity levels. By establishing their organization's position in this framework, software professionals and their managers can readily identify areas where improvement actions will be most fruitful.

Many software organizations have found that this framework provides an orderly set of process improvement goals and a helpful yardstick for tracking progress. Some acquisition groups in the US Defense Dept. are also using this maturity framework and an associated SEI evaluation method called the Software Capability Evaluation to help select software contractors.

Maturity Framework

Exhibit 1 shows the SEI's software process-maturity framework. The SEI derived this empirical model from the collective experiences of many software managers and practitioners. The five maturity levels

- reasonably represent the historical phases of evolutionary improvement of actual software organizations,

- represent a measure of improvement that is reasonable to achieve from the prior level,
- suggest interim improvement goals and progress measures, and
- make obvious a set of immediate improvement priorities once an organization's status in the framework is known.

While there are many aspects to these transitions from one maturity level to another, the overall objective is to achieve a controlled and measured process as the foundation for continuous improvement.

Assessment

The process-maturity framework is intended to be used with an assessment method. A process assessment is a review of an organization's software process done by a trained team of software professionals. Its purpose is to determine the state of the organization, to identify the highest priority process issues, and to facilitate improvement actions.

The assessment process facilitates improvement by involving the managers and professionals in identifying the most critical software problems and helping them agree on the actions required to address these problems[2]. The basic objectives of an assessment are to

- learn how the organization works,
- identify its major problems, and
- enroll its opinion leaders in the change process.[3]

In SEI assessments, five or six projects are typically selected as representative samples of the organization's software process. The guiding principle for selecting projects is that they represent the mainstream software business for the organization.

EXHIBIT 1 The SEI Process-Maturity Framework

Level	Characteristics	Key Challenges	Result
5 Optimizing	• Improvement fed back into process • Data gathering is automated and used to identify weakest process elements • Numerical evidence used to justify application of technology to critical tasks • Rigorous defect-cause analysis and detect prevention	• Still human-intensive process • Maintain organization at optimizing level	Productivity & quality
4 Managed	(Quantitative) • Measured process • Minimum set of quality and productivity measurements established • Process database established with resources to analyze its data and maintain it	• Changing technology • Problem analysis • Problem prevention	
3 Defined	(Qualitative) • Process defined and institutionalized • Software Engineering Process Group established to lead process improvement	• Process measurement • Process analysis • Quantitative quality plans	
2 Repeatable	(Intuitive) • Process dependent on individuals • Established basic project controls • Strength in doing similar work, but faces major risk when presented with new challenges • Lacks orderly framework for improvement	• Training • Technical practices (reviews, testing) • Process focus (standards, process groups)	
1 Initial	(Ad hoc/chaotic process) • No formal procedures, cost estimates, project plans • No management mechanism to ensure procedures are followed, tools not well integrated, and change control is lax • Senior management does not understand key issues	• Project management • Project planning • Configuration management • Software quality assurance	Risk

SEI Process Assessment Procedures (*Cont.*)

On-site Period The on-site assessment period is an intense four "half-days": The team members are involved for more than half of each 24 hours, generally starting at 7:30 a.m. and not concluding until 10:00 or 11:00 p.m. No one has time to perform normal duties during this phase.

While this is a potentially stressful activity, the extensive training prepares the team members to make a highly productive effort and to build the cohesion and team spirit required to achieve consensus on the complex issues encountered. The dedication and enthusiasm of the assessment team also significantly contributes to their credibility to the organization and to acceptance of the findings.

Exhibit 2 shows the flow of the on-site activities during SEI process assessments. Each on-site assessment starts with a presentation to the manager, staff, and all the assessment participants. This meeting covers the assessment ground rules, assessment principles, and the schedule.

The assessment team then meets in closed session to review the questionnaire responses in preparation for the first round of discussions with project leaders. Project managers and functional experts are interviewed to clearly determine the key issues behind their responses to an SEI questionnaire.[4]

Next, a private discussion is held with each project leader to clarify any issues identified by the assessment team during its review of project responses and to request explanatory materials, if appropriate.

Next, a full day is devoted to discussions with software practitioners from selected technical areas such as requirements and high-level design, and code and unit test. Typically, about six professionals are selected from across the organization for each functional area. These functional area representatives are selected with the following criteria:

- Be considered an expert in the technical area by his or her peers.
- Be assigned to, and working on, one or more mainstream projects at the site (not necessarily a project included in the assessment).
- Be considered an opinion leader in the organization.

A second round of individual project leader meetings is then held to review the supporting materials, resolve remaining issues, and review the preliminary assessment findings. On the last day, a findings briefing is presented to senior management and all the assessment participants.

The final assessment activity is the preparation and presentation of a written report and recommendations to the site manager and staff. The recommendations highlight the assessment team's view of the highest priority items for immediate action. Following the assessment, the organization prepares and implements an action plan. In accordance with the agreement, the SEI reviews and comments on these plans.

References

1. W.E. Deming, *Out of the Crisis,* MIT Center Advanced Eng. Study, Cambridge, Mass., 1982.
2. R.A. Radice et al., "A Programming Process Study," *IBM Systems J.,* No. 2, 1985, pp. 91–101.
3. D.H. Kitson and W.S. Humphrey, "The Role of Assessment in Software Process Improvement," Tech. Report CMU/SEI-89-TR-3, Software Eng. Inst., Carnegie Mellon Univ., Pittsburgh, 1989.
4. W.S. Humphrey and W. Sweet, "A Method for Assessing the Software Engineering Capability of Contractors," Tech. Report CMU/SEI-87-TR-23, Software Eng. Inst., Carnegie Mellon Univ., Pittsburgh, 1987.

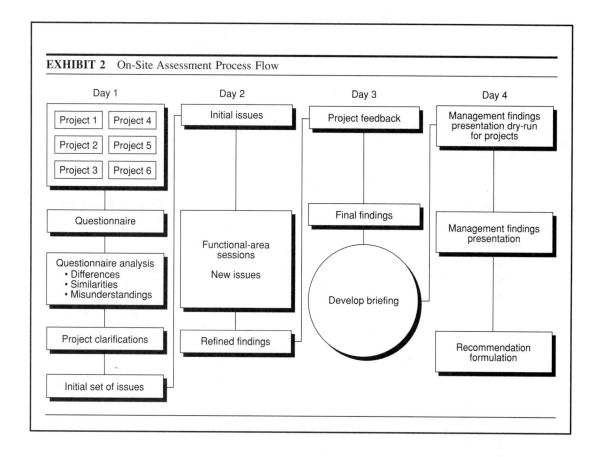

EXHIBIT 2 On-Site Assessment Process Flow

SEI trained them in its assessment method. These two-day training programs were held at the SEI, where the entire assessment team was familiarized with the assessment process and prepared for the on-site period.

• The on-site assessment was conducted.
• A detailed, written report of the assessment findings and recommendations was prepared and a briefing on the recommendations was delivered to the SED management team and all the assessment participants. In both assessments, the SED manager invited senior corporate executives to attend the briefing. Because he did not know the findings in advance, this involved some risk. However, the added understanding provided by these briefings contributed materially to the launching of a Hughes corporate-wide

process-improvement initiative modeled on the SED's work.
• The SED developed and implemented an action plan based on these recommendations.

Maturity Levels

In 1987, the assessments focused on the responses to the level 2 and level 3 questions: Because the assessment period is intentionally limited to four days, we decided to devote our attention to those areas most pertinent to the organization's perceived maturity level. This was possible because the SEI assessment process uses the questionnaire to help focus on the most informative interview topics.

In the 1990 assessment, the team briefly reviewed the level 2 responses and then interviewed the project representatives on the questions at levels 3, 4, and 5. In areas where the project responses differed or where the response pattern was atypical, the team requested more information. Because these discussions were on Tuesday afternoon and the additional materials were needed by Thursday morning, the representatives were told to bring only available working materials and not to prepare anything special.

As a consequence, we believe the team determined an organizational maturity level with a fair degree of accuracy in both the 1987 and 1990 assessments. There is, of course, the possibility that some questions were not discussed in sufficient detail to identify all misunderstandings or errors.

1987 ASSESSMENT

The first SEI assessment of six Hughes projects was conducted November 9–12, 1987. The final report, including recommendations, was presented in January 1988.

Recommendations

The assessment team made seven recommendations.

Quantitative Process Management

The assessment team found that the professionals working on the assessed projects gathered a significant amount of data on many aspects of the process. While this was important in moving the organization toward a managed software process (level 4), much of the long-term potential value of this data was lost because it was kept in multiple, disparate databases. Furthermore, the lack of a central location for this data made it difficult for project managers and professionals to know what data was available, what data should be gathered, and how it could most effectively be used for product and process improvement.

The team recommended that the SED establish the goal of achieving quantitative process management. To establish the foundation for statistical process management, this goal should include:

- Establishing a centralized database to include current and future data on cost estimates, cost experience, error data, and schedule performance. Additional process data should be included as it is gathered.
- Establishing uniform data definitions across projects.
- Augmenting the process definitions to include those key measures and analyses required at each major project milestone, together with appropriate responsibilities.
- Providing the resources needed and the responsibility assignments required for gathering, validating, entering, accessing, and supporting the projects in analyzing this data.

Process Group

The team recommended that the SED establish a technical group to be the focal point for process improvement. This group's initial tasks would be to lead the development of action plans for accomplishing the assessment team's recommendations, to lead, coordinate, and track the implementation of the action plans, and to establish the centralized process database.

Requirements

The team found that the SED generally was not involved in early system definition. Whenever software considerations were not integrated into systems engineering early in the system-definition phase, the software specifications often were ambiguous, inconsistent, untestable, and subject to frequent last-minute changes. Because in general the quality of a software product cannot exceed the quality of its requirements, the team perceived this as a critical problem.

The team recommended that the SED be involved in the specification development for all new Hughes software-intensive projects. It also suggested that systems-engineering groups attend applicable software-engineering courses.

Quality Assurance

Although the existing software quality-assurance organization at Hughes performed several necessary functions, it suffered from widely different views of its usefulness and could not fully contribute to the software-development process because it was understaffed and its personnel were not adequately trained.

To strengthen the role of SQA, the team recommended a training program that would include software-engineering principles, Hughes standard procedures, phases of the life cycle, and the functions of SQA personnel. It was also recommended that the value added by SQA be clarified for program management so it could better understand the need to allocate resources to it.

Training

The team found that Hughes had a comprehensive, company-sponsored software-engineering training program. However, the team also found that certain training categories were either not available or not being used adequately. Key examples were training for assistant project managers, review leaders, and requirements specification.

The team recommended that Hughes review its software-training requirements. The review was to conclude with plans for restructuring the current training programs, providing new subjects, creating a training priority structure, and using new training methods as appropriate. It was also recommended that Hughes consider a required training program.

Review Process

Although Hughes had made provision for technical reviews during the development process, they were not performed uniformly across all projects. So the team recommended that Hughes reassess its current review practices and determine how to assure a consistent and uniform review practice at appropriate points in the software-development process. The objective was to improve product quality, reduce reliance on testing, and improve overall project predictability and productivity.

Working Relationship

During the assessment, the working relationship with the Defense Dept.'s Defense Contract Administrative Services department was often identified as ineffective or counterproductive. It was thus recommended that the SED work to improve this relationship.

Actions Taken

Within two months of the January 1988 recommendations briefing, Hughes developed an action plan to implement the recommended improvements. As predetermined, the assessment site coordinator was the primary author for the action plan, although many people contributed to the decision and approval process.

Because implementation of the proposed actions was estimated to require a 2-percent increase in division overhead rate, it took three more months (until June 1988) to get the action plan and required funding approved by Ground Systems Group management. In so doing, top management became committed to the improvement program.

For the most part, the 1988 action plan was implemented on schedule and under budget. It took 18 months and was completed just one month before the 1990 reassessment.

Action Plan

The 1988 action plan began with a one-page summary of the assessment life cycle and the projects assessed. It then listed the goals and put the action plan in the context of a Ground Systems Group organizational improvement strategy.

The plan then detailed five improvement tasks, written as process-requirement specifications:

- Form a software-engineering process group.
- Implement quantitative process management.
- Fill in the gaps in training.
- Standardize an effective review process.
- Move toward a software-engineering discipline.

Exhibit 3 shows a part of the plan's wording. As the exhibit shows, the plan specified testable conditions for each task that, if met, would satisfy the recommended process improvements. The plan also avoided specifying solutions, to allow implementation flexibility.

EXHIBIT 3   Section 3 of Hughes SED 1988 Action Plan. The Action Plan Lists Tasks as Process-
Requirements Specifications in the Context of the Ground Systems Group

3.1   FORM SOFTWARE ENGINEERING PROCESS GROUP

3.1.1 Summary of the SEI Findings. Decentralization of the software organization into geographically isolated projects and even into separate product line divisions has impaired progress in software-technology development. Such decentralization has already affected quality-indicator data collection leading to multiple, disparate databases.

3.1.2 Requirements. The following are necessary attributes of the desired solution.

a. An organizational entity, the software-engineering process group (SEPG), exists and has the following attributes:

• serves as the focal point for software process improvement
• leader has technical credibility and influence
• staff is experienced
• initial staff size is three people
• eventual staff size is 2 percent to 3 percent of software developers
• staff is rotated every 2 to 3 years

b. The SEPG performs the following functions:

• lead development and implementation of the SEI action plan
• define/improve technical and management software practices
• lead definition of standards for software processes/products
• establish and maintain the software-process database
• initiate the definition, collection, analysis of process data
• facilitate periodic assessment of software-engineering process

• identify and promote the organization's technology needs
• establish requirements and plans for training
• research, develop, and transfer new technology
• define requirements for process automation (i.e. tools)
• facilitate periodic management reviews on state of practice

3.1.3 Responsibilities.
Manager, Software Engineering Division, forms SEPG and assigns SEPG leader, approves SEPG charter, provides funding for SEPG activities, and periodically reviews SEPG progress. Leader, Software Engineering Process Group, develops SEPG charter, develops and implements plans to accomplish 3.1.2, and recruits and selects full-time technical staff for the SEPG.

3.2   IMPLEMENT QUANTITATIVE PROCESS MANAGEMENT

3.2.1 Summary of the SEI Findings. Although data on projects is collected, it is kept in multiple, unrelated databases. The lack of a central focal point for data makes it difficult to know what data is available, what data should be gathered, and how it can be most effectively used for product and process improvement.

3.2.2. Requirements. The following are necessary attributes of the desired solution:

a. A centralized database exists that has the following attributes:

• standardized data definitions across all projects
• fed by all projects

EXHIBIT 3 *(Cont.)*

• sufficient data element types to statistically manage the software-development process

b. Software process and product standards exist that specify when and what data to collect to be able to statistically manage the software-development process.

c. Software process and product standards exist that specify analyses to be performed at each project milestone, together with appropriate responsibilities, to be able to statistically manage the software-development process.

d. An organization exists (SEPG) that provides the following services:

• gathers, validates, and enters data into the database
• controls access to the database
• supports projects in analyzing the data

e. Formal means exist to enforce these requirements.

3.2.3. Responsibilities.
Leader, Software Engineering Process Group, assigns responsibility for 3.2.2a through 3.2.2.d, ensures implementation of 3.2.2.e.

3.3 FILLS GAPS IN TRAINING PROGRAM

3.3.1 Summary of the SEI Findings. Although there is clear evidence of commitment to training, there are unfilled gaps in certain areas, opportunities for more effective training, and not enough required training (as opposed to optional training).

3.3.2 Requirements. The following are necessary attributes of the desired solution:

a. A report based on review of current training needs and training effectiveness exists and isused to modernize the existing training program. The report contains the following:

• recommended restructuring of current training program
• unfilled gaps in training curriculum
• training priorities
• recommended changes to existing training methods

b. A training curriculum exists that contains all training that is currently defined plus the following additional training subjects:

• associate program manager (APM)
• review leader (for internal reviews)
• use of engineering techniques in software development
• understanding and using software practices and procedures
• how to write good software-requirements
• how to test at the software-requirements level
• how to test at the unit level
• software quality assurance
• practical guide to the use of performance analysis

c. A directive exists that specifies training requirements in terms of specific subjects versus job position and that these training requirements be considered in annual performance evaluations.

3.3.3 Responsibilities.
Leader, Software Engineering Process Group, leads the effort to accomplish 3.3.2.a, 3.3.2.b, and 3.3.2.c. Manager, Software Engineering Division, approves and enforces the training practice developed as a result of 3.3.2.c.

EXHIBIT 3   *(Cont.)*

3.4   STANDARDIZE AN EFFECTIVE REVIEW PROCESS

3.4.1 Summary of the SEI Findings. While Hughes does include provision for reviews during the development process, reviews do not appear to be uniformly performed across projects.

3.4.2 Requirements. The following are necessary attributes of the desired solution:

a. Review standards exist as part of the directive system. They include the following:

• overall review practice (i.e., what reviews, when, who is responsible)
• specific criteria to be used in each review
• procedures for conducting reviews
• required data collection and reporting from reviews

b. Required training curriculum includes review-leader training.

3.4.3 Responsibilities.
Leader, Software Engineering Process Group, leads the effort to accomplish 3.4.2.a and 3.4.2.b. Manager, Software Engineering Division, approves and enforces the standards developed as a result of 3.4.2.b.

3.5   MOVE TOWARD SOFTWARE-ENGINEERING DISCIPLINE

3.5.1 Summary of the SEI Findings. Software engineering is not uniformly treated as an engineering discipline. There are several aspects to this problem, including lack of early software involvement in systems definition, lack of the use of experimentation (i.e., prototyping) as an engineering tool, and skipping software development steps when schedule pressures increase. On several of the projects studied, software engineering is appropriately addressing these systems-engineering concerns, and software engineering is treated as an engineering discipline; however, on other projects, this was found not to be the case.

3.5.2 Requirements. The following are necessary attributes of the desired solution:

a. Software-development plans for all new projects include an approved budget and task for software-engineering participation in system design and software-requirements specification.

b. System engineers are invited and attend appropriate software-engineering training classes.

c. All required software-development steps are carried out, regardless of schedule pressure.

3.5.3 Responsibilities.
Software Associate Program Managers (APMs) implement 3.5.2.a and 3.5.2.c.
Manager, Software Engineering Division, ensures 3.5.2.a and 3.5.2.c. Leader, Software Engineering Process Group, leads the effort to accomplish 3.5.2.b.

Two of the SEI's recommendations were not included in the action plan because they involved organizations not under SED control. The first, to strengthen SQA, dealt with a function that was in another division of Hughes. Although the SED was striving to regain a centralized SQA function that would be under its control, it had not yet achieved that reorganization and therefore could not guarantee the outcome. (Later, the SED did achieve a centralized SQA organization.)

The second recommendation not included, to improve relations with Defense Contract Administrative Services, again dealt with an organization over which the SED had no control. To negotiate an effective interface with the DCAS was not something Hughes could guarantee, so it was excluded from the action plan. (However, an effective interface was later negotiated.)

The action plan then estimated the labor for implementation to be 100 man-months over 18 months, divided into six major functions:

- process-group leader: 8 percent,
- process definition: 6 percent,
- technology development: 28 percent,
- quantitative-process management: 41 percent,
- training: 16 percent, and
- review-process standardization: 1 percent.

Budget cuts later reduced the 100 man-months of labor to 78. Not included in these estimates were other direct charges for such things as computers, office space, and training facilities, and the existence of certain services such as training and central computer facilities.

Process Group

In June 1988, the idea of an SEPG was relatively new at the SEI. Although the concept was well-understood, the implementation was assumed to require that certain roles be organized into a separate function focused on process-technology improvement.

At first, Hughes didn't understand the process-group concept very well, so it tried to implement this SEI approach literally. Also, Hughes' experience with centralizing technology improvement was that, over time, walls of miscommunication developed, leading to just the opposite of technology transfer.

However, on further examination, it was found that the SED, a high level 2 organization with significant progress toward level 3, already had formal roles in place for many process-group functions. All but three functions (action-plan implementation, technology transfer, and development of a required training policy) were either in place or being formed independently of the action plan. Hughes just didn't call it a process group.

To implement the action plan, Hughes issued a bulletin that created the process group, named the existing major functions, and named the person responsible for each function. The bulletin was enlightening to those who understood both what already existed and the SEI's concept of a process group because it made the concept tangible.

The process group, however, was not yet complete. Three key additions brought it all together as an effective focus for process improvement:

- Technology steering committee. Although the technology steering committee already existed, Hughes did not fully understand its role as a process-group driving function. Given the newly established functions and responsibilities, the process group did not have one person as a leader but instead was directed by the technology steering committee. Thus, it became the committee's job to develop technology road maps, assess current technology, evaluate the overall direction, and make general technology-policy decisions.
- Technology management. Hughes' practices and procedures addressed people management, project management, resource management, and management of other *things,* but not management of *technology.* One of the first improvements was to formalize the management of technology, as with any other corporate resource. This was done through brainstorming and consensus decision making. The plans were recorded as a new practice, technology management.
- Technology transfer. A new job function, head of technology transfer, was created and staffed with a full-time person. It was soon clear that the establishment of this function was the most profound action in the entire improvement process. It is not clear if the very positive effect of this action was due to the person's abilities, the existence of the function, or just the timing—but without a doubt this function had more effect than any other single improvement.

Among other things, the head of technology transfer coordinated self-assessments, developed a questionnaire glossary, became the local expert in the SEI maturity questionnaire, became a member of the Software Productivity Consortium's technology-transfer advisory group, developed an SPC technology-transfer plan, briefed senior management on the state of process maturity, maintained a database of technology used on each project and an awareness of what technology each project needed, facilitated technology transfer among projects, ran a special-interest group on process improvement, supported the corporate-wide technology-transfer program, and served on the practices and procedures change-review board, the training policy committee, and the technology steering committee.

Two other additions to the process group that were very helpful were a training committee to periodically review training requirements and their effectiveness and a special-interest group on process improvement. These groups met as needed to find and fix process problems.

Quantitative Process Management

Before the 1988 action plan, the SED collected "quality indicators" in response to a company-wide push for total quality management. These indicators were error or defect counts, categorized into types, shown in bar graphs with descending importance, and used in postanalyses to isolate where improvement was needed. Each project collected its own data in its own format.

The new approach called for senior management to be briefed every month on the health of each project. To do this, information was collected from each project and compiled into a report that included the project's accomplishments, problems, program trouble reports, quality indicators, scope changes, resource needs, and lessons learned. Also presented were plots of actual versus planned values over time to show the project's schedule, milestones, rate chart, earned value, financial/labor status, and target-system resource use.

The SED implemented a new, division-wide quantitative process-management function and selected one person to be its champion. It standardized the data collected and the reports produced with it, centralized its error-and-defect database, and established a technology center for process-data analysis.

This effort firmly ingrained error-and-defect data collection and analysis into the Hughes culture. It provided the capability required for level 3 maturity and serves as a foundation for future improvement. But time and budget constraints caused it to fall short of achieving all the goals. Some capabilities not achieved are

- collecting historical data to support predictions,
- projecting analyses within the context of division-wide data,
- automating data collection and reporting, and
- optimizing data collection based on business needs.

Training Gaps

The SED also implemented an organizational policy for required training. Although a policy for required training was not achievable the first time it was tried in 1985, by 1988 the time was right to make it work. (Hughes made training a job requirement, not a promotion requirement, thus solving the equal-employment-opportunity problem that stalled the 1985 effort.)

The company's thrust in continuous measurable improvement and total quality management, combined with the SED manager's personal belief in training resulted in a new policy that required training for all software engineers in the division. To support the new requirement, the SED implemented a training-records database that recorded the training status of each employee yearly, at about the time of performance appraisals, and it established a training committee to periodically review training requirements and effectiveness.

Before the 1988 action plan, the SED's internal formal training classes included 17 on modern programming practices, 51 on programming languages and CASE tools, and three on job-specific topics. Enrollment was first-come, first-served. Although training was encouraged and well attended, it was not required.

Although the action plan suggested specific additions to the training program, the SED surveyed its employees to establish what new training was needed. Based on that survey, it added classes on project management, internal reviews, requirements writing, requirements- and unit-level testing, and quality assurance. All these courses had been developed and conducted several times by the 1990 reassessment.

The training programs were open to all engineering functions. Attendance was advertised to and encouraged for all engineers. As of November 1989, 20 percent (174) of the attendees at the training classes were from organizations outside the SED.

Standardized Reviews

Before the 1988 action plan, Hughes had established an overall technical-review practice, review criteria, review reporting, data-collection procedures, and the requirement to have a quality-evaluation plan for each project.

Despite these practices, the assessment revealed that the review process was inconsistent. The 1988 action plan included a standard procedure for conducting reviews as well as the training of review leaders in how to conduct reviews. Both were completed in 1989.

Software-Engineering Discipline

The 1988 action plan required that software engineers be involved in the system-engineering process, that system engineers become more involved with software, and that software engineers use traditional engineering techniques such as prototypes and experimentation.

The SED could not require that the system-engineering organization implement these changes because system engineering was not under its control.

Instead, the plan required that the SED participate in the system-engineering process, with the realization that some system-engineering organizations might be reluctant to accept its help. In those cases where software engineers were involved with system design, considerably fewer problems occurred and better products resulted.

1990 REASSESSMENT

Early in 1989, Hughes asked the SEI to conduct a second assessment of the SED. The SEI's resources are limited and it can conduct only a few assessments per year, but the opportunity to evaluate a major software organization at two points in its process-improvement program interested the SEI greatly.

The findings and recommendations from the second assessment indicated that substantial improvements had been implemented. From level 2 in 1987, Hughes had progressed to being a strong level 3, with many activities in place to take it to level 4 and 5.

Improvements included the formation of a process group, key training actions, and a comprehensive technical review process. The assessment concluded that Hughes had achieved a strong position of software-process leadership and had established the foundation for continuing process improvement.

The assessment team also found that the professional staff was committed to high-quality software work and that it demonstrated disciplined adherence to the established process.

Findings

The SEI made five basic findings in the second assessment:

- The SED's role in the Ground Systems Group. The software-engineering process was constrained by lead program managers' misunderstandings of software issues.
- Requirements specifications. The SED had become involved in specifying software requirements for some, but not all, projects.
- Process data. The SED had made substantial progress in gathering data, but the progress still required solidification. For example, it needed more assistance for data application and analysis.

(Although data analysis at the project level was maturing, division-wide data analysis was limited.)

- Process automation. The SED had improved its CASE technologies, but the team found that improvement in six areas would reduce the drudgery and labor of recurring tasks: unit-test procedure generation, execution and analysis of regression tests, path-coverage analysis, CASE-tool evaluation, tool expertise, and tool- and method-effectiveness evaluation.
- Training. Training was identified as an organizational strength. However, the team found that additional training was needed to help the projects effectively use the process data being gathered.

Recommendations

The team made six recommendations.

Process Awareness
Enhance the awareness and understanding of the software process within lead divisions and Ground Systems Group management.

Process Automation
Establish a project-oriented mechanism to assess tool needs and effectiveness, develop or acquire automation support where needs assessment justifies its use, provide ongoing information on CASE availability and capabilities, and make tools expertise available to the projects.

Process-Data Analysis
Expand the process-data analysis technology to include error projection, train employees to analyze project-specific process data, develop a division-wide context for interpreting project-specific data, and ensure that process data is not used to evaluate individuals.

Data-Collection/-Analysis Use
Optimize process data collection and analysis to best benefit product and business results.

Requirements Process
Continue efforts to increase participation in the software-requirements process, update SED bidding practice to require SED input and participation in requirements generation, and increase the skill level of software engineers in writing requirements.

Quality Assurance
Ensure adequate SQA support for SED software efforts. In particular, it should ensure that Ground Systems Group SQA practices are consistently applied on all efforts in which the SED is responsible for the software and that the level of SQA effort is sufficient to support each project's needs.

ASSESSMENT COMPARISON

The SEI has compiled data on all the assessments it has conducted in its *State of the Software Engineering Practice*[2]. Exhibits 4 and 5 detail the two Hughes assessment results compared with the state-of-the-practice data for level 2 and level 3 questions. (Because there was insufficient data on level 4 and 5 questions at the time of the state-of-the-practice report, we cannot include this comparison.)

To provide a valid comparison between the two SED assessments, we used the same SEI questionnaire in both assessments. In 1987, the SED met the level 2 criteria in all important aspects. As Exhibit 4 shows, of the six projects assessed, there were only four negative answers to two of the 12 key level 2 questions. In other words, of 72 answers, 68 were yes. In 1987, the SED could not answer yes to many key level 3 questions, as Exhibit 4 also shows. Exhibit 5 shows the more interesting changes in the key level 4 questions between the two assessments.

We drew several conclusions from these results. First, in 1987 there was not agreement among projects on some organization-wide questions. For example, in Exhibit 4 questions 1.1.7, 1.2.3, and 1.2.5 concern the total organization, not individual projects. In all cases, these responses should have been 0 percent. Similarly, in Exhibit 5, questions

EXHIBIT 4   Comparison of Responses to Level 2 and Level 3 Questions (Percentage of Positive Responses)

Question		1987 assessment	1990 assessment	Average Response (From State of the Practice)
Level 2				
2.1.4	Is a formal procedure used to make estimates of software size?	50	100	33
2.2.2	Are profiles of software size maintained for each software configuration item over time?	83	100	36
Level 3				
1.1.7	Is there a software-engineering process group or function?	50	100	69
1.2.3	Is there a required software-engineering training program for software developers?	50	100	44
1.2.5	Is a formal training program required for design- and code-review leaders?	0	100	12
2.4.13	Is a mechanism used for controlling changes to the software design?	50	100	100
2.4.19	Is a mechanism used for verifying that the samples examined by software quality assurance are truly representative of the work performed?	33	100	69
2.4.21	Is there a mechanism for assuring the adequacy of regression testing?	33	80	23

1.3.4, 2.3.1, 2.3.8, and 2.4.2 relate to the entire organization. Here, the numbers should have been 0 percent for the first three and 100 percent for 2.4.2.

Second, the analysis and error-projection activities asked about in the level 4 questions typically are difficult and require extensive training and support. Because the intent is to focus attention on the key error causes, to build understanding of these critical factors, and gradually to establish the means to control them, considerable data analysis and experience is required before proficiency can be expected.

LESSONS LEARNED

Hughes learned 11 important lessons from the SED process-improvement effort, listed here in order of importance.

Management Commitment

The path to improvement requires investment, risk, time, and the pain of cultural change. Delegation is not strong enough to overcome these roadblocks. Commitment is. Process improvement should be tied to the salary or promotion criteria of senior management.

EXHIBIT 5   Comparison of Responses to Level 4 Questions (Percentage of Positive Responses)

	Question	*1987 Assessment*	*1990 Assessment*
1.3.4	Is a mechanism used for managing and supporting the introduction of new technologies?	16	100
2.2.5	Are design errors projected and compared to actuals?	16	20
2.2.6	Are code and test errors projected and compared to actuals?	16	20
2.2.14	Is test coverage measured and recorded for each phase of functional testing?	83	100
2.3.1	Has a managed and controlled process database been established for process metrics data across all projects?	50	100
2.3.2	Are the review data gathered during design reviews analyzed?	16	100
2.3.3	Is the error data from code reviews and tests analyzed to determine the likely distribution and characteristics of the errors remaining in the product?	16	20
2.3.4	Are analyses of errors conducted to determine their process-related causes?	83	100
2.3.8	Is review efficiency analyzed for each project?	50	100
2.4.2	Is a mechanism used for periodically assessing the software-engineering process and implementing indicated improvements?	83	100

Pride Is the Most Important Result

Improvements are one-time achievements, but pride feeds on itself and leads to continuous measurable improvement. When the whole organization buys into the improvement and sees the results unfold, it gains a team esprit de corps and from that, pride. Hughes' people pulled together to improve the entire organization's software process and they all share in the success.

Increases in Maturity Decrease Risk

Another, important benefit (and goal) of process maturation is decreased risk of missing cost and schedule estimates. The two concepts of risk and process maturity are closely coupled. As an organization matures, its performance in meeting planned costs and schedules improves.

The indicator the SED uses for cost risk, and the indicator for which there is historical data available, is a cost-performance index, which is calculated as CPI = BCWP/ACWP, where BCWP is the budgeted cost of work performed and ACWP is the actual cost of work performed.

The CPI has shown a steady improvement, from 0.94 in July 1987 to 0.97 in March 1990. In other words, in July 1987 the SED averaged about 6 percent actual costs over budgeted costs; in March 1990 it had reduced this average to 3 percent. This 50-percent reduction nets Hughes about $2 million annually. These values are averages for all SED projects at the time.

When considering all the direct labor, support, overhead, travel, and equipment costs for the assessment and improvement costs, these first-year benefits are five times the total improvement expenditures.

Assuming that the Hughes maturity is at least maintained, these financial benefits should continue to accrue. Furthermore, the improved contract performance makes Hughes' estimates of software cost more credible during contract negotiations.

The Benefits Are Worth the Effort and Expense

When the improvement effort was begun in 1988, Hughes was not sure what the benefits would be, other than achieving the next higher level on the process-maturity model. However, Hughes received a handsome return on its investment: The quality of work life has improved, and the company's image has benefited from the improved performance.

The SED has experienced very few crises at the Ground Systems Group facility since applying a mature process to each project. Although volatile requirements continue to be a persistent engineering problem, the effect of shifting requirements on cost and schedule is under control and reliably predictable.

A less quantifiable result of process maturity is the quality of work life. Hughes SED has seen fewer overtime hours, fewer gut-wrenching problems to deal with each day, and a more stable work environment. Even in the volatile aerospace industry in California, software-professional turnover has been held below 10 percent.

Software Technology Center Is Key

A software technology center works most effectively when most of the development, project management, administration, technology development, training, and marketing are housed in one organization.

The size and focus of such a central organization makes it possible to afford, for example, an SEPG that focuses on technology improvement, a full-time person in charge of technology transfer, an organization-wide data-collection and -analysis service, independent software research and development, and a CASE center. All these are important contributors to improving process maturity.

A Coherent Culture Exists at Level 3

A coherent organizational culture results from the cumulative effect of a long-lived organization with a common purpose, environment, education, and experience base. You can quickly sense the nature of an organization's culture when you hear people speaking in the same technical language, sharing common practices and procedures, and referring to organizational goals as their own.

At level 3, Hughes found that the common culture helped foster an esprit de corps that reinforced team performance. In fact, Hughes concluded it needed to achieve a common process across the organization, to establish an organization-wide training program, and to enable buy-in of organizational goals. Although it is difficult to precisely phrase a question to determine if an organization does or does not have such a positive culture, an assessment team can agree whether or not team members experienced it during an assessment.

A Focal Point Is Essential

Disintegrated, asynchronous improvement is not only inefficient but also ineffective for solving organization-wide problems. Although there is still the need for cell-level improvement teams, there must also be an organizational focal point to plan, coordinate (integrate), and implement organization-wide process improvements. The SEI calls this focal point an SEPG. Hughes calls it the technology steering committee, others might call it an engineering council. Whatever the name, there must be a focal point.

Technology Transfer Is Essential

The establishment of a technology-transfer function was judged the most profound of the actions taken.

Software-Process Expertise Is Essential

In 1987, the SEI questionnaire and a few SEI professionals were all the expert help there was. Now there is a growing literature on software process, a draft capability maturity model, and an improved draft questionnaire. Many SEI people are experts in software process, and even more people in industry have become experts in software process[1].

To understand and use the available knowledge, process-improvement teams must become process experts and they must be able to interpret the assessment questionnaire in the context of the organization. For example, the SED wrestled over the ambiguity of the phrase "first-line managers" in the questionnaire. In the Hughes organization, "manager" is used only for the third promotion level and above in the line-management hierarchy, but this isn't what the SEI meant. After discussions with the SEI over the meaning of the phrase, Hughes concluded that it meant the first supervisory position for software engineers, a position Hughes called group head.

Because group heads did not sign off on schedules and cost estimates, Hughes considered changing their practices to require the heads to do so. However, Hughes found that some software projects have eight people, while others might include an entire lab of 250 people with several sections and many groups. It thus did not always seem appropriate to have group heads approve schedules and cost estimates.

Hughes finally concluded that "first-line manager" in the Hughes culture meant associate project manager, the person who is in charge of software development on a project (no matter what level), and the one who negotiates and approves schedules and cost estimates with the program manager, documenting those agreements in a work authorization and delegation document. Hughes SED thus translated the question "Do software first-line managers sign off on their schedules and cost estimates?" as "Do associate project managers approve work authorization and delegation documents?"

An Action Plan Is Necessary

An action plan based on process-maturity assessment recommendations will not necessarily move an organization to the next stage of maturity. Assessment recommendations come from a brainstorming and consensus-building team process that, because of the nature of the process and the time limitations, can address only the top priority recommendations (about 10 out of 36 in the last assessment). Furthermore, action plans tend to not include many people-oriented changes (such as getting people to buy in on changes) that are needed for progress.

The Only Ones Questioning the Value of
Level 2 Are Those Who Have Not Achieved It

To an organization that has achieved it, level 2 capabilities seem obvious and indispensable. It is simply a natural, responsible way of conducting business.

When compared with those of the general population of SEI-assessed organizations, it is clear that the 1987 Hughes improvement efforts started from a very strong base. Based on the SEI data, the Hughes process in 1987 was in approximately the 90th percentile of all organizations studied[2].

It is also clear that given sufficient management emphasis and competent, skilled, and dedicated professionals, significant improvement in software process is possible. Improvements like those made at Hughes' SED can significantly help a software organization's overall business performance. The SEI assessment of Hughes' SED formed the bases for a sustained improvement effort.

Finally, improvement is reinforcing. As each improvement level is reached, the benefits are demonstrated and the opportunities for further improvement become clear.

References

1. W.S. Humphrey, *Managing the Software Process,* Addison-Wesley, Reading, Mass., 1989.
2. W.S. Humphrey, D.H. Kitson, and T.C. Kasse, "The State of Software-Engineering Practice: A Preliminary Report," Tech. Report CMU/SEI-89-TR-1, Software Eng. Inst., Carnegie Mellon Univ., Pittsburgh, 1989.

SEI CAPABILITY MATURITY MODEL'S IMPACT ON CONTRACTORS

Many government agencies, led by the Department of Defense, are assertive in demanding better software development within their own organizations and from private industry. The most notable effort concerns the five level Capability Maturity Model (CMM) developed for the government by the Software Engineering Institute. This model includes procedures for "assessments" and the somewhat controversial "evaluations." In a letter dated September 25, 1991, the Department of the Air Force, Rome Laboratory, Griffiss Air Force Base, notified selected computer software contractors who bid for and work on US government contracts:

> We wish to point out that at some point in the near future, all potential software developers will be required to demonstrate a software maturity Level 3 before they can compete in ESD/RL [Electronic Systems Division/Rome Laboratory] major software development initiatives . . . Now is the time to start preparing for this eventuality.

Industry has reacted with both favorable and unfavorable opinions. The letter has generated or at least accelerated major new undertakings by contractors, but also may have caused some fear and turmoil. Studies concerned with using the CMM purport to demonstrate software product improvement at reduced cost. Criticisms include the model's questionable suitability, its lack of a requirement for Total Quality Management techniques, and the associated intrusion by evaluation teams in the private corporate domain. Nevertheless, companies are responding to this government initiative.

The recent general emphasis on software engineering within the contracting environment, with specific emphasis on CMM compliance, is the most pervasive effort to improve software processes that we've seen in our more than 30 years of continuous association with software development. Only time will tell whether this undertaking will actually produce major positive results or whether its current high visibility will be allowed to gradually fade. But undoubtedly the government *can* cause major changes in the software contracting industry and, if it continues with the spirit and intent of the above quote, probably will.

SOFTWARE PROCESS MATURITY

Software Process Maturity is a model developed by the Software Engineering Institute (SEI) at Carnegie Mellon University. This model attempts to quantify a software organization's capability to consistently and predictably produce high-quality software products.

Historically, software efforts emphasized products such as operating systems and new languages or techniques such as transaction processing. Today, software pervades all aspects of life, but the "expert" consensus is that software development methods are generally very poor. Software engineering has emerged to bring engineering principles and discipline to what has traditionally been an art or craft.

The US government—more specifically, the Department of Defense (DoD)—has always been a major software purchaser and has contended with poor software, missed schedules, and high costs.

Article by Hossein Saiedian and Richard Kuzara. © 1995 IEEE. Reprinted, with permission, from (*IEEE Computer;* 16–26; January/1995).

An unpublished review of 17 major DoD software contracts found that the average 28-month schedule was missed by 20 months, one four-year project was not delivered for seven years, and no project was on time[1]. In 1982, the DoD formed a joint-service task force to analyze its software problems. Initiatives included establishing the SEI and developing the well-known Ada Program. But recent years have seen an order-of-magnitude growth in software size and complexity, making it impossible to upgrade current software techniques without a fundamental process change.

In 1984, the SEI was established to address the DoD's need for improved software. Data collected by the SEI indicated that most US software-development organizations do not possess or use a defined, shared development model[2]. As a result, the Software Process Maturity Model was developed for DoD and industrial-software organizations. The Air Force asked the Mitre Corporation to participate in this effort, and the SEI-Mitre team produced a questionnaire and framework for evaluating organizations on the maturity of their software processes. This effort combined previous industry work with W. Edward Deming's principles and Walter A. Shewhart's process management concepts (described in Deming's book, *Out of Crisis*).

In 1991, the SEI produced the Capability Maturity Model. The CMM serves as a framework to continuously evolve and improve the related SEI questionnaire. A Questionnaire Advisory Board has been established to review SEI work and determine whether proposed changes to this work are suitable. To balance the needs and interests of those most affected, this board includes both US industry and government members.

Capability Maturity Model

The CMM is a five-level model (see Exhibit 1)[3]. The model is designed so that capabilities at lower stages provide progressively stronger foundations for higher stages. Each development stage—or "maturity level"—distinguishes an organization's software process capability.

EXHIBIT 1   Capability Maturity Model Levels

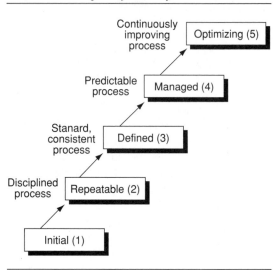

The CMM and the associated questionnaire have two major uses: assessments and evaluations[1]. With assessments, organizations use the maturity model to study their own operations and identify the highest priority areas for improvement. Results form the basis for an organization's self-improvement action plan. Acquisition agencies use the maturity model to identify qualified bidders and monitor existing contracts. Results help develop a risk profile that augments the traditional criteria used to select the most responsive and capable vendors.

CMM Levels

For easy reference, the five CMM levels have been abbreviated as initial, repeatable, defined, managed, and optimizing. These levels have been selected by the SEI because they[1]

• reasonably represent historical phases of evolutionary improvement,

• provide achievable improvement steps in reasonable sequence,

• suggest interim improvement goals and progress measures, and

- provide immediate improvement priorities once an organization's status in this framework is known.

Generally, the levels are characterized and distinguished as

1. *Initial:* While there are many degrees of management control, the first step is to roughly predict schedules and costs. This level has been described with many different catchy phrases such as "ad hoc," and "chaotic." Bollinger and McGowan[4] refer to it as "really not even a level at all, but the logical equivalent of an F—a failing grade." Until the process is under management control, orderly progress in process improvement is not possible.
2. *Repeatable:* The organization has achieved a stable process with a repeatable management control level by initiating rigorous project management of commitments, costs, schedules, and changes.
3. *Defined:* The organization has defined the process as a basis for consistent implementation and better understanding. At this point, the risk of introducing advanced technology is greatly reduced.
4. *Managed:* The organization has initiated comprehensive process measurements and analysis. This is when the most significant quality improvements begin.
5. *Optimizing:* The organization now has a foundation for continuously improving and optimizing the process.

Key Process Areas

Each CMM level except Level 1 includes key process areas (KPAs) that identify where an organization must focus to raise software processes to that level. (Because KPAs are the requirements for achieving a maturity level, no KPAs are defined for achieving Level 1.) When an organization collectively performs the activities defined by KPAs, it can achieve goals considered important for enhancing process capability. All KPAs include both project and organization responsibilities, but primarily the project is responsible for addressing many KPAs. Exhibit 2 shows the KPAs for each maturity level. Each KPA is subdivided into (1) goals, (2) commitment to perform, (3) ability to perform, (4) activities performed, (5) measurement and analysis, and (6) verification of implementation. (Additional details are available in Paulk et al.[3])

Each area except goals is further defined by specific statements applicable to the area. These statements are used to judge whether the specific contract or project meets the expressed criteria. Judgments are performed by working-level personnel and first-level management who control performance on the contract. For statements to be considered met, "hard evidence" demonstrating verification of statement intent must be provided.

EXHIBIT 2   Key Process Areas by Maturity Level

Level 5: Optimizing	Defect prevention Technology-change management Process-change management
Level 4: Managed	Quantitative process management Software quality management
Level 3: Defined	Organization process focus Organization process definition Training program Integrated-software management Software product engineering Intergroup coordination Peer reviews
Level 2: Repeatable	Requirements management Software project planning Software project tracking and oversight Software subcontract management Software quality assurance Software configuration management

Basically, hard evidence refers to a philosophy statement about how something is done and evidence that the philosophy is consistently performed. An evaluation team will require hard evidence when judging the CMM level of a company or contract. What appears to be hard evidence to some, may not be to others. For example, a project may use a programmer notebook to specify exactly how a code inspection must be performed, but this alone is probably insufficient as hard evidence. In addition, a report for each inspected code module should specify a check or verification block for each code inspection step and should contain verification-personnel signatures along with the dates that steps were performed.

This stage's end result is to identify the specific statements within each KPA that are or are not currently being accomplished. For those being accomplished, hard evidence is identified and collected. This serves to guide the next process improvement stage: developing action plans to address process deficiencies.

Assessments

A software process assessment is initiated by an organization to help improve its software development practices. The assessment is generally conducted by six to eight of the organization's senior software-development professionals and by one or two coaches from the SEI or from an SEI-licensed assessment vendor. The assessment is typically conducted in six phases[1]:

1. In the selection phase, the organization is identified as an assessment candidate, and the qualified assessing organization conducts an executive-level briefing.

2. In the commitment phase, the organization commits to the full assessment process when a senior executive signs an assessment agreement.

3. In the preparation phase, the organization's assessment team receives training, and the on-site assessment process is fully planned. All assessment participants are identified and briefed. The maturity questionnaire is filled out at this time.

4. In the assessment phase, the on-site assessment is conducted in about one week. Then the assessment team meets to formulate preliminary recommendations.

5. In the report phase, the entire assessment team helps prepare the final report and present it to assessment participants and senior management. The report includes team findings and recommendations for actions.

6. In the assessment follow-up phase, the assessed organization's team, with guidance from the assessment organization, formulates an action plan. After approximately 18 months, the organization should do a reassessment to assess progress and sustain the software process improvement cycle.

The assessment represents a major resource commitment by the organization and can be accomplished only with senior management's honest commitment and involvement. The assessing organization treats the assessment and its results as confidential information. The organization being assessed controls the assessment information and its exposure.

Evaluations

In contrast to the voluntary, confidential assessment process (described above), a software capability evaluation (SCE) is typically conducted by an outside organization such as the government or a software contractor. It is intended to help the acquisition agency understand the management and engineering processes used by a bidder. It is assumed that the bidder will submit to the SCE process if it wishes to win the contract on which it bid.

Organizations that are candidates for an SCE first complete a maturity questionnaire. An evaluation team visits the organization and uses the maturity questionnaire to help select representative practices for a detailed examination. This examination generally consists of interviewing the organization's personnel and reviewing the organization's software-development-related documentation. By investigating processes used in the organization's current projects, the team can highlight specific records for review and quickly identify potential risk areas. Potential risk categories[1] considered include the likelihood that

- the proposed processes will meet the acquisition needs,
- the organization will actually install the proposed processes, and
- the organization will effectively implement the proposed processes.

The SCE is a very judgmental process, and it is mandatory that all organizations for a single contract be evaluated consistently. The SEI believes that the SCE method provides the needed consistent criteria and method.

Evaluations require significant time, travel, and other resources. The acquisition agency and its evaluation team spend many weeks preparing for and performing evaluations. The organization being evaluated is significantly impacted if it is interested in a successful evaluation. It will expend much effort emphasizing its strengths. Its personnel will be warned and briefed. Documentation and files will be organized and made ready. During the evaluation, interviewed personnel will be under great pressure to respond honestly but with properly chosen words. Some may feel that if they answer incorrectly, they'll be responsible for losing the contract. This is not to imply that organizations intentionally deceive evaluation teams, but the organization and its personnel can be expected to present the most favorable image possible.

What the CMM Does Not Address

The CMM is based on the premise that major software-development problems and, hence, causes for software project failures are managerial rather than technical. The CMM applies process management and quality-improvement techniques to software development and maintenance and therefore models organizational process improvement. The CMM, however, is not an exhaustive model or "silver bullet." It does not address several software management and engineering practices important

for successful projects. For example, the CMM does not yet directly address expertise in a particular application domain; advocate specific tools, methods, or software technologies; or address issues related to human resources (such as how to select, hire, motivate, and retain competent people). Neither does it address issues related to concurrent engineering, teamwork, change management, or systems engineering. The authors of the CMM Version 1.1 acknowledge the above deficiencies in Paulk et al.[3]

There are other maturity models besides the CMM. One notable example is Capers Jones's model, considered by some as comparable or even superior to the CMM and purported to be widely used in the commercial sector. The ISO standard 9001 specifies quality assurance guidelines for software-system design, development, installation, and servicing. Since the CMM has its roots in government systems and defense-oriented software industry areas, it makes certain assumptions that may not be true in the commercial sector. This has prompted certain companies, such as Digital, to extend the CMM and make it applicable to their own process improvement efforts.

INDUSTRY OPINIONS

As might be expected, opinions about the CMM and its associated assessments and evaluations include pro and con, with many shades of gray. Favorable opinions run from a lukewarm "it's better than nothing" to the rousing "achieving maturity saves millions." Unfavorable opinions typically cite individual deficiencies in the SEI model but do not appear to prove that it is worse than no model at all.

Favorable

One of the most detailed—and, apparently, carefully controlled—studies on implementing the SEI model concerns an assessment, actions, and reassessment at Hughes Aircraft's Software Engineering Division[5]. The SEI assessed six Hughes projects during November 9–12, 1987. The

Case Studies of Hughes and Raytheon's CMM Efforts

The software community has reached a stage where it has begun to formally define the software development process and the most effective ways to improve it. Several new "maturity" models have been proposed, but without quantitative evaluations it will be difficult to truly assess their impact. The SEI Capability Maturity Model is no exception. In fact, only a few quantitative studies have been conducted to evaluate the CMM's capability to improve the quality and predictability of software development, as well as its cost-effectiveness and return on investment. Following is a summary of two major case studies that offer concrete figures for CMM efforts at Hughes and Raytheon.

What They Accomplished

Hughes Aircraft's two-year program to raise its Software Engineering Division from level 2 to level 3 cost the company roughly $400,000 (75 person-months) from 1987–1990, a 2-percent increase in division overhead. This was allocated among six major functions:

- process-group leader (8 percent),
- process definition (6 percent),
- technology development (28 percent),
- quantitative process management (41 percent),
- training (16 percent), and
- review-process standardization (1 percent)[1].

Hughes calculated that its initial return on this investment amounted to $2 million annually based on a 50-percent reduction (from 0.94 to 0.97 percent) of its cost-performance index (budgeted cost of work performed/actual cost)[1-2]. The business value of this investment was 4.5:1[2]. Hughes' CPI continued to improve through 1992, climbing from 0.97 to 1.02, to the point where projects as a whole were under budget[2]. Hughes attributes these savings to the new processes' early detection of defects, which substantially reduced rework costs. According to Herbsleb et al[2]. savings at each stage for rework amounted to about

- 44 percent for preliminary design,
- 96 percent for detailed design,
- 83 percent for coding,
- 60 percent for unit tests, and
- 58 percent for integration tests[2].

Raytheon's numbers are even more remarkable. Investing almost $1 million annually in process improvements, Raytheon achieved a 7.7:1 ROI (a $4.48 million return on $0.58 million) and 2:1 productivity gains (see Exhibit 3)[3]. Although allocation patterns change with perceived need, in 1992 funds were allocated as follows: policy and procedures, 18 percent; training, 23 percent; tools and methods, 30 percent; process database, 29 percent. Staffing is predominantly part-time and totals about 15 people per year, with one or two full-time personnel. Raytheon states that it has eliminated $15.8 million in rework costs (from 41 to 11 percent) on 15 projects tracked between 1988–1992 (see Exhibit 4).

How They Accomplished It

These two case studies also lend substance to the types of process improvements deliberately left unspecified in CMM Version 1.1. Despite being tailored for specific business environments, the two process improvement plans share family resemblances based on the CMM model. Because the model requires senior management buy-in, the companies adopted a top-down approach, establishing what is commonly called a Software Engineering Process Group (SEPG) to develop, coordinate, and track the process improvement plans. The SEPG works to standardize policies and procedures, oversees

Case Studies of Hughes and Raytheon's CMM Efforts (*Cont.*)

EXHIBIT 3 Average Increase in Productivity on 18 Raytheon Projects (Measured in Equivalent Delivered Source Instructions Per Person-Month). Figure Courtesy of *IEEE Software*

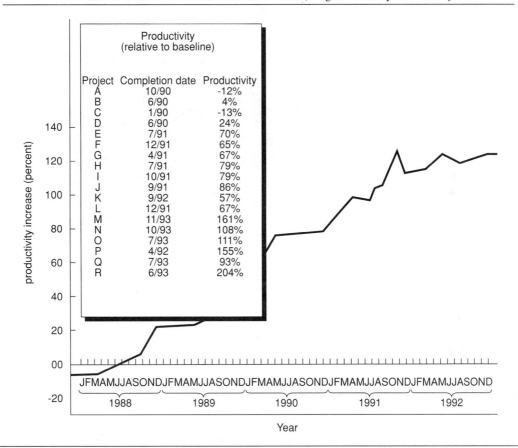

Productivity (relative to baseline)		
Project	Completion date	Productivity
A	10/90	-12%
B	6/90	4%
C	1/90	-13%
D	6/90	24%
E	7/91	70%
F	12/91	65%
G	4/91	67%
H	7/91	79%
I	10/91	79%
J	9/91	86%
K	9/92	57%
L	12/91	67%
M	11/93	161%
N	10/93	108%
O	7/93	111%
P	4/92	155%
Q	7/93	93%
R	6/93	204%

the various technical working groups (TWGs) implementing process improvements, and provides a centralized organization-wide database for process-data analysis[1]. As reflected in the cost allocations, the two initiatives focused on three key areas.

Quantitative Process Management

Hughes standardized uniform data definitions across projects and used them to track cost esti-mates, actual costs, errors, and schedule perfor-mance. Information was compiled in a monthly report for senior management that included

the project's accomplishments, problems, program trouble reports, quality indicators, scope changes, resource needs, and lessons learned. Also presented were plots of actual versus planned values over time to show the project's schedule, milestones, rate chart, earned value, financial/labor status, and target-system resource use[1].

Case Studies of Hughes and Raytheon's CMM Efforts (*Cont.*)

EXHIBIT 4   Raytheon's Savings on 15 Projects Due to Reduced Rework Costs. Figure Courtesy of *IEEE Software*

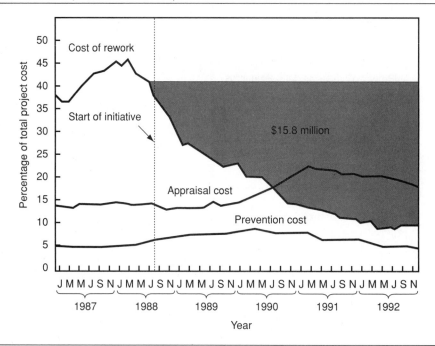

Similarly, Raytheon's TWG for metrics issues adopted Mitre's Management Metric set for identifying "systemic problem areas in a development process" and created the Process Data Center to support "proposal writing, quarterly reviews, software-capability evaluations, and specific studies such as the predictive models necessary to achieve level 4 maturity"[3]. The TWG also provided standardized spreadsheet templates to facilitate metrics collection by project members.

Technology Development
Hughes' technology steering committee formalized technology management practices and procedures, and created a job function called head of technology transfer. Among other things, the head of technology transfer monitored process maturity, "maintained a database of technology used on each project and an awareness of what technology each project needed," and became involved in various corporate-wide programs relating to technology development, process maturity, and training.

Raytheon established a similar tools-and-methods working group that focused on evaluating tools and environments and on process automation. The program has

sponsored the evaluation of alternative CASE products, the cost-benefit analyses used to justify their purchase, the training to

Case Studies of Hughes and Raytheon's CMM Efforts (*Cont.*)

instruct the developers in their intricacies, the integration of individual tools to provide a seamless environment, the inevitable tailoring to specific projects, and the generation of manuals for various types of users[3].

Training

Both Hughes and Raytheon place heavy emphasis on training, with Hughes going so far as to make training a job requirement instead of a promotional requirement. In response to SEI recommendations and an employee survey, Hughes supplemented its classes on programming practices, languages, and CASE tools with classes on project management, internal reviews, requirements writing, requirements- and unit-level testing, and quality assurance[1]. Hughes opened these courses to engineering functions outside of its Software Engineering Division and reported a respectable non-Software Engineering Division attendance of 20 percent. Hughes believes that this enhanced training program contributes heavily to the "coherent organizational culture" achieved at level 3[1].

Raytheon sponsors a comprehensive training program, with courses conducted during work hours (564 courses in 1992). Overview courses are designed to provide general knowledge about some technical or management area and are scheduled periodically. Detailed courses are often tailored for specific projects and scheduled accordingly. Like Hughes, Raytheon reports "a definite culture shift in the area of training[3]."

Although the ROI reported above (and elsewhere) suggests that CMM more than pays for itself, it can also be argued that corporations are more likely to report successful results than negative ones. To establish a more thorough understanding of the CMM's impact, we need a more extensive project-base (for example, 50 projects) to quantitatively, statistically, and comparatively report the results. It is probably too early in the evolution of the CMM to perform this type of study.

—Hossein Saiedian, University of Nebraska,
and Scott Hamilton, *Computer* Staff

References

1. W. Humphrey, T.R. Snyder, and R.R. Willis, "Software Process Improvement at Hughes Aircraft," *IEEE Software,* Vol. 8, No. 4, July 1991, pp. 11–23.

2. J. Herbsleb et al., "Benefits of CMM-Based Software Process Improvement: Initial Results," Tech. Report SEI-94-TR-13, Software Engineering Institute, Carnegie Mellon Univ., Pittsburgh, Aug. 94.

3. R. Dion, "Process Improvement and the Corporate Balance Sheet," *IEEE Software,* Vol. 10, No. 4, July 1993, pp. 28–35.

assessment team made seven recommendations on quantitative process management, process group, requirements, quality assurance, training, review process, and working relationship. (See sidebar on overleaf.)

The Hughes Software Engineering Division was assessed at Level 2 maturity. In early 1988, Hughes developed an action plan to implement recommended improvements that required 100 labor staff-months over an 18 month period. Budget cuts later reduced the labor staff-months to 78. In early 1989, Hughes requested that the SEI conduct a second assessment, which the SEI performed in 1990. Hughes had progressed to a strong Level 3, with many activities preparing it for Level 4 and 5.

Hughes has identified many advantages resulting from its improved software development processes. And perhaps more importantly, Hughes contends that improvement costs have been more than offset by a positive net return. Specifically, "The assessment itself cost Hughes about $45,000, and the subsequent two-year program of improvements cost about $400,000 . . . Hughes estimates the resulting annual savings to be about $2 million[5]." (Humphrey, Snyder, and Willis[5] wholeheartedly favor the SEI model and its results and provide a deeper analysis of the above figures.)

Even though the CMM model is relatively new, there are other success stories. In early 1988, the Software Systems Lab at Raytheon's Equipment Division initiated a process improvement program[6]. An initial assessment, based on the SEI questionnaire, found that the lab was slightly below "repeatable" (Level 2) and four areas needed improvement: documented practices and procedures, training, tools and methods, and metrics.

In 1992, a follow-up analysis of six major Raytheon projects spanning three years showed substantially decreased rework costs since the start of the process improvement program. More specifically, Raytheon saved about $9.2 million of its nearly $115 million in software development costs. The approach chosen to quantify the software improvement initiative's effect was based on Phil Crosby's "cost of quality" idea (from his book, *Quality Without Tears*), which distinguishes the cost of doing something right the first time from the cost of rework. This approach used four major development-cost categories:

1. performance costs associated with doing it right the first time (such as developing the design or generating the code),
2. nonconformance rework costs (such as fixing code defects or design documentation),
3. appraisal costs associated with testing the product to determine if it's faulty, and
4. Prevention costs incurred trying to prevent faults from degrading the product.

Nonconformance, appraisal, and prevention costs are accepted as the cost of quality. However, the primary objective is to significantly reduce nonconformance costs, which clearly was accomplished (as witnessed by the $9.2 million savings). As stated in the referenced article, "In terms of the SEI's maturity levels, we believe we're now a solid Level 3, on our way to Level 4. About 25 percent of our software engineering staff is actively involved in process improvement, and our initiative has good visibility at all levels of management. . . ."

As another example, the first Air Force center to perform a software engineering process self-assessment was the Aircraft Software Division (LAS) of the Oklahoma City Air Logistics Center at Tinker Air Force Base[7]. In the late 1980s, LAS struggled with the need to implement a strong, effective process improvement program, and in 1989 LAS was introduced to the SEI methods. The SEI helped assess LAS, which was challenged with developing a process-improvement infrastructure to correct the assessment findings and increase its organizational maturity. LAS established a management steering team and technical Software Engineering Process Group (SEPG).

By late 1992, LAS had implemented 44 improvements. Return-on-investment information gathered for 18 of these improvements reported $462,100 invested with $2,935,000 returned, for an ROI ratio of 6.35 to 1. In fact, LAS continued collecting such data, making a strong case for its process improvement program.

Further benefits include improved communications and accuracy. LAS officials believe that the improvement program has made process improvement a daily business priority. Employees actively seek improvement opportunities. Customer satisfaction, a primary LAS goal, has increased directly because of process improvement efforts. LAS is a leader in achieving the Air Force decree that all of its software organizations perform a self-assessment by 1994 and reach an SEI maturity Level 3 by 1998.

Unfavorable

As might be expected, not all opinions about the SEI and CMM are favorable. Documented concerns address specific details of the CMM, assessments, and evaluations. There is a consensus regarding the need for software engineering improvement, but there is disagreement on specific issues.

The SCE, which represents intrusion into the contractor's previously "private" environment, generates controversy. A common theme is that this evaluation is being applied in many different ways and that the SCE method taught departs significantly from the one published[8]. The SCE method taught is based on CMM version 0, which identifies eight KPAs and has never been published. Although version 1 with 13 KPAs is the published version, the SEI apparently will wait for the next version before updating its SCE method (due in 1996).

At the Software Capability Evaluations Workshop (held July 16-17, 1992 in Pittsburgh), five speakers from government and Mitre described SCEs they had conducted or observed. No two speakers described the SCE method the same way (see Card[8] for many differences). Furthermore, even when the same method is applied, SCE results can vary greatly. In one case, two SCE teams evaluated the same organization only a month apart and got different results for 15 of 85 questions.

Common concerns expressed by five industry representatives during the aforementioned workshop included

- different SCE methods,
- questionable SCE team qualifications and training,

- SCE teams intimidating personnel,
- SCE teams not providing timely feedback,
- fuzzy compliance criteria,
- cost of supporting frequent SCEs, and
- discrepancies between Software Process Assessments (SPAs) and SCE results.

One Air Force representative observed that in seven of 14 cases, an SPA rated an organization higher than an evaluation did. This was attributed to misguided improvement efforts and poor contractor integrity. Government and industry representatives both contended that because SPAs often give different or misleading answers, they should be replaced by SCEs. But many industry representatives felt that because SPAs offered a more cooperative approach and covered more issues, they were useful for process improvement.

This thinking illustrates the common misconception that SCEs and SPAs must agree. Actually, they need not always yield the same rating. SCEs evaluate an organization's ability to perform the specific tasks required for fulfilling a contract; SPAs assess an organization's general maturity. An SCE result can legitimately differ from an SPA result if, for example, the organization bids on a contract outside its usual business sphere. As summarized in Exhibit 5 (see Paulk[3] for details), SPAs and SCEs differ in motivations, objectives, and results ownership. These in turn lead to

EXHIBIT 5 Comparison Between Software Process Assessments and Software Capability Evaluations

Software Process Assessments	*Software Capability Evaluations*
Used by organization to improve software process.	Used by acquisition organization for source selection and contract monitoring.
Results to organization only.	Results to organization and acquirer.
Assess current practice.	Substantiate current practice.
Act as catalyst for process improvement.	Assess commitment to improve.
Provide input to improvement, action plan.	Analyze contract performance potential.
Collaborative: organization members on team.	Independent evaluation: no organization members on team.
Apply to overall organization, not individual.	Apply to performance for particular contract.

differences in the information collected and outcomes formulated. For instance, while SPAs are performed in an open, collaborative environment, SCEs are performed in a more audit-oriented environment, and objectives are tied to monetary considerations because team recommendations help select contractors[3].

Pyzdek[9] presents arguments against the SEI and its somewhat rigid CMM. In this article, Pyzdek contends that there is no "right" way to improve software quality: Every organization must come up with its own approach. This implies that no single mandated approach is right, although the CMM comes close. This article also states, a quality improvement solution imposed from the outside is by definition not the answer. And the CMM is certainly from the outside. The counterargument is that the *methods* for achieving CMM levels can be chosen by the organization; it is only the *criteria* that are defined from the outside.

Another confusing major area has been the relationship between the CMM and Total Quality Management (TQM). Exhibit 6 shows the implied relationship between the CMM and TQM. According to this figure, while TQM principles may affect all of an organization's projects, the CMM affects only software development projects. Silver[10] claims there are several CMM flaws. He says the CMM

- ignores TQM and processes' cultural dimension,
- confuses processes' infrastructure and activity dimensions,
- institutionalizes quality assurance and process groups,
- poorly implements statistical process control,
- delays useful process improvement activities,
- doesn't account for parallel, interdependent, and continuous improvement of all KPA activities,
- provides no quantitative process-performance metrics, and
- ignores software support.

Silver[10] expands on each failing and argues that the CMM's major flaw is its failure to recognize TQM, a criticism stemming from the belief that TQM should serve as the foundation for quality.

EXHIBIT 6   Relationship between Capability Maturity Model and Total Quality Management

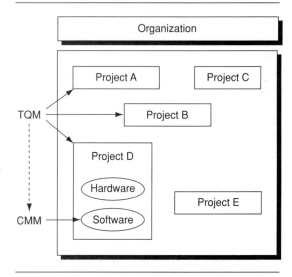

Another article concludes that "while the SEI has developed a truly outstanding program for performing process assessments, both its assessment and the SCE program are seriously flawed by their reliance on the SEI's unproven process-maturity model. Furthermore, the methods by which the SCE program determines numeric process-maturity scores for organizations are so riddled with statistical and methodological problems that it appears unlikely that such ratings have any meaningful correlation to the actual abilities of organizations to produce high-quality software on time and within budget."[4] Bollinger and McGowan also criticize the process-maturity questionnaire of 101 yes/no questions on various software engineering-process issues. Each maturity level requires a minimum number of yes answers, which must be backed by documented evidence. The questionnaires represent about 10-20 percent of collected information; structured interviews and other methods are used to gather the remaining information.

Most companies (approximately 80 percent of companies assessed) are currently at Level 1. Consequently, the Level 1 category includes a very broad organizational range, from organizations totally incapable of producing software to those with excellent bottom-line development track records. Some companies are rated at Level 1 because they miss important Level 2 questions, even though they may be able but are not allowed to affirmatively answer many or all of the questions required for a higher level. If an organization misses more than one of the 12 key questions for entry to Level 2, it fails the entire test regardless of how well it can answer the other questions. Therefore, the rating is viewed by some as quite arbitrary.

Humphrey and Curtis[11] responded to several faults identified by Bollinger and McGowan[4]. One interesting statement from this response contradicts planned government contract award procedures: "The fact is that the Software Engineering Institute instructs Software Capability Evaluation auditors not to base their contract-award recommendations on maturity grades for software vendors." But this article's opening paragraph states, one government organization is intending to mandate that bidding vendors be at Level 3. Whatever the intention, prudent software vendors must assume that certain levels will be mandated or at least will become the de facto standard for bidder selection.

This assumption is supported by an article published in *Signal* (the official journal publication for the Air Force Communications and Electronics Association) stating, "The general consensus among those interviewed is that the SEI model eventually would become the process standard over other models in existence, primarily because it is being promoted by the Defense Department."[12] This consensus and other information in the article came from interviews with commercial, defense, and government companies of varying sizes. These interviews also identified industry complaints about the evaluation process. Evaluation teams have conducted evaluations inconsistently among contracts, and the process maturity determination has varied among evaluations. Different results have been reached by different teams at the same time or by the same team at different times. (Many of these comments about the DoD are applicable to other organizations, as other government departments and organizations in other nations are—or are considering—implementing the CMM.)

Another industry complaint questions some government agencies' ability to select vendors and manage software projects. Many DoD program managers do not have a software background and are not held accountable for their programs, often being rotated to another assignment before program completion.[12] This sometimes results in a Level 2, 3, or 5 organization being managed by a "Level 0" government bureaucracy. However, there is some optimism that DoD is becoming more educated about the CMM and that improvements in this area are forthcoming.

Another complaint about the CMM and the resultant SCE is that the evaluation team may come from a company that, itself, is a bidder on government software projects (hopefully on projects unrelated to those projects evaluated). Hence, companies may be reluctant to welcome the evaluation team, fearing that the promise of confidentiality may be subverted.

One nearly universal complaint is that moving from level to level can cost hundreds of thousands or even millions of dollars. Since the government mandates levels and simultaneously selects bidders using lowest cost as a significant criterion, this creates a very real dilemma. In addition, government financial assistance is probably not forthcoming during this time of reduced budgets. Although the ROI may eventually become positive, organizations can incur expenses and reduced profits for years before increased efficiency offsets the cost.

RECENT INSIGHTS

We discussed the CMM's impact with several companies. However, many companies are reluctant to divulge specific material. To protect the interests of companies from which information *was* obtained, we've omitted company names and other revealing details. Furthermore, since we usually spoke with one knowledgeable manager at each company, our results do not necessarily represent the official company position.

It is difficult to determine whether a company is using the CMM in a serious effort to improve software development or merely to be competitive on upcoming government contracts. The former is driven by product quality, the latter by near-term business considerations. Both motives can be valid simultaneously in a single company.

Beliefs vary as to whether and when a specific CMM level will become a requirement for bidding on government contracts. One opinion is that requiring a specific CMM compliance level is against the principles under which the CMM was developed and, therefore, compliance can only be used as one criterion for bidder selection. But it is probably dangerous to rely on this assumption, since a specific maturity level may have very heavily weighted criteria. Another possibility is that those responsible for bidder selection may rightfully view increasing CMM levels as increasing their ability to mitigate "risk," an important factor in bidder selection since it affects bidder ranking.

Companies also reported that achieving a higher CMM level is a very complex process. However, since most companies are at Level 1, we discuss experiences related to progressing from Level 1 to Level 2. Since process improvement is essentially level independent, insight gained from these experiences should be applicable for promotions to other levels. Nevertheless, we must stress that we uncovered no information on the relative effort needed for each level promotion. There are no known guidelines that indicate, as a function of efforts required to achieve Level 2, the amount of additional effort required to achieve Levels 3, 4, and 5.

Implementation Approaches

Meetings, meetings, and more meetings seem to be the norm for beginning to achieve the first CMM level increase. Since the companies we interviewed were in the formative stages of imple-

menting CMM principles, they expected action and results to replace planning and meetings (hopefully rapidly). But meetings to assess progress will likely continue, because the companies we queried had not yet experienced the action or implementation stage.

CMM software development principles, like most software engineering principles, stress initial analysis and design. Companies reported that CMM-mandated processes were more likely to succeed when implemented in phases, with significant initial analysis and design efforts.

One company obtaining new major contracts is initiating them with CMM Level 2 principles even when these principles are not mandated for those specific contracts. The reasoning is that future assessments or evaluations will require certain projects to be at the specified CMM level, and establishing new contracts on a solid CMM foundation will improve the company's overall posture. A parallel effort involves identifying some key current contracts and making them comply with CMM Level 2.

It may appear that there is high potential for a conflict of interest when a company is assessing itself. But honesty is rewarded, as a self-assessment is often followed by an external, impartial evaluation (an SCE). Moreover, because of the personnel involved (line personnel and first-level management) the focus tends to be on technical and practical issues. Consequently, the CMM goal of improved product quality can indeed offset the temptation to present a facade for near-term contract awards.

Benefits and Impacts

Published studies of software engineering improvements measured by the CMM indicate significant cost savings or profit return. This implies that software testing and maintenance costs were reduced, since the software better meets verification and validation requirements.

In their analysis of CMM-compliance costs, companies distinguished (1) one-time costs of achieving a higher CMM level from (2) continuing costs of performing software engineering at that higher level.

The latter may actually represent a cost reduction when compared to software production costs at a lower CMM level. Some studies have even shown that the one-time cost of achieving a higher level are quickly recouped by the significant savings of producing software at the higher CMM level.

Companies reported that process improvement works best when both employees and employer agree to accept the required extra effort and expense. One of many possible arrangements is to have some meetings or training conducted during lunch hour, with the employer providing lunch. Other variations and employer/employee compromises include "shared time," when training is done on 50-percent company time and 50-percent employee time.

Much has been said about how an employer or company benefits from implementing the CMM, but little has been stated about how employees benefit. The techniques learned are useful professional skills. The higher CMM level in which the employee works, the more valuable the employee is to the computing industry. This type of expertise can be very marketable. In addition, employee pride and management respect should not be overlooked as an employee benefit, reward, or motivating force.

The companies we questioned agreed that reputation with their customers is primarily based on product quality and agreeable interface with those customers. There is little argument that higher CMM levels should lead to better quality software and therefore better company reputation. However, CMM compliance may also change the manner in which a company interacts with its customers. For example, the formalism of higher CMM levels will make ad hoc contractor responses to volatile customer demands more difficult, but will contribute to more reliable and mutually beneficial contractor-customer relationships. Fortunately, the most compelling argument is also a very simple one: Higher quality software at lower cost along with improved company reputation should be a very potent formula for winning and keeping contracts.

Since no approach that enforces improvements will be universally acceptable in all aspects to all concerned, the CMM, on balance, can be considered a very successful model, particularly when combined with TQM principles. What may be less certain is whether the costs of attaining and maintaining a CMM level will be recouped through reduced software production costs and more efficient software engineering practices. Published studies (some cited in this article) report that process improvement based on the CMM more than pays for itself. However, we can safely assume that far more studies will report a positive outcome than a negative outcome. Few companies will be willing to publish their process-improvement failures. Nevertheless, with continued strong sponsorship by the DoD, there will likely be an increasing number of companies that base their software process improvement efforts on the CMM.

References

1. W.S. Humphrey, "Introduction to Software Process Improvement," Tech. Report CMU/SEI-92-TR-7, Software Engineering Institute, Carnegie Mellon University, Pittsburgh, June 1993.

2. H. Krasner et al., "Lessons Learned from a Software Process Modeling System," *Comm. ACM,* Vol. 35, No. 9, Sept. 1992, pp. 91–111.

3. M. Paulk et al., "Capability Maturity Model for Software, Version 1.1," Tech. Report CMU/SEI-93-TR-24, Feb. 1993.

4. T.B. Bollinger and C. McGowan, "A Critical Look at Software Capability Evaluations," *IEEE Software,* Vol. 8, No. 4, July 1991, pp. 25–41.

5. W.S. Humphrey, T.R. Snyder, and R.R. Willis, "Software Process Improvement at Hughes Aircraft," *IEEE Software,* Vol. 8, No. 4, July 1991, pp. 11–23.

6. R. Dion, "Elements of a Process Improvement Program," *IEEE Software,* Vol. 9, No. 4, July 1992, pp. 83–85.

7. W.H. Lipke and K.L. Butler, "Software Process Improvement: A Success Story," *CrossTalk,* Nov. 1992, pp. 29–39.

8. D. Card, "Capability Evaluations Rated Highly Variable," *IEEE Software,* Vol. 9, No. 5, Sept. 1992, pp. 105–106.

9. T. Pyzdek, "To Improve Your Process: Keep it Simple," *IEEE Software,* Vol. 9, No. 5, Sept. 1992, pp. 112–113.

10. B. Silver, "TQM vs. the SEI Capability Maturity Model," *Software Quality World,* Vol. 4, No. 2, Dec. 1992.

11. W.S. Humphrey and B. Curtis, "Comments on 'A Critical Look,' " *IEEE Software,* Vol. 8, No. 4, July 1991, pp. 42–46.

12. D.L. Johnson and J. Brodman, "Software Process Rigors Yield Stress, Efficiency," *Signal,* Vol. 46, No. 12, Aug. 1992, pp. 55–57.

Discussion Questions

1. Humphrey's model simultaneously provides both for assessment for self improvement and for management evaluation. How might these dual roles for measurement be in conflict? What could management do to ameliorate this situation?

2. At Hughes Aircraft, the budget for process improvement was significant (100 work-months) and was cut during the course of the project. What does this suggest for organizations who wish to take on one of these projects?

3. Saiedian and Kuzara note in more than one location in their article that the industry will likely see a bias toward favorable, rather than unsuccessful, case studies of such changes as adopting the CMM process. How might this bias be overcome by researchers in order that the industry could benefit from the lessons of failed changes?

Appendix

Case Studies

Case 1

RIVERVIEW CHILDREN'S HOSPITAL

On Thursday, February 15, 1990, Louis Bernard, the Assistant Executive Director of Finance at Riverview Children's Hospital in Toronto, reviewed the latest financial statements from the new computerized financial system. His fears of a slower than expected implementation were confirmed. The fiscal year-end of March 30 was fast approaching and the new system was not ready for the external auditors who would begin their audit in mid-April. Even though the implementation was already eight months late, Louis was tempted to delay the system implementation until after the audit.

RIVERVIEW HOSPITAL BACKGROUND

Founded in 1899 as a "Home for Incurable Children," Riverview Children's Hospital had developed over the years into a modern 87-bed children's facility providing long-term care and rehabilitation for infants, children and young adults. Riverview patients were chronically ill, physically handicapped children who were educable. The most common afflictions were: Cerebral Palsy, Spina Bifida and Muscular Dystrophy. Officially classified as a chronic care hospital, it had become one of the most respected paediatrics facilities in Canada. Riverview currently enjoyed a three-year accreditation status, the highest award granted by the Canadian Council on Hospital accreditation. (See attached Mission Statement - Exhibit 1.)

Since his arrival in 1987, Mark Thompson, the Executive Director, had guided Riverview towards enhancing its leadership role in providing services to its target population. Recently, Riverview had expanded into providing long-term acute care for eight ventilator-dependent children. This program required special approval from the Ministry of Health to fund the additional staffing and specialized equipment requirements. Additionally, many other programs had been expanded or enhanced since Mark Thompson's arrival at Riverview to replace the previous Executive Director who was removed by the board of trustees.

This case was prepared by Bradley J. Dixon under the supervision of Jim A. Erskine and Duncan G. Copeland of the Western Business School. Copyright 1991, The University of Western Ontario.

This material is not covered under authorization from Can Copy or any reproduction rights organization. Any form of reproduction, storage or transmital of this material is prohibited without written permission from Western Business School, The Universtity of Western Ontario, London, Canada N6A 3K7. Reprinted with permission, Western Business School.

EXHIBIT 1   A Statement of Mission

Philosophy

Riverview Children's Hospital is committed to providing high quality Inpatient and Outpatient services for physically disabled children and young adults through ongoing programs of rehabilitation, health care, education and research. This care involves the family or guardian, and is provided in an environment serving the whole person to promote optimum individual growth, development and integration into the community.

Structure and Role

Riverview Children's Hospital, an 87-bed Chronic Care facility, shall operate within the requirements of the Ontario Public Hospitals Act and strive to:

- Assess and meet each patient's physical, mental, spiritual, social, recreational and educational needs.
- Promote an atmosphere of caring support to patients, their families, staff and volunteers.
- Liaise with other health services to fulfil its role in providing a continuum of care to the community.
- Encourage research and scholarly works to enhance the quality of life for the disabled.
- Provide education and training for health care personnel and the public.
- Exclude service for the management of those conditions which primarily require ongoing critical and/or diagnostic services of an Acute Care Hospital.

More than 95% of the operating budget of $10 million came from the Ontario Ministry of Health. The 1989 fiscal operating deficit of $200,000 was funded by the Riverview foundation which had grown into a sizable ($20 million in assets) foundation that supported disabled children through grants to Riverview and other institutions.

Riverview, like all public hospitals, was run by a board of trustees. The board had always consisted of a large majority of women, as women had started Riverview when they were driven from the board of a major children's hospital more than 90 years ago. The board took an active role in the administration of the hospital and met regularly with the hospital executive management group.

The board had several committees that also met regularly to set policy and review management decisions: the Executive Committee, the Joint Planning Committee and the Finance and Audit Committee. The Finance and Audit committee met every month and comprised nine board members, three of whom were Chartered Accountants.

In April 1987, Riverview had been given the responsibility for managing the eventual closing down of another chronic care children's hospital 20 kilometres north of Riverview in Thornhill, Ontario. The Thornhill Heights Hospital had been privately owned and the physical condition was deemed too inadequate by the Ministry of Health to warrant continued operation. The Ministry purchased the facility and gave the management team at Riverview the responsibility for managing the Thornhill Heights facility until it was closed. The phase out period was estimated to be at least 5 to 7 years.

Louis Bernard

Louis obtained an undergraduate degree in Business Administration in 1982, joined a major accounting firm and received his Chartered Accountant designation in 1985. At the accounting firm, Louis had the opportunity to learn about healthcare accounting as an external auditor of hospitals and medical supply companies. Through his accounting firm's consultancy practice, he was given the opportunity to become the interim Finance Director at Riverview in April 1987. The opening at Riverview had arisen from the recent dismissal, by the hospital board, of the previous Assistant Executive Director of Finance who had held the position for less than nine months. In August 1987, Louis was offered the position of Assistant Executive Director (A.E.D.) of Finance.

The Assistant Executive Director of Finance was responsible for all facets of the finance function at Riverview: Treasury, Accounting, Auditing, and Office Management (see Exhibit 4). When Thornhill Heights was acquired in April 1987, a part-time A.E.D. of Finance was hired. In the fall of 1987, the part-time contract was not renewed and Louis was given the finance responsibility for both facilities. Louis spent between one and two days per week at Thornhill.

Finance and Computer Departments

As the Assistant Executive Director of Finance, Louis Bernard was responsible for all aspects of financial management at Riverview and Thornhill. At Riverview, his staff consisted of 7 people organized into two departments, Accounting and Materials Management (see Exhibit 2). Three Thornhill staff reported to Louis, the accounting clerk, the payroll clerk and the receptionist. Job responsibilities, educational background, employment history and Louis' comments on the staff are detailed in Exhibit 3.

The computer and communications department was formed in January 1989 at the same time that a computer room was being constructed to house the new computer hardware. Wilma Lo was promoted to Computer Coordinator reporting to Mark Thompson who was overseeing the new system implementation. Previously, Wilma was the Word Processing Coordinator and reported to Louis Bernard. The computer vendor's technical staff were favourably impressed with Wilma Lo's enthusiasm and felt that she could manage the computer

operations. As the computer coordinator, Wilma was responsible for the operations and the technical management of the new computer system in addition to her current word processing support and telephone system management responsibilities. Wilma felt overextended by her new responsibilities.

"I feel I am so busy all the time, there is so much going on. I never have the time to do anything right. There is so much to learn about the new computer, I have never worked with such a large system before. Working with the new computer is enjoyable, there wasn't much challenge in my job of providing support for all the word-processing users. Now the Word Processor users always phone, often at awkward times, and expect me to come running to solve their problems. Mark tells me to not worry about them too much, but I used to be a word-processing clerk, they are my friends."

Wilma Lo also maintained the telephone system and reported to Louis Bernard who had overall responsibility for the telephone system. The telephone system was not a big part of Wilma's job, but Louis felt that her priorities were not always logical.

"Whenever I asked Wilma to make a minor change to the telephone system, it would be done immediately, even if I specifically mentioned that this could wait. I thought her service was great, until my staff complained about Wilma's service. I realized she was doing everything I asked because I was the Assistant Executive Director and her former supervisor."

The computer department at Riverview should logically have reported to the A.E.D. Finance, but Louis had no time or desire to manage it at that stage. In Canada, hospital computer departments usually report to the A.E.D. Finance, except the largest (500 plus beds) hospitals, where a Chief Information Officer would manage the computer department. Louis felt that Wilma Lo, the computer department coordinator, was in over her head, and Mark Thompson was having to spend more time than he would like managing her and

EXHIBIT 2 Organizational Chart

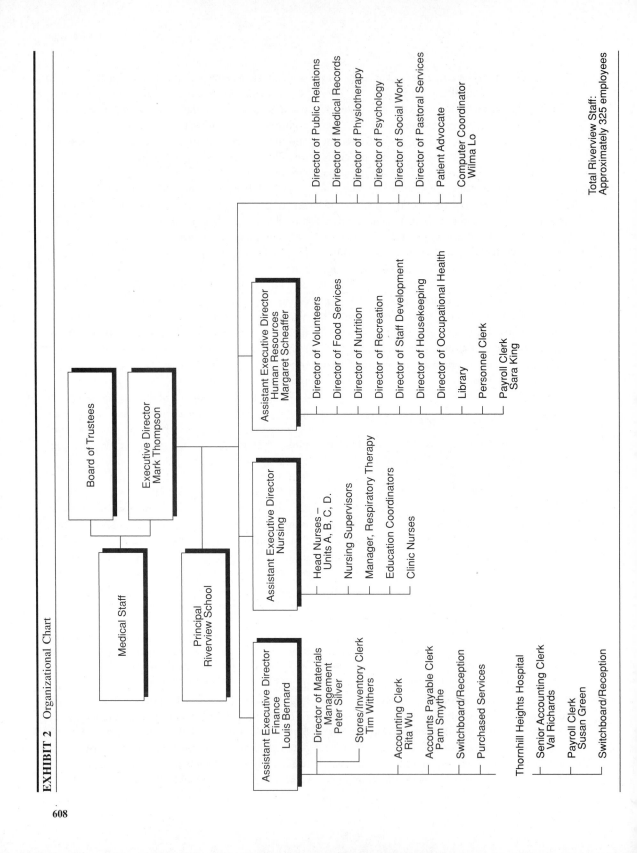

Board of Trustees

Executive Director
Mark Thompson

Medical Staff

Principal
Riverview School

Assistant Executive Director
Finance
Louis Bernard

- Director of Materials Management
  Peter Silver
- Stores/Inventory Clerk
  Tim Withers
- Accounting Clerk
  Rita Wu
- Accounts Payable Clerk
  Pam Smythe
- Switchboard/Reception
- Purchased Services

Thornhill Heights Hospital

- Senior Accounting Clerk
  Val Richards
- Payroll Clerk
  Susan Green
- Switchboard/Reception

Assistant Executive Director
Nursing

- Head Nurses –
  Units A, B, C, D.
- Nursing Supervisors
- Manager, Respiratory Therapy
- Education Coordinators
- Clinic Nurses

Assistant Executive Director
Human Resources
Margaret Scheaffer

- Director of Volunteers
- Director of Food Services
- Director of Nutrition
- Director of Recreation
- Director of Staff Development
- Director of Housekeeping
- Director of Occupational Health
- Library
- Personnel Clerk
- Payroll Clerk
  Sara King

- Director of Public Relations
- Director of Medical Records
- Director of Physiotherapy
- Director of Psychology
- Director of Social Work
- Director of Pastoral Services
- Patient Advocate
- Computer Coordinator
  Wilma Lo

Total Riverview Staff:
Approximately 325 employees

EXHIBIT 3   Biographical Details of Employees and Louis Bernard's Comments on Employees

---

Louis Bernard's comments on the performance of selected employees are shown in *Italics*.

RIVERVIEW CHILDREN'S HOSPITAL

Sarah King - Payroll Clerk

5 years at Riverview
High School Education
Previous experience in Payroll Department in Industry
Poor Management Skills, Not detail-oriented, Weak comprehension skills, learned by copying procedures
Good worker, but progressively poor attendance record,
Increasingly becoming flustered and missing details.
Part-Time Assistant was necessary because of work load.

Rita Wu - Senior Accounting Clerk

6 years at Riverview
High School Education
Runs the current micro-computer accounting system
Relatively Independent, did not need much direction.
Learned the new system well
Responsible for General Ledger and Management Reports

Pam Smythe - Accounts Payable Clerk

6 years at Riverview
High School Education
Recently received Hospital Accounting Course Certificate
Not too confident - tends to hesitate
Procrastinates-Somewhat Insecure about the system

Peter Silver - Materials Management Supervisor

15 years at Riverview
College in Portugal
Community college - High marks - Transcript posted on wall.
Not a delegator - runs the department very tightly
Workaholic, tries to do everything
Never used computer before but learns quick

RIVERVIEW CHILDREN'S HOSPITAL

Tim Withers - Stores Inventory Clerk

10 years at Riverview
Educated in Ireland
Very laid back - likes to visit with the sales representatives
Prompt - arrives and leaves on time
Recent heart attack

---

the computer problems. Louis remarked that he would need an Accounting Supervisor to look after the office and the day-to-day accounting issues before he could even consider managing the computer department.

Louis was concerned that the organizational structure of the administration departments did not make sense. Louis felt that the payroll department should not report to the same manager as the personnel department. More than seventy percent of a hospital's costs are salary expense. Proper audit and control practices dictate that the person who enters the hours worked into the system should work in the accounting department.

"However, I am not sure I would want Sarah King, the payroll clerk, reporting to me anyway. I

EXHIBIT 3   *(Cont.)*

Wilma Lo - Coordinator of Computer and Communication Department

7 years at Riverview
Diploma in computers from DeVry institute
Formerly supported the secretaries with their Word Processors
Chosen (based on recommendations from ICS personnel) to head computer department.
Very busy worker, but poorly organized.
Writes copious notes, but takes time for her to comprehend
Management skills are lacking - does not prioritize well.

THORNHILL HEIGHTS HOSPITAL

Val Richards - Senior Accounting Clerk

19 years at Thornhill
Bookkeeping training
High School Education
Knows Everyone, Friendly
No computer experience

Susan Green - Payroll Clerk

5 years at Thornhill
High School Education
Was Junior Clerk in Payroll Department at Large Employer
Intelligent, Learns Quickly

EXHIBIT 4   Assistant Executive Director of Finance Job Responsibilities

---

The Assistant Executive Director of Finance is responsible for all facets of the finance function at Riverview and Thornhill: Treasury, Accounting, Auditing and Office Management.

Treasury responsibilities include:

Negotiate revenue from the Ministry of Health.
Manage the Cash and Investments of the Riverview Hospital and Foundation.
Prepare Capital Assets Budgeting.
Advise the board of the financial implications of decisions.
Oversee all donations, bequests and estate matters.

The Accounting and Audit responsibilities include:

Submit financial Statements to Board of Trustees.
Produce quarterly reports to the Ministry of Health.
Ensure the accounting system is current and accurate.
Establish policies and procedures to prevent errors and fraud.

The Office Management Responsibilities include:

Ensure smooth functioning of all financial procedures.
Respond to questions and requests from the departments.
Manage the telephone system and photocopiers.
Supervise office staff.

have had numerous incidents with her and I do not have much confidence in her abilities. Once I even pushed to have her fired, but the A.E.D. of Human Resources, Margaret Scheaffer, protects her staff and supported Sarah.''

PURCHASING THE NEW SYSTEM

Louis had been involved in the process of purchasing a new computer system soon after his arrival in 1987. Even though he did not have any experience installing computer systems, Louis was interested in introducing a hospital financial system into Riverview.

A computer evaluation committee had been formed to decide which computer system to purchase. The committee consisted of Mark Thompson, the three Assistant Executive Directors, the Director of Medical Records and Wilma Lo.

There were six reasons for purchasing a system to replace the existing micro-computer based accounting system and to automate other areas of the hospital. First, the existing system was inadequate and could not provide the department managers with anything beyond basic reports outlining the departmental expenses. Because the system had not been designed for hospitals it could not produce the necessary statistical and budgeting reports that the department managers needed in an increasingly cost-conscious health care environment. Good management reports are important to enable managers to control costs.

Second, the Canadian Hospital Association had just finished the Management Information Systems (MIS) guidelines. These guidelines covered how management information should be recorded, managed and disseminated in hospitals. While the guidelines were just recommendations, it would only be a matter of time until adherence to MIS guidelines would become a prerequisite of receiving Hospital Accreditation.

Third, the payroll deposits and earning statements had been processed by an off-site computer service bureau which cost $1300 per month. To update payroll and personnel information involved filling out forms that were couriered to the service bureau where they were entered into the computer. The entire process was slow, error prone, and cumbersome.

Fourth, the existing micro-computer system, purchased in 1982, was running out of capacity and increasingly breaking down. The computer would have to be replaced or upgraded soon.

Fifth, the Executive Director realized that proper financial systems were an important factor that the Ontario Ministry of Health would consider before allowing Riverview to expand programs. The Ministry of Health encouraged all hospitals to install financial systems that would support the management of a hospital, in addition to simply maintaining the accounting ledgers. Louis felt that Riverview's installation of a new system had been a consideration in the recent approval of the new program for ventilator-dependent children.

Finally, the management of patient information was entirely manual. The patient record, a binder that contained a record of all treatments, diagnoses and progress reports for a patient, was located in a central records room. Computerized patient care information would enhance productivity, reduce errors, and move Riverview into the 1990s by providing greater analysis of treatment outcomes, faster access to medical histories by medical staff, and automatic output of the mandatory statistical reports for various governments.

In late Autumn 1987 a consultancy firm specializing in Hospital Systems had been retained to prepare a needs analysis report of Riverview's systems requirements. After much discussion with the computer committee, the report was the basis of a Request For Proposal (RFP) which was sent to several computer system vendors in May 1988. The 195-page RFP was analyzed by the vendors who responded with elaborate proposals, addressing each question in the RFP. The proposals were reviewed by the committee with assistance from the consultants. A short list of three vendors was selected in June 1988. After numerous visits to other sites and further analysis of the proposals submitted by the vendors, a system was selected in August. A contract for purchasing the Hardware,

Software and Implementation services for $499,000 was finally signed in November 1988 with a major computer hardware vendor, Integrated Computer Systems (ICS).

ICS proudly advertised that they were the only single source healthcare systems vendor in Canada. ICS were responsible in the contract for managing the training, hardware installation, software implementation and hardware support for Riverview. Louis was impressed that the training and implementation costs were lower than other vendors' proposals. The hardware to be installed at Riverview was a ICS-A1 mainframe computer with 25 terminals connected to the computer.

The software comprised two parts: the first part was the patient-care system which automated the patient information flow and computerized the Medical Records department. The patient-care software was developed by ICS in their Winnipeg office and the software trainers were ICS employees. The second part was the financial system which automated the Materials Management, Payroll and Accounting departments. The financial system consisted of many inter-related sub-systems, or modules (see Exhibit 5), that had to be implemented in a coordinated fashion. There were few connections between the financial and patient-care systems; each system could be implemented independently of the other. The financial software was sold by ICS but written by Dovetail Software, a London, Ontario-based software firm, under contract to provide hospital financial software exclusively to ICS. The Dovetail financial software was one of the most advanced hospital financial systems in Canada. The software's many features, coupled with the fiscal control from the disciplined procedures the software required, made Dovetail software popular with larger, 400-plus bed, hospitals.

Implementing the System

A schedule for implementing the financial modules was agreed upon in the contract between the computer vendor and Riverview's computer committee (see Exhibit 6). The computer hardware was installed in the computer room during January and February, 1989. A project manager was appointed in March 1989 and the 10-week implementation schedule was initiated. As executive director, Mark Thompson would oversee the entire project and liaise with ICS. Louis would direct the financial system portion and the Director of Medical Records would manage the patient-care system portion. The expected date for the financial system to be fully operational or 'Live' was early July. The patient accounting system would be implemented after the financial system. The entire implementation was expected to take 6 to 7 months.

The implementation budget, to cover project management and miscellaneous technical support expenses to get the system 'Live', was $64,000. This amount was included in the negotiated contract price and was estimated to cover a 6 to 8 month implementation. Riverview relied on ICS to employ the appropriate project management candidate. ICS, in turn, sub-contracted Sharon Picalle from a computer consultancy firm in March 1989. Sharon had worked extensively with ICS computers and had project management experience in the banking industry. This was her first project working with patient-care and hospital financial software. Sharon reported to both Venkat Halambi, the support manager at ICS, and Mark Thompson at Riverview. Venkat actually employed Sharon but any major decisions that Sharon referred to him were made after consultations with the ICS marketing account manager for Riverview.

After a few days on the job, Sharon realized that Wilma Lo, the Computer Coordinator, was not understanding the computer system and would require extra training and technical support. Sharon asked Venkat to provide an ICS technical support person to spend extra time with Wilma Lo to help her understand the system and enable her to solve the minor technical problems that invariably arose. The technical support person was billed to the project at $480 per day for time spent solving problems where ICS had determined they were not at fault or responsible. Fortunately for Riverview, there was not another system being

EXHIBIT 5   Financial System Modules

General Ledger and Budgeting

The purpose of this application is to maintain and report the financial data arising from the operation of the hospital and its various departmental units. This system assists in cost control through more timely financial reports, prepared with less clerical effort.

The system provides an on-line auditing capability that allows the users and auditors to easily track the movements of data to and from the general ledger accounts.

The general ledger system accepts input transactions automatically from other applications, such as accounts payable, accounts receivable, payroll, purchasing and inventory control. Users can also input transactions manually, and inquire about the status of any general ledger account. The system allows use of the new chart of accounts described in the MIS Guidelines for Canadian Hospitals. A user-defined chart of accounts is also allowed.

The system generates financial reports as specified by the user. It can provide comparative reporting by period, by departmental unit or any other desired basis. The system also provides consolidated financial statements for the hospital.

The system monitors actual expenditures against the budget for the hospital and all departments. It generates monthly budget variance reports for each department and cost centre.

Accounts Payable

The purpose of this application is to assure the proper receipt of goods, to support the orderly payment of supplier accounts and to assure authorization of payments. This system allows the hospital staff to have current information on volume of purchases and minimizes the time required to find the status of a supplier order. It also helps the hospital staff to avoid missing supplier discount dates.

The system regularly prints a list of invoices or accounts which should be paid. The user can make modifications to this pre-payment register. When a user is satisfied, the system prints the required cheques.

The user can, at any time, request the printing of a single cheque, which is charged against a specified general ledger account (e.g., an expense account). The user could also write cheques manually and enter the details, which the system uses to keep all account balances up-to-date. The system keeps track of outstanding cheques and performs a reconciliation with the monthly bank statements.

The system generates purchase analysis reports by department, product type and supplier. It can also produce other useful reports such as product price histories and supplier delivery performance. On-line inquiry to all accounts payable information is available.

Payroll

The purpose of this application is to maintain time and attendance data for all hospital personnel and calculate the payroll. This system minimizes the clerical effort required to produce the payroll and other labour statistics. The system can generate a report of payroll costs and full-time equivalents used by department, cost centre and job description. It can produce consolidated reports for the hospital. It can also produce reports which monitor vacation days, sick leave, overtime hours, etc. by employee.

Time and attendance data for all full-time and permanent part-time staff are entered from time sheets. The system can handle multiple pay cycles. Some employees are paid on a weekly basis; others can be paid bi-weekly,

EXHIBIT 5 *(Cont.)*

semi-monthly, etc. The hospital is a multi-union environment. The system should be flexible, allowing changes to union contracts and pay scales to be made with a minimum amount of effort.

In most cases, employees are paid through an automatic funds transfer to their bank accounts. The system can also issue cheques for those employees not on automatic deposit.

The system automatically prints Record of Employment forms for terminated employees. The system retains certain information on terminated employees for retroactive and reference purposes.

The system has the capability to calculate vacation pay, sick pay, bonuses, etc.

Purchasing

The purpose of this application is to oversee the acquisition of commodities, parts, supplies and any other material goods required by the hospital. The system captures requisition data from multiple departments, assists in the preparation of purchase orders and monitors the receipt of goods received.

The normal flow of operation within the purchasing application is:

1. A purchase requisition is created within a hospital department. This requisition is sent to the purchasing department for approval and creation of a purchase order.
2. The purchasing department will review the requisition. They will, when necessary, select the appropriate vendor. They may negotiate prices and discounts. They will ensure that delivery is for the required date. Once they approve the requisition, they will enter it into the computer.
3. The computer will generate the purchase order. A copy of this purchase order will be sent to the supplier. The system also automatically produces stock purchase orders based on inventory reorder points and economic order quantities.
4. The supplier will deliver the goods.
5. The receiving department will count the items received. Their receipt will update the inventory control and open purchase order records.

Inventory Control

The purpose of this application is to control the issue and stocking levels of most hospital stock items, including medical and surgical supplies, sterile supplies for nursing units, re-usable linen items, dietary material and utensils, pharmaceutical supplies and paper supplies. The system attempts to prevent stockouts, while minimizing inventory carrying costs.

The inventory control system maintains a file of all stock items, including newly purchased, re-usable and manufactured items. The system records all requisitions and issues. Details of supplier orders and receipt of goods are automatically received from the purchasing system. It assists in physical inventory taking, and upon authorized clearance makes any necessary adjustments to the file.

The system calculates order points and quantities for all items. It regularly generates a report of all items near their order level.

The system prints product item catalogues for departments to use when requisitioning items from stores or non-stores.

The system allows for multiple stores locations. It maintains cart profiles for the multiple supply carts found throughout the hospital. It also provides information for charging supplies usage to the various cost centres.

The system allows on-line inquiry for inventory item status and purchase order status.

EXHIBIT 6   Implementation Schedule - Financial Modules

Task #	*Weeks*									
	1	*2*	*3*	*4*	*5*	*6*	*7*	*8*	*9*	*10*
1a. Initiate Team Formation	X									
1b. Identify Dovetail Modifications Define Modifications for:										
a) Accounts Payable	X									
b) General Ledger	X									
c) Financial Reports	X									
2. Analysis of Modifications Requested										
a) Develop Specifications		X								
b) Provide Cost Estimates			X							
c) Provide Implementation Estimates			X							
3. Acceptance of Modifications										
a) Priorities				X						
b) Approval				X						
c) Signoff/Acceptance				X						
4. Revise Implementation Plan Revise Due to Modifications					X					
5. Consultation For User Training										
a) Core Trainers Assigned	X									
b) Develop Training Plan	X									
6. Customization & Programming										
a) Programming Commences					X	X	X			
b) Testing						X	X	X		
c) Incorporate in System							X	X	X	
d) Documentation Changes Made						X	X			
7. User Training Implement Training Plan						X	X	X	X	
8. Determine Conversion Methodology Manual vs. Tape-To-Disk		X								
Internal vs. Contracted		X								
9. Prepare Conversion Data										
a) Define Conversion Specs.			X							
b) Review & Cost Conversion Specs.			X							

installed at the same time. The technical support person was available to spend the extra time Wilma needed to learn the system.

Training for the first financial module (General Ledger) started in April. The users complained to Sharon that the training was too rushed and after talking to the Dovetail trainers Sharon realized that the days allocated for training in the contract had been cut roughly in half. Sharon learned from ICS's marketing department that the training days

EXHIBIT 6   *(Cont.)*

Task #	1	2	3	4	5	6	7	8	9	10
						Weeks				
10. Perform Conversion										
a) Write Conversion Programs				X						
b) Test Validity of Programs				X	X					
11. Test Accounts Payable										
a) Test for Integrity of Data						X				
b) Test Scripts						X				
12. A/P Acceptance										
Evaluate and Accept A/P							X			
13. Test General Ledger										
Test for Integrity of Data						X				
Test Scripts						X				
14. G/L Acceptance										
Evaluate and Accept G/L							X			
15. Test Financial Reporting										
Test for Integrity of Data							X			
Test Scripts							X			
16. Financial Reporting Acceptance										
Evaluate & Accept Financial Reporting								X		
17. Test Payroll										
Test Integrity of Data							X			
Test Scripts							X			
18. Payroll Acceptance										
Evaluate & Accept Payroll									X	
19. Live Implementation										
a) Provide Conversion Coverage										X
b) Prepare For Operations										X
c) Implement Plan (See 4)										X
20. System Shakedown										
Allow Time Post-Implementation to Resolve any Problems								X	X	
21. Post-Implementation Review										
a) A/P										
b) G/L										
c) F/R										
d) Payroll/Personnel										

had been reduced because Riverview, at 87 beds, was less than half the size of all the hospitals that had purchased the system to date. Sharon reviewed the training days' shortfall with Mark Thompson and Louis. Louis felt that the training he attended for the General Ledger module did not seem rushed. He wondered if days recommended by Dovetail were actually needed. Louis felt that Sharon should be able to help the staff with implementing the system. Sharon, Mark and Louis agreed to keep to the original training plan rather than incur costs of $650 per day for a Dovetail trainer for the extra 30 days that were cut.

In May it became apparent to Sharon that the frequency of computer problems was not decreasing. Wilma Lo was still having trouble with the computer system, although the technical support person was spending 2 to 3 days per week at Riverview assisting Wilma. The computer was constantly going down, inconveniencing the users. Louis was not surprised when Sharon mentioned to him that she was postponing the second training sessions until the end of May to correct the hardware problems. The system 'Live' date was delayed by one month to July.

Many difficulties were created for Sharon by Riverview staff's lack of familiarity with computers. Although Sharon was spending extra time working with the staff the users still complained that there was not enough time to learn the system. Sharon found that she had to be increasingly assertive and persistent to ensure that users completed any assigned project tasks. Payroll was the most complicated of all the financial systems and it became apparent to Margaret and Louis that the payroll clerk, Sarah King, would not be able to handle going live until sometime in the fall. Louis was disappointed that Riverview would not be able to realize the monthly savings from implementing Payroll earlier.

During June several of Louis's staff mentioned that they felt increasingly uncomfortable working with Sharon. Louis saw Sharon only a couple of times per week, and always asked how things were going. Sharon was positive about the system, the staff, and the prospects for going live with everything but payroll in August. Louis increasingly wondered why Sharon was spending so much time to manage this project. Louis knew that the $64,000 budget was based on a part-time project manager.

Shortly after completion of the training sessions in June, Tim Withers, the Stores Inventory Clerk, suffered a major heart attack. Tim would be off work recovering until October. Peter Silver, the Director of Material Management, was taking holidays in September. Louis realized that the Material Management module implementation would be delayed until November. Summer holidays interfered with the implementation plans of the other financial modules as well. Louis agreed with Sharon that the live dates for the other financial modules would have to be pushed back to October.

Louis' concerns about the amount of time Sharon was spending were realized in early July when he received a invoice from ICS for $59,000 for the implementation costs to date. The invoice did not provide a breakdown of the hours spent and Louis requested, through Mark Thompson, that a breakdown be provided. Eventually, the hour totals revealed that over 400 hours, or 50 days, of billable technical support were charged between March and June. Louis and Mark met with Sharon and representatives from ICS and expressed their concern with the amount of the bill. Sharon felt confident that the implementation would not be delayed further.

Louis noticed that Sharon's style was becoming more controlling, demanding and aggressive. Sharon annoyed Margaret, the A.E.D. of Human Resources, by her manner during meetings to discuss the payroll implementation. Louis learned that Wilma felt she was being treated 'like a child' by Sharon. The situation reached a crisis in late August when ICS submitted an invoice for $20,000, which included an additional $15,000 charge over the remaining budget to cover extra implementation costs. Louis refused to pay the $15,000. Louis, Margaret and Mark Thompson met to discuss the project and Sharon's role. They felt Sharon's handling of the project was inadequate and Mark Thompson told ICS not to renew Sharon's contract, effective September 1.

The New Project Manager

At the end of August, Louis approached John Deans, the Dovetail trainer for the Accounts Payable and General Ledger modules, about assuming the project management responsibilities. Louis and John had developed a good relationship from working together on the General Ledger module over the past several months. Dovetail prepared a proposal that outlined the implementation dates, the project management days, and the extra training required (see Exhibit 7).

The Riverview board was very concerned about cost overruns. Louis was concerned how the board would react to a request for an additional $32,000 to cover project management costs. After discussions with Mark, Louis rearranged the computer budget by deferring a software purchase for a year. Louis was able to find enough funds to pay for the extra project management costs without requesting additional funds from the board. John Deans was appointed project manager in mid-September.

John realized how concerned Riverview was with their expenses. Riverview had a strict policy regarding overtime, and employees mentioned that several years back people had been asked to take unpaid leave in order to meet the budget. John submitted status reports every week detailing the days spent to date and was careful not to spend any unnecessary time at Riverview.

During October, John's visits focused on getting the general ledger and payroll system live. The payroll system live date of December 1 was delayed until January 1, 1990 because of problems in obtaining the specialized forms and making custom modifications to the software. Delaying the implementation of payroll past January 1 would cause more complications from converting tax and benefit deductions that were based on a calendar year.

The implementation of the general ledger went smoothly and by the middle of November the closing balances from the old system were transferred to the new system, reconciled and financial reports were prepared in time to be included in the 1990 budget packages for distribution to department managers by the end of November. The managers would review their results and prepare a budget which was to be submitted to finance by mid-January. Then the entire finance department faced 4 or 5 very busy weeks to consolidate the data, review and prepare preliminary pro forma statements for budget meetings, then revise the statements and prepare final reports, meanwhile performing the required daily duties.

Each time John visited the hospital he would check with the accounting and materials management staff to inquire about how the implementation was going and was always told that everything was going as planned. John's schedule of training and consulting at three other hospitals prevented him from travelling to Riverview during most of November and early December.

After an absence of 5 weeks, John arrived at Riverview on December 18. Louis told John that it appeared that everything was progressing as planned and the Accounting and Material Management staffs were not having any major problems. Louis acknowledged, however, that he was not confident that everything was going as well as his staff let on. Louis remarked that he had been too busy to spend time down in Materials Management to learn what was really happening. John spent the morning investigating the status of the system and generating computer reports. After analyzing the computer output John realized things were not going as planned and arranged a meeting with Louis.

"Louis, there are three concerns that I have with the system. First, the accounts payable invoices for November are not entered into the new system. Pam assured me, the last time we talked, that she was right on schedule. She has not spent any overtime doing this. Second, the Materials Management department is not looking at their daily

EXHIBIT 7 Proposal for Project Management and Training

This proposal is for the balance of the training required, the implementation assistance, and the project management required to implement the system successfully to meet the target dates.

Based on our daily rate of $525.00, the cost would be $32,025 excluding travel and lodging costs. We estimate our travel and lodging expenses to be approximately $150 per day. We look forward to discussing the details with you to ensure that we mutually understand the project requirements.

TRAINING REQUIREMENTS

Training required to implement Dovetail is outlined by module below:

Material Management: **6 - 9 Days**

Refresher training at both Thornhill and Riverview is highly recommended due to the delays between the original training and the implementation date. Recommended training is 2-3 days per site.

Implementation support is recommended when system goes live. This support is usually requested by hospitals and has proven extremely valuable to eliminate implementation problems and minimize future system issues. Suggested support is 2-3 days when system is going live.

Management Information: **2 - 3 Days**

Outstanding training in Management Information will cover payroll and other complex reporting. This training would be scheduled over the next few months as data become available on the system.

General Ledger and Accounts Payable:
1 - 2 Days

Implementation support and review are recommended for these modules. This time would be scheduled concurrently with the implementation date.

Payroll and Personnel Training: **19 Days**

There are five outstanding tasks before the payroll system can go live. The major items and their associated training days include:

Test with subset of 25 employees	5 Days (Riverview Only)
	4 Days (Thornhill Only)
Department Head Training	1 Day
Parallel Payroll	5 Days
Miscellaneous Payroll Functions	3 Days
Review outstanding issues	1 Day

Operations Training: **5 Days**

Consideration should be given to scheduling 5 days of operations training, 2-3 days when the system goes live and the remainder after several months of operation.

PROJECT MANAGEMENT

Schedule

In order to project the number of days required for project management, a summary schedule was developed based on conversations with hospital personnel coupled with past experience at other hospitals.

Key Milestone Dates

G/L, A/P Implementation:	1-Oct-89
Material Management Live:	1-Nov-89
Conversion of Payroll Data:	?-Nov-89
Payroll/Personnel	1-Dec-89

EXHIBIT 7   *(Cont.)*

Projected Days Required

The days required for project management are listed below. These days are based on the above schedule and our previous experience with implementing Dovetail. These days are our best estimate and are, therefore, subject to mutually agreed revisions as the project progresses.

September	5 Days
October	9 Days
November	5 Days
December	3 Days
January	1 Day
TOTAL: 23 Days	

Project Management Approach

Dovetail is committed to working with our customers towards the common goal of a smooth implementation of the Dovetail System. We believe that communication among all people involved in the implementation is vital. We will strive to keep communication open and as up to date as possible.

Successful projects are implemented in an environment of cooperation, communication and team work. We believe that Dovetail's project management skill will be a positive addition to this implementation.

---

computer reports, and I believe the inventory balances are not accurate; they blame the delays in entering Purchase Orders into the system. This leads me to believe that they are not managing their inventory or their module well. Third, the payroll will not be able to go live January 1, because the programmer who was writing the software to convert the files from the service centre to the new computer is very sick with pneumonia and nobody else will be able to finish the job in time."

Louis and John discussed the problems and arrived at an action plan to correct the problem. Louis agreed to encourage Pam Smythe, the Accounts Payable clerk, to spend time entering November's invoices into the system and to speak with Peter, the materials management manager, about his module. John mentioned that he would arrange for the Dovetail Materials Management trainer to come and review the system with the Materials Management staff as soon as possible.

In January, John worked with Pam to enter the November Invoices into the system. Louis talked with Pam and realized that his earlier requests for working overtime went largely ignored because the staff thought they would not get paid for overtime. Louis assured them that they would get paid overtime.

Entering the invoices was complicated by the elapsed time since the goods had arrived and the many errors in purchase orders. Invoices could only be entered against a purchase order previously entered into the system, and then only when the order was marked by the receiver as having been received. When the system was notified that the goods had been received, a liability was created for the value of the goods as per the Purchase Order. The invoice was entered into the system, and if it matched the liability exactly, a cheque was produced. In the conversion, all the Purchase orders, receipts, and invoices were entered for one month as a parallel to ensure that the old and the new systems were matched and this also provided an accounting 'trail' for the auditors to follow.

THE DECISION

By Monday, February 12, all the November Invoices were entered and matched to the purchase orders. The system was ready for the first month end to be run overnight. The month end failed because Material Management had not run their month end first. After investigating further, John found that the Materials Management manager did not know how to run a month end and thought that accounting was responsible for starting the run.

After both the Inventory and Accounts Payable month ends had been run on Tuesday evening, Louis requested the computer to generate the first set of financial statements Wednesday morning. The financial statements were worse than Louis imagined. First, the Accounts Payable Liabilities for November were $1.4 million, not even close to the current system's liability of $50,000. Additionally, the Inventory value was shown as over $1 million dollars when it should be about $70,000. Finally, three months of inventory issues had been entered into November's expenses.

After a long discussion with John, Louis realized he could either parallel the system for four months from November to February or start fresh after the Audit and the year end stock count sometime in April.

Louis spent most of Wednesday and Thursday working with the statements trying to understand the magnitude of the errors. His main concern was inventory, where there were some obvious mistakes, like photocopier paper inventoried at about $1 per sheet. With 200 items in inventory, correcting errors would require at least a half hour per item just to investigate the problems. Some of the discrepancies arose from mistakes on Purchase Orders or the corresponding goods receipts. With about 800-900 purchase orders generated over the past four months, it could take a couple of weeks of analysis to sort out the purchase order problems. If all the Accounts payable invoices were entered, the program to match invoices to purchase orders would help materials management to find a lot of the problems. To date, only November invoices had been entered into the system; it could take Pam Smythe 40 to 50 hours to enter a month's invoices.

Louis felt that his odds were "50-50" of being able to balance the statements to the old system in

time. Louis did not feel confident that even with all invoices, purchase orders, and receipts entered and checked that all the errors could be found before the audit started in April. Louis wondered how the work would get done. Should he attempt to utilize temporary employees who would know nothing about the system, or spend the money and utilize the Dovetail trainers, at $650 per day, or should he rely on his staff to work enough overtime at an overtime rate of about $20 per hour?

Louis was concerned that delaying the implementation would prolong the frustration until next May or June. Louis knew the morale of the staff working with the new system was not good. The accounting staff had just finished working on the budget, a very busy time of the year. Wilma Lo was in especially bad shape; she was irritable, constantly blaming everyone else for each petty incident, and Louis noticed during one coffee break that she was shaking when she held her cup. The system was constantly going down, Louis believed that Wilma was too preoccupied to schedule preventive maintenance to catch problems in time. Pam Smythe was frustrated with all the obstacles in both the new and the old systems. Louis was also worried about how much longer Tim Withers would be able to handle the stress, given his heart condition.

Louis wondered if the current micro-computer system would be able to last much longer. During the last month, the micro-computer had been broken for six days and there were a number of corrupt files on the disk which was overloaded. To work around the problems, Pam Smythe was having to trick the system into producing Accounts Payable cheques.

Louis knew that the Audit would keep his accounting staff very busy during the month of April, and it would be a messy and difficult audit if based on the old system. Louis could not imagine which was worse, trying to implement the system during April while doing an audit or implementing the system now. If he continued to implement the new system, and the systems did not balance by March 30, his Audit would become extremely complicated; the fees could double from the typical bill of $15,000. The auditors would not regard a botched implementation lightly. They could cast Louis in a most unfavourable light in the Management Report that was prepared by the Auditors for the Finance and Audit Committee.

Louis questioned why he had not known about the problems earlier, and wondered what changes were necessary to prevent this lack of communication from recurring?

The Finance and Audit committee would not be pleased with another delay in the system implementation. Implementing in April would push computer implementation expenses into another fiscal year, something Louis was sure the Board would want to avoid.

Louis had to make a decision soon; the Finance and Audit Committee of the board of directors was to meet on Tuesday, February 20. They expected an update on the status of the system implementation.

Case 2

GOURMET-BY-MAIL
POINT-OF-SALE
SYSTEM

The phone was ringing again. Steve Polidaro, head of the MIS department stared at it, willing it to be silent. The complaints came in an almost constant stream. They might slow for some period but they never stopped completely. The franchisees were furious that one year after the roll-out of the new point-of-sale system, the cash registers in their stores were still not functioning properly. Steve sighed and reflected on the events of the past couple of years.

HISTORY OF GOURMET-BY-MAIL

Gourmet-By-Mail was started in the mid-1930s in California. It started as a small gourmet retail food store and eventually evolved into a 1300 location business by 1985. The company branched out into the mail-order gourmet food business in 1950 to serve customers that were unable to get to the retail stores. The company was closely held by the

Myers family. Alan Myers remained at the helm throughout with his closest advisors also being family members. Myers' strategy was to continue to open retail stores modeled after a new store which was opened in 1968. Given the shift in emphasis from mail order to retail locations, the name of the company was changed to GBM.

The late 1980s brought about a host of changes for the company. Shortly after Myers' death, the company stock hit an all-time low. In 1985, the board at GBM elected to bring in a new president and CEO, Otis Nelson. Nelson was highly regarded by the industry as a miracle-worker having just completed a turnaround for a troubled fitness equipment company.

Nelson promptly made moves to reposition the company as a specialty retailer of gourmet foods. He closed about 300 unprofitable stores and earmarked $20 million for expansion and remodeling of the most profitable stores. The company developed its own line of GBC prepackaged dinners. During this time, GBM had cultivated an extremely loyal base of customers, and its goal was to continue to increase its market share.

This case was prepared by a student under the direction of Professor Chris F. Kemerer as the basis for class discussion rather than to illustrate either effective or ineffective handling of an administrative situation.

Nelson began an innovative program of selling franchises in 1987. His motive was to finance expansion and create a new spirit of entrepreneurialism within the company. Many of these franchise stores were offered to former GBM employees. The reasoning was that these were people that best knew the GBM business. The company offered financing to the new owners and a very high visibility, high quality marketing program. A franchise store typically increased its sales by 60% in its first year. Due to this extraordinary increase, management aggressively pursued expansion efforts on the franchise scene.

In 1990, a leveraged buy out was completed by the Seattle-based Grant Corporation. The Grant Company brought in Michael Samuelson to be the new president. Otis Nelson remained CEO and was elected Chairman of the Board. The Grant Company waited patiently as sales slowly increased over the next several years. To decrease the amount of debt that the company had amassed over the past years due to the LBO, the Grant Company decided to hold an initial public stock offering in 1992. By doing this, they decreased the amount of debt that GBM carried by more than 50 percent. At the hands of the new president, the company continued to grow. Mr. Samuelson's philosophy was to pursue only projects that would affect the company's bottom line. For example, employees had been asking for direct deposit of their paychecks for years. Although management viewed this as a worthwhile project, they kept moving it to the bottom of the priority list since it was something that would not immediately show up in the sales or profit numbers for the company.

Since the new management team has taken over, the number of GBM outlets in the United States has more than doubled to 2270. Future projections plan for this number to reach 4000 by the year 2000. No one main competitor exists since it has been the company's main strategy to buy out any potential rival chains. For example, California Creations and Epicurean Delites were acquired in 1991 and 1993, respectively. The last acquisition occurred in 1994 with GBM acquiring approximately 400 La Parisian Patisserie outlets in the US. See Exhibit 1 for the company's financial data over the last several years.

ORGANIZATION OF THE COMPANY

The company's organizational structure was based on a traditional hierarchy. See Exhibit 2 for the organizational chart. The president, Mr. Samuelson, led the organization with heads of all departments reporting directly to him. Department heads included Richard Swindell, VP and General Manager. Swindell had come with Samuelson from the specialty foods industry. Walter Polin, VP of Legal Counsel had joined GBM in 1988 when Otis Nelson was at the helm. Paul Dravis, VP of Distribution & Production had been running since 1985. Samuelson hired John Livingston, VP & CFO, fifteen months ago. Charles Randolff, VP of New Business Development had previously worked for the competing Health Foods, USA. Steve Polidaro, VP of Management Information Systems had joined the company six years earlier when the company was under the management of Nelson.

The relationships between the departments at GBM tended to be very competitive. The department heads vied for the president's positive attention and recognition. Every quarter, the financial numbers for each department were analyzed and recognition for good and bad performance was made public throughout the organization. The solid performers had the entire three-month period to bask in their success while the poor performers had to endure embarrassment for that same period.

The president of GBM ran a no-nonsense operation that was solely profit-driven. He was renowned for being very resistant to employee requests and expectations that would require any type of change. Mr. Samuelson denied requests for flexible work hours or "flex-time" because he said he did not believe in it. The policy of Friday being dress-down day, which was relatively common and becoming accepted by an increasing number of companies was not permitted at GBM. No policy

EXHIBIT 1

Balance Sheet (In Millions)

Assets	6/31/95	6/25/94	6/26/93	6/27/92
Cash	$ 1.16	$ 1.16	$ 50.72	$ 4.20
Receivables	$ 35.07	$ 27.93	$ 15.96	$ 12.39
Inventories	$ 148.05	$ 99.65	$ 72.98	$ 61.95
Prop, Plant & Equip	$ 118.86	$ 77.81	$ 63.21	$ 55.86
Other Assets	$ 354.80	$ 283.50	$ 286.13	$ 284.03
Total Assets	$ 657.93	$ 490.04	$ 488.99	$ 418.43
Liabilities	6/31/95	6/25/94	6/26/93	6/27/92
Accounts Payable	$ 55.13	$ 40.43	$ 30.35	$ 42.74
Accrued Expenses	$ 15.54	$ 15.65	$ 13.34	$ 18.27
Income Taxes	$ 3.68	$ 3.47	$ 6.83	$ 6.30
Current Liabilities	$ 159.18	$ 119.91	$ 135.24	$ 86.73
Long Term Debt	$ 211.37	$ 142.38	$ 228.17	$ 220.82
Total Liabilities	$ 444.89	$ 321.83	$ 413.91	$ 374.85
Equity	6/31/95	6/25/94	6/26/93	6/27/92
Common Stock Net	$ 0.42	$ 0.42	$ 0.32	$ 0.11
Capital Surplus	$ 208.53	$ 202.44	$ 135.66	$ 105.00
Retained Earnings	$ (1.16)	$ (40.22)	$ (64.89)	$ (61.53)
Other Equities	$ 5.25	$ 5.57	$ 6.30	NA
Shareholder Equity	$ 213.05	$ 168.21	$ 75.08	$ 43.58
Total Liab & Equity	$ 657.93	$ 490.04	$ 488.99	$ 418.43

Annual Income (In millions)

Fiscal Year Ending	6/31/95	6/25/94	6/26/93	6/27/92
Net Sales	$ 706.55	$ 573.62	$ 476.18	$ 413.28
Cost of Goods	$ 440.06	$ 357.74	$ 302.72	$ 267.54
Gross Profit	$ 266.49	$ 215.88	$ 173.46	$ 145.74
Sell Gen & Admin Exp	$ 155.51	$ 129.15	$ 113.72	$ 103.64
Inc Bef Dep & Amort	$ 110.99	$ 86.73	$ 59.75	$ 42.11
Non-Operating Inc	$ (8.30)	$ (7.14)	$ (14.18)	$ (7.14)
Interest Expense	$ 20.69	$ 24.47	$ 34.65	$ 37.59
Income Before Tax	$ 82.01	$ 55.13	$ 10.92	$ (2.62)
Prov for Inc Taxes	$ 33.92	$ 24.05	$ 5.88	$ 4.41
Net Income	$ 48.09	$ 31.08	$ 5.04	$ (7.03)

for tuition reimbursement existed for employees who were interested in furthering their education. Once during a yearly employee meeting, an employee asked why, if the company was doing so well, didn't GBM "share the wealth." Mike Samuelson's response was,

"You've all got jobs, don't you? I don't see any prospective layoffs in the near future either."

THE MIS DEPARTMENT

The structure of the organization within the MIS department was a traditional hierarchy. See Exhibit 3 for an organizational chart of the MIS department. The department was headed by Steve Polidaro and was split into two general classifications of hardware issues/support and applications programming. The hardware group managed the purchase, installation and maintenance of all computers (mainframe, mini and PCs) and peripherals. This group also maintained the networks and associated applications at all company locations. The applications group was split into three subgroups: (1) administrative applications, (2) distribution applications and (3) retail applications. In each subgroup, there were lead analysts, analysts, programmer/analysts, and programmers.

Andy Bender managed the administrative applications group, which had six employees. This group supported all administrative and human resource functions including payroll and insurance. All applications were designed for the mainframe.

Distribution applications was managed by Donna Costa and was the largest subgroup with 15 employees. Distribution was a key function within GBM and was heavily supported as indicated by the number of employees. All applications were mainframe-based.

Ted Ashton headed the ten person retail applications group. Retail was responsible for all applications that supported sales and retail operations. For many retail applications projects, the end-users were the managers of the retail stores. This included the Point-of-Sale or POS system. Most of the applications in retail were mainframe-based

but as PCs were becoming more of a commodity item, more applications were being written to run on the PC platform. The POS system included programs to run on PCs and programs to process batch data on the mainframe. Ashton had a strong background in mainframe programming but had little experience with PCs and PC-based applications.

As expected, the retail applications group had frequent interaction with the retail stores. Many retail application programs were designed for use by the store managers. There were two types of GBM retail stores. The original stores were the corporate stores which were managed and run by employees of GBM. Managers of the corporate stores received their paychecks from corporate headquarters. Corporate stores were constrained by what headquarters wanted for them rather than what they themselves thought would best serve their needs. Once, in a system specification meeting, Ashton said,

"I'm not really interested in whether the corporate stores like the way we design this or not. We really know better than them what they need. Besides, they work for us so they'll do it the way we tell them."

The newer franchise stores were an unfamiliar entity. Since these stores were privately owned and run, the owners had a much larger stake in trying to get things done in a way that would make their jobs easier. It had been difficult for corporate headquarters to adjust to this unfamiliar line of thinking. The MIS department was still trying to get used to the difference in dealing with the franchise stores.

HOW THE NEED FOR A POS SYSTEM EVOLVED

As the company grew, it became more difficult to manage the processing of data from the increasing number of stores. Management decided to create a standardized, computer-based POS system. They expected that a POS system would make record keeping and information processing at the corporate office easier. In addition, a POS system would make operations at the store level more efficient.

EXHIBIT 2

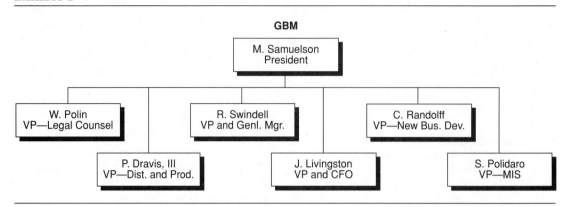

Before the point-of-sale system was created, there was very little standardization in daily operations from store to store. Corporate stores were using two different basic types of cash registers. The POS system would require standardized hardware at each store. This would make supporting register operations easier since the support staff at corporate only had to be trained on one system rather than several.

Maintaining current prices and price changes on items in the stores typically took up 50% of the store employees' time. Employees spent much of their time placing price tags on every item. In addition, price change information was communicated to the stores weekly so it was not as timely as the store managers would have liked it to be.

Nearly all of the record keeping at the store level had to be done manually. Sales history information was kept on paper. Records of inventory levels had to be kept manually. Timely reports on pertinent sales information were unavailable to the managers. Delays were inherent with this predominantly paper system.

The POS system would include a bar-code scanner, which would allow employees to scan product prices. The scanning system would also help in maintaining accurate inventory on-line. Reports that managers wanted but previously had no way of obtaining would be available on a timely basis. On-line stores had more accurate pricing information since this data was updated nightly.

Before POS, the primary way that corporate headquarters received sales information from the stores was via paper. To get the store data into the GBM mainframe for processing, computer operators had to key the data into the mainframe system at headquarters. The POS system provided a nightly "polling" or gathering of data that eliminated the need for re-keying data and thereby eliminated the opportunity for human keying errors in the data.

WHAT THE SYSTEM DID

The POS system was a menu-driven DOS-based application. Use of a mouse or other pointing device was still uncommon in the stores so menus were manipulated by using the arrow and enter keys. The POS system performed several very important functions. Primarily, it was the cash register for the store. RFS, a third-party vendor located in California, developed and supported the actual cash register and sales functions of the system. Other GBM-designed features and functions were integrated with the cash register functions through "hooks" in the RFS code. These hooks were a type of placeholder within the RFS code that allowed the GBM functions to be included. The RFS register functions were initiated from batch files on the PC. Within these batch files, RFS provided empty sections for the GBM programs to be started.

The POS system kept real-time data on pricing, sales history and inventory data. Reporting functions to summarize this data were available. At any time, a manager could run a report and find out exactly how much of an item was in stock or had sold this week or month.

The POS system also kept track of employee and payroll data. The register functioned as a time-clock system where the store employees could punch in and out. Reporting functions were available to the store manager.

The system facilitated daily communication with corporate headquarters via nightly polling sessions. Each register had a link to the corporate office via a modem and phone line. Each day before leaving the stores, the manager would close out and back up the data on the register. The last function in this daily process was for the register to enter a polling mode. The register would wait in this mode until corporate headquarters dialed in and connected with it each night to do the data transfers.

Headquarters initiated polling operations at 11:00 P.M. each night. Different polling sessions ran from four different polling machines. Each polling session corresponded to one of the four time zones in the United States. Portions of these sessions often overlapped in the hours they were running but the entire polling process was completed by 5:00 A.M. so mainframe processing could begin.

Data transfers were done in both send and receive directions. All the daily sales and payroll data were transferred from the stores to corporate headquarters for mainframe processing. Then, any new product and pricing data was transferred from corporate headquarters to the stores. Any program updates and fixes were also transferred from headquarters to the stores during this nightly polling session.

After the stores were polled each night, the polling network transferred all of the store data to the corporate mainframe for processing. Mainframe programs to analyze sales, trends and predict product demand were scheduled to run after polling was completed. The polling process typically took 15–30 seconds per store when no program updates were being sent. With approximately 1200 corporate stores, polling was taking close to three hours per time zone to complete. Polidaro and Ashton were aware that as new stores were opened, time for the entire polling operation was gradually taking longer.

The corporate POS system was completed in 1991. The price tag on the final system was $7 million to develop and install. While the executives at GBM were pleased with the effort, the corporate stores were thrilled. A manager of a store in Louisville, Kentucky said,

> "I had fewer pricing errors in ringing up sales, I could be pretty sure that my inventory numbers were correct and price changes from corporate took effect immediately. Sure it took some time to get all the employees familiar with our new way of doing things. But once trained, they saw the value in it as well. For example, whenever we got new products in, the system automatically had the correct prices already in the register. Since we were unfamiliar with the new items, it was very helpful that the system already had the information for us. The POS system sure made my life a lot easier!"

FRANCHISEES REQUEST SIMILAR SYSTEM

After seeing how much more efficient the corporate stores had become, the franchisees recognized their need for a similar system. They began to express their wishes to management. Management viewed POS as an opportunity to placate the franchisees. In the past, the franchisees had often felt like second-class citizens when it came to corporate making an effort to meet their requests. For example, there had been rumors circulating among the franchisees that preferential treatment was given to the corporate stores when it

EXHIBIT 3

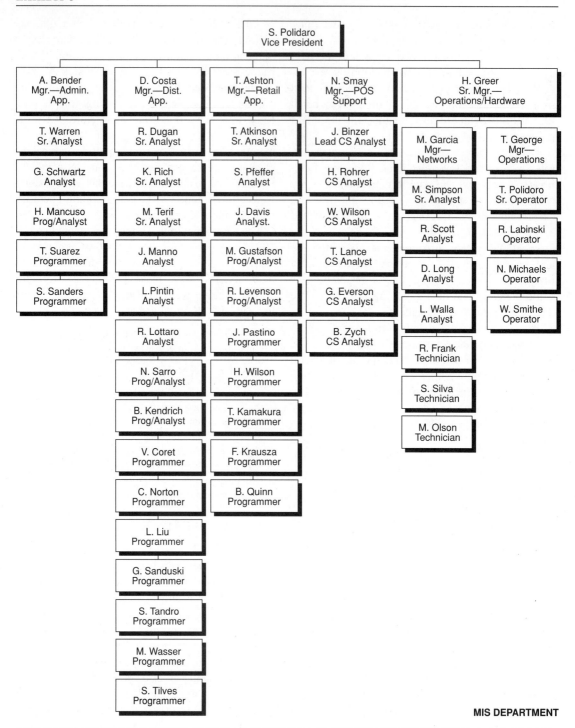

MIS DEPARTMENT

came to providing the stores with products to sell. The franchisees were pleased that corporate was making an effort to meet their needs. Corporate had committed to the POS system with little resistance and this made the franchisees feel more secure.

A POS system for franchise stores would be similar to that used by the corporate stores but there were some differences. It had been unnecessary for the complete sales history to be maintained at the corporate store level. These data were uploaded from the corporate store registers nightly and kept on the mainframe system. However, the franchise stores required that this data be kept at the store level. The reason for this was that franchise stores functioned more independently than the corporate stores and the store managers had far more leeway in the day-to-day operations of their businesses. Another consequence of the difference in store operations was that the franchisees also expected more detailed reports would be made available to them. The sales history files were used in almost every register operation.

In many cases, franchise stores had the option of overriding suggestions that came from corporate headquarters where the corporate stores did not. An example of this was in the area of placing orders for products. Corporate could suggest a quantity and franchise stores could either accept or change the quantity. Another example was in pricing. The pricing information that franchisees received from headquarters could also be accepted or changed. Corporate stores did not have an option in either of these cases. After closer inspection of what franchise stores would need in a POS system compared to what corporate already had, it appeared that about 75% of the functions in the POS system would need to be modified, some extensively.

Coinciding with the time of the franchise request, there was a rapid change in user expectations from software. As the franchise stores were realizing their need for a similar POS system in 1991, the popularity of the new Microsoft Windows-based applications was growing. The arrival of this technology created a general users' expectation of more easier and more user-friendly software programs. Although corporate POS functioned adequately, it was a DOS-based application and as time passed, it began to "show its age."

FRANCHISE POS DEVELOPMENT TEAM

Initially, eight people were assigned to the franchise POS project, three of them being analysts. Judy Davis had been with the company for six years since obtaining her bachelor's degree. She worked primarily on mainframe applications. Susan Pfeffer had been with GBM for seven years after working at a local bank for three years. She worked on a mix of mainframe and micro applications and had been involved in the corporate POS effort. Terry Atkinson had been with the company for nine years, having accepted an offer immediately after obtaining his undergraduate degree. He was a talented designer and programmer who knew in detail the technical specifics of hardware and coding. Terry had led the corporate POS effort and was the natural choice to head the franchise POS development effort. One programmer said,

> "Terry's background in the POS system was solid but unfortunately a lot of times, he got too confident in his knowledge and took shortcuts. Sometimes program and test walk-throughs were cut short or eliminated altogether to save time. This happened more frequently toward the end of the effort."

The outcome of rushing through established procedures often resulted in missing documentation. In addition, four programmers were assigned to the franchise POS project. They were Ralph Levenson, Hannah Wilson, Justin Pastino and Michelle Gustafson. Ralph, Hannah and Justin were new to GBM, all being hired within the last year and a half. Only Michelle had worked on the corporate POS system. Michelle was very technical and knew the most about the polling of the registers. She provided almost exclusive support for the existing polling network.

FRANCHISE SYSTEM DEVELOPMENT BEGINS

In April 1993, MIS management committed to developing a POS system for the franchise stores. Since MIS management was still under the impression that only minor modifications to the corporate POS system code were necessary, they settled on what they believed to be a conservative date for beginning the roll-out of the franchise POS system. The target date was the last quarter of 1993.

The corporate POS system had been developed entirely using the Microsoft C language. In 1992, Microsoft Visual C was becoming very popular and was the version of the compiler found on most of the developer's desktop PCs.

When writing to the register screen, the standard way to write to a screen in a C program did not work. The POS register hardware required a special set of graphics routines for their display functions. Calls to routines from a third-party software package had to be done in the POS system source code. Using this method had worked quite well for the corporate system. Now, several years later, new versions of the software had been released making the older version that GBM had used outdated and obsolete. Since using a newer version of graphics software would require almost an entire rewrite of some programs, the decision was made to continue to use the older version. Due to the outdated software, each time problems were discovered in the graphics routines, the GBM programmers were forced to find a way to "work-around" the problem. The preferable way of having the vendor fix the bugs was not an option since the software version GBM was using was no longer actively supported by the developer.

It was difficult for the developers to test the code they were writing since the register screen-writing routines were hardware specific and would not run properly on their PCs. The test lab was located on a different floor of the building. It contained six registers; three were permanently configured with the programs for corporate POS and three were permanently set up to run the franchise POS system. Some of the larger retail stores had two registers that were networked together. Testing this configuration required two of the test registers at a time. When asked about the testing setup, one programmer said,

> "Anytime I have something to test, I have to find a free test register. If it's a program for a two register system, I have to connect the registers with the network cables and boot the network software. Then I compile the code under the old Microsoft C compiler and try to run it. If it doesn't run, there is no way to interactively debug the programs. I have to edit the code, put in some print statements to try to find the problem. It is a time-consuming process and a real pain."

The passage of time and the relatively short life cycle for new PC processors made hardware advances fairly frequent. The corporate POS registers were based on an Intel 80286 processor. By the time the franchise system was being developed in 1993, the new registers were based on the Intel 80386 processor, which was much more powerful than an 80286-based machine. Other PC features such as hard disk drive sizes and access speeds had also changed. The difference in hardware platforms was another difference between corporate and franchise POS systems.

Several times, the network support staff had chosen to modify the source code of the SoftNet network polling software. This was necessary so the software would properly support GBM's network configuration. Due to these custom modifications, the prospect of upgrading to the latest version of polling software was very unappealing. The version of the polling software that GBM was using had become so outdated that the SoftNet company no longer supported it. Upgrading all stores and polling machines was such a large project that management kept putting it off.

Throughout 1993 as development efforts progressed, the retail applications group became so busy that they pulled Michelle into programming full time. She no longer had time to support the polling network so management passed it over to the hardware support group. In retail, support of the polling network had started as a small part of the POS effort, but had grown into a project that was no longer manageable by the group. Matt Garcia, the manager of the hardware support group said,

> "Retail managed the polling network up to this point. Now my group has to get involved and support something that had gotten way out of hand. I hope Retail realizes that I have other projects to manage besides this."

FRANCHISE POS RELEASE

The November 1993 release date for the franchise POS system came quickly. At this point, the quality control group was still testing the system so MIS pushed the release date back to February 1994. Their reasoning was that this would be plenty of time to finish final quality control procedures. When the February date arrived, POS support was still finding problems. During the executive staff meeting, Steve Polidaro again told Mike Samuelson that the release date would have to be pushed back, this time to March 1994. The other departments had a field day with the MIS department's situation. Rich Swindell and John Livingston antagonized Polidaro about the missed deadlines every chance they got and Mr. Samuelson was starting to become impatient. As the March 1994 date quickly approached, QC was still discovering new bugs. Polidaro was embarrassed by having to give the same excuse repeatedly. Against his better judgment, he made a decision and told Ashton to begin the installation of the system in April 1994.

The roll-out was scheduled to be done in groups of 100 stores per week. Using this schedule, MIS expected all retail stores to be live in within 12 weeks. As the roll-out began, the POS support group was inundated with problem reports immediately. The manager of POS support sometimes worked 14 hour days just to keep up with the calls. The telephone support staff was increased from five to 15 over six months just to manage the problem phone calls.

Michelle and Terry endured most of the grief of the late, then prematurely released system. Management made more demands on them and their time. Michelle carried a beeper for emergencies so the POS support group could reach her. Michelle said,

> "When I first got my pager, I thought it was kind of neat but after franchise POS, it seemed to be going off ALL THE TIME! I wasn't getting enough sleep at night and the more time I put in, the more time management expected me to put in."

In June 1994, things were not getting any better and there did not look like there was an end in sight. Michelle submitted her resignation. It was two months after the beginning of the franchise POS roll-out. She took a position with a bank which would provide her with more regular hours. Terry followed her out the door shortly after, having secured a senior consulting position with a "big six" accounting firm.

Repair efforts on the franchise POS system continued for the next eight months through the rest of 1994 and into 1995. Over this period, up to six people at once in retail applications had been allocated to fix problems with the system.

The system continues to be used and repaired as problems are discovered and reported from the field. One person is dedicated full-time to delegating the problems with the system to programmers and analysts. Three people are working on problems full-time and other employees are involved but these people are typically spending some of their time on other projects as well.

GBM's relationship with the register vendor has become very strained. Some of the problems that cropped up in the franchise system had to do with hardware disk space, memory constraints, and general incompatibility with the RFS code as the size of the GBM code grew. GBM and RFS spent a lot of time blaming each other as problems arose. At one point, a frustrating problem with the registers locking up prompted Ted Ashton to call the RFS contact person and say,

> "Kim, we never had these problems with the old RFS software, what in the world did you guys change that screwed everything up!"

Kim became furious and fired back,

> "You guys are making changes too. How do you know it's not your problem?"

The pricing and sales history files for the franchise stores that must be kept on the registers have continued to grow over time. The design team neglected to plan for a way to archive or off-load some of the older, unused history data. As a result, from time to time, some of the franchise stores are pushing the limits of the capacity of their register hard disk drives.

Due to the franchise stores being added to polling process, polling is now taking up to five hours to complete. As more franchise and corporate stores are added to the fast-growing company, the polling process is having problems handling the additional load. The schedule of mainframe processes that run after polling had to be shuffled. The polling process sometimes takes longer than anticipated due to program updates and fixes that must be sent out. The method that was used in the past to keep track of failed polling sessions had proven unacceptable as the number of stores grew.

In January 1995, eight months after franchise POS roll-out began, Mike Samuelson called a meeting between Steve, Ted and the other department heads to decide what to do. Eight months after initial roll-out, the franchise POS system was still not stable. Samuelson wanted Polidaro and Ashton to commit to a "guaranteed" solution to the problem.

WHAT NEXT?

Steve Polidaro reflected on all that had happened so far. He thought over what his options were. He thought about continuing to fix problems and trying to get the system stabilized. Based on past experience and how stable he guessed that the franchise system was at this point, he estimated that this would require some commitment of time and resources over the next 12 months, which would take them into 1996. Steve also felt that the test register facilities had to be upgraded immediately if they were going to continue the fixing process.

Steve also thought about tackling certain sections of the POS system such as upgrading the polling network, changing the display routines for the register screens, or trying to make the system a Windows-based application. Then he thought about designing the entire system over again from scratch.

This would entail everything from the design stages and forward. Steve thought,

"We already have so much time and resources into this, I can't stand the thought of starting over. But, I want to do what's right."

Steve sighed as he sat back to try to decide what to do next.

Case 3

DIAND'S EXECUTIVE INFORMATION SYSTEM

This case was prepared by Professors Sid L. Huff and Duncan G. Copeland of the Western Business School. Copyright 1993, The University of Western Ontario.

"People here are becoming aware that personal computers can be used to do more than just compose memos or process electronic mail," said Bruce Handel. "In addition, the ADM* I report to does not believe that our PCs are being used to their full potential. We've got to do more to allow

_____

*Assistant Deputy Minister—roughly equivalent to a vice-president in the private sector.

senior management to make the best possible use of the data holdings of the department."

Handel, Director of the Client Services Directorate within the Informatics Branch of DIAND, the Department of Indian Affairs and Northern Development, knew for some time that the department's central computer systems held a great deal of information which might be of use to the senior managers—if only they could access it easily and efficiently. To date, however, the PCs on their desks did not allow them easy access to the central databases. Senior managers rarely attempted to use their personal computers for much more than sending and receiving electronic mail, and for occasional word processing. Some did not use PCs at all.

Handel thought that it should be possible to develop an Executive Information System, or EIS, for senior management to access and analyze the central data—as well as information brought in from outside the department—using their own desktop PCs. Jim Moskos, a project manager within Handel's area, was charged with developing an EIS for the department. Moskos had created a DIAND EIS conceptual architecture, and was proceeding to build the EIS itself following a prototyping approach. Now that an early prototype of the system had been created and demonstrated, and the EIS idea promoted to the executive team at a recent offsite meeting, Handel realized that expectations were building among the senior managers for the full EIS. He believed that, if the EIS was successful, it had the potential to substantially alter the way the department managed its affairs; its impacts would be far-reaching. But many questions remained. What exactly would its impacts *be*? Was the design of the EIS appropriate for the target user group's needs? Would senior management fully accept and use the system? How would the remaining technical challenges be overcome? And, once senior management did have direct, hands-on access to the department's data, what would they think about the quality and quantity of that data? What if it turned out that the data they discovered they really wanted, wasn't there?

DEPARTMENT OF INDIAN AFFAIRS AND NORTHERN DEVELOPMENT

DIAND was one of the 33 ministries of the Canadian government. It was created in 1966, initially, to lead the development of services for Canada's native peoples. In 1993, the Department consisted of nearly 4,000 staff (down from 6,200 eight years earlier), and controlled a total budget of $4.6 billion. The Department defined its mission as "working together to make Canada a better place for First Nations and Northern peoples." Among other things, department responsibilities included:

- Fulfillment of the lawful obligations of the federal government to native people arising from treaties, the Indian Act and other federal government legislation, including:
  —Administration of Indian reserve lands;
  —Administration of the elections of First Nation councils;
  —Management of registration of entitlement to Indian status and First Nation membership;
  —Administration of the funds of First Nations and the estates of certain individual Indians;
- Provision for the delivery of basic services (such as education, social assistance, housing, and community infrastructure) to status Indians and Inuit communities;
- Assistance to Indians and Inuit to acquire employment skills and to develop viable businesses;
- Negotiation of the settlement of accepted native land claims;
- Providing support for the government's ongoing constitutional efforts, primarily in areas relevant to native people.

DIAND also held various responsibilities for managing and administering northern Canada development, through both direct action as well as through a transfer of funding to the governments of the two northern territories.

The department interacted with its clients mainly through the elected leaders of Canada's 604 different native bands and their organizations.

These ranged from the Popkum, consisting of only eight people, to the Six Nations with a total membership of over 16,000.

DIAND itself was headquartered in a large, modern office building at 10 Wellington Street in Hull, Quebec, just across the Ottawa River from downtown Ottawa. However, much of the department was decentralized: over 65% of DIAND's employees worked out of nine regional offices, which supplied a wide variety of services to a culturally, economically, and geographically diverse collection of native and northern peoples throughout the country.

In the summer of 1993, as part of a government-wide initiative to restructure and streamline government operations, DIAND initiated a reorganization which resulted in both staff reductions as well as in responsibility assignment changes. Following this reorganization, the department comprised five major sectors: Corporate Services, Claims and Indian Government, Lands and Trust Services, Northern Affairs, and Policy and Strategic Direction. Each sector was headed by an Assistant Deputy Minister. Informatics Branch, which included Bruce Handel's Client Services Directorate, was part of the Corporate Services sector. Operationally, the entire department was headed by a Deputy Minister, who reported to the Minister, an elected member of Parliament charged with the responsibility for Indian Affairs and Northern Development. A departmental organizational chart is given in Exhibit 1.

EXHIBIT 1   DIAND Organization Chart

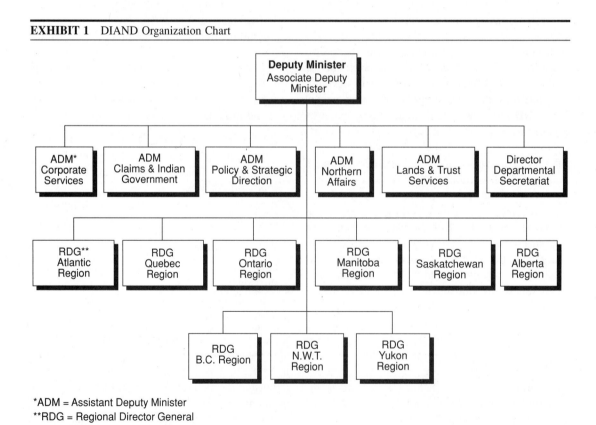

*ADM = Assistant Deputy Minister
**RDG = Regional Director General

DIAND had, over the years, acquired a reputation as being an especially well-managed department that was a good place in which to work. In each of the previous two years, DIAND had been a co-winner of an award given to the best-managed department of the federal government. In the current year, DIAND was the sole winner of this award.

DIAND'S ENVIRONMENT AND STRATEGY

DIAND functioned in a highly politicized and volatile environment. In recent years, serious frictions had arisen in the relations between the government and native people. One incident, in the summer of 1990, resulted in an armed standoff between the army and a native group at Oka, Quebec, which lasted for 77 days. Such incidents received a great deal of attention in the news media. Given this sort of environment, DIAND was viewed as a particularly challenging department to manage. The Government of Canada looked to the department not only to manage ongoing relations with native people, but also to be prepared to provide informed and timely advice, together with background information, in the event of crisis situations. Frequently, DIAND managers would find themselves scrambling to pull together up-to-date information, from wherever they could get it, in order to be able to respond to the issues of the day.

Overlaid on the day-to-day management of native issues, DIAND's long term strategy centered on the principle of devolution. Devolution referred to the ongoing transfer of administrative authority, responsibility, and resources directly into the hands of native bands. Until the onset of devolution, services were provided to native bands and individuals through programs managed by the department. For example, when it was decided to build and run a school on a native reserve, DIAND would administer and pay for the building of the school, hire and pay teachers to teach there, and so forth. Under devolution, these kinds of activities were being transferred to the control of the bands and tribal councils. DIAND still provided the necessary funding to the bands, but, under devolution, the elected representatives on the various band councils controlled the use of the funds.

Devolution was an ongoing process. Some bands had taken over the administration of nearly all the services DIAND had previously managed for them; others continued to rely on the department for such services. But the trend was clear: over time, the department was becoming more a provider of funds than a direct provider of services. DIAND's role was evolving from that of a service provider, into that of a funding organization (with an accountability to Parliament for the expenditure of public funds).

Juxtaposed against devolution was the notion of the fiduciary responsibility of the Government of Canada to aboriginal people. While the legal issues were very complex, it was often the case that the government (in effect, the department) continued to hold responsibility for such things as management of monies, lands, and native estates, even as much of the decision making authority over these things was being transferred to the native bands. As it pursued devolution, then, the government often found itself walking a difficult line between meeting the legitimate needs of various Indian bands, being charged with paternalistic behaviour by the client group, and trying to uphold the ongoing responsibilities of the Government of Canada to native peoples.

In order to uphold its fiduciary responsibilities and to properly understand the situation on the reserves, the department needed to gather various information from the bands, about local conditions, how the transferred funds were spent, the demographics of band members, and so forth. Prior to devolution, much of this needed information was gathered and transmitted to regional offices by DIAND staff. As devolution proceeded, however, the department was becoming ever more dependent on the First Nations and councils themselves, rather than DIAND personnel, for feeding needed information into the department. In many instances, local band governments were less than enthusiastic about gathering all sorts of data, filling out forms and communicating this information to the department.

Devolution created an opportunity for departmental downsizing. In the past, the department enjoyed larger-than-average increases in its annual operating budget. That was changing. The pressure to reduce the department's staffing level and administrative expenses stemmed from two sources. The fact of devolution clearly meant that fewer people should be required within the department itself to provide and administer services, since much of this work was being transferred to the bands. Furthermore, the government, generally, was under great pressure to reduce expenses in order to better manage its large and growing debt; this reality affected DIAND as well as all other government departments.

In October 1993, Canadians elected a new government. Aboriginal issues were a major priority in the election platform of the new government. Nonetheless, Jean Chretien, the incoming Prime Minister, mentioned during the election campaign that he might even consider doing away with DIAND altogether—in effect, completing the devolution mission in short order.

INFORMATION SYSTEMS AT DIAND

Information systems work in the department was centred in the Informatics Branch (IB), and within IB was organized into two "directorates," under the overall leadership of Jim Phillips. The Client Services Directorate, headed by Bruce Handel, was responsible for developing and maintaining the department's information systems applications. The Operations and Technical Services (OATS) Directorate, headed by Kate Dobson, held responsibility for operating the department's central computers and networks.

Phillips came to the department in 1987, after leading a team that designed and installed a sophisticated local area network throughout the Canadian Parliament buildings. Phillips inherited an IS group in disarray. He commented:

> At that time, we had some serious morale problems within the branch, and our relations with the rest of

the department were poor. We had experienced many of the same problems that occurred in IS departments in many companies: long backlogs of requests, inadequate attention to users' needs, and poor communications with our clients. We approached the development of information systems in a traditional manner—following a structured development methodology, and coding our applications in COBOL. Our application priorities were determined by the information needs of the program managers which were mainly tied back to their areas of accountability.

As the devolution process unfolded in the latter part of the 1980s, it became clear that DIAND's approach to designing, building and modifying its information systems was too cumbersome and stodgy to be able to handle the rapid changes that were occurring. Phillips explained, "The department was no longer program driven; we had become First Nation driven. Vertical information systems designed for stand-alone programs were just too isolated and rigid."

Informatics Branch, under Phillips's leadership, made some important changes in their approach to building and maintaining information systems for the department. In an effort to move away from the well understood but less productive COBOL programming environment of the past, they adopted the fourth generation programming language called PowerHouse. PowerHouse was sold and supported by the Ottawa-based, international software firm Cognos Ltd. A short time later they also adopted a computer-assisted software engineering (CASE) tool called Excelerator, to aid in the "front end" of system design and development. Training was provided to the development staff in both PowerHouse and Excelerator.

In late 1989, an effort was launched to better understand the future needs of the department for information systems and services. Several consulting firms were hired to lead an intensive systems planning process. A series of Strategic Business Analysis (SBA) and Business Requirements Study (BRS) projects were undertaken as a first step toward defining DIAND's complete set of information and applications requirements. With the help of the consultants, all areas of the department engaged in the creation of structure charts, data-process matrices, and functional decompositions of their operations. The work was time-consuming and difficult for both users and the systems staff. The documentation produced from the study was voluminous. For example, the document describing just one BRS, concerned with Band Support and Capital Management, was nearly 300 pages long.

In the end, there was substantial dissatisfaction with the results. Users were frequently unhappy because they felt they were being asked to put a lot of their time and energy into something that they did not fully understand or see the rationale for. Nor were the systems people fully satisfied. The studies' emphases on business processes produced results that quickly became obsolete.

Every change in DIAND's operating procedures would be reflected in changes in the process logic documented by the studies. Keeping the studies' results up-to-date proved to be an impossible task.

Furthermore, the new software tools were less than had been originally hoped. Jim Moskos, a Client Services project manager, recalled: "We wanted advanced software development tools because of the promise of rapid development, but we didn't know what we were getting into. We ended up choosing tools, and not examining our overall development approach. While we were drawing great pictures with Excelerator, and also building programs more rapidly with PowerHouse, we had really not automated our analysis. Also, Excelerator was not integrated with PowerHouse, so automatically generating code from our plans was not possible."

As a result, the department decided to adopt a new approach. Moskos was familiar with an approach to systems planning and development called "Information Engineering." The Information Engineering approach formalized the connection between an organization's strategic plans and its information systems. Strategic Management Statements either explicitly or implicitly formed

the business rationale for the existence of each data entity in a strategic data model, which then became the basis for all information systems development.

Following a consulting study, DIAND decided to adopt the Information Engineering approach. They recognized, however, that shifting to an Information Engineering methodology would render the work done in the earlier business process studies largely worthless. Handel and Phillips knew that they had used up a lot of goodwill among their user clientele in the department in the course of conducting the earlier studies, and did not relish at all the thought of approaching them with the need for even more, but different, studies.

With those concerns in mind, IB set out to develop a strategic data model for the department. A separate group within DIAND, called Quantitative Analysis and Statistical Research (QASR), headed by Janet Hagey, was given overall responsibility for guiding the development of the strategic data model. Hagey's staffing was increased by 5 people to provide the necessary manpower, and strategic data modelling began across the department. The Information Engineering era at DIAND had begun.

THE EXECUTIVE INFORMATION SYSTEM—GENESIS

As Bruce Handel thought about the evolving role of information systems in DIAND, one thing kept occurring to him. While they had made some important strides recently, essentially all their efforts were targeted at improving the operational capabilities of the department. Data modelling and information engineering would, he hoped, allow them to create a sound, lasting data architecture for the department. Case tools and prototyping development methods were allowing them to become much more efficient in creating new application systems. As appropriate and worthwhile as these efforts might be, they did not directly assist the *senior management* of the department. Conceivably, at some point in the future, DIAND could end up with a collection of high-quality integrated databases and efficient operational-level systems, and yet still have its senior managers functioning with traditional briefing books, file cabinets full of paper, and so forth.

Nonetheless, Handel was not at all eager, initially, to launch some sort of project aimed at providing computer access to the senior executives in the department. Handel elaborated:

> The notion of an EIS has been around for several years, but I had not accepted it as a reasonable undertaking for the department, primarily because I didn't feel we had adequate data. I've seen too many examples of systems that look good, but didn't have any substance to them. In those cases, people seem to be enamoured with the technology, but then stopped using it. A lot of money could be wasted.

In the past, problems of inadequate data within the department had been handled by layers of analysts and executive assistants, who would receive reports from the computer systems, and massage the raw data into a form usable by the executives. Gaps and inaccuracies in the computer-based data could be recognized and handled by these individuals, before the summary reports ever got to senior management.

Today the situation was changing. Handel continued:

> So far, we have concentrated our efforts in Indian Affairs in the past several years in building the data bases and the applications. It's not yet complete, but we have made a lot of progress. In the fall and winter of last year, Alan Williams (the Assistant Deputy Minister for Corporate Services) started to talk more about personal computers, and the extent to which they were being effectively used to manage the department. At the executive level they were used primarily for e-mail, and some small amount of word processing. When we thought about the pool of corporate data that *did* exist, we started to realize that our computers were not being used to their full potential. We have an awful lot of transaction data that is collected regularly, but executives do not have easy access to it. But it wouldn't make sense to just try to plug them into the existing transaction systems, because senior managers are not interested in transaction-level data, only in summarized information.

Furthermore, Handel knew that there were numerous other sources of information "out there," not on DIAND's computers, but potentially accessible electronically—for instance, Statistics Canada data, or on-line commercial databases, or even the nightly news! There were still other sources of information which could be converted to an electronic form, for example, documents such as briefing notes in the department. But there would be no sense in digitizing such information if the potential users of the information, the senior managers of the department, could not access it through their computers.

Handel decided it would be appropriate to investigate further the possibility of creating some form of executive information system within the department. His sense that the time was right was reinforced during a recent meeting between Handel and the Deputy Minister, Dan Goodleaf. Handel explained:

> We were meeting with the Deputy Minister to discuss our informatics plan. As we proceeded through the various items in the plan, he commented, 'This is interesting, we will have systems for this, that, and the other thing.' And then without any prompting from us, he said, 'It would be very useful if we could put all this together, and I could go to my computer and use it to find the state of affairs with respect to a particular band or with respect to a particular issue.' I was able to say, 'As a matter of fact, that's the very subject of the next project on the list.' I told him a little bit about what we had planned for the EIS. Then the very *next* project on the list concerned integration of certain subject data bases. While normally this would not be something that the Deputy Minister would think much about, I was able to make the point that unless we have good, reliable, consistent data, the EIS that we just talked about would have very limited value.

Following discussions with his boss, Jim Phillips, Handel decided to task Jim Moskos to lead a project to investigate the feasibility of an EIS, and, if feasible, to develop an EIS for DIAND.

JIM MOSKOS

Jim Moskos joined DIAND in 1988, after leaving a partnership position in a Toronto-based consulting firm. Since joining the department, Moskos had taken responsibility for a number of important informatics initiatives. It was Moskos who first argued that the department should adopt the data-driven approach to systems development, which resulted in a major change in the department's overall systems philosophy and methods. During the 1992 United Way campaign, Moskos headed a project to develop an impressive, state-of-the-art multimedia system to showcase aspects of United Way's services as well as the department's progress in the campaign. The display featured animated graphics, text, voice, and full-motion video technologies, all together in one PC. It was displayed in the entrance foyer to the building for all to see. As it turned out, the commercially available hardware and software for creating such a display was in rudimentary form, so Moskos spent some late nights writing detailed, low-level code to make the various pieces of equipment work with each other. In the end the system did work, and generated much interest and enthusiasm for the potential of new information technology.

A short time later, a second multimedia system was built for use in a departmental information fair, to advertise and promote the services of the Informatics Branch. This time the system also included a touch-screen feature that allowed the users to plot their own path through the displayed information. Handel observed that this system was the first direct exposure most departmental senior managers had to the fact that the computers could be used for much more than just handling e-mail and doing word processing.

A third multimedia application was also developed by Moskos and his team, this time to support a major policy presentation the department made to a cabinet committee of the federal government. Through these projects, the department gained experience in nontraditional uses of information technology, and other outside Informatics Branch were coming to recognize that IB possessed the technical talent to do much more than develop traditional transaction systems.

As they plotted strategy for the EIS project, Handel and Moskos knew that it would be important to obtain strong executive sponsorship. Handel had already gained a strong endorsement from Alan Williams. Williams was known as an aggressive, competitive manager who was constantly trying to move the department ahead. When Handel broached the EIS subject with him, his response was, "Go for it. Let's take a risk. Let's see if we can really move the yardsticks here."

As Jim Moskos pointed out, however, that meant that Williams' credibility was also on the line with the project. Moskos recalled the conversation:

> When we developed the original conceptual plan for the EIS and sent it to Alan, he attached his own note to it saying, 'Here we go again, doing something the government has never done before. Wish us luck,' and sent it on to the Deputy Minister. If we fall down, he's going to look pretty bad. So that shows he has a lot of faith in us, and it puts a lot of pressure on us.

Handel felt that they should also solicit advice and assistance from one of the regional executives. Consequently, he approached Gerry Kerr, the Regional Director General for the Atlantic Region, and asked him to become involved in the project. Kerr readily accepted. Kerr had a keen appreciation for the potential of information technology, and Handel felt that he would be an excellent source of ideas for the EIS. Williams and Kerr, then, became the official evaluators of the planned EIS prototypes.

Having agreed to take on the EIS effort, Moskos set up a small team of IB staff to work on the project. The first challenge they faced was trying to figure out what capabilities a DIAND EIS should provide. Handel commented:

> The key is to design the system around the job functions of the senior executive. However, it wouldn't have made sense to sit down with people like Alan Williams and Gerry Kerr, to take them through a data modelling session. Rather, we simply went and sat in their office on a number of

occasions and talked to them about their jobs. As our concepts evolved, we've gone back and forth with them, always bringing the discussion back to their jobs. We've had to continually caution against becoming enamoured with the flashiness of the technology. We keep asking, 'What do you do? What comes in your mailbox? What does your boss ask you? How do you have to respond? What is the nature of the telephone calls you get? What sort of demands does the Minister place on you? And, by extension from all this, what information do you need to do your job? How can we make it easier for you?'

At the same time as Moskos and Handel were working to understand what a DIAND EIS should do, Moskos's team was investigating the existing EIS technological options. The first thing they did was to investigate existing commercial EIS packages. The two primary competitors in this market were Commander (sold by Comshare Inc.) and Pilot (sold by Pilot Software Inc.). These types of EIS packages were usually termed "EIS shells." They provided a software framework which a company could tailor somewhat to fit their own situation. However, after examining the capabilities of these EIS shell products, Moskos decided that they should develop their own system, not base it on an off-the-shelf package. He explained:

> The reason we decided to build rather than to buy was because we couldn't get the kind of functionality we wanted in some of the other systems, which are just shells. It seems the centerpiece of many of the off-the-shelf systems is the data analysis and statistical analysis tools for crunching numbers, displaying graphs and so forth. But a significant part of our system is turning out to be the text retrieval component, and the access to video. Another important feature we need is a bring-forward capability. It is very important to our executives that they be able to quickly assemble various data—text, charts, some comments they type in, and so forth—to drop these "objects" of information into a folder and forward it on to someone else and say, 'Here are my thoughts, and some of the pieces of information, get back to me by such-and-such a date with a briefing note for the Deputy Minister.' The existing off-the-shelf systems just don't have that functionality.

Moskos continued:

> The shell packages are also quite expensive. We only expect to spend about $225,000 including salaries this year on our project. Putting up a commercial EIS shell with all the associated infrastructure can often end up being a million-dollar exercise. Also, we have got to be able to react very quickly to put in new capabilities. That's a given. Every time we review the system with Alan and Gerry, there is something new. It's getting finer, but it's also getting more complex, and we have to be able to deliver it. To me this means initially we have to have a robust object-oriented language that I can use to implement components quickly, and also maintain fairly easily. That would not necessarily be the case with a shell. And I think it probably would have taken more time to try to develop and integrate the pieces that people really want, such as text retrieval and video capability, into the existing shells than it will have taken simply to build the system ourselves from scratch.

THE DIAND EIS TECHNICAL ARCHITECTURE

After a number of discussions, Moskos evolved a technical architecture for the EIS. He designed it to operate within the Windows environment, on a DOS-based PC. Windows, a product of Microsoft Inc., was a popular graphical user interface, or GUI. It allowed users of an IBM-type PC to utilize screen icons and a mouse, among other things, rather than laboriously typing cryptic commands on their keyboards. Moskos planned to make extensive use of recently-added capabilities of Windows, features such as "Object Linking and Embedding," and "Dynamic Data Exchange," which allowed software developers to hook together various subsystems under Windows, so they could easily interchange data and work together seamlessly. Moskos also settled on a language called Visual Basic, another Microsoft product, to create the integrating "glue" for the system.

A couple of core principles underlay the EIS's architecture. One was the briefing book metaphor. Moskos and Handel knew that departmental executives relied heavily on briefing books, essentially text documents prepared by their staff, for information. Consequently, Moskos thought it would be a good idea that the EIS be centered around the notion of a briefing book. Within the EIS, a briefing book would be an electronic "space" for holding various pieces of information about a particular subject. The pieces of information—chunks of text, graphs, charts, tables of data, and even video clips, would all be represented within the briefing book by icons of their own. The manager could use his or her mouse to click on any of these icons, to call up the associated information onto their screen. Furthermore, objects within a briefing book, or an entire briefing book of information could be electronically mailed to other users.

Another key concept in the EIS was the centrality of textual information. As Moskos had observed, text is the dominant medium of information with which the executives work. Charts and tables drawn from departmental data, while important, are less commonly used by most senior managers. Thus, he reasoned, the EIS had to provide excellent access to textual information electronically. Moskos selected a "text engine," named Fulcrum, to be part of his system. Using Fulcrum, an EIS user could search a text database, select entries using keywords, cross reference selected entries with others in the database, perform similarity searches, and so forth. Furthermore, Fulcrum was designed to be used within the Windows environment. Moskos put it as follows:

> Fulcrum is the engine we chose for our full text searching. It has an excellent similarity algorithm capability, and also has good hooks into Visual Basic. Senior managers will want to be able to phrase their queries to the text data base the same way they would speak to an executive assistant, for example, 'Bring me the briefing notes associated with Davis Inlet, and also housing.' Fulcrum also has the capability of automatically indexing the documents. A person doesn't have to manually construct a set of key words for each document. It would also be possible to set things up so that the user could do more complex searches—for example,

to search for documents in which one word occurs within, say, five words of some other word. However, that requires making the user interface more complicated, and I don't want to do that. I want to keep things as simple as possible for the users.

A third part of the EIS architecture, one Bruce Handel knew really added to the system's "pizazz," was the capability of accessing and displaying full-motion video clips on the user's screen. Handel explained:

> One of the things that came out very early, from Gerry Kerr, was that he wanted to be able to treat all forms of information the same. What he gets now is, for example, a video clip from the CBC News, 15 briefing notes, and some graphs from his staff. That is typical of the basic information source from which he has to make decisions for the Deputy Minister. He said, 'If my system can't handle all of that, what good is it to me?' So we want to provide a capability for the executives to search for any kind of video from the video library, and to be able to combine that sort of information together with other information such as text or data and to be able to use it themselves or forward it on to others. What we want to do is to have the user think of a video clip as just another object in a folder.

Jim Moskos commented on the costs associated with including video capabilities in the EIS:

> Those users who want to be able to capture and enter video information into the database will have to have a $1200 video co-processor board installed in their PCs. However, users who only want to be able to view video will not need any additional hardware. Video data will be stored on a server on the LAN, not on the local PC storage devices. Another problem we have at this point is that the existing communication lines to the regional offices run at 9600 bits per second, so sending a five-megabyte video clip across one of those lines would not be very viable. However, within headquarters we have a high speed LAN, and we will have T1 links to all the regions within a year. It is important to note that we are not talking about interactive video, simply sending video clips one-way over the network, so the communications demands shouldn't be prohibitive.

Jim continued:

> Regarding the video, I don't think it's going to be used a great deal, but Alan and Gerry have said that it's the sort of thing that, when they really need it, it will be wonderful to have. For example, when the Atlantic Region picks up a local New Brunswick newscast that probably wouldn't make its way to Ottawa for a day and a half, they would be able to get that video to the Deputy Minister with a note and other supporting information to explain the situation. They feel that will be extremely powerful.

Additional discussion of the EIS conceptual architecture, together with some example EIS prototype screens, is shown in Exhibit 2.

TWO PHASES

The project plan for the EIS targeted two major phases for the system's development. The first phase was to be one year long, and was broken down into three sub-phases. At the end of each sub-phase, a new prototype of the system would be made available to Alan Williams and Gerry Kerr. Their comments and feedback on the prototype would be gathered and injected into the development of the following versions. At the end of the first phase, it was planned to provide the executive cadre (the Deputy Minister, all Assistant Deputy Ministers, and ADM Executive Assistants) with a functioning version of the EIS, containing the data, text and video tools.

In Phase Two, additional capabilities would be added, and the development team would examine the feasibility of migrating the EIS down one level in the organization, to the Directors General, those located in the regions as well as in headquarters.

A project Gantt chart is shown in Exhibit 2.

In September 1993, Jim Moskos and Bruce Handel were invited to attend an offsite meeting of all DIAND senior managers—both headquarters and regional executives. This was the first time that all the senior managers of the department became aware of the EIS project. The demonstration of the EIS prototype generated considerable

excitement in the room. However, both Handel and Moskos knew very well that all they had so far was an early prototype. Many of the capabilities of the EIS had been "mocked up" for the demo, to give the executives a sense of what the final system would look like. There was still a long way to go.

HOW DO YOU SPELL "SUCCESS"?

In the Conceptual Design Document for the DI-AND EIS, a number of different advantages that stem from the use of an EIS were mentioned, including the following:

- An EIS can enhance the way executives think about their business by affecting their "mental models," i.e., their understanding of the organization and its environment, as derived from past experience;
- It can improve management processes through leveraging the organization's time better, allowing more people to share important information more quickly;
- It can direct organizational attention toward issues that really matter, thereby exerting far-reaching effects on the organization's goals and directions;
- It can provide managers with access to a large pool of organizational data, allowing them to "poke around" and to explore at their leisure, including during off-hours.

The DIAND EIS Project Plan document put it this way:

> A system like the one described would fit seamlessly into the DIAND office of tomorrow. EIS reports could be cut-and-pasted into our new Windows-based e-mail and word processing systems. Executives would have the capacity to retrieve all documents based on a specific set of criteria, or review video footage of recent events. The DIAND EIS will be the cornerstone which will allow senior management to leverage the department's robust information infrastructure, to insure timely and informed decisions are made on key issues.

EXHIBIT 2 EIS Project Gantt Chart

EIS Project Plan as of April 16, 1993

Task name	Resources	Status
Project Initiation		
Present and review project plan	PM	
Perform initial regional visit	PM	r
Define project boundaries	PM, PC, UIS	r
Complete prototype one		
Design user interface	PM, UIS, PC	r
Develop desktop graphic design	CGA	r
Develop and code desktop	PM, UIS, PA, PC	r
Design desktop tool suite	PM, UIS, PC	Cr
Develop tool graphics	CGA	r
Create test data environment	PA, PM, DBC	Cr
Test prototype one	user, PM, UIS, PC	Cr
Complete prototype two		
Analyse user testing results	PM, UIS, PC, PA, DBC,	r
Create modified design	PM, UIS, PC, DBC	r
Create infrastructure		
Design communications model	PM, DBC	r
Design query database model	PM, DBC, AN1, PA	r
Implement comms and database	PM, DBC,PA, AN1	r
Develop and code prototype two	PM, UIS, PA, DBC,	r
Test prototype two	user, PM, PC	r
Complete final version		
Analyse user testing	PM, UIS, PC, DBC	r
Create modified design	PM, UIS, DBC	r
Develop and code final version	PM, UIS, DBC, AN1	r
Test final version	user, PM, UIS, PC	Cr
Prepare documentation	PC, PA, AN1	r
Implementation		C
Install HW and SW for all users	PM, PA, PC, DBC,	r
Train users	PM, PC, AN1, AN2	r
Migrate to production	PC, AN1, DBC, PA	Cr
Provide 1 month extended support	PM, DBC, AN1, AN2	Cr

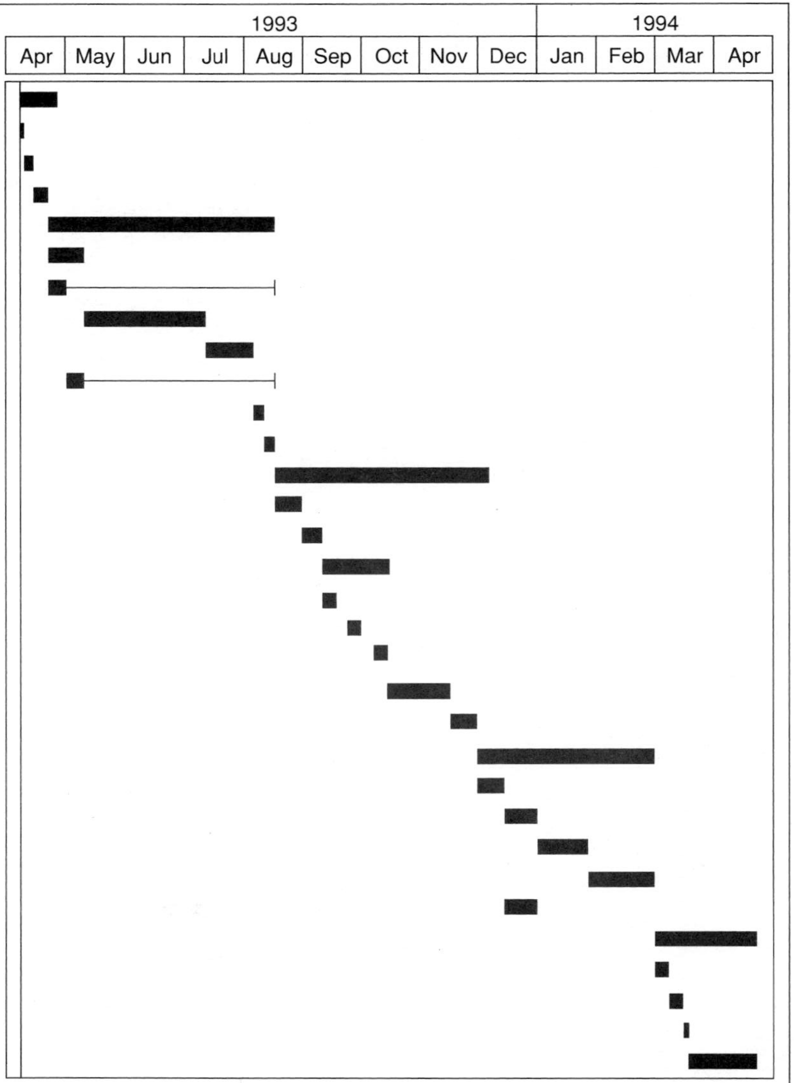

643

Bruce Handel commented:

The EIS will give our senior executives much more flexibility, a lot more versatility, and also a lot higher degree of timeliness of information, as opposed to having the same thing done through an executive assistant.

Jim Moskos added:

Another thing that we are going to be able to do is allow them to look at one piece of information and relate it to other pieces of information, something that was very difficult to do until now. That sort of analysis might entail a week's worth of work today. But if this could be done more quickly using the EIS, important trends or relationships can be discovered without placing a huge strain on the resource pool.

Sandy Foot, president of Systems Interface and an advisor to the project, also observed:

As far as text retrieval goes, the EIS will be miles ahead of what senior managers have now. The fact is, the executives are probably making all kinds of decisions now without doing a really thorough search of all briefing notes that might be relevant, simply because it would take too long to do so. People in different parts of the department rarely look at each other's briefing notes, which reinforces the "stovepipe" situation in the department. This system will improve upon that dramatically. With the system, it will be possible for everybody to see everybody else's briefing notes (subject to security considerations).

In summing up what he thought it would mean to be successful with the EIS project, Bruce Handel put it this way:

The department exists for two purposes: to flow money, and to process information. We're demonstrating with our operational systems that we can expedite the flowing of money: financial systems, transfer payment management systems, and so on. The challenge here is to expedite the processing of information.

Once this is implemented, I think it's going to cause the officials of the department to think about the overall organization of the department, and the job functions. The organization overall is still a "stovepipe" organization. But we find now that issues are not stovepipe issues. I think the system is going to facilitate dealing with issues in that way. And as an extension to this, I think people are going to question how the department is organized. It's going to lead them to think about different organizations within the department, to effect efficiencies in the way we do our business.

People are going to have access to powerful data summaries at all levels of the organization that they never had before. If we are to be successful we are going to have to have our senior executives be willing to do their jobs differently. They probably all believe they spend too much time on work now, so the last thing they think they'll want is something that's going to cause them to have to spend even more time. In other words, they've got to be able to *change* the way they spend their time. That's going to be a measure of success. I presume they will only do it if they find this thing to be truly useful.

In October 1993, as Bruce Handel and Jim Moskos were flying back to Ottawa from Amherst, Nova Scotia, following another round of discussions about the EIS with Regional Director General Gerry Kerr, they once again debated the open questions surrounding the future of the DIAND EIS: What, really, would its impact *be*? Was the design of the EIS appropriate for the target user group's needs? Would senior management fully accept and use the system? How would they deal with the remaining technical challenges? And, once senior management did have direct, hands-on access to the department's data, what would they think about the quality and quantity of those data? What if it turned out that the data they discovered they really wanted wasn't there?

EXHIBIT 3   Excerpt from DIAND EIS Conceptual Design Document

EIS CONCEPTUAL MODEL

Executive Desktop

The Executive Desktop is an object oriented desktop which runs as an application under Microsoft Windows. The desktop would supersede Windows Program Manager and contain only the desktop objects needed by the executive. Each executive can have his or her most common tools available plus the tools and objects provided by the EIS.

The desktop will allow for the automation of repetitive tasks at all levels e.g., gathering of E-mail, or the updating of a request for information on a given subject. These will be accomplished by an EIS agent. The purpose of the EIS agent is to allow the executive to create a mental model of his or her work environment. This model can be evolved as different issues arise and others disappear.

The EIS application under Windows 3.1 will consist of the application window with a toolbox along the top of the screen which contains the 5 tools used to request information and the desktop objects as shown below:

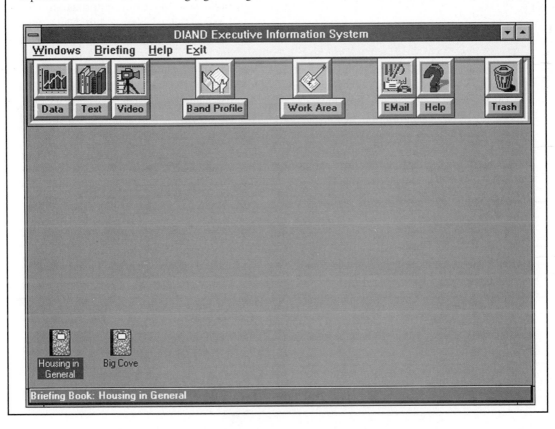

EXHIBIT 3 *(Cont.)*

Tools and Objects

The Executive desktop contains both tools and objects as follows:

Tools	Objects
Statistical Viewer (Data)	Document
Textual Viewer (Text)	Folder
Video Viewer (Video)	
E-Mail	
Help	

Tools:

The tools are divided into query and communications groups.

There are four query tools:

• The *Statistical Viewer* allows the user to construct and launch a query "document". A dialog will appear which will allow the senior executive to build a query from a set of predefined data structures. The resulting query can be saved to the desktop as a document for future queries. An existing query "document" may be modified by dropping it on the Statistical Viewer Icon which will then display the dialog box containing the query. The resulting new query can be saved as a new document or onto the original query document. The statistical query document can be launched from the desktop or from the tool. It will result in graph which could be printed, filed or mailed to another individual.

• The *Textual Viewer* gives the manager the capability to construct a query in a natural language form for textual information, e.g., "Tell me about problems with Davis Inlet and Housing". When selecting the Textual Viewer Icon a dialog box appears allowing the senior manager to select the collections which he or she would like to search and build a natural language query. Collections would include; briefing notes; E-mail; and clippings. An existing textual query document may be dropped onto the Textual Viewer Icon for modification. The textual query document may be launched from the desktop. It will place the textual query and receive a weighted list of documents that most closely meet the composition of the query. The senior manager would be able to view the documents of interest and print, file, or mail any component of it.

EXHIBIT 3   *(Cont.)*

- The *Video Viewer* facilitates the building of queries for searching and viewing of stored video media related to issues of interest. The senior manager would enter a query in natural language in the same fashion as the textual viewer e.g.; "Show me CBC footage on Big Cove", "drop it" on the Viewer Icon and receive a list of video clips that match the query specifications. The resulting clips could be viewed on screen or mailed to other interested parties. As in the other tools a video query can be saved as a document which can be launched from the desktop or from the tool.

- The *Help Tool* will allow for context sensitive help at any place in the EIS.

There is one communications tool:

The *Communication tool* would allow the user to take the results of any query and forward the information to any E-Mail enabled party, again the "Drag and Drop" Approach would be used.

Objects

The other components of the EIS system are: *documents,* and *folders.* Documents are predefined queries for data, text or video information. Folders contain query documents for given issues or subjects.

Documents

A document is created using the appropriate tool. Once the senior manager has created a document it is stored on the desktop or in a file folder. A senior manager may receive or send a document via E-mail to other senior executives using the EIS.

Folder

A folder is an object for storing query documents. A file folder may be setup via issue or any related subject. A file folder containing all of its documents may be received or sent via E-mail to other senior executives to run on their desktop.

Query Forms

Data	SQL Syntax for the query used to determine the data results in the frame; or various combinations of check boxes & radio buttons that will build the query for the user; Options for the graphing of data, if applicable (line, pie, or column graphs); Options for tabular display, if applicable
Text	Natural language/Boolean syntax for the text results desired; if more than one result comes back, might put up a result list where the user can pick which result(s) to include in the frame (or all of them)
Video	User would be able to search on a given topic, author or date. If more than one video file is selected, the frame would display a set of standard playback buttons to allow the user to flip back and forth through the images; in other words, the frame would be "live" on screen. When printed, the images in a frame would be attached to the back of the report.

EXHIBIT 4   Selected Screens from DIAND EIS Prototype

EIS opening screen, showing buttons for query tools, band profile tool, work area, electronic mail interface, EIS help, and "trash" (delete). Also shown are two briefing book icons, for briefing books previously created by this user.

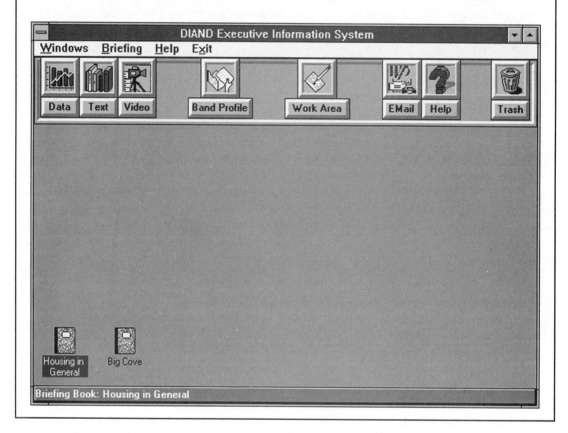

EXHIBIT 4   *(Cont.)*

Creating a new briefing book: a new briefing book named Education on Reserve was created, and the results of a text query ("Education on Big Cove Reserve") placed in the new briefing book.

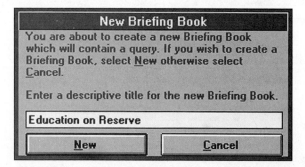

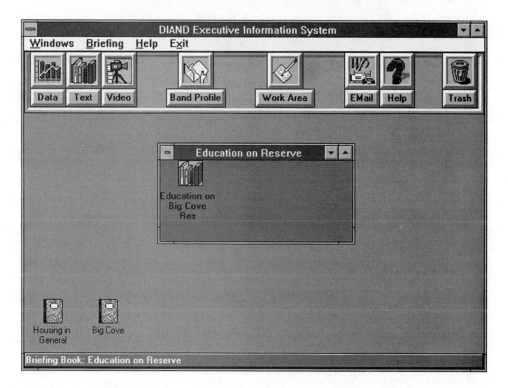

EXHIBIT 4   *(Cont.)*

Results of a data query, showing output as numerical information and also as a bar chart.

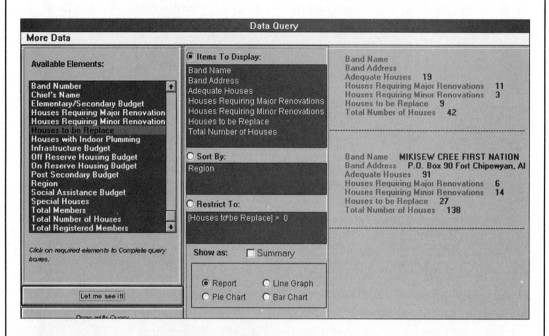

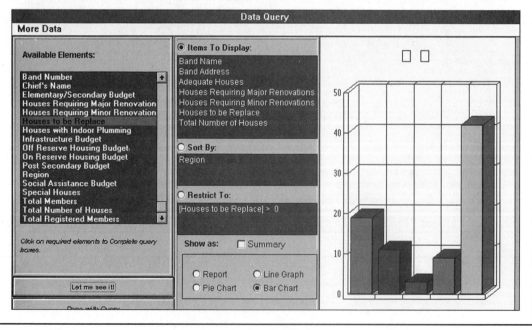

EXHIBIT 4 (*Cont.*)

Execution of a text query, showing the query, a list of documents found by the EIS containing related information, and the detailed text of one of the documents.

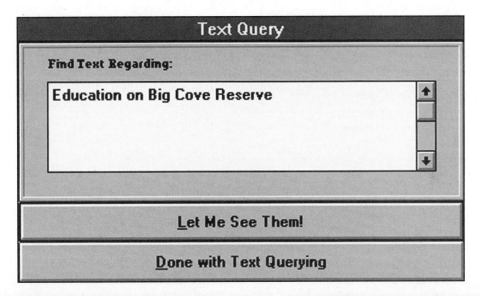

EXHIBIT 4   *(Cont.)*

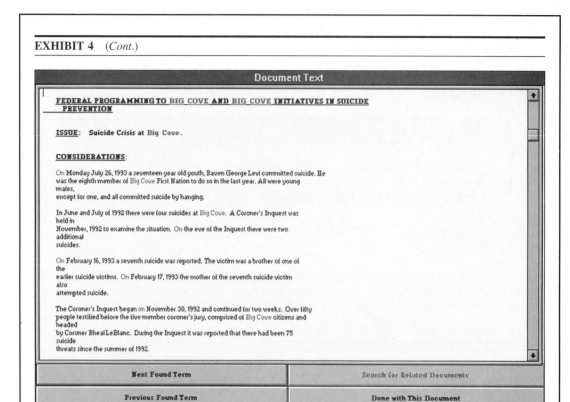

Document Text

FEDERAL PROGRAMMING TO BIG COVE AND BIG COVE INITIATIVES IN SUICIDE PREVENTION

ISSUE: **Suicide Crisis at Big Cove.**

CONSIDERATIONS:

On Monday July 26, 1993 a seventeen year old youth, Raven George Levi committed suicide. He was the eighth member of Big Cove First Nation to do so in the last year. All were young males, except for one, and all committed suicide by hanging.

In June and July of 1992 there were four suicides at Big Cove. A Coroner's Inquest was held in November, 1992 to examine the situation. On the eve of the Inquest there were two additional suicides.

On February 16, 1993 a seventh suicide was reported. The victim was a brother of one of the earlier suicide victims. On February 17, 1993 the mother of the seventh suicide victim also attempted suicide.

The Coroner's Inquest began on November 30, 1992 and continued for two weeks. Over fifty people testified before the five member coroner's jury, comprised of Big Cove citizens and headed by Coroner Rheal LeBlanc. During the Inquest it was reported that there had been 75 suicide threats since the summer of 1992.

Next Found Term	Search for Related Documents
Previous Found Term	Done with This Document

Illustration of the EIS interface with Wordperfect Office, the department's internal electronic mail and office productivity system. Screens show one EIS user placing the results of certain text queries, data queries, and video clips in the work area, then forwarding to another manager, with a short note attached, as a "bring forward" item.

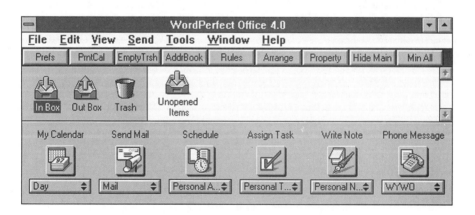

EXHIBIT 4 *(Cont.)*

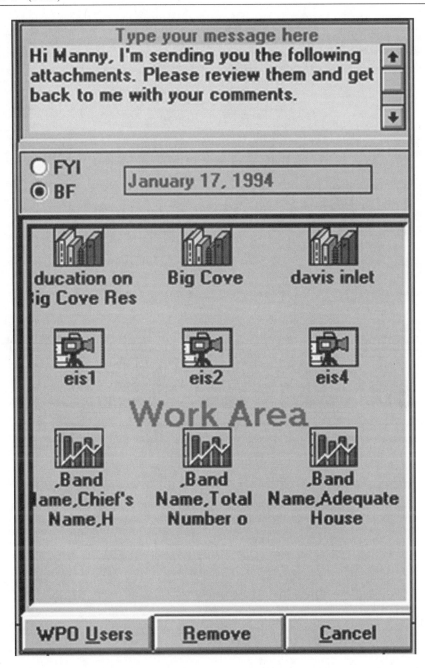

EXHIBIT 4 *(Cont.)*

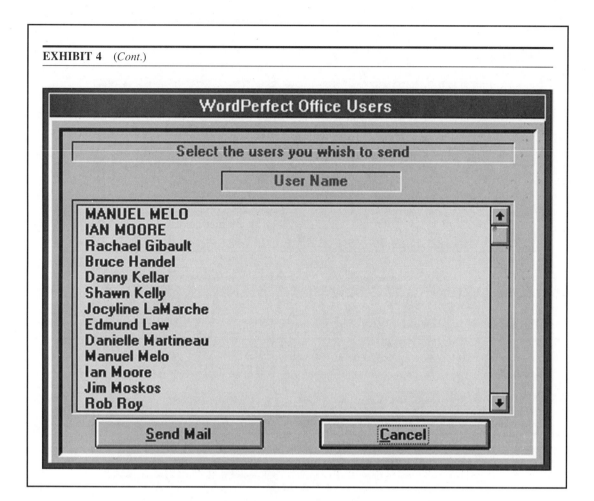

Case 4

STRATEGIC DATA
MODELLING AT DIAND

"Oh God!" exclaimed Bruce Handel as he hung up the telephone and turned to face Janet Hagey. "The Minister just greeted an important Chief by the wrong name."

Handel had recently been appointed the Director of the Client Services Directorate, Informatics Branch for the Department of Indian Affairs and Northern Development (DIAND). He had been meeting with Hagey, the Director of Quantitative Analysis and Socio-Demographic Research, to discuss some information systems problems facing the department; this made the telephone call all the more timely. A day earlier, the Minister of the Department, about to leave to visit an Indian community in western Canada, had requested a printout of First Nation information from DIAND's computer database. Unfortunately, the First Nation had held an election a few months earlier, and the names of the Chief and other First Nation officials in the printout were incorrect. No one in the First Nation had told the Department of the changes, and no one in the Department knew of the election. The Minister, duly informed by the printout, then proceeded to greet the First Nation Chief warmly, but used the wrong name. While the error might seem minor, relations between the government of Canada and First Nations had never been as sensitive. Such mixups simply created problems, serving to place the Minister, and by extension the entire Canadian government, in an even worse light in the eyes of the country's Native peoples.

Handel explained, "Furthermore, the kind of problem encountered by the Minister is just the tip of the iceberg, although it gets a high profile. The integrity of all the data DIAND relies upon is suspect. Our mission in DIAND is changing. More and more of the actual work of this Department is being passed to the First Nations themselves, through our strategy of devolution. With fewer DIAND staff in the field, it is becoming harder and harder to get our hands on accurate data about Indians and their communities. But we still have critical responsibilities on behalf of Native people that we must uphold, and doing so requires good, reliable data. Our information systems, therefore, are becoming ever more critical to us. Unfortunately, our past system development practices have not prepared us very well for the challenges we now face.

We're now trying to turn the corner. In the past year, we've adopted a completely new approach based on the concept of information management, recognizing that DIAND's data resource is fundamental to fulfilling our responsibilities. Information management is concerned with both information content, a business issue and the information conduit, the technical infrastructure. This change is a quantum leap for us. We have great hopes that the new approach will solve a lot of our problems. It had better."

DEPARTMENT OF INDIAN AFFAIRS AND NORTHERN DEVELOPMENT

DIAND, created in 1966, was one of the 33 ministries of the Canadian government. By 1991, the Department involved the efforts of almost

4,000 people and an operating budget of $3.5 billion. The Department defined its mission as "working together to make Canada a better place for First Nations and Northern peoples." Specific Departmental responsibilities included:

- Fulfillment of the lawful obligations of the federal government to Aboriginal people arising from treaties, the Indian Act and other federal government legislation;
- Administration of Indian reserve lands and elections of First Nation councils, registration of entitlement to Indian status and First Nation membership, and administration of the funds of First Nations and the estates of certain individual Indians;
- Provision for the delivery of basic services (such as education, social assistance, housing, and community infrastructure) to status Indians and Inuit communities;
- Assistance to Indians and Inuit to acquire employment skills and to develop viable businesses;
- Negotiation of the settlement of accepted claims relating to Aboriginal title not dealt with by treaty or other means, or relating to past non-fulfillment of government obligations;
- Support for the ongoing constitutional development regarding, among other matters, the definition of the rights of Canada's Aboriginal people;
- Provision of transfer payments to the governments of the Yukon and the Northwest Territories to assist them in providing public services to territorial residents in accordance with the Yukon and Northwest Territories Acts and other agreements;
- Support for the balanced development of the North, through management of natural resources, protection and management of the environment (including Arctic seas), fostering of economic and employment opportunities for northerners, and funding of social and cultural programs;
- Fostering political development of the two northern territories and the coordination of federal policies and programming for Canada's north.

DIAND's assorted responsibilities were administered through four programs. The objectives of the **Indian and Inuit Affairs Program** were: (1) to support Indians and Inuit in achieving their self-government, economic, educational, cultural, social and community development needs and aspirations; (2) to settle accepted Native claims through negotiations; and (3) to ensure that Canada's constitutional and statutory obligations and responsibilities to the Indian and Inuit peoples were fulfilled. The objectives of the **Northern Affairs Program** were: (1) to promote the political, economic, scientific, social and cultural development of the northern territories; (2) to assist northerners to develop political and economic institutions which enable territorial governments to assume increasing responsibility within the Canadian federation; and (3) to effectively manage the orderly use, development and conservation of the North's natural resources in collaboration with territorial governments and other federal departments. The **Transfer Payments Program** provided grants to assist the governments of the Yukon Territory and Northwest Territories in the provision of a full range of public services for their residents. Finally, the **Administration Program** was charged with ensuring the efficient and effective management of DIAND and its programs in a manner that was responsive to its mandate, ministerial and parliamentary priorities and the overall needs of its clients.

DIAND interacted with its clients mainly through the elected leaders of Canada's 603 different First Nations and tribal councils. These ranged from the Popkum that consisted of only eight people to the Six Nations with a total membership of over 16,000.

DIAND itself was headquartered in a large, modern office building at 10 Wellington Street in Hull, Quebec, just across the Ottawa River from downtown Ottawa. However, much of the department was decentralized: over 75% of DIAND's employees worked out of ten regional offices, supplying over 400 different services to a culturally, economically, and geographically diversecollection of Native and northern peoples throughout the country.

DIAND was organized into six major sectors, each led by an Assistant Deputy Minister reporting to the Deputy Minister,[1] plus a number of staff and regional functions. An organizational chart is given in Exhibit 1. Both the Informatics Branch and Quantitative Analysis and Socio-Demographic Research were part of Finance and Professional Services, of which Alan Williams had recently been named Assistant Deputy Minister.

DIAND'S STRATEGIC DIRECTIONS

For the past several years, DIAND's strategy had centered around two principles: devolution and downsizing. **Devolution** referred to the transfer of administrative responsibility and accountability, together with the resources for the delivery of services, to First Nations, and, in the North, to territorial governments. The principal force behind the move to devolution was the desire of Native people to gain more control over their own affairs.

In contrast to devolution was the concept of the fiduciary responsibility of the Canadian government to the aboriginal people. This responsibility was derived from a number of sources, principally statutes and treaties, and could be extremely difficult to interpret in the context of the activities carried out by DIAND. The Indian Act was one clear source of this fiduciary responsibility, for example, in the areas of management of monies and lands and the administration of estates. DIAND was held to account by the courts for any failure to discharge its functions in these areas, as it was in the Guerin decision of the Supreme Court of Canada. Another source of possible fiduciary responsibility was the developing legal concepts related to aboriginal rights issues, as in the Sparrow decision which dealt with the aboriginal right to fish and the responsibility of the federal government to protect this right.

The legal issues were extremely complex, and while the department pursued the devolution of its

---

[1]Deputy Ministers comprised the senior management of the civil service, supporting the respective portfolio accountabilities of federal cabinet ministers who were elected members of parliament.

activities, it constantly found itself walking a difficult line between meeting the legitimate needs of various First Nations, being charged with paternalistic behavior by the client group, and trying to uphold the ongoing responsibilities of the Government of Canada to its Native peoples.

Legalities notwithstanding, devolution was proceeding. For example, in the area of education, DIAND in the past had held responsibility for building and maintaining First Nation schools, hiring and paying teachers, and so forth. Under devolution, DIAND transferred educational funding to individual First Nations. Building schools and hiring teachers was carried out by the First Nations themselves, not DIAND. As time passed, the department was becoming more a provider of funds than a direct provider of services. As a result of devolution, the nature of the department's information needs was changing. Furthermore, as devolution proceeded, the department was becoming ever more dependent on the First Nations and councils themselves, rather than DIAND personnel, for providing needed information.

Downsizing referred to the planned reduction in the size of the department, as part of the government's policy of restraint. It was consistent with efforts to reduce the costs of doing business within the public service. In the past, the department had enjoyed larger-than-average annual budget increases. Now, to ensure that as much of the increasingly scarce financial resources as possible were available to its clients, DIAND was seeking means to streamline its operations.

DIAND'S POLITICAL ENVIRONMENT

The political environment within which DIAND conducted its business had never been more uncertain. In 1990, relations between Native people and the federal government were especially strained. As Canadians struggled to redefine their constitution, many Native people felt bitter about being largely left out of the process. Elijah Harper, a Native Member of the Provincial Legislature in Manitoba, succeeded almost singlehandedly in

EXHIBIT 1

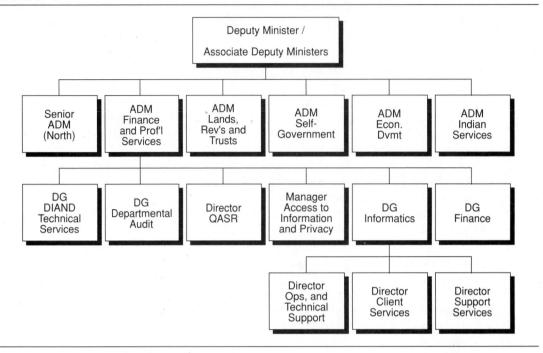

blocking the Meech Lake Accord constitutional plan from being passed in that province, resulting in its collapse nationwide. Tensions erupted in July 1990, in the form of an armed standoff at Oka, Quebec, that lasted 77 days. Smaller disturbances at the nearby Kahnawake and Akwesasne reserves, among other flashpoints, further underscored the strained relations.

In reacting to these events, Prime Minister Mulroney addressed the House of Commons on September 25, 1990, saying:

"I would like to outline the course my government plans to follow to preserve the special place of our first citizens in this country, based on their Aboriginal and treaty rights recognized in the Constitution. The agenda will have four main pillars: land claims; the economic and social conditions on reserves; the relationship between Aboriginal peoples and governments; and concerns of Canada's Aboriginal peoples in contemporary life."

At the same time, DIAND staff recognized that a number of the First Nations with which they dealt were rapidly becoming more skilled at influencing the government, the media, and events generally. Previously isolated First Nations were now able to stay closely in touch with outside affairs through information technology. Also the political skills of the First Nations were increasing: First Nation leaders knew "what buttons to push to make things happen in Ottawa," as one DIAND staff member put it.

DIAND's management knew that the nature of the relationship between First Nations and the Department was sure to change as a result of these pressures, although they could not anticipate whether they would take the form of an amendment to Canada's constitution or amendments to legislation and regulation. Further, they had no way of knowing the specific nature, timing, and scope of the coming changes.

INFORMATION SYSTEMS AT DIAND

Bruce Handel's Client Services Directorate had primary responsibility for the analysis and design of DIAND's information systems. The Operations and Technology Support Directorate, also part of the Informatics Branch, was responsible for operating the department's computer and telecommunications systems.

DIAND began its Informatics initiatives approximately 25 years earlier, using a service bureau computer and developing basic transaction processing applications in the COBOL programming language. As the department's needs grew, a decision was made in 1981 to move most of the computer processing in-house. In 1985, a request for proposal was issued, and the decision was made to purchase a number of Hewlett-Packard minicomputers—three for headquarters and one for each regional office connected through a commercial packet switched network. By 1991, most of the applications that previously ran on the service bureau computer had been successfully migrated over to the HP facilities.

In 1987, Jim Phillips was appointed Director General of the Informatics Branch, after having spent the previous six years heading a team that designed and installed a sophisticated local area network throughout the Canadian Parliament buildings. Phillips commented, "The situation today is a far cry from what we had when I arrived. Then we had some serious morale problems within the Branch, and our relations with the rest of the department were poor. We had experienced many of the same problems that occurred in IS departments in many companies: long backlogs of requests, inadequate attention to users' needs, and poor communications with our clients. We approached the development of information systems in a traditional manner—following a structured development methodology, and coding our applications in COBOL. Our application priorities were determined by the information needs of the program managers which were mainly tied back to their areas of accountability."

In 1985, Bill C-31 was passed and had immediate and dramatic effects on the number of applications received for Indian status. Bill C-31 ended gender discrimination in the Indian Act and required DIAND to reinstate women who, as a result of marrying a non-Indian, had lost their status. The department had been unable to accurately forecast the impact of this legislation due to a lack of information on the demographic composition of the clientele. Harry Swain joined DIAND as Deputy Minister in 1988 and immediately sought to remedy these inadequacies. The Quantitative Analysis and Socio-Demographic Research unit was founded as a result.

As the devolution process unfolded in the latter part of the 1980s, it became clear that DIAND's approach to designing, building and modifying its information systems was too cumbersome and stodgy to be able to handle the rapid changes that were occurring. Phillips explained, "The department was no longer program driven; we had become First Nation driven. Vertical information systems designed for stand-alone programs were just too isolated and rigid."

Alan Williams, the Assistant Deputy Minister responsible for Finance and Professional Services, listed the new information issues from a DIAND manager's perspective: "What type of data do I need now? Why is it needed? Where can I get it? Who can give it to me? Is it reliable? From my perspective, the problems aren't technical, they're people. My challenge is to get my colleagues to think about these issues, and then demonstrate the support available from Informatics to help them improve the service they provide."

It was clear that the department's strategy for application development was not supporting its mission. Neither the systems nor the underlying data were sufficiently integrated to provide the access to information demanded by devolution. Furthermore, the tools being used to develop systems were constraining the staff's productivity.

ADOPTION OF NEW SYSTEM DEVELOPMENT TOOLS

Phillips decided to commit the Informatics Branch to building future applications using state-of-the-art systems development tools that promised improved productivity for both programmers and analysts. The first step was to adopt a fourth generation programming language (4GL), to be used for future development work. In 1987, the PowerHouse 4GL, sold and supported by the Ottawa-based Cognos Ltd., was adopted by the department. PowerHouse was a strong competitor in the 4GL market, and its adoption at DIAND promised to relieve programmers of the tedium of coding in the procedural, third generation CO-BOL. "It was a morale booster," commented Phillips. In adopting PowerHouse, DIAND established an important ongoing partnership with Cognos. The fact that Cognos's head office was just a few blocks away from DIAND's headquarters was a helpful aspect of this relationship.

A short time later, a computer-assisted software engineering (CASE) tool, named Excelerator, was selected for use in the department. Excelerator was an "upper CASE" tool, in that it was aimed at supporting the system design process (the "front end" of the overall system development process). Excelerator could be used to document the overall design of a system in the form of graphical diagrams and charts. However, there was no link between Excelerator and PowerHouse. Programmers would have to use the diagrams produced by Excelerator as "blueprints," then code their systems by hand using PowerHouse.

Once the decision had been made to adopt these development tools, training had to be provided for the staff. DIAND contracted with Cognos to provide a series of training courses, and eventually just about every systems analyst and programmer in the department received training in Power-House, and many in the use of Excelerator as well.

While the tools had been improved, the basic approach to systems development remained unchanged. The traditional systems development life-cycle approach guided systems creation in the Department. Systems analysts would conduct lengthy discussions about information needs with users, in order to understand thoroughly the details of specific department procedures. The emphasis in this activity was strongly focused on information *processes*—how things were done, who required what information, what they did with it, what data needed to be kept on hand, what was passed on to other people, etc. In designing a new information system, a systems analyst's job was, basically, to develop a "map" of the relevant processes, which could serve as a guide to developing the detailed computer software to automate certain information aspects of the process. The processes were documented using text descriptions as well as techniques such as flowcharts, data flow diagrams and the like (which could be quickly produced and modified using Excelerator). Users were asked to verify the correctness of this process documentation, after which no further changes were allowed. The design documentation was then used as a guide in writing the code for the application systems being developed, after which the completed system was returned to the user for testing and acceptance.

INFORMATION SYSTEMS PLANNING

For many years DIAND's approach to developing systems had been responsive to the needs of the day. Little had been done in the way of longer-term systems planning. As the importance of information systems in the Department grew, the need for a long-term systems plan became evident.

In late 1989, several consulting firms were hired to lead an intensive systems planning process. A series of Strategic Business Analysis (SBA) and Business Requirements Study (BRS) projects was undertaken as a first step toward defining DI-AND's complete set of information and applications requirements.

The SBA took a high-level view of the various user areas across the entire department. Each BRS took a more detailed view, with the goal of generating a plan at a level of detail sufficient to begin system development. The projects had two objectives. The first was to provide users with insight into the effectiveness of their current business processes in meeting their business objectives; the second was to highlight potential application initiatives, and to provide a "running start" at systems development.

With the help of external consultants, all areas of the department engaged in the creation of structure charts, data-process matrices, and functional decompositions of their operations. The work was time-consuming and difficult for both users and the systems staff. The documentation produced from the study was voluminous. For example, the document describing just one BRS, concerned with Band Support and Capital Management, was nearly 300 pages long.

In the end, there was less than universal satisfaction with the results. Users were frequently unhappy because they felt they were being asked to put a lot of their time and energy into something that they did not fully understand or see the rationale for. When the Informatics staff responded by saying, in effect, "trust us, this is important," it often failed to set the users' minds at ease. The complexity of the approach made it difficult for many users to make meaningful contributions or to comfortably verify the conclusions. Nor were the systems people fully satisfied. The study's emphasis on business processes produced results that became quickly obsolete. Every change in DIAND's operating procedures would be reflected in changes in the process logic documented by the study. Keeping the study's results up-to-date proved to be an impossible task.

The strategic system planning project generated an unforeseen byproduct. As users in the department were required to think through and help document their operating procedures in great detail, a number of them discovered new potential uses for computers in their own areas. This resulted in a dramatic spike in demand for new applications from users, and a concomitant request for millions of additional dollars in the systems

development budget. Even with additional funding, however, Informatics could not possibly satisfy all the requests for new systems. This created even more frustration on the part of the user community.

The funding issue aside, the department's need for flexible, integrated systems required that it base its future applications upon a well-designed data base. The planning process, however, was oriented more towards documenting processes than data requirements; a strong database design was not forthcoming from the planning process. Further, the plans that did emerge from the SBA and BRS activities did not lend themselves to rapid systems development—the primary reason for converting to the 4GL/CASE tool development environment in the first place.

Jim Moskos, a Client Services project manager, recalled: "We wanted advanced software development tools because of the promise of rapid development, but we didn't know what we were getting into. We ended up choosing tools, and not examining our overall development approach. While we were drawing great pictures with Excelerator, and also building programs more rapidly with Power-House, we had really not automated our analysis. Also, Excelerator was not integrated with Power-House, so automatically generating code from our plans was not possible."

In mid-1990, Informatics turned to the Cognos product line for a solution to their problem. They adopted the PowerDesign methodology for Rapid Application Development, and Cognos's new PowerCase as a CASE tool standard, replacing Excelerator. These new tools were intended to further improve both development productivity and the quality of the end product. PowerDesign segmented applications into components that could be delivered to users throughout the development process. Further, the integration of PowerDesign with PowerCase and PowerHouse facilitated relatively easy modifications based on feedback received from users after the application had been tested in production. This feature effectively allowed for iterative prototyping of applications, which increased both system quality and user satisfaction.

SHIFT TO A DATA-DRIVEN APPROACH

Moskos was familiar with an approach to systems planning called information engineering, and when a seminar on the subject was offered in Toronto, he attended. The seminar, entitled "Bridging the Gap Between Strategic Planning and Information Systems," was conducted by the Dallas-based Information Engineering Systems Corporation (IESC). The information engineering approach formalized the connection between an organization's strategic plans and its information systems. Strategic Management Statements either explicitly or implicitly formed the business rationale for the existence of each data entity in a strategic data model that became the basis for all information systems development.

Two information engineering concepts seemed particularly relevant to DIAND. The first addressed the importance of the explicit alignment of the overall mission and purpose of an organization with the activities of the information systems function. The second was the use of data normalization techniques that systematically produced a minimal set of data requirements that were directly linked to the mission and purpose of the organization as justification for their existence. From the basic data, other useful variations and combinations could be derived when needed. The "business rule linkage" acted as a safeguard against the impulse to collect and store redundant data.

Stemming from Moskos's enthusiasm for the Information Engineering philosophy and approach, the department decided to investigate the concept further. Two consultants from IESC, joined by two other consultants from Systems Interface, an Ottawa-based consulting firm with a long relationship with DIAND, were hired to perform an audit of the Department's approach to system development in November 1990. Their findings indicated:

- The new 4GL/CASE approach to systems development and the supporting technical architecture were forward-looking, robust, and compatible with the Information Engineering methodology;
- The application design and construction approach embedded in PowerDesign were data-driven and compatible with Information Engineering concepts.
- The strategic planning and problem analysis procedures employed in the SBA/BRS projects were process-driven and not compatible with the PowerDesign methodology.
- There was a need for executive management participation in information resource management issues.
- DIAND's data administration function needed to be a business-oriented activity that directly supported the mandate for managing information as a strategic asset, while the database administration function needed to be a technology-oriented activity supporting the application design and development and information resource delivery mandates with Informatics. Since the two activities were different, they should be staffed differently and managed separately.
- Informatics required "upper CASE" tools and a corporate data dictionary compatible with the middle and lower CASE tools provided in the Cognos software engineering environment.

The consultants' recommendations included:

- Develop an interim corporate data dictionary and set of PowerHouse applications to support strategic data modelling activities and information systems planning. Transfer from Excelerator to the new dictionary all the data models developed during the SBA and BRS projects.
- Initiate a pilot project to develop a high-level Strategic Data Model for DIAND comprised of interested members of user area throughout the Department to familiarize them with data modelling concepts.
- Develop and publish new procedures and clearly defined roles for the data administration and database administration functions.
- Seek organization-wide support for, and establish at the Deputy Minister/Assistant Deputy

Minister/Director General level, a DIAND mandate for information to be managed as a strategic asset of the organization, with full participation and commitment at this senior management level.

• Establish a permanent data administration function at the highest level practical within DIAND, commensurate with the mandate for managing information as a strategic asset.

The results of the consultants' study were received with mixed emotions by DIAND staff. The recommendations embodied many worthwhile suggestions, in particular the confirmation that the Information Engineering, data-driven approach to planning and developing the Department's information systems was the right way to proceed. However, shifting to an Information Engineering methodology would render the work done in the earlier SBA/BRS studies largely worthless. Handel and Phillips knew that they had used up a lot of goodwill among their user clientele in the Department in the course of conducting the earlier studies, and did not relish at all the thought of approaching them with the need for even more, but different, studies.

THE STRATEGIC DATA MODEL

In accordance with the November 1990 consultants' report, which identified the need for a high-level strategic data model and called for a separation of the data administration and database administration functions, a two-week information engineering strategic data modelling session was held in February 1991 under the direction of Quantitative Analysis and Socio-Demographic Research. This assignment was a marked shift in responsibility for Janet Hagey's group, which was fully occupied managing the demographic statistics required by the Department. "We certainly didn't have any idle resources ready to accept the data modelling responsibilities," said Hagey. "But it doesn't take you very long doing quality control on the back end in data analysis before you realize that you need to fix up the front end in data collection."

Session participants were members of DIAND's Information Management Working Group, a collection of directors drawn from across the department's divisions. This group existed to address data-related issues within DIAND, but was operating without a conceptual framework to support its mandate to provide advice on the rationalization of data and systems. The information engineering methodology filled this void.

The objective of the strategic data modelling session was to produce a first-cut model which would specify the information that DIAND's Indian Affairs Program required in the long run to meet its mandate and to serve as a framework for managing its information. A total of 236 data entities and their relationships were described, as well as the strategic management statements that supported the entities. The high-level model is described in Exhibit 2.

With the aid of Information Engineering Systems Corporation (IESC) and their IE:Expert CASE tool the data modelling sessions recorded strategic management statements, their source and all linked data entities. For example, a strategic management statement related to DIAND's devolution mandate was "Activities Self-Government" which involved the development, negotiation and implementation activities required to establish structures that recognized the cultural, organizational and regional differences among Native peoples and increase Indian control, decision-making and accountability. Data entities linked to this statement were those required to support the information needs of the related policy, liaison and administrative functions of the department.

The February session also identified five functional areas of DIAND's business: Delivery, Expenditure, Players, Accountability and Authority. Their relationship to the high-level model is depicted in Exhibit 3 and their own data models are included in Exhibit 4.

THE PILOT STUDY

With the strategic data model completed, the issue facing its sponsors was what to do next. The lacklustre results of the Strategic Business Analysis and

EXHIBIT 2   DIAND Strategic Data Model

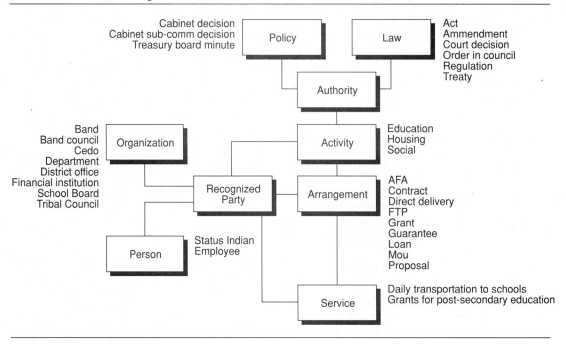

Business Requirements Studies indicated that another department-wide initiative would be unwise. Prototyping the new systems development approach seemed sensible, but the choice of the target application was important. It needed to provide DIAND with significant benefits, yet two of the most critical systems—those that registered status Indians and their lands—were clearly too big to ensure a quick, demonstrative success.

It was widely recognized within DIAND that the completeness and accuracy of existing information about Indian First Nations was unsatisfactory. Roger Gagnon, ADM for Lands, Revenues, and Trusts, managed many of the Department's obligations to Native peoples. He observed: "In the old days we delivered services to individual Indians, but with devolution we deal with Indian governments in the form of First Nation councils. Nevertheless, it is important to note that our responsibility is to both individuals and First Na-

tion councils. The range of sophistication of the First Nations determines their preparedness to accept responsibilities under devolution and thus the timing of its implementation. Devolution cannot be a hands-off administrative process if it is to be an honourable process. We cannot devolve services without devolving responsibilities, and we must make sure that they are ready to make informed decisions. We must build the capacity to transfer the responsibilities properly, and the first step is a good data base. We must manage our information resources just like we manage our financial and human resources. Unfortunately, this view is not shared by all my colleagues."

Reporting to Roger Gagnon was Gregor MacIntosh, Director General of the Registration, Revenues and Band Governance Branch. "I have accompanied the Minister on his visits to First Nations," noted MacIntosh. "He will ask for various profile information about a First Nation,

EXHIBIT 3   Five Functional Areas

such as how much it spends on education, and typically we can't give him a very good answer. The department spends nearly $4 billion each year but can't tell the Minister much of what he needs to know."

The development of a First Nation profile system had acquired a new urgency as Native issues, and by association DIAND, attained heightened prominence on the national agenda. While such an application seemed ripe for strategic data modelling, its complexity was daunting for a pilot project. Accordingly, a subsystem of the First Nation profile was identified that could serve as a foundation for the larger system.

The Statutory Requirements Information Management System (SRIMS) was chosen. An existing version of SRIMS recorded and reported information on the leadership of Indian First Nations, and the types of legislative activities enacted by these councils including by-laws, elections, and treaty obligations. The SRIMS redesign included distrib-

uted features to make it accessible to Band Governance field officers.

During the autumn of 1991, Janet Hagey assigned one full time and one part-time staff person to lead detailed data modelling sessions with Band Governance employees. During eight half-day sessions the information engineering discipline obliged participants to consider all the data elements needed to satisfy DIAND's information requirements without, as Gregor MacIntosh put it. "collecting a lot of data we don't need—as we usually do." Exhibit 5 contains an entity-relationship diagram from one of these sessions.

"The SRIMS sessions confirmed that data modelling is very labour-intensive," said Janet Hagey. "I estimate that I will need at least five or six full-time people leading modelling sessions next year if we are to make real progress. In a downsizing environment, making the case for staff increases to people who have never heard of information engineering will be a challenge, to say the least."

EXHIBIT 4 Players, Accountability, Expenditure, Delivery, Authority

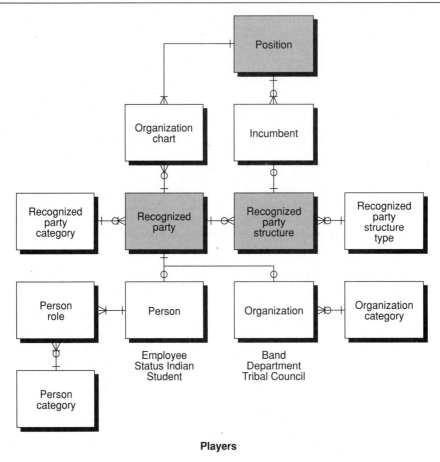

Players

THE FUTURE

Bruce Handel and his colleagues in Financial and Professional Services were in a delicate position. They, and perhaps they alone, understood that their information modelling efforts represented the foundation for a more daunting initiative. The larger goal was the dynamic reengineering of DIAND's business processes, in order to ensure continual alignment with the department's changing mandate and environment. Productivity and throughput became meaningful concepts only when applied to a current and consistent depart-

mental vision. They knew that the investment in new technology and methods would yield significant value only when the information available to top management was closely aligned to the strategic direction of the department. The strategic application of information technology was merely an enabling mechanism.

"Information engineering and our new systems development environment are necessary, but not sufficient criteria for the Department's successful transition. Even if we secure funding to support continued modelling sessions, entity-relationship

EXHIBIT 4   *(Cont.)*

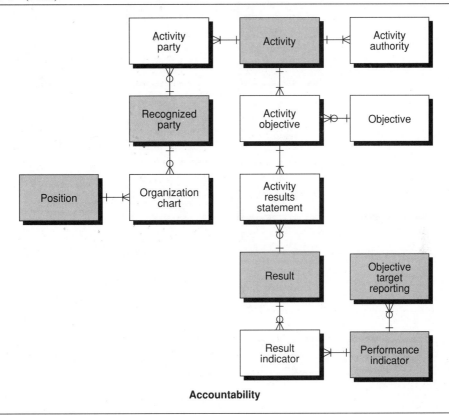

Accountability

diagrams alone do not constitute a stable information platform. Devolution is not conducive to collecting the information we are going to need—and we need it more than ever before. Somehow we've got to find a way to convince people who heretofore have only paid lip service to data as a strategic resource," confided Bruce Handel.

"I have no fears," added Alan Williams, ADM for Finance and Professional Services. "We've got good people working on it. We've got crap today. It can only get better."

EXHIBIT 4 (*Cont.*)

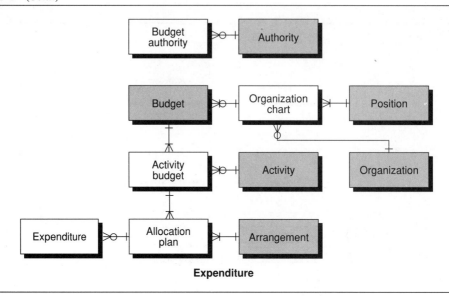

Expenditure

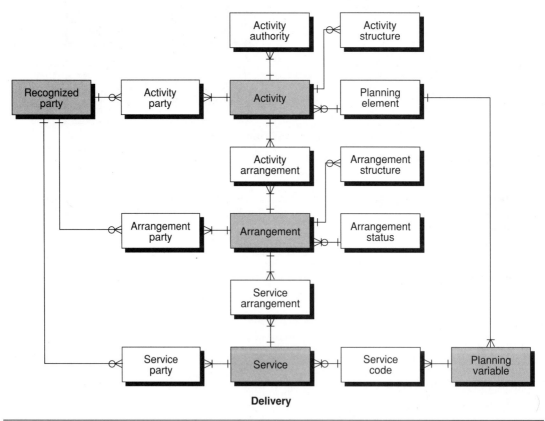

Delivery

EXHIBIT 5

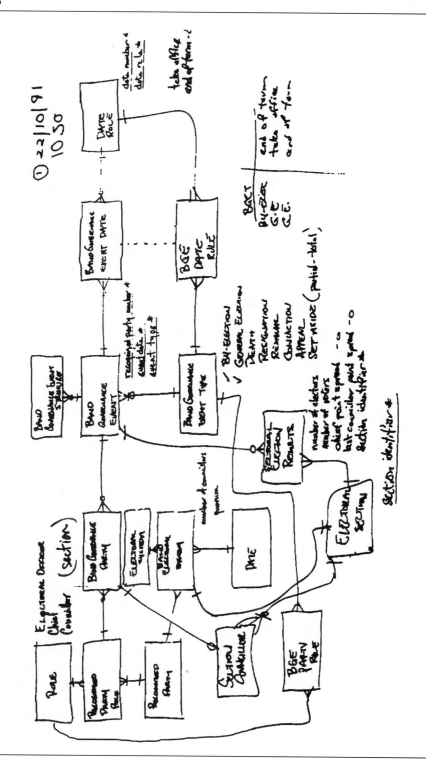

Case 5

WINDEMERE TRUST COMPANY: REBUILDING THE MIS INFRASTRUCTURE

Alan Bartt, the recently hired Senior Vice President of Information Systems for Windemere Trust Company[1], left the three-day management committee meeting in Toronto on April 29, 1989 feeling pleased. His proposal for getting rid of the existing computers, bringing in a totally new hardware platform and re-developing all of the company's software systems using "state-of-the-art" CASE (Computer Assisted Software Engineering) tools had been well received. With the strong support of Frank Scannell, the company's new CEO, he had received general approval to pursue the dramatic new directions his plans entailed. Now all he had to do was deliver the results. The four hour plane flight back to Vancouver would give him some time to think about how he should proceed.

COMPANY BACKGROUND

Windemere Trust Company, incorporated in Calgary in 1962 as Calgary Savings and Trust, was the sixth largest trust company in Canada, with assets of $3.6 billion, and net profit of $24.4 million in 1988. Windemere Trust Company, and Windemere Capital Markets, a merchant banking firm, were wholly owned by the holding company Windemere Trustco Inc., which in turn was 83%

This case was prepared by Debbie Campeau and Professor Sid L. Huff of the Western Business School. Copyright 1993, The University of Western Ontario.

[1]Disguised name.

owned by another holding company, Windemere Financial Corp. Ltd. A life insurance firm, Regina-based Northwest Life, was also 45% owned by Windemere Trustco Inc. Other companies in the Windemere Financial Corp. group included real estate development firms in Canada and the US, a manufacturing firm, and a New York merchant banking company.

Windemere Financial Corp. was the business empire which had been created 27 years ago by James Taylor, who at age 60 was still quite active in the company's affairs. Five other members of the Taylor family also held key positions in the organization. The Taylors had developed a reputation in the financial services industry as sharp, entrepreneurial, innovative deal-makers. At the height of Wall Street's most controversial raids, the New York Times had published a list of the most successful corporate takeover artists; the Taylors received top billing.

They routinely innovated with new investment vehicles, often taking chances other financial institutions refused. For example, one family member had been instrumental in the initial financing of the cellular telephone firm Cantel Inc. in Canada in 1984, when few people thought it had a chance. Recently, Windemere Financial sold its share of Cantel, netting the company $240 million.

The firm had grown to include five primary business groups: the Savings Division, Trust Services and Mutual Funds, the Equipment Financing Division, the Real Estate Financing Division, and Treasury and Investment. The company also owned a US leasing operation and a real estate assets business. The latter was currently being managed by a sister company, and was scheduled to be phased out within a few years.

Savings Division (Savings)

The Savings Division was the largest division in Windemere, with over 300 employees working in 36 branches in 24 cities across the country. The bulk of the branches were located in southern Ontario, Manitoba, and British Columbia. Deposits made by the Savings Division's clients formed the primary pool of funds used by the lending divisions.

In keeping with its mission statement, Windemere Savings did not usually try to compete head-on with the large Canadian banks and trust companies. The Savings Division's customers were older, with an average age of 57. Most dealt with other financial institutions as well as Windemere. Most of the deposits held by the company were term deposits with terms of one year or longer; only 10% were demand deposits. Relatively few customers held chequing accounts. Furthermore, Windemere did not operate a network of automated teller machines (ATMs); all customer transactions took place in branch offices during business hours.

Trust Services and Mutual Funds (TS/MF)

This division employed 39 people, and operated in four main areas: mutual fund loans, mutual fund management, corporate and personal trust services, and personal tax services. Mutual fund loans (loans made to individuals or organizations to buy shares in mutual funds) totalled $35 million in 1989, but were declining due to the availability of lower market interest rates. Three mutual funds were managed by the division. The largest, Windemere Realfund, was valued at $120 million and was composed primarily of real estate assets. Windemere Income Fund was valued at $6 million, and Windemere Growth Fund at $9 million. Corporate and Personal Trust customers were developed through relationships with other divisions, and through the acquisitions of other trust businesses. A recently acquired "H&R Block type" operation in Alberta was the vehicle for providing Personal Tax services.

Equipment Financing Group (EFG)

The Equipment Financing business, comprising 20% of Windemere's assets and employing 225 people, was rapidly growing. In 1988 the company handled the third largest volume of all similar firms in Canada. Most of the business was in small (under $25 million) and medium ($25-100 million) sized investments. Small ticket items represented 15% of the portfolio, with an average size of $7 thousand, while mid-ticket items with an average size of $70 thousand made up the rest. Computer equipment and trucks each represented 25% of the portfolio. The division's customers were typically vendors, as opposed to end users of the equipment.

Real Estate Financing Group (REFG)

Forty-one percent of Windemere's assets were accounted for by the REFG, which operated five offices in three regions, and employed 119 people. While the division currently offered both commercial and residential loans, residential financing was being phased out. Sixty percent of Windemere's commercial loans were regular fixed rate mortgages, while 20% were construction loans, with floating interest rates and yielding twice the net interest margin of the fixed rate loans. Commercial loan customers tended to be established, mid-sized developers or owners.

Treasury/Investment Division (Treasury)

This group was responsible for managing the asset-liability matching of Windemere, maintaining its liquidity levels, managing the investment portfolio of bonds, preferred shares and stocks, managing the company's foreign exchange position. In addition, Treasury provided corporate investing and money management services. The division's investment portfolios totalled $545 million in 1988.

FRANK SCANNELL

Frank Scannell had been asked to join Windemere as President and CEO in February 1988, following the resignation of Darryl Williams, who had served as President since 1983. Scannell had started his career in banking, but prior to joining Windemere, he had managed a large paper and envelope company, Docutech Inc., for 15 years, and the Canadian operations of a US leasing company before that.

Scannell had a strong customer orientation that he hoped to instill at Windemere:

"I believe that if things are not being driven by customers, they're probably not being done very well. All of our businesses need to be more customer-focused. In my view, one of our corporate mistakes is that we've been running around doing deals, while failing to build good customer relationships or even understanding who our customers were."

In the short to medium term, his focus was less on achieving high levels of growth and more on improving the alignment of the organization with its current businesses. Since joining the firm, Scannell had made a number of changes to his top management team. In addition, he had moved some of the company's executive offices from Vancouver to Toronto. Some senior managers and a few staff people, 120 in all, worked out of the offices at 20 Adelaide Street East, while the main company operations, including 430 people, worked in the main administrative offices at 222 Hornby Street in Vancouver. The remainder of Windemere's 800 employees were located in various regional sites and branches across the country.

Scannell was a strong believer in the value of information systems and the competitive advantage a firm could achieve through efficient and innovative use of information technology. In his previous company, Scannell had been instrumental in introducing sophisticated on-line operational systems, at a time when competitors were locked into older batch-style systems. This move had provided the company a key competitive advantage for a number of years.

Scannell frequently used a personal computer, both at home and in his office, and felt that using a PC was both useful and fun. In his view, "there are all sorts of things you can do with a personal computer, and the more you do the more it makes you think of other ways to use the technology. You just develop a sense of it, and you actually start to think about the business differently."

While many of his peers in the industry also had PCs on their desktops, in most cases these machines were rarely turned on, serving more as "desktop jewellery" than valuable hands-on tools. Not in Scannell's case.

"At a recent board meeting, one of the board members was giving me the needle, saying that I had a computer on my desk, but did I ever really use it? When I told him that I had prepared the entire board presentation myself, including the graphs and charts as well as the overheads and text, he couldn't believe it. But it's far easier to do it that way than to sit and scribble with a pen."

Scannell also made significant use of electronic mail within the company, using the IBM PROFS system through a terminal in his office which was connected into one of the company's mainframe computers. While the other executives had rarely used electronic mail before his arrival, they do now.

"When I walked in the door, they quickly found that it was hard to get the messages I sent them without a screen. In a number of cases, one of the other senior managers would ask me about my reply to a memo they sent me, and I said I had answered it three or four days ago. Then I said, 'I guess you'd better get a screen in your office or you'll never know what the answer was, because I don't even remember now.'"

Within about a month the other senior executives had become regular users of PROFS.

He viewed information technology as a key strategic factor in the company:

"I regard it a strategic and critical on an ongoing basis for all of the business units. We don't have any other equipment. We're not going to gain much competitive advantage from redecorating our offices. Information is our only product; therefore information systems are critical."

Prior to Scannell's arrival, the situation had been quite different. The information systems department had been thought of (when it was thought about at all) as a "back room" operation, whose role was to run the computers and software that processed the firm's transactions.

INFORMATION SYSTEMS AT WINDEMERE TRUST

When Frank Scannell arrived at Windemere, the Information Systems group consisted of 80 people (out of a total of approximately 800 in the entire company), all located in Vancouver. The Vice President of Information Systems reported to the company Controller. The IS group was split evenly between the operations staff, whose main task was to operate the computers located in the firm's data centre, and the development and administrative staff, mainly systems analysts and programmers, who developed new systems or maintained existing ones. Most of the system development staff actually reported within the business units, but also had a dotted line relationship to IS. The

Savings Division had the largest of these development groups, 20 people in all. The other business units had smaller IS groups, of a few people each.

The Information Systems department budget for 1988-89, including costs incurred by the central IS group (but excluding the costs of the satellite development groups) was $5.2 million.[2] Exhibit 1 illustrates the breakdown of the IS budget.

HARDWARE AND APPLICATION SOFTWARE

Windemere's original computer was a Microdata minicomputer. Acquired in 1976, it was quite an advanced system for its time. It featured a built-in relational database management system, and it was

---

[2]The overall systems-related expenses for the entire company amounted to about $10 million in 1988–89.

EXHIBIT 1 Consolidated Information Systems Budget

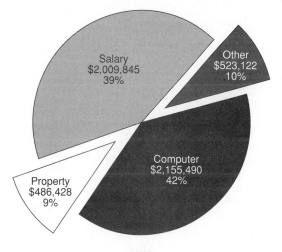

Information Systems Consolidated Budget

Salary $2,009,845 39%

Other $523,122 10%

Property $486,428 9%

Computer $2,155,490 42%

1989

(Source: Windemere Trust Co. documents)

quite easy to make changes to the applications that ran on it (e.g., to produce a new report).

Some time later, following the lead of other major financial institutions, a corporate decision was made to standardize on IBM as the company's primary vendor. Over time, additional computers were acquired and added to the Vancouver data centre. By the spring of 1989, two IBM 4381 mainframes, three IBM System/36 midrange machines, plus the original Microdata mini ran the bulk of the company's application systems. In addition, various personal computers had been purchased by individuals or groups to assist with their processing. The existing hardware array, together with the major application software systems, are illustrated in Exhibit 2.

According to an Assistant Vice President in the Real Estate Financing Group, the company had,

---

EXHIBIT 2   Hardware Platform and Applications

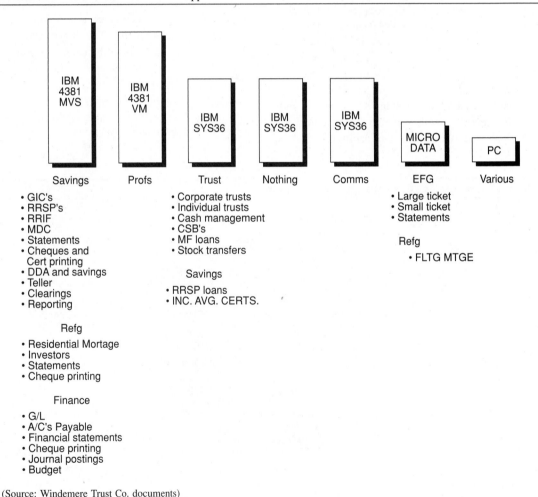

(Source: Windemere Trust Co. documents)

for a number of years, intended to sell the Microdata computer—its only non-IBM hardware—and convert the applications that ran on it to IBM equipment. However, the Microdata was still there and running; the transfer was continually put off.

Some of the computer systems, such as the original Microdata applications, had been developed by Windemere's own staff, but most had been purchased as packages from outside software firms, then extensively modified by company IS staff. Requests from the business groups for new applications were frequently of an emergency nature, because the firm operated in such a fast-moving, reactive fashion. The IS staff usually felt that they had insufficient time to develop new required applications in-house. Furthermore, nearly 80% of the IS programmers and analysts were kept busy maintaining the existing applications, leaving few people available to develop new ones. Systems consulting firms were often hired to handle specialized tasks or to fill the manpower gaps.

In 1987, a major project was launched to convert the company's IBM 4381 mainframe from DOS/VM to the MVS operating system.[3] The project cost over $1 million, and required the conversion of over 600 programs, as well as significant staff training and changes to other computer operating procedures. Twenty eight staff had worked on the project for over a year starting in October 1987. In terms of time and budget, the project was a success: the final cost was only 3% over budget, and the conversion had been completed on time, although some overtime was required to finish it.

---

[3]The DOS operating system was a relatively simple system for controlling and managing the basic computer hardware. It was targeted by IBM at smaller organizations with simpler processing requirements. The MVS operating system provided a much more powerful and sophisticated environment, though it cost more to lease from IBM, and was far more complex to use. It also consumed a much larger share of the computer's power. IBM targeted MVS at large organizations with complex and extensive data processing needs.

Another major project had been under consideration when Scannell joined the company. In conjunction with a major consulting firm, the IS staff had developed a plan for the creation of a new leasing system for the Equipment Financing Division. According to Scannell, however, the proposal was

". . . perhaps the most amazing I'd ever read. I was told that our present system was about to collapse in a heap, although it wasn't entirely clear why this was so. So we were going to build a new leasing system, which was ill-defined, and we were going to spend between $5 and $10 million doing it. We were going to give that money to a consulting firm who had proposed to us to build the system, although they insisted that any overages would be on our account. They said 'we think it can be done, for these sorts of numbers, and we'll give it our best shot.' It was preposterous!"

Shortly after Scannell expressed his concern about the proposal, the consulting firm's senior management decided to withdraw it.

The business units were also dissatisfied with the current information systems. In the TS/MF group, the systems had been developed by consultants. None were adequately documented, and most were outdated and unreliable. Year end processing in 1988 had required significant overtime and "bandaid" solutions to complete. In the Real Estate Financing Group, the systems were running on two different machines: most of the applications ran on the 4381, but the floating rate mortgages had to run on the Microdata, since the 4381 package could only handle fixed rate mortgages. In the Equipment Financing Group the problems were less serious, although the leasing system needed to be replaced. In addition, the Microdata minicomputer lacked the capacity to expand as the business grew.

The problems in the Savings department reflected the historical lack of customer focus throughout Windemere. All of the applications were product- rather than customer-centred. There was no single customer file. If, for example, a customer held both a GIC (Guaranteed Investment Certificate, a form of term deposit) and an RRSP

(Registered Retirement Savings Plan) with Windemere, and came into a branch to ask about the status of both, the teller would have to enter the GIC system, key on the customer's name and extract the necessary information, then exit the GIC system and enter the RRSP system, and repeat the process. This was a nuisance for customers, but more importantly it made it extremely difficult to analyze activities by customer, something necessary for developing customer-driven policies and products. The Savings division also had over 300 requests outstanding for maintenance and enhancements to existing systems.

The Treasury group had no applications running on the company's computers, but did make use of some packages that ran on computers of an outside computer bureau. The financial systems such as the general ledger, consolidated reporting, accounts payable and the like were also outdated and were not integrated with any of the company's other business systems.

As Scannell became more familiar with the information systems in place in the company, and with the IS group, he became increasingly dissatisfied. He reached the conclusion that the job being done by the IS staff was "completely unsatisfactory, and at colossal cost." He felt that the IS staff suffered from a serious lack of understanding of the businesses Windemere was in, that they had blinders on and were only interested in playing with their computers, not in supporting the real needs of the business.

After discovering this, Scannell called a meeting of the IS staff, confronted them with his perceptions, and asked their advice as to what ought to be done to improve things. The IS people put together a proposal, but it was not to Scannell's liking:

"They wanted to substantially increase the IS staffing from 10% of the company headcount, and spend a whole lot more money. There was not the first glimmer of anything being cost justified. So they wanted to about double the expenditures, and it was going to be 24 months down the road before anything came out of the trough."

THE JAMIESON REPORT

As his frustration grew over the state of IS in the company, and the apparent inability of the IS group to address the problems he saw, Scannell decided that a major shakeup was needed. Late in 1988 he hired a Toronto consultant, Lawrie Jamieson, to examine the IS area and make recommendations. Jamieson spent two weeks talking to people in the company and studying the existing systems and procedures in the IS department. Jamieson's report argued, among other things, that the company should reduce it's IS staff to about 20 people, from the 80 currently in place, and should migrate nearly all the application systems onto a network of microcomputers. Jamieson also criticized the IS operation for a complete lack of leadership.

While Scannell liked Jamieson's recommendations and felt they were reasonable, the Information Systems staff was quite upset and angry at the report and at the job Jamieson had done. They felt he had been unprofessional, closed minded from the start, and that he had decided before even talking to any of the IS staff what his recommendations were going to be. The staff attributed many of the IS problems to the unwillingness of top management in previous years to invest in IS. They felt that the turnover at the executive level that had occurred in the late '70s and early '80s had resulted in an overcautious attitude towards IS and a lack of the necessary expenditures. The IS people would develop ideas and plans for new projects, only to see them shelved following a change in senior management or a backing away by them when the time came to expend major funds.

One of the IS staff put it this way:

"That report was an insult to the people who had spent 8 or 10 years here doing their damnedest to improve systems. Jamieson told us that we were all stuck in a closet, didn't know what the business was about, that we were all mainframe bigots. He asked very few questions, rather came in and told us what the solution was going to be. He was totally unprofessional."

During this time, Scannell was actively recruiting for a new IS executive, someone who would be made a Senior VP and who would report directly to himself. Eventually he found Alan Bartt, at the time an executive with a major bank in the US.

ALAN BARTT

Bartt was hired in February 1989, and made a Senior VP with the official title of Chief Information Officer (CIO). He moved his family to Vancouver in April and purchased a home there.

Bartt had worked for a large, aggressive U.S. bank for 19 years before joining Windemere. He described his job there as organizational troubleshooting. He had moved through various parts of the bank's organization, fixing problems and starting up new ventures. He had no formal training in IS, but had learned a great deal about information technology and financial applications in the context of the bank's businesses. For example, when the bank set up a separate financial agency a few years ago, Bartt was charged with drafting the specifications for the agency's general ledger and profit reporting systems. Later he created and headed the Treasury operation for the new company. In the course of his years of experience there, he felt he "had probably touched every form of banking and financial product that exists, although not necessarily to a great depth."

When Bartt came on board, he found. . .

". . . the civil service. It was an incredibly fragmented, 1960s approach to IS, very bureaucratic, with lots of motherhood activities, lots of analysis, but nothing being delivered. The budget at the start of the year was just over $10 million, half of which went to run the ongoing operations. The IS head count was phenomenal. The move to MVS was simply a technology-driven 'must-have.' There was no justification for it in terms of the business. The business units also controlled their own system development staff, which was fine with me in principle except that there was no data architecture in place so these people often ended up heading off in tangential directions.

"The IS staff didn't understand the business, and there had been no attempt by the other executives to incorporate IS into the strategic planning process of the business. In fact, there had been little in the way of strategic planning at all until this past year. It was a catch-44: twice as bad as a catch-22."

Bartt believed the opportunities for making major improvements in IS at Windemere were so numerous that it was like "picking up jewels off the floor." Consequently, during the negotiations that preceded his joining the firm, he concurred with Scannell that the IS budget could be substantially reduced from the $10 million to which it had grown. They agreed on a reduction target of about $5 million annually.

THE RELIGION SESSION

A few weeks after he arrived, Bartt called a one-day off-site meeting of all his IS staff. The purpose of the meeting was, as he put it, to 'get religion.' Bartt had two main objectives in mind. First, he wanted to deal with the ill will that had been stirred up by the Jamieson report and associated events, to try to turn his staff's attitude around and to convince them that IS was going to become a key part of the company's strategy.

Bartt himself didn't dismiss the Jamieson report; quite the contrary, he felt that

"the IS people were totally defensive, they couldn't stand up and look in a mirror at themselves. There were some pearls in the report, but Jamieson had managed to get everyone's back up in IS, while the rest of the business just said 'see, I told you so.' "

At the meeting, Bartt proposed a "ceremonial burning" of the Jamieson report. His purpose was to "amputate the preoccupation with history" on the part of his staff. However, as it happened, this humorous comment also helped him win his staff's respect and support, which he knew he would need in order to accomplish the job ahead. As one IS staffer put it, "When Alan suggested the ceremonial burning, I thought, 'He's in!' "

The second objective of the meeting was to get his staff to brainstorm about what they would do with IS if there were no financial barriers to worry about. In the course of this free-wheeling discussion, Bartt laid out his initial thinking about how IS should be done in Windemere.

"We're in an extremely volatile environment: multi-currencies, multi-business groups, multi-legal environments, multi-countries, multi you-name-it. We need to have a dynamically scalable computer environment. We need to be able to ramp up, ramp down, amputate, to really have 'LEGO computing.' This implies we have to distribute our computing to the smallest possible size. We may even want to distribute the data bases across multiple machines. We have to go to a small box because large machines exhibit extreme "lumpiness" in their cost behaviour. You want to open a new branch in Winnipeg, with five people in it, and we're at the limit of the 4381? At that point there's no easy way to expand just a little. The next step is to bring in the plumber[4], get a 3090, and expand the data centre, which would cost millions. All this for one five-person branch? Ridiculous!

"Scalable computing would also provide better control over costs, and better product profitability accounting. The scalable approach is the ultimate in managing the business, never mind the technology.

"Also, we don't want to buy software packages from someone else. When you do that, you're buying someone else's problems, not buying what you really need, and you usually have to make massive modifications afterward anyway. No one is going to get a competitive edge by buying packaged software.

"Furthermore, we don't want to go near procedural languages any more. I don't want to hear the word 'third' ever again.[5] Think about an architectural firm: when they have to design something, architects don't get out their pads and pencils any more today, they go straight to their CAD systems. They generate drawings, show them to their customers, and say 'Do you like it? If not, let's sit down here at my workstation and I'll change it.' That's what we have to do. So, we have to go to a full CASE [6] approach to developing systems. No more COBOL. From now on, everything will be done using CASE tools."

BARTT'S IS VISION

During the weeks following the meeting, Bartt pulled together what he had learned about the company and its IS operations, and developed the key elements of his vision for the future of IS in Windemere:

- the IS head count would be reduced from the current 80 people to a much smaller number, possibly as few as 20 staff, much as Lawrie Jamieson had recommended. The goal was an IS staff budget of $2 million per year, which, Bartt argued, could be achieved by having 20 very good staff (he referred to them as "rocket scientists") at $100,000 per person. All the data centre people would be let go, and many of the other staff as well. The data centre would be disbanded.

- the present hardware would be sold, and a network of minicomputers would be installed throughout the company to take its place. The key considerations behind the selection of the new hardware platform were scalability, and responsiveness in system development. Bartt had decided that the new IBM AS/400 minicomputers would serve his purposes well. Among other advanced features, these machines offered good security facilities, and a built-in relational database management system. (See Appendix 1 for more information on the AS/400.) The AS/400 machines would be located in company offices, not in a special data centre, and would be operated by regular employees. The smallest of the AS/400 machines, the model B10, would

---

[4]to set up the water cooling system for the 3090 system

[5]in reference to 'third generation languages,' such as COBOL.

[6]CASE is the acronym for Computer Aided Software Engineering.

be used wherever possible, to provide the smallest (and cheapest) capacity increment as additional machines were added to the network.

- the AS/400 machines would be connected together in a token-ring network, so that one machine could provide disaster recovery and backup support for another. Networking would also allow databases to be distributed across various machines in the future if that was required.
- all the existing software applications would be rebuilt from the ground up, using CASE tools. Future applications would also be developed using CASE tools (a brief discussion of CASE is provided in Appendix 2).
- all user documentation for the new systems would be created and maintained on-line, in the form of context-sensitive help screens like those used in modern microcomputer packages. "I don't ever want to see paper documentation again," Bartt told them.
- prototyping and user-driven application development approaches would be used for developing all new information systems, as well as for rebuilding the existing systems. This would insure a high degree of user involvement in the design and creation of systems, something both Bartt and Scannell thought was crucial.

Finally, Bartt wanted to accomplish all this in 18 months: to have all the systems rebuilt using CASE tools and running on the AS/400 hardware platform, by the end of the following December.

THE TORONTO MANAGEMENT COMMITTEE MEETING

Bartt knew he had to sell his vision to the other senior managers. The occasion he used was a three-day off-site management committee meeting in Toronto, held in late April about two months after he joined the firm. Bartt took charge of the entire second day of the meeting, using part of it as a tutorial session on the basics of information technology, and part to lay out his IS vision. Scannell commented:

When Alan brought up the idea of going to a network of AS/400s, I had never even *heard* of an AS/400! But now the plan is that by the end of 1990, he'll take all the existing hardware and put it into a dumper. And the people who are maintaining the current equipment can drive the dumper to the dump. Then they can go to the beach.

The other thing Alan introduced us to, which sounded absolutely unbelievable to everyone there, is this business of CASE tools. Nobody at the meeting had ever heard of CASE before. Alan's explanations, using CAD and word processing analogies, make a lot of sense, but people there simply didn't know this sort of thing was even possible.

Bartt's presentation at the management committee meeting was a big success. In Frank Scannell's words, it was "a show stopper - he left us panting." By the end of the day, Bartt had convinced the other senior executives of the viability of his ideas, and had received their concurrence and support for his plan.

SYNON/2

Bartt and his staff had been referred to Synon 2 as the best CASE tool for the AS/400 platform. As it turned out, because the AS/400 was a new machine in the computer marketplace, Synon 2 was also the *only* CASE tool available at the time. The vendor, Synon Inc., a British company, had its North American headquarters in San Francisco, and also had an office in Toronto. As part of their promotion, Synon claimed it would build any system a purchaser wished within a maximum of 90 days on a consulting basis, using the Synon/2 toolkit and Synon staff. Bartt thought it would be a good idea to take them up on that offer.

THE ET&A SYSTEM

Bartt felt that, in a perfect world, he would have begun the task of redeveloping the company's systems with the core money market system, since that system was connected to many others, thus formed a kind of information hub for the firm's systems. However the rest of the company couldn't wait, and expediency more than anything else drove the decision of where to begin. The existing system in the most dire condition was the ET&A (Estates, Trusts and Agency) system in the Trust Services and Mutual Funds Division. Because the ET&A system was in such bad shape, and because the division itself was losing customers and doing poorly, Bartt and others felt they had nothing to lose by starting with it.

The ET&A system was a key one for the division. Ever since the Vice President in charge of the division, Murray Taylor, joined the firm in July 1988, he had had nothing but headaches with the ET&A system.

The ET&A system ran on an IBM System/36 computer, originally located in the division's Hamilton office. Most of the past programming and other work was being done by outside consultants, who turned over frequently. Soon after Taylor joined the firm, it was suggested that the System/36 be moved to Vancouver, since that was where most of Windemere's IS staff were located. That way, he felt, they would be better able to maintain the systems running on it. While moving the computer to Vancouver would cost his division $25,000, he believed it would save money in the long run, so the move was made in October. A telecom link was installed so that the users in the Hamilton office could use the system just as before. However, problems continued. Response time was painfully slow. Worse, transactions would occasionally, inexplicably be lost. Taylor commented,

> a clerk would make an entry, the entry would show up in the general ledger file, but when it was supposed to be transferred to the client screen it would disappear. And it wasn't consistent. Nobody could figure out what was happening. And that was just one example.

When the Vancouver IS people started examining the systems, they found there was no documentation, so they had to spend the first few weeks documenting the existing software. After this was done, they discovered the system had insufficient capacity to handle the coming year-end processing. The company wouldn't be able to close its books on time! A major effort was launched, including adding hardware capacity and hiring more consultants, and with lots of overtime and added costs they were able to make it through the year-end.

The problems with the ET&A system didn't stop at year end, however. Taylor continued,

> My employees are having to work three times as hard, and take abuse from me as well as our customers. We've had to add staff to clear up problems on a manual basis being created by the system. We bought a software package called a Debugger, but even with that we still were not able to sort it out. Our January statements came off perfectly, no 'problem. We thought maybe we had it licked. Then with the February statements, bang, we ran into problems again.

Bartt had discussed with Taylor the possibility of using the ET&A system as the first project in his systems redevelopment plan. Bartt had also proposed that they use a particular development methodology which requires heavy user involvement in creating the requirement specifications for the new system. Furthermore, Bartt wanted the staff from Synon, the CASE tool vendor he had selected, to lead the development effort.

The redevelopment of the ET&A system would achieve multiple goals. It would serve as a training ground for key Windemere staff to learn how to use Synon/2, by working with the vendor's staff and observing their practices. It would also provide the opportunity to become more familiar with the new AS/400 hardware. It would provide a trial of the user-centred development methodology. And, of course, it would produce a new ET&A system for Taylor's division.

Taylor was very enthusiastic about Bartt's plans. "It's like you telling me the messiah's coming; it's my only answer today," he said. He explained further why he thought the new system would be so valuable:

One of the benefits I'm led to believe of CASE tools on the AS/400 is that I'm not going to need support for a system that is up and running. The computer itself will run all the time, in a regular office, not an expensive data centre. As for the CASE tool benefit, suppose I want to make a minor change to a client file. With the CASE tool and the modular aspects in which the programs are written, I should be able to make that kind of a change easily, without having to search through the program for all the places where references to that client file are made. I just have to find the one little place in the client module where I need to make the change, take half a day to do it, and plug it back in. I don't need programmers, I don't need support people, or anything. There would still be programmers for the company, but I wouldn't need a dedicated IS staff of my own in my department. Today I have a staff of three people — an operator, a programmer, a backup programmer, and 40% of a manager for those people. Once this new system is up and running, I won't need any of those people, rather all I'll need is to be able to call on a corporate programmer for a half a day of his time once in a while.

If I can get this new set of systems, it will not only solve my problems, but it will give me the capability to take an organization which has been uncompetitive for years, to an organization which would have a major advantage over the competition. I would be able to go out and get more new business because, if you said to me, can you do this this way, I would be able to go back to my programmers and in a half a day or two days have a program written to do it. If you said that to CIBC or Royal Trust, who have a big-box mainframe orientation, they would have to line it up in their queue of things that they want to do and then when they finally get down to it, it would still be a major expense for them to do. This is going to move me out to the edge of the envelope!

IMPLEMENTATION DECISIONS

As Alan Bartt flew back to Vancouver, he felt confident his proposals, when fully implemented, would alleviate Windemere's system-related problems, and would provide a superior foundation for supporting the firm's future business needs. However

he knew he still had to deal with several important issues. Perhaps the most important of these concerned the need for major staff reductions.

Under the new systems configuration, Alan thought that the number of IS staff could be reduced by as many as 60 people. One of his major concerns, however, was how to manage this reduction, and what its implications were for the interim period of systems changeover. In particular, Alan was concerned about how to keep the data centre staff from leaving Windemere before the changeover had been made. The data centre would be closed after the changeover, but had to be kept operating efficiently until that time.

A second issue on his mind was the choice of an initial project. He knew a lot was riding on the success of the first project undertaken using CASE tools on the AS/400 platform; he wanted a "big win." Synon would shoulder the bulk of the responsibility for the first system, since they would lead the project. The ET&A system was not Bartt's first choice, but it was undoubtedly the "squeakiest wheel" in the company at the time.

Another issue concerned user participation in the redesign of the company's systems. Given the time horizon under which he wanted to operate, Alan was concerned about whether he would be able to involve system users in the development process. One alternative solution that he had been considering was the concept of surrogate users. Surrogate users were professional consultants with knowledge of the business requirements who were hired to provide the system specifications to the designers. Because they were professional systems consultants, they understood the system development process better than most users, and could provide the information more quickly and accurately. The downside of using surrogate users, however, was that while they were familiar with the type of business involved, they did not have full knowledge of the company and its idiosyncrasies. Thus, systems developed with surrogate users would not be fully tailored to the organizational environment. Also, some of the benefits of high user involvement in the system development process would be lost when surrogate users were employed for this purpose.

Finally, Bartt was concerned about properly managing the great amount of change that the IS staff who would be remaining would be expected to undergo. He knew that their world was shifting violently around them, and that a great deal was being asked and expected of them in a short time period.

While he pondered these issues 32,000 feet above Winnipeg, Alan Bartt also wondered what other things might trip him up as he started down the road to implementing his IS vision in Windemere.

APPENDIX 1: THE AS/400 COMPUTER

IBM's Application System/400 minicomputer family is a new addition to the IBM product line, announced in the fall of 1988. Described in the industry as a "revolutionary" product, the AS/400 incorporates several important features.

Single-Level Addressability:

This feature of the AS/400 allows users to operate as if all of their applications were resident in one very large main memory. Users do not have to know the physical location of files in the system, and programmers do not have to manage the allocation of storage space.

Consistent Interface:

The AS/400 utilizes a standard interface to all programs. Thus, the operation of function keys and other commands is consistent across all applications. From the users' perspective, therefore, the training received for one product can more easily be transferred to other AS/400 products.

Fully Integrated Relational Database:

A relational database function is built into the architecture of the AS/400. This releases the programmers from having to be concerned about the physical organization and storage of the data. While database management systems are frequently added to other

computers also, in the form of an extra purchased software package, in the AS/400 it comes built in. Among other advantages, this makes it more efficient, able to process data in the databases more quickly.

Distributed Database:

IBM announced that the AS/400 would be capable of supporting 'distributed' database applications. In such applications, a database could be spread out across different machines in a network, making it possible to place components of the database closest to where they will be most heavily accessed (to minimize communications costs), yet still allow users to view the database as a logically integrated structure. The distributed database capabilities of the AS/400 were not included in the initial release of the computer, rather were left for future development by IBM.

OS/400:

The AS/400 operating system, OS/400, includes many applications not part of traditional operating systems. Graphics capability, the relational database, basic office applications and an interactive "help" system are all integrated into OS/400.

SAA:

SAA (Systems Application Architecture) is a major IBM project whose objective is to develop a set of standard interfaces across families of previously incompatible IBM computers, to make it easier to interconnect these systems. To date, the three major platforms in the SAA "family" are the 370-architecture mainframes (including the 4381 and 3090 computer lines), the PS/2 microcomputers, and the AS/400 midrange computers. The AS/400 is the first computer system to have been designed from the beginning with SAA in mind.

Family of Sizes:

Seven different models are available in the AS/400 family. The smallest of these, the B10, supports from 4-16 megabytes of memory, and about one billion bytes of disk storage capacity, and is designed to support from 8-24 concurrent users. The largest AS/400 model, the B70, supports 32-96 megabytes of memory, up to 38.4 gigabytes of storage, and 172-400 concurrent users.

APPENDIX 2: CASE AND CASE TOOLS

CASE is an acronym for Computer Assisted Software Engineering: using computers to help automate the creation and maintenance of software. CASE tools provide the necessary software to automate parts of the applications development process. For instance, CASE tools are available to draw data flow diagrams, provide project management support, and generate code. Although industry experience with CASE tools has been limited, one of the leading CASE vendors, Synon Inc., has claimed that it can develop any application within 90 days using its Synon/2 package of CASE tools.

The idea of using a computer as a software design and production tool is not new. In the early days of computing, special programs called assemblers were written to allow programmers to write programs in a way that was easier to learn and more flexible and productive than the "machine language" that computers actually use. The assemblers would translate programs from the more flexible form (termed "assembly language") into machine language. Somewhat later, high level languages such as Fortran and COBOL were developed, making the programming task still easier, and programmers more productive.

However, attempts to continue the push to still more flexible and productive programming and system building tools stalled, and for many years, through the 1960's and 1970's the third generation language COBOL (COmmon Business Oriented Language), latterly augmented with additional tools such as on-line editors and code libraries, became the widely accepted standard for application development.

In the late 70's, some further progress was made, in the form of "fourth generation languages," or 4GL's. These new languages allowed programmers to write programs in a still more flexible and condensed form, improving productivity somewhat further. However, 4GLs had some shortcomings of their own. First, 4GL packages were quite costly. Also, the programs produced using them tended to be very inefficient, hence required greater computer horsepower to run them (as compared to the same programs written by a programmer in COBOL). Furthermore, no single 4GL clearly dominated the market, so there was the problem of which 4GL vendor to choose. If the chosen vendor turned out to have a short life, the investment made in applications built using that vendor's 4GL would be in serious jeopardy. Finally, 4GLs failed to produce a *major* productivity improvement in system development for most firms, rarely much more than 5-10% for most uses.

Other recent developments have helped to automate the "back end" of the system development process (programming, testing, maintenance) still further. Programs called code generators were developed to simplify the laborious task of writing out the detailed lines of COBOL code required in each new program, many of which were nearly identical from one program to another. A code generator is essentially a shorthand way of producing a COBOL program: the user can write a program using the concise syntax of the code generator, then the generator produces the corresponding, but far lengthier and more verbose, COBOL program. The COBOL program is then translated into executable form using the normal COBOL compiler (translator). Other back-end tools include software packages to assist in program testing and debugging; tools that help maintain libraries of reusable code modules; tools to assist in maintaining documentation, and so forth.

Assemblers, compilers, 4GLs, code generators, etc. all address the back end of systems development. Until quite recently, there were very few tools for improving the front end of the process: analysis and documentation of user requirements, system design and specification, project planning, data base design, and so forth. Much of this work is inherently graphical, and relies heavily on various types of diagramming methods. Computers traditionally have not been very good at handling such graphical information. However the advent of powerful and relatively inexpensive "desktop workstations" has changed things. These workstations can be used to run CAD (Computer Aided Design) software for architects and machine designers, so that today even very small design and architectural firms are able to make use of these computer-based tools. The same desktop workstations can be applied to automating the front end of the systems development process. In fact, automating the front end of system development bears much similarity to automating machine design using CAD: both are mainly processes requiring the creation and labelling, and subsequent modification, of drawings - -tasks that used to be laboriously done on paper (the architect's hand-drawn blueprint, the system designer's logic flow diagram). Front-end tools are now available to automate the creation, handling and modification of the drawings that constitute the design of an information system. Furthermore, some front-end CASE tools have been integrated with other back-end tools, specifically code generators, so that in some instances the system developer can generate COBOL code directly from the diagrams created during the front-end analysis and design steps.

The entire process of using computer-based tools to automate system design and development is today referred to as CASE, or Computer Assisted Software Engineering. There are numerous vendors of CASE tools, and the market for such tools is growing rapidly, at over 30% per year. Vendor offerings can be categorized as one of two types: CASE toolkits or CASE workbenches. Toolkits are more focused, addressing only a portion of then overall development life cycle. Workbenches are sets of integrated CASE tools (sometimes referred to as I-CASE) that address the entire cycle, from planning and design through code generation, testing and maintenance. As yet, the CASE workbenches are less popular than the toolkits: they are more expensive to buy, take longer to learn, and generally are not equally effective at the different development cycle stages. The problem with toolkits is that they are not integrated, so transferring the information from one toolkit to another is cumbersome and often must be handled manually. However, toolkits are less expensive and usually more effective for the narrower task they do address.

Case 6

TRAVELERS INSURANCE: PROCESS SUPPORT THROUGH DISTRIBUTED TECHNOLOGIES

Nearing delivery of a new workers' compensation workstation, Doug LaBoda, Vice President of PC Claim Systems at Travelers Insurance, reflected on the process of developing systems with leading-edge technologies:

My experience has been that you can't design the whole thing from start to finish at the very beginning, that you've got to have some part of your solution based on pieces that are not yet there. And hopefully you're close enough to the developers [of tools] to know that it's around the corner or it's coming or whatever. That's really the way that, I think, the successful leading edge applications get rolled out quickly, because if you wait until that's all proven you won't be leading edge. You won't have the competitive advantage that we think this is going to deliver in a workers' compensation market, because somebody else will have beaten you to it.

The development team had experienced a variety of frustrations in their efforts to deliver a workstation that combined a number of immature technologies, including object orientation, distributed data bases, and client-server architectures. In particular, they found it difficult to estimate dates of completion, because they lacked experience on which to base their estimates. Problem diagnosis was also challenging in an environment where, when something went wrong, hardware, operating system, application software, or communications software could all be at fault.

Nonetheless, the 1850 persons who would be using the system and the PC Claim managers who had championed its development applauded the workstation design. They predicted that it would significantly improve the productivity of the field office staffs and the quality of the service they provided to their customers. As pilot tests indicated that the productivity improvements were real, Mike Costigan, Vice President of Workers' Compensation Claim, observed:

This is a home run. It's not a single.

BACKGROUND

The Travelers Group was formed on December 31, 1993, through the merger of Primerica Corporation and The Travelers Corporation. Although Primerica acquired The Travelers, the new corporation retained the Travelers' name and logo—a red umbrella—because marketing research indicated that it was one of the best recognized consumer names in the United States. With combined revenues of $20 billion and an asset base of over $100 billion, Travelers Group represented a new breed of financial services firms in the United States offering a broad range of services. Its investment banking unit, Smith Barney, was the second largest investment banking and securities brokerage firm in the country; Commercial Credit

provided consumer financial services through 768 branch offices; Primerica Financial Services was the largest issuer of individual term life insurance in the United States; and Travelers Insurance unit offered commercial and personal insurance lines.

Travelers Insurance operated largely independently of the parent corporation with assets of about $40 billion and revenues of around $7 billion, it had four divisions: Property-Casualty Commercial Lines, Property-Casualty Personal Lines, Managed Care and Employee Benefits, and Financial Services.[1]

The Commercial Lines Department was the largest of the divisions and Workers' Compensation provided two-thirds of the revenues of that division. Travelers was the market leader in workers' compensation, insuring 50% of the Fortune 500, and administering claims for many self-insured firms. The company renewed well over 90% of its workers' compensation accounts each year and was growing the business rapidly.

Workers' compensation was mandated and regulated by both federal and state laws. Its purpose was to protect workers who were injured at their place of employment or elsewhere in the course of doing their job. It covered medical costs, lost wages and benefits, rehabilitation expenses and other costs associated with an accident or illness. Workers' compensation claims varied from small and short-term, such as the cost of X-rays following a fall on a parking lot, to large and long-term, such as lifelong medical costs and wage and benefit expenses for a worker who was permanently disabled on the job.

In the early nineties, even as workers' compensation insurers were facing pressures from rising medical costs and rate regulation, most of their customers were experiencing dramatically increasing workers' compensation expenses. By 1994 workers' compensation often comprised as much as 70% of a firm's insurance premiums. Consequently, Travelers had stepped up efforts to help customers develop

---

[1]In January, 1995, the Managed Care and Employee Benefits unit will be merged with a similar unit of MetLife. The resulting organization to be known as MetraHealth will be an independent company jointly owned by The Travelers and MetLife.

cost reduction and control strategies. The company was also emphasizing national accounts, in which large firms would self-insure and use Travelers as their claims administrator.

Because laws governing workers' compensation varied by state, Travelers administered claims locally at 51 field offices. Travelers supported its highly skilled, well-trained branch work force with a number of innovative information systems. The company was the only insurance carrier that had a single integrated 800 number for telephone reporting of accidents and injuries. This included a host-based medical bill management system that among other things, checked for double billing and determined the appropriate amount to pay on a given bill. The company had rolled out, in early 1993, a national online pharmacy preferred provider organization, which enabled an enrolled pharmacist to enter a customer's prescription information and learn whether it was covered by workers' compensation. Management believed that continued success in the workers' compensation market required identifying additional innovative applications of information technology that would enable them to increase customer service while cutting costs.

INFORMATION TECHNOLOGY AT TRAVELERS

The Information Systems Department (ISD) at Travelers Insurance defined its mission as follows:

> . . . to work with the businesses to implement technology and information-based capabilities that enable and sustain competitive advantage and superior service, and to master technology and technique in order to provide desired capabilities rapidly and operate them effectively.[2]

Both ISD and its business partners espoused a division of labor that entrusted technology and its support to ISD. One IS manager explained:

---

[2]Information Systems Department Mission Statement, March 1993.

> We don't want our business customers to need to know the technology, or be responsible for the technology. Their job should be paying claims, or selling insurance, and not worrying about the backups for last night, or what software is on their machines. (Steve Grace)

ISD staffed to meet these expectations. Each business unit had a systems division that focused on applications and development and maintenance. Staff of the business unit systems division reported to the business but maintained a "heavy dotted-line" relationship with central IS. A strong central IS unit supported the divisional units through development of the communications infrastructure, research and development of new technologies, and support for mainframe and distributed systems. An 800-number provided round-the-clock computer operations support to headquarters and field office personnel.

ISD prided itself on its well-trained professional staff. IS employees organized by teams for individual projects. The teams were transitory, so that they could acquire expertise and then reuse it in future projects. In many projects a core team was supported by experts who came and went as needed. Transfers between central and divisional IS and across units within divisions and central IS were common. IS managers credited the frequent transfers with helping them understand the capabilities that existed across ISD and with facilitating a camaraderie that encouraged mutual dependence between divisional and central IS.

Travelers had traditionally been strictly an IBM shop, but had introduced elements of open systems as it implemented distributed systems. ISD prided itself on being at the leading edge of technology and typically had 20-40 persons experimenting with hardware, operating system, telecommunications and other infrastructure technologies that were not yet mature enough to be applied to the business. This enabled management to move quickly when they sensed that business needs would benefit from new technologies. For example, the company had started to move toward increased use of personal computers and distributed systems as early as 1985—well before client-server architectures became fashionable.

Like other units at Travelers Insurance, ISD had experienced significant downsizing in recent years. A collapsing real estate market in the late eighties and high payouts to victims of Hurricane Andrew in 1992 had depleted cash resources, leading to large-scale cost-cutting initiatives. As a result the department had fewer hierarchical layers than had previously been the case. IS staff were encouraged to think of career growth in terms of increased skills and competencies rather than managerial advancement. Technical ladders ensured opportunities for financial growth apart from managerial advancement.

WORKERS' COMPENSATION WORKSTATION PROJECT

In 1989, Mike Costigan, Vice President of Workers' Compensation Claim, and Jack Gardner, a former IS manager who had become a technical advisor to Commercial Lines management, persuaded the head of Commercial Lines, Chuck Clark, to undertake reengineering of the workers' compensation claims process. Travelers had traditionally charged premium prices for its services. Intensified competition, however, suggested that, in the long-run, this was not a viable strategy. The company had invested heavily in training field office personnel, and had developed a highly skilled, competent work force. Costigan indicated that this would not be sufficient to retain the company's leadership position in the workers' compensation market:

> In the late 1980s, Travelers took a look at its workers' compensation claims management, and we restructured our entire workers' compensation delivery system. We made the commitment, both resource-wise and financially, to jump ahead of the competition. Having done that, and put the right human resources in place, the right training in place, we now had a tremendous additional expense base, or cost base. And in doing that we asked how could we become more effective and more efficient. Through technology and the use of systems. It wasn't just better sameness. It was, step out of the box and look at the concept. And I believe the foundation to that is technology. You have to give people the opportunity to see what improvements they can make in work flow and office structure with the technology.

A case in workers' compensation was initiated whenever an individual filed a claim requesting compensation for a work-related injury. Travelers was notified of the claim through its centralized 800-number from which the claim would be forwarded electronically to the appropriate case manager. Processing involved collecting necessary information on expenses and lost compensation and then providing reimbursements to the claimant and other appropriate sources. It also involved communicating the status of the case to the employer and state and federal agencies. The case was closed when all payments had been made, no more expenses were expected to be filed, and all relevant parties had been notified of the disposition of the claim. Thus, small cases could be completed in a few days, but cases involving major disabilities could continue for months or years.

Branch office personnel had been using terminals connected to a mainframe at corporate headquarters in Hartford, Connecticut to record key steps in case processing. The system performed adequately for accounting purposes, but was highly structured to accept limited amounts of data in a predetermined sequence. Thus, it was not valuable in helping case managers process claims or in providing information on claims to supervisors and branch managers.

In December 1989 Costigan and Gardner assembled a field design review team, consisting of seven branch office managers. The team examined claims processing work flows, focusing, in particular, on the role of the company's 700-plus case managers. The team met several times a month in the early phases of the project. They were encouraged to think "out of the box," and members who suggested that some ideas "couldn't work" were challenged to explain why not.

The field design review team worked with a core reengineering team to establish a vision and define needs for system support. The core reengineering team was primarily responsible for defining information systems requirements to support the field team's vision, but some members of the team visited other insurance companies to collect ideas to advance the vision. The core reengineering team had a technical project manager, Paul Reid, and a business project manager, Linda Robison. Maureen Hesney, who was then responsible for PC Claim Systems, Mike Costigan and Jack Gardner championed the project and worked closely with the teams. Exhibit 1 shows the initial project team composition.

The goal of this project was a productivity increase of 15–20%. This meant that case managers who typically handled 150–180 cases at a time might be able to handle 200 or more. Accomplishing this goal required finding ways to significantly reduce paperwork and keep case managers organized. Case managers processed large volumes of paperwork for all but the very simplest cases. They sent and received information from claimants, employers, doctors, nurses, hospitals, and other medical care providers, lawyers, and state and federal agencies. Reading, writing, filing and retrieving this paperwork was time-consuming and error-prone. The field design review team suggested that much of this information could be exchanged and stored electronically.

In May of 1990, the teams submitted initial findings and recommendations in order to secure funding from the business unit and resources from ISD. By the end of 1991, the core reengineering team had compiled a book specifying the requirements for a case manager's workstation. The book, which was referred to as the *gray book* due to the color of its cover, defined the vision for the workers' compensation reengineering project, identified the expected impacts on the field offices, and presented a thorough cost/benefit analysis. Exhibit 2 summarizes the nature of the expected benefits of the Workers' Compensation Reengineering Project.

Central to the reengineering was the concept of "the new case manager." According to this concept, case managers should be highly skilled and self-sufficient, with a set of automated tools that permitted them to function autonomously and efficiently. Key features of the proposed system included a di-

ary that would serve to remind case managers of action items, a letters and forms capability that would enable sending out a form letter with a single command or permit customization of letters, electronic referrals, a sophisticated notes capability to track the status of a claim, and an inventory checking capability. The workstation specifically addressed needs of national accounts by documenting the unique communications requirements of each account and measuring compliance with those requirements. Exhibit 3 presents an overview of the capabilities of the case manager's workstation.

As part of the process of defining systems requirements, systems personnel produced an initial prototype of the system using a graphical user interface[3] product that accessed the host system. The tool was intended to front-end the existing system, and it resulted in an improved transaction processing system. While the prototype represented a far superior system, management felt it did not fundamentally reengineer the process. Linda Robison explained:

> It was a prettier system [than the existing host-based system], but I don't think it was a significantly more functional system, as far as being more of a decision support system to case managers.

Based on her reading of the trade literature, Maureen Hesney suggested that object technologies might provide the capabilities that the case manager workstation required. She sought out a consulting firm with experience in object-oriented (OO) systems development.[4] The consulting firm provided an early prototype. The prototype

---

[3]A graphical user interface, usually referred to as a GUI, is a software product that provides a friendly interface to individual users of the system. A GUI uses icons to describe options. Users typically point to an icon using a mouse and then click to activate that function.

[4]Object-oriented systems are distinctly different from traditional systems in that they encapsulate data and operations into objects. Individual objects can then inherit properties from other objects. These encapsulation and inheritance principles are expected to reflect business processes in a way that commonalities across and within systems can be easily identified and replicated.

EXHIBIT 1 Workers Compensation Re-engineering Project Organization

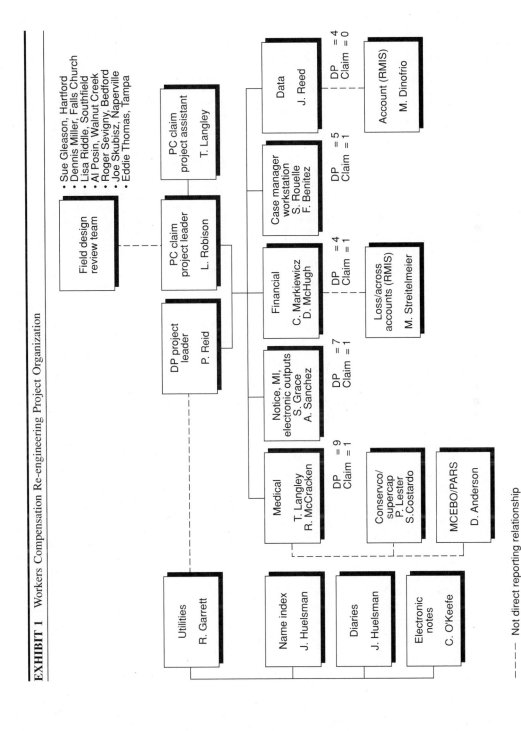

- Sue Gleason, Hartford
- Dennis Miller, Falls Church
- Lisa Riddle, Southfield
- Al Posin, Walnut Creek
- Roger Sevigny, Bedford
- Joe Skubisz, Naperville
- Eddie Thomas, Tampa

Field design review team

PC claim project leader
L. Robison

PC claim project assistant
T. Langley

DP project leader
P. Reid

Data
J. Reed

Account (RMIS)
M. Dinofrio

DP = 4
Claim = 0

Case manager workstation
S. Rouelle
F. Benitez

DP = 5
Claim = 1

Financial
C. Markiewicz
D. McHugh

Loss/across accounts (RMIS)
M. Streitelmeier

DP = 4
Claim = 1

Notice, MI, electronic outputs
S. Grace
A. Sanchez

DP = 7
Claim = 1

Medical
T. Langley
R. McCracken

DP = 9
Claim = 1

Conservco/ supercap
P. Lester
S. Costardo

MCEBO/PARS
D. Anderson

Utilities
R. Garrett

Name index
J. Huelsman

Diaries
J. Huelsman

Electronic notes
C. O'Keefe

----- Not direct reporting relationship

689

EXHIBIT 2   Anticipated Benefits of the Workers' Compensation Workstation

---

1. Shorten time between date of injury and date of claim resolution and eliminate over-payments.
2. Reduce unallocated expenses by automating filing of state forms and form letters.
3. Establish a strong competitive position through fully-automated telephone reporting capabilities and medical bill review.
4. Establish the best customer service in the business.
5. Maintain consistent, quality level of execution.
6. Improve financial controls.
7. Provide information to customers that demonstrates the value of Travelers' Loss Payout Reduction Services.

---

provided a glimpse of the capabilities that an OO system could utilize to provide a flexible and powerful set of desktop tools for a case manager. Linda Robison described the team's reaction:

> It was like night and day. They forced us into ten years from now, instead of just five years from now.

While the prototype generated initial enthusiasm for pursuing an OO solution to the workstation project, there were concerns about the technology. Paul Reid explained:

> One by-product [of the prototype] was a much more distributed application. More information was needed on the servers to have access to your full inventory and be able to get all your cases at a glance. It called for us to stretch our thinking about the amount of distributed application, and frankly, that's a much riskier application.

The technical complexity of the project led to intensive discussions within the team and with

Costigan and Hesney about the potential benefits and risks of the object solution. Reid expressed reluctance because of concerns that the immaturity of object technology would make it difficult to control. Moreover, ISD did not have relevant expertise:

> The traditional environment at Travelers is IMS, MVS, COBOL. We understood data modelling—the tasks that you went through were very cut-and-dry. You didn't have to wonder "Have I got the right technology here, do I know enough about it?" With this project, we didn't start out understanding object oriented. We had gotten conceptual training on it. We had taken classes, but we didn't really have any practical experience with it. Both object-oriented and OS/2 are hardly things where lots of people have lots of experience. SQL Server was a new data base technology for us. There were so many new things we were working in that we needed to build or hire a lot of skills, and we needed to find those skills quickly.[5]

ISD noted, however, that OO had two important benefits: (1) much faster maintenance and changes, and (2) reusability. Costigan and Robison noted that faster change would ensure long-term competitiveness. Reusability appealed to top managers who sensed that the claims processes for auto, property and casualty, and liability would eventually need to be reengineered. Ultimately, the core reengineering team, with support from Costigan, Hesney and top management in Commercial Lines and ISD, made the decision to adopt an object-oriented approach to developing the case manager's workstation.

BUILDING THE INFRASTRUCTURE

The strategy for distributed computing at Travelers was called "industrial strength distributed computing." This meant distributing the hardware and

---

[5]Object-oriented systems are distinctly different from traditional systems in that they encapsulate data and operations into objects. Individual objects can then inherit properties from other objects. These encapsulation and inheritance principles are expected to reflect business in a way that commonalities across and within business processes can be easily identified and replicated.

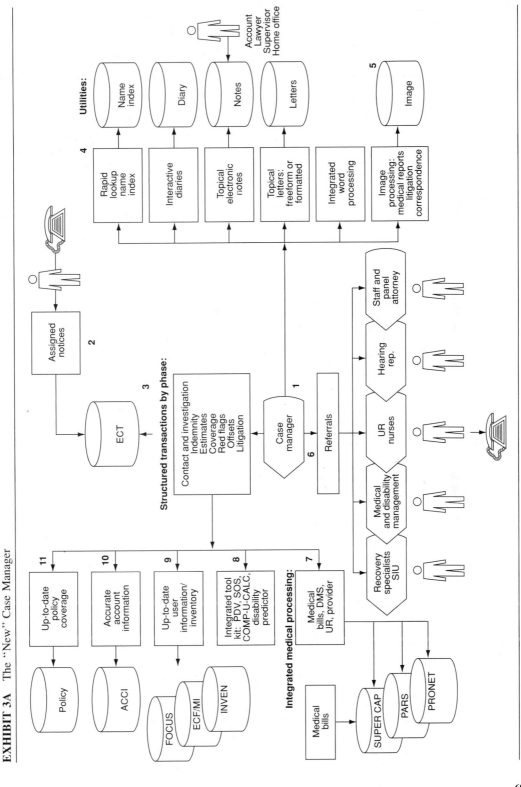

The following text corresponds to the chart shown on the prior page.

1. The Case Manager, responsible for structuring the job, is at the center of the workflow.
2. Newly assigned notices automatically appear as part of a Case Manager Roster.
3. Structured transactions organized by the phases of claim management have a consistent look and feel.
4. Integrated utilities are available. They provide: Rapid lookup based on name or Social Security number combined with the ability to select the correct claim and access the necessary transaction.

   A Diary facility that provides the ability to move from the diary directly to the activity required (e.g. when a diary is selected that says an estimate is due, estimate screen processing is automatically initiated).

   Topical Electronic Notes with a simple subject index are written and accessible to all key parties involved with a claim (Case Manager, Defense Attorney, Accounts, Supervisor, Investigators, Recovery Specialist.)

   Topical letters which are either free-form or completely system formatted. Sent letters can be viewed and reprinted.

   A complete word processing package.
5. Image processing will be integrated in the future for critical items such as medical reports and litigation correspondence. Preferred goal is to replace paper with electronic communication.
6. Electronic referrals to 'experts' facilitate the Case Manager's communication with Recovery Specialists, Investigators, Medical Representatives, Disability Management staff, Utilization Review, Nurses, Hearing Representatives, Staff and Panel Attorneys.
7. Medical bill review and repricing will be fully integrated into the Case Manager Workstation. Utilization review and disability management and follow-up will be streamlined by integration of PARS.
8. An Integrated Tool Kit packages a number of PC-based software packages which are relevant to the particular phase of a claim. These tools include a Present Day Value calculator, SOS, a Comp-U-Calc facility that calculates indemnity payments based on indemnity state, lost time and average weekly wage, and a Disability Predictor. Other tools will also be added.
9. An up-to-date claim roster listing claims by Case Manager is available. The Case Manager's User Management Information system supports review of the claim inventory by date of loss, estimate size, referrals, red flags, etc. (Refer to Section 4, Impact on Claim Office, Performance Management Systems).
10. Accurate account information is available. This includes summaries of account subsidiaries and locations, contacts, special account agreements, and problems.
11. Up-to-date policy coverage information is available, including a list of all claims registered under a particular policy.

---

software, but retaining centralized support. In the second quarter of 1992 a Distributed Systems Management (DSM) team was formed within the Distributed Environment Division of central ISD to develop the necessary tools for centralizing management of distributed systems. As DSM developed tools, they would hand them over to Distributed Systems Management Support (DSMS), a centralized unit responsible for 24-hour monitoring and support of distributed systems. Steve Grace, head of the DSM team, described the advantages of centralized distributed systems management as follows:

- permits development and deployment of sophisticated tools and techniques to monitor hardware and software problems
- reduces systems administration costs through economies of scale
- enables around the clock support and expedites resolution when problems occur
- permits systems division personnel to devote their efforts to providing solutions to business problems, and also reverses the trend of infringing on business partners to do distributed system support functions.

Grace's team developed probes that would enable DSMS to constantly monitor distributed systems. He described the vision for centralized monitoring:

> I need to be able to distribute applications transparently, to know when things break at a remote site before the user calls. Multi-window screens make it difficult for a [remote] IS professional to know what's wrong, so I need to be able to see their screen from Hartford. I need to understand the business application and to know what part of the machine is broken. This is the role of the probes.

Another key capability that Grace's team was developing was electronic distribution, installation, and configuration of all software. Electronic distribution and installation had two advantages. First, it meant that software could be installed on servers at headquarters and then sent out to field offices, and simply plugged in by a designated user. Second, updates to software could be accomplished simultaneously at all sites. Travelers could actually provide better service without the expense of local experts.

Grace believed that effective support would enable one person to support thirty servers, as compared to the average of one person for every two servers in divisions that were supporting their own servers. With centralized support ISD calcu-

lated annual costs to support a server at between $1200 and $1800. The industry average was $26,000 per server.

Grace's team focused on the workers' compensation workstation as a model of future systems. As development work commenced on the workstation, DSM was developing protocols to enable centralized support of the system. The workers' compensation workstation would place two servers in each of the 51 field offices, and top IS managers stated that centralized support was critical to the cost-effectiveness of the system.

THE DEVELOPMENT PROCESS

Because the system was broad in scope, development was divided into three phases. Most functionality was to be delivered in Version 1, which was scheduled to be piloted by July, 1993 with full roll-out by the end of the year. Versions 2 and 3 would provide additional functionality, such as litigation and enhancements to existing capabilities. The target completion date was sometime in 1995.

Although they worked closely together, Linda Robison and Paul Reid had distinctly separate responsibilities for delivering the system. Robison focused on changes in work flows. She was responsible for reviewing prototypes, clarifying design issues with the field design review team, communicating with field offices, designing and conducting field office training, and managing change requests. Reid was responsible for technical project management. He coordinated the efforts of the developers and clarified requirements for teams that were developing the necessary technical infrastructure.

In addition to Robison and Reid, Mike Costigan and Doug LaBoda, who replaced Maureen Hesney in 1992, and Mike Costigan viewed the Workers' Compensation Workstation as their top priority. They communicated with Commercial Lines and ISD management respectively to secure the necessary resources and commitment for the project.

REENGINEERING PROCESSES

Robison viewed her primary responsibility as working with field office personnel to define the requirements and prepare for implementation. She conducted teleconferences twice a week with the field design review team and held monthly teleconferences with all other branch managers to update them on the status of the project and secure their feedback. She occasionally visited field offices, usually with other members of the core team, to discuss the objectives and design of the system. These indepth discussions both prepared the way for system implementation and provided useful feedback.

As the design evolved, it became clear that Robison would have to devote much of her time to explaining the need for the process changes that the system would entail. She observed that early tests of the system revealed that field office personnel would not be resistant to the technology. However, they were likely to resist changes in their work processes. The system was intended to empower case managers to meet customer needs, but it did so by standardizing processes, thereby restricting their choices for action:

> I've been focusing my time on how to make changes. Some of them will occur naturally as a result of the implementation of the workstation. Others are more difficult because it's a culture change. We're moving from an organization that said, "This is your shop; you run it as you see fit," to one of being very prescriptive and directive.

Mike Costigan supported Robison's efforts to define and communicate the vision to all the field offices. His discussions with field office personnel focused on the capabilities that the system would provide:

> My commitment is that if you take this system and you learn it, within six months after it being in your office, 50% of the paper on your desk will be gone. And if you learn it well, within one to two years, all of the paper on your desk will be gone. That's my commitment. That's my guarantee.

Costigan participated in the teleconferences with the field design review team and branch managers.

He also included a demonstration of the system prototype at the national field office manager's conference in May, 1992. In discussions with field office personnel, he emphasized the importance of standard procedures for generating the benefits of the system. He found that some field office staff, especially support staff, questioned the reason for reengineering. He explained:

> My purpose in reengineering is to grow our business and increase profitability. I want to be able to maximize on new business. Again, I want to grow our workers' compensation business. I'm pretty adamant about that.

TECHNICAL DEVELOPMENT

Paul Reid was coordinating the systems development efforts of 22 developers and 10 business people. He met regularly with the field design review team to demonstrate prototypes and get further feedback on the design of the system. The distributed nature of the project required that he split the development staff between host development and workstation development. The host was designed to hold the primary database and control the servers. The workstation was designed to be the user interface. Workstation code was written in C++, an object-oriented language.

Due to the lack of OO expertise on staff, Travelers split responsibility for development with the consulting firm that had designed the prototype. The consultants worked out of their offices in New Jersey, joining the development team in Hartford for major monthly or bimonthly team meetings. Reid found that the consultants had a helpful understanding of OO technology, but their lack of familiarity with the business and their inexperience with projects as large as the present project proved to be a handicap. Travelers gradually phased out the ten consultants who started with the project team in 1992, until only one remained with the project at the end of 1993.

PC Claim Systems experienced greater success with efforts to develop OO skills internally. Approximately eighteen inhouse professionals acquired OO expertise through classes, mentoring, independent study, and on the job training. Doug LaBoda organized nonthreatening tests of their skills to determine the current training needs of each individual. Ultimately, inhouse staff was able to take primary responsibility for workstation development, as well as ensure the needed expertise for maintaining and enhancing the system over time.

The development team was challenged by immature and changing technologies. Early on, the team found that its C++ compiler was not satisfactory. Nonetheless, they were reluctant to change, because of the new uncertainties that would introduce:

> We were having a lot of problems with the compiler and the learning curve associated with debugging and trying to figure out what was wrong with the application. It was almost like a mystery trying to correct problems. If you were able to correct it, it was like luck. It wasn't a science. Switching to Borland was the turning point. There was a lot of hesitancy from everyone to do that because it was such a risky thing to do. But to me, in hindsight, it gave us a whole new set of tools that were better. (Ron Calabrese, Technical Director)

ISD also wrestled with the decision on the LAN and client operating system. UNIX had become well established for distributed processing but Travelers had no resident UNIX experts. While PC Claim staff had little experience with OS/2, central IS had been working with OS/2 for several years. Thus, technical staff elected to use OS/2 in order to minimize the number of new technologies deployed in the project. It was clear that the number of workstations in some growing offices would eventually exceed the limits of OS/2, but key decision makers felt that initial reliance on OS/2 would permit them to acquire UNIX expertise more gradually. During the life of the project one California office grew from 70 to 130 persons. Technical staff determined that OS/2 was not adequate for that office and revisited the operating system decision. Ultimately, they decided to move UNIX into just three offices and to leverage OS/2 expertise in the remaining offices.

The distributed database was the riskiest part of the system. The architecture called for storing data at both the host and servers. Centralized data was needed for management information while local data was needed to provide case managers with immediate access to their files. Data would be updated centrally when new claims were called in through the centralized 800-number and when medical bills were processed for repricing (the determination of how much to pay on medical claims). Locally, case managers updated their files as they processed mail and received calls. These local updates were copied immediately to the central data base. The volume of updates moving from the host to local servers, however, was so great that centralized updates had to be queued for transmission to the servers. The system was designed so that updates to local servers would take place, on average, one minute after host updates.

The decision on how to distribute the data between host and server was largely based on how the objects were conceptualized:

> I hate to think of the number of times we talked about data encapsulation and tried to isolate the data from the application. But we were constantly revisiting that, that whole concept of how distributed you want this thing to be and what do you want the application to do, and do you really care whether the data is coming local or from the host. All those sort of issues don't seem to go away. (Paul Reid)

Early in the project, Reid realized that the OO learning curve was steeper than originally estimated. Scheduled delivery dates started to slip. They informed members of the field design review team and other business partners of the technical challenges as schedules were pushed back.

Disappointed by the delays, business managers nonetheless remained committed to the decision to adopt OO. Acknowledging her role in the decision, Robison noted:

> I think I had some influence, but not the knowledge. What do I know about OS/2, about object oriented, about CICS and IMS? I think that I was probably less concerned about the risks and I had the trust.

THE ROLL-OUT

In February, 1993, the equipment for the new system was moved into the three pilot offices: Bedford, New Hampshire, Southfield, Michigan, and Hartford. Staffs at those three offices were given workstations to replace their terminals, and they started to interact with the existing system through a graphical user interface. Each workstation was equipped with a mouse and connected to an on-site server. Although limited new functionality was provided, the change generated enthusiasm for the workstation. Staff responded positively to the mouse and the windows.

Pleased with the response to the hardware installation, Mike Costigan urged nation-wide deployment of the new hardware and operating system to familiarize all field staff with the technology. The roll-out continued through 1993. The pilot provided an initial successful test of the architecture. DSM's plug-and-play capability successfully enabled servers to be configured at headquarters and sent out to local sites, where a designated user plugged them in.

A scaled-back Version of 1 of the workstation software was installed in Southfield, Michigan in December, 1993. Exhibit 4 shows the main menu screen and the screen for reviewing individual cases as it rolled out with Version 1. The system still had a variety of bugs, but the Southfield staff agreed to use the system in production and to talk with development staff daily to discuss problems, design flaws, and needed enhancements. The development staff made almost weekly improvements to the system, which were installed in Southfield from Hartford by DSMS.

The system was installed in the other two pilot offices in February, 1994. While most of the promised functionality for Version 1 was available on the system, it was not reliable. In particular, data integrity was sometimes an issue. Pilot office staff reacted to the system with a mixture of hope and disappointment:

> Everybody recognizes the benefit that they're ultimately going to see in being able to be more efficient, to work more quickly and produce a better product, to have the new system do for them a lot of things that they now have to do manually, to eliminate steps in doing things, to give them better availability of information they need to do their day-to-day work. We realize our job as a pilot is to identify and correct problems. Yet seeing it not function as it ultimately will is frustrating. (Roger Sevigny, Bedford branch manager)

Despite problems with the system, Mike Costigan pushed for nation-wide roll-out of the system. Systems staff explained the risks of moving ahead, but he made the decision:

> I knew that this was the largest and most complex system design ever undertaken at the Travelers. We're enhancing in production. Some would say that's a little dangerous, but at the same time, with this type of newness to the technology, it's not something you can do a whole lot of study in a test environment. You do, at some point, have to put it out there in real life, which we've done, and find out. We're moving very aggressively. If it works, it works. If it doesn't, it doesn't. You can't take the chance with something this good, not to get it out there. As long as everybody is willing to understand the down side and the up sides, that's the way we'll go.

Robison designed the training for all 1850 field office personnel. She used a train-the-trainer approach, bringing 2–5 persons form each office to headquarters for one week of training on the system and on how to teach it. Worker's Compensation, PC Claim Systems, and DSMS all participated in the training program. Office trainers received the training one week before the system was installed in their offices. They had the option of training their office staffs in either a production or test environment.

By July, 1994, all field office personnel had received initial training on the system, and Version 1 had been installed in all the offices. Staff had the option of using parts of the new system or turning it off and using the old. Most attempted to use it, but the majority reverted back to the old system after experiencing technical problems. Sevigny noted that personnel were starting to go through

EXHIBIT 4A

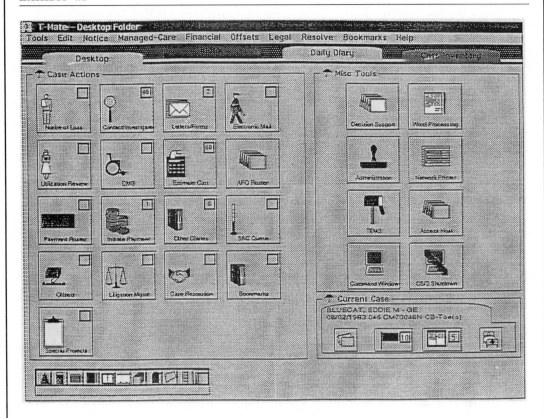

The main screen for the workstation has a menu along the top, key activities reflecting major activities from Exhibit 3, displayed as icons on the left, icons for important tools on the right and a toolbar at the bottom. The toolbar remains on the screen at all times and permits immediate access to the following capabilities: Special Account Instructions, Calculator, Calendar, Notes, Add Diary, Directory, Letters & Forms, TEMS, State Regulators, File Cabinet, and Host Access.

the refresher training and they would not resist using the new system once it worked properly.

By the fall of 1994, Travelers had invested $25 million in hardware and 70 man-years of development time for the workers' compensation system. Despite technical problems, utilization of the system was increasing. Development staff continued to work out bugs in the system. In September, 1994, Doug LaBoda indicated that ISD had organized four focus teams that would resolve the remaining four categories of problems with the system. ISD felt confident that they would meet the most recent target date of November 1994 for full implementation of Version 1.

EXHIBIT 4B

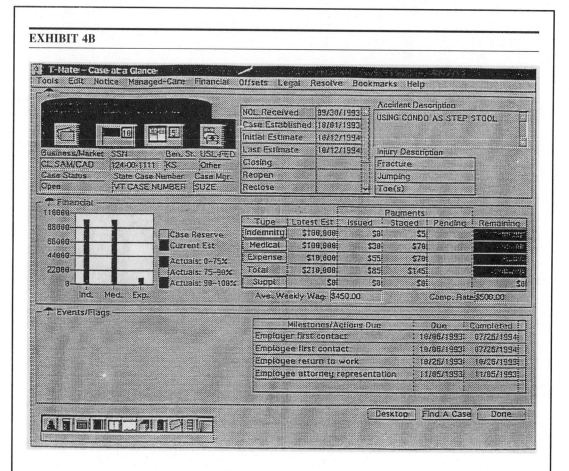

The Case-at-a-Glance Screen displays general, financial case management information about a case. This screen can be used to review or update case status. Menu line at the top of the screen and tool bar at the bottom permit easy access to other system functions.

INITIAL ASSESSMENT OF THE WORKSTATION

In the offices where staff regularly used the new workstation, initial reactions to the system were very positive. Management indicated that the system was making much more valuable information available to them and to many of their customers who had online access to their workers' compensation records. Case managers said they could process their work much faster, and the workstation helped them organize their day. One noted that the workstation demanded more sophisticated case managers. It required that they write custom letters without the support of a transcriptionist. They also had to deal with inquiries from well-informed customers who had online access to their cases. Support staff reported that they felt more professional. The workstation gave them access to much more information about the cases, so they could respond to questions from the field that they had formerly turned over to case managers.

Field office staff speculated about the long-term effects on staffing. Eventually, the system might reduce the need for support staff, because many of their tasks had been automated. It also might reduce the need for supervisors since the workstation performed some of their duties, such as checking whether necessary forms had been filed and payments made. Staffing effects, however, were likely to evolve slowly because workers' compensation cases were frequently long-lived. Initially, only new cases would have histories on the new system. Old cases would still be heavily dependent on paper-based files.

Early experience with the workstation indicated that the centralized support was working as planned. Field office personnel were delighted with the responsiveness of the individuals doing the trouble-shooting. Diane Niedzwiecki, a supervisor at the Bedford office, reported:

> The support people have been very helpful. If we don't call the right person, they get the right person. They know what they are doing.

Niedzwiecki, along with Connie Compagna, another supervisor, were the designated users in the Bedford office. DSMS called one of them as soon as the system went down—even if it was the middle of the night. When this happened, they had to go to the server and reboot. Everything else was taken care of at headquarters. The server went down periodically immediately after installation, but by September 1994, Niedzwiecki observed that it had been months since the system had gone down.

The workstation would be enhanced in versions 2 and 3, and while some suggestions from users were implemented immediately, others were held for later versions. Ultimately, all branch staff would be required to use the workstation. Because the data in the system were mission critical, management could not turn off the old interface until they were confident that the workstation was reliable. In the meantime, running two systems simultaneously was contributing to the technical challenges.

Costigan and Robison were assessing the business value of the workstation through productivity measures developed prior to implementation. To better understand the source of productivity improvements, they could monitor system use from headquarters. Monitors could determine whether certain capabilities were underutilized, thus alerting PC Claim managers to the need to provide additional training on the system. For the most part, the monitors showed only the usage of various system capabilities for an entire office. In order to understand how the system was impacting individual case managers, however, they could also monitor the work of a single individual.

LOOKING AHEAD

The workers' compensation workstation had significant implications for the technology infrastructure at Travelers as well as for the workers compensation area. Technologies chosen for the project, such as OS/2 and C++, were expected to become *de facto* standards for the division. The probes and protocols developed to support the distributed system were already being reused on other systems across the company. There was some concern that the technologies would not be capable of handling all the functionality that was planned for the system, but key staff felt that the capabilities of the technologies would expand as quickly as they needed them.

The business benefits of the workers' compensation workstation project were expected to easily justify the investment in the system. Estimates of the payback period ranged from two to five years, but the system was expected to have non-quantifiable benefits as well. Doug LaBoda observed that part of the benefit was in the adaptability the system provided:

> Change, hopefully, is going to come faster. By having the application in place in advance of your competitors, you can change with the market more rapidly. If you wait until [the technology] is tried and true and then come up with your application, you won't be ahead of your market, and for that

period of time that you don't have that application, you're still going to be operating in a slower to change environment as well. So I think you pay the price twice. So that's what I think you get for the pain and the suffering that we're getting trying to be leading edge.

In addition to the business benefits, ISD managers anticipated benefits from reusing the skills, technology, and even the code to redesign auto, property, and liability systems. Initial efforts to reuse the code on an auto system stalled as it became clear that many of the objects in the workers' compensation workstation would need to be redesigned before they were usable in another context.

> We have a lot of concepts, like the desktop activities that go into icons, concepts like diaries and navigation from diaries and notes. Many of these business functions and concepts are clearly reusable, but they will need some amount of work to take the [workers' compensation] flavor out of them. (Paul Reid)

Reid observed that redesigning for reuse would require the efforts of key people who were needed to complete enhancements of the workers' compensation system. He noted that some redesign would be undertaken in order to gain the fast, easy maintenance, that had been promised for that system. Costigan had agreed to fund the redesign:

> When we changed something, we haven't been smart enough, because of the current architectural design to see what impact it's had on something else. I think now that we are a lot better in object-oriented, we will have to bite the bullet and

sit down and do an architecture redesign. In order to have the type of system to lead us into the future, I don't think we're going to have an alternative.

Other lines of business at Travelers were looking at reuse of the concepts, development methodology, frameworks, and expertise acquired through the workstation project. Opportunities for code reuse were not evident, but key developers from the workers' compensation workstation team provided a framework for OO development to another division and acted as mentors to individuals in that division who were attempting to acquire OO skills. Ron Calabrese noted some of the challenges in designing for reuse:

> There's a very strong hesitancy in the corporation about this whole concept of reuse. It's very much an uphill battle. It is funded, but it's continually being challenged and checked. That's because the real benefit to the corporation is, obviously, supporting the business and coming up with the right reengineering strategy to make us more productive.

In the meantime, Doug LaBoda was focused on both building and retaining workstation developers, while ensuring comparable rewards for staff who supported COBOL systems:

> My experience has been that the new stuff is really always where the people want to go. We have to make them understand that the traditional world has as much value as that world. You can't fool them. They look at things like who's getting promoted, who's getting the opportunities, where's the recognition going. If you don't have that balance, that's the signal they're going to listen to.

Case 7

MICROSOFT CORPORATION: OFFICE BUSINESS UNIT

On March 30, 1990, Jeff Raikes, general manager of the Office Business Unit (OBU), glanced out the window one last time as the rain began to fall softly on the Douglas Firs at Microsoft's beautifully landscaped Seattle campus. The peacefulness of the setting contrasted sharply with the turmoil of the software development projects in the applications division.

One recent project, Opus, had been particularly difficult. Opus, Microsoft's code name for the Word for Windows[1] word processor development, had finally been shipped on November 30, 1989 after over five years of development. With the completion of the Opus project, two major issues arose: (1) what the follow-on project should be; and (2) how the development process's speed and effectiveness could be improved.

Although the schedule slipped significantly from the originally projected ship date (see Exhibit 1), Word for Windows (known internally as WinWord) received significant critical acclaim. It was Microsoft's first word processor to be rated higher than archrival WordPerfect by the influential computer journal, *InfoWorld*. Sales exceeded Microsoft's projections.

Harvard Business School case 691-033

This case was prepared by Geoff Gill under the direction of Professor Marco Iansiti as the basis for class discussion rather than to illustrate either effective or ineffective handling of an administrative situation. Reprinted by permission of the Harvard Business School.

[1]Windows was an operating system written by Microsoft for the IBM PC which provided an easy-to-use graphic user interface, allowed convenient data sharing and switching between different application programs, and enabled programmers to write larger applications than with DOS.

MICROSOFT HISTORY

Microsoft Corporation had its roots in a company called Traf-O-Data that Bill Gates and Paul Allen founded in 1973 when Gates was only 16 years old. Gates had started programming when he was in junior high school and, by the time he was in ninth grade, local Seattle companies were employing him as a programmer after school hours. Gates and Allen formed Traf-O-Data in an unsuccessful effort to market software that generated summary traffic flow statistics derived from a rubber tube strung across a road. The software ran on an Intel 8008, the first 8-bit microprocessor[2] ever developed.

In 1974 Gates was graduated from high school and began attending Harvard College. He did not stay there long, however. Early in his college career, he wrote a BASIC interpreter[3] for the first commercial microcomputer, the Altair, developed by a startup called MITS. The entire development required only four weeks even though Gates had to write the program without even seeing the Altair, working only from an emulator that Allen had developed. Soon after the program was completed, Gates and Allen reached an agreement with MITS to sell Gates's version of BASIC and Gates dropped out of Harvard to work full time with their company, which they renamed Microsoft. The Altair computer took off and Gates's implementation of BASIC became a standard. Over the

[2]A microprocessor was a single chip that contained all the essential circuitry for a computer's central processing unit (CPU). The 8008 chip was a predecessor of the Intel 8088 that was used in the IBM PC.

[3]An interpreter allowed a user to program the computer using simple English-like commands.

EXHIBIT 1   Actual vs. Projected Schedule

Report Date	Estimated Ship Date	Estimated Days to Ship	Actual Days to Ship
Sep-84	Sep-85	365	2,187
Jun-85	Jul-86	395	1,614
Jan-86	Nov-86	304	1,400
Jun-86	May-87	334	1,245
Jan-87	Dec-87	334	1,035
Jun-87	Feb-88	245	884
Jan-88	Jun-88	152	670
Jun-88	Oct-88	122	518
Aug-88	Jan-89	153	457
Oct-88	Feb-89	123	396
Jan-89	May-89	120	304
Jun-89	Sep-89	92	153
Jul-89	Oct-89	92	123
Aug-89	Nov-89	92	92
Nov-89	Nov-89	0	0

next several years, Microsoft developed programs for a series of computers, including the Apple II and the Osborne portable computer.

Microsoft's big break came in 1980, when IBM chose it to develop the operating system for its personal computer. The result was MS-DOS (Microsoft Disk Operating System), a copy of which accompanied virtually every IBM and IBM-compatible personal computer (PC) sold.[4] IBM also worked with Microsoft to develop a BASIC and several other computer languages. DOS and the languages gave Microsoft a large, solid customer base on which to grow. And grow it did. From 1980 to 1989, Microsoft annual sales increased from less than $1 million to over $800 million (see Exhibit 2). The company's employment grew from 45 people to over 4,000. In 1988, Microsoft's sales passed Lotus Development Corporation's (the maker of the 1-2-3 spreadsheet),

---

[4]In this case, PC refers to any IBM or IBM-compatible personal computer. Microcomputer is the generic term for any single-user computer.

EXHIBIT 2   Financial Information ($ Millions)

	Fiscal Year Ending		
	6/30/89	6/30/88	6/30/87
Net Sales	804	591	346
Cost of Goods	204	148	74
Gross Profit	599	443	272
Research and Development Expense	110	70	38
Selling, General and Administrative	247	186	107
Non-Operating Income	9	(4)	(6)
Interest Expense	0	0	0
Income Before Taxes	251	184	121
Provision for Income Taxes	80	60	49
Net Income	171	124	72

Source: *The Wall Street Journal,* May 21, 1990, p. A4, reprinted with permission.

making Microsoft the largest personal computer software company in the world.

Profits and stock price increased as well. In 1989, Microsoft's return on sales was over 15%— the highest of any major software company. Microsoft also had an aggressive employee stock ownership plan, and it was estimated that over 200 Microsoft employees had been made millionaires by increases in Microsoft's stock value. Gates, himself, had become the microcomputer industry's first billionaire.

By 1989, the approximate size of the personal computer software industry was $9 billion. While sales growth in the industry had been spectacular in the early 1980s, growth slowed somewhat in subsequent years, from a 30% yearly growth rate in 1987, to a 15% rate in 1989. Competition intensified, as the number of products on the market increased. Moreover the products themselves were becoming increasingly complex, incorporating more advanced features, and integrating with a greater variety of hardware and operating system environments.

During the 1980s, Gates almost singlehandedly determined Microsoft's technical direction (Allen, his cofounder left Microsoft in 1983 for medical reasons). After seeing results of research involving a graphical user interface (GUI) performed at Xerox's Palo Alto Research Center (PARC), Gates became convinced that this type of interface would become the standard in the industry.[5] For this reason, Microsoft started to develop a similar interface for the PC. The resulting program, Windows, added an additional layer of software between DOS and applications programs. Windows provided a set of utilities that allowed applications programs to work together in a user-friendly graphical environment. First released in 1985, Windows was slow to catch on. Microsoft continued to improve the program incrementally, and by March 1990, Windows had gained significant mo-

mentum with approximately 2.5 million of the 40 million PCs installed, having Windows.

Although the languages (compilers and interpreters) and operating systems for PCs formed the core of its business, Microsoft soon began to move into the applications software market. In the 1980's, software could roughly be divided into three categories. Operating systems were the programs (like MS-DOS) that controlled the low-level operations of the computer (such as reading data from disks). Compilers and interpreters translated computer languages that were made up of English-like commands into machine language (series of 1's and 0's) that the computer could understand. Applications were the programs that end users typically ran (such as spreadsheets and word processors) to do specific tasks.

In 1983, Microsoft became the first software company to develop software for the Macintosh, and, by 1990, Microsoft was the major applications developer for it. Microsoft Excel was the dominant spreadsheet in the Macintosh market (with approximately a 90% market share) and Microsoft Word for the Macintosh was its dominant word processor (with 65% unit share and 80% revenue share).

Microsoft was not able to achieve the same market dominance in PC applications as it had in its other markets. Both its high-end word processing software (PC Word) and spreadsheet (PC Excel) were the second most popular products in their respective markets. Although these were successful products, they had yet to overcome their entrenched rivals (WordPerfect and Lotus 1-2-3). On the other hand, Microsoft was the only software company to compete successfully in all three segments, and was one of the few companies to have more than one market-leading application. By 1990, applications products accounted for over half of Microsoft's revenue (see Exhibit 3 for a list of Microsoft's major products and their market shares in 1990).

Microsoft's products were not all a result of internal development. Gates actively sought out small companies with advanced technology. In fact, MS-DOS was an extension of SCP-DOS, a product developed by Seattle Computer Products

---

[5]In 1984, Apple introduced the Macintosh which employed GUI concepts and was widely praised as being fun and easy to use.

EXHIBIT 3   Microsoft's Product Line and Market Shares (estimated for 1990)

Product Line	Sales ($ millions)	Market Share[a]	Market Rank
IBM PC Operating Systems	$300	98%	1
MS-DOS, PC-DOS	130	91	1
OS/2	56	5	3
Xenix	14	2	4
Windows (requires DOS)	100	15	2
PC Languages	95	70	1
C	50	65	1
Pascal[b]	10	35	2
FORTRAN	35	92	1
PC Applications	430	9	2
Excel (windows spreadsheet)	120	15	2
Multiplan (spreadsheet)[c]	10	1	8
Word (word processor)	250	30	2
Word for Windows	50	6	6
Macintosh Languages	17	80	1
C	9	85	1
Pascal	2	55	1
BASIC	6	95	1
Macintosh Applications	140	25	1
Excel (spreadsheet)	70	90	1
Mac Word (word processor)	70	80	1

[a]Market share was defined as the percent of sales in the particular product category. For example the market share of Word for Windows was defined with respect to all PC wordprocessors (but not including Macintosh word processors). It should be mentioned that the market shares for PC operating systems total over 100% because all Windows systems must have DOS as well.

[b]Borland was the leader in this category with Turbo Pascal with approximately $20 million in annual sales and a 60% market share.

[c]Lotus dominated this category with 1-2-3 Release 2.2 with $230 million in sales and 1-2-3 Release 3.0 with $120 million in sales annually. Borland's Quatrro Pro was also a player in this category with $60 million in sales.

---

that Microsoft purchased and adapted to the IBM PC. Although adapting and extending a product developed outside Microsoft was quite common, Gates usually preferred to perform the development of strategic products in-house.

MICROSOFT ORGANIZATION

In 1990, Microsoft was divided into two groups: applications and systems (languages and operating systems). The Applications Division was headed by Mike Maples, who reported directly to Jon Shirley, the president and COO. Under Maples, there were six groups: Applications Strategy and five business units. Four departments comprised Applications Strategy, which provided central resources to all the business units. The resources ranged from programming tools and common subroutines to a User Interface Laboratory where the process by which test subjects learned and used software could be observed and recorded. Because these central resources were available on a voluntary basis, there was wide variability to the extent that the business units and even individual projects used them (see Exhibit 4 for a partial organization chart).

All the business units were organized similarly, each specializing in a particular applications area. Jeff Raikes was the general manager of the Office Business Unit (OBU) which developed and marketed all of Microsoft's high-end word processors (PC Word, Mac Word, and Word for Windows). Under Raikes, the departments were organized by functional responsibility. Quality Assurance (also known as Testing) tested all the software for bugs and errors in the documentation. User Education

EXHIBIT 4   Microsoft Organization Chart, 1990

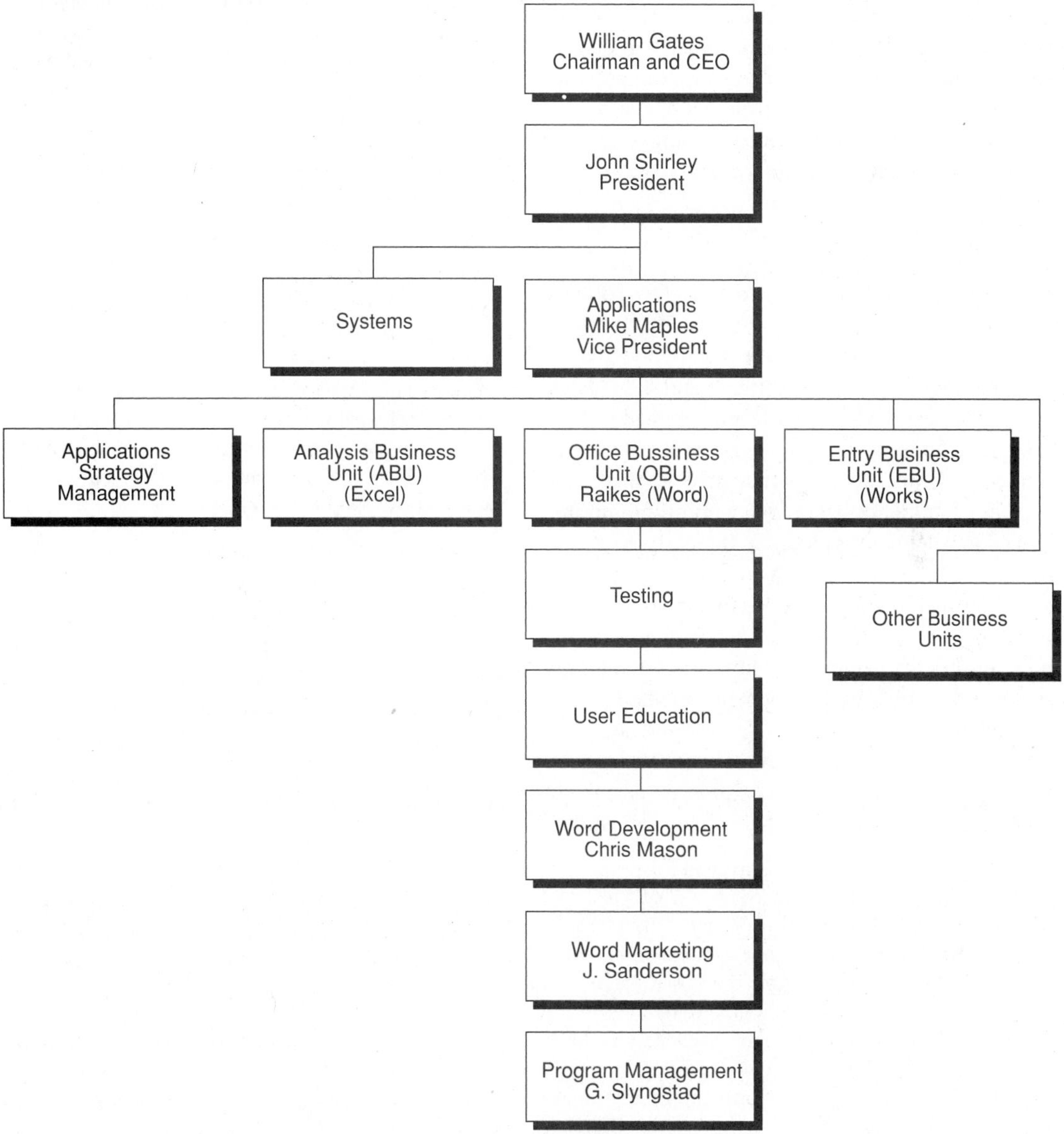

William Gates
Chairman and CEO

John Shirley
President

Systems

Applications
Mike Maples
Vice President

Applications
Strategy
Management

Analysis Business
Unit (ABU)
(Excel)

Office Bussiness
Unit (OBU)
Raikes (Word)

Entry Business
Unit (EBU)
(Works)

Testing

Other Business
Units

User Education

Word Development
Chris Mason

Word Marketing
J. Sanderson

Program Management
G. Slyngstad

wrote the documentation. Development, under Chris Mason, was responsible for developing the software. Product Marketing and Program Management also had separate departments. The other business units were responsible for different applications such as spreadsheets and databases.

The business unit organization had been instituted in August 1988 in order to help the Applications Division manage its growth. Prior to 1988, the entire division had been organized on a functional basis—so that there was only one department for each in the division as opposed to one for each business unit in the division. Raikes commented on the change: "At Microsoft, we have a process of on-going organizational change—it helps to maintain a small company feel and team focus."

Evolution of the Development Process

In Microsoft's early days, there were few colleges or universities that offered degrees in computer science and computers were relatively scarce. Finding programmers was difficult and, like Gates, most of the early Microsoft developers had little or no formal training in computers. Many had been trained in other fields (particularly in math and science), but had fallen in love with programming.

The development process in the early days was more informal and there was less emphasis on schedule methodology and software architecture. Perhaps because of their lack of formal training, most of these developers did not follow the highly structured software development methodologies created by the Department of Defense and large corporate MIS departments. They often developed software without a formal specification or design. In 1990, stories about legendary developers abounded:

> There was one guy who could type at 80 words a minute. That's pretty impressive, but what's really impressive was that he actually wrote code at that speed. He'd write a 10,000 line application in two days, then if it didn't work, he'd throw it out and start again from scratch. He'd go through this process two or three times, until he ended up with a working program. Not only did it take him less time to do this than if he had sat down and tried to think

everything out in advance, but the program that resulted was better too. Because he had implemented the same program several times before, he knew how to avoid all the pitfalls so his code became very clean.

One of Microsoft's early developers described his own views about software design:

> I design user interfaces to please an audience of one. I write it for me. If I'm happy I know some cool people will like it. Designing user interfaces by committee does not work very well: they need to be coherent. As for schedules, I'm not interested in schedules; did anyone care when *War and Peace* came out?

Raikes described some of the problems of relying too much on such star performers:

> There are a lot of problems with relying on individual superstars: (1) they are in very short supply; (2) someone has to maintain and update the software they've written (which often doesn't interest them) and often other people have difficulty understanding their code; (3) sometimes they don't understand what the market wants; and finally if you try to put several of them on the same project you get real problems with design decision—"too many cooks spoil the broth."

During the early to mid-1980s, Microsoft was often criticized for writing software which was technically excellent but difficult to understand and hard to use. In an attempt to make Microsoft more responsive to the market, in the early 1980s Gates began to hire marketing specialists, both from other software firms and also directly from MBA programs. Many of the new arrivals were not technical experts, but their mission was to reorient Microsoft to focus on the customer.

To help bring a more coherent perspective, a program management function began to evolve. Jabe Blumenthal, a marketing assistant who became the first program manager, described the evolution of the function in more detail:

> In early 1984, we began to work on a spread sheet for the Mac. I got involved and became a sort of service organization for the development group. I

helped document the specifications, do the manual reviews, and decide what bug fixes were important and what could be postponed to a later release. While I didn't make the design decisions, I made sure that they got made. The process worked out really well, so they decided to call it something and institutionalize it.

Raikes described the purpose of the program management function:

> Program Management was introduced to formalize design, coordinate product creation functions (development, testing, and user education), and perform support functions (such as manual reviews, and competitive product evaluation).

In 1990, several people shared leadership for the development of a new product: the project lead and the technical lead from the development group, the program manager from Program Management, the product manager from marketing, the on-line lead and print-based lead from User Education, and the localization lead from the international division. These people were supposed to work as a group, with no one person having total authority. The project lead was responsible for overseeing the product development effort including handing out programming task assignments, scheduling, and coordinating the development effort. The technical lead had final say in all technical decisions, code reviews, and programming standards. The product manager handled all the marketing issues such as competitive analysis, positioning, packaging, and advertising. The program manager's job was to integrate and coordinate the efforts of everyone involved in the project. Program managers were also directly responsible for the concept and specification of the product. The on-line and print-based leads handled the user education functions and the localization lead oversaw the customization of the program for various international markets.

A team of about a dozen developers was usually dedicated to each major development effort, and was responsible for writing the code. Microsoft managers were quite proud of the small size of their teams. Other major competitors would use much larger teams often including more than one hundred programmers for major applications. Microsoft's cost per line of code developed was significantly lower than the industry average, which was about \$125 in 1989.[6]

Despite the fact that he had a key role in the development of the system, Blumenthal felt that the process had many problems:

> The problem is that they did not copy a lot of what caused our effort on the Mac spreadsheet to be successful. We had a small group, I regarded myself as a service organization, and I was best friends with the developer. Now program management owns the product; they write the spec and throw it over the wall. The product managers don't know much about the realities of development, and the developers don't know the competition. The program managers have become a bottleneck—they make all the decisions, and the developers act as if they have no responsibility for the product.

Chris Mason, the development manager of the Office Business Unit (OBU), however, described a different interpretation of the development process:

> While Microsoft has become somewhat more formalized, the basic truth is that developers still have ultimate control of the process. If they want to check in a piece of code, there is no way we can stop them. There comes a time in every development project where the development manager says 'no new features shall be added,' but if the developer feels strongly, there is not much the manager can do. Microsoft has a deep underlying philosophy that people know what they are doing and will try to do the right thing.

Despite the changes in the development process, Bill Gates remained a constant factor, actively involved in every major development project. He attended design meetings periodically, reviewed design specifications and project schedules, and read many of the periodic status reports. Although

---

[6]Rules of thumb for programmer productivity in the industry averaged over a project typically ranged between 5 to 10 lines of code per day. These measures were considered very rough guidelines.

many people at Microsoft had experienced his sometimes harsh critiques, there was universal respect for his technical expertise and ability to forecast where the computer industry was heading.

THE DEVELOPMENT OF WORD FOR WINDOWS

Microsoft introduced its first high-end word processor for the PC, "PC Word", in late 1983. The product received only lukewarm reviews, and its sales were mediocre by Microsoft's standards. In September 1984 Gates, convinced that a key opportunity was being squandered, prompted the development of a new revolutionary word processor. The new product was going to run on the Windows operating system (at that time in development), and was going to exhibit some extremely innovative features to make Microsoft the leader in PC wordprocessing. Gates gave three people, John Hunt, Andrew Hermann, and Lee Arthurs, responsibility for the project which was code named Cashmere. Greg Slyngstad, who later became program manager for Cashmere, describes the start of the project:

> Gates put three real hotshots on the project. Hunt, who had single-handedly written the first version of PC Word, became the project manager. Arthurs, who had a Ph.D. in psychology, was responsible for user interface and documentation. Hermann had been at Wang and was supposed to know the word processor business inside and out.

In giving the Cashmere team its assignment, Gates directed that they "develop the best word processor ever," and that they complete the project as soon as possible—preferably in less than a year. Thus, the project was scheduled to be completed by October 1985. Not much progress was made, however, in the first year of the Cashmere project. Hunt brought on a couple of software developers to prototype software and he, Hermann, and Arthurs wrote several papers suggesting the features to be included. Their original concept was to integrate a uniform user interface and data structures for multiple purposes at the lowest level. In

other words, they planned to structure the program and data so that it integrated seamlessly into other types of applications such as spreadsheets and databases. Not only would the new product be able to interface with other applications, but it would include some of the same types of features that these applications included so that the distinction between product categories would blur. Some of the specific features to be included were electronic mail, document protection (so that other people would not accidentally destroy someone's documents), facilities to build mail lists, and primitive spreadsheet capabilities.

By the beginning of 1986, the scheduled ship date was still approximately a year away, and Gates began to put pressure on Hunt to get some visible results. Eventually the pressure got to be too much for Hunt and he left the project in July 1986.

When replacing Hunt, Gates decided to use the program manager concept which was being developed at the time. Three Microsoft veterans were brought in: Doug Kurtz, the PC Word development lead, took over the same role for Cashmere; Lars Dormitzer, a well regarded developer, assumed the technical lead role; and Slyngstad became the program manager. A new marketing manager, Jeff Sanderson, was also brought in. As a new team member recalled:

> We all thought that the project was much farther along. Although Hunt had written a bunch of papers describing features that he wanted, there was no comprehensive specification of what would be in the product. We ended up throwing everything that had been done out, and started from the code used in Word for the Macintosh. We were a year behind schedule from the first day we started.

At this point, the project was renamed Opus. A new team of developers was formed. Due to a shortage of experienced developers, the new team was almost entirely staffed with new hires. Very few of the developers had had experience with other Microsoft projects.

During the second half of 1986 and the first half of 1987, a lot of effort was spent writing a new specification for the product. As time passed, however, pressure built up on the team to show visible results. The schedule continued to slip into 1988, and the pressure increased to a disturbing level. Sean McDermott, who was a software development engineer (SDE) on Opus at the time, recalled this period:

> We were under a lot of schedule pressure. Some managers seemed to regard the schedule as a contract between them and the developers. Furthermore, when development came up with a new schedule, management questioned every estimate.

Upper management kept up the pressure. During one meeting in early March 1988, one manager indicated that he felt that the Opus team was the worst in Applications Development. Chris Mason, the OBU development manager, recalled the effects of the constant schedule pressure:

> Opus got into a mode that I call "Infinite Defects." When you put a lot of schedule pressure on developers, they tend to do the minimum amount of work necessary on a feature. When it works well enough to demonstrate, they consider it done and the feature is checked off on the schedule. The inevitable bugs months later are seen as unrelated. Even worse, by the time the bugs are discovered, the developers can't remember their code so it takes them a lot longer to fix. Furthermore, the schedule is thrown off because that feature was supposed to be finished. These problems aren't unique to Microsoft—every company in the industry faces them.

In April 1988, Dormitzer had to take a medical leave of absence. McDermott, who had less than two years of experience, was made technical lead. Although McDermott was relatively young and inexperienced for such a position, the job required a very detailed knowledge of the program, and no one with more experience had the required knowledge. McDermott was also an outstanding technical contributor. Two months later, Kurtz, who had tired of the continual pressure, took a leave of absence from Microsoft. Dormitzer, who had recovered somewhat, came back to take the development lead.

Over the next several months, progress was made on Opus. All the required features were coded (though not debugged) and the team declared that the "Code Complete" milestone was reached in October 1988. Code Complete meant that all that remained to be done was to debug and optimize the code for performance. This phase was called "stabilization," and once the code had stabilized (all known bugs were fixed and performance was adequate), the product could be shipped. For scheduling, Microsoft used a rule of thumb that the stabilization phase typically lasted three months.

It soon became clear that Opus was not likely to follow the three month rule. Although developers were fixing bugs quickly, the testers seemed to find new bugs just as quickly (see Exhibit 5). During this period, Dormitzer did his best to lead the project, but his illness had not fully abated.

EXHIBIT 5   Data from Opus Portmortem

Statistics	
Size of shipped product	852,576 bytes[a]
Number of lines of program instructions (code)	249,000
Total development time spent (including part-time members)	55 person-years
Number of lines of code present at "code complete"	209,000

One "byte" corresponds to a unit of computer memory storage roughly comparable to that required by one character of text.

asm = assembly language code.

EXHIBIT 5 (*Cont.*)

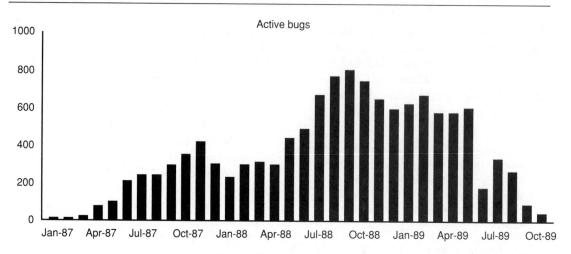

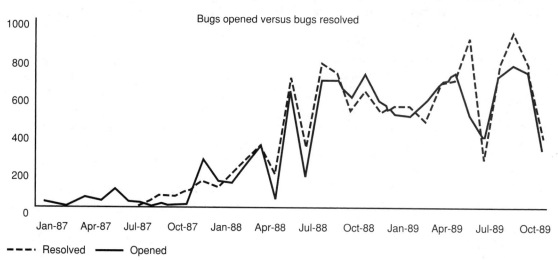

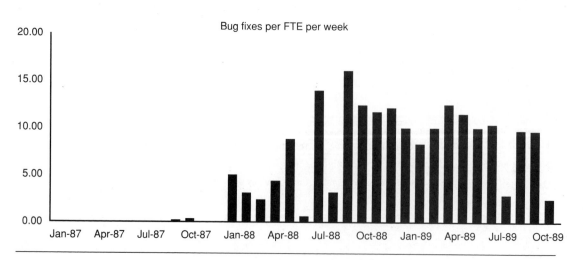

Eventually, Mason responded by making McDermott acting development lead in addition to his technical lead responsibilities. At that time, McDermott had been at Microsoft for three years.

McDermott recalled the stabilization period:

> Not having a technical lead who could concentrate on technical issues definitely cost us. The size, speed, and memory usage of Opus could have been made better than it was if the technical lead had not spent the last 18 months as development lead or covering for sick and burned out development leads. The team at this stage had 15 developers, six programmer assistants and seven interns during this period. No one lead could possibly keep tabs on what each person was working on.

Despite the troubles, the Opus program began to stabilize. During the spring of 1989 the number of active bugs remained relatively constant, but, during the summer, an initiative emphasizing the quality of changes rather than the quantity of changes was instituted. For the first time, testing was invited to development code reviews, and ownership of the code was stressed. By late fall of 1989, the program had stabilized and Word for Windows version 1.0 was released on November 30, 1989 (see Exhibit 6 for a project time line).

Word for Windows' Market Reception

Despite the long delay in the Word for Windows (WinWord) development, only one other company, Samna, had been able to release a full featured word processor for Windows earlier. While it was too early to gauge the customer reception accurately, early signs were very encouraging. One particularly encouraging sign was the reception in the industry press. Reviews in computer magazines and journals wielded great power over the marketplace perceptions, and the reviews had been universally favorable. WinWord was described as easy to use and incredibly bug-free for a first release. Many magazines rated WinWord higher than any other word processor for the PC. (See Exhibit 7 for a description of competitive products.) In response to WinWord's success, WordPerfect announced that it was developing a word processors to run under Windows. WordPerfect for Windows was scheduled for release in February 1991.

WinWord Postmortem

While the WinWord development project had been an extreme case, its problems were not unusual at Microsoft (or for any software development project at any company). In order to learn from the mistakes of previous development projects, Microsoft had instituted a policy of reviewing every project on its completion. The review entailed gathering many statistics on the project as well as holding a series of meetings with project participants in which their views on the project were discussed. While the exact type of statistics varied somewhat from project to project, typically they included estimated versus actual schedule over the course of the project, bug counts over time, code size over time, and milestones scheduled versus actual completion.

These statistics and summaries of the discussions from participant meetings were collected in a document called a postmortem, which was then distributed to all managers in the business group as well as to senior managers. Most postmortems were about 25 pages in length, but the Opus document ran over 100. Extensive statistics had been collected on the project (including those in Exhibits 1 and 5).

IDEAS FOR IMPROVING PRODUCT DEVELOPMENT

There were many views on the best way to prevent scheduling fiascos like Opus from recurring. While some of the ideas focused on improvements in the development process, others focused on Microsoft's approach to project management, or on its development strategy.

Process

While the majority of developers enjoyed Microsoft's informal approach, some felt that a more structured development process would substanially

EXHIBIT 6   Time Line of the Cashmere/Opus Project

Cashmere/Opus leadership

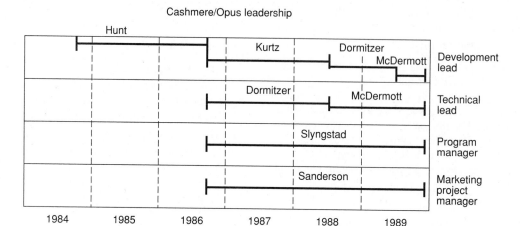

Cashmere/Opus events

Date	Event
8/84	Winword project begins
8/85	Coding begins
9/85	First demonstration to Bill Gates
11/85	Coding work intensified
1/87	Testing work begins
4/87	Specification discussed with Bill Gates
6/87	Revised specification distributed
10/87	Addendum to final specification distributed
12/87	Visual freeze: the way the program looks to the user is officially established
2/88	Presentation to Bill Gates; additional features added
3/88	Addendum to final specification distributed
6/88	Almost all features reported to be "working to some degree"
7/88	Addendum to final specification distributed
8/88	Feature complete: no more features added after this point
10/88	Code complete
3/89	Performance optimization declared complete
10/89	Word for Windows is officially announced
11/89	Word for Windows ships

improve the company's development performance. This would include relying on more formal project phases and strict milestones, as well as the implementation of formal structured methodologies for software development. Among the developers, McDermott and Mason were advocates of a more structured approach.

McDermott, having lived through the Opus project, had strong views about the causes of its problems:

A major problem was the lack of an early, clear direction and specification. While we need some flexibility to respond to new information and market changes, from the time development work begins, the major features should be down.

McDermott believed that the development process should have two major clear phases: concept development and implementation. In the first phase, a product concept would be carefully

---

EXHIBIT 7   The PC Word Processing Software Market

Word processing software was the largest segment of the applications software market for IBM PCs and compatibles. Over $800 million was spent annually on professional word processors, the high end of the word processor market. This market segment was dominated by a few players, all of which were character-based in 1990.

WordPerfect, Version 5.1

WordPerfect version 5.1 was the latest in a long line of updates of a highly successful product. WordPerfect had the largest share of the word processor market at 45%. In product comparisons, WordPerfect generally won on the number of features it had and the wide variety of printers it supported. WordPerfect was also available on a wide variety of non-DOS computers including the Apple Macintosh, Digital Equipment Corporation's VAX line, and IBM mainframes. Although WordPerfect was character based, Word-Perfect Corporation had announced that a Windows version was under development and was expected to ship in the first quarter of 1991.

Word for DOS, Version 5.0

Microsoft's original high-end, character-based wordprocessor for DOS had first been released in 1983, but had not received good reviews in in-

dustry magazines or achieved much market success. Since then, however, Microsoft had continually improved the product to the point where it was rated on a par with WordPerfect, and much higher than any other word processors. Word's market share had improved correspondingly and was now the second highest at 30%.

Wordstar, Version 5.5

Wordstar Corporation had first developed a word processor for the CP/M computer market (a predecessor of IBM/DOS). Dominant in the CP/M market, it had translated its software to run under DOS in 1982, and had quickly become the market leader. Since that time, however, its updates had not kept pace with the rest of the market and the product had fallen behind technically. Its market share in 1990 was 12%, well below the market leaders.

Displaywrite 4

IBM's entry in the word processing software market was generally considered to be an inferior product to either of the two market leaders. Its limited market success (10% share) was attributed to IBM's dominance in the hardware market. Its market share had been declining for several years.

---

investigated, leading to a complete specification. Once the specification was down, everyone would buy in and implementation would follow without interruptions or delays.

Mason had a different opinion. He had written documents proposing a different approach to improving Microsoft's software development process. He called it "Zero Defects":

> Our goal should be to have a working shippable product every day. This means that when a programmer says a feature is done, it is totally

complete: all error and boundary cases work, all interactions with the rest of the product work, and test code and documentation have been checked in.

In this mode of development, the project would begin with a brief period of time in which senior team members would lay out the basic architecture of the software application, breaking it down into several sets of desireable features. These feature sets would then be prioritized. The software coding process would focus on each feature set in a sequential manner. The code would be written in "object-oriented" modules, each of which could be tested independently.

After each module was completed, work would proceed to the next module. This would allow the product to evolve in a controlled fashion, gradually adding subsets of features under the scrutiny of the project's management. This would imply substantial flexibility in the product's specification, since feature sets could be added at any time before (or after) the shipping date. Conversely, this process would also allow meeting virtually any shipping date, with a clear tradeoff between time-to-market and available features. Among the major costs of this approach, however, would be sacrifices in speed and program efficiency: the modularity in the code would make the application substantially slower and larger (in memory usage).

Project Management

Some of the program managers at Microsoft felt that changing the structure of the development process would not be enough to improve things substantially. They felt instead that the root cause of Microsoft's problems was in its approach to project management. The current approach lacked focus and control.

Some program managers felt that their role and position in the organization ought to be strengthened substantially. Their role should evolve to one of "software designer," in charge of conceptualizing and specifying the full range of features and characteristics of the product to be developed. The developers would then simply implement their design in code.

Several program managers emphasized that this approach was consistent with the opinion of several industry experts who felt that the character of the best software applications had changed in recent years. They felt that developing outstanding software now required a much greater attention to detail rather than sheer performance: attention to how the individual features fit together into a well designed, "coherent" product that was attractive, reliable, and fun to use.

Most developers were strongly opposed to turning program managers into designers, however. With a few exceptions, current Microsoft program managers had not previously been developers. The developers thus felt that program managers simply did not have the level of technical sophistication that was required to really understand the potential of a software development project.

Development Strategy

Other managers emphasized Microsoft's lack of a uniform strategy at the business level as the fundamental problem. They focused on the need for coherence across similar applications, to create economies of scale in development as well as a common "look and feel" in the products.

In 1990, Microsoft was actively writing applications to run on several different operating systems: the main ones were MSDOS, MSDOS with WINDOWS, and the Macintosh. Independent teams would be dedicated to the development of an application for each system. For example, there was a team for Word for the Macintosh, a team for word for DOS, and a team on Word for Windows. Keeping up efforts aimed at different operating systems was putting considerable strain on Microsoft resources. A set of suggestions thus focussed on code sharing within the Applications Division. Different programs required similar components, such as drop-down menus, macro languages, and graphics. Previously written software could often provide similar functionality to a large portion of the routines developed in a typical project. This would create development efficiencies as well as a more consistent user interface across different programs.

On the other hand, as Mason described, sharing code on Opus had cost more time than it saved:

> On WinWord trying to share code with MacWord was a tremendous source of delay. We took a whole bunch of MacWord code at the very beginning—which was fine. The problem came when the Opus made slight changes to optimize the code for WinWord—or just changed it because they felt that

the way the MacWord people had done something that was "brain-dead." Then the MacWord people would announce that they had found a whole bunch of bugs in the code they had given Opus. To get those fixes, Opus would then be required to make the same changes so that it was compatible with WinWord. This happened about three or four times. Not only did it delay WinWord by maybe six months, but it probably delayed the release of MacWord version 4.0 by about eight months. To share code, you can have only one set of source code and one group of people modifying it. Sharing 80 percent of the code in a project is good, 20 percent is a nightmare.

Recognition of the code-sharing problem had led to the "core code" approach. In this approach, almost all of the functionality of an application was written in "generic" code which would be shared by the teams working on each individual operating system platform. The Excel business unit had used the approach and Pete Higgins, the general manager, felt that the long term reduction of the development effort would be worth the substantial hiatus in product improvements. No new Excel application had been introduced for a

full two year period. Raikes felt that there were also other drawbacks to this approach:

> A risk with the core code standardization approach is that the software tends to get written for a lowest common denominator platform. For example, if you are writing for a PC and a Macintosh, you will tend to use only the features that are common to both. This means that it's difficult to write software that uses all the capabilities of either. Because of this, you may not come out with the best software on either machine and the way the market is today, you need the best software to compete.

OPTIONS FOR THE NEXT VERSION OF WINWORD

After a lot of thought, Raikes had boiled down future WinWord project possibilities into two basic options.

The first option involved introducing a new WinWord version (version 2.0) in as rapid a time period as possible. He was pleased with the product's market reception, but he felt that it could use some performance improvements, a few important bug fixes, and the addition of a few features. This

---

EXHIBIT 8 Word Processor Operating Environments

	Macintosh		IBM PC and Compatibles		
Operating System	*Mac/OS*	*DOS*	*DOS*	*OS/2*	*OS/2*
Layered Product[a]	—	—	Windows	—	Presentation Manager
Interface Type	GUI[b]	Character	GUI	Character	GUI
MicrosoftWord Processor	Word for Macintosh	Word for DOS	Word for Windows	—	—
WYSIWYG[c]	yes	no	yes	—	—

[a]The layered product is an add-on to the basic operating systems which provides a more uniform and easy-to-use user interface. The Mac/OS was designed from the ground up to provide such capabilities, whereas DOS and OS/2 do not. For this reason, Microsoft has developed Windows for DOS and the Presentation Manager for OS/2 to provide similar capabilities.

[b]GUI stands for Graphical User Interface, where the user gives commands to the computer by using a mouse to point to icons on a graphics screen.

[c]WYSIWYG stands for What You See Is What You Get. It refers to applications where the screen display closely resembles printed output.

was a common strategy at Microsoft. In many cases, it was only when the second version of a new application shipped that its sales really took off–many key customers would wait for the inevitable product improvements before committing to new software. The goal would be to ship WinWord 2.0 in slightly more than one year, or about when WordPerfect had announced it would enter the Windows market. This would involve a highly focused effort, and Raikes doubted that it could be combined with the major improvements in development process and strategy suggested above.

The second option was to postpone the introduction of WinWord 2.0, but use the project to substantially improve the product development process in his business unit. He could experiment with freezing the product's specification, as suggested by McDermott or with Mason's modular approach. Additionally, he could focus the team on "core code" development. Word for DOS, MacWord and WinWord would be rewritten so that 80% of the code was common and only a small part was machine specific. Raikes expected that working on these improvements would add substantial delays to the shipment of WinWord 2.0, ranging from one to two years. Perhaps most important, it would add substantial uncertainties, since these approaches were relatively novel at Microsoft.

In each option, a team of approximately ten programmers and four programmer assistants would be assigned to the project. This was Microsoft's standard team size and had been chosen because Microsoft's management felt that it was the largest practical team. Raikes was uncertain about having enough resources to emphasize more than one project, since there was a limited number of outstanding, experienced developers available.

As Raikes considered his options, his primary goal was clear—he wanted Microsoft to surpass WordPerfect and develop the best-selling word processing software in the world. Achieving such a goal would be difficult, but Raikes felt that if he chose the correct development option and managed the project well, it was possible.